W9-ATN-022

THE BLUE GUIDES

Shaoxing: moon gate

BLUE GUIDE

CHINA

Frances Wood

Photographs by Susan Benn
Maps by András Bereznay

A & C Black
London

W W Norton
New York

First edition 1992

Published by A & C Black (Publishers) Limited
35 Bedford Row, London WC1R 4JH

ISBN 0–7136–3027–2

A CIP catalogue entry for this book is available from the British Library

Published in the United States of America by
W W Norton & Company, Incorporated
500 Fifth Avenue, New York, NY 10110

Published simultaneously in Canada by
Penguin Books Canada Limited
2801 John Street, Markham, Ontario L3R 1B4

ISBN 0–393–30888–X USA

The publishers and the author have done their best to ensure the accuracy of all the information in *Blue Guide China*; however, they can accept no responsibility for any loss, injury or inconvenience sustained by any traveller as a result of information or advice contained in the guide.

Please write in with your comments, suggestions and corrections. Writers of the best letters will be awarded a free Blue Guide of their choice.

Frances Wood studied Chinese at Cambridge (1967–72); joined a worker-peasant-soldier class in Chinese history at Peking University (1976), and obtained a PhD in Chinese architecture from London University. She first visited China in 1972 and began to lead tours there in 1977, later accompanying three Parliamentary delegations, and from 1980 began to travel more extensively. She has translated Chinese fiction (Dai Houying, 'Stones of the Wall, 1985), written children's and general books ('Companion to China, 1988), and on Chinese illustration, gardens and architecture. She is Curator of the Chinese section of the British Library.

Printed and bound in Great Britain by
William Clowes Limited, Beccles and London

PREFACE

This Blue Guide is the result of trips to China made over a period of nearly 20 years, wearing, as the Chinese would say, a variety of different hats. The most useful include a year's residence in Peking, a dozen or more visits as guide or guide-lecturer accompanying groups organised by China Travel Service, and the most recent trips which I have made with friends.

Dates have been included occasionally in the text to indicate the time of my last visit, where things appear likely to change. The size of the country and the slow pace of travel there have made it impossible to dash back and check everything. Politics have also complicated tourism for 1986–87 saw a tremendous increase in activity anticipating a tourist boom. After the massacre in Tianenmen on 4 June 1989, seen on television throughout the world, the large number of new hotels opened unfilled. 1987 was also a year in which much was promised: very detailed maps marking sites of interest appeared on sale in most cities and piles of bricks outside temple walls indicated reconstruction everywhere. Quite a number of the designated sites had not yet officially opened when I rushed to see them and the absence of tourist revenue over the last three years may well delay their opening.

Putting China into a single volume presents problems: places have been omitted and maps are necessarily very small-scale. However, as the vast majority of travellers visit China on organised tours which cover many towns across the country, division by region, for example, would mean carrying several volumes. As few visitors spend more than a few days in any place, extravagant detail would add pounds to their luggage. It is to be hoped that in the future travellers to China will begin to spend longer in especially interesting towns and areas and find it easier to explore on their own: then the Blue Guide can be expanded and divided.

I have tried to include enough detail to be of use to long-stay visitors and, particularly, to try and encourage them to visit surrounding sites (Chengde and Tianjin from Peking, for instance, and the wealth of tiny towns in the Yangtse delta that are easily accessible from Shanghai). I hope, too, that those on package tours will find accessible sites they might prefer to and afternoon officially designated 'shopping' or 'free' and dare to take a bus or taxi. I have not included the wealth of material on police stations, very cheap dormitory hotels and travel details included in the Lonely Planet or Rough Guide series which are ideal for the back-packer. The slightly less-adventurous traveller should find that resorting to the services of the China Travel Services office (for booking and buying train or air tickets) will involve a modest fee but saves much time trying to comprehend the railway timetable, hanging about in stations or re-visiting airports.

Moving about in China is not easy: buying train tickets in a station (bellowing through a knee-high pigeon-hole) is a difficult business (see Travel within China, pp 77–78) complicated by the absence of return tickets and regulations about not buying tickets more than eight hours before departure, but it can be resolved. I often think travel is easier for those who do not speak Chinese. They can get away with being in the wrong place, with buying tickets at the wrong time (for the regulations are in Chinese) and, as the entire nation is trying to improve its English, there is always someone longing to help.

Getting around towns can also be difficult. Though Peking has all its major streets labelled in pinyin romanisation, Tianjin's street-names are entirely in characters, while in places like Kunming, only the major central streets are named in pinyin which makes it difficult for me to plan and describe the classic Blue Guide itineraries through major towns. I have tried to do so, as far as possible, but owing to the size of many cities and their widely dispersed temples, taxis are often the best solution, especially if time is short.

I am grateful to everyone involved in the production of the guide: Andras for trying to make the best of my frequently totally Chinese maps, Gemma for enduring the wait, and Tom for making it look like a Blue Guide and putting up with me losing Kashgar and worse. Helen Espir has helped enormously by generously sharing what she knows and has seen, and by explaining the railway timetable, and K who likes to take his time in temples has been galloped round more cities than I can count. All the mistakes are mine.

CONTENTS

8 CONTENTS

Maps and Plans

THE GROWTH OF CHINA FROM 1900 B.C. TO 1110 B.C.

N

YELLOW SEA

Anyi

Huang he

Chiang jiang

Xia Principality in 1900 B.C.

Added during the Xia dynasty

Boundary of China during the Shang dynasty in 1300 B.C.

Extent c. 1110 B.C.

HISTORY

Recent Western views of Chinese history have emphasised the agrarian nature of Chinese society, borrowing from Mao's stress on the peasantry. In fact, the breakdown of the highly organised, centrally controlled society is a relatively recent phenomenon, dating back to the mid 19C when Qing rule began to crumble. For most of China's history, the civilisation is better viewed as one that was highly organised and technological, with a well-maintained system of roads, staging posts, canals and government granaries. Technologically, China's superiority begins in the Shang dynasty with the sophisticated bronze industry and later saw the development of cast iron (by the 4C BC), porcelain (6C AD), paper-making (c 2C BC), printing (by the 7C AD), as well as gunpowder and firearms (10C AD) and textile technology which played an important part in exports of silk (to Rome in the 3C BC).

Another view of Chinese history is that of the traditional historians of China. The first great historian was Sima Qian (died c 90 BC) whose 'Shi ji' (often translated as Records of the Grand Historian) recounted the history of China from the earliest times to the Han. In works such as this events and stories are mixed to the point that David Hawkes, discussing some of the Shang legends, has said that the method could either be characterised as the 'historicisation of myth' or the 'mythicisation of history'.

If Chinese historiography begins in the Han, it was to continue throughout the succeeding millennia with ever greater significance. Each dynasty compiled the official history of its predecessor (which it had overthrown), based on the massive imperial archives. Someone recently described peasant China as a 'vegetable civilisation' but a better description of medieval China would be a 'paper civilisation' with a passion for documentation. Though it antedated the invention of paper, the first documented ruling house of the bronze age already possessed a script which was used to record events on bones which were carefully stored as an official archive.

The earliest inhabitants of China so far unearthed lived at Lan tian (Shaanxi province), 600,000 years ago. China's civilisation, however, begins with the **neolithic** era in which there were two major cultures with strong local variations. The **Yangshao** culture, characterised by the use of a red earthenware, sometimes decorated with swirling black designs, was mainly concentrated in the W of China, whilst the **Longshan** culture, characterised by the use of fine, wheel-made, burnished black pottery, was more eastern. In Henan, Longshan cultural layers overlie those of the Yangshao and the Longshan exhibits more characteristics that were to be developed in the subsequent bronze age. Longshan settlements were surrounded by walls of tamped (pounded in layers) earth, a technique also used in architecture. Their ceramic forms included tripods and tall libation cups (forms that were to continue in Shang bronzes). Late in the Longshan culture there is evidence of the use of divination.

Chinese historiography begins with the gods, legendary figures who invented all the techniques and implements useful to man, but the first 'dynasty' recorded is the **Xia**. As yet, no cultural remains have been unearthed that are definitively of the Xia though some suggest that a late Longshan group may have been the Xia. Archaeology and history unite in the **Shang** (c 16C BC–c 1066) which is divided into three phases exemplified by three major sites: early Shang at Erlitou (c 2000–1500 BC), middle Shang at Zhengzhou and late Shang at Anyang (all in Henan province). Sometimes known as the Yin in Chinese (the remains of one of the Shang capitals at Anyang are known as 'The Wastes of Yin'), the

Shang rulers inhabited palaces in considerable walled settlements which included suburbs where specialised industries (bone, bronze, pottery) were concentrated. The Shang palaces were apparently constructed using similar techniques to those seen in the neolithic Longshan, with hard, well-prepared tamped earth floors, but there were also stone pillar-bases, sometimes with bronze plates on them as a protection against damp. The Shang aristocracy used fast horse-drawn chariots with bronze fittings for hunting and warfare, which were both amongst the activities listed in their oracle bone divination records.

The rulers appear to have been shamans of a sort, consulting the gods on the outcome of military campaigns, hunts, illnesses and other natural events. In this oracular consultation they used prepared bones (scapulae of oxen, ventral shells of turtles). Shallow grooves were carved on the bones and heat applied to produce a T-shaped crack which was 'read'. The questions and answers were later inscribed on the bones in the first written language of any complexity to have been seen in China. The script comprises some 5000 characters which include simple graphs, more complex signs for abstract ideas and phonetic symbols (of which only 1500 have been deciphered with certainty, partly with the aid of the Shuo wen dictionary of c AD 100). Characters also appear cast on Shang bronzes (although it was during the succeeding Zhou dynasty that bronzes were widely inscribed). The excavated Shang bronzes that survive are almost all from tombs and formed part of sets of 'ritual' bronzes, presumed to have been used for food and wine sacrifices to heaven and then buried with nobles whose spirits were assumed to continue with the same sort of rituals after death.

The Shang aristocracy constructed enormous underground graves in which the coffin of the deceased was accompanied by sets of ritual bronzes wrapped in silk and filled with offerings of food and wine, chariots, complete with horses and drivers and, in some cases, dozens of human sacrifices. The human victims may have been prisoners of war, captured in some of the Shang campaigns against their neighbours. Major sacrifices were held on fixed dates when dead kings were commemorated and records of these enable archaeologists to construct a genealogy of the Shang kings, as well as providing evidence of a form of ancestor worship which was to survive as a major form of family worship throughout traditional China. Other aspects of Shang worship which were to continue were the cult of a supreme god, controller of natural forces and the political fate of rulers, and of gods of the compass points and mountains.

The Shang rulers were eventually overthrown by the **Zhou**, a warlike group with effective chariots and harnesses who came from the W (Shaanxi province) of the Shang kingdom. The Zhou continued many of the Shang practices like the ritual use of bronze and jade, the same sort of burials (though not on quite the same barbaric scale), but they discontinued oracle bone divination. At first, most Zhou texts were inscribed on bronzes, later on silk and strips of bamboo and wood.

The chronology of the Zhou is complicated: a fundamental break occurred in 771 BC when the Zhou were forced to move their capital from the Wei Valley E to Luoyang. Nomadic tribes were pressing forward in the W, threatening the old capital. Throughout succeeding centuries dynasties attempted to establish their capitals reasonably, but not dangerously, near the significant frontiers. Being near was important, to ensure that frontier garrisons were adequately supplied and supported; being too near meant that the capital might have to be evacuated, as the Han discovered when they had to move their capital several times.

The move of the capital, the survival of historical records and the gradual breakdown of centralised rule are reflected in the traditional divisions of Zhou rule which appear in the chronological tables:

Western Zhou 1066–771 BC } these two deriving their names
Eastern Zhou 770–256 BC } from the move of the capital

Subdivisions of the Eastern Zhou:
Spring and Autumn Period 722–481
Warring States Period 403–221 BC

The *Spring and Autumn Period* takes its name from an historical record of
the same name which describes events in the state of Lu, for which the
last entry is in 481. A text of commentary on these annals is called the
'Zuo zhuan' and Chinese historians sometimes use the two names
together as a name for the period.

The *Warring States Period* also derives its name from a document, the
'Zhan guo ce' or Records of the Warring States. The name reflects the
breakdown of Zhou power as separate states, derived from fiefs, grew in
power and began to fight each other for supremacy. The Shang had ruled
a smaller area without delegation but as the Zhou expanded their territory (NE to Peking and Shandong, S to the Yangtse plains), it became the
practice to enfeoff noble families with cities, towns or regions. The gift
was commemorated by the presentation of inscribed bronzes, cowrie
shells, chariots, weapons and animal sacrifices. Within the earthen banks
that demarcated their lands, the ruling house performed the major
sacrifices but held power through the size of its chariot army.
    The regional separation into separate states is reflected in strong
regional art forms: bronzes of the northern and 'metropolitan' areas cast
with strong, plain interlaced dragons whilst those of the S are covered in
more complex, smaller scrolling decoration. Jades, too, show regional
variations similar to those of the bronzes with dragon heads in the N and
spiralling forms based on dragons in the S.

CHINA UNDER THE HAN

ARAL SEA

Lake Balkhash

N

Palimbothra

▓▓▓ The Empire of the Han in 100 B.C.
\\\\ The Empire of the Han in 100 A.D.
——— Boundary of the Empire of the Tang in 750 A.D.
------- The Silk Road

It was during the 6C that iron began to be worked in China, cast into mass-produced agricultural implements which were improved during the Qin and Han. Europe was not to see cast iron until the late Middle Ages but, owing to long experience in the bronze industry, metallurgical progress was rapid in China: steel was made in the 1st–2C AD, thanks to the perfection of a double-action piston bellows. Agricultural improvements led to the growth of cities and trade between the states which did not, however, bring them closer together for each state had a different form of currency (cast bronze coins sometimes in the shape of knives or ploughs reflecting the agricultural economic base), slightly different writing styles and different systems of weights and measures.

Administering these and the other affairs of each ruling house was a growing official class of ministers, scribes, officers and specialists. The growth of the literary official as distinct from the military officer is reflected in a change in use of the term 'shi' which originally meant a knight (or 'gentleman' at arms) but came to mean an educated gentleman. Confucius was a representative of this class, having served as an officer in the State of Lu, and though his expressed views on political morality and public ethics were to dominate Chinese thought from the Han, he was not widely known during and immediately after his lifetime. Another philosophical theory that was to play an important, though short-lived part, in the unification of the separate states was *Legalism*.

AND THE TANG DYNASTIES

YELLOW
SEA

Chang'an Luoyang

EAST CHINA
SEA

PACIFIC
OCEAN

SOUTH CHINA
SEA

Unification of China under the Qin. The Legalists, one of whose major writers was Han Fei (or Han Fei zi, died 234 BC), saw law as order (rather than arising out of custom or common practice in the settlement of disputes). Their aim was to substitute the customary rights and privileges of the old society by an all-embracing legal system including collective responsibility, impartial rewards and punishments and uniformity of weights and measures. The system was adopted by the ruler of the Qin state—who by 221 BC had conquered all the others—to unify China for the first time. This was not a purely military process; he unified the weights and measures, introduced a standard copper coin (round with a square hole in the middle) which remained the standard until the 20C, and he imposed the Qin writing style, a standard cartwheel gauge, began the development of a road and canal system and pulled down the walls of the separate states whilst building the Great Wall on his northern frontier. In order to 'unify' thought, in 213 he ordered the destruction of all works except those on medicine, agriculture and divination (the 'burning of the books') and the execution of some 400 opponents of his regime. The human expense of the construction of the roads, canals and Great Wall by workers on corvée labour (a form of government service similar to military conscription by which able-bodied men had to work on government projects for a specified period each year), as well as his expensive military campaigns in Central Asia and Vietnam, took their toll.

Uprisings began and the dynasty did not long survive his death in 210 BC. In 206 BC Liu Bang, the leader of one of the insurgent rebel bands managed to defeat the Qin army, overcome his rivals and proclaim himself emperor of the Han dynasty. The Han was one of the most significant and long-lasting dynasties in Chinese history and the pattern of a ruthless unification followed by a stable 'golden age' was to recur in Chinese history. It illustrates the danger of fragmentation which haunted all of China's rulers, for the size of China and the strength of local loyalty made centralised government difficult.

Han dynasty: 206 BC–AD 220. The 'golden age' of the Han is subdivided into two major periods: *Western Han* (206 BC–AD 23) and *Eastern Han* (AD 25–220). The two major periods represent the different sites of the capital, first in Chang'an (modern Xi'an) in the W, later in the eastern city of Luoyang. The brief intervening period is known as the *Wang Mang interregnum*, for Wang Mang attempted to set up a new dynasty and to improve economic and social conditions by returning to theories of a past 'golden age' mostly based on myth. Wang Mang is characterised as a 'reformist' rather than a 'modernist' and struggles between reformists and modernists persisted during the Han and, to some extent, throughout Chinese history. The relative positions were taken on the basis of texts and reflect the supreme importance that the Chinese have always given to the written word and its interpretation. The possibilities of interpretation and varying positions taken up on the basis of interpretation reflect an aspect of the nature of the written language which Jacques Gernet called 'the first shorthand in history'.

The Han reformists based their position on texts written in the old script that had survived the Qin emperor's burning of the books, whilst the modernists used texts copied out in the modern script. Arguments over variant characters and passages have raged ever since. The desire to set down the approved text of the Confucian classics that no-one could dispute provoked a Han emperor to have them carved in stone in AD 175. Despite the Wang Mang interregnum, the Han dynasty established the basis of the Chinese system of bureaucratic government and bureaucrats' education which persisted until 1911.

Also important was the Han expansion into the western desert and the establishment of trade routes across the deserts of Central Asia. Along these silk was exported to Rome and fine horses for the imperial cavalry were brought to China from Ferghana as well as luxury foods such as grapes, pomegranates, walnuts, sesame, onions, coriander and cucumber. China's expansion S of the Yangtse also began in the Han when expeditions were sent to the Kingdom of Dian (around Kunming in Yunnan), to Vietnam, Burma and the Nanyue kingdoms of the Guangdong area where commanderies were set up.

The establishment of a centralised bureaucratic government was based on the Confucian ideology of paternalistic rule by superior, educated and moral men. An imperial university was set up in 124 BC. Within a hundred years it had 3000 students. The curriculum consisted entirely of the Confucian classics with forms of examination being held at court (based on the Confucian texts) to select 'men of talent' to govern. The Han bureaucracy was smaller than that of later dynasties; local officials did not penetrate below the level of towns of a reasonable size from where they collected the agricultural taxes (in products as varied as raw lacquer and silk as well as grain) that supported the imperial government.

The government also controlled by monopoly important products such as salt (mined in Sichuan province) and iron. As under the Qin, apart from producing agricultural goods as tax, men were compelled to do military and corvée labour service to maintain roads and mines and construct grand imperial buildings. This control of taxation and labour was based on an efficient system of data collection and the Han censuses are still considered to be remarkably accurate.

The extent of the Chinese bureaucracy can be seen in the surviving records of the administration. Many of these have survived in the dry desert of Gansu province, at the western extremity of the Great Wall. The Han, particularly under Wu Di (the 'martial emperor'; 141–87 BC), waged a series of campaigns against their northern neighbours the Xiongnu tribes (sometimes identified as Huns), and gained control of much of Central Asia, extending the Great Wall west. Having established control of Gansu, it was necessary to garrison the Wall. The garrison records consist of documents written on thin strips of wood and bamboo. Inscribed with ink and brush, top to bottom, these were then tied together and rolled up for storage. They describe the daily tasks of these distant garrisons—inspecting the woodpiles kept to fire the signal beacons, clearing stray dogs and reporting on local conditions to superior officers.

Despite the economic strains of maintaining the garrisons in the W and launching military campaigns which included an occupation of much of Korea, China's population flourished during much of the Han and the census of AD 2 revealed a population of nearly 60 million with cities of up to a million inhabitants. Technological progress continued with the use of the breast-strap harness (first seen in the Warring States), the improvement of iron tools so that an ox-drawn iron plough became commonplace, the introduction of the donkey from the West and the invention of the wheelbarrow (the Chinese wheelbarrow places the load directly above the wheel so that though the barrow is difficult to balance, it is a most effective means of transport). Ceramic tomb models of the Han illustrate both town and country life: rural farmhouses with tiled roofs contrast with grand watchtowers constructed with wooden brackets to support the tiled roofs; fish ponds full of fish, ducks and geese; figures play boardgames, oxen pull carts.

Houses (also depicted on the tomb bricks lining underground burial chambers) had a series of courtyards with the main hall raised on a stone platform and an open verandah in front. Despite the wealth that was being created by the merchant class, the Han saw the first laws controlling merchant activities. The introduction of the government monopoly on salt and iron was one (for these were most profitable). In succeeding dynasties the attempt to control these commodities is balanced by the wealth of the merchants who dealt in them, like the Ming salt merchants of Anhui. Merchants were also forbidden to wear silk, to ride horses or to carry arms and these restrictions were extended in later dynasties, effectively preventing the merchant class from rising in society except by educating its sons to become bureaucrats, rather than merchants.

Though Confucianism triumphed as the state philosophy in the Han, it was not unchanged, nor was its supremacy unchallenged by Taoist and other cults which were taken up at court. A major aspect of Han thought was interpretation by means of the Five Elements (wood, metal, fire, water and earth) and yin and yang (dark, female, weak versus bright, male, strong) by which all living things can be classified. Dong Zhongshu (1C BC), a leading figure in the establishment of the imperial university to train future government officials, linked historic events in the Confucian classics to the Five Elements. Critics, such as the rationalist Wang Chong, attacked the superstition, and particularly the reliance on portents and omens, that had crept into Confucianism.

In the Eastern Han, as under the Western Han, initial stability gave way to the growth of huge estates (with the consequence that many peasants became landless) and expensive military campaigns which led in turn to higher taxes, turning more peasants off the land. This pattern is another that was to be repeated throughout China's history as dynasties gradually lost control of the economy through corruption or incompetence. When large numbers of peasants became landless, they easily grouped into anti-dynastic armies and, though it was rare for peasant leaders to establish a dynasty themselves, they often paved the way for others.

As the Eastern Han lost control, picturesquely named, millenarian peasant bands rose up throughout China, notably the Yellow Turbans, the Red Eyebrows and the Five Pecks of Rice Band (inspired by magical Taoism), and the Han fell. In this case, no single leader emerged to reunite China and a period of disunion followed, rather like the earlier 'Warring States'.

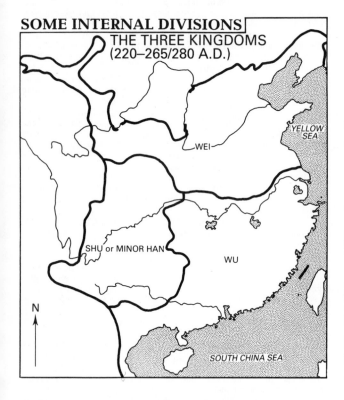

SOME INTERNAL DIVISIONS

THE THREE KINGDOMS (220–265/280 A.D.)

YELLOW SEA

WEI

SHU or MINOR HAN

WU

N

SOUTH CHINA SEA

Period of Disunion: 220–581. Fourteen different short-lived dynasties and 16 'kingdoms' were established in this period when China was divided, with different rulers in different parts, and almost constant warfare. According to one view, the population dropped by 30 million between AD 156 and 280 but it is likely that the drop was not entirely due to the casualties of war but to the not-unrelated fact that thousands or millions were forced to leave their land and were no longer registered. Between the 3C and the mid 5C a migration S to the Yangtse by dispossessed northerners and the development of this fertile area led to a subsequent increase in population in the Yangtse delta.

In this period when Confucianism with its view of the moral ruler, governing by grace of heaven and maintaining the welfare of his subjects, was clearly somewhat irrelevant, Buddhism with its path to salvation and sense of abstract continuity in the endless cycle of rebirths made great progress. It was brought to China by foreign missionaries such as the Parthian known in China as An Shigao (late 2C) and the prolific translator Kumarajiva (late 4C) who had an Indian father and a Kuchean mother.

In the late 4C Chinese Buddhists began to make lengthy journeys to the Indian homeland of Buddhism to collect sutras, bringing them back to China for translation. The first of these was Fa xian who returned to Nanjing in 414 after a 15-year journey which he later described in detail. The work of translating the sutras was monumental, for there are 1662 works in the Chinese Buddhist canon, most of them translated

IN c. 535 A.D.

WESTERN WEI

EASTERN WEI

YELLOW SEA

LIANG

N

SOUTH CHINA SEA

by the early Tang dynasty. It was frequently a bi- or tri-partite interpretation with a Central Asian monk (who knew Sanskrit) giving a verbal translation which then had to be translated verbally into Chinese. There were varying approaches to translation, some favouring literalness, others trying to achieve a more polished style which would appeal to the literary Chinese. Though he devoted much of his life to translation, Kumarajiva is supposed to have said that reading sutras in translation was like eating rice that someone else had already chewed.

There was also a renewed interest in Taoism, both philosophical and alchemical. Groups of intellectuals gathered to drink wine, write poetry, play the lute and discuss Taoist philosophy in what were called 'pure debates'. One of the most famous of these groups was the 'Seven Sages of the Bamboo Studio' who met in the late 3C. There was a growing interest in Taoist immortality through bodily means: by diet, abstinence, sexual practices and breathing exercises and through the often explosive or poisonous alchemical search for an elixir of life. Recipes for such an elixir appeared in Ge Hong's 'Bao pu zi', compiled in the early 4C.

The period, with its military heroes and wily strategists, has also provided rich material for later folklore and literature. The **Three Kingdoms** (220–265) was later depicted in the 'San guo yan yi' (Romance of the Three Kingdoms) by Xia Naian of the 14C. The ruler of the state of Wei, Cao Cao, figures as a grand strategist from the N but the most exciting characters (in fiction and folklore at least) came from Shu, in present-day Sichuan province. Liu Bei ruled with his generals Zhang Fei and Guan Yu (the latter was eventually deified as the God of War in another example of the mythicisation of history), and his prime minister, Zhuge Liang, a strategist of inventive genius. Much of Sichuan is associated with grand battles involving these god-like figures.

Another ruling house to leave a lasting impression, at least on the landscape, was the **Northern Wei** (386–534). A non-Chinese people, the Wei (thought to be of Turkic or Tungusic origin) first established their capital at Datong in the northern province of Shanxi where they financed the carving of the huge cave-temple complex at Yungang (460–494), with massive Buddha figures and highly-decorated caves based on the carved rock temples of India and the giant Buddha at Bamiyan. When the Wei moved their capital SE to Luoyang, near the Yellow River in Henan province, they started work on another great cave-temple complex in the cliffs of Longmen in 494.

Reunification under the Sui dynasty, 581–618. Just as the first Qin emperor united the separate states in 221 BC into a short-lived empire characterised in folklore as ruthless and tyrannical, the first emperor of the Sui reunited the country and gained a similar position in folklore as a brutal tyrant. In both cases it is partly the 'golden age' that followed their necessarily rigorous regimes that colours the traditional view.

The father of the first emperor of the Sui was forced to change allegiance from one small ruling house to another and his father-in-law was forced to commit suicide. Born in 541, he was brought up for the first 12 years of his life by a Buddhist nun, in separate quarters from his parents. He remained committed to Buddhism all his life, making huge donations to Buddhist monasteries after some of his murderous rages. Consciously or unconsciously, he followed the Qin pattern of setting up a complex legal system which was enforced with draconian severity and he ordered major works on the existing canal system, bringing grain to his capital and his armies (the beginnings of the Grand Canal). 5.5 million conscripted labourers worked on this and the extension of the Great Wall, whilst over a million men were sent to subdue the ruler of Korea (who inflicted an ignominious defeat on this vast army). The first Sui emperor was succeeded in 604 by his son who may well have ordered his father's death and who, in turn, was murdered in his bathhouse in 618 by the descendants of the Wei ruling house which had been almost wiped out by his father.

Though chronologies list the Tang dynasty as following immediately upon the Sui (618–907), it took 10 years for the Li family to establish control after the murder of the second Sui emperor.

The Tang dynasty, 618–907. The Tang dynasty is viewed as another 'golden age' in which Chinese culture flourished with a solid economic base for the prosperity of the country, based on an early enforcement of the 'equal field' system by which all eligible able-bodied males were supposed to receive almost 5.7 hectares (14 acres) of land. Only one-fifth of this could be permanently held; this was known as 'mulberry land' for long-lasting investment crops like mulberries to feed silkworms, could be planted there as opposed to annual tax crops like grains. At the begin-

ning of the Tang the reimposition of the system was essential to re-establish cultivation on abandoned land and to provide the tax income
required by the government.

A vast revenue was needed to support the growing bureaucracy, for
the Tang restored the old Han system and refined it into an enormous
pyramid with the emperor at the top, served by his imperial Chancellery,
imperial Secretariat and Department of State Affairs. The last supervised
six ministries (of officials, finance, rites, army, justice and public works).
There were also nine 'offices' and five 'bureaux' as well as the Board of
Censors who reported on the officials. These ministries and boards were
grouped around the imperial palace in the centre of the capital. The rest
of the country was divided for administrative purposes into 15 circuits,
350 prefectures and 1500 counties, the last administered by local magistrates at the lowest level of the imperial civil service. As the system was
based on that of the Han, so were the newly-revived civil service exams
which still, in theory, meant that a career in the bureaucracy was open to
all. In fact, the long years of schooling required eliminated the poor and
positions could still be bought.

Nevertheless, from the Tang onwards, upward mobility in China was
via the civil service exams and a civil service career. Merchants, whose
wealth could not improve their low social status, were forbidden by law
from taking the exams. They first invested in land (to change their status)
and on that basis they could educate their sons to become officials.
Towards the end of the Tang the merchants' investment in land, together
with the increasing wealth of the aristocracy (who were exempt from
taxes), meant that there was ever less land for distribution and, in consequence, ever fewer tax-paying peasants.

For the first 200 years the Tang saw expansion. The agricultural centre
shifted south as wet rice cultivation developed with new planting techniques producing greater yields and new tools suited for use in paddy
fields. Rice, transported along the expanding canal network, was stored
in massive imperial granaries at canal junctions to alleviate famine.
Through military campaigns and diplomacy, Chinese influence was
extended out into the NW, along the Silk Route, and good relations were
established with the Tibetans. The Koreans and Japanese, forced to
accept the cultural domination of China with its complex government
system, elegant architecture, flourishing literature and marvellous handicrafts combining in an extremely elegant lifestyle, borrowed all these
institutions and techniques.

The capital of the Tang, Chang'an (today's Xi'an) covered an area far
greater than that delineated by the surviving Ming city wall. The markets
of the capital were strictly controlled and the citizens lived in walled districts which were closed at night. Apart from the local population, a considerable number of foreign traders from the Middle East also lived in the
city and had their own mosques, Zoroastrian and Manichean temples.
They came to trade in silks, porcelain and other luxury goods and, in turn,
they brought luxuries—pearls, arab horses for the emperor's games of
polo, grapes and melons, precious stones, silver and gold vessels.

One woman rose to power during the Tang, the Empress Wu (reigned
660–705), traditionally characterised as a despot, like the later Dowager
Empress Cixi. Both seem to have ruthlessly eliminated potential rivals
(poisoning many of their close relatives) though both were patrons of
Buddhism. Despite her popular reputation, the Empress Wu promoted
the examination system (decreasing the possibility of purchase of office)
in order to recruit independent administrators and break the power of the
aristocracy.

By the middle of the 8C imperial power was declining; Tang armies
were defeated by the Arabs in Central Asia, losing control of the westernmost end of the Silk Road in 751. In 755 the dynasty was almost over-

thrown by the *An Lushan rebellion*. An Lushan (of Central Asian origin) was a general, favoured by the concubine Yang Guifei. He led an army to take the capital city and proclaimed himself the new emperor. The Xuanzong emperor (reigned 712–756) fled the city, taking Yang Guifei with him but, on the way to exile in Sichuan, his bodyguards insisted on strangling her. The rebellion was put down but the emperor never recovered, abdicating in favour of one of his sons. The flight to Sichuan with its tragic finale and the romantic misery of the bereaved emperor have been favourite subjects for poets and painters ever since.

Towards the end of the Tang, when the economy was in crisis, a great persecution of Buddhism took place (841–46), following the eradication of the Manichean Church. The persecution, which returned 260,000 monks and nuns to secular life, was fundamentally an attack on the great wealth of the Buddhist Church which owned vast estates and was exempt from taxes. Though the Buddhist Church never regained its position as a powerful landlord, it remained an important popular faith.

As the economy began to founder and more and more peasants became landless, the Tang began to collapse in a series of rebellions and, in the endlessly repeated pattern, China was again divided. The great legacy of the Tang was both governmental and cultural. The pattern of imperial government was established, to change little in succeeding centuries, and the poetry of the dynasty is still considered China's greatest.

The two best-known poets of the period are Li Bai (Li Po in Wade-Giles) and Du Fu (Tu Fu). The former is known as a great drinker and his best-known poem describes drinking with the moon and his shadow for company. Du Fu is regarded as a more profound observer for his poems reflect the misery of exile (he fled to Sichuan during the An Lushan rebellion and was sometimes out of favour with his bureaucratic superiors) and, occasionally, the sufferings of the poor at the gates of rich men's mansions.

The wealth of individual aristocrats of the Tang has survived as hoards (buried during the An Lushan rebellion when the court fled from the capital) have been unearthed with sets of silver and gold chased tableware and pots of expensive medicaments. The recent discovery of imperial donations to the Fa men Temple outside Xi'an includes fine porcelain, tea implements of silver, and robes of silk gauze. Though few paintings that can definitively be ascribed to the period have survived, the beginnings of the great landscape style can be seen in the wall-paintings of the Dunhuang caves and tomb frescoes and their furnishings of ceramic models have supplied illustrations of court dress of the time (including the new mid 8C fashion for loose dress based on Central Asian styles and said to have been popularised by Yang Guifei, concubine to the Xuanzong emperor), gentlemen playing polo and court entertainments.

Perhaps the greatest contribution of Tang China was the invention of woodblock printing which took place some time before the mid 9C. Paper, an essential prerequisite for the technique, had been discovered in the early Han and was apparently in quite widespread use by the 5C as the mass of Buddhist manuscripts on paper discovered at Dunhuang testifies. During the height of the Tang, government departments used millions of sheets of paper every year.

One of the documents discovered at Dunhuang was a printed copy of the Diamond sutra with a colophon that dated its printing to AD 868. The work, printed on separate sheets of paper pasted together to form a scroll some 7.5m long, is preceded by a beautifully cut frontispiece of the Buddha preaching. Though it is clearly the product of a mature industry, few other dated examples have been found to illustrate the development of the technique. It is probable that some of the small Buddha figures, printed in long series on paper scrolls, (also found at Dunhuang) may have helped to furnish the inspiration for the repetition of texts.

Whatever the source, printing quickly spread from Buddhist centres to the outside world and examples of printed calendars of the early 10C have been found at Dunhuang (privately printed in defiance of a government regulation which stipulated that calendars should be official publications). By the Song a whole range of works were printed for wider circulation—histories, poetical works, technical and medical books—though great religious printing enterprises also continued.

Period of Division: Five Dynasties and Ten Kingdoms, 907–960. The period of division following the collapse of the Tang is known as the 'Five Dynasties and Ten Kingdoms'. The Five Dynasties were short-lived military dictatorships in the N of China whilst the Ten Kingdoms coexisted more peacefully in the S.

The Song Dynasty, 960–1279. The Song dynasty was founded by the leader of the Imperial Guard of one of the Five Dynasties, Zhao Kuangyin. One of his first actions was to concentrate the best troops in the imperial capital rather than on the periphery. This was done in order to abolish the 'warlordism' (seizure of local control by military commanders) that had helped to destroy the Tang and kept China divided into the Five Dynasties. He also gathered more bureaucratic power into his own hands rather than trust powerful and potentially threatening ministers. The examination system continued to be the method of entry into the civil service but during the Song the exams were held more regularly and high standards were established by regulations controlling possible corruption.

The Song, in contrast to the expansionist Tang when the capital was filled with foreign traders and artisans, was a period characterised more by productive introspection. As it involved both philosophical and artistic retrospection, with ceramics and jades made in the form of Shang and Zhou bronzes, it was a true 'revival'. Confucianism was re-evaluated in

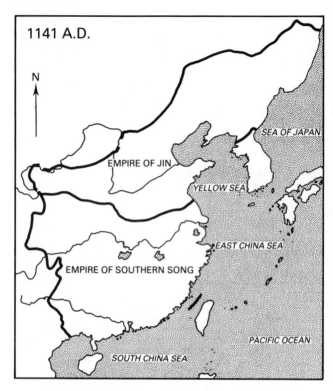

1141 A.D.

N

EMPIRE OF JIN

SEA OF JAPAN

YELLOW SEA

EAST CHINA SEA

EMPIRE OF SOUTHERN SONG

PACIFIC OCEAN

SOUTH CHINA SEA

the light of social change and of Buddhist influence. Ouyang Xiu (mid 11C) continued the work begun by the great Tang thinker Han Yu. He re-examined Confucian concepts and deplored the divorce between political function and culture: politics without culture was corrupt, culture without politics, meaningless. More philosophers sought to identify the natural order and find man's place in the cosmos, basing themselves on the Confucian classics, Buddhist metaphysics and finding a dualism between order and spirit.

Zhu Xi (1130–1200) used a metaphysical approach in his re-examination of Confucianism. He ascribed to all things their own pattern (li) and their own 'matter' or 'essence' (qi). In a complex scheme, he fitted the varying theories of yin and yang (femaleness, darkness, submissiveness versus maleness, light and strength), and the five elements (essences of manifested nature: metal, air, fire, water, wood) to the li and qi, incorporating a cyclical theory of chaos and order (which owes something to Buddhism) into a comprehensive view of the nature of things. This was combined with the adoption of Confucius' disciple Mencius' view of human nature as essentially good (dropping the opposite view of Xun zi, the 3C BC philosopher whose tough legalist philosophy was adopted by the Qin emperor). Zhu Xi's belief that man's essential goodness can be cultivated, his essential li developed from his rather chaotic qi, also owes something to Zen Buddhist ideas of self-cultivation towards enlightenment. Despite the metaphysical input Zhu Xi's neo-Confucianism was essentially conservative, preserving the family as the basis of society and the paternal figure of the emperor as the father of his people.

Geography, map-making, archaeology, mathematics, astronomy and historiography all made great strides during the Song, whilst the expansion of overseas trade (in well-made boats with nautical compasses) and major agricultural innovations in the form of new, faster-growing rice strains, all served to assist the development of an advanced economy and an urban society.

A major figure, reflecting the new idealism of the bureaucracy, was Wang Anshi (1021–1086) who attempted drastically to reform the economy in the face of changes. The population of China increased steadily during the Song and began to concentrate in growing towns, leaving a smaller number of registered payers of the agricultural tax to support the government. Wang Anshi abolished the corvée labour system, replacing it by further taxation which, in conjunction with his graduated tax system (based on the productivity of the soil) and a system of government loans to peasants, meant that the tax burden fell more heavily on the rich. He brought the government further into the economy by setting up government pawnshops and establishing a system by which the government purchased local goods for redistribution elsewhere, thus stabilising commodity prices. He also expanded the number of government schools to prepare students for the civil service exams, widening the possibilities of a bureaucratic career. He was bitterly opposed by the more conservative bureaucrats in government and by the rich and was forced to resign in 1076 when conservatives managed to reverse many of his policies.

Trade within the empire grew and merchant trade guilds expanded into a country-wide network, eventually building their own inns or hostels throughout China. The growth of local trade was accompanied by the increasing use of proto-banknotes, promissory notes on paper. These were issued both by the government and by large merchant houses because both faced the problem of moving large sums of bulky copper cash coins about the country. The government, which in previous periods had received virtually all its taxes in the form of grain, cloth, lacquer and other raw materials, was beginning to take more taxes in the form of money.

Foreign trade overland was difficult but the sea trade from southern coastal ports (most notably Quanzhou and Ningbo) flourished. Silks and porcelain were shipped in long, narrow boats to SE Asia, Korea and Japan and the boats returned loaded with spices, ivory, luxury timbers and medicinal herbs.

Some idea of the activity of the capital is gathered from Zhang Zeduan's narrative scroll 'Going Up the River on the Eve of the Qing Ming Festival' (late 11–early 12C), a portrait of Kaifeng. It depicts the bustling streets with their open-fronted shops and the variety of road traffic: officials with 'eared hats' on horses, the characteristic Chinese wheelbarrow (with the weight over the central wheel), loaded carts, ladies in sedan-chairs with brightly-patterned curtains, pedlars with loaded baskets on carrying poles. Many of the buildings have a verandahed upper storey and the internal courtyards behind the shops can be seen.

The way that the women are concealed within the sedan chairs is an indication of the increasing enclosure of women which was reinforced by the then-new practice of foot-binding. Originally an upper-class fashion, it gradually spread to all but the very poor who depended upon the work of women as well as men. When girls were about 7, their feet were tightly wrapped in wet strips of cloth, bending all but the big toe underneath the sole of the foot. A small block of wood was bandaged in under the heel to enable the victim to walk.

The division of the Song into the **Northern Song** (960–1127) and **Southern Song** (1127–1279) reflects the forced move of the capital from Kaifeng on the Yellow River, S to Hangzhou. The move was forced by increasing military power and threat from northern peoples, most notably the Khitan, Jurched and Tanguts (and, later, the Mongols). The Khitan, who were also of Mongolian origin, founded the *Liao dynasty* in N China (947–1125), but were later driven W by the Jurched and set up the

Western Liao dynasty (1124–1211) in eastern Turkestan. The Jurched, of the Tungusic language group, founded the *Jin dynasty* in N China (1122–1234), coexisting with the Tanguts (who spoke a language of the Tibetan group) whose Xi xia kingdom dominated NW China from 1038 to 1227. Continuing the threat from the N, the Mongols swept all aside, including the Khitan, Jurcheds and Tanguts, and finally overthrew the Song in 1279, establishing the Yuan dynasty.

The Mongol Yuan Dynasty, 1279–1368. Though non-Chinese dynasties had been ruling the N of China for some time, the rise of the Mongols swept them and the Song rulers aside. The sudden rise of the Mongols in the 12C and their conquests of central Asia, China and eastern Europe remains a matter of debate. It has been suggested that Central Asia suddenly became drier and less hospitable to these nomads but this theory has not stood close examination. Others suggest that a purely nomadic society such as that of the Mongols suffered from economic instability for nomadism without pastoralism could not provide the grains needed to supplement the milk and meat diet, nor could nomads produce the iron that was essential to their horsemanship for both stirrups and arrows had to be purchased from sedentary mining communities. The need for these commodities, it is suggested, forced the Mongols into conquest.

The sudden change in Mongol history was probably a combination of such factors and the divided and unstable nature of the neighbouring countries and the rise of a charismatic leader in Chinggis (or Genghis) Khan (c 1167-1227). Orphaned as a child, he later subdued all the other Mongol clans and groups and began the apparently inexorable conquering expansion. His army of 130,000 was far smaller than that of the Chinese but his troops were extremely well-disciplined. The Mongol army was said to practise 'hunting' techniques, groups of cavalry encircling enemy forces like herds of deer, and sudden manoeuvres, drawing the enemy into pursuit and then suddenly wheeling to confront them with their longbows.

Chinggis divided his ever-growing empire between his sons but relied on local advisors to assist in day-to-day local government, using the Uighur Turks in Turfan (and borrowing the alphabetic Uighur script to write Mongolian for the first time) and Chinese advisors in N China. It was Khubilai Khan (1215–94), a grandson of Chinggis, who supervised the conquest of S China, overthrowing the Song dynasty and establishing the Yuan dynasty. The name means 'first', 'beginning' or 'fundamental principle', and it was the first time that a dynastic name was chosen for its meaning (all previous ones were either surnames or placenames of significance). As Chinggis Khan had realised, 'the empire is conquered on horseback but it cannot be governed on horseback' and the Chinese system of government through the imperial offices and their subordinate ministries down to the local magistrate was continued.

The description of Mongol China contained in 'Marco Polo's Travels' is detailed, including mention of the regular grid-pattern of the street layout of Peking, the markets, craftsmen's guilds and pleasure boats on the lake at Hangzhou, the silks and myriad bridges of Suzhou, the use of paper money, the collection of customs tariffs during transport of goods, systems of household registration and the posting of names of inhabitants at the door of every residence. Significant omissions in the text include the Great Wall, footbinding, tea and tea-drinking, printing and the peculiarities of Chinese language and script. As all placenames are rendered in Persian (rather than Chinese or Mongol forms) it has been suggested that this vivid account was based on a contemporary Persian guidebook compiled for the numerous Persian travellers and merchants journeying to China, rather than personal decoration.

The Mongol capital was established in the N, in Peking, where, though previous small capitals had existed in the area, an entirely new city was built to the Chinese city planning ideal with walls enclosing a central palace surrounded by a grid system of streets. The tamped earth walls enclosing the city had one Mongol aspect in the enclosure of pasture land to the N of the city proper. By making use of the Yellow River, the Grand Canal was extended N to reach Peking and supply the capital with grain from rice-producing south China.

The Mongols kept themselves separate from the Chinese, with the barrier of their non-Chinese advisors between them. Khubilai promoted the state cult of Confucius and eventually re-established the examination system, but the Mongols at this time adopted the Tibetan form of Lamaist Buddhism and patronised Buddhist monasteries and temples.

The first papal envoys came to China during the Mongol era (when travel across Europe and Central Asia was relatively free). One of the reasons for papal interest was the relative strength of Nestorian Christianity amongst the Uighur Turks and Mongols, Khubilai's own mother being amongst the believers. Papal envoys who reached China included John of Montecorvino who died in Peking c 1328, having spent some 30 years in the city from where his successor took a letter from the Khan to Pope Benedict XII; Odoric of Pordenone (c 1286–1331), the first European to mention Lhasa; and John of Marignolli who arrived in China c 1342. In the light of Marco Polo's account, it is interesting that Odoric of Pordenone wrote a rather sober account of China (borrowed and embroidered by Sir John Mandeville) which did include mention of footbinding and the long fingernails of the scholar-class as well as details such as the use of cormorants for fishing.

Two cultural developments which took place during the Yuan, reflecting how little Chinese culture was affected by alien rule, were the rise of the Chinese drama and the first appearance of novels, a published form probably based on the narrative style of travelling story-tellers.

After the death of Khubilai's successor, Temur, no Mongol ruler managed to control warring factions within the Mongol nobility and, as old family rivalries were multiplied by new ones, the Mongol hold on China weakened. As with other dynasties in decay, there were other symptoms. Paper currency was over-issued, causing serious inflation. A disastrous change in course of the silted Yellow River flooding an area of more than 7000 hectares was seen as a significant omen of the withdrawal of the heaven-given 'mandate to rule'. Armed uprisings of landless peasants began in the 1320s; civil war between Mongol nobles broke out in 1328 and the secret society of the White Lotus, a millenarian Buddhist sect, led a peasant rebellion in central China as did another 'restore the Song' peasant secret society, the Red Turbans. In the past, peasant uprisings had helped to bring dynasties down (or served as decisive indicators of decay), only to be followed by the victorious establishment of a new aristocratic ruling house rising out of the chaos. The rebellions at the end of the Yuan were different for the founder of the Ming dynasty was actually an impoverished member of just such a peasant army who rose to supreme power.

Ming Dynasty, 1368–1644. Zhu Yuanzhang, founder of the Ming ('Bright') dynasty, was born into a poor tenant family in Fengyang, Anhui province in 1328. When he was 17 his entire family succumbed to the effects of famine and disease and he entered a Buddhist monastery as a novice. He joined the Red Turbans where he quickly distinguished himself and, despite his poor background and lack of formal education, soon became the leader of a disciplined army which attracted wide support until he managed to drive the Mongols back to the Gobi Desert. Though a formidable and capable leader in his early years, in later life, he became increasingly cruel. Chinese historians have compared him to Liu Bang, the founder of the Han, who also rose from obscurity to establish a grand dynasty.

Zhu Yuanzhang and his supporters, having overthrown an alien

CHINA DURING THE MING AND THE QING DYNASTIES

Lake Baikal

SEA OF JAPAN

Peking ●

● Hancheng

YELLOW
SEA

Nanjing ●

EAST CHINA
SEA

Guangzhou (Canton)
● Macau

PACIFIC OCEAN

NAM

SOUTH CHINA SEA

The Empire of the Ming in 1415
Boundary of the Empire of the Qing in 1760
Boundary of vassal states in 1800

dynasty, looked back to the great Chinese dynasties of Han, Tang and Song as models. In the first years of his administration, Zhu Yuanzhang allowed peasants to return to the land (as in the 'equal field' system) and recover it for agriculture without paying taxes. When taxes were imposed, they were collected twice yearly (the 'summer tax', mainly of winter wheat, was collected in the 8th month and the 'autumn grain' was collected after the main rice crop of the centre and south). Taxes were also collected in the form of silver and bolts of silk and the government maintained its monopoly taxes on tea and salt. Corvée labour service was required from adult males. Like the Yuan government, the Ming began by issuing paper money but soon reverted to metal coinage to prevent inflation.

In the early Ming, the government system of the Song was revived but in the later years of his reign Zhu Yuanzhang abolished the post of Prime Minister, assuming a more autocratic role than previous emperors, a practice which was to continue throughout the dynasty. In his direct handling of the many memorials to the throne and issuing of edicts, he was assisted by Grand Secretaries, and the Grand Secretariat came to serve as a kind of imperial cabinet, above the Six Ministries. Though there had been eunuchs at court from the Tang, in the Ming and Qing they assumed far more power in the Inner Court than they had had before and were often in conflict with the bureaucrats (of the Outer Court).

The civil servants were still selected by examination according to a system that was continued to the end of the Qing. There were first district exams to qualify candidates to enter for the prefectural examinations which offered the lowest degree level, xiu cai ('flowering talent'). Xiu cai degree-holders were exempt from corvée labour and certain forms of legal punishment. The next level of exams was held at the provincial capital where exam candidates were locked into individual cells in examination compounds. One in a hundred (or less) would pass and become eligible to take the highest level exams in Peking. Success there (after being locked into a similar complex of cells, formerly located to the W of the Friendship Store) meant achieving the title 'presented scholar' (jin shi), being presented to the emperor and appointed to a post.

In 1369 Zhu Yuanzhang decided to establish his capital in Fengyang, Anhui, his home town and the place where he had begun his rebellion against the Yuan. For six years work was carried out on the palace and city walls, and the tiny plot where his parents had been buried was enlarged into an imperial mausoleum, larger than any succeeding imperial mausoleum of the Ming or Qing and largely destroyed at the fall of the Ming. It was soon decided that Nanjing was a more suitable site for a capital and work began there on the construction of his palace and his own tomb.

The system of naming emperors was changed in the Ming: Zhu Yuanzhang is known as the Hongwu emperor ('Vast Martial Power'), a term which was originally used as the name of a year period. From the Han it had been customary for emperors to assume an imperial name but their reigns were frequently divided into several 'reign periods', with equally auspicious names which were changed to avert disaster or to try and improve events. For example, the ninth ruler of the Tang dynasty is known as the Xuanzong emperor. Xuanzong is a posthumously awarded dynastic title meaning 'Powerful Ancestor'. His surname, that of all the Tang ruling house, was Li, which is not reflected in any of the names by which he is now commonly known. His reign is divided into two reign periods: Kai yuan or 'Opening and Beginning', 713–742, and Tian bao, 'Favoured of Heaven', 742–756.

The reign periods were not of any ordained length. Sometimes a reign name would be changed suddenly after a natural disaster in the hope that heaven would be placated; the Xuanzong emperor's successor changed his reign name every two years for no particular reason. From the reign of Zhu Yuanzhang, in the Ming, it became the practice to have a single reign name for each reign, although emperors still had a variety of other names ranging from their real name to their posthumous title.

Zhu Yuanzhang may have had good reason for his paranoia in later life;

having set up his sons as princes in different parts of China, he appointed his grandson as his successor. One of Zhu Yuanzhang's sons, Prince of Yan, who controlled the north from his base in Peking, led an army against his nephew on the death of the dynastic founder, captured Nanjing and proclaimed himself the Yongle (Eternal Joy) emperor. He proceeded to remove the capital to Peking, for it was strategically more sensible to have the capital nearer the Great Wall, source of the greatest external threats from the non-Chinese tribes in Mongolia and Manchuria. There were some who felt that the feng shui or 'good luck' of the site of Peking had been exhausted with the conquest of the Mongols and the razing of their capital but the Yongle emperor found feng shui experts who thought otherwise and constructed the grand capital with its central 'forbidden city' or palace. The layout of today's streets and lanes in Peking is the same as it was in the early 15C (except for the ring roads) and the city, constructed on a flat plain, surrounded by fine walls and filled with a checkerboard of streets surrounding the imperial palace and government buildings, with imperial altars on all four sides, was considered to represent the ideal of the Chinese city plan according to principles which dated back to the Zhou period.

Technological progress during the Ming included the perfection of blue and white porcelain, which was to play an important role in China's export trade, and improvements in both silk and cotton looms, which also produced valuable export commodities. Agricultural machinery was improved and new crops like peanuts, maize, sorghum and the sweet potato, introduced by the Portuguese and the Spaniards, improved peasant livelihood.

For intellectuals, knowledge was spread widely through a massive increase in the printing industry (where the perfection of multi-coloured woodblock printing led to the production of fine illustrated albums and painting manuals). The output was enormous and included a great number of works on agricultural techniques, military science and medicine. One of the finest is the 'Tian gong kai wu' (Creations of Nature and Man) which illustrates ceramic, textile and paper production, smelting and forging and the production of carved jades from the search for the raw material (by diving women). Geography, philology and hydrology made great progress: the geographer Xu Xiake spending much of his life travelling throughout China, tracing the source of the Yangtse and the Xi jiang and publishing the results, whilst others produced works about foreign countries (Korea, Japan, Vietnam, Central Asia and Tibet).

Philosophically, the Ming was a period of 'reinforcement' of Song neo-Confucianism, although there was a move away from the reading and interpretation of texts (as advocated by Zhu Xi, 1130–1200) and a stress on personal conduct. The most famous thinker of the period is Wang Yangming (1472–1528) who developed Mencius' idea of 'innate goodness' which has to be rediscovered by stripping away egoistical thoughts and desires. Against the purity advocated by Wang Yangming, the expanding urban class was provided with a new wealth of popular literature in the printed editions of Fujian. The two most famous examples are 'Xi yu ji' (Journey to the West; c 1570), a fantastic and amusing version of the pilgrimage to India of the Tang monk Xuan zang who, in the novel, is accompanied by a pig (representing human failings and desires) and a magical monkey; and the 'Jin ping mei' (Plum Blossom in a Golden Vase; 1619), a novel of manners, describing the life and loves of a Shandong merchant.

It was during the Ming that much of the Great Wall, which was regarded as a a crucial defensive barrier against northern barbarians, was faced with brick. The Ming was not, however, at the outset, an inward-looking dynasty for during the reign of the Yongle emperor a series of grand maritime expeditions were launched under the command of the eunuch admiral Zheng He from Yunnan. Between 1405 and 1433 seven expeditions set out to the Persian Gulf, SE Asia and the E coast of Africa. The expense of the expeditions was one reason for their cancellation and the Chinese never regained the same status as a maritime power.

Towards the end of the Ming, considerable damage to the economy was inflicted by Japanese pirates and by official inactivity in the face of a huge rise in smuggling and dealing in contraband by both Chinese and Japanese (brought about by unenforceably rigid official policies on trade and the intense demand for Chinese products such as silk in Japan). The government still profited from the trade with Japan, Korea and the Dutch; a 17C writer, Gu Yanwu, stated that tax levied on only 20–30 per cent of goods shipped by sea paid for half of the state's expenditure at the end of the 16C. However, on the seas, piracy was almost uncontrollable and the Ming government was also forced into a very expensive war against Japan which invaded Korea in the last years of the 16C.

External threats (also from the Mongols) and ethnic uprisings in Guizhou were matched by chaos within the palace, largely as a result of feeble emperors surrounded by rapacious eunuchs (there were said to be 100,000 of them, effectively controlling the ministries, by the end of the Ming period). In 1620 the Taichang (Exalted and Glorious) emperor was poisoned by the eunuchs who controlled his imbecilic heir and when scholars of the ancient Donglin academy, calling for a return to strict Confucian ethics, attempted to curb the eunuchs, many were killed.

As peasants were driven from their land in the last decades of the Ming when, with the government coffers empty, disastrous famines notwithstanding, taxes were exacted with increasing ferocity, they once again banded together in anti-dynastic armies. Led by a peasant from Shaanxi, Li Zicheng (1606–45), the peasant army entered Peking. Abandoned in his palace, the last Ming emperor fled to Coal Hill (just behind the palace) and hanged himself from a tree. Li Zicheng's peasant army did not manage to gain control of the whole of China for the Manchus, a non-Chinese group from the NE who had been progressively absorbing the Chinese system of government in preparation, swept down in their place, capturing Peking in 1644.

The Qing Dynasty, 1644–1911. The Manchus, who established the Qing ('Pure') dynasty, were descendants of the Jurched who had established the Jin dynasty in N China (1122–1234), and Nurhaci (1529–1626), effectively the founder of the Qing, first proclaimed a 'later Jin' dynasty in 1616. He was chief of the Aisin Gioro clan and one of his major contributions to the success of the Manchu conquest was the organisation of the scattered tribes into a proto-state, and the formation of the Eight 'Banners' or companies of warriors, each with a distinctive banner. All Manchus were registered under their local banner and taxed, conscripted and mobilised according to the needs of the new state. Breaking tribal divisions and establishing his own clan as the leading family, Nurhaci built up a strong basis for a disciplined army. He also used captured Chinese civil servants to help him set up a bureaucracy in his capital in Shenyang.

Though Nurhaci died in 1626 during a campaign against the Ming, his son, Abahai, continued his efforts, and it was he who proclaimed the new Qing dynasty in 1636 (before the total subjugation of China). Abahai's son, though young and in the control of his uncle as regent, finally presided over the seizure of power in China. The Manchus' adoption of Chinese methods of rule through their Chinese advisors was significant: they had no desire to be seen as mere 'policemen' as Arthur Waley described the earlier Mongol rulers of China. The conquest of China took decades for groups of Ming loyalists held out in Yunnan and Taiwan. The north fell fast but the last Ming stronghold, the island of Taiwan, was not captured until 1683, owing to the fierce resistance of Zheng Chenggong (Koxinga) and his family. The Qing also pursued a policy of conquest in Turkestan, Mongolia and Tibet, areas which had fallen out of Chinese control.

Despite their tactical adoption of Chinese methods, the Manchus were keen to remain separate: Manchus were forbidden to marry Chinese women and various occupations (like trade) were forbidden to them. All Bannermen were allocated land and a stipend for life. They remained different in appearance for they wore their own costume and their women never bound their feet. Chinese men had to follow the Manchu male custom of shaving the front of the head and braiding the rest of the hair into a long plait, instead of the Ming hairstyle of a bun (which was seen as a sign of resistance).

In government, the tiny minority of Manchus managed to retain control for 400 years. Military power underlaid the successful maintenance of internal peace for much of the period. As under the Ming, the emperor retained ultimate control over all details of government, whilst the lower levels of government (from the Six Ministries downwards) were jointly staffed by Chinese and Manchus, just as there were three Chinese Grand Secretaries and three Manchu. The provincial administrations were similarly mixed, with the Manchus also working with a number of Mongols. The dual administration meant complexities of translation in the early years when Manchu was the official Court language. It was eventually superseded by Chinese (which became the sole language of the administration) but to the end of the dynasty all court documents relating to the imperial house were produced in both Manchu and Chinese.

The first 150 years of the Qing saw a huge expansion of Manchu power throughout Central Asia as far as Lake Baikal and the borders of Nepal. Great care was taken to obtain and retain the loyalty of major Mongol and Tibetan leaders who were entertained in specially-built Lamaist temples in Chengde and Peking. One of the major campaigns of the Qianlong emperor was that of 1791, carried out against the Gurkha tribes of Nepal to punish their incursions into Tibet. After military campaigns, areas such as Yunnan and Xinjiang province (the 'New Border') were colonised by Chinese settlers and by the military. Towards the end of the 18C revolts of the colonised ethnic peoples became more and more frequent as Chinese officials in the distant areas grew increasingly corrupt. Campaigns to quash the rebellions drained government finances.

However, under the early Qing rulers China prospered and expanded. The most prominent of these were the Kangxi (Vigorous and Splendid) emperor (1654–1722) and his grandson, the Qianlong (Lasting Eminence) emperor (1711–99). It was the Kangxi emperor who in his youth had directed the capture of south China from the last Ming loyalists. Soon after that he was involved in the settlement of border disputes with the Russians, signing a treaty of peace in 1689, before personally leading an army into Outer Mongolia and Turkestan. He made six tours of inspection to south China, particularly to examine water conservancy projects, and was concerned with improving communications via the Grand Canal and with making the Yellow River safe.

The Kangxi emperor supervised the construction of the Summer Palace at Chengde, about 150km NE of Peking, the Bi shu shan zhuang or 'Mountain Village Where You Can Escape the Heat', a hunting park dotted with pavilions and pools, surrounded by the eight 'outer temples' in the Tibetan style. Here he entertained Mongolian and Tibetan leaders. It was the Kangxi emperor who appointed Jesuit missionaries to run the Imperial Board of Astronomy and he made use of Jesuit missionaries like Gerbillon as interpreters during negotiations with Russia. Jesuits and Chinese made maps for the Kangxi emperor, showing the areas of his new conquests, and Matteo Ricci made copper engravings of maps, drawings of military scenes and illustrated editions of the emperor's poems. Viewed popularly in China as something of a poly-

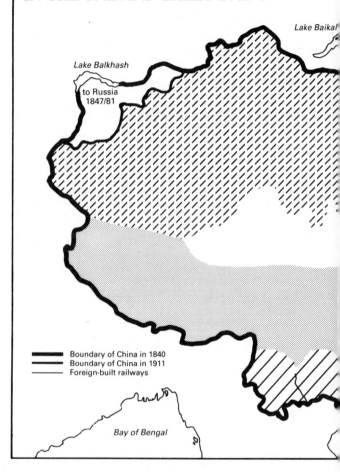

FOREIGN PENETRATION TO CHINA IN THE 19th AND EARLY 20th C.

Lake Baikal

Lake Balkhash

to Russia
1847/81

Boundary of China in 1840
Boundary of China in 1911
Foreign-built railways

Bay of Bengal

math, the Jesuit Matteo Ripa (1628–1745) in his 'Memoirs' voiced a more jaundiced view: 'The emperor supposed himself to be an excellent musician and a still better mathematician, but though he had a taste for the sciences¡he knew nothing of music and scarcely understood the first elements of mathematics …'.

Though he had 28 children who survived infancy, the only son born to the empress (rather than a concubine) was apparently mentally unstable and was incarcerated at his father's order, leaving the succession a matter to be fought over after the emperor's death. Yin zhen, fourth son of the emperor (by a palace maid), cultivated the friendship and support of influential courtiers including the head of the Peking garrison, the Bannerman Lungkodo. Though it is thought that Kangxi named Yin ti (his 14th son, whose mother was the same palace maid) as his successor, Yin

to Russia 1858

to Russia 1860

KOREA
independent 1895
to Japan 1910

Peking

Tianjin

Port Arthur to Russia 1898 (1905 to Japan)
Wei hai wei
to G.B. 1898
Jiaozhou
(Kiao chow) to Germany 1898

EAST CHINA SEA

Shanghai

N

Taiwan
to Japan 1895

Spheres of influence in 1911

/////// Russian

\\\\\\\ Japanese

XXXXX German

British

///// French

Hong Kong
to G.B. 1841
Leizhou wan (Kwang chow wan) to France 1989

SOUTH CHINA SEA

ti was commanding border armies in the northwest so Lungkodo and Yin zhen seized power and Yin zhen ruled under the reign name of Yongzheng (1678–736). He was reasonably successful in controlling official corruption (by offering financial rewards), thereby improving the state's financial position. He named his fourth son his heir, though the nomination was kept secret until after his death, to prevent quarrels.

The Qianlong emperor (reigned 1736–96) personally led many military campaigns, particularly in central Asia, Burma and Vietnam, which—with the exception of the central Asian campaigns—were not very successful and enormously expensive. They virtually wiped out the government reserves, leaving China quite unable to withstand foreign encroachments in the succeeding century. Another intimation of the impending problems of foreign relations was the attitude of the emperor and his court to the embassy of Lord Macartney sent to open China to foreign (or at least British) trade (1792–94). The emperor was not completely unaware of the possible consequences of his refusal to grant a single concession for he instructed his officials in Canton to try and prevent other European merchants from allying themselves with the British.

Like his grandfather, the Qianlong emperor made use of the special talents of the Jesuit missionaries (who seem to have spent more time ingratiating themselves with the Court and teaching European sciences and arts than gathering converts, a fact which contributed to the dissolution of the order in 1773). He particularly favoured the painter Castiglione, and Father Benoit who contributed the 'European' palaces and Italianate gardens to the emperor's summer palace (the 'Old Summer Palace'), the Garden of Perfect Brightness on the outskirts of Peking.

One of the Qianlong emperor's greatest projects, the compilation of a vast collectanea in 36,000 manuscript volumes, the 'Si ku quan shu' (Complete Collection of the Four Treasuries), intended to preserve rare works from oblivion, involved a vast literary inquisition on a scale not to be repeated until the Cultural Revolution of the 1960s. Provincial officials were required to collect rare works for inclusion but all works submitted were also scrutinised for anti-Manchu sentiments. Hundreds of volumes were destroyed; the authors and their families killed (or subjected to posthumous disgrace).

Towards the end of his reign, corruption amongst officials was rising, unchecked, the economy drained by military campaigns and the traditional cycle of peasant uprisings heralding the end of a dynasty was beginning.

Local officials' embezzlement of funds intended for flood prevention work led to the calamitous change in course of the Yellow River (1855) when it broke its banks and moved from the N to the S of the Shandong peninsula (a distance described by Jacques Gernet as that from London to Newcastle). This occurred during the disastrous Taiping ('Great Peace') uprising of 1850 to 1864. The Taiping rebels were led by Hong Xiuquan who mixed idealistic Confucianism with Christianity which he had learnt from an American missionary in Canton. Hong Xiuquan looked back to a golden age of equal land distribution and forward to greater equality between the sexes. Calling himself Jesus' younger brother, he wanted to create a 'Heavenly Kingdom of Great Peace' in China where all would be brothers. Some of the early practices of the Taipings were 'egalitarian' for captured spoils were shared equally.

The vague Christianity of some of the Taiping ideas was supported at first by missionaries and foreigners but they eventually decided, as the Taipings established themselves in Nanjing and moved to threaten the Qing, that their trading interests were better served by the dynasty that they knew. In the end, the Taipings were crushed by a combination of imperial forces and the foreign-led 'Ever-victorious Army', commanded at first by an American, Frederick Ward, and subsequently by General Gordon (later of Khartoum). There was also a long and damaging rebellion in northern China in the mid 1800s (the Nian rebellion), and a moslem uprising in the northwest (1862–73) which was crushed savagely.

These took place during the period in which control of imperial power had passed into the hands of the Dowager Empress Cixi ('Motherly and Auspicious'). Born in 1835 into a Manchu family of the Bordered Blue Banner, she entered the palace in 1851 as a concubine to the emperor whose only son she bore, consequently raising her status. The emperor died in 1861 and Cixi, together with the senior consort, acted on her son's behalf. There were eight official regents but Cixi personally held the imperial seal required for all edicts and, using the pretext of their weakness over the British and French invasion of 1860, Cixi managed to get one regent executed and the rest punished.

When her son died of smallpox in 1875, she chose her younger sister's son as the heir-apparent in a flagrant breach of protocol (the decision was

N ←

PACIFIC OCEAN

Boundary of China in 1911
New boundaries in 1933
The main thrust of the Long March 1934–35
Under Communist control from 1936
Japanese occupation (greatest extent 1944)
Note: Taiwan occupied by Japan in 1895

CHINA 1911–1944

SEA OF JAPAN

MANCHURIA
Independent under
Japanese control
from 1931

EAST CHINA SEA

Shanghai

Nanjing
Wuhan
Peking

Yan'an

Chongqing

Guangzhou

SOUTH CHINA SEA

Lake Baikal

MONGOLIA
Autonomous 1911
Independent 1921

TANNU TUVA Independent 1921

From 1928 under Russian influence

TIBET
Autonomous 1912

Claimed by G.B. from 1914

Lake Balkhash

Bay of Bengal

not hers to make) and practice (new emperors were supposed to be chosen from the generation after that of the late emperor to avoid confusion of relative positions within the imperial clan). Even when the new Tongzhi emperor reached his majority, she continued to manoeuvre her associates into positions close to the emperor. In 1898, when the young emperor began to associate with reformers pledged to modernise and reinvigorate China in the face of foreign incursion and evident incapacity to face the 20C, she had him imprisoned in the new Summer Palace which she had been improving (apparently with money designated for, and badly needed by, the Navy).

Weakened by the endless series of rebellions and by an increase in population which food production was not matching, the mid Qing also saw a series of disastrous wars with foreign powers anxious to open China to foreign trade: the first Opium War with Great Britain (1840–42), the Arrow War (or Second Opium War) with Britain and France (1856), the Sino-Japanese War (1894–95) and skirmishes with Russia.

Cixi seems to have been, at best, contemptuous of foreigners, and, at worst, is thought to have given support to the Boxers (originally an anti-dynastic movement which concentrated its later efforts on the massacre of foreign missionaries). When the Boxers reached Peking, a Japanese diplomat was murdered by Chinese troops and the foreign diplomats requested military protection from their governments. As an eight-nation army assembled on the coast, the empress asked all foreign diplomats to leave and the German minister was killed by imperial troops. It became clear that the Court was actively supporting the Boxers and the siege of the foreign legations in Peking was laid both by Boxers and imperial troops. When the Allied army finally arrived, the empress dowager fled to Xi'an, issuing edicts in the emperor's name taking the blame for everything. A protocol was signed by which the Chinese government paid reparation for the loss of life and Cixi eventually returned to Peking and began to give a series of receptions for foreigners who were charmed by the 'old Buddha'.

The Qing dynasty did not long survive the death of Cixi in 1908. Its downfall was finally achieved by an uprising which declared a Republican government in 1911. This Western-influenced movement was the result of more-than-50-years' search for a new pattern of society which had been forced on China by Western encroachment. During the late Qing this had had a profound and disastrous effect, although it had begun several centuries before.

Modern China. From the end of the 18C, it was clear that China, closed, conservative and uninterested in trade, was bound for a clash with the brash, expansive, mercantile West. China has not always been closed to the outside world yet even during the cosmopolitan Tang dynasty foreign policy was conducted on the basis of 'tribute'. Missions came from the rulers of surrounding countries such as Burma and from the Japanese and Korean courts, and all acknowledged China's superiority by presenting their 'tribute' on a regular basis.

The earliest Western visitors to China were papal envoys during the Yuan, followed by the Jesuit missionaries to the early Qing. The latter were anxious not to upset the Chinese for they felt that pleasing the emperor was the best way into China. Their success, achieved through astronomic, mathematical, architectural and painterly skills, was such that they provoked considerable jealousy amongst those like the Franciscans who accused them of succumbing to idolatry, and their attitude was diametrically opposed to that of the European traders who arrived in the 17C.

Both the Dutch and the British first traded through their East India Companies, behind which lay government power. From 1757 the Chinese authorities restricted all foreign trade to the city of Canton.

Foreign traders were not even allowed to reside in Canton throughout the year; they had to retreat to Portuguese Macau outside the trading season. They were not permitted to bring their wives or any foreign women into Canton; they were only permitted to live on a narrow strip of river shore and compelled to trade with a limited number of licensed traders.

Frustration with restrictions led to the embassies of Lord Macartney (1792–94) and Lord Amherst (1816) which sought to open the rest of China to trade and diplomacy. Both missions foundered for the Chinese insisted that European envoys should behave in the same way as envoys from surrounding states bringing tribute, and this the European dignitaries refused to do.

The 19C saw continuous pressure, often enforced by gunboats, to concede the opening of the whole of China to foreign traders, missionaries and diplomats. A triangular trade between Britain, China and India (in Chinese tea and porcelain and Indian cottons) was costing Britain silver but a solution to the drain of silver was found in the form of opium—specially grown in India for (illegal) shipment to China. There had previously been no addiction problem in China where opium was used medically as a painkiller. The silver drain was reversed when the British also started tea plantations in their colony of India, supplying the demand for tea which had previously been met by imports from China. The two Opium Wars (1842, 1856) were waged by the British in defence of their illegal opium traders and forcibly opened China to trade and foreign residents. The European powers subsequently divided China into 'spheres of influence', with the French strongest in the areas bordering on Vietnam, the Germans effectively controlling Shandong and the British strongest along the Yangtze and in Shanghai.

One of the effects of this foreign invasion was to demonstrate to intellectuals the need to modernise though there was profound disagreement throughout the late 19C and early 20C on the best methods. Supporters of the Reform Movement of 1898 sought Confucian 'self-strengthening', combined with the adoption of Western technology and educational methods. Many of their proposals—the adoption of foreign arms-manufacturing and boat-building techniques, foreign language study and study abroad—were implemented in the first years of the 20C after the Boxer uprising. One of the students who went abroad to study, supported by his brother who had emigrated to Hawaii, was Sun Yatsen (1866–1925) who studied medicine in Hong Kong and, to some extent influenced by foreign ideas, developed his Three People's Principles. These were Nationalism (aimed both against Western imperialists in China and the Qing government), Democracy (not a Chinese concept) and 'People's livelihood', a policy of economic reform involving the redistribution of land (which could be said to have its roots in traditional Chinese reforms) and control of capital. He founded a 'Revive China Society' in 1894 but was forced to flee China after an unsuccessful rising against the Manchus in Canton in 1894.

A stronger anti-Qing organisation was the Tongmenghui (United League) which was behind the finally successful rising against the Qing in 1911. Sun was in America, raising funds, at the time but returned to China to be elected provisional President of the Republic of China in 1911. He was forced to resign in favour of Yuan Shikai, a general who had betrayed the 1898 reformers to the Dowager Empress. Yuan was in command of one of the regional armies established at the end of the Qing. Yuan died in 1916, just after declaring himself emperor, and, though Sun Yatsen held power in Canton (his ancestral base), the rest of China came under the control of other regional army generals, like the late Yuan Shikai. From 1916 until 1949, in effect, China was divided between these 'warlords'.

The Nationalist Party (Kuo-min-tang in the Wade-Giles romanisation,

KMT for short, Guomindang in pinyin) was led by Sun until his death in 1925 when he was succeeded by a young general, Chiang Kai-shek (1887–1975). Chiang had divorced his first wife and converted to Christianity in order to marry Song Meiling, daughter of a Christian Chinese who had spent years in the USA and whose son and sons-in-law were amongst the richest and most powerful people in early 20C Shanghai. He had studied at a military school in Japan and become commandant of the KMT's crucial Whampoa Military Academy in Canton. Chiang Kai-shek used his military position to seize power in the KMT through the Canton coup in 1926, after the death of Sun Yatsen.

The Chinese Communist Party was founded in 1921. At its third congress in 1923 it was decided to unite with the KMT in the struggle against the warlords, a decision upheld by Moscow. The 'united front' did not survive long for in 1926 Chiang expelled the Communists from the KMT. During the 1927 'Northern Expedition', when Chiang Kai-shek led his army N against the warlords to establish a Nationalist capital in Nanjing, the Communist-led workers of Shanghai who had seized the city for the army were turned on and massacred by underworld gangsters at Chiang's instigation. The Communist Party was driven underground. Mao Zedong retreated to the countryside to work amongst the peasants though others, faithful to Moscow's instructions, tried to rise up in the cities, where they were doomed to failure.

By cultivating the peasants, particularly in remote areas, seizing and redistributing land and running educational programmes, Mao became convinced that a movement based amongst the peasantry was possible. It took him many years to convince other members of the Communist Party and Mao's rise to the chairmanship was an intense struggle in which he displayed considerable ruthlessness in the elimination of opposition, a trait which was to persist after 1949.

In 1930 Mao and the military specialist Zhu De founded the Jiangxi soviet. On the borders of several provinces, high in mountains, both administratively and physically remote, the Jiangxi soviet was supported by local peasants after land redistribution and new marriage laws were enacted. In his determination to get rid of the Communists whom he saw as a greater threat than the warlords, Chiang Kai-shek launched five massive encirclement campaigns and finally drove the Communists out of the soviet area in 1934. Turning defeat into a moral victory, Mao led his troops off and away on the Long March.

Starting out with some 100,000 soldiers, after a journey of 9500km (6000 miles) on foot, the Red Army reached an equally inaccessible mountain fastness in Yan'an (N Shaanxi province) with only about 8000 survivors, a year after they had set out. There were serious factional struggles during the March, against Zhang Guotao and with the 'Twenty-eight Bolsheviks' (Communist Party members who had studied in Moscow and still adhered to the anti-guerrilla warfare line of the Comintern) at Zunyi. It was at Zunyi in 1935 that Mao emerged as the unchallenged leader of the Chinese Communist Party and his policy of guerrilla warfare was upheld.

From 1936 to 1945, Yan'an was the headquarters of the Chinese Communist Party and the base both for guerrilla warfare and for the land reform, social reform and educational programmes that were to form the basis of Communist Party policy after 1949. Mao's army, though ill-equipped, was strongly disciplined, an almost unprecedented thing in China where most soldiers were regarded as little better than bandits. The army was used to help peasants in educational programmes, in agriculture and in building works.

A further blow came with the Japanese occupation of Manchuria in 1931 (where the last Qing emperor, Henry Aisin Gioro Pu yi was enthroned as puppet ruler) and the full-scale Japanese invasion of China in 1937. By the end of the year, much of the north of China, Shanghai and the Yangtse valley and Nanjing had fallen to the Japanese who treated the inhabitants of Nanjing, in particular, with unbelievable savagery, soldiers indulging (with the tacit approval of their officers) in an orgy of rape and murder that left 200,000 to 300,000 civilians dead. Chiang Kai-shek's government fled, first to Wuhan where the order was made to breach the Yellow River dykes to stop the Japanese advance, a measure which achieved its tactical end but killed hundreds of thousands of Chinese peasants. The Nationalists continued their flight W to Sichuan where they established a new capital in Chongqing.

By its failure to resist the Japanese advance and by its secret agreement with the Japanese to withdraw Chinese troops from the province of Hebei, the Nationalist government began to lose the support of the intelligentsia. By contrast the smaller Red Army, mobilising peasants for support in information-gathering and back-up guerrilla attacks in the NW, was offering a stronger resistance to the Japanese. Intellectuals began to leave the cities, making their way to the tiny mountain town of Yan'an. Even the warlords were disappointed in Chiang Kai-shek: as early as 1936, Chiang was seized and held prisoner in Xi'an by two of them, Zhang Xueliang and Yang Hucheng, who demanded that he stop the civil war against the Communists and mobilise instead against Japan. Negotiations involved Communist leaders including Zhou Enlai and Chiang was finally released, promising to purge the KMT of pro-Japanese members, release political prisoners and prepare to resist Japan.

A KMT leader, Wang Jingwei, conducted secret negotiations with the Japanese and left Chongqing for Nanjing to proclaim a rival, Japanese-supported, puppet 'Nationalist government' in 1940. In the following year, the second 'united front' between the Communists and the KMT, set up after the Xi'an incident, collapsed when the KMT army which had been skirmishing with the Communist forces, turned on the Communist New 4th Army of 10,000 men, of whom 1000 managed to escape, 2000 were killed and the rest were taken prisoner and held in KMT concentration camps.

With the entry of the USA into the Second World War, the KMT was supplied with American advisors and arms and financial support. Despite this, Chiang Kai-shek's regime failed to lead resistance against Japan and nearly 60 of the KMT generals joined the Wang Jingwei regime where they were instructed by the Japanese to fight the Communist guerrillas. General Stilwell was sent by Roosevelt to be Chiang Kai-shek's chief of staff but reported that the KMT army was 'underfed, unpaid, untrained, neglected and rotten with corruption…'. Despite a successful publicity campaign, masterminded by his beautiful wife, which painted Chiang as a clean-living simple man without a single vice, a devout Christian and moral man, there was appalling corruption in the KMT and an economic crisis with consequences recalling the downfall of many a previous dynasty.

Uncontrolled inflation meant hardship for all but a failure to provide any relief after a drought in Henan (1942–43) led to the deaths of between 2 and 3 million. A group of American observers travelled to Yan'an to look at the Communist resistance to Japan where the enthusiasm and organisation provided a telling contrast with Chongqing (though for this positive report, many were later to fall foul of Senator Macarthy).

After Japan's defeat in 1945, despite efforts at mediation by the Americans and continued pressure put by Stalin on the Communists to lay down their arms and join the Nationalists, civil war finally broke out in 1946. In 1947 the Communist armies, which had been actively carrying out land reform to ensure the support of the people in the countryside, turned from guerrilla tactics to strategic offense. The separate armies attacked KMT troops in pincer movements and, as they went, captured an enormous number of weapons from the KMT army which was being supplied both by the USA and the Soviet Union. Between 1948 and 1949 they gained decisive victories and on 1 October 1949 Mao stood on the great Gate of Heavenly Peace in Peking and proclaimed the Communist victory: 'The Chinese people have stood up…'.

Chiang Kai-shek and his followers had made preparations, removing treasures from the Palace Museum (which are now exhibited in Taibei) and gold to Taiwan where they set up the Nationalist government.

The task faced by the Communists in 1949 was a daunting one. For a hundred years China had been torn by wars with foreign countries and finally the Japanese invasion and civil war which had devastated agriculture and industry. Many of the factory-owners and managers, who at least had industrial experience, had fled to Hong Kong or Taiwan and foreign industrialists all left by the early 1950s.

Most experts agree that the Communists defeated the KMT for a combination of reasons: the skilful enlistment of the peasants through land reform and the involvement of the intellectual class which threw itself behind the war against Japan and the war against corruption in a 'nationalist' or patriotic movement; the powerful and visionary leadership of Mao Zedong, the effective collapse of the KMT, internally corrupt and unable to control inflation. In the first years after 1949 there was unity in the task of national reconstruction.

Amongst the first laws to be passed were the Land Law, giving men and women equal rights to hold land and involving the seizure of land from landlords which, in some parts of China was carried out with savagery, and the Marriage Law, outlawing arranged marriage. The central government presided over the remnants of a military organisation, for local government in the early years was organised on the basis of military regions. In government and in the takeover of industrial enterprises a triple alliance was instituted, consisting of trustworthy survivors of the previous administration (in factories this could include the factory owner if he had stayed behind), army representatives and party members.

Between 1951 and 1952, whilst China felt itself severely threatened by the Korean War, mass movements were organised throughout the country, to bring the entire population into the struggle against KMT supporters, to clean out corruption in the Communist Party and to bring its members into line, and to clean up 'undesirable' elements.

In agriculture, land reform cut the land into small pieces which were individually worked by peasants who were encouraged to form 'mutual-aid teams', pooling resources such as animals and ploughs. By the early 1950s these small teams had been largely reorganised into rural co-operatives which were larger than the teams. In 1956 the collectives were regularised (by household) when it was stipulated that they should consist of 300 households in flat areas, 200 in hilly areas and 100 in true mountains (where households were few and far between). They were subdivided into brigades of 20–40 households, often reflecting the size of the previous 'mutual-aid teams'. In effect, most collectives were old villages.

In industry, the Soviet model and Soviet aid were of early significance. The Soviet Union had not been quick to recognise Mao's victory. Nevertheless, Soviet loans and expertise were essential, particularly in redeveloping heavy industry. The Soviet management model was followed, as was the Soviet system of five-year plans, and a large number of Soviet technical experts came to China to set up plant.

The major movements of the 1950s and 1960s, the *Great Leap Forward* (1958) and the *Cultural Revolution* (1966–76), were launched with the aim of transforming the economy and purifying the Party, in the context of Soviet models which Mao increasingly felt to be inefficient and corrupt. Not all Chinese Party leaders agreed with him; some resisted, only to be dismissed (examples include Minister of Defence Peng Dehuai in 1959 for opposing the Great Leap and for continuing to advocate close ties with the USSR as Mao prepared to break off relations, and Liu Shaoqi, Chairman of the People's Republic, 1959–69, for opposing the Cultural Revolution).

The *Hundred Flowers* movement of 1957 was a prelude to the Great Leap: 'It is correct to let a hundred flowers blossom and a hundred schools of thought contend. Truth develops in the struggle with falsehood…Good things and good men develop in comparison with and in struggle against bad men…We people in the Communist Party know too little of our opponents…'. In response, intellectuals called for a loosening of Party control, a return to the work of legal reform, and called for academic freedom until, in June, appalled at the flood of criticism it had unleashed, the Party turned on them in an 'anti-rightist movement'. Nearly 10 per cent of the students at Peking University (the nation's most prestigious university) were denounced as 'rightists' and sent to the countryside for years of manual labour as a corrective.

Mao then turned to rural and industrial reforms, proclaiming the foundation of the People's Communes, far larger collective units of local government than the previous collectives. It was envisaged that the commune would replace the family, providing communal meals and childcare to release more women for manual work. A further plan was for all communes to set up some form of industry, most commonly smelting plants to produce iron for farm tools. Mao called this ruralisation of industry 'walking on two legs', joking that Stalin only had one leg, which was heavy industry. In retrospect, though some aspects of the commune (widespread medical provision and the ability to organise a greater number of people to carry out irrigation and road-building) were positive, there were many disasters. Apart from serious accidents, the success of the Great Leap was compromised by the falsification of production figures. Local officials concealed problems with impossibly high figures causing the central authorities to set next year's projections even higher. These factors combined with natural disasters in the 'three disastrous years' of the early 1960s when harvests failed and millions starved.

This new and unorthodox pattern of development together with Chinese attacks on Soviet foreign policy threatened Russia's traditional leadership of the Communist world. In 1960 all Soviet loans were frozen, projects abandoned and technicians withdrawn. Forced to readjust in the context of the disastrous harvests and Soviet withdrawal, the communes were reduced in size and centralised control of industrial enterprises was lessened. In 1961 private plots were reintroduced as an incentive to peasants to produce more for free sale.

Whilst Liu Shaoqi (who had succeeded Mao as State Chairman in 1959) and Deng Xiaoping attempted to correct the worst excesses of the Great Leap and to improve the food supply, Mao went into semi-retirement. In 1965 he returned to the task of purifying the Communist Party which he saw as thoroughly corrupt, launching the Cultural Revolution against 'revisionists' and 'capitalists'. The campaign was so-named, taking the Marxist term 'culture' to cover all aspects of social organisation that were not part of the economic base, for Mao felt that after the industrial and agricultural base had been socialised, it was necessary to transform culture. It was wrong to study anything that did not have a direct connection with socialist transformation, it was wrong to read old novels or to watch Peking opera; the new culture should reflect nothing but the new society.

In launching the Cultural Revolution, Mao made great use of four people (later caricatured as the 'Gang of Four'): Yao Wenyuan, Editor-in-chief of the 'Shanghai Liberation Army Daily'; Zhang Chunqiao, a propagandist and critic; Wang Hongwen, a young worker who rose to prominence during the Cultural Revolution in Shanghai, and Mao's third wife, an ex-film star called Jiang Qing.

Mao's first wife, Yang Kaihui, had been executed by the KMT in 1930, leaving two small sons; he then married He Zizhen who accompanied him on the Long March. He was still married to her when Jiang Qing arrived in Yan'an from Shanghai but he soon divorced He Zizhen to marry Jiang Qing. As became quite clear during the tele-vised trial of the Gang of Four (1980–81), Jiang Qing used the terror of the Cultural Revolution to eliminate those who knew her past or who had offended her.

Mao called on the young to 'Bombard the Headquarters' and for some years, the Cultural Revolution was an attack by the young on the old; students virtually seized power in many parts of China and were able to ransack houses and torture elderly writers, professors and intellectuals. Specialisation and expertise were regarded with suspicion and virtually all office workers and administrators, ballet-dancers, musicians, surgeons, specialists from museums, and teachers had to spend years in backward parts of the countryside, doing heavy manual work in order to understand the struggles of the peasants and the dignity of labour.

Schoolchildren were sent off to the countryside in the same way whilst many cities were 'ruled' by armies of young Red Guards who quarrelled amongst themselves and fought pitched battles in the city streets. The army was brought in to end street violence in 1968. All institutions, whether factory, office or school, were run by 'revolutionary committees' consisting of representatives of army, party and 'masses' seeking to achieve the goals of the Cultural Revolution: the elimination of corruption and favoured position and the establishment of absolute egalitarianism in the age of the 'new socialist man'. There were no more private plots in the countryside, no free markets, all was for the community, not the individual. There were no bonuses in the factories, only moral incentives. In education, the universities were reopened to 'worker-peasant-soldier' students whilst the children of intellectuals were positively discriminated against. The goal of education was to produce socialists, not specialists.

On 9 September 1976 Mao died. Just under a month later the 'Gang of Four' was arrested (on 6 October) by the army guard unit appointed to the State Council (the highest administrative body of the state, which co-ordinates the work of the ministries). Within months the policies of the Cultural Revolution were abandoned, to great popular relief. Mao's long-time opponent, Deng Xiaoping, quickly emerged as the *de facto* leader of the state and put into practice the economic reforms that were pioneered in his native province of Sichuan by Hu Yaobang and Zhao Ziyang. The major priority was the development of the economy and to this end financial incentives (bonuses) were introduced in factories; land was once more allocated to peasant families and the family was made the basis agricultural production unit. Throughout the early 1980s the economy made great progress, particularly in agriculture where bustling free markets improved the quality of city life and made many peasants comparatively rich.

By the end of the 1980s, however, the economy was increasingly troubled by rising inflation and a lack of control. There were serious shortages of power and fuel and a threatened shortage of grain (which peasants were abandoning in favour of cash crops). Deng Xiaoping's economic liberalism was not matched by political or cultural relaxations and intellectuals, as well as city workers (more strongly affected by rising inflation than the peasants), joined students in their call for democracy and an end to corruption. Though basic economic policies including the 'open door' to foreign investment and overseas trade remain, the movement for greater democracy was bloodily suppressed in Peking's Tiananmen Square on 4 June 1989.

CHRONOLOGICAL TABLE

Shang	c 1600–1066 BC	
Zhou	Western Zhou 1066–771 BC	

	Eastern Zhou 770–256BC
	                Spring and Autumn Period
	                722–481 BC
	                Warring States Period
	                403–221 BC	

Qin	221–206 BC	
Han	Western Han 206 BC–AD 23	
	Eastern Han 25–220	
Three Kingdoms	Wei 220–265	
	Shu 221–263	
	Wu 222–280	
Western Jin	265–316	
Eastern Jin/ Sixteen Kingdoms	Eastern Jin 317–420	
	Sixteen Kingdoms 304–439	
Northern and Southern States	Southern States	Song 420–479
		Qi 479–502
		Liang 502–557
		Chen 557–589
	Northern States	Northern Wei 386–534
		Eastern Wei 534–550 Northern Qi 550–577
		Western Wei 535–557 Northern Zhou 557–581
		Western Wei 535–557 Northern Zhou 557–581
Sui	581–618	
Tang	618–907	

	Later Liang 907–923
	Later Tang 923–936
	Later Jin 936–946
Five Dynasties	Later Han 947–950
	Later Zhou 951–960
	Ten Kingdoms 902–979
Song	Northern Song 960–1127
	Southern Song 1127–1279
Liao	907–1125
Western Xia	1032–1227
Jin	1115–1234
Yuan	1279–1368
Ming	1368–1644
Qing	1644–1911
Republic	1912–1949
People's Republic	1949–

Emperors of the Qing dynasty (1644–1911)

Shunzi	reigned	1644–1662
Kangxi		1662–1722
Yongzheng		1723–1735
Qianlong		1736–1795
Jiaqing		1796–1820
Daoguang		1821–1850
Xianfeng		1851–1861
Tongzhi		1862–1874
Guangxu		1875–1908
Xuantong		1909–1911

CHINESE RELIGION AND BELIEFS

The two major indigenous systems of thought in China, Confucianism and Taoism, arose at about the same time in the 5C BC. Neither was originally a 'religion', Confucianism being a reiteration of current moral values which became the basis of the imperial cult and Taoism a system of belief based upon a harmonisation of man with the natural order. Taoism, in particular, saw a split between the original philosophy and a developing popular religion closely associated with alchemy which sought to find an elixir of long life. Both added to the gradual growth of a mixed 'popular religion' (which came to dominate popular belief after the Tang dynasty).

Two non-indigenous religions came to play an important part in Chinese life. Islam, which entered China soon after its inception, was largely concentrated in the far northwest (Xinjiang province) but uprisings, uncertainties and persecutions in that area led to massive migrations so that Chinese Moslems can now be found scattered throughout China (though they are still most numerous in Xinjiang and the northwest). Buddhism, which entered China during the Han dynasty (206 BC–AD 220) permeated Chinese life to a great extent, achieving its greatest power during the Tang dynasty when it was ruthlessly suppressed by Tang emperors concerned about the wealth and power of the great monasteries and temples. It survived the suppression though it never reached the same heights and many of its deities and tenets were incorporated into popular religion.

Confucius is a Latinised version of *Kong fu zi* (Master Kong) used by the Jesuit missionaries to China in the 17C. Confucius was born in Qu Fu in the State of Lu in 551 BC and what little is known about his life is mainly gleamed from the 'Lun yu' (usually translated as the Analects), a collection of his statements collected by his disciples, probably after his death. He is thought to have become Chief of Police in the state of Lu but to have left suddenly in 497. Explanations for his precipitate departure vary; some suggest it was because he disapproved of the arrival of singing girls whilst his most famous disciple Mencius (c 372–288 BC) suggests that it was because the State of Lu failed to observe the proper rites (or ritual). He travelled, attempting to influence other rulers but, unsuccessful, eventually returned to Qu Fu where he died in 479 BC. The Analects are full of detail about the Master, how he avoided dark purple and maroon silk for collars and cuffs and did not wear red or violet informal robes, how he lifted his gown and held his breath when he entered his master's hall and ate sparingly (though the only rule he set himself with regard to alcohol was to stop drinking before he became confused). The impression is that of a rather pedantic and extremely fussy person (who could not sit if his mat was not straight and would not talk in bed) although D.C. Lau (who has translated the Analects), describes him as 'a man whose life was full of joy'. The 'joy' he lists—eating coarse rice and drinking water, eschewing wealth immorally gained and going swimming in spring 'with five or six adults and six or seven boys…and then to go home chanting poetry'—are rather the joys of a scout master.

Confucius is associated with a group of texts, the Five Classics (*Shi jing* or 'Book' of Songs, *Shu jing* or 'Book of Documents', *Yi jing* or Book of Changes, *Chun Qiu* or Spring and Autumn Annals and the *Li ji* or Record of Ritual) and the Four Books: the Analects, the Mencius and two chapters from the Li ji: Great Learning and the Doctrine of the Mean. A later classification of relevant texts lists Thirteen 'Classics': the Five Classics (with the Chun qiu counting as three when accompanied by three major commentaries on it including the Zuo zhuan), the Analects, the Mencius, the *Xiao jing* or Classic of Filial Piety (a 3C or 2C BC reworking of elements in the Li ji), the *Er ya*, a 3C BC collection of glosses on the texts, forerunner of later Chinese dictionaries, the *Yi li* (Ceremonials and Rituals) and the *Zhou li* (Rituals of Zhou, a Confucian reconstruction of the supposed governmental system of the early Zhou dynasty of almost 1000 years before). The inclusion of texts relating to the early Zhou (11–8C BC) is important for Confucius used to insist that he was not an innovator, simply that he wished to return to the great era of the Duke of Zhou (Zhou gong). The duke was the brother of the king who overthrew the Shang dynasty (in either 1122 or 1027 BC) and who effectively consolidated Zhou rule.

The ideas which Confucius expressed were those current during his lifetime, with his own stress on the duty of rulers to set an ethical example. Though he acknowledged the existence of heaven and the spirits, he did not often discuss the afterlife or the spiritual side of human experience. In order to return to the order of the golden age of the past, he believed it was important for all to recognise their place in society and to act accordingly. One of his most famous tenets is: 'Let the ruler be a ruler and the subject a subject; the father a father and the son a son'. This idea of making a concept into reality (with the ruler acting in accordance with the theory of rule) was later greatly expanded in 'the rectification of names'.

Order in society did not stop with the relationships between ruler and subject, father and son, for his concepts of subordination (common at the time) included the absolute subordination of women, not only to their husbands but also to their sons. Correct relationships between men and women were not only dependent on acceptance of subordination but also governed by contemporary rules of propriety. These rules were elaborated over the centuries, to the point that a Ming work on the correct running of a household contained a map with marked paths through the maze of courtyards to be used either by men or by women. If they adhered to these paths, they would not meet, which was proper, for in extended family groups there were people in different kinship relations who should not enjoy encounters. A Confucian dilemma was that of whether it was proper for a man to rescue his sister-in-law (whom he should not touch) from drowning by holding out his hand to her.

The concept of government by ethical example and of the 'gentleman', versed in literature, music and the rites, were the most important ideas developed by Confucius. These were set in the context of two ideas: those of 'the Way' and of virtue. D.C. Lau suggests that for Confucius, 'the Way' is virtually synonymous with 'Truth' in Western religion and philosophy and that virtue is conferred by heaven but must be cultivated in order to govern properly. Neither of these were original ideas but were current at the time. As he laid little stress on rewards after death, for Confucius the pursuit of morality was a duty to be undertaken for its own sake. Men who did so were 'jun zi' or gentlemen, the rest were 'small men' (effectively synonymous with rulers and subjects). The major attribute of the gentleman was 'benevolence' (*ren*), a word stretched infinitely to encompass 'do as you would be done by', loving others and not exploiting small men inappropriately. Loving others was set against the background of the family system and one's first duty of love and loyalty to the immediate family. An interesting passage in the Analects occurs where someone mentions a man known as 'Straight' because he reported his father to the authorities for stealing a sheep. Confucius retorted that in his village it was 'straight' to stand up for your relatives.

A further stretching of 'benevolence' took it to include the rites (ritual, including sacrifices, which expressed ancient views of morality). Other aspects of the gentleman include his attention to the study of literature and music and other gentlemanly skills like archery, charioteering, writing and mathematics. But it is above all the gentleman who has cultivated 'ren', courage, reliability, reverence and respectfulness and righteousness, who is fit to rule. The two major relevant passages in the Analects state: 'Guide them by edicts, keep them in line with punishments and the common people will stay out of trouble but will have no sense of shame' but 'Guide them by virtue, keep them in line with the rites and they will, besides having a sense of shame, reform themselves' (D.C. Lau, 'The Analects', Penguin, 1979).

The success of Confucianism in China lay in its theoretical stimulus to 'good government' and its usefulness as a philosophy for the bureaucracy which was growing as China moved from fragmentation to centralised government. It provided a theoretical basis for the traditional idea of the 'mandate of heaven' by which a ruler governed and which could be withdrawn if he failed to set a fine moral example. The collapse of enfeebled dynasties in natural disasters and peasant uprisings (both either exacerbated or directly inspired by the failure of central government to protect the livelihood of its subjects) were explained in terms of the withdrawal of heaven's mandate from an unfit ruler.

The subjects that a Confucian gentleman was expected to master became the basis for the examinations for entry into the imperial bureaucracy (first established during the Han dynasty). Candidates memorised vast tracts of the Confucian classic books and practised writing essays of commentary on these works; their education was liberal but not necessarily very practical as a preparation for government. Though the basic texts (the foundation of the examination 'syllabus') remained unchanged for 2000 years, commentaries grew. During the Song (960–1279) there was a massive renewal of interest in the Confucian texts, a revival of interest in the past (which extended to archaeology and the decorative arts) and a re-examination of the Confucian texts in the light of a new era. This movement to re-examine the Confucian texts and theories is known as Neo-Confucianism.

Interestingly, there is no term for 'Confucianism' in China; what we would call 'Confucian scholars' are simply known as *ju* or scholars. The dominance of the literati in traditional China was such that the physical attributes of the scholar (paleness, weakness to the point of anaemia and long fingernails) were those of all the heroes of novels and dramas, whilst tall, strong robust men were generally villainous or 'small' in heroic terms. Aside from cultural heroes, some of the ideas associated with Confucianism (though not in fact innovations of the Master) which have survived longest in China include filial piety (which is not only a moral but also a legal duty in contemporary China where it is an offence for people to fail to take care of their elderly parents) and veneration for education. The importance of family loyalty (mentioned by Confucius in connection with informing on a sheep-stealing parent; see above) was also written into the traditional legal system; families were also held responsible for errant members and disgrace could affect an entire group. The same principle persists in China; in 1949, people were given class labels on the basis of parental status. These were hard to shake off and families are still communally disgraced by a single offender. One of the grimmest reminders of family responsibility is the fact that today families are expected to pay (a tiny sum) for the bullet used to kill a condemned family member.

Taoism, whose major philosophers lived at about the same time as Confucius, can be seen as the antithesis of his views though some of the terms used are the same for the historical background was identical. The first figure is Lao zi (c 570–490 BC), said to have been an archivist and 'keeper of the lacquer grove' (lacquer—the sap of an indigenous tree—was an important, taxable product, protecting the timber of buildings and used as a water-, heat- and acid-proof covering for food vessels). He is traditionally viewed as the author of the 'Dao de jing' (Classic of the Way and of Virtue; Tao te ching in Wade-Giles), a somewhat mystic collection of passages (probably a composite text dating from the 3C BC and which, according to a recent discovery, should probably be renamed the De dao jing). Part of the mysterious quality of the work derives from the fact that it attempts to describe the indescribable, the 'dao'. Many of the descriptions are essentially non-descriptions in the form of 'without it, X would not be X': 'Without what makes it full, a valley might run dry, Without what makes it settled, earth might sink', and so on.

The 'dao' is the source of all life, the hidden principle. An ideal human state exemplifying the 'dao' is that of a baby, soft and supple, attributes that are borne out by mention of the contrast between a living person, 'supple and weak' and a 'hard and stiff' corpse.

A more accessible text is that of the 'Zhuang zi', also probably 3C BC but attributed to Zhuang zi (c 369–286 BC). A wonderful collection of parables, metaphors and poetry, the 'Zhuang zi' conveys more of the Taoist ideal of suppleness in fitting in with natural patterns. For example, Zhuang zi was found cheerfully singing and drumming on an upturned bowl (a babylike state) after the death of his wife. He explained to a shocked visitor that: 'Man's being has its seasons, its sequence of spring and autumn, summer and winter. If someone is tired and gone to lie down, we do not pursue him with shouting and bawling. She whom I have lost has lain down to sleep for a while in the Great Inner Room. To break in upon her rest with noise of lamentation would but show that I know nothing of nature's sovereign law...' (Arthur Waley, 'Three Ways of Thought in Ancient China', London 1939).

Another major concept in Taoism was that of 'wu wei', non-action or inaction, the opposite of Confucian activity.

Later Taoism divided into various schools, some more contemplative, seeking to learn from nature by retirement from the world into mountain retreats, some more active in the pursuit of an elixir of life. The former contemplatives are considered by Joseph Needham, author and 'overseer' of the fascinating and encyclopaedic 'Science and Civilisation in China' (Cambridge University Press) to have practically reached Darwinian ideas of natural selection through their earnest contemplation of nature in the search for its essential 'pattern' to which they sought to cleave. He has also found much of interest and amusement in the alchemical searches for the elixir of life (which involved some unfortunately explosive accidents). The search for eternal life had its roots in earlier Chinese belief that physical immortality (or the preservation of the body after death) conferred longer life on the soul. Chinese burial practices included the use of jade (in the Han, jade 'bodysuits' of hundreds of tiny plaques joined by gold and silver wire) which was believed to preserve the body, as well as various forms of preservation and occasional deliberate mummification. The Taoists took the matter further, eating gold and poisons like cinnabar and setting off on sea voyages to Penglai, the islands of the immortals.

In simple terms, the two major ways of thought can be seen as contributing to the traditional concept of the scholar. In his early life, he devoted himself to study in preparation for the exams which led to a place in the imperial bureaucracy and government service; in his leisure and when he retired, he would (ideally) retreat to a mountain cottage to drink wine, write poetry (full of natural imagery), paint and practise calligraphy. A popular saying in China which sums up the different ways of thought and their relevance to stages in life, refers to the gentleman as 'Confucian in office, Taoist in retirement and Buddhist as death approaches'.

Confucianism was very much to do with life and though Taoism dealt with the fact of death, its matter-of-fact approach did not allow for the consolation of ceremonial, which Chinese Buddhism provided. I use the term Chinese Buddhism for the philosophy of the North Indian founder of the faith, Sakyamuni (c 566–c 486 BC) was a rather bleak, distinctly unceremonial and reclusive search for enlightenment through abstention from desire.

Buddhism was transformed gradually in China. It seems to have arrived, via Central Asia, before or during the Later Han (AD 25–220) but its influence grew after the period of disunion that followed the fall of the Han, when the official 'Confucian' ideology of the guiding centralised state had clearly failed. After the re-establishment of central power under the Sui (581-618) tension between the state and the growing Buddhist monasteries was accompanied by tension between family worship (ancestor worship, antedating but sanctioned by Confucius) and the seclusion of the monastic system, integral to Buddhism. For the state, the wealth (and consequent economic power) of the tax-free monasteries was an economic threat; similarly, seclusion in a monastery, which meant that an individual could not carry out the essential duty of feeding and caring for the ghosts of his ancestors, was a real threat to the social order.

Several major persecutions of Buddhism, particularly under the Tang (618–907), meant that China never became a Buddhist state, though Buddhism entered and contributed to popular beliefs, especially those concerning death and the afterlife. When Buddhist texts were first translated into Chinese (in large numbers from the mid 2C AD), translators borrowed from existing Taoist ideas of eremitism, meditation (Taoist contemplation of nature) and Taoist magic ritual (associated with Buddhist Tantrism), all of which have been discussed at length by Erik Zurcher in his 'Buddhist Conquest of China' (Leiden, 1959).

The greatest contribution of Chinese thought to Buddhism was the development of the Chan (Japanese Zen) School which, in simple terms, provided the possibility of sudden enlightenment to the lay person, against the prevailing theory that enlightenment was only available to those who withdrew from family life into a monastery. Popular religion made most use of the power of Amitabha Buddha who presided over the 'pure land' or Western Paradise, where pure souls might find a haven after death. The Buddhist holy mountain of Jiuhua shan in Anhui, dedicated to Ksitigarbha, the Boddhisattva who led souls to the Western Paradise, sees many two-part funerary services in which the Boddhisattva Ksitigarbha first 'judges' the soul of the dead and then the Boddhisattva Amitabha receives the soul in paradise.

Other aspects of popular belief drew upon a variety of sources: Taoist priests presided over the choice of a site (and auspicious date for works to commence) for buildings and tombs, according to the *feng shui* system. Feng shui (literally 'wind and water') texts date back to the Han but the system certainly antedates the texts. It prescribes the siting of buildings, oriented southwards, with hills to the N and water nearby, all eminently practical aspects overlaid by *post-facto* textual justification and the use of the geomancer's compass, marked with the hexagrams and trigrams also used in the classic of divination, the 'Yi jing'. Geomancy, whilst practised all over China, seems to have been strongest in the south, probably because of the practice there of secondary burial. In the north bodies were buried once, under rounded mounds, which can still be seen in the fields. Graves in the south were more elaborate affairs, with horseshoe-shaped walls protecting the mound. It was common practice to bury bodies for a period of a year or two in temporary graves; then they were dug up, the bones scraped clean and sometimes crushed (by relatives; another filial duty), placed in small ceramic urns with elaborately decorated lids and buried in a second, permanent grave. Geomancers were also often responsible for the erection of pagodas on hilltops (to avert local disasters) and are still used widely in Hong Kong, not only in the siting of new buildings but in the periodic rearrangement of office furniture to improve a company's fortune.

The eight trigrams (which provide all possible combinations of a series of three broken and unbroken lines), were used in divination, using the 'Yi jing' and a handful of milfoil sticks, are not the only numerical group of significance in China. The somewhat mysterious Ten Heavenly Stems are combined with the 'Twelve Earthly Branches' to form the 60-year cycle, the Chinese equivalent of our century. Traditional dates were always written in the form of a stem and a branch, indicating where they came in the 60-year cycle (though not in which cycle the date fell). Personal horoscopes were cast in the form of stems and branches as well as the 12-year cycle represented by 12 animals and were used to judge the suitability of marriage partners. The 12 animals are the rat, ox, tiger, hare, dragon, snake, horse, sheep, monkey, cockerel, dog and pig (1948 was a rat year).

Taoist priests also carried out exorcisms and provided spells for all sorts of events, most notably in the case of disease. Magical formulae were written on pieces of paper which were burnt and the ashes made into a sort of tea to be drunk by the patient; another example of the view of the power of words in China.

Christianity, whose 19C and 20C missionaries made valiant attempts to wipe out such superstitions, was said by one expert to have arrived too late in China, when the popular pantheon was already overcrowded with a deity for every occasion and every social group. The Jesuits, the first major group of missionaries to arrive in China (in the last years of the 16C), sought to influence the emperor and the court, believing that the whole of China would then follow. Other groups of Catholic missionaries followed, jealous of the Jesuits' success at court (which was mainly won by skilful calendrical and mathematical calculation, cannon casting and artistic and architectural skills).

The Rites Controversy which raged in the 18C over whether or not ancestral rituals could be performed by Christian converts (Pope Clement XI in 1715 and Pope Benedict XIV in 1742 said not) was largely responsible for the decline of Jesuit influence, followed by the suppression of the order in 1774. They achieved a small popular success in that Matteo Ricci did join the Chinese popular pantheon as the patron saint of watchmakers. The Jesuits were succeeded by the Lazarists but the greatest influx of Christian missionaries, now including non-Catholics, came after the enforced opening of China to the outside world after the Opium Wars in 1860. Converts were made, although the faith has only survived in any strength in the coastal treaty ports, and medical missionaries opened the first western hospitals in China (most notably the Rockefeller-funded Peking Union Hospital which, until it reassumed the name in the 1980s, was previously the Peking No. 1 Hospital). Some strange small sects survive, notably a group of ranters in Fujian who are subject to public order complaints as they shout loudly during services.

In contemporary China religion is not outlawed by the constitution, but preaching is. There are sizable Christian communities in the old treaty ports and Christianity is currently enjoying something of a vogue amongst the young. The Catholic church has been split; the Protestant groups banded together soon after 1949 and formed a 'patriotic' organisation, with a first loyalty to the state; whilst some Catholics did the same, others insisted on the primacy of the Pope and have suffered imprisonment in consequence.

Islam is still strong, mainly in the northwest, but it is Buddhism in its popular form that remains the most widely followed religion. Even during the Cultural Revolution both Islam and Buddhism gained some strength from the support of overseas co-religionists whilst Taoism, a uniquely

Chinese system of belief, suffered, especially because of superstitious practices like making spells and talismans. Today there is a growth in study of philosophical, if not religious Taoism. Confucianism, similarly, declined with the end of the traditional state but many of its tenets, particularly those relating to family observances and respect for authority and education, persist.

ART, CRAFT AND ARCHITECTURE

Painting

Though wall paintings have survived in tombs and cave temples, the fragility of most Chinese painting together with the painters' training, which consisted largely of making exact copies of great works of the past, make the attribution and dating of paintings in China extremely difficult. Chinese painting is usually done on paper or silk, using a brush and, frequently, black ink alone. The ink was made from soot or lampblack, mixed with animal glue and scents such as musk or camphor to hide the smell of the glue. The ink was then pressed into moulds, often impressed with delicate designs—good inksticks could be extremely expensive and valued as heirlooms. Brushes were made of animal hairs glued into bamboo (occasionally enamel or porcelain) tubes. The hard inkstone was ground and mixed with water on an inkslab, made of slate or jade, carved with a shallow depression at one end. Depending on the amount of water mixed, the ink would be solid and black or a thin grey wash; shades of black and grey are found in traditional paintings.

Painting manuals contained examples of mountains, huts, bamboos, pines, figures and other essential elements of the classic painting. The amateur would copy these endlessly until he had mastered every detail and only then would he feel confident that he could combine such elements into his own painting. Innovators who developed the possibilities of the ink and wash include *Ni Can* (1301–74) with his 'dry brush' style, *Liang Kai*'s impressionistic portraits (13C), his near-contemporary, *Mu Qi*'s 'Six Persimmons', similarly simple and impressionistic, *Shi Tao* (1630–1707), whose 'Ten-thousand Ugly Ink-blots' starts with splashes which are combined into a long landscape scroll (Suzhou Museum), and *Zhu Da* (or *Ba da shan ren*; 1626–1705) whose solidly blocked fish and brooding birds form dark abstract forms on the white paper.

Very few paintings which can be attributed with certainty survive from before the Song. Exceptions include the silk scroll from the Han dynasty Mawangdui Tomb (Changsha) and the wall paintings at Dunhuang, dating from the Tang, which show the beginnings of a great landscape style in the background to paintings of the life of the Buddha. Literary reference provides more information on the development of traditional ink and wash painting: *Xie He*'s 'Gu hua pin lu' (Classification of Ancient Paintings) of the 6C AD described the principles which included composition and placing of elements, transmission by copying ancient models, accurate use of colour and accurate depiction and the first and most important principle of 'spirit resonance' by which the painter had to 'become' the subject before he could paint it.

There were various groups of painters in China: those who were paid for their paintings (craftsmen), amateurs and educated gentlemen like the Tang painter *Yan Liben* who devoted himself to painting whilst holding a variety of official positions—Senior Secretary of the Peerage Bureau, President of the Board of Works and Minister of State.

During the Song two major 'schools' of Chinese painting emerged, one based upon the Imperial Painting Academy set up (on the basis of previous academies) by the Hui zong emperor (reigned 1101–26). The favoured style in the Academy was delicately naturalistic, depicting birds and flowers on silk album leaves. Every feather of the bird, every petal and leaf of each flowering branch was painted with minute attention to detail of appearance and, in the pursuit of accuracy, jewel-like coloured pigments were used. This 'academic' style continued in favour throughout succeeding centuries, co-existing with the very different 'literati' style. This latter was more scholarly in theory, basing itself on such essays as Xie He's. It was both style and subject matter which distinguished the academic and literati painters; the former concentrating on natural detail in birds and flowers, the latter expressing the grandeur of nature in lofty monochrome mountain scenes.

Guo Xi (c 1020–90), himself a major landscape painter, described the painter's methods for depicting depth and distance which help in the reading of a landscape with its various viewpoints (a technique quite distinct from that of the Western landscape, viewed from a fixed spot). First is *jin yuan* (near distance) where the viewer looks across a flat ground into the distance; next, *shen yuan* (deep distance) where the viewer appears to be standing on a raised area in the foreground; and, finally, *gao yuan* (high distance) where the viewer looks up from the foreground to towering mountains. These principles are best expressed in hanging scrolls although they are also used to provide a series of landscape foci in handscrolls. To aid the viewer to take the appropriate viewpoint, a tiny figure is often included in the foreground and landscapes often include small huts with scholarly recluses enjoying wine or music, attended by small boy servants or figures approaching these rustic retreats on donkey-back, again with a small boy carrying a qin (zither) or rolls of paper for painting.

Because of their fragility and the fugitive nature of the colours, Chinese paintings were never intended for permanent display. Handscrolls and albums were kept closed in damp-proof camphorwood boxes until friends came round and then they would be unrolled and enjoyed in company, the landscapes of handscrolls gradually unfolding as they were unrolled. Even hanging scrolls would be put up only when visitors arrived or on special occasions. Great care would be taken to choose the right painting for the occasion, with huge calligraphic scrolls of auspicious characters reserved for birthdays and paintings reflecting the seasons hung as appropriate.

Other types of painting include the decorative ancestral portrait. Often produced in pairs (husband and wife), these were usually posthumous paintings of the deceased dressed in wonderfully lavish silken clothing with, in the case of men, all their official regalia. Another type, scorned by the literati, less colourful than the academic paintings but just as detailed, is the 'genre' painting, depicting bustling street scenes and events. The best known example is the 11–12C handscroll by *Zhang Zeduan*, 'Going Up the River on the Eve of the Qing Ming Festival', depicting the busy streets of Kaifeng in ink and wash. In the Ming there was a fashion for a sort of combination 'genre' and academic painting of children at play, showing every detail of the children's faces, clothing and top-knotted hairstyles as well as their games, but using colour (unlike Zhang Zeduan). In the Qing imperial events were often depicted in this colourful, detailed style and there are many examples in the collections in the Gu gong (Forbidden City Museum in Peking, where the original of the Zhang Zeduan painting is also held). The oldest paintings in the imperial collection (pre-Ming) are only displayed in October when the weather conditions are best, being neither too hot nor too damp.

Painting is still immensely popular in China, and remains an amateur enthusiasm as well as an art-school speciality. Two major painters of the 20C have helped to bring a new vitality to brush painting: *Qi Baishi* (1863–1957), whose strong black brush-strokes are combined with equally strong splashes of colour, and *Xu Beihong* (1896–1953). Xu studied in Paris in the 1930s and was a master of both Western oils and traditional Chinese brush painting, painting the galloping horses (1944) that were popular in the West in the 1950s. Like Qi Baishi, he combines colour with his strong brush strokes in many of his paintings. There are a number of Xu Beihong's paintings in the Shanghai Museum and a special museum devoted to his work (with models of his studio) in the N of Peking.

Ceramics

There were two major ceramic types during the neolithic period, a fine-grained reddish earthenware associated with the Yangshao culture (5th–3rd millennium BC), sometimes decorated with mainly black pigments in geometric and animal designs (seen in the neolithic village of Banpo, outside Xi'an), and a fine black burnished ware made on the wheel produced by the Longshan culture. Particularly in the Longshan, the forms of ceramic vessels, including a high-footed cup and many forms of tripod, appear to anticipate the succeeding bronze age forms.

During the bronze age (c 1500 BC–4C BC), ceramics were used in daily life though they were subordinate in ritual (and therefore in burial) to bronzes. Even so, during this period there was a technical breakthrough in the manufacture of stonewares. The clays used for stoneware can be fired to a higher temperature than earthenware and at these higher temperatures they fuse to form a relatively impermeable (waterproof) body which is harder and more resilient than earthenware. The stonewares were often partially glazed with a transparent glaze on the shoulder of vessels. Green lead glazes appeared in the Han when ceramics were very widely used in burial. Models of houses, granaries, farmyards with pigs in their sties and watchdogs curled up inside the gate, human figures playing board games, all made in low-fired earthenware covered with a green lead glaze, were placed in tombs to accompany the spirit to the next world.

In the period after the fall of the Han such models were still made, although often in the olive-glazed stoneware characteristic of southern China and known as Yue ware after the southern kingdom of Yue (SE China). Water-droppers (for use with inksticks and brushes in calligraphy or painting), chicken-headed ewers and shallow dishes, sometimes carved with a simple lotus flower design symbolising Buddhism (which had just entered China), were also common Yue ware products.

The same period saw the gradual development of porcelain, which first appeared in Sui tombs. Made from special clays (which vary slightly from north to south China though they are always feldspathic), porcelains are high-fired, with the glaze fused completely with the body, translucent (if the body is thin enough) and make a musical note when struck. During the Tang, plain, white porcelains were used as practical, durable and non-porous containers for food and drink. They were also exported in great quantities and have been found at contemporary sites in Egypt and along the African coast. Porcelain remained a mystery, first to Arab travellers and later to westerners, until the early 18C when Böttger managed to make porcelain at Meissen.

Tang funerary ceramics were very different from the elegant monochrome porcelain. Following the Han tradition, models were still placed in tombs to accompany the spirit but whilst the Han stressed ordinary life (with an accent on agricultural production in the farmyard and fishfarm models), the Tang—the great age of overseas trade, elegance and wealth—stressed these even in burial models. Made of earthenware, splashed with blue, green, yellow, brown and cream glazes, Tang funerary models are of all-female orchestras, fat fashionable court ladies (reflecting changes in current fashions and the devastating effect of the concubine Yang Guifei on the female form), officials in high hats, and camels and horses, representing the trade with central Asia. Some of the horses had real horsehair tails and manes. These funerary models were mass-produced in piece-moulds, and produced as matching sets. There were sumptuary regulations, just as there had been during the Han, forbidding excessive consumption at funerals and restricting both the number of figures and their maximum height (about 30cm), but these regulations were frequently broken, as museum exhibits testify.

In the period between the Tang and Song, the most notable ceramics were those produced by the northern dynasty of the Liao (947–1125; founded by a Mongolian group). Surviving Liao ceramics are funerary earthenwares, using the same palette as the Tang but in rather eccentric elongated shapes of a particular elegance. They include elongated ceramic versions of the leather water-bottles used by nomadic horsemen.

The Song was one of the great periods of ceramic production with a multitude of kilns, north and south, producing a variety of ceramics from stonewares to porcelain in distinct types of kiln: most notably coal-fired mantou (or steamed bread bun) kilns in the north, and long 'dragon kilns' in the south, built up hillsides and invariably wood-fired. Porcelain production was beginning to concentrate in the south where the best clays were to be found and translucent vessels with a glassy glaze with a blueish tinge (qingbai or blue-white in Chinese) are characteristic of the south whilst northern porcelain, often known by its kiln name of Ding, was a creamy colour, frequently with moulded designs. Ding bowls were fired upside down on bare rims which were later bound with dark brown copper bands, providing an elegant contrast with the cream coloured body. Another major northern ware used the same techniques of production: wheel-thrown plates and bowls were pressed onto moulds carved with floral designs and then covered with an olive green glaze. Known to the Chinese as 'green ware' (sometimes further distinguished by its kiln-name), the European name of celadon was first applied by the French, borrowing the name from a character who wore green-grey clothing in 'Astrée', an 18C French play by D'Urfé.

Southern green wares (or celadons) of the Song were also covered with an iron-oxide glaze but their blue-green colour reflects different physical conditions in the kilns. Other northern wares whose glaze colour was also based on iron oxide, were the grey blue Ru ware, crackled Guan and the grey-blue suffused with purple known as Jun. Ru is extremely rare, produced at the northern imperial kilns (in Kaifeng) where manufacture was interrupted after only a few years when the north of China was invaded and the court fled S to Hangzhou (1127). Only some 30-odd examples are known and most are in collections outside China.

Before widespread excavation of kiln sites (mainly after 1949), it was thought that ceramic kilns specialised in one particular ware and, indeed, traditional Chinese connoisseurs often referred to ceramics by the name of the kiln as an indicator of type. Excavation has revealed a more complex picture: though kilns did tend to produce more of one kind of ware, in northern kilns specialising in white wares, for example, numbers of black and green shards have also been found. Thus, though black-glazed wares are often known as Jian wares (after a kiln in Fujian province), black glazed shards have been found in a large number of other kiln sites. Jian wares were very popular in Japan where they are known as temmoku. The majority of those that found their way to Japan were probably produced in Fujian whose ports saw a vast volume of trade with Japan (and Korea and SE Asia) during the Song. Dark-toned, Jian wares were dominantly large tea bowls, used in the Japanese tea ceremony, with a glaze that was subtly spotted with silver ('oil spot') or streaked with dark brown ('hare's fur'). These effects were also produced by manipulating iron oxide in the glaze. The way that the thick glaze gathered in drips near the foot was also much appreciated by the Japanese who like the combination of haphazard unevenness of surface with the perfection of body form.

With one major exception, most Song ceramics relied for their dramatic effect on their elegant form and the monochrome glaze. The moulded designs on some northern vessels remains a subtle, underglaze effect. The exception is known as Cizhou ware (after the Cizhou kilns in Hebei), a stoneware covered with a cream glaze and surface-decorated either by carving down through the slip to the greyer body beneath or by painting, usually in dark brown, sometimes red and green, floral designs or scenes from novels and folk stories.

The overall decoration of Cizhou wares may have been one inspiration for a major development in ceramic taste which occurred during the Yuan, the development of 'underglaze blue' or 'blue and white' wares. Other Yuan ceramics continued Song styles although the vessels tended to be rather more massive, compared with their slim and elegant predecessors. The technique of blue and white underglaze painting—using cobalt on the body of the vessel (over a white slip) before covering with a translucent glaze and firing the vessel—was a complicated one, particularly because porcelain is fired at such high temperatures that many colouring materials behave unpredictably. Previously, coloured glazes had been applied to earthenwares or stonewares which are fired at lower temperatures. During the Yuan, at the same time as experimenting with cobalt blue, the Chinese potters also tried to used copper to produce an underglaze red effect but the results, which can be seen in many museums, were unsuccessful for the red is often greyish; copper did not behave as predictably as cobalt.

The origins of blue and white are complex for the cobalt was imported from the Near East (Chinese native cobalt contained a lot of manganese which was difficult to control and was not used until methods of purification were perfected in the 15C), and many of the designs painted on vessels were taken directly from the incised floral scrolls on Near Eastern metalwork. This has led some to assume that the technique itself originated in Persia. However, the major feature was the use of porcelain; whilst other nations could use cobalt on earthenware, none but the Chinese could make porcelain at this time, and there are also the experiments in underglaze red which were conducted in China. It must be concluded that this was a Chinese invention based on imported cobalt and imported metalwork designs, facilitated by the 'pax mongolica' which reigned from China across the Gobi into the Near East, allowing free trade through the Mongol dominions. Almost as soon as the technique was perfected, huge blue and white vessels began to make their way back across Central Asia to Turkey and Persia where there are impressive collections of early 14C Chinese blue and white in the Topkapi Museum in Istanbul and at the Ardebil shrine.

Throughout the Yuan and the Ming blue and white was improved. The achievements can be seen in the contrast between the thick, heavy vessels of the Yuan with their uneven spotted blue decoration and the tiny, light and translucent bowls of the Chenghua period (mid 15C) with their pure sky-blue floral scrolls.

Though blue and white porcelain dominates Ming ceramics, the same period also saw the deliberate revival of Tang dynasty 'three-colour' earthenware, imitating Tang funerary wares. The Ming palette was different from the yellow, browns and greens of the Tang, preferring purple and blue with some yellow and green, but the style of glazing earthenware was the same. This type of ware was used for pots as well as in roof tiles and the last of the funerary models (for paper substitutes were being used in increasing numbers).

Towards the end of the Ming, when ceramic control was very good and some fine blood-red pieces were being made (in contrast with the Yuan failure to produce red at high temperatures), the beginnings of the last great innovation in Chinese ceramics can be seen. This was the use of overglaze enamel colours. Unlike underglaze colours which, because they had to endure the high temperatures of firing porcelain, were restricted to a few minerals, overglaze decoration was done on finished porcelain. After painting, the vessel was fired a second time at a very low temperature, sufficient to soften the glaze surface and allow the colours to adhere, but not hot enough to affect the pigments used, making a much wider range of colours possible. In late Ming examples blue and white underglaze designs were often further embellished with overglaze enamels. This made ceramic production complicated for porcelain, with or without underglaze blue designs, was made in Jiangxi province at the small town of Jingdezhen, the porcelain capital of China for hundreds of years. Jingdezhen was well inland and porcelain was brought to the coast by water. Enamelling was often done in Guangzhou, on the coast, hundreds of kilometres away. As the export trade developed in the 17C and 18C, plain porcelain vessels were shipped to Guangzhou for enamelling according to European orders but the early blue and white export wares had to be made inland, in Jingdezhen.

The colours of enamels allowed for all sorts of landscape scenes, interiors, portraits, animals, birds and flowers to be painted in a variety of colours on pieces of porcelain. In the early period, at the end of the Ming, the enamels were translucent, the white of the body showing through, but in the first years of the 18C new colours were first employed, a pink (made from gold) and a solid white which meant that enamel painting could achieve a new, non-translucent solidity. During the Qing monochromes were also popular with numerous reds, turquoise, coffee and cream, 'peach bloom' (pink shading to green), 'tea-dust' (a sort of olive green-brown) and ceramics imitating lacquer, jade and wood. Forms were equally varied: from tall teapots in the form of auspicious characters to duck-shaped tureens and imitations of Meissen openwork baskets in porcelain.

Bronze and Metalwork

During the Shang and the Zhou (16C BC–221 BC) elaborately cast bronze vessels were used in ritual worship and burial. No substantial evidence has yet been unearthed of a period of development which scholars assume must include a phase of wrought-metal work. In the earliest Shang site (Erlitou near Luoyang), bronze vessels cast in pottery piece-moulds have been found and it is this technique that is characteristic of all subsequent bronze age production. Multi-part moulds inscribed with designs that were to cover the body of the bronze were luted together and filled with molten bronze (a different alloy from that use in western Asia). The inevitable breaks in pattern where the mould parts joined were exploited in decorative projecting flanges. Lost wax (cire-perdue) does not appear to have been used until about the 5C BC.

Some of the vessels produced reflect late Longshan ceramic forms—tripods, jugs, tall libation cups. The vessels are all food and wine containers and, during the Shang, there was complex animal decoration: sometimes the whole vessel is in the form of an animal (or animals), the surface is decorated with small animals in low relief and covered in an overall scrolling pattern between them. Thus a vessel in the form of two rams may have pairs of birds on the neck, wings on the shoulders and curly dragons lower down with serpent-like scales between them. Most Shang bronzes bear several *taotie* 'monster' masks, with a pair of high relief eyes, beneath curling horns, and sometimes pointed, elfin ears, with a snarling upper jaw beneath the eyes. Sometimes a raised flange forms a sort of nose between the eyes. The significance of the *taotie* is not known though in bronzes used in burial it may have acted as a protection against evil spirits.

Bronzes were frequently produced in matching sets (rarely found in western museums where they appear as individual items); the display in the treasury in the Xi'an Provincial Museum emphasises this aspect. It appears that they were used in life, to offer food sacrifices to the gods, and that they were later buried with their owner who could continue his offerings in the other world.

In the succeeding Zhou period, inscriptions appear quite frequently on bronzes, sometimes commemorating the gift of land or a victory. Later Zhou bronzes were sometimes inlaid with copper or gold in the increasingly linear decorative style that was to continue into the Han.

Bronzes were still produced in the Han, but their forms were simpler and the use of ritual bronzes appears to have been dying out as the Confucian state came into being. Bronze was still used for mirrors (with one highly polished surface and a decorated back) into the Tang period. With the taste for archaic, archaeological forms in the Song, Ming and Qing, more bronzes were made, imitating the Shang and Zhou forms but now used as flower vases rather than significant objects of ritual.

Gold and silver were used most notably during the Tang, for chased vessels, often of silver inlaid with gold are common, but gold and silver never occupied the position of opulence that they do in the West. They were used in jewellery and in filigree hair-ornaments worn by women, but it is thought that the Tang vogue for chased silver was due to the presence of Near Eastern silversmiths in the Tang capital of Chang'an.

A later metalware form, developed during the Yuan and perfected in the Ming, was cloisonné enamelling. A plain bronze vessel was covered in tiny wire shapes (outlines of lotuses and other flowers and leaves), glued on with rice paste. Thick enamel colours were painted in between the wires (which served to separate the colours) and the vessel was fired at a low temperature, after which the surface was polished to make the colours and the fine golden wires shine. The vessels are richly coloured in a sort of stained-glass effect.

Sculpture and Carving

Much sculpture in China is associated with religion and ritual. The Qin emperor's tomb outside Xi'an is known for its larger-than-life earthenware soldiers in three armies and other ceramic and bronze sculpture. From the Han dynasty, tombs were fronted by stone sculptures: carved stone columns with leonine figures around the base and supporting a square inscription at the top and great figures of elephants, horses and lions which were developed into the major spirit roads of the Tang-Qing, including numbers of human figures. The interiors of Han tombs were either painted, lined with bricks or stones, stamped or carved with figures and animals or constructed of stone imitations of timber constructions. The great Buddhist cave temples are filled with life-sized or larger stucco statues, as are Buddhist, Taoist and Confucian temples. Wooden or lacquer figures, often of the Buddha and his disciples, and smaller bronze figures used as altar-pieces fill the temples of China.

In contrast, carving of semi-precious materials including jade, ivory and wood, is frequently not religious. Tiny carved figures were carried in the sleeve, larger pieces placed in the home, on wooden stands or in specially constructed pieces of furniture with multiple shelves intended to display bibelots. Scholars used jade brushrests in the form of pointed rows of mountains, carved ivory or bamboo wristrests when writing, and they set small carvings of mountains with trees, tiny figures and pavilions in jade or other hardstones on their painting tables for inspiration.

Many neolithic cultures used jade but only in China did it survive the stone age to become significant as a material believed to have the magical property of preserving the body after death and as symbolic of Confucian virtues: unbending, translucent (honest) and musical (when struck). Jade is a name given to two hardstones, jadeite and nephrite, similar in appearance but chemically distinct. Neither was found in traditional China, and jadeite was only imported from Burma in the 18C AD. The nearest source of nephrite was Central Asia and the use of nephrite from the neolithic period is surprising, suggesting that there must have been trade routes as early as the 3rd millennium BC, bringing nephrite thousands of kilometres to China. Jade is a hard material (nephrite is 6.5 on Moh's scale) and cannot be cut by a steel knife without an abrasive so it must have been extremely hard to work in the Stone Age. From well before the Han, it was used for adornment, carved into decorative plaques for belts or sewn onto the clothing or suspended from a silken girdle. Later pieces were often 'pocket pieces', in the form of small animals. In the Qing, jade-carvers, producing decorative pieces for display, made use of the different colours in a single stone to carve a floral spray in green with a tiny brown grasshopper or used a piece that shaded from green to white to carve a tiny Chinese cabbage.

Lacquer

Produced from the sap of *Rhus verniciflua*, a tree native to China (and later introduced to Korea and Japan), lacquer was first used well before the Han as a timber preservative for it has the unusual property of hardening in the damp. During the Han, before the invention of porcelain, lacquer was widely used on a fine wooden base to make practical food vessels—plates and double-lugged cups. At that time lacquer was one of the materials (like silk and rice) used for tax purposes. Coloured with various substances—mercury sulphide, iron oxide and cadmium, producing red, black and yellow—Han artists used it as a paint on lacquered vessels, tracing sinous cat-like animals, mist-shrouded mountains and swirling scrolls of cloud.

Carved lacquer was a comparatively late discovery, emerging in the Yuan, after lacquer had fallen behind porcelain as a major material for eating utensils. Again using a wooden base, many layers of lacquer were painted on, mainly in red, sometimes with interspersed yellow or black layers used as markers or to provide contrast. The lacquer was then carved, to some depth, when it was of a rubbery consistency. As the colour red is associated with good fortune in China, red lacquer pieces of the Ming and Qing were auspicious presents, frequently associated with marriage.

Textiles

Silk was known to the Shang (although a cut cocoon has been found at a neolithic site, perhaps suggesting earlier use) and has survived in traces in burial when silk fabrics were used to wrap bronzes. Though little survives from the early period, literary accounts mention the use of linen and hemp for clothing, and fur pelts, with silk reserved for ceremonial garments. Most garments were made from plain twill, satin or gauze weave silk but there was one type of tapestry weaving, called *ke si,* which was traditionally done by men and used for imperial clothing.

As little has survived, evidence for changes in dress style has to be drawn from wall-paintings in tombs and ceramic tomb figures although some examples of Tang silks and articles of clothing have recently been unearthed in the Gobi desert. Major changes in styles of dress can be seen in the Tang and the Qing. In the Tang there was a development from the high-waisted, tight-bodiced female dress to the looser robe, combined with large turban-like hats and padded-toed shoes (almost upholstered at the toe end). Loose, V-necked, crossover gowns, belted at the waist, worn over under-trousers (for both men and women), were worn in the Song, Yuan and Ming, and it was in the Qing that the Manchu style of high-necked crossover garments, sometimes with a high collar, was introduced. As before, clothing was multi-layered, with perhaps several gauze undergowns beneath a thicker embroidered outer gown. It was common, both in the Qing and earlier periods, for women of the higher classes to wear wraparound pleated skirts under their gowns, whilst working women commonly wore a shortish jacket and trousers for convenience of movement.

Architecture

As Chinese builders have always relied on timber as the primary structural material, their buildings have been relatively short-lived. The earliest surviving timber building is the small hall of the Nan chan Temple on Wu tai shan (618–782) and other pre-Ming examples are extremely rare. Material for the history of Chinese architecture has to be gathered elsewhere: from excavated foundations (from the neolithic period onwards) and architectural items such as tiles and pillar bases (Warring States onwards), and most usefully Han tomb models, stone tomb components in architectural forms and tomb bricks with carved pictures of courtyard houses and city gates.

From the late neolithic, house floors were carefully prepared from tamped earth with postholes for the timber columns supporting the roof. From the Warring States, at the latest, roofs were covered with ceramic tiles and circular end tiles at the eaves bore stamped decorations.

By the Han, a characteristic timber-frame, post-and-beam construction was used. Upright timber columns supported cross-beams which were placed one on top of the other, in diminishing size, to create a pitched roof in a series of steps. On top of the cross-beams, eaves purlins were laid and roof-tiles placed on these. From the Han, at the latest, Chinese eaves projected quite a way beyond the front row of timber columns, presumably to protect them from rain. The projecting eaves with their heavy load of tiles (the roof was made heavier in the north by an insulating couch of mud laid on the roof below the tiles) required support in the form of brackets projecting beyond the columns, taking the load of the eaves. In the Han these were quite simple with a W-shaped bracket on a block above the column, but by the Tang the eaves brackets had developed into complex pieces of joinery, strong structural members under the eaves. The eaves of Tang buildings already seem to show a slight uplift at the corners, anticipating the fancifully curved eaves still seen in southern China. On the tiled roof, decorative circular end-tiles finish the eaves and the ridge of the roof was built up and finished with an incurving 'owl's tail' at each end of the ridge. As the folklore relating to buildings developed, these owls' tails were transformed into water-bearing dragon heads, apparently eating each end of the ridge and performing the dual function of frightening evil spirits and protecting the building from fire. The circular end tiles often bore auspicious designs, sometimes lions' heads with bared teeth, or dragons (associated with water) or auspicious characters. On grand buildings the four corners of the roof were protected near the eaves by a little series of ceramic animals: lions, dragons and frightening mythical beasts, best seen on the roofs of the Forbidden City in Peking.

Even in the neolithic buildings at Banpo near Xi'an, the characteristic orientation of houses to the S is seen. Though some variations are found in the neolithic, the practice of orienting major buildings towards the S soon became universal. Orientation, siting and plan are all affected by the theory of *feng shui* ('wind and water') or geomancy, whose texts claim an ancient history but do not seem to antedate the Han. Geomancy has its roots in practicality: major halls and buildings are always oriented towards the S, to make the most of the sun, and closed to the cold winds of the N. Ideally, a building, or a city, should be protected to the N by hills and should have a water-supply to the S.

The universality of the courtyard plan in Chinese architecture (whether domestic, religious or imperial) has no such scriptural justification and must presumably arise from a desire to enclose possessions and, in the case of domestic architecture, women. Buildings generally consist of a series of courtyards, the main halls oriented to the S, with strict balance on either side of the central axis and with more 'public' areas inside the gate, private apartments (whether of a family or monks) to the rear. It is common for writers on Chinese architecture to stress the similarity between the enclosed rectangle of the courtyard plan and the ideal walled city.

Chinese settlements were surrounded by a wall from the late neolithic period (at Banpo there is no wall but a defensive ditch). In subsequent periods they were as subject to geomantic considerations as were houses. The ideal rectangular plan was only possible in the N and NW (Peking and Xi'an are good examples); the hillier topography of the S made rectangular city walls difficult (as is clear from the plan of Nanjing). Imperial or administrative buildings were ideally sited in the centre of the city, with a drum tower and bell tower to announce the hours of the day and the time when the city gates were opened and closed. During the Tang market areas were strictly controlled and the city divided within itself into walled 'wards' which were locked up at night. By the Song these inner walls had almost all disappeared and markets were deregulated to a large extent.

Though it is a very late example of a system which dates back in theory to the Zhou, Peking is (or was, until recently) the best example of the town-planners' ideal: protected to the N by mountains, open to the S, with a river drawn in from the NW to make a moat and provide water, the city was surrounded by a regular, rectangular wall pierced by huge gates and had, at its heart, the imperial palace, surrounded by government buildings. The most prominent road (until the widening of Tiananmen Square and the construction of Chang'an jie) was that leading S from the imperial palace (today's Qianmen wai dajie), on the central axis. Peking's streets were a perfect grid, with neat, S-oriented courtyard houses set between them.

The buildings in a courtyard complex, whether domestic or religious, have an uneven number of *jian* or bays (defined by the upright columns) and division into rooms is usually made on the basis of the bay, although a three-*jian* building may be undivided, divided into three rooms or two.

Southern courtyard house: Lu Xu's house, Shaoxing

The uneven number of bays gives a natural prominence to the central bay which, in the main wing of a domestic building, is used as a reception room and ancestral shrine for family worship. The disposition of the limited amount of furniture reflects the balance of rooms: a centrally placed table is flanked by a chair on either side. Domestic buildings in north China almost invariably had a built-in brick platform (*kang*) which was used as a seating platform by day and a bed by night. The hollow *kang* could be heated from underneath by a small stove (or sometimes the flue from the cooking stove was led underneath it). The *kang* was covered with straw matting and, in Shanxi province, a brightly-painted black oilcloth. *Kang* furniture, ideally of a dark hardwood, consisted of small, very low tables and silk cushions arranged to form a couch; in poor houses, the folded bed-quilts served the same purpose. *Kang* are fast disappearing as Western furnishing styles have become more popular and they take up too much space (which is now being filled with wardrobes, armchairs, couches and coffee-tables). Possessions were traditionally stored in wooden chests.

Much is made of the similarity between grand and minor buildings, in plan, orientation and construction. To some extent, the difference is, indeed, a matter of degree, although a vital element of construction, the *dou geng* or bracket, was forbidden in domestic architecture according to the sumptuary laws of the Qing (and maybe previous dynasties).

Another major distinction, more marked in domestic that in grander buildings, is that of regional variation. Temples vary less in both plan and construction but houses can be very different. In Anhui province and much of the S, houses appear to be solid (rather than open courtyards) though they are built around an internal courtyard with only a small opening in the roof for ventilation and shade. In central and southern China, gable-end walls are built up and stepped or curved (an elaborate curve with two uptilted ends is called 'arched cat's back') and perhaps painted with black and grey landscape scenes in cartouches along the edge of the gable. In Sichuan, farmhouses are often thatched, white-washed and dark-timbered with strong L-shaped brackets supporting the overhanging eaves. In the NW loess areas (around Xi'an and Yan'an) troglodyte courtyard houses are carved out of the loess and their window and doorframes painted black with a thin red outline. In the N, eaves are less up-turned, buildings are stronger and plainer, though there is a greater use of colour (green roofs, red-painted timber), perhaps to compensate for the lack of natural colour during the long winters. In the south, roofs are up-tilted and colours are restricted to dark browns and greys and white. In the ideal house-garden complexes of Suzhou and other small towns of the Yangtse delta, these colours provide a perfect background for plants and the up-tilted roofs seem to echo the curving forms of nature. The curve of southern roofs compared with the relative straightness of the north remains a mystery; early 19C western writers, whose knowledge of Chinese history stopped with the nomadic Mongols, suggested that it was because the Chinese used to live in tents from which they had inherited curved roof-ridges.

Temple layout. The characteristic temple plan involves elements from Indian architecture that have been sinicised—the pagoda and the *pailou* (or archway). Temples generally have a 'spirit wall' outside the main gate (in domestic buildings, this is found inside the main gate) to prevent the ingress of evil spirits which can only travel in straight lines. Beyond, there may be a *pailou* (a free-standing decorative archway of timber with extensive bracketing supporting a tiled roof) and a gateway into the first courtyard. This first gate may hold the figures of temple guardians: in Buddhist temples there are four guardians, two on either side of the gateway or hall. The guardian of the east has a white face and carries a spear; the guardian of the west has a blue face and carries a lute (at the sound of which all the world listens); the guardian of the south has a red face and carries an umbrella 'of chaos'. If he raises it, universal darkness ensues; if

Eaves bracketing at the Jin ci, near Taiyuan

he points it downwards, it produces earthquakes and thunderstorms. The guardian of the north has a black face, two whips and a panther-skin bag in which he keeps a white man-eating rat (which turns into a white, winged elephant when released from the bag). One sometimes carries a pagoda. There is an equivalent Taoist quartet, found near the entrance gate to Taoist temples: generals who assisted Tang and Song emperors and who hold a pagoda, a sword, two swords and a spiked club.

The first courtyard normally contains a pair of small tower-like build-ings, the bell and drum towers (equivalent to those found centrally in walled towns), used to mark special events and the hours of the day. In the first hall of the temple there is usually a figure of the fat 'laughing' Buddha, one of the manifestations of Maitreya, the Buddha of the Future (who is elsewhere depicted sitting in a more solemn style, always with both legs pendant). Behind the Maitreya figure, facing the main hall, is another guardian figure, Wei tuo, dressed as a general. In the main hall or halls there is frequently a trinity of three: the historic Buddha (Sakya-muni), flanked by Amitabha of the Western Paradise and the Buddha of Medicine with Guan yin (Avalokitesvara) behind the screen at the rear of the trinity, often depicted on a rock above the sea, holding a small flask. The major trinity can vary somewhat—it can consist of the past, present and future Buddhas and the attendant Bodhisattvas vary: Samantab-hadra may appear, on his white elephant, or Manjusri with lion. Side or subsidiary halls contain figures of different Bodhisattvas and deities.

Towards the rear of the temple, the hall that is used for worship usual-ly has mats or circular patchwork cushions laid out on the floor. If there is a library building, it is often two-storeyed and found at the rear of the temple, with the monks' living quarters, dining rooms and kitchens.

Drama

Chinese drama, known popularly in the West as 'Peking Opera', is a rel-atively recent development. The combination of spoken monologue, singing, formalised gesture and stunning acrobatics appeared in its mature form during the Mongol Yuan dynasty. There are a great variety of regional operas, each subtly different from the next, and regional pride is considerable. The characteristically high-pitched tone of the singing voices makes it sometimes difficult for Western visitors to appreciate and the repertoire of gestures needs explanation. A leg raised high may indi-cate departure on horseback, fingers run, riverlike, down a long beard to indicate worry, and so on. Not all gestures are so obscure: I remember a Sichuan opera in which a doll 'baby' was vigorously beaten to death but a large number of women were 'murdered' by a mere pointing finger which caused them to leave the stage. The stories are frequently based on heroic 'historic' characters or Confucian love affairs (where pursuit of examination success or devotion to elderly parents ranks higher than sim-ple love). Until quite recently, all women's roles were taken by male singers such as Mei Lanfang.

LANGUAGE AND SCRIPT

The Chinese script presents an immediate barrier to the Western traveller for it is non-alphabetic. Whilst it is quite possible to learn the different symbols of the Greek or Cyrillic systems in order to be able to read street names in Greece or Russia, the Chinese script requires a mastery of several hundred characters before you can begin to 'get by'. Even then, the characters used in place names, temple names and street names are frequently recondite or archaic and would involve a knowledge of several thousand characters, at least.

In many places, street names are written up in roman script in the romanisation system known as *pinyin* which has been taught in all Chinese schools since 1958. This will enable travellers to read simple maps, at least in city centres (in Kunming, for example, only a few central streets are named in pinyin, and in Tianjin, previously labelled in pinyin, the new street signs are only in characters, alas). Station names are similarly rendered, which is useful, though it should be remembered that these, often involving ancient characters, are romanised for the benefit of a not-tremendously-literate population, unfamiliar with the nearly 40,000 characters contained in the 18C Kangxi dictionary, rather than for the few thousand foreign visitors.

The Chinese script developed out of a form of picture writing (possible examples can be seen on some of the pottery vessels from Banpo near Xi'an, c 5000 BC) but by the second millennium BC, writings on shell and bone, recording oracular divination, illustrate a development towards a genuine script which reflected the complexities of language. One of the major methods of expanding the script was the rebus (or pun), borrowing a similarly pronounced 'picture' character to write words whose meanings were not easy to represent graphically. Thus the verb 'to come, to arrive', pronounced 'lai', was rendered by the use of the character (a graphic representation) for a stalk of wheat which was also pronounced 'lai'; the number 10,000 (pronounced 'wan') was indicated by a drawing of a sort of scorpion which was also pronounced 'wan'.

Though the oracle bone script was very much a beginning, it has been largely deciphered, thanks to the existence of a dictionary, the 'Shuo wen' (Explanation of Writing) which was compiled in about AD 100 when the script was still comprehensible. When the 'Shuo wen' was compiled, during the Han, the form of script commonly used was basically similar to that used today so that contemporary Chinese can read a Han text aloud quite easily, though they might not be able to understand the classical language.

The 'Shuo wen' also revealed a further development of the script through its classification by 540 'radicals' (214 of which are still in current use). Radicals were parts of characters, particularly those which had been developed through the rebus system, which signified an element of meaning. Thus characters which incorporate radical 61, 'heart', usually mean something to do with emotions, feelings or thoughts, and those with the water radical usually have watery meanings. The remaining part is often referred to as the phonetic though, again, it only offers a hint of how to pronounce the word.

The question of pronunciation is linked to that of the relationship between the script and the spoken language and the development of dialects or languages in different parts of China. The fact that it was largely meaning that was conveyed in the script, rather than pronunciation, meant that the written word could be commonly used to communicate throughout the vast land mass where people spoke dialects or

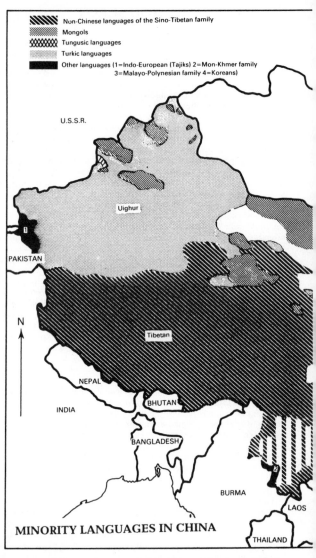

▨	Non-Chinese languages of the Sino-Tibetan family
▨	Mongols
▨	Tungusic languages
▨	Turkic languages
■	Other languages (1=Indo-European (Tajiks) 2=Mon-Khmer family 3=Malayo-Polynesian family 4=Koreans)

U.S.S.R.

Uighur

PAKISTAN

N

Tibetan

NEPAL

INDIA

BHUTAN

BANGLADESH

BURMA

LAOS

MINORITY LANGUAGES IN CHINA

THAILAND

languages that were mutually unintelligible. Thus, while a local official in south China might need a couple of interpreters to speak to local people, he could write a letter to them and to his superiors in Peking that, as long as it wasn't read aloud, could be understood in both places.

Some have argued that this loose relationship between script and speech 'allowed' dialects to develop; others feel that the gradual spread of Chinese culture throughout the land mass and its incorporation of local cultures meant that these, and their different languages, influenced local developments. Linguistic maps of China show a strong north–south divide, the south (the provinces of Hunan, Jiangxi, Zhejiang, Fujian, Guangdong and Guangxi) being further subdivided by six language regions. In the north, 'Mandarin' (as the Portuguese translated the Chinese term 'guan ha' or official language, using their own verb 'mandar', to rule) is supposed to be spoken everywhere but the Mandarin of rural Sichuan and Shaanxi, for example, is pretty hard for a native of Peking to understand. However, the difficulties are insurmountable for a northerner in a Cantonese area: it has been said that the languages are as different as English and Dutch; only the odd word is mutually comprehensible.

THE CHINESE DIALECTS

The question of the origin of such divergence is discussed particularly in reference to Cantonese. The far south was one of the last areas to be colonised by the Chinese, in the Tang dynasty (when parts such as Hainan Island were used as places of banishment for political exiles) and Cantonese, which has more tones than Mandarin and more varied endings to words, is often regarded as closely preserving Tang-dynasty pronunciation and has been used in the reconstruction of the rhyme scheme of Tang poems (which, when read in today's Mandarin, no longer rhyme). Its relative archaism has been explained by some as preservation through isolation (rather like Pennsylvania Dutch) and by others as the result of its use by non-Chinese peoples of the south who preserved what they learnt, rather than letting the language develop naturally as in the north.

Whatever the reasons for divergent developments, the spoken language of the north, in particular, is relatively poor in sounds, which can lead to confusion, even for the Chinese. For example, the pocket dictionary 'Xin hua zi dian' lists 27 characters pronounced 'chang'. These are subdivided by four different 'tones' (even, rising, falling and rising, falling), but even so the chances of misunderstanding, for non-standard speakers especially, are quite high. This is particularly the case when monosyllables are used: I have been given sugar (tang, rising tone) instead of soup (tang, even tone); a friend was dragged to the fish (yu, rising tone) market when he wanted to buy jade (yu, falling tone), and even Chinese children, used to calling their mother ma (even tone) are surprised at their first sight of a horse (ma, falling and rising). Many words are, however, bisyllabic now (though this was not the case in the past), which reduces the problem to some extent and, of course, they are all distinguished in the written language by different characters.

The grammar of Chinese is simple as the language is uninflected. One of the problems that I have encountered in writing temple and street names has been that of word division, which remains a rather fluid notion. In the modern spoken language, referred to as *putong hua* (common speech) rather than Mandarin or *guan ha* these days, words are constructed of a number of elements. In the written language, each character is separately written so that 'word division' is not reflected except grammatically, but when writing in romanisation the problem arises. One answer is to separate every part of compound words: thus Tian an men guang chang (Tiananmen Square). Another is to join them all up: Tiananmenguangchang, creating something of a mouthful. I have tried to separate elements in a sensible manner. Thus temples, where the full name is given in romanisation, are separated into the name of the temple and then the word for temple (usually si, sometimes miao). I have separated words for village (cun), town (zhen), and county (xian). Street names have been divided by name and the word for street: Renmin lu (People's Road), Zhongshan lu (Sun Yat-sen Road), Chang'an jie (Avenue of Eternal Peace). Some long streets are divided into sections, usually into Northern, Central, Southern, or West, Central and Eastern sections (bei, zhong, nan; xi, zhong, dong) and I have separated these elements.

I have used the pinyin system of romanisation (developed in China, 1958), rather than the Wade-Giles (developed by two English scholars in the 19C) since it is used throughout China—where there are station names or street names in romanisation, this is the system you will see (though I cannot guarantee that the word division or juncture will tally with mine).

As with Wade-Giles, pronunciation rules need to be learnt and a rough guide follows:

a as in 'bar'
b (Wade-Giles p) as in 'bar'
c (Wade-Giles ts'), initial consonant, ts as in 'its'
d (Wade-Giles t) as in 'dog'
e as in 'her'
f as in 'far'
g (Wade-Giles k) as in 'go'
h as in 'her'
i varies according to the preceding consonants: pronounced 'ee' unless preceded by c, ch, r, s, sh, z, zh, when it is pronounced 'er' as in 'her'
j (Wade-Giles ch) as in 'jingle'
k (Wade-Giles k') as in 'kill'
l as in 'lad'
m as in 'man'
n as in 'man'
o as in 'or' in 'lord'
p (Wade-Giles p') as in 'pick'
q (Wade-Giles ch') as 'ch' in 'chick'
r (Wade-Giles j), an unrolled 'r'
s (Wade-Giles s, ss, sz) as in 'Sunday'

sh   as in 'shift'
t   (Wade-Giles t') as in 'tuck'
u   either 'oo' as in 'fool' or, with umlaut, as the German ü
[no v]
w   as in 'wall'
x   (Wade-Giles hs) between 'ss' and 'sh'
y   as in 'yellow'
z   (Wade-Giles ts, tz), 'ts' as in 'its'
zh   (Wade-Giles ch), 'j' as in 'jingle'

There is a slight complication to the pinyin system: vowel combinations like i and a (as in tian, heaven), are not pronounced quite as the individual vowels but sound more like 'eh' in combination. Thus tian is pronounced 'tien'. Similarly, o in guo (country) is pronounced in the standard manner but when followed by ng, as in zhong (middle), is rather longer; thus Zhongguo (the 'middle' country, or China) is pronounced 'joong-guohr'.

Near Shaoxing: nature improved by calligraphy

GLOSSARY

AMITABHA BUDDHA, luminous and of infinite life, who rules over the Western Paradise (an important concept in late popular Buddhism as it offers the consolation of an 'after-life' in heaven)

APSARA, Buddhist 'goddess', appear in Buddhist paintings as flying women

BODHISATTVA, technically a future Buddha, in popular Chinese belief a being who has attained enlightenment and could enter nirvana, a state of non-being, but who has chosen to stay in the world of men to alleviate suffering

BUDDHA, the founder of Buddhism, Sakyamuni, was an Indian prince whose sheltered upbringing meant that the sufferings of ordinary people came as a painful revelation. His meditations on suffering and eventual attainment of enlightenment (overcoming human failings, most notably desire) and nirvana, formed the basis of later belief and practice. Buddhism entered China during the early Han dynasty (206 BC–AD 220) and was of the Mahayana school which stressed the attainment of Bodhisattva-hood (qv) though it was eventually much changed to encompass Chinese ideals of family worship and duties. Sakyamuni, the 'historic Buddha', is widely represented in Chinese temples, usually seated in the position of meditation (with crossed legs) and wearing a simple cloth thrown over one shoulder. His various manifestations are also represented: the most popular form in China is Maitreya, the Buddha of the Future, who is usually represented seated with his feet flat on the ground (and who also appears as the fat, jolly, welcoming Buddha beyond the four guardian figures at the entrance to Buddhist temples

CHAN BUDDHISM, the Chinese term for Zen (Japan), a form of Buddhism developed in China. The stress on 'sudden enlightenment' through meditation (rather than a lifetime of monastic textual study) meant that lay persons, who remained in the home and carried out their filial duty to parents and ancestors, could achieve enlightenment

DAGOBA, see PAGODA

DAOISM, see TAOISM (the former pinyin, the latter Wade-Giles romanisation)

FENG SHUI, or GEOMANCY, a view of natural forces developed in early times, first recorded in Han dynasty texts with eccentric names like the 'Mysteries of the Blue Bag' [universe]. The Chinese term is composed of the words for wind and water. Geomantic texts held that natural forces in all areas could be harnessed for good or evil and that building, whether of tombs or dwellings, should attempt to harmonise with natural forces. Thus pagodas were often constructed on hilltops after natural disasters such as floods, to placate and divert the local forces, and the sites for tombs were selected by geomantic specialists (often Taoist priests) using a special compass with 'good' and 'bad' directions marked. Tomb-building was a complex matter, particularly in the south where geomantic beliefs were strongest. There, secondary burial was practised. Bodies were first buried in temporary tombs, then exhumed by relatives (after a couple of years), the bones scraped and broken, and rehoused in ceramic funerary urns (tall, lidded jars). The final burial place, often a family tomb housing many urns, was the one that required careful siting in order to preserve the prosperity of the family.

The geomantic rules concerning building and planning were based on practicalities. Southwards orientation and siting near water, as well as axial balance, all antedate geomantic texts and are clearly practical. Later refinements included the erection of a spirit gate inside or outside the main entrance (to prevent the entrance of evil spirits who could only fly in straight lines) and a height limit on the spires of missionary churches (to prevent interference with good spirits which fly at approximately 30m above ground)

GUAN, means hall or is otherwise used as a suffix denoting 'institution' as in *tushuguan* (charts and books institution or library), *meishuguan* (arts institution or gallery), *jinianguan* (memorial hall or museum) and *bowuguan* (myriad things institution or museum)

GUANYIN, the Bodhisattva (*qv*) who hears the cries of the world, the Chinese translation of Avalokitesvara, a Bodhisattva who became associated with mercy and succour of those in distress, a bringer of sons. Through these attributes the Bodhisattva came, in China, to assume semi-female form and is one of the popular images in temples. Patron of Putuo shan

GUOMINDANG, Wade-Giles KUOMINTANG (KMT), 'National People's Party', founded by Sun Yat-sen in 1900, though it did not acquire the name until 1911. On Sun's death in 1926, Chiang Kai-shek assumed leadership of what is often referred to as the Nationalist or Republican Party

JIE = avenue; see LU

KSITIGARBHA (Dizang wang), the Bodhisattva who judges souls after death and determines their fate, patron of Jiuhua shan. He is depicted wearing a sort of crown, of lotus-petal-shaped lappets

LU = street, sometimes divided into *bei* (north), *zhong* (middle), *nan* (south), *xi* (west), *dong* (east), sometimes into numbered sections (yi = one, er = two, sa = three), sometimes preceded by terms such as *huan* (circular) as in Bei huan lu , North Circular Road). See also JIE

LOHAN (LUOHAN) or ARHAT, disciples of the Buddha

MANJUSRI (WENSHU), the Bodhisattva of wisdom, patron of Wutai shan, usually depicted with a lion

MIAO, see TEMPLE

PAGODA (probably derived from an Indian name for a temple complex), used for the tall tower-like buildings usually associated with Buddhist temples but also constructed free-standing on hills outside towns. The Chinese word is *ta* (possibly derived from a Sanskrit term).

The original Indian form was known as a *stupa* in Sanskrit, a domed reliquary building. An elongated version of the squat original form is preserved in the Lamaist stupas (*dagoba*) found in Peking temples and on Wutai shan. Chinese pagodas were first found in Buddhist temples of the Han dynasty, either on the central axis as storehouses of precious relics (such as the ashes of abbots or religious texts), or paired on either side of the main axis, more reminiscent of the tapering towers (*gopura*) that encircled later Indian temples (such as the 17C Madurai Temple). The use of elegant single pagodas, tapering structures usually of wood, sometimes brick, on hills outside towns, was related not to Buddhism but to the pseudo-science of feng shui (*qv*) which held that the natural good fortune of an area could be adjusted by such construction. Thus they were often built after diastrous floods, for example

PAILOU, 'triumphal arch', free-standing wooden, sometimes stone, gateway, set on the approach to temples, palace gardens and tombs. These were also traditionally erected in honour of 'virtuous widows' (who had committed suicide rather than survive their husbands)

SAMATABHADRA (Puxian), the Bodhisattva of pervading goodness, patron of Emei shan, usually depicted riding a white elephant

SHAN = mountain or hill

SHENG = province

SHI = city

SI, see TEMPLE

TA, see PAGODA

TAOISM, a Chinese system of belief based on the ideal of man's attunement with nature. The antithesis of Confucianism which stressed organisation and the supremacy of human order, Taoism stressed non-action, the contemplation of nature and acceptance of the flow of natural events. The major texts of Taoism are the writings of Zhuang zi (late 4C BC), charming fables, and the more esoteric Lao zi (3C BC), the 'Dao de jing' (Classic of the Dao, 'the Way' and power). Recent archaeological discoveries suggest that the order of the books should ben reversed and it should be known as the 'De dao jing'.

TEMPLE: Buddhist temples are called *si*, Lamaist temples *gong*, Taoist temples *guan* and those dedicated to Confucious or other official cults, *miao*. The layout of all is similar. Outside the gate is a spirit wall and there may be a pailou. In the first, gate hall are guardian figures (in Buddhist temples of the four celestial guardians of the four directions); then, (in a Buddhist temple), facing the visitor, comes the fat, smiling figure of one of the manifestations of Maitreya, the buddha of the future, behind whom is the serious, military figure of Weituo, a guardian of the faith. In the first courtyard of a temple of any denomination are usually drum (left) and bell (right) towers (echoing their presence within city walls). Halls and courtyards succeed one another, dedicated to different deities, and the living quarters are almost invariably to the rear

XIAN = county, a lower administrative level than province

PRACTICAL INFORMATION

Approaches to China

By air: most major airlines have direct flights from their capital cities to China, usually to Peking. There are also direct flights to Shanghai from Fukuoka, Hong Kong, Los Angeles, Nagasaki, New York, Osaka, San Francisco, Tokyo, Toronto and Vancouver, Singapore and Moscow.

By train: it is possible to travel to China from Europe by rail, taking the *Trans-Siberian train* from Moscow. There are two through departures per week, one by the Chinese train (leaves Moscow on Tuesdays, Peking on Wednesdays), one by the Russian (leaves Moscow on Mondays, Peking on Saturdays). The former takes 6 days to get to Peking via Mongolia (Outer and Inner), the latter 10 days via Siberia and Dongbei (Manchuria). It is generally advisable to travel on the Chinese train as it is better staffed and cared for.

Mealtimes on the train are a bit changeable and timings very difficult to work out as stations (in the former Soviet Union) all run on Moscow time (despite the intervention of several time zones in Siberia) whilst the train runs on its own time. There is a Russian dining car for the first part of the journey (with a vast menu, most of which is 'off'), a Mongolian one in Mongolia and a Chinese one attached at Erlian on the Chinese border. You need to provide yourself with transit visas in advance and, if travelling on the Chinese train which passes through Mongolia, you have to get the Russian visa before the Mongolian one when leaving Peking and when leaving Europe, the Chinese before the Mongolian (as the Mongolian authorities seem keen to know that you can get across their border).

Specialist travel companies like Regent Holidays, Bristol, offer an alternative rail route from Russia to Northern Xinjiang, obviating the need for a Mongolian transit visa.

From Hong Kong, there are a variety of ways of entering China. There are direct flights to Shanghai, Kunming, Peking, Tianjin and many other destinations. There are at least three flights a day to Guangzhou (whence there are numerous departures to all Chinese cities). It is also possible to travel to Guangzhou by train, boat or hydrofoil.

Group travel. Most tourists visit China in groups. Group travel is most commonly arranged by tour operators with *Zhongguo guoji luxingshe* (China International Travel Service; aka Luxingshe or CITS). A growing number of other organisations in China provide the same service as CITS. The most prominent as yet is the *China Youth Travel Federation* (which does not restrict itself to young people).

CITS arranges a variety of itineraries, most for general tourists, some with specialist interests (birdwatchers, railway enthusiasts, etc). CITS provides all the in-China service—booking trains, 'planes and boats, arranging hotels and buses— and (usually) a 'national guide' normally from the CITS headquarters in Peking. This guide accompanies the group throughout the tour, as well as one or more 'local guides' in each place visited.

Variations in the price of otherwise similar tours occur when the overseas travel company offers extras such as a sinologist or specialist accompanying the group, more expensive accommodation in Hong Kong and, occasionally, more expensive hotels within China. It is, in general, impossible to know in advance in which hotel a group will stay in each city unless special requests and bookings have been made, and these will cost more than the standard hotels.

Individual travel: a number of people visit China as individual tourists. This can be done quite independently or with varying degrees of prearrangement. Those intending to make all their own arrangements are advised to consult guides written especially for individual travellers, of which the most complete is 'China: a travel survival kit', by Alan Samagalski, Robert Strauss and Michael Buckley, Lonely Planet, 1988 (2nd edition). Those who cannot face the mobs at station booking offices and the uncertainty of obtaining hotel rooms or air flights or whose time is restricted, can opt for an individual package tour (for any number), arranged in advance, usually through CITS. Within China, CITS will book hotels, make travel arrangements and supply guides (usually a new guide in each place, with no 'national guide'). This method can be useful for those who wish to extend a business trip.

Travel agents: lists of travel agents specialising in China can be obtained from Chinese embassies and tourist offices.

Travel within China

Rail: China's railway network is not very extensive, considering the size of the country but, where convenient, train travel is relaxed and pleasant. There are three to four classes: hard seat (narrow wooden benches, crammed with passengers), hard sleeper (triple-tiered wooden-slat bunks filling an entire carriage with no separate compartments; cool in summer but noisy), soft sleeper (four luxurious bunks to a compartment, bedding provided as well as vacuum flask and teacups). For short journeys, there are some carriages which have soft seats (on the trains from Hong Kong to Guangzhou, for example), but these are comparatively rare. There are also different sorts of train: *te kuai* or 'very fast', *zhi kuai* or 'fast', *kuai ke* or 'fairly fast' are the main categories (with others like 'mixed' or 'local' which are probably irrelevant to all but the most impoverished backpacker). All trains have numbers and the smaller the number the faster the train (and the fewer stops). All long-distance trains have dining cars which provide lunchboxes, once of returnable, reusable tin, now white expanded polystyrene which litter the rail-lines like a covering of snow.

Individuals may encounter some difficulties in using trains as the timetable is immensely complicated (and only in Chinese) and there is no such thing as a return ticket in China. Tickets may be purchased not more than 8 hours before departure. If time allows it is possible to get CITS (which usually has a desk in large hotels) to buy rail tickets for a small extra charge which avoids multiple trips to the station. Prices for foreigners are considerably higher than for local people (with Overseas Chinese in the middle). This sliding scale is widely applied: on planes and boats, in hospitals and in entrance charges to many museums, for example.

Air travel is expanding fast in China. Until recently there was only one (state-owned) airline, *CAAC* (Civil Aviation Administration of China), but deregulation has been introduced and a number of independent airlines have sprung up. Air travel is roughly similar in price to soft-class train travel. Airline booking offices are usually some distance from airports so the same principle (of using CITS) applies as with rail tickets. There are sometimes two classes (on flights from Hong Kong, for example) but usually only one.

Boat travel: owing to the scarcity of railway lines, especially along the Yangtse River and the coastal areas of Fujian and Guangdong provinces, boat travel is fairly convenient if slow. Booking offices are usually close to the docks. There are various classes on most passenger boats which make overnight journeys: second class is the most luxurious, with two beds and washbasin, then there are various sizes of dormitory cabins and finally the equivalent of 'hard seat' on the trains. There is rarely a 'first class', I think because there are few single cabins.

Roads: more roads are now being built in China, including a number of 'motorways' (as these are cheaper than building new railway lines). The pace of road widening and improvement is, however, slow and road travel is currently subject to problems of excessive traffic of a very varied nature. Buffalo carts, overloaded bicycles, tourist coaches and army trucks do not mix well on the predominantly narrow roads of the country-side. The only foreigners to drive in China are long-term residents for international driving licences are not acceptable and would-be motorists must pass the Chinese driving test (which involves a very serious medical check-up and basic maintenance). Thus there are no cars for hire without a driver.

Most tourists will do much of their sightseeing in Japanese mini-buses or larger coaches, and *taxis* may be hired by the day (or for longer or shorter periods). In major cities, many taxis now have meters but there is normally a day rate for taxi hire, which includes petrol. On common routes (Jingdezhen to Nanchang, for example) you may not have to pay the return fare if the driver can arrange to pick someone else up. If taxis are hired for overnight journeys (to go to Wutai shan from Taiyuan, for example), you will have to pay for the driver's overnight accommodation and meals. It is still the practice for most Chinese to have a siesta after lunch; taxi-drivers will not usually insist on it but it is worth bearing in mind.

Though in some of the major cities taxis can be picked up anywhere (if they show an orange light on the roof), they are very scarce. It is best to go to any hotel that serves foreigners if you want to hire a taxi. They are not always easy to obtain there: methods of payment of taxi-drivers vary and when they are being paid a fixed monthly wage (with no incentive to work overtime) they may become extremely scarce towards the end of the month, reappearing on the first of the next month. There are also often queues at 8–9 am and 2 pm, when business people set off for their meetings.

There is a considerable network of local and long-distance *buses* which, because they are the cheapest form of travel, are most popular. City buses are usually jammed with passengers, as are the long-distance buses where luggage has to be piled on the roof. Buses are economical but very uncomfortable.

Bicycles can be hired in most cities (enquire at the hotel desk) though they are not always hired out in very roadworthy condition and may require a first stop at a roadside repair shop. If you do hire a bicycle: the Chinese drive on the right and everyone has priority over bicycles. Buses pull in to bus-stops through the bicycle traffic. At traffic lights the usual rules apply (though the green and yellow lights shining together mean that you can, in theory, turn left across traffic) but no-one pays much attention to them. Though everyone does, it is forbidden to carry passengers or an umbrella whilst cycling and fines can be imposed on the spot by the traffic police.

Formalities and Currency

A **visa** is required. Visitors on official business should receive an invitation from their host organisation and obtain their visa from the nearest Consulate but visas can be obtained easily and cheaply on arrival at all major airports. Take a passport photograph. Tourists travelling with a group will usually be included on a group visa arranged by their travel agent; individuals can also get a travel agent to obtain a tourist visa for them. Tourist visas, normally for one to three months, are easily obtained in Hong Kong at the China Travel Service office at 77 Queen's Road Central, and other tourist agencies. There are varying rates according to how fast you want the visa (the minimum time is something like 5 hours, the standard time a couple of days). Extensions may be applied for in China, at the local Public Security Office (not through CITS).

Health: no inoculations or vaccinations are required but those against typhoid, cholera and polio may be recommended, as may malaria pills for the extreme south (Guangdong and Yunnan); consult your physician. It is important to take any medicines you require with you although Chinese hospitals in major cities are generally of a high standard and many physicians speak some English.

Medical insurance is essential as you will be expected to pay for any treatment. As Chinese food is generally prepared on the spot, few tourists suffer from stomach upsets though it is wise to be prepared and, in the light of a recent massive outbreak of hepatitis, to avoid shellfish, particularly if you are a long way from the sea. The great epidemic of hepatitis which affected thousands in 1988 occurred in Shanghai (which is virtually on the coast) when night-soil boats were used to bring shellfish to the city from outlying islands. Many tourists suffer from colds in China so it is quite a good idea to take cold relief preparations or you can try Chinese cold cures.

Water is treated in the major cities but in the countryside, smaller towns and on trains, unboiled water should not be drunk. The Chinese always boil water before drinking it, a sensible precaution which dates back to before the days of sewage treatment but which is still universally observed. They do not drink cold water themselves but nowadays accept that foreigners do. Hotel rooms should be provided with a vacuum flask full of hot (boiled) water and, increasingly, a carafe of cool boiled water (usually the remains of what was in the flask).

Voltage: 220/240 volts, 50 cycles AC.

Customs: visitors entering China are given a customs declaration which lists items brought into China (cameras, watches, radios, cassette-players, etc). The authorities are extremely concerned that these items should not make their way into the hands of local people without a very high import tax being paid. For that reason, loss of any item listed should be reported to the local police otherwise the customs officials at your point of departure can be very difficult. It is forbidden to take weapons, explosives, pornography and anti-Chinese propaganda into China.

Currency: the Chinese have a non-convertible currency known as *renminbi* ('people's currency') of which the major unit is the *yuan* (c 10 yuan to £1). This is subdivided into 100 *fen*. There are coins of 1, 2 and 5 fen. There is a subdivision of the yuan into 10 fen (known as a *jiao* on banknotes but popularly referred to as a 'mao') and there are notes of 1 jiao (10 fen), 2 jiao (20 fen) and 5 jiao (50 fen). When foreign visitors exchange money they are given 'Wai jiao hui' or *Foreign Exchange Certificates* (FECs) instead of renminbi. These are issued in the same denominations as renminbi (notes of 1 yuan, 2 yuan, 5 yuan, 10 yuan, 50 yuan and 100 yuan), though amounts of less than 1 yuan are given in renminbi.

This dual system of currency was introduced in 1980, apparently to try and avoid the development of a black market, but it created an instant black market in FECs. These may be used by Chinese citizens to purchase imported goods (which, if they use renminbi, are subject to a huge import duty). Many tourists will be approached by black-marketeers (many from Xinjiang but, since all Chinese would like to have FECs, even monks have been known to ask for them) offering 1½ to 2 times their face value. Apart from the obvious danger of getting arrested, it is unwise to accept since most places that tourists go (hotels, taxis, restaurants, shops) will insist on their using FECs and you could well end up with a vast amount of effectively unusable currency.

When foreigners leave China their remaining FECs will be changed back into foreign currency (against production of an exchange slip from a bank); renminbi above 1 yuan will not be exchanged. It is wise to be careful in accepting change as large amounts of renminbi may well be offered but these present the same problem: they are difficult to use and impossible to reconvert into foreign currency on exit. For this reason, when you change money try not to accept notes of over 10 yuan in FECs as you may find it impossible to get change. The system is fairly maddening as most Chinese are very keen to get hold of FECs and obtaining the correct change can become a nightmare. It was announced that the system would be abandoned in 1986, which caused a brief slump in black-market prices, but this has not yet happened.

Most travellers will find it convenient to change their money at the Bank of China branches in (virtually) all hotels. Friendship stores also have exchange counters (run by the Bank of China) and there is no variation in rate of exchange between the Bank itself, hotel or Friendship Store counters.

Postal services: most hotels have post-office counters which sell stamps, postcards and newspapers. From Peking and major cities, postcards and letters sent airmail take about 1 week to reach their destinations but from more distant parts this may be considerably longer. If you wish to mail parcels, this may be possible in your hotel though you may have to go to a post office. You will need to provide (or purchase in the post office) all the wrapping materials. Do not wrap a parcel before going to the post office as the officer will need to examine the contents. Chinese postal authorities are fairly tough on regulations (no letters to be sent inside parcels, for example). For those receiving parcels: these have to be collected from the post office or branch and a small fee (plus any duty) must be paid.

The major hotels offer telephone, telex and, increasingly, fax facilities, as many of their clients are businessmen. Local phone calls are free (or 5 fen if dialled from a public call box). It is possible to direct dial major Chinese cities.

It is difficult for tourists to receive mail in China. Letters and cables should be directed to them, c/o Luxingshe or CITS, mentioning the number of their tour. Long-stay business people do not suffer from the same problem although those on shorter trips would be advised to establish an address and telephone number (with their host organisation or Embassy Commercial Section if willing) before leaving.

Time difference: China is 7 hours ahead of London (GMT), 13 hours ahead of New York and summer times alter these figures slightly. China adopts a summer time in June (one hour ahead of standard time) and, despite a number of time zones, Peking time is standard throughout the country. In the far west, in Gansu and Xinjiang, in order to accommodate the different hours of sunlight, visitors will find that they are served breakfast at 9 am (instead of the amazingly early starts in eastern China). The Chinese generally adopt fairly early hours, frequently with a long lunch break (c 11.30–2 pm) including a siesta. Chinese restaurants usually close by about 8 pm and banquets start between 5 and 6 pm, finishing before 9 pm.

Hotels and Restaurants

Hotels: there are various grades of hotel though tourists will normally only see the luxury and semi-luxurious categories. There is little official grading and, indeed, the semi-luxurious hotels quite often also comprise dormitory accommodation for the backpacker. These two types accommodate most foreign visitors, though backpackers will no doubt patronise the cheaper hotels used by ordinary Chinese travellers who do not have the FECs or 'connections' to get them into the luxury or semi-luxurious hotels.

Most of the luxury hotels are recent constructions, built since 1980, often with a certain proportion of foreign investment (and many run as joint ventures). Rooms in these hotels (which are bookable from abroad) may cost several hundred US dollars a night, in contrast with the average of 50–60 yuan a night in middling hotels (outside Peking and Shanghai). The rooms are luxurious, with Western or Japanese bathroom fittings, and the hotels boast bars, several restaurants (usually with one serving non-Chinese food) and 'business centres' as well as the usual post office and bank counters, souvenir shops and hairdressers.

The semi-luxurious hotels are in the majority. Some are newly constructed; most are the old hotels built during the 1950s, originally to accommodate Soviet advisors and technicians. A considerable number have been modernised in the last five years so that much of their interior approaches the luxury class (and prices follow suit) though as fewer are foreign-managed, their bars close early in Chinese tradition and Western food is more basic. Even after modernisation, rooms are invariably twin-bedded (and for members of tourist groups, prices are calculated on room-sharing so a supplement must be paid if a room is to be occupied by a single person). They all have their own bathroom, desk, armchairs, telephone, vacuum flask and carafe of water, teacups, and almost invariably a television.

Group travellers eat together (and should try and arrive together at the appointed mealtimes when the food will appear) and the usual pattern is a Western-style breakfast (toast and jam, eggs, coffee) with Chinese lunch and dinner (unless visitors have made separate requests in advance). Strict vegetarians and those on special diets may find Chinese food difficult (as mainly vegetable dishes often have a few prawns or a little pork for flavouring and pork is the dominant meat) and should express their needs well in advance through their guide as well as perhaps bringing some emergency rations.

Virtually all hotels have a bank counter, post office and hairdressers as well as souvenir shops which also sell basic toiletries as well as some imported goods (photographic film, alcohol and cigarettes, etc). At times of pressure, tourist groups may be accommodated in 'Chinese' hotels which may have a surprising number of beds per room and lack some of the facilities listed above.

Restaurants: the national hobby of the Chinese is eating. Each region has its specialities which can be found in restaurants in most major cities. Tourist groups will be taken to some restaurants although their food there will be ordered in advance. If you wish to eat out separately, it is best to organise this through the guide and meals are usually booked by a fixed price per head.

Food: there is a saying that the Cantonese will eat everything with four legs except the table and everything that flies except an airplane; this is also broadly true of the other culinary regions of China but it fails to insist on the delicate flavours used to produce splendid dishes from the very wide source of raw materials. For those who enjoy food but are squeamish, it is better not to ask what it is that you are enjoying unless you are sure you can stomach answers like sea slug, beef tendon or worse.

Ordinary Chinese families eat simple meals most days: a breakfast of unflavoured rice porridge with salted and pickled vegetables, lunch of soup noodles and dinner of rice with some pork, eggs and vegetables in one or two dishes. On feast days and in restaurants they will eat a variety of dishes, just as tourist groups will do at lunch and dinner.

Food is divided into two broad categories: rice or wheat (the latter in the form of noodles, pancakes, casing for ravioli and dumplings or flat pancakes), both of which are sometimes rather misleadingly listed in English-language menus as 'food', and 'dishes' of meat, eggs, fish and other seafood cooked in different ways with varying seasonings.

It is important to remember that, for the Chinese, food is not only a matter of survival and enjoyment but it is also closely connected with traditional views on health. Chinese medicine lays great stress on the importance of balancing the two major aspects of life, the yin and yang (crudely translated as the dark, female, negative aspect and the light, strong, masculine aspect respectively).

Foods are divided into 'yin' and 'yang' types. Yin or cooling foods (often pale and light in colour) include cucumber, crab, beancurd, green tea and oranges. Yang or warming foods include meat, apricots, sugar, black tea, chilli, ginger and wine, all of which are regarded as stimulating, almost irritant. Most dishes will consist of both types of food, to maintain the balance, and people with various ailments will be recommended by traditional medicine practitioners to eat or to avoid certain foods.

The aesthetic aspect of food is also important; without necessarily resorting to excessive decoration, colours should be varied and attractive, a few slivers of carrot or green pepper improving the appearance of a dish.

Though four major culinary regions are usually described, the major distinction is between north and south China and is based on the 'food' divisions. N of the Yangtse, the traditional staples are wheat, maize and millet, used for porridges or in the form of flour as the basis for noodles and pancakes. S of the Yangtse, rice has long been the staple food and the variety of crops (and the year-round growing season) means that the southern cuisine is more varied than that of the north.

Northern food is more robust than that of the south, more dishes are slow-cooked, braised and stewed and many are flavoured quite strongly with spring onion and garlic. Mongolian and Moslem influences mean that mutton is quite common, used in spicy kebabs (kao yang rou), in 'hamburgers' eaten in sesame buns, and in shuan yang rou or 'Mongolian hotpot'. This, a convivial winter dish popular throughout the north, is a kind of fondue: water is boiled in a special copper vessel with a central chimney and paper-thin slices of mutton, spring onions, noodles and cabbage are held in it, then dipped in spicy sauces. Many solid steamed bread rolls (mantou) are eaten as the staple and though most people eat large mantou, steamed and stuffed with pork, cabbage, onion and garlic (baozi), there are more delicate open-topped steamed ravioli in Peking called shaomai. The most famous dish of Peking is Peking duck, a force-fed meaty fowl carefully roasted so that the skin is crisp and the flesh moist. It is eaten in slices, wrapped up in thin pancakes with sliced spring onion, cucumber and a sweetish sauce and is also best in winter.

The food of eastern China (roughly Jiangsu, Zhejiang, Anhui, Fujian, Hubei and Jiangxi provinces, all of which are largely S of the Yangtse), is more delicate, with much use of fish and shellfish (both freshwater and marine) and more sugar in sauces than elsewhere. This is one of the areas most subdivided, with specialities from each major town. 'Sweet and sour' dishes—flavoured with sugar (tang) and vinegar (su), thus tangsu *rou* is sweet and sour pork, *tangsu yu,* sweet and sour fish—originate here but, by contrast, there are also simple steamed fish, crabs and tiny elvers (in season). As Shanghai was once a city of very rich men, food had to be of the best and the tradition is continued. Shanghainese, in particular, are sweet-toothed and, apart from the sweet flavour of local dishes, also enjoy Western puddings and cakes from the French tea rooms on the Huaihai road.

By contrast, western Chinese food is strongly spiced and often very peppery. Hunan and Sichuan are the major provinces (also Guizhou and Yunnan) and the Hunanese Mao Zedong was so fond of hot food that he had peppers baked into his bread on the Long March. Though chilli is used, one of the major flavouring agents is Sichuan pepper, small red peppercorns that provide a crunchy texture and an almost lemony flavour. Some of the most famous Sichuan dishes have odd names: *mapo doufu* (pock-marked old lady's bean curd) is a beancurd dish with a chilli and crunchy pepper sauce, and *mayi shangshu* (ants climbing trees) is a hot dish of minced pork and rice noodles. Other notable dishes include tea-smoked and camphor-smoked duck and beef with ground rice.

Southern food is extremely delicate in flavour and immensely rich in ingredients. Fish and seafoods are popular and fish-farming is a major industry in the south. Food is cooked quickly (stir-fried and blanched) so that vegetables remain crisp and flavours distinct. As in the eastern area, simple steamed fish is popular, steamed with only a little ginger and spring onion and perhaps basted with a light stock. A major Cantonese speciality is *dim sum* ('dot hearts'), a huge range of steamed and fried snacks including spring rolls, tiny stuffed dumplings of all sorts (like the *shao mai* of the north), usually served in bamboo steamers. Dim sum restaurants are noisy lunchtime meeting places: waiters rush about with trolleys piled with steamers shouting their wares and guests are charged by the number of steamers piled on their table.

Eating out: in ordinary Chinese restaurants, the menu is chalked on a blackboard and tables are crowded so that many diners have to share a table and may wait, standing over anyone who looks as if he might be finishing, to snatch his stool. Grander restaurants have printed menus and somewhat more attention is paid to decoration. Most tourists can arrange to eat out, booking a table through their guide and specifying the amount to be spent per head and some of the dishes. It is often a good idea to mention a few dishes and allow the restaurant to decide upon the rest and the order in which they are served.

In the Chinese tradition, a cold plate begins a formal meal: lightly pickled vegetables, sliced beancurd, liver, beef and chicken each with different sauces. These are often (especially for tourists) arranged in the form of a phoenix, goldfish or butterfly, with dyed and carved radishes and turnips for extra decoration. Then follows a series of dishes of pork, chicken, duck, fish, a little rice and finally a soup. Soup is regarded as a digestif in China so it comes at the end of the meal. Sometimes some slices of fresh orange or watermelon round off the meal. There is no final sweet course; such sweet northern dishes as 'toffee apples' (apple and banana in batter covered with toffee) will arrive at any point in the meal and everything has to stop whilst the toffee apples are dipped in cold water to set them individually.

Traditionally, the Chinese do not drink with meals for the soup provides enough liquid. Alcohol was drunk on separate occasions, with a few dishes of peanuts or pickles. The Western habit of drinking with meals has now become common practice at banquets, though not for ordinary diners. At banquets, guests are provided with three glasses: one tumbler for beer, mineral water, orangeade, or, increasingly, Coca Cola, a small wineglass for 'ladies wine', traditionally a sweet red grape wine, and a tiny wineglass for a 'white spirit', usually Maotai. Toasts can be sipped from any of these but the white spirit glass should be drained and held upside down. The traditional toast is 'gan bei' (meaning a dry glass).

The white spirits—which vary throughout China as each region makes its own, of which it is very proud—are distilled from various grains, usually sorghum or millet and they are all extremely strong. The most famous, Maotai, comes from Guizhou where it is made from spring water and sorghum. It appears in a white opaque glass bottle (which some have rudely suggested makes it look like lavatory cleaner).

Etiquette: this matters most at banquets but in general the Chinese are fairly relaxed and informal. On informal occasions, when dishes are placed on the table, diners help themselves directly with their own chopsticks. Many Western visitors feel that this is unhygienic (and it is probably more unhygienic with clumsy chopstick users poking about and dropping things) and serving spoons are usually provided.

The late Party Secretary Hu Yaobang (died 1989) agreed with this view and suggested that knives and forks were perhaps more hygienic. He also abandoned the Mao suit (Sun Yat-sen suit in Chinese) in favour of Western suits before he fell from power...

At banquets, serving chopsticks are placed before the host (and the host on each table if there are more than one). The most important thing to remember at a banquet is that if you are a guest you must not start eating until your host has served you. If you are the host, you must serve your most important guest at least with the serving chopsticks. If you are not very good at using chopsticks, it should be enough to touch the serving chopsticks, then everyone can begin eating. The same is true of toasts. No-one should drink until the host has first proposed a welcoming toast, then people can drink or propose more toasts at will. Guests at a banquet should take care to arrive after their hosts and depart before them (soon after the slices of fresh fruit indicate the end of the meal); if you are the host, then you must arrive before your guests and depart after them.

The Chinese are fairly relaxed about Westerners' hopelessness with chopsticks but you could bear in mind that whilst it is not considered impolite to hold your bowl close to your mouth (and thus avoid accidents) it is considered bad manners to put your fingers in your mouth to extract bones, etc. This should be done with chopsticks if possible and you can forget everything your mother said about sitting up straight for it is quite easy discreetly to extract a fishbone with chopsticks if you have your face practically on the table. As river fish are full of bones, crayfish are served in their shells and Chinese poultry is served chopped up into little pieces, bones and all, getting rid of bits can be quite a problem.

Local delicacies (some listed by place, others by province as the boundaries vary) include:

Peking: Peking duck, Mongolian hotpot, kebabs, *shaomai* (small dumplings).

Xi'an: Yangrou shuijiao (mutton ravioli, a Moslem version of the shuijiao or jiaozi dumplings filled with pork, onion and cabbage) that are eaten all over the north of China. One of the most famous dishes of Xi'an, yangrou paomo, is a mutton, vegetable and noodle soup poured over broken flatbread, and has been described as 'haggis stew, noodles and digestive biscuits'. There is a very good crunchy pepper sauce to be found in Xi'an (similar to that of Sichuan).

Xinjiang, Gansu (the Silk Road): mutton kebabs and *kao baozi* (buns stuffed with mutton and onions) and pilau rice with apricots and sultanas, also noodle soup with mutton and peppers (*la tiaozi* with *la zirou*) and, in summer, fresh grapes and Hami melons.

Sichuan: in tourist hotels the food is underspiced. Those who like spiced or hot food are recommended to order separate dishes: *huiguo rou* (spiced stewed pork), *maopo doufu* (hot beancurd). Specialities include smoked duck (*xiangsu ya*), *gongbao jiding* or *gongbao rouding* ('palace' chicken or pork, cubed and fried with chillies and peanuts), sizzling rice with pork (where a pork and vegetable sauce is poured over crispy rice and the noise of sizzling should be deafening).

Kunming in Yunnan: *Yunnan huotui* (Yunnan ham), *rubing* (a mild cheese, often fried and an unusual dish in milk-abhorring China), *qiguo ji*, a boiled chicken with medicinal ingredients.

These include the little brown rubbery caterpillar-like sticks of Cordyceps fungus. The life-cycle of this parasitic fungus is appalling (involving moving into a caterpillar and eating it up from the inside out) but it is an important ingredient in Chinese medicine, apparently producing a natural antibiotic. As part of the delicately boiled chicken soup, it is interesting if chewy.

Another famous dish from Kunming is *guoqiao mian* (crossing the bridge noodles), a boiling meat broth with side dishes of finely sliced chicken, duck and pork, scallions, rice noodles and seasonal vegetables which are all dropped into the broth to cook.

The dish was supposed to have been invented by the wife of a poor scholar who locked himself away in order to prepare for the imperial examinations. Anxious to maintain his strength, his wife prepared meals for him but they all got cold as she walked across the bridge to the island where he had his study. She finally discovered that if she made a soup, poured a fine layer of oil on top of it and kept the other ingredients aside, the broth stayed hot until she crossed the bridge.

Shanghai: 'drunken chicken' cooked in Shaoxing wine, *shizi tou* or lions' heads (large pork and cabbage meatballs), smoked fish, braised sea slugs and shrimps fried in egg white (*furong*). From October to December is freshwater crab season. The crabs are eaten dipped into a vinegar, ginger and scallion dip. In spring, elvers.

Yangzhou: Yangzhou fried rice.

Hangzhou: West Lake fish with vinegar.

Guangzhou: dimsum.

General Information

Climate: the vast area of China means that there is a variety of climates. The subtropical south and southwest are subject to heavy rain in the summer months which are also uncomfortably hot (over 30°C). Even the northern cities like Xi'an and Peking have temperatures in the 30s and some quite heavy rain and humid weather in July and August. Winters are equally extreme in the north (with temperatures descending to -5°C on average in Peking, and -20°C in Harbin). A compensating factor in the northern winter is the lack of precipitation and bright blue sunny skies.

Buildings in the north are also well-heated from mid November to March (at least in places where tourists are likely to stay like hotels and restaurants and trains) whilst places on or south of the Yangtse like Shanghai and even Guangzhou, where the temperature can descend to around freezing, have little or no central heating. Cold weather can be a problem in Hong Kong hotels in December–January as they are designed only for heat and provided with air-conditioning but not heating. It is generally true that late September to early November is the ideal time to visit most of China; rainfall should be light or non-existent and temperatures warm but comfortable.

Spring (late March–April–May) is also often recommended though the weather is more changeable at this season. The changeover period when the central heating is abrupty switched off or before it is switched on (March, early November) can be cold in the north as little or no attention is paid to the weather conditions, only the date. Certain areas (Tibet, the Silk Road) virtually close down for the winter from November to April.

The popularity of October means that hotels and sites tend to be crowded and difficulties can occur. It is also true that the world's weather is getting less predictable so it may pour with rain all October (when it shouldn't).

Clothing: as most trips to China involve a lot of walking and travelling (many itineraries rush groups from place to place every two days or so), clothing should be comfortable and practical. All hotels offer laundry services but they are not always very quick; if your schedule is tight you should check before handing your clothes over. Usually clothing handed over early in the morning will be returned the same evening but in damp areas like Mount Emei where clothes are dried on washing lines they can take several days to dry. Business travellers who are likely to have to attend formal banquets should take a suit but neat and tidy shirtsleeves are acceptable in the height of summer. In general it is more important at a banquet to be neat and tidy than excessively well-dressed, for both women and men.

In changeable seasons like spring, it is best to take clothing that can be worn in layers for warmth if necessary. A light mackintosh and a change of footwear are recommended in case of rain. In the coldest months of winter, warm outdoor clothing is most important. Hotels are usually very well-heated so a warm outdoor coat, warm footwear, hat and gloves are more important than warm indoor clothing.

Public holidays: the major public holidays are 1 January, the Spring Festival (which, because it is fixed by the lunar calendar is a movable feast marking the beginning of the Lunar Year, usually late January to early February, 1 May (International Labour Day) and 1 October, National Day. For Spring Festival, most Chinese have up to a week off (time to visit their families) and about three days off around 1 May and 1 October.

There are other holidays for sections of the public: Women's Day on 8 March, Children's Day on 1 June and Army Day on 1 August. On these days, parades or large meetings for the relevant group are sometimes held. 1 May and 1 October see the public parks decorated with pot plants, red lanterns and fairground attractions such as stalls where you can shoot at tin ducks, and giant chessboards to illustrate games by celebrated players.

These are usually the two traditional forms of Chinese 'chess'. *Xiangqi* closely resembles Western chess but is more closely associated with battle formations. Known certainly since the Tang dynasty, possibly earlier, Xiang qi is not as ancient as *Weiqi* ('Go' in Japanese, 'Othello' in the UK), a game played with white and black counters on a checkerboard. It was listed, along with playing the lute, calligraphy and painting, as one of the pastimes of the traditional gentleman.

The traditional festivals of the lunar calendar begin with the *Spring Festival.* Preparations begin some days in advance when the house is thoroughly cleaned and New Year pictures (*nianhua*, traditionally coloured woodblock prints of auspicious scenes and guardians for the doors) pasted up. The stove was smeared with honey for the God of the Stove/Kitchen God was supposed to make an annual trip to heaven to report on the household activities and the honey is varyingly intepreted as intended to sweeten his tongue or to stick his lips together. Debts had to be paid by Spring Festival as part of the 'clean sweep'and fire-crackers let off to scare away evil spirits. The day itself was and is one of visiting friends and relations, eating sweets and peanuts and melon-seeds.

The *Lantern Festival* followed soon after (15th of the 1st lunar month) when more fire-crackers were let off and children were taken to buy lanterns (in Peking, the Lantern Market or Deng shi ran across Wangfujing: the northernmost crossroads is called Dengshi kou). These lanterns, fashioned out of paper or silk, in the form of animals, boats, insects or just great round red balls, were lit by a small candle inside and small children can still be seen carrying their great red globes through the night.

The *Qingming* (pure and bright) *Festival* follows on about 5 April. This is a festival of the dead when people go out to sweep, weed and tidy up their ancestral graves and to make offerings of paper money there. The festival is officially a remembrance of the revolutionary dead when schoolchildren are taken to martyrs' memorials and instructed in their heroism but the traditional grave-tidying has undergone a revival and streamers of yellow paper can be seen all over the graves in the countryside.

The 5th day of the 5th month (usually late May–early June) is the *Dragon Boat Festival*, celebrated in different ways throughout China. It was more of a southern festival and in south China and Hong Kong it is marked by races between decorated dragon-prowed boats. In the north it is mainly marked by the sale of *zongzi*, sweet sticky rice and dates wrapped in triangles of dried leaves. The origin of the festival is said to be the suicide of the upright official (and major poet) Qu Yuan in c 288 BC. Having warned his ruler of the appalling state of national affairs, his warning went unheeded, indeed he was criticised so he committed suicide. He was greatly admired by the local people who did not want fish to eat his body (for that would have distressed his soul) so they threw bundles of sticky rice into the river for the fish.

The *Mid-autumn Festival* falls on the 15th day of the 8th lunar month (the autumn equinox, usually late September), when people gather to admire the full moon, to eat and to make presents of moon cakes which are stuffed with bean paste and sometimes eggs and stamped on the outside with auspicious characters.

A great number of charming old festivals have vanished now: the 3rd month when hats and hairpins were changed, cool summer hats and jade summer hairpins exchanged for winter gold ones and warm hats; the tying of tiny silk tigers, mulberries and gourds onto the back of children's heads at the Dragon Boat Festival (to prolong life); the 'laying down of needles' (7th day of the 7th month) when needles were floated on a bowl of water and the clarity of the shadow cast indicated whether a small girl would be good at embroidery or not. This coincided with the 'bridge of magpies', said to be formed on the same day so that two stars, representing parted lovers (the herd boy and the spinning girl), could cross the Milky Way that divided them. Some seasonal traditions still persist like the viewing of seasonal flowers in the parks and the flying of kites on windy spring days.

Opening times: Museums are often closed on Mondays. Otherwise they are normally open from c 10.00 to 17.00. Some also close at midday (from c 11.30–13.30). It should also be noted that many sites have a 'last ticket' time, in the case of the Ming tombs and Forbidden City this is at 16.00.

Some larger sites (Forbidden City, Buried Army, Lama Temple) require separate tickets for separate halls, if an (expensive) all-inclusive ticket is not available.

Mosques occasionally require female visitors to wear trousers and long sleeves; shoes are always removed outside prayer halls.

BIBLIOGRAPHY

History
Jacques Gernet, *A History of Chinese Civilisation*, Cambridge, Cambridge University Press, 1972
Witold Rodzinski, *The Walled Kingdom: A History of China from 2000BC to the Present*, London, Fontana, 1984
Two elegantly written, highly readable chronological histories.

Jessica Rawson, *Ancient China*, London, British Museum, 1980.
The most up-to-date comprehensive description from the Stone Age to the Han; useful for archaeological sites and ancient capitals.

Jacques Gernet, *Daily Life in China on the Eve of the Mongol Invasion 1250–1276*, Stanford, Stanford University Press, 1970
Describes Hangzhou and Kaifeng, in particular.

Frank Ching, *Ancestors: 900 Years in the Life of a Chinese Family*, London, Pan, 1989
A Chinese-American journalist described his ancestors, officials from the Wuxi area.

Cesar Guillen-Nunez, *Macau*, Macau, Hong Kong, Oxford University Press, 1984
A history of the Portuguese colony which, unlike Hong Kong, preserves many elegant colonial monuments.

Kong Demao and Kong Delan, *The House of Confucius*, London, Hodder and Stoughton, 1988
Autobiography of the last descendant of Confucius to inhabit the family mansion in Qufu.

Lettres edifiantes et curieuses par des missionaires Jésuites 1702–1776, Paris, Garnier-Flammarion, 1979
The first detailed accounts of China seen through Western eyes.

L.C. Goodrich, *The Literary Inquisition of Ch'ien-lung*, New York, Paragon reprints, 1966 [1935]
The dramatic and murderous 18C inquisition which recalled the Burning of the Books (2C BC) and anticipated the paranoia of the Cultural Revolution, raising the question of the possibilities for change in a long-lived culture.

Jonathan D. Spence, *The Death of Woman Wang*, Harmondsworth, Penguin, 1979
Drawn from 17C sources which reveal peasant life.

Jonathan D. Spence, *Emperor of China: Self-portrait of K'ang-hsi*, Harmondsworth, Penguin, 1974
Based on contemporary letters and court memorials.

Marina Warner, *The Dragon Empress*, London, Cardinal, 1974
Very well-illustrated account of the life and times of the Dowager Empress Cixi (1835–1908).

Modern History
Edgar Snow, *Red Star over China*, Harmondsworth, Penguin, 1978
First published in the late 1930s, Snow's was the first book to describe the (then) young Communist leaders such as Mao.

Jonathan D. Spence, *The Gate of Heavenly Peace, the Chinese and their Revolution 1895–1980*, Harmondsworth, Penguin, 1982

Spence uses individuals—poets, writers, thinkers—to illustrate the introduction of reformist ideas.

Sterling Seagrave, *The Soong Dynasty*, London, Sidgwick and Jackson, 1985
The family of a poor Chinese convert to Methodism. His daughters married Sun Yat-sen, Chiang Kai-shek, and his Minister of Finance. Useful background for the Republican period.

Zhang Xinxin and Sang Ye, *Chinese Lives: An Oral History of Contemporary China*, London, Macmillan, 1986
Depressing but varied introduction to the citizens of post-Mao China and their values.

Lynn Pan, *The New Chinese Revolution*, London, Hamish Hamilton, 1987
The post-Mao era described in detail.

Barbara Tuchman, *Sand against the Wind: Stilwell and the American Experience in China*, London, Futura, 1981
The American General, sent to assist Chiang Kai-shek, wrote his own account of Chinese corruption.

W.H. Auden and Christpher Isherwood, *Journey to a War*, London, Faber, 1973
The civil war through literary eyes.

Flora and Fauna
E.H.M. Cox, *Plant-hunting in China*, Hong Kong, Oxford University Press, 1986 [1845]
Reprint of a history of botanical adventure.

Zhai Ji, Zheng Guangmei, Wang Huadong and Xu Jialin, *The Natural History of China*, London, Collins, 1990

Rodolphe Meyer de Schauensee, *The Birds of China*, Oxford, Oxford University Press, 1984

Roy Lancaster, *Travels in China*, London, Antique Collector's Club, 1988

E.H. Wilson, *A Naturalist in Western China: With Vasculum, Camera and Gun*, London, Cadogan Books, 1986 [1913]
Wilson flung himself into all three activities, at some personal risk.

Literature
Arthur Cooper, *Li Po and Tu Fu*, Harmondsworth, Penguin, 1973
Translations of the two great Tang poets: in the Penguin Classics series which contains other Chinese volumes.

Lao Tzu, *Tao Te Ching*, translated by D.C. Lau, Harmondsworth, Penguin, 1963
The major Daoist classic.

Mencius (1970) and *The Analects of Confucius* (1979) translated by D.C. Lau, published by Penguin, the major Confucian classics.

Ezra Pound, *The Classic Anthology Defined by Confucius*, London, Faber, 1984
Pound's translations of the *Shi jing*, Book of Songs, eccentrically convey the rhythms of monosyllabic classical Chinese.

Cao Xueqin, *The Story of the Stone*, translated by David Hawkes and John Minford, Harmondsworth, Penguin, 1973–84
The Dream of the Red Chamber in a multi-volume translation of great elegance and accuracy.

Occasionally, recent novels from China are published in translation, most notably the works of Zhang Xianliang and Zhang Jie; Dai Houying and Wang Meng are to be recommended.

Travel

Barry Till, *In Search of Old Peking*, Hong Kong, Joint Publications, 1982

Pan Ling, *In Search of Old Shanghai*, Hong Kong, Joint Publications, 1982

L.C. Arlington and W. Lewisohn, *In Search of Old Peking*, Hong Kong, Oxford University Press, 1991 [1935]
In the latter case, much has been lost since 1935.

Marco Polo, *The Travels*, Harmondsworth, Penguin, 1958
For the 13C armchair traveller.

Judy Bonavia, *A Guide to the Yangzi River*, Hong Kong, China Guides Series, 1985
One of a series, each covering a small area in considerable detail; useful for travellers to a single destination.

Joe Cummings and Robert Storey (editors), *China: A Travel Survival Guide*, South Yarra, Lonely Planet, 1991
Indispensable for the back-packer, filled with details of the whereabouts of police stations and the protocol of hotel dormitories but resolutely anti-culture.

All About Shanghai, introduction by H.J. Lethbridge, Hong Kong, Oxford University Press, 1983 [1935]
Detail for travellers and residents in the mid 1930s.

Peter Hopkirk, *Foreign Devils on the Silk Road*, Oxford, Oxford University Press
The gripping story of the race for buried treasure on the old Silk Roads at the turn of the century.

Peter Fleming, *News from Tartary*, London, Futura, 1983 [1936]
Across the Gobi desert

Ella Maillart, *Forbidden Journey*, London, Century, 1983 [1937]
Ella Maillart was compelled by necessity to travel with Peter Fleming; their accounts are complementary.

Mildred Cable and Francesca French, *The Gobi Desert*, London, Virago, 1984 [1942]
Account by intrepid lady missionaries.

S. Schatzky and R. King, *Coping with China*, Oxford, Basil Blackwell, 1991
Contains all practical details.

Art

Margaret Medley, *The Chinese Potter*, Oxford, Phaidon, 1978

Mary Tregear, *Chinese Art*, London, Thames and Hudson, 1980

Ann Paludan, *The Imperial Ming Tombs*, New Haven and London, Yale University Press, 1981
Particularly recommended to those with time in Peking to visit the lesser-known tombs; with a supplement for bird-watchers.

Ann Paludan, *The Chinese Spirit Road: The Classical Tradition of Stone Tomb Statuary*, New Haven and London, Yale University Press, 1991

Indispensable guide to tombs and sculpture.

S.J. Vainker, *Chinese Pottery and Porcelain: From Prehistory to the Present*, London, British Museum, 1991

Roderick Whitfield and Ann Farrer, *Caves of the Thousand Buddhas: Chinese Art from the Silk Route*, London, British Museum, 1990
The BM's collection of paintings and banners from Dunhuang.

Frances Wood, *Chinese Illustration*, London, British Library, 1985
The history of printing and book production as seen in the British Library collections.

Yu Zhuoyan, *The Palaces of the Forbidden City*, New York, Viking, and London, Allen Lane, 1984
Beautifully illustrated and very detailed account of the most important building of late traditional China.

Ji Cheng, *The Craft of Gardens*, New Haven and London, Yale University Press, 1988
Early 17C work on garden design.

Norah Titley and Frances Wood, *Oriental Gardens*, London, British Library, 1991
The Chinese section contains illustrations of the desired effects achieved in gentlemen's gardens.

Nancy Schatzman Steinhardt (ed.), *Chinese Traditional Architecture*, New York, China Institute in America, 1984
Descriptions of major buildings.

Along the Ancient Silk Routes: Central Asian Art from the West Berlin State Museums, New York, Metropolitan Museum, 1982
For the western-most sites on the Silk Routes: artefacts removed by German archaeologists.

Rose Kerr (ed.), *The T.T. Tsui Gallery of Chinese Art: Chinese Art and Design*, London, Victoria and Albert Museum, 1982

Craig Clunas, *Chinese Furniture*, London, Bamboo, 1988

Craig Clunas, *Superficial Things: Material Culture and Social Status in Early Modern China*, Cambridge, Polity Press, 1991

Rose Kerr, *Later Chinese Bronzes*, London, Victoria and Albert Museum, 1990

Rose Kerr, *Chinese Ceramics: Porcelain of the Qing Dynasty*, London, Victoria and Albert Museum, 1986

Thought

Fung Yu-lan, *A Short History of Chinese Philosophy*, New York, The Free Press, 1966

Bob Whyte, *Unfinished Encounter: China and Christianity*, London, Collins, 1988
Particularly strong on recent events.

Jacques Gernet, *China and the Christian Impact*, Cambridge, Cambridge University Press, 1985
The early history of missionary activity.

Kenneth Ch'en, *Buddhism in China*, Princeton, Princeton University Press, 1973

Lucid account of the faith and its Chinese transformation.

J. Prip-Møller, *Chinese Buddhist Monasteries: Their Plan and its Functions as a Setting for Buddhist Monastic Life*, Hong Kong, Hong Kong University Press, 1967 [1937]
Useful guide to the layout and the history of many well-known temples.

C.K. Yang, *Religion in Chinese Society*, Berkeley and London, University of California Press, 1977

General
Joseph Needham, *Science and Civilisation in China*, Cambridge, Cambridge University Press, 1954– (in progress)
Dr Needham's monumental work is accurately titled: the section on architecture and engineering is particularly useful but those interested in any aspect of Chinese scientific history will find all the information they need.

Philip Snow, *The Star Raft: The Chinese Encounter with Africa*, London, Weidenfeld and Nicolson, 1988
Scholarly work with much information on traditional Chinese geographical knowledge, attitudes to the outside world and the great early 15C navigator, the eunuch admiral Zheng He.

Edward H. Schafer, *The Golden Peaches of Samarkand: A Study of T'ang Exotica*, Berkeley and London, University of California Press, 1963
Extravagant imports into Tang China, from ermine to lychees; one of Professor Schafer's fascinating books on the period.

K.C. Chang (ed.), *Food in Chinese Culture*, New haven and London, Yale University Press, 1977
A scholarly history of the most important aspect of life in China.

S. Robert Ramsay, *The Languages of China*, Princeton, Princeton University Press, 1987
The language and its many dialects.

Samuel Couling, *The Encyclopaedia Sinica*, Hong Kong, Oxford University Press, 1983 [1917]
A good source of biography and descriptions of cities and institutions (up to 1917).

Denis Twitchett, *Printing and Publishing in Medieval China*, London, Wynken de Worde Society, 1983
The invention of paper and printing in China and the rapid growth of the industry.

Lynn Pan, *Sons of the Yellow Emperor: The Story of the Overseas Chinese*, London, Secker and Warburg, 1990
The Chinese diaspora: of interest to visitors to Guangdong and Fujian.

I CHINA

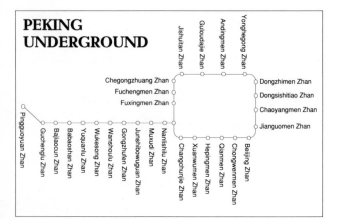

PEKING UNDERGROUND

Jishuitan Zhan
Guloudajie Zhan
Andingmen Zhan
Yonghegong Zhan

Chegongzhuang Zhan
Fuchengmen Zhan
Fuxingmen Zhan

Dongzhimen Zhan
Dongsishitiao Zhan
Chaoyangmen Zhan
Jianguomen Zhan

Pingguoyuan Zhan
Guchenglu Zhan
Bajiaocun Zhan
Babaoshan Zhan
Yuquanlu Zhan
Wukesong Zhan
Wanshoulu Zhan
Gongzhufen Zhan
Junshibowuguan Zhan
Muxudi Zhan
Nanlishilu Zhan
Changchunjie Zhan
Xuanwumen Zhan
Hepingmen Zhan
Qianmen Zhan
Chongwenmen Zhan
Beijing Zhan

1 Peking

PEKING, China's capital, lies at the edge of a plain which stretches south to comprise much of Hebei, Henan, Shandong and Anhui. Peking itself is close to a semi-circle of mountains, the foothills of the Mongolian plateau, which surround the plain to the W, NW and N, in which the Great Wall was built to protect the open plain. Though smaller states established their capitals in the Peking area (whose earliest inhabitants include 'Peking Man' of c 500,000 BC), the city has only been a dynastic capital since the early 15C. It was then that the name *Bei jing* (Northern Capital) was first applied to the city and it has been used ever since, with the exception of the brief period of Chiang Kai-shek's Nanjing government (1928–49) when it was renamed *Bei ping* (Northern Peace).

The spelling Peking reflects a peculiar early Jesuit romanisation which assigned a 'k' to the sound value 'j' (Nanjing-Nanking, Beijing-Peking) but I continue to use it for to non-Chinese (and even to some literary Chinese) it is a name with resonance and historical associations.

Somewhat ravaged by city-planners who tore down the city walls and continue to flatten the traditional low grey-roofed courtyard houses in favour of blocks of flats, and spoiled by careless industrial development to the W and E in particular, the city nevertheless contains a multiplicity of monuments.

Airport: the city's airport is to the NE, some 30km from the city centre. It is China's major airport, with several international flights daily and departures to all other airports in China.

Railway: the station (one of the Ten Great Buildings put up in 1958) with its twin towers is in the SE part of the city centre. Trains leave for all parts of China, as well as for the Soviet Union (Trans-siberian). The Trans-siberian is in fact two trains: the Chinese one departs on Wednesdays and takes the shorter route via Mongolia (five days to Moscow) whilst the Russian train leaves on Saturdays and goes via Manchuria.

Hotels: there are innumerable hotels in Peking; as with most other centres, the newer hotels are generally built in somewhat inaccessible high-rise suburbs. Notable hotels include the old *Peking Hotel* in Chang'an jie, just next-door to the Forbidden City (the best site). Made of three (soon to be four) parts, based on the old Wagons-lits Hotel with additions in the 1950s and 1970s (the fourth part is a luxury hotel to the W of the rest, under construction), the hotel is difficult to get into and not the most efficient but its location makes up for any deficiencies. The bars and coffee-shops on the ground floor are useful meeting places.
   The first 'joint-venture' hotel in Peking was the *Jianguo*, on Chang'an jie, some blocks E of the Friendship Store in the diplomatic quarter of Jianguomen wai. Reasonably conveniently situated, the Jianguo set the pace for Chinese hotels (which largely failed to keep up) and later joint-ventures. It is an ugly building but service is generally good. The *Xiangshan* (Fragrant Hills) *Hotel* (see below), designed by I.M. Pei, is by far the most interesting hotel architecturally but it is amazingly distant from anything except the Fragrant Hills. The new white block of the *Bejing International Hotel* on Chang'an jie, well-situated not far from the railway station, is said to be managed by Zhao Ziyang's daughter.

Getting about: Peking is large and its monuments are unfortunately rather scattered. The enterprising could use *buses* (cheap, somewhat infrequent and incredibly crowded—difficult to get both feet on the floor at once and since the conductors sometimes have to use force to get people in and the doors shut, you can end up with dusty footprints up your back). Many maps include bus routes and mark the stops clearly. Unfortunately, though pinyin is used on street-name signs, it is not used on bus stops so accurate counting is required.
   It is probably easiest to use *taxis* for the far-flung sites. Taxis can be found at all hotels (though they can be scarce at busy times or if methods of payment for the drivers do not make it worth their while to turn up for work). They can also be flagged down in the street, if you can find one. It is easier to take them from hotels as staff often speak a bit of English and can help to explain your destination.
   I have arranged groups of monuments on the assumption that taxis are taken from hotels.

History. In the hills to the W of Peking is Zhoukoudian where the first relic of 'Peking Man' (a wisdom tooth) was discovered in 1921 by Otto Zdansky. In 1927 Birger Bohlin unearthed another tooth and ten years later, further excavations by Teilhard de Chardin, Franz Weidenreich and W.-C. Pei unearthed the remains of some 40 individuals, including the famous crania which were lost in 1941 in transit to the United States. The first major settlement in the area was probably near the Zhoukoudian site, SW Peking but at some time during the Zhou, the major settlement, referred to in literature as *Ji* (Reeds) was sited in the SE suburbs of present-day Peking.

Western Zhou tombs with elaborate ritual bronzes have been unearthed at Liulihe, S of Peking. During the Warring States period, Ji was the capital of one of the northern states, Yan (which means 'swallow'; the name *Yanjing* or Capital of Swallows—appropriate as swallows nest under the eaves of tall buildings including the halls of the Forbidden City and the surviving gates and fly at dusk—is still often applied to Peking).

According to the great Han historian, the city of Yan under the Qin dynasty (221–206 BC) was a thriving market with goods traded from Shandong and Hebei and as far away as Korea. Its northern site meant that Peking, known in the Tang dynasty as *Yuzhou*, was used as a base for expeditions against Korea. With the end of the Tang, the gradual encroachment of northern, non-Chinese people (which was to culminate in the Mongol Yuan dynasty some 300 years later) was reflected in Peking's history. The Khitan, a semi-nomadic, Mongolian-speaking people from the area around Chengde, NE of Peking, who adopted the dynastic name of Liao (and ruled the north of China from 907 to 1125), established their capital in Peking in 936, calling it instead *Nanjing* (Southern Capital) as it was S of their ancestral home.

In 1125 Peking was taken by yet another of the northern tribes, the Jurched, also an Altaic people but whose linguistic affiliations were Tungusic, rather than Mongolian. They had lived a more settled life than the Khitan, fishing, hunting and cultivating the river valleys of N and E Manchuria (Dongbei). The Jurched assumed the dynastic name of Jin (Golden) and ruled the north from 1125 to 1234, pushing the Song dynasty further S by their capture of the capital of Kaifeng in 1126. This move followed the unsuccessful Song policy of trying to regain power by pitting 'barbarian against barbarian' which had involved a treaty with the Jurched to expel the Khitan. Nothing now remains visible of the Jin city, in the SW of today's Peking.

The Jin were, in their turn, driven out by the Mongols who took Peking in 1215 and built a new capital, known to them as *Khanbalik* (City of the Khan) and to the Chinese as *Dadu* (Great Capital). The Yuan (Mongol) city had high earth walls, parts of which can still be seen along Xueyuan lu in the NW of the city (near the academic suburb) and also along the road to the Great Wall, to the NE. In keeping with their nomadic origins, the Mongols enclosed a huge area within their city walls, space for their horses to graze. The southern wall of the Yuan city ran roughly along the same line as that of the Ming and Qing 'Tartar City' (Xuanwumen xi da jie–Qianmen dong da jie with Qianmen in the centre) but the northern wall was far to the N of the later city wall.

During the Yuan the checkerboard arrangement of city streets was laid out which survives to this day although the city was pretty much destroyed in the battles at the end of the Yuan. The description of the capital in Marco Polo's 'Travels' probably reflects something of its appearance and grandeur, even if Marco Polo cribbed his material from a Persian guidebook. '...Built in the form of a square...enclosed by earth ramparts...the whole interior of the city is laid out in squares like a chessboard with such masterly precision...All the way down the sides of every main street there are booths and shops of all sorts. All the building sites throughout the city are square...and on every site stand large and spacious mansions with ample courtyard and gardens...In the centre of the city stands a huge palace in which is a great bell; in the evening this peals three times as a signal that no one may go about the town...'.

His description could well have stood for Peking some 500–600 years later though the spacious mansions were crowded in by little low grey houses, still built to the courtyard plan on small square sites determined by the checkerboard of the streets. 19C Chinese guidebooks to Peking refer to the tiny lanes (known as 'hutong' or 'barbarian alleys', a name which no-one has successfully explained though some suggest it refers to the Mongol—non-Chinese—foundation of the city), as being as fine and numerous as hairs on a cow.

The first Ming emperor established his capital in Nanjing (after a first tentative attempt to set it up in his home village in Anhui), centred on his own power base. However, his successor (not his heir but another of his sons who assumed control) had been enfeoffed in Peking and decided to move the capital there in 1402. Not only had it been his personal power base but a major factor in the transfer of the capital was its relative proximity to the major threats to Ming control (which still came, like the Khitan and Jurched, from the N and NE). It was military strategy which determined these shifts of capital: during the Han and Tang the greatest threat came from the NW, hence the maintenance of their capital in Xi'an. Peking was close enough to the Great Wall to be able to maintain its garrisons and morale of the border guards; Nanjing was too distant.

The site of Peking is geomantically 'good', with its open plain to the S and E (well supplied with water led from the Yongding River) and its almost encircling mountains to the N, protecting the site from evil, northern influences. There was, however, some doubt that the 'good luck' of the site might be exhausted with the downfall of its previous occupants and the bloody, destructive battles that had nearly destroyed it. The Yongle emperor (reigned 1402–24) consulted geomancers and even the major philosophers of the day about his decision and they felt able to reassure him.

The Ming city walls, which were most unfortunately demolished during the Great Leap Forward (1958) but whose form can be traced through street-names referring to the ancient gates, were set to the S of the Yuan walls. The street-names with the suffixes -men nei or -men wai indicate 'within X gate' or 'outside X gate' respectively. With the exception of those in the Forbidden City, the only gates left standing are the Desheng men (Gate of the Victory of Virtue) in the NW, Dongbian men (Eastern side Gate) in the SE (seen from the railway) and Qian men (Front Gate) just S of the Forbidden City. The high, grey-brick-faced walls were similar to those that still surround the Forbidden City, broader at the base but still wide enough for several horsemen to ride abreast along the top, between the battlements.

This part of Peking was known as the Inner City (and, later, by foreigners, as the Tartar City or Manchu City), in contrast with the southern part of the city (a broader, W–E rectangle which enclosed the main shopping areas and the Temple of Heaven) which was walled (in earth ramparts in 1524 and faced with brick in 1543) and known as the Outer or Chinese City. The Inner City, with the Forbidden City in its centre, contained all the government buildings and imperial granaries, as well as housing areas whilst the southern, outer city, was the commercial, theatrical and entertainment sector, though also containing several major buildings of imperial significance such as the Temples of Heaven and Agriculture. Though the Forbidden City, in particular, saw constant additions as required as well as constant rebuilding of its halls as a result of fire through the Ming and Qing dynasties, with 22 major fires between 1421 and 1891 (some caused by lightning, others by fireworks and other

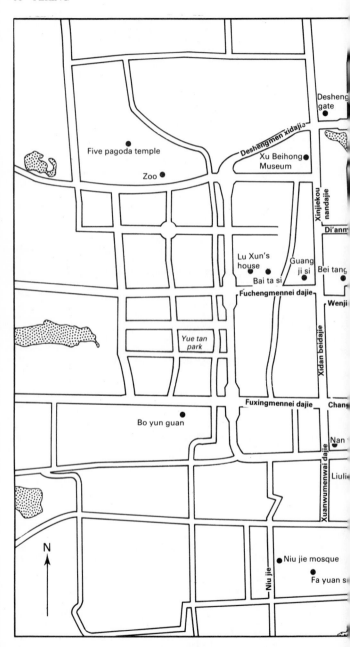

Deshengmen gate

Deshengmen xidajie

Five pagoda temple

Zoo

Xu Beihong Museum

Xinjiekou nandajie

Di'anm

Lu Xun's house

Bai ta si

Guang ji si

Bei tang

Fuchengmennei dajie

Wenji

Xidan beidajie

Yue tan park

Fuxingmennei dajie

Chang

Bo yun guan

Nan

Xuanwumenwai dajie

Liuli

N

Niu jie

Niu jie mosque

Fa yuan s

PEKING

Andingmen xidajie

Bell tower

Confucian temple

Lama temple

Drum tower

Gulou Dongdajie

beidajie

n xidajie

Bei hai

Dongsi

jie

Jing shan park

Zhongguo meishuguan

Dong si mosque

Chaoyangmennei dajie

Chaoyangmen beidajie

Beichizi dajie

Forbidden City

Dong tang

Wangfujing dajie

Zhongnanhai

Ri tan park

Imperial archive

Peking Hotel

Friendship Store

jie

Jiangguomennei dajie

an

Tian an men square

Great Hall of the People

Historical Museum

Observatory

ng

Old Legation quarter

Railway station

Chongwenmen dongdajie

nang

Chongwenmennei dajie

Qianmen dajie

Chongwenmenwai dajie

Yongdingmennei dajie

Temple of Heaven

accidents), the palace remained basically the same throughout the two dynasties, as did the layout of the city of Peking.

The old walled 'inner' city of the Ming and Qing, despite being a relatively recent construction, is held up as the classic example of Chinese town-planning theory, traditionally ascribed to such classic works as the 'Kao gong ji' (Record of Trades) of the Warring States period. The city should be rectangular in plan, surrounded by a wall, with its palace in the centre, close to government buildings; its geomantic situation was also important and Peking's site, according to Father De Groot, is 'perfectly in accord with the principles of geomancy' (though the flatness of the northern plain made such siting easier than in the case of, say, Nanjing).

The nine gates in the city's outer walls were explained in terms of the significance of the number nine, the number 'with greater prestige than any other' in north China (Hong Kong and the south favour eight for its pronunciation in Cantonese rhymes with the word for 'wealth'). All sorts of legends grew up around the perfect city and its construction. The major theme concerns a strange, eight-armed small boy called Ne zha (who could ride dragons and 'stir up' the sea) who passed the town planners puzzling over their designs (apparently unable to get the city right). Flapping his arms in his oddly-shaped red coat, he suggested that they copy him for a solution. Thus the central southern gate is Ne zha's head, the two wells at the gate, his eyes, its subsidiary flanking gates, his ears. The two northern gates are his legs and his eight arms the other gates, E and W. The Imperial Way from the southern gate to the palace is his alimentary canal and the Imperial (Forbidden) City contains his viscera whilst the streets which cross Peking with such regularity are his ribs.

Although Peking is not perfectly aligned on a N–S axis (due to the westwards declination of the magnetic compass needle after AD 1050), its basic orientation and the regularity of the street-grid is such that its inhabitants still commonly eschew the use of 'right' and 'left' in giving directions or descriptions, preferring to use the points of the compass.

The greatest changes to the city came after 1949, when Tiananmen, the Gate of Heavenly Peace, the national emblem, was rebuilt for parades and the great square in front of it (Tiananmen Square) opened up for the same purpose. With the clearance of the square and the construction of the major avenue running E–W through Peking, traversing the square, the pivot of the city was altered. The main 'imperial way' had run S to the southernmost gate of the Chinese or Outer City (today's Qianmen da jie), in the traditional manner but the major axial route in today's Peking is the E–W Chang'an jie.

During the Qing, whenever the emperor processed S from his palace to the Temples of Heaven and Agriculture, along the Imperial Way, shops were closed and shuttered for no commoner was allowed to see him. All the major streets were lined (as they are today) with shops but the old shops had richly carved wooden frontages, horizontal boards carved with plum blossom, lotuses, meander and other patterns, a few of which can still be seen. The shops faced outwards onto the street but behind the shopfronts were courtyards just like those of dwellings.

One further loss, with the disappearance of the city walls and the gradual demolition of vast tracts of the low, grey-roofed courtyard houses that filled in Marco Polo's checkerboard of streets, is the view of the city which, to 19C and early 20C visitors was a 'rus in urbe', the trees planted for shade in every courtyard affording a view to Pierre Loti (in 1901) of 'Peking at my feet, like a forest'. A British 'student-interpreter' (trainee diplomat) in 1885 wrote of looking down onto the city from the wall in summer when 'very little was to be seen of the houses, so thickly are trees planted about them. Indeed, Peking might seem to be a green wood, surrounded by a high wall...nothing can be seen of the squalor and dirt of the streets and houses.'

To most visitors, Peking today is a modern city filled with concrete blocks of flats and anonymous administrative buildings; an impression that grows by the day. Even ten years ago the area between the Zoo and the University was still rural, with low peasant courtyard houses standing in green cabbage fields, but now the road out to the Summer Palace is lined with the same concrete blocks of flats that fill the city proper. There are a few islands of traditional houses and shops left (from Qian men to Liulichang and around the 'Back Lakes' just S of Gulou xi dajie) but much of the city's historic architecture, ancient sites and its grand city plan survive only in the street names.

Tourists are not often allowed much time in Peking, just the couple of days needed to see the Forbidden City, Great Wall and Ming tombs and perhaps the Temple of Heaven and Summer Palace. Longer stays in the city can provide a wealth of temples and sites, with an increasing number of 'houses of the famous' being opened to allow a view into the otherwise enclosed courtyard houses.

A.   The Forbidden City

Tourist groups are usually taken through from S to N, along the main axis then to the E through the 'treasury' to the garden at the rear. They rarely have time to see the private apartments open on the W side of the main axis, nor to pause in the museum display areas—these latter routes could take several visits.

At the heart of the inner city, the 72-hectare enclosure of the **Forbidden City**, filled with red-walled, yellow-roofed halls, served both as the centre of the imperial administration and as a home for the imperial family and retinue.

Its name in Chinese, Zi jin cheng, is slightly complicated. 'Jin cheng' means 'Forbidden City' and entry was indeed forbidden to all except members of the imperial family and those on official business (who were only admitted to the front halls). The character 'zi' refers to the pole star (ziwei star), at the apex of the heavens where the supreme deity lived in his palace; the emperor, son of heaven, therefore lived in the earthly equivalent. The usual contemporary name for the Forbidden City is the Gu gong or Ancient Palace.

The front half of the palace, the more 'public' area, consists of three broad axes with wide open courtyards and large halls. The rear part, the imperial dwelling area, is more tightly packed with smaller courtyards surrounded by lower buildings, a garden and a maze of open corridors. The Palace was inhabited by the last Emperor of the Qing, the Xuantong (Proclaiming Unity) emperor Henry Aisin Gioro Pu Yi, until 1924 although some of the southern parts of the Forbidden City (the great halls connected with imperial ritual and government) were opened to the public in 1914, three years after the overthrow of the Qing dynasty and the establishment of the Republic.

The palace is surrounded by a *moat* 52m wide (constructed in the Ming); the excavated earth was piled up to the N of the moated palace to form *Mei shan* (called 'Coal Hill' by 19C foreigners, probably mistaking the character 'mei' [beautiful] for that which means coal). Vital things like the palace's water-supply had already been laid out by the planners of the Yuan palace, leading water from a pool to the NW through the western part of the palace, across the wide front courtyard inside the Wu men (Meridian Gate) where it is named the Golden Waters (Jin shui) and crossed by five white marble bridges.

On either side of the front part of the palace are two parks. On the left is *Zhongshan* (Sun Yat-sen) *Park*, once the site of the Ming dynasty altar to the earth and harvests.

The altar is a square white marble terrace filled with differently coloured earths (white—west, green—east, black—north, red—south and yellow—centre) symbolising the imperial control of China's earths from all quarters with their colour associations part of the major system of 'five elements'. The emperor made twice-yearly sacrifices in spring and autumn to pray for and to give thanks for the harvest.

PEKING—FORBIDDEN CITY

1 Wu men
2 Marble bridges
3 Tai he men
4 Tai he dian
5 Zhong he dian
6 Bao he dian
7 Qian qing men
8 Qian qing gong
9 Kun ning gong
10 Imperial garden
11 Shen wu men
12 Watchtowers
13 Wen hua dian
14 Wen yuan ge
15 Archery pavilion
16 Kitchens
17 Cheng xian dian
18 Jing ren dian
19 Cheng qian gong
20 Zhong zui gong

N ←

21 Feng xian dian
22 Huang bao dian
23 Ning shou gong
24 Yang xing dian
25 Le shou tang
26 Yi he xuan
27 Shou an gong
28 Wu ying dian
29 Xian ruo guan
30 Ci ning gong
31 Yang xin dian
32 Yong shou gong
33 Yi kun gong
34 Ti he dian
35 Chu xiu gong
36 Tai ji dian
37 Ti yuan dian
38 Chang chun dian
39 Nine dragon screen

N of the altar is the *Hall of Prayer* which was later (1928) dedicated to Sun Yat-sen. N of the Hall of Prayer is the *Hall of Halberds* where sacrificial implements were kept, including 72 halberds used in the protection of the altar. Just inside the entrance to the park is a white marble pai lou (ceremonial gateway) with blue tiled roofs, the *Ketteler Memorial* which used to stand in Chongwenmen da jie (known as Hatamen Street by foreign residents).

Baron Clement August von Kettler (1853–1900), German Minister (Ambassador) to China, was going to the Zongli yamen (Tsungli yamen in Wade-Giles), the imperial 'foreign ministry', to protest about the growing menace to the foreign legations of the Boxer movement, when he was murdered by Boxers on 20 June 1900. His memorial bears inscriptions in Chinese, German and Latin, expressing the emperor's regret. It used to stand on the spot where he was killed, but it was moved to its present location in 1918.

The park to the right of the entrance to the Forbidden City is now known as the Workers' Cultural Palace (Gong ren wen hua gong) but was previously the Temple of the Imperial Ancestors. Yongle established it here in 1420 and was rebuilt in 1544. Ceremonies in honour of ancestors were held here by both Ming and Qing emperors on New Year's Day and other important occasions such as weddings and coronations. Though it is now a public park, it is interesting to note that the ashes of celebrated leaders (Zhou Enlai, Zhu De, etc) are laid out here for the masses to file past (the equivalent of lying-in-state but it happens after cremation): thus its connections with the souls of the dead are retained.

Tiananmen and the Square. Tiananmen (Gate of Heavenly Peace) lies well S of the moat and the truly 'forbidden' city, yet it marked the outer limit of the imperial domain and the emperor would rarely sally forth through the gate. Before the widening of the square, the ministries of the imperial government lay on either side of the Imperial Way that led S through the Qianmen (Front Gate), still visible on the far side of the square. To the E were the Ministries of Rites, Works and War and the Astronomical Office; to the W, the Ministry of Justice, the Office of Sacrifices and the Court of Censors.

In front of Tiananmen stands the *Monument to the People's Heroes* (1958), a granite obelisk on a double terrace. The inscription to the N is in Chairman Mao's calligraphy and reads: 'The peoples' heroes are invincible'. To the S is a longer inscription in the neater, more clerical hand of Zhou Enlai.

The low relief carvings depict: (E) Lin Zexu destroying chests of opium in Canton, 1842 and the Taiping uprising, 1851; (W) the guerrilla war against Japan, 1937–45) and the Nanchang uprising, 1927; (N) Communist troops cross the Yangtse (1949), and (right) provision of grain for the troops and (left) 'Long live the Liberation Army'; (S) the uprising against the Qing in 1911, the 4 May demonstration against the terms of the Versailles Treaty (1919) and the 30 May demonstration in Shanghai against the English and Japanese (1925).

The monument is appropriately sited for the square has seen many of the early 20C demonstrations, such as that of 4 May 1919. As I write, it has just seen its bloodiest suppression, that of the students and citizens supporting a movement for greater press freedom and democracy on 4 June 1989.

Beyond the monument is the **Mausoleum for Chairman Mao** built by 70,000 volunteers in ten months (October 1976–August 1977). It is built in the 'national style' (related to the 1958 Great Hall of the People to the W and the Historical Museum to the E), flat-roofed with rather Egyptian columns and a narrow line of yellow tiles along the roofline. The 13 pine trees from Yan'an recall Mao's 13 years there (1936–49); the interior is lavishly decorated with a huge tapestry of hills and rivers based on a design by the contemporary painter Huang Yongyu, marble floors and a crystal coffin containing the embalmed body (visitable but with changing opening times).

Just S of the Mausoleum, or Maosoleum, is the barbican gate, the *Qian men* (Front Gate) which used to stand in the wall separating the inner and outer cities. Like other fine gate structures in Peking and elsewhere (Xi'an for example), its grey brick base is topped with a tiled roof and timber-framed gatehouse.

The W of the square is largely occupied by the *Great Hall of the People* where large government assemblies meet; to the E is the **Historical Museum**, one of the most important displays (arranged chronologically) in China. Western experts continue to argue over the validity of the displays: are the objects real or clever facsimiles? As this is rarely made clear by labels it remains a question of the pull of Peking versus the non-metropolitan authorities (though the best exhibits are, for reasons of conservation, almost all facsimiles, with the originals stored in better conditions).

Tiananmen (the Gate of Heavenly Peace), the entrance to the Forbidden City, is another massive gate with the same wooden gatehouse and a roof of imperial yellow tiles. In front of it runs the *Jin shui*, the Golden Waters stream that flows through the palace and the gate is approached over five low marble bridges leading to the five openings in the gate.

The central opening was previously reserved for the emperor, though empresses could pass through it on their wedding days and the three top candidates in the highest civil service exams left the palace through it after accepting their honours. Princes and members of the imperial family used the gates to either side whilst those furthest to the left and right were only opened when the emperor held court and then civil officials used the E gateway, and military officials the W.
   The gate is now decorated with one of the rare surviving portraits of Mao Zedong (whose image whether graven or painted has disappeared from most other public buildings) and two signboards reading (W) 'Long live the People's Republic of China' and (E) 'Long live the great unity of the peoples of the world'. The gate is now used as a stand for high officials to view occasional parades in Tiananmen Square (and has recently been opened to foreign visitors for a high price).

Inside the Tianan Gate there is a longish walk (through a courtyard lined with low office buildings) to the *Wumen* (Meridian Gate) in the walls of the Forbidden City proper, just inside the moat. The *walls* are nearly 8m high, 8.6m broad at the base and 6.6m broad at the top.

With a core of rammed earth, the walls were unusually solid in construction, having a triple layer of bricks on either side, finished with mortar to give a smooth surface. The bricks used on the outer surface were made in Linqing in Shandong province and are 48 x 24 x 12cm, each (of the 12 million used) weighing 24kg.

It is at the Meridian Gate that visitors buy their entrance tickets to the Palace complex. Many of the separate exhibition halls inside the Palace (Clock Hall, Treasury, Garden of the Palace for Tranquil Longevity, etc) have separate ticket halls and tickets must be bought each time (except by group members) (1989). Visitors may only enter the Forbidden City through the Meridian Gate though they may leave either by the same gate or through the northernmost gate (Shenwumen) or by the southern of the two eastern gates, the Donghuamen (rather a pleasant walk).

The **Meridian Gate** was built in 1420 and substantially restored in 1647 and 1801. It is unusual in that it is constructed with two wings stretching S on either side.

During the Qing the emperor would stand on the wall in the gatehouse above to receive prisoners of war after military campaigns, to issue proclamations or to present the almanac on the 1st day of the 10th lunar month. Inspection parades were held before the gate three times a month in the emperor's absence (if he was in the palace, his tri-monthly acceptance of memorials from his officials was held in the Hall of Supreme Harmony to the N). During the Ming, punishment of officials (by beating) was carried out to the eastern side of the imperial way in front of the Meridian Gate.

Inside the Meridian Gate is a vast paved courtyard through which the Jin shui (Golden Waters) flow in a balustraded channel spanned by five marble bridges. At the far end of the courtyard the *Gate of Supreme Harmony* (Taihemen, rebuilt in 1890) leads to the courtyard in front of the **Hall of Supreme Harmony** (Taihedian, one of the 'three great halls'). The courtyard—like the others with a central, marble imperial way, the rest paved with similar grey bricks to those that surface the surrounding wall—is the largest in the palace and was very much part of the ceremonial significance of the Hall of Supreme Harmony.

As court paintings of the Qing show, the emperor sat on his throne, high up in the hall (which is raised on a three-tiered platform) and his officials were lined up in the vast courtyard below. White stone slabs laid in the grey bricks of the courtyard indicated where the imperial guard should stand and foot-high bronze markers in the shape of mountains (inscribed with degrees of rank in Chinese and Manchu) indicated where officials of each rank should be.

The *platform* on which the hall stands stretches back; indeed all of the three great halls stand on it. It is known as a 'Sumeru terrace' after the multi-tiered mythical mountain of Buddhism and, whilst most major buildings are raised on stone platforms, triple tiers are rare except in imperial buildings (including the Temple of Heaven). The balustrades of the terraces are lavishly carved, in this case with cloud scrolls on the post capitals (elsewhere in the Forbidden City, variant decorations are found on balustrades and post capitals) and the drainage channels end in elaborate gargoyles in the form of *chi* (hornless dragons). There are two rows of steps leading up to the hall and a central 'stair slab', an elaborately carved ramp of white marble over which the imperial sedan chair was carried. This one is carved with dragons chasing pearls amongst clouds over mountains.

The dragon is the symbol of the emperor (as well as an auspicious, rain-bearing beast) and the pearl is variously explained as a symbol of purity or of (rain-heralding) thunder. In other parts of the Forbidden City there are differently decorated stair slabs: the phoenix, symbol of the empress, is found on that before the Palace of Inheriting Heaven in the NE corner of the inner court (where women lived) and is also used as a ceiling decoration in the same area.

The vast hall (2730 square metres) is a nine-bay construction (11 bays if you include the narrower side verandas) with a double-eaved, hipped roof covered in yellow tiles.

At either end of the main ridge is the open-mouthed dragon (*chi wen*), apparently swallowing the end of the ridge; the *chi wen* is supposed to be a particularly watery child of the dragon whose damp presence would protect a building from fire. This gives the ridge the characteristic form of the Ming-Qing. Along the ridge at the eaves end is the equally characteristic row of tiny animals in the same yellow-glazed tile: they comprise dragons, phoenix, lions, scaled lions, 'sea horses', fire-eating beasts, scaled oxen, and a winged human figure with an animal face leaning on a sword, and are often enclosed between another chi wen and, at the eaves end, a human figure riding a chicken (possibly the legendary tyrant Prince Min of Qi who was hanged from the eaves as a lesson to others). Below, the brackets supporting the painted tie-beams are reduced in size but increased in number (when compared with the magisterial bracketing of Tang and even Song buildings), almost forming a decorative frieze above the tie-beams. The internal and external timbers are painted, here in the multi-coloured *he xi* style used in the grandest halls. A similar style, also found in grand halls, is the *xuan xi* (which is less angular, incorporating more rounded forms); the Suzhou style, found predominantly in garden pavilions and women's living quarters incorporates realistic flowers and genre scenes in cartouches.

Inside the hall, the floor is paved with hard dark tiles known as 'metal bricks' (as they produce a metallic sound when struck), produced for the palace in the Suzhou area and ferried up the Grand Canal. The timbers are of nan mu (*Phoebe nanmu*) from Sichuan province, the huge logs destined to form single columns in the great halls floated by river to the Grand Canal, taking 3–4 years *en route*.

The columns (and external timbers) were (and still are) coated in a thick protective mixture of hemp, clay, tong oil and pigs' blood, then painted red in the traditional manner, using a bunch of paint-soaked rags rather than a brush. The layers could be seen during repairs in 1976 and where the coating is damaged, it is still possible to see the half-inch-thick hemp and clay mixture.

Peking: the Forbidden City

Above the red columns, the ceiling is painted mainly in green and gold in the *he xi* style with angular cartouches enclosing golden imperial dragons in different forms. There is a fine coffered ceiling. The columns surrounding the raised throne are painted gold with dragons in relief and the same dragon motif is seen on the golden screen behind the throne and on the carved and gilded throne itself.

The hall was relatively rarely used: the emperor would proceed southwards from his apartments in the 'inner court' on New Year's Day when all his officials would wait below with the court orchestra as the emperor cracked his 10m-long red silk whip. He would also attend ceremonies here at the winter solstice, his birthday, when the list of successful candidates in the imperial exams was published, and at the beginning of a major military campaign.

Behind is the *Hall of Perfect Harmony* (Zhonghedian), a charming and elegant square building with a hipped pavilion roof topped by a roof pommel. It was restored in 1627 and 1765 and now contains various of the imperial sedan chairs.

In both the Ming and Qing it was a place of preparation before major ceremonies: the emperor would read the scripts of memorials to be presented to him and inspect the grain and agricultural implements he was to use in ceremonies in which he inaugurated the agricultural year by ploughing a ceremonial furrow and planting seed in the Temple of Agriculture in the S of the town. During the Qing it was decided that the imperial genealogies (known as the *yu pu* or jade lists) should be revised every ten years and the emperor read the revised versions here.

Behind is the **Hall of Preserving Harmony** (Baohedian), rectangular in plan, with a double-eaved hip and gablet roof. Its previous names were 'Hall of Respectful Care and Contentment' in the early Ming, and 'Hall of Establishing Supremacy' during the late Ming. It was given its present name in the early Qing. Its interior appears lighter than that of the Hall of Supreme Harmony for, using a Song and Yuan technique called 'without pillars', several of the interior columns were 'missed out', creating a wider, more open effect.

The emperor sometimes assumed his imperial robes here before proceeding by sedan chair to the Hall of Supreme Harmony. He also held banquets here and held the examinations for the title of 'jin shi' (presented scholar), the highest level of the three-tiered exam system.

Behind the hall there is a fine view of the rear garden of the palace area and the external gardens around the *Bei Hai* (North Sea) *Lake* with the white stupa. The *stair slab* behind the Hall of Preserving Harmony is the largest in the entire palace.

Carved from a single slab of marble, it is decorated with a classic scroll border enclosing dragons in clouds above mountains and waves (representing the earth). The great slab of marble came from Fang shan (also known as Shijing shan) some 48km away and, weighing over 200 tons, took some 20,000 men 28 days to drag it to its present position. Some said that it was moved in the depths of winter when water was thrown on the roads to form slippery ice to facilitate the task.

The galleries that surround the courtyards beside the Three Great Halls were used as stores for such items as ceramics, winter and summer garments, furs and weaponry (and in a translation of the Abbe Grosier's 1785 account in the 'Guide Nagel' inappropriately rendered as 'shops').

Behind the Hall of Preserving Harmony is a wide courtyard whose walls mark the boundary between the inner and outer courts. Beyond is the truly 'Forbidden' city where only the thousands of eunuchs (nearly 1500 were dismissed in 1922 when the last emperor's tutor, Sir Reginald Johnston discovered that some were secretly selling off palace treasures for their own profit), maids and members of the imperial family were allowed. Most tourist groups are led eastwards to the treasury but I will complete the central axis and then describe the western and eastern ones.

Immediately N of the Hall of Preserving Harmony is the *Palace of Heavenly Purity* (Qianqinggong), first built in 1420 but three times destroyed by fire (last reconstructed, apparently using many of the original timbers in 1797). This, with the Hall of Union (Jiaotaidian) and the Palace of Earthly Tranquillity (Kunninggong), forms the 'Three Palaces' (paired with the Three Great Halls) and was, in the Ming, the living area for the emperor and empress: hence their position on the central axis.

The side wings of the courtyard before the Palace of Heavenly Purity contained the emperor's clothing (E in the *Hall of Accomplishing Uprightness*), his office and study (W, in the *Hall of Industrious Energy*), a secretariat staffed by scholars from the Hanlin Academy ready to answer queries on the emperor's behalf (E end of the southern gallery) and the classroom of the heir to the throne (W end of the southern gallery). To the N were the imperial apothecary, the chief eunuch's office and the treasury office.

The emperors slept here until Yongzheng (reigned 1723–36) moved to the Hall of Mental Cultivation, Yangxindian, in the courtyard immediately to the W. The palace was henceforth used for greeting foreign emissaries. The emperor also received congratulations from his own officials on his birthday in this palace and gave banquets, notably the 'thousand old men banquets' held in 1722 (the 61st year of the reign of Kangxi) and 1785 (the 50th year of Qianlong) when 3000 men of all ranks over the age of 60 were invited and presented with walking sticks.

There is still a throne in the centre of the hall as well as huge mirrors and carved cupboards (under restoration, 1988).

From the Yongzheng reign until the mid 19C, a custom inaugurated by the Yongzheng emperor to avoid unseemly factional struggles over a death-bed was to make a second copy of the name of the designated heir and place it in a box behind the horizontal board (inscribed with the characters for 'upright and pure in mind'). The emperor carried the other copy on his person.

Beside the throne, similar in design though somewhat more ornate than those in the Three Great Halls, apart from the cloisonné incense burners, are two cranes (symbols of longevity) bearing lotus leaves in their long beaks with spikes to hold candles. It was the practice for dead emperors to be laid out temporarily in this Palace before being moved to Coal Hill and thence to the two Qing tomb enclosures outside Peking.

Outside, tubs of dwarf pomegranate trees have been placed along the imperial way approaching the Palace whose name-board (blue with gold characters and frame, hung under the upper eaves) is inscribed in both Manchu and Chinese, unlike those of the Three Great Halls where only Chinese is used.

Behind the Palace of Heavenly Purity is the smaller *Hall of Union* (Jiaotaidian), built in 1420 and restored in 1655. In design and position (between the two grander halls) it echoes the Hall of Perfect Harmony, Zhonghedian, in the outer court. It also has a pyramid pavilion roof culminating in a golden roof pommel but lacks the verandah of the former.

This used to be the throne room of the empresses, where they received homage on the main festivals of the year, until the 18C when the imperial family moved their living quarters to halls on the W and E (the latter axis favoured by women). During the reign of the Qianlong emperor it became the practice to store the imperial seals here in caskets. These, the equivalent of the imperial signature, were of great value and importance. They can still be seen, their caskets covered with yellow silk damask covers.

The hall contains much calligraphy by the Qianlong emperor and two clocks, a chiming clock produced in the palace (late 18C) and a clepsydra of c 1800. Above the throne is a tablet inscribed with the two characters *wu wei* (refrain from action), one of the Taoist ideals.

Behind is the *Palace of Earthly Tranquillity* (Kunninggong) with its relatively simply decorated interior, the official residence of the empress though during the Qing she no longer actually lived here.

It was, however, used as a bridal chamber for most emperors who would spend the first three nights after the wedding in the eastern 'warm' chamber of the Palace where the bed, surrounded by a carved wooden frame, was hung with silken curtains embroidered with the traditional theme of the 'hundred children at play' (often seen in Ming paintings and in New Year prints).

The Palace is supposed to be decorated in the Manchu style: with long wooden 'kang' lining the walls, some with yellow silk cushion-seats.

The kang or brick bed (a hollow brick platform which could be heated by braziers from underneath) was a standard fixture against the southern or outer walls of traditional houses throughout north China but the Manchu, coming from the extremely cold northeast, often had kang platforms all round the room, not just under the windows. In both the Forbidden City and the Summer Palace (yi he yuan), low wooden platforms are used instead of the crude brick platforms of ordinary homes and their disposition reflects Manchu taste.

Manchu taste can also be seen in the filigree corner decorations of the plain ceiling panels (not unlike the cut-work decoration found on Tibetan tents) which stand in marked contrast to the overall painting of the Chinese-style rooms (on the eastern axis).

The 'Last Emperor', Henry Aisin-Gioro Pu Yi (1906–67), was meant to spend his wedding night here in 1922 in what he described as 'rather a peculiar room: it was unfurnished except for the bed-platform which filled a quarter of it and everything about it except the floor, was red' (the Chinese colour for good luck, always used at weddings). There were 'red bed-curtains, red pillows, a red dress, a red skirt, red flowers and a red face…' since the bride was clad entirely in the auspicious colour. Pu Yi, supposed to be keener on ants than women, 'decided that [he] preferred the Mind Nurture Palace [Hall of Mental Cultivation, Yangxindian] and went back there.'

The western part of the Palace (once the empresses had moved out) was used for sacrifices to Chinese and Mongolian gods and has a sort of kitchen where sacrifices were made and food for offerings prepared (including 1300 pigs for the kitchen god, annually). Once the food offerings had been made to the spirits, they were eaten by the participating human beings, including the emperor and empress.

Behind the Palace of Earthly Tranquillity are the northernmost galleries (with the imperial apothecary and pharmacy, eunuchs and treasury offices), the right-hand one now housing a display of the Last Emperor's possessions including his toys.

Pu Yi was declared heir to the throne on the death of the Guangxu emperor in 1908. He was only two (and not the correct heir; his nomination was one of the Empress Dowager Cixi's last attempts to retain power) so he was brought up in the Palace.

Between the galleries is the *Gate of Earthly Tranquility* which leads straight in to the **Imperial Garden** (Yu huayuan). The major (but not the only) garden in the Forbidden City, it was laid out in the Ming and remains little changed (quite a number of the trees are thought to be original). It is 80m by 140m and, sparsely provided with the water that is an integral part of the traditional Chinese garden (there are two lily pools beneath the Pavilion of Auspicious Clarity in the NW corner and the Jade Green Floating Pavilion in the NE corner—a balanced pair), the garden focuses on buildings, rockeries, trees and *pen jing.*

On the central axis is a long path leading to a gate, the *Tian yi men* (First Gate of Heaven, a name commonly found in temples) which cuts the vista, offering a glimpse of two pines twisted together. Beyond is the major building of the garden, the *Jin'an dian* or Hall of Imperial Peace. The simple grey First Gate of Heaven, made of finely ground grey bricks, is flanked by two bronze *qilin* (mythical beasts, often identified with unicorns, they have the bodies of deer, horses' hooves, ox tails and single horns; these are variant beasts with flaming manes). *Qilin* are said to be only visible when a wise ruler is on the throne. Behind the *qilin* are two meteorite-like rock clusters mounted on carved stone pedestals, some of the many interesting rocks including fossil tree-trunks, a cluster of fossilised sea-slugs and more common lake rocks from near Wuxi, which are mounted as *penjing* ('pot scenes') on finely-carved stone bases throughout the garden.

Apart from the central axis, the buildings are arranged in pairs, E and W, like the two pavilions over pools. Their names are frequently paired, too: just S of the two pool-pavilions are a pair of pavilions that are cross-shaped in plan, to the W the *Pavilion of a Thousand Autumns* and to the E the *Pavilion of Ten Thousand Springs.*

The major rockery (there are several) is set against the back wall, just to the E of the gate. It is high enough for the *Pavilion of Imperial Prospect* on top of it to afford a view of the outside world.

For the women of the imperial family, this was probably their only view of the outside and the rockery's position, against the wall, is typical: Chinese fiction and legends are full of lovers' meetings and rockeries, the woman, forbidden to leave the house, climbing up to speak to her lover who is outside on the road. At festivals where it was traditional practice to ascend hills (like the Mid-autumn Festival in the eighth lunar month when the full moon was viewed from high places), the imperial family would climb up this artificial mountain (the Hill of Piled Excellence).

A notable feature of the garden is the widespread use of pebble-patterned pavements with many-coloured stones laid in different patterns or forming horses, pots of flowers, figures from opera and even a depiction of the bridge and bronze oxen at the Summer Palace.

A double gate leads to the outer part of the Palace, just inside the northernmost gate (*Shenwu men*, Gate of Martial Spirit). It is composed of the *Gate of Inherited Light* which is flanked by two gilt bronze elephants on carved stone pedestals, the elephants' legs, like those in the Potala at Chengde, uncomfortably bent the wrong way at the knee (and on this basis they may be assumed to be 18C). In the outer wall is the *Gate of the Pursuit of Truth*, the inner rear gate of the Forbidden City, leading out to the broad road that runs between the inner and outer walls. At either corner of the outer walls, the complex corner towers can be clearly seen at this point.

The incredibly complex arrangements of double-hipped roofs and gablets in the corner watchtowers create the effect of 'floating eaves'. One Peking legend has it that, when the builders of the Forbidden City were absolutely stumped by the corner towers, they were assisted by the sudden appearance of an old man carrying a beautiful birdcage made of straw with an incredibly complicated roof. The old man who provided the model for the solution of the problem was Lu Ban, the legendary patron saint of carpenters and builders.

Returning to the division between the inner and outer courts, behind the *Bao he dian* (Hall of the Preservation of Harmony), the small building in the NW corner of the courtyard was the office of the Grand Council. Beside it a small gate leads to a long corridor which runs between the Three Rear Palaces (on the right) and the living quarters of the Qing emperors (on the left).

The *Hall of Mental Cultivation*, built in the Ming, became the living quarters of the emperor from the Yongzheng reign period (1723–36) when the Yongzheng emperor decided not to live in the Palace of Heavenly Purity where his father had resided for more than 60 years. The hall is H-shaped in plan (with the H on its side); the emperors used the front part for their office and the rear part for their bedroom. S of the hall, the long gallery was the dining room of the inner court. There were no fixed times for meals for emperors, whose food was brought to them as required, wherever they were. As they spent much time here (after Yongzheng), the dining room was most conveniently situated. The side halls to E and W housed Buddhist shrines. The galleries outside the courtyard were the duty rooms of the eunuchs.

In front of the gate leading to the hall is a large jade tablet, the centre, which is in the form of a *bi* disc, pierced and surrounded by carved five-clawed dragons (five-clawed dragons were 'imperial', 'ordinary' dragons were three-clawed). Inside the gate is a screen, hiding the interior from view and preventing the ingress of malevolent spirits (who were believed only to be able to fly in straight lines). Such screens, known as 'spirit walls', are commonly found in domestic architecture.

The hall itself has a variant roof, the front part covered with a 'rolled pitched roof', curving smoothly over the ridge, without the raised line of upstanding roof tiles found on other roof ridges in the Palace. The three-bay front hall has a central throne room which is, however, more businesslike in arrangement than other throne halls in the palace for bookcases curtained in black and blue silk line the walls on either side of the throne.

The western bay (the 'Room of the Three Rarities') was where the emperors summoned their grand councillors. The front part of the bay has an unusual floor of blue and white ceramic tiles and a huge painting opposite the door (by the Jesuit Giuseppe Castiglione and Jin Tingbao, 1756) involves a trompe l'oeil depiction of the floor tiles and window lattices, apparently extending the room. The Qianlong emperor used to keep three extremely rare pieces of calligraphy by Wang Xizhi (see Shaoxing), Wang Xianzhi and Wang Shun in the room, hence its name.

The Qianlong emperor was a great connoisseur in the arts although some now find it hard to forgive his habit of inscribing his (extremely rare and valuable) paintings himself. Whilst this was a common practice and could enhance the value and interest of a painting, showing who had owned it and what they thought of it, the Qianlong emperor's inscriptions, in a large, bold hand, were often placed centrally (most connoisseurs would inscribe the margins only), tending to spoil the overall design.

The room is light and pleasant and a fine example of imperial interior design.

The room on the E of the main throne room with a rare carpet on the floor (carpets were more often placed on kang platforms) was the one in which the Dowager Empress Cixi used to control the infant emperors on the throne (Tongzhi, reigned 1862–75 and Guangxu, reigned 1875–1908). Even when they grew up, these emperors could never quite escape her despite a brave attempt by Guangxu in 1898, prompted by a series of memorials addressed to him (but frequently intercepted) by Kang Youwei (1858–1927).

Kang's ideas on constitutional monarchy and 'national self-strengthening' based on Confucian ideals were advanced in the face of China's clear weakness in the face of Western and, more humiliating, Japanese threats and the emperor was keen to support them. For 100 days, plans were made to create modern armaments factories in China, to found modern universities (including Peking University) and to begin to teach science and politics and abandon the traditional examination system based on literary classics. However, the Dowager Empress intervened to imprison those reformers she could catch (Kang Youwei fled abroad) and the emperor whom she kept under house arrest until his somewhat suspicious death in 1908.

The throne in the western room shows how she controlled affairs. Behind it hangs a yellow silk curtain, concealing another chair behind where the Dowager Empress sat listening whilst affairs of state were discussed. The large, rather horrible piece of calligraphy to the right is by her.

A corridor links the front and back parts of the hall. The rear rooms are all provided with kang (hollow platforms to be heated from underneath) and the furnishings are largely as they were during the Guangxu period (1875–1908). Pu Yi, the last emperor, also lived here but, despite his interest in Charlie Chaplin and his frequent assumption of Western clothes (including pink spats) probably had little lasting effect on the decoration. On the far W of the rear hall is the *Hall of Festive Joy* where concubines and palace maids 'waited' and to the E is the *Hall of Manifest Compliance* used as a bedchamber by the manifestly uncompliant Dowager Empress Cixi whenever she stayed with the emperor.

Behind the Yangxin dian are the 'Six Western Palaces', reached from an alleyway that runs from the NW corner of the Yangxin dian.

They were fundamentally used as residences by the empresses, secondary wives, widows and children from the mid 17C. Like the Yangxin dian, they are furnished much as they were in the late 19C when the last empresses, concubines and children of the imperial family lived here.

First, on the left, immediately NW of the Yangxin dian is the *Taiji dian* (Hall of the Ultimate Principle), originally named the Palace of Infirmity; later, because the Zhengde emperor of the Ming (reigned 1506–22) was born there, his son renamed it Palace of Initiating Auspiciousness in 1535 and it was given its present name during the Qing. It has a pleasant shady courtyard full of trees and a large spirit-wall (screen) of glazed tiles.

Immediately behind it is the *Hall of Manifest Origin*, built in the late Qing, with an extension at the back to form a stage visible from the Palace of Eternal Spring which lies to the N. The *Palace of Eternal Spring*, without a stage, was originally the residence of Concubine Li of the Tianqi emperor of the Ming (reigned 1621–28) and later used by the Dowager Empress when she was acting as Regent for the infant Tongzhi emperor in the mid 19C. It was she who had the stage installed so that plays could be performed for her. The concubines of the Guangxu emperor and Pu Yi also lived here. The dark hardwood throne with its yellow and blue embroidered cushions stands in front of a screen painted with bamboo and birds, lightening the somewhat oppressive gloom of the furniture.

The walls of the corridors surrounding the palace building have an unusual series of paintings illustrating scenes from the great novel 'Hong lou meng' (Dream of the Red Chamber/Story of the Stone by Cao Xueqin, c 1760). As the book contains many episodes relating to the life of women inside a grand but declining household, the subject is most appropriate to the setting. Probably painted towards the end of the 19C, the paintings make consderable use of western painting styles (perspectives, trompe l'oeil).

Immediately E of the Palace of Eternal Spring, on the other side of the alley, is the *Palace of Emperor's Assistance* which has the most lavish 'hanging curtain partitions' of openwork carved hardwood. These partitions, like great swags of flowers and foliage, are found in various interiors in the Forbidden City, usually placed between columns. The palace also has very lavish door plates and handles decorated with bat motifs (a rebus for wealth) and stylised characters meaning longevity.

N of the Palace of Emperor's Assistance is the *Hall of Manifest Harmony* which has a particularly fine ceiling painted in the Suzhou style, with landscapes, floral and genre scenes amongst the gilt dragons and enclosing geometric and curvilinear forms.

The northernmost of the Six West Palaces is the **Palace of Gathering Excellence** and it is perhaps the most lavishly decorated. Built in 1420, it was last refurbished in 1884 for the 50th birthday of the Dowager Empress Cixi who lived in for the next ten years. It is a five-bay hall with a single-eaved hip and gablet roof and stands in a broad courtyard with two old cypresses. The bronze dragons and deer in front of the terrace date from 1884. The ceiling inside is painted in the Suzhou style. In the central bay is a wooden platform (with a carpet: this arrangement was more common than placing a carpet on the floor) in front of a mirrored screen behind the throne which is surrounded by the usual impedimenta of incense burners, ceremonial fans and high tables with pots of jewelled flowers. The partition doors on either side are of rosewood, the lower panels carved with bamboo and magnolia, the upper panels containing silk paintings made by senior officials enclosed within glass.

To the W was the Empress Dowager's sitting room and beyond that, separated by a large mirror carved with the characters for good luck and longevity, her bedroom. The bed, with its double curtains and marvellously variegated quilts is splendid. The upper parts of the lattice windows incorporate the Buddhist swastika (which goes the other way from that of the Nazis and is a symbol of good fortune) and circular motifs made up from bats and the character for long life, again. In the eastern side rooms are asymmetrical open display cabinets and a gaudy ivory 'dragon boat' model.

Leaving the Palace of Gathering Excellence, immediately to the E are the imperial garden and the northern gate of the Forbidden City. In the parallel series of 'Six Eastern Palaces', most of the halls are now filled with displays of objets d'art, many, though not all, from the old imperial collections (such as remain after Chiang Kai-shek had many of the treasures moved with him to Taiwan in 1949).

These and the major display of historical relics in the side halls to the E and W of the Three Great Halls could be visited together. Starting from the S, on either side of the raised sumeru platform on which stand the Three Great Halls (Supreme Harmony, Perfect Harmony and Preservation of Harmony), in the galleries that were once imperial storehouses for porcelain, furs, tea and other essentials, is a display of 'historical art', a chronologically arranged display which covers early man to the late 19C. Not particularly linked to the imperial family, their collections or imperial buildings, it is, in effect, another historical museum, of a high standard.

Behind the Hall of Preservation of Harmony, to the E of the gate that leads into the Palace of Heavenly Purity, is a small side gate. This leads to an alleyway that runs N and gives access to the Six Eastern Palaces. The first (southernmost) buildings to the right (E) of the alley, not strictly part of the Six Eastern Palaces, are the *Zhai Gong*, or Hall of Abstinence, where the early Qing emperors would come to fast for a day before proceeding to the Temple of Heaven or the Altar of the Earth (in the NE suburbs), and the associated Hall of Sincere Respect. Fasting apparently meant 'total abstention from wine, music, hot and spicy foods, as well as onions and garlic'.

In these and the next building, the *Jing ren gong* (Palace of Great Benevolence), are displays of bronze vessels, arranged in chronological order and including items from the old imperial collections.

The Jing ren gong was where the Kangxi emperor was born to the 15-year-old empress Xiaokang in 1654. Both the Qianlong and Daoguang emperors lived here as heirs-apparent and Zhen Fei, the beloved Pearl Concubine of the Tongzhi emperor (said to have been killed at the Dowager Empress Cixi's order), also lived here for a time.

The next building to the N is the *Palace of Inheriting Heaven*, a residence for concubines. It has a fine ceiling decorated with paired phoenixes (symbols of women, as opposed to the male dragon). It also used to contain Buddhist shrines for the concubines to worship. In the winter, birdcages with songbirds and aquaria were stored here. It now houses a display of ceramics, which is continued in the *Yonghe gong* (Palace of Eternal Peace), immediately to the E. The Yong he gong was once the residence of the imperial concubine Jin Fei (1874–1924), older sister of the Pearl Concubine.

N of the Jing ren Gong is the *Zhongcui gong* (Palace of Gathering Essence), used as the residence of the heirs-apparent in the early Ming. It has fine bamboo carving on the partition doors and unusually early *xuan zi* style painted decoration on the inner eaves. Most of the surviving *xuan zi* painting is Qing, this is Ming in date.

Immediately E of the Zhongcui gong is the *Jingyang gong* (Palace of the Great Yang) with a single-eaved hipped roof (similar to that of the Tang dynasty Foguang si on Wutai shan) and a wonderful ceiling painted in the Suzhou style with a paired crane motif.

The next hall to the S of the Palace of the Great Yang is the Yong he gong (see above) and S of that is the Yanfu gong (Palace of Prolonged Happiness).

If you then return to the courtyard behind the Hall of the Preservation of Harmony and take the gate to the E, opposite you is a gateway that leads to the *Hall for Worshipping Ancestors* (Juxian dian) in which there is now a large display of clocks and watches.

Originally a Ming construction, the large H-shaped hall was renovated in 1676, 1679, 1681 and 1737. During the Qing it was used to hold ancestral tablets (small painted wooden tablets on which the names of the deceased were inscribed and which 'represented' them). The tablet of Nurhaci (1559–1626), founder of the dynasty, was placed in the front part of the hall, those of his ancestors behind. The lower panels of the outer doors have a curly gold outline pattern on them, known as the *ruyi* pattern. As with the curled jade 'sceptres', S-shaped carved jades about 30cm long, known as '*ruyi*' sceptres, the term is somewhat baffling. The characters used mean 'as you wish, according to your wishes' so the intention when presenting a jade *ruyi* or decorating a door with the *ruyi* pattern is to hope that wishes will come true.

The crossbeams above are painted in a particularly decorative version of the *xuan zi* style and the interior columns are gilded. The clocks displayed include a massive Chinese clepsydra of great complexity, one where bronze buckets slowly drain downwards, raising a tiny gilt tongue-shaped baton (representing ivory *aide-mémoires* held by officials during imperial audience) held in the hand of a tiny figure near the bottom—a massive construction though the actual part telling the time requires binoculars. There are inscriptions in English which reveal that many of the enormously elaborate 18C and 19C timepieces were made abroad, in France, England, Switzerland and other places and were presented by foreign envoys (shades of the 'mechanical toys' brought by the Macartney mission of 1793). They grow increasingly elaborate: birds in gilded cages, elephants, pheasants, vases of flowers, some (like the Chinese clepsydra) with a tiny wristwatch somewhere in the composition.

S of the Hall for Worshipping Ancestors is a vast empty space stretching southwards to the front wall of the Palace. The *Arrow Pavilion* is the only building to break the view. Not strictly a pavilion, it is really a hall with a grand hipped and gabled roof and a large number of columns supporting the eaves boards of the surrounding verandah (reducing the number of intercolumnar brackets, reversing the normal Qing style). In this huge open space, the once-nomadic Manchu emperors rode their horses and practised archery and, in the Arrow Pavilion, tested the martial skills of examination candidates.

In the NE corner of the great open space is a small gate leading to a courtyard with a fine nine-dragon screen of coloured ceramic tiles on the right. This and the series of buildings on the left, known as the *Palace of Tranquil Longevity* (Ningshou gong), were built by the Qianlong emperor in 1722–26 as he intended to retire and spend his declining years here.

There were buildings on the site (dating from 1689) but he constructed his garden and the associated buildings and screen to cut himself off from the outside world. He only retired there in 1795 and spent the next four years (before his death) in this palace. In 1889 the deserted buildings were reoccupied by the Dowager Empress Cixi and it was from here that she fled to Xi'an in 1900 when European troops entered Peking to relieve the siege of the foreign legations that had been laid by Boxer rebels (with at least tacit support, if not more, from the court).

The *Gate of Imperial Supremacy* on the right leads to the courtyard in which stands the *Hall of Imperial Supremacy* (Huangji dian), approached by a raised stone walkway. This now contains a painting exhibition.

Ming and Qing paintings from the imperial collections are displayed in the hall, except during the month of October when some of the very early paintings are displayed. This only happens in October when the weather conditions (dry and fine, neither too hot nor too cold nor too damp) are appropriate.

The early paintings include a wonderful scroll of oxen, said to be Tang in date, the famous scroll by Zhang Zeduan (late 11–early 12C), *Qing ming shang he tu*, 'Going up the river on the eve of the Qingming festival', a lively depiction of daily life in the bustling capital of Kaifeng at the time, and many other significant works. After the death of the Dowager Empress in 1908, her coffin lay in state here for over a year, awaiting an auspicious day for burial.

Behind the Hall of Imperial Supremacy is the *Ningshou gong* (Palace of Tranquil Longevity), on the same stone platform. The painting exhibition is continued in here and in the galleries to W and E that run around the courtyard. Behind, the *Gate of Spiritual Cultivation* (Yangxing men) leads to a small area with three axes, built as the private living quarters of the Qianlong emperor.

To the W (left) is the entrance to the charming **Garden of the Palace of Tranquil Longevity**, built by the emperor.

It is long and narrow, but perfectly designed to provide a series of pavilions and views in a restricted space (a clever example of the sort of garden that was associated with grander domestic buildings of the north). Its northerness is seen in the use of colour—all the pavilions are painted red and green with Suzhou style painting under the eaves (southern garden architecture is monochrome so as not to compete with the plants which, in the north, are absent in winter).

Inside the *Gate of Spreading Happiness*, on the right is the *Pavilion of the Carpenters' Square* (a name redolent of simplicity and unworldliness) and on the right is the most notable pavilion, the *Pavilion of the Ceremony of Purification* with the maze-shaped channel in the floor, a 'cup-floating stream', other examples of which can be seen in the Tanzhe Temple outside Peking and at Shaoxing.

That at Shaoxing is the 'original' version, where the famous calligrapher Wang Xizhe (321–379) is supposed to have originated the 'party game' of floating a wine cup along a meandering stream on whose banks his friends sat. When the cup floated in front of one, he would have to compose a poem—or, as a forfeit, drink the cup of wine thus creating an atmosphere of literati conviviality. Here, lacking running water, huge vats were used to store well-water which was poured along the channel.

Rockeries with hidden steps and paths complete the first courtyard of the garden which stretches back through four more with intervening halls. (The central part has not been openrecently but if it is possible to walk right through the garden, the rear building, the *Study of Peaceful Old Age*, has a very interesting interior with a small stage and the most extraordinary trompe-l'oeil wall and ceiling paintings, with a grape arbour on the ceiling and bamboo fencing concealing further buildings on the walls).

The central axis of this NE corner of the Forbidden City is occupied by a series of charming low halls of a domestic character which now house some of the palace treasures. As it is normal to exit through these halls, first go to the far end of the courtyard where you will find the *Changyin ge* (Pavilion of Pleasant Sounds), the largest of the theatrical stages in the Forbidden City. It houses an exhibition of photographs of palace actors in opera costume, props and costumes and some unusual manuscript playscripts.

This stage was built by Qianlong, though he rarely visited it; it was used far more frequently by the Dowager Empress Cixi when she lived in the adjoining halls. Though a troupe was maintained within the palace, in the late 19C famous actors from outside such as Mei Lanfang (who died in the 1950s after many performing visits outside China) were also invited to perform here. In China, theatrical performances were associated with festivals (whether popular or restricted such as guild celebrations) and this was also true in the Forbidden City.

Performances were given at birthdays, ceremonies of granting titles or the accession to the throne as well as at the annual festivals of the Beginning of Spring, Mid-Autumn, New Year and many others. For the 60th birthday of the Dowager Empress, performances lasting 6–7 hours were performed over two periods of a week.

The pavilion is a three-storey building, with the stage on the central floor as the upper and lower floors were used for special effects (people or backdrops ascending and descending. Opposite is the two-storeyed *Yueshi lou*, the imperial viewing building.

On the way back to the central axis, note the unusual pillar in the corner of the courtyard with a little grey 'palace building' with arched openings on top of it. Its position suggests to me that it is a chimney though others have suggested that it is a dovecote.

The treasury is housed in two charming halls on the central axis of this corner of the Forbidden City: the *Hall of Spiritual Cultivation* (Yangxing dian) and the *Hall of Pleasurable Old Age* (Leshou tang), both of which are built on the small scale and decorated in a very different way from the grand halls of the outer court.

They contain palace treasures, many of which are self-explanatory: gold ingots, golden bells (cast in 1715 using 422kg of gold), 18C jade musical stones (imitating those of the Shang dynasty), gold and silver vessels from the imperial table and a wonderful collection of translucent 'spinach' green jade elegance (which look like vichyssoise). The stupa-shaped reliquary of cloisonné was made in 1777 to contain the hair of Qianlong's mother on her death. There is armour with gilded and silver links, there are silken robes, countless necklaces of interestingly mixed stones in subtle colours (and great use of baroque pearls), head-dresses of kingfisher feathers, mats made from plaited strands of ivory (cool to sleep on in hot summers, used by the Yongzheng emperor in the old Summer Palace, Yuanming yuan) and a lot of *pen jing* (pot scenes) of jade, amethyst, rose quartz and other semi-precious stones carved into flowers and leaves. There is a huge block of jade weighing some 5 tons, carved in the Qianlong reign with scenes of the Great Yu 'taming the floods' and controlling China's rivers.

The buildings themselves are very much domestic, the rear hall with a screen made up of irregular openwork display panels (Qianlong intended it as a library) and with a low upper storey. The ceilings are painted in the Suzhou style.

As you leave the Hall of Pleasurable Old Age, you pass a small well-cover (a 30cm-high ring of stone with a metal bar through it). This is known as the *Zhen Fei jing* or 'Well of the Pearl Concubine' for she was supposed to have been drowned in it in 1900 as the Dowager Empress fled the Palace as the western troops entered the city. The concubine, only 25 when she was unceremoniously bundled down the well (supposedly for trying to encourage the Emperor to stay in Peking and face the consequences of Cixi's support for the Boxers), must have been remarkably slender.

Just beyond the well is gate that leads out of the inner wall of the Forbidden City. As you walk W towards the northern gate, notice the wonderful long corridors that run down between great red walls.

The SE corner of the Forbidden City, from which the Donghua men (Eastern Flowery Gate) exit gate leads out to Nanchizi Street, is the library and cultural section of the palace. From the N, a small back gate leads into the enclosure and the first hall (to the N) is the *Wenyuan ge* (Hall of the Literary Abyss), built in 1774–76 by the Qianlong emperor to house one of the copies of the vast imperial collectanea, 'Si ku quan shu' (Complete Treasury of the Four Storehouses), a huge manuscript encyclopaedic work in 36,000 volumes containing containing copies of some 3450 works.

A similar building is to be found in the Bi shu shan zhuang in Chengde, and in Shenyang (Wensu ge) and all are said to be modelled on the Tianyi ge Library in Ningbo (q.v.) though, as the latter is a southern construction with uplifted eaves and the imperial versions are all rather solid northern constructions, the similarity is spiritual rather than demonstrable. However, all have pools and rockeries around them (to help prevent fire), and all are two (or more) storeys high.

Just S of the library building is the H-shaped *Wenhua dian* (Hall of Literary Glory) where the emperors would come once a year for a reading from the Confucian classics. A wall, with a main gate in the S, surrounds the whole.

On the other side of the Palace, W of the *Taihe men* (Gate of Supreme Harmony) is a parallel series of buildings including the **Wuying dian** (Hall of Military Eminence).

During the Ming this was a place where the emperor 'could purify himself by fasting and separating himself from his concubines'; during the period when the peasant leader Li Zicheng took Peking at the very end of the Ming(1644), he directed his affairs of state from this hall.

Its name is well-known to bibliographers for, during the Qing, it housed the palace printing establishment (known by the name of the hall) where imperial editions were prepared and printed. Unusually, for virtually all of China's publishing up to the mid 19C was by the woodblock technique, a font of copper moveable type was prepared in the Wuying dian in order to print another massive collectanea (this time more of an encyclopaedia for it was composed of extracts from former works, arranged by topic), the 'Gu jin tu shu ji cheng' (Synthesis of Books and Illustrations of Ancient and Modern Times), printed in an edition of 64 in 1728. The work consisted of 10,000 volumes covering all sorts of subjects, thus the font was massive, comprising over a quarter of a million pieces of copper type. As traditional printers might have guessed, the use of moveable type proved unwieldy and the method was not repeated in the Wuying dian (and such was the value of the copper that the font was soon melted down and used for coinage).

B.   Central Peking (within walking distance of the Peking Hotel)

The Forbidden City used to be surrounded by another, larger rectangular enclosure some six times the size of the Palace proper, which contained granaries, parks for rearing sheep and cows, storehouses, residences of princes and high officials and the numerous craftsmen who worked both on the upkeep of the city itself (carpenters, masons, painters, brick-makers) or in the imperial workshops producing such goods as clocks and watches, clothing, glasswares, metalwares, jewellery and ceramics. The ceramics were usually porcelains made in Jingdezhen in Jiangxi province and shipped, undecorated, to the Palace where overglaze enamel decoration was applied.

The outer walls of the 'imperial city' have largely disappeared except to the S where a high red wall with a yellow ceramic tile top extends from beside the Peking Hotel (E) to the western end of the *Nan hai* (Southern Sea) *Lake*. To the W, the whole area around the *Zhong hai* (Middle Sea— also the name applied to the Mediterranean) and the *Nan hai*, known collectively as ZHONGNANHAI, is closed to the public and, as in the past, houses the supreme government organs and the official residence of the Head of State. Thus when protestors gather in Peking, whether they are peasants or students or whatever, they frequently sit outside the ornamental gates of the Zhongnanhai in the hope of presenting their petitions to the Head of State, as they would have waited to present petitions to the Emperor or his high officials in the past.

A narrow road, Nanchizi, runs along the eastern side of the Forbidden City. At the end where it meets Chang'an jie, it is entered through an archway in the red wall, indicating that it was once a closed part of the extended 'imperial city'. Not far up Nanchizi, on the E side of the road is the yellow-roofed **Imperial Archive** (Huang shi cheng).

Built in 1534, rebuilt under the Qing and recently restored, it is an interesting fire-proofed brick-vaulted building with a roof of the imperial yellow tiles. As the Chinese had always set such store by documents and history (and the Qing, though originally non-Chinese, adopted Chinese methods of government and traditions), it was essential to guard imperial archives against fire. The 'Shi lu' (True Records), used in compiling dynastic histories and therefore not necessarily 'true' but rather reflections of the official view, were kept in the archive, as were imperial edicts. Official biographies were compiled for each emperor. During the Qing paperwork proliferated as all official records of this sort were written out both in Chinese and Manchu (though towards the end of the dynasty, Manchu was increasingly abandoned).

The Ming and Qing imperial archives have, unfortunately, been separated between Taiwan and Peking and the vast majority of those that remain in Peking are now housed in a separate archive building. The imperial archive still contains some of the copper-covered chests in which the archives were originally stored on a long stone platform and there is an exhibition of various types of archive material including examples of imperial annotations in vermilion ink. Other documents displayed in the enclosure include charming paintings, half-architectural, half-decorative, of buildings visited and used as temporary residences by the emperors on their tours of inspection of the south in the 18C, and of imperial parks.

A little further up Nanchizi, also on the eastern side but further off the road along narrow lanes, is the Pudu si (Temple of Universal Rescue; closed, 1988).

The third major turning on the right (E) up Nanchizi, Dengshikou xi jie (Western Lantern Market Street) leads to WANGFUJING (Well of the Princely Mansion), one of the main shopping streets in Peking. In Dengshikou xi jie there is a Bank of China building on the left (N) and just beside it a narrow lane runs N. The first house (on the left, W) was the home of Lao She (1899–1966), one of the great writers of the 20C. The house, still inhabited by his painter widow and daughter, is not yet open to the public though it may be in future as it appears on tourist maps.

Lao She was the son of an impoverished Manchu bannerman. Under Nurhaci (1559–1626), the Manchus organised themselves into 'banners', military groupings into which all villagers and tribes were recruited. The 'banners' were effectively garrisons but they carried with them their wives and families—some of the former village settlements on the northern outskirts of Peking preserve the banner names, such as Lanqi ying (Blue Banner Barracks). A member of the imperial guard, Lao She's father was killed in 1900 during the siege of the foreign legations by the Boxers.

Lao She, who later worked as a Chinese-language tutor in London University's School of Oriental and African Studies, is very much a Peking novelist. His most famous work, 'Luo tuo xiang zi' (Rickshaw Boy; 1936) is about a rickshaw puller in the city, gradually worn out and forced into poverty; but some of Lao She's most charming work is autobiographical and describes life in old Peking in wonderful detail.

Continue E to the crossroads with Wangfujing and turn N into Wangfujing. The Jesuits' *Eastern Church* (Dong tang) is a little way up on the E side of the road (it is now a primary school).

The present building dates from the early 20C but it stands on the site of Adam Schall von Bell's house, where he died in 1666. Verbiest, his successor as Director of the Board of Astronomy and Mathematics, took it over on behalf of the Portuguese Jesuits and built St. Joseph's Church on part of the site. Destroyed in the early 19C, this was said to have been built in the Ionic style and to be the most beautiful church in Peking. After the suppression of the Jesuits, Portuguese Lazarists took over the church but they were expelled in 1811, only to return in 1860. They then built another church on the site with an altar of Naples marble and red sandstone pillars with gilt capitals but this was destroyed by the Boxers in 1900.

If you turn S into Wangfujing from Dengshikou xi jie, the second major turning on the left (E) is JINYU HUTONG (Goldfish Lane), still lined with low grey houses typical of Peking domestic architecture. The whole area, between Wangfujing and Dong dan (the next major road to the E) still retains some of the flavour of old Peking.

When wandering in hutongs, look out for the remains of ornamental doorways. These often have cut-brick panels on the pilasters, frequently in the form of a hanging basket of flowers, sometimes with the Buddhist swastika (a symbol of good fortune). At the base of the door, the jambs used to stand in rather fine carved stone bases, sometimes rounded (drum-shaped), sometimes rectangular, and often carved. Though most houses have simple grey-tiled roofs, either with a built-up ridge or the 'rolled' ridge, some have tiny decorated circular end tiles (impressed with little gaping tiger faces or dragons) along the eaves and some have cut-bricks in the form of auspicious characters inset in the ridge.

Occasionally you will see a glazed drainage tile (in the form of an inverted triangle) at the eaves. Note the varying ways in which the tiles are laid—though uniformly grey, they are not uniform in shape. Some are semi-cylindrical, some in flatter curves. The latter are often laid in alternating rows, one row serving as a gutter, the next built up on a couch of grey clay. It is almost impossible to see inside the courtyards: doors are kept closed and there may be a spirit wall inside the gate, but occasionally you can catch a glimpse of a cluttered interior court. Though demolition is proceeding apace, it was possible to get a good view of courtyards from about the fourth floor of the Heping binguan (Peace Hotel), the first building on the left (N) in Goldfish Lane (Jinyu hutong).

You can return to Chang'an jie and the Peking Hotel either by walking down Wangfujing or Dong Dan and then back westwards along Chang'an jie.

If you continue to the end of Goldfish Lane, you reach Dongsi nan da jie, one major intersection S of the crossroads named Dongsi (Eastern Four) because four large pailou or triumphal arches in brightly-painted wood (one across each street at the intersection) used to stand there. They were matched by four more to the W, at the intersection known as Xisi (Western Four) just beyond the Beihai Park.

If you turn left up the main road (Dongsi nan da jie), after three turnings on the left you will find the **Dong si Mosque** on your left on the main road. Also known as the *Faming si* (Temple of the Propagation of Brightness), it was first constructed in 1356 and restored in 1447, when the costs were borne by Chen You, a Moslem military commander.

Covering an area of 10,000 square metres, its main constructions include the prayer hall, a pair of subsidiary teaching halls, a library and a pool for purification. It is said to preserve a mixture of Ming and Islamic building styles. The rear part of the main hall is brick-vaulted (a form found commonly in northern mosques (in Peking's Niu jie Mosque for example), creating a characteristically low-ceilinged, broad hall and the interior is richly carved and gilded, with Koranic texts.

The mosque contains many relics, including a Yuan manuscript Koran, the 1468 bronze finial of the minaret and an inscribed stele in both Chinese and Arabic dated to 1579, recording the 1447 restoration.

Opposite the mosque is a substantial church, closed to the public and about which I have been able to gather no information.

The entire block S of the Peking Hotel, stretching westwards to include the area now covered in the northern part by the Historical Museum and bounded to the S by Qianmen dong da jie, to the E by Dong dan gongyuan (Dong dan park) and Chang'an jie to the N, used to be the FOREIGN LEGATION QUARTER, beseiged by Boxer rebels in 1900. As you walk through it, you can still see plenty of older Western buildings.

The first foreigners to occupy a building in the area were the Russians in 1727, when they were permitted to maintain a permanent ecclesiastical mission according to the terms of the Treaty of Kiachta (or Kiakhta). This was negotiated by Savva Lukitch Vladislavich, the 'Illyrican Count', who went as ambassador to China in 1725 to announce the death of Peter the Great and the accession of Catherine. In Peking he accomplished little but his treaty, signed on the border, regularised trade contacts, fixed borders and opened the ecclesiastical mission which occupied the area subsequently used for the Russian Legation (on the N side of Dongjiaomin xiang, W of

Zhengyi lu). The area had formerly contained the internal customs house and Dongjiaomin xiang means Lane of Contact with Eastern Peoples, some say because traders from outside Peking came here to do business. During the Cultural Revolution, when some embassies were still housed in the area, the streetname was changed to 'Anti-imperialist Street'.

After the Russians, the French and British opened their legations in the area (the British immediately to the N of the Russians and the French further E, on the corner of Dongjiaomin xiang and Taijichang da jie). It is said that they chose the area, not because the Russians were there but because of its proximity to the Six Boards (ministries) of the Qing government, lining what is now Tiananmen Square. They naturally assumed that the Chinese 'foreign office' would be conveniently close but the Chinese, incensed that the foreigners had not accepted their offers of land outside the city, created a new office to deal with foreigners (the Zongli yamen, its full name of Zongli geguo shiwu yamen meaning 'Office in Charge of the Affairs of All Countries') in 1860 and set it to the NE of the expanding Legation Quarter, off Dongdan da jie.

Until 1900 the area included many Chinese houses between the embassies but after the Boxer seige destruction of the Legations (and at the insistence of the victorious foreign powers), all Chinese dwellings were cleared and the spaces filled with more legations, banks, hotels, Kierulf's stores (much favoured by the Manchu nobility and their trains of concubines) and other essential offices.

The area used to be surrounded by a glacis and Dongdan Park was once the polo ground, bounded on the E side by Hatamen Street (Chongwenmen nei da jie) and on the W by 'Avenue Yamato'. The slightly curving Dongjiaomin xiang (which runs just N of and roughly parallel to Qianmen dong da jie) was once called Legation Street.

Along it were (from the E): the German compound and German barracks and the Belgian Legation to the S with the Post Office next to a Catholic church (whose twin spires can still be seen) on the corner of Rue Marco Polo (now Taijichang da jie). Turning up (N) Taijichang da jie, on the right was the French Barracks and the Peking Club (still used as the International Club in the early 1970s) and, on the left, the French Legation and a Customs building (this, I think, is now occupied by the Chinese People's Association for Friendship with Foreign Countries).

Along Chang'an jie, but set back beyond the glacis, were the Austrian Legation, the Italian Legation and the huge area of the British Legation (which was built from 1860 in the grounds of a princely mansion belonging to Prince Liang, who could no longer afford to maintain it). This is now largely covered by the Historical Museum. S of the British Legation, on the N side of Legation Street at its westernmost end was the Russian Legation (reasonably acceptable in 1860 but considered uncomfortably close by the British after 1917). The United States barracks and Legation were on the S side of Legation Street at the western end, near Qian men. The Wagons-lits Hotel was on the corner of Rue Meiji and Wall Street (Zhengyi lu and Qianmen dong da jie respectively). By 1976, with the exception of the large Soviet Embassy, all embassies and their personnel were moved to two new settlements at Jianguomen wai (near the International Club and Friendship Store) and Sanlitun in the NE (near the Changcheng, Great Wall, Hotel).

Behind the Forbidden City is the separate entrance to **Jing shan Park** (Jing shan, Scenic Mountain, is the contemporary name for the artificial hill built with the earth excavated from the moat of the Forbidden City and formerly known as Mei shan, Coal Hill to early Western visitors).

It stands on the site of an imperial garden of the Yuan dynasty but was made into a hillock, or a series of five ascending hillocks, under the Ming. In the mid 18C the Qianlong emperor had pavilions built on the hillocks and fruit trees planted on the slopes, giving rise to an alternative name, the Garden of 100 Fruit Trees. The small enclosure was also said to have been stocked with hares, rabbits and singing birds.

Opposite the southern gate is the *Qiwang lou* (Tower of the Beautiful View), dedicated to Confucius. The central pavilion on top of the hill is called the Wanchun ting (Pavilion of Ten-thousand Springs—spring as a season); the Buddha figure is recent. From here, to the S you get a useful overview of the Forbidden City with its long axes of main halls in the centre and the tightly-packed rear private buildings.

To the N is the broad *Drum Tower* (Gu lou), built in 1420 in a similar style to the major gates in the city walls with a broad brick base and a wide hall, its columns beautifully painted, above. It marks the centre of the Yuan capital of Dadu and stands on the site of the first drum tower built in 1272. Drum towers (once found in all major towns) housed huge drums to beat the hours through the day and night (traditional Chinese hours were two hours long).

Behind it, slightly to the NE, is the *Bell Tower* (Zhong lou). First built in the early Ming, it was burned down and the present building is mid 18C. Its great bell, used to mark the closing of the city gates in the evening, is no longer in place. It is narrower with a taller base than the Drum Tower and is made of grey brick.

On the W side of Jing shan, at the base, is the *Dagaoxuan dian* (Great, Tall, Dark Hall) built by the Ming Jiajing emperor (reigned 1522–67) and containing a Taoist temple, as its name implies. The emperors used to come here to pray to the Yellow Emperor (a legendary ruler of China, 2698–2598 BC, whose benevolence was recognised by the appearance of *qilin*—Chinese unicorns—and phoenix) for rain. The temple is closed to the public (1988).

At the foot of the hill, on the E side, is the tree from which the last Ming emperor (Chongzhen) is said to have hanged himself in 1644. As the troops of the rebel leader Li Zicheng entered the palace, the emperor is said to have fled to the hill behind and bidden farewell to his family before taking off his boots and hanging himself.

N of the hill is the Qianlong period *Shouhuang dian* (Hall of Imperial Longevity), where the portraits of previous emperors used to be kept (it is now part of the Peking Children's Palace).

Immediately to the W of Jing shan, the road (Wenjin jie) crosses a lake, called *Zhongnanhai* to the S (closed to all but government employees) and *Beihai* to the N. The broad bridge looks a place of good omen now but, according to Peking legend, there used to be a ghostly donkey-driver who offered lifts here and then tipped his victims into the lake to drown. Tucked into a corner on the northern side of the street, just beside the bridge is the main entrance to the **Beihai Park**.

The northernmost of the three lakes that formed part of the gardens associated with the Forbidden City (until the end of the Qing, these were, of course, well inside the imperial city so not easily accessible to the masses), the Beihai Lake is the focus of a public park which includes the Round Town Peninsula, the ancient site of the Altar of Silkworms (now a children's park) and a group of garden buildings constructed during the reign of Qianlong in the NW corner.

The park occupies a site that was used as a garden by the Liao emperors (907–1125) although the lakes were not dug out until the succeeding Jin dynasty (1115–1234) occupied Peking. Khublai Khan chose this area as the site for his palace, which he built in the small enclosure on the S bank of the lake now known as the 'Round Town'. At the beginning of the 15C the Ming divided the lakes, separating Beihai from the double Zhongnanhai and, when the old Yuan palace was in ruins, the White Dagoba was built on the circular island (Qiong hua, Hortensia Island) (1651). Qianlong made many improvements to the garden in the mid 18C, though the area was damaged in 1900 when Western Allied troops sacked the palace area during the suppression of the Boxers.

The present bridge (presumably no longer haunted) crossing the southern end of the Bei hai where it joins the southern lakes was built in 1956.

Immediately inside the gate is the entrance to the **Round Town** which encloses a courtyard with fine white pines and cypresses (said to be Liao or Jin in date) and a small blue-tiled pavilion (1745). This houses a huge 'black jade wine bowl' carved with mountain streams, dragons and fish.

The bowl is said to have been presented to Khublai Khan in 1265 and inscriptions in its praise are housed in the pavilion. According to one account, it was lost at the end of the Yuan and rediscovered in the early years of the Qing in a small temple where it was used for pickling vegetables.

Behind is the *Chengguang dian* (Hall of Inherited Lustre) which houses a white jade Buddha brought from Burma in the last years of the 19C.

The British Minister, O'Connor, was received in the Round Town when he presented his credentials to the Guangxu emperor in 1893 (instead of the more usual hall in the Zhongnanhai) and it was used as a prison for Cao Kun, last President of the Chinese Republic in 1924–26. Imprisoned by one warlord, Feng Yuxiang (the 'Christian General', said to have baptised his troops with a hosepipe) who occupied Peking in 1924, he was released by another, Zhang Zuolin (the 'Old Marshall', ruler of Manchuria from 1911 until he was blown up in a train in 1928 by the Japanese Kwantung Army which was taking over his area of command).

N of the Round Town is a bridge leading to the circular **Hortensia Island** (so-called because eating hortensia was supposed to confer immortality), dominated by the *White Dagoba* (Tibetan-style stupa). A pair of pailou stand at the end of this bridge (and the other which leads to the eastern shore of the lake). The inscriptions on the pailou read 'Accumulated moisture of heaven' and 'Piled clouds'.

The White Dagoba towers over the major lower buildings: those immediately at the end of the bridge form the *Yongan si* (Temple of Everlasting Peace), also built in 1651 and, together with the dagoba, constructed to celebrate the first visit by a Dalai Lama to Peking. Pavilions inside the temple pailou contain stone-carved inscriptions written by the Shunzhi and Yongzheng emperors recording the construction of the temple and other buildings. Behind the eastern pavilion is a large rock inscribed with the characters *Kunlun* (Chinese for Sumeru, the Buddhist holy mountain).

Over to the W is the two-storey *Qingxiao lou* (Pavilion of Felicitous Skies) where the Qianlong emperor used to come with his mother on the 8th day of the 12th month (January) to watch skating parties on the lake (the ice smoothed with flat-irons so as not to trip the imperial guards as they performed). Above is the White Dagoba, a Tibetan inscription meaning 'the all-powerful ten' on its S side, opposite a small square building covered with multi-coloured glazed tile Buddha figures. Inside is Yamantaka, one of the 10 'irate protectors', Lamaist guardians of the faith.

On the northern side of the island, the *Yilan tang* (Hall of Rippling Waves) and associated buildings are now occupied by a restaurant (Fangshan or 'Imitation delicacies' fandian) which is famous for its 'imperial' cuisine, especially the petits fours faintly resembling miniature 'wowotou' the great indigestible lumps of maize flour eaten by peasants.

It is said that on the Dowager Empress's flight to Xi'an in 1900, when she was terribly hungry on her hurried journey, a peasant served her wowotou, the only food he had. As she was famished, she enjoyed them greatly and, when reinstated in the Palace, ordered her cook to make them. Knowing she would be unlikely to enjoy them quite as much in her more comfortable surroundings, he made tiny wowotou using light water-chestnut flour instead of heavy maize.

Round to the W of the island, one of the major buildings is the *Yuegu lou* (Tower for the Inspection of Ancient Scripts), a crescent-shaped hall where 400 stone tablets inscribed with the calligraphy of great masters of the past (including the 'three Wangs', Wang Xizhi, Wang Xianzhi and Wang Xun of the 2C AD) are set into the walls. These, the best possible selection made by the scholars of the imperial academy (the Hanlin or Forest of Brushes Academy), were chosen for the Qianlong emperor.

The eastern shore of the Bei hai leads past the site of the imperial boat house to where the Hall of Imperial Silkworms and the Altar of Silkworms used to stand (now a children's park).

Two stone terraces (altars) were used for examining mulberry leaves before giving them to the silkworms (which were kept in houses along the outer walls) and where offerings were made to the God of Mulberries. During the 3rd lunar month empresses (or their deputies) used to come and make offerings to the Goddess of Silkworms, for sericulture was supposed to have been invented by Xi ling, wife of the Yellow Emperor (in 2602 BC). In fact, a silk cocoon, apparently partly cut in half (presumably by human agency) was discovered in 1927 in a neolithic Yangshao site of c 5000–4000 BC; thus the actuality of sericulture may antedate the legend.

If you walk on, past the northern gate, the group of buildings clustered in the NW corner of the park were mainly built in the mid 18C by the Qianlong emperor although they were later favoured by the Dowager Empress Cixi in the later 19C. The easternmost is a walled enclosure, a tiny garden filled with pools, bridges and pavilions with names such as *Playing the Lute Studio, House of Rare Paintings* which indicate Qianlong's hand and interests. The garden, a very fine example of a northern garden, built in a small space and filled with brightly coloured pavilions and piled rocks, is called the *Studio of the Restful Mind* (Qingxin zhai). It was restored a few years ago (though it has sometimes been closed since).

Many of the other buildings are now used as exhibition halls and places of popular entertainment but they were previously (immediately W of the garden): the *Pavilion of 10,000 Buddhas* (behind) and *Xiaoxi dian* (Small Western Sky), a temple group with (behind) a three-storeyed building covered with green and yellow glazed tile Buddha figures and the *Nine-dragon Screen* (similar to that in the Forbidden City), a huge screen wall covered with glazed-tile dragons, built in 1417 in front of a temple (which no longer exists). Next (to the W) is the walled enclosure of the *Pine Hill Library* (Songpo tushuguan) containing three halls: the Hall of Crystal Waters, Porch Where Orchids are Washed (on the 5th of the 5th lunar month at the Dragon Boat Festival) and the Hall of Joyful Snow, a name taken from one of Wang Xizhi's poems. The poet and calligrapher was apparently describing a snowstorm in verse when snowflakes began to fall, hence his joy.

On the lake shore, in front of what is now a children's science museum, are the *Wulong ting* (Five Dragon Pavilions), five little pavilions built out in the lake in the form of a curved dragon's spine. Against the western wall is an open-air cinema, once the *Great Western Heaven Temple*, with glazed tiling inscribed with Buddhist texts. The building is unusual in construction with four pailou, one on either side, and a massive roof frame supported by four rows of columns.

Returning to the main gate by the western side of the lake, the buildings just outside the SW corner of the park used to be the *National Library* (founded in 1910).

The library has now been largely rehoused in a new, air-conditioned tower block beside the Zizhu yuan (Purple Bamboo Park) in the NW of the city, not far from the major university campuses. Some of the rare books are still in the old library building (1989). Behind the library, there was (until 1900) a famous temple which used to contain a 1.5m red sandalwood Buddha figure and where Peking's Lamaists used to come and worship every year on the 8th day of the 1st lunar month; all that now remains of the temple is in the name of the small street N of the Library, Zhantansi jie (Red Sandalwood Temple Street).

Immediately W of the southern entrance to the Beihai Park are the Bei Tang (Jesuit, or Northern Church), Guangji si (Temple of Universal Rescue), the White Pagoda Temple (Miaoying or Baita si) and the residence of Lu Xun.

The **Bei Tang** or Northern Church is at Xishikkowu, just to the N of Xi'anmen da jie, W of the old National Library building, up a narrow lane leading N from the main road. Its twin spires and grey and white-painted wedding-cake façade are clearly visible.

This is the third 'Northern Church'. The first was built after a grant of land within the imperial city from the Kangxi emperor in 1693 and consecrated in 1703. The group of French Jesuits, sent to China by Louis XIV (including Fathers Gerbillon and Bouvet), gained favour with the Kangxi emperor by acting as interpreters during the negotiations with Russia over the Treaty of Nertchinsk (1689; allowing the Russians to build a fort there and fixing a river boundary) and by making astronomical calculations. They persuaded him to sign an 'edict of tolerance'. The gift of land for a church was made, however, after they had cured him of a serious illness by using the newly discovered quinine (sent from Pondicherry by a fellow Jesuit).
  During the reign of Yongzheng the Jesuits fell from imperial favour and, following the suppression of the order (1773), despite Louis XVI's Lazarist mission (intended to take over the Bei tang), the church land was sold to a mandarin in 1827 and the build-

ing demolished. The Conventions of Peking (1860) included a stipulation that Catholic mission property should be returned so a new building was erected on the old site in 1867—including the stone steps of the former cathedral and a wrought-iron grille of the period of Louis XV.

This second cathedral was the subject of fierce arguments with the Chinese who objected to the height of the spire. The Chinese believed that good spirits flew at a height of 30m and therefore no towers should be built that might impede their passage. This second church was therefore built with an impressive triple arched façade but nothing much in the way of a spire. No sooner was the church finished, however, than it had to be abandoned because the Dowager Empress Cixi had decided to live on the shore of the Zhong hai (she had to leave her apartments in the Forbidden City on the marriage of the Guangxu emperor) and she did not want the church nearby. Li Hongzhang (1823–1901), one of the 'modernising' officials (associated with modern arsenal, steamship and naval projects and the establishment of modern naval and military academies) negotiated with Monsignor Favier and the site on which today's Bei tang stands (still within the imperial city but in an area near stores) was selected. The third building was consecrated in 1889.

The old Bei tang had been used as a store for Cixi's possessions and Pierre Loti described a visit during the plunder of the city by the allied armies after their defeat of the Boxers in 1900: 'Imperial robes of heavy silk brocaded with gold dragons lie on the ground...we walk over them, we walk over carved ivories, over pearls and embroideries galore...This church, so full of pagan riches, has kept its organ intact, altough it has been silent for thirty years. My comrade mounts with me to the gallery to try the effect of some hymns of Bach and Handel, while the African chasseurs, up to their knees in ivories, silks and court costumes, continue their task of clearing things out below' ('The Last Days of Peking', translated from the French, Boston, Little Brown, 1902).

The building was destroyed in 1911. Meanwhile, the third Bei tang had been beseiged by the Boxers at the same time as the Foreign Legation Quarter to the SE and 400 Chinese Christians were killed assisting Italian and French soldiers to defend the church (which was relieved by Japanese soldiers).

Though it was made into a school during the Cultural Revolution, the Bei tang has now once again been restored to the Peking Catholic Patriotic Association (Beijing shi tianzhujiao aiguo hui) and during 1985 it was extensively restored and reopened on 24 December 24 1985 and the Bishop is Fu Tieshan.

The Gothic façade (its twin towers were increased in height after 1900) is cheerfully painted and the interlaced columns of the vaulted interior are striped red and black, creating a Strawberry Hill gothic effect. Much of the stained glass has survived intact. Outside, the gardens and the Grotto of Our Lady (a wonderful mixture of Lourdes and Chinese garden rockeries) have been restored and the twin Chinese pavilions have been rebuilt to house imperial stelae. Some of the pieces of imperial calligraphy (such as the red board inscribed in gold by the Kangxi emperor with the words 'Profoundly true origin') are replicas. The church is now open to visitors and worshippers.

W of the Bei tang is one of the major temples in Peking, the **Guangji si** (Temple of Universal Rescue). Take Xi'anmen da jie W until you reach Xida bei da jie and turn right (N). The next crossroads is Xi si (West Four), paired with Dong si, where once four pailou stood across the roads. Take the turning on the left (W), Fuchengmen nei da jie. The temple, behind green arched gates in a grey brick wall, is on the N side of the street.

The site has been occupied by a temple since the 12C (when it was the temple of West Liu village in the northern outskirts of Zhongdu, the 'Middle Capital'). It was rebuilt in the Yuan and again in 1457 and expanded in 1466, 1584 and 1694. It has seen three disastrous fires, the last in 1934 when the main and rear halls were largely destroyed and the Ming edition of the Tripitaka (Buddhist scriptures) and a white sandalwood Buddha figure (a gift from abroad) were also destroyed. Major restorations were undertaken in 1952 and 1972.

The façade of the temple, aside from its great doors, has an inscription in yellow lozenges reading 'the wheel of the law turns eternally', and the gates open onto a very spacious courtyard. On the main axis are a gatehouse, the Hall of Heavenly Kings, main hall, Guanyin Hall and library. Inside a courtyard on the western axis is a triple-tiered white marble ordination platform where ordination ceremonies were performed which include the shaving of monks' and nuns' heads and the burning of little piles of incense on the scalp: these scars persist for some time and a triple or double row of tiny burn marks on a shaved head can indicate that the person is no longer a novice but has been ordained.

Inside the main hall, the most important thing is the very rare painting on the back of the screen behind the altar. This monochrome of the Buddha expounding the Law is by the 18C artist Chuan Wen and is a 'finger painting' (or a finger and fingernail painting).

Eccentric painting implements have a considerable history in China and are particularly associated with Chan (Zen) Buddhist painters. Some of the earliest Tang Chan painters used to paint with the end of their long hair, as well as fingers. Chuan Wen's large painting is wonderfully vigorous, crowded with lively figures.

In the *Guanyin Hall* behind, there is a Qing 'thousand-eyed, thousand-armed' (omnipotent) Guanyin; a smaller copper figure of the deity on a lotus flower (Ming), and a great number of gifts from Buddhists abroad.

The temple is the headquarters of the Buddhist Association of China and is therefore visited by an enormous number of Buddhist pilgrims (mainly from Japan and Southeast Asia).

A little further W along the same street (also on the N side), a middle school now occupies the remains of the *Lidai diwang miao* (Temple of Generations of Rulers). The temple was used by both the Ming and Qing emperors to house the ancestral tablets of long-dead rulers—those of their personal ancestors were kept in the imperial palace.

This secondary temple echoes traditional practice: families usually kept the tablets of the last three generations in their home, to include these recent ancestors in family worship; if the family were rich enough to possess an ancestral hall in the village they stored the tablets of long-dead, long-forgotten ancestors there. There were sometimes differing viewpoints and tablets were removed and replaced according the prevailing view: Kubilai Khan's tablet moved a couple of times during the Qing. The temple was built in 1530 and restored in 1729. A white marble balustrade in front of the main hall is said to be a fairly rare example but the school is not open to visitors.

Further E, just past the next crossroads (with Taipingqiao da jie to the S), on the N side of the road, is the huge white dagoba of the **Miaoying si** (Temple of the Miraculous Response), familiarly known as the **Baita si** (White Dagoba Temple). It is reached by a narrow lane off the main road (which is usually impenetrable to motor traffic).

The temple was first built in 1271 and a Nepalese temple designer, Arniger, assisted in the construction. A large temple which stood in front of the dagoba was one of the major constructions of the reign of Khubilai Khan (1264–95), and the dagoba remains the largest standing Yuan construction in Peking.

The *dagoba*, which dominates the temple, is 50.9m high, standing on a lotus-petal base, which (to quote the official guide) 'is surrounded by five "king kong" hoops that make the square base grow into the round pagoda body much naturally. The body of the pagoda is like a huge upside-down almsbowl…' and is made of brick faced with white stucco. At the top, beneath the copper finial, a wooden canopy covered with copper, has a sort of copper-link fringe from which hang 36 aeolian bells.

The great pagoda was built to house relics, which must have been added to during later repairs for when the dagoba was being restored in 1978, some scriptures and other items (including coins of Han to Qing date were found in the umbrella-shaped crown, placed there in 1754. In 1457 and 1465 the dagoba was restored; during the 1465 restoration brick niches were built round the gallery to hold lanterns at festivals.

The sculpture of two deer supporting a wheel of the law at the top of the steps to the gallery symbolically represents the Buddha's sermon given at

Benares (and is commonly found in Lamaist art). The dagoba courtyard is at the end of the axial line of low halls, forming the temple, in which is a collection of Buddhist (Lamaist) sculpture, scriptures and robes.

These include a fine series of cast-iron lohan figures (Ming), some small gilt-bronze lamaist deities on lotus-petal bases (Ming), a thousand-eyed, thousand-armed Guanyin in bronze (Qing), Qing tangkas, embroidered silk boxes, 'Five-Buddha hats' in velvet and 'patchwork' robes of silk damask (the patchwork effect symbolised the poverty and lack of possessions of a monk; in rich silks it is somewhat incongruous).

A little further W along the main road (Fuchengmen nei da jie) is **Lu Xun's House** (Lu Xun guju; open 9–4, closed Mondays), at 21 Xisantiao hutong, just N of the main road (but the approach is visible from it).

Lu Xun (1881–1936; see Shaoxing, his birthplace) is still celebrated as the greatest Chinese writer of his time. He was born into a declining family of landlords and officials and, after a classical education, went to Japan to study medicine. There, faced with (tiny) Japan's triumph over Russia in 1905 (following her humiliation of the enfeebled giant of China in the Sino-Japanese War, 1894–95), he decided to abandon medicine (which could only cure individuals) in favour of literature which could rouse thousands. He was a major participant in the New Culture movement which followed the 4 May uprising of 1919 and which advocated writing in *baihua* ('plain language', the language of the masses rather than the extremely restricted classical language of the official class which had hitherto dominated).

His satirical short stories, some based on his childhood reminiscences, and his equally pointed essays are still justifiably popular. His greatest stories are, perhaps, the 'Diary of a Madman' (whose persecution mania illustrates the violent and unsympathetic nature of late imperial China) and the 'True Story of Ah Q', a hopeless labourer, symbolic of China's self-inflicted hopelessness.

Lu Xun occupied this small house between 1924 and 1926, though his mother stayed on here into the early 1930s. It is a good example of a simple courtyard house. Entered by a gate in the SE corner of the courtyard (most courtyard houses in Peking had their entrance at this point, though grand houses and houses in other places were entered on the central axis; this variation represents a Peking version of *fengshui*), the courtyard is surrounded by buildings (not all houses have a southern wing, sometimes the southern part of the courtyard is simply enclosed by a wall).

The southern wing was the reception area, with the kitchen in the SW corner. The two side wings (E and W) are both two-jian—or two-bay—constructions (which is also common) whilst the southern and northern wings are three bays wide. The two lilacs in the front courtyard are said to have been planted by Lu Xun himself. The northern wing is unusual in that it has an extra room built on at the back, at Lu Xun's order: this was his bedroom and study where he wrote the collections of essays entitled 'Wild Grass' (Ye cao) and 'Wandering' (Pang huang). Known as "the tiger's tail", Lu Xun himself called it 'the green study' for it looks out onto the back courtyard with its well and plum trees. The dark wood furniture and simple possessions in the house (washbasin, vases, brushes, alarm-clock) are said to he just as they were when he lived there and they give a good idea of interior decoration in the 1920s.

E of the house is a new building housing a *Lu Xun Museum*, filled with photographs (and paintings where these are lacking) illustrating Lu Xun's life and career: translations of his works, copies of the Jules Verne novels ('Voyage au centre de la terre' and 'Autour de la lune') that he translated into Chinese, and some of his possessions including Han bronze mirrors.

C.   The Back Lake Area

The 'Back Lake' area (Hou hai) includes Song Qingling's house, Mei Langfang's house, Guo Moruo's house, Mao Dun's house, the Gongwang fu, Huguo si, Desheng Gate, Guanghua si, and the Bell and Drum Towers.

The long strip of three joined lakes (Xi hai, Hou hai and Qian hai: West Sea, Back Sea and Front Sea) lying NW of the Forbidden City, formed an area that was favoured by high officials for their residences.

Just E of the top NW corner of the old city walls stood the Desheng men (Gate of the Victory of Virtue), now rather isolated by wide motorways and roundabouts. Built in 1439, it was rebuilt under the Qing.

A double gate (a third part was lost during the construction of the underground railway beneath in 1969), it is similar to others in that it appears somewhat grey, blank and fortified to the N but open and pavilion-like to the S. It is known as the Arrow Tower because of the 82 small square openings for defensive archers that pierce the outer wall (and was the only 'arrow tower' of the nine old gates of Peking). There is an exhibition of ancient coins in the gate tower (open 9–4, closed Mondays).

Despite the endless destruction of small courtyard houses, the GU LOU XI DA JIE, which leads diagonally SE from the Desheng men, remains a rather good example of an old street, lined with low houses and shops. It leads to the Drum Tower (with the Bell Tower visible just behind to the NE).

N of the Drum Tower, the second turning on the left off Gulou bei da jie leads to the *Zhuyuan bingguan* (Bamboo Garden Hotel) which also has a fine Cantonese restaurant. The garden with its piled rocks and somewhat Westernised buildings was once the residence of Kang Sheng (died 1975), head of the Secret Police for many years and not everyone's favourite person.

Song Qingling's House, open only occasionally, lies on the northern shore of the Hou hai/Back Lake, best approached by turning E along Houhai bei yan from Deshengmen nei da jie. The great red gates announce that it was once a princely mansion (fu), (said by some to be the birthplace of the last emperor Pu Yi) and some of the outline of the garden can still be seen (in the heaped and piled rocks and pools) but Song Qingling built herself a modern house in the grounds.

Song Qingling (1892–1981) was the middle daughter of Charlie Soong, a Shanghai comprador who had been converted to Methodism when he went to the United States in his youth. His eldest daughter married into China's richest banking family, Song Qingling married Sun Yat-sen, his youngest daughter married Chiang Kai-shek and his son T.V. Soong was Minister of Finance, Premier and Minister of Foreign Affairs in his brother-in-law Chiang Kai-shek's government as well as being governor of the Central Bank of China. In this wealthy group, Song Qingling was the idealistic exception, marrying the 'Father of New China' when he was nearly 50 and she 30 years younger. Despite the involvement of the rest of her family in the Nationalist Government (and various money-making schemes) she sided more closely with the Communist Party and remained in China after 1949, taking an interest in welfare work and childcare, founding, amongst others, a major children's hospital in Shanghai and the China Welfare Institute.

Inside the modern house where she lived there is a display of her possessions (fascinating dresses and shoes), photographs of her life, from the delicate, rosebud-lipped bride of Sun Yat-sen to the handsome dowager with her hair scraped back into a bun; photographs of her persian cats with one blue and one brown eye (a prized feature often portrayed in Suzhou embroidery) and the rather ghoulish scene of her final admission into the Communist Party on her deathbed.

As with Lu Xun, who never joined the Communist Party during his lifetime (claims were made during the Cultural Revolution that his application had been lost in the post), looking at the prone woman with unseeing eyes and a drip, one wonders whether she actually wanted to join.

Continuing SE along the lake, the entrance to the Guanghua si (Temple of Great Transformation) is set back from the lakeside road. This is the only one of the several temples once situated in the area to survive.

More famous was the Longhua si (Temple of Civilising Influences) with a pagoda that once stood at the western end of the lake. The lakes at the time were known as the Shicha hai (Ten Temples of the Sea) and were supposed to have been dug out during the Ming in the hope of recreating a scene reminiscent of the south with its rice paddies and lotus pools. The Longhua temple is supposed to have owned a small paddy field where homesick southerners would come to smell the flowering rice. This and other temples, together with the lakes, were said to have been constructed in the Wanli period (1573–1620) by an official from Shaanxi province.

Festivals were held on the lakes including the annual 'washing of the horses' from the imperial stables which took place on the 6th day of the 6th month. At the Zhonghua festival on the 15th of the 7th lunar month (when ancestral graves were swept), lanterns made from lotus leaves (candles glowing through the green leaves), artemisia lanterns and paper lanterns in the form of lotuses, were floated on the lake.

The *Guanghua Temple* (said to have been in good repair in 1935), was closed in 1988 but preparing to open to the public. Repaired in 1634 by a eunuch, whose work is commemorated in a stele in the main courtyard, the temple takes its name from a legend about a wandering monk who finally took up residence on the wasteland here in the Yuan dynasty.

For 20 years he meditated and lived on rice supplied by local people. He only ate half the rice he was given, saving the rest to build a temple. His frugality impressed people who started to make donations and since the rice he did not eat was 'transformed' into a temple, it gained its present name.

S of the lake (on Qianhai xi jie) is the Gongwang fu. If you are on foot, it is best reached by returning to Deshengmen nei da jie, turning S and taking the first turning on the E (Yangfang hutong), the second turning on the right (S) which is Liuhu jie and then the first on the left (E).

Opposite a monument to a soldier who died saving a child from the frozen lake quite recently, is a gate and the high wall of the **Gongwang fu** (Mansion of Prince Gong; closed 1988 but under restoration and likely to be opened soon although John Minford reported in 1982 that it was used for residential purposes by the Ministry of Public Security which may be difficult to dislodge). If it is ever opened it should be well worth visiting as it is reputed to be the mansion on which Cao Xueqin based his 'Dream of the Red Chamber' of c 1760 (the best translation is by David Hawkes and John Minford, 'The Story of the Stone', Penguin).

The mansion had belonged to the Manchu bannerman who rose to become the favourite and confidant of the Qianlong emperor, Heshen (1750–99). He rose to power through his military career (putting down various Moslem rebellions in Yunnan and Gansu) and was rewarded with such privileges as being allowed to ride on horseback through the Forbidden City (all others except elderly high statesmen were required to dismount) and the gift of the mansion. He was also in charge of arrangements for the Macartney mission to the emperor in 1793 (and was treated by Dr Gillan, the mission's doctor, when he fell ill with rheumatism). The mansion was later owned by Prince Gong (1833–98), sixth son of the Guangxu emperor, who was largely responsible for the establishment of the Zongli yamen (which dealt with the newly-arrived foreign ambassadors) in 1861.

There is no suggestion that Cao Xueqin, the impoverished author of the 'Dream of the Red Chamber', actually lived in the mansion (it is thought that he may have lodged with relatives not far away, near the Bei hai) but, as a member of an aristocratic family—his grandfather had been an imperial Salt Commissioner and had entertained the Kangxi emperor on his trips to the south where the Cao family's ancestral home was (in Nanjing)—he was likely to have been familiar with some of the other Manchu nobility.

The Gongwang fu garden has various pavilions that bear the same names as those used by Cao for his Rong family mansion and Zhou Ruchang has carefully traced the plans of the imaginary mansion and garden and finds them remarkably similar to that of the Gongwang fu. The mansion and its garden occupy an area of about 300 hectares. The mansion is constructed with three axes or series of courtyards, the buildings beautifully decorated and the garden full of piled rock mountains, pools and pavilions.

Just SW of the Gongwang fu is the ex-residence of Guo Moruo. It is on the W side of a narrow street which runs N from just opposite the N gate of the Bei hai Park, off Di'anmen xi da jie. There is an impressive gate and plaque but the residence is not (late 1988) open to the public as yet; the soldier at the gate said that it would be in a year or so.

Guo Moruo (see Leshan, Sichuan) 1892–1978 was a poet, pantheist, novelist, archaeologist, epigrapher, historian, playwright, literary critic, cultural administrator and tireless apologist for whatever seemed safest to defend.

Returning to Di'anmen xi da jie, go W to the next crossroads with Deshengmen nei da jie to the right (N); turn up Deshengmen nei da jie (N) and take the first turning on the left (W), Huguosi jie.

Not far along on the right (N), No. 9 is the old *Home of Mei Lanfang* (open 9–11, 1–4, closed Mondays), the greatest 20C exponent of Peking Opera, a specialist in female roles (which were traditionally performed by men although this is now changing).

Born into a theatrical family, Mei Lanfang (1894–1961) saw the development of a more modern style of Peking Opera, in a sort of equivalent of the 'bai hua' or 'plain speech' movement in literature. He popularised new stories and frequently gave virtuoso performances of the most striking extracts from longer operas. He travelled abroad, meeting many fellow-performers and impressing Bertolt Brecht with his miming and ability to convey a wealth of information through simple gesture.

His house, a fine courtyard house of some elegance (note that the main hall and side wings have verandas in front and are raised on low stone platforms) is a good example of the better class of courtyard house and contains a small exhibition about his life. The house is entered from the SE, which accords with a Peking variant on fengshui and two small side courtyards are entered through moon gates. The main wing (northern wing of the first courtyard) has some painting on the beams which indicates that it was once a house of someone of high status.

A little further along the street is the crumbling hall of the **Huguo si** (Temple to Protect the Country). Once a Mongol prince's palace under the Yuan, the mansion was transformed into a temple in his honour (after he had been disgraced, committed suicide and been rehabilitated—shades of contemporary China).

The temple used to be famous for its fairs (on the 7th, 8th, 17th, 18th, 27th and 28th days of every month) where curios, calligraphy, paintings, food, flowers, birds, insects and fish, entertainers and fortune-tellers were to be found. It operated in parallel with the Longfu Temple (which lay just N of Dongsi xi da jie: the next street to the N is called Longfusi jie but the temple is now covered by the Renmin shichang, a huge department store) where fairs were held on alternate days. In both, the seasonal flowers were most spectacular (and when I went to look for the Huguo si it was almost hidden under piles of seasonal cabbage in November).

On the far side of the lakes, over to the E, is the residence of the great novelist Mao Dun. From the Drum Tower (Gu lou), take the road running due E, Gulou dong da jie, and at the second crossroads take the road running due S, Nanluogu xiang. **Mao Dun's House** is on the N side of the second turning on the left (E), 13 Houyuanensi hutong. This is a simpler courtyard dwelling than that of Mei Lanfang, without the red-painted columns and beam painting, but it is a very characteristic Peking dwelling. Entered from the SE, the main courtyard has a southern building with sofas, used as a reception room. The rooms to the N and in the next courtyard were those used by Mao Dun and his family until his death in 1981.

Born in 1896, Mao Dun was an active participant in the 4 May New Culture movement and also served as secretary to Mao Zedong for a time during the 1920s. His most famous work is 'Midnight', a long, 'Zola-esque' novel about the shadowy business world of Shanghai in the 1930s, which first appeared in 1933. After 1949 he served as Chairman of the Writers' Union and, for a time, Minister of Culture.

The main hall of the first courtyard is raised on a stone platform and is a three-bay building with *er fang* (literally 'ear rooms', or small subsidiary rooms added to either end of a building) on either side. There is some fine cut-brick decoration to the main wing in the courtyard, which also has a verandah but the side wings are plain. Inside the main hall are photographs of the author (looking sinister in a tie and dark glasses in the May 4 period) and stills from films of his works. To the left of the building is a tree and beside that a great water-pot (many houses in Peking did not have their own well so water had to be purchased daily from the water-carriers most of whom were from Shandong province).

In the reception rooms of the front court are his eyewash cups, a tin coffee-pot, a magnifying glass and English-Chinese dictionary. One of the rooms, presumably used as a reception room at the time, has an unusual carpet on the stone flagged floor, sofa and armchairs and a lacquer smoking set. The little red plastic-covered books are his membership cards for the Communist Party and credentials as a delegate to various of the National People's Congresses. Fountain pens that he used to write his manuscripts in the 1950s are on display, as are the seals (chops) that he used and a National tape-recorder he used when writing his memoirs late in life.

In the courtyard behind is the five-bay wing where Mao Dun lived after his wife died in 1970. He suffered from arthritis and other ailments of the elderly as is obvious from the 12 bottles of medicine and teaspoons laid out ready for use. His old man's padded waistcoat is visible, as is a Snowflake-brand fridge (which, in the 1970s would only have been accessible to the rich and famous). There is also a rather terrible old towelling vest which, I presume, falls into the well-known Chinese archaeological category of 'revolutionary relics'. These are the ex-possessions of great revolutionaries which are often worn and old to demonstrate the simplicity and frugality of the true revolutionary.

D.   East of the Forbidden City

Due E of the Forbidden City are the Art Exhibition Hall, the Fuwang fu and the Zhihua si.

The *Art Exhibition Hall* (Zhongguo meishuguan) is a great yellow-tiled building with a central tower which lies on the N side of Wusi da jie, just before it reaches Wangfujing.

If you are travelling along Wusi da jie from Coal Hill and the N gate of the Forbidden City, the road bends slightly to the N and a large, oldish red-brick building is on the left (N) just after the bend. Today the centre of the Cultural Relics Publishing House (Wenwu chubanshe), this was the original home of *Peking University*.

Built on the site of the Temple of Horses in 1898, the Imperial University (as it was known at its founding) was renamed Peking University in 1911. Its students played a major part in the demonstrations of the May 4 Movement 1919, inspired by the treachery of the Versailles Treaty which, instead of allowing China to recover the old German concession areas in Shandong, gave Japan 'a special interest' in them. Japan had been an ally of the Western powers in the First World War, hence the concession; but the students were not only enraged by the Western powers, they were also appalled that the Chinese warlord government had accepted the terms (in return for a massive loan). The Chinese had not officially participated in the World War though a considerable number of 'coolie labourers' had served close to the front lines and many hundreds died.

It was in this building that Mao Zedong had worked as a junior library assistant in 1918, when his mentor Li Dazhao was librarian. In 1953, the University moved from the cramped building to the spacious campus of the American missionary foundation, Yenching (Yanjing) University in the NW suburbs.

The Art Exhibition Hall has no permanent exhibition but it is worth watching to see what is on.

Continue along Wusi da jie (which then beomes Dongsi xi da jie) past two major crossroads. At the third, turn left, up Chaoyangmen bei xiao jie, and left again to find the *Fuwang fu*, once the mansion of the 13th son of the Kangxi emperor, Yinxiang (1686–1730), later that of the 9th son of the Daoguang emperor, Prince Fu (1845–77). (Not yet open to the public in 1988, it is said to be the best preserved of Peking's princely mansions.)

Returning to the main road, Chaoyangmen nei da jie, at the crossroads turn S down Chaoyangmen na xiao jie and take the third turning on the left (E), Wenfangjia hutong. At the end of the lane, turn right into Xiaobeifang hutong and then take the first right, Lumicang hutong (the name means Storehouse of Glutinous Rice, and between 1644 and 1654 81 granaries were constructed here to store rice used to pay government officials).

On the right (5 Lumicang, N side of the lane) is the *Zhihua si* (Temple of the Transformation of the Intellect), built by a eunuch, Wang Zhen in 1443. It first served as a family temple and used to house a statue of Wang Zhen placed there in 1457.

He purchased a copy of a Ming printing of the tripitaka with all of its notes which were housed in the main hall. In 1742 a Qing official removed Wang's statue but the printed volumes still remain in the temple. The dark-blue, almost black tiled roofs of the temple halls have been frequently restored but are said to retain a Ming style. Inside the Rulai (Buddha of the Future) Hall are some fine carved wooden Buddha figures and there is also a revolving library to store the Buddhist sutras (in a side hall). The ceiling of the Rulai Hall was removed by the monks in the 1930s and is now in the Nelson Atkins Museum in America. There is a display of ceramics in the temple; open 9–4.

E.   East Central Peking

S of the main W–E avenue (Chang'an jie in the centre of the city), Jianguomen nei da jie, between Dong dan crossroads and the road that leads S to the railway station, is the **Yu Qian si** (Temple to Yu Qian), on Xibiaohou hutong (which runs parallel with the main street, just to the S). The temple was not open to the public in late 1988.

Yu Qian (1398–1457) was a native of Hangzhou. In 1449, when a Mongolian group attacked northern China, the Zhengtong emperor (1436–50) personally led the campaign against them but was defeated and taken prisoner. Officials in the capital, Peking, panicked, but Yu Qian, who was Minister of War, personally took charge and led the local people to defend themselves. When the emperor was freed to return to Peking, Yu Qian was branded a traitor and executed in 1457. He was posthumously reinstated in 1466 and his residence was made into a temple.

Proceeding E along the main road (Jianguomen nei da jie), after the right-hand turning to Peking Railway Station (S), the **Observatory** comes into view on the S side of the road; a square grey brick platform with strange bronze implements on the roof. This is the old Jesuit observatory (Guanxiang tai). Opposite, on the N side of the road, was the site of the examination halls (Gong yuan), now covered by the buildings of the Chinese Academy of Social Sciences, the highest scholarly body in the humanities—not an inappropriate covering). (One of the lanes leading N is called Gongyuan xi hutong, Lane West of the Examination Halls.)

The huge area of 8500 individual brick cells was built at the beginning of the Ming occupation of Peking (1420s) on the site of the Yuan dynasty Ministry of Rites. Every three years, during the third lunar month, graduates of the first stage of the imperial exams would arrive in Peking to take the next degree. They had to change into fresh clothes and were then locked into their personal cells for three days (and the intermediate two nights). Despite such precautions, some candidates appear to have found ways of cheating: in the Forbidden City collection there is an entire gown completely covered with the texts of the Confucian classics for reference purposes and in the British Library there are two very fine silk gauze squares, similarly inscribed. The traditional examinations in the classics were no longer held after 1900 and the cells were demolished in 1913.

The Observatory terrace stands on the site of earlier observatories. The Jin brought astronomical instruments that they had captured in Kaifeng, the Northern Song capital, but it was Khubilai Khan who established the observatory in this place. He appointed two astronomers to recalculate the calendar which was faulty (perhaps because the lunar calendar needs intercalary periods to be inserted every so often). Moslems were later put in charge of the observatory, to be supplanted by the Jesuits in the 17C. Notable Jesuit astronomers such as Ricci (1553–1610), Schall von Bell (1591–1666; Director of the Board of Astronomy) and Verbiest (1623–88; made Director of the Observatory in 1669), impressed the Kangxi emperor with the accuracy of their calculations (particularly in their prediction of an eclipse whose accuracy surpassed that of the Moslems).

Verbiest published a couple of Manchu-Chinese-Latin accounts of eclipses witnessed during his stay in Peking (of which there are copies in the British Library). In 1674, after he had already cast a number of cannon, Verbiest was commanded to produce a new set of five astronomical instruments for the terrace; a sixth was said to have been presented by Louis XIV. Their subsequent history, and that of the Ming pieces previously in use, is somewhat confused. Some were removed to Potsdam in 1900 (but some were returned in 1919), some moved to the observatory in Nanjing in 1933.

The Peking Observatory was restored in 1983 and the instruments now in place are said by some to be the originals, though which originals is uncertain. The 'Zhong guo ming sheng ci dian' says that they include two-thirds of the original Ming pieces (the remaining third being replicas) but, unless that is a misprint, that fails to explain what happened to Verbiest's Qing pieces.

The layout in 1935 (for those who can distinguish an armilla from an altazimuth) was as follows: NW corner: Quadrant (dragons) of 1674, then (moving S along the western wall), Celestial globe (1674), in the SW corner an Ecliptic armilla (1674). Moving E along the southern wall, W to E after the ecliptic armilla were: Altazimuth (1674), Theodolite (1715), Sextant (1674), Zodiacal armilla (1674). On the northern wall, between the Quadrant (dragons) and the steps, was a New armilla (1744), and none of these was Ming in date. There are exhibitions on the two interior floors, about astronomy. (The captions are all in Chinese and astronomy is not my strongest subject, but knowledgeable visitors will find the illustrations helpful.)

From the top of the Observatory (assuming that the high-rise mania has slowed a little), to the S you should be able to see the grey brick tower of the fortified corner tower of the old city walls, standing on the SE corner. The Tonghui River flows beneath it. To the NE (outside the point where the Jianguo [Establish the Country] Gate once stood), beyond the motorway, are the tower blocks of one of the two diplomatic quarters of Peking. Behind them are the lower embassy buildings, stretching E from the motorway.

On the far side of the motorway, on the N side of the main W–E road, Jianguomen wai da jie, are the *International Club* (provided for diplomats but the restaurants are open to all foreigners; I'm not sure about Chinese) and, beyond that, the *Friendship Store*. This is larger than most other Friendship Stores and sells items for tourists (clothing, embroideries, silks, jade, lacquer, jewellery, carpets, antiques, ceramics, etc) as well as foodstuffs for the diplomatic corps. There is a small flower, bird and goldfish shop inside, too.

N of the Friendship Store, in the diplomatic quarter, is the Ritan (Temple to the Sun) Park and, further N, the Dongyue miao (Temple of the Eastern Peak).

Ritan Park, formerly called the Chaori tan (Altar for Worship of the Sun), was built in 1530 on a piece of land formerly owned by Xiao Ying of the imperial guard which, during the Ming was known as 'Protector of the Brocade Robes'. Court astrologers are said to have recommended the purchase of the land as its area was appropriate. The form of the enclosure is interesting for the walls enclose a horseshoe-shaped area with a straight side to the W. It is entered from the NW corner by a triumphal arch inscribed 'Gateway to the worship of the (sun)-spirit. The small courtyard enclosing low buildings immediately inside the archway was the disrobing pavilion where the emperor changed robes for ceremonies. To the E were a bell tower, a repository for musical instruments, sacrificial vessels and carpets and, in the NE corner of the enclosure, another enclosed courtyard with the Hall for Spirit Tablets and a kitchen and a smaller walled enclosure to the rear where the sacrificial animals were slaughtered. In the centre of the whole is a red circular wall enclosing a low square altar platform of white marble. The wall is pierced by small gates to N, S and E and a triple gateway to the W.

Ceremonies of homage to the sun were carried out before sunrise on the 15th of the 2nd lunar month at the spring equinox, when the emperor came on alternate years (with official deputies in the intervening year) to worship the spirit tablet of the sun (placed on the altar) and offer up the animal sacrifices.

The park now houses a restaurant much favoured by diplomatic families.

Almost due N of the Ritan Park on the N side of Chaoyangmen wai da jie (the major road reached by taking the road that leads N from the park: turn left at the junction with the main road), is the **Dongyue miao** (Temple of the Eastern Peak), with its ornate green and yellow-tiled pailou on the S side of the road. The temple is closed (1988) but as an officially protected site may well open soon.

It is the largest temple of the alchemical sect of Taoism in north China (which may well account for its tardy reopening as philosophical Taoism is acceptable in contemporary China but superstitions and alchemy are not). The founder of the sect, Zhang Daoling (AD 34–156) used to charge five measures of rice for every case of sickness successfully treated by his spells and the practice gave its name to the Five Pecks of Rice Band of Sichuanese Taoist rebels who, together with the Yellow Turbans (another Taoist rebel group from eastern China) virtually brought the Han dynasty down in the early 3C.

The temple, named after Tai shan (the Taoist holy mountain in Shandong), was founded in 1322 but burnt down in 1698 and re-established in 1761. Though the temple buildings are Qing in date, the central axis is siad to preserve the Yuan style. Another description of the temple ('In Search of Old Peking', Arlington and Lewisohn, Peking, 1935) says that it is dedicated to the legendary Huang Fei Hu, deified for his rebellion against Zhou Xin, the tyrannical last emperor of the Shang dynasty (though elsewhere, Huang Fei Hu is identified with the Buddhist God of Hell). Confusions over the origins of the temple probably result from the fact that it was effectively a multi-deity temple. Buddhist temples have different halls dedicated to different deities though they retain a basic unity.

The Dongyue miao was a Taoist department store with different halls dedicated to immensely different deities and sects, each with separate feast days. In the second courtyard of the main axis were the 72 'Chiefs of Department', each responsible for some human action or force of nature (deities of seas, rivers, mountains, thunder, various animals, those that supervised official rank, riches, literature or various sins). Other deities whose effigies stood in company with others or in separate halls in the temple include the Fangsheng si, 'a kind of Inspector of the Cruelty of Animals Society from whom one can obtain good marks by setting free caged birds, or even fish', the Spirit of Plagues and Boils (suitably afflicted), the Goddess of Birth (surrounded by small plaster dolls) and the Xianbao si, 'a kind of Lost and Stolen Property Office' where lost or stolen articles could be retrieved by drawing lots of thin numbered slips of bamboo. A chest of drawers nearby contained printed slips (with numbers corresponding to those on the bamboo slips) which bore rough directions on how to find the missing article. There was a deity worshipped by actors, the God of Literature, the Goddess of Smallpox and another who looked after children's eyesight (she was depicted holding a spare set of eyes), shrines for travellers (where the fox, weasel, snake, hedgehog and rat were worshipped for their ability to exorcise evil spirits and protect travellers) and there were various kings of hell.

A separate shrine was that of Lu Ban, patron saint of carpenters and builders (also masons, bricklayers, house-painters and paperhangers) and members of the trade guild (named after Lu Ban) would hold annual ceremonies here on Lu Ban's birthday, as would other guild members whose patron deities were enshrined in the temple.

On the eastern outskirts of town, just S of the towering new *Great Wall Hotel* (Changcheng fandian), is the green-tile-roofed **Agricultural Exhibition Hall** (Quanguo nongye zhanlanguan). This is one of the Ten Great Buildings (which include Peking's Railway Station, the Great Hall of the People and the Historical Museum) constructed during the Great Leap Forward (1958).

They were mostly built in a new 'national style'. Exemplified by the Railway Station and the Agricultural Exhibition Hall, this involved the use of (western) concrete below and 'Chinese' tiled roofs above. The major theorist of this new style was Liang Sicheng (son of the great reformer Liang Qichao, who studied architecture at the University of Pennsylvania and pioneered architectural history in China, rediscovering the Tang dynasty Fo guang Temple on Wu tai shan) who was later strongly criticised for the 'wastefulness' of the Chinese roofs. Liang was in a political and aesthetic no-win situation for not only was it difficult to solve the problem of transition from timber-frame to concrete frame but the rising slogan of post-Great Leap architecture was 'Utility, economy and, if possible, beauty'.

There is a large salesroom in a corner of the site which has one of the widest selections of porcelain in Peking.

F. Northeast Peking

The NE corner of town includes the Imperial Academy (Guozijian), Confucian Temple and City Museum (Shoudu bowuguan), the Lama Temple (Yonghe gong) and Bolin si.

A small street running W off Yonghegong da jie in the NW corner of the old walled town is called GUOZIJIAN JIE. On it lie the old Imperial Academy (Guozijian or College for the Sons of the Nation) and the Confucian Temple. It is the only street in Peking (and perhaps in the whole of China) which still has a number of pailou (triumphal arches) standing across the road. Great timber constructions painted in blue, green, red and gold, with high stone bases, such arches stood in many places in China's towns and cities (in Peking there were groups at Xi si, Dong si, Dong dan and Xi dan). They were sometimes erected in commemoration of virtuous widows (who had committed suicide on the deaths of their husbands), sometimes merely as decoration. Here they mark the importance of this narrow, tree-lined lane with its collection of major educational establishments.

At the western end of the road is the **Guozijian**, now housing the capital's main library (distinct from the National Library), which was the most prestigious school in the land from the Yuan to the Qing.

Founded in 1306 under the Yuan (and some of the cypresses are said to date from that period), in the first years of the Ming it was known as the School of the Beiping Commandery but it was renamed College for the Sons of the Nation in 1404.

The present buildings date from different periods. The *pavilion* behind the Yilun tang, used as the office of the director, was built in 1528 and the great hall in the centre, the *Bi yong* (Hall of Sovereign Harmony), which stands in the middle of a circular pool (once filled with carp and lotuses), was built in 1784 under the Qianlong emperor. It is approached through a triple arch covered in yellow tiles which bears an inscription from the Confucian Analects: 'All under heaven benefit from instruction'.

Here the emperors used to come in the 2nd month every year and cross the marble bridges, sit in the hall in front of a Five-mountain screen and expound upon the Confucian Classics. The courtyard walls were set with 190 stones engraved in 1794 with the texts of the Confucian Classics (comprising over 630,000 characters); these have now been moved into halls specially built in 1956. The Guozijian is not now normally open to foreigners (unless they have a library ticket).

E of the Guozijian is the **Confucian Temple** (Kong miao or Wen [Literary] miao) which also houses the **Peking City Museum**. This is an ideal temple to visit for it seems to be off the usual beaten track and is therefore very tranquil. (Open 9–4, closed Mondays.)

Founded in 1302 under the Yuan, it was first rebuilt in 1411 and frequently restored during the Ming (under Wanli—1567–73—the halls were tiled in green). During the Qing the same process of restoration and improvement continued (and under the Qianlong emperor, most of the halls were retiled in yellow). The main hall was expanded in 1904, though its bracketing is still in the heavy and simple Yuan style.

The temple's *spirit wall* is on the far side of the street. In the *first courtyard*, amongst the old trees are numerous stelae engraved with the names of successful examination candidates throughout the centuries from the Yuan to the late Qing. On either side of the first great gate, some of the 'stone drums' (or replicas of them) are exhibited.

These are problematic stones, with rather illegible inscriptions said to date from the Zhou (770–221 BC), and to have been lost and rediscovered in the Tang. Despite their weight, they were carted about by fugitive emperors (the Song), dragged back to Peking in 1192 and placed in the Confucian Temple in 1307. It is said that the originals were removed by the Nationalist government in 1933 but that the facsimiles were carved in the 18C at the order of Qianlong to preserve the fading inscriptions. These are in da zhuan or 'great seal script' (the second major style in the development of the Chinese script after that found on oracle bones of the Shang) and record episodes in a hunting expedition along a riverbank led by the Duke of Qin (who may have lived c 375 BC).

Inside the gate the main courtyard has ten (closed) yellow-tiled *stelae pavilions*, whose stelae record famous victories and conquests of the Kangxi, Yongzheng and Qianlong emperors. The *main hall* (Dacheng dian, Hall of Great Perfection), is huge, nine bays broad, five deep, raised high on a 'moon platform' of white marble with white marble railings. It is closed (1988) but contains (or contained) the spirit tablet of Confucius and his major followers, beams of teak from Burma and Indo-China and special straw matting presented from south China.

On either side of the courtyard, the side wings contains exhibitions. On the W is a very interesting permanent display relating to the history of Peking, from Peking Man to recent times (all explanatory material in Chinese). It includes a number of architectural relics (drainage tiles, roof tiles, etc). The E wings house temporary exhibitions. One of the most fascinating (early 1980s) related to the work of a Peking antiquarian who had rescued the most extraordinary collection of ancient and not so ancient bronzes from scrap-metal collection points. In 1988 there was an exhibition of 'women revolutionary martyrs' containing touching blurred photographs and some sad little garments amongst the artists' impressions of often-terrible fates.

Worship in the temple took place in the spring and autumn with the 27th day of the 8th lunar month (Confucius' birthday) seeing the greatest festivities. After 1911, under the Republic, the worship of Confucius declined for a while but was officially reinstated in 1934, to be abandoned again in 1949.

At its E end, the lane runs into Yonghegong da jie and the entrance to the **Lama Temple** (Yonghe gong or Palace of Harmony) is virtually opposite.

Built in 1694, it originally served as the palace (or mansion) of the Kangxi emperor's son who became the Yongzheng emperor. In 1725 it was converted into a temple (because, according to custom, the palace of a prince who ascended the throne could not be inhabited by his descendants, hence, also, a lot of the movement around the Forbidden City). Stelae in the front courtyard, inscribed with inscriptions by the Qianlong emperor, refer to this custom. The Yongzheng emperor was not the heir-apparent (so he could not have known that his palace would have to be abandoned as such) as he was the fourth son of the Kangxi emperor. The heir-apparent showed signs of mental instability which led to an unseemly scramble for power amongst his brothers, which the Yongzheng emperor won.

The temple was first used by the imperial family to house ancestral portraits (and the roofs of major halls were tiled in yellow). In 1744 it was made into a Lamaist temple. It covers a considerable area and has five major courtyards. Partly because of the impropriety of some of the Tantric statues (which are now usually covered with white and yellow silk scarves arranged rather like nappies [diapers]) and partly because of the rather wild behaviour of some of the Tibetan lamas, as late as 1935 visitors were warned never to allow themselves to be alone with a lama. Arlington and Lewisohn warned, 'In former days the Yong he gong had a very bad reputation for assaults on foreigners and sometimes the complete disappearance of solitary sight-seers. Even in quite recent times there have been numerous authentic cases where single foreign visitors have undergone very unpleasant experiences there. As recently as 1927, one of the authors was enticed into one of the buildings on the pretence of being shown some rare ornaments and nearly had the door closed on him. When he pulled out his revolver...the lama at once let go of the door explaining that he had only closed it because he did not want the Head Lama to see him showing visitors around. He was, however, not content with this explanation and reported the man's action to the Head Lama and had the pleasure of seeing him give the rascal a good thrashing until he shouted for mercy.'

In the 1930s, 'Devil dances' were still performed in the temple at the end of the 1st lunar month (the Tibetan New Year) but even then, apparently, the police had ordered the omission of 'the more exciting and horrible parts' (where a doll made of dough and filled with a red liquid was torn up and chewed in a representation of human sacrifice).

The long approach to the temple used to be lined with the dwellings of the lamas. Beyond the spirit wall and pailou, the temple proper is entered through the *Chaotian men* (Gate of Shining Glory) which leads to a court-yard in which there are *bell* and *drum towers* on either side, then a pair of Qianlong-period bronze lions standing between two open *stelae pavilions*. These contain inscriptions in Chinese, Manchu (left), Tibetan and Mongolian (right) with Qianlong's account of the foundation of the tem-ple. Throughout the temple there are examples of the curious great pine poles found in Lamaist temples.

The *first hall* is not very different from that in any Chinese Buddhist temple: it contains the Four Heavenly Guardians, ranged on either side, a 'fat' Maitreya (Buddha of the Future) facing S with Wei tuo, defender of the faith, standing behind, looking N. Though the temple is generally Chinese in architectural style, it may be noted that this hall's façade is reminiscent of some of the Eight Outer Temples at Chengde and the mosque in Cow Street. With three arched doorways, the rest of the façade is filled in with planking and painted deep red. This style appears to be associated with 'non-Chinese-ness'.

In the *second court* is a fine incense burner (they are all very good in this imperially favoured temple), with flattened lions floating in a brocade sea (dated 1746), which stands in front of a double-roofed *pavilion* over a stelae inscribed with the history of Lamaist Buddhism, again in the four languages—Chinese, Manchu, Tibetan and Mongolian. Another bronze incense burner in the form of the Buddhist holy mountain, Sumeru, stands in front of the *Hall of Eternal Harmony* with its three Buddhas (past, present and future) and 18 luohan figures.

The Lama Temple is the best place I have found for hearing the aeolian bells which hang from the eaves of halls and pavilions: the wind seems frequently to rustle through the bamboos and move the little bronze bells.

At the S end of the *third courtyard* is the *Yongyou dian* (Hall of Eternal Protection) with the Buddha of Medicine (favoured by Lamaists) on the left of the Buddha of Longevity. Opposite is the cruciform *Falun dian* (Hall of the Wheel of the Law) with Tibetan stupa (dagoba) shaped roof decorations. This was the centre of religious devotion in the temple. It contains a 6m bronze statue of Tsongkhapa, 15C founder of the Yellow Hat sect of Tibetan Buddhism. Paintings of his life cover the walls.

Tsongkhapa's sect gradually achieved supremacy over the older 'Red Hat' sect in Tibet and this ascendancy continued after the establishment in 1578 of the title of Dalai Lama (head of the Yellow Sect, based in Lhasa, as opposed to the Panchen Lama who was head of the Red Hats and whose base was Shigatse or Rikaze).

Behind, on the main axis, is the three-storey *Wanfu ge* (Tower of Ten-thousand Happinesses). There are numerous side buildings beside and behind the Hall of the Wheel of the Law, to which we will return. The Wan fu ge was built in 1750 (and in 1988 was closed for a massive rebuilding) and is linked to two side pavilions by 'flying corridors' (bridges at the second-storey level).

The height of the building was determined by the massive (18m) Maitreya figure inside. Said to have been carved out of a single trunk of either cedar or white sandal-wood, when I last saw it (prior to the 1988 closure of the hall) it was black with dust and, visible only from below as the upper galleries were unsafe, was an awesome sight, in keeping with the rather terrifying nature of Tibetan Buddhism.

The only form of banditry currently practised in the Lama temple is the proliferation of entrance tickets: many of the rear side halls containing treasures require separate tickets. On either side of the Falun dian are two dark-roofed halls: to the left the *Jietai* (Ordination Platform) *Building* and to the right the *Panchen Building*, constructed to house the 6th Panchen Lama when he came to pay his respects on the occasion of Qianlong's 60th birthday in 1780. This contains a silver and gilded statue of the Panchen himself and a variety of gifts and objects used in (Tibetan) daily life.

These range from cups, bowls, inlaid chopsticks, butter churns (tall, very narrow, cylindrical churns), snuff bottles, silver altar-pieces, Qianlong's throne, robes, Tibetan musical instruments including conch shells and long trumpets, sculpted and padded hats, bird and flower paintings and a collection of modern Japanese offerings of little flags and fountain pens.

Against the wall just NE of the Panchen Building is the *Zhaofo Building* which contains a beautifully carved phoebe nanmu niche with dragon columns, all-over floral scrolling and hanging lotus-bud bosses.

S of the Panchen Building, in the eastern side hall, the images include those of some of the fiercer defenders of the Lamaist faith, including Yama the bull-headed 'God of Death' and Lha mo, the 'terrible goddess', the Tibetan equivalent of Kali.

Leaving the Lama Temple, turn S (left) down the main road and take the first lane on the left which leads around the southern end of the temple and then turns up N, taking you to the nearby **Bailin si** (Temple of the Cypress Grove). Founded in 1347, it was enlarged during the Ming and Qing and an inscription was writtn for it by the Kangxi emperor: 'Forest of ten thousand ancient cypresses'.

The temple houses the woodblocks used to print an edition of the Buddhist Tripitaka (canon), called the 'Dragon Tripitaka' published in a woodblock edition between 1733 and 1738 in 7240 fascicules. They were printed from 79,036 woodblocks of which 78,230 survive. This is the earliest surviving set of woodblocks for the Tripitaka to survive in China.

Apparently the temple was used as a 'summer retreat' by lamas from the Lama Temple. As it is only next door it is difficult to imagine what they managed to retreat from at such proximity.

Immediately N of the Yonghe gong, on the far side of the Andingmen dong da jie motorway, is the *Ditan gongyuan* (Park of the Altar to the Earth), of which little remains bar the enclosure of the altar; it is hardly worth the trip.

Originally, the Ming emperors had worshipped at the Altar to Heaven and Earth (in the Temple of Heaven enclosure in the S of the town) but in 1530 the Jiajing emperor was persuaded by his court astrologers to build a separate Altar to the Earth on the site of an old temple in the NE suburbs (just outside the city walls). It apparently remained a modest affair until the Jiaqing emperor (reigned 1796–1821) decided to completely remodel the altar. The entire area was squared (for the earth was believed to be square whilst heaven was round, as is clearly expressed in the Temple of Heaven). Otherwise, the layout was not dissimilar to that of the Ri tan (Temple of the Sun).

Approached from the W through a pailou, the double-walled square enclosure contained a hall of abstinence where the emperor fasted and changed his robes before participating in the annual ceremonies, a bell tower, storehouses and a slaughterhouse for animal sacrifices, a Hall of the Imperial Gods where imperial spirit-tablets were housed (until used for firewood by soldiers in the 1930s). The altar itself was a two-tiered square structure of white marble, surrounded by a moat. The emperor came annually to perform ceremonies very similar to those performed in the Temple of Heaven except that here they were performed at the summer solstice.

G.   Northern suburbs: Xihuang si, Dazhong si

Not far to the W of the Ditan (Temple of the Earth Park), on the far side of the Andingmen wai da jie (the main road leading N from the Anding men or Gate of Peaceful Pacification), about 800m W of the site of the gate was the *Russian Cemetery* (not found, 1988).

This used to belong to the old Russian Mission which occupied the site now covered by the large Soviet Embassy, filling the angle of the extreme NW corner of the old city wall. The area was first occupied by Albazin prisoners brought back to China in 1685 after Kangxi had been out to suppress border incursions on the Amur River. They remained in this area though they gradually intermarried with the Manchus and in 1858 the Russian Ecclesiastical Mission was moved here from the old Legation area. The Mission buildings were destroyed in 1900 when the Boxers murdered hundreds of Chinese Christians who had taken refuge there.

Aside from Russians in the cemetery, there was a memorial to eight Sikhs, one British Attaché, three soldiers including Captain Brabazon and 'The Times' correspondent T.W. Bowlby who died as prisoners 'treacherously seized in violation of a flag of truce on the 18th September, 1860' (though apparently Captain Brabazon's body was never found).

The **Xihuang si** (Western Yellow Temple) is off Huang si lu, NW of An ding men.

There was a temple on the site from the Liao but it was destroyed in 1643 when the rebel leader Li Zicheng and his troops arrived to attack Ming Peking. The history of the present structure dates back to 1652 when the Shunzhi emperor had it restored for the 5th Panchen Lama on his official visit. There were two parts to the temple: the temple proper was called the East Yellow Temple (Dong huang si) and the residential quarters were called the Xi huang si (West Yellow Temple). Under Kangxi, the temple was further restored and used as a residence for Tibetan and Mongolian Lamaist dignitaries on official visits.

In 1708 the 6th Panchen died of smallpox and, though his ashes were returned to Peking two years later, the Qianlong emperor ordered the construction of a white stupa in his memory in one of the temple courtyards. The temple continued in use, serving as a stopping place for Mongol merchants en route for Peking and the 13th Dalai Lama stayed here in 1908.

The *Hall of Guardians*, with four fierce figures, still stands, and the remains of the **Eastern Temple** can be seen in the pillar bases but the major surviving construction is the white *stupa*. Raised high on a platform, the central dagoba in the Tibetan style is surrounded by four lesser stupas in the Chinese style and the whole is surrounded by a white stone railing. The Chinese-style stupas are covered with carved Buddhist texts. The central dagoba has a fine gilded crown and the base is finely carved with lotus flowers, Buddha figures, lohans and landscapes with scenes from the life of the Buddha. The carvings were badly damaged by foreign troops in 1900.

If you are in a car (or on a bicycle), between the two temples you could make a small detour northwards to see the *Jimen stele*. This stands on a small remaining portion of the old Yuan earthen wall, to the W of Xueyuan lu (which runs N from the North Circular Road, at the major intersection W of Beitaipingzhuang). The stele has inscriptions in the hand of the Qianlong emperor with the four-character phrase 'A haze of trees at the gate of Jin' on one side and a seven-line poem on the reverse commemorating the site of Jin (a town of the Warring States period said to have stood here).

The Yuan wall, an earthen rampart stretching far N of the Ming and Qing city walls, runs for some way along the W side of Xueyuan lu (which leads to many of the educational institutes built in the NW suburbs: the name means Academy Road).

NW of the Yellow Temple, on the western part of the North Circular Road (Bei san huan xi lu), just E of the junction with Haidian lu, is the **Juesheng si** (Temple of the Enlightened Life), better known as the **Dazhong si** or Great Bell Temple (now housing the *Guzhong bowuguan* or Museum of Ancient Bells).

The temple was built in 1733. In 1743 a famous bell cast in 1406 was brought here from the Wanshou si just to the W and the temple gained its present name. The temple is of considerable size and emperors came here to pray for rain and carry out other Buddhist observances.

Its great bell was cast in the Hanjing foundry, just inside the Desheng Gate. It is almost 7m high, 22cm thick at the lip with a circumference of 3.3m and it weighs 46.5 tons. There are 17 Buddhist texts cast on the surface of the bell, including sutras and dharani (incantations) with over 227,000 characters. When struck (like most Chinese bells, it has no clapper but was struck on the outside) it resonates for more than 2 minutes. Underneath is a small seated figure in bronze.

A common legend related to bell casting is applied to this bell (and others): the craftsman was failing to produce a perfectly resonant bell until his daughter threw herself into the molten metal, sacrificing herself for her father's work.

The temple now houses a small museum of bells with examples from the Song onwards displayed in its halls and courtyards (open 8.30–5.30, closed Mondays).

H.   Northwest Suburbs

Peking's NW suburbs include the Zoo, Exhibition Hall, Xu Beihong Museum, Dahui si, Qi Baishi's Tomb, Wanshou si, Wuta si, Yuan ming yuan, the Summer Palace and Xi shan

Baishiqiao lu leads N from the **Peking Zoo** (on Xizhimen wai da jie), not too horrible a zoo and often visited for its pandas.

It occupies an area which was a Qing imperial park, renovated by the Qianlong emperor for his mother's 60th birthday (1751) and again by Cixi. In 1902, when the Viceroy of Shanxi returned from a trip to 17 different countries, he brought back a collection of animals from Germany which were a present for Cixi. They were housed here and the park was renamed 'The Park of Ten-thousand Animals'. In 1908 the zoo was opened to the public though it was badly neglected during the civil war period (leaving only a one-eyed ostrich, 12 monkeys and a few old parrots). Since 1949 the zoo has, however, been restocked with native fauna and some animals acquired from abroad through exchanges.

The zoo is next door to the Russian-style *Exhibition Hall* (Zhanlanguan) with its star-topped spire (similar to the Shanghai Exhibition Hall) and Russian and Qiaozhou restaurants.

Due E of the Exhibition Hall, just N of the junction called Xinjiekou (where Xizhimen nei da jie meets Xinjiekou bei da jie) is the new **Museum** devoted to the life and works of the painter **Xu Beihong** (1895–1953). There used to be a museum in his old house near the railway station but this was demolished in 1957 and the new museum at Xinjiekou was opened a few years ago. The museum's display begins with Xu Beihong's birthplace, Yixing, famous for its little brick-red teapots. It includes replicas of two rooms in his old house—one of which is the painter's studio. Xu Beihong studied painting in France in 1918 and became one of the first Chinese successfully to master oil-painting techniques. His oil-covered easel contrasts with the desk which is covered with Chinese brushes. The curtains are of Chinese 'lan bu' or blue cotton, indigo-dyed cloth with wax-resist patterns, here restricted to a border.

There are some fine oil paintings and numerous sketches in the western style, many of which were done in Paris. His most famous paintings, however, are the galloping horses in monochrome ink wash (in the Chinese style) first painted in 1941 and which became extremely popular in the west in the 1950s. The works exhibited demonstrate his mastery of both Chinese and western techniques with some very charming sketches, particularly of his small son asleep.

A major intellectual figure of the 1930s, he painted portraits of distinguished vistors to China like the Bengali poet and philosopher, Tagore. As a result of his stay in France, he romanised his name himself, often signing his works 'Peon' (for Beihong). The museum is open 9–11, 1–4, closed Mondays.

Returning to the Zoo and Exhibition Hall area, on the corner of Xi zhi men wai da jie and Baishiqiao lu is the *Capital Stadium*, built in 1968. At the southern end of Baishiqiao lu, on the W side of the road, is the **Zizhuyuan gongyuan** (Purple Bamboo Park) and the double-towered new *National Library Building*.

The park was the site of lakes and a canal built in the Yuan dynasty by the engineer Guo Shou, in order to regulate the flow of water from the Jade Fountain and the Bai River into the city of Peking. During the Qing, 'travelling palaces' were built here so that members of the imperial family travelling back to the city from the Summer Palace by boat could stop and rest. The lakes remain but the only old building in the park is the nine-storey Ming pagoda.

The main road crosses a small stream. Just beyond the stream, on the E side of the road, is a small lane which leads behind the stadium and the Zoo to the **Wuta si** (Five-pagoda Temple).

During the reign of the Yongle emperor of the Ming (1403–25), an Indian monk called Pandida presented the emperor with five golden Buddha images and a model of the Diamond Temple at Boddhgaya. The Zhenjue si (the formal name of the Five Pagoda Temple) or Temple of the True Enlightenment was built on this site to house the precious relics. In 1473 a five-pagoda building, modelled on the Diamond Temple model, was constructed in the middle of the temple. Apart from this five-pagoda structure which still stands, the rest of the temple suffered damage inflicted by foreign troops in both 1860 and 1900.

The building has a square base covered with bas-relief carvings. There are five stepped, tapering Indian-style pagodas on the top with a rather incongruous Chinese-style glazed tile pavilion in the centre (with images of the Buddha's footprints). The interior of the square base has a stone staircase leading up to the top. The bas-relief carvings on the exterior are divided into seven bands: the upper five have multiple images of the Buddha in different positions (particularly varying the positions of the hands, in the set of gestures known as mudra); below are bands of lotus petals, Sanskrit characters and Buddhist symbols: celestial guardians, the wheel of the law, vases of flowers and various animals like lion, garuda (human-headed bird) peacock, elephant and horse.

Due W of the Five-pagoda Temple is the **Wanshou si** (Temple of Ten-thousand Longevities). It is on the northern bank of the same small canal that runs past the Five-pagoda Temple, just outside the NW wall of the Purple Bamboo Park. It is most easily reached by going all round the outside of the Purple Bamboo Park (the Zizhuyuan lu runs along the S wall, take the first turning on the right (N) and the temple is visible in the little lane that runs off to the E).

It is said to have been built in 1577 by Feng Bao, a favourite eunuch of the Ming Wanli emperor, and once housed the bell that is now in the Great Bell Temple. This temple was also used as a resting place by the Dowager Empress as she made her stately way to the Summer Palace. The temple has not been open to the public in recent years though in 1987 an attendant said that there were plans for a '.Dragon Museum' to be installed here and opened in the Dragon Year (1988–89). On a 1986 map of Peking the temple is sub-titled Zhongguo xiandai wenxue guan or Hall of Chinese Contemporary Culture.

A 1935 description of the temple describes a piled stone rockery in the eastern courtyard from which the Dowager Empress used to survey the scenery. There was also a stele with an inscription by the Qianlong emperor (in Chinese, Manchu, Mongolian and Tibetan) recording the history of the temple. It seems that, though Feng Bao was favoured by the Wanli emperor, he fell from grace in 1584 when he was stripped of his titles and had his property confiscated on the grounds of arrogance and excessive power.

Returning to Baishiqiao lu and heading N, the road is lined with great educational institutes for this area of Peking is the academic centre, with Peking University and Qinghua University to the N. The *Minzu xueyuan* (Minorities Insitute) is on the left, medical and agricultural institutes on the right. About half-way up the road is a suburban settlement which still bears its village name of *Weigongcun* (Duke Wei's Village)—as late as 1976 it was surrounded by fields.

Just S of Weigongcun, a road to the right (E) leads to the great hall of the **Dahui si** (Temple of Great Wisdom), commonly known as the **Dafo si** (Great Buddha Temple). Founded in 1513 by Zhang Xiong (another powerful eunuch), the the temple's great hall with its double roof is the only surviving building and, despite repairs in 1757, still retains its Ming-style timber construction. There was a huge bronze Buddha in the hall which was taken away by the Japanese during their occupation of Peking in 1937 and replaced by a wooden figure. The wall-paintings and stucco figures of the 18 lohans are, however, Ming. The wall paintings illustrate stories of the potential achievements of ordinary people who devote their entire lives to good (Buddhist) works.

At the northern end of Weigong cun, a road to the left (W; Weigongcun lu) leads past a housing estate close to the main road. There, amongst the blocks of flats and visible from the road, is the concrete tump of the *Grave of Qi Baishi* (1863–1957) and his wife.

Born into a very poor family, Qi Baishi learnt the craft of seal-carving as a child and only in later life managed to survive as a painter, becoming, with Xu Beihong, one of the most famous of China's 20C painters. Working in the traditional style with ink and brush, he added bright splashes of colour. His paintings frquently include groupings of objects (books, candles and jugs of wine, chrysanthemum flowers and small wine-cups) in the literati tradition (they recall Li Bai's poems on drinking), or unusual animal and vegetable groupings with a great fondness for shrimps and minnows. Immediately attractive, they are enhanced by his characteristic calligraphy and a variety of simple seals (which he cut for himself).

Qi Baishi's old house at 13 Lipingche hutong, just N of the Minzu gong (Palace of the Minorities) on the western part of Chang'an jie, is shown on maps but is not yet open formally; and the courtyard will require considerable renovation before it becomes an attractive site.

After crossing the (third or inner) North Circular Road (Bei san huan xi lu), Baishiqiao lu is renamed Haidian lu and leads through the eastern edge of the old village of *Haidian* (Sea of Lakes). It was previously an important stage on the road to the Summer Palaces and also served as a provisioning point. It was surrounded, not only by the palaces to the N, but also by many great country seats of high officials.

The centre of the village can be reached by turning left at the fork in the road just beyond the Haidian Hospital (on the left). There used to be some rather well-carved façades to the shops and houses lining the main street, particularly N of the main department store and on the narrow street to the right near the new 'supermarket'.

Continue along Haidian lu to the next large intersection, Zhongguancun. Haidian lu turns sharp left and runs along past the southern wall of **Peking University**. This part of the university is fairly new, with grey brick dormitory blocks built in the 1950s, but at the bottom of the hill, Haidian lu turns right (N) again and runs past the main gates of the university which are more impressive, with fine stone lions.

The university stands on the site of two mansions, one of which was owned by He Shen (who also owned the Gongwang fu near the Back Lakes just N of the Bei hai Park). The other was the Shao yuan (Ladle Garden) which belonged to the painter Mi Wanzhong (late 16–early 17C). A poet and calligrapher as well as a painter, he used to paint scenes of his garden on lanterns (a practice which became extremely fashionable at the time). The rather luxurious new dormitory block for overseas students is called Shao yuan in commemoration of Mi's garden.

He Shen (1750–99) was a Manchu soldier of relatively poor origins. His sudden acquisition of the ear and favour of the Qianlong emperor in 1775 is still somewhat inexplicable (and scurrilous stories are generally discounted). He was instantly grant- ed various important military positions and led some successful campaigns (though he had to be recalled from the mission to suppress a Moslem uprising in Gansu as he was doing so badly). His power was paramount, especially as the emperor became increasingly senile, even after Qianlong's 'retirement' in 1796 (when he did not in fact relinquish the reigns of power but left them in He Shen's hands). He Shen amassed a fortune and a vast collection of treasures, some of which were kept in his 'villa' at Haidian.

The gardens surrounding the villa still stand (though nothing much remains of any 18C building), with pools, hills and tiny lodges for porters and a 'stone boat', a version of that in the Summer Palace (a simple carved stone platform without the Mississippi riverboat superstructure), still stands by the main lake.

As he was in charge of the arrangements for the visit, He Shen welcomed Lord Macartney to his country villa in 1792. Early in the 1920s Yenching University, set up by American missionaries to provide an education in English to Chinese students, built its campus on the site of the two gardens, adding a 'pagoda' (actually a water- tower) and the earliest group of dormitory buildings (grey brick with green roof tiles) near the lake. In 1953, when the missionary university had removed itself to Harvard, Peking University (founded in 1898) was moved from the cramped 'red house' at the back of the Forbidden City out to this spacious site and building work continued, though the lake area remains as a pleasant rustic garden.

Beside the 'Nameless Lake' in the University grounds is a *memorial to Edgar Snow* (1905–72), the American journalist who in 1936 first gave the world a detailed account of China's communist leaders in Yan'an in 'Red Star Over China'. Some of his ashes were scattered by the lake.

Opposite the main gate of Peking University, on the other side of the road are the remains of another gate which used to lead to the Qinghua yuan of Li Wei, a distant relative of the Wanli emperor of the Ming who was the first to build a villa and gar- den in the Haidian area.

At the northern end of Haidian lu there is a T-junction. To the W the Yiheyuan lu leads to the (new) Summer Palace, to the E, to the Yuanming yuan or 'Old Summer Palace'.

Beyond lies *Qinghua University*. This, now paired with Peking University but slight- ly stronger in technical and scientific subjects where Peking University is famous for the humanities, was started in 1911 (financed by some of the American part of the Boxer indemnity, paid in reparation for the damage and loss of life sustained by Americans during the Boxer uprising) as a preparatory institution for students about to go abroad to study.

The **Yuanming yuan** (Garden of Perfect Brightness) is sometimes known as the *Old Summer Palace*. Not strictly older than the series of imperial gardens to the W (now known as the [new] Summer Palace), the garden seems older today for after its destruction by British and French troops in 1860, it was never rebuilt, whilst the Dowager Empress continued to spend vast sums on the 'new' Summer Palace every time it was damaged by foreign troops (1860 and 1900). There are ambitious and expensive plans to rebuild the Yuanming yuan which to the western eye would be a terrible pity as the area is now one of romantic ruins. Reconstruction would run the risk of creating a Qianlong 'theme park'.

The Yuanming yuan was made up of three gardens in an enclosure about 10km in circumference. All were established by Qing emperors (beginning in 1709) and were traditional Chinese gardens with lotus pools, piled rocks and over 140 pavilions. There were considerable apartments, banqueting halls and a library building, the Wenyuan ge (Pavilion of the Source of Literature), built, like its pairs in the Forbid- den City and the Summer Resort at Chengde, to house a copy of the imperial col- lectanea, 'Si ku quan shu' (Complete Treasury of the Four Storehouses).

Nothing now remains of the (major) Chinese part of the garden; what was not burnt down by looting French and British troops in 1860 was probably carried away for building materials by local peasants. There are traces of rockeries, the remains of pools and, in what was the northern part of the Garden of Everlasting Spring, the remains of the *Xiyang lou* ('Western Buildings', often described as the 'European Palaces').

Constructed between 1747 and 1759, these stone buildings were all made to the designs of Jesuit fathers (Sichelbarth, Benoist and the painter Castiglione), who also acted as foremen during the building operations. Though only a few pieces remain, the Jesuits themselves recorded the fruits of their labours (which 'could stand comparison with Versailles and St Cloud' they said) in a series of engraved 'views' (an almost complete copy of which is held in the British Museum, the Bibliothèque Nationale in Paris has a complete set and reproductions have been published).

The 'European Palaces' included a pavilion with music rooms, a labyrinth, an aviary, a gazebo, five kiosks and the major 'Palace of the Calm Sea' with fountains, as well as a theatrical representation of the scenery near Aksu (Xinjiang) with moving stage scenery (made for Xiang fei, a favourite Uighur concubine of the emperor who suffered from homesickness).

The stone animals which spouted the 'pyramid of water' forming the fountains in front of the Palace of the Calm Sea are gone but a huge open seashell in stone remains (this was the centre of a tiered group of fountains). Father Benoist, who designed the fountains, spent much effort on the production of a water clock using the 12 animals which represent the 12 two-hour long 'hours' of the traditional Chinese day (as well as representing the 12-year cycle). The rest of the stone remains, columns encircled by flower swags and arches with acanthus leaf bases (which almost look as if they have been turned upside-down) are in what one Chinese guidebook calls the Barock style and which is elsewhere described as 'Jesuit colonial architecture' (of the type found in Argentina and Paraguay).

In the SE corner of the old garden area is a small *museum* relating the history of the garden(s) and including a model reconstruction. There is also a collection of carved stones gathered from other sites. Some of the most curious include depictions of Darwin, Erasmus and Democritus; these were originally carved for the old National Library of Peking and, since the library has largely vacated its original site, have been brought to this small 'stone-carving museum'.

The history of the destruction of the Yuanming yuan in 1860 (when British and French troops were sent to Peking to force ratification of the Convention of Peking, opening China to diplomatic representation) still creates conflict. A recent French PhD thesis sought to blame the British entirely, to the point of accusing them of misleading the French troops about the route to the Summer Palace. It would seem, however, that blame must be equally apportioned: in the British Library, as well as a tiny jade-covered Buddhist work, volumes of fine illustrations of imperial costume and ritual items generally assumed to have been removed from the Old Summer Palace, there is also a lacquer-bound volume of Qianlong's own calligraphy which the Library purchased from the General de Montaubon (who had led the French troops to the site in 1860). During the sack of the palaces, certain of the better items were kept aside for Queen Victoria and Napoleon III, before ordinary soldiers were allowed to help themselves, after which the area was set on fire.

To the W, the 'new' **Summer Palace**, better distinguished by its Chinese name **Yihe yuan** (Garden of the Preservation of Harmony), suffered the same fate but was rebuilt in 1888 by the Dowager Empress Cixi (allegedly with money that should have been spent building up the Chinese Navy). The Yihe yuan covers an area of 290 hectares, with the vast Kunming Lake to the S and the Wanshou (Ten-thousand Longevities) Hill to the N.

Before the Yuan dynasty the hill was known as Weng shan (Jar Hill) and a small lake beneath it, fed by a number of springs on the hill, was also known as Weng shan Lake. One of the Jin emperors constructed a 'travelling palace' (or temporary residence) here in 1153.

In the Yuan the lake was dredged by the engineer Guo Shoujing and the spring waters diverted to the Tonghui River. During the Ming the area was cultivated, springs filling paddy fields and lotus and water-chestnut pools; the aquatic scenery that resulted compared in poems to the West Lake at Hangzhou. During the Ming the imperial residence here was rebuilt and the area named the Garden of Wonderful Hills (Haoshan yuan). Famous men wrote poems about it—Wen Zhengming

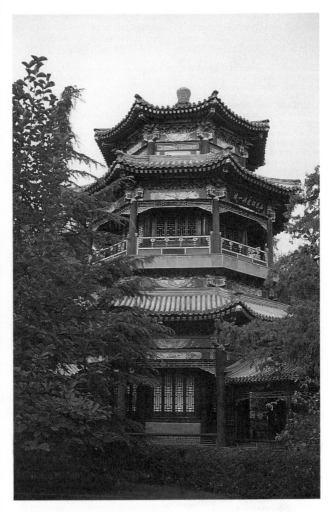

Peking, the Summer Palace

(1470–1559; a famous painter, pupil of Shen Zhou), wrote: 'A spring lake in the setting sun, orchids moving with the gentle flow, Buildings within the shadow of heav-
en tower above and below', and a contemporary poet, Yuan Zhongdao, in his 'Ten
Notes on the Western Hills', described the area thus: 'When summer is at its height,
the hibiscus blooms for miles like a tapestry, its fragrance wafted afar by the breeze.
Men and women gather by the flowing water, filling their wine cups to the brim.
What can be more delightful?' (Liu Zuohui, an horticulturalist of the Peking Municipal Bureau of Parks and Gardens notes that by hibiscus, he means lotus and there are
still plentiful lotus flowers in the lake.)

    As the area had been compared to the West Lake at Hangzhou, it is not surprising
that the Qianlong emperor, who loved to travel to the south (making six southern
trips during his reign and sending his gardeners S to study landscape gardening),
should choose to build himself a garden here. In 1749 work began on his Qingyi yuan
(Garden of Clear Ripples), enlarging the lake and building up mountains. The lake

was renamed Kunming hu (Vast Bright Lake, a name derived from a legendary lake of that name supposedly created near Xi'an under the reign of the legendary emperor Yao, 2357–2258 BC), and Jar Hill was renamed Longevity Hill (Wan Shou shan). The buildings constructed at his orders totalled 3000 jian (bays, sometimes 'rooms'). Construction was completed in 1764.

The name of the hill, and many of the buildings on it—the Hall of Benevolence and Longevity (where the emperor held court), the Hall of Happiness in Longevity (residential)—were given in honour of the emperor's mother's 60th birthday (60 was considered a major achievement, the marker of venerable old age).

Unfortunately, the many pavilions and their treasures were ransacked and destroyed in 1860 (at the same time as the destruction of the Yuan ming yuan) by British and French troops, leaving only the Bronze Pavilion (to the right of the central group of buildings on Longevity Hill) and the Sea of Wisdom Temple (of brick and tile, behind the major group on Longevity Hill) standing. A poet of the period, Wang Kaiyun, wrote of the desolate garden: 'Jade fountain laments and Kunming mourns, Alone, the bronze ox guards the thistles and thorns, In the hills of blue iris the fox calls in the night, Neath the bridge of soft ripples fish weep at the sight'.

In 1886 the Dowager Empress Cixi rebuilt the imperial garden and called it Yihe yuan (Garden of the Preservation of Harmony). After its second destruction by foreign troops in 1900 she had it rebuilt in 1902, personally visiting the site with great frequency and demanding progress reports every five days. She spent the summers there (rather than in the more distant Bi shu shan zhuang at Chengde), dragging the Guangxu emperor with her (in case, left to himself, he made a further attempt at reform after the failure of the 1898 reform movement) from the flowering of the mangolia to the withering of the chrysanthemums.

Cixi either travelled by road (with a retinue of over 1000) which meant instant road repairs and restoration of all possible 'resting places' (? comfort stations), or by boat which meant a total eradication of all duckweed for the water surface had to be 'mirror-smooth' for her. When she arrived in 1905, 458 eunuchs were lined up to greet her. Every day 100 separate dishes were served at the two main meals of the day (with 20–50 dishes for light refreshment in between). The dining table in the Hall of Happiness in Longevity (on the NE corner of the lake, where Cixi usually stayed) was designed to hold 100 dishes in set patterns. The wardrobe she kept in the Summer Palace (in 3000 chests) contained robes reflecting the change of the seasons, embroidered with wintersweet, peonies or wisteria for spring, lotuses for the summer and chrysanthemums for autumn, with every accessory embroidered to match. A 348-member opera troupe was permanently installed to perform for her in the theatre in the Dehe yuan (Palace of Virtue and Harmony, just E of her residence). On her birthdays, extravagance was unbridled: theatrical performances lasted for days, banners, garlands, lanterns, flowers, flags and ribbons decorated the buildings and trees and chrysanthemum flowers were strewn underfoot (chrysanthemums are the flowers of longevity).

The unfortunate Guangxu emperor died here (mysteriously) on 14 November 1908 and Cixi died the next day. When the Qing dynasty was overthrown in 1911 the garden remained the property of the last emperor, Pu Yi, but the grounds were opened to the public for a small fee. In 1924 it was declared a public park though the ensuing decades of warfare and invasion left it in a somewhat dilapidated state until its restoration after 1949. As before, people come in crowds to view seasonal flowers: the fine almond, cherry and plum blossom on the northern slopes of the hill in late winter, wisteria and peonies in spring, lotuses in the lake in August and chrysanthemums in autumn.

On major public holidays, the park is decorated much as it might have been for Cixi's birthdays: with lanterns and flags and special displays of pot plants and (one 1 May when the spring blossoms had already fallen) tiny flowers made of pink (lavatory) tissue twisted into every tree.

Most tourist groups visit the Eastern Halls, make a slight detour to the N to the Xiequ yuan (Garden of Harmonious Interest) and then follow the covered walk along the N shore of the lake as far as the Marble Boat. Those with a little extra time could walk around to the Back Lake area (quieter and more restrained) or walk the entire circumference of the lake to be able to look back at Longevity Hill.

The architecture and decoration of the Summer Palace is much as it was after its last major restoration in 1902 (although the timberwork is constantly repainted). A grand *pailou* (ornamental arch) stands across the approach road (the two-character inscriptions on either side mean water and hills), with lesser versions inside the entrance (the *East Palace Gate*). This eastern gate (opposite which stands a protecting screen wall) was formerly restricted and used only by members of the imperial family (lesser mortals used the N Gate). The low buildings on either side of the gate were for the duty officers. The pair of bronze lions sitting on stone pedestals on either side of the gate date from the mid 18C (Qianlong's Garden of Clear Ripples). They are virtually identical with pairs in the Forbidden City and are usually described as male (with embroidered and tasselled ball under one paw) and female (with a cub under one paw).

I have heard guides explaining that the cub is suckled through the mother's claws but can find no authority for this statement and the representation simply looks to me like well-observed cat behaviour. I have yet to hear a guide mention the fact that the phrase 'the lion plays with the embroidered ball' is said by Professor Wolfram Eberhard of Berkeley to be a metaphor for sexual intercourse.

The stone stair slab leading up to the gate, carved with a dragon and cloud design, is also mid 18C and was brought here from the ruins of the Yuanming yuan.

At the far end of a courtyard filled with cypresses and a pailou, is the single-storeyed, grey-tile roofed *Hall of Benevolence and Longevity*, where the Dowager Empress used to conduct state affairs (at first from 'behind the screen' but after the abortive 1898 reform, she held the Guangxu emperor a virtual prisoner and sat on the yellow-silk cushions of the throne herself).

The hall was built on the site of the Hall of Diligent Government which was also used as an audience hall in the 18C. In the middle of the courtyard is a bronze qilin (sometimes translated as a Chinese 'unicorn' though this, and many, but not all, examples have two horns) with cloven hoofs, scaly skin, 'the head of a dragon', the tail of a lion and deer's antlers. Bronze dragons and incense burners stand on the terrace in front of the hall. The furnishings are as they were when Cixi sat on the throne—rows of enamelled cranes with lotus-leaf candle-holders, cloisonné enamel incense burners and heavily carved dark Victorian furniture.

Behind the hall is a rockery through which a path winds to the next building, the *Hall of Jade Billows*. Like all the other buildings in the 'eastern palaces', this had a simple unglazed grey tile roof although the tie-beams are painted (in the Suzhou style, also found in the Forbidden City). The relative simplicity of these single-storeyed buildings imparts a sort of 'Petit Trianon' rusticity to the imperial summer retreat (and is also to be seen at Chengde).

The Hall of Jade Billows was the residence of the Guangxu emperor and, from 1898 until his death, effectively his prison. The interior furnishings, including the carved red sandalwood table and chair, the dais, screens and ornamental fans are all of the period. Behind the main hall were (left) the bedroom with the original bed-hangings and quilts, (centre) the wardrobe and (right) a dressing room. In the western and eastern side buildings in the courtyard it is possible to see a brick wall built right through the buildings; to prevent the emperor escaping, for these side wings had front and rear entrances.

From the Hall of Jade Billows, go to the lakeside and turn N (right) when you will pass the *Xijia lou*, the two-storey Pavilion of Beautiful Sunsets which looks W, offering an uninterrupted view of sunsets over the lake.

The next courtyard to the right (N) is that of the *Lodge of the Propriety of Weeding* (another rustic note), used as a residence by empresses from the 18C. The southern gate to the courtyard is a fine example of an interior gate of the 'hanging flower' (chuihua) type with elaborately carved pendant bosses. On either side of the gate are stone-carved calligraphic slabs, moved from the ruined Huishan Garden (destroyed in 1860).

Behind the Lodge, connecting the rear part of the Hall of Happiness in Longevity with the Garden of Virtue and Harmony (with its stage), is a covered gallery, with lattice windows in the southern wall and quaintly-shaped (teapot, persimmon, diamond, peach) glazed windows in the N wall. The Dowager Empress would sit on her gold lacquered throne in the Hall of Health and Happiness, watching the performances on the three-level stage. On either side of her throne (which is decorated with a scene of the hundred birds paying homage to a phoenix) is a pair of gilded cages with clockwork birds inside, 'presents from a foreign power' as a Chinese descriptive work notes. The stage closely resembles those in the Forbidden City and Chengde but is larger than either. The principle is the same: action took place at the central level and whilst angels and good spirits could descend from above, devils could rise from below.

Due N of the stage courtyard, a little way up the hill, on the way to the Garden of Harmonious Interest, is the *Pavilion of Blessed Scenery*, a large building with an interesting roof made from three juangpeng ('rolled-up mat') ridges.

Here, where there is an open view of the lake, the Dowager Empress used to come to watch the moon and the rain and sometimes entertain the families of foreign ambassadors. In 1948, when the People's Liberation Army had encircled Peking, negotiations with the KMT on the peaceful hand-over of the city were conducted here.

Beyond, to the NE, is the 'garden within a garden', the *Xiequ yuan* (Garden of Harmonious Interest), built in 1751 as a fairly faithful representation of the Jichang yuan (originally called the Huishan Garden) at Wuxi.

In his preface to the poems on the eight scenes of the Huishan Garden, the Qianlong emperor wrote: 'The garden is the oldest villa garden in south China. My imperial forebears renamed it the Garden of Ease. In 1751, when I was on a tour of inspection in the S, I was much attracted by its quiet beauty, so brought back a detailed drawing and had a likeness of it produced at the eastern foot of Longevity Hill...'. In 1811, the garden was rebuilt and renamed the Garden of Harmonious Interest.

Centred on a lotus pool, surrounded by covered walks and low, open, grey-roofed buildings, there is a low white stone bridge at the eastern end of the pond (copied from the bridge in the Wuxi garden). The white stone arch at the end of the bridge bears the characters for 'Know your fish' in the calligraphy of the Qianlong emperor.

The lowness of the bridge enables passers-by to see the fish below clearly but the inscription refers to a famous story about the philosopher Zhuang zi (4C BC) and the logician Huizi (who often appears to serve as the straight man for Zhuang zi's playful wordplay). Walking over a bridge, Zhuang zi remarked on the happiness of the minnows darting below. Hui zi asked how, since Zhuang zi was not a fish, could he know what made a fish happy? Zhuang zi replied, 'You are not I so how can you know that I do not know what makes a fish happy?' Hui zi insisted that his argument still stood—if he could not know because he was not Zhuang zi then because Zhuang zi was not a fish he could not know what a fish felt. Zhuang zi returned to the beginning of the conversation, 'You asked me how I knew what made fish happy so you already knew that I knew it. And I knew it just by standing here on this bridge.'

In the NW corner of the garden is a 'gorge' of rough, rockery stones, through which water (from the Back Lake outside the little garden) tumbles into the lotus pond; it is called the *Jade Zither Gorge* as the sound of the water is said to resemble zither music. The Dowager Empress favoured this little garden and there is a strange surviving photograph of her, elaborately dressed and coiffed, sitting in a boat amongst the lotus leaves in the middle of the pool (the photograph was used as the basis for a scene in Bertolucci's 1988 film, 'The Last Emperor').

Returning to the lakeside, the Lodge of the Propriety of Weeding (see above) is just at the NE angle of the lake. Immediately to the W of the lodge is the *Hall of Happiness in Longevity*, a large complex of two court-yards and various side wings. This was the residence of the Dowager

Empress Cixi from spring to autumn during most of her last years. The courtyards used to be full of magnolias (and therefore especially lovely in March and April when they flowered) but almost all were destroyed in 1900 except for one white and one purple magnolia (the latter standing just behind the hall).

S of the hall, on the lake, is the jetty (an open hall called the *Hall of Affinity between Wood and Water*) where the Dowager Empress would disembark if she had arrived by boat; on either side of it the lakeside is lined by a whitewashed walkway, its walls pierced with fanciful double-glazed windows (in which candles would be set at night). The eastern courtyard of the Hall of Happiness in Longevity is planted with peonies; in the northern wall, a moon gate is shaded by wisteria. The moon gate led to the apartments of the chief eunuch, Li Lianying (died 1911).

The hall itself was lavishly furnished with dark, carved wooden tables and stands (supporting giant double-peach incense burners that look like gilded cottage loaves). The coloured glass chandeliers were installed in 1903 and are said to be 'the first electric lamps in China'. The west 'inner' chamber was Cixi's bedroom and the saffron stain bed-curtains and multi-coloured quilts are original, as are most of the heavily carved pieces of furniture. The E inner chamber with its 'kang'-like wooden benches and low kang tables (short-legged tables made specially for use on kang/brick beds) is a good example of Manchu interior design and was used as a breakfast room by the Dowager Empress.

In the main courtyard there is a huge boulder standing on a marble pedestal carved with waves. It is called 'Blue Iris Hill' and is said to have been found in Fangshan (not far from Peking, where the marble used in the construction of the Forbidden City came from) by a stone-loving official called Mi Wanzhong. He wanted to move it to his garden in Peking but the effort was too costly and the stone was abandoned half-way. Years later, the Qianlong emperor heard of it and ordered it to be dragged along frozen waterways to his garden.

An adjoining courtyard NW of the Hall of Happiness in Longevity (reached through a moon gate), beyond a square pool, is the *Fan Pavilion*, built high up above a rockery on the mountainside. Constructed in 1888, it is a simple building in the shape of a fan, with fan-shaped windows and a terrace in front made of radiating marble slabs (which resemble the ribs of a fan). It is a charming little building, occupying a site where the 18C imperial family kept their pet fish and birds.

From the Hall of Happiness in Longevity, the long *promenade* runs all the way along the N shore of the lake. It was first built in 1750 and late reconstructed (and keeping its paintings fresh is an unending Forth-Bridge task). Four pavilions break up the long covered walk: *Retain the Good, Living with the Ripples, Autumn Water* and *Clear and Far Pavilion*. All the beams and lintels of the covered walk are painted in the Suzhou style, with elaborate cartouches enclosing flower paintings, genre scenes, landscapes and scenes from mythology and literature. Some of the 14,000 paintings are quite odd: I once discovered a scene of tattooing.

Halfway along the promenade, in the centre of the southern slope of Longevity Hill, a group of buildings rises against the hill, quite distinct from the eastern palaces for all their roof are tiled in yellow (sometimes with a green border). The timber-frame halls were built in 1886 (restored in 1902) whilst the solid, tiled buildings are those put up by the Qianlong emperor in honour of his mother's 60th birthday (1750).

At the lakeside is an elaborate pailou, the *Arch of Gorgeous Clouds and Jade Eaves*, beside which is a row of 12 lake stones in fantastic shapes each supposed to resemble an animal, either real or mythical. Behind that is the *Gate that Dispels the Clouds*, beside which stand two bronze lions cast in the Qianlong reign and considered the finest in Peking. Beyond the gate is a courtyard with a square pool over which is the *Golden Water Bridge* (echoing the layout of the Forbidden City); beyond that is the second *Palace Gate* which opens onto the courtyard in front of the *Hall that Dispels the Clouds*. In the hall, the Dowager Empress sat on the nine-dragon throne to receive congratulations on her birthday.

The innumerable presents offered to her are displayed in the rear rooms, still with their yellow paper slips, 'Respectfully presented by your lackey…'. The rear chambers are divided by some fine lattice work. The hall contains a portrait of Cixi by the Dutch artist Hubert Vos painted in 1905 when she was 71. Richly dressed, holding a silk-embroidered fan in her long claw-like nail-protectors of gold, the Dowager Empress looks exceedingly young for her years. It was Sarah Pike Conger, wife of the American Ambassador (who met the Dowager Empress a number of times) who found the artist.

Behind, on a massive 21m stone platform (reached by stepped side walkways and a final double staircase on the platform itself), is the *Foxiang ge* (Tower of the Fragrance of Buddha). The three-storey octagonal structure with four tiers of eaves dominates the group but there are important buildings on either side. To the E is the *Zhuanlun cang* (Revolving Archive). In its courtyard is an elaborately carved stele inscribed in the Qianlong emperor's hand, 'Kunming Lake, Longevity Hill' (with an account of the building of the garden on the reverse). Twin pavilions with green-tiled roofs flank the stele. Behind is the *main hall* which, unusually for northern China, has three little glazed-tile figures (representing, left to right: happiness, emolument and longevity) on the roof-ridge. The pavilions contain revolving sutra libraries (architectural in form) which once held books: classical works and Buddhist sutras. The main hall was used for prayers.

To the W is a courtyard surrounded by green-tiled pavilions. A *bronze pavilion* is raised on a high, balustraded platform of carved white marble in the centre.

Similar to the bronze pavilions on Wutai shan and in Kunming, this is a miniature version of a timber-frame building but made entirely of cast bronze. It was cast in 1750 (some say under Jesuit supervision), is 7.55m high and weighs 207 tons. All the details of carved timber doors and end-tiles, roof-ridge monsters and bracketing are perfect imitations of the normal timber construction though the lattice windows are missing. In the past, Lamaist monks were summoned to the tiny pavilion to recite scriptures and pray for the emperor and empress on the 1st and 15th of every month.

The pavilion survived the destructions of the surrounding palaces though nothing remained of its contents except the bronze offerings table (again modelled on wooden prototypes). In 1945 the Japanese were preparing to take this (and a bronze jar which stood in the courtyard) to Japan but they were abandoned in Tianjin and later restored to the Summer Palace.

On the central axis of the hill, behind the Tower of Fragrance, is a strangely stepped, rockery path leading to an archway of glazed tiles, which leads to the brick and stone *Sea of Wisdom Temple* (Zhihuihai). This is an 18C construction which, with its arch, survived the fires that destroyed most of the buildings of the Summer Palace, although many of the small glazed tile Buddha figures which cover the temple have had their heads smashed (by foreign troops). The temple building is yet another example of a 'beamless' brick-vaulted hall (like those in Nanjing, Taiyuan and Wutai shan). Entirely covered with mainly green and yellow tiles, most in the form of small niches containing a seated Buddha, the roof is also elaborately decorated with tile dragons and dagobas. On the roof there are blue and purple tiles amongst the green and yellow and the elaborate ridge is more like that of a southern Chinese temple.

Down beside the lake, almost at the end of the long gallery, is a small *pavilion* (Building Where the Colours of Lake and Hill Merge) which stands just before the group of buildings known as the *Pavilion for Listening to Orioles* (Tingli guan). In front of it, jutting out into the lake is the small *Fish Amongst the Pond-weed Pavilion* (Yucao xuan) from where the Dean of Peking University, Wang Guowei, drowned himself somewhat prematurely in 1928 'in despair at the state of the country, then on the

verge of going "red"' (as was reported in 1935). The Pavilion for Listening to Orioles is reached by a flight of steps beyond a garden of bamboo
and begonia.

First built in the 18C and rebuilt in 1892, the pavilion group includes a small stage
which fell into second place when the far larger stage in the Garden of Virtue and
Harmony (Eastern Palace) was built. The pavilion is now used as a restaurant and
sales area mainly for foreign tourists.

On the hillside above the Pavilion for Listening to Orioles is the *Strolling
Amidst Paintings Complex* (Huazhong you), centred on a two-storeyed
open octagonal pavilion with rockeries and a serpentine covered walk
behind. Smaller octagonal pavilions stand at either end of the walkways
and from them further covered walks lead down to the base of the main
pavilion. The whole complex is a very interesting one, making use of the
varied topography of the hillside to create an effect of studied irregulari-
ty. Qianlong and his courtiers used to drink wine and compose poems
here, looking over the lake though, according to an official guide, Cixi
'turned these pavilions into a place of debauchery and merrymaking'. A
flight of steps leads to a white stone archway with a stele; beyond is a
Buddhist 'hall of fasting' with galleries leading up and down the hill. The
courtyard behind, surrounded by a whitewashed wall, has a 'hanging
flower gate' at the eastern end which leads to the western summit of
Longevity Hill and the Pavilion of the True Concept of Lake and Hill.

At the far western end of the long gallery is the 'Marble Boat' officially
known as the *Boat of Purity and Ease*. The marble base was built in 1755
and it had a Chinese-style timber superstructure. This was destroyed in
1860 and rebuilt in 1893 when the Dowager Empress (with her usual
exquisite taste) ordered a western style superstructure and waterwheels
so that Qianlong's marble boat became a Mississipi paddle-steamer with
stained glass windows. Mirrors are positioned on each floor, to reflect
scenes of the lake.

Immediately N of the marble boat is a small creek, crossed by a stone
bridge with an open pavilion above it, known as the *Bridge of Floating
Hearts*. In the creek, below, a miniature metal paddle-boat was found,
the 'Yonghe' (Eternal Peace), a gift from the Japanese to the Dowager
Empress who used to cruise on the lake in it.

The Back Lakes and the northern slopes of Longevity Hill were badly
damaged and have been less restored than the rest of the Summer
Palace. They are also less popular with visitors and rather attractive in a
very different, less decorated manner. Of the Hall of Pines, Xumi Temple,
Pavilion of Fragrant Rocks and Ancestral Seals, 'Four Great Regions',
Temple of the Emergence of Virtue, Hall of Painted Fragrance and Temple Where Clouds Gather, only the main hall of the latter, the glazed tile
pagoda and the Pavilion of Fragrant Rocks and Ancestral Seals (built in
1890) remain. The slopes are planted with early-flowering prunus.

The *Temple Where Clouds Gather* is not far below the Sea of Wisdom
Temple. Only one of the three great bronze Buddhas in sculpted niches
now remains (mid 18C) but the temple courtyard is quiet and filled with
pines and cypresses. Over to the E is a gate, reminiscent of a city gate,
with a pavilion-like building above a castellated grey brick wall; this is
the *Gate of Exuding Pleasure*. Further E, rising above the trees (many of
which are early flowering fruit trees) is the glazed tile pagoda (*Pagoda of
Many Treasures*), an seven-storey octagonal pagoda more than 16m high.

Along the N side of the bottom of the hill runs the **Back Lake**, also
known as the **Suzhou Creek**. Crossed by fine bridges, lined with angular
brick walls and stone embankments, this was once an extraordinary
'model' marketplace. Shops were built along both sides of the creek, in
imitation of a canalside market in Suzhou (Jiangsu province). When the
Qianlong emperor and his retinue arrived, eunuchs would dress up as

shopkeepers and merchants and play at buying and selling to entertain the imperial passers-by. A fine three-arched stone bridge crosses the canal or lake at the point where the toy shops were in the 18C. N of the bridge is a mock mountain of rock stones from Lake Tai (Wuxi) and N of that is the *Northern Gate* of the Summer Palace, built as a two-storeyed structure by Qianlong whose mother used to watch cavalry practice of the guard outside the palace from this gate.

The lake itself has dykes and a long bridge leading to the small round island near the E bank. The dykes—the major one being the *West Dyke* which almost cuts the lake area in two—were built in imitation of the dykes on the West Lake at Hangzhou at the order of the Qianlong emperor. They serve to enhance the sense of space by breaking up the expanse of water. This is also done decoratively: the dyke is planted with willows and mountain peach and pierced by high, arching stone bridges (the elegant *Jade Belt Bridge*) and small, pavilion-topped bridges (the *White Silk Bridge* and *Mirror Bridge*). The Jade Belt Bridge on the West Dyke and the similar *Bridge of Embroidered Ripples* (in the far SE corner of the lake where the emperors arrived by boat) are amongst the best examples of Qing stone-carving, very elegant, with fine, high arches (which, reflected in still water, form a 'full moon' circle) and carved balustrades.

The other major bridge is the 17-arch bridge from the eastern shore to South Lake Island. Near the E end of the bridge, close to the main E entrance to the Summer Palace, a fine, life-sized bronze ox looks out over the water.

A long inscription on its side refers to the Great Yu's taming of the floods, for the ox was cast in 1755 after the Qianlong emperor had ordered the expansion of the lake. The inscription includes the lines: 'the Great Yu harnessed the rivers, the iron ox spread his fame...the broad-backed ox, broad as the universe, keeps the river dragons at bay, and crocodiles and turtles...the divine ox shall keep the floods of the Kunming lake under rein'.

Somewhere on the E side of the lake, all guidebooks (except Nagel) state that the *Tomb of Yelu Chucai* (1190–1244) can be seen though I have never yet found it. He was a descendant of the Khitan royal family and became Ghenghis Khan's advisor on Chinese-style administration, industry and taxation, teaching the Mongols how to utilise the Chinese economy (a foreign thing to semi-nomadic horsemen).

Just beyond the ox is an unusually large, open, octagonal double-roofed pavilion, called either the *Spacious Pavilion* or the *Eight-sided Pavilion*. When Cixi went to the island for banquets, the sedan chairs would wait here, with imperial officials. The pavilion holds some stelae with poems by the Qianlong emperor and responses by scholars. The bridge, paved with stone slabs, has 500 stone lions, 'no two alike', on the balusters, each sitting on a little brocade mat.

The island, which is surrounded by white marble balustrades, is called the **Dragon King's Island** and the *temple*, reached through a fine small pailou, contains an image of the Dragon King (who, like the Great Yu, is always associated with the control of water, and an alternative name for the temple is the Temple of Beneficial and Blessed Rain). On the northern side of the island, built on a high, heaped stone rockery, is the *Hall of Forbearance and Humbleness*. During Qianlong's reign there was a three-storey building modelled on the Yellow Crane Tower in Wuchang (Wuhan), where, it is said, the imperial family watched naval exercises on the lake.

The lake is extremely shallow (the navy must have used flat-bottomed boats) with a swimming area and many row-boats for hire, as well as larger boats used to tow tourist groups about. In winter it is a popular area for skating (and the hill with its pavilions looks magical when covered in snow) and in summer, for swimming. 26 August, the anniversary of the day in 1969 when the elderly Mao Zedong swam in the Yangtse with assembled bodyguards, sees the entire lake filled with schoolchildren, swimming in convoys and attempting to wave clenched fists (when they usually sink).

I. West and South of the City

One of the routes to the Summer Palace, Lanqingchang nan lu (South Indigo Factory Road) runs alongside the JINGMI CANAL which takes water from the Kunming Lake to the old moat running around the southern city. At *Balizhuang*, due E of the Forbidden City, is the *pagoda* of the **Cishou si** (Temple of Benevolence and Longevity), all that now remains of the temple.

The temple was founded in 1576 in honour of the mother of the Wanli emperor, on land formerly belonging to one of the Zhengde emperor's eunuchs. The temple fell down in the late Qing, leaving only the pagoda (and there was a record factory built around it in the 1970s). A 13-storey, octagonal construction with a close-eaved top, it is 50m high. The carved brickwork of the base and body of the pagoda is particularly fine and there are marvellous celestial guardian figures beside the doors on the central part of the body.

On the North Circular Road (here called Xi san huan bei lu) which runs parallel to the Indigo Factory Road, nearly due E of the pagoda is one of the few interesting modern buildings in Peking. The *dormitory blocks* of the Peking Art School (clustered around a small pagoda about which I can find no information) are built of dark grey brick with window and roof details recalling traditional domestic architecture in an economical but elegant manner.

Sites to the W of the city include Yuetan Park, Boyunguan, Tianning si, Li Dazhao's House, Nan Tang (Ricci's Tomb), the Niujie Mosque, and the Fayuan si.
  Due W of the Altar to the Sun Park (Ritan gongyuan) is the parallel **Park of the Altar to the Moon** (Yuetan gongyuan; on the W side of Nanlishi lu which runs N–S between Fuchengmen wai da jie and Fuxingmen nei da jie). The *Altar* was built in 1530, oriented towards the E (the triple gateway is on the eastern side), with a square white marble altar in a circular enclosure. To the N is a *Bell Tower*, to the NE the *Jufu dian* or robing hall. The major sacrifices took place in the autumn, between 6 and 8 pm. The moon tablet was apparently yellow and offerings of white jade and yellow silk were laid before it and then white sheep, oxen and a white pig were sacrificed.

The park was used in 1979 as a home for da zi bao ('big character posters' of protest). These had been plastered along the walls on Chang'an jie near the Xi dan crossroads (W of the Forbidden City) during what proved to be the first of many movements calling for democracy which followed the end of the Cultural Revolution and the Downfall of the Gang of Four in 1976. This was the 'Democracy Movement' which flared up in 1978–79 when students and young artists and poets called for a 'fifth modernisation', that of political reform and greater democracy following Deng Xiaoping's reform and 'liberalisation' of the economy through his 'four modernisations' (of agriculture, industry, science and technology, and national defence).
  One of the first to put up a political poster in 1978, Wei Jingshen, was arrested on a charge of treason and is still in prison. His arrest, with that of other young protesters, coincided with Deng Xiaoping's decision that all posters whould be moved from the centre of town to the rather hidden Altar of the Moon Park. Though that first Democracy Movement was suppressed, student movements have continued to erupt throughout the 1980s, leading to the downfall of Hu Yaobang (1988) and the massive protests in May 1989 which have resulted in the downfall of Zhao Ziyang, Hu Qili and the arrest of some 40 professors, academics and workers.

Almost due S of the Altar to the Moon Park is the **Boyunguan** (or *Baiyunguan*; the second, more modern pronunciation is better-known to the younger generation which includes all taxi-drivers), the Temple of the White Clouds, the major Taoist temple in Peking. It stands on Binhe lu which is N of Baiyunguan jie, just W of Xibian men and just S of the main E–W road, Chang an jie (here called Fuxingmen wai da jie).

It was the centre of one of the major Taoist sects, the Quan zhen pai (Total Truth

Sect), founded in 1167 in Shandong by Wang Chongyang. He is said to have died here in 1227 at the age of 80 and under one of his various sobriquets, Chu Ji (Control of Means) is the patron saint of the temple. His sect stressed purity of action and thought (rather than recourse to alchemy and potions). It also required that its monks remain celibate which was by no means the case in other sects. The temple is said to have been founded in 739, well before the birth of its founder, and to have changed its name three times before 1394 when it acquired its present name.

The temple is of considerable size and the surviving buildings are late Qing or later (and, sadly, not very distinguished). The temple is the Headquarters of the Taoist Association and is inhabited by elderly Taoist monks who still wear their hair in the style which was normal for Chinese men before the Qing (and the imposition of the queue or plait), in a bun, fixed on top of the head by a silver or jade hairpin.

Inside the first courtyard the similarity of all temple plans becomes apparent: there are bell and drum towers (just as in a Buddhist temple) and temple guardian figures in the hall at the far end of the courtyard. In the 2nd courtyard is the *Yuhuang dian* (Hall of the Jade Emperor). The incense burner in front of it is said to be late 16C. Inside the hall is an image of the Jade Emperor and paintings of Toist sages (paralleling the Buddhist saints or lohans). Peaches and cranes, symbols of longevity, a particular goal of Taoists (though common to Chinese folklore) abound. Other Taoist decorations (which, with the sculptures of Taoist deities, are all that mark this as a Taoist rather than a Buddhist temple) include the lingzhi or magic fungus, and the eight trigrams, used in divination.

In the third courtyard are a bronze bell and bronze horse which were moved from the Dongyue miao (in E Peking). The hall is the *Laolu tang*, containing a Ming drum painted with a dragon. The next courtyard houses the hall dedicated to the founder of the sect (who is buried beneath it) and the figures are said to be mid 18C. The great offering bowl was a gift from the Qianlong emperor and comes from Xinjiang. Behind is a courtyard with the two-storey *Siyu dian* (Four Great Men Hall), dedicated to the four major protectors of Taoism who hold a pagoda, sword, two swords and a spiked club and who are said to have assisted the Tang and Song emperors. In the hall above are the 'three pure ones', the Jade Emperor, Dao Jun, controller of the yin and yang, and Lao zi, one of the major Taoist philosophers. This hall also contains a Ming (mid 15C) woodblock edition of the 'Dao zang' (complete Taoist scriptures).

Behind, in a garden is the *ordination platform* (again, similar to that found in some Buddhist temples such as the Jie tai si (Ordination Platform Temple) outside Peking. This example has niches around it in which ascetics would fast and meditate.

Major temple festivals included the 19th of the 1st lunar month when the eight Taoist immortals were supposed to descend from heaven at midnight. Horseraces of various sorts were subsequently held on a nearby piece of land when, as one guidebook of 1935 noted, 'a veritable orgy of gambling succeeded a few days of religious worship'.

The *pagoda* of the **Tianning si** (Temple of Heaven's Will) is S of the Boyunguan, just outside Dong an men, to the W of Binhe lu. The temple (which has disappeared) was an old foundation, dating back to the Northern Wei (5C). The pagoda was built during the Liao (907–1125) and is similar in style to that of the Cishou Temple, an octagonal, 13-storeyed 'close-eaves' brick construction, 57.8m high. It has very fine carvings of guardian figures and Bodhisattvas on the central part of the body.

The **Baoguo si** (Protect the Nation Temple) is E of the Tianning si Pagoda, just S of Xuanwu yiyuan (a park), reached by taking the small turning to the N of Guangan men nei da jie beside the Xiaoxing luguan (Small Star Hotel). The temple was founded under the Liao and was in poor condition by the Ming. However, because the younger brother of the Chenghua emperor's mother became a monk there, the temple was rebuilt in 1466. The western part of the temple contains a hall dedicated to Gu Yanwu (1613–82), a leading scholar of the early Qing who spent his life trying to demonstrate the emptiness of Song Neo-Confucianism and to revitalise Confucianism, and frequently stayed in the temple. (Not open, 1988.)

N of the Baoguo si, in a narrow lane to the W off Tonglinge lu which runs S from Chang'an jie immediately opposite the Minzu gong (see below) is the *House of Li Dazhao* (1888–1927).

'Father' of Chinese Communism, he was Director of the Peking University Library when the young Mao Zedong worked there as a library assistant (1918) and Professor of History in the same university. With Chen Duxiu (Dean of the Faculty of Letters) he founded and contributed to various journals ('New Tide', 'Weekly Critic' and 'New Youth') which spread Marxist ideas amongst students and intellectuals. He was captured in 1927 in the garden of the Soviet Embassy in the Legation Quarter by the secret police of the warlord Zhang Zuolin, and executed. (The house is marked by a plaque but not yet open to the public, 1988.)

The *Minzu gong* (Palace of the Minorities), is a giant white and green tiled building which used to house an exhibit on the national minorities of China and a shop where minority costumes and handicrafts could be purchased but which recently seems to be given over to exhibitions of refrigerators and electric fans—this may change.

In the next lane to the N is the old *Women's Teacher Training College* whose students were particularly active in the 4 May Movement of 1919, a very unusual role for young women at the time.

S of Li Dazhao's house is Peking's major mosque. To reach it continue S down Tonglinge lu until it reaches a T-junction with Xuanwumen xi da jie; turn right (W) and take the first major turning S (left) which is Changchun jie. This runs into Niu jie at a T-junction. Turn right (still S) and cross the major road (Guang'anmen nei da jie) and soon you will see the mosque's grey carved-brick spirit wall on the right and the minaret and green trees of the mosque enclosure on the left. The name of the street, Niu jie, means 'Cow Street', in deference to the Moslem avoidance of pork, and the whole area around the mosque is full of Moslem shops of all sorts, Moslem primary schools and men wearing little white crocheted skull caps (not to be confused with the white cotton caps worn by almost all who handle food).

The **Cow Street Mosque** is the largest and oldest in Peking. Founded in 996, it was restored in 1442 and 1696. The mosque is constructed in the Chinese timber style but the arrangement of the buildings and some of the decoration reflect Islamic influence. The main *prayer hall* is (like the mosque in Dong si, NE Peking) covered by three linked double-pitched roofs, and a hexagonal pavilion-style roof. It is oriented W–E and the interior is broad but low-ceilinged, filled with columns and carpets. There are five 'naves', with differently treated ceilings, some coffered, some with open beam ceilings. The columns and the coffered ceilings are decorated in the 'Arabic style' with Chinese flowers mixed in with Arabic inscriptions. The *mihrab* is beautifully carved and thought to be Ming. The *tower* beside the entrance is the 'moon-watching tower', Chinese-style, hexagonal in plan, used for making the astronomical calaculations (for which the Arabs were famous in China until supplanted by the Jesuits in the 17C).

The minaret is in the centre of the courtyard in front of the prayer hall; it is a square, double-eaved pavilion and before it is the Hall of Veneration of the Scriptures where two Arabs came to preach during the early Mongol period and where the holy books are stored. On either side of the minaret stand stelae pavilions housing stelae with funerary inscriptions in Arabic dated to 1280 and 1283 (commemorating the two Arabs who were buried here) and an inscription in Chinese and Arabic of 1496 on the history of the mosque. The mosque is open to visitors but it is an active centre of worship.

Not far E is the **Fayuan si** (Temple of the Source of the Law), one of Peking's pleasantest and quietest temples. It was famous for the lilacs which grow in the courtyards.

In my inherited copy of Arlington and Lewisohn's 'In Search of Old Peking' (published by Henri Vetch of the French Bookstore in Peking, 1935) is an old newspaper cutting from the English-language 'Peiping Chronicle' of Tuesday, 27 April 1937 which reads: 'The Fa Yuan Su in Hsi Chuan Hutung, outside the Hsuan Wu Men, is noted for its lilacs, which are in full bloom at this time of the year. The abbot of the temple has issued invitations for a reception to be held at 6 o'clock this afternoon to view the lilacs.'

To reach the temple from the mosque, continue S down Niu Jie and take the first turning on the left (E). Go straight across the main road (where on your left you will see the strange pale green five-domed building of the *Islamic Association of China*) and the lane will lead you straight to the Fayuan si, on your left, with its spirit wall on your right.

Historically, the oldest temple in Peking, it now houses a *museum of Buddhist relics* of the area (which is being expanded to cover the whole of China) and the Buddhist 'College' where young novices are taught the rudiments of the faith (and they can sometimes be heard chanting in their classrooms which line the rear courtyards).

In 645, when the Tang Taizong emperor returned from his unsuccessful campaign in Korea, he founded the temple to placate the souls of his soldiers who had died far away. The temple, which was completed in 696, was then called Minzhong si (Temple of Grief for the Loyal). Its name was changed many times; the first time during the mid 8C An Lushan rebellion, when it was renamed 'Temple of Heaven's Will'. As it was dedicated to the memory of long-dead soldiers, it was not really maintained after the end of the Tang: the Huizong emperor of the Song was imprisoned here when he was captured by the Jin in the 12C, and during the Jin (in 1173) it was used as an examination hall, not for the Chinese bureaucratic exams but for those who were to take the examinations in the Tungusic language of the Jin themselves. They, unlike their Mongol conquerors and successors, maintained a dual administration, with dual languages and scripts. In 1734 the temple was given its present name and established as a Buddhist college.

The present buildings are not very old, few probably even dating back to the 18C, but the layout reflects the original plan. In the first courtyard are *drum* and *bell towers*. In front of the drum tower is a tree that was of a considerable size when the Qianlong emperor visited the temple in 1780 (and which was frequently visited by one of the eight eccentric painters of Yangzhou (a group which included Gao Qipei of the early 18C), Luo Pin. The tree is called a Wenguan guo (Fruit of Literature and Officials).

At the end of the courtyard is the *Hall of the Heavenly Kings*, a solidly built hall with two arched windows framed in white carved stone and an arched door in the centre of the solid façade. In front of the hall is an iron incense burner (probably 1730) with the Eight Trigrams on its body, which are more usually associated with Taoist fortune-telling. The pair of bronze lions are similar to those found in the Yihe yuan (Summer Palace) and are mid 18C. The bronzes in the hall are all Ming.

The gilded fat Maitreya Buddha (of the Future) faces you as you enter the hall. Behind him are fine figures of the four heavenly kings and behind them, facing the main hall, is Wei tuo, defender of the faith; the latter all bear traces of gilding and are very beautifully cast. Behind is a courtyard with a number of elaborate Ming and Qing stelae on stone turtles (with accounts of the restorations and history of the temple).

The *Daxiongbao dian* (main hall) stands on a high stone platform and is a five-bay constuction, now with glass where its lattice windows would have been. In front of it is a tall iron incense burner with a pavilion-shaped cover and a date of 1575. Inside the hall is a plaque suspended from the beams with an inscription in the hand of the Qianlong emperor reading 'The true source of the vast ocean of Buddha-truth' (in four characters), to the left a bell and to the right a drum. The bell was cast in the Forbidden City in 1531. The three figures, 'the three sages of the Huayan or Garland sect', are the historic Buddha in the centre with the Bodhisattvas Manjusri on his right and Samantabhadra on his left. The gilded stucco figures (with a wooden skeleton) are Ming in date and rare in Peking temples, whilst the wooden lohan figures along the side walls are slightly later (Qing). In the centre of the hall two stone pillar bases carved with flowers are preserved. These are Tang (726) in date, relics of the original foundation and appear not to have been carved from local stone (the imperial interest in the temple probably meant that excellent materials were brought from distant parts).

Behind this main hall is a *pavilion*, said to resemble the Pavilion of Ten Thousand Springs in the rear garden of the Forbidden City in construction, standing on what is popularly known as the *Minzhong Platform*. In it are displayed some of the treasures of the temple—stone-carved records and scriptures from 757 to 1909 and some Tang sculptures only recently discovered during restoration work. Into the outside walls are set stone carvings from the Tang to Qing. In the courtyard is a stone incense burner (1793), with a double pavilion roof, a rare form amongst stone incense burners. Behind is a stone 'alms bowl' on a stone base, carved with dragons and other fabulous beasts amongst waves. According to a local history of the Qing, this was once in a nunnery near Xihua men but was removed by the Qianlong emperor to the Beihai 'Round Fort' and only recently moved here. Two stele bear images of Guanyin (1589) and the Chan Damo or Bodhidharma (1591) which were in the nearby Shangan Temple which fell down.

Behind is the *Great Pilu* (Vairocana Buddha, the Buddha of All-pervasiveness or Light) *Hall* with a 4.6m-high bronze Vairocana Buddha sitting on a double round lotus base with tiny Buddhas in each petal, and the Buddhas of the Four Directions below. The group was cast in the Ming.

Behind this is the *Dabei tang* (Hall of Great Compassion), now housing an exhibition of gifts from Buddhists overseas, and behind that is the *Cangjing ge* (Sutra Store Hall or Library) in front of which stands a gingko tree over 100 years old and two flowering crab-apples planted in the 18C, about which many poems have been written. The three Buddha figures in the upper hall are Ming in date, made of lacquer on a wooden frame. In the hall, examples of Ming and Qing woodcut editions of the Buddhist canon (Tripitaka) are displayed. On the lower floor is an exhibition relating to the famous Buddhist monk and doctor of the Tang, Jian Zhen (688–753), who travelled to Japan during the Tang dynasty (see Yangzhou, Fajing si) and settled in Nara to teach. Of the four central lotus-petal-carved pillar bases in this hall, two are fairly recent (and made of 'green stone'), but the other two are differently carved and are thought to date from the 1031 rebuilding.

Small halls to either side of the main axis are now being developed as a *museum of Buddhist art and history*. A major section is devoted to the stone-carved sutras of Fang shan (not far SW of Peking, the source of most of the marble in the Forbidden City). The museum is still being built up so its displays may well change.

Amongst the other items on display is a cloisonné reliquary of the Qianlong period (mid 18C) which houses a piece of Xuan zang's skull. When the famous Buddhist pilgrim died in Xi'an, he was eventually buried in the Xingjia si but his tomb was apparently violated in the 9C during the rebellions that marked the downfall of the Tang and a piece of skull was taken to Nanjing. It was buried beneath the Baoen Temple which was, in turn, destroyed during the Taiping uprising in the mid 19C. Japanese excavators rediscovered the relic in 1943 and broke it up; one piece eventually reached the Fayuan si in 1950 (from a temple near the Beihai Park).

There are Buddhist paintings of the Ming and Qing, a variety of northern and southern editions of the Tripitaka, musical instruments, ritual implements (including those used in Lamaist worship) and a variety of figures.

Almost due N of the Fayuan si is the **Nan Tang**, the Southern Cathedral. It stands on Xuanwumen dong da jie, not far E of the junction with Xuanwumen wai da jie. To reach it from the Fayuan si, return N up Niu jie to Guang an men nei da jie and turn right (E) along that. The second major turning on the left (N) is Xuanwumen wai da jie. Turn left (N) and continue to the next major intersection (with Xuanwumen xi da jie (left) and Xuanwumen dong da jie (right). Turn right and the Nan Tang with its grey baroque façade is visible, set back from the N side of the road.

The cathedral was built on the site of the house in which Matteo Ricci lived from 1601 to 1610. The German Jesuit Adam Schall von Bell took over from Ricci as head of the mission and inherited his residence. In 1650, having impressed the new Qing Kangxi emperor with his astronomical skills, Schall obtained permission (and even a financial contribution) to build a church on the site. Finished in 1703, the church burnt down in 1775 and though the Qianlong emperor offered money for repairs, the coincidental suppression of the Jesuits made rebuilding complicated.

During the Jiaqing emperor's suppression of foreign missionaries, Portuguese Lazarists were sheltered here after being driven out of the Eastern Church but their last missionary Pires (tolerated for his astronomical skills) died there in 1853. In 1861, when all church property was returned to the foreigners, French Lazarists under Monsignor Mouly had the church rebuilt within a year and dedicated to the newly proclaimed dogma of the Immaculate Conception. The Nan Tang was destroyed in 1900 during the Boxer uprising when hundreds of Chinese Christians were killed or burnt alive.

The present building dates from 1904. It is the major Catholic church in Peking, with a baroque-ish façade of plain grey brick. The interior is filled with square columns with Corinthian capitals, painted to look like marble. Outside is a a Chinese garden-style rockery grotto filled with plastic flowers and lanterns and a statue of the virgin.

Permission to visit the grave of Matteo Ricci (which is in the N of the city, unfortunately sited within the Peking Communist Party School which does not welcome casual foreign visitors) must be obtained here in writing.

Ricci's Tomb is inside the *Peking Party School* at Erligou dong kou, on Chegongzhuang da jie, just E of the intersection with Zhanlanguan lu. It is a concrete-covered mound, all that remains of the old ecclesiastical burial ground known as Cha la. The Wanli emperor of the Ming gave the Jesuits this piece of ground when Ricci died in 1610, although it was covered by a Buddhist temple built by a palace eunuch (who had recently been condemned to death and his property confiscated). It was used until 1704 to house the bodies of other Jesuits including Schall, the painter Castiglione and Verbiest (at whose funeral the Kangxi emperor's father-in-law and five high officials represented the emperor). It was later transferred to the care of the Russian mission but in 1861 it was handed over to the French Lzarists. It was looted by the Boxers in 1900 who destroyed the great statue of St Francis Xavier and the imperial marble stelae on tortoises' backs.

Just W of the Nan Tang, (on the W side of the crossroads) beside the *Xuan wu Gate* (which used to stand at the intersection of the two main roads) the *imperial elephants' stables* were once to be found.

Elephants were sent as tribute gifts from neighbouring small states such as Burma and Vietnam as early as the Tang dynasty. The imperial elephants of the Tang were used in one of Bai Juyi's poems in which he compared the wise and noble rule of the previous emperor (when the elephants had enjoyed good health) with the terrible conditions currently prevailing which were reflected in the elephants' poor condition. The Ming emperors built the elephant stables in 1495 to house yet more gifts from Burma and Vietnam.

There were said to be six rows of eight large stables, surrounded by a trench, and a small temple to the 'tutelary deity of elephants' was provided. The elephants took part in ceremonial processions and used to pull the emperor's carriage when he went annually to the Temple of Heaven. Their keepers used to charge the public admission to see the beasts and the annual washing of the elephants in the nearby moat (on the 6th day of the 6th lunar month) was a popular sight. The keepers made a little extra money by selling the dung which was supposed to make hair glossy and to soothe cuts on the shaven heads of men who had the front of the head shaved whilst the long queue hung behind).

The last elephants were presented in 1873. One escaped in 1884, causing absolute chaos in the neighbourhood until it was recaptured in an alley, and it was decided to stop using them in imperial processions. The rest are thought to have died slowly of starvation as so little money was allocated for their upkeep (a fate which the Tang poet would have seen as clearly illustrating the decline of the Qing imperial house). The buildings which housed China's first Parliament (1912–24) were put up on or near the site of the old elephant houses.

The *Xuan wu Gate* (Gate of the Proclamation of Military Strength), also known as the *Shunzhi men* (Gate of Direct Rule) the westernmost gate in the southern wall of the northern, Manchu city, was always considered unlucky for it stands in the 'cutting-off-of-life' quarter according to geomantic belief.

For the same reason, the main door to houses in Peking was always sited in the SE corner of the courtyard and unimportant buildings like storehouses and kitchens were sited in this dangerous quarter.

The unluckiness of the gate was reinforced by the fact that condemned criminals were led through it to the old execution ground which was due S of the gate, at the next major crossroads, which is known as Caishikou (Vegetable Market Corner). As the execution ground was near the Vegetable Market, a common curse in late traditional Peking was to suggest that someone should go to the vegetable market (or, in other words, 'go hang').

J. South of the City

This Rte takes in Liulichang, the Temple of Heaven (Tian tan), the remains of the Altar of Agriculture, Taoranting Park and China's first 'theme park' the Daguanyuan.

LIULICHANG, or Glazed Tile Factory Street, is a narrow road which runs W–E across Nanxinhua jie (which runs N–S from Xuanwumen dong da jie and Qianmen xi da jie). It was for hundreds of years the centre of the antiquarian book trade and antique shops in general. In the last few years it has been rebuilt as a 'Qing dynasty shopping street' with brightly painted façades concealing the antique shops behind. A possible walk through some of the smaller lanes of Peking, lined with courtyard houses, takes you from the Qianmen shopping area to Liulichang.

Starting from Tiananmen Square, head S for the great double *Qian men* (Front Gate) at the southern end of the square. The road that leads due S is Qianmen da jie, one of the busiest shopping centres in Peking. To the right (W), running parallel to the main street, is a narrower lane, also lined with shops but here, and in the lanes running W, many of the shopfronts are of brightly-coloured tiles or beautifully carved wood. The third lane on the right is called Dashanlan and it is lined with shops.

It takes its name from the wooden gates (lan) which used to stand at the end of the street so that it could be closed at night against thieves and looters. This whole area was a rather louche place in the late Qing, the centre of the theatre world (and no respectable ladies were allowed into theatres) as well as being full of restaurants, teahouses and shops.

Take this turning and note the wrought-iron work and carved headboards of the old shopfronts. There is a famous old pharmacy, the *Tong-ren tang* (founded in 1669), on the left. The coloured and carved stucco shopfronts in a sort of western style date from after 1900 (for parts of the area were burnt after the Boxer uprising). As the lane leads into a residential area, the high grey walls of courtyard houses, pierced by gates with little tiled roofs, succeed the shops.

Though little can be seen of the houses behind the walls, some have handsome stone bases for the doorposts, circular and carved like drums or square and carved with flowers. Some gates have cut-brick work on the pilasters and some of the roof-ridges bear decoration.

This area is one of the best in Peking for hearing flocks of pigeons with pigeon whistles ('aeolian flutes') attached to their tails which hum as the wind rushes through them. The wheeling flocks of pet pigeons produce an almost electrical humming as they fly. You can often see 'pigeon lofts' built out of old packing cases suspended beneath the eaves of the houses.

If you continue to follow Dashanlan, it will bring you to Nanxinhua jie a little to the S of the point where Liulichang crosses the street so turn right

Peking shopfronts, Qianmen district

(N) until you reach the crossroads, marked by the gaily-painted carved pailou-like structures in front of the restored shops. It is possible to wiggle through the hutongs to reach Liulichang precisely (though directions are difficult as the hutongs, unlike the main streets, do not have pinyin street names): not far beyond the point where the shops give way to houses, turn right and then left and this lane should bring you to YANSHOU JIE (The Street of Extended Longevity, a name reminiscent of the Peking novels by Daniele Vare written in the 1920s) which runs at an angle of 90 degrees to Liulichang. Turn left (S) into Yanshou jie and Liulichang is the first 'major' turning on the right (W).

During the Ming Liulichang was the site of a workshop producing coloured glazed tiles for the Forbidden City. Before that the area was a suburban village called Haiwangcun (Village of the King of the Sea) for in the late 10C, when the area was crisscrossed by creeks, a local entrepreneur set up a business involving boats ferrying grain around on the creeks. His extortions were such that he became known as the king of the sea. In 1770 a Liao (10C) tomb was found in the area, testifying to the village name.

When the Ming Yongle emperor decided to make Peking the capital, the works begun on the imperial city required a second glazed tile factory (there was only one, in the eastern suburbs, managed by a native of Shanxi, the province famous for its tiles) and one was established at Liulichang, hence its present name. The glazed tile works were abandoned and destroyed at the end of the Qing but in the meantime the area had become a popular market which, by the beginning of the Qing, began to specialise in books and antiques, articles sought out by scholars, men of taste and would-be men of taste (who followed 'style manuals' when decorating their studies with fashionable paintings, objets d'art and the appropriate books). Peking's book-sellers congregated in Liulichang and printers also set up shop in the area. Perhaps the most notable printing enterprise in Liulichang was the production in 1792 of the major trilingual (Manchu-Mongolian-Chinese) dictionary.

A major fair was held in the first two weeks of the lunar New Year when 'curios ... could be picked up at very reasonable prices'. As Arlington and Lewisohn describe: 'Here Manchu princes and high Chinese officials used to stroll up and down looking into the shops and inspecting the old books and pictures' and the art shops still sell fine papers, brushes, ink-stones and other 'articles of the scholar's table' to calligraphers and painters.

The *Rongbao zhai* (Studio of Glorious Treasures) on the W side of the street still produces fine woodblock prints of paintings by famous contemporary masters, most notably Qi Baishi, which are a reasonably-priced substitute for a real painting. Visits to the workshop where the woodblock prints are produced from multiple pear-wood blocks, can be arranged through the China Travel Service.

The street used to be charming if rather run-down, with carved wooden shopfronts and courteous elderly gentlemen who served customers with great discretion. The area has now been 'restored'; the shops rebuilt in the Qing style, their newly carved and painted wooden boards hung in front of traditional-style buildings made of concrete instead of timber.

The effect is rather that of a film set but it closely resembles 19C paintings of Peking shops (examples can be seen in the Museum of Peking History in the Confucian Temple/Wen miao in the NW of the city) so that, whilst it is not a real reconstruction of Liulichang, it is an accurate representation of an imaginary 19C Peking shopping street.

Due S of Liulichang, on Taiping jie, beside the southern city moat, is the **Taoranting gongyuan** (Carefree Park). During the Yuan it was an area of temples but in the Ming, more ceramic kilns were set up here. The *'Carefree Pavilion'* against the northern wall of the park was built in 1695 by the Minister of Works, Jiang Zao, and the two characters 'tao ran' inscribed in gold on the board hanging from the eaves are in his calligraphy. They are taken from a verse by the Tang poet Bai Juyi: 'Let us wait until the chrysanthemums are golden and the home-brewed wine is ready, then together we will be drunk and carefree'. The same characters are carved in stone on the southern wall of the pavilion.

The area was made into a public park in 1952 with two wooden structures moved from the Zhongnanhai area (W of the Forbidden City, the new 'forbidden' area inhabited by China's leaders)—the *Yunhui lou* (Cloud Painting Tower) and the *Qingyin ge* (Pavilion of Clear Sounds). It is also said that the great wooden arches (pailou) that used to stand at the crossroads of Dong dan and Xi dan in the N of the city were moved here but, if they were, they have long since disappeared. The *Cibei an* (Hermitage of Benevolence and Pity) in the park (E of the Carefree Pavilion) is a Yuan dynasty foundation, one of the many temples that stood here at the time. It houses two stone pillars (chuang) dated to 1099 and 1131 inscribed with Buddhist texts.

During the years before and after the 4 May Movement (1919), Li Dazhao (1888–1927), the Professor of History at Peking University who was one of the first to propagate Marxism in China, hired a temple building for meetings which were attended by Mao Zedong and Zhou Enlai, amongst others.

W of the Taoranting Park, also on the edge of the southern city moat, in the SW corner of the southern city, between Zuoan men and Nancaiyuan jie is Peking's first 'theme park', the *Da guan yuan* (Garden of the Great View) constructed in the mid 1980s according to the description of the mansion and garden in Cao Xueqin's 'Hong lou meng' (Dream of the Red Chamber/Story of the Stone). (Not seen.)

It is ironic that it should have been constructed in this SW corner of the city when the probable real model for the garden, the Gongwang fu, in the Hou hai/Back Lakes

Peking: a ceiling in the Temple of Heaven

area to the N of the Forbidden City, is still under restoration and there is no definite opening date.

One of Peking's greatest temples, **Tian tan** (the Temple of Heaven), is also in the S of the city, immediately E of Qianmen da jie which leads S to the Yongding (Eternally Stable) Gate. The enclosure, square to the S, with a rounded wall to the N (the earth is said to be square, the heavens round in traditional Chinese cosmology) is almost 6.5km from N to S. A smaller inner wall in the same form encloses the temple buildings and the whole enclosure is planted with fine cypresses which are, unusually, planted in straight lines, like ranks of soldiers.

The major entrance is to the N and it leads to a series of buildings: the Qinian dian (Hall of Prayer for Good Harvests), the smaller Huangqiong yu (Imperial Heavenly Vault) and the circular white marble Altar of Heaven, all linked by a high stone causeway.

The two halls are exceptional in that they are circular in plan with cone-shaped roofs covered in wonderful dark blue tiles topped with a golden ball. The plan derives from the traditional view that the heavens were circular; the roof colour (the blue of the sky) is also symbolic.

First built in 1420, the enclosure was then known as the Temple of the Earth and Heaven but in 1534 it was renamed Temple of Heaven for the Jiaqing emperor had built the three other altars (of earth, sun and moon: Ditan, Ritan, Yuetan).

As its relative size might suggest, the sacrifice at the Temple of Heaven saw the

most important of the imperial observances, during both Ming and Qing. On the day
before the winter solstice the emperor proceeded (in his elephant-drawn chariot) to
the temple, with a retinue of some 2000. Entering by the northernmost of the two W
gates, he went straight to the smaller of the two circular halls (Huangqiong yu) to
burn incense and prostrate himself before the ancestral tablets there. He then
returned in his chariot to the Hall of Abstinence (a blue-roofed hall, rectangular in
plan) which stands against the inner wall of the enclosure, to the W, between the two
circular halls. He spent the night 'in fasting and meditation, his eyes fixed on a life-
size brass image—said to be that of a certain eunuch of the Ming dynasty who had
changed his earthly for an ethereal form—and implored his spirit to intercede with
Heaven ...' (Arlington and Lewisohn, 'In Search of Old Peking', 1935).

The next day, the emperor, dressed in plum silk robes with a black hat and blue
silk boots, went to a yellow silk tent erected in the grounds, and to the circular, triple-
tiered white marble altar where animal sacrifices were offered, together with bundles
of silk and jade. The tablets of the imperial ancestors were brought to the altar to 'participate' in the sacrifice. In this ceremony, the emperor spoke directly to the heavens
of all the events of the previous year. In the first month he returned to the Temple of
Heaven and, in the larger of the two circular halls, prayed for heaven's favour in the
coming year and for a good harvest.

The northernmost of the two circular halls, the *Qinian dian*, was built in
1420, restored in 1751 and again in 1889 after it had been struck by lightning. It stands on a circular triple-tiered platform (identical to the Altar of
Heaven) with eight flights of steps.

The hall is 30m in diameter and 37.5m high. 28 columns of *Phoebe nanmu* from Yunnan support the roof (in which no nails were used). The four central columns (18m
high) symbolise the four seasons whilst the other 24 represent the 12 months and the
12 hours into which the Chinese divided the day. The red columns are decorated with
dragons and the roof timbers are brightly painted (with, amongst other things, the
imperial dragon and empress' phoenix). In the centre of the floor is a circular stone
with interesting veining: this is known as the dragon and phoenix stone. The thrones
in the hall were used for the imperial ancestral tablets which were brought here
when the emperor came in the 1st lunar month before being returned to the
Huangqiong yu where they were normally stored.

A door on the E side of the Qinian dian enclosure leads to a covered way to the
sacrificial kitchens, slaughterhouses and other essential offices. Just SW of this covered walkway is a pile of rough stones known as the 'Seven Meteorites' (which they
are not); prayers for rain were said to have been made to them).

Red gates pierce the walls that enclose each of the halls: the next hall to the S is the
smaller *Huangqiong yu*, 15.5m in diameter and 19m high, with a cone-shaped
blue-tiled roof with a gilded ball on top; the roof supported on eight columns.

The vault was built in 1530 and was restored in 1752. The blue-topped wall that surrounds it is said to produce an acoustic phenomenon: people on either side of the
enclosure standing close to the wall can apparently speak to each other without raising their voices (although there are so many people trying to do so that I have never
experienced the phenomenon).

Through the gates to the S is the *Altar of Heaven*, a triple-tiered circular
platform with white marble balustrades. It is approached through four
white stone triple gates with stone 'clouds' piercing the upright columns.

The stones of the terrace are carefully organised to add up to multiples of 9 and 81,
lucky numbers for the Chinese. The top terrace, for example, has a circular stone in
the centre, surrounded by nine stones which are, in turn, surrounded by 27 stones,
and so on until the magic number of 81 is reached in the outermost circle. There is
also said to be an echo effect if noises are produced in the centre of the terrace (but,
again, the cumulative effect of many tourists trying to achieve it tends to reduce the
chances of success).

Built in 1530 when the outer walls of the altar were covered with blue tiles, the
altar was enlarged in 1749 when the white marble balustrades replaced the blue tiles.
It was here that the sacrificial animals and bundles of silk were burnt, to send them
up to heaven.

Immediately W of the Temple of Heaven was the **Altar of Agriculture**
(Xiannong tan), a slightly smaller enclosure which has not survived
intact. Now set off Xiannong tan jie (which runs parallel to Qianmen da

Peking: double-phoenix ramp in the Temple of Heaven

jie), between a sports stadium and the Taoranting swimming pool, all that survive are the small *Altar of Agriculture*, the *Terrace for Watching the Ploughing* (where the emperor watched everyone else after he had ploughed his eight furrows) and two halls: the *Qingcheng gong* (Palace of Celebration of Achievement), where the empress awaited the emperor, in order to congratulate him on his achievements, and the *Dasui dian* (Hall of the Year God).

The enclosure actually contained a number of halls devoted to different deities (so 'Xiannong tan' or Altar of Agriculture is a rather restricted name). For example, sacrifices to the year god (represented by the planet Jupiter) were carried out in a special courtyard and hall on the last day of the year and the two southernmost altars

(Altar to the Spirits of the Earth and the Altar to the Spirits of Heaven), were surrounded by separate shrines to wind, cloud, rain, thunder, mountains, rivers and seas. The small square altar which gave the complex its name was dedicated not just to agriculture but also to the 'first agriculturalist'.

The southern part of the enclosure (Altars to Earthly and Heavenly Spirits) was built in 1420 and the rest added in 1530. The emperor would come every spring to plough a small plot, to inspire his subjects and to initiate the agricultural year. The emperor then sowed rice (other officials who came with him to plough their own plots sowed four varieties of millet). All the emperor's implements—plough, harness, trowels and even the oxen that pulled his plough—were yellow, the imperial colour but also the colour which represented the earth. The emperor would plough eight furrows, the official in charge of the Board of Finance followed on his right wielding a whip whilst the Viceroy of the Metropolitan Province on his right bore the box of seed. Lesser persons ploughed 18 furrows and 'finally some aged peasants completed the work'.

It is ironic that Arlington and Lewisohn, writing in 1935, should comment gloomily about the Temple of Heaven, 'It is doubtless only a matter of time, before the whole place will be razed to the ground and converted into a municipal swimming-bath or a stadium, or some other equally utlitarian structure' for such has been the fate of the next door temple, instead.

2 Excursions Outside Peking

Excursions outside Peking include the Great Wall, the Ming Tombs, the Qing Tombs, Tanzhe and Jietai Temples, Fragrant Hills, Wanping, Zhou kou dian and the Yunju Temple at Fang shan.

A. The Great Wall

China's greatest monument can be seen in many places, most notably at Shanhaiguan, on the coast N of Peking and at the Jiayuguan fortress in the distant NW province of Gansu, but most people probably visit the Wall from Peking. The most popular spot is at **Badaling**, some 50km N of Peking (and it can be reached by car, taxi, several public buses, tourist bus or train from Yongdingmen Station in the S of the city).

Known for some centuries to foreigners, the Wall received some recent publicity when it was said (inaccurately) to be the only man-made structure distinguishable from the moon. Dr Johnson commented on it in 1778: 'He talked with an uncommon animation of travelling into distant countries; that the mind was enlarged by it, and that an acquisition of dignity of character was derived from it. He expressed a particular enthusiasm with respect to visiting the wall of China. I catched it for the moment and said I really believed I should go and see the wall of China, had I not children of whom it was my duty to take care. "Sir, (said he) by doing so, you would do what would be of importance in raising your children to eminence. There would be a lustre reflected upon them from your spirit and curiosity. They would be at all times regarded as the children of a man who had gone to visit the wall of China. I am serious, Sir".' There is also a Chinese saying (sometimes attributed to Mao Zedong), to the effect that there is no great man who has not been to the Great Wall.

Known to the Chinese as 'wanli changcheng', the 10,000 li fortification (a li or Chinese mile is about 530m), it is in fact considerably longer than that. Including a secondary 'outer' wall, built during the Han dynasty, it is some 20,000 li or about 10,000km long, though it has been estimated that if all the bits were added to the original Qin Wall, it would be 50,000km long.

The history of the Wall begins in the 7C BC when the State of Chu built a defensive wall and this fortification was copied by others of the Warring States (Qi, Zhongshan, Wei, Zheng, Han, Qin, Yan and Zhao), some of whose walls were several thousand li long. The first emperor of the Qin, who unified China in 221 BC, had a great deal of work done on the present Wall, extending it to some 10,000 li (and that was when it acquired its present name). The Han, an expansionist dynasty, extended the Wall right out into the Gobi Desert to protect its far-reaching territory but also to

The Great Wall at Badaling

provide a means of military communication. All the way along the Wall small fortresses were constructed and their garrisons maintained a constant supply of brushwood to fire signal beacons which could instantly transmit the news of military emergencies (through fire and smoke signals). A quantity of wood and bamboo slips used by Chinese garrison commanders to record events in and around their fortresses have been unearthed in the dry sands of the Gobi Desert to provide a picture of frontier life (with much checking of brushwood piles and counting of logs).

The greatest periods of construction of the Wall were the Qin, Han, Jin and Ming, for various reasons. During the Jin and Ming dynasties (1115–1234 and 1368–1644 respectively), the Wall was strengthened and extended because of a real threat from the north, beyond the Wall. The Jin was eventually overthrown by the Mongol Yuan dynasty (from beyond the Wall) and the Ming empire was overrun by the Manchu, again, from N of the Wall. Thus it was not particularly effective, partly because its enormous length made it impractical to garrison effectively. The fact that the Tang, for example, did not do much to maintain the Great Wall reflects on the contemporary perception of threat which, to the Tang, came from the W, not the N.

Most of what we see today reflects Ming improvements to the Wall. Originally made of tamped earth, much of it was faced with brick in the Ming. Those who worked on the Wall included soldiers, men on corvée duty (corvée labour being a form of taxation paid through performance of public works by all able-bodied men) and criminals (the latter especially in the 'exile' area of Gansu province). They built a Wall that was some 6.7–7.9m high, 6.4m wide at the base and 5.5m wide at the top. Its width meant that up to five horsemen could ride abreast along it and it served as a military road through difficult terrain. 10,000 small beacon towers were built along the Wall, and 12 military garrisons controlled its total length from the watchtowers and secondary fortresses (like that at Badaling near Peking or Jiayuguan in Gansu).

On the way to Badaling, the road to the Wall passes beside a fine stone gateway, the *Guojie ta* (Tower that Straddles the Road) at Juyongguan (pass). Built in 1345, the square gate has a flat roof which may once have had a stupa on it.

Inside are fine bas-relief stone carvings of Buddhist figures and inscriptions of Buddhist dharani or incantations in Chinese, Sanskrit, Tibetan, Uighur, Mongolian (in the 'Phags-pa' script of 42 alphabetic symbols, invented by a young Tibetan lama for Khubilai Khan in an unsuccessful attempt to supplant the modified Uighur alphabet for writing Mongolian) and Tangut (or Xi Xia, the language of a Tibetan people who set up an independent kingdom in Gansu in the 11C and whose script, which is not fully deciphered, was based on Chinese characters).

Near the Juyonggan Gate and Badaling is *Qinglongqiao Station* on the Peking–Kalgan (Zhanjiakou) railway. This was the first to be built entirely with Chinese funds and was completed in 1909 by Zhang Tianyun who had studied engineering at Yale. A statue on the station platform commemorates the chief engineer and there is a railway museum nearby (not seen; open 8.30–4.30).

Another section of the Great Wall has been opened near Peking: this is at **Mutianyu**, to the NE. Roughly the same distance from Peking as Badaling, the Wall here is a stiff climb (there is a funicular) and, as a less well-known site, is a more peaceful place to visit for Badaling is jam-packed with coaches, tourists (and insufficient lavatories unless you brave the old Chinese public ones where nobody queues except upwind). On the other hand, the gateway and fort at Badaling stand amongst impressive hills, the view of the Wall there is wonderful and it is easier to combine this stretch of the Wall with a visit to the Ming Tombs or the Juyongguan Gate.

Take 300mm + 1,4 x

B.   The Ming Tombs

The **Ming Tombs**, known to the Chinese as the **Shisan ling** (Thirteen Tombs) lie c 48km N of Peking, on a road which branches off that which leads to the Great Wall (hence a brief visit to the tombs is usually combined with the Great Wall for tourist groups).

The founder of the Ming dynasty is buried near his capital of Nanjing but of the total of 16 Ming emperors 13 are buried in what was once a huge enclosed area N of Peking. The Jingtai emperor who ruled from 1449 to 1457 (during the time that his brother, the Zhengtong emperor, had been taken prisoner by the Mongols) was regarded as an usurper and buried in the Western Hills (see below) and it is not known where the second Emperor of the Ming, who was quickly dethroned by his uncle (the Yongle emperor), was buried.

As soon as Yongle had decided to move the capital to Peking he had geomancers decide upon a suitable site for the imperial tombs. These 'mountain cockroaches', as some called them, chose a valley some 5km long N–S and 3km wide, bounded to the N by hills. The site is very beautiful and when you stand high on the ramparts of a tomb, you can see the yellow-tiled roofs and red walls of the stele towers of other tombs amongst the tall trees, arranged in a semi-circle against the hills.

The size of the area and its quiet beauty make the Ming Tombs one of the pleasantest outings from Peking. Two of the tombs have been officially opened to the public, one has been extensively excavated (Ding ling) and the other has been restored above ground level (Chang ling); the other tombs are open but untouched and are marvellously quiet places to visit and to picnic in (tidily).

The general layout of the tombs is similar and has its roots in previous tomb design; it was also continued in the two groups of Qing tombs (see below).

The tombs consist of two major, linked parts. The front courtyard is square in plan (representing the earth) and contains buildings above the ground where ritual implements were stored and rituals took place (on the birthdays of the deceased and traditional days of tribute to ancestors). Behind, enclosed by a high rampart, is the circular tomb mound (representing heaven) with a high stele tower in front of it. The tombs were grouped together in the valley which was itself enclosed (the remains of the wall could still be seen in 1920) and whose approach was indicated by a series of stone monuments.

As you approach the tombs, the first sight is of the great stone *pailou* (1540). Built entirely of white marble, with a superstructure which perfectly reproduces the details of a timber and tile roof construction, it has extremely fine carved column bases with three-dimensional lions and makara (serpent gods of Indian origin, later associated with Buddhist mythology), above bas-relief carvings of more lions, dragons and makara. Even the background to the bas-relief panels is carved with damask-like patterns.

Beyond the pailou is the *Great Red Gate* which stands at the proper entrance to the valley and its tombs, and which was once set in the enclosing walls. In design and colour similar to buildings in the Forbidden City, the gate was probably built in 1425. Its central opening was for the defunct emperor in his coffin, living emperors used the doorway on the left. It was at this point that all attendants had to dismount and make the rest of the journey on foot.

500m further along the road is the double-roofed, four-doored *stele pavilion*, flanked by four highly carved stone columns. The pavilion houses the largest memorial stele in China, standing on a stone tortoise.

Apparently stone tortoises as stele bearers were first used during the 6C AD though their use was restricted to the three highest grades of officials and the imperial family. The tortoise was a symbol of longevity. It was also common from the end of the Han to decorate the tops of stele with some intertwined, bottle-horned dragons who were considered to bring benefit.

The giant stele bears the names of the Ming emperors buried in the necropolis and, although it is dated 1425, it was not put in place until 1435. The carved columns with clouds piercing the top (beneath the lion or qilin seated on a canopy) are similar to the pair (also Ming) which stand beside the Gate of Heavenly Peace (Tiananmen) at the S end of the Forbidden City. The columns are thought to be based on Han dynasty pillars which were used to signal staging posts in the imperial postal system but by the Ming they are certainly more decorative than indicative.

Beyond the stele pavilion is the famous 'spirit road' lined with carved stone figures. The road is curved, apparently to confuse evil spirits who could only fly in straight lines. The whole series of figures is now somewhat hidden by the orchards that line the road (photographs taken early in the 20C show the stone figures in a completely barren landscape).

First are a pair of carved stone columns with dragons all over them and rather stubby tops—these are symbolic beacons; they are followed by pairs of animals (in double pairs, one standing, one sitting): lions (Buddhist guardians), xiezhai (with leonine heads, horses' bodies and symbolising justice), camels, horses, elephants and qilin (augurs of wise rule). These are followed by human figures: four warriors, four civil officials and four imperial councillors. The officials wear the uniform of a President of one of the Six Boards (effectively a Minister), with badges of office embroidered on the front and back of their robes. They hold carved stone versions of the ivory boards which were used to write notes on matters to be raised in audience with the emperor. The last four figures are also officials but higher in rank, members of the imperial Grand Secretariat and they have flat-topped embroidered hats.

At the end of the avenue is a *Dragon and Phoenix Gate* with stone lintels topped with what look like versions of the Buddhist Wheel of the Law.

The tombs all have different names, which have no connection with the several names of their inhabitants. I shall first describe the two tombs which are generally open to the public and visited by tour groups, then the others in chronological order.

The first tomb is some 4km beyond the last gate. This is the **Chang ling** (Long-lasting Tomb) where the Yongle emperor was buried in 1424, with his empress who had died in 1407. Chang ling is not always on the tourist itinerary, if time is short, but it is very much to be recommended for its above-ground architecture. The tomb is approached through a yellow-roofed triple gate which leads to a courtyard, in the middle of which stands the *Gate of Heavenly Favours*, with a stele pavilion on the right housing a stele with inscriptions dated 1659, 1786 and 1804 recording penalties for felling timber in the area and dates of repairs.

Though the tomb was built for the Yongle emperor (reigned 1403–24) during his lifetime, the succeeding Qing dynasty made attempts to maintain the necropolis of their forerunners, probably for superstitious reasons (for it was believed that the disturbed souls of the deceased could influence events negatively).

Beyond the gate is the main courtyard of the *Hall of Heavenly Favours*. On either side of the path are small green and yellow-tiled 'buildings', actually ovens in which paper offerings were burnt. The great hall is one of the largest traditional buildings in China (only very slightly smaller than the Hall of Supreme Harmony in the Forbidden City). The triple-terraced marble terrace on which it stands is the earliest example of the type. Similar to the later versions in the Forbidden City (where construction began some years after the Yongle emperor began his tomb), this has dragon-topped pillars,bottle-horned dragon gargoyles and a fine carved slab in the centre of the staircase with dragons writhing above waves.
  The interior of the hall is exceptionally grand with huge columns of cedar (brought from Sichuan province on a journey that probably took some three years and thousands of unlucky labourers to drag them here). 10m high and 1m in diameter, these great columns are now unpainted (they may well have been painted red in the past) though the ceiling panels are painted in green, gold and blue. Their sombre colour adds to the grandeur of the hall (which is now unfortunately guarded by attendants in bright 'Ming costumes' and filled with a small exhibition of Ming artefacts, 1988).

Sir Reginald Johnston, tutor to the last Qing emperor, records how a descendant of the Ming royal house carried out his last ancestral sacrifices in the hall in 1924 before following Pu Yi into exile.

Behind the hall a triple doorway leads to another courtyard. A narrow screen door of wooden panels set between high white marble columns with qilin sitting on top (these columns, without the doors, can be seen in many of the ruined Ming tombs), stands in front of the great white marble 'altar' table with five marble versions of ritual bronze vessels, symbolic of those used in the rituals carried out in the Great Hall. Behind the marble 'altar' is the *stele tower*. Built above the battlemented circular brick wall that surrounds the tomb mound, it resembles a city gate with solid red walls and yellow tiled roof. At its base is a tunnel which leads up to the paved walk that runs around the battlements. Above, in the tower is the stele simply engraved with an inscription that states whose tomb it is. The *tomb mound*, which gives no indication of where the body actually lies (to confuse robbers), is thickly planted with pines and thujas. Walking round the ramparts, above the persimmon trees and fields below, you can see the yellow tiled roofs of other stele towers in the distance.

The **Ding ling** (Stable Tomb) is that of the Wanli emperor (died 1620) and two empresses, both called Wang. One was a concubine who bore the heir to the throne so that she was raised to the status of empress.

The tomb was excavated in 1956–58. The undergound chamber is open to visitors and there are halls of exhibits in the front courtyards. The discovery of the undergound chamber was fortuitous (and the amount of luck required helps to explain why none of the other tombs has yet been excavated). When archaeologists were examining a weak spot in the encircling wall they found a tunnel. This was not the entrance to the undergound chamber for it led to a dead end but, fortunately, the builders' instruction on how to find the burial chamber (inscribed on a small stele) had been left in the tunnel. Such instructions were apparently left by the original builders for those who would have to open the tomb when the emperor actually died and was to be buried in it. The stele should have been removed after the funeral. The tomb chamber was bricked up and beyond the brick wall was a pair of marble doors. These were extraordinarily difficult to open as they had been closed by a special buttress which fell against the doors as they were closed.

Like the Chang ling, Ding ling has three front courtyards forming its rectangular 'earth-shaped' section. Beyond the triple entrance gate are the remains of the *Gate of Heavenly Favours* and the *Hall of Heavenly Favours*. In the third courtyard, on either side of the marble altar are *exhibition halls*.

The west one contains mainly the effects of the emperor and that on the E those of the empresses. The emperor's several hats include one of black velvet studded with gems and pierced Munster-like with a great jade pin (for use when travelling), with rows of curtain-like tassels and beads for audiences, a plumed black iron helmet and a gold gauze hat with dragons. There are wooden models of furniture, gold, jade and miniature pewter vessels and wooden figurines, rolls of brocade, silver and gold ingots cast in Wanli's reign, a jade belt and a number of *meiping* blue and white porcelain jars. The empresses' possessions in the tomb include hairpins and jewellery, silken skirts and jackets, jade belt pendants, copies of the phoenix crowns decorated with kingfisher feathers stuck on paper and more jade and gold vessels.

The *tumulus* can be entered from the front or rear of the mound behind the stele tower (traffic problems sometimes dictate a one-way flow from either entrance). Beyond the antechamber are the great marble doors with the hole in the floor behind them where the heavy stone prop fell into place as the tomb was sealed. The chamber is beautifully constructed with carefully worked stones that fit neatly together without any cement. The main corridor leads to a major coffin chamber (with crude copies of three coffins on a raised stone dais) and there are side corridors leading to parallel side chambers (also with stone coffin platforms but which were empty). The main corridor has three stone thrones and huge blue and white porcelain vats which were filled with sesame oil to serve as 'everlasting' lamps (which had gone out as the oxygen was depleted). The side chambers had entrances with the same self-locking doors, leading to the outside—it is assumed they were there for any wives of the emperor who survived him and had to be buried here later. Paintings on the walls depict the construction of the tomb (which took six years and cost more than half a million pounds, using a corvée workforce of 600,000 men). The grave mound, like the front courtyards, planted with pines and thujas, has been tidied up considerably.

The other tombs are (W to E): Si ling, Zhao ling, Kang ling (behind Ding ling), Tai ling, Mao ling, Yu ling, Qing ling, Xian ling (just W of Chang ling), Jing ling (E of Chang ling) and Yong ling. In chronological order they were built as follows:

Xian ling (Offering Tomb) is the burial place of the Yongle emperor's sickly son, the Hongxi emperor (who died having reigned for barely a year), and his empress. The unlucky emperor's tomb (some 700m NW of Chang ling) is also geomantically rather odd for a small hill (Jade Table Mountain) intrudes on the axis of the tomb, splitting the entrance gate and sacrificial hall from the altar table courtyard and the mound. Little remains of the first courtyard, though the stele tower is in good condition. The mound is unusually elongated (hog's back shape) with thujas on top and Chinese oaks on the lower slope. These are extraordinary trees with huge leaves that seem to grow straight from the trunk creating the impression that they were drawn by a child (they can be found in many of the overgrown tombs).

Jing ling (Scenic Tomb) is the tomb of the Xuande emperor (died 1435) and his empress. It lies to the E of Changling and, like the Xian ling, is one of the smaller tombs. The tortoise stele that stands in front of the tomb

Great Wall

Ming tombs

N

Airport

Summer Palace

Bada chu   ● Peking University

Tanzhe si
and Jietai si

Marco Polo Bridge

0   km   10

Fang shan

PEKING AND ENVIRONS

has been surrounded by village buildings but behind, the double courtyard and long mound (also similar in shape to that of the Xian ling) are in
quite good condition. Though the sacrifical hall is now only visible
through its pillar bases, it was still intact in 1931. The stele tower is built
on a terrace with a steep approach ramp and side ramps running up to the
battlements on either side.

Yu ling (Lucky Tomb) is the burial place of the Zhengtong emperor (died
1464) and two empresses. It lies W of Xian ling and is reached by a small
cobbled road which runs N from a bus stop. It is rather isolated (with no
nearby village) and very quiet. The Zhengtong emperor's reign was
interrupted in 1449 when he was taken prisoner by the Mongols after a
military defeat and only managed to regain the throne from his brother in
1457. His tomb houses two empresses' bodies, in defiance of tradition for
one of the empresses had not borne a son (and should therefore have
been excluded). Beyond the tortoise stele are three arched bridges crossing a stream. The two courtyards are in ruins though there is a fine marble slab carved with mountains and clouds (the lack of dragons is quite
restful) leading to the platform of the sacrificial hall.

Mao ling (Flourishing Tomb) is that of the Chenghua emperor (died

1487) and three empresses, who also represent the major break in tradition for one was son-less and two were buried in the tomb after the emperor (which in previous periods of Chinese history was extremely unusual as it was considered unlucky to re-open a tomb—only tough characters like the Tang empress Wu were prepared to overrule the geomancers). It lies quite close to the main road, just W of the Yu ling and is not in terribly good condition.

Tai ling (Peaceful Tomb) is the burial place of Hongzhi (died 1505) and one empress. It lies just W of Mao ling and is in poor condition with the first courtyard open to a village, though the small offering oven is still in place.

Kang ling (Healthy Tomb) is the burial place of the Zhengde emperor (died 1521) and one empress (died 1535). It is one of the prettiest tombs, situated just SW of Tai ling (it was common for sons to site their tombs as near as possible to those of their fathers). Just beyond Mao ling a small path on the left leads through a persimmon orchard and across a river to the tomb which is rather tucked away. There is a wonderful view from the front of the tomb to distant mountains through the orchards. The tomb mound (whose ramparts also offer spectacular views) has a smaller group of mounds on top, said by some to represent children surrounding their father.

Yong ling (Eternal Tomb) is the burial place of Jiajing (died 1567) and three empresses who predeceased him. It is the easternmost of the tombs, reached by a road off to the right of the main tomb road which branches off some time before the Chang ling is visible. One of the best preserved of the 'ruined' tombs, it is also rich in wild flowers, handsome trees and birds. The marble slab leading to the platform on which the Gateway of Heavenly Favours once stood has a phoenix and dragon carved on it; this is the first appearance of the empress's symbol alongside that of the emperor in the Ming tombs. The proportions of the tomb are generous: there are wide steps and a broad ramp beside the equally broad stele tower whose workmanship is far more careful than that found elsewhere.

Zhao ling (Shining Tomb) is that of Longjing (died 1572) and three empresses and it is reached only by foot, through the fields SW of Ding ling (from the lower part of the parking area there). Here there is also a triple bridge over a stream behind the tortoise stele (parts of a finely carved wall surround this) and (once) an impressively raised gateway. The triple doorway of the second courtyard is still largely intact and though the stele tower was said to have been burned down by Li Zicheng's troops in 1644, it was restored.

Qing ling (Celebration Tomb) is that of the Taichang emperor (died 1620) and three empresses who predeceased him.

Taichang died a month after ascending to the throne. As he had not had time to prepare his own tomb he is buried in someone else's. Conveniently, when the Zhengtong emperor was taken prisoner by the Mongols in 1449, his brother, the Jingtai emperor who was placed on the throne instead, prepared a tomb for himself. When the Zhengtong emperor was restored to the throne in 1465 Jingtai was denounced as an usurper and his imperial tomb was destroyed—above ground. Thus the Qing ling's sub-structure dates from about 1450 and the superstructure was added in 1620–21.

Like the Xian ling, there are two parts to the tomb, divided by a small hill. The Qing ling lies W of the Chang ling (second tomb on the right). The tortoise stele is to the left of the main road, the entrance gate and sacrificial hall and mound to the right. The stele tower is slightly unusual in that it has two small side ramps and a staircase up to the terrace and the walkway round the grave mound is also slightly different in arrangement and has stone 'gates' which led to the mound. These have recently fallen over but were in place in 1971. (The mound also has a 'very well-developed' drainage system.)

Ann Paludan, whose loving and detailed guide to the area is indispenable to the serious Ming tomb visitor ('The Imperial Ming Tombs', Yale, 1981) is a keen student of tomb drainage and reports that 'this is the first tomb to show a complete system of drainage in both mound and courtyards' and she illustrates some of the drain covers.

De ling (Virtuous Tomb—though Piet Van der Loon, former Professor of Chinese at the University of Oxford, would massacre me for that translation: he prefers the Latin term *virtus* which includes an element of masculinity and strength quite lacking in 'virtuous') is the burial place of the Tianqi emperor (died 1627) and his empress who strangled herself at the orders of the last Ming emperor as Li Zicheng's rebel troops entered Peking marking the downfall of the dynasty. At the very farthest point E in the necropolis E of Chang ling (beyond Yong ling), this is a very beautiful tomb. Set quite high, with a marvellous view of the valley below from the gate and tortoise stele, its small size is belied by the spacious courtyards. The tortoise stele on its stone platform is in good condition, beautifully carved with turtle, prawn, fish and crab on the corners of the base. The tomb is built on rising ground, the second courtyard higher than the first and the crumbling stele tower set in front of an oval mound. As Ann Paludan says: 'Although it has no particular architectural interest, De ling is beautiful … a place of utter peace and many birds.'

Si ling (Meaningful Tomb) lies far to the W, strictly outside the imperial necropolis. It was originally a concubine's tomb, part of a complex of concubines' and imperial children's cemeteries in the area, and it was opened to receive the bodies of the last Ming emperor, Chongzhen, and his empress in 1644. The tomb and the concubine cemeteries are not easy to find: take the road W off the main road just beyond the dragon and phoenix gate (at the N end of the spirit way of animals). At a T-junction within sight of the hills, turn left and follow the road along the hills W past the remains of concubine cemeteries and round to the Si ling. Originally it had no tumulus but one was added, with a surrounding wall. All that survives today is the tumulus, the marble altar and its altar objects and a stele standing on a charmingly carved square base (instead of the usual imperial tortoise).

C.   The Western Hills

The **Western** or **Fragrant Hills** (Xiang shan) are 20km NW of Peking, beyond the Summer Palace. On the way to the Xiang shan are the Wofo si (Temple of the Sleeping Buddha) and the tomb of the Ming Jingtai emperor.

The **Tomb of the Jingtai Emperor** is 4km from the Summer Palace, off the main road at the point where the *Jade Fountain Pagoda* (standing on a hill in a military area which was once an imperial palace for the Jin and a garden for the Kangxi and Qianlong emperors of the Qing) is to the left and a village (*Niangniangfu*) and an army camp on the right. A ditch between these two leads to the stele pavilion of Jingtai's tomb.

The Jingtai emperor usurped the throne in 1449, when his elder half-brother, the Zhengtong emperor, had been captured by the Mongols. On Zhengtong's restoration he was disgraced and possibly murdered (he died suspiciously soon after). Denied a place in the Ming necropolis (Shisan ling; see above), the Jingtai emperor was reinstated in 1475: thus his stele is inscribed with the characters for the name of the dynasty and he himself described as 'reverent and peaceful'.

His tortoise stele stands in a small square pavilion with a painted beam and glazed tile roof (the only Ming stele pavilion to survive in Peking).

Inside the simple three-bay gatehouse is an enclosure which is rectangular to the S and curved to the N (thus incorporating both the square earth and circular heaven symbols). No buildings remain inside the enclosure, no hall or stele tower, just a simple grave mound with the characteristic earth cone on top.

The **Wofo si** (Sleeping Buddha Temple) is not far beyond. At a crossroad, a road leads N to the temple. (The road to the S leads to one of the Eight Great Sites [Badachu], that to the SW leads to the Xiang shan/Fragrant Hills Park.)

The temple was founded during the Tang, expanded in 1320–1331. Owing to its proximity to the imperial parks and gardens, various Ming and Qing emperors presented sutras and built halls and pagodas in the temple. The last major rebuilding was in 1734.

The temple is entered through a glazed-tile pailou gateway at the end of an avenue of fine old cypresses. Beyond is a bridge over a pool with the bell and drum towers on either side and in the first hall are statues of the Heavenly kings. In the second courtyard are two old Bodhi trees, *Shorea robusta*, said to have come from India: in front of the hall a Qianlong-period incense burner, inside the Maitreya (Future) Buddha with guardian figures and a Wei tuo (protector) behind. In the next hall are the Historic Buddha with Amitabha and the Buddha of Medicine and Guan yin behind (with luohans on either side). The great sleeping Buddha in the fourth hall is of lacquered bronze (over 5m long) and was cast in 1321.

That, at least, is the literary account, but many believe that the present figure is a later copy. The image is that of the dying Buddha, about to enter nirvana (rather than simply sleeping: the name of the temple should be more accurately translated as the Reclining Buddha Temple) and it is surrounded by smaller figures of Bodhisattvas, and giant shoes presented as offerings to the Buddha.

From the earliest period, the Buddha's feet or footprints have been used as symbolic representations of his presence. The soles of his feet were traditionally believed to have been different from those of ordinary mortals, imprinted with 108 symbols of good fortune (including conch shells under each toe).

There are E and W axes to the temple: the buildings to the W were used by the Ming and Qing emperors as 'travelling palaces'; those on the E were the monks' dwellings, kitchens and refectory.

Just NW of the temple is the *Yingtaogou yuan* (Garden of the Cherry Valley) where there was once a Taoist hermitage (founded in 1442, enlarged in 1486), of which nothing now remains. In the park are the *Bailu yan* (Cliff of the White Deer) where a sage was said to have landed during the 10C, flying in on a white deer. A cave where Taoist hermits meditated can be seen along with several pavilions.

S of the Temple of the Sleeping Buddha (on the road that eventually leads S to the Eight Great Sites), is the round fort, *Tuan Cheng*, built in the mid 18C by the Qianlong emperor. It was built to help prepare troops for military manoeuvres during uprisings in the SW: all that now remains is a small watchtower.

The **Fragrant Hills Park** lies beyond. It has long been a park, used as a hunting ground by emperors ever since the 12C.

In the 18C it was walled for, as game was scarce, 'horse deer' (*Cephus elaphurus*) were brought from Manchuria. The many temples and pavilions built here were damaged by the French and British armies in 1860 and by the Allied army at the end of the Boxer uprising (1900).

Just outside the walls on the left of the path is the new *Xiang shan Hotel*, designed by the American Overseas Chinese architect I.M. Pei in 1983.

Certainly the most striking modern building in China as yet, it is an interesting if slightly antiseptic mixture of the southern (Suzhou) garden-house complex and the grandeur of Chengde. Great flat white walls (Chengde without the red) surround a group of buildings linked by moon-gates and with other garden-like windows; most grouped around gardens and pools. The management has no doubt changed since I visited it soon after opening when the administration was the usual friendly, lethargic shambles at odds with the pristine elegance of the polished white halls. The hotel's distance from the centre of town makes it inconvenient for tourists but it would be an ideal conference centre.

Beyond is the entrance to the hilly park. Inside, along a path which leads first W then N, is the **Zhao Miao** (Luminous Temple), built by the Qianlong emperor in 1780 in the Tibetan style (recalling Chengde's outer temples, in particular the Xumifushou Temple).

Like the latter, it was constructed for visiting Tibetans, in particular the Panchen Lama, for him to use whenever he visited Peking (and its distance from the centre makes his use of the Huang si or Yellow Temple as a stopping place more explicable).

Like the temples in Chengde, it has a 'false' façade, with blind windows in the Tibetan style, breaking the monotony of the wall. The nearby seven-storey *Glazed Tile Pagoda* also resembles that at the Xumifushou Temple. Octagonal in plan, it has 56 bronze bells suspended from the eaves.

The *Jianxin zhai* (Pavilion of Introspection) is N of the Luminous Temple. Built in the reign of the Ming Jiaqing emperor (reigned 1522–1567), it was enlarged later. This is a courtyard residence built in the 'southern style'. In the centre of the courtyard is a semi-circular pool in which spring water spouts from a stone dragon head. The pool is surrounded by a covered walk.

Due S of the Pavilion of Introspection and the Zhao miao is the *Xiangshan si* (Fragrant Hills Temple), founded in 1186 and rebuilt in 1312. The Kangxi emperor of the Qing used it as a 'travelling' or temporary palace and it was again enlarged in 1745. Little remains but the stone terraces of what was once a huge temple for it was burnt down in 1900.

S of the temple are the remains of the *Shuangqing bieshu* (Two Springs Villa) where the two springs are named in the Qianlong emperor's calligraphy. The villa was used by Mao Zedong and others in March 1949 to plan the Red Army's crossing of the Yangtze River to liberate south China. He moved directly from this spot to Zhongnanhai (immediately W of the Forbidden City, still the residence and official centre of government) in November of the same year.

The highest peak in the park, the **Xianghu feng** (Incense Burner Peak) is in its western corner, 557m above sea level and crowded with visitors in the autumn when the leaves (of the Huanglu smoke tree) are red.

Outside the N gate of the Xiang shan Park is the **Biyun si** (Temple of the Azure Clouds), built against rising ground with the Diamond Throne Pagoda (a white marble version of the Wutai si, an Indian-style building with five tapering, stepped pagodas on top) visible above the trees.

There was apparently a Buddhist convent on the site in 1330. In the early 16C a group of eunuchs had the temple enlarged, planning to be buried there, but the work was later abandoned. The Diamond Throne Pagoda and Luohan Hall were built in 1748. Sun Yat-sen's body lay in the pagoda from 1925–1929, when it was transferred to his grave outside Nanjing, and a small commemorative museum is housed in the back halls of the temple.

The *Gate of Heavenly Guardians*, which stands beyond a bridge over a ravine and two Ming stone lions, contains fine figures of 1513, some 5m high. In the first courtyard are the bell and drum towers and a hall with a Ming figure of Maitreya (the Buddha of the Future). There is a pool in the centre of the second courtyard and two octagonal pillars carved with sutras: behind is a hall with a Buddha image and plaster figures (the upper register depicts Xuan zang's pilgrimage to India during the Tang dynasty).

On the S side of the third courtyard is the *Luohan Hall* (modelled on that at the Lingyin Temple at Hangzhou) with 500 lacquered carved wooden figures, a group of seven saints and a tiny figure of the monk Jian gong carved on a roof beam (making 508 figures in all). In the same courtyard is the *Puming juemiao Hall* where Sun Yat-sen's body lay. Behind is the *Diamond Throne Pagoda*, nearly 35m high with an interior staircase.

Inside are buried Sun Yat-sen's clothes and hat (repeating the old tradition that if bodies could not be found, clothing would be buried; in this case, Sun Yat-sen was not lost but, as the Father of the Nation, Peking wanted to keep a little of him, symbolically).

On the roof are two small dagobas with five square 13-storey close-eaved pagodas. The whole is covered with fine carvings of Buddhas, heavenly guardians, dragons, phoenix, lions, elephants, etc. Behind are hills, woods and a spring.

The **Eight Great Sites** (Bada chu) are eight temples situated on three hills, S of the Western Hills. They have long been closed as they are in a military area also peppered with villas, to which the Politburo retires in times of crisis (like June 1989). The sites are listed in the 'Zhong guo ming sheng ci dian' (Dictionary of Famous Sites, 1982) and Nagel's Guide (1979 edition) though they still not open to foreigners. In case the Politburo ever moves out, they consist of:

1 *Changan si* (Temple of Everlasting Peace), founded in 1504, described by Arlington and Lewisohn in 1935 as 'completely in ruins' but by Nagel's Guide as housing a fine gilded Guan Yu (God of War) figure of the Ming and a Niangniang Hall dedicated to a version of the Bodhisattva Guanyin, here as a giver of children to the childless. The figure was (is?) flanked by minor female deities who protected children from illness. There are two Yuan dynasty trees in the first courtyard, white-barked dragon-claw pines.

2 *Lingguang si* (Temple of Divine Light), founded in the 7C, destroyed by the Allied armies in 1900, when a box was found in the ruins of the pagoda which contained a Buddha tooth, for which a new pagoda was built in 1959. There is also a pond with enormous goldfish said to be over 100 years old.

3 *Sanshan an* (Three Hills Nunnery), founded in 1442, reconstructed in 1597 and 1786. It is popularly known as the Ma Family Nunnery (presumably because some nuns of the Ma family resided there. A great 'Jade stone' in the doorway of the main hall is called the Water and Cloud Stone because of its veining.

4 *Dabei si* (Temple of Great Compassion), founded during the Song, with an interesting stone entrance gate carved with animals, both real and mythological. The luohan figures in the first hall are said to be the work of a famous Yuan dynasty (1279–1368) sculptor, Liu Yuan. Behind the main hall are two gingko trees said to be 800 years old.

5 *Longwang tang* (Dragon King's Temple), founded in 916, restored in 1180 and frequently during subsequent dynasties. Its name comes from a spring which pours out of the mouth of a carved stone dragon's head.

6 *Xiangjie si* (Temple of the Fragrant World), the major temple of the group, was founded in 619 and restored in 1426, 1678 and 1749, the last restoration under Qianlong who built himself a garden and a 'travelling palace' here, gave the temple its present name and wrote an inscription on the temple's history which has been carved on a stele. It is said by Nagel's guide that it is now 'a rest-home for primary school teachers'.

7 *Baozhu dong* (Precious Pearl Cave), a temple which existed before 1326. Nagel says it is approached through a fine wooden pailou (in 1935, Arlington and Lewisohn recorded that there had once been a pailou which had since disappeared).

8 *Zhengguo si* (Temple of Buddhahood), founded in 620, destroyed in 1900. Traditionally believed to be the home of a hermit of the Tang dynasty, Lu Shi, who came from the south and lived in a cave here.

Arlington and Lewisohn also describe the *Tiantai si* (Monastery of Exalted Heaven), 'about one-and-a-half-hour's walk' from site No. 7, which contains a mummified figure.

S of the Bada chu, near the village of *Moshikou* is the *Fahai si* (Temple of the Sea of the Law), founded in 1439 and paid for by the eunuch Li Tong.

Despite later repairs it is said to preserve the early Ming style of building. The internal ceiling beams of the gate were painted in the early Ming and there are Ming frescoes of Buddhist deities on the walls of the main hall (not seen).

In the eastern suburbs of Peking, along the road that runs S from the Zoo (Sanlihe lu), to the W is the *Diaoyutai guo binguan* (State Guesthouse of the Angler's Terrace). Here state visitors stay in villas in the extensive grounds. The Queen of England, George Bush and Mikhail Gorbachev are among recent state visitors. Some groups of tourists may get to stay in the complex.

According to tradition, the Zhangzong emperor of the Jin (reigned 1190–1209) used to fish here where the Jin poet Wang Yu had 'built a terrace and lowered his fishing line'. During the Yuan the area was a park; during the Qing, the Qianlong emperor had one of his innumerable 'travelling palaces' here. The gardens are laid out as they were in the Qing and many of the trees date back to that period.

At the bottom of the road, where it joins Changan jie (here called Fuxingmen wai da jie), are the great grey buildings of the *Academia Sinica*, the Chinese Academy of Science (on the E side of the road). Some km along Fuxingmen wai da jie, out beyond the built-up area, is the cemetery of *Babao Shan* where the ashes of prominent citizens are placed.

D.   Southwest of Peking

SW of Peking are the 'Marco Polo Bridge' or Lugouqiao, the site of the finds of Peking man at Zhoukoudian, the two temples—Tanzhe si (Temple of the Pool and the Mulberry) and the Jietai si (Temple of the Ordination Platform). Further on are the Yunju si (Temple of the Habitation in the Clouds) and nearby Shijing shan/Fang shan (Stone Sutra Mountain).

The 'Marco Polo bridge', known to the Chinese as **Lugouqiao** (Bridge Over the Lugou River) is 16km W of the Guang'an men in the SW of the city.

The main road out of the city through the site of the Guang'an men is called Guang'an men wai da jie, then Lugouqiao lu. It crosses the river once known as Lugou, now as the Yongding. The stone bridge (replacing previous pontoon bridges which were always being washed away) was built between 1189 and 1192.

There is a description of the bridge in Marco Polo's 'Travels': '...it is quite 300 paces long and quite eight paces wide...all of grey marble very well worked and well founded'. Though he mentions stone lions, he fails to mention the 140 balusters each with a little stone lion on top or the stone elephants at either end of the bridge (nudging the parapets with their foreheads).
Marco Polo is supposed to have seen the bridge in 1276 (hence its name for foreigners) but his description which, as usual, misses the most striking of the bridge's decorative features, could well have been copied from elsewhere. One of the arguments against Polo's having seen things personally (and the likelihood that he copied his account from Persian travel books) is his use of Persian names (never Chinese or Mongol), and he calls this bridge *Pulisangin*, from the Persian 'pul' for bridge and 'sang' for stone.
At either end of the bridge are stele pavilions housing a stele describing restoration work of 1698 and one describing the morning moon on the bridge as one of the 'eight views of Peking'.
The bridge gained a 20C notoriety as the site of the 'Marco Polo Bridge incident' of 7 July 1937 which provided the Japanese with a pretext for the invasion of north China. The Boxer Protocol of 1901 had allowed the establishment of a Japanese garrison in the area which had been holding manoeuvres by the bridge. Claiming that a soldier was missing, the troops attempted to search the small walled town of Wanping at the E end of the bridge. The Chinese garrison commander refused to let them in so they bombarded the town, occupied it, and commenced their total invasion of China from the N.

There is a small museum, *The Chinese People's Anti-Japanese War Memorial Hall*, at 10 Chengnei Street, Wanping (closed Mondays; open 8–11, 1–4.30), commemorating the incident. There is also a *Museum of the History of the Marco Polo Bridge* beside the bridge.

It is possible to climb up onto the walls of **Wanping** from where you can look down into the courtyard houses below. Houses in the town (and throughout these western suburbs out to the Ordination Platform Temple, Jietai si) often have rather wonderful lattice windows, some with auspicious characters and symbols worked into them, some with the five–pointed star of the army.

Beyond the bridge (48km from Peking) is **Zhoukoudian**, where Teilhard de Chardin found relics of Peking Man (of 300,000–500,000 years ago) in 1929.

Animal bones were associated with the early-man remains; it is also clear that fire was used in the caves. Teeth marks and breaks on some of the bones have led some to suggest the practice of cannibalism but it is also likely that animals were responsible.

Peking Man, otherwise known as *Sinanthropus pekinensis, Pithecanthropus pekinensis* and *Homo erectus pekinensis*, walked upright, had a considerable cranial capacity and used stone tools, lived mainly by hunting and cooking meat but also ate nuts. Some of the limestone caves on *Longgu shan* (Dragon Bone Hill) where the excavations were carried out can be visited.

A second group of early inhabitants have been distinguished: Upper Cave Man (of some 50,000 years ago). Upper Cave Man also worked bone and antlers into needles and necklaces and seems to have had a reasonably complex burial ritual (the Upper Cave remains seem to be those of a burial).

There is a *museum* at the site, illustrating both the finds of the site and the life of its earlier inhabitants and the development of man in general.

120km (75 miles) SW of Peking are the remains of the **Yunju si** (Temple of the Habitation in the Clouds) and the **stone sutras of Fang shan**. The temple was founded during the Sui (6C) and almost completely destroyed by the Japanese during the War (1937–45). All that remains in this beautiful mountain site is a group of stupa pagodas. These include a group of four beautifully carved stone 'relic' pagodas or stupas with fine figures on each of its facets, dating from the Tang, surrounding a 30m Liao dynasty (907–1125) pagoda. There are also six Liao brick pagodas.

When I visited the site in 1984 with some of the first foreign visitors, apart from the modern buildings housing stone slabs and offices, there was nothing remaining of the temple save the pagodas and stupas. However, an article in the 'China Daily' of 7 November 1987 states that a 'restoration' of the temple is under way, which has so far included 'work on the Vairocana, Mahakaruna and Devajara Halls totalling 1500 square metres.' It may be very sensitively undertaken but to the English eye, at least, the ruined stones, grass, wild flowers and surrounding mountains were extremely lovely and in no need of further restoration.

The founder of the temple, a monk called Jingyuan, began the work of carving the Buddhist sutras on stone, in imitation of the imperial carving of the Confucian classics on stone (a practice which began in the Han and was intended both to allow rubbings of the text to be taken before the development of woodblock printing and to lay down the 'authorised' version of the text). Carving of the sutras continued after his death, up to the Ming, and 4915 slabs were carved. Rubbings of the texts are still taken in the traditional manner (by inking the slab, spreading a sheet of fine paper over it and pounding it with a soft cloth pommel).

Though many of the sutra stones are now in the modern buildings beside the pagodas, they were originally housed in caves on top of the nearby *Shi jing shan* (Stone Sutra Mountain), across the railway line. It is possible to climb the picturesque mountain and see the caves where the slabs were stored.

Due W of Peking, beyond the enormous cement and steel works of Shijing shan, are two marvellous temples in the southern part of the Western Hills. The lower one, 35km from Peking, is the **Jietai si** (Temple of the Ordination Platform). It is on the slopes of *Ma'an shan* in the Mentougou area and was founded in 622. Its famous ordination platform was constructed during the Liao (907–1125) by a monk called Fa Jun. With the exception of the platform (which in its present form dates from the Ming) and some funerary stupas, the surviving buildings are Qing in date (and have been extensively restored in the early 1980s. Below and beside the temple is a 'cemetery', a group of finely carved funerary stupas in stone and brick (most imitating timber construction), dating from the Liao, Yuan and Ming, standing amongst white-barked pines against the red walls of the temple.

The present buildings are not intrinsically very interesting (and their sculptures are all modern), though the courtyard layout is very pleasing, as is the surrounding scenery. The trees in the courtyards are famous and they include 'pagoda pines, sleeping dragon pines, living pines and nine dragon pines'. A poem states: 'The Tanzhe Temple is famous for its spring, the Jietai for its pines'. One of the most famous of the pines has died and its original site is marked by a stone tablet on the left of the hall behind the main hall. It was known as the 'moving' pine because it was said that if one of its branches was touched, the entire tree would shake.

The *Ordination Platform* is some 3m high and must have been reached by temporary timber or bamboo structures when used (as it was annually). It is made of white marble in three tiers and carved with hundreds of figures, some c 1m high. It was used both for an annual gathering of local monks who came to hear their superiors preach from the terrace and also for ordination ceremonies of novices. Young monks and nuns who had served their novitiate would gather together, their heads freshly shaved. Part of the ceremony included the placing of rows of little piles of incense on their bald heads. These were burnt, leaving the classic marks of the true monk in the row of dotted scars on the shaved scalp.

The **Tanzhe si** (Temple of the Pool and the Mulberry) is 45km from the centre of Peking, beyond the Ordination Platform Temple, on the *Tanzhe shan* (Pool and Mulberry Mountain) from which it takes its name, near Mentougou. The foundation is immensely old, dating back to the Jin (265–316); a popular saying describes its antiquity as being greater than that of Peking itself. The present buildings date from the Ming and Qing.

The forest of stupas below the temple includes funerary stupas from the Jin to the Qing and forms a marvellous approach to a temple which offers some wonderful views and venerable trees. It is built against a steep mountain slope, each courtyard towering over the next. On the central axis is a pailou archway, the gatehouse (or 'mountain gate'), the Hall of Heavenly Kings, and the main hall, behind which was the Hall of the Three Sages which no longer survives. Beside it stands the 'imperial tree', a gingko, some 30m high with a span of 6–7m. It is said to date from the Yuan and its 'imperial title' was conferred by the Qianlong emperor of the Qing in the mid-18C. On the other side of the site of the hall is another tree, 'the emperor's wife', said to put forth a new branch every time a new emperor was born.

The highest point on the central axis is reached in the Vairocana Hall. The main hall is tiled with imperial yellow tiles with yellow ridge acroteria for the temple enjoyed especial imperial favour under Khubilai Khan (whose daughter was buried here) and Qianlong who built a 'travelling palace' in the eastern axis of the temple (in which visitors can still stay overnight).

On the western axis is a modest ordination platform and Guanyin Hall (amongst others) whilst the western axis is composed of more domestic courtyards. Amongst them is a 'cup-floating pavilion' (similar to that in the Forbidden City), called the *Yilan ting* (Pavilion of Ripples). The floor has a curling groove where water from the Dragon Spring was led in and imperial guests would float winecups and play a forfeit game which involved composing a line of poetry if a cup floated towards them.

There is a marvellous view of mountains from the high *terrace* of the temple which is one of the most beautifully sited in China.

This was the temple that the novelist Ann Bridge (the pen-name of Lady O'Malley, whose husband served in the British Embassy in Peking during the 1920s and 1930s) used as the major setting for 'Peking Picnic' (1932). It was common practice at the time for Peking residents to take themselves off to the temples of the Western Hills during the hot, humid summer. 'Nothing is stranger to the new-comer to China than this custom of temple authorities of throwing open their sacred precincts to European visitors. A courtyard or two, or three, according to their needs, is let off to each party, and there with their beds, food, chairs and servants they establish themselves for a day or two.'

Some famous Peking residents like Sir Reginald Johnston, tutor to the last emperor, hired temples on a long-term basis and spent much time there; temporary visitors in the 1930s were recommended to 'take bedding and provisions'. Ann Bridge's characters first spend a night in the Jietai si which, at the time, was—like the Tanzhe si—still a practising religious centre. She describes how the visitors moved on to the Tanzhe si to view the 'imperial' gingko and its 'wife', how 'the whole temple was full of the gentle voice of water', the hillsides planted with thujas, and the cemetery below the temple where Khubilai's daughter the nun was buried. The story continues, involving a bandit attack in this idyllic setting, and an escape up the mountainside which you can re-run if you take the novel with you.

E.   Tombs of the Qing Emperors

The two groups of **Tombs of the Qing Emperors**, the Dong ling (Eastern Tombs) and Xi ling (Western Tombs) are c 125km and 135km from Peking (in opposite directions as their names suggest). Their distance makes a day trip something of an ordeal: the Eastern Tombs can be seen by making (quite) a detour on the road to Tianjin. It is best to see the Ming tombs first for the Qing tombs, though beautifully sited, are almost parodies of those of the Ming.

The Eastern Tombs were the first to be used (by the first and second Qing emperors) and the first tomb in the Western group is that of the (third) Yongzheng emperor who died in 1735. Thus the Ming practice of sons building their tombs adjacent, or close, to those of their fathers, was broken in the Qing. The tombs themselves are much smaller than those of the Ming, with funny little stumps of mounds, though some of the preceding halls are extremely grand, and the bridges and streams of the Eastern Tombs are relatively elaborate. The carving of the spirit way figures is far cruder than seen in the Ming tombs.

The **Eastern Tombs** (Xi ling) are in *Zunhua xian* (county), N of the road that runs between Ji xian and Zunhua, set against the foothills of the Changrui Mountains.

The journey now takes some 3–4 hours depending on traffic problems; it is extraordinary to think that in 1924 the Japanese Railway Guide stated that it took nearly a week to reach them from Peking, 'on four days of which crude native means of transport or horses have to be used'.

Five emperors are buried here: Shunzhi (the first Qing emperor, died 1661), Kangxi (the second Qing emperor, died 1722), Qianlong (the fourth emperor, died 1799), Xianfeng (the seventh emperor, died 1861) and Tongzhi (the eighth emperor, died 1875) as well as 14 empresses (including the Dowager Empress Cixi (died 1908) and 136 concubines. The whole cemetery area (which was previously enclosed as a forbidden area) covers 48 square km and is ideally sited to accord with fengshui beliefs with hills behind to the N and a flat plain with a river (the Xida he), from which a canal was led, in front.

Three tombs have been restored and opened to the public: those of the Qianlong emperor (the Yu ling or Fortunate Tomb), his empress and concubine Rong (the Yufei or Fortunate Concubine's Tomb) and the pair of tombs in which the Empress Dowager Cixi and the senior consort Cian were buried (known as the Cian and Cixi Tombs).

Cian was the empress of the Xianfeng emperor (died 1862), though Cixi, originally a lowly concubine, was raised in rank when she bore the emperor's only heir, the Tongzhi emperor (died 1875). As he was a child when he succeeded his father, the two women acted as his regents (having got rid of the official regents) though the less ambitious Cian was seen as being under the thumb of the ruthless Cixi (and was widely believed to have been poisoned by her when she died in 1881).

The enclosure is entered through a stone archway, beside which is the *Zhaoxi Tomb* (of a concubine), and behind which is a great red gate and a robing hall. Behind that is a stele pavilion and the spirit road then leads to the row of stone statues and the dragon and phoenix gate. This spirit road leads directly to the tomb of the Shunzhi emperor (*Xiao ling* or Filial Tomb). Off to the right (E) are the *Hui ling Tombs*, those of the Tong zhi emperor and a concubine, illustrating the common Qing practice (at variance with that of the Ming emperors) of constructing paired but separate tombs for emperors and their concubines. To the left of the main spirit road, a subsidiary line of stone animals sandwiched between another stele pavilion and stone gateway leads to the *Yu ling Tomb* of the Qianlong emperor and (further to the left) the *Cixi and Cian Tombs*, with the *Ding ling* (Secure Tomb) of the Xian feng emperor at the far left (W) end approached by yet another small spirit way.

In plan, the tombs are similar to those of the Ming emperors—rectangular in front (representing the earth), circular behind (representing heaven). Each is preceded by a tortoise stele in a pavilion, the base surrounded by a fish, crab, prawn and turtle emerging from the waves, and a smaller stele or stone horse instructing officials to dismount for, as in the Forbidden City and the Ming tombs, they had to proceed on foot. The arrangement of water (which had to lie in front of the tomb according to the fengshui belief) is very elegant, with flattish triple bridges of white marble crossing broad expanses of water.

In the long rectangular courtyard in front, the *Sheng'en dian* (Hall of Great Compassion) stands in the centre with (unlike the Ming tombs) side wings for the display and inspection of grave goods, for Lamaist prayers and kitchens (described as 'pastry and food halls') on either side of the courtyard. A gateway leads to the rear courtyard where, behind the gate with its qilin-topped pillars, a stone altar with stone 'ritual vessels' stands before the stele tower in front of the burial mound itself.

Though the Qianlong emperor's tomb has a grassy mound, the later mounds are rounded, asphalted tumps (not the rustic, tree-covered hills of the Ming emperors) and below, the 'underground palaces' are also treated in a different manner. Far less effort was expended in concealing the entrance to the burial chamber, but far more on decorating its stone walls and doors with very fine low relief carvings of Buddhist figures and Buddhist inscriptions. This Buddhist theme is even carried over into the official figures of the spirit ways who wear Buddhist rosaries instead of carrying the ivory tablets used by officials at court and depicted in the figures at the Ming tombs. The attention paid to the decoration of the inner chamber (contrasted with the simple brick vault of the Ming tombs) recalls earlier burial traditions as can be seen in, for example, the Tang royal tombs near Xi'an.

The tombs of Qianlong and Cixi were robbed by soldiers of a minor warlord, Sun Tianying, in 1928, when it is said that the body of Cixi was frighteningly well-preserved. Manchu nobles went to the scene of desecration and reburied the bodies but it was too late to recover much of the jewellery.

The last emperor, Pu Yi, who was then in nearby Tianjin, is said to have been enraged by the news that some of the pearls from Cixi's phoenix crown had found their way onto the toes of Mme Chiang Kai-shek's shoes. Cixi's jewellery was legendary; Sir Edmund Backhouse (1873–1944), a peculiar adventurer who purchased some fine palace editions for his alma mater, Oxford University, attempted to sell guns that he did not have, and claimed to have slept with every notable of the late 19C from Verlaine and Oscar Wilde to Cixi herself, also claimed to possess a jacket made entirely of huge pearls that had belonged to Cixi.

There are, however, a very wide range of items on exhibit in the hall of Cixi's tomb and other halls: fine robes, some of which display a slightly European influence, most notably a spring robe embroidered with wisteria and decorated with imported butterfly lace panels. Some of the garments, worn by the deceased, are very tattered. There are small gilt-bronze Buddhist images (in the Tibetan or Lamaist style), altar sets, food-serving dishes and compartmented trays for sweetmeats, a great collection of unguents and medicines including bear fat and tiger-bone ointment (for the hair?) in a porcelain jar decorated with birds amongst roses. Dominoes, playing cards and theatrical robes are displayed with a stern notice describing Cixi's luxurious and spendthrift habits, as is a stuffed Pekinese dog wearing a blue and purple damask jacket. Cixi had many dogs, mostly small Pekinese or Lhasa terriers, all with their own wardrobes and all of whom had their portrait painted.

There is also a fascinating collection of turn-of-the-century Western cigarette packets, and cigarette cards—Muratti's after-lunch cigarettes (London and Manchester), Duke's Cameo cigarettes (with cards) and a tin of King Whiff extra-length high-grade Virginia cigarettes. Clocks in glass domes were made in France and imported by Allman and Co. of Shanghai and Hong Kong or Kieruff's of Peking. There are tattered garments of the Qianlong emperor and some dirty old hada (white scarves traditionally presented by and to Lamas), earrings, hairpieces, strings of pearls, jade ruyi sceptres, a 'good-luck hat' which looks like an army cap that has seen better times, sedan chairs, military uniforms and weapons and many locks and hinges from the boxes that held the grave goods.

The **Western Tombs** are 120km SW of Peking, 15km W of Yixian below the Yongning Mountains.

There used to be a railway line to Lianggezhuang (until 1906 forbidden to the public) to enable the court to get to the tombs in 5 hours (followed by an hour's donkey ride). The site was chosen at the order of the Yongzheng emperor in 1730, despite the existence of the earlier Eastern Tombs complex—Yongzheng's successor, the Qianlong emperor, decided to be buried next to his grandfather at the Eastern Tombs. Qianlong suggested that emperors should henceforth alternate between the two sites but this practice was not followed.

Interred at the Western Tombs are the Yongzheng (died 1736, buried in the Tai ling or Peaceful Tomb), Jiaqing (died 1821, buried in the Chang ling or Flourishing Tomb), Dao guang (died 1851 and buried in the Mu ling or Admiration Tomb) and Guangxu (died 1908, buried in the Chong ling or Lofty Tomb) emperors, as well as their consorts and a number of concubines, in 14 tombs altogether. The area covers some 100 square km and was surrounded by a wall 21km long.

The tombs and the associated Lama temple have red walls, yellow-tiled roofs, whilst those of the wives, princes and concubines have red walls and green tiled roofs (reflecting a distinction that can also be seen in Peking's architecture). The main tomb is that of the Yongzheng emperor, to which the spirit road with its animal figures and stele gate leads. With the exception of the tomb of the Daoguang emperor, the other tombs are all similar in construction.

The major tomb, the *Tai ling*, is approached through a great red gate, with a robing hall inside and a 30m-high stele pavilion with a yellow-tiled roof. Beyond is the row of carved stone animals and a small hill which serves as a 'spirit wall'. The dragon and phoenix gate lies behind the hill, embellished with dragons and clouds in carved glazed tilework. Inside the tomb enclosure, the main hall, with brightly painted ceilings and gilded pillars, is flanked by side halls and small stoves for burning offerings. In the mound behind the stele tower, the Yongzheng emperor was, unusually, buried with his empress and concubines.

The *Mu ling*, the westernmost of the tombs, also holds the bodies of the Daguang emperor and his three empresses. His grave had originally been constructed in the Eastern Tomb Cemetery but, after one empress had been buried there, the tomb was flooded (apparently construction had been skimped) so another tomb was started in the Western Tombs Cemetery. It is rather small, lacking a stele pavilion, row of stone animals and stele tower. The main hall is built of unpainted nanmu cedar with carved windows, beams and ceiling. The wood is fragrant so it is said of this hall, filled with carved dragons, that 'ten-thousand dragons are gathered, puffing out incense from their mouths'.

The most recent grave, that of the Guangxu emperor who died in 1908, was not begun until 1909 and he was buried there with his empress in 1915, well into the Republican period. The tomb is small, lacking stele pavilion and avenue of animals, and the workmanship is poor, with nails used on the timber structure of the hall. However the setting, with silver and lohan pines and a surrounding orchard, is very pretty.

Also in **Yixian** (the nearest town) is a temple, the *Kaiyuan si*, founded during the 26th year of the Kai yuan reign period of the Tang (738).

Shijiazhuang, c 230km SW of Peking, is the capital of Hebei province. The town grew with the railways from the late 19C to become the Crewe of China, standing at the junction of three main lines. It has major textile factories and is also the current site of *Norman Bethune's Grave*.

Bethune (born 1980) was a Canadian surgeon who made significant contributions to thoracic surgery and volunteered as a doctor, first in Spain during the Civil War. There he realised the importance of quick treatment and mobile blood-transfusion units, to prevent wounded soldiers dying unnecessarily from shock and blood loss. He continued these methods, as far as possible, in China where he arrived in 1938. Unfortunately, he died in the same year of septicaemia, after cutting himself during an operation, illustrating the pressures under which front-line surgeons worked. He was first buried elsewhere, but his body, together with the of the Indian Dr Kotnis, who had also volunteered to work with the Red Army, was moved to Shijiazhuang for the convenience of visitors.

12km N of Shijiazhuang, in **Zhengding**, is the *Longxing Temple*, famous for its colossal bronze Guanyin figure (more than 22m tall, cast in the late 10C), and its revolving library (similar to that on Wutai shan).

3 Tianjin

Tianjin is one of the major maritime ports of China, c 120km SE of Peking. It lies on the Hai River, at the junction with the Grand Canal, some 30km from the coast (at Tanggu).

Opened to foreign trade in 1860 by the Convention of Peking, separate foreign concessions were quickly opened in the city, Austrian, Italian and Russian and Belgian running W to E along the north bank of the Hai River, Japanese, French, British and German running W to E along the south bank. After the First World War the German and Austro-Hungarian Concessions were renamed 'Special Districts' and reverted to Chinese control. The closeness of the concessions and their retention of separate control (as opposed to the mixed 'International Settlement' of Shanghai) has meant that the separate areas are still architecturally distinct. The British Concession has its solid bank buildings and the Scottish baronial of Gordon Hall, château-like roofs and towers characterise the French Concession and strange modernistic buildings are to be found in the ex-German Concession.

Tianjin, now a sprawling industrial centre whose size (with over 7 million inhabitants in the entire municipal territory) has been acknowledged in its status which is equivalent to that of a province, suffered greatly in the 1976 Tangshan earthquake. In the past decade, however, its recovery has been dramatic, largely owing to the appointment of a new mayor, Li Ruihuan, an ex-carpenter, who has thrown himself successfully into the task of reconstruction and developed a strong sense of local pride in recent achievements.

Dangerous as it is in days of political ups and downs to single out personalities, Li Ruihuan has had the most extraordinary effect on the city. He was locally born in 1934 and worked as a construction worker in Peking from 1951 to 1965, joining the Communist Party in 1959. His bureaucratic career started in 1965 but took off after 1971. He was then based in Peking (where he was concurrently secretary of the Party Committee of the Peking Construction Timber Plant, deputy secretary of the Party Committee of the Peking Bureau of Building Materials, Vice-chairman of the Peking Capital Construction Commission, Director of the headquarters of the Peking Capital Construction Commission. Vice-chairman of the Peking Trades Union Federation, a permanent member of the All-China Federation of Trades Unions and a member of the Standing Committee of the Fifth National People's Congress). In 1981 he moved to Tianjin where he became a member of the Standing Committee of the Communist Party of Tianjin, Deputy Mayor, Party Secretary, Acting Mayor and Mayor of Tianjin (this list, which I assume should be understood to represent a sequence of posts, was taken from the 'China Daily').

The date of 1981 is important because it represents the turning point in Tianjin's history when the devastation of the 1976 earthquake was finally tackled with a massive restoration programme, improving the city's housing stock, streets and public buildings without destroying its 19C–early 20C treaty port style.

Since the Tiananmen massacre of 1989, Li has been moved away from Tianjin, to higher office in Peking, in control of censorship.

Airport: there are daily flights to Hong Kong, Guangzhou and Peking, and less frequent departures to Chengdu, Harbin, Nanjing, Xi'an and Urumqi (mostly two flights a week).

TIANJIN

- Da bei yuan temple
- Wanghai lou
- Xinkai lu
- Dongmalu
- Hai River
- Xinhuochang lu
- Jianguo lu
- Wenhua jie, Folk art Museum
- Nanmalu lu
- Railway station
- lu
- Heping lu
- Old Nankai University
- Erwei lu
- Nanmenwai lu
- Jie fang qiao
- Duolun lu
- Hebei lu
- Anshan lu
- Binjiang
- Dagu
- lu
- Fine art Museum
- Jiefang lu
- Weijin lu
- Xinxing
- Shengli
- Yingkou
- Tai'an lu
- Gordon hall
- Astor House hotel
- Tianjin Hyatt
- Guizhou lu
- Tianjin Canting/Kiessling and Bader's tea rooms

Railway: the station is on the N bank of the Hai River, just opposite the iron bridge that leads to the French Concession on the S side. Tianjin is very conveniently reached from Peking by frequent trains which take 90 minutes (and a day trip from Peking is recommended).

Hotels: the best old hotel is the Astor House Hotel in the British Concession, 199 Jiefang bei lu, its timbered halls and dining rooms, dark wood double staircase and original entrance left intact whilst the back entrance (now the main reception area) has been internationalised, as have the rooms. Its Chinese name is (and always has been) Lishun fandian or Profit and Success Hotel. Just down the road are the twin towers of the odd-looking Tianjin Hyatt (complete with Presidential suite), virtually the only new building to despoil the city, and opposite the Astor House Hotel is the Tianjin No. 1 Hotel, 198 Jiefang bei lu, another old colonial building housing a cheaper hotel.

Tianjin's history is surprisingly short for it stands on an area that was originally under water and only gradually silted up to become inhabitable. It was first mentioned as a trading port during the Song dynasty, growing during the Ming (and being surrounded by a wall in 1404) when it was apparently colonised by people from Anhui (presumably because opportunities were lacking in that province which has been described as the Appalachians of China) and the Tianjin dialect is said to reflect this migration. In the 18C the river-port town was extremely prosperous as was noted by members of the first Dutch embassy in 1655: '…surrounded by sturdy walls over 25 feet high with watchtowers…the town has many temples; it is thickly populated and trade is very brisk…because all the boats which go to Peking, whatever their port of origin, call here…'.

The first European settlers were Anglo-French troops in 1860 (after the Treaty of Tianjin, 1858, was ratified in Peking, 1860) and the concession areas soon sprang up S of the Chinese town on both sides of the Hai River. In 1870 Tianjin was, in the eyes of Europeans, 'disgraced by the Tianjin massacre' when ten Sisters of Charity (mostly French with one Irish and one Italian sister), two Lazarist priests and an entire congregation mainly of Chinese orphans were killed by a mob which also claimed a Russian merchant (Protopopoff) and his wife, a French merchant (M. Chalmaison) and his wife and the French consul. It was said that the riot started as a result of the belief that the Sisters of Charity kidnapped Chinese orphans for sinister purposes (there was a Chinese belief that railway lines required human sacrifice), though in fact the mob first attacked the French Consulate so it may be considered as generally anti-foreign. Twenty or more Chinese were beheaded as a result, a considerable amount of money was awarded in recompense and the Prefect and Sub-prefect of Tianjin were 'banished to the Amur province, with hard labour'.

Life for foreigners in pre-Liberation (or pre-Japanese invasion) Tianjin was luxurious, with pastries and hot chocolate served in Kiessling and Bader's Restaurant as violinists played Strauss amongst the palms, bands playing in Victoria Park, Gordon Hall illuminated like Harrods for the coronation of George VI, the Empire Cinema (where the violinist from Kiessling's also performed), shops like those of Shanghai— Whiteway, Laidlow and Co., Aux Nouveautes in the French settlement—and the whole governed (in the British settlement at least) by regulations. Chinese nursemaids (amahs) required non-transferable passes before being allowed into Victoria Park with their small white charges and were to note 'That the cenotaph being a memorial to the dead, Amahs must exercise the greatest vigilance to prevent the children under their care from playing on the Cenotaph steps, or from touching any flowers or wreaths that may be deposited thereupon'. No dogs or bicycles were allowed although 'this Rule does not preclude wheeled toys for children such as bicycles, wooden horses, etc'. Regulations covered everything from the running of Aerated Water Factories (first in the long list of licensed premises' regulations in the 1920 'Municipal Handbook') to 'the maximum quantity of loose straw which may be stored in a Chinese house or shop at one time is TWO piculs' (their capitals) and, in re bicycles, brakes, bells and lights were required and 'Furious riding' was forbidden on the roads of the Concession.

Tianjin was a centre for traditionalist Chinese secret societies and anti-foreign movements in the 19C (whilst Shanghai tended to conceal more of the modern anti-colonialists); the White Lotus Society (Bailian hui), a secret society of long-standing which dated back to well before the Ming, was, and some say still is, strong in the area. The Ming founder was associated with the White Lotus, a millenarian popular society influenced both by Buddhism and Manicheanism, though once he became emperor he turned on secret societies for they were almost invariably anti-imperial. The Manichean influence on the White Lotus is clear in its vocabulary and stress on 'light' and the name of the Ming dynasty (Ming means 'bright' or 'shining') and the Buddhist influence is clear in the name of the society and its enthusiasm for a non-canonical Buddhist work, the 'Mu niu' (Taming the Ox) classic where the illustrations depict a black ox slowly turning white as it is tamed by a small boy, implying the possibility of the taming of the self or self-cultivation. The White Lotus were active throughout the late 19C and early 20C, capturing rice-laden junks on the Grand Canal and setting fire to the Standard Oil Company's storage tanks in 1929 and, under cover of the confusion, seizing grain from the old imperial granary. The shorter-lived but more terrifying Boxers, who rose against the imperial dynasty in 1900 but quickly (with imperial assistance) turned their murderous attention to the foreign community in the north of China, were also active, and perhaps connected with the White Lotus movement in Tianjin and the surrounding countryside.

The 'Japanese Railway Guide' for 1924 noted that: 'situated on a large sandy plain, without hills or mountains to relieve the view, [Tianjin] has scarcely any place in its neighbourhood noted for the beauty of natural scenery, nor has it many temples or other works of ancient art as its importance only began with the opening to foreign trade in 1860'. It is, however, a neat and compact treaty port with the most varied foreign architecture to be seen (and many treasures perhaps to be found: I have spent days searching for the expressionist factory of A. Faust and Co., but so far have failed to run it down).

Sites to visit in Tianjin include the Mosque, the Museum, the Dabeiyuan Monastery and the Wenhua jie area with the Tianhou gong Temple and Folk Art Museum. These completed, Tianjin is small enough for fascinating walks through the British, German and French Concessions, in particular.

A.   North Tianjin

The Mosque, the Dabei yuan, Wenhua jie, the Wanghai lou and
  Santiaoshi Museum are all in the N of the city and could be seen in a
  rather full morning's taxi ride.

The Mosque, **Qingzhen da si**, is in the NW corner of the old Chinese city, just off Dafeng lu, near Xiaohuo xiang. The streets are incredibly narrow and the car may have to park some 100m away from the wrought-iron entrance to the mosque. Founded in 1703, it is a well-preserved example of a Chinese mosque, with minaret, entrance hall, prayer hall, study hall, side rooms and washing pool. The prayer hall is oriented E–W and its size is achieved through a four-roof construction with a complex pavilion-like roof at the rear, all with unusually upturned eaves for a northern building. Inside the two little pavilions are boards bearing the characters for 'looking at the moon' and 'time for sound' indicating the importance of time (for prayers) and the noisy call to prayer for Moslems.

The windows and much of the timber of the mosque is very beautifully carved with floral designs (following the tradition of not depicting the human form), combining this islamic tradition with a Chinese woodcarving tradition.

The Dabei yuan Temple is on the far side of the narrow Ziya he (Ziya River). Between the mosque and the temple is the *Santiaoshi bowuguan* (Santiaoshi Museum) in the centre of the old industrial quarter of Tianjin where, in the 17C and 18C, before the arrival of foreigners, metalwork and machinery of all kinds was produced, contributing to the trading and industrial reputation of Tianjin.

In 1926 the Fujuxing factory was set up in the area, producing watercarts (important in those pre-sewer days: the Japanese 'Railway Guide' noted in 1924 that 'the lower-class natives depend mostly on the river for their drinking water…almost any day there may be seen along the river many wheelbarrows, each loaded with a water barrel…), 'ox-headed' planing machines, oil-presses and other pieces of machinery that were exported to other provinces. Apprenticeships were encouraged. The original equipment and workshops have been preserved as part of the museum.

Beyond the Industrial Museum is the **Dabei yuan** (Temple of Great Compassion) at No. 26 Tianwei lu, the largest and best-preserved Buddhist temple in Tianjin. It consists of two parts, the old temple (founded not long before 1669; since Tianjin is a relatively new city, its temples do not trace their foundation back to the 3C as so many others so) and the new temple, founded in 1940. The 1940 extensions (including the 'Hall of Heavenly Doorkeepers', Mahavira (or Great) Hall and the Dabei Hall) were made after Tan Zu, a monk and noted calligrapher, had collected contributions. Despite severe damage during the 1976 earthquake, the temple was restored in 1980 and many of the old pine trees survived.
    The temple used to contain a holy relic, part of Xuan zang's cranium (see Xi'an, Big Goose Pagoda and Fayuan si, Peking) which was apparently presented to the Nalanda Temple in India in 1956 (though there is still a Hall of Xuan zang's cranium in the Dabei yuan). The western courtyard houses the headquarters of the Buddhist Association of Tianjin and a Cultural Relics Hall which displays the best Buddhist relics found in the Tianjin area. Made of bronze, iron, wood and stone, they date back to the Nan bei chao (420–581).

Also on the N side of the Ziya River, just S of the major bridge which crosses it just S of the point where the Grand Canal joins the river, is the *Wanghai lou* (Sea-watching Tower) or *Notre Dame des Victoires* (Shengmu desheng tang). It stands just to the N of a smaller bridge across the Hai River, the *Shizi lin qiao* (Bridge of the Forest of Stone Lions).

The cathedral was built by the French Lazarists in 1869 and burnt down during the Tianjin massacre (known more delicately in Chinese as the 'Religious incident at Tianjin') in the following year. In 1897 it was rebuilt with money from the Qing government demanded in recompense by the foreign settlers, only to be burnt down again in 1900 during the Boxer Uprising. The current building is the third, built in 1904 and is said to be very similar to the earlier constructions with stained glass and very pretty floor tiles inside (it was not possible to get in in late 1987).

One of the most spectacular rebuilding efforts of the post-earthquake administration under Mayor Li Ruihuan is the **Wenhua jie** which is on the W side of the Hai River, just S of the Sea-watching Tower. The area is similar to (but larger than) the Liulichang area of Peking, an old shopping centre with traditional Chinese shops (rather than the grand foreign department stores of Heping lu, previously Asahi gai/Rue du Chaylard). It is quite prettily restored and, as a pedestrian area, pleasant to wander in.

It lies to the side of one of the major temples of Tianjin, reflecting its maritime and riverine situation, the **Tianhou gong** (Hall of the Heavenly Empress).

According to legend, the Heavenly Empress (sometimes known as Niang-niang, the Good Mother) was a local sailor's daughter who saved her father from a shipwreck. A temple was built in her honour where sailors would bring a model of their ship to pray for her protection. It is interesting to note that Nagel's guide (very extensive and impressive and compiled in the late 1960s) states that 'the temple still existed in 1936 but has now disappeared' for it was rebuilt (on the original site) in 1985.

The temple, apparently founded in 1326, now houses a very interesting folk museum (not quite finished in 1987). The main hall has a statue of Tianhou with Buddhist figures and there are the usual temple guardians in the first gate hall (thus the mixing of established and popular religions). Surrounding the inner courtyard are a number of small exhibition halls (they were rather oddly numbered in 1987, requiring an eccentric course around the court; this may have changed). The first hall contained gongs and bowls (also to be struck) and other implements once used in the temple and a mud sculpture of a construction worker apparently trying to extract a dragon from a stone. There are a number of other smaller brown 'mud people' (ni ren), tiny figures which used to be made on the streets by local pedlars and were an acclaimed speciality of the Tianjin streets.

Brian Power, brought up in Tianjin, describes in his haunting book about a Tianjin childhood ('The Ford of Heaven', London, Peter Owen, 1984) how the pedlars made the figures:

> The high back wall of the granary formed one side of the marketplace. Against this wall, the acrobats, story-tellers, magicians and conjurors performed…Next to the conjurors sat a row of men making little figures about 6 inches high out of different coloured clay mixed with water. The figures were called ni ren in Chinese which meant 'mud men'. You could ask for anything you wished, an opera singer, dancer, mandarin or warrior. Some of the ni ren makers were especially good at making soldiers. They would watch the foreign soldiers parading in the streets and within minutes they could make a lifelike figure of the commanding officer. Sometimes they got into trouble with the police over their caricatures and were banned.

The ni ren were apparently the invention of a man named Zhang in the 19C (they are also mentioned favourably by Pierre Loti in 'Les Derniers Jours de Pekin', 1901) and his descendants still make them, though political constraints rather than customers have tended to dictate the subjects in recent years.

In the museum are mud figures showing the dramas and entertainments (acrobats, stilt dancers) performed on the day sacred to the Heavenly Empress (23rd day of the 3rd month of the lunar calendar). There are also examples of the woodblocks of Yangliuqing, one of the major centres of popular colour printing in China.

From the 16C this village near Tianjin became one of the major centres producing brightly coloured 'New Year Pictures' (nianhua) which had their origin in the pictures of door gods and seasonal calendars that people pasted up on their walls at the New Year (following a great spring cleaning). By the early 17C Yangliuqing was producing some 20 million pictures a year (in two editions—spring and autumn—with particular care being devoted to the spring or New Year pictures). The pictures were produced from multiple woodblocks in bright colours (and production in the traditional manner has now been moved to Changchun jie in Tianjin itself; the workshop can be visited by arrangement through China Travel Service).

Smaller items of folk art on display in the museum include hair ornaments (of a sort of felt), kites (a known Tianjin speciality), papercuts, spinning tops and other toys, and in the second hall there is a lovely collection of the model boats presented to the Heavenly Empress, all painted with big eyes on the prow (to ward off evil spirits). There are high-backed sea-going junks. like those that can still be seen on the coast. There is a nice fire engine and a large display of items relating to traditional shops: big blue jars in which soy sauce was sold, biscuit moulds, toffee (crab) apples, a pedlar's portable stove and models of the 'goubuli' baozi that are the most famous delicacy of Tianjin.

The name of these meat-stuffed dumplings means 'dogs wouldn't touch them' and is sometimes said to refer to the dumplings themselves (food for the poor) and some-times to the hideousness of the man who is said to have invented them. The major outlet for them today is the Goubuli restaurant near the corner of Binjiang lu and Xin-hua bei lu in the shopping centre.

The shop signs on display used to hang down from carved wooden shopfronts and are sometimes self-explanatory—shoes and pipes—some-times mysterious: a wooden fish or a child and fishes means a medicine shop, a string of coins and silver ingots means a sort of primitive bank (money shop), a double gourd means a doctor's establishment.

There is a model of a marriage procession and examples of all sorts of items associated with marriage from the red bridal-gown with red scarf to caver the face, and children's clothing including tiger shoes, pig shoes and patchwork 'hundred family' jackets where different family members donate different bits of cloth and the garment is supposed to convey a hundred years of life on the child. The little metal lockets children wore around their necks were also called 'hundred family' for the same reason but they were often shaped like Chinese locks to 'lock' the child to life. There is a child's tiny abacus and a copy of the 'San zi jing'(Three Char-acter Classic, by which children learned to read through memorising a series of three-character phrases about Chinese history and folklore) and some examples of the funny backless aprons that tiny children wore in hot summers.

There is a small household temple to hold the household gods, equip-ment used by geomancers in siting houses (compasses and textbooks), garments of all sorts and a huge variety of cricket-cages in which prized fighting crickets were kept (especially during winter). Cricket-cages were, and are, often made of gourds with finely carved lids. Birdcages, also displayed, are of equal importance to bird-lovers and often highly decorated and provided with tiny porcelain water and seed pots. There are teapots and tea-nests, locks and keys and a fine handwarmer—a small metal container with a handle and an openwork top, to be filled with charcoal and slipped carefully into long sleeves on cold days.

B. West Tianjin

Over in the W of the city is the old *Nankai daxue* (Nankai University) where there is a classroom display of photographs and relics associated with Zhou Enlai who studied there from 1913 to 1917. In order to avoid confusion with the new campus of Nankai University (due S of the old one), ask for Zhou Enlai jinian guan on Nankai er wei lu.

Not far from the old Nankai University, on Nanmen nei da jie is the **Guangdong hui guan** (Guangdong Guildhall). To reach it from Nankai, turn left along Nankai er wei lu and take the second major turning on the left. The Guildhall is a little way up the road, on your right. It is the largest and best-preserved guildhall and 'locality' temple in Tianjin (in the 1920s, the Zhejiang, Fujian, Jiangsu and Shanxi merchants also had fine guildhalls). Serving as a trade centre for locals of Guangdong province, the guildhall was very beautifully constructed, in the southern style. It has a gate, main hall and a particularly well-preserved stage (for guild dramas and local operas to be performed). The ceiling is in the 'chicken coop' style and the four characters *Tian guan ci fu* (May the heavenly officials bestow good fortune) are painted on the back wall.

The hall has recently been closed as a theatre museum is being installed in it.

The **Fine Art Museum** (Yishu bowuguan) is on Jiefang lu (77 Jiefang bei lu) in the old French quarter. The street used to be called Rue de France until it crossed Bristow Road (today's Yingkou dao) the border of the British Concession, when it turned into Victoria Road. The museum (founded in 1928) is in a grand old building which is not entirely suited to its present function. The permanent collections on display include a great number of ni ren or mud men figures, many by the Zhang family, and a considerable display of Yangliuqing woodblock new year prints. There is also a major display of silhouette shadow puppets made from coloured donkey skin.

Some of the other collections of the museum which are shown in special or temporary exhibitions include Tianjin carved bricks (used to decorate doorways), woodcarvings, contemporary paintings and seal carvings, ancient bronzes, ceramics, jades, seals, calligraphy and painting.

A walk that takes in the French, British and German Concessions with their varying architecture, passing by the Fine Art Museum, can start from the Station itself. There is only one major problem, which is that the streets all have handsome new road names, in Chinese characters only.

The street signs of Tianjin were due for an overhaul: when I first went in 1975 they were obviously pre-Liberation for they had characters and the 1918 system of zhuyin zimu (alphabet to indicate the sound), a strange forerunner of the pinyin romanisation system (used on Peking and Shanghai street-signs) with odd, angular symbols not unreminiscent of Japanese hiragana. It is a great pity that pinyin is not included on the new street signs for it means an awful lot of counting blocks. However...

Leave the railway station by the main entrance and walk straight down the approach road which takes you to the river. Diagonally opposite is a bridge with huge curved iron girders, *Liberation Bridge* (Jiefang qiao), built, according to the French authors of the Nagel guide, by French engineers in 1903 (others suggest the Austrians built it). Cross the bridge and carry on straight ahead, away from the river. This is Jiefang lu (formerly the Rue de France in the French Concession) and the first building, on the right-hand corner of the road, facing the river, was the *Imperial Hotel.*
   On the NW side of the next crossroads (the NW corner with Binjiang dao) was the *French Club.* On the SW corner of the next crossroads (Haerbin dao) were the *French Municipal Council Offices* and on the SE corner of the next crossroads (Chifeng dao) is the **Fine Art Museum**. On the NW corner of the next-but-one crossroads (Yingkou dao) was the *Tianjin General Post Office* and, opposite it (SW corner), the *Yokohama Specie Bank.*
   Yingkou dao, formerly Bristow Road, marked the beginning of the British Concession. On the E side of the road, a yellow and red brick building with bulging balconies was the *Russo-Asiatic Bank.*
   Continuing down Jiefang lu, on the E side of the road (on the corner of the second lane on the E side) was the *Chartered Bank of India, Australia and China*, next, *Jardine & Matheson*, with *Butterfield & Swire* a tiny bit further down on the same side and the *US Consulate* opposite Swire on the W side of the road. Just before the *Astor House Hotel* (with a modern, plastic-fronted branch of the Hong Kong and Shanghai Bank in front of it), were the *Tientsin Press* (E) and the British Municipal Council in the bizarre *Gordon Hall*, a dark, battlemented castle-like building, put up in 1887 (in the year of Queen Victoria's jubilee).

This was not only the British Municipal Council Office (where the regulations against furious bicycle riding were promulgated) but also the police station, law court and concert hall and assembly room. It was described by its clergyman designer as 'Victorian Tientsin' in style though others said it recalled a prison hospital on the outskirts of Edinburgh. It took its name from General Charles George 'Chinese' Gordon who (though later to serve in the imperial forces against the Taiping rebels; see Shanghai) had served as a captain in the Royal Engineers in 1860 and had surveyed and fixed the boundaries of the British Concession. In 1900, when the Boxer rebellion threatened, the British community took refuge in Gordon Hall.

Next to Gordon Hall (opposite the Astor House), is the tiny *Victoria Park* where there used to be a Chinese pavilion which served as a bandstand and which was the social centre for British children, their wooden horses and their amahs. It was opened for Victoria's jubilee, like Gordon Hall. Just S of the Astor House Hotel, also on the E side of the road, was the *Tientsin Club* (which could not bring itself to admit the deposed emperor Henry Aisin Gioro Pu Yi even as a 'special member' during his stay in Tianjin (1925–30) though he was invited to guest nights).

You could consider returning to the river along the Bund at this point where you would pass the old *British Consulate* (on the corner of the fourth turning on the left), the old *Hong Kong and Shanghai Bank* building (on the S corner of the fifth turning on the left, Yingkou dao), with the old *Customs House* on the N corner and the *French Consulate* on the N corner of the next turning on the left.

Alternatively, from the Astor House Hotel, turn right (W) along the next main road (Tai'an dao) and diagonally opposite, on the S corner of Tai'an dao and Zhejiang lu is the old Protestant *Church of All Saints*, now some sort of storehouse (its back entrance is No. 11 Tai'an lu). Behind you is the immensely long façade of the huge *Kailan Mining Administration Building* (controlling the British-owned coalmines near Tianjin) and next to it the *British Consul's Residence*, a peculiarly stepped building with a colonnaded verandah and strange octagonal tower.

Continue S down Zhejiang lu (this is two streets to the W of Jiefang lu/Victoria Road). It ends on a wide open space with a roundabout. On your left, facing the roundabout is the old *Kiessling and Bader's Tearooms* (known prosaically in the Cultural Revolution as the Tianjin Canteen although it still served chicken Kiev and ice-cream with chocolate sauce), Qisilin canting, in Chinese. If you haven't already eaten, you could take coffee (and perhaps a beef stroganoff) here.

The road diagonally opposite Zhejiang lu on the far side of the roundabout is Machang dao (previously known as Racecourse Road, which is what Machang dao means) which used to mark the border between the British and the German Concessions. It is lined with grand buildings of all sorts. You could follow Machang dao as it twists SW, heading back N perhaps along the fifth turning on the right (N), Yunnan lu. Yunnan lu crosses two roads and then reaches a crossroads where three roads meet. Turn left here up Guizhou lu (and you should see the onion domes of another church—closed in 1987—at the top of Guizhou lu). On the far side of the church, the main road running W–E is Shengli lu and was Elgin Avenue. Take the road running NE (in front of the church), Binjiang dao, which will take you to the major shopping street (ex Asahi Road/Rue du Chaylard), Heping lu. You could look at the huge old shop buildings along Heping lu and the Zhang Garden (now the offices of the Tianjin Daily) where the last emperor Henry Aisin Gioro Pu Yi lived (from 1925), enjoying 'flush lavatories and central heating'. Or continue straight up Binjiang lu (N) which will take you to Jiefang lu (second on the left after Heping lu) and the bridge leading to the railway station.

There is more walking that can be done in the German Concession, and indeed, all the concession areas, but the lack of pinyin street signs makes it difficult to direct people. For those with a good sense of direction or an ability to retrace their steps, the old Chinese town is N, bordered by the Bei ma lu, Nan ma lu, Dong ma lu and Xi ma lu. The Japanese settlement was bordered by Duolun dao. Shengli lu, Jiangzhou dao and the river; the French settlement was bordered by Jianzhou dao and Yingkou dao; the British settlement by Yingkou dao and Machang dao; S of Machang dao was the German Concession. The buildings in some parts offer clues—Scottish baronial, French château and German expressionist—although there are traces of southern colonial and international bank styles that cross boundaries.

4 Chengde

Chengde, previously known to Chinese as *Rehe* (Warm River) and to Western visitors as *Jehol*, is a small town, about 200km NE of central Peking. Very early in the Qing dynasty the emperors established first a small royal lodge, then the great 'Summer Mountain Retreat' in a vast walled enclosure surrounded by eight 'outer temples'.

Hotels: there are two hotels for foreigners in Chengde: the Chengde binguan in the centre of town on the main street and the Bishushanzhuang Hotel which is opposite the main entrance to the Imperial Summer Resort (and therefore preferable for the town itself is not very interesting). The former is reached by a No. 7 bus from the railway station, the latter by a No. 6 or 8.

Railway: the obvious way to reach Chengde is by train from Peking, a journey of some 5 hours, passing sections of the Great Wall. Chengde is an ideal weekend trip from Peking, a minimal 'weekend' visit involving an early Saturday morning departure, and leaving Chengde just after lunch on Sunday.

The Imperial Summer Retreat was begun in 1703 by the Kangxi emperor, the expansion of a tradition linking the now-established Manchus with their past life of mounted hunting expeditions. Early in his reign Kangxi had built small lodges (including one near Chengde in 1677) in the north where the court established itself for hunting expeditions and archery competitions. These annual northern trips were more than merely sporting for they were also used to forge links with other northern groups such as the Mongols who inhabited border regions of great strategic importance. The use of the Summer Retreat as a diplomatic centre was continued in the reign of the Qianlong emperor who constructed the extraordinary 'outer temples', some in the Tibetan architectural style, deliberately chosen to impress visiting Tibetan and Lamaist dignitaries.

To the NW of the town, a great walled enclosure, its surrounding wall 10km long, with a lake area surrounded by palace buildings and pavilions, the rest wild hills for hunting, was constructed over an 80-year period (with further later additions in succeeding reigns) and named Bi shu shan zhuang, 'The mountain village where you can escape the heat'. Sometimes confusingly known as the 'Summer Palace', confusing since there are two 'summer palaces', old and new, in Peking, the Imperial Summer Resort at Chengde was the home of the court for virtually six months of every year during the reigns of the Kangxi and all succeeding emperors until 1820. In that year the Jiaqing emperor died in the Resort, probably of an apoplexy though legend had it that he was struck by lightning. The death, by whatever means, was regarded as a portent of bad things and the Resort was avoided for some decades afterwards.

The belief that bad luck was associated with the resort was reinforced when the Xianfeng emperor fled Peking as French and British troops approached in 1860. He stayed at Chengde even after peace was restored, refusing to grant an audience to foreign envoys (one of the conditions of the peace treaty) which would have involved the humiliation of their not performing the humble kotwow (kneeling, forehead on the ground in front of the emperor). Devoting himself, instead, to 'excesses', he, too, died in the Resort in 1861.

The relationship of Chengde to the Peking summer palaces is interesting. The 'Old' Summer Palace, Yuan ming yuan (Garden of Perfect Brightness) was built, with the help of Jesuits, by the Qianlong emperor in the mid 18C on the foundations of garden palaces built by the Kangxi and Yongzheng emperors and sacked in 1860 by British and French troops. The 'New' Summer Palace, Yi he yuan (Garden of the Cultivation of Harmony), was laid out mainly by Qianlong on the basis of earlier (12C, Yuan and Ming) gardens, sacked in 1860 and then rebuilt in 1888 by the Dowager Empress Cixi who favoured it above all others. All were used by the Emperors during the hot summer months but the longest periods were spent at Chengde during the 17C and 8C, when the whole court decamped.

The resort almost fills a valley in the hills of southern Manchuria through which the *Warm River* flows to the W and a smaller stream to the E of the enclosure. The surrounding hills with their strangely-shaped rocks (most prominently the phallic *Club* or *Anvil Rock* to the E) form part of the whole of the garden enclosure. It is here, where an entire valley has been taken over for imperial pleasure, just as in the vast golden palace in the centre of Peking with its endless series of halls and dazzling white court-yards, that you sense the amazing scale of the grandeur of imperial China at its height in the early Qing.

The Jesuit Matteo Ripa (1682–1745) who lived in Peking from 1711–23, described the surroundings:

> It is situated in a plain surrounded by mountains, whence flows a tor-rent…A hill rises gently from the plain, its side studded with buildings des-tined for the Emperor's followers. and a copious spring of water forms a noble lake…the plain, the slopes and the hill are thickly covered with foliage; and the filberts, corianders, pears and apples, though growing wild, have so delicious a flavour that they are served on the Emperor's table. The plain, the slopes and the hill are so extensive that it took me an hour to make the tour of the inclosure on horseback…

The Kangxi emperor himself (his words 'reassembled' by Jonathan Spence) described the coolness and freedom of the Chengde area:

> …it is when one is beyond the Great Wall that the air and soil refresh the spirit: one leaves the beaten road and strikes out into untamed country; the mountains are densely packed with woods 'green and thick as the standing corn'. As one moves further north the views open up, one's eyes travel hun-dreds of miles; instead of feeling hemmed in, there is a sense of freedom. It may be the height of summer but there is dew on the trees, and some of the leaves are turning yellow already, as if it were late autumn; you have to wear a fur jacket in the mornings, even though in Peking it is so hot that you hesitate about having the eunuchs lead the consorts out of the palaces to greet you on your return.

In the great imperial valley even the emperor could recapture the outdoor freedom of his hunting ancestors:

> There is tea, made from fresh snow on the little brazier slung between two horses. There is the perfect flavour of bream and carp from the mountain streams, caught by oneself in the early morning…There is venison, roasted over an open fire by a tent pitched on the sunny slope of a mountain; or the liver of a newly killed stag, cooked with one's own hands (even if the rain is falling), and eaten with salt and vinegar….

The Imperial Enclosure.

The **Imperial Enclosure** covers an area of over 5.5 square km, and is sur-rounded by a battlemented wall 10km long. Most of the buildings (con-structed between 1703 and 1790) are concentrated in the E of the enclosure, near the lakes, and they fall into two major categories: palace or domestic and garden buildings. To the W, the hilly area to the left of the main gate is allowed to remain wild, for hunting.

The **Palace Enclosure**: situated in the SE of the whole enclosure, this originally consisted of three virtually parallel 'palaces'. The 'eastern palace' (to the E) has since disappeared (it lay within the small Dehui men or Gate of Assembled Virtues and led to the long dyke of the triple Lake Heart Pavilion). The main surviving palace building is the **Zheng gong** (Main Palace). The outer gate, *Lizheng men* (Gate of Beauty and Upright-ness), serves as the main entrance to the whole enclosure now. There are three openings in the gate: the central one, which is paved with white stones, was reserved for the emperor and close family members, just as in the Forbidden City in Peking. Where the two stone lions stand outside the gate there were once stone notices requiring officials to dismount (just as at the Qing imperial tombs) or descend from their sedan chairs.

Inscriptions throughout the palace are either in Chinese or the five languages

(Manchu, Mongolian, Tibetan, Chinese and Uighur) used out of politeness to the envoys from border areas who were frequently entertained here. A further gate lies inside the Gate of Beauty and Uprightness and beyond is a courtyard where officials and envoys from the borders awaited their audience with the Emperor. All of the courtyards in the palace are relatively small, surrounded by simple, low, buildings, almost domestic in appearance. The simple plan and careful axial balance, with matching side-wings and main halls oriented to the S, are characteristic of domestic architecture in north China though the floors and materials of this 'simple' complex are luxurious and frequently expensive. Nevertheless, the whole retains a feeling of an imperial country retreat, if compared with the pomp of Peking.

Beyond is another major gate, the *Bi shu shan zhuang men* (Gate of the Mountain Village Where You Can Escape the Heat, the humble name for a summer palace echoing the relative simplicity of the architecture), from where the emperors, seated on soft cushions, watched archery contests and saw officials. The major activities at this gate are described in four lines of poetry by the Qianlong emperor: On return from the hunt, officials kowtow on the steps; In the autumn with bows lightly held, the noblemen's arrows hit the target; as the moon grows to a circle.

Behind is a courtyard planted with 42 old pines, the *Courtyard of the Tranquil Heart and Honour to Sincerity*. The *Main Hall* (on the N side of the court), the most important in the palace, is deceptively simple, single-eaved, with seven bays. It is raised on a stone platform and the timber used in construction (including the carved ceilings) is cedar, brought thousands of kms from western China (the hall is sometimes called the Cedar Hall). The floors are paved with polished, patterned, marble-like rock but the simple grey eaves tiles are in contrast to the imperial yellow glazed tiles of the Forbidden City. Side rooms are lined with bookcases originally constructed to hold a copy of the 10,000-volume 'Gu jin tu shu ji cheng' (Synthesis of Books and Illustrations from Ancient to Modern Times), printed, at imperial order, using copper movable type in 1728.

The work was an encyclopaedic collection of quotation and reference, most interesting for its technical features. Movable type was experimentally used in China in about 1040 but was (given the nature of the Chinese script) not an economical advance on the system of carving whole pages onto woodblocks. The experimental imperial printing of the 'Tu shu ji cheng' involved a font of over 250,000 pieces of types, of such value as metal that it was never reused but melted down for coinage.

In the smaller courtyard behind, the small main hall was named 'Compliance with Clarity and Freedom from Worries' by the Kangxi emperor but renamed 'Study of the Four Branches of Knowledge' by the Qianlong emperor. The 6th Panchen Lama was received here in 1779. The main building in the courtyard behind is a long, 19-bay hall, 'A Thousand Years of Brightness', which divides the public, front part of the palace from the private imperial living-quarters behind (the same layout is found in the Confucian Family Mansion in Qu Fu, Shandong). In this hall banners and weapons were laid out before the emperors went out (progressing from the private quarters at the rear to the front gate) on hunting expeditions in the nearby hills.

In the courtyard behind ('Refreshed by Mist-covered Waters') were the *living quarters*. In the main hall were thrones and Buddhist shrines and the room to the far left was the emperors' bedroom where the Jiaqing and Xianfeng emperors died. The concubines' and wives' apartments are connected to the bedroom. Behind is a two-storey building, 'Landscape Amid Clouds and Mountains', with a mock mountain in front of it in which a series of steps allows you to reach the upper storey, and behind this is a decorative 'hanging flower' gate which leads to the park.

If you leave from this gate, just to your left is the *Tame Deer Slope* where the Père David deer that used to roam the park came to be fed. These peculiar animals, Elaphurus davidianus, named by Père Armand David (1826–1900), a Lazarist missionary and naturalist, were extinct in China by about 1900. Manchu accounts of the 18C say that they lived in the Kokonor area and also in Manchuria and they were first described in French by David. He saw a herd of some 120 in the imperial hunting park, Nan yuan, S of Peking, but they certainly also existed in Chengde. They had disappeared from the Nan yuan by 1900; killed and eaten by park-keepers and by the local population whenever they could, and the same fate must have overtaken those at Chengde. The Dukes of Bedford had a herd and recently presented some 20 of them to the Chinese government for reinstatement in the Imperial Resort. In late 1985 they were kept in an enclosure just behind the Wenjin ge library building in the NE of the park (easily located by smell) and it is to be hoped that they will be allowed eventually to roam more freely in the park. They are large, peculiar-looking animals with reindeer-like horns and a donkey's tail and the popular Chinese name for them, 'four dissimilarities', is appropriate. They say that the horns are like deer horns but it is not a deer, the head is like a horse's head but it is not a horse, its body is like a donkey's but it is not a donkey and the hooves are like a cow's but it is not a cow.

There are exhibits of imperial possessions—bronzes, ceramics and jades—in some of the halls of the main palace.

To the E (right) is a smaller, parallel place enclosure of low, grey-tiled courtyards called the *Pine and Crane Study* which was inhabited by Qianlong's mother. To the E of that, the eastern palace which has since disappeared was where the Qianlong emperor received Lord Macartney in September 1793.

There, the English aristocrat shared a display of tightrope walking and wrestling with six ambassadors from Outer Mongolia and was shown the lake area of the park. His description serves to introduce it:

> We rode about three miles through a very beautiful park, kept in the highest order, and much resembling the approach to Luton in Bedfordshire; the grounds gently undulated and chequered with various groups of well-contrasted trees…an extensive lake appeared before us, the extremities of which seemed to lose themselves in distance and obscurity…The shores of the lake have all the varieties of shape which the fancy of a painter can delineate…one marked by a pagoda, or other building, one quite destitute of ornament, some smooth and level, some steep and uneven and others frowning with wood or smiling with culture…One thing I was particularly struck with, I mean the happy choice of situation for ornamental buildings. From attention to this circumstance they have not the air of being crowded or disproportioned; they never intrude upon the eye but wherever they appear always show themselves to advantage, and aid, improve and enliven the prospect…

The **Lake Park**. Macartney's description is a sensitive one of an ideal Chinese garden (combining water, buildings and plants with interest) and as the David Deer have returned from Woburn, they, too, may have felt a similarity noted by Macartney to 'the soft beauties of Woburn' ('An Embassy to China…the journal kept by Lord Macartney', edited and with an introduction by J.L. Cranmer-Byng, Longman, 1962).

Entering the park from the rear of the palace, walk along the western (left-hand) shore of the lake, past the major islands, to the far end of the lake where a small stream continues N. As you walk alongside the stream, soon, on your left, you will find the **Wenjin ge** (Pavilion of Literary Delights), one of the imperial libraries. Built to house one of the four original sets of the vast imperial manuscript collectanea, 'Si ku quan shu' (Complete Treasury of the Four Storehouses), which was completed in 1785 (this copy is now in the National Library, Peking), the two-storey library building was once surrounded by other buildings whose foundations can still be seen.

Like all the other buildings constructed to hold the imperial collectanea (which comprised 3470 titles copied out in some 36,300 slim volumes), the building was based on the privately-owned Tianyi ge library in Ningbo although a comparison of the two reveals the fundamental differences between northern and southern styles of building. The Tianyi ge has dark-tiled roofs with upswept eaves whilst the Wen jin ge is a solid little northern building with straight eaves. However, for fire protection, it is set on a high stone platform (and originally surrounded by water) with a stone rockery in front of it, just like the setting of the Tianyi ge. The Qianlong emperor wrote a poem about the Wenjin ge which began: 'The Tianyi ge had a pool in front of it and piled rocks to the south, The Wenjin ge was modelled on it and stones were piled up into a mountain; there are peaks and a gully and the sound of the qin floats over the water...

The building appears from the outside to consist of two storeys though inside there are three. It was originally roofed with black glazed tiles (which would have looked closer to the dark tiles of the Tianyi ge) but when part of the roof fell down in 1866 it was reroofed with grey unglazed tiles in the northern domestic style. In 1980 it was handed over to the town and it is intended that a reprint of the original collectanea (published in late 1987) will be housed in the building.

Beyond the library, further N, almost at the northern wall of the enclosure, is the *Liuhe ta* (Pagoda of Six Harmonies), all that remains of the grandest of the Buddhist temples constructed within the park in 1751. Its name recalls the pagoda at Hangzhou and southern inspiration is widely found throughout the park.

Returning to the lake, it is possible to cross a bridge to the central island where the *Yanyu lou* (Misty Rain Tower) is based on a southern building, on the South Lake near Shanghai. On the far side of the lake, the three-storey tower rising above lower buildings (called *Jinshan si* or Gold Mountain Temple) is also modelled on the Shangdi ge (Gods' Pavilion) at Zhenjiang on the Yangtse. Both of these are no doubt the result of the Qing emperors' many tours of inspection of the luxurious south where they frequently stayed in beauty spots which they had recreated in the drier, colder north.

A copper-engraved volume produced by the Jesuit Matteo Ripa (1711–12) contains illustrations of all the major sites at Chengde with accompanying poems in Chinese and Manchu by the Kangxi emperor. Of the Jinshan si, he says: 'A mountain suddenly rises from the lake, flat-topped with a three-roofed pavilion; To the north is the hall of the supreme god, above are layers of cloud, below is azure water; To ascend it is like climbing a magical peak, the north is enclosed in banks of cloud, to the open south, scenes merge into a view'.

The Eight Outer Temples.

These are best visited by taxi (half a day if you hurry) as they are some distance apart.

The eastern temples are, in general, earlier than the western, so it is convenient to start with the Puren si. In the past there were 12 temples, but these eight are all that remain today. Built between 1713 and 1779, their religious significance to the emperors was, as noted, subordinate to their political usefulness in wooing the adherents of Lamaist Buddhism in the border regions of Mongolia and Tibet.

Puren si (Temple of Universal Love). Built in 1713, for Kangxi's 60th birthday (the only one of the outer temples to date from his reign), the Puren si was said to have been built for the Mongol princes who had expressed a wish to attend the celebrations. Building temples for them meant that they could continue their Lamaist devotions whilst in Chengde. Built in the Chinese style, to a Chinese plan, typically expressed as 'temple guardians and seven halls', nothing remains of any Tibetan elements, said to have been present in the past, in painted ceilings and Buddha images.

Pushan si (Temple of Universal Goodness). Little remains of the temple, built at the same time and for the same reasons at the Puren si. All that does remain and surviving photographs reveal a Chinese-style temple of several courtyards.

Pule si (Temple of Universal Joy). Sometimes called the Temple of the Round Pavilion, after the form of its Pavilion of the Rising Sun, the Pule si was built in 1766–67 for the western Mongols who came each year to pay homage to the emperor. A Tibetan advisor was employed in the construction of the temple. Oriented E–W (which is almost unheard of in Chinese temple architecture), the front part of the temple is, nevertheless, reasonably Chinese in design. The gateway, however, has arched doors with carved stone lintels, in a form which is widely seen in the outer temples at Chengde and also in 'minority' buildings in Peking, like the Lama Temple and also the Cow Street Mosque. Owing nothing obvious to Tibetan architecture, the form may be Islamic in inspiration, though the lotus carvings are Buddhist. Before the gate, on either side of the stone lions, are the tall pine poles or 'banner masts' which are a feature of Lamaist architecture. In the Hall of Heavenly Guardians (behind the gateway), the façade of wood with its arched doorways repeats the form of the stone gateway in timber.

The most striking features of the temple are to be found in the third courtyard which is filled with a circular, double-roofed Pavilion (of the Rising Sun), reminiscent of those in the Temple of Heaven in Peking. The circular pavilion with its spectacularly carved, gilded, ceiling is still a Chinese form but it encloses a strange columnar construction in the form of a cross, a three-dimensional representation of the mandala of Samvara, a protective Tantric deity. The circular enclosure is part of the scheme, as is, apparently, the orientation of the temple, all recommended by the Tibetan advisor. From the back of the temple, it may be noticed that it is oriented in a direct line with the peculiar Anvil Rock ahead.

Anyuan miao (Temple of Distant Peace). This temple was constructed in 1764 by the Qianlong emperor for the tens of thousands of western Mongols that he had brought to Chengde as part of the complex manoeuvres of control in the desert area of Xinjiang.

In Yili (near Yining), Turkic princes had ruled until Mongol tribes established themselves in the 17C. They became converts to Lamaist Buddhism through the neighbouring Tibetans. Qianlong was, like Kangxi before him, worried about this alliance and began to re-establish Islam in the area, moving groups of people and destroying major Lamaist temples.

The Anyuan miao was modelled on one of the temples in Yili which had been destroyed, apparently a Tibetan-inspired building of three storeys surrounded by a high wall. These two elements are virtually all that survive of the original temple. In plan, it consists of two square enclosures separated by a wall, the whole forming a great rectangular enclosure. The first enclosure, through the gate, is filled with trees; behind, in the second court is the main hall. Apparently, the second court also enclosed numerous low buildings which have since disappeared. The hall is supported on 60 columns, the lower part of the exterior columns hidden in an apparently solid but actually non-load-bearing red-painted wall. A narrow roof above the red wall is surmounted by a double roof covered with yellow and black glazed tiles, with a tiny ceramic stupa in the centre of the ridge. Inside, galleries surround the hall which has a gilded figure of Ksitigarbha (Bodhisattva who presides over the underworld) and the caisson ceilings are richly carved with phoenix and dragons.

Guangyuan si. Nothing remains of this small temple built in 1780, just to the E of the Puyou si, though it was apparently built in the Chinese style.

Puyou si (Temple of Universal Help). The temple was built in 1760, inside the walls of the Puning temple. Nothing remains now but the surrounding wall, a terrace with a square pavilion and small side buildings all with green and yellow tiled roofs.

Puning si (Temple of Universal Peace). One of the grandest of the outer temples, this was the first to be built by the Qianlong emperor in Chengde, in 1755.

Though it anticipated the event by some four years, it was built to celebrate the pacification of the Yili area and the bloody suppression of the Jungar Mongols (who were already destroying themselves in fratricidal struggles). Fearful of Russian intervention, the emperor ordered forced resettlement of the area and its occupation by penal colonies. Much of the temple design was based on that of the oldest Tibetan temple, the Sam-yas (although apparently the Panchen Lama, who visited the temple, failed to recognise its inspiration).

Chengde: one of the elephants at the Xumifushou miao

Built against a hill, to the NE of the palace enclosure, the temple rises towards the back. It consists of two parts, the front in the Chinese style, the back in a parody of the Tibetan. In the first part, the most impressive building is the *Da xiong bao dian* (Precious Hall of the Great Hero, referring to the Buddha's demon-conquering powers) in the centre of the second courtyard of the 'Chinese'-style front part. The walls are covered with paintings in the Tibetan style. Steps lead up to the rear, Tibetan part of the enclosure where a major hall, the *Mahayana Hall*, stands on a high platform, five storeys high with a complex roof formed of four lower square gold-tiled roofs topped by a larger central square roof. It contains a massive wooden figure of the thousand-armed Guanyin, 28m high with two 12m attendants. The walls of the hall are covered with niches where pilgrims used to place tiny Buddha figures.

In front and beside the Mahayana Hall are numerous smaller buildings in the Tibetan style: solid, whitewashed constructions with blind windows in the Tibetan style (tapering rectangles). The solidity of many of these subsidiary buildings and the fact that their windows are simply decorative give the feeling of a stage set. Though the Chinese emperors adopted the Tibetan style of building to make their Mongol and Tibetan visitors feel at home, the theatrical effect of the false façades suggests that there was a slightly hollow ring to the Chinese desire to please.

Xumifushou miao (Temple of Happiness and Longevity in Mount Sumeru). The temple was built for the 6th Panchen Lama when he came to visit the Qianlong emperor who was celebrating his seventieth birthday in 1780; it is said to have been inspired by the Panchen's residence, Tashilumpo at Shigatse in Tibet. One of the most lavish of the outer temples, rendered quickly obsolete as the Panchen died soon afterwards in Peking, it is also built against a hill, the enclosure terminating near the summit with a glazed turquoise and yellow pagoda. Inside the gate is an almost garden-like area, containing the stele describing its construction in a pavilion, and a rustic path of uneven stones leading to a stone and tile pailou (decorative gateway) flanked by two stone elephants with uncomfortably bent forelegs. These recall the gilded elephants at the rear of the Forbidden City in Peking which are also anatomically incorrect in the forelegs. Behind is a great square enclosure surrounded by a high red wall pierced with Tibetan style windows. The enclosure is almost entirely filled with a four-storey (17m high) square building with a gilt roof, its four ridges embellished with sinuous crawling dragons. The red wall is lined with wooden galleries and the central hall is galleried within and without. There is a grand central gilded ceiling with dragons but the caisson ceilings elsewhere bear Sanskrit characters. Immediately behind is a small pavilion with a roof ridge decorated with a pair of ceramic deer and a central sun, in imitation of the gilt figures on many temple roofs in Tibet.

To the right, behind the main hall, is a three-storey building with a decorative wooden façade, the *Jixiang faxi dian* (Hall of the Law and Good Fortune), built as a dwelling for the Panchen Lama. Surrounding buildings (now in disrepair) were for his attendant monks. At the rear of the enclosure is the pagoda, the tile-clad tower rising from an open, octagonal base. The pagoda is not unlike the tiled pagoda at Xiangshan, just outside Peking.

Putuozongcheng miao (Temple of the Putuo Sect). Otherwise known as the Potala Temple for its most striking feature is the great red wall at the back, based on the Potala Palace of the Dalai Lamas in Lhasa, the temple was actually built for Mongols from the Kokonor area and Eleuths who came to pay their respects to the Qianlong emperor on his sixtieth birthday (1770) and his Dowager Empress on her 80th birthday (1771). Construction began in 1767 and was finished in 1771.

A further reason for celebration through temple construction was the return of many exiled Central Asian Torguts from Astrakhan and Russian influence. The Qianlong emperor was worried about Russian influence in Central Asia (just as he was beginning to be concerned about the East India Company's activities in North India) and any anti-Russian feeling was seized upon. The temple, which covers a greater area (220,000 square metres) than any other at Chengde, consists of an open front area, dotted with trees and irregularly-disposed Tibetan-style buildings (many solid and unusable), dominated by the massive red-walled enclosure at the back, further up the hill. The stele describing its foundation states that it was based on the Potala

Chengde: the Potala Temple

palace but, though the great red wall at the back does recall the Potala, the latter is a more solid building whilst the Chengde version encloses a Chinese-style pavilion; and the open area in front owes little to the Tibetan original. The irregular placement of buildings is, however, very un-Chinese so the whole is perhaps best considered as a 'rendering' of the Potala. As in the Xumifushou Temple, many of the small, white-washed buildings with Tibetan-style windows, sometimes topped with pepper-pot dagobas (Tibetan stupas), are solid and unusable, presenting, once again, a theatrical effect.

From the gate a path leads through the stele pavilion and a second gate, through a glazed-tile pailou into the wooded, rocky area dotted with whitewashed buildings. Above looms the great red wall of the mock Potala, whose Tibetan-form windows are mostly blank and purely decorative. From its terrace there is a fine view of the wide enclosure below and the back wall of the imperial palace enclosure. As in the Xumifushou Temple, the red wall encloses a double-roofed square building in the Chinese style. Inside, a central gilded ceiling is surrounded by a caisson ceiling and the main columns are painted red. No central Buddha figure survives but a series of smaller figures and pieces of altar furniture stand in the centre.

Shuxiang si (Temple of the Statue of Manjusri). Built in the purely Chinese style, the Shuxiang si was constructed between 1774 and 1776, based on the temple of the same name at Wutai shan (in Shanxi province).

Wutai shan, the northern Buddhist holy mountain, was dedicated to Manjusri, the Boddhisattva favoured by Lamaist Buddhists and was a major centre of pilgrimage for Mongolian Buddhists, thus its cult was important to Chengde where temples were built for Lamaist dignitaries. The mother of the Qianlong emperor, a devout Buddhist, had made a pilgrimage to Wutai shan.

The gate-building (*Shan men* or Mountain Gate) is interesting for its stone carving. On either side of the entrance are two stone 'windows', arched and with stone-carved lattice. Whilst other examples of such carving over doorways and windows in Chengde usually involve the Buddhist lotus emblem, the carvings here are more geometric (and reminiscent of furniture decoration). Many of the original buildings in the enclosure are now in ruins, but the seven-bay main hall with its double roof covered in imperial yellow tiles still stands. Inside are three gilded Manjusri figures with flame mandorlas. The Bodhisattva is characteristically depicted riding a lion. Behind the hall is a mountain garden with rocks and pines.

Guang'an si (Temple of Great Peace). Nothing remains of this temple. It was constructed to the W of the Shuxiang si in 1772 in honour of the 80th birthday of Qianlong's mother (when the Ten-thousand Buddha Pavilion in Peking's Beihai Park was also built). It was apparently built in the Tibetan style with none of the ideal Chinese axial balance.

Luohan tang (Hall of the Lohans). Nothing remains of this hall, built in 1774, although some of the gilded statues of the 500 lohans may still be seen in the Puning si.

5   Shenyang

Shenyang, capital city of Liaoning province, was formerly known as *Mukden* (in a Western variant of its Manchu name). In 1625 it was declared the first capital of the Manchus who were to conquer all of China and establish the Qing dynasty in 1644. And, as the 'Japanese Railway Guide' noted, like all the major centres in NE China, it 'occupied a most advantageous position in regard to railway facilities...'. It was also, like Changchun, economically involved with beans, its chief products being bean-cakes and bean oil. The 'Guide' contains a long section on the

SHENYANG

Zhaoling/Northern tomb

Huanghe lu

Chongshan lu

Beiling lu

Xiaobei lu

N

Shifu lu

Shengli lu

Nanjing lu

Imperial Palace●

Railway station

Liaoning guest house

Nurhaci's tomb/Eastern tomb

organisation and management of 'you fang' or 'oil-manufactories' which used horses or donkeys to power the bean-cracking machines.

Nurhaci (1559–1626), founder of the Qing dynasty, was born into the Aisin Gioro clan which held the hereditary chieftainship of one of the Juchen tribes. The Juchen or Jurched were of Tungusic stock: the Tungus were tribes inhabiting eastern Manchuria (or Dongbei as the Chinese call it, a name meaning the North-east) and lived by a combination of hunting and agriculture (which included pig-raising). Though the Chinese built palisades, ditches with embankments planted with willows, to divide Manchuria into the region controlled by China and that beyond, the whole area was naturally an undivided plain, inhabited by various settled tribes. Nurhaci was later to forbid the use of the term Nuzhen (Juchen or Jurched in Western usage) because it smacked of Chinese suzerainty (the first character in Chinese means 'slave') which he spent his life overcoming, preferring Man zhou (Manchu), a term whose origins are obscure.

Through a combination of marriages (to the daughter and granddaughter of two of his rival chiefs) and warfare through which he united the major Jurched tribes against the Chinese (who had killed his father and grandfather in battle), Nurhaci rose to prominence in the Liaodong peninsula. He extended his control by developing trade with the Chinese in the highly prized medicinal root ginseng (which was locally produced) and in horses, establishing a sound local economy. He also set up the beginnings of a state bureaucracy which used a new system of writing the Manchu language (based on the Mongol alphabet). Classic Confucian works were translated into Manchu and a captured Chinese official, Fan Wencheng, advised Nurhaci on the establishment of his administration. He regrouped the Manchus into companies of warriors called 'banners' into which all warriors and their dependents were registered, taxed, conscripted and mobilised as necessary. He moved his capital to Shenyang in 1625, when the building of his palace began. On his death in 1626 he was succeeded by his eighth son Abahai (1592–1643), who began the preparations for the conquest of north China. This was finally achieved in 1644 under Dorgon

(1612–50, the 14th son of Nurhaci) who officially only acted as regent for Abahai's small son.

Monuments relating to Nurhaci's capital are the most important sites in Shenyang today.

The old **Imperial Palace**, originally named *Shengjing gong* (Palace of the Prosperous Capital), renamed *Travelling Palace of Upholding Heaven* in 1644 when the Manchu capital was moved to Peking, stands in the centre of the old city of Shenyang. Covering an area of 60,000 square metres, it was begun in 1625 and basically completed in 1636, though additions were made in the 18C. It consists of a walled enclosure surrounding over 300 'rooms' in ten courtyards grouped in three axes. The central axis, entered through the *Daqing* (Great Purity) *Gate*, leads through the main hall, the *Chongzheng* (Esteem Government) *Hall* to the *rear palace* (from the *Fenghuang* or Phoenix Tower) where the Nurhaci and his family had apartments.

The eastern axis is most typically Manchu in architectural disposition for a long courtyard is filled with ten regularly spaced pavilions, the *Shi wang* or Ten Kings' Pavilions where the heads of the Eight Banners and the Two Kings of the Left and Right Wings (in other words the highest placed officials and chiefs of the Manchu administration) had their own offices. At the northernmost end of the enclosure is the octagonal, double-roofed *Dazheng dian* (Hall of Great Government), used for ceremonial. The *Chongzheng Hall*, on the central axis, was built in 1632. The roof is tiled in yellow with a green border and decorated ridge whilst the ceiling is painted with 'flying clouds and pouring water'. Between two dragon pillars is a gold dragon screen and throne where the emperor was to discuss military or governmental affairs and receive foreign ambassadors and the envoys of the minorities such as Tibetans and Mongolians. It was here that the name of the dynasty (Qing, meaning pure and bright) was proclaimed in 1636, and whenever emperors stayed in Shenyang on trips to the north, government matters were discussed in this hall.

The tallest structure in the palace is the three-storey *Fenghuang Tower* which acts as a gate marking the entrance to the 'inner' *Qingning Palace* where the emperor and his family had their private apartments; it was also the place where imperial banquets were held and military campaigns were planned. When the court was moved to Peking in 1644, and the Manchus 'entered the passes' (the term used to mean entering China proper from outside the Chinese pale), palace archives and seals relating to the beginnings of Qing rule were kept here. Behind the *Fenghuang Tower*, on the same axis, is the *Qingning Hall*, standing on a stone platform 3.8m high, at the northern end of the courtyard. The empresses used the eastern side of the hall (in Chinese practice they would probably have been on the W) and ancestral and other ceremonies were held in the western side, under the supervision of shamans, at dawn, midday, dusk and on festival-days. In the SE corner of the courtyard is a pole topped by a tin measure where grains used to be set out to feed the sparrows and other birds.

The most important building on the western axis of the palace is the *Wensu ge* (Hall of the Source of Culture), built in 1782 to house one of the first four sets of the 'Si ku quan shu' (Imperial Collectanea; 'Complete Collection of the Four Treasuries', a manuscript edition of some 3450 works; see Peking, Hangzhou and Chengde where other copies were housed). This library building is somewhat different from the others in that it has a stage in front, though, like the others, it is said to be modelled on the private library, Tianyi ge, in Ningbo. Inside the hall is a plaque with the inscription (written by the Qianlong emperor): 'The flavours of the ancient and modern are contained within; plucking from it is to explore the ten-thousand phenomena and the deep blue sea. With rites and music, respect for fundamentals is celebrated from the Three Rivers to the Milky Way and the vast oceans'. There is also a stele in a pavilion to the E of the Hall with a Chinese-Manchu inscription commemorating the establishment of the Hall.

In the suburbs of Shenyang are two imperial tombs and a temple. The *Shisheng* (True Victory) *Temple* (also known as the *Huang si*, Imperial Temple, and the *Huang si*, Yellow Temple—both 'huangs' being second tone but written with different characters), is in Heping qu on Huangsi lu and was the most substantial Lamaist temple in Shenyang before 1644. It was built in 1638 and substantially restored in 1726. It covers an area of over 5500 square metres and contains some imposing buildings.

The **Tomb of Nurhaci**, true founder of the Qing, is c 11km NE of the city and is known as the *Fu ling* (Fortunate Tomb) or *Dong ling* (Eastern Tomb). Built against the Tianzhu mountains with a river in front, in an area thick with conifers, it was started in 1629 and finished in 1651 (though later embellishments were added in the 18C). The area enclosed by its surrounding wall is 194,800 square metres. In front of the gate is the usual notice to dismount (also found at the other Qing tomb enclosures); inside is an avenue of paired animals: camels, lions and horses. On either side of the stele tower are buildings originally intended to serve as stores for ceremonial vessels and materials used in sacrifices. There is a 'lacquer vessel' store, a 'sacrificial animal' store, a document store and so on.

The tomb itself lies beyond, within a fortified-looking wall which encloses a three-storey tower. This 'Square City' with its corner towers stands in front of the 'Jade City', the circular enclosure with the tree-covered mound beneath which the emperor, empresses and concubines are actually buried. Like the other Qing tombs, it was forbidden for anyone to enter the tomb enclosure during the life of the dynasty (unless they came officially to make sacrifices and offerings on birthdays and festivals).

The similar **Zhao ling** (Clear Tomb), also known as the *Bei ling* (Northern Tomb), is in the northern suburbs of Shenyang and contains the bodies of Abahai and his wife. It is the largest and best-preserved of the Qing tombs that lie 'beyond the passes'. It was built between 1643 and 1651 with additions and alterations by the Qianlong and Kangxi emperors who were incapable of leaving anything alone. Before the gate are stone lions, stone bridges (crossing the waterway required by fengshui beliefs), mounting stones (where visitors were required to dismount) two pavilions (one for robing and one for sacrifices) and a finely carved pailou (archway) in black Liaoyang stone. In the avenue of paired animals beyond, the horses are said to have been modelled on Abahai's favourite mounts. In the 'square city' is the Long'en Hall with a curtained bed in one alcove, another containing the spirit tablets of the emperor and his wife, as well as various items of furniture (incense burners, palace lanterns and candle-holders).

6 Harbin

Harbin (properly rendered in pinyin as *Haerbin*), on the banks of the Songhua or Songari River, capital of Heilongjiang, China's northernmost province, is, like Changchun, a city that grew with railways. For the 'Japanese Railway Guide to Manchuria' (1913) it was 'a child, bred, reared and supported by the Chinese Eastern Railway'.

By 1933 the child had grown and, according to Carl Crow, in his 'Handbook to China', '...It now has a population of about 200,000, half Chinese and half Russian, thus having the largest European population of any city in Asia…'. The Russian population of Harbin was enormously swelled by the influx of White Russian refugees from the 1917 revolution. Yet even before the expansion of 1917, the 'Japanese Railway Guide' states that 'every visitor who does not already know Russian will soon wish he did'. The continuing attraction of Harbin is its Russian-ness, stucco buildings perfectly resembling those of Leningrad lining the streets and the onion domes of Orthodox Churches visible above. One of the best areas for wandering is the old *South Riparian Quarter* on the S bank of the river, around Youyi lu, Shangzhi and Zhongyang da jie.

There is still a considerable (but rapidly aging) White Russian population left in Harbin and another aspect of Harbin's history is seen in *Ping-fang qu*, in the Japanese Germ Warfare Experimental Base where quite horrific experiments were secretly carried out on Chinese people, during the Second World War. Bubonic plague was injected into some victims whilst others contributed to knowledge of how the body behaves at extreme temperatures by being frozen alive (the results were eventually useful in early open-heart surgery) or by being roasted alive, which has not advanced the cause of science at all. The establishment was not dissimilar to those in some German concentration camps (and, as with various German scientists, some of the 'scientists' were protected after the end of the Second World War by the US government which was interested in some of their results).

Today, Harbin is famous for its Ice Festival, held annually from 1 January till early March. Ice sculptures of doubtful aesthetic value (Mickey Mouse is tending to replace Chinese dragons) are created, some with lanterns inside them, some that can be climbed by children and slid down, are set up in the Zhaolin Park. The Sungari also freezes over and can become a road (bearing the load of lorries when it is 1m thick).

7 Beidaihe

Beidaihe, on the Hebei coast, is a seaside resort favoured by foreign diplomats since the last years of the 19C. In those days foreign missionaries also came to Beidaihe for their summer holidays, nowadays, though foreign diplomats still come, they are vastly outnumbered by Chinese visitors. In the summer, when sea-bathing is most popular, it is virtually impossible for a Chinese person without 'connections' to find a place to stay, and the beaches are completely covered with people.

Six hours by train (N on the line to Shenyang) from Peking, it is a pleasant place, preferably out of season unless you are very keen on crowds. Apart from new hotels and shops, the older buildings still retain something of the flavour of the past. In Ann Bridge's novel 'Four-part Setting' (1939), Beidaihe is the setting for a tale of restrained romance, with bungalows 'half-hidden in the native growth of bushes and small trees, mimosas and thorns…', convenient cover for kisses 'amongst the polygonums'. After shopping for 'such articles as cannot well be left to the discretion of their Number One Boy' in the shopping centre, 'an untidy row of shacks, a sort of tumble-down tin-town, in which the big shops from Tientsin and Shanghai open ephemeral branches for the summer season', holidaying foreigners would return to their bungalows where the verandah 'ran the whole length of the bungalow; a dining table stood at one end; rush chairs with cushions, a bridge table and gramophone occupied the centre—the further end was littered with tennis racquets, a fishing rod and other sporting gear.' 'It was the custom in Beidaihe to lunch in negligées in one's own house' so they donned kimonos and espadrilles after a sitz bath and recuperated from shopping over cocktails on the verandah.

A rather less ephemeral branch of the famous Tientsin/Tianjin restaurant, *Kiesslings*, originally run by Austrians, still exists in Beidaihe, serving coffee, bread and cakes. The accommodation available includes some of the old bungalow buildings (Diplomatic Guesthouse, Xishan Guesthouse).

From Beidahe it is possible to visit *Shanhaiguan*, 50km N, the point where the Great Wall tumbles into the sea. Nearby is the *temple* dedicated to Meng Qiang nu, the legendary wife of a man who was conscripted during the Qin (221–206 BC) to build the Great Wall.

He was away for many years and her family threatened to marry her again so she set off to try and find her husband. She finally discovered (at Shanhaiguan) that he had died during his corvée service. On hearing the news, her tears made the wall fall down. Her devoted search for her husband is the subject of many popular stories and operas (and it is said that one of the best playwrights and opera-writers of the 20C, Wu Zuguang, has just written a new version of the tale. As he is a forthright critic of contemporary arts policies and lack of freedom, it is likely to cause a stir, if he ever manages to get it performed).

In the temple there are paired inscriptions outside the main hall: 'the waves of the sea break break break break break break'; 'the floating clouds drift drift drift drift drift drift '. The rear hall is devoted to Guanyin.

8 Shanghai

SHANGHAI, China's largest city with a population of 10.8 million (1982) living in an area of 6100 square km, lies on the Huangpu River, in the Yangtse delta. The small seaport, surrounded by a circular defensive wall built in 1553 to prevent raids by Japanese pirates, was recognised as a port with trade potential and forcibly opened to foreign trade at the end of the First Opium War in 1842. It quickly attracted entrepreneurs and a poor reputation, of which the term 'to shanghai' (first used in 1871), meaning 'to drug or otherwise render insensible and ship on board a ship lacking hands' is an illustration. Its early growth as a treaty port was steady but saw a dramatic increase during the First World War when European trade was disrupted. Its prosperity in the 1920s and 1930s is demonstrated in the grand office buildings that line the riverfront and its reputation as 'the wickedest city in the world'.

The Japanese invasion and occupation of Shanghai in 1942–45, during which foreign residents were interned, marked the beginning of the end of Shanghai as a treaty port. Most foreign firms left after 1949 although the last foreign factory, a Swiss-owned aluminium mill, was not taken over until 1960.

Shanghai is one of China's three 'municipalities', with the equivalent status to a province, and is still a major port and industrial area. Though many modern high-rise blocks are now being built amongst the earlier banks and office buildings of Shanghai's heyday, the city still retains much of its 'European' appearance.

Airport: there are both domestic and international departures from the airport (Hongqiao or Rainbow Bridge Airport, named after the suburb immediately to the S) which is 15km W of the city centre. International flights connect Shanghai with Japan and Singapore. A CAAC bus runs between the airport and the CAAC office at 789 Yan'an Road (near the Shanghai Exhibition Centre).

Hotels: the older hotels in Shanghai are of considerable interest. On the Bund (Zhongshan lu), overlooking the Huangpu, is the *Peace* (Heping) *Hotel* (170 Nanjing xilu) which has two buildings: that on the S side of the road was formerly the Palace Hotel whilst the taller building on the N side was Sassoon House, comprising office buildings of the Sassoon family and the old Cathay Hotel, built in 1930. Noel Coward stayed there soon after the opening in 1930 and, suffering from influenza, is said to have completed the draft of 'Private Lives'. Though the rooms have been refurbished (which involved the removal of much of the British bathroom porcelain and the chaise-longues in curtained alcoves which used to grace the rooms), the corridors are unchanged, with dim '30s light-fittings and armchairs (1987). The hotel is still famous for its bar and the pre-war swing played every night by a slightly middle-aged group of gentlemen.

Just to the N of the Peace, on the N side of the Suzhou Creek which joins the Huangpu, is the *Shanghai Mansions* (Shanghai daxia), formerly Broadway Mansions, which was also built in 1934, as an apartment hotel with small suites for long-term residents. A tall, block-like '30s building, it affords a fine view of the Bund area from the top floor and used to have a band playing in the evening led by Howard 'Zing' Wu with 'Shorty' on the piano. This hotel has also been refurbished and little of the original interior remains.

In the centre of the city is the *Overseas Chinese Hotel* (Huaqiao fandian) which is dwarfed by its next-door neighbour, the 24-storey *Park Hotel* (Guoji fandian, 170 Nanjing xilu) which was advertised as 'ready for occupancy September 1934'. Then it boasted that it was the tallest building of the Far East, with 205 luxury furnished rooms, apartments and unfurnished flats, and it still has an amazing art deco dining room high above the Nanjing Road.

W of the central district is the *Jing'an Guesthouse* (370 Huashan lu), near the old 'Bubbling well' which gave the name to the road that is now known as Nanjing xilu. Set behind a large and beautifully-kept lawn with pretty gardens, it stands in what used to be a smart residential area.

In the old French district is the *Jinjiang Hotel* (57 Maoming lu), a huge complex of castellated towers originally constructed, like the Shanghai Mansions, as an apartment hotel. A flight of steps sweeps up to the entrance of the main building, and the lifts, with their clock-dials, used to figure in Chinese films of the 1950s when pre-liberation luxury was depicted, (1985: the Jinjiang has been refurbished; much of the lobby has been buried).—S of the Jinjiang Hotel is the *Ruijin Guesthouse* (118 Ruijin erlu), once a private house, said to have been owned by Chiang Kai-shek's brother-in-law. It has dark wooden panelling, '30s furniture and black-tiled bathrooms as well as a garden.

Major foreign hotel chains are constructing hotels in Shanghai (Sheraton has already opened a hotel in the far SW suburb of Xujiahui and the Hilton is in a slightly more central location) and there are a number of Hong Kong joint-venture hotels but these are mainly in the outer suburbs.

LUXURY: *Huating Sheraton*, 1200 Caoxi bei lu, tel: 386000, telex: 33589
Xijiao binguan, 1921 Hongqiao lu, tel: 379643, telex: 33004
Xijiao dongyuan, 1591 Hongqiao lu, tel: 372170
Shanghai Hilton, 250 Huashan lu, tel: 563343, telex: 33612

FIRST CLASS: *Longbai* (Cypress) *fandian*, 2419 Hongqiao lu, tel: 329388, telex: 33288
Donghu Guesthouse (not yet open in 1987; Du Yuesheng's old residence), 167 Xinle lu, tel: 370050
Peace Hotel, 20 Nanjing dong lu, tel: 211244
Ruijin Guesthouse, 118 Ruijin lu, tel: 372653, telex: 33603

STANDARD: *Chengqiao Hotel*, 2266 Hongqiao lu, tel: 329220
Hengshan Hotel (under renovation, previously *Picardie Mansions*), 534 Hengshan lu, tel: 377050, telex: 33009
Jing'an Guesthouse, 370 Huashan lu, tel: 563050
New Garden Hotel, 1900 Hongqiao lu, tel: 329000
Overseas Chinese Hotel (Huaqiao fandian), 104 Nanjing xi lu, tel: 226226
Park Hotel, 170 Nanjing xi lu, tel: 225225
Qichong tian binguan, 627 Nanjing dong lu, tel: 220777, telex: 33907
Shanghai Hotel, 505 Wulumuqi bei li, tel: 312312, telex: 33295
Shanghai Mansions, 20 Suzhou bei lu, tel: 244186, telex: 33007
Xingguo Guesthouse, 72 Xingguo lu, tel: 374503, telex: 33016

Passenger boats depart from the numbered quays on the Bund (Zhongshan lu, near the junction with Dongmen lu leading E from the old Chinese city) and the advance booking office is at 22 Renmin lu, near the quays. The *railway station* is in the N of the city, near the junction of Henan bei lu and Tianmu lu.

Situation and history: it was Shanghai's position in the Yangtse delta that first attracted Europeans looking for a trade port. The Yangtse flows through much of China's richest and most fertile territory, from Sichuan province in the west, through the silk, tea and rice-producing delta to the sea. The river brings much silt with it, as the early Western port engineers discovered in the latter part of the 19C, and this has shaped Shanghai's history. The name Shanghai means 'on the sea' or 'beside the sea', and though this name has only been used from the Song dynasty (before that it was probably almost non-existent, described as 'part of Hua ting county'), it may well be that Shanghai used to be nearer the sea. Literary accounts describe how the Suzhou River (originally known as the Wusong River) was much wider in the Tang but had shrunk to less than half its width by the Song and continued to narrow as more silt was brought down through succeeding centuries until it became the narrow flow that the European inhabitants of Shanghai knew as the Suzhou Creek. Another, older name for the Suzhou or Wusong River was the Hudu, and the first character, hu, became the literary name for Shanghai, which is still used in, for example, railway timetables.

By the Song dynasty Shanghai had acquired the name *Shanghai zhen*, or Market Town by the Sea, and in 1292, under the Yuan, it was elevated to the status of county town. As trade, notably with Japan, in silks and tea grew during the succeeding centuries, Shanghai's key position, situated at the head of the Yangtse which, with its tributaries, flowed past all the most important silk- and tea-producing towns of the delta, meant that it became one of China's major ports. Coastal traffic was officially controlled and boats from the north were allowed no further S than Shanghai (and vice versa) so that it became an interprovincial entrepôt. Incursions by Japanese pirates in the early 16C led to the walling of the town for protection. Though the city walls were demolished in 1912, the ring road circling the 'Chinese' town in the SE of the city still indicates the form of the enclosure and the roads that led out from the gates are named for them. Shanghai's steady growth as a local port with a volume of trade probably equal to that of London in the 19C was, however, interrupted by Western trading interests which eventually came to shape the modern city.

Though trade was dramatically to affect the city, the first foreign 'influence' came from the Jesuit missionaries of the 16C. One of Ricci's converts was Xu Guangqi (1562–1633), a native of Xujiahui (which means Xu Family Village), now part of metropolitan Shanghai but then a village within Shanghai county. Xu, who was baptised Paul in 1603, had left his native village to become an official in Peking, working first in the Board of Rites, later in the Imperial Library. He was the highest-ranking Chinese official to convert, and family land was later given to the Catholic Church which established an observatory and cathedral in Xujiahui.

A century later, when foreign traders had established themselves in some discomfort in Canton and Macau, confined to a narrow strip of coast, compelled to deal with imperially-appointed merchants, they began to cast about for more favourable sites. An East India Company report of 1756 notes that Shanghai is a desirable place for trade, owing to its protected site away from the typhoons of the coast and its pivotal point of access to the tea and silks of the hinterland. An East India Company vessel, the 'Lord Amherst', made an exploratory trip up the Huangpu in 1832, and though Mr Lindsay, who headed the commercial mission, managed to see the local official in charge, there was no question at the time of opening Shanghai to trade. Lindsay was very enthusiastic about Shanghai's potential, despite his frosty reception, counting the junks in the river whose numbers suggested that Shanghai was, even then, one of the world's busiest ports, hoping for a market for British woollens in the colder western provinces of the upper Yangtse and concluding that, …considering the extraordinary advantages which this place possesses for foreign trade it is wonderful that it has not attracted more observation.'

Under Chinese restrictions of foreign traders even observation was difficult, but the Treaty of Nanking, imposed upon the Chinese after defeat in the First Opium War (1842), negotiated after British warships had sailed up the Yangtse, past the point near Shanghai where the Huangpu joined the great river, succeeded, where commercial missions had failed. Shanghai, Canton, Amoy (Xiamen), Fuzhou and Ningbo were not only opened to trade but British consuls and the families of both merchants and consuls were to be admitted (women had not previously been allowed into the 'factories' in Canton and Macau). According to land regulations negotiated with the senior Chinese official, the Daotai, after the treaty, foreigners were still not allowed into the walled city but were allocated a plot of land immediately N of the city, reaching up to the Suzhou river, with anchorage extending some 300m across the Huangpu. The area allocated was bounded by ditches which, with the exception of the Suzhou River, have since been filled in. Amongst the earliest works initiated by Captain George Balfour, the first consul, were drainage works, which were to continue for as one of Shanghai's historians remarked: 'Within the memory of the present writer the positions now occupied by the Russian and German consulates were under water, and the Bund foreshore was unfilled, the tides coming up to the footpath.'

Embankments were constructed on the tidal foreshore, a process known by the Anglo-Indian term 'bunding' which gave the waterfront road its name. Struggles with water marked much of Shanghai's early foreign history. Not only did the foreshore need strengthening, but the drinking water supply required urgent attention. At first, local water was taken out by ship and settled with alum, then boiled before consumption, until a water company working under contract to the Shanghai Municipal Council began to supply piped and chlorinated water in 1883.

Struggles with the silt of the delta were another problem. As the estuary is tidal, silt not only flows downstream but is also sucked upstream with the tide. From the 13C various forms of flood gates had been set up at the mouth of the Suzhou Creek to prevent the inflow of silt, and the main channel, the Huangpu, was endlessly scoured to prevent it silting up and inhibiting the passage of deep-draught ships which often had to wait for the tide before they could enter the channel. Between 1905 and 1930 Dutch and Swedish hydraulic engineers supervised the dredging of nearly 26 million cubic metres (34 million cubic yards) of mud from the Huangpu shipping channel. The subsoil of the riverbank gave cause for considerable worry, as Lanning describes: 'What Shanghai is built on we now know with some degree of certainty and detail. When our first iron bridge was in course of construction in 1871 on the site of the present Garden Bridge (over the Suzhou Creek on the Bund), visitors to the Public Garden were astounded one afternoon to see it bodily sinking before their eyes. Its collapse and disappearance gave the first serious object lesson regarding the foundational value of Shanghai subsoil' (1920).

Perhaps because of the problematic subsoil, the first British buildings in Shanghai were based on those of Canton: bungalows and offices of no more than two storeys with open verandahs, mostly built by workmen brought up from Canton. A major priority with the early British settlers was sport; a racecourse was built at the western end of Park Lane (later the Nanjing Road) and excursions were made into the flat surrounding countryside of the delta, to shoot snipe. Later, the racecourse was moved W, along the Nanjing Road, to the area now occupied by the Renmin Park and the square, despite the fact that the area had been occupied by Chinese graveyards and much local opposition was encountered. The 1904 map of Shanghai shows the racecourse with swimming baths and cricket ground within its circular enclosure.

Balfour's major tasks were to open Shanghai to foreign trade and to establish the rules by which foreign traders could lease land, providing they allowed former owners to visit their ancestral graves. Foreign representatives had long been trying to establish a right of 'extraterritoriality' in China which, in the words of an early colonial legal expert, Sir Francis

Piggott, once Chief Justice of Hong Kong, meant that: '...the foreign sovereign enforces the duties of his subjects, representing the oriental sovereign *pro hac vice*, but does not protect their rights, except in the single instance of disputes amongst themselves.' In other words, foreign residents had to observe local laws but did not need to attend local courts. Consular courts were set up in 1842, and in 1863 the British Consul established the Mixed Court, a 'tribunal for the decision of cases in which foreigners were either directly or indirectly interested...in which due attention to foreigners' interests might be secured by the presence of their representatives, while the jurisdiction of the native authorities was left untouched.' It acted as a police court, when a Chinese officer tried cases involving Chinese in the Settlement that had been brought by the police, whilst in criminal cases brought by foreigners against Chinese, a Chinese magistrate delivered judgement in the presence of a Consular Assessor.

By the end of 1843 there were 11 foreign firms based in Shanghai—mainly British and American businesses formerly based in Canton—and by 1849 there were 175 foreigners resident in Shanghai. The position of the Americans was different: never directly associated with the unpleasant business of Opium Wars and subsequent treaties, they established themselves in Hongkou on the N bank of the Suzhou Creek, though in 1863 their settlement was merged with that of the British to form the new 'international settlement', under the control of the Shanghai Municipal Government which had formerly only controlled the British Settlement. Japanese had also begun to settle in Hongkou (where rents were lower than in the British Settlement on the S side of the Suzhou Creek), and the French, who had arrived in 1846 (although according to an English writer, their trading interests consisted of only one shopkeeper), negotiated the lease of a separate plot of land S of the British concession (between the British and the Chinese city).

In the early days, up to 1890, foreign firms traded mainly in tea, silk and (illegal) opium. Whilst these were the major commodities of interest to foreign traders, Shanghai's importance as a port of transshipment is evident in the fact that overseas imports in the first 100 years almost always exceeded exports by about 10 per cent per year. Until 1900 Shanghai had a virtual monopoly of world trade in tea and silk but, as with other agricultural goods like rubber and sugar, the monopoly declined and a more varied trade pattern emerged in the 20C. An early visitor to Shanghai was Robert Fortune, a well-known plant-hunter. In the early 1850s he travelled in China on behalf of the British East India Company collecting tea cuttings and information on tea-growing in order to set up rival plantations in India, precisely in order to break China's monopoly of tea production. Silk exports declined partly because of changes in fashion and partly because the Japanese began to make determined efforts to overtake China as a silk producer and introduced mechanisation to the detriment of the handicraft methods of the Chinese.

The import of opium, whose consumption had long been known in China but whose spread was promoted by the early foreign traders, was officially banned by the Chinese, but it continued to be brought into Shanghai illegally on foreign ships. This posed a problem for the British Consuls who were caught between Chinese law which prohibited it and British law, which did not. The first British Consul, Balfour, acted decisively against those ships whose manifests showed chests of opium but, nevertheless, it was well known that there were often as many as six ships loaded with opium anchored at Shanghai.

In the first decade of foreign residence in Shanghai the life of the trader varied between the frenzied activity of the early summer silk-buying season, complicated by the slowness of communications with the home markets (seven weeks by sea until the telegraph line through Siberia was set up in 1871), and the relative quiet of the rest of the year. A visitor in the late 1850s stated that it was: '...the most rowdy and disreputable place imaginable...the bulk of the population is composed of a number of lively spirits who drive about in pony traps the whole day and call themselves brokers, but whose occupation, like Othello's, is apparently gone...California in its worst days could not have been worse than Shanghai today.' The entry 'Sink of Iniquity' in Couling's 'Encyclopaedia Sinica' (1917) refers to '...an expression used by the Duke of Somerset in Parliament in 1869...the accusation was against the commercial morality of the place.'

Residents took exercise by shooting pheasant, teal and woodcock in the mud-flats, and riding, although there were complaints about the condition of the ponies which was such that in 1852, a 'man and horse race, 50 yards there and back, was won by the man.' Class distinctions were already apparent for the regatta featured '...mainly...merchant crews...'.

A source of material on the early social life of Shanghai is the 'North China Herald' which commenced publication on 3 August 1850, its 'northern-ness' being relative to Canton, the first foreign base in China, reflecting the inward-looking attitude of the foreign residents. Serving less than 150 residents, the 'North China Herald' describes performances of amateur dramatics in the New and Imperial theatres which included an operatic burlesque extravaganza entitled 'Roofscrambler' and something else called 'Bombastes Furioso'. The Northern Lodge of Freemasons held its first meeting in 1849 and the first bachelor's ball was held in 1850, although dancing was difficult due to the lack of female partners.

The original Catholic settlement at Xujiahui, established in the 17C, had suffered from persecution and the church became a temple to the god of war. It was later returned to the French but meanwhile, in 1848, the foundation stone of a new cathedral was laid. In the same year a wooden Protestant Episcopalian church was built, though its roof fell in within two years and it was decided that it must be replaced with something more substantial, which was to be one of Gilbert Scott's earliest commissions in 1862. Missionaries arrived with the first traders: Dr Medhurst of the London Missionary Society conducted a service in the British Consulate in 1843, Dr W.J. Boone of the Protestant Episcopal Mission in 1845, bringing Miss Fay, the first unmarried American lady to come to China; the Church Missionary Society in 1849; Dr M.T. Yates of the Southern Baptist Convention also arrived in 1849, and others came from the Northern Presbyterian Church and the Southern Methodist Episcopal Mission.

In 1853 Taiping rebels took nearby Nanjing, and the foreign community in Shanghai had to consider its defence. Opinion amongst the foreign community was divided for the leader of the Taiping rebels, Hong Xiuquan, had learnt something about Christianity, apparently from the Rev. Issachar J. Roberts of the American Baptist Missionary Union in Canton, and believed that he was Christ's brother. The editor of the 'North China Herald' supported the Taiping rebels against the imperial forces, as did many missionaries. But when Nanjing fell and, suddenly, an army of the 'Small Sword Society' (Xiao dao hui), a branch of the Triad secret society from Guangdong province, taking advantage of the turmoil caused by the Taiping, seized the Chinese city of Shanghai in September 1853, the foreign community felt forced to take action. An international group, the Shanghai Volunteer Corps, was formed, and its first action, the Battle of Muddy Flat, was to clear an encampment of imperial troops which had been made within the boundaries of the International Settlement. The Small Sword Society was finally driven out of the Chinese city in 1855 and the Taiping rebels never managed to enter the city but the incidents had a considerable effect on Shanghai's development.

The Shanghai Municipal Council, comprising British, French and American representatives, was inaugurated on 11 July 1854. It immediately formed new committees such as that of 'Roads, jetties and police' and adopted a set of 'Land Regulations'. These recognised Chinese sovereignty over the land of the settlement and that all land leases should be conducted with the Chinese through the renter's own consul. One of the effects of civil disorder had been a huge number of Chinese refugees arriving in the settlement, seeking safety. It was therefore agreed that Chinese should be allowed to lease buildings in the International and French settlements, thus completely altering the nature of the settlements and laying a new pattern for Shanghai's development.

As a result of the disruption caused by the Small Swords' occupation of the Chinese city and the powerlessness of the Chinese Daotai who, like thousands of other Chinese, had been forced to seek refuge in the British Settlement, the regulation of customs and collection of customs duties had lapsed completely and the Daotai agreed with the foreign Consuls that they should appoint customs inspectors henceforth, to collect customs duties due to the Chinese government. Thus the basis of the Chinese Maritime Customs, staffed by foreigners answerable to the Chinese government, was set in 1854. Many famous figures served in the Chinese customs, including Sir Thomas Wade (co-inventor of the Wade-Giles romanisation system and a considerable sinologist) and Sir Robert Hart, whose name is virtually synonymous with the Chinese Customs Service for which he worked from 1863 until his death in 1911. In 1864 the Customs Service employed some 1000 Chinese and 400 foreigners. By 1916 the numbers had swelled to 6325 and 1321 respectively, the foreigners by then representing some 20 nationalities.

The Second Opium War or Arrow War of 1856 was ostensibly the result of an insult to the British flag on a Chinese-owned ship, the 'Arrow', in Canton, but it offered the British, French, Americans and Russians an excuse to press the Chinese imperial government for further opening of the country. The 'Arrow' was boarded by a Chinese patrol looking for pirates, who lowered the British flag and arrested 12 Chinese sailors. The Consul's request for an apology was refused; British forces from Hong Kong seized the forts outside Canton; the Chinese set fire to the British 'factories'; an Anglo-French forced attacked Canton; an Anglo-French force set out from Shanghai, making for Peking but settling instead in Tianjin where the Treaty of Tianjin was signed in 1858 which considerably expanded the provisions of the Treaty of Nanjing (1842). Another 'unequal' treaty, forced upon the Chinese on a fairly flimsy pretext, this finally 'opened' the interior of China, with ten new treaty ports (mostly on the Yangtse), better conditions of travel and residence in the interior for missionaries and traders, and permanent diplomatic representation in Peking for Britain, France, Russia and the United States. Opening more ports along the Yangtse to foreign trade led to an increase in Shanghai's importance as the starting point and headquarters of up-river ventures.

Oddly, against this background of deliberately-applied pressure, there was considerable co-operation between imperial forces and foreign volunteer forces in the final campaigns against the Taiping rebels (1860–64) in the towns of the Yangtse delta. The 'Ever-Victorious Army', led first by Ward, an American (killed in 1861), later by the British General Charles Gordon who was to die in Khartoum, was paid for by worried Chinese merchants resident in Shanghai. Many thousands of foreign troops, British, Indian and French, released from 'operations in the north' (or sacking the Summer Palace in an effort to enforce the Treaty of Tianjin), also joined the imperial forces against the Taiping rebels.

The Chinese refugee population which had arrived in the foreign settlements as a result of the Taiping upheavals numbered nearly half a million, as against approximately 570 foreigners including 300 British, 60 Indians and about 120 Americans (and 74 women). This ratio of Chinese to foreigners was maintained as Shanghai's population gradually increased, most dramatically between 1910 and 1940 when the foreign population rose from some 10,000 to 60,000, many of the new arrivals consisting of Japanese (who arrived in large numbers after the defeat of

China in the Sino-Japanese War of 1894–95 and numbered 20,000 in 1936), White Russians fleeing the Bolsheviks (15,000 in 1936) and some 5000 Germans and Austrians, many of them refugees from Hitler.

The latter half of the 19C saw the physical development of Shanghai with road improvements, the advent of gas street-lights, attempts to establish a railway in 1865–77 which met with hostility from the Chinese who were unwilling to give up land and anyway regarded railways as interfering with local spirits, the introduction of modern cotton mills and the extension of the settlement to allow for industrial development up the Huangpu beyond Hongkou, and the construction (on underground rafts) of the grand edifices, office blocks in the commercial centre and mansions along Bubbling Well Road, that still dominate the Shanghai skyline.

Many of the names associated with the early trade and later industrial development of Shanghai are still significant in the Far East. Jardine & Matheson and Butterfield & Swire, Scottish trading companies, were typical, trading in tea and silk (and opium) as well as a variety of other goods like bristles and leather, horsehair and cotton piece-goods, as well as dealing in insurance and shipping and land and house agencies. The varied nature of their dealings and their stress on intelligence made them able to cope with the changes in trade patterns. Other major names were those of the Sassoons and, later, Hardoon.

Both of these were Jewish families from Baghdad but whilst the Sassoons had been trading in cotton (and opium) in India and first arrived in Shanghai in 1844, Silas Hardoon was originally employed by the Sassoons and later made his own fortune. Sassoon House and the Cathay (now Peace) hotel, still stand, as does the old Sassoon home, 2409 Hongqiao Road (next to the Zoo), a half-timbered, mock-Tudor mansion set in extensive grounds which the Gang of Four (including Jiang Qing, a connoisseur of luxury) used for meetings during the Cultural Revolution; in the late 1970s it became the Shanghai office and residence of the British Petroleum representative. Hardoon House was a 26-acre complex including a Buddhist temple (now demolished; the site is occupied by the Shanghai Exhibition Hall). Rising through rent collection to make a fortune in opium and property, Hardoon had married an Eurasian who was a devout Buddhist and paid for the printing of massive Buddhist canon, whilst her husband paid for the construction of the Beth Aharon synagogue in the 1920s. His funeral consisted of both Chinese and Jewish obsequies. Another grand mansion that still stands (though nowadays occupied by the Number One Children's Palace) is that of the Kadoorie family; a pink and white classical structure of considerable size, which once included a billiard room with several full-size tables.

On the Bund, the Customs House and the Hong Kong and Shanghai Bank building (now occupied by the Municipal Government), the Bank of China building and the pointed peak of the Peace Hotel express in stone the wealth of Shanghai in the 1920s and '30s. It was during this period that the separate existence of the Chinese majority was most strongly felt. The small park on the Bund, laid out (beside the bridge over the Suzhou Creek) by a Scottish gardener, had a list of regulations which included a prohibition against dogs and, originally, Chinese, except for those accompanied by their foreign employers (this was a let-out clause for the Chinese amah or nanny). The regulation was later amended to allow in well-dressed Chinese, but the privacy of the park was strictly guarded by the foreign minority. To a great extent, foreigners and Chinese led separate lives, although they lived in close proximity.

For foreigners, as for Chinese, Shanghai was a luxury shopping paradise, with the finest ladies' silk underwear to be found in Yates Road (Shanxi lu), entire trousseaux of the finest hand embroidery from the Door of Hope Mission on Nanjing Road which took in child prostitutes, antiques and silks in Nanjing Road, the best tailors on Avenue Joffre (Huaihai lu) in the French Concession, rugs and carpets in Bubbling Well Road, furniture from such emporia as the Charming Artistic Furniture Co. on the Route des Soeurs, and Parker pens in the middle section of Fuzhou Road, without straying into the red-light district full of young girls, all described as natives of Suzhou (where traditionally the prettiest women with the most seductive voices originate), also on the Fuzhou Road.

Residents, keen to maintain a European life-style, were supplied with

Shanghai: Nanjing Road

aerated water from Watson's Mineral Water Company (327 Jiangxi lu), canned goods from Sun Sun Co. (470 Nanjing Road) and Tai Kong Canned Provisions (377 Nanjing Road), milk from dairies like the Model Dairy Farm, Steys Dairy Farm and Ice Factory and the Yah Shing Dairy on the western outskirts of the city; Moutrie's supplied pianos proof against the ravages of the tropics and kept them tuned, and cars were supplied and maintained by the Central Auto Supply Co. (411 Avenue Foch) or the Foo Lai Tyre and Rubber Repair Co., on Park Road. Madame Soloha, a clairvoyant, maintained two consulting rooms on Bubbling Well Road and Wah Kee Avenue and a number of dentists (Dr John Hoh, Dr K.L. Kormilitzina and Dr T.P. Lews, amongst others) advertised their services. Many of the names of pre-war Shanghai—the department store Lane Crawford, the bookseller and publisher Kelly and Walsh, as well as Watson's Mineral Water—are still well-known in Hong Kong, whence they decamped after the Anti-Japanese War and the Communist takeover. The Sikh guards employed by many Hong Kong jewellers also recall the turbaned Sikh policemen of pre-liberation Shanghai.

The dual nature of Shanghai in 1937, a year in which over 20,000 corpses were collected from the pavements of the International Settlement alone, was described by Christopher Isherwood:

> Seen from the river, towering above their couchant guardian warships, the semi-skyscrapers of the Bund present, impressively, the façade of a great city. But it is only a façade. The spirit which dumped them upon this unhealthy mud-bank, thousands of miles from their kind, has been too purely and brutally competitive. The biggest animals have pushed their way down to the brink of the water; behind them is a sordid and shabby mob of smaller buildings…
>
> Nevertheless the tired or lustful businessman will find here everything to

gratify his desires. You can buy an electric razor, or a French dinner, or a well-cut suit. You can dance at the Tower Restaurant on the roof of the Cathay Hotel, and gossip with Teddy Kaufman, its charming manager, about the European aristocracy or pre-Hitler Berlin. You can attend race-meetings, baseball games, football matches. You can see the latest American films. If you want girls, or boys, you can have them, at all prices, in the bath-houses and the brothels. If you want opium you can smoke it in the best company, served on a tray, like afternoon tea. Good wine is difficult to obtain in this climate but there is enough whisky and gin to float a fleet of battleships. The jeweller and the antique dealer await your orders, and their charges will make you imagine yourself back on Fifth Avenue or in Bond Street. Finally, if you ever repent, there are churches and chapels of all denominations.

Apart from the destruction of Japanese bombing which was already evident in the poorer, Chinese city, exacerbating the appalling conditions in which many Chinese were living, their numbers swelled by refugees from Japanese invasion, Auden and Isherwood were taken to some of the factories in Hongkou:

In the accumulator factories, half the children have already the blue line in their gums which is a symptom of lead poisoning. Few of them will survive longer than a year or eighteen months. In scissors factories you can see arms and legs developing chromium-holes. There are silk-winding mills so full of steam that the fingers of the mill-girls are white with fungus. If the children slacken in their work the overseers often plunge their elbows into the boiling water as a punishment. There is a cotton mill where the dust in the air makes T.B. almost a certainty…In this city the gulf between society's two halves is too grossly wide for any bridge. There can be no compromise here. And we ourselves, though we wear out our shoes walking the slums, though we take notes, though we are genuinely shocked and indignant, belong, inescapably to the other world. We return, always, to Number One House (the British Ambassador's private residence) for lunch.

In the early days of foreign trade the Chinese comprador was an essential member of any trading house. Many compradors became rich in their own right and as Shanghai prospered in the period during and after the First World War when European manufacturers presented little competition, many set themselves up as independent entrepreneurs. Some of today's 'national bourgeoisie' such as Rong Yiren, whose family fortunes were based on Shanghai cotton mills, are the descendants of these breakaway compradors though others, who made their money from opium, gambling, prostitution and extortion, also made fortunes in the 1920s and '30s. Du Yuesheng, who controlled much of the vice in the French Concession, was described in the Shanghai 'Who's Who' as '…most influential resident, French Concession, Shanghai. Well-known public welfare worker. 1932, councillor, French Municipal Council…', with a string of respectable directorships. Du Yuesheng, a board director of the Red Cross, was also a leader of a Shanghai secret society, the Green Gang, which in 1927 he unleashed upon workers and communists in Shanghai, securing the city for Chiang Kai-shek and the Kuomintang.

The protective nature of foreign concessions meant that underground political movements could thrive, partly because of the possibilities of escape across boundaries, for there were separate police forces in the International and French settlements. The acute problems of workers in the Shanghai factories and natural antipathy to the contrasting luxury of the life of Shanghai's foreign residents also made Shanghai an obvious site for the secret founding meeting of the Chinese Communist Party in July 1921. The meetings were held in 106 Rue Wantz (now 76 Xingye Road) in the French Concession, the home of one the 12 delegates, who are said to have stayed in the empty girls' school in Rue Auguste Boppe (127 Taicang lu). The meeting was not without incident; the French police interrupted it and the delegates scattered, to re-group in a house-boat on the Nan hu, 100km SW of Shanghai. From this small and inauspicious beginning Communist influence grew in Shanghai, as students and intellectuals began to oppose the foreign domination of their city.

In 1925, when a Communist labour representative was killed in a Japanese-owned cotton mill, thousands of students demonstrated against Japan in the International Settlement on 30 May and many were arrested by the police. Thousands of sympathisers gathered outside the police-station and a British police officer ordered his men to fire on the crowd, killing ten. Communist-organised reaction included a strike, although the most successful strike was in Hong Kong (it lasted 16 months) and was combined with a boycott of all British goods from Hong Kong in Canton.

Protected, to some extent, from events in the rest of China by extra-territoriality, the Shanghai Volunteer Corps and police were, however, mobilised in 1913, 1924, 1925 and 1927 as warlord armies fought battles near the city. In 1926 Chiang Kai-shek launched the Northern Expedition, taking the Kuomintang army from its base in Canton to seize territory from the Northern warlords. At the beginning the Kuomintang and the Chinese Communist Party were nominally united and Communist Party activists did much preparatory work, organising strikes and mobilising peasants and workers in support of the troops. In Shanghai, as elsewhere, armed volunteer workers led by Zhou Enlai, amongst others, took control of the Chinese city in anticipation of the arrival of the Kuomintang troops. On 12 April 1927 the Kuomintang army arrived but it disarmed the workers and, with help from Du Yuesheng who mobilised the underground 'Green Gang' in return for obtaining the government opium monopoly, arrested and executed all known Communists who could be found, driving the rest underground and effectively beginning the civil war that was to last over 20 years. The Shanghai Volunteer Corps was fully mobilised to defend the International Settlement but all the fighting took place in the Chinese city and suburbs.

The arrival of Chiang Kai-shek brought changes to Shanghai: the Mixed Court was abolished in favour of entirely Chinese courts which could try Chinese and 'non-Treaty' foreigners like Germans and Russians. Chinese were finally admitted to the public parks though, as Davidson-Houston notes, 'The problem of admitting Chinese to public parks was solved in 1928 by making a small charge, which limited the numbers to a tolerable level. Most of the clubs, however, were still closed to them, as foreigners felt strongly that some refuge must be left where they could retain something of the atmosphere of home' (which also meant that few clubs admitted any women, foreign or otherwise).

The Japanese invasion of Manchuria in 1931 had repercussions in Shanghai where progressive Chinese were quick to react. A boycott of Japanese goods was organised and a mob attacked a group of Japanese monks in January 1932. This led to a battle between Japanese and Chinese troops in the Zhabei (Chapei) district to the W of Hongkou where most Japanese were resident. Japanese planes dropped incendiary bombs on the crowded quarter of Zhabei and the Shanghai Volunteer Corps was mustered to protect the International Settlement until May when an 'armistice' was signed. Throughout the succeeding years there were anti-Japanese incidents but Shanghai flourished as never before. Visitors from all over the world came to shop and stare at such sights as the Great World Amusement Centre, described by Joseph von Sternberg in the mid 1930s:

> On the first floor there were gambling tables, singsong girls, magicians, pickpockets, slot machines, fireworks, bird cages, fans, stick incense, acrobats and ginger. One flight up were the restaurants, a dozen different groups of actors, crickets in cages, pimps, midwives, barbers and ear wax extractors. The third floor had jugglers, herb medicines, ice-cream parlours, photographers, a new bevy of girls, their high-collared gowns slit to reveal their hips, in case one had passed up the more modest ones below who merely flashed their thighs; and, under the heading of novelty, several

N

Huangpu river

Zhongshan

lu

Shanghai Museum
donglu

Yu garden

Zhonghua

nanlu

Henan

Zhongshan

Sichu

Dongfeng Hotel

donglu

Fuzhou

Jinling

Renmin

lu

Zhejiang

lu

Zhonghua

Huaihai donglu

Great World

zhonglu

People's
Square

Yan'an

Xizang nanlu

zhonglu

Weihai lu

Site of the first
meeting of the Chinese
Communist Party

Shanghai Exhibition Centre

Yan'an
zhonglu

Jinjiang Hotel

zhonglu

Sun Yat-Sen's home

Ruijin

Fuxing

Shanghai Art Theatre

nanlu

Shaanxi

Yan'an

Changshu lu

Hengshan lu

Jing an temple

Huaihai

Xujiahui Roman Catholic Cathedral

Yan'an xilu

Huashan lu

Shanghai Zoo

Long hua pagoda

rows of exposed toilets, their impresarios instructing the amused patrons not to squat but to assume a position more in keeping with the imported plumbing. The fourth floor was crowded with shooting galleries, fan-tan tables, revolving wheels, massage benches, acupuncture and moxa cabinets, hot-towel counters, dried fish and intestines, and dance platforms serviced by a horde of music makers competing with each other to see who could drown out the others. The fifth floor featured girls whose dresses were slit up to the armpits, a stuffed whale, story tellers, balloons, peep shows, masks, a mirror maze, two love-letter booths with scribes who guaranteed results, 'rubber goods' and a temple filled with ferocious gods and joss-sticks. On the top floor and roof of that house of multiple joys, a jumble of tightrope walkers slithered back and forth, and there were see-saws, Chinese checkers, mahjong, strings of fire-crackers going off, lottery tickets and marriage brokers.

The Great World was one of the scenes of bloodshed early on in the Anti-Japanese War (1937–45) in Shanghai. The Japanese had provoked various incidents (by trying to enter the Chinese military airfield at Hongqiao, by demanding the withdrawal of all Chinese troops from Shanghai and by fighting) and the Chinese began a clumsy retaliation by air on 14 August 1937, first dropping a huge bomb on the Bund end of the Nanjing Road and then dropping two on the Great World. In the two incidents 1740 were killed and 1873 wounded. These accidents confused the flow of refugees, first fleeing into the city from the skirmishes outside, now fleeing out of the city away from bombing.

Throughout the next five years the Japanese increasingly insisted on control in Shanghai, in 1938 demanding that senior administrative posts, including that of Deputy Police Commissioner, should be given to Japanese, and they took control of the Customs. In 1941 the chairman of the Japanese Ratepayer's Association inexplicably tried to shoot J.H. Keswick, British chairman of the Shanghai Municipal Council, at a special General Meeting of Ratepayers, and on 8 December 1941, just after Pearl Harbour, the Japanese shelled the British riverboat HMS 'Peterel', killing seven and wounding seven. The attack on the 'Peterel' provides an early evidence of the threat on Shanghai in J.G. Ballard's novel 'Empire of the Sun'.

Life for most foreigners, however, continued much as usual until 1943, and is neatly described by Christopher Isherwood (1937):

It is the Ambassador's turn to give an official garden-party. The preparations are elaborate. They require the co-operation of the ladies of the British colony, the Seaforth Highlanders, the Embassy staff. Invitations are sent out. The drinks and cold buffet are organised...Next morning, the local newspaper will carry photographs of the most distinguished guests. Out on the lawn, the Scottish pipers play their airs.

Everything goes off like clockwork. It is a beautifully contrived charade, the perfect image of another kind of life—projected, at considerable expense, from its source on the opposite side of the earth...But gaily as the charade-players laugh, and loudly as they chatter, they cannnot altogether ignore those other, most undiplomatic sounds which reach us, at intervals, from beyond the garden trees. Somewhere, out in the suburbs, machine-guns are rattling.

And the Chinese were subject to persistent humiliation and terror. The refugee situation grew increasingly acute, with currency devaluation adding to the misery of those compelled to live in refugee camps on 'family bunks' or those who had to pay rent to live on a mere landing or in a room subdivided by sheets. Many of the 20,000 corpses picked up in 1937 were those of the homeless who had simply frozen to death in the streets.

In January 1943 all enemy nationals were interned by the Japanese in seven enclosures. Ironically, the same month saw the signing of a treaty between the British and American governments and that of Chiang Kai-shek in Chongqing, ending all extra-territorial rights and giving up the concessions. 8000 were interned, as life outside continued, murders and brutality the order of the day. Collaborators were murdered, there were reports of human flesh being sold as food became scarce, and Japanese bombers flattened parts of the Settlement and the French Concession. Yet such was the resilience of the Shanghainese, both foreign and Chinese, that within a year after the defeat of the Japanese (1945), despite civil war raging across China, the proportion of China's foreign trade passing through the city had almost doubled the pre-war figure.

On 25 May 1949 Communist troops peacefully entered the city and established a new, military government. In the first months foreign governments were keen to recognise and accept Mao's new regime for British commercial investments alone were thought to be worth £300 million. The Korean War of 1950, however, marked the beginning of the end although the Communists themselves were keen to maintain Shanghai's flourishing economy. The new Chinese government preferred to deal direct with governments rather than commercial intermediaries, and one by one the foreign trading houses shifted their bases away from Shanghai, often to Hong Kong. The government embarked upon an ambitious retraining programme for the thousands of prostitutes suddenly abandoned by their clientele, turning them into respectable cottonmill workers and eradicating venereal disease.

Shanghai did not visibly change much at first: the European buildings were reallocated and occupied by offices of the municipal government and, though Shanghai's port has recently been overtaken by Ningbo which is being developed as a deeper draught container port, Shanghai has remained a major manufacturing centre, a centre recognised throughout China as producing high-quality, well-designed goods. Shanghai enjoyed a brief further fling of leadership during the Cultural Revolution when a series of strikes in 1967 led to the formation of the 'Shanghai People's Commune' under the leadership of Zhang Chunqiao and Yao Wenyuan, later to be vilified as members of the 'Gang of Four', and a young worker, Wang Hongwen (later also classified as a member of the 'Gang'), rose to sudden prominence.

A. The Bund

The *Shanghai Mansions* (Shanghai daxia), formerly Broadway Mansions, a 22-storey red-brick building with art deco detailing, faces S down the Bund, standing on the northern bank of the Suzhou Creek opposite the Baidu Bridge, known to foreign residents as 'Garden Bridge', an iron structure built in 1906 to replace the wooden one, infamous during the Japanese occupation for all Chinese crossing it had to bow low to the Japanese soldiers on duty there.

On the other side of Changzhi lu, towards the Huangpu River, a series of consular buildings used to stand. Only the *Russian Consulate* remains, under repair (1987, after being occupied for years by the Seamen's Club; now the Russians have asked to occupy it again) for beside it, the American and Japanese consulates have disappeared under a new hotel (Hai e fandian), opposite the run-down Pujiang Hotel, once the prestigious Astor House Hotel (palm garden, cuisine under French chef, Trocadero tearoom at back).

Crossing the iron bridge, the river side of the Bund (Zhongshan lu) is still a garden, the riverside promenade that was once forbidden to dogs and Chinese, except those accompanying Europeans. Its entrance (for which, as with all gardens in China, there is a small fee) is in the bus station to the S.

Near the entrance to the garden is the pier from which the Huangpu pleasure steamers leave, twice a day (at 8.30 am and 1.30 pm) for a 3-hour trip up the Huangpu to its confluence with the Yangtse and back. Tickets can be purchased at the pier (28 Zhongshan dong lu, tel: 211098) and the first-class ticket, 15 rmb (1987), includes

snacks and a conjuring show if the docks pale. The trip passes the international passenger terminal, the container port, and the site of the Wusong fort, before reaching
the confluence of the muddy brown Huangpu and the clearer, salty water of the
Yangtse estuary. The best part of the trip is the view of the grand buildings of the
Bund on the return.

Immediately opposite the Shanghai Mansions, on the S side of the bridge,
is the old enclosure of the *British Consulate*, with trees and lawns and
flower beds as well as low stone buildings (replacing the original building
that was burnt down in 1870), the windows hung with tattered blue-and-
white awnings. There was a church in the NW corner and until a few
years ago the Shanghai Friendship Store was housed in the old consulate
so it was possible to enter. The *Friendship Store* is now in a huge new
building just around the corner (40 Beijing dong lu).

According to old maps, the building on the N side of Beijing lu and the Bund was the
Masonic Club.

Going S along the Bund, between Beijing lu and Zhenchi lu stood the
Yokohama Specie Bank, the Bank of China, a square skyscraper which
once housed the German Club and stands next to the green-tiled pyra-
mid-tower of the *Peace Hotel* (formerly Sassoon House and the Cathay
Hotel) which is on the corner of the Bund and Nanjing lu. Across Nanjing
lu is the annexe to the Peace Hotel, once the Palace Hotel.
     On the river side of the Bund, opposite the Peace Hotel, there is a wide
open space, one of the best places in Shanghai to watch elderly citizens
performing their graceful taijiquan morning exercises (from c 6.30 am).

Here once stood the Parkes Monument commemorating Sir Harry Parkes (1828–85),
British consul at Canton who 'distinguished himself' in the Arrow (or Second Opium)
War (1856) and became Commissioner at Canton after the capture of the city.
Between 1862 and 1865 he was consul in Shanghai.

The next turning off the Bund (S of Nanjing lu) is Jiujiang lu. Some 500m
along Jiujiang lu, standing back from the road, next door to a solid man-
sion-block now housing the Huangpu district government, is the small,
red-brick *Cathedral of the Holy Trinity*, built to designs of the distinguished British architect, Sir Gilbert Scott in 1866. It is said that his original designs would have cost too much so they were pared down in
Shanghai. A mixture of gothic windows and almost romanesque patterning in grey and red brick, the cathedral has not been used for worship for
years and is now under restoration (1987).

Retracing your steps to the Bund, the major buildings, mainly housing banks and
commercial institutions, were as follows: 33, British Consulate; 31, Yokohama Specie
Bank, the China Textiles Export Corporation, once the Jardine & Mathieson head-
quarters; 29, Banque de l'Indochine, 27, Benjamin & Potts (brokerage house); 26,
Mercantile Bank of India and Danish Consulate; 24, Japanese Chamber of Com-
merce; 22, Bank of China; 21, Nederlandische Handel Maatschappij; 20, Banque
Belge pour l'Etranger and Credit Foncier; 18, Chartered Bank of India, Australia and
China and Credit Foncier d'Extreme-Orient; 17, North China Daily News, also the
Canadian Trade Commissioner and the British Chamber of Commerce; 15, the
pinkish-yellow Russo-Chinese Bank; 14, Bank of Communications, the rusticated
stonework of the Customs House; 12, the classical façade and dome of the Hong
Kong and Shanghai Bank (now the seat of the Shanghai Municipal Government); 7,
Commercial Bank of China; 6, P & O Banking Corporation; 3, Shanghai Club, with
the longest bar in the world (over 30m long), now the Dongfeng Hotel; 1, Philippine
National Bank.

The **Shanghai Museum**. The Museum is easily reached from the Bund, as
it stands at 16 Henan zhong lu, near the junction with Yan'an dong lu
(which ends at the Bund). The high, pointed red-brick building was originally the headquarters of the Zhong Hui Bank which was set up in 1929
by Du Yuesheng and others. Du Yuesheng, associate of Chiang Kai-shek
and the 'Green Gang' of underworld thugs, chief of the illegal opium
trade, was president. The characters Zhong hui can still be seen

Shanghai: the Bank of China

engraved in the glass windows on the ground floor, and the building, with its open hall and galleries, retains the feeling of a grand banking hall.

The museum was established in 1952 and is unusual in that it reflects the history of collecting in China. Apart from the Gu gong in Peking whose 'founding collection' was that of the emperors (although it also includes later purchases and excavated items), the Shanghai Museum is the only museum in China to be based firmly in collection rather than excavation. The museum still obtains items from notable collections, as Nien Cheng describes in 'Life and Death in Shanghai' when, after her porcelains had been returned to her in 1979 (after confiscation in the Cultural Revolution and processing by the 'Bureau for Sorting Looted Goods'), the Shanghai Museum approached her asking to buy 15 pieces. Despite the difficulties of exhibiting paintings and sculpture in a bank, its displays are also the best-designed in China, the work of a staff-member of great talent. To date, the sculpture display and the bronze galleries have been redesigned; the ceramic gallery is the next to be transformed.

The *Bronze Gallery* on the first floor displays one of the great collections of bronzes in China; formerly grouped in strict chronological order, the collection is now arranged in a rough chronological order but grouped by type. The display includes a rare 'transparent mirror' of the Western Han which can both reflect an image and also display the designs cast on the reverse when a strong light is beamed on the reflecting surface. The display includes a section on bronze technology and cast designs.

The *Ceramic Section* on the second floor (where the gift shop is also situated) is fundamentally chronological but includes a final section reflecting contemporary production from famous kilns.

On the third floor, the gallery of *paintings* reflects the wealth of the collection but, owing to the fragility of Chinese paintings and the fugitive nature of the ink, very few of the paintings of the pre-Ming period are original; copies are displayed instead, to give a reflection of the development of pictorial art in China without harming fragile originals. Also on the third floor is a small *sculpture* exhibit; the first to be redesigned, with a chronological arrangement of the sculptures set against peach and ochre silks. A large number of the exhibits have English-language captions as well as Chinese.

B.   The Chinese City

Though the walls encircling the Chinese city were torn down in the first year of the Republic (1911), the form of the city is still indicated by the roads Zhonghua lu and Renmin lu.

Take Sichuan lu, cross Renmin lu (the road then changes its name to Lishui lu) and a large carpark appears on the left; this marks the entrance to the narrow grid of shopping streets surrounding the Yu yuan (Mandarin Garden) and the Huxinting Teahouse. To the left of a tall yellow-tiled building, the Shanghai lao fandian, a narrow path which runs under part of the Shanghai lao fandian leads, with a series of left turns, to the open square beside the pool across which a zig-zag bridge (now in pink concrete) leads past the teahouse. On the far side of the pool is the Yu yuan, behind it (approached from the back exit to the garden across Anren jie) is the Chenghuang miao (Temple of the City God); the whole area used to be part of the City God Temple Enclosure.

The *Huxinting Teahouse* (Pavilion in the Heart of the Lake), a five-sided building of two storeys with exaggeratedly upturned eaves to the grey-tiled double roof, was constructed in 1784 using money donated by a group of blue-cotton-cloth merchants. Originally used for cotton broking (the original regulations forbade the practice of medicine and fortune-telling as well as selling tea on the premises), the pavilion became a teahouse in the reign of the Guangxu emperor (1875–1908),

Shanghai: the Yu yuan

and remains a popular teahouse today. The bridge was built in its zig-zag form because of the Chinese belief that evil spirits could only travel in straight lines.

Opposite the teahouse is the entrance to the **Yu yuan** (Garden of Content), originally built by Pan Yunduan, an official who, though a native of Shanghai, had held high office in Sichuan province. Construction lasted from 1559 to 1577, and the garden was built for his father. It is a very characteristic southern garden, combining pools, rockeries, winding walkways and pavilions, creating an illusion of space and depth within a small area. A rather exaggerated feature is the dragon walls; grey overlapping tiles, reminiscent of the scales of a dragon, on top of the whitewashed dividing walls are finished off with dragon heads. The huge pock-marked rock standing in front of the *Yuhuatang* (Hall of Jade Magnificence), said by connoisseurs to fulfill all the desired qualities of a garden rock, being zhou, shou and tou (rough, craggy and holey), is said to have been destined for the imperial gardens. The Huizong emperor of the Northern Song (reigned 1100–26) sent 'notorious' rock-collectors to south China in search of treasures but this particular prize was shipwrecked in the Huangpu and was dredged up by Pan Yunduan for his garden.

The Yu yuan has a particular place in Shanghai's history, recalled in the *Hall of Heralding Spring* (Dianchun tang), for the Small Sword Society, a branch of the Triad secret society from the south, used the hall as their headquarters (1853–54), during the unrest of the Taiping uprising. Led by a Cantonese (ostensibly a sugar-broker but suspected of opium trafficking), Liu Lichuan, the Small Swords captured the Chinese city during the Taiping uprising, forcing the Chinese Daotai to flee into the British concession. Relics of the unsuccessful attempt to overthrow the dynasty in the shadow of the Taipings are displayed in the hall.

The detailed woodcarving of the timber doors and lattice windows, seen at its best in the *Sansui tang* (Three Ears of Corn Hall) which is carved with rice, millet, wheat and fruit, is exceptional but other details are also beautifully observed; note the curved fish carved on stone drain covers. Opposite the Sansui tang is a stone-carved essay on the garden by its builder; calligraphy and literary reference being essential features of the traditional Chinese garden.

The S part of the garden, called the *Inner Garden* (Nei yuan) was a later (1709) addition to the Yu yuan. In the centre of the E wall of the Yu yuan, between the original and inner gardens, is an exit into Anren jie; on the other side of the road is the old *Chenghuang miao* (Temple of the City Gods), built on the foundations of the 15C Jinshan miao, a temple built to commemorate the legendary general Huo Guang. The ceremonial archway, stage and main hall of the temple have been restored though the temple is a shadow of what it was when it was a centre of fairs and markets and seasonal flower shows: plum-blossom in early spring, followed by orchid displays and chrysanthemums in autumn.

To the N of the Chinese city, in the block bounded by Sichuan nanlu, Jiangxi lu, Renmin lu and Jinling dong lu, rises the spire of *St. Joseph's Catholic Church* which stood on Rue Montauban (Sichuan nan lu).—To the NW, at the crossroads of Xizang lu and Yan'an lu, stands the restored wedding cake tower of the old *Great World Amusement Centre*, now the Shanghai Youth Palace.

C.   Frenchtown

Stretching W from a narrow strip of waterfront, bounded on the E by Avenue Edouard VII (Yan'an lu) and the Avenue des Deux Republiques (Renmin lu) which runs along the northern edge of the Chinese city, the **French Concession** is at its most distinctively 'French' further W, the roads lined by plane trees (still associated in the Chinese language with the French), the windows of many buildings shuttered (in contrast with the tattered awnings of the old International Concession).

Whilst the commercial and banking sectors were concentrated in the International Settlement, apart from the smart shopping streets like Huaihai lu (Avenue Joffre), the French Settlement was largely residential. The streets are lined with narrow 'terraced' lanes interspersed with solid bourgeois houses with mansard roofs and shutters similar to those on the outskirts of any French town.

The central section of Avenue Joffre (Huaihai lu) used to be known as 'Little Russia' for it was here that most of the White Russian refugees congregated, including the bar hostesses (almost a White Russian monopoly) and such famous figures as the singer Alexander Vertinsky (whose great recorded hits included 'Magnolia' and 'The Mad Organ-grinder'). The section of Huaihai zhong lu just S of the Jinjiang Hotel is still full of cake shops, like the famous *Laodachang* on the corner of Maoming lu which advertises 'cake à la française' and sells wedding cakes, lemon-meringue pie, apple pie and ice cream and coffee. On the opposite corner is the *Cathay Theatre* (a cinema).

N, up Maoming lu, is the *Jinjiang Hotel*, a towering complex with herringbone brickwork and inset stone panels. Opposite the Jinjiang Hotel was the Jinjiang Club, formerly the Cercle Sportif Française, with ballroom, bars and huge swimming pool surrounded by wicker basket chairs. This has, unfortunately, been taken over by a Japanese concern and a modern tower-block hotel is being built in the beautiful, once extensive, garden.

Further N along Maoming lu is the *Shanghai Art Theatre*, formerly the Lyceum Theatre, opened in 1931 by the British Consul for the Amateur Dramatic Society. Along Changle lu (which crosses Maoming lu beside the Shanghai Art Theatre), on the corner with Shaanxi nanlu, is the *Hong fangzi* (Red House Restaurant, 37 Shaanxi nanlu), formerly Chez Louis, a restaurant specialising in western food—minestrone, chicken Kiev, stroganoff and soufflé Grand Marnier (during the Cultural Revolution you had to bring your own Grand Marnier).

Turn left down Shaanxi nanlu and take the first turning on the right, Xinle lu, with the green onion domes of what must have been the Russian Orthodox Church, on the corner with Xiangyang beilu. Turn left down Xiangyang beilu (which runs beside Xiangyang Park, on the left), to Huaihai zhong lu.

S of Huaihai lu down Shaanxi nanlu, at the point where it intersects with Yongjia lu, on the left is the *Wenhua gongchang* (Culture Square), formerly the greyhound racing centre or 'Canidrome', opened in 1928. NW of the Canidrome, at 7 Xiangshan lu (formerly Rue Molière), is the old *home of Sun Yat-sen* (he moved in 1920), with a garden behind in which he met delegates from the Communist Party. The two-storey house is said to be preserved as it was during his life, with the addition of interesting photographs, and 'most' of the items on display are original. It may be visited by appointment.

NW of Sun Yat-sen's house, at *76 Xingye lu*, is the grey-brick building where the first congress of the Chinese Communist Party was held in June 1921. The building is interesting, with its forbidding, windowless façade embellished with fine red, almost armorial tile work over the dark red door. Inside are the 12 chairs, teacups and ashtrays supposedly used by the delegates until the police raid forced them to move outside Shanghai. A small exhibition commemorates the history of the Communist Party and the fate of the 12 delegates (two later collaborated with Japan and almost all later clashed with Mao).

At the E end of Yan'an dong lu, near the Jing'an Guesthouse, 64 Yan'an dong lu, is the main *Children's Palace*, once the Kadoorie family residence, viewed by appointment only. Though there are 12 other 'children's palaces', places where children of working parents can go after school and where their special talents can be developed, this one is run

Shanghai: the Soviet-built Exhibition Centre

by the Municipality and the children selected because of their abilities. Music, painting and sports activities predominate, with special classes in academic subjects to promote talent, all in the grand rooms and fine garden of the pink, classical Kadoorie mansion.

Further E along Yan'an dong lu (1000 Yan'an zhong lu) is the *Shanghai Exhibition Centre*, built to Russian designs in 1955 (and virtually identical with the Beijing Exhibition Centre). The steel spire is topped by a red star and the huge enclosure of over 8360 square metres is built in the garden of what was once the Hardoon House. The exhibition halls contain displays of Chinese modern technology and light industrial products with a special display of locally produced arts and crafts which are sold at counters in the display area.

D.   The City Centre

Opposite the Jing'an Park, off Nanjing xi lu is the **Jing'an Buddhist Temple**, known to foreign residents of the past as *Bubbling Well Temple*, though its name, which dates from 1008, means Tranquil Peace Temple.

According to literary records, its history goes back to the Warring States period (238–251) but the original temple was situated on the N bank of the Wusong (or Suzhou Creek) and was moved to its present site in 1216 because the site was flooded. The new site was near the 'Bubbling Well'. This spring, called 'the eye of the sea' and 'the sixth spring in the world', was surrounded by a stone railing in the Qing but covered over after Liberation because it impeded traffic flow. The temple fell into ruins and the present buildings date from the Guangxu period of the Qing (1875–1909); they have been thoroughly restored recently.

Three main halls, with side buildings enclosing three courtyards, are constructed in the characteristic southern style: yellow-washed walls pierced with decorative circular openwork tile windows, and façades of dark-painted wood are topped with grey-tiled roofs. The ends of the eaves are curved and topped with openwork tile decoration whilst large fish acroteria curl on the straight ridges. Before Liberation the temple was famous for its abbot, 2m (6 feet 7 inches) tall, with a very wealthy wife, 'seven concubines and his own White Russian bodyguard'. There is a piece of stone-carved calligraphy in the temple, dating from 1183, written by the Guangzong emperor (reigned 1190–95) before he ascended the throne, as a celebration of the library of the scholar Qian Liangchen; the stone was moved to the temple when the library building was destroyed.

Further E along Nanjing xi lu is the great open space of RENMIN GUAN-CHANG (People's Square) and RENMIN PARK, the roughly circular form of the whole indicating that this was once the racecourse. On the E side of the square is a long dark building with a clock tower, once the club building, now the *Shanghai Library*, with one of the finest collections in China. Serving as a municipal library, the collections range from the general to a notable collection of 'shan ben' (rare or antiquarian volumes) that is second only to that in the National Library in Beijing.

This was the site of Shanghai's third racecourse, the first lying between Henan zhong lu and Jiangxi zhong lu and Nanjing dong lu (this was opened in 1851 and abandoned in 1853 when land prices in the area rose after the Small Swords uprising). The second was immediately to the E of the third, the curve of Hubei lu indicating its form. The grandstand was immediately next-door to the present Number One Department Store.

Again because of rising land prices, the racecourse was moved in the early 1860s, the acquisition involving a dispute over graves on the site which lasted more than 30 years. A memorial archway to Xu Yuanlai's wife (recorded in the local annals of 'chaste widows and virtuous women') stood inside the racecourse until Liberation, as the family refused to move it. When it was damaged, a director of the Race Club Board called Moller paid for its repair. Moller and his brother are described in a recent Chinese publication as 'out and out adventurers' whose house (now housing the Shanghai Municipal Committee of the Communist Youth League, 30 Shaanxi nan lu), was 'a building in a convex and concave shape with a spired roof and said to be in the Norwegian style', its garden filled with the graves of horses and grey-hounds, 'benefactors who helped the Moller brothers to become millionaires' through racing.

Huangpi bei lu runs beside the Shanghai Library and running between Huangpi bei lu and Chengdu bei lu is Jiangyin lu (parallel with Nanjing lu) where you can find the *Flower and Bird Market*. On the other side of the park, at 328 Xizang zhong lu, near the junction with Jiujiang lu is the old American *Baptist Church*, built in 1929 and still functioning.

Opposite Renmin Park on Nanjing lu are the two fine 1930s hotels, the *Guoji fandian* and, next door to it (No. 170), the *Huaqiao fandian* (Park Hotel) with a dining room which has a view over the park.

The next block E along Nanjing xi lu is the *Number One Department Store*, formerly the Sun Department Store; further along, on the corner of Zhejiang lu, is the *Number Ten Department Store*, formerly the Wing On Department Store and further down, again, the *Shanghai Number One Clothing Store* which used to be the Sincere Department Store.

The surviving cosmopolitanism of Shanghai is as evident on the Nanjing lu as on Huaihai lu; opposite the junction with Jiangning lu (with

Nanjing xi lu) is the *Number One Xibiliya* (Siberian) *Fur Shop*, and on the junction with Tongren lu is the *Shanghai Kafei* (coffee) *House*.

E.   Excursions

The old Jesuit centre of **Xujiahui**, the Xu family village, as its name implies, was once a village some distance from the old walled town of Shanghai. One of the members of the Xu family, Xu Guangqi (1562–1633), convert and pupil of the Jesuit Matteo Ricci, left land for the Jesuits to establish a seminary, observatory and church in Xujiahui, now a suburb in the SW of the city, where the Sheraton Hotel has been built, together with comfortable blocks of flats for 'returned Overseas Chinese'. The Jesuit settlement, known to foreigners as Siccawei or Zikawei, was founded in 1848 and the *Cathedral of St. Ignatius* was built in 1906 with its twin 50m spires and space for 2500 worshippers. The observatory is still in use. The cathedral is on Caoxi lu, just S of the Xujiahui roundabout (the terminus of the No. 15 bus from Nanjing lu and the No. 26 from Huai-hai lu). As with other religious buildings, there is no official entrance fee or opening times but the doorkeeper will admit visitors, and crucifixes and religious tracts can be purchased in lieu. The newly restored cathedral includes 'stained-glass' windows made from plastic by the pastors who worked in a plastics factory manufacturing umbrella handles during the Cultural Revolution (1966–76).

Just SW of the cathedral, in a park which is either called *Guangqi Park* or *Nandan Park*, on Nandan lu, is the *Tomb of Xu Guangqi* (a mound with a modern bust of Xu Guangqi in front of it).

The **Longhua Pagoda and Temple**, S of Xujiahui, lie in an area that was used for as a prison and execution ground, mainly for Communists in the pre-Liberation period by the Kuomindang and which is commemorated by a memorial on the W side of Caoxi lu. The pagoda is said to have been first built in the Three Dynasties (238–251, contemporary with the Jing'an Temple). It is an octagonal, seven-storey structure of wood and brick, with up-turned 'flying' eaves of grey tiles. The brick foundations date from the Song (977).

The temple buildings were founded in 687, according to literary records, and have been rebuilt many times. Those that stand today date mainly from the Guangxu period of the Qing (1875–1909). Similar to those of the Jing'an Temple, they include a Maitreya Hall, Hall of the Heavenly King, Grand Hall, Three Sage Hall and Abbot Chamber.

The area, and the temple in particular, has long been famous for its peaches, described in a couplet: 'a riverside village surrounded by willows, ten li [Chinese miles] of red peaches'. Visitors come especially to see the peach-blossom in spring.

On Anyuan lu, in NW Shanghai, the **Jade Buddha Temple** (Yu fo si) is a very late establishment (1882), set up by a monk from Putuo shan to receive a gift of white jade Buddhas from Burma, which were originally housed in the Jiangwan Temple. The temple was abandoned after the 1911 revolution but restored between 1918 and 1928. Of little architectural interest (except as a late version of the other southern-style temples in Shanghai), the major features are the two Buddha figures: that on the lower floor is a reclining figure less than 1m long, whilst upstairs is a seated Sakyamuni image, almost 2m tall, embellished with semi-precious stones. The temple is now fairly active with a number of monks in attendance, partly to cope with the tourist trade, partly for the faithful.

Hongkou Park, known to previous residents as Hongkew Park (laid out in 1905 in the Japanese quarter of the city), now, apart from rowing boats on the lake and the occasional autumn chrysanthemum display, houses the *Tomb of Lu Xun* (1881–1936) which was moved here in 1956, and a *Lu Xun Exhibition Hall*.

One of China's great modern writers, of short stories and satirical essays, Lu Xun was a pioneer of the baihua or plain-speech movement of the early 20C, attempting to break away from the stultified and incomprehensible prose of the ruling class and write in the plain language of ordinary people. A reformer, determined to change China for the better, Lu Xun spent some years in Shanghai (1933–36), living in a small three-storey red-brick house on Shanyin lu (No. 9, Luxincun), now open to the public. On the ground floor are the reception room and dining room; on the first floor, his study with writing desk and rattan chair by the window, and bedroom. On the third floor was his small son's room and a guestroom where Qu Qiubai often stayed. This was the house in which Lu Xun died.

In Hongkou Park his grave is marked by a seated statue and an exhibition hall detailing his life and work which, apart from his own writing, included active promotion of woodcuts as an art form and the revival of the dying woodblock fine-art printing industry.

In the western suburbs, bordering the Wusong River (Suzhou Creek) is **Zhongshan Park**. Laid out in 1914, it was known to the foreign residents of Shanghai as Jessfield Park. It contains impressive flower beds, notably of roses and peonies, and borders the campus of the old (missionary-founded, English-language) St. John's University, now the *Huadong zhengfa xueyuan* (East China Politics and Law Institute). Many of Shanghai's progressive entrepreneurs, including Rong Yiren, graduated from St. John's before 1949.

Shanghai Zoo. Situated near the airport on Hongqiao lu, the site used to be that of the golf course which was converted into a zoo in 1954. Covering over 80 hectares, this is one of the most pleasant zoos in China as the animals have a considerable amount of space to themselves. Species include Giant panda, Golden monkey, Red-crowned crane, Northeastern tiger, Asian elephant, Chinese alligator and Red pandas, which are particularly recommended as they make the most of the space available.

9 Suzhou

Suzhou lies in the S of Jiangsu province, on the Grand Canal, and is most famous for its silk and its gardens. Lying in the low, flat Jiangnan ('South of the Yangtse') area, the city, like Shaoxing, has been compared to Venice for it is criss-crossed with canals. The comparison is not particularly helpful for both Shaoxing and Suzhou, though important cultural centres, are more reminiscent of small country towns; their narrow canals lined with low, grey-tiled and whitewashed houses with steps leading down to the water where women wash clothes and vegetables. The town is less full of canals than it was in the past as many have been filled in, partly to improve road communications and partly for reasons of hygiene; thus, in more ways than one, the town has lost some of its atmosphere. Silk is produced in the neighbouring countryside and brought to the town for spinning and weaving and Suzhou houses the national Embroidery Research Institute. Though the famous gardens date back to the 10C, the most significant periods of garden building were the Ming and Qing when rich officials retired to the picturesque town, a centre of cultural activity (and of the publishing trade) and built themselves house-garden complexes for their old age.

The prettiness of the old town is reflected in folklore; in the saying that 'there is heaven above, on earth, Suzhou and Hangzhou'. Hangzhou's beauty is primarily scenic, Suzhou's man-made: the old whitewashed, grey-tiled houses of the town lying amid green rice-paddy and sparkling water, the green and peaceful gardens hidden behind white walls. Tradi-

Suzhou: hump-backed bridge

tionally, too, China's prettiest women come from Suzhou and the local dialect is regarded as particularly charming when spoken by women.

Railway: Suzhou is an hour away from Shanghai on the Shanghai–Nanjing line. The *station* is in the N of the town on Chezhan lu. The frequent trains to Shanghai and Nanjing make this the simplest means of access (and there is no airport).

Hotels: the main hotels for foreigners are the Nanlin Hotel, 21 Gunxiu fang (just N of Youyi lu), and the Suzhou Hotel (which houses the Suzhou branch of the China Travel Service) at 115 Youyi lu in the SE corner of the town (some 20 minutes from the railway station by taxi). In the very centre of the town is the Lexiang Hotel, 18 Dajing xiang, mainly reserved for Overseas Chinese. The first two are quite convenient, however, for they are close to the most perfect garden, the Wang shi yuan, and another, less frequently visited, the Cang lang ting, and the Twin Pagodas.

The town of Suzhou was first laid out by He Lu, king of the state of Wu which controlled the area in the 6C BC during the period of division (the Warring States). He is credited with digging canals to control the low water-table and floods of the Yangtse delta and digging a moat to surround the walled town. As late as the 1920s the walls, pierced with water gates, still stood (4km E to W and 5.5km N to S) and the city was often approached by boat (from Hangzhou, Yangzhou and Shanghai), the piers being located outside the Panmen gate in the SW corner of the wall. Boats are still used as a major form of transport between villages in the area. When He Lu died in 496 BC, according to tradition, his son Fu Chai buried him on Tiger Hill, W of the town. The great historian of the Han, Sima Qian (died c 90 BC), visited the town and was impressed by the beauty of its buildings.

Throughout the succeeding centuries Suzhou attracted many of the refugees who fled fighting in the north, and its economic importance was enhanced by the construction of the Grand Canal which made use of He Lu's Hangou canal (from Yangzhou to Huaiyin, linking the Yangtse and the Huai rivers) but extended water links from the Sui capital of Luoyang to Hangzhou (passing by Suzhou) in the south and Zhuoxian (near Beijing) in the north. This great burst of canal construction, which brought the rice and silk of the south to the north and to the Sui capital, took place between AD 605 and 611 and involved several million labourers.

Suzhou silk, made from silk cocoons raised in farms in the surrounding districts and fed on the low mulberry bushes that you will see lining paddy fields, was always highly prized. A 13C dandy of Hangzhou who would call his tailor instantly if there was anything wrong with the hang of his gown, wore shoes and stockings 'of fine satin and Suzhou silk'. The unreliable Marco Polo described the inhabitants of 13C Suzhou: 'They live by trade and industry, have silk in great quantity and make much silken cloth for their clothing.' He also described the canals and bridges that filled the town: 'there are fully 6000 stone bridges, such that one or two galleys could readily pass under them', and, despite the exaggeration in the number of grand bridges, it is clear from this and from other accounts that the shape and form of the city has not changed since.

During the Ming, when Suzhou became a fashionable cultural centre, a Mecca for retired officials, the silk industry adopted very intensive production methods. Workers were hired by large contractors as they could not afford their own machinery for spinning and weaving and, at the mercy of the contractors, they would queue up in their hundreds at dawn, hoping for a day's work. A rebellion in 1626, known as the 'Rebellion of the Five' as it was led by five workers, did little to improve their lot and stone-carved stelae from 1715, 1734 and 1822 have been found with edicts forbidding silk-workers to strike. In contrast to the Dickensian conditions of the silk-workers, one of the members of Lord Macartney's embassy to China (1792–94) described the town as: 'the school of the greatest artists, the most well-known scholars, the richest merchants, the best actors, the most nimble acrobats, is also the home of delicately-made women with tiny feet. It rules Chinese taste in matters of fashion and speech, and is the meeting-place of the richest pleasure-seekers and gentlemen of leisure in China.'

In 1860 the Taiping rebels captured Suzhou with ease and established themselves. Their leader, Li Xiucheng, lived in a grand house (now the Historical Museum) and a nearby garden was a grand mansion taken over by the Taipings.

The city was filled with famous gardens, built from the 10C to the late 19C (12 are now open to the public). The greatest concentration of private gardens is in Suzhou, built by retired generals, officials, scholars and painters, adjoining houses. The aesthetic of the Chinese garden, so influential in Japan (and thence reaching the West), is different from that of the West. For the Chinese it is an integration of dwelling, other buildings (built to admire aspects of the scene), water, freely available in watery Suzhou, rocks piled up into 'mock mountains' and, finally, plants. A garden must contain all of these elements and, since they were constructed within a crowded city, there is an element of miniaturisation in what is essentially intended as a microcosm of nature. The contrast with the great landscaped parks of the 18C English is complete. Though the Chinese sought to imitate nature, they did so in a tiny, confined space, by means of controlled views, rather than the great expanses of the English parklands. They sought the opposite in architecture, as in gardens: rather than a single great vista, they created a series of views and scenes, like a series of handscrolls being opened one after another. Another vital ingredient in the Chinese garden is poetry and calligraphy.

Poetry and quotation were the final touch to a garden (for a full account of how pavilions were named see Chapter 17 of the famous 18C novel by Cao Xueqin, 'The Story of the Stone', translated by David Hawkes, Penguin Books, 1973). Though the names of garden buildings seem simply charming—Pavilion of the Pagoda's Shadow, Retreat Among the Bamboos, Kiosk Where One Awaits the Hoarfrost, Pavilion of Distant Perfume—they are almost invariably literary in origin, quotations from famous poems which are appropriate to the building and its surroundings. The names were inscribed over the doors, and names for rocks or appropriate quotations were carved into the rocks themselves. Some gardens (like the Cang lang ting) make a special feature of calligraphy carved in stone and set into the garden walls so that the whole, with its allusive names and beautiful calligraphy becomes a sort of literary quiz-game where visitors must guess the origin and significance of a name.

The **Wang shi** (Master of the Nets) **Garden** is at 10 Shijin jie, virtually opposite the Suzhou Hotel. It is the best garden to visit first for its tiny size makes it easiest to grasp and it contains all the essential garden features.

It was originally the home of Shi Zhengzhi, an official of the Southern Song, when it was known as 'Fish Shade'. It later fell into disrepair. Its current name was adopted in the late Qing (1875–1908) and is obviously related to the former since the 'master of the nets' is a fisherman.

The garden lies to the W of the house and the entrance from Shijin jie is actually a back entrance to the whole enclosure which covers 8 mou (1 mou is 2.7 hectares or 6.6 acres). The garden, with its surrounding halls, is centred on a small pool surrounded by buildings, rocks, pines and a very old wisteria. Entering from the back, through a small courtyard which leads to the Staircase to the Clouds Hall, you are led to the right and approach the pool through one of two halls, the *Hall of Gathered Emptiness* or the *Verandah for Looking at the Pines and Studying Paintings* (the latter has a wonderfully carved wooden façade which can be fully opened to the view or closed so that the greenery and water is

Suzhou: the Wang shi Garden

glimpsed through wooden lattice). As you approach the central scene through these elegant halls, the principle of 'framing a view' is apparent. The halls and buildings have carved and pierced dark wood windows and doors and hanging screens carved with sinuous vegetation which frame the view beyond.

The pool is clear: lotuses and waterlilies were restricted in garden pools for the surface of the water was best left clear so that its varying moods, reflecting clouds and overhanging plants or stirred by wind, could be appreciated. On the right is a small six-sided *Pavilion* with exaggeratedly up-turned eaves, perched on rocks and with an elegant 'goose-neck' railing to sit against. The pavilion is called 'The Moon Sinks and the Wind Gets Up', suggesting that you can sit there and admire the reflection of the moon and the ripples of the wind on the water. In the back of the pavilion a mirror is set, to provide the illusion of a further view beyond.

The little pavilion sits against a whitewashed wall which is pierced with windows affording a view of the courtyard on the other side, full of plants, rocks and more buildings. The window openings are themselves decorative, made of plaster-covered wire, so that the view beyond is seen through a decorative lattice, another aspect of 'framing a view', creating the desired effect of walking past a series of paintings.

The Master of the Nets is an ideal garden to begin with, both because of its small size and because it still contains the ideal combination of house (including a library near the Shijin jie entrance) and garden, the latter including a vegetable plot to the W. Notice the paved stone floors, sometimes prettily made out of pebbles forming patterns and pictures, and the raised stone beds for seasonal flowers like roses and peonies; also the pot plants (including some fine cacti) and pen jing or 'pot scenes' where tiny plants are combined with volcanic rocks to create a truly miniature landscape. These can be moved around the garden and its buildings, stored when dormant and brought out when at their best.

The **Canglang ting** (Pavilion of Dark Blue Waves) is not far from the Master of the Nets. Turn left onto Shiquan jie and take the first left (Wuquequiao long); the entrance to the garden is across a bridge over a broad stream. This is one of the oldest of Suzhou's gardens.

In the late Five Dynasties (907–960) one of the military officials of the state of Wu-Yue, Sun Chengyou, had a villa on the site, which later fell into ruins. In the middle of the Northern Song Su Wuqin built a garden which was famous for its natural scenery and it was later inhabited by Han Shizhong (1089–1151), a noted military commander whose wife helped him in his military career by caring for his soldiers and even beating drums in battle. He led many successful campaigns against the northern invaders who were threatening the court and also suppressed banditry in south central China. Nevertheless, he was a supporter of Buddhism and Taoism and gave himself the name of 'the gentleman who lives in cool purity' though he had many honorific titles conferred on him by the grateful ruling house. He asked to be relieved of the post of Military Commissioner and retired in 1140 to a life of unpolitical peace. He greatly enlarged the garden which later came to be owned by a Buddhist temple.

The garden was rebuilt in 1697 and the entrance and the bridge over the stream date from that time. Further major renovations were carried out in 1874.

The name of the garden was suggested by Su Wuqin (or Su Zimei), who had owned it in the Northern Song. Himself a poet, he took the name from a passage in the 'Chu ce' (Songs of the South, by the 3C BC poet, Qu Yuan) where an old fisherman says that if the dark blue waters are clean, he washes his hat ribbons, if they are dirty, he washes his feet. The phrase came to stand for necessary adaptation to circumstances and a relaxed attitude, and the name recurs in other gardens.

The garden makes use of the water outside, in another favourite garden technique, 'borrowing a view'. This means making use of an external feature (a technique which can be seen in the Summer Palace at Peking where external pagodas set on hills form a focal point seen from within the garden). A number of pavilions and walkways offer views of the water outside, like the tiny *Watching Fish Pavilion* on the SW corner and the larger *Water Verandah* just to the W of the entrance. Within the garden the central focus is a 'mountainous area' of lake rocks, bamboos and trees, with the Dark blue waves pavilion perched on high. Inside the main entrance are several inscribed stelae with poems by Su Zimei and a bird's-eye view of the garden carved in stone. Stone carvings of calligraphy are a great feature of this garden, set in the walls of covered walkways around the central hillock and in other buildings, emphasising the importance of poetry and calligraphy in a Chinese garden.

At the back of the garden, in the N, is the *Mountain View Tower*, from which the hills SW of the town can be seen. Between this and the central mountain are a number of buildings including the *Five-Hundred Sages Hall* with portraits of eminent men. As with the richly carved front entrance of the Master of the Nets Garden, there are a number of carved bricks (grey bricks carved in high relief, a speciality of architectural decoration in Suzhou, also to be seen in Guangzhou and, in lower relief, in Peking).

Just N of the Cang lang ting, near the Suzhou Medical School, is the *Ke yuan* (Suitable Garden, also known as the Le yuan or Garden of Joy). This was part of the larger Cang lang ting Garden in the Song dynasty and was rebuilt as a separate garden in 1767. It used to house the Suzhou Library and now contains a pool surrounded by pavilions and dark groves and a winding walkway.

Returning to Shiquan jie, turn left and, at the junction with Renmin lu, turn left and go S down the main road. Not far down on the right is the **Confucian Temple**, almost totally rebuilt in 1864 after destruction during the Taiping uprising. It was originally a Song building (1034), and the only surviving early hall is the Ming (1506) main hall, seven bays wide, with fine brackets under the eaves and a moon terrace in front. In the temple several very important stone carvings are preserved. One is the map of the town (then called Pingjiang) dating to 1229, the earliest city map in China; the other is a star map of 1247, not the earliest star map

SUZHOU

from China (there is a 10C example on paper from Dunhuang now in the British Library), but one of the earliest to survive.

Continuing down Renmin lu, take the second major turning on the right, Xi er lu, and at the T-junction at the end of the road you are opposite the **Ruiguang Pagoda**. Though founded in AD 241, the present building dates from the Song (1119–25) and is seven storeys, 43m, high, octagonal in plan, with a brick core and wooden verandahs. Though the top finial and the eaves decorations are missing, the fine Buddhist carvings at the base remain. The pagoda was popularly believed to be associated with the well-being of the imperial family and in the 18C the mother-loving Qianlong emperor covered it with lanterns to provide light for his mother's soul after her death. When the pagoda was restored after the Cultural Revolution a Buddhist column in silver decorated with pearls, presented by the wife of an official in 1013, was found.

N of the Ruiguang Pagoda is the 'beamless hall' of the *Kaiyuan Temple*, all that remains of the original temple complex.

Built in 1618, this is one of several examples (others are on Wu tai shan, near Nanjing, in Taiyuan) of the type. A practical solution to the increasing deforestation of China in the Ming and consequent shortage of building timber, the beamless or brick-vaulted hall does not seem to have survived the Ming or enjoyed widespread acceptance. This was originally the temple library (and as a fireproof building was most suitable for the purpose; the only later example I know is the Qing Archive Building associated with the Forbidden City in Peking). It is in two-storeys, like the Wu tai shan example, with five doors. The brickwork is decorative.

Turning right down Dong da jie, the road curves round to the W. The *Panmen Gate* stands at the SW corner of the city, the only surviving part of the old city wall. The gate in its present form (restored in 1978) dates from 1351, standing over the moat that surrounds the town. Over the moat is one of the handsome hump-backed bridges that use to be legion in the town.

To return to the hotel area retrace your steps to the Ruiguang pagoda, take Xi er lu (leading E from the pagoda) to Renmin lu, turn left and take the second major turning on the right, Shijin jie.

Another itinerary that can be made on foot from the hotel area includes the Twin Pagodas, the Yi Garden, the centre of town and the Xuanmiao Taoist Temple.

From Shijin jie, go N up Fenghuang jie. After the second crossroads the next turning on the right is Dinghuisi xiang and the *Twin Pagodas*, all that remains of the original twin-pagoda temple which, from the name of the street (Street of the Temple of Certain Wisdom), was presumably originally named the Dinghui Temple.

Indeed there is a reference in the late 19C Suzhou gazetteer: '...in the Yongxi period of the Song (984–988), Wang Wenhan built two identical brick pagodas and that was how it got its popular name'. They were in fact built by Wang and his brother apparently in honour of their teacher (for both were successful in the bureaucratic exams) and are identical in every detail. Octagonal, seven-storeyed, they stand over 30m high and are relatively rare as identical twin pagodas are not often found in China, although in the Indian temples that provided the distant model for Buddhist there were always twin towers. In Chinese temples these have gradually become the twin bell towers that stand in the first court of most temples whilst pagodas have generally developed into 'single' structures. They are careful copies of timber constructions, with upturned eaves and supporting brackets all in brick.

There are doors on four of the eight faces, with brick lattice 'windows' on the other four. Both are topped with iron Ksatriya spires (said to be based on monastery flagpoles surmounted by gilt pearls, symbolising Buddhism itself), nearly 8m high. During restoration after Liberation, on the second storey, an inscription was found recording repairs in 1135 and stating that they were built in 982, a date which conflicts slightly with the 19C account and therefore baffles the literary-minded compilers of the 'Zhong guo ming sheng ci dian', but I would have thought the near-contemporary account would be more reliable.

Turn back to Fenghuang jie and, at the junction with Ganjiang lu, turn left and follow the road, crossing Renmin lu (the major N–S artery), then take the second turning on the right, Xinchun xiang. The **Yi yuan** (Garden of Happiness) is on your right.

Built in the late 19C on the site of the house of one of the ministers of the Ming period, Wu Kuan (1436–1504), also a noted poet and calligrapher, the garden is part of a major complex: separated by a narrow lane (called 'Minister's Lane') from the dwelling area to the S and with a large ancestral hall originally lying to the W. The official who rebuilt the garden in the late 19C is said to have spent 200,000 ounces of silver on it and, apart from gaining inspiration from other gardens, used famous and much admired rocks from three gardens that had been abandoned. The garden itself is built around a pool surrounded by rocks and broken into three parts by a crooked bridge virtually across the centre and a narrow bridge of rocks to the W.

The garden is entered from Renmin lu through a broad, empty courtyard with a pebble-patterned floor. Then the path winds westwards through courts and buildings until the crooked walkway that runs along the E bank of the pool, pierced with stucco openwork windows, is reached. The major viewing point for the central pool is the *Lotus-root Fragrance Hall* with its dark lattice façade which can be folded back to reveal the whole scene. On the far W side of the garden is a 'dry boat' (an open, rectangular pavilion built out into water) which provides a view back across the rocks that narrow the main pool.

Return to Renmin lu, go left and take the first turning on the left. At the junction turn right and the *He yuan* (Crane Garden) is at 4 Hanjia xiang.

It is a late Qing official's private garden. With a small central pool surrounded by rocks and a crooked covered walk, an entrance hall, the Four-sided Hall overlooking the pool, a library and main hall at the back, it is less full than many other gardens, the halls standing relatively clear of the rocks and water.

Returning to Renmin lu, turn left (N) and take the third turning on the right, a pedestrian road called Guanqian jie which leads to the **Xuanmiao Taoist Temple**, which lies on your left, behind the Friendship Store and Antique Store. First constructed in the 4C AD, it once covered a far larger area than it does today. The main *Hall of Three Pure Ones* dates to the Song (1179) when it was designed by the younger brother of the famous painter Zhao Boju. This hall and the great entrance gate which leads to it are all that survive of the early temple; the hall is the largest early Taoist building in China. It is 45m by 25m, nine bays wide and six deep, with a double roof with strong brackets supporting the up-turned eaves. The internal roof structure has curved 'moon' beams. There is a finely carved platform for the three deities in gilt stucco which are also thought to be Song. Outside the hall the carved stone railings with their human and animal figures have been much restored but the carvings on the SW corner are thought to be Song in date.

Though the temple was wrongly identified as Buddhist in the 1924 'Japanese Railway Guidea', the market function of this central temple was still apparent at the time: 'The temple is a favourite resort of the people of the city and in its compound, besides tea-houses, variety shows, photographers, etc., are open-air stalls where various articles are sold. The street in front of the temple is one of the busiest…'.

If time allows, three further gardens can be reached on foot: the Huan xiu shan zhuang and Yi pu to the W or the Ou yuan to the E.

The **Huanxiu shanzhuang** (Village Encircled by Splendid Mountains) is at 280 Jingde lu which is the W continuation of Guanqian jie (on the other side of Renmin lu). It is very near the *Embroidery Research Institute* (visited by appointment and usually included in tourist itineraries) where the most extraordinary, almost painfully fine, double-sided embroideries are produced, with different pictures on either side of a piece of translucent silk gauze (sometimes the back and front of a kitten or a puppy). It is also possible to see the production of *kesi* woven silk tapestry, once widely used in imperial clothing and previously always done by men whilst the embroidery is generally a women's craft. Still highly prized in Japan and used to mount Tibetan tankas, the last time I visited the Institute the *kesi* loom was still being used by a man.

The Huan xiu shan zhuang was built as an official's private residence in the Qianlong period (1736–96), on the site of a Five Dynasties garden and a Ming villa; with the exception of the Autumn Mountain Residence, most of the other buildings had disappeared before 1949. This small garden is one of the most 'mountainous' and is a complex maze of mountain and water. The piled rock mountains are said to have been constructed by the famous mountain-maker, Ge Yuliang, in the Qianlong period. Constructed in a tiny space (about 2.4 hectares), mountains are the major feature, with a twisted figure-of-eight water channel as the secondary feature, sometimes appearing in deep gullies beneath the piled rocks which are ascended by steps. There is a charming zig-zag bridge in the SW corner, low over the water.

Just to the NW of the Huan xiu shan zhuang, across a small canal, off Wuqu fang (which runs along the W side of the canal) at Wenwu nong is the **Yi pu** (Garden of Skill), built in the Ming and later owned by Wen Zhenmeng, great-grandson of Wen Zhengming (1470–1559) a local painter, one of the most prominent figures responsible for the growth of Suzhou as an artistic and cultural centre.

Significantly for art historians, Wen Zhengming is one of the first Chinese painters and calligraphers whose work has survived in reasonable quantity. When his great-grandson owned the garden, it was known as the Physick Plot, presumably because it was planted with medicinal herbs. Consisting of an almost equal area dedicated to house and garden, the garden contains a pond (the focal point) with a rockery beyond, best viewed from the house. Though the garden is thought to preserve most of its late Ming–early Qing features, a painting by the Kangxi-period (1662–1723) artist Wang Hui reveals that the Waterside Pavilion was a simple platform at the time with a pavilion to the W which had, apparently, disappeared before 1949. The major water surface is broken by waterlilies and also by two low bridges, one low on the water, zig-zagging across a corner, the other very slightly arched but still low. Though the pool, with its built-up centre, provides the main focus of the garden, a moon gate (circular opening in a wall) leads to a further courtyard in the SW corner so that the whole of the garden is not visible all at once—a major feature in Chinese garden planning.

To reach the **Ou yuan** (Paired Garden), near the Zoo in the NE corner of the city, continue E along Guanqian jie to the junction with Lindun lu. Turn left along Lindun lu and take the fourth turning on the right, Liuzhi xiang. When you reach the outer moat, the Ou yuan is on your right, at 6 Xiaoxinqiao xiang. The space is mainly occupied by fine buildings, and the garden gets its name from the fact that there are two separate garden areas to the E and W of the dwellings.

The proportion of building to garden, particularly in the W, where the garden area is very small, is more reminiscent of the north of China where small garden plots were often associated with grand houses. The domestic buildings are characteristic of Suzhou, with whitewashed walls and façades consisting almost entirely of dark wooden lattice backed with white window paper. The rockeries in the western garden are very varied, not only consisting of the characteristic pitted pale-grey lake rock but also the more solid chunks of 'yellow rock'. In the centre of the pool in the western garden is a charming open pavilion called, appropriately, the Pavilion Between Mountains and Water. The long pool surface is broken again to the N by a low zig-zag bridge. The entire complex is set between water to the N and S.

In the N of the city, reached by a No. 2 bus (going N up Fenghuang jie) from the E side of the Nanlin Hotel, getting off at the sixth stop on the corner of Xibei jie and Lindun lu, are the Suzhou Museum, the Beisi Pagoda, and two major gardens, the Zhuo zheng yuan and Shi zi lin.

The **Shi zi lin** (Forest of Stone Lions) is on Yuanlin lu, which runs N–S off Shilinsi xiang, a turning off Lindun lu, just S of its junction with Xibei jie. It is 'one of the four great gardens' of Suzhou and the one that is perhaps most in the Chinese taste, more inaccessible to Europeans unless they are very fond of the pitted, oddly shaped lake rocks that are the major feature of the garden.

It was originally constructed in 1342 as a back garden of a temple built by a monk to commemorate his master. Four famous garden designers were involved and the garden's name is taken partly from the Lion Cliff where the Zen master had lived, partly from the significance of lions as guardians of the Buddhist faith, and partly from the fact that the stones are considered to resemble lions. There is a picture of the garden by one of the best-known of all China's painters, Ni Can (c 1301–74), obviously made soon after it was completed. While some appreciated the garden greatly, the later writer Shen Fu in his 'Six Records of a Floating Life' (1809) said that the 'most famous place in Suzhou itself' reminded him of a heap of clinker 'covered with moss and ant-hills, without the least suggestion of the atmosphere of mountains and forests', and added, 'In my humble opinion there is nothing particularly wonderful about it'.

One of the larger gardens, despite its name, it also contains a considerable central pool, crossed by a zig-zag bridge which passes through the Pavilion in the heart of the lake and also featuring a stone boat. The buildings which lie N–S along the side of the garden (and through which it is entered) are particularly fine, with delicate lattice tracery set under the eaves of walkways and pavilions and a multitude of differently shaped doors cut through the whitewashed walls. It is said that the last private owners of the garden were relatives of I.M. Pei, the Chinese American architect who built the Xiangshan Hotel (Peking) and the new Bank of China building (Hong Kong) as well as sections of the Louvre in Paris and many buildings in the USA.

Just N of the Shi zi lin, on Xibei lu, is the grand *Mansion* once inhabited by Li Xiucheng, leader of the Taiping rebellion, when Suzhou was the Taiping headquarters in 1860.

It was originally the residence of the adjoining Zhuo zheng yuan, taken over and converted for the Taiping 'King' and, with the defeat of the rebellion, used as his headquarters by Li Hongzhang who was in charge of suppressing the Taipings.

Parts of the original have been destroyed, though the main axis remains impressive with double gate, main hall and back hall. The courtyards on either side of the main axis were those built by the Taipings. Behind is a garden on which noted craftsmen worked and which still includes a Mountain-viewing Tower and Magnolia Pavilion. The stone lions in front of the main gate, the lattice windows of the double hall and the painted beams all date from the Taiping era.

The building now houses the *Suzhou Museum*. Exhibits are arranged chronologically and refer to local excavations and finds. They stress the canal-building and related technology and, later, silk technology. Three of the stelae forbidding strikes are displayed in the museum, as well as rubbings of the early town and star maps.

Immediately E of the Museum is the **Zhuozheng yuan** (translated as either the Humble Administrator's Garden or the Plain Man's Politics Garden). This is considered the greatest of all the Suzhou gardens and it is certainly the largest. It is therefore better to see the smaller gardens first to enable one to see how the simple can be expanded into the complex.

It was laid out in the mid 16C by a retired censor Wang Xianchen and the name, appropriate to a retired official, was taken from an earlier writer who said that in cultivating a garden one met one's daily needs and that is what is meant by 'the politics of the plain man'. Wang's son later gambled away the family fortune and the garden was sold many times in the succeeding centuries.

The garden is laid out in two major parts, E and W, separated by a wall, and water is a major feature in both. The major water area is broken up by islands. The central part contains a large hall, the *Hall of Distant Fragrance* (named for lotuses planted nearby whose fragrance is supposed to waft towards the hall), which faces an island on which stands the *Hall of the Scent of Snow and Rosy Clouds*. The island is linked by zig-zag bridges to a central dyke, to the W, which is viewed from the *Magnolia Hall* on the S side of the garden. On the far side of the dividing dyke, which is crossed by a covered walk, a smaller, more irregular pool is created by a a triangular island, linked by low bridges to the N bank. The dividing wall between E and W is pierced with openings and the eastern part of the garden is less full of rocks and buildings, almost bare in comparison with the rest.

A painting of the garden by Wen Zhengming (1470–1559) shows that more of the banks beside the water were left as natural earth than is apparent today where most are rock-covered. There are also fewer water plants in Wen Zhengming's depiction.

To the right, along Xibei jie, is the *Beisi* (North Temple) *Pagoda*, all that remains of a former temple complex, traditionally said to date back to the Three Kingdoms (220–280) though the present structure is fundamentally Song (of the Shaoxing reign period, 1131–63). It is a nine-storey, octagonal pagoda, 76m high, with a brick base and external structure of brick and wood with a wooden staircase which can still be ascended. The grey-tiled roofs of each storey are sharply up-tilted in the southern style and climbing the pagoda to get close to the eaves is a good way of seeing southern architectural structure close to. Below is a teahouse.

Just outside the town, to the W are two more gardens, the Liu yuan and the Xi yuan. These can be reached by taxi or a No. 2 bus going W from just beside the Nanlin Hotel (alighting at the seventh stop). A road leads N from Fengqiao lu and the Liu Yuan Garden is to the right (E), the Xi yuan to the left (W) on the first crossroads (Liuyuan lu).

The **Liu yuan** (Garden to Linger In) is one of the largest in Suzhou, comparable with the Zhuozheng yuan.

It was originally one of a pair of gardens, E and W, laid out by a Ming official, Xu Shi-tai. In 1800 a new garden was built on the ruins of the old E garden and, since the owner at the time was surnamed Liu, it was called the Liu Garden. As the surname and the character meaning 'to linger' are pronounced in the same way, the garden gradually acquired its present name as a pun.

There is a pool in the centre of the garden, surrounded by rocks, with a further rocky area to the W and a mixture of building, courtyard and rocks to the NE. The garden is entered through the substantial ancestral hall (the domestic buildings were to the E of this but no longer exist) which ends in a stone platform looking out over the pool. Characteristically, the water is broken up: to the right is a tiny island, *Xiao penglai* (Miniature Island of the Immortals), reached from a rocky promontory by a crooked bridge. In the far left-hand corner a channel, crossed by several small bridges, leads off towards the covered walkway that runs along the W and N sides of the pool.

To the E of the central pool is an area that is as naturalistic as is possible in the man-made world of the Chinese garden whilst the more complex eastern side of the garden includes the *Hall of the Spirits of the Five Peaks*, surrounded by rocks, the tiny *Place where I Read Books* overlooking a rockery and close to the *Hall of Tall Trees and Springs* with the small *Pool for Washing Clouds*. There are several small courtyards in this part of the garden, with calligraphic inscriptions over the door, decoratively paved floors and raised beds of bamboo or single massive lake rocks in the centre of the small enclosure, providing a rich series of small spaces. Opposite the *Hall of Mandarin Ducks* in the far NW corner of the garden is the *Cloud Cap Peak*, a huge, single lake rock, pitted with holes, remarkable for its size (for many of the rockeries are skilful concoctions of much smaller stones).

The **Xi yuan** (West Garden) was originally the pair of the Liu yuan, built as part of his private garden by Xi Shitai in the Ming. This part of the garden was later given by his son (an official of the Board of Works) to a Buddhist temple. During the Taiping uprising (1860), which destroyed so many buildings in Suzhou, the temple was burnt down and subsequently rebuilt in the late 19C. The *Jiechuang* (Vinaya Pillar) *Temple*, though obviously late, is considered a fine example of southern temple building with its grand halls with upturned eaves, and the Hall of 500 Lohans, built as a copy of the Lohan Hall of the Lingyin Temple at Hangzhou, is important as the model was subsequently destroyed. The garden area is now to the W of the temple. It consists mainly of a large pool with a small six-sided pavilion in the centre, reached by zig-zag bridges.

Further outside the town to the W are the Hanshan Temple and Tiger Hill, best reached by taxi or tourist bus. For the intrepid: take a No. 4 bus from beside the Nanlin Hotel (heading N) to its terminus inside the Changmen Gate. Outside the gate on the other side of the moat is a bus station. From there you can take a No. 6 to the Hanshan Temple (alight at the fourth stop) or a No. 5 to Tiger Hill which is the terminus.

The **Hanshan Temple** stands opposite a fine hump-backed bridge on a canal, the *Maple Bridge*.

The temple itself was founded under the Liang (502–557) but takes its present name from one of two famous monks of the Tang dynasty who are said to have lived here. Hanshan (Cold Mountain) was an early 7C Chan (Zen) Buddhist monk and poet, 300 of whose poems survive. He was very friendly with another monk, Shide, and stone-carved depictions of the two in the temple show a couple of tubby and jolly men with slightly wild hair and dishevelled robes. The temple was, like the Jiechuang Temple and so many others, destroyed in the Taiping uprising and subsequently rebuilt, mainly in the late 19C.

Recent rebuilding, particularly of the entrance, is evident for the photograph in the 1924 'Japanese Railway Guide' shows a western influence to the contemporary gateway which was curved with a sort of Dutch gable effect and decorated with lozenge designs in different coloured bricks, rather different from the yellow-washed walls of today. One of the most famous aspects of the temple was its bell which has been returned to the bell tower: a Tang poem by Zhang Ji (inscribed in Wen Zhengming's calligraphy on a stone preserved in the temple) entitled 'Anchored at night by the

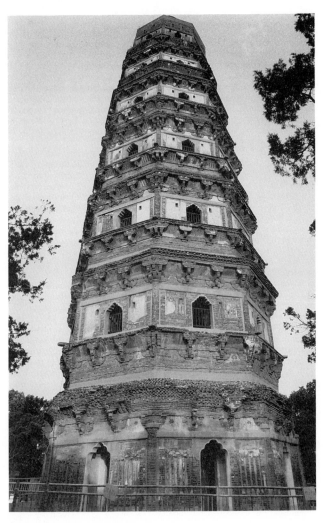

Suzhou: pagoda on Tiger Hill

maple bridge', includes the lines: 'The moon sinks, the crow calls and the night is filled with frost; under the Maple bridge, the glare of lanterns prevents sleep. Outside Suzhou is the Hanshan Temple, in the middle of the night I can hear its bell from my boat'. The original bell was lost and the Ming copy was taken away by the Japanese; the writer and reformer Kang Youwei (1858–1927) wrote a poem in reply, some 1000 years later (also inscribed on stone in the temple): 'The sound of the bell is over the eastern sea; cold silence fills the Hanshan temple'. The bronze bell now hanging in the bell tower was cast in 1905 by a Japanese as a gift to the temple.

NW of Suzhou is TIGER HILL, a multiple scenic spot.

It is varying described as having been the site of the 'travelling palace' (or alternative palace) of the kings of Wu during the Spring and Autumn Period, or the imperial mausoleum of He Lu, founder of Suzhou and King of Wu. The hill derives its name from the legend that a protective tiger appeared on the hill three days after He Lu was buried. Others say that the hill is in the shape of a crouching tiger, hence the name. In the Eastern Jin (317–420) villas were built here, later a temple, called Tiger Hill Temple. In the Tang the temple had to change its name for 'tiger' (hu) appeared in one of the names of the founder of the Tang dynasty and the character was therefore declared taboo.

This practice of outlawing characters that occurred in imperial names was common in the Tang and later dynasties; it made life difficult for writers and could even bring a sentence of death if ignored, even inadvertently. It also became a forger's weapon: documents would be prepared using the common 'substitute' characters used to avoid the taboo characters in the hope of providing a false date. The temple regained its name in the mid Qing.

A path starts at the bottom of the hill with the first gateway, crosses a bridge and leads up to the second gateway known as the *Broken Beam Hall* because of the oddly shaped, 'moon' beams used inside; it was originally constructed in the Tang and rebuilt in 1338. Beyond it, to the right of the path is a huge boulder split in two—according to legend this was when He Lu tried one of his swords on it (the swords of the period made in Suzhou were famous).

Passing a restaurant on your left, and the 'pillow rock' where the monk Shengong is said to have rested, a path to the right leads to the *Zhenniang Tomb*, said to be that of an honourable widow of the Tang dynasty who was to be sold as a concubine after her husband's death but committed suicide to avoid the disgrace. Ahead, slightly to the right, is a plateau covered with stones, called the *Thousand Men Stones*; according to one legend they are the followers of He Lu, incarcerated with him when he was buried (as had been the custom). To the right is a lotus pool, to the left, the *Pool of Swords* is a deep cleft in the rock, surrounded with rocks covered with calligraphy (the largest inscription beside the cleft reads Tiger Hill Pool of Swords). This is said to be the tomb of He Lu, buried with his huge collection of swords, hidden beneath the water.

Crossing a bridge, the path winds up to the leaning *Pagoda* of Tiger Hill. Built between 959 and 961, it is the earliest Song pagoda surviving but preserves many Tang features (especially in the interior which is painted). Built of brick in imitation of wooden construction, it is octagonal, seven-storeyed and stands 47.5m high with an incline of some 3m. In 1957, when repairs were carried out to strengthen the pagoda and prevent further inclination, workmen found sutra caskets and a record of the date of construction (now housed in the Suzhou Museum). A tapering cone in form, the pagoda is valued for the particular closeness of the brick construction to wooden architecture, both internal and external.

Surrounding temple halls on the hill are all late 19C, dating from after the Taiping destruction.

Beyond the Hanshan Temple, c 7km outside the town is the **Lingyan Hill and Temple**. The hill is covered with springs and oddly-shaped stones, the larger ones identified as resembling 'drums' or animals, the smaller, fine-grained stones used as inkstones (for grinding ink for painting and calligraphy). These were (according to Mi Fei, the famous 11C painter) slowly roasted after being cut to shape, which coloured them purple. The hill is still a very popular burial place; hundreds of tombs can be seen on the slopes.

The existing **Lingyan** (Cliff of Spirits) **Temple** was built on the ruins of one of the Qianlong emperor's 'travelling palaces', specially built or converted for one of his six, immensely expensive tours of inspection of the Yangtse Valley (1751–84).

The fact that the emperor (and his grandfather before him) stayed here underlines the Chinese appreciation of the site with its strange stones and pretty springs. The old temple and 'travelling palace' were destroyed in the destructive Taiping uprising in 1860 and rebuilt after 1927.

The temple, perched on top of the hill, contains a *Hall of Heavenly Guardians*, a bridged courtyard with a pool and a large central hall with lohan figures. The temple and its pagoda were said to be originally Song in foundation, rebuilt in the Ming and heavily restored in 1980. The pagoda's wooden interior was destroyed by lightning in 1600 though the brick exterior was unharmed. It is a tapering, pointed, almost rocket-like structure.

10 Hangzhou

Hangzhou is the capital of Zhejiang province, which, with its numerous waterways and rice-fields, contains most of the features which gave rise to the appellation 'land of rice and fish', applied to the region 'south of the Yangtse' (Jiangnan). Fish were caught in rivers and streams and reared in special pools set amongst the irrigated paddy fields. The towns and villages of the Jiangnan area are criss-crossed by waterways and filled with riverine streets and hump-backed bridges of great charm. Hangzhou lies on the bank of the Qiantang River, which winds its way to the sea (the Bay of Hangzhou), c 100km to the E. To the W of the city is the West Lake, and the city marks the southern end of the Grand Canal (a section built in the Sui dynasty). Set in the fertile Yangtse delta area, the surrounding farmlands produce rice, hemp, silk cocoons and fish. The local tea, Longjing or 'Dragon Well', is one of the most famous in China. Long famous as a beauty spot, the West Lake of Hangzhou has been painted and praised in poetry for centuries.

Airport: the new terminus, some 16km outside the town, was completed in 1972 for President Nixon's first visit to China. There are daily flights from Beijing and Guangzhou, flights every day except Thursday from Shanghai and less frequent arrivals and departures from Fuzhou, Guilin, Hefei, Hong Kong, Nanjing, Ningbo, Shenyang, Tianjin, Wuhan, Xiamen and Xi'an.

Railway: the station is in the W of the town; Hangzhou is some 4 hours by train from Shanghai. It lies on the Ningbo–Shanghai line and is a major terminus on the eastern route S from Shanghai, with frequent trains.

Boat: it is not uncommon now for tourist groups to arrive in Hangzhou from Suzhou by steamer, a method of travel also possible for individuals. The boats arrive in the NW of the city, near the long-distance bus station.

Hotels: the major hotels are grouped around the lake. The most prominent is the Shangrila Hotel on the NW corner of the lake (2 Yuefen lu) with the attached Xiling Guesthouse just behind it. The local office of the China Travel Service is in the Shangrila Hotel. Others include the Huaqiao (Overseas Chinese) Hotel (92 Hubin lu) on the E side of the lake, the nearby Dahua Hotel (185 Nanshan lu), and a number of guesthouses around the shores. The Shangrila Hotel is taken as a starting point for excursions.

Hangzhou does not have a very long history for it took time for the river to silt up and enclose the West Lake, once an inlet off the estuary. By the 6C AD, when the S part of the Grand Canal was built (to reach the plentiful supplies of rice from the Hangzhou area), the city was walled, though it was still frequently threatened by flood as the lake waters flowed out into the river. The latter is itself raised every month by the famous Hangzhou bore when strong tides force the river water back inland. At the autumn equinox, usually around 23 September, the Hangzhou bore is most spectacular, with a wall of water, at its highest some 7m high 75km downriver from Hangzhou. It is said to roar as thunderously as the Niagara Falls.

From this early period, the lake was divided by a sandbank linking the small Gu shan Island (opposite the Hangzhou Hotel) with the northern shore. During the Tang, the first dyke (the Bai Causeway) was built with bridges with locks to control the flow of water. The dyke was strengthened by a famous poet, Bai Juyi, who was an official serving as governor of Hangzhou in the early 9C (and it is still called after him). A later dyke, creating the 'western inner lake' running N to S, was built by another famous poet, Su Dongpo, when he, in turn, served as Governor between 1089 and

1091. This second dyke is named for him, Su Dyke. Just prior to Su Dongpo's period of service, during the Five Dynasties period (907–978) when Hangzhou was ruled by the independent kings of Wu Yue, pagodas and temples were built around the lake and one, the Liu he ta (Pagoda of Six Harmonies) still stands (much restored) on the banks of the Qiantang river; this was constructed in the hope of subduing the threatening bore. Hangzhou's development was vastly encouraged when it was chosen as the capital of the Southern Song, after the court had been driven from the capital, Kaifeng, by the invasion of the north in 1126.

Though Hangzhou was reduced to ruins by the Taiping rebellion in 1860–62 and all its major temples and buildings were destroyed, there are numerous accounts both in Chinese and western languages testifying to its magnificence in previous centuries. Odoric of Pordenone (1286–1331), who visited the city in the early years of the 14C, had never seen 'so great a city'. He described how it was crammed with buildings: 'houses of ten or twelve storeys high, one above the other' and 'eleven thousand bridges'. A surviving plan of the city from 1274 shows the ramparts surrounding the town, c 16km long and doubled on the river side, to protect the town from naval attack. A central Imperial Way ran from the Imperial palace in the north to the altars to heaven and earth in the south. The population at the time was over one million and Marco Polo noted the Mongols' imposition of household registration by which all the inhabitants had to list at the door those who lived within, scratching out the names of the dead and adding those of the newborn.

The multi-storeyed houses (extremely rare elsewhere in China and during later periods), crammed into the walled city, were very vulnerable to fire. Fires broke out almost every other month in the early years of the 12C until a fire-prevention system was established with watch-towers provided with scythes, hatchets and buckets. There was plenty of water for fighting fires for the city was criss-crossed with canals which, in the early years of the Southern Song, were lined with stone balustrades to prevent drastic numbers of drunken revellers from falling in. Ten great markets supplied the huge population with food: cereals, fish and pork were the staples but the rich could enjoy lotus seeds, 11 varieties of apricots, pears, paw-paw, shellfish, venison and other luxuries.

Such was the sybaritic life of the rich in Hangzhou that there were petshops selling fish for pet cats and items for cricket cages and it seems that some people even used to dye the coats of their pet dogs and cats with pink balsam leaves crushed with alum (a preparation normally used by women to tint their fingernails). One man was said to have covered the floor of his house with tiles inlaid with silver. The tender jasmine flower was brought in from Fujian province to scent the houses of the rich. There were restaurants and teahouses near the Imperial Way but the lake itself was a major pleasure area, its surface covered with boats for hire, boats full of sing-song girls, jugglers, operatic performers and musicians, restaurant and teahouse boats, with tiny boats paddled by peasants selling snacks amongst the grander barges. There was a special area for male prostitutes outside the New Gate.

Despite the conspicuous consumption of Southern Song Hangzhou, a 13C account summarises Hangzhou's enduring attraction to the Chinese (the reason that it attracted so many famous poets as Governor): 'Green mountains surround on all sides the still waters of the lake. Pavilions and towers in hues of gold and azure rise here and there. One would say a landscape composed by a painter. Only towards the east, where there are no hills, does the land open out, and there sparkle, like fishes' scales, the bright coloured tiles of a thousand roofs' (Jacques Gernet, 'Daily life in China on the Eve of the Mongol Invasion', Stanford University Press, 1970).

During the Ming Hangzhou remained a trading centre, visited by many foreigners, and it was then that the silk industry began to flourish in the town. In the Qing it was a popular place for Chinese tourists who used simple woodblock guidebooks with illustrations of the temples and pagodas in the lakeside hills.

It was during this period that the major sights of the area were classified according to traditional practice: tourist sites were supposed (ideally) to have ten 'prospects' and this love of numbers persists in Chinese in, for example the 'Ten Great Buildings' of the Great Leap Forward in Peking. As with so many other placenames in gardens, the view is associated with an activity or a season at which the prospect is at its best. One of the ten is some distance from the lake: this is the Twin Peaks Piercing the Clouds, two hills by the side of the road to the Lingyin Temple. The others surround the lake: Lotuses Stirred by the Breeze from the Distillery (just S of the Yue Fei temple), Spring Dawn at the Su Causeway (in the centre of the causeway crossing the lake from N to S), Observing the Fish at the Flower Harbour (in the Huagang Park at the SW corner of the lake), Reflection of the Moon Above Three Deep Pools (the three stone pagodas rising from the lake near the Island of Little Oceans), Setting Sun by Thunder Peak Pagoda (S tip of the lake shore), Sound of the Evening Bell Below Southern Screen Hill (by the Jingci Temple, whose bell has since disappeared, near the SE corner of the lake), Listening to the Orioles in the Willows (in the Children's Park on the E side of the lake where the orioles would be silenced by today's children), Snow on the Bridge (by the Brocade Belt Bridge on the Bai Causeway at the NE corner of the lake) and Autumn Moon on the Lake (on Gushan Island).

Hangzhou was favoured by the Kangxi and Qianlong emperors (much of whose clothing was made from Hangzhou silk brocades). The Qianlong emperor built a palace on the Gushan Island in the lake. It included the Wenlan ge Library housing one of the second series of manuscript collectanea, 'Si ku quan shu' (Complete Library of the Four Storehouses). There were four sets of the collectanea made for library buildings in Peking (one for the Forbidden City, one for the Old Summer Palace), Chengde and Shenyang, and a subsequent three sets were copied for Hangzhou, Yangzhou and Jinjiang. The Wen lan ge on the island in the lake was looted during the Taiping occupation of Hangzhou (1860–62), when a local man, Ding Bing (1832–99), whose family library had been destroyed in 1860, realised that volumes from the imperial library were appearing on the open market. He bought as many as he could and persuaded a Shanghai bookseller to enter Hangzhou (still in the hands of the Taipings). The bookseller pretended that he was piously 'rescuing' paper with characters on it to prevent it being used for unsuitable purposes, and managed to acquire many more volumes of the 'Si ku quan shu'. This custom, known as 'Respectfully cherishing paper with characters on it', like the use of 'taboo characters' (usually those in the names of the reigning emperor) illustrates the traditional Chinese preoccupation with words and their elevation to an almost sanctified position. Ding Bing eventually built a library on the site of the old one though the Hangzhou copy of the 'Si ku quan shu' remains incomplete, with odd volumes scattered throughout the world.

Like the library, many of Hangzhou's famous temples were rebuilt in the late 19C and early 20C; little ancient architecture remains.

Circuit of the lake.

Turning right out of the Shangrila Hotel, past the small bridge that links the W tip of Gushan Island to the shore, the red-walled *Temple to Yue Fei* appears on your right.

Yue Fei (1103–42) was a general of the Southern Song, a character whose extreme loyalty (to an effete ruling house) has elevated him to almost god-like status. Countless stories are told about him and, as a popular hero, he is commemorated in opera, popular fiction and iconography. As the N of China was invaded, Yue Fei led a peasant army to defeat the Jin (the Jurched, ancestors of the Manchus, who established the Jin dynasty in north China, 1122–1234) in 1140 at Yancheng. He was keen to proceed with the recapture of the whole of north China for the Song but he was ordered to withdraw. It is thought that his army was seen as even more of a threat to the enfeebled Song than the invaders. The prime minister, Qin Hui, had Yue Fei imprisoned and later executed with his adopted son, whilst the court concluded a treaty of vasselage with the Jin. Yue Fei was later buried by the lake and, in 1221, a temple to his memory was built by the grave.

The present buildings, rebuilt after the Taiping destruction, date from the last years of the 19C and were thoroughly restored in 1979. In front of the temple is a three-arched stone gateway with four characters, 'Jade blood, cinnabar heart', and behind is a huge, double-eaved gate building which leads to the large courtyard, at the far end of which is the main hall. This contains a recent statue of Yue Fei made in the local art school, above which is the inscription: 'Return our mountains and rivers'. On either side are four stone carved characters (written by Hong Zhu of the Ming): 'Ultimate loyalty to the country,' which Yue Fei's mother is supposed to have tattooed on his back before he went off to battle (a scene which can be found in popular cartoon strip woodblocks of his life). The wooden ceiling of the hall is painted with white cranes, symbols of eternal life. Subsidiary halls on either side of the courtyard commemorate two faithful followers of Yue Fei, Niu Gao and Zhang Xian, and members of his family.

To the left of the temple, *Yue Fei's Tomb* is approached by a small avenue of stone statues: lions, rams, horses and officials. There are also over 100 stone stelae including Hong Zhu's four characters (Ultimate loyalty to the country) whose inscriptions relate to Yue Fei, some, in extravagant characters, based on his own hand. The most famous is Yue Fei's own poem, written in prison, in the calligraphy of Wen Zhengming (1470–1559). The central tumulus is that of Yue Fei; on the left is that of his adopted son, Yue Yun. They are surrounded by a stone railing and

HANGZHOU

planted with pines. There are four kneeling figures in iron, their hands bound behind their backs facing the tomb: they represent Yue Fei's persecutors, Prime Minister Qin Hui, his wife Zhang Jun (a general jealous of Yue Fei's success), and Wan Qixie (said to be the prison governor). An inscription reads: 'Loyal bones are gloriously buried in a green mound, the sycophants are cast in iron'. The figures were cast in the first years of the 19C.

An earlier group was cast in 1503 but they were lost by 1731 when a new set was cast. Because of their deteriorating condition, they were replaced by the present group. In the past it was customary for visitors to the temple to spit on the figures (which may have caused the rapid deterioration); a notice requests today's visitors to refrain for reasons of conservation and hygiene. The use of iron for the statues of villains is significant. Stone, a permanent material, was restricted to statues of 'good' people. Iron figures were often re-cast, the melting-down process indicating that these 'bad' images (and therefore the souls of those they represented) were impermanent.

The road past the temple leads W to the *Hangzhou Botanic Gardens*, built in 1956 on the site of a 5C temple (whose buildings were only removed in 1964). There is a spring, the 'Jade Spring', rising in a square, stone-railed pool, long famous for its large, red and black goldfish, still raised there. Goldfish of all sorts form one of the sights of the gardens which are also famous for their many varieties of bamboo, the herb garden and extensive collection of trees and plants.

Returning to the lake, you pass the site where lotuses are best viewed (one of the Ten Prospects), on your right, then the *Su Causeway* leads across the lake from opposite the Yue Fei Temple. Walking along the Su Causeway, in the centre of the lake, on your right is the *Island of Small Seas*, with its four pools. Just S of the island the three stone *pagodas* rise from the lake (one of the Ten Prospects: Reflection of the Moon Above Three Deep Pools). This is the point on the Su Causeway at which you should be viewing the spring dawn (another of the Ten Prospects) which might conflict with reflections of the moon. Just before you reach the end of the causeway, on your left is the *Huagang* (Flower Harbour) *Garden* where (according to the rules of prospect) you should observe fish, and the park is full of goldfish pools. The garden is said to have been built originally by a eunuch of the Song dynasty.

At the end of the causeway turn left. On your right you will find the *Jingci* (Pure Compassion) *Monastery*, at the foot of the Nanping Hill. Founded in 954, it was originally called the Hall of the Eternal Brightness of the Compassionate Sun, but acquired its current name in 1139. The main hall was restored in 1960. The sound of the Jingci Monastery's bell at evening was one of the ten 'prospects', heard no more. Poets praised the sonorous quality of the bell but the 'Japanese Railway Guide' says: 'being struck at dawn it was supposed to wake up everything within hearing'. A famous monk of the Song, Daoji, was commemorated in one of the halls, and there used to be a well called the 'Timber Transporting Well' because when timber was short during reconstruction, Daoji got drunk and slept for three days, waking to find the required timbers had appeared in the well.

Opposite the Jingci Monastery is a promontory, DIEZHAO SHAN (Sunset Hill) and on the lakeside is a column which marks the site of the *Lei feng* (Thunder Peak) *Pagoda* which collapsed in 1924.

Built in 975 by Prince Qian of Wuyue, constructed from brick and timber, it was a major landmark, even after being burnt down by Japanese pirates in the 16C in case it was used as a watchtower to warn of their approach. The brickwork of the seven-storey pagoda survived for hundreds of years despite the depredations of superstitious peasants and trophy-hunting tourists who removed bricks. The peasants scattered brick dust on their fields, believing that it would bring the good fortune of a fine crop (through the benevolence of the Buddha), or sprinkled it in drinks, for their health.

Suddenly, on 25 September 1924, 'on a still afternoon the pagoda sank into a shapeless mound of bricks'. When it collapsed, it was discovered that many of the bricks were hollow and contained small rolled-up pieces of paper printed (by woodblock) with an illustration and the Chinese translation of a Sanskrit Buddhist text, 'Sarvatathargatadhishthana-hridaya-karandamudra-dharani-sutra' (a short text, despite the promise of the title), believed by early Chinese Buddhists to act as a protective charm. These tiny scrolls are amongst the earliest examples of printing in the world. It is not known how many scrolls were walled up in the pagoda; legend states that the pagoda was constructed from 84,000 bricks (a symbolic number in Buddhist legend) and that there must, in consequence, have been 84,000 scrolls. There were certainly a considerable number (one is displayed in the Zhejiang Provincial Museum on Gushan Island) but there is also an incredible number of fakes which still circulate. The British Library acquired a genuine copy in the year of its discovery and the Library of Congress and the National Library of China also have genuine examples. It is interesting to note the description of the pagoda in the 'Japanese Railway Guide', published a year before the collapse, accompanied by a photograph of an indistinct, stubby tower: 'the pagoda is so thoroughly ivy-mantled that no trace of the material of the original building is visible'.

One of Hangzhou's most famous stories (often performed as an opera) is 'The White Snake'. A white snake which could turn itself into a beautiful woman to ensnare young men was eventually trapped in the foundations of the pagoda. At the end of the story is the warning that when the pagoda falls, the river bore fails to appear and the West Lake dries up, the snake will be released ... So far only one of these conditions has been met.

Following the road around the lake, towards the W side, a park with drooping willows is the 'Listening to the Orioles In the Willows' prospect and N of that is the Children's Park. In the top NE corner of the lake is the Bai Causeway, creating a small inner lake and leading to Gushan Island. There are two bridges on the causeway. The first, near the lake shore, is the 'Interrupting Bridge' (Duan qiao), where the white snake first entrapped her young lover (before being buried under the Thunder Peak Pagoda). Walk across the Bai Causeway to **Gushan (Lonely Hill) Island**.

The first building on the eastern tip of the island is one of the Ten Prospects, *'Autumn Moon on the Lake'*. During the Tang dynasty there was a 'lake-watching pavilion' here which was extended in 1699, during the reign of the Kangxi emperor. An 'Imperial Books Pavilion' anticipated the later arrival of the Wenlan ge Library in the reign of the Qianlong emperor. In front of this a stone platform was constructed for viewing the autumn moon over the tranquil lake. The area was expanded in 1959 when, according to one account, 'garden workers knocked down the high wall of the Hardoon Garden, occupied by the imperialist'.

This is presumably Silas Aaron Hardoon (1847–1931), the industrialist and financier of Shanghai, who might well have come here from nearby Shanghai, although Nagel's guide mentions 'A European house, which was to be the palace of Prince Henry of Prussia' which was built on the ruins of the imperial residence constructed here by the Qianlong emperor in the 18C.

On the building by the stone platform are the words: 'Through the lattice comes the fresh breeze of summer and the rays of winter sun; rolling up the blinds, the bright moon appears before the mountains, behind are mountains and mountains'. Nearby among the piled rocks are cassia trees and wisteria and the area is one of which poets of the past wrote: 'The vast lake is like a mirror; the moon is at its best in autumn'.

Turn right along the path along the inner lake, towards the N of the island. On the far side of a small 'Nine-bend (crooked) Bridge' is the *Pavilion* where the cranes were released and the tomb of the bird-loving poet Lin Hejing (967–1028).

The pavilion was first built in the Yuan, in memory of Lin, a native of Hangzhou who lived on Gushan Island for 20 years, planting plum trees and rearing cranes (both symbolic of long life), to the point that he was said to 'have married a plum and had a crane for a son'. It is said that if he was out when friends called, his servant would send a crane out to fetch him.

On the wall of the pavilion is the calligraphy of the Kangxi emperor (modelling his style on the Ming calligrapher Dong Qichang) and the stone-carved poem by the 5C writer Bao Zhao, 'Dancing Cranes'; plum trees are planted nearby for this is the place in Hangzhou where plums are to be appreciated.

Further along the northern shore of the island is a small pavilion marking the Cloud Spring, then a monumental archway in memory of Sun Yat-sen, and, at a bend in the path, a memorial to the messengers of the People's Liberation Army during the Liberation War, called the 'Chicken-feather Letter Memorial'.

In the past, messages sent by post horse were marked 'urgent' by attaching a chicken feather to them. During the guerrilla war against first the Japanese, then the Nationalists, the Communist armies' messengers were often young boys, and since their work was dangerous, all messages were effectively 'chicken-feather letters', after which they were named.

Close to the Xiling Bridge which leads from the western tip of the island to the shore, on the shore side is a pavilion marking the *Tomb of Su Xiaoxiao*, a beauty of the 5C who met her lover, he on a black horse, she in a painted lacquer sedan chair, here by the pines of Xiling.

Turning back to the W and S shore of the island, on the N side of the slope is a small stone pagoda, alternatively called the *Huayan jing ta* (Pagoda of the Garland Sutra) or the Pagoda of the Xiling Seal-engraving Society for it lies in the garden behind the headquarters of the Seal-engravers' Society of Zhejiang (Xiling she) on the island. It was built in 1903 when the society, which encourages research into and the practice of seal-carving, was founded, and is just over 10m high. It is carved with the text of the Buddhist Garland sutra but because of its situation amongst trees, engraved rocks and plants, is viewed as a 'scenery-enhancing' rather than a strictly religious pagoda. Beyond the Seal-engravers' headquarters, amongst the ruins of the 18C imperial gardens are, from W to E, a restaurant, the antiquarian section of the Zhejiang Provincial Library (modern works are kept elsewhere), much of which was built in the 1940s, and the *Sun Yatsen Park*. The park is formed of part of the old imperial garden with ancient cypress trees, considerably antedating Sun Yatsen.

Slightly set back, between the park and the Zhejiang Provincial Museum, is the *Pavilion of Literary Waves*, built by Ding Bing in the last decades of the 19C to house the 9000 or so volumes of the copy of the 'Si ku quan shu' deposited in the old Wenlan ge by the Qianlong emperor in 1782–87, that he had rescued after the library's destruction during the Taiping uprising. Ding's 9000 volumes represent about a quarter of the original.

Next to the Pavilion of Literary Waves is the **Zhejiang Provincial Museum**. Apart from important exhibits relating to the history of Hangzhou (including the brick from the Leifeng Pagoda with its tiny paper scroll, copies of early stone-engraved maps of the town and woodblock illustrations of the ten 'prospects' as well as much information on the history of silk technology in Hangzhou), the museum contains important exhibits from elsewhere in the province. Notable are the finds from Hemudu which include 7000-year-old cultivated rice (the earliest so far discovered in China) and fascinating remains of early wooden construction. There is also the skeleton of a whale, beached in Zhejiang, interesting because from the Song dynasty, if not before, such events were often associated with disaster. When a whale was beached in 1282, a terrible fire in the town which ensued was blamed on people who, rather than try to rescue the whale, had cut it up for meat.

Next to the museum are the remains of the Shengyin Temple constructed by the Qianlong emperor.

The hill behind the Hangzhou Hotel.
Turn right out of the hotel, taking the lakeside road towards the Yue Fei Temple. Before you reach the temple, on your right, is the *Tomb of Qiu Jin* (1879–1907), the woman martyr from Shaoxing, whose remains were eventually moved here after 1911. An early member of Sun Yatsen's anti-Manchu Republican movement, she had abandoned her husband and children to help organise an uprising in Zhejiang when she was executed by the Qing government forces.

Behind the Yue Fei Temple a path leads up towards the hills behind. Up on the hill are a number of caves. First on the left is the *Yanxia dong* (Cave of Twilight Mists), full of small Buddhist figures, including icons of the Bodhisattva Guanyin and 16 lohans dating from the 10C and later. Just beyond, on the right of the path is the *Tomb of Niu Gao* (1087–1147), another Song general, who followed Yue Fei in his campaigns against the Jin, and who died of poisoning. Up to the left, beyond, is the *Ziyun* (Purple Cloud) *Cave*, surrounded by trees and offering a fine view of the lake. Up to the left, near the summit, is the *Huanglong* (Yellow Dragon) *Cave* where a spring gushes from a stone dragon's head into a pool. Pavilions have been constructed nearby and a stele beside the pool bears the inscription: 'where there is a dragon, there are spirits'; nearby the famous 'square' bamboo grows. There was a Taoist temple here and the buildings have recently been restored.

Returning to the main path, at the eastern end of the hill is the *Bao Chu* (Protect Chu) *Pagoda*, sometimes known as the needle pagoda because of its sharply tapering form. First built between 968 and 975, the pagoda is said to have been constructed when Prince Qian Sichu was held prisoner by the Song court at Kaifeng; it was erected by his mother and brothers in the hope of divine intercession for his return. It has been restored in 998–1003, 1789 and 1933. It was a mixed timber and brick construction (though none of the timber has survived), hexagonal in plan, seven storeys and approximately 30m high. It once formed a sort of pair with the Lei feng pagoda on the opposite, S bank of the lake, but it alone remains as one of the major focal points around the West Lake.

To return to the hotel, either retrace your steps or take the lakeside road beneath you (to the right).

The pavilions in the centre of the lake.
The only way to reach the lake centre is, naturally, by boat. Boats depart from Gushan Island (opposite the hotel), or from the Flower Harbour (Huagang) Park in the SW corner of the lake or from just N of the Children's Park on the E side of the lake. Between Gushan Island and the larger Small Seas Island are two small islets. The western one is an earth mound, formed by dredged mud (dredged on the instructions of an official called Ruan and now known as *Ruan's Island*); the eastern one, which can be visited, is called the *Pavilion at the Heart of the Lake* (previous names included Pavilion of Pure Joy and Pavilion where the Herons Flap their Wings) and was first constructed in 1552. The present building, with its double eaves and yellow-tiled roof, was built in 1953. It was described by a poet: 'Returning after long travels, the solitary pavilion sits between water and clouds; open on all sides, to one side the city, the rest is mountain'.

The *Island of Small Seas*, beyond, consists of four enclosed pools, enclosed by dredged mud in 1607, with the first pavilions put up in 1611 and the crooked ('nine bend') bridge in 1727. Just S are the three small stone stupa-like 'pagodas', facing the Wo xin xiang yin (Reflections of my Heart) Pavilion on the island. They are said to have been first set up by the Song poet Su Dongbo when he was Governor, to warn against the planting of water-chestnuts and gorgon fruit here, to avoid clogging up the lake. The original pagodas were lost and those that still stand date from 1621. They stand about 2m high with hollow, bulbous bodies. When the moon is full they have a candle placed inside and the openings are covered with paper so that they seem like three small moons joining the reflection of the full moon in the lake. A poetic description of the scene runs: 'The moon floats on the water, the three pools are bright; on the boats at night, there is singing and dancing as people cross the mirror'.

One of the members of Lord Macartney's embassy (1793) described an excursion on the lake, full of pleasure-boats: 'We had a splendid yacht, and another made fast to it to serve as a kitchen: the dinner...consisted of at least a hundred dishes in succession...the water was as clear as crystal. Vast numbers of barges were sailing to and fro, all gaily decorated with paint and gilding and streaming colours; the parties within them apparently all in pursuit of pleasure...'.

The Lingyin Temple.

In the hills to the W, beyond the Botanic Gardens, is the **Lingyin** (Spirit Retreat) **Temple**, one of the most famous Chan (Zen) temples in China, founded by an Indian monk, known in Chinese as Huili, in 326. Huili was particularly impressed by the rocky formation to the left of the path that leads to the temple and which is known as the Fei lai feng, the 'Peak that Flew'.

Huili said: 'This is a small peak of the Grdhrakuta (Vulture Peak) Mountain in India; when did it fly here? When the Buddha was alive there were many miracles.' In the 10C the temple was twice enlarged and had 72 halls and 3000 monks. It was destroyed in the Taiping rebellion, rebuilt in the early 20C, though the main beams of the main hall collapsed again in 1924, and a disastrous fire in 1936 further reduced it. The present buildings were reconstructed in 1956 and again in 1970, after the Cultural Revolution.

Inside the gate a path leads to a small covered bridge, the *Chun cong ting* (Pavilion of the Gurgling Stream in Spring), beside which (on the left) is a small stupa, called *Sir Li's Pagoda*, said to contain the remains of Huili, the Indian founder of the temple. A path beside the stream to the left leads to three caves: Dragon Depths Cave, Jade Milk Cave and Green Forest Cave. You can either take the path straight to the temple (on the right-hand side of the stream) or, better, walk on the left side of the stream, along the cliff of the 'Peak that Flew' where there are over 380 Buddhist images carved in the rock, dating from the Five Dynasties, Song and Yuan periods (10–14C). The largest is a very fat Maitreya (in his 'laughing Buddha' form), of the Song, and the majority of figures date from the Yuan. The whole forms the most important group of Buddhist rock carvings in southern China.

The *Temple*, which faces the stream, consists of an entrance hall with guardian figures, and a Great Buddha Hall behind. The entrance hall has a double-eaved roof and contains the standard icons: the four protective guardians, two on either side, a fat, laughing Maitreya welcoming visitors, and, behind him, the Weituo guardian figure. The Maitreya is said to be 18C; the Weituo figure is said to be Song and carved in camphor wood. On either side of the entrance hall are two stone sutra pagodas, dated 969. Across a broad courtyard is the triple-roofed Great Buddha Hall which, though fundamentally dating back only to 1956, is an impressive building and is flanked by two early multi-storeyed stone pagodas. The central gilded wooden Buddha figure inside the hall was made in 1956. The temple is a very active one, visited by enthusiastic pilgrims and local worshippers.

Outside the temple, on the cliff opposite is the *Cuiwei Pavilion* (cuiwei is a poetic word for the iridescent green of hillsides), first built in the Southern Song in memory of Yue Fei. The whole area is a pleasant, if crowded, place in which to wander. A cable-car (one of the first in China) can take visitors to the summit of the Northern Peak, and the *Taoguang Hermitage* (the name is taken from that of a Tang period hermit) to the NW, was celebrated by the poet Wei Fangtai in 1724:

A stone-paved pathway hidden deep in myriad bamboos
Tempts me to climb with an old friend to meditation's home,
Suddenly, as we unbar the gate, our eyes delighted see
Beyond the lake, the city's smoking hearths; beyond the river, hill.

(Translated by A.C. Moule)

Dragon Well Tea and Tiger Spring.

S of the Lingyin Temple, W of the lake, is the area in which Hangzhou's most famous tea, Longjing or Dragon Well, is grown and dried. The tea-producing areas can be visited (by appointment, arranged through China Travel Service). The scenery is wonderful, with green hills, pickers dressed in bright blue and pink bending over the dark-green bushes, and the simple process of drying the tea-leaves is interesting. The processing is brief and the leaves remain intact, to open out like privet leaves in hot water and produce a refreshing, fresh-tasting, leafy green tea.

The best spring water for making Dragon Well Tea (the combination is described as the 'two superlatives') is found in the *Tiger Spring*, to the SE of the tea-growing area, midway between the lake and the Pagoda of Six Harmonies on the Qiantang River. In the teahouses there you will see people floating light Chinese coins on bowls of spring water for it has a strong surface tension and notable meniscus (curving up from the edge of the bowl). The spring is said to have arisen in 819 when a monk lived here, suffering from a lack of water. One day two tigers leapt from the earth and a spring bubbled up. The spring is called the 'Third Spring Under Heaven'.

Pagoda of Six Harmonies (Liuhe ta).

The pagoda stands beside the railway bridge across the Qiantang River, high on a hill. It was first built in 970 in an effort to subdue the River bore and has long served as a landmark, with a lantern on its tip to help sailors. It was built beside the Liuhe (Six Harmonies) Temple, which has long since disappeared, leaving its name to the pagoda. It has been constantly rebuilt throughout its history (in 1121, 1153, 1163, 1524, 1735 and 1900).

Octagonal in plan, it is almost 60m high and though, from the outside it appears to have 13 storeys, internally it has only seven. The core is of brick, the exterior wooden. A spiral staircase inside enables visitors to climb to the top. The internal brickwork is decorated with birds, flowers and animals.

To the E of the pagoda, the hill between the river and the lake, the *Yuhuang* (Jade Emperor) *Hill*, used to be covered with temples. On the lake side was the Song Altar of Heaven and Field of Eight Trigrams where the Southern Song emperors ploughed their ceremonial furrow to inaugurate the agricultural year. The form of the fields can still just be seen and, like the Lingyin Temple area, this is a pleasant area for walking (and less crowded).

The **Mosque**, called the *Fenghuang si* (Phoenix Temple), is in the S-central area of the town itself, at No. 325 in the central section of Zhongshan lu. It is easily reached on foot from the Children's Park on the E side of the lake. Take the road leading E (away from the lake) opposite the park (Kaiyuan lu) which, with a slight wiggle at the end, arrives at the major N–S road, Zhongshan lu. Turn right and not far down on your right is the mosque. Founded in the Tang, it is one of the 'four great' mosques in China and has been much restored. The surviving great hall is a Yuan brick structure with vaulted roof, and carved brick decoration.

The **Grand Canal** can be seen to the N of Huancheng bei lu (to the right of the junction with Zhongshan bei lu), in the N of the city. It leads N.

11 Wuxi

Wuxi, which stands on the edge of *Lake Tai* (Tai hu), some 48km W of Suzhou in Jiangsu province, is an old city whose origins as a small country town go back to the Han. Its name, which means 'no tin', is said to derive from the fact that during the Zhou and Qin periods tin (xi) was extensively mined on Xi shan (Tin Hill) in the western suburbs but the supplies became exhausted during the Han (Wu xi shan shan wu xi: 'there is no tin on "no tin" town's Tin Hill' is a local tongue-twister) when the town grew up. As with many of the towns in the area, the Grand Canal passes through the centre and one of its gardens, in particular, excited imperial interest in the 18C. In the early 20C it became a centre for silk production using modern machinery, with 45 filature factories. It is also known for the production of clay figurines.

Railway: Wuxi is on the main Peking–Shanghai line with frequent express trains. The station is in the NE of the city.

Hotels: most foreigners stay in hotels beside Lake Tai, some 20 or more minutes from the town. The Taihu Hotel is the oldest (though it now has a new luxury building); the Hubin Hotel was built in 1978 and a strange addition, the Shuixiu Hotel, was 'assembled' in 1980. It is apparently a prefabricated Australian hotel with koala bear, kangaroo and wattle curtains.

Lake Tai: one of the largest freshwater lakes in China, Lake Tai is best known for the curiously-shaped rocks it produces; limestone boulders scoured and holed by the action of the water. The Huizong emperor of the Song dynasty (reigned 1101–26) was an enthusiastic petromane who almost brought the country to bankruptcy with his extravagant expenditure on stones. The celebrated painter Mi Fei (12C) had a huge stone that he bowed to deeply every morning and addressed as his elder brother.
  Though not all garden stones came from Lake Tai (for volcanic and ore-bearing stones were also appreciated for their varying textures and colours), many of the best did and they can be seen in all the gardens of Suzhou, especially the Shizi lin (Grove of Stone Lions). Lake stones were supposed to be 'holey, slim and leaky', pierced through with holes and, ideally, balanced on a narrow base, flaring outwards, the heavier top on its slim foot apparently defying gravity. Connoisseurs spent hours scraping the stones, scouring their hollows and, occasionally, resorting to chisels to improve a little on nature. The 12C 'Yun lin shi pu' (Stone Catalogue of the Cloud Forest) describes Lake Tai stones hauled up from the lake as 'huge specimens, up to 50 feet high, with a colour range from white through pale blue to blue-black...the most desirable have tortuous, rugged contours, and abundant hollows.' According to the translation of the Swedish sinologist Osvald Siren, small surface cavities 'are called arbalest pellet nests' (by which he may mean the type of swallows' nests used for birds-nest soup).

Opposite the Taihu Hotel is a promontory called *Guitou zhu* (Turtle's Head Peninsula), because it apparently looks like a turtle's head. Reached by pleasure boat from below the hotel, it is a favourite spot for Chinese tourists. Beside the Hubin and Shuixiu Hotels is the bridge linking the promontory with the lakeside road (Huanhu lu) and next to this is the *Li* (Worm-eaten) *Garden*, which some guidebooks ('hideous circus', 'tatty affair', 'concrete labyrinth') would consider an appropriate name (though they never seem to translate it).

It was made between 1927 and 1930 out of two gardens, the original Worm-eaten Garden and the Yu zhuang (Fishing Village) gardens. The 'worm-eaten' bit takes its name from a part of the lake which was originally known as Li hu (Worm-eaten Lake) but is now known as Wuli hu (Five-Mile Lake). Li hu, in turn, is said to derive its name from Fan Li, the great statesman of the state of Yue at the end of the Spring and Autumn period who retired here to relax on a boat. It is not enormously to be recommended except for a view of the lake, if the crowds permit.

San shan (Three Hills) *Island* in the lake, a former haunt of bandits, can be reached by boat.

On the road towards town from the Taihu Hotel is the **Mei Yuan** (Plum

Garden), named for the plum trees in it, though in the late Qing it was known as the Xiaotao yuan (Small Peach Garden), belonging to a scholar called Xu Dian. In 1912 it became the private garden of a family called Song who planted the plum trees, which are particularly beautiful in flower in the early spring. Autumn visitors need not despair for wonderfully scented cassia (*Osmanthus fragrans*) bushes are another feature of the garden. Amongst the many pavilions, the *Songbin tang* (Hall Where the Praises of the State of Bin are Chanted) was built from nanmu (a cedar) wood and the three-storey brick *Nianqu* (Contemplation of Effort) *Pagoda* was built by Song Zongjing and Song Desheng, two major industrialists, to commemorate their mother's 80th birthday. It affords a view of the distant lake.

To the W of Wuxi city is **Xihui Park**, constructed in 1958 by linking the Xi shan (Tin Hill) and the famous Hui shan (Generosity or sometimes, using another 'hui', Wisdom Hill). On the small (74.8m) *Xi shan* is the 16C *Longguang* (Dragon Brilliance) *Pagoda and Temple*; on the much more lofty (328.9m) **Hui shan** are nine peaks (sometimes known as nine dragons), as well as the 'second spring' in the world.

So named by Lu Yu of the Tang (who, in his 'Cha jing' or Classic of Tea, paid as much attention to the ceramics in which tea was served—did the colours enhance the colour of the tea or not?—and the water from which tea was brewed, as the primary raw material itself), the spring produces water that is sweet and 'thick', with the same sort of meniscus as found in the spring at Hangzhou. The Huizong emperor of the Song gave the spring water a form of 'royal warrant' declaring it a 'palace product'.

Also on Hui shan are a Song dynasty *bridge* (the Jinlian, or Golden Lotus, bridge), the seal-script inscription 'Ting song' or listening to the pines by the Tang calligrapher Li Yangbing, and the beautifully carved Tang and Song 'sutra pillars' outside the gate of the *Hui shan Temple*. That to the N side of the gate dates from the Tang (876) and has the Dharani sutra carved on it; the Song pillar is to the S of the gate and, like the Tang one, is just over 5m high with dharanis carved on it.

One of the most famous gardens in China now forms part of the Xihui Park. This is the **Jichang yuan** (Attachment to Freedom Garden) which so impressed the Qianlong emperor on one of his visits to the south that he commissioned a copy of it for the Yihe yuan (Summer Palace) in Peking, the Xiequ yuan (Garden of Harmonious Interest), built in 1750. It is interesting to compare the two, if you can, for they provide the best possible example of the difference between northern and southern garden styles. The plans are fairly similar, centred on water surrounded by covered walks and verandahs, but the narrow columns and lightly up-turned eaves of the south give way to more solid construction with thicker columns and heavier roofs with little upturn to the eaves in the northern Xiequ yuan.

The Jichang yuan stands on the site of a Yuan dynasty monastery which became a garden in the Zhengde period (1506–22) of the Ming. It was originally called Fenggu xingwo (Temporary Nest in Phoenix Gully). The garden is fundamentally divided into two parts: east and west. Water and surrounding walkways are the focus of the eastern part; piled rocks and 'mock mountains' dominate the west. The higher parts of the garden afford views over the hills of the surrounding park in a garden design technique called 'borrowing a view', commonly used in the small gardens of the Yangtse delta towns.

12 Yixing

Yixing is a small town on the W of Lake Tai in Jiangsu province, on the opposite side of the lake from Wuxi. It is best known for the production of small pottery teapots and other items made most commonly from a dark, brick-red clay. The pottery is still made in Dingshu zhen, some 20km SW of Yixing town. Also SW of the town are a number of curiously-shaped karst caves which are frequently visited.

Hotel: the Yixing binguan (Yixing Guesthouse) is on Renmin lu in the S of the town. This is the only local hotel in which foreigners are supposed to stay.

Travel: Yixing is not on a railway line and is best reached by bus (c 2 hours) or car from Wuxi which is on the railway, intermediate between Zhenjiang and Suzhou. Dingshu zhen and its potteries, as well as the karst caves may be reached by public bus or car from Yixing.

Set in beautiful scenery of lakes, canals, rivers and paddy-fields, the Yixing area has long been famous for its beauty. During the Warring States period (403–221 BC), the ex-minister of the State of Yue, Fan Li, came to live in Yixing (which was then known as Jingqi, a name which was changed during the Qin dynasty, 221–206 BC, to Yang xian; the name Yixing dating from the Song, 960–1279) because of its beauty and he brought a lady, Xi Shi, equally well-known for her attractions, with him. Fan Li is supposed to have produced ceramics at Yixing and is therefore worshipped as the patron deity of potters.

Another legend credits the beginnings of the local ceramic industry to the arrival of a monk who offered 'riches or honours'. Ridiculed by the townspeople, he led them to a cave where clay of brilliant colours was found. This account first appeared in print in the late 16C in the 'Yang xian ming hu xi' (Account of the Famous Teapots of Yang County) by Zhou Gaoji. At the time of its publication, Yixing was already known for its production of utilitarian objects such as flowerpots for the local tea bushes and drainpipes.

It was during the 16C that local kilns began to produce the characteristic small teapots, water-droppers and decorative objects that are now known as Yixing ware. Another Chinese name for the ware is 'purple sand', in reference to the dominant colour which is a dark red (produced by a high level of iron in the clay), although green, grey, buff and black clays are also used. All the clays are locally found and the wares were fired in multi-chambered dragon kilns built up the local hills and fuelled with local timber. In the past, the multitude of waterways meant that transport of the wares to nearby centres like Shanghai, Nanjing and Suzhou, was easy and cheap.

It is the not only the colours that distinguish Yixing wares; they are also very amusingly shaped. Tiny teapots may look like teapots, often further embellished with incised calligraphy or drawings, or they may be made in the form of melons, pumpkins, peaches, gnarled tree-stumps or bundles of books wrapped in cloth. In other small pieces, the varying colours of local clays are used to produce three-dimensional 'still-lifes', baskets with yellow peanuts, grey crabs and green leaves in them, or life-like walnuts, sweet chestnuts and snail-shells. Some of the plain teapots have speck-led finishes or tiny gilt spots on their surface. Though virtually all other Chinese ceramics are anonymous products, many Yixing pieces were signed with the seal of the potter, a tradition which continues today.

There is a *Confucian Temple* in Yixing, said to contain fine statuary (closed for renovation). It stands behind a fine white stone pailou or arch, dated to 1627. The temple is also said to be 17C.

On Heping jie is an old house, used as a residence by the Taiping 'king' Yang Fuqing after the capture of Yixing in the mid 19C. It still con-tains painted decoration of the Taiping period including murals depicting agricultural scenes, discovered in 1958.

Dingshu zhen.

Reached by bus or car from Yixing (some 20km away), Dingshu zhen is the centre for contemporary ceramic production, with some 25 factories, many of which still make domestic articles such as drainpipes and flower-pots whilst the Zisha (Purple Sand) factory continues to produce the highly-prized tiny teapots. Stalls selling flowerpots, teapots and teasets as well as some of the small decorative pieces, line the streets of the town and the Pottery Exhibition Hall may be visited. To visit a ceramic factory, it is necessary to make arrangements through China Travel Service.

Tourist buses leave from Dingshu zhen for the various karst caves in the locality. These include the *Zhang Gong Cave*, 22km SW of Yixing, reputedly a place where various eminent Taoists lived and cultivated 'the way', notably Zhang Daoling of the Han dynasty and Zhang Guolao of the Tang, hence its name: Duke Zhang's Cave. It consists of an inner and outer chamber, covering 3000 square metres. There are over 72 caves in all, including smaller chambers. The main inner chamber is said to hold 5000 visitors and on holidays, it may appear to do so.

The *Linggu dong* or Spirit Cave is 6km beyond the Zhang Gong Cave, near a major tea plantation. This contains, amongst many varied stone formations, a large white stone 'screen', 17m high and 5m wide, which was discovered and praised by the Tang dynasty poet Lu Guimeng when he came to Yixing to buy tea.

The *Shanjuan Cave*, also 25km SW of Yixing, is divided into three levels and, as it is partly water-filled, can be visited by boat. Some of its scenic highlights have been embellished with stone-carved calligraphy, includ-ing one piece dated AD 850 and another by the noted calligrapher of the Liang (502–557), Tao Hongjing.

13 Putuo shan

Putuo shan, Potala Mountain, is one of the islands in the Zhou shan archipelago, off the coast just S of Shanghai. Since the 10C it has been celebrated as one of the four Buddhist mountains (the others are Wutai shan in Shanxi, Jiuhua shan in Anhui and Emei shan in Sichuan). These sacred mountains are places where Bodhisattvas appeared; Putuo is the abode of the Bodhisattva Avalokitesvara or Guanyin in Chinese. The mountain home of Avalokitesvara was named Potalaka in Sanksrit, trans-lated by sound into Putuo in Chinese. The palace in Lhasa, Tibet, histori-cally the home of the Dalai Lama, is called the Potala for the same reason as the Dalai Lama is believed to be a reincarnation of the Bodhisattva Avalokitesvara.

Boats: Putuo is reached by boat, overnight from Shanghai (departing c 7 pm, arriving c 6 am; in 1986 a cabin for two cost less than 20 yuan) or a 4-hour trip from Ningbo.

Transport: the island is small and there is little motor traffic. It is wise to bring as little luggage as possible as there is no certainty of finding any motor transport at the jetty and you may have to walk (c 20 minutes) along the stepped path to the hotel. There are tourist minibus trips (starting from the W side of the Pu ji Temple) to the Foding (Universal Wise Sovereign) Mountain, Fayuchan Temple, Fanyin Cave, Zizhulin, and other temples en route.

Hotel: Xilei Hotel, behind the Puji Temple.

Tourist Office: on the W side of the Puji Temple; information may also be obtained in the hotel.

The **Zhou shan archipelago** is very beautiful; small green islands with beaches of clean, pale sand rise from a clear blue sea (if you travel in the spring to autumn period; Gutzlaff in February 1831 found the weather 'generally dark and stormy'). The first view of Putuo Island from the jetty is of a low, yellow-painted temple building ahead, a naval settlement with elderly submarines and sailors playing basketball to the left and the green island behind. For the missionary Gutzlaff (whose 'zeal never failed'), who arrived in late winter, the island first appeared '...barren and scarcely habitable, but as we approached it, we observed very prominent buildings, and large glittering domes. A temple built on a projecting rock, beneath which the foaming sea dashed, gave us some idea of the genius of its inhabitants, in thus selecting the most attractive spot to celebrate the orgies of idolatry'.

The spot was also attractive to the East India Company, which set up a factory on Zhou shan, the major island of the archipelago, in 1700 (from where Cunningham, the Company doctor, visited Putuo and acquired a couple of woodblock-printed books from the monks which he sent to the collector, Sir Hans Sloane in 1703; they are now in the British Library). Attempts to enter China proper from the archipelago failed and the Company had to retreat to Canton. The British continued, however, to seize Zhou shan occasionally (1840, 1842 and 1860).

Putuo's significance is said to date from 847 when a vision of the Bodhisattva appeared to an Indian monk meditating in the Chaoyin cave. In 916 a Japanese monk, who had taken a figure of Guanyin from the sacred mountain of Wutai in Shanxi, passed the island en route for Japan. A sudden typhoon blew up and he was unable to continue. He retired to a rustic hut in the Purple Bamboo Grove, and the episode of divine intervention is commemorated in the temple called Bukenqu guanyin yuan (Hall of the Stopping of Guanyin). From the Song dynasty, the monks adhered to the Chan (Zen) sect, and many of the temples are named chan si (meditation temple).

The Bodhisattva Avalokitesvara, in early Indian belief, was associated with compassion and the full Chinese name—Guan shi yin—is a translation of one of Avalokitesvara's epithets: 'the one who hears the cries of the world'. The Indian deity was, if anything, masculine, but in China Guanyin was gradually transformed into a sort of female icon (though ambiguous, for sculptures never reveal bound feet), as the association with compassion was conceived of as a female virtue. The childless and the sick still pray to Guanyin and miracles of healing were soon reported from Putuo island. It is still quite common to find very sick people on the boat from Shanghai, amongst the tightly packed crowds of ordinary tourists.

Among the tourists, many of whom come on package tours from Shanghai and are led by a whistle-blowing guide across the island, wearing identical peaked caps, are a number of pilgrims, some monks and nuns from other Buddhist centres but often groups of middle-aged and elderly ladies carrying yellow cotton bags. The pilgrim bags, decorated with woodblock prints of lotuses (symbols of Guanyin) and Guanyin images, are stamped with the seal of the temple in each temple the pilgrims visit. In order to get a monk or nun to stamp the bag a payment must be made (large sums required from foreigners).

The buildings on the island, of which there were said to be 218 occupied by over 2000 monks and nuns in 1949, have suffered throughout the centuries from pirate attacks and the island is thought to have suffered badly during the Cultural Revolution, presumably because it was such a charming place to visit, even for Red Guards on a rampage. It is therefore not of

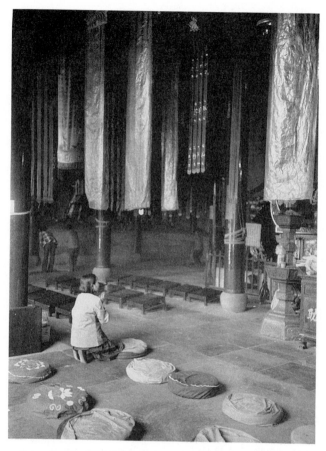

Putuo shan: temple interior

any great architectural significance but it is a very pretty island indeed and a great place to walk, particularly if you avoid the main paths which can get crowded. For that reason, and since the island is only 8.6km N–S and 3.5km W–E, after describing the route from the jetty to the hotel, I will simply list places to see and suggest that you make your own itinerary, avoiding the worst of the crowds.

From the jetty, the path to the village at the centre of the island, where the Puji Temple and the hotel are situated, leads off to the right (away from the naval base). Passing the *Haiyan pailou* (Monumental Arch on the Edge of the Sea), a modern construction, the path, lined with stalls selling religious and secular souvenirs, breaks away from the road, to the left, leading up over a hill in a series of shallow steps. The slopes are planted with small tea bushes and certain old trees (the trees on Putuo are wonderful; it is a mercy that Red Guards did not include tree-felling in their acts of desecration) appear to have achieved some sort of sanctity for joss-sticks are placed beneath them. As the path descends through the trees, buildings appear on either side, dormitory hotels with washing hung in the windows. Ahead is an open area with a large pool crossed by a stone bridge and embellished by an octagonal pavilion with upturned eaves, the whole dominated by the main temple on the island, the *Puji* (Universal Succour) *Temple*, surrounded and filled with magnificent trees. Like most of the temples on the island and throughout Zhejiang province, it is yellow-walled with grey tiled roofs. First mentioned in 1699, it contains nine main halls and 36 other buildings. On the main axis are the Hall of the Heavenly Kings, the Hall of the Universal Penetration of Wisdom, the Library and the Abbot's Hall. The hotel lies behind the temple.

Across the bridge is a small pagoda and beyond that, the sea. A major group of buildings lies on a promontory to the right: the Zizhulin (Purple Bamboo Grove), the Chaoyin Cave (where the presiding Bodhisattva first appeared) and the Hall of the Stopping of Guanyin.

The *Purple Bamboo Grove* is named after the purplish colour of the rock formation and the bamboo leaf patterns that are said to be visible in the rocks; it was here that the Japanese monk lived after he failed to transport his Guanyin figure to Japan.

The *Chaoyin* (Wave Sound) *Cave* is famous for the thunderous sound of breaking waves. During the Song and Yuan it was a common place for suicide so in an attempt to prevent people throwing themselves into the sea a pavilion called the No-suicide Pavilion was constructed here. It has since been destroyed.

Around the promontory, heading W towards the jetty, is the *Nantian men* (Gate to the Southern Heavens), on another rocky promontory.

N from the Puji Temple, at the far left of the beach is the *Chaoyang* (Facing the Sun) *Cave*, in the past surmounted by a three-storey building. Beyond, to the N, is another long beach (the Thousand-pace Beach) with a concrete tank, presumably for defensive purposes, parked in the dunes and, on the right-hand side of the road, first the Cultural Hall, which contains a small exhibition of very few local relics and, further on, set back from the road on the left, the *Dacheng* (Mahayana) *Nunnery*, which no longer seems to be restricted to the female sex.

At the far end of the beach is another of the major temples, the *Fayu* (Rain of Buddha Truth) *Temple*, founded in 1580 as the Sea wave nunnery. Destroyed by fire, it was rebuilt in 1699 and much restored in succeeding centuries. It stands high on a stone platform. On the main axis are the gate (from whence you climb), the Bell Tower, the Jade Buddha Hall, the Guanyin Hall, the Jade Tablet Hall, the Mahavira Hall, the Library and the Abbot's Hall. The Guanyin Hall is also called the Nine Dragon Brackets Hall because of the complexity of the roof construction. In front of the temple is a pool fed by streams from the hills behind.

On a large promontory projecting to the E from the temple is the *Fanyin* (Sanskrit Sound) *Cave*.

From the Fayu Temple a stepped path leads to the summit of the *Foding* (Universal Wise Sovereign) *Mountain*, 291m above sea level, affording a marvellous view of sea and islands. The major temple at the summit is the *Huiji* (Favour and Succour) *Temple*, originally merely a stone pavilion, gradually built up from 1793 to 1907 into a complex of four main halls with painted beams, seven smaller halls and six pavilions. To the left of the temple is a famous 'goose-ear oak' tree of some rarity. There is a beacon on the summit to aid navigation at sea. The tea grown on the mountain slopes is called 'Buddha's tea'.

The village, to the N of the Puji Temple, with its public washing place (like the lavoir in a French village), surrounding walls and narrow streets lined with small restaurants serving delicious fresh fish and marvellous shrimps (better than the food in the hotel) is well worth visiting.

14 Ningbo

Ningbo, c 20km up the Yong River from the coast, was China's greatest port from the Song to the end of the Ming, trading mainly with Japan and Korea. The position of the port was ideal, close to the ceramic-producing areas of Jiangxi and Zhejiang and the tea- and silk-producing southern provinces, whose products were transported to Ningbo by sea or river. Its natives were, and still are, known for their trading abilities, and the city is now being developed as a major container port, with help from one of its best-known native sons, the shipping magnate Sir Y.K. Pao (died 1991).

Airport: there is one flight a day to Shanghai (except Thursdays) and two flights a week to Hangzhou and Peking respectively (1987).

Railway: the Shanghai–Ningbo line was one of China's earlier railways, rights to build being granted to a British firm in 1898, though the construction was transferred to two Chinese firms in 1905. The Japanese Government Railways Guide to China (1924) says of the Shanghai–Hangzhou–Ningbo line: 'This railway now connects Shanghai and Hangzhou'. The Hangzhou–Ningbo link still appears incomplete in the map drawn for Carl Crow's 1933 'Handbook for China'. Today there are four trains a day via Hangzhou to Shanghai. The station is in the S of the city, just to the W of Changchun lu, 5 minutes by car from the two hotels.

Hotels: the two major hotels in Ningbo are the Huaqiao (Overseas Chinese) fandian on Liuting jie, which has been newly redecorated and refurbished and is by no means restricted to Overseas Chinese, and the Ningbo fandian, just to the W of the Huaqiao

Ningbo: the waterfront

fandian, a tall new building, visible across the bridge. The China Travel Service office is on the ground floor of the Ningbo fandian.

Bus stations: buses to the Baoguo Temple leave from the Northern Bus Station (Daqing nanlu, near the passenger boat dock). Buses to the Tiantong si leave from the Eastern Bus Station, on the eastern side of the river, Shuguang lu.

Passenger boats: the passenger ferry piers are on the W side of the Yong river, near the Northern Bus Station. Tickets may be obtained from the general office on the N side of the Xinjiang qiao (Xinjiang Bridge). There are boats every day to Putuo shan (4–5 hours) and to Shanghai (overnight).

Though a small town was built in the hills to the S, capital of the kingdom of Yue during the Warring States period (435–221 BC), Ningbo's period of glory was from the Song to the end of the Ming. During the 9C the local governor built a series of locks and canals to drain the area and in the 12C a protective breakwater was constructed on the coast. During the succeeding centuries, when China's foreign-trade emphasis shifted from the overland silk routes to the coast, ships plied between Japan, Korea and Ningbo, loaded with celadon wares from Zhejiang and, later, blue-and-white ceramics from Jingdezhen in Jiangxi, silks from the Yangtse delta and locally-produced salt, for which the Japanese paid in gold and silver. Coastal fisheries have flourished for hundreds of years. Traditional products of continuing importance include bamboo shoots (which can be seen in the markets in spring, great fat shoots, the size of a large loaf of bread), and dark-wood furniture inlaid with coloured pieces of shell.

In the Tang and Song the town was named Mingzhou and renamed Ningbo ('Calmed Waves') at the beginning of the Ming. The town was subject to frequent attacks from pirates and, as late as 1924, was still surrounded by 'strong walls', encircling the old town (to the SW; now replaced by Yongfeng lu, Lingqiao lu, Changchun lu and Wangjing lu). One of the best-known defenders of the nearby coast from pirates was Qi Jiguang (1528–88), a famous military strategist and author of 'Ji xiao xin shu' (A New Treatise on Tactics), a work in which he recommended that soldiers drill in the traditional martial arts, as part of their training. Even the idea of training soldiers was a new one, for the Chinese traditionally believed that, just as you did not waste good iron by making it into nails, good men did not become soldiers who were regarded as little better than brigands. Despite his high military position, Qi Jiguang is said to have been dominated by his wife who is supposed to have taken command of a coastal fort surrounded by pirates.

Outside the walled town, on the N side of the Yao River (across Xinjiang Bridge), was the foreign concession area, for Ningbo is known as the first area in which foreign traders settled. The Portuguese Fernando de Andrade and George Mascarenhas reached Ningbo c 1517 and by 1533 a Portuguese trading colony was flourishing there until Ferdinand Mendez Pinto landed. Mendez Pinto (c 1509–c 1581) travelled widely in the Far East, visiting Japan in the uplifting company of St. Francis Xavier, but, by contrast, arriving in Ningbo in 1545 with (according to the 'Encyclopaedia Sinica') 'a troop of other desperadoes'. They plundered tombs on a nearby island and, after a shipwreck, were taken prisoner by the Chinese, 'thrown into a pond and almost devoured by leeches', and were eventually sentenced to a year of corvee labour on the Great Wall. Saved by the arrival of the conquering Manchus, Mendez Pinto was said to have made a subsequent trip to China which was 'less full of excitement'. The behaviour of the desperadoes, together with the 'insolence and licentiousness of the colonists', provoked an attack by imperial orders in which over 1000 Christians, nearly half of them Portuguese, were killed and many ships burnt.

During the 18C and early 19C the British East India Company made several attempts (1701, 1736, 1755, 1832), to settle in Ningbo, only to be prevented by imperial edicts restricting all but the Russians (who maintained a small establishment—a priest, three curates and five or six language students—in Peking from 1727, as well as trading posts on the Russo-Chinese frontier), to seasonal trade at Canton. In 1840 British warships blockaded Ningbo and the British entered the city in 1841; it was one of the ports opened to foreign trade by the Treaty of Nanking in 1842 after the Opium War. A British consulate, post office and other port buildings were constructed in the northern part of the city, outside the walls, and in the early years of the 20C the non-missionary foreign population was about 60. Ningbo was never a very important centre of foreign trade, post 1842, for Shanghai's growth eclipsed it, but in the mid 1980s the Chinese began to develop a computerised cargo port along the river when Shanghai's silted channels provided insufficient draught for huge container ships.

Ningbo's most famous monument is the **Tianyi ge**, a private library constructed between 1561 and 1566. Its name means 'Pavilion of Heaven's First Creation'; a name deriving from a traditional saying that 'heaven first created water' which, together with the brick and tile involved in its construction, was intended to protect its contents from fire. The library is easily reached from the Huaqiao Hotel: turn right out of the hotel and take the first major turning on the right (Changchun lu, which runs alongside a long, river-like pool). The two-storey building is visible at the end of the next turning on the right, effectively behind the hotel.

Despite fire dangers, it is fundamentally a two-storeyed, six-bay timber structure, with the dark-tiled, upturned eaves characteristic of southern architecture. Within the gate is a small courtyard; the library is behind, with a pool and rockery (complete with tiny garden pavilion) in front of the library. The rockery and pool were constructed during the Kangxi period (1622–1723) by descendants of the original owner, Fan Qin.

Fan Qin (1506–85) passed the third-degree exams in the capital in 1532 and later became vice-president of the Ministry of War. He retired to Ningbo with a library of Ming editions (both woodblock printed and manuscript) which included items purchased from other famous collectors like Feng Daosheng, heir to the Wanjuan lou (Ten-thousand Fascicle Pavilion) Library and Fan Dazhe.

The Tianyi ge is the oldest surviving private library building in China (private as opposed to temple library, for Buddhist temples have sutra halls), and said to have inspired the Qianlong emperor (reigned 1736–96) to construct the Wenyuan ge (Pavilion of the Deep Pool of Learning) in the Forbidden City in Peking, to house the new manuscript imperial collectanea, for he sent an official to inspect the Tianyi ge in 1774. The Wenyuan ge, a building in the northern style, perfectly harmonising with surrounding buildings in the Forbidden City, bears no resemblance to the Tian yi ge, except that it has two storeys and a rockery in front of it; it was presumably a mainly spiritual inspiration. The Emperor knew of the Tianyi ge through the collection of material for his great collectanea, 'Si ku quan shu' (Complete Library of the Four Storehouses or Branches of Literature), which was begun in 1772 when an imperial edict went out ordering provincial authorities and private book collectors to supply rare books for copying into the collectanea. Fan Mouzhu (1721–90) sent in 638 items of which 473 were described in the imperial catalogue and 96 were actually copied in the collectanea. The emperor was so impressed with the collection that he wrote two poems celebrating rare items, and presented two sets of paintings commemorating Qing military conquests and a set of the printed imperial encyclopaedia 'Gu jin tu shu ji cheng' (Synthesis of Books and Illustrations of Ancient and Modern Times) to the library.

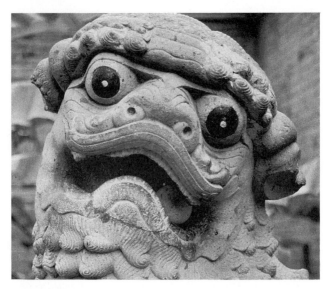

Ningbo: a lion in the garden of the Tianyi ge

In keeping with Fan Qin's fear of fire, his descendants maintained strict rules forbidding the use of fire and artificial lighting in the library; they also guarded against theft. No books could be removed from the library and the doors were locked with a series of keys held by different branches of the family (all of whom needed to be present to open the door). Unfortunately, considerable losses were incurred during the Taiping rebellion (1853–64) and it is said that British forces removed some of the gazetteers, for which the library is most famous, in 1840. A catalogue of 1808 lists 4094 items in 53,799 fascicles (excluding the 10,000 fascicles of the Imperial Synthesis), but a catalogue of 1889 lists only 2065 items, of which a mere 1270 were complete. By 1930 only 310 items were complete (out of a total of 962 titles in 7991 fascicles). Most of the surviving works (and others subsequently recovered) are now held in the Zhejiang Provincial Library in Hangzhou, although a few items are displayed in the Tianyi ge now.

All southern book-collectors had problems other than fire to worry about, most notably damp and bookworms. In the library, a piece of limestone was placed beneath each book case to prevent damp, camphor-wood box-cases were made for precious items for they absorbed damp and were insect resistant. In the Tianyi ge a special herb was also placed in the book cases to prevent worm attacks. It was also traditional to 'air' books in the early spring (before the atmosphere became humid).

Beside the library building (in the N of the compound) is the *Zunjing ge* (Pavilion of Respect for the Classics), moved from the Ningbo Confucian temple in 1933 with a number of Song and Yuan stelae from the temple. The enclosure is quiet and shady with bamboos growing by the rockery and pool; the whole enclosed by whitewashed walls.

Surrounding the Tianyi ge, between Chanchun lu and Jiefang nan lu, with the Yue hu (Moon Lake) in the centre, is the oldest quarter of Ningbo, well worth wandering in. The large houses, enclosed by whitewashed walls topped with grey unglazed tiles, are the crumbling remnants of its former commercial glory, built for the rich burghers of the Ming and Qing dynasties. They are characteristic of the SE: their gable-end walls are either curved into what the Chinese call 'arched cat's back' gables or else 'stepped'. Where you can see into the courtyard, two-storeyed buildings with wooden verandahs surround the court, the woodwork often carved.

Through the lanes, work your way N to Zhongshan xi lu, a main road crossing the old town, where the *Drum Tower*, now incongruously furnished with a modern electric clock, stands back from the road, up Gongyuan lu, which leads to a park. Returning to Zhongshan lu, turn left and take the second major turning on your right (Kaiming jie), lined with shops and small restaurants. At the bottom of the road, near the bent T-junction where the right turn leads to Jiefang lu, the *Tianfeng Pagoda* used to stand. It is mentioned in all guidebooks but had been knocked down in 1986. It may, however, be rebuilt, so a description of its history and former appearance is included here. First built during the Tang dynasty, the most recent interior brick structure was fundamentally of the Yuan (1330), though the outer wooden galleries were destroyed by fire during the Qing (1798). During a complete restoration in 1957 relics were found at the very top of the pagoda. The pagoda was octagonal and seven-storeyed; c 30m high.

From the site of the pagoda, return to Kaiming jie. Turn left then take the right turning that leads back to Jiefang lu and follow the narrow streets westward until you reach the Moon Lake, which is crossed by Liuding jie, on which the Huaqiao Hotel stands.

Another area in which to wander is the old *Foreign Concession*, N of the Xinjiang bridge, close to the waterfront and quays, where the crumbling Western-style buildings contrast with the crumbling Chinese mansions of the old city.

From Ningbo it is possible to visit two temple complexes, Baoguo si to the NW, and the Ayuwang si, Wufo ta and Tiantong si to the SE. They can be reached by taxi or bus.

The No. 11 bus (from the Northern Bus Station) takes approximately 45 minutes to reach the **Baoguo si** (Temple to Protect the Nation), 15km outside Ningbo in the Lingshan Hills. A waterfall on the tree-covered hill against which the temple is built, descends from a dragon's head spout. The temple itself is laid out in the standard pattern with the Heavenly King Hall, the Mahavira Hall (the Hall of the Great Hero, one of the titles of the Buddha), the Guanyin Chamber and the Library on the main N–S axis, with the monks' accommodation, reception rooms and the bell and drum towers on either side. The *Mahavira Hall*, though restored, is the earliest surviving wooden building, not only in Zhejiang province but the whole of the Yangtze delta area, dating from the Song (1013). Despite restoration, the interior, in particular, preserves early features in the chunky *dougeng* brackets and the crescent-moon-shaped beams. There are three caisson ceilings, also solidly constructed in the Song style (consider, in comparison, the Qing dynasty caisson ceilings in the halls of the Forbidden City, Peking, where the structural parts have been miniaturised and multiplied into a filigree decoration). The external appearance of the halls is typically southern, with strongly up-turned double-eaves and decorated ridge.

The *Ayuwang Temple* or *Asoka Temple*, some 20km E of Ningbo and reached from the Eastern Bus Station, is not itself architecturally distinguished but is famous for its tiny carved wooden relic pagoda, of uncertain date. Only some 15cm high, it is said to contain a relic of Sakyamuni. Legend has it that it was dug up in the late 3C and was believed to be one of the 84,000 reliquaries made by King Asoka (the Indian king, first major patron of Buddhism, who ruled c 274–237 BC). The reliquary is square, carved with Buddhist scenes in high relief and surmounted by four flaring tips with a central spire. Its date is uncertain but literary records recount pilgrimages made to see the relic by famous monks such as Jian Zhen of the Tang (who travelled to Japan). (Account taken from 'Zhong guo gu ta' by Luo Zhewen, 1985.)

Not far from the Asoka Temple is the *Wu fo ta* (Five Buddhas Pagoda) and 100m further E is the *Tian tong si* (Temple of the Heavenly Child), founded in the late 3C, famous as a Chan (Japanese Zen) centre in the Tang and Song, attracting such famous Japanese monks as Eisai (1141–1215) and his disciple Dogen (1200–53) who introduced the Rinzai teachings (based on those of the Chinese Chan master Lin Ji) and Soto Zen respectively. Eisai also introduced tea-drinking to Japan on his return from China. The buildings that survive today are not architecturally remarkable.

15 Shaoxing

Shaoxing, a small town some 100km W of Ningbo, is one of the prettiest and most unspoilt towns in China. Criss-crossed with canals, filled with whitewashed houses, quite a number of which are now open as museums commemorating the lives of their famous inhabitants, its narrow streets and hump-backed bridges often impassable to motor traffic, it is quiet and relatively unmodernised, its tranquillity belying its traditional reputation for producing more corrupt government servants than anywhere else in China. The strength of the belief that all natives of the town were scheming shysters was such that one of its most famous recent inhabitants, the writer Lu Xun (1881–1936), would often only admit to coming from Zhejiang province, without specifying his home town.

The town is equally well-known for its rice-wine, Shaoxing jiu, which, like Japanese sake, is drunk warm and tastes pleasantly of glue. As it improves with age, local people are said to bury sufficient jars at the birth of a daughter to celebrate her wedding.

Hotel: Shaoxing fandian on Huaishan lu in the W of the town. One of the most attractive hotels in China, it uses old buildings (formerly a merchants' guild headquarters) set around paved courtyards full of plants. A fish-pool lies at the back of the hotel and the dining room (in what must have been the rear hall) is reached by a raised walkway which passes over a pool with fountains. The hotel has been restored and expanded, but with some care.

Railway: Shaoxing is on the Ningbo–Shanghai line, just over half-way from Ningbo to Hangzhou. There are four fast trains a day.

The legendary founder of the Xia dynasty, Yu the Great, is supposed to have been buried S of the town. He is supposed to have ascended the throne as first emperor of the Xia in 2205 BC, after taming the dragons who lived underground and caused floods—hence his sobriquet, 'tamer of the floods'. The Xia dynasty, recorded in China's literature, remains a puzzle to archaeologists for no sites that can be definitely ascribed to it have yet been discovered. During the Warring States period the capital of the state of Yue was in Shaoxing; Gou Jian, ruler of Yue, fought long battles against the neighbouring state of Wu throughout the 5C BC, only overcoming the ruler of Wu by the stratagem of sending a beautiful woman to him so that his energies were dissipated, and in 473 BC Yue annexed Wu.

The town grew rapidly during the Southern Song (1127–1276) when the imperial capital was moved to nearby Hangzhou, and very scanty remains of six imperial tombs of the Song have been found SE of the town in Zangong shan. In succeeding centuries Shaoxing's reputation for sharp practice grew: in Ming dramas clerks were usually from Shaoxing and there was a popular saying that Shaoxing had 'hills but no wood, water but no fish and men but no righteousness'. It may have been pressure of population that drove Shaoxing's inhabitants out into the empire to buy magistracies and make money elsewhere for in 1820 it was the fourth most densely populated prefecture in China. Together with natives of Ningbo, men of Shaoxing dominated the native banks or 'money shops' of 18th and 19C Shanghai: indeed, the first money shop had been opened by a Shaoxing charcoal merchant in the 18C. All of Suzhou's cloth-dyers and most of the soy-sauce merchants were from Shaoxing and in 1892 15 per cent of all county jail wardens in China were from Shaoxing. Jail warden was a position of great possibilities with prisoners' families only too willing to pay for privileges.

SHAOXING

Railway station
Chezhan lu
Xiada lu
Jiefang lu
Shengli lu
Shaoxing Hotel
Dashan pagoda
Zhou Enlai's ancestral home
Laodong lu
Ba zi bridge
Hongbu lu
Nan hou jie Beihou jie
Xinjian lu
Renmin lu
Xu Wei's studio
Lu xun Museum
Luxun lu
Shen Garden
Ying tian pagoda
Yan'an lu
Qiu Jin's house
N
Jiefang lu
Xinjing lu
East Lake

Tomb of the Great Yu

The charm of the town belies its unsavoury reputation: E.H. Parker, a visiting British Consul, wrote in 1884: 'The country realises to the full the "willow pattern" ideal of China. Stone bridges of elegant shape are seen or passed every few minutes...there seems to be little means of intercommunication except by boat...many of the small ones are worked with the feet'. The bridges and boats can still be seen; there are even rubbish boats in the canals. Small boats are still worked by an oar from the back, lazily moved by one foot by boatmen who wear the distinctive Shaoxing hat of squashed black felt, strongly reminiscent of Chico Marx's hat.

Starting from the hotel, turn left into the road that passes below the hilly park in front of the hotel, turn left, right and left again into Guangming lu. Soon, the *Dashan (Great Good) Pagoda* will be visible on the left. It is a six-sided, seven-storeyed pagoda, 40m high, and was first built in 504 when it was part of the Da shan Temple (whose ruins are now covered by the largest department store in the town). The present structure dates from the Ming (1403) and a major restoration was carried out after 1949.

At the T-junction with Jiefang bei lu turn left and the right along Laodong lu where **Zhou Enlai's Residence** can be found on the left.

Zhou Enlai (1898–1976) was a long-time revolutionary who finally became China's Premier. His 'ancestral home' was in Shaoxing, where his family was thought to have arrived during the Ming. As one of his Qing dynasty forebears lived for 91 years, and his wife for 100, their home was afterwards called Baisui tang (the Hundred-year Hall). Zhou Enlai studied at Nankai University in Tianjin and in Paris, where he

Shaoxing: canal-side houses

joined the China Socialist Youth League. A pragmatic man, with great diplomatic skills, he worked both underground and above during the 1920s–1940s. He was one of the most important negotiators over the Second United Front against the Japanese (1937) and negotiated the release of Chiang Kai-shek after the Xi'an incident (1936). His personal contact with Shaoxing seems to have been minimal: one guidebook describes at length a visit he made in 1939, concluding that 'although he only spent four or five days in Shaoxing, he did a great deal of revolutionary work.' Thus the house must viewed as a place where Zhou Enlai may have slept.

The original building was a Ming construction but its dilapidation was such that an entirely new building was constructed on the site after 1949. Entered by a lacquered black door in the centre of a three-bay entrance building, with its narrow 'heaven-well' courtyard inside leading to other halls separated by paved courtyards, it is a typical Shaoxing structure. The halls now house a museum commemorating Zhou Enlai's life.

Continue E (the road's name changes to Changqiao zhi jie) until you reach a T-junction with Guangningqiao zhi jie. Turn right here and you will soon reach one of Shaoxing's oldest bridges, the *Bazi qiao* (Bridge in the Shape of the Character for 'Eight'). The flat-topped stone bridge was built between 1201 and 1204. Beside it is a Catholic Church (under some sort of restoration, 1986).

Walk W back along the house-lined canal. People come out on to the path to start their little clay stoves with a tall stovepipe to get the charcoal glowing, and wash vegetables in the canal as small boats of all sorts pass. Continue W along the canal until you reach Xinjian bei lu and turn right (S) until you reach Lu Xun lu and turn left into it. The new buildings on your left house the **Lu Xun Museum**, and his *House* lies behind.

Lu Xun (whose real name was Zhou Shuren) was born into a landlord family in Shaoxing in 1881 and some of his childhood memories are recounted in his short stories, most notably 'Gu xiang' (Ancestral Home) where his playmate is an agricultural labourer's child of great charm and imagination, called Run tu. Run tu's son later ran the Lu Xun Museum. True to Shaoxing's traditions, Lu Xun's grandfather had been sentenced to death for attempting large-scale bribery in the provincial examinations and his father was an opium addict, who frequently sent his small son out to collect expensive and useless medical concoctions which failed to cure his T.B. Watching his father die, Lu Xun had determined to become a modern doctor, and went to Japan to study. Whilst he was there his class was shown lantern slides of Chinese being executed for their part in the Russo-Japanese War of 1905 and he began to feel that China's ills were not to be cured by a single doctor but, perhaps, by literature.

Returning to China, Lu Xun was a major participant in the movement to simplify the written language, a movement which gained momentum and political significance after China's post World War One humiliation at Versailles, when Japan was granted control over the German concession in Shandong province. The May 4 Movement (as it was called, after a patriotic demonstration) tried to transform China through simplifying literature and making it more accessible to a greater public. Lu Xun's own short stories are characteristic of May 4 literature and his sharp, bitter and satirical essays indicate his firm political commitment to reform. He saw much interfactional struggle in his life and the tragic sacrifice of many of his young students and, though sympathetic to the Communists in their anti-Japanese stance and lack of the corruption that was increasingly obvious in Chiang Kai-shek's regime, he never actually joined the Party. Many observers consider that he would eventually have fallen out with the Communists over literary policy but he died of T.B. in 1936 before he had a chance to do so. He is perhaps the most respected literary figure in modern China.

The museum contains a large display of photographs, editions of works by and about Lu Xun, and some relics, including his tiny gown and shoes. The family house, in which Lu Xun was born, is a large series of dark buildings grouped around courtyards, characteristic of grander buildings of the region. It has a vegetable garden at the back and quite a lot of typical furniture.

On the other side of the road is the *Sanwei shushi* (Three Flavour Study), the traditional private school which Lu Xun attended as a small boy until his grandfather's disgrace in 1893 and his father's death in 1897 made schooling too expensive.

A little further along Lu Xun lu (c 400m), on the right is one of the several houses in Shaoxing with fragmentary remains of murals of the Taiping kingdom (1850–64) which raged in the south of China, threatening the Qing dynasty. The houses are not formally open to the passing public but the gate-keepers will sometimes let curious visitors in for a moment.— Back on Lu Xun lu, almost opposite the Museum is a small turning on the right, Chunpo long, which leads southwards to Yan'an lu.

At the T-junction with Yan'an lu turn left, and take the next turning on the left, Yanghe long, where you will find the *Shen Garden*. This was a famous garden of the Shen family during the Southern Song (1127–79), of which only a corner still survives. It is particularly the garden buildings that have disappeared for the small gourd-shaped pool in the centre is original, as is the stone slab bridge and 'mock mountain'. The poet Lu You (1125–1210), another of Shaoxing's famous sons, wrote a poem about the garden where he used to meet his wife, and there is a small exhibition on his life and work in a new building beside the garden. The paved paths, the (modern) bamboo fencing and the flowering trees of the small, peaceful garden are not without charm.

Returning to Yan'an lu, turn right and walk back W until you reach the junction with Jiefang nan lu. Ahead is the second famous pagoda of Shaoxing, the **Yingtian** (Heaven-answering) **Pagoda**. This was originally part of a temple founded under the Song. The whole was destroyed during the Taiping uprising (1850–64) and rebuilt afterwards.

Turning right up Jiefang nan lu, heading N, past the crossing with Lu Xun lu, a small lane on the left, Qianguan xiang, leads to Dacheng long, where the **Qing teng shu shi** (Green Vine Study) lies. Perhaps the most perfect example of domestic architecture surviving in China, this was the home of the extraordinary poet-painter-calligrapher-dramatist Xu Wei (1521–93), who also murdered his wife.

His paintings are remarkably modern and free, and his calligraphy has been described as 'turbulent'. Some of his dramas are still performed and 'strike a very modern note' for his heroines attain military and academic distinction which was hardly common at the time. The murder of his third wife was extraordinary: his protector, a general whom he served as secretary, was thrown into prison in 1565, and Xu Wei seems to have suffered a nervous breakdown or period of dramatic insecurity approaching paranoia, for he became suspicious of his wife and beat her to death. His biography contains the mysterious information that he had previously 'destroyed his own testicles'. Condemned to death, his sentence was commuted to seven years imprisonment. The tiny house is, by contrast, exceedingly tranquil.

Approached through a garden with a rockery, full of bamboos, the building's whitewashed façade is pierced with two doors, one a circular 'moon gate'. The house consists of two main rooms, the southern one with a pool beneath the window, overhung with creepers. In the other room is a small exhibition of Xu Wei's work and that of the late Ming painter Chen Hongshou, who later lived here. The second room opens onto a small walled courtyard with pen jing and pen cai (pot 'scenes' and bonsai).

Returning to Jiefang lu, turn left and head N. The third major turning on the left is Guangming lu which leads back to the hotel.—It would be possible to include a visit to Qiu Jin's house, which lies behind the Ying tian pagoda, before Xu Wei's studio. Otherwise, it is well-combined with the Yu ling (Tomb of the mythical Emperor Yu), either by car or by bus. If the latter, take the No. 2 bus from the corner of Fuheng jie and Jiefang lu (heading S) and get off at the Ying tian pagoda, continuing on foot down Jiefang lu and turning right into Hechang tang; Qiu Jin's House is on the right. To get to the Yu ling, return to the bus stop and take a No. 2 in the same direction to the Yu ling, outside town.

Qiu Jin's House, another example of local domestic architecture with whitewashed walls, dark wood and narrow, stone-paved courtyards, was once the home of a famous woman martyr, born here in 1875, who was executed in 1907. The house was formerly the 'villa' of the Ming scholar, Zhu Xu.

Qiu Jin reacted violently against the contemporary subjection of women, unbinding her feet and abandoning her children and husband (to whom her marriage had been arranged by her family) to go to Japan and study in 1904. There she met other Chinese students, anti-Manchu radicals determined to overthrow the decaying Qing government and establish a progressive government. Qiu Jin seems to have been almost overwhelmed by possibilities, working with activists who made bombs and practising martial arts. A photograph survives of her, taken in Japan, where she wears a man's suit and flat cap, a costume she continued to wear on her return to China where, in 1907, she became director of a progressive girls' school near Shaoxing. She continued her revolutionary, anti-Manchu activities, for which she was beheaded.

Inside the house, which is set against a hill on the outskirts of the town, is an exhibition commemorating Qiu Jin's life.

The **Tomb of the** (mythical) **Emperor Yu**, subduer of the floods, lies 4km to the SE of the city, and whilst there have been buildings on the site since the 6C, those that stand today are modern: many buildings are said to be of the Qing, the great hall was rebuilt in 1934 and there was extensive rebuilding in 1986.

The 'tomb', if a mythical subduer of floods can be said to have a tomb, consists of a stone tablet, engraved with the three characters, 'great Yu's tomb', written by the Nan Daji of the Ming, standing under a very new pavilion with up-turned eaves. Nearby is the temple complex with a meridian gate, sacrificial hall and great hall on the main axis, built against a hill so that the buildings to the back on their high stone platforms tower over those at the front. The temple is not of great architectural interest but the area, with its canals, streams and pools where fish are farmed, is typical of the 'land of rice and fish', as the area is named.

The *East Lake*, 3km E of the town (at the end of the No. 1 bus route, which also passes down Jiefang lu before heading E along Renmin lu), is a well-known scenic area, with the lake lying beneath a towering cliff. Dykes and hump-backed bridges cross the lake and boat-trips take you through natural openings in the cliff. It is also possible to climb up the cliff for a view over the lake and surrounding countryside.

14km SW of Shaoxing (at the end of the No. 3 bus route, which starts from

The Orchid Pavilion outside Shaoxing

the corner of Jiefang bei lu and Shengli lu, just NE of the hotel) is the **Lan ting** (Orchid or, more technically, Epidendrum, Pavilion), a place of pilgrimage for Chinese calligraphers for, on the site (or somewhere nearby, the exact site is now unknown) China's greatest calligrapher, Wang Xizhe (321–379), held a party with 40 friends in 353.

Visiting the Lan ting, the complexities of China's view of her own past are made concrete. The exact site of the original pavilion is unknown, but people are quite happy to visit an approximation. At the party sacrifices were made to dispel bad luck and the gentlemen then sat, floating small cups of wine on the pool's surface. Whenever a cup of wine floated in front of a guest, he had to compose a poem on the spot or pay the forfeit of drinking the wine. At this gathering, 26 people wrote 37 poems and Wang Xizhe wrote a preface to the collection. The collection was carved in stone, and thus his calligraphy has been preserved and prized for hundreds of years. The event itself inspired the construction of garden pavilions with stone floors carved with maze-like runnels which were filled with water so that groups of friends could play the same drinking and writing game. Examples can be seen in the Tanzhe Temple outside Peking and in the Forbidden City (the 'cup-floating stream' in the garden of the Palace of Tranquil Longevity). The resonance of the Orchid Pavilion for the Chinese is enormous.

Inside the entrance, on the left, is a pavilion covering a stele with the two characters for 'swan pool' carved on it. They are said to have been written by Wang Xizhe and his son. Wang Xizhe had just written 'swan' when he was told that a message from the emperor had arrived so he rushed off, leaving his son to write 'pool'. The eponymous pool lies behind the pavilion.

Crossing the pool, the *Orchid Pavilion* is to the left (the building is modern). The inscription was badly damaged in the Cultural Revolution but was originally by the Kangxi emperor. Straight ahead is the *Liushang tang* (Floating Cup Pavilion), and behind it is a stele inscribed with the Kangxi emperor's preface to the Lan ting poems. To the right, surrounded by the 'Ink Pool' (said to have been the place where Wang Xizhe washed his brushes) is the *Zuojun ci* (General's Temple, for Wang held military office), plastered with stones carved with calligraphy by the famous.

Rice and water landscape near Shaoxing

16 Nanjing

Nanjing, capital city of Jiangsu province, situated on the lower reaches of the Yangtse, has been a city of major importance for 2000 years, serving as the capital of the southern kingdom of Wu (229–280), the Eastern Jin (317–420), the Southern States of the Nan bei chao era (420–589), the early period of the Ming dynasty (1368–1420), the Taiping Heavenly Kingdom (1851–64) and the Chinese Republic (1911–49). As wars were fought around and over Nanjing, the city suffered considerable devastation throughout the centuries but many relics remain, including substantial portions of the massive city wall.

Airport: the airport is S of the city. As a major centre, there are flights to many Chinese cities throughout the week.

Railway: the station is in the N of the city and is on the main Peking–Shanghai line, as well as the branch line to Tongling in Anhui province. Beware of the station taxi-drivers, some of whom are bandits; the fare to the centre should not be much more than 5 yuan (1987).

Hotels: the two main standard tourist hotels are the Nanjing fandian, 259 Zhongshan bei lu, and the newer Dingshan fandian, 90 Chaha'er lu (the latter is rather distant for walking purposes). There is a very new luxury hotel, the Jinling fandian, towering over the central roundabout at Xinjiekou.

Surrounded by hills, situated on the south bank of the Yangtse at a point where the river narrows, now marked by the huge Nanjing River Bridge (constructed in the 1960s, beginning with Soviet aid which was suddenly withdrawn in 1960), Nanjing has long been viewed as strategically well-placed. The first settlements of c 7000 BC were those of the Beiyinyang neolithic culture, characterised by reddish pottery, stone tools and evidence of cloth weaving. A large number of Beiyinyang burials were discovered near the Drum Tower in the centre of the city in 1955. Subsequent bronze age settlements of the Shang and Zhou have been found on both sides of the Yangtze. During the Warring States period (770–221 BC), an early arms factory, using raw materials from the surrounding hills, made swords during the late 5C BC for the three 'warring' states whose borders lay near Nanjing. The site of the sword factory is now occupied by the Chaotian gong Temple-museum. A walled town was built in 333 BC when the leader of the state of Chu overthrew the Yue kingdom.

The town, built to the W of Nanjing (just beside the communications tower), was first known as Jinling (Golden Hill), a name preserved in Jinling Hotel, amongst other contemporary institutions, later as Shitou cheng (Stone City) and centred on Qingliang Hill (now the Qingliang Park). It is said that Qin shi huang, Emperor of the Qin, the 'Great Unifier', came to Nanjing in 210 BC and was told by a geomancer that a new emperor would arise in Nanjing. Paranoid, the Qin emperor saw this as a threat to himself and ordered earthworks to be dug to alter the fengshui of the area. Despite his precautions, many (albeit short-lived and usually regional) future rulers later arose in Nanjing.

Sun Quan (AD 185–252) established the state of Wu (one of the Three Kingdoms, 220–280), moving his capital to Nanjing in 229, constructing a new walled city on the site of the previous 'stone city'. Part of his sandstone wall can still be seen in the W of the city, overlaid by the 14C Ming city wall. It was during Sun Quan's reign that Kang Senghui or Samghavarman, a Sogdian Buddhist missionary and translator of Sanskrit sutras into Chinese, arrived in Nanjing, bearing a Buddha relic, for which Sun Quan built a temple. Sun Quan's successors as rulers of Wu were less effective than he and the state was overthrown in 280 by the Western Jin rulers based in Luoyang, to the north.

In succeeding centuries the confusing rapidity of the rise and fall of local dynasties was evident in the Nanjing area. The Western Jin were overrun by western barbarians in their capital, whereupon a member of the Jin ruling house, who had been governing the Nanjing area, proclaimed the Eastern Jin with Nanjing as capital. The Eastern Jin failed to regain control of the invaded northern territory and failed to deal successfully with the influx of distressed refugees from the N, yet Nanjing became a cultural centre, graced by the presence of the painter Gu Kaizhi, c 344–406 (whose work survives in rare, later copies, including examples in the British Museum and the Freer Gallery in Washington), the wonderful but rarely translated poet Xie Lingyun and the calligrapher Wang Xizhe, associated with the Lan ting Pavilion near Shaoxing. Buddhism continued to flourish in this period of disunion with the arrival of the great translator, Fa Xian. One of the reasons for the attraction of Buddhism was that it filled a spiritual vacuum as Confucian orthodoxy appeared to have failed to effect governmental cohesion.

In 420 one of the Eastern Jin's generals, Liu Yu, seized power and established the Liu Song dynasty, which lasted 60 years. With the exception of its founder, this dynasty was characterised by brutal and extravagant rulers and savage wars with the Northern Wei which ruled China north of the Yangtse. It was overthrown by a general who, in 479, established the Southern Qi dynasty (479–502), like the Liu Song, nasty, brutish and short-lived. The material remains of the Southern Qi include a beautiful series of tombs at Danyang, 70km E of Nanjing. Avenues of large carved stone animals stand in the fields, the chimera, in particular, beautifully curved and feline, in great contrast with the stubby, solid animals of the later Ming tombs in the outskirts of Nanjing. There is also a series of Buddhist caves, filled with substantial stone figures, the walls carved with smaller figures in niches, at Qixia shan, 20km E of Nanjing. Though the caves were added to during succeeding periods, as late as the Ming, 1000 years later, they were founded by a hermit called Ming Sengshao in the late 5C, under the Southern Qi.

Once again (and the pattern is characteristic of disturbance when military power is all), the ruling house of the Southern Qi was overthrown by a general who established the Liang dynasty (502–577), retaining Nanjing as his capital. As was often the case in Chinese history, the first emperor of the Liang was a man of vision and accomplishment, setting up state-funded colleges for free education, promoting trading links to obtain exotic products from the S, and building avenues and canals and palaces in Nanjing. Towards the end of his life the first emperor of the Liang became a fanatical Buddhist, apparently withdrawing to the contemplative life in one of the many temples he had constructed and from which he had to be ransomed to return, reluctantly, to government. He funded the first publication of the complete collection of Buddhist scriptures (the Tripitaka), wrote on Buddhist ritual, and is frequently depicted in the frontispieces to southern Buddhist works, in earnest discussion with Buddhist monks. Towards the end of the Liang, a rebellion led by a general called Hou Jing caused incredible destruction and, with a population already pressed by the arrival of refugees from the equally turbulent north of China (fleeing to the grain-rich south), led to a famine in which up to half the population died of starvation.

The Liang dynasty staggered on for a few years until, in its turn, it was overthrown by yet another general who founded the Chen dynasty (557–589). Though the Chen dynasty managed to regain a small amount of territory from the Northern Qi, it was defeated in further attempts by the Northern Zhou, which was soon to be overturned by the founder of the Sui dynasty (581–618) which finally reunited China, the discrepancy in dates between the founding of the Sui and the downfall of the Chen indicating that the process was a lengthy and bloody one. As Nanjing had been the capital city of southern China virtually throughout the period of division (since the end of the Han dynasty in 220), the first Sui emperor presumably regarded the city and its inhabitants as potentially threatening and he ordered the city to be razed. No longer a capital, Nanjing managed to retain its position as a cultural centre and a major southern city. At the end of the Tang, when China was once again fragmented, it was made the capital of the Southern Tang dynasty (937–975), which was overthrown by the Song dynasty which, once again, reunited China.

Nanjing's next great period of importance came with the establishment of the Ming dynasty (1368–1644). The first emperor of the Ming, Zhu Yuanzhang, came from a very poor family in Anhui (though he later said that his family had moved there from the Nanjing area), and, typically faithful to his native place, first established his capital at Fengyang in Anhui. After six years of palace building (and the construction of a tomb complex for his parents which still stands), he was advised to move his capital to Nanjing, which he did in 1356 where, after capturing the S and proclaiming the Ming (bright) dynasty, he built a second palace and surrounded the city with a huge wall. After his death, he was officially succeeded by his grandson but one of Zhu Yuanzhang's own sons, who had been appointed to rule the Peking area, seized power and, in 1420, moved the capital to Peking, leaving much of Nanjing, including his father's palace, in ruins. During the late Ming the Jesuit missionary Matteo Ricci finally obtained permission to reside in Nanjing in 1599.

Nanjing was to be a capital twice more: first when the Ming dynasty fell to the invading Manchus and a Ming prince proclaimed the Southern Ming dynasty with Nanjing as its capital (partly in an attempt to revive the creative spirit of Zhu Yuanzhang, partly because the N was in the hands of the Manchus). The Southern Ming only lasted from 1664 to 1662. The last episode (leaving out the anti-Manchu Taiping leaders whose major base was Nanjing) came in 1912, during another period of division, when the Republic of China was proclaimed, with Nanjing as its capital, whilst those in favour of a constitutional monarchy, led at first by General Yuan Shikai, held on to power in Peking until 1928. Nanjing then became the capital of China but the external threat of the Japanese and the internal threat of the growing Communist Party meant that little power was actually concentrated in Nanjing. Nevertheless, the city today, its streets lined with plane trees and solid Western-style government buildings with the great monument to Sun Yat-sen in the hills, retains an architectural flavour of the 1920s and 1930s. The contemporary municipal government offices occupy the old government buildings of the Republic, and Beijing lu (W of Xinjiekou) is the old diplomatic quarter. Though Nanjing's buildings did not suffer drastically during the Japanese invasion, the occupation of Nanjing was one of the bloodiest episodes of the Japanese invasion. It is estimated that 400,000 civilians died between 1938 and 1945, many raped and butchered in a horrifying manner. When Chiang Kai-shek's Nationalist government fled W to Chongqing, the Japanese set up a puppet government under Wang Jingwei (who died in Tokyo in 1944, though his collaborationist colleagues, including Zhou Fuhai and Chen Gongbo who had both been founding members of the Communist Party in 1921, were executed).

A. From the Zhonghua Gate to Xinjiekou

The CITY WALL of Nanjing is not the regular rectangle required by traditional Chinese town-planning theory. As the terrain is hilly and also surrounded by areas of water, like many southern city walls, that of Nanjing, built over a 20-year period by the first Ming emperor in the mid 14C, follows the contours of hill and pool in an irregular manner. Its full length was over 33km and it was the longest city wall in the world. The average height from the ground is 12m and the wall is roughly 7m broad at the top. A number of sections survive: along the Xuanwu Lake in the N, and on the southern edge of the Zijin hills, and in the S of the city. There, the most impressive gate, the *Zhonghua men*, still stands and has been restored.

The original name of the gate was Jubao (Massed Treasure) and the name Zhonghua, one of the words for 'China', was first used for the gate in 1912. This is a well-fortified gate constructed from stone and grey clay bricks with three inner gates, covering an area of over 15,000 square metres. There are several narrow tunnel-like openings in the solid defensive walls and smaller side tunnels in which soldiers could

NANJING

be hidden. As with the bricks that form the floors of the Forbidden City in Peking, many of the grey bricks used in the Nanjing wall and gates are stamped with the name of the kiln where they were made and they come from several surrounding provinces. It is possible to climb up onto the grassy wall to the E side of the Zhonghua Gate and walk quite a way.

Back on the main road (Zhonghua lu) inside the gate, head N towards the city centre. Take the first major turning on the right (Changle lu) and then the second turning on the left (a lane called Dongpailou) which leads up to an open stretch of water (black mud as the canal was being drained in spring 1987). On the far side of the water is Zhanyuan lu.

Turn left and at No. 128 is the **Taiping Museum**. The museum, which commemorates the anti-dynastic uprising of 1851–64, is located in a residence used by one of the Taiping 'Heavenly Princes', as the leaders were known. This was the headquarters of the 'Eastern Prince' Yang Xiuqing, and it incorporated an old garden, the *Zhan* (Enthusiasm) *Garden*, which had formerly belonged to the first Ming emperor and later to his general Xu Da. Centring on a pool surrounded by piled rocks, pavilions and walkways, the garden also contains two notable pieces of calligraphy, a single vigorous character 'tiger' (hu) and the name of the garden in the calligraphy of the Qianlong emperor.

The museum itself is laid out in three parts, the last two rooms being part of the same hall. Exhibits include copies of many documents, maps of the progress of the Taiping armies which from their stronghold in Nanjing even threatened Peking, seals and coins cast with the name of the Heavenly kingdom of Great Peace (Taiping tianguo), used as currency during the period. There are Taiping soldiers' and officers' uniforms and, in the second room, weapons. Many of the texts displayed outline the Taiping ideology which included attempts to redistribute land and establish equality in marriage and the abandonment of the Confucian classics as the basis of education. In the last room there are accounts of contemporary rebellions, like that of the Small Swords who attacked Shanghai, and references to the internal divisions amongst the Taiping leaders and to the foreign army that helped the Qing armies finally to destroy the Taipings. The display is updated as new discoveries are made; the recent restoration of the tomb of Lindley (an adventurer who helped the Taipings) in a London cemetery is marked by a photograph.

Due E of the Taiping Museum (on the E side of Chiangjiang lu, behind No. 30 Meiyuancun) is a new *museum* commemorating Zhou Enlai who stayed in Meiyuancun (1946–47) as a leader of the Communist Party delegation which attempted to negotiate a peace settlement with the KMT government after the defeat of Japan. The new museum building of brick (to harmonise with surrounding 1940s Western-style buildings), and window details faintly reminiscent of the Shanghai house where the Communist Party first met in 1921, won a national architectural prize in 1991.

Back on Zhan yuan lu, turn left, bear left (the road running alongside the canal is called Gongyuan lu). Soon the entrance to the newly restored **Fuzi** (Confucian) **Temple** can be seen to the left. Founded in 1034, the temple was destroyed by fire not long after but rebuilt and the huge examination hall complex was built nearby.

The present buildings are said to date from 1869 though there has been recent rebuilding. The halls contain a small exhibition of local folk arts: paper cuts and various embroidered articles like children's tiger hats and 'cloud collars' with pendant lappets for women.

The area around the Confucian Temple is being thoroughly rebuilt in traditional southern style (and is interesting to compare with the northern style of shopfronts found in restored areas such as Liulichang in Peking and Qu Fu in Shandong). White-washed walls with stepped gables, dark painted woodwork and dark grey tiles, up-turned eaves and decorated ridges are all characteristic of southern building and the restoration of a popular shopping area is not without sensitivity.

Opposite the Confucian Temple at the end of Baishiba jie, against the city wall, is the *Bailu* (White Heron) *Park*, originally owned by the Ming general Xu Da. The pavilions were all destroyed during the Taiping occupation but the park has been restored (1951).

Retracing your steps from the Confucian Temple, past the Taiping Muse-

um, and back to Zhonghua lu, turn right up Zhong hua lu and walk until
you reach the junction with Jianye lu (W) and Baixia lu (E). (This is a
major junction where most buses turn left and then right, heading for
Xinjiekou.)

Turn left along Jianye lu and take the fourth major turning on the left
(Mochou lu) where you will find the **Chaotian gong** (Heaven-facing
Palace), a Confucian temple with a fine entrance.

Temples had been built on the site since AD 390, but the present buildings were built
in 1865 as a government school and centre for Confucian worship. Covering a considerable area, the Chaotian gong includes many gateways (with different names),
bell and drum towers, covered walks and halls. It is now used as a municipal museum, with a display of artefacts locally unearthed, from Shang bronzes to Qing calligraphy (by the ever-active Qianlong emperor).

Perhaps the most notable relics are those of the famous 'porcelain pagoda'. Built in
the early 15C by the Ming Yongle emperor in a moment of filial piety to honour his
mother, the Baoen (Debt of Gratitude) Pagoda stood in a temple of the same name
which was an earlier foundation. The pagoda was clad in white-glazed brick, each of
the eaves covered in green tiles and the whole surmounted by a golden dome.
Destroyed in the Taiping period, the pagoda was a marvel to foreign visitors such as
Nieuhoff (1623):

> In the middle of the plain stands a high steeple or tower made of Porcelain
> which far exceed all other workmanship of the Chineses in cost and skill;
> by which the Chineses have declared to the world the rare ingenuity of
> their artists in former ages. The tower has nine rounds and a hundred
> eighty four steps to the top; each round is adorn'd with a gallery…The out-
> side is all Glaz'd over and painted with several colours, as green, red and
> yellow…Round about all the corners of the galleries hang little bells, which
> make a very pretty noise when the wind jangles them: the top of the tower
> was crowned with a pineapple, which (as they say) was made of gold…This
> wonderful pile (as they inform us) the Chineses built at their own charges…

The pagoda was also included in Longfellow's 'Keramos':

> And yonder by Nanking, behold
> The Tower of porcelain, strange and old,
> Uplifting to the astonished skies
> Its ninefold painted balconies,
> With balustrade of twining leaves,
> And roofs of tile beneath whose eaves
> Hang porcelain bells that all the time
> Ring with a soft melodious chime…

Leaving the Chaotian gong and its relics (the porcelain pagoda was seen
as the symbol of Nanjing by early foreign visitors), turn left into Mochou
lu and then right into Chaotiangong xi lu (lined with small shops and
stalls). The street soon changes its name to Tangzi jie. At No. 74 on the
right *wall paintings* of the Taiping kingdom survive (they were rediscovered in 1952). The house was taken over by one of the members of the
entourage of the 'Eastern Prince' Yang Xiuqing and pictures of animals
(deer and horses and peacocks), flowers and the magical lingzhi fungus,
as well as the famous watchtower used by the Taipings, were painted on
the walls (not by an amazingly skilled artist).

Turn right out of the house and follow Tangzi jie until it reaches a T-
junction with the busy Hanzhong lu; turn right and walk (or take a No. 5
or a No. 18 bus in the same direction) to Xinjiekou, the main roundabout
dominated by the Jinling Hotel tower.

B.   To the Drum Tower and Xuanwu Lake

The next major roundabout N of Xinjiekou (reached by foot from Xinjiekou or by a No. 35 bus going N up Zhongshan lu), is that of the **Drum
Tower**, which dominates the open space. First constructed in 1382 by the
first Ming emperor, it has been much restored since. Built on a brick and
stone platform (once pierced by three tunnels), the upper part of the

tower is a double-roofed, grey-tiled wooden structure which once housed a number of sets of drums, mainly used to mark the watches of the night but also to sound the alarm or welcome visiting dignitaries. There is a fine view of the city from the top of the tower.

NE of the Drum Tower (approached from Dazhongting jie, the first turning on the right N of the roundabout) is the **Bell Pavilion**, first built in the Ming but destroyed in the early part of the reign of Kangxi (1622–1723) and rebuilt in 1889. It contains a massive bronze bell (estimates of its weight vary from one ton upwards), cast in 1388.

One of the largest bells in China, the folktale attached to it is the same one found associated with all large bells: the bellsmith, failing to achieve the appropriately musical tone, or distressed by cracks during casting, was in despair until his daughter threw herself into the molten metal; the resulting cast was perfect.

From the Bell Tower, continue E towards the city walls, behind which lie the **Xuanwu Park and Lake**. The area bounded by the lake to the N, Beijing lu to the S and Zhongyang lu to the W, was the old diplomatic quarter of the Republican period (1912–49) and contains some solid buildings. Xuanwu Park consists mostly of lake (15km long).

The lake was important as a water source to the many dynasties occupying the area and it was known by a variety of names until the Song period (960–1279, when it was used for naval exercises) when a black monster was seen to emerge from the water and the lake was renamed Xuanwu ('dark warrior'), after the turtle that presides over the N (for the lake is also in the N of the city). In the centre of the lake, linked by dykes, is a series of small islands which, under the Republic, were named for the continents—the state archives were housed on 'Australia', for a while.

C. Xinjiekou to the Museum and the Ming Palace

Take a No. 5 or a No. 9 bus E along Zhongshan dong lu to the **Provincial Museum** (321 Zhong shan dong lu). The museum was founded in 1933, at the instigation of Cai Yuanpei (a major scholar, friend of Qiu Jin of Shaoxing and Dean of Peking University during the May 4 period) amongst others, and built in 1950 in the traditional style. It houses the major provincial collection and includes a wonderful Han dynasty 'money tree' and a jade body suit (of the early Han), amongst other exhibits arranged in chronological order.

In the early 1980s the museum was mysteriously closed (it still closes on Mondays) because the director, who had fallen out with his colleagues and provincial superiors, committed suicide inside the museum; his family, resenting his treatment, refused to allow the body to be moved for some time. His action, committing suicide in the place where his problems had occurred, was utterly traditional. During the Qing a whole section of the legal code was devoted to the act of 'pressing a person into suicide'. It was not uncommon for a person who felt that they had been wronged and who could find no redress to commit suicide in the home of the wrongdoer, who was then held responsible by the courts. The end of the museum director's case is not known but it is a fascinating insight into the prevalence of traditional views in modern China.

If you walk from Xinjiekou to the museum, at the large junction with Taiping lu turn left into Taiping bei lu and then take the first on the right, Changjiang lu (which, further E, becomes Hanfu jie). On your left you will soon find the old *Kuomintang Government Buildings* (at No. 292, seat of the Republican government). The garden in which the buildings are situated was once the headquarters of the leader of the Taiping Uprising (1853). All that survives of the extensive house-garden complex is a 'stone boat' (or pavilion built out over water) in the western garden, in this case very closely modelled on a boat.

At the end of Hanfu jie turn right, along Xihua gai, back to Zhongshan dong lu and E to the museum.

Just before you reach the Provincial Museum a park which crosses the main road indicates the site of the old *Ming Palace*. To the left it is simply an expanse of grass, but to the right there are finely-carved marble pillar bases indicating the siting of previous buildings, five small marble bridges crossing a pool, the remains of an impressive gate (the Wu men or Meridian Gate) and, beyond, five more marble bridges. The park has been planted with trees which cover the area once dominated by buildings. When Zhu Yuanzhang first built his palace in Nanjing in the early 14C it consisted of three major courtyards with massive buildings raised on platforms and, on either side of the axis, an altar to the earth and a temple to his ancestors, with ministries in the first courtyard.

D. Zijin shan

This itinerary is best covered by car or bicycle.

Beyond the museum, outside the city walls, the E of Nanjing is dominated by the ZIJIN SHAN HILLS. This huge area of tree-filled park is full of sites of interest. In the W is the modern *Tomb of Liao Zhongkai and He Xiangning*, his wife. Built in 1935, the tomb has lion-topped columns echoing the Liang dynasty tomb columns in the vicinity, though the tomb itself is a bun-shaped stone mound with a stone tablet in front of it. Liao Zhongkai was a Cantonese closely associated with Sun Yat-sen; he was assassinated not long after Sun's death (in 1925). His body was brought to Nanjing for burial in 1935 and his wife, a well-known calligrapher and painter, was buried with him in 1972.

N of the tomb, on top of a hill, is the *Zijin shan Observatory*, still the largest in China. Founded in 1934, it still displays copies of the bronze Ming and Qing astronomical instruments cast for the early Jesuit astronomers who worked from the observatory in Peking for the Qing emperors in the early 18C.

SE of the observatory are the remains of the **Tomb of Zhu Yuanzhang**, founder of the Ming dynasty and the only Ming emperor to be buried in the vicinity of Nanjing (the tombs of the others are outside Peking).

Zhu Yuanzhang began the construction of the tomb in 1381, 18 years before he died. In the following year the Empress Ma, known as the 'filial empress', died and was buried in the tomb which was thereafter known as Xiao ling (the filial tomb). Construction of the tomb, surrounded by a wall over 22km long, was completed in 1383. The tomb has been badly damaged and now consists of two main parts, the approach and the tomb proper.

The tomb is approached from the SE; the indirect line of approach partly forced by the terrain, partly due to the traditional belief that evil spirits could only travel in straight lines and therefore an angle in the approach road would throw them off course. The great walls surrounding the enclosure have vanished, leaving only the entrance, the stone archway called Xiamafang (Place Where Officials Dismount from their Horses), with, some 700m behind it, the Dajin men (Great Golden Gate) with its three arches and, close behind, the Sifang cheng (Square City), a brick structure with a huge stone tortoise stele inside, inscribed with a long description of Zhu Yuanzhang's accomplishments (erected by the Yongle Emperor, his son).

From the Square City the path turns W and is lined with a magnificent series of stone animal sculptures (just like the spirit way to the Ming tombs outside Peking).

Each animal type occurs in two pairs: two sitting lions are followed by two standing lions, two 'couchant' camels are followed by two standing camels, and so on. The animal figures are between 1.5m and almost 4m high and they include lions, rather doggy xiezhi (described in a guidebook as 'fabulous sheep said to be able to gore wicked men during fights between the good and the evil'), camels, elephants, qilin (often translated as 'unicorn', scaled and hoofed quadrupeds), and horses.

Beyond the horses the path turns N, past two carved columns, through the avenue of figures, military and civil officials (over 3m tall), before twisting again until the tree-lined approach to the tomb itself leads N.

This originally consisted of a walled enclosure containing a major hall, with an enclosed walk leading to the tower in front of the vast mound in which the emperor was buried. Today little remains of the structures, save the stone floors and pillar bases and small stone bridges over dry waterways. Even the huge tower fronting the mound has lost its wooden superstructure (though the enclosure has recently gained a herd of spotted deer to the E). In front of the mound, the original great hall was destroyed in 1853 and replaced by a much smaller building (built in 1865, restored in 1873) which stands incongruously amongst the broadly-spaced stone pillar bases of the original floor. The carved stone ramps are still very fine and much planting of ornamental flowering trees enhances the rather desolate enclosure.

E of Zhu Yuanzhang's tomb is the **Sun Yat-sen Mausoleum**.

Sun died in 1925 and his body was laid out in the Biyun Temple in Peking's Western Hills. A competition was held to construct a grand tomb and it was won by Lu Yanzhi (Y.C. Lu), a graduate of Cornell University School of Architecture whose 'untimely death robbed the renaissance of its most promising Chinese exponent'. It was originally intended to display Sun's embalmed body in a crystal coffin but mortuary technology was not up to the task and a recumbent sculpture lies over Sun's remains.
  Borrowing from the Ming tomb nearby, the tomb, whose white marble and blue tiled roofs symbolise the white sun and blue ground of the Kuomintang flag, is approached through a series of walks, steps and archways, the first of which bears the characters bo ai (universal love), the next the phrase 'the world belongs to all', and a stele pavilion. Beyond this is a huge flight of white marble steps leading to the tomb itself, which is carved inside with the Republican constitution in Sun's own hand. The seated figure was carved by a Polish sculptor resident in Paris, Landowski, and a Japanese artist also contributed to the construction of the huge tomb which took some three years to complete.

To the E of Sun Yat-sen's Tomb is the *Linggu* (Spirit Valley) *Pagoda*, constructed in 1929 at Chiang Kai-shek's suggestion and designed by an American architect, Henry Killam Murphy, who was architectural advisor to the Chinese government in the 1930s (and teacher of Lu Yanzhi who designed Sun Yat-sen's Tomb).

It would appear that the pagoda was intended to be part of a 'Revolutionist's Memorial' (commemorating the 1911 Republican revolution), in which 'purely Chinese architectural features were carried out in reinforced concrete construction'. Only the pagoda, with its blue and green glazed tiles and 'full Chinese colour scheme, red columns with polychrome entablatures...in permanent cement colours built in without the use of paint' (H.K. Murphy in 'China', ed. H. Farnsworth Macnair, Berkeley, University of California Press, 1946) stands today.

Just S of the concrete pagoda is the *Wuliang dian* or 'Beamless Hall' (which was incorporated into the Revolutionist's Memorial area by restoration in the 1930s), a Ming structure built entirely of brick.

This is relatively unusual in China where timber remained the fundamental structural material. During the Ming timber shortages were acute and several of these brick-vaulted halls were built (another fine example is on Wutai shan and there is one in Taiyuan), but the practical solution to the timber shortage did not catch on. The hall was part of a temple that originally stood in the tomb area of Zhu Yuanzhang. When the first Ming emperor began the construction of his tomb he had the temple pulled down and rebuilt to the E. The hall was originally named the Wuliang shou fo dian (Hall of the Buddha of Eternal Longevity) and its present name, Wuliang dian, involves two entirely different characters pronounced in the same way as the 'wuliang' meaning 'eternal' or 'boundless'.

Just NW of the hall is the small (now concrete) *Tumulus* of the 6C monk Bao zhi (the tomb is called Zhigong ling or Duke Zhi's Tomb), and to the NE is the *Tomb of Deng Yanda* (1895–1931), a close supporter of Sun Yat-sen who opposed Chiang Kai-shek and was therefore executed.

There is, apparently, a completely reconstructed Ling gu Temple now standing S of the pagoda, with monks and some precious relics of the Tang dynasty Buddhist pilgrim Xuan zang.

There are a large number of tombs, particularly of the Ming period, scattered around Nanjing, some inaccessibly tucked away in factories and housing estates (listed in Barry Till, 'In Search of Old Nanking', Hong Kong, Joint Publishing, 1982), but two are reasonably accessible by car (or by No. 11 bus from the Drum Tower, descending at the terminus, Yingtuo cun, and walking back towards Nanjing, when they can be found on the right). They stand on the Ningqi lu, between Bancang cun and Yingtuo cun.

The first that you encounter (if you head NE along the Ningqi lu) is the *Tomb of Xu Da* (1332–85).

Xu Da was a famous general, a native of Fengyang in Anhui (close to Zhu Yuanzhang's home, a factor which must have brought them closer for trust in traditional China was often established on the basis of kinship or 'native place' ties). He fought alongside Zhu Yuanzhang from 1353, taking Peking with considerable restraint (allowing no pillage) and leading armies out across the Gobi Desert to pursue the Mongols.

His tomb is characteristic of the non-imperial tombs of the Ming, with a tumulus (with a stone in front of it simply saying that it is Xu Da and his wife's tomb) at the back, preceded by a small 'spirit way' of carved stone figures and a tortoise stele. In the non-imperial Ming tombs, the first figures are usually a pair of horses with attendants, the solid little figures enlivened by the carving of the animals' saddles. These are followed by a pair of sheep, a pair of tigers, military officials and civil officials.

Li Wenzhong's Tomb is a few hundred metres further along the road. He was a virtual contemporary of Xu Da, also a general in the Ming army but noted for his scholarly tastes. His funerary stele was inscribed by the first Ming emperor himself and stands out of line with the spirit road. One of the first figures (the horse and attendant) is missing from the spirit way but a large slab of stone to the right appears to be the half-finished raw material for the missing figures. The presence of this block has led to the suggestion that figures for such tombs were perhaps carved in situ.

E. Trips Outside the City

The King of Borneo's Tomb. The tomb of the visiting King of Borneo who died in Nanjing in 1408 was discovered in 1958. It lies off the Ning dan gong lu, outside the city walls to the S (beyond Ande men). From the Zhonghua Gate it is only a couple of kilometres, and marked by an almost invisible sign on the main road. It is some distance off the main road, to the W, beyond a hamlet. The first glimpse of the tomb, which is set against a small hill, is the tortoise stele. The figures of the spirit way are almost hidden by trees and undergrowth and are almost identical with those in other non-imperial Ming tombs.

The King of Borneo was only 28 when he died, after arriving in Nanjing with his wife, brothers and sisters and children in 1408 on a tribute mission. Apparently, Borneo had been sending tribute to China since 977, and when the first Ming emperor assumed power, he sent envoys out to foreign countries, including Borneo, in order to re-establish the old tribute system. The then king was apparently not very willing to acknowledge Chinese superiority but was, by 1371, persuaded.

On the way to the King of Borneo's Tomb, outside the Zhonghua Gate, the road passes *Yuhua tai* (Terrace of the Rain of Flowers) where, according to legend, during the reign of the pious Buddhist ruler Wu Di of the Liang (502–557), a monk preached on the hill to such effect that a rain of flowers fell upon his audience. The flowers then turned into little coloured pebbles (which are still offered for sale there in saucers of water). Under the Kuomintang the area was used for executions and possibly 100,000 Communists died on Yuhua tai, now commemorated in a great stone monument.

Qixia Temple and the Liang Tombs. About 15km NE of Nanjing is the

Qixia Temple, founded in 483, though the surviving buildings are basically of the very late Qing (1908), apart from some stone carvings. Carved into the hill are almost 300 caves and niches, the earliest dating back to the mid 5C.

A monk was said to have been reading the 'Wu liang shou jing' (Sutra of Eternal Longevity) when a Buddha appeared against the hill and the character for 'hall' also appeared. Although the monk in question (Ming Sengshao) died soon after, his son began the carving of the Buddhist caves, most notably the 'Three Saints Hall' (Sansheng dian, which is also, confusingly, known as the Wuliang—Eternal—dian) with its 10m figures of the Buddha and attendant bodhisattvas. Unfortunately, many of the figures in the niches (which were still being carved as late as the Ming) were damaged during the Taiping rebellion and late 19C restoration was almost as harmful.

To the E of the Great Buddha Hall of the temple itself is a small stone *Pagoda* (Sheli ta), said to date from 601 but restored during the Southern Tang (937–975). Octagonal, 15m high, with five storeys, the carving is lively, in the Tang style, with scenes of the life of the Buddha near the base, then a series of small figures supporting the pagoda, above them a circle of lotus petals surmounted by architectural details interspersed with carvings of the guardians of the four quarters and a pagoda-like top with stone-carved eaves details.

Beside the road to Qixia si there are a number of *Tombs* of the Liang dynasty (502–557) only a few kilometres outside the city. Standing in green fields, these tombs are recognisable from the tall (sometimes fluted) columns and the solid but curvy winged lions carved with cloud patterns, their mouths open in a snarl. The tombs are those of Xiao Jing, a cousin of the Emperor Wu Di who served as an official and died in 528, and the Emperor's younger brother, Xiao Dan, who died in 522 and whose tortoise stele bears characters carved from the calligraphy of the great master Wang Xizhi. Further on there are two more tombs of brothers of the Wu Di emperor, with similar assemblages of winged lions, tortoise stelae and lion-topped columns. The sinuousness of some of the lions and the scrolling lines of the patterns that cover them stand in marked contrast to the other great group of funerary figures to be found in Nanjing, the stolid, almost naive non-imperial Ming figures.

17 Yangzhou

Yangzhou in Jiangsu province, situated near the junction of the Grand Canal, some 80km NE of Nanjing, is one of the historic towns of the Yangtse delta area. It is a charming city with many canals and bridges and spectacular domestic architecture though it is particularly famous for its gardens and cultural connections, both intellectual and popular.

Travel: Yangzhou is not on the rail network, nor does it have an airport. It is most easily reached by bus from Nanjing (about 2½ hours on one of China's first dual carriageway motorways), or Zhenjiang (usually less than 1 hour including the crossing of the Yangtse).

Hotels: the Xiyuan fandian (West Garden Guesthouse) on Fengleshang jie is said to have been constructed on the site of one of the villas laid out for the Qianlong emperor's visits to Yangzhou. The emperor's boat was said to have moored on the section of moat that runs through the garden. Next door is the multi-storeyed Yangzhou bingguan (Yangzhou Hotel).

Yangzhou's recorded history begins with construction of the town of Hanjiang and canal construction in 486 BC. For many hundreds of years, particularly after the construction of the Grand Canal linked Yangzhou with the Sui capital at Luoyang in the 7C, Yangzhou was extremely prosperous and, as the 'Japanese Railway Guide' (1924) has it: 'The place has always been known as one of pleasure and gaiety...In the palmy days of Yangzhou, it was said that a man having once entered the city in search of pleasure would find himself unable to leave it until he had squandered his all'. When the Sui Emperor linked Yangzhou by canal to his capital in Luoyang he celebrated the link by arriving in a flotilla of gloriously decorated dragon boats which were pulled along the canal by teams of beautiful girls.

At the fall of the Song in the 13C the Grand Canal was in disrepair; Yangzhou's fortunes declined, and with them, the gardens that had been famous from the Tang dynasty. Marco Polo claims to have been governor of Yangzhou which he described as 'great and prosperous', with a population of 'idolators' but his further account of the city where 'accoutrements for horses and men-at-arms are produced…in great quantities' hardly tallies with Yangzhou's fame as a cultural centre whose handicrafts included lacquered pottery, carved jade, embroidery and painting. If he was indeed governor, he was remarkably out of touch since he concluded that, beyond the men-at-arms and their accoutrements, there was 'nothing else here worthy of note'.

At the beginning of the Ming the Grand Canal was restored and with it, Yangzhou's prosperity, based not only on silk and rice but also on salt. Salt was a major item of taxation in traditional China and much of the salt trade was controlled by merchants from Anhui province, who lived in Yangzhou in large numbers, constructing elegant houses and gardens for themselves. Yangzhou was one of the major stopping points for the imperial tours of inspection of the south in the middle to late 18C; whenever these occurred the salt merchants vied with each other to build lavish gardens and villas to accommodate the imperial visitors.

The gardens of Yangzhou are, in general, smaller in scale than some of those in Suzhou and more invariably associated with houses and temple buildings. In some, the garden area is far smaller than the residential part. Chen Congzhou has written of the mixture of influences in Yangzhou's architecture and garden design, combining forms from Anhui with aspects of northern design. He states that some of the garden areas of the Yuanming yuan ('Old Summer Palace') in Peking used a Yangzhou design method, and the smallness of the garden areas also recalls the private gardens of the north. The rockeries and rather solid pavilions are also reminiscent of the north whilst the domestic architecture, with its stepped and curved gable end walls, is firmly of the south.

Aside from its domestic architecture, much of which is well-preserved despite destruction over the centuries—during the fall of the Ming and the Taiping uprising in particular—Yangzhou is also famous for a group of painters, the 'eccentrics of Yangzhou' whose work was said to have been excluded from the imperial collection on the grounds of its unconventionality. The eccentrics are often numbered as eight but the actual number must be taken as more flexible, representing a group of painters, associated with the cultural centre of Yangzhou and characteristically bold in their approach. Gao Qipei (1672–1734) grew a fingernail and specialised in 'finger-painting', which we normally associate with pre-school children. His incredibly sparse paintings include a wonderful series of album leaves now in the Nanjing Museum. A water-buffalo in a pool is depicted: the top of its head and horns sketched lightly, a single splash of paint to indicate its rump. In another leaf, duckweed (a series of dark splodges of paint, laid on with the finger tip) serves as an attraction for three prawns and a shoal of tiny minnows, scratched in with his fingernail. Hua Yan (1682–1786) used brushes in his 'Wutong Tree and Squirrels' (in the Palace Museum collection, Peking, rather contradicting the traditional view of imperial disapproval though the painting may have been acquired later). Charmingly lively squirrels painted with tiny furry strokes dash about in branches which have been painted with a softer, wetter brush.

Another, earlier, master who lived in Yangzhou, was Shi Tao (also known as Dao Ji), 1642–c 1717. A very distant relative of the Ming imperial family, Shi Tao became a Buddhist monk with the fall of the Ming, adopting the Buddhist name Dao Ji. He was one of the most innovative of all China's painters, perhaps his best-known painting being the long landscape scroll, now in the Suzhou Museum, sometimes known as the '10,000 Ugly Ink-dots'. Shi Tao himself describes in a colophon how he 'splashed the ink' and how the spots would annoy the great masters. Beginning with splashes of ink thrown across the paper, he built up a landscape, straggling lines linking the blots to form mountains and trees. Shi Tao also painted marvellous album leaves (there are examples in the Shanghai Museum) with funny little figures dwarfed by mountains. The association of these major masters with Yangzhou serves to emphasise its position as a centre of culture in the area.

In popular culture, Yangzhou gives a name to a form of recitation or story-telling, *Yangzhou ping hua*. In the 18C, platforms were set up along the streets near the town gates and performers would re-enact entire novels in narrative form; each performer specialising in a specific genre of story. Performances of this type still take place in Yangzhou. There is also a form of local opera, *Yang ju*.

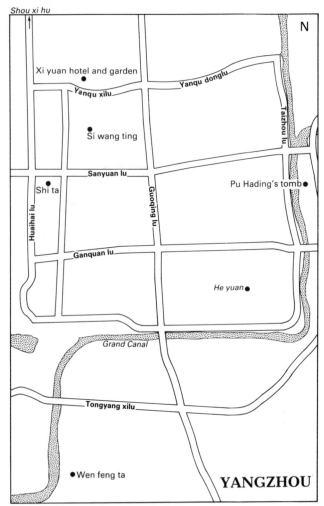

Some of the major sites of Yangzhou lie just outside the town, to the NW and are best visited by car.

Sui Yangdi ling (Tumulus of the Sui Emperor Yangdi; reigned 605–617). The emperor visited Yangzhou three times, in 605, 606 and 612, celebrating the construction of the Grand Canal. He died 'of excesses' in Yangzhou and was first buried elsewhere. This tumulus was constructed in 622 but it soon fell into disrepair. In 1807 a local scholar had it tidied up and a new stone bearing the emperor's name was carved by a contemporary calligrapher, Yi Bingshou.

Returning to Yangzhou, 3km outside the town, to the NW, are the ruins of the **Tang city wall**. During the Tang the town was divided into two parts, one containing the administrative offices (yamen) and one enclosing dwellings. The site is that of the former, administrative enclosure; the other is buried under today's buildings to the SE. Excavations of the site have yielded many burials, ceramics, building materials (tiles and bricks) as well as sites of carved bone and smelting workshops.

In the SW corner of the Tang ruins is the *Guanyin Hill* (Guanyin shan) with stone steps leading to the top where all the buildings are late Qing or later (though there was a tower here during the Sui on whose ruins a temple was built during the Song).

Just W of the Guanyin shan is the **Daming si** (Great Brightness Temple). It was founded during the Great Brightness reign period of the Liu Song dynasty (457–465), hence its name. It is also sometimes known as the *Qiling si* (Temple of the Home of the Spirits) after the Qiling Pagoda that was constructed here in 601. When the Qing Qianlong emperor visited the temple in 1765 he wrote, in his own hand, the name Fajing si (Silence of the Law Temple). The surviving buildings all date from the late Qing (after the Taiping rebellion so it must be assumed that the temple was damaged or destroyed at the time). In the main hall are three Buddhas; behind them is Guanyin on his island in the sea, and there are 18 lohans on the side walls, all 'finely carved in clay'. One of the side buildings contains an exhibition on the life of the Tang dynasty monk Jian Zhen.

A notable feature of the temple is the *Jian Zhen Hall*, built by the Japanese in 1973. The hall is modelled on the main hall of the Toshodai Temple in Nara (Japan) built by Jian Zhen after his arrival in Japan in 753. Jian Zhen (688–763) was a monk of the Daming si who went back to Japan with two monks who had come to seek a master (required to impose discipline on the lax Japanese Buddhist community). It took five attempts at the sea voyage before he succeeded on the sixth voyage and he is commemorated by a dry lacquer statue which still stands in the Toshodai Temple. He is credited with introducing, not only Chinese Buddhist discipline but also medicine, language, architecture, sculptural techniques and printing to Japan. Memorial activities were held in Yangzhou, jointly sponsored by the Chinese and the Japanese in 1963 for the 1200th anniversary of his arrival in Japan. The clean lines of the hall, reminiscent of the Tang buildings on Wutai shan in distant Shanxi, are characteristic of the Tang and there is an elegant cedarwood sculpture of Jian Zhen in the hall, as well as murals commemorating his life and work.

Just E of the Daming Temple is the **Shou xi hu or** 'Narrow West Lake', an area of park and garden with a long, thin stretch of water in it which is indeed narrower than Hangzhou's West Lake. It has been, as Chinese guidebooks have it, a favourite 'scenic spot' since the Six Dynasties (AD 222–589). The area contains many of the sights of Yangzhou.

The *Bai ta* or White Dagoba (a dagoba is a Tibetan-style stupa) is modelled on that in the Beihai in Peking and it is said to have been constructed by a rich salt merchant, anxious for imperial favour, after the Qianlong emperor had remarked that a dagoba, like that in the Beihai, would improve the scenery of the Narrow West Lake area.

The *Five-pavilion Bridge* (Wuting qiao) in the Narrow West Lake Garden was built in 1757 over a lotus pool, also at the expense of a local salt merchant in anticipation of one of the Qianlong emperor's visits. It is not unlike a three-pavilion bridge in the imperial park at Chengde (Hebei) but it is more complex in construction. The willow-shaded dyke on the W side of the lake is called the 'Long Dyke' and the pavilion in the middle bears the inscription 'Spring willows over the dyke'.

The **Xu yuan** (Xu Garden), with its *Listening to Orioles Pavilion*, with marvellously carved woodwork in the interior, is at the N end of the dyke. In front of the pavilion are two iron cauldrons, supposedly used to control the flow of canal water during the Liu-Song era. The *Pingshan tang* (Mountain-flattening Hall), on a hill in the garden, very near the Daming Temple, was first built in 1048 by Ouyang Xiu, (1007–72), a famous man of letters who was governor of Yangzhou and who often came to the hall to drink and write poetry. He looked out over the scenery from his vantage point where he was on the same level as the surrounding hills, hence the name of the hall. The present building dates from the late Qing (post-Taiping period).

There is a *Temple to Ouyang Xiu* nearby, containing a stone-carved, painted statue of the writer. To the SE of the Pingshan Hall is the *Pingyuan lou*, a three-storey, late Qing structure; views from each floor are said to demonstrate the theories of perspective advanced by the Song painter Guo Xi. The flowers on the ancient trees in the courtyard are said to be the legendary Red Jade flowers which first attracted the Sui emperor to Yangzhou.

The **Xiao Jin shan** (Small Golden Hill) is an island in the lake, dotted with Qing-period pavilions and rockeries (though there were said to be garden buildings on it as early as the Liu-Song period). It is named after the Golden Hill at nearby Zhenjiang which it is said to resemble. At the W extremity of the hill is the flat *Diaoyu tai* (Anglers' Terrace) where the Qianlong emperor is supposed to have fished, and at the S end of the lake is the *Rainbow Bridge*, a stone structure dating from the Qing (restored after Liberation) which replaces an original wooden bridge of Ming date.

On the moat which leads to the E off the Narrow West Lake are three gardens and the imperial jetty (where Qianlong's barge was moored) beside the Xiyuan Guesthouse. The jetty consists of a charmingly rustic group of white-walled, thatch-roofed buildings set amongst trees. Immediately E of the Rainbow Bridge is the **Xi yuan** (West Garden), built in 1751 which, apart from rockeries and old trees, includes the *Imperial Inscription Pavilion* (Qianlong) and a spring, the 'fifth spring under heaven'. The **Hong yuan** (Red Garden) is to the E of the West Garden and is thick with pen cai (bonsai) plants in marvellous pots; this, in turn, leads to the **Yechun yuan** (Beauty of Spring Garden).

Immediately S of the moat is a group of buildings: the Shi ta, Siwang ting and the Wenchang ge.

The **Shi ta** (Stone Pagoda) on Shita lu (which intersects with Huaihai lu, leading S from the Hong Garden; take the second turning on the right) was built within a temple in 840. It was originally outside the city walls and was moved to its present position in the Southern Song period (1127–1279). Many of the small Buddha figures on the pagoda were recut in the Qing. It is a five-storeyed, six-sided construction with a stone platform inside and finely carved railings on the upper register carved with animals including dragons, phoenix, oxen and horses. The stone-carved architectural detail includes upturned eaves and tiles.

Walking due E, along Shita lu, you pass a Tang dynasty Gingko tree and arrive at the *Wenchang ge* (Promoting Literature Pavilion) at the intersection with Wenhe lu.

This used to stand in front of the Confucian Academy of Yangzhou (and was one of a pair), dating from the Ming (1585). The academy, or college, was established at the order of the first Ming emperor who, being of very low birth, was a great egalitarian and believed in educational opportunities for all, hence his promotion of educational establishments. The present structure, all that remains of the Confucian academy, is late Qing. It is a three-storeyed, octagonal wooden pavilion, the lower storey faced with brick.

Walking N up Wenhe lu, the first turning on the right (Xianxue jie) leads to the *Siwang ting* (Pavilion of the Four Views). This was also part of an educational establishment: the Provincial College.

The college was also established at the order of the first Ming emperor. The pavilion was said to have been used for astronomical observation. Built in the Ming (1559), restored in the Qing, it is a three-storeyed, octagonal tower of complex timber construction (the four pillars of the lower storey lead right up to the top). It was used as a lookout by the Taiping army that took Yangzhou, hence its present name.

From the Xiyuan Guesthouse, the Tianning Temple, Museum and Shi Kefa Memorial are easily reached. Turn right along Yanfu xi lu and the

Yangzhou Museum is on the left. It is housed in the temple complex dedicated to Shi Kefa (1601–45), a loyal official in Yangzhou when the Qing seized power. He refused to surrender Yangzhou, attempted to commit suicide and was arrested and executed. His body was never found but his belt of 20 pieces of jade was buried (and rediscovered in 1979 when the tomb was restored) and the temple in his memory (Shi Kefa ci) built in 1772. Two fine gingkos grow in front of the main hall; his tomb is behind on Plum Blossom Hill. The buildings now house the museum with exhibits referring to the 'eight eccentric' painters and their followers.

Behind is the *Tianning si* (Temple of Heaven's Will). This was built on the site of a villa, and in 418 a famous Nepali monk came here to translate Buddhist sutras. It was destroyed in the Song, rebuilt in the Ming and, when the Qianlong emperor came on his southern tours, Cao Yin, a high official and grandfather of the famous novelist Cao Xueqin (1716–64; author of 'The Dream of the Red Chamber', otherwise known as 'The Story of the Stone'), ordered the block-printing of presentation volumes of the 'Complete Tang Poetry' (amongst others) to be undertaken in the temple. The emperor stayed in the temple on his trips south, when his barge was moored on the moat nearby. The gate, three halls and some side buildings are all that remain.

SW of Yangzhou is the **Wenfeng ta** (Pagoda of the Literary Peak), best reached by car. It stands by the old Grand Canal and was built in 1582. Constructed of a mixture of timber, mud and brick, it is octagonal in plan and six storeys high, marking the point where Jian Zhen set off for Japan.

The famous **salt merchants' houses** of Yangzhou are mostly to be found in the E of the town, around Dongguan jie. One of Yangzhou's most famous 'gardens' the Ge yuan, also on Dongguan jie, is an example, for these gardens were essentially part of a dwelling. Dongguan jie runs parallel to Yanfu dong lu (the eastwards continuation of Yanfu xi lu), immediately to the S. The **Ge yuan** is traditionally supposed to have been the home of the famous painter Shi Tao but in the mid 19C it was remodelled by a rich salt merchant, Huang Yingtai. The bamboos of the garden have leaves that are supposed to resemble the three simple strokes of the character 'ge' (which means single, self), hence the name. There is an almost equal area of building to that of garden. The buildings are beautifully carved and detailed, the garden lovingly designed, full of rockeries and winding paths. There are moon gates, flat stone zigzag bridges in corners of the pool and high-piled groups of curiously-shaped stones from nearby lakes.

Not far from the Ge yuan is the Tomb of Puhading. Go E along Dongguan jie until you reach the main road, Taizhou lu, which runs alongside the eastern moat. Turn right (S) and just beyond the next crossroads, on the right (across the moat, immediately S of Jiefang qiao or Liberation Bridge) is the **Huihui tang** (Moslem Hall). Here there is a mid-Qing mosque and the *Tomb of Puhading* (Behao Alding), a Moslem teacher who died in Yangzhou in 1275. According to an inscription, he was a 16th generation descendant of the Prophet and he was buried here in an 'Arab style' (according to a Chinese source) rectangular building with a vaulted ceiling, the actual grave in the centre of the floor, the walls carved with Koranic inscriptions between floral scrolling. Nearby are other graves of noted Moslems of the Song and Ming periods. There is also an historical exhibition on the friendly relations between China and Arab countries.

Near the SE corner of the city is the **He Yuan**, named after a later owner, a late Qing (19C) official called He Zhengdao who enlarged and rebuilt it. An alternate, possibly earlier name is Jixiao shanzhuang (Mountain Village of Sighs). It is entered from a small lane, Xuning men jie (opposite Xuning men Bridge, close to the SE corner of the city and moat). The garden is divided into two parts and buildings occupy more of the ground than open, garden spaces. There is much light, southern lattice in the buildings, many two-storeyed with open verandahs, though some of the smaller pavilions are slightly heavy and northern in feel, such as the *Chixin ting* (Pavilion in the Heart of the Pool).

Rocks and grand old trees are important features and the smallness of the garden courtyards, combined with the rather bare garden areas, combine to hint at northern influence which is said to have resulted from northerners coming to Yangzhou to work in gardens as well as the Yangzhou workers influencing northern gardens.

If you follow the Xuning men jie round to the N and W, you will find the tiny *Xiaopangu Garden* on Dashu gai. This is a late 18C construction and once belonged to a governor-general of the city. The small area is cunningly divided into two, to provide more separate 'views' on either side of the tile-covered walk that divides the space. There are fine details, stone tables and seats beside a whitewashed wall against which a small prunus grows and a wonderful peach-shaped moon-door, framing a view.

If time allows, other small gardens that can be seen in Yangzhou include the *Yi Pu* (Pleasure Garden), the garden-house of the Li family, at the western end of the Ge garden on Dongguan jie; the *Yi Lu* (House of Joy), once the home of the silver merchant Huang Yizhi, in Jijiawan; the garden and house of another salt merchant (19C), the *Yu yuan* (Remaining Garden) and the Chen family's *Wei pu* (Luxuriant Garden) on Fengyuan gai. These are similar in style and detail to the more famous gardens and well worth visiting for their architecture, as well as the gardens.

18 Zhenjiang

Zhenjiang, on the south bank of the Yangtse, is a convenient point from which to visit Yangzhou. Zhenjiang itself, like Yangzhou, owes its past prosperity to the opening of the Grand Canal in the 6C, under the Sui. This connected it (and its silk and rice production) to the capital in Luoyang, further N. Marco Polo praised its silk, especially the golden fabrics sold by rich merchants. It was a foreign concession town, with French and British consulates established. The latter can still be visited (it stands at the corner of Bo xian Park) as it now houses the local *museum* (open daily, 8–11.30; 1.30–5). The most interesting exhibits are the preserved body of a local scholar, buried holding his examination certificate in his hands, and the anchor of the 'Amethyst'.

This was a British gunboat sent up the Yangtse in April 1949 with supplies for the British Embassy in Nanjing. It was an unfortunate moment to choose for the Communist forces launched their attack across the Yangtse at the very same time and the 'Amethyst' was caught in the battle. Attempts to rescue the ship, by sending other gunboats and a third secretary (later to become a distinguished ambassador) from the Nanjing Embassy to negotiate with the Communist forces failed and it was months before the 'Amethyst', which had suffered some losses, managed to sail back to the coast.

The American novelist Pearl Buck (1892–1973), who brought Chinese rural life to millions in the West through 'The Good Earth' (1931), grew up in Zhenjiang. Her chldhood home is now part of the Zhenjiang Semi-conductor Factory and the school she attended (and where she subsequently taught) is now the Zhenjiang Middle School.

Though Zhenjiang is now a busy commercial centre, its setting on a rocky outcrop is attractive and there are temples and other sites of interest in the surrounding hills.

The *Ganlu si* (Sweet Dew Temple) is in the NE of the town. There has been a temple on the site since the 5C though successive structures seem to have suffered from constant destruction and the surviving buildings are Qing in date.

On top of the hill is a pavilion, the *Lingyun ting* (Soaring Clouds Pavilion), considered to be one of the finest anywhere by such diverse figures as the outstanding Song painter Mi Fei (1051–1107) and the Qing reformer Kang Youwei (1858–1927). Not far away is the *'First Scenic Stele under Heaven'* in the E wall of the temple, said to have been carved to commemorate the fact that the 6C Liang emperor considered this spot to be the first (or best) scenic place under heaven. The stele has suffered multiple destruction, like the temple; the current one dates from the 18C.

Nearby is the *Iron Pagoda* (Tie ta) which was erected to commemorate a noble of the Tang dynasty in the Tianbao era (825–826). Iron was used in its construction: hence its name. The original was destroyed at the end of the Tang; a replacement erected during the Southern Song was blown over in 1582. Its successor has also suffered from wind and lightning and only the base and first two storeys date from the Song; the top was added later.

Mi Fei's Tomb. The tomb of the famous artist of the Song (1051–1107), noted for his use of flat blobs of ink to delineate mountains, is on Huanghe shan. Mi Fei's (or Mi Fu's) *zi* or 'style' (name taken at the age of about 20) was Mi Yuanzhang and his tomb is known as *Mi Yuanzhang mu*. He had always loved the Helin si (Goose Grove Temple) at Zhenjiang and was buried near it. In front of the tree-covered mound is a stone altar and a stele.

Jin shan (Golden Mountain) in the NW suburbs was originally an island in the Yangtse. By the end of the Qing silting had joined it to the shore. The **Helin si** on the ex-island was built against the hillside, pavilions and halls rising above one another; it was locally described as the 'mountain within a temple'.

Founded in the Eastern Jin (317–420), the temple has had various names throughout its history, 'Golden Mountain' referring to the fact that gold was mined on the hill during the Tang dynasty. The Qianlong emperor named it Jiangtianchan si (Meditation Temple by Hills and River) on one of his southern journeys. The Song poet and official Wang Anshi wrote: 'Many halls rise in serried stone ranks, windows open on all sides to the winds; suddenly I see a bird rise in flight and feel frightened by the void'.

On the W of the hill is the 'First Spring Under Heaven'. It was first graded as No. 7 by Lu Yuping of the Tang but shortly afterwards Liu Bochu awarded it first place (on the basis of the taste of the water boiled for tea). A stone railing surrounds the spring, there are pavilions around it and the calligraphy describing it as the 'first Spring' is by the Qing calligrapher Wang Renkan.

Also on Jin shan is the *Cishou* (Benevolence and Longevity) *Pagoda*. Originally one of a pair known as the *Zunci* (Amassing of Benevolence), traditionally supposed to have been built in the 6C although archaeological and literary evidence places them in the Tang dynasty (618–907), this, built on the ruins of the northern one of the pair was last rebuilt in 1900, some say to celebrate the 65th birthday of the Dowager Empress Ci Xi, hence the addition of 'shou' or longevity to the name.

Jiao shan (Scorched Hill) is NE of Zhenjiang, on the banks of the Yangtse. It is famous for its scenery, views from pavilions overlooking the river and its ancient trees which reputedly include a Six dynasties (222–589) pine, a Song dynasty cassia and a Ming gingko. The *Dinghui Temple* (Settling of Wisdom, a name given by the Qianlong emperor), was founded during the Eastern Han (AD 25–220), destroyed and rebuilt through the centuries, the last major rebuilding occurring after the Taiping uprising (1850). Repairs since Liberation have 'preserved the Ming style' and it is a major Buddhist centre of the Yangtse delta area.

On the eastern slope of the hill are the remains of the *fortifications* against the English, built during the Opium War (1842) and reinforced in 1845 and 1874. The fortifications were severely damaged by the Taiping rebels in 1853 and, after rebuilding, were used from 1880 as an astronomical observatory.

19 Guangzhou

Guangzhou, known in English as **Canton**, the capital of Guangdon province, is a major river port situated at the northern end of the Zhu jiang (Pearl River) delta, close to the South China Sea but protected from coastal typhoons by its inland position. Its riverine communications with the hinterland are good, for three tributaries of the Pearl River—the Dong jiang, Xi jiang and Bei jiang—converge at Guangzhou. The city covers over 92 square km and is densely populated with more than 2 million people living in the city itself and another 5 million in the surrounding counties, giving an average density of 420 people per square km.

Apart from the intrinsic interest of an incredibly lively and populous city, by nature worlds apart from staid Peking, Guangzhou is currently the focus of interest within China because of its proximity to and close links with Hong Kong: it has rather taken over from Shanghai as the fashion centre of China in the broadest sense. Its architecture reflects its dual history as a southern Chinese centre (southern buildings at some of their most flamboyant are the temple at Fo shan and the Chen family ancestral hall) and the first major (pre-Opium War) foreign settlement (overgrown mansions on Shamian Island and arcaded shopping streets, out of northern Italy via Portugal and its empire).

Airport: the *Baiyun Airport* is N of the town, 12km from the centre. If you are organising your own transport beware of appalling traffic jams if you have to cross the city to reach the airport—consult the hotel desk and leave plenty of time. Probably the busiest airport in China, the Baiyun is both an international and a domestic airport. International flights arrive from and depart to Bangkok and Singapore (twice weekly), Melbourne and Sydney (once a week). Flights to and from Hong Kong are not strictly described as 'international' although customs formalities are conducted as if they were; there up to three flights per day. Flights to the rest of China are plentiful. If you are stuck in Hong Kong, trying to get on a rare direct flight to China, it may be best to book first to Guangzhou and then on to your destination (all of which can be done in Hong Kong), even if it means an overnight stay in Guangzhou.

Railway: the station is in the north of the town, at the N end of Renmin beilu. The main line N from Guangzhou connects with lines to Fujian, the west, northwest, north and northeast though distances may make travelling by a rail a slow business. Many groups enter and leave China by rail for Hong Kong, a journey of a couple of hours in a comfortable train with air-conditioning and videos.

Buses: long-distance bus travel is a new and cheap means of transport in China. The long-distance bus station is just W of the railway station and may be useful in emergencies (though it takes 24 hours to get to Xiamen, for example); a new means of relieving tourists of surplus funds is highway robbery which has occasionally been reported in Guangdong province.

Boats: the terminal for boats to Shanghai and Fujian is on the E of Yangjiang lu on the riverfront, and further down is the hydrofoil terminus (for Hong Kong). The journey is rather slower than the train and not as interesting, as spray conceals any views.

Hotels: there are an enormous number of hotels in Guangzhou as it receives a vast number of extra visitors for the twice-yearly international trade fairs (May and October). At these times, rooms are very difficult to find (and it may be wise for international travellers to book in advance from Hong Kong is possible). The trade fairs, once China's only channel for trade with the outside world, have to some extent been supplanted by direct trade at the provincial level and this spreads the burden slightly. During recent decades the fairs have occasionally been abandoned in favour of year-round trade in the city, but for the moment they seem to have been re-established.

Many hotels are concentrated around the Liuhua Park, just S of the railway station. These include: the *China Hotel*, the *Dongfang Hotel* and the *Liuhua Hotel*. Just E of the station, along Huanshi dong lu are the *Baiyun Hotel* (the tallest building in

Guangzhou, with a quite-pretty open-air lobby area) and the *Garden Hotel*. For non-trade visitors, hotels near the river are more attractive, set in the centre of town. The *White Swan Hotel* is the grandest. It has ruined Shamian's waterfront by taking over a fantastic view of the river and its traffic, now best seen from the lobby atrium (and many of the rooms). The *Guangzhou Hotel* (again, 'first class') is just E of the White Swan, on Haizhu Square, overlooking the river. The *Aiqun Hotel* is also on Yanjiang lu (the waterfront road), between the White Swan and the Guangzhou Hotel.

Guangzhou has had many histories. An independent neolithic culture (whose artefacts, characterised by earthenware pots with all-over stamped designs, some of which are intriguingly close to later bronze designs, can best be seen in Hong Kong) was overlaid by a distinctive, southern version of the Longshan (Black Pottery) culture. As yet, there is no evidence of a continuous bronze-producing culture in SE China. Lack of evidence is no basis on which to hypothesise, but traditionally the province of Guangdong and the neighbouring southeast was regarded by northern Chinese from the cultural heartland of the Yellow River as non-Chinese. An American scholar has described SE China, Hainan and the adjacent Vietnam as 'a linguistic and cultural Balkans in which relatively recent arrivals are intermingled with very ancient groups'. The distinctive language of Guangdong province, Cantonese, which appears to preserve many archaic forms (such as more tones and endings) now lost in northern dialects, has also been used to explain the gradual colonisation of the south. Xia Nai, the foremost archaeologist of 20C China (died 1986), believed that the archaism of the language was preserved because it was learnt by local people whose fundamental cultural affinities were more with the people of Vietnam than with the northern Chinese. Imported as a 'foreign language' in the Tang dynasty, it did not develop as it was to in the north, but preserved Tang dynasty endings (which have been used to recreate the rhymes of Tang poetry, lost in northern speech). Another theory about the archaism of Cantonese is that it was preserved by frontiersmen, far from their cultural heartlands, rather like Pennsylvania Dutch.

The south was colonised by the Qin emperor in the 3C BC and the Han dynasty proclaimed nine provinces in the area, sending colonists and magistrates to enforce Chinese rule. Their hold on the south was, however, precarious and with the end of the Han Chinese sovereignty retreated though it was more firmly re-established during the Tang. For the Tang, the south was both a source of exotica—glossy purple stone for inkstones came from W of Guangzhou, cinnabar, coral and, above all, pearls; cinnamon, cardamom, rosewood, oranges, tangerines and limes, bananas and lychees, camellia, hibiscus, francolins and parrots—and also a place of exile. Though the major posts (office of the Legate at Guangzhou) were filled by favoured officials, many lesser posts were filled by exiles who had offended the court, Though they hoped to return to the north, many died early of tropical disease and left behind despairing poems, sometimes acknowledging the beauty of the sub-tropics, but filled with nostalgia for home. Song Zhiwen, banished by the Tang empress Wu, wrote:

> Climbing figs sway in the blue air
> Arenga palms veil the cyan moss ...
> Hugging the leaves, the dusky langurs whistle
> Biting on blossoms, the kingfishers come ...
> Yet my glossy black hair will shortly become white
> My loyal-vermilion heart has already turned to ashes.
> Then how shall I ever head out on the homeward road
> To work the shears on my old garden's weeds?

(From E.H. Schafer, 'The Vermilion Bird: Tang Images of the South', Berkeley, University of California Press, 1967.)

During the Tang, Guangzhou developed as a major south coast port, attracting overseas traders and, like Quanzhou in Fujian, acquiring a sizeable Moslem population. Communications with the interior were improved during the Song as roads were built and Guangzhou became less a place of exile, more a trade centre.

During the Qing, as Westerners began to arrive in China, many approached through Guangzhou (including the British Macartney mission in 1793 which first requested permission to enter China from the coast of Guangdong). The British East India Company, granted royal permission to trade with China in 1609, established a factory in Guangzhou (Canton) in 1684 (though the Portuguese had arrived in 1516 and the Dutch about 100 years later). Foreign traders were restricted to the shoreline of the city of Guangzhou and at first were not allowed to reside in Guangzhou throughout the year, being compelled to retreat to Macau which was also the only place in which the families of merchants and missionaries were allowed to live before the Opium Wars. Without any civilising influences, the young Englishmen who went out as 'supercargoes' (a name given to those in charge of East India Company affairs abroad) tended to behave rather like schoolboys on the loose. William Hickey (1749–c 1830), the diarist, was sent out to work for the Company after squandering much of his money. He described his friend Bob Pott's approach to washing the dishes in Guangzhou: 'I never suffer the servants to have the trouble of removing a tea equipage, always throwing the whole apparatus out of the window or downstairs. They easily procure another batch from the steward's warehouse'.

The waterfront at Guangzhou in the late 18C and early 19C was dominated by the fine 'factories' of the various East India Companies; two-storey European-style buildings, flying national flags, built of timber at first, though this was soon superseded by rusticated stonework, colonnades and open verandahs. Here the supercargoes lived and worked, trading only with Chinese-government-appointed traders in tea, any porcelain to survive Bob Pott, silk and luxury goods, paying for these first in silver bullion and increasingly with opium. William Hickey described the waterfront in 1769:

> The view of the city, as you approach it, is strikingly grand, and at the same time must always surprise strangers. The scene upon the water is as busy a one as the Thames below London Bridge, with this difference, that instead of our square-rigged vessels of different dimensions, you there have junks … About half a mile above the city suburbs … is a wharf, or embankment, regularly built of brick and mortar, extending more than half a mile in length, upon which wharf stands the different factory or place of residence of the supercargoes, each factory having the flag of its nation on a lofty ensign staff before it. At the time I was in China, they stood in the following order: first, the Dutch, then, the French, the English, the Swedes, and, last, the Danes. Each of these factories, beyond admirable banqueting, or public, rooms for eating, etc., having attached to them sets of chambers, varying in size according to the establishment. The English being far more numerous than any other nation trading with China, their range of buildings is much the most extensive … with a small garden and every sort of convenience. Besides the factories which belong to the East India Company, there are also others, the property of Chinese, who let them to Europe and Country captains of ships, merchants and strangers whom business brings to Canton. For several years there has been an Imperial flag flying before a factory occupied by the Germans. The Americans (whom the Chinese distinguish by the expressive title of Second Chop Englishmen) have also a flag.

(From the 'Memoirs of William Hickey', edited by Peter Quennell, London, Century, 1975.)

Relations with the Chinese deteriorated as Western traders chafed at their restriction and confinement (both physical and economic). Couling defines 'Opium War' in his 'Encyclopaedia Sinica' thus: 'a question-begging epithet … The seizure of the Opium by Commissioner Lin was the occasion of the war, but the causes were the insults, indignities, oppressions and injustices of all the years during which the British and others

Guangzhou: 'treaty port domestic' architecture

had sought legitimate trade with China', and he reflects the view of the expansionist West of the 19C. The Chinese could well define the Opium War in similar terms but stressing instead the continuous provocation of expansionist Westerners who did not understand the traditional Chinese control of foreigners and trade, the frequent, sometimes murderous, brawls of Western sailors and the determination of Western traders (the British in particular) to pay for their purchases with addictive and illegal opium. The East India Company had the monopoly of opium cultivation in Bengal and the opium was shipped to China and traded illegally. In 1839 Lin Zexu (see under Fuzhou) was appointed Opium Commissioner in Guangzhou and destroyed 20,000 chests of the drug there, provoking the despatch of a British expeditionary fleet in 1840. The fleet blockaded ports, besieged Guangzhou and occupied Shanghai, forcing the Chinese to open more ports to trade through the Treaty of Nanjing (1842).

The Second Opium War, or Arrow War (1856), also took place in Guangzhou. When the Chinese authorities boarded a Chinese-owned ship, the 'Arrow', which was flying the British flag (to enable it to sail into all Chinese coastal ports), in search of pirates, the incident was described as an insult to the flag. The British Consul in Guangzhou, Sir Harry Parkes, ordered the occupation of the city by 1000 British troops. The incident was a useful pretext for revising and expanding the Treaty of Nanjing by means of the Treaty of Tianjin (1858) which gave foreigners the right to a permanent Minister in Peking and further freedom to travel and settle in the interior.

Parkes acquired the sandbank or mudflat known as Shamian (Sand-bank) Island in the Pearl River in 1859. This was to become the major foreign settlement in Guangzhou and the best surviving collection of colonial buildings is now there as the factories have disappeared.

Though the city was much marked by foreign influences, and retains many of the arcaded shopping streets that are found in so many ex-colonial towns, after the 1911 revolution it became an important nationalist

GUANGZHOU

Bus station • • Railway station

Liuhua Hotel

Orchid Garden

Huanshi

Tomb of the Prophet's Uncle •

Jiefang

Yue xiu Park

Dongfang Hotel

Zhen hai lo

Renmin beilu

Huanshi xilu

Liuhua lu

Dongfeng xilu

Dongfeng

Jiefang

Renmin beilu

Liu rong temple

Chen Family Ancestral temple

Zhongshan balu   Zhongshan qilu   Zhongshan liulu   Zhongshan

wulu

Huai sheng Mosque

xilu

Longjin donglu

Renmin

zhonglu

lu

Huifu

longjin xilu

Hua lin temple

Dade Guangzhou Hotel •

Dishi fulu Xialiu Roman Catholic Church

Heping lu   Wen hua gong yuan

Renmin nanlu

Yide lu

Yanjiang lu

Liuer san   lu

White Swan Hotel

Shamian Island

Zhu Jiang

(Pearl River)

centre, particularly since Sun Yat-sen returned to the city to found the KMT in 1923, after the 1911 revolution failed really to establish democratic government. The prestigious Whampoa Military Academy was founded in the suburbs in 1924 (with Chiang Kai-shek as Head, Zhou Enlai as political commissar and the Russian General Galen as advisor) to improve the quality of leadership in the Nationalist Army. In 1923 the Peasant Movement Institute was set up by the Communist Party in the former Confucian Temple in the E of the town and in 1925 the workers of the city went on strike in support of the Hong Kong workers who were themselves on strike against the British. Chiang Kai-shek, who had had his base in Guangzhou, from where he set out on the Northern Expedition in an attempt to take the rest of China (in 1927), had some 5000 workers killed in the city in 1927.

In recent years, with the establishment of the 'Special Economic Zone' at Shenzhen, which lies between Guangzhou and Hong Kong, there has been a tremendous increase in Hong Kong influence in Guanzhou. Businesses cross the border, goods from Hong Kong are found in Guangzhou, and Hong Kong fashions are quickly copied. In the evenings, when the hubbub of traffic is less, many of the streets of Guangzhou hum with the sound of sewing machines as Hong Kong-style garments are run up, and the incredible increase in the volume of traffic is partly due to the number of trade vehicles supplied from Hong Kong. Such is the increase in traffic that the jams are worse than anywhere else in China and, in an effort to alleviate them, second, upper tiers of roads are being constructed over already crowded roads (near Shamian, for instance).

Shamian Island and the Market.

The *White Swan Hotel* is on the waterfront of **Shamian**. Behind it is the old island with its colonial buildings crumbling slowly in the damp; a small, quiet place to walk and admire colonial architecture. Under the vast banyan trees were the French Consulate (E tip), a British Consulate on the main street, Protestant and Catholic churches, a masonic lodge and several bank headquarters. In the past, the gates beside the bridges of the tiny island were closed every night at 10 pm. On the quay on the far side of the bridge at the E end of the island a stone *stele* used to stand, commemorating striking Chinese workers killed by foreign bullets on the very spot in 1925. In 1987 this was buried under building works but it might resurface.

Take the northern bridge from Shamian to the mainland (to Liuer san lu). A little to your right you will find the entrance to the QINGPING STREET MAR-KET which fills all the small streets N of Liuer san lu to heping lu.

For those with strong stomachs, indifference to animal suffering and a total lack of interest in ecology and the protection of endangered species, it is possible to pass through the food section of the market and reach the bonsai and antiques section to the N. I have never made it much beyond the first, medicine section (as the sight of the edible kittens beyond is too much) but I understand that there are some hand-some pots for sale and reasonable prices can be achieved by bargaining. I expect it is possible to reach the appropriate section from the N.

Retreating to Liuer san lu, turn left, heading towards Renmin lu. The *Wenhua gongyuan* (Cultural Park) is on the left. In the early evening this is packed with people watching open-air entertainment which includes traditional forms like puppet shows and acrobats as well as space-invaders machines.

As the streets and all forms of public transport in Guanzhou are impossi-bly packed and distances are considerable, especially in the humid heat, it is better to visit other sites in groups by taxi.

Roman Catholic Cathedral, Peasant Institute and Martyrs' Memorial Park; Yuexiu Park and the Museum (W and NW).

The *Roman Catholic Cathedral*, or *Shi shi* (Stone Room) is at 56 Yide zhong lu. It stands in the grounds of the old Chinese Viceroy's palace (destroyed in an attack by French and British troops in the Arrow War or Second Opium War).

Building started in 1860 to designs in the Gothic style by the French architect Guillemin, and finished in 1880, though the cathedral was consecrated in 1863. The land was granted to the French in recompense for 'losses in the interior' incurred dur-ing the Arrow War and was described by J.A. Turner in his 'Kwang Tung, or Five Years in South China' as 'a fine Gothic building, which, with its magnificent granite spires, towers nobly above the dead level of the native houses, a grand example of "music in stone".' It was undergoing repairs, especially to a leaking roof, in 1987.

The **Peasant Institute,** where Mao Zedong was a tutor in 1925–26, is on Zhongshan lu, section 4. It was housed in the former Confucian Temple of the Ming period, portions of which remain; the rest of the dormitories and schoolrooms are those used by many of the great figures of the com-munist Party—Mao Zedong (who was head of the Institute in 1926), Zhou Enlai, Qiu Qubai, Guo Moruo and Peng Pai—until the school was closed when Chang Kai-shek turned on the Guangzhou workers in 1927. There is a rather wonderful display of revolutionary relics of peasant students and blurred photographs of associated events.

A little further E along Zhongshan lu (section 3) is the *Memorial* to the 5000 workers killed when Chiang Kai-shek suppressed the Guangzhou workers' movement. This was built in 1957 and consists of a grand gate and paved way which leads to a huge tumulus surrounded by a marble wall.

In the centre of **Yuexiu Park** (in the N of the town, just E of Jiefang bei lu) is the 28m-high **Zhenhai lou** (Pavilion Guarding the Sea), built in 1380 on a high point behind the town. It was intended as a watchtower for during the early Ming, 'dwarf pirates' (as the Japanese were known) were a tremendous nuisance to China's coastal towns. According to one account, it was burnt down and rebuilt in 1686 and it was certainly restored in 1928 when much of the five-storey timber structure was replaced by concrete. From the pavilion there is a fine view of the city, described rather oddly by Geil in 1911 as 'a most eclectic omelette into which many eggs have

Guangzhou: the Chen Family Ancestral Temple

been broken'. He appears to have been referring to the 'winding alleys' which have been 'modified by the foreign trader' and affected (physically less) by the 'cross-current produced by the foreign missionary'.

The pavilion now contains exhibits from the city museum. These include good tomb models from local tombs; items relating to foreign trade in the Sui and Tang and to the development of industry in the Ming and Qing (when Guangzhou was a silk centre, thanks partly to the support of an Overseas Chinese, Chen Qiyuan who, in 1872, introduced machine-reeling). There is an extensive display devoted to the history of foreign repression in the area.

The park has been a convenient resting place for local tombs of notables which have had to be moved because of new building. They include the tomb of one of the last members of the Ming royal house who held Guangzhou for 40 days against the Qing in 1646 (moved here in 1955) and that of Wang Xing (1615–59), a local Ming loyalist who held out until 1659 but committed suicide when his food ran out.

Guangzhou's Temples.
Just off the western part of Zhongshan lu, section 7, is the **Chen Family Ancestral Temple** (Chenjia ci), which now houses an exhibition of local crafts (*Guangdong minjian gongyi yuan*). The ancestral temple, built in 1890–94 with funds collected from members of the Chen clan from 72 counties in Guangdong province, is a marvellous example of the highly decorated architecture of the south. In plan it resembles temples in Macau, with a long front hall and courtyards on several parallel axes behind, the whole forming a long, broad (but rather shallow) rectangle. Northern temple complexes tend to concentrate on an emphatic central axis and are deep rather than broad in plan. The façade and roof of the first building are lavishly decorated with cut-brick work and fantastic glazed-tile figures—operatic scenes, masses of gods and goddesses crowded on roofs and in grey tile panels. Inside, the same lavish decoration is found, combined attractively with sombre timberwork. The openness of the halls of the interior is also characteristically southern and practical for ventilation is essential in the humid climate. There are some fine, massive pieces of temple furniture but the halls are mainly occupied by exhibits of locally produced Shiwan pottery (often figure pieces with a dark body and somewhat curdled glaze), carved peach stones and mother-of-pearl.

Due S of the Chenjia ci is the *Hualin* (Flourishing Grove) *Temple*, founded in 526 and visited by the famous Indian monk Bodhidharma, inspirer of Chan (Zen), soon after its foundation. The present buildings date from the Qing and the most notable feature is the group of 500 lohans in the main hall which is said to include Marco Polo in a broad-brimmed hat (to the right of the altar, at the far end).

To the W of the Hualin Temple is the **Huaisheng si** (Cherish the Sage) **Temple**, Guangzhou's mosque (at No. 56 Guangta lu). It is said to have been founded by one of the Prophet's uncles during the Tang dynasty and thus to be the earliest Moslem foundation in China. Its *minaret*, known as the 'smooth pagoda' (for it is different from many pagodas, and indeed from many Chinese minarets, in that it has no marked eaves and is, in fact, smooth), is Islamic in form (and now rather dependent on concrete). Though the mosque contains early stone stelae, it was burnt down in the Yuan and the buildings are recent.

N of the mosque are the two major temples of Guangzhou, the Liurong Temple (and Hua ta pagoda) at 87 Liurong lu and the Guanxiao si at 109 Guangxiao lu.

The **Liurong** (Six Banyan Trees) **Temple** was founded in 537 to house some of the ashes of the Buddha which had been brought back to China by a monk called Tanyu, uncle of one of the founders of the Liang dynasty (502–557), The ashes were placed in the *Hua ta* (Decorated Pagoda). Originally contemporary with the temple, the pagoda was burnt down in the 10C and rebuilt in 1097. During repairs in 1980, bricks with Northern Song inscriptions were discovered. The octagonal, nine-storey pagoda is 57m high; the bronze finial dates from 1358. There are extra floors (17 in all) concealed within the pagoda which has a spiral staircase to the top.

Owing to the proximity to the Pearl River and the marshy ground, the foundations of the pagoda had to be built on nine linked stone ring wells; a construction technique called 'plum-blossom piles' because the linked wells looked like the petals of plum blossom. The temple had several changes of name throughout its history but in 1099 the famous poet, painter of bamboo and calligrapher Su Dongpo (temporarily in disgrace and exiled southwards) visited the temple and, struck by the banyan trees, inscribed the words 'six banyans'. His calligraphy, carved on wood, now hangs over the gateway and has given the temple its name.

The major buildings include the *Guanyin Hall* and the *Hall of the Sixth Patriarch* (of the Chan or Zen school of Buddhism). In the Hall of the Sixth Patriarch is a bronze figure of the Sixth Patriarch, cast in 989, and three 6m-tall bronze Buddha figures cast in 1663. In the Guanyin Hall there is a 4m Guanyin figure, cast at the same time as the Buddhas.

The **Guangxiao** (Glorious Filiality) **Temple** is said to have been founded during the Han dynasty though at that time it was the palace of a southern king.

Its gardens were developed during the Three Kingdoms period when the place was owned by a high official whose family turned it into a temple on his death. Many Indian monks came to preach in the temple before and during the Tang dynasty; the Sixth Patriarch, Huineng, was ordained here in 676, later to found the 'Southern School' of Chinese Buddhism. Though the temple was once far larger, with 12 great halls and six minor halls, amongst other buildings, the grandeur of the original enclosure is still evident.

Most of the buildings date from the last major repair of 1832 though the huge *main hall* with its unusual tapering rhomboidal pillars is still very striking. Behind the main hall are two important pagodas: the small (6.7m) seven-storey stone *Jingfa Pagoda*, built in 676 over a hair of Huineng, the Sixth Patriarch, and the *Dongtie* (Eastern Iron) *Pagoda* which is almost identical in height, and made of gilt iron with 900 niches for Buddha figures.

Guangzhou: bicycle-/footbridge

During the Cultural Revolution, when the major Buddha figures were destroyed, they were found to contain within them smaller wooden figures dating from the Tang dynasty (now in the museum). Most Buddhist figures contain further relics, whether sutras or figures, but these were particularly important because of their early date.

N of these temples, on the other side of Jiefang bei lu from Yuexiu Park, is the *Lan yuan* or *Orchid Garden*. It occupies part of the site of the old *Moslem Burial Ground* which can be reached by walking round the outside of the park (turn right and right again) to the NW. The graveyard is said to contain the tomb of the Prophet's uncle, builder of the mosque, which is housed in a small stone building surrounded by ordinary tombs and banyan trees.

The Orchid Garden contains more than 10,000 pots of orchids with varyingly ornate blooms and names like Silver-bordered Bodhisattva or Great Phoenix Tail, but it is also a quiet and pleasant garden full of pools and bamboos, where you can also drink orchid tea.

Foshan (Hill of the Buddhas), 20km NE of Guangzhou, is a town that has been famous since the Song dynasty for its ceramic production (Shiwan ware), although excavations reveal that production flourished in the Han dynasty. The most characteristic wares are figurines in reddish clay covered in thick grey-blue glaze. It is possible to visit the ceramic factories by arrangement with China Travel Service. The factories are divided; most of the kilns produce both utilitarian wares (drainpipes, flowerpots) and figures.

The **Zuci miao** (Ancestral Temple) is in the S of the town. Founded in the Northern Song, it was extensively rebuilt in 1372 (and many times in subsequent years).

Dedicated to the worship of the Emperor of the North or Xuandi, Lord of the Black Pavilions of Heaven, the temple is a Taoist foundation (with no connection with the Confucian ancestral cult; it is called the Ancestral Temple because it is the oldest temple in Foshan).

A warrior king, Xuandi was rewarded for his demon-slaying with honorific titles and positions, and is often represented with a turtle and snake (symbols of the north for Taoists).

The surviving buildings, covering an area of 3000 square metres, date from the Ming and Qing and are most notable for the extraordinary elaboration of timber carving and roof decoration. Covered in Shiwan ceramic figures, illustrating famous scenes from history and folklore, the over-decorated roofs are characteristic of the southern provinces—a 'triumph of the artisan' according to the 'Zhong guo ming sheng' (Dictionary of Famous Sites in China).

20   Ji'nan

Ji'nan, capital city of Shandong province in east China, is a city with a long history incorporating neolithic sites and 19C German architecture. Its name means 'South of the River Crossing' and it is c 5km south of the Yellow River.

I have romanised it rather pedantically: few guidebooks bother with the apostrophe but it is important to distinguish the two sounds (without the apostrophe it could well signify the sounds 'jin' and 'an' and would be pronounced differently).

The name dates from the 3–4C AD when Ji'nan was part of a commandery of that name. At that time the Yellow River flowed N of the peninsula, much as it does now, but it has changed its course many times over the centuries as it overflowed from its silted bed. The silt that it carries down from the loess highlands gives it its name, Yellow River, and the disastrous changes of course caused by the silt have given rise to another name for the river, 'China's Sorrow'. The major changes of course took place in the Shandong area where it neared the sea; the last distastrous change was in 1851 when it shifted its mouth from S to N of the peninsula (a distance of some 350km), flooding everything in between.

Ji'nan has long been a major trading centre; its city walls (no longer extant) were built during the Ming, and, after the Germans obtained rights to build the Shandong railways in 1898, the city was opened to foreign trade in 1906 (for once without a treaty consequent upon some foreign incursion). It is famous for its natural springs, around which gardens have been constructed, has a particularly interesting provincial museum and not far away is the earliest known pagoda in China.

Railway: Ji'nan is on the main route S from Peking (to Shanghai and Nanjing) and the railway station is of particular interest as it is a German construction more appropriate to Bavaria.

Airport: the airport is to the W of the town. There are daily flights to Peking; flights three days a week to Nanjing, Qingdao and Hefei; flights every day except Tuesdays and Fridays to Shanghai, to Xi'an, Zhengzhou and Yantai five days a week and less frequent departures for Dalian and Lianyungang.

Hotels: the main hotels for foreigners are the Ji'nan Hotel at 240 Jingsan lu, not far S of the railway station, and the Nanjiao Guesthouse on Maanshan lu in the southern suburbs, not too far from the Thousand-Buddha Cliff but a long way from anywhere else.

Sites to visit in Ji'nan are rather spread out and best visited by taxi or tourist bus. The town itself is not picturesque in a Chinese way but contains much German and Japanese architecture of the late 19C and early 20Cs, much of it solid administrative building, all in the European style favoured by the Japanese at the time.

German influence in Shandong province dates from the occupation of Qingdao in 1897. The harbour had long been coveted by Germany and it is said that the gunboat 'Iltis' which went down in a typhoon off the coast of Shandong on 23 July 1896 might have been making for Qingdao. 77 of the 89 crew went down with the ship, singing to the Kaiser and the flag as they sank; the accident was commemorated in a 'handsome monument on the Bund at Shanghai' which no longer stands.

As in so many other cases, the murder of two German missionaries (Fathers Nies and Henle) in Shandong gave the Germans the pretext they sought 'for violent action' and they used three warships under the command of Admiral Diederichs to take Qingdao on 14 November 1897. Prince Henry of Prussia was sent to take command after a farewell banquet in Kiel where the Kaiser made his notorious reference to the 'mailed fist' ('fahre darein mit gepanzerter Faust'). Under such duress, the Chinese were compelled to sign a treaty, leasing c 50,000 hectares (about 193 square miles) of land around Qingdao and allowing a considerable 'sphere of influence' in the province. The Qingdao–Ji'nan railway was built by the Germans and completed in 1904.

Japan's interest in the area was no doubt as old as that of Germany, if not older, but her real chance came in 1914, when the First World War broke out. Acting under her treaty of alliance with Great Britain, Japan demanded that German warships at Qingdao be disarmed and eventually declared war, capturing Qingdao in November 1914. At the end of the war Japan's interests in the area, part of her 21 demands made to President Yuan Shikai in 1915, were recognised by Russia, Great Britain, France and Italy and Japan took over the old German 'concessions'. Recognition was a complex affair: in return for a massive loan, Yuan Shikai had conceded Japan's demand for control of Shandong, Manchuria (Dongbei), Inner Mongolia and the SE coast and Yangtse valley (though he had refused to agree to purchase 50 per cent of China's munitions from Japan or to employ Japanese 'advisors' throughout the Chinese administration). This had some influence on the Western powers at Versailles though the Chinese delegation there fiercely contested Japan's 'rights' in Shandong. Failure to resist the Japanese demands led to the wave of nationalist demonstrations known as the May 4 Movement (beginning with a demonstration by Peking students on 4 May 1919) which had a profound effect on subsequent Chinese cultural development. Nevertheless, the Japanese reigned in much of Shandong until the end of the Second World War as their architectural remains demonstrate.

The site of the old *city walls* of Ji'nan, built in the Ming, can be traced in the course of the moat that still runs around the N of Da ming hu Park and along Baotuquan lu (W) and Heihuquan lu (S). Two of the 72 springs said to rise in the area which gave Ji'nan a reputation for cleanliness and healthfulness (quoted in the 'Japanese Railway Guide' of 1924 which also praised the 'generally salubrious' climate), can be found at the SW and SE corners of the old city wall. The *Baotu quan* (Fountain Spring) just outside the SE corner of the old city, is the 'first' of the 72 springs and illustrates an interesting variation on northern garden design.

As greenery is lacking for much of the year in the cold north, the bubbling surface of the pool in which the spring rises is made the focus of the garden. Water surfaces are also important in southern gardens (where they should not be too much obscured by lily leaves to allow for the sight of clouds reflected and the play of wind on the surface), but in a northern garden on an overcast day when trees are bare, the constant bubbling of a spring and movement of water provide a major focus.

The focus of the **park** (which actually contains some 16 springs) lies in the three springs that rise in a squarish pool surrounded by stone railings. The spring was first mentioned in the Spring and Autumn Annals with reference to a meeting of nobles which took place here in 694 BC and in the notes to the 'Classic of Water' the spring is described as 'bursting forth, bubbling as if turned by a wheel'. On the N side is a pavilion, the *Luoyuan tang* (Hall of the Source of the Luo), first built in the Song, rebuilt in the Qing, which is decorated with a couplet inscribed by the calligrapher and painter of the Yuan period, Zhao Mengfu (1254–1322; best known for his paintings of horses) which reads: 'Clouds and mist in damp vapours, glory unfixed; the sound of the waves thunders in the Lake of Great Brightness'.

In the SW corner is the *Guanlian ting* (Pavilion for Viewing the Waves) over a central stele which reads 'Baotu quan', with two other inscriptions, 'Wave pavilion' and 'The first spring'. The stone-carved inscriptions all date from the Ming and Qing. On the eastern side is a bridge with a teahouse. The bridge is called 'Bridge of Arriving Cranes' and the teahouse 'Looking at Cranes'.

In the E of the garden area (which contains a fine bonsai garden with many little old conifers grown in lovely blue and white pots), is the *Hall to Commemorate Li Qingzhao*. Built in 1956 and restored in 1980, the hall was constructed 'in the ancient style, but using steel frame and concrete'. In the halls surrounding the courtyard are portraits and extracts from literary accounts of the life, and the works of one of China's most famous woman poets, Li Qingzhao (1084–1151). There are also poems and paintings by famous modern persons including Ye Shengtao (who died in 1988 at a very venerable age, a short-story writer, educationalist and children's writer, associated with the vernacular fiction that developed after the May 4 Movement of 1919) and the polymath (or jack of all trades) Guo Moruo (see Leshan, Sichuan).

Li Qingzhao, born in Ji'nan, married the scholar and poet Zhao Mingcheng. She was herself an accomplished poet and painter and she helped her husband to compile the 'Jin shi lu' (Record of Bronze and Stone), a compilation of inscriptions on the afore-mentioned bronze (vessels) and stone (stelae). When her husband died in 1129, Li Qingzhao's most famous ci (poems) were composed—breaking new ground for the ci had been more commonly used to praise courtesans than to commemorate conjugality.

The ci is a verse form with different line lengths, its most important characteristic being that the poems were intended to be sung and were written to well-known tunes, the music dictating the rhythm.

Not far S of the Baotu quan is the **Shandong Provincial Museum** at 103 Wenhua xi lu, partly housed in a pleasant old temple. The exhibitions undergo occasional rearrangement and, when last seen, the sculpture exhibit was particularly fine, with many very early Buddhist carvings, many originally free-standing shrine-like pieces with inscriptions on the back (as opposed to sculptures hacked out of cave temples). Many date back to just after the Han dynasty, revealing the speed with which Buddhism travelled to the eastern extremity of China. The sculptures vary from competent pieces in the Indian style to cruder, livelier pieces presumably by local sculptors, incorporating (often in the lower registers) linked figures that recall the low-relief stone carvings in Han tombs of the area which are particularly well-known. The exhibit has been arranged by type of sculpture rather than being part of the usual wide-ranging chronological display.

It is hardly surprising that a noted epigrapher, Zhao Mingcheng (husband of Li Qingzhao), should be associated with Ji'nan and Shandong, for the low reliefs of local Han tombs have long been admired. The tombs were lined with stone blocks, carved with mythological scenes of deities and dragons in the heavens, men banqueting or driving chariots in the earthly realm and strange fish- or serpent-tailed monsters in the lower depths. In content (mythological or baronial), these contrast strongly with the contemporary tomb bricks (of clay) made in Sichuan (best seen in the Chongqing Museum, also in the Sichuan Provincial Museum in Chengdu) which frequently depict scenes of daily life including salt-mining, agriculture and hunting. The tombs were based on the same principle, underground and lined, but the stone slabs of Shandong provide a more frieze-like decoration than the squarer, more pictorial Sichuan bricks. Originals and rubbings from these Han tombs are to be found in the museum.

One of the most famous series of exhibits is that of the excavations at Longshan and Dawenkou, two neolithic sites in the province. Longshan zhen (Dragon Mountain Village) in Shandong, where a neolithic site was first discovered in 1928, has given its name to a group of later neolithic sites, the 'Lungshanoid (or black pottery) cultures' (which have, incidentally, given rise to what archaeologists call 'the Lungshanoid problem').

Characterised by a strange burnished black pottery, often fashioned into tripod shapes, the Longshan (or Lungshan in Wade-Giles romanisation) culture seems to anticipate the bronze age in vessel forms and use of scapulimancy. The 'Lungshanoid problem' was that of the relation between what appeared to be two cultures in the Chinese neolithic, the red pottery culture (sometimes called Yangshao) and the black pottery culture (or Longshan culture). The fact that some sites have conveniently been sandwiched between a red pottery stratum and a later bronze age stratum led some archaeologists obsessed with neatness to assume that this was the pattern of development everywhere in China. As more neolithic sites are uncovered, the pattern has become less simple and there is now a greater stress on regional development rather than the simple relation between the two early sites.

The Longshan remains from Shandong have been dated to c 5000–2000 BC and comprise the famous thin, wheel-made, burnished black pottery wares, large numbers of stone and shell implements apparently designed for agriculture rather than hunting (in contrast with the mainly hunting tools of many Yangshao sites) and pig, dog, cattle and sheep bones, indicating widespread domestication and settled agriculture. Scapulimancy, jade-carving, class-distinctions manifested in different types of burial and some form of ancestor worship, apparently conducted by specialised persons, all indicate a fairly highly-developed, settled way of life anticipating many forms that persisted in the subsequent bronze age.

The Dawenkou remains, typographically associated with sites in northern Jiangsu, were unearthed in 1959. They probably date from between 4000 and 2000 BC and are of the 'Lungshanoid' type though they show a development from red pottery to a wheel-made, black polished type.

Other important exhibits include the inscribed bamboo slips from a Han tomb at Yinque shan (Silver Sparrow Mountain). These include a full calendar for the year 134 BC (which provides a date for the entombment), the text of the 'Sun Bin bing fa' (Sun Bin's Art of War), lost for some 1700 years, and other military and philosophical texts. Written with a brush and ink on thin strips of bamboo which were threaded together, these represent the earliest form of 'book' in China, antedating the use of paper (which was known at the time but clearly not in common use). There is also a fine set of 406 wooden tomb figures (which have lost their paint) from the tomb of the 10th son of the founder of the Ming dynasty, enfeoffed as 'King of Lu' (Lu is the old name for Shandong). He died at 19 in 1389 and his tomb, which was near Qu Fu, was excavated in 1970–71.

The museum was the first provincial museum to be opened after Liberation (in 1956). It incorporates a natural history and geology exhibition hall.

The **Heihu quan** (Black Tiger Spring) is on Heihuquan dong lu, at the SW corner of the old city moat. It has been known by that name since before the Jin (1115–1234) and it rises in a cave from which it emerges through three stone tigerhead spouts. A Ming poem on the 72 springs of Ji'nan describes it: 'Twisted stones in the water mansion where all is green, green; the depths are dark and murky like the lair of a tiger. At midnight when the cold wind blows, the stone splits: one resounding crack and the moon is dark'.

Nearby 14 more springs rise forming a stream; these include the *Pipa Spring* (which emerges from holes in grey rock and is said to sound like the stringed pipa—a sort of lute—at night), the *Jizhong* (Deep In a Gully) *Spring* which rises to the surface in a square pool and is also known as the Waterlily Spring, and the *Nine Women Spring* (where nine fairy women were supposed to come at night to bathe and wash silk).

500m away is the *Five-Dragon Pool* (Wulong tan) formed by five springs where the king of a barbarian country was said to live in the Tang dynasty. The northern wall of the old city enclosed the *Daming hu* (Lake of Great Brightness), entered from Daminghu lu. The name was originally used in reference to another lake, further to the N, now covered by streets, so during the Jin (1115–1234) the name was transferred.

Describing the old city of Ji'nan in the Qing, Li Fenggao wrote: 'Waterlilies on four sides, willows on three, half the city is mountain, the other half lake'. The park incorporates several small gardens including the *Xia yuan* (Distant Garden) built in 1909 in the S, in the NW the *Xiaocanlang* (Small Blue Waves Garden) built in 1792 which offers a view of the distant Thousand-Buddha Mountain. This was described in the late Qing novel 'The Travels of Lao Can' (or Ts'an) by Liu E as being 'like a screen painting 10 miles long with a thousand Buddhas painted by a Song master'. The little pavilions are beautifully made, models of the sort of places that scholars used to entertain their friends in. One is carved with the words of Li Fenggao and there are other inscriptions carved in stone by Qing scholars including Ruan Yuan and Liang Tongshu.

On the island is the *Lixia ting* (Historic Pavilion) where the Tang poet Du Fu is supposed to have met Li Yong, a calligrapher and local official, at a meeting commemorated in a poem. The present pavilion, successor to Song, Yuan and Ming buildings (which were on a different site), dates from the Qing. On the gate are lines from Du Fu's poem, written by the Qing calligrapher He Shaoji: 'This pavilion stands to the right of the sea; there are many famous men in Ji'nan'. Inside the pavilion are portraits of Du Fu and Li Yang and behind the pavilion is a couplet by Guo Moruo (see Leshan, Sichuan and above): 'Willows in the spring wind, music from all sides. Lotus in the autumn moon, great brightness'.

On the S side of the lake is the *Memorial Hall to Xin Qiji* (Xin Qiji ji nian ci).

Xin Qiji (1140–1207), a native of the nearby town of Licheng, was a famous ci poet of the Southern Song. He was also an official and an anti-Jin patriot (opposing the invasion of the north by the Jin and the failure of the Song to resist). He was banished for his memorials to the throne criticising its weakness in repelling the invaders.

The 'hall' was built in 1961 (rebuilt in 1980), like the Li Qingzhao memorial hall 'in the style of an ordinary house' with two courtyards, exhibition halls filled with commemorative calligraphy by famous contemporary figures. The main inscriptions are by Chen Yi (1901–72, an outstanding military commander, general of the New Fourth Army, later mayor of Shanghai) and Ye Shengtao (see Li Qingzhao Memorial Hall, above).

The main hall's pillars are embellished by lines written by the omnipresent Guo Moruo which refer to loyalty to the Song through a thicket of classical allusion: 'Iron columns and the bronze pipa continue the song of Su Dongpo to the east of the Great River, Beautiful celery and tragic millet hope that the Southern Song can fly south with the wild goose.' Without following every reference in this over-crammed couplet, suffice to say that celery is first associated with beauty in the 'Lu shi chun qiu' (Spring and Autumn Annals of Master Lu), a late Zhou (c 1066–221 BC) text.

The *Pearl Spring* (Zhenzhu quan) on the N side of Quancheng lu is said to bubble up like pearls in its square pool.

In his 'Record of the Pearl Spring', Wang Chang said: 'The spring rises from sand, suddenly gathers, suddenly disperses, suddenly stops, suddenly continues, suddenly speeds, suddenly slows. In the sunlight the larger bubbles are like pearls, the smaller like seed pearls, rising from the depths.' The site of the spring used to be occupied by a government office and in the Chenghua reign period of the Ming (1465–87) one of the members of the royal family built a residence by the spring. In 1666 it became a government office and later a military headquarters. In the 'Gu ji ming sheng ce dian' (Dictionary of Famous Sites), a line from Liu E's late Qing novel 'The Travels of Lao Can' is used in reference to this spring (which gathers with others to flow into the Daming Lake) and others in Ji'nan: 'A spring in every house, willows hanging over every home.'

The *Nanda si* (Mosque) is in Libai si jie. The name of the street can be translated either as 'week' or 'religious devotions' and is often used in reference to Moslems with their daily prayers at fixed hours. The mosque was founded in the Yuan and last restored during the Republican period (1911–49). The main hall, part of a large complex, is raised on a 4.2m-high platform and composed of three linked parts. The roofs are black-tiled and the windows in particular are highly decorated, incorporating arabic inscriptions.

On the southern outskirts of the city, 2.5km from the centre, is the **Thousand-Buddha Mountain** (Qianfo shan), not far from the Nanjiao Hotel.

Legend has it that the mythical Emperor Shun ploughed the soil here. Shun, successor to Yao, is supposed to have reigned from 2317–2208 BC, and was held up as an example of filial piety (despite the fact that his father kept trying to kill him as he preferred his second son). He is supposed to have had double pupils to his eyes, and to have invented the writing brush. Together with the Emperor Yao he is, in the words of Sellars and Yeatman, generally considered to be 'a Good Thing'.

A group of Sui carvings made between 581 and 600 are reached up 300 steps behind the *Xingguo si* (Temple of the Flourishing State), founded 627–649. The main carvings are on a cliff above the temple though there are others in the Dragon Spring and other caves below. In the eastern courtyard of the temple are sculptures of the Emperor Shun and his two wives (Yao's daughters). Nearby is a Ming pavilion, the *Lan ting* (Viewing Pavilion) which affords a view of the city, Daming Lake (like a mirror), and the Yellow River (like a belt), according to a Chinese guidebook.

Not far from Ji'nan, a few km WNW, is the town of *Li cheng*. In the surrounding county are a number of Buddhist sites, some of whose carvings can be seen in the provincial museum in Ji'nan.

The *Big Buddha Head* (Dafotou zao xiang) is on **Fo hui shan** (Buddha Wisdom Mountain), 3.5km N of Ji'nan. The head, 7.8m high and 5.35m wide, was carved in 1035. There are Ming inscriptions on the W and two small pagodas carved on the E wall of the cave.

Carvings at the *Dafo si* (Big Buddha Temple) may be found on the southern slopes of the **Qing tong shan** (Bronze Mountain) in Li cheng county. The temple has disappeared but there is a Tang Buddha figure 9.05m high, with smaller attendants. On the platform in front of the Buddha are stone incense burners and altar table, as well as three much-respected old cypress trees.

In the SE of Li cheng county is the **Longdong shan** (Dragon Cave Mountain). It is said that the Great Yu ascended the mountain to request that the dragon help him control the waters and the cave has long been a place that local farmers came to pray for rain. Inside the cave is a spring, where the dragon is supposed to live; on either side of the entrance is the couplet 'True spirit and the forest springs thickly up, spiritual achievements borrow from the primeval chaos'. Below are the remains of the *Sage Longevity Hall* whose name and a record of imperial order for its construction was perhaps inscribed by the Song dynasty poet, bamboo painter, calligrapher and official Su Shi (Su Dongpo). Stone carvings on the mountain date from the mid 6C to the Tang (first rather straight and narrow, growing increasingly sinuous in the Tang).

On **Qinglong shan** (Green Dragon Mountain), near Linbu cun in Li Cheng county, is the earliest extant stone pagoda in China, the *Simen ta* (Four-Door Pagoda). Originally thought to have been constructed in 544 (according to an inscription inside), restoration of the top part in 1972 revealed a date of 611. 15m high, it is constructed from large slabs of stone and is a square building with arched doors in each side, hence the name. It has a decorative crown and a central stone pillar inside carved with Buddha figures.

NW of the Simen ta on **Baihu shan** (White Tiger Mountain) is the more decorative *Longhu ta* (Dragon Tiger Pagoda), possibly Song in date and associated with over 200 stone-carved figures from early Tang to Ming. They include emperors, officials, monks, three princesses, horses and figures of commoners apparently carved as part of a rain-seeking cult. On *Lingjin shan*, all that remains of the Nine-Pagoda Temple (Jiuta si) is the *Nine-Pagoda Pagoda*, a 13m-high Tang dynasty pagoda with nine little pagodas of great charm on the roof.

21   Tai shan

Tai shan (the Honourable Mountain), in Shandong province, has a religious significance that goes back beyond Confucianism and Taoism to the earliest cults. It is otherwise known as the Eastern Peak and is the most significant of the Five Holy Mountains loosely associated with the imperial cult and Taoism (and not to be confused with the Four Buddhist Mountains).

Buses: Tai shan (and the town at its foot, Tai'an) can be reached by bus or car from either Ji'nan or Qu Fu (it is about 70km from both).

Train: Tai'an is on the main line from Ji'nan to Nanjing and Shanghai and slower trains stop there (it is just over an hour by rail from Ji'nan).

Hotel: The Tai shan Guesthouse is c 5km from the railway station, near the bottom of the central route up the mountain. A new guesthouse has been constructed on the summit; it is said to be quite attractive.

The **Five Holy Mountains** are Tai shan, the eastern and most important for all life (like the sun) was thought to emanate from the E; Heng shan (southern) in Hunan, Hua shan (western) in Shaanxi, Heng shan (northern) in Shanxi and Song shan (central) in Henan. They represent the five 'directions' sacred to the Chinese (north, south, east, west and centre) and their connections with emperors had something to do with this. The emperor came to be viewed as the son of heaven, a representative of heaven on earth, and he lived at the centre of his realm. Every so often, he would 'beat the bounds' of his domain by visiting the mountains on the edge of it, to commune with gods.

Mountains in general were seen as the abode of gods and spirits, particularly those associated with rain, whose timeliness and sufficiency was essential to the maintenance of the agricultural order upon which the livelihood of all (including the emperor who lived off agricultural taxes) was based. The association of mountains, whose summits are cloud-covered, with rain and rain-bearing dragons is logical. The size and weight of a mountain was also considered important in maintaining the stability of the earth and preventing earthquakes. The emperor's right to rule was conveyed by heaven and depended upon heaven's pleasure: if all was well, the people well-fed and content, then heaven allowed the emperor to continue. Manifestations of heaven's displeasure were earthquakes, disastrous floods and droughts, all of which were seen to be connected with mountains. Thus the emperor would pay his respects to mountains and, since the Five Mountains in particular were considered to be gods in their own right, effectively attempt to rule together with the mountains.

According to Sima Qian (died c 90 BC), the great historian of the Han period, as early as the Zhou the Five Mountains were regarded as the equals of the three dukes and in 725, the emperor granted Tai shan the title of King Equal to the Sky (tian qi wang). In 1101, the mountain was promoted to emperor.

There were numerous imperial visits to Tai shan throughout the centuries though the great imperial ceremonies of feng (sacrifice to the earth, performed at the base of the mountain) and shan (to the sky, performed at the summit), were last carried out in 1008. It is said that when the first emperor of the Qin came to sacrifice here in 219 BC, he had had to shelter from a storm on the way down and was so grateful to the tree he had stood under that he made it an officer of the fifth rank.

Aside from the imperial cult, celebrated in stelae, there were an enormous number of local and popular cults relating to Tai shan. Houses built in traditional Peking had the first stone in the foundations inscribed with the name of the mountain as a protection against falling down and blind alleys in the capital often had a 'Tai shan' stone set up in them to deter evil spirits. The easternness of the mountain, its source of life, meant that emperors prayed to Tai shan for sons and many childless women (some sadly elderly) still make pilgrimages to the mountain, offering incense and money at special shrines. One of the favoured deities of the mountain is the 'Princess of the rosy clouds' (Bixia yuan jun), who became a sort of northern, roughly Taoist equivalent of the Bodhisattva Guan yin (the popular Buddhist 'goddess of mercy' who lived on the southern Buddhist mountain, Putuo shan). With the princess, two other females are often depicted, one holding an eye in her hand. She is 'the eye maiden' (Yan jing niang niang) and is worshipped by those with eye problems. It was also believed that the souls of the dead gathered at the foot of Tai shan and that the mountain presided over their fate like the Buddhist Ksitigarbha at Jiuhua shan in Anhui. The cult of the eastern peak was such that most cities had a Dongyue miao (Eastern Peak Temple) with statues of judges and depictions of the torture of hell, where people would make offerings in the hope of avoiding them, in a Taoist borrowing from popular Buddhism.

Near Tai'an, at the foot of the mountain in *Dawenkou cun*, the remains of an important late neolithic site were discovered in 1959. The remains are sufficiently distinctive to be described as a 'culture' (the Dawenkou culture) though they are of the Longshanoid type (see Ji'nan, Rte 18).

7.5km E of Tai'an are the remains of a *ming tang* (bright or sacred hall) recorded in the Han histories as having been built by the Wudi (martial) emperor of the Han (reigned 140–86 BC) after a trip to Tai shan. The ming tang was a sacrifical building specific to the Han dynasty: a hall that had to be surrounded by water and an enclosure that reflected both the circle and the square and which was used for all sorts of sacrifices and acts of worship. As the ming tang remains a slightly mysterious edifice, the circular mound and quantities of Han tiles and pots unearthed here are of great interest to Han historians.

The major building in Tai'an is the **Dai miao** (Tai shan Temple, using an old name for the mountain, 'dai'), constructed for the use of emperors coming to make sacrifices and offerings to the mountain. There was apparently a temple on the site in the Han, rebuilt in the Tang and Song (in 1122, it was described as having 813 buildings and rooms), and in all succeeding dynasties. The temple is entered through a great pailou, *Dongyue fang* (Gate of the Eastern Peak), built in 1672 at the order of the Kangxi emperor. It is very much a conglomerate of beliefs, including many stelae commemorating imperial venerations as well as separate Taoist halls devoted to the 'wife of the mountain', a deity who 'appeared much later than her husband' which must have been inconvenient. She is commemorated in a hall at the rear of the temple.

In a back, side courtyard is the *Temple of Yanxi*, a Taoist who lived on the mountain and who was linked to the cult of the mountain in the Tang dynasty. The great main hall, *Tianpei dian* (Hall of Heaven's Associate) is on the main axis, beyond a courtyard filled with stelae which include one commemorating the mountain's elevation to emperorhood (1013). One of the most important stelae, carved in 209 BC recording a visit of the second emperor of the Qin, is in the E courtyard: though only a minute fragment of the original seal-script inscription was discovered in 1815 to have survived the fires that destroyed its 'protecting' temple which originally stood on the summit. Two Ming bronze lions stand in front of the nine-bay main hall which was first built in 1009 and despite much restoration since is said to preserve the Song style. It stands on a carved white stone platform and the roof is covered with yellow-glazed tiles. Inside is a wall painting, supposed to be Song in date, illustrating the mountain, its peaks, clouds, animals and spirits.

In the rear courtyard are two metal 'pagodas' the bronze 'pavilion' and the 'iron pagoda'. They originally stood elsewhere (the bronze pavilion on the summit of the mountain) but were moved here in the early 1970s, presumably for reasons of preservation). The bronze pavilion was cast in 1615 to house a figure of the Princess of the Rosy Clouds; the casting imitates wooden architectural construction perfectly. 4.4m high, 3.4m wide, it is one of several examples of cast bronze pavilions surviving in China. The iron pagoda was cast in 1533, a hexagonal, 13-storey tower, though only the three lower 'floors' survive today.

The second courtyard of the temple was, apparently, once lined with cubicles serving as 'judgement' seats (presumably used in ceremonies linked to significance of the mountain's judgement of souls) and the ancient trees in the side courtyards are said to have been planted by the Martial Emperor of the Han in 110 BC.

The **mountain**, stepped like all holy mountains in China, is now provided with a cable car. In contemplating your ascent (which will take 4–5 hours for the middling fit), bear in mind that for larger western feet (even those of ladies), the 5500 narrow, unstable steps are more uncomfortable to descend. Ascent may leave you breathless but descent tends to paralyse the thigh muscles for days: if possible, I would use the cable car for the descent. The cable car to the summit starts about half-way up the mountain at the *Zhongtian men* (Gate of Middle Heaven) which can be reached by bus.

The mountain begins with a stone pailou, the *Daizong fang* (Gate of the Mountain Ancestor), built in the mid 16C, rebuilt in 1730, bearing the inscription 'Yi tian men' (First Gate to Heaven). Beyond, to the right is the *Laojun tang* (Hall of Prince Lao or Lazi).

One of the major writers of the early Daoist faith, Laozi is depicted in the hall with two disciples, one of whom may be the mysterious disappearing frontier guard who prompted him to write the 'Dao de jing' (Classic of the Way and of Virtue). He was said to have been tired of the world and had set off on an old buffalo to escape when he met a guard at the frontier. After earnestly requesting him to return to philosophy, the guard disappeared. The fact that a recently excavated example has the two parts of the work in the reverse order means that we should now consider calling it the 'De dao jing' (Classic of Virtue and the Way), which is a bit like having to reverse the order of the books in the Bible.

In the courtyard of the temple are two stelae under the same capital (the *Mandarin Ducks Stelae* or Yuanyang bei) with poems and lists of names dating from 661 to 698.

Just beyond, to the right of the main path, is the *Wangmu chi* (Pool of the Heavenly Queen) in the forecourt of a small *nunnery*. The pool is one of the 'scenic spots of the mountain' and the founding date of the nunnery is uncertain—a poem of the Wei (3C AD) suggests that there was a house, rather than a temple, nearby. There is now a two-courtyard temple of 'Ming-Qing' date. In the main hall is a statue of the Xiwang mu (Queen Mother of the West, the major female deity in Taoism); in the hall behind is a statue of the famous Daoist immortal Lu Dongbin.

He was a real person, born into an official family in 755. When he was 20 he went to Lu shan and met a dragon who gave him a magic sword which enabled him to fly. He devoted the rest of his life to various magical feats and practices around which count-less legends have grown up.

The real starting point for the mountain is the *Hongmen guan* (Hall of the Red Gate; built 1626), just NW of the Pool of the Heavenly Queen (and it is here you buy your ticket for the ascent). There was an earlier gate here but its dates are uncertain. The name is taken from the reddish stones nearby which appear to form a natural arched gate. The western hall is dedicated to the Princess of the Rosy Clouds, the eastern one used to be dedicated to Amitabha Buddha.

N is the *Wanxian lou* (Tower of the Myriad Spirits), built over the path in 1620, restored in 1954. Stone-carved inscriptions are set into the walls, some mentioning the clumps of bamboo that surrounded the tower: 'Slow grow the ancient bamboos; rooted in Tai shan'. To the right, just below the tower is the *Tomb of the White Mule* (Bailuo zhong), said to be where the white mule that had carried the Tang emperor Xuan zong up and down the mountain in 726 dropped dead after finishing its task: the emperor posthumously gave it the title of general and had it buried here with pomp.

N of the Wanxian lou, on the W side of the path is a two-character inscription with an incomprehensible first character followed by the character for the number two. The first character is made up of parts of the characters for moon and wind and refers to a four-character phrase, 'moon and wind without limit', which means that this spot is one of unrivalled scenery. The inscription was carved in 1899 by a scholar from Ji'nan, Liu Yangui.

Passing a memorial to the martyrs of the liberation struggle, the next building is the *Doumu gong* (Temple of the Goddess of the Great Bear), lived in by Taoist nuns. Its date of founding is uncertain but it was rebuilt and given its present name in the Jiaqing reign of the Ming (1522–67). Outside the gate is a Ming dynasty locust tree (*Sophora japonica*) called the 'Sleeping Dragon Locust' because of the way it sprawls on the ground. The temple has three courts and three halls, the first court with trees and a pool. In the hall of the second court there used to be ceiling paintings of the 'mother star' and her 12 daughters. In the back courtyard, the Princess of the Rosy Clouds was worshipped.

1km N of the Doumu gong, off to the E of the main path is a narrow gully, the *Stone Sutra Ravine* (Jingshi yu) where the text of the Buddhist Diamond sutra has been carved on the rock face. This has been further carved by later calligraphers including Guo Moruo (see Ji'nan and Le shan in Sichuan) who wrote in 1961 'written by men of the Northern Ji' (ie 550–577). An anonymous Ming calligrapher also carved a passage from the Confucian 'Da xue' (Great Learning) beneath the sutra.

Further up the main path is the *Hutian ge* (Pavilion of the Teapot Sky), apparently given this name in 1747 because the surrounding peaks create the impression of being in a teapot and looking up at the sky. Originally constructed in the Ming, the inscription on the gate reads 'When you have reached the Teapot Mountain, you are half-way to the summit, near the place of extreme and multiple good fortune'.

To the N of the Teapot Sky Pavilion, a stone gate marks the *Huima ling*, the 'mountain where the horses turn back', said to be the place where the Xuan zong emperor of the Tang (reigned 713–756; some say it was the Zhen zong emperor of the Song, reigned 998–1023) had to dismount and leave his horse for it could not negotiate the twists and turns above. Not far above is the *Zhongtian men* (Gate in the Middle of the Sky), also known as the *Ertian men* (Second Celestial Gate), marking the half-way point (and the cable car for those who are flagging). It is also the point where the main path (eastern) and the longer (infinitely less crowded, almost temple-less and with good views) western path start. The stone gateway is a Qing construction; nearby is a large stone whose patterning is said to resemble that of a tiger. The Qing epigrapher Wu Dahui carved the seal-script character for 'tiger' on it and it is called the 'Reclining Tiger Stone'.

If the weather is fine, the peak can be seen from here: if there is rain and mist, 'the yellow peak returns home to the clouds'. The path leading upwards towards the summit crosses the *Yunbu qiao* (Step Over the Clouds Bridge) which spans a stream flowing down from above.

In the words of a Ming poet, Chen Fengyu, 'The hundred foot cliff is locked into the kingfisher mist; the jade dragon hangs down in the emptiness. When the sun shines in the 6th month, there is often flying rain and when the wind is still there is the sound of stringed instruments'. Beside the bridge is a pavilion with the couplet: 'Lean on the stone railing and watch the flying spray, then cross the cloud bridge and greet the noble pine'.

Above is the *Wusong ting* (Five Pine Pavilion) where the first emperor of the Qin is said to have sheltered from a storm in 219 BC and gratefully ennobled the pine tree (as an official of the fifth grade; it is only since the Tang dynasty that this has been mistranslated as 'five pines'). The current three trees were planted in 1730. There is an old pine to the W of the five-bay pavilion which is said to appear to be stretching out its hand in welcome; another candidate for the original title of 'the pine that welcomes guests', endlessly depicted in paintings in restaurants and waiting rooms. On the W of the path, a little above, is the *Chaoyang dong* (South-facing Cave), dedicated to the worship of the Princess of the Rosy Clouds and there are two poems by the Qianlong emperor inscribed in vast characters on a rock opposite.

At the *Pine Tree Mountain* (Duisong shan) the path turns sharply and the summit is visible. A stone gateway, *Shengxian fang* (Gateway to the Ascent to Immortality), leads to a steep stairway with the *Nan tian men* (Southern Heavenly Gate) at the top. First constructed in 1264, this was called the 'building where one can touch the void'; the stone carved verses read: 'The gate opens up the nine clouds and leads to the famous places of the three heavens; ascending tens of thousands of steps we can see and are close to a thousand peaks.' To the W of the gate on a stone is a Yuan dynasty inscription, 'the heaven's gate inscription' composed by Du Renjie, written by Yan Zhongfan. It is apparently a protest against the evils of 14C society (and was buried during the Qianlong reign and rediscovered in 1956).

The summit is a mere 1km from the gate and the 'Dictionary of Famous

Sites in China', noting this, immediately cites the words of the the the Tang poet Li Bai in his poem in praise of Tai shan: 'In a long breath at the heavenly gate, the fresh wind comes from a thousand miles away'.

The *Temple of the Princess of the Rosy Clouds* (Bixiayun jun ci), the focal point for pilgrims, is on the southern slopes of the summit.

From 1759 until the fall of the Qing, the emperor would send an official on the 18th day of the 4th lunar month each year to make an offering here. First built in 1008–16, it was enlarged in the Ming and Qing. In order to resist the winds and also the danger of fire from thunderstorms, it was roofed with iron tiles (and iron acroteria) and there is much brickwork. In the main hall, the figure of the princess is of bronze. There are even two bronze stelae, dating from 1615 and 1625. This use of metal in construction and decoration is unique in China.

There is a *Temple to Confucius* (founded very late, in the late 16C) just below the Bixiayun jun ci, the stone terrace of which was used as an observatory.

The summit of Tai shan is effectively enclosed in the *Yuhuang* (Jade Emperor) *Temple*; the peak itself, carved with the two characters for supreme summit, surrounded by a balustrade in a courtyard of the temple, is called *Tianzhu feng* (the Pillar of Heaven Peak). In Chinese popular religion (the mixture of Taoism, Confucianism and much earlier beliefs), the Jade Emperor is the supreme ruler of heaven and is depicted as an emperor in an imperial hat with bead curtains hanging down by his face.

Outside the temple is the 'Stele with No Words', traditionally supposed to have been put in place by the First Emperor of the Qin in 219 and the text weathered away by the winds and rains of the summit; historians consider it more likely that it was erected by either the Wu or the Zhang emperor of the early Han. On the *Daguan feng* (Peak of the Great View) is the stone-carved inscription (whose characters, cut into the rock, have been gilded) ordered by the Tang Xuanzong emperor in 726 when he ennobled the mountain. In it, the emperor describes his difficulties in ruling and how his officials persuaded him to carry out the two major sacrifices at the foot and summit of Tai shan and 'all was as it should be'.

SE of the Jade Emperor Temple is the *Riguan feng* (Peak for Watching the Sunrise) where thousands of visitors, who have stayed overnight in the rather rough hotel (there is apparently a new guesthouse) and hired padded coats, watch the sun rise through the clouds, one of the sights of Tai shan. It was here that the Song emperor Zhenzong performed the *feng* ceremony in 1008. In 1747 two jade boxes were unearthed beneath the platform, containing slips of jade inscribed with texts of prayers to the mountain. S of the Riguan feng is the *Zhanlu tai* (Platform for Surveying Lu) from where the state of Lu (southern Shandong) could be viewed, clouds permitting.

Those who wish to walk down the mountain could take the longer, emptier (of buildings and people) western path from the cable car station, past the *Heilong tan* (Black Dragon Pool) and (near the bottom) the *Puzhao si* (Temple of Universal Clarity), built against the mountain and famous for its Six Dynasties (222–589) pines.

The temple (a Buddhist centre) was said to have been founded during the Six Dynasties, expanded during the Tang and rebuilt in the Ming. In the main hall is a bronze figure of Sakyamuni, the historic Buddha, and behind is the main Six Dynasties pine. In the three-bay hall beside the pavilion at the back of the temple, Feng Yuxiang, the 'Christian warlord', used to stay between 1932 and 1935.

Feng Yuxiang (1882–1948) was one of the warlords who had command of a northern army but who more-or-less allied himself with the Nationalist cause as long as it was led by Sun Yat-sen. He was given a post in the Nationalist (KMT) cabinet though he retained his own power-base as a 'new national warlord' though he challenged Chiang Kai-shek in 1929, allying himself with Wang Jingwei in a rival KMT government. He was called the 'Christian marshall' not, as S.J. Perelman who had trouble with Chinese names, suggested, to distinguish him from Feng the Jewish marshall, but because he was a Christian convert and he used to baptise his troops with a hosepipe. His *tomb* is on the western slopes of Tai shan for, though he was a native of Anhui, his power-base was in the north. The tomb is near the Dachong Bridge which he built in the early 30s when staying here. There is a bronze statue of Feng in front of the tomb and an inscription by Guo Moruo reading 'Mr Feng Yuxiang's tomb' as well as the single character wo ('me') in the general's own hand.

22   Qu Fu

Qu Fu, one of the most charming country towns in China, had a traditional importance quite out of proportion to its size for it was the birthplace of Confucius, the First Sage Under Heaven. Slightly difficult to get to as the descendants of Confucius managed to protect the feng shui of their ancestral graveyard and force the railway into a detour away from Qu Fu, the small walled town lies on the Shandong plain some 100km S of Ji'nan, the foothills of mountains just visible in the distance. The tiny town is entirely dominated by the enormous Temple to Confucius and the Mansion of his descendants which occupy its centre.

Railway: Qu Fu is c 13km W of Yanzhou which is on the main line from Beijing to Nanjing (via Ji'nan). There are few taxis at the station but hordes of minibuses which will take you to Qu Fu in 20 to 30 minutes for about 50 yuan. It is also possible to drive from Ji'nan.

  Getting away from Qu Fu can be a bit difficult as train tickets are sold at Yanzhou Station no more than 8 hours before the train departs—unless you want to spend much of your time going backwards and forwards to Yanzhou, it is easiest to ask the hotel to book a ticket for you for a small surcharge. As Yanzhou is an intermediate station, it is not usually possible to buy anything other than a hard seat ticket; if you want a sleeper, you will have to negotiate once you get on board the train.

Hotels: the most romantic place to stay is inside the Mansion itself: the Kong fu Hotel run by Luxingshe. There is also a luxury hotel which is not much more expensive, the Queli Hotel, just opposite the Mansion. It is worth visiting as it is rather beautifully designed, a most unusual feature of contemporary hotel building in China. It combines fairly modern lines with the low roof line and grey colours of the houses around it.

Confucius, said to have lived from 551 to 479 BC, was a teacher who was ignored in his own time, but who has had the most profound effect on Chinese culture over the last 2000 years.

His father died when Confucius was young and he was brought up simply by his mother. He is thought to have held various positions in the government (Keeper of Granaries, Director of Public Pastures) but he failed in his ambition to achieve high status (from which position he could have tried to restore the old moral codes of the State of Zhou) in his home state of Lu (in Shandong) so he moved from state to state, attempting to influence rulers towards a higher moral standard. His teachings and some small details about his life and character are known through the 'Lun yu' (Analects), a collection of anecdotes and quotations apparently compiled long after his death by the disciples of his disciples. From the Analects he emerges as a man of finicky habits (unable to sleep if his mat was not straight) but great determination ('He's the one who knows its no good but keeps on trying').

  His mission in life was to 'restore the old order' (a slogan used to attack Defence Minister Lin Biao in the early 1970s), to re-establish the virtuous ways of the State of Zhou which he felt were ignored. He was not an innovator, he proposed ideas which were current (but in his view ignored) but in the hagiography that has grown up around him, all these ideas have become his own.

  Fundamental to his theories were views on government, gentlemen and learning. Looking back to a past golden age when everything was perfect, he stressed the need for moral government in which the people could have confidence. The concept of heavenly approval was important; a ruler was sanctioned by heaven and if he ruled badly heaven's mandate could be withdrawn. Symptoms of the withdrawal of the heavenly mandate were natural disasters and such is the pervasive nature of Confucianism that the earthquake of 1976 which immediately preceded the death of Mao was viewed by many peasants as a heavenly portent. One story from the Analects tells of Confucius meeting a woman weeping by the road side. He leaned out of his carriage and asked her what was the matter. She told him that her son, husband, father and uncle had all been killed by a tiger. Confucius questioned the wisdom of her staying in such a dangerous place but she replied that the government was good. Confucius turned to his disciples and said, 'Bad government is worse than a tiger'. His views on what constituted good government included 'humaneness', the importance of ritual as a reinforcing agent and the importance of people knowing their position and behaving appropriately. 'Let the ruler be a ruler, the son a son...' is one of his famous dicta and it illustrates his stress on social stability running through from the ruler to conduct within the family. If people failed to behave appropriately (and here ritual was an important underpinning), chaos would ensue.

He has been much criticised in recent decades for his conservatism which incorporated views current at the time. The position of women, within society and within the home, was subordinate: a woman should obey her father, her husband and her son; this was all part of knowing her place. He stressed the importance of proper behaviour: a man should not touch his sister-in-law, to the point where it was inappropriate for him to save her from drowning if that meant hand to hand contact (I suppose a bargepole might not have offended the proprieties).

The ruler should be a 'gentleman', well educated in the classic books which, in time, became known as the Confucian Classics. He should also be humane, 'love others' and behave with 'courtesy, diligence, good faith and kindness. If you behave with courtesy then you will not be insulted; if you are generous then you will win the multitude; if you are of good faith then other men will put their trust in you; if you are diligent then you will have success and if you are kind then you will be able to command others'.

Confucius' stress on education was, in the Han dynasty, to form the basis of the civil service exams for which gentlemen had to learn (effectively by heart) the Classics, a syllabus which remained relatively unchanged until the first years of the 20C. Music and ritual were the outward signs of appropriate behaviour, means of showing respect to the living and the dead. The service of ancestral spirits was practised at the time and was part of Confucius' view of the world—he stressed the importance of filial devotion: 'When the father is alive, you see only the son's intentions. When he is dead, you see the son's actions. If for three years he makes no change from the ways of his father, then he may be called filial'. This three-year period became institutionalised as an appropriate length of time to mourn a parent.

Confucianism as the state cult was adopted during the Han, persisting until the 20C. Its adoption meant that the descendants of the Sage became 'the first family under heaven', of almost greater status than the imperial family for dynasties came and went whilst the Kongs endured (and still exist).

The name 'Confucius' is a late 16C latinicisation of Kong Fuzi (Master Kong), invented by Jesuit missionaries who were enormously impressed by the benevolent despotism of Confucian rule, seeing China as ruled by a class of philosophers schooled in ancient texts. Such were their enthusiastic reports that Confucius has been described as 'the patron saint of the Enlightenment' though Protestant missionaries were less impressed: James Legge (1814–97,) who translated the Confucian Classics, said 'He gave no impulse to religion. He had no sympathy with progress'.

Though the ideas he expressed may simply have been those of any 6C BC conservative, the longevity of the legacy of Confucianism is quite extraordinary. Even today his stress on filial piety is felt as it is, for example, against the law to neglect elderly parents and old people's homes are for those with no surviving relatives, and in education, rote learning still plays an important part. It is interesting that the Teachers Training College was established in Qu Fu (rather than in the provincial capital, Ji'nan) early this century when, though Confucius' influence was finally waning, it was as if the air of Qu Fu was specially conducive to education. And, during the 1930s, both Chiang Kai-shek and the invading Japanese sought to get the Kong family on their side, to help legitimise their regimes.

The story of the family and, in particular, the last of the Yansheng Dukes to live in the Mansion, is told by Kong Demao, a 77th generation descendant now in her 80s (whose brother, the last of the Yansheng Dukes, now lives in Taiwan) in 'The House of Confucius' (Hodder and Stoughton, 1988). It is a charming account of a strangely privileged yet isolated childhood amongst the dust and ghosts of 76 generations; a rather tragic tale of the intrusion of the 20C (in the form of vacuum flasks, wellington boots and political intrigue) on the backward stronghold of the 'first family under heaven'.

Qu Fu (the name means 'winding hill' and was first glossed in the 'Li Ji' or Book of Rites, c 2C BC), was the capital of the state of Lu from c 1060 to 249 BC, although earlier settlements have been revealed by archaeological excavation of sites of the Da wen kou and Longshan neolithic cultures (c 4000 BC). Though Qu Fu continued as the seat of local government, the present major buildings, including the Temple, Mansion, and Drum Tower, mostly date from the Qing (although the present layout existed during the Ming).

On the central axis of the small walled town is the Temple to Confucius, with the Mansion to the NE (adjoining the rear part of the temple enclosure). The Drum Tower is at the SE extremity of the Mansion's wall; N of it are, on the right, the Yan hui Temple and, outside the town, to the N, the 'Forest of the Exalted Sage' or graveyard of the Kong family. Much of the centre of the town (around the Drum Tower) has been extensively renovated. The two-storeyed grey brick buildings with their gaily-painted timber fronts concealing banks and restaurants, are recent constructions, modelled on Qing shopfronts (like those that have been reconstructed on Liulichang in Peking and at Wutai shan in Shanxi). The reconstruction is, however, quite tasteful and appropriately northern in architectural style.

The **Temple to Confucius** (Kong miao) has been described as 'one of the three great classical architectural complexes in China' (along with the Forbidden City in Peking and the Imperial Summer Resort at Chengde). Architecturally, it is related to the imperial complexes for it is very much of the north: the buildings are solid with sedate roof-lines (not the light, upward sweep of the south) and colour is important: roofs are imperial yellow or green, columns are red-painted. It is a long, rectangular enclosure, over 1km long from N to S, the first part consisting mainly of a series of narrow courtyards dominated by a series of gates. A central courtyard houses the 13 stele pavilions, crowding the narrow space and beyond are three parallel series of courtyards, long rather than narrow.

The first temple was constructed in 478 BC on the site near the Sage's family home, where his disciples commemorated Confucius. It is said that it was originally merely a three-room building where Confucius' possessions (clothes, cap, musical instruments, carriage and books) were kept until in AD 539 an emperor of the Eastern Wei dynasty renovated the building and set up a statue of Confucius for worship. From then on, rulers made it their business to maintain and improve the temple (to help legitimise their right to rule) and 15 major reconstructions, 31 minor reconstructions and several hundred minor renovations have been recorded in the last 2000 years.

The main *S gate* in the town wall of Qu Fu was the first approach to the temple. It is known, hyperbolically, as the '10,000 ren palace wall' (a ren being an ancient measure equivalent to 2.5 metres), a reference to one of Confucius' disciples Zi Gong who said: 'If one compares a man's learning to a palace wall, then Confucius' palace wall must be a good many ren high'. The four-character inscription over the gate was set up by the Qianlong emperor in the mid 18C.

Not far N of the town wall is the first gateway of the temple. Of carved stone, it has four stone drums bearing octagonal pillars with one-horned beasts sitting on lotus thrones. The gateway is known as 'Striking of Gongs and Sounding of Musical Stones' (a reference to the major musical instruments of Confucius' time when L-shaped stones of varying sizes hung on a great wooden frame were struck like a giant musical chime).

Beyond is the *Lingxing Gate* (the Ling star is the 'star of literature' in the Great Bear and Confucius is also traditionally viewed as a 'literary star'). The gate, built in 1754 (to replace a timber construction), has four stone pillars, iron crossbeams, red walls and a yellow tiled roof. The *side gates*—named (left) The Way that Has Predominated Through Ancient and Modern Times, and (right) Virtue Equal to Heaven and Earth—to this first courtyard have some rather impressive, early-looking stone lions. Two free-standing gates follow, the *Gateway of the Original Ether of Supreme Harmony* and the *Archway of the Temple of the Exalted Sage*.

Behind them is a gate set in a wall, cutting off the first grassy courtyard. This is the *Gate of the Timeliness of the Sage* and it leads into a paved courtyard filled with cypresses, which has a stream, the Bi River, running through it, crossed by three stone bridges. On the left is a modern pavilion covering two stone figures dating from the Eastern Han (AD 25–220). These formed part of the approach to the tomb of the Prince of Western Lu, situated c 4km SE of Qufu, and were moved here after 1949 for safekeeping.

Beyond the Bi River bridges is the *Gate of Augmenting the Truth* (which leads to a narrow courtyard beyond).

The gate was first constructed in 1018 at the order of the Song Tianxi emperor and enlarged in 1504 during the reign of the Hongzhi emperor of the Ming. The name of the gate is taken from a line in the Analects: Man can augment the truth.

Inside the gate are two Yuan dynasty (1271–1368) stelae: the four-sided one on the right is inscribed with the 'Chronicles of Qu Fu county', that on the left is the 'Epitaph of a gentleman recluse' and was moved to the temple for safekeeping when the Cultural Revolution broke out in 1966.

Next comes the *Gate of the Great Mean* (meaning 'the middle way' or avoidance of extremes, a cornerstone of Confucius' views on belief and behaviour). In the Song dynasty this was the main gate to the temple though the present structure is Qing in date. Its previous function as the main entrance may be gathered from the two L-shaped, green-tiled corner towers (first built in 1331) that stand on either side of the wall (and outside to the right is the Bell Tower of Qu Fu).

In the next courtyard is a central gate, the *Gate of the Unity of the Written Language*, with two side pavilions, and behind is the 'lofty' *Kuiwen* (Worship of Literature) *Pavilion*.

First constructed in 1018, the pavilion was then called 'Pavilion of Libraries'. It was reconstructed in 1191 at the order of the Jin dynasty emperor Zhangzong and given its present name. It has a triple roof, is three storeys high and, last rebuilt in 1504, has survived remarkably well. When much of Qu Fu was destroyed by an earthquake in the reign of the Kangxi emperor (1654–1722), the pavilion was quite undamaged, as is recorded in a stele on the terrace. There are two Ming stelae pavilions in front of the Kuiwen Pavilion and four huge Ming imperial stelae.

The small courtyards to each side of the courtyard are called 'abstention lodges' where visiting emperors would retire to fast and bathe before participating in ceremonies of sacrifice to Confucius.

In the next courtyard are the 13 *stelae pavilions* (reminiscent of the stelae pavilions in the Temple of Confucius in Peking). They were constructed to hold a total of 53 imperial stelae recording imperial visits, imperially sponsored repairs and gifts of lands or titles to members of the Sage's family. The earliest are Tang in date and the latest of the Republican period (1914–19). In the same courtyard, along the northern wall and in the southern corners are stelae recording sponsorship of repairs and gifts made by the nobility and gentry.

Side gates (on the E, the *Gate of the Search for Purity*, on the W, the *Gate of the Spectacle of the Virtues*) lead to the town. In the N wall of the courtyard are five gates, four side gates subordinate to the central *Gate of Great Achievements*. The gate on the far W is the *Gate of He who Heralds the Sage* and on the far E, the *Gate of Succession of the Sage*.

'Great achievements' was Mencius' pronouncement on Confucius. Mencius (c 372–288 BC) was perhaps the most famous of Confucius' pre-Han followers whose assertion that human nature was essentially good became a prime tenet of later Confucianism.

The row of five gates marks a division within the temple, from the series of wide but narrow entrance courtyards to the three parallel courtyards beyond.

The Gate of Succession of the Sage leads to the eastern courtyards where sacrifices were offered to five generations of Confucius' ancestors (just as the eastern wing of the Forbidden City in Peking contains the ancestral hall) whilst the Gate of He who Heralds the Sage leads to courtyards where Confucius' father and mother were worshipped. The central axis comprises halls where Confucius himself was worshipped.

Immediately behind the Gate of Great Achievements is a long courtyard full of cypresses and various types of pine (some with twisted bark that spirals up the trunk, some with stippled bark), with a tall vermilion pavilion called the *Apricot Altar*, by tradition the place where Confucius instructed his disciples.

The actual site of the original Apricot Altar is unknown but in 1018 the 45th generation descendant, Kong Daofu, renovated the temple and rebuilt the Great Hall to the N of its original site. The latter was covered with an altar, apricot trees were planted around it and it was named the 'apricot altar'. A pavilion was constructed over the altar during the Jin (1115–1234) and a stone tablet with calligraphy by a Jin scholar, Dang Huaiying. The present building dates from 1596 and survived a great fire in 1724.

Behind the Apricot Altar is the main hall of the temple, the *Hall of Great*

Achievements. Built on the grand scale, its most notable feature is the series of 28 stone columns carved with dragons which support the lower roof of the double-roofed hall. Each 6m column is carved from a single block of stone and stands on a base of double lotus flowers. They were carved in 1500. The back and sides of the hall's lower roof are supported on 18 octagonal columns decorated with polished low-relief carvings of dragons amongst clouds. The ten columns in the front of the hall are sculpted in bas-relief with pairs of dragons surrounded by clouds and pearls and are unique (though they recall the wooden columns with twisted dragons on the Shengmu dian in the Jin ci near Taiyuan, Shanxi province). When emperors came to the temple, these columns were concealed behind yellow cloths to prevent imperial jealousy (for there are no such carved stone columns in the Forbidden City). The original statues of Confucius, his four companions (Yan Hui, Zheng Shen, Kong Ji and Mencius) and 12 disciples were destroyed during the Cultural Revolution and replaced in 1984.

The main hall has yellow tiles on its roof but the sides of the courtyard are lined with green-tiled, red-columned side wings where Confucius' disciples were once worshipped. These now contain a display of some of the 2000 stone stelae (the earliest dating from the Western Han) preserved in the temple.

Worship of the disciples dates back to AD 72 when the Yongping emperor of the Han came to Qu Fu to venerate Confucius. He also made sacrifices to 72 disciples. In 647 the Zhenguan emperor of the Tang decreed that 22 more disciples should be included in venerations and succeeding rulers have 'expanded and re-shuffled' the disciples so that there are numbered as 172.

Just inside the Gate of Great Achievements (on the right) is a cypress surrounded by a fence. This is supposed to be the 'Cypress Planted by the Hand of the First Teacher' and its flourishing or withering was supposed to reflect the fortunes of the Kong family and the imperial house.

Behind the main hall is the *Inner Hall* for the worship of Confucius' wife, Qi Guan, its columns and ceilings painted with phoenixes (symbolic of the female, as the dragon is for the male). Qi Guan, mother of Confucius' son Kong Li, was first worshipped separately in 1018.

Behind is the *Hall of the Relics of the Sage*, containing 120 carved stone plaques depicting events in the life of Confucius, from his mother praying for a son on Nishan Hill to his disciples at his grave. The carvings were made in the late 16C from Song paintings. There are also stone-carved copies of Gu Kaizhi's 4C painting of Confucius the travelling teacher, a portrait of Confucius by the Tang painter Wu Daozi and a seal-script inscription by the great Song painter Mi Fu.

The eastern axis entered from the Gate of the Succession of the Sage contains the *Hall of Poetry and Rites*, said to have been where Confucius instructed his son Kong Li in the study of poetry (through the 'Book of Songs')—'If one has not studied poetry. one cannot express oneself'—and ritual—'if one does not study the rites, one cannot strengthen one's character'. The present hall was built in 1504 and the courtyard contains a Tang dynasty cypress and two Song dynasty gingko trees. Each year the female tree still produces the nuts which formed the vital ingredient in 'Poetry and Rites Gingko', a dish served at banquets in the Kong family mansion next door.

Nearby is a gate which leads east to the Kong family mansion and, behind the Hall of Poetry and Rites is a well, said to have been used by Confucius.

E of the well is a small wall, 'The Wall of Lu', said to have been where the ninth generation descendant of Confucius concealed copies of the Confucian classics during the 'Burning of the Books'.

The first emperor of the Qin, Shi huang di (? 159–210) was extremely anti-Confucian, preferring the more brutally practical philosophy of legalism. He took his persecution of Confucius and all things Confucian to a degree seen later in the literary inquisition of Qianlong (late 18C) and the Cultural Revolution. He is supposed to have insisted on the burning of all books (and scholars) associated with Confucianism (and unknowingly created a scholarly controversy that raged during the Han based on 'reconstructed' versus 'survived' texts of Confucian works). After the books were concealed in the 'Lu Wall', they were forgotten until 154 BC when Liu Yu (son of the Jingdi emperor, enfeoffed as Prince Gong of Lu), decided to make extensions to his palace which involved demolition of part of Confucius' original home. During demolition, 'the rustling of silks and the clinking of bamboo slats' was heard inside a wall and the hidden documents discovered. The present Lu Wall (an unfortunate name to the English middle classes) was built later to commemorate the event.

Behind the Lu Wall are three small gates set in a wall enclosing the courtyard of the *Temple for Adoring the Sage*. This stands on a high platform and was built in 1723 by the Yongzheng emperor for the worship of five generations of Confucius' ancestors who had posthumously been granted high rank.

The rear western wing of the temple is the place where Confucius' parents were venerated and where musicians prepared for the major rituals. Entered through the *Gate of He who Heralds the Sage* (on the western side of the N wall of the courtyard of the 13 stele pavilions, the first hall on a high brick terrace is the *Hall of Silks and Metals* (meaning string and percussion instruments). The front of the building was where the musical instruments used in ritual in the temple were stored (some of them can now be seen in the museum at the rear of the Mansion). Musicians and dancers used to practise on the terrace in front of the hall.

Behind are three gates leading to the *Hall of He who Heralds the Sage*. The five-bay hall has a green glazed-tile roof and stone supporting pillars carved with pairs of dragons chasing pearls. The original hall was a Song construction but the current building dates from 1724.

The hall was built in honour of Confucius' father Shu Lianghe, a minor official who was elevated to the nobility (in retrospect) because of the achievements of his son. In 1008 he was named Duke of Lu and in 1330 he was granted the additional title of 'he who heralds the sage'.

On the same terrace, to the rear, is the smaller, three-bay *Hall of the Wife of the King Who Heralds the Sage* (meaning Confucius' mother, Yan Zhengzai who died when her son was 24). She was ennobled with her husband (in 1008, entitled 'First Lady of the Sage of Lu' and in 1330, 'Exalted Wife of the King Who Heralds the Sage'). The hall was first constructed in 1330.

The **Kong Fu** or *Confucian Mansion* is just to the NE of the Temple, approached by Queli Road, the narrow street lined with souvenir stalls that runs along the eastern wall of the temple. Descendants of the Sage are said to have lived here for over 2500 years (77 generations), though the first 'mansion' was further S on Queli Road.

Along Queli Road, at the southern end is the *Queli Gate* (most recently renovated during the Republican era though there was formerly a Han dynasty timber construction carved with flowers) with the words 'Que li' on a horizontal board in the centre. Que means stone tower (and two stone towers used to stand at the southern end of the road) and li is an old word for street.

Further N up Queli Road, the **Bell Tower** straddles the road. It was first constructed in 1302, in the style of a city gate with the green-tiled tower rising above a stone arch. The huge bronze bell inside (1.5m high) was rung to mark ceremonies in the adjoining temple and at dawn every day to mark the rising of the sun, except in the 12th lunar month when it was rung both at sunrise and sunset.

Beyond the Bell Tower is the *gate* of Confucius' former dwelling, with grey roof tiles and a lintel decorated with animals. Such gates were only permitted by sumptuary law to the highest ranks of the nobility and places the Kong family on a par with the imperial family. Inside the gate is a stele incribed 'In praise of the Gate of the Former Dwelling' in the handwriting of the Qianlong emperor.

The present **Mansion**, E of the site of the 'former mansion', was constructed here during the reign of the first Ming emperor (1368–98) and was extensively renovated and enlarged during the Qing.

The major inhabitant of the Mansion was always the Yansheng (Extending the Line of the Sage) Duke, the oldest male direct descendant of Confucius. The title 'Yansheng Duke' was conferred in 1055 and remained unchanged until 1935 when Chiang Kai-shek changed it to 'State Master of Sacrifices to the Exalted Sage and First Teacher'. The status of the Yansheng Duke rose throughout imperial history from the rank of a 5th grade official in the 10C, to a grade-one official under the Ming (1368–1644), second only to the Prime Minister. During the Qing, further privileges such as being allowed to ride a horse inside the Forbidden City (all others were called upon to dismount at the gates of all Qing imperial buildings), exemption from taxes and corvée labour and the power to preside over its own court of law, raised the position of the Yansheng Duke until he was effectively on a par with the Emperor. This is illustrated by the marriage of a daughter of the Qianlong emperor to the Yansheng Duke in 1772. The princess was born with a mole on her face which, fortune-tellers predicted, would bring misfortune unless she was married into 'a family more illustrious than either the nobility or the highest of officials'. The Qianlong emperor had to marry her to the Yansheng Duke, the only other person in China allowed to walk with the emperor along the Imperial Way.

There was a complication for Manchus (such as the imperial family) were not allowed to marry Chinese (such as even the Kongs) so she first had to be given in adoption to an official's family. Her dowry included 20 villages (and the taxes collected therefrom), several thousand trunks of clothing and jewellery, jasper ruyi (S-shaped carved objects sometimes, unhelpfully, called 'sceptres' which were used as presents: ru yi means fulfillment of wishes so they serve both as symbols of good wishes and approval), 27 metres of satin and many pelts. The Qianlong emperor was most amused by one gift amongst the thousands of wedding presents, a small gold axe sent by a magistrate 'for future imperial grandchildren to crack walnuts' (the 18C present for someone who has everything).

The mansion divides into three major parts: the front or formal and administrative section, the rear part where the family lived, and beyond that the garden. There are also the normal three parallel axes running through the front and rear: the western wing included the reception rooms for important guests, studies and rooms where the rites were learnt, whilst the eastern wing included the family temple and ancestral hall (just as in the Forbidden City) and apartments for various dependant relatives.

The *main gates* are painted black with red borders (a colour scheme more common around Xi'an) and have fine brass knockers as well as the inevitable pair of calligraphic inscriptions reading 'Sharing happiness with the whole nation, the peaceful, prosperous, respected, glorious mansion of the Duke' and 'As long-lived as the heavens, the house of the learned sage of moral excellence'. The two small gates beside it are supposed to mark the entrance to the original mansion which in the early 20C was a place where a small girl of the 77th generation used to play amongst relics supposed to have belonged to the sage himself, a dilapidated (it would be after 2500 years) carriage and a zither.

Inside the gate to the main mansion is a wide courtyard: the narrow building to the W was the *Hall for Sending Memorials to the Emperor*. On the E was the carriage house which dealt with rather more mundane communications. Beyond is the *second gate* inscribed 'Gate of the Sage' and beyond that a *screen gate* with four black pillars standing on eight stone drums and carved beams terminating in flower buds (a form of decoration often found on internal gates which were known as 'hanging flower gates'). This screen gate was kept closed except when emperors visited and then it would be opened with a 13-gun salute. Above the gate is an inscription by the Ming Jiajing emperor (1507–66) which reads 'Bestowing Double Glory'. The same courtyard is lined with buildings housing six administrative departments (modelled on the six ministries of the imperial government).

The Department of Rites was in charge of ancestral worship, the Department of Seals of jurisdiction and edicts, the Department of the Hundred Households was responsible for security and the administration of the burial ground; the others were the Departments of Music, Letters and Archives, Rent Collection and Sacrifical Fields. These Departments or minor ministries were housed in the side wings of the courtyards of the Great Hall and the second and third halls, the Department of Letters and Archives (which has, since the Cultural Revolution, begun publishing an immense series of archives), for example, to the W of the second hall.

In the *Great Hall*, behind the Gate of Double Glory, the Yansheng Duke, sitting on a wooden chair covered by a tiger skin, proclaimed edicts and administered the affairs of the family.

The Kongs owned vast tracts of land in different parts of China and received the taxes due on the land: 650 hectares were personally owned and some 24,000 further hectares were set aside for the peasants of Qu Fu to work. There was a Department of Punishments in the mansion (and a goose-winged pitchfork, a gold-tipped jade baton and a tiger-tail baton that had been presented by emperors to help inflict punishments for unpaid taxes or misdemeanours that fell within the family's jurisdiction). On the table in front of his seat were brushes and writing materials and the seal of authority. Ranged around are banners and signs used in public processions which say 'Silence' and 'Make Way'.

Behind the Great Hall is the *Second Hall* where the Duke gave audience to officials of the fourth rank and higher and where children were examined in rites and music under horizontal boards inscribed 'Respectfully inherit the cause of the sage' and 'Poetry, literature, music and the rites'. Vertical tablets in the hall include one reading 'happiness and longevity' written by the Daoguang emperor (reigned 1797–1821) and one with the character for 'longevity' written by the Dowager Empress Cixi (there are similar inscriptions by her in the Summer Palace outside Peking).

Linked to the Great Hall by a covered way, there is a red-lacquered bench in the corridor, known as Yan Song's bench.

Yan Song was a Prime Minister of the Jiajing reign period of the Ming and his daughter married a 64th generation descendant of Confucius. Owing to trouble at court, Yan Song was to be tried and he came to Qu Fu to beg his son-in-law to intercede. As the Yansheng Duke did not want to interfere, Yan Song sat interminably on the bench waiting for an audience.

In the *Third Hall*, behind, the Yansheng Duke attended to less important family matters and those involving the vast retinue of servants. When the last generation inhabited the mansion (and there were only four family members), there were 500 hereditary servants. The central room now contains sedan chairs used by the family: the red one used by the Yansheng Duke within the mansion, the green one used for trips outside.

Behind the Third Hall is the *Gate to the Inner Apartments*, marking the division between the public areas and the private, which could almost be described as the masculine and the feminine areas.

Visitors came to the front halls; administrative work and official family cults (such as ancestral venerations which were carried out in the two halls on the eastern axis of the front part of the mansion, the Hall for Cherishing Ancestral Kindness and the Hall to Requite Ancestral Kindness), all took place in the front of the mansion but only family members and trusted (mainly female) servants were allowed to pass into the rear part of the mansion. Even the water-carrier had to pour his sweet well-water into a trough that ran through the wall, just W of the gate.

This strict seclusion could cause problems as Kong Demao (of the 77th generation) recalled. When a fire broke out, only 12 of the 500 hereditary servants were allowed into the rear apartments to try and put it out with the result that it burnt for three days, destroying seven buildings (shades of the impropriety of rescuing your sister-in-law from drowning persisting into the 20C).

The first hall in the Inner Mansion is the *Front Reception Hall*, where relatives were received and wedding and funeral ceremonies conducted.
The eastern room contains a set of furniture of dark tree-roots, presented
by the Qianlong emperor, and a dinner service (for banquets were held in
this hall).

196 different dishes might be served at a single banquet including 'gold and silver
fish' served on a special plate shaped like two fish and coloured white and yellow,
'lilac beancurd' (beancurd carved and arranged with a beansprout, said to resemble
a lilac blossom) sea-cucumber, shark's fin and duck (known as the 'big three') and
glutinous rice.

The room on the far western end of the Front Reception Hall was used as
a study by the 76th Yansheng Duke (died 1919).

To the E of the Hall, reached by a very narrow passageway, is the
Tower of Refuge, a tall, narrow, windowless tower, built to preserve the
Yansheng Dukes from attack. It has, apparently, never been used, except
by an owl who lived there when Kong Demao was a child, like the hordes
of crows that roosted (and still do, together with the big blue-backed
magpies) in the trees of the mansion and temple's courtyards.

Behind the Front Reception Hall is a small gate which leads to the two-
storeyed *Front Main Building* (Qiantang lou), where the women of the
76th and 77th generations lived, whilst the 77th Yansheng Duke (who
was born after his father died) lived in the hall behind (the *Rear Main
Building*, Houtang lou).

The eastern central room of the Front Main Building was the bedroom of Madame
Tao, wife of the 76th Yansheng Duke, a terrifying figure to the small Kong Demao
and her sister (who, together with their brother, the heir, were the children of Concubine Wang, a secondary wife, taken because Madame Tao had borne no children
that survived). The two small girls had their bedroom in the easternmost room and,
until her death, their mother's room was the inner western room, where her photograph hangs on the wall.
    Madame Tao appears to have poisoned Concubine Wang just 17 days after she
gave birth to the posthumous heir to the Dukedom in 1919. Concubine Wang had
originally come to the mansion as her servant and, despite her position as mother of
the Duke's children, whenever the Duke was away, Madame Tao would whip her
with a special whip she kept for the purpose.
    Ostensibly an ardent Buddhist, officially in charge during the infancy of the 77th
Duke, Madame Tao was Qu Fu's equivalent to the intriguing and all-powerful Dowager Empress Cixi. A secondary concubine of the Duke, Madame Feng lived in the
western inner room, almost a prisoner until she died in 1928, a year before her perse-
cutor, Madame Tao. The building where the women lived is decorated with a motley
collection of ancient and modern gifts and decorative objects, as is the Rear Main
Building where Kong Decheng, the 77th Yansheng Duke (who is still alive, in Taiwan) lived.
    A sad picture of his childhood is painted by his elder sister Kong Demao-she, her
elder sister and the young Duke rattling around in the dusty mansion. The little boy's
solitude increased unbearably as his sisters were married off and went to live in
Peking. Kong Deqi, the eldest sister, died at the age of 25 after a terribly unhappy
marriage to a useless, debt-ridden and unfaithful husband (who lost all his teeth the
day he bought a car and immediately crashed it into a telegraph pole as he hadn't the
faintest idea how to drive), who had been carefully selected for her by Madame Tao.

The Rear Building has been left as it was in 1940 when the Yansheng
Duke departed for Chongqing (and later Taiwan) during the Japanese
invasion), decorated in a 'mixture of Chinese and western styles', with
rounded 1930s sofas mixed with congratulatory pieces of calligraphy sent
for Kong Decheng's wedding in 1936. A picture of plum blossoms on the
wall was painted and presented by the famous Peking opera singer Mei
Lanfang (1894–1961), one of the greatest 20C male singers of female roles
who did much to promote Peking opera after Liberation.

The wedding of the Duke, reflected in the furnishings and presents was a mixed Chi-
nese-Western affair, the bride in a white wedding gown and high heels, the groom in
a long gown and mandarin jacket. Five orchestras led the marriage procession and
three Chinese operas were performed in the town. The courtyard in front of the Front

Reception Hall was filled with tables spread with auspicious foods—pine-kernels and longans (symbolising the early birth of sons and daughters)—branches of pine and cypress (symbolising eternal youth) and 'happiness salt'. As the bride dismounted from the red bridal sedan chair, hordes of reporters in western suits rushed forward, flash-bulbs popping. She then made her way to the Rear Building to change into a Chinese bridal dress, a red cheongsam with red satin shoes, and sat cross-legged on the bridal bed waiting for her husband who still had to sit through several hours of ceremonies in the Front Reception Hall.

W of the Rear Main Building is a Buddhist *chapel*, and just S of it, on the western axis, is the *family school* where the Yansheng Dukes were trained in their duties, in calligraphy and couplet-writing, as well as in standard school subjects (which, in the 1920s, included English).

Behind the Rear Building is the *garden*, known as the 'Iron hill garden', first constructed in 1503 and reconstructed when the Qianlong emperor's daughter married the 72nd generation Duke. Fairly typical of northern gardens, with water, artificial stone mountains, free-standing twisted rock formations on raised stone bases, bridges and pavilions, there is a 400-year-old cypress with five trunks and a juniper growing in the centre.

There is also a small *museum* displaying items from the Mansion which is extremely interesting. There are ritual bronzes in specially made silken boxes and a wealth of clothing, from children's garments to those of older women, all showing the bold mixing of colours that characterises Chinese costume and jewellery.

A short walk N of the town is the **Forest of the Exalted Sage**, the Confucian family burial ground. Walled, grassy and full of the indistinct hillocks that are the grave mounds of thousands of long-forgotten Kongs, it is a marvellous (and on a cold November day, empty) place to wander in.

Turn left out of the Mansion and walk along the road until you reach the *Drum Tower*. This, like its pair, the Bell Tower, was constructed in the Ming, on a solid brick base. The timber pavilion on top housed the drum which was struck to mark the sunset and also used when important ceremonies were carried out in the Confucian Temple.

At the Drum Tower turn left (N) and the road will take you straight out of the northern city wall towards the burial ground. It is about a 20-minute walk through fields and a village. Pedicab drivers will harass you to be bicycled though it is hardly worth it if you enjoy walking along relatively traffic-free roads. You will soon see the stone *Gateway of 'Eternal Spring'* which straddles the road. Built in 1594, the six stone columns are topped back and front by 12 stone lions, the lintels and columns carved with dragons, phoenixes, qilin (Chinese unicorns), horses, deer, flowers and clouds. Over the central gate are two dragons playing with a pearl whilst carvings of phoenixes flying towards the sun can be seen over the side gateways.

Just before you reach the gateway, two square *pavilions* with green-tiled roofs are set on either side of the road, each containing a stele. The eastern one was put in place in 1594 and is inscribed 'The divine road of Confucius, first teacher of sagely accomplishments' and that on the W is dated 1595 and commemorates the renovation of the forest and temple.

The 'forest' is surrounded by a 7km wall (3m high and 5m thick) enclosing an area of 2 square km, filled with graves since it has been used since the Han dynasty. There are over 100,000 trees of all sorts for apparently Confucius' disciples collected exotic trees to plant here. These include cypress, japonica, oaks, elms, scholartrees, pistachio, hackberry, maple, poplar, willow and cherry.

At the end of the 'divine road' is a decorative *archway* in front of the main gate. The archway, or pailou, is a timber construction painted in red, blue and gold, with a green-tiled roof. The inscription reads 'Forest of the supreme sage'. The pailou was first erected in 1424 and rebuilt during the Qing. Behind is the *Gate Tower*; the red railings protecting a collection of stone tablets recording renovations and restoration works at the forest and ceremonies held in commemoration. Inside the gate, a long stone-flagged path leads to a *watchtower*, built in 1732, with guardian stone lions. You can climb this for a view over the flat fields to Qu Fu and the grassy 'forest' below.

Running W from the gate is the *imperial carriageway* (previously exclusively used by emperors coming to offer sacrifices); 200m along the carriageway, on the N side is a stone *gateway* inscribed in red characters 'Zhu river bridge'. Beyond is an arched stone bridge over the river. This leads to the area where Confucius and his son are buried.

Apparently (or according to legend) Confucius chose this place for his burial, stating that the fengshui was good. His disciples objected because there was no flowing water (according to fengshui beliefs, tombs should have a hill behind, to the N, and a river or stream flowing in front, just like any other building), but Confucius said that sooner or later someone would make good this deficiency. Legend continues to relate that during his intensive persecution of Confucianism (by burning books and scholars), the First Emperor, Qin Shi huangdi, attempted to decrease the influence of Confucianism by trying to destroy the fengshui of Confucius' tomb. He ordered that a river be dug through the burial ground, thus inadvertently improving the fengshui he was trying to destroy.

Just NE of the bridge is a small courtyard and the *Hall of Deliberation*, behind which is another small courtyard where visitors assumed ritual clothing before sacrifices to Confucius. In a third courtyard was the 'divine kitchen' where sacrificial animals were slaughtered.

Due N of the Zhu River Bridge is the *Hall of Sacrifices*, approached by an avenue of carved stone columns, tigers, griffins and guardian figures (one pair dates from the Song, the other from the Qing). Behind the hall is the *tumulus* that now marks what is supposed to be the tomb of Confucius. In front is a large stone tablet of 1443 reading 'Tomb of the prince of literary excellence and sagely achievements', with a smaller Song stele behind.

Nearby to the E is the tomb of Confucius' son, *Kong Li*, who 'died before his father, without making any noteworthy achievements'. S of Confucius' tomb is that of his grandson, *Kong Ji*, who was said to have been an active promoter of his grandfather's cause. W of Confucius' tomb is a three-bay building said to mark the site of the little hut that Zi Gong, one of his disciples, built to watch over the grave. Most of his disciples were said to have observed the current custom of watching over the grave for three years, the pious Zi Gong stayed on for another three.

The graveyard is still used by direct descendants; when I last visited it, a Mrs Kong had been buried only a day before, the brilliant pink, white and silver paper flowers of her burial wreath the only colours to be seen.

As the graveyard has been in use for over 2000 years, many of the graves are unmarked and unknown but some groups may be distinguished.

Taking the main road that crosses the westernmost bridge over the Zhu River, to the left (when facing Confucius' tomb), on the extreme W is a group of *Ming tombs*. Continuing round, almost due N of Confucius' tomb is the memorial archway and group of stone animals marking the grave of '*Madame Yu*', the daughter of the Qianlong emperor (reigned 1736–96), who married the 72nd-generation Yansheng Duke. Her only child, a daughter, was buried outside the forest (female descendants were not allowed inside the forest, only wives). Nearby is a huge stone stele marking the grave of *Kong Shangren* (1648–1718), a 64th generation descendant and author of the drama 'Taohua shan' (The Peach-blossom Fan, an opera based on events in Nanjing, 1644–45, as the Qing took over), ranked as one of the greatest dramas in the Chinese language.

Kong Shangren served as an official but was dismissed from office in 1699 and spent much of his time in his 'Lonely Cloud Villa' NE of Qu Fu where he wrote and instructed some 700 descendants of the sage in rites and music. He also wrote literary essays commemorating his official service on Yellow River conservancy work and a statistical work on the number of people in 16 provinces who were aged 70 or more in 1688.

Near Kong Shangren's tomb, on the E side of the graveyard, is the tomb of the *76th Duke* and the awful *Madame Tao*. The grave also includes Madame Wang, mother of the 77th generation who was (against the strict rules that concubines could not be included in clan graves) reburied there, to the joy of her small son.

The **Temple of Yan Hui** (Yan miao) is just inside the northern city wall, on the E side of the road leading to the Confucian burial ground.

Yan Hui was Confucius' favourite disciple and was therefore worshipped by emperors visiting Qu Fu along with his master. The founder of the Han dynasty (reigned 206–194 BC) is said to have founded the temple which was extensively restored in 1326 and then in the Ming and Qing. In 1330 he was posthumously awarded the title of Fusheng Duke of the state of Yan and the temple is sometimes known as the Fusheng (Return of the Sage) miao.

Said to have been built on the site of Yan Hui's house in Humble Alley, the temple covers 56 hectares with wide courtyards full of old conifers; the main buildings arranged on the central one of the three axes, culminating in the *Hall of the Sage Returned* and the *Hall of Yan Hui's Wife* behind (echoing the arrangement in the Temple of Confucius). Notable features of this grand, empty enclosure are the well in the first courtyard, said to have been used by Yan Hui, now covered by a pavilion also covering a stele inscribed 'The well of Humble Alley' by the Kangxi emperor of the Qing. Inside the gate to the second courtyard (which once contained side buildings for storing sacrificial implements) are two stele pavilions with stelae commemorating renovations in 1441 and 1509.

The *Main Hall* is, like the hall in the Temple of Confucius, supported by stone columns carved with dragons.

The side halls of the courtyard were once used for the worship of Yan Hui's descendants who included Yan Zitui (c AD 531–590), a 34th-generation descendant who wrote the 'Moral instructions for the Yan Family', a remarkably Confucian document on family conduct. Similar works were written by many Confucians, though this is the earliest surviving example: a Ming work on the same subject contains a map of a house with separate paths marked for men and women of the family so that they should not meet by chance.

Yan Shigu (581–645) was famous for his annotations to the history of the Han dynasty and Yan Zhenqing (709–785) was a famous calligrapher who raised an army with his brother to help suppress the An Lushan rebellion of 755.

The eastern building now contains a display of locally excavated neolithic and early Zhou ceramics, illustrating the local development of the Longshan type of neolithic culture. From the second courtyard, an eastern gate, the *Gate of Watching Advancement*, leads to the eastern axis where in the *Hall for Withdrawal and Introspection* there is a Ming stele with an image of Yan Hui seated. The parallel western axis contains halls devoted to the worship of Yan Hui's father and, behind, his mother.

Outside the city wall, to the NE, is the **Zhou Gong miao** (Temple to the Duke of Zhou), a smaller temple than that of Yan Hui but equally tranquil and filled with fine cypress, juniper and pistachio trees.

The Duke of Zhou is a semi-historical figure, fourth son of King Wen of the Zhou who assisted his brother, King Wu, in the suppression of the Shang dynasty (late 11C BC) and the establishment of the Zhou. He is credited with the formulation of the regulations by which the Zhou ruled and is therefore described in Chinese textbooks as 'the most famous politician of China's ancient slave-owning society' (as close to a 'Good thing' as a slave-owner could get). In AD 1008 he was granted the title 'King of Cultural Regulations' by the Song emperor and his temple was built on the site of an earlier temple built by his son in the 11C BC (and such restored in succeeding dynasties).

The *main gate* is a decorative wooden structure with a grey tiled roof. On top of the tall wooden columns are glazed figures of heavenly warriors seated on drums and over the western gate is an inscription 'Regulating the rites and creating music' whilst that over the eastern doorway is translated as 'Ability to make the warp and woof of the universe'. The main building, the *Hall of the First Sage*, has inscriptions by the Qianlong emperor.

The huge horizontal tablet reads 'Diligently practising illustrious virtue' and the seal reads 'imperial calligraphy of the Qianlong emperor', who is also responsible for the antithetical couplets on the pillars praising 'the eternal influence on governmental and social regulations established by the Duke of Zhou and the illustrious spiritual model he provided for Confucius' (who sought to bring contemporary rulers back to those golden days of regulations).

Set into the NW wall of the building is a Han dynasty depiction of the Duke (described in a Chinese guidebook as 'the only extant portrait of the Duke of Zhou in China', omitting to mention that it was made nearly a millenium after his death). The figures are replicas of those destroyed in the Cultural Revolution and comprise the Duke of Zhou in the centre with Bo Qin, his filial son, to the E and Bo Qin's servant to the W. The servant has a board on his back with a few maxims from the Duke for his son.

The Duke of Zhou was supposed to have feared that Bo Qin might occasionally show a lack of prudence in directing the affairs of the state of Lu so he had a trusted servant carry the inscribed board on his back and turn round whenever his young master needed an exhortation.

Sacrifices used to be offered on the broad terrace in front of the hall which is now surrounded by inscriptions from 1008 onwards written in praise of the Duke of Zhou.

On the W of the road out to the Confucian burial ground (NW of the Temple of the Duke of Zhou) is a high mound called the 'Terrace for gazing towards father' where Bo Qin would sit and look westwards thinking of his father.

Another somewhat legendary site, 4km E of Qu Fu (in the NE corner of **Jiuxian** village) is the *'Tomb' of Emperor Shaohao*, said to have been the son of the Yellow Emperor and a first ancestor of all the Chinese people.

His divine status meant that the 'tomb' was improved throughout the centuries, most notably by the Huizong emperor of the Song, who had it bricked over like a pyramid in AD 1111, and by the Qianlong emperor who ordered 421 cypresses and four junipers to be planted there in 1748 after a personal visit.

A carved stone pailou of 1739 leads to the *Hall of Sacrifices* with an inscription by the Qianlong emperor and the flattened pyramid of the tomb. Just to the S are two massive stone tablets lying face down, the only remains of the 'palace' built in 1012 to commemorate Shaohao's father, the Yellow Emperor. The tablets were intended to be carved on site but the Song dynasty was driven from north China before this could happen.

Some 30km SE of Qu Fu is **Ni shan Hill** where Confucius' mother prayed for a second son (as her first had been too sickly to participate in the essential task of a son, the maintenance of the ancestral sacrifices).

Her wish was granted but Confucius was said to have been so hideous at birth that his father abandoned him on Ni shan Hill where he was reared by a tigress and kept cool by an eagle that fanned him with her wings. These phenomena convincing his father that the child was exceptional, the child was allowed back home.

There is now a temple on the hill and the place is also famous for its ink-stones which were obviously appropriate souvenirs for Chinese visitors to the home of the effective founder of the Chinese bureaucracy.

23 Zibo

Zibo, 160km W of Ji'nan, is a very ancient city, incorporating the site of the capital of the state of Qi in the Spring and Autumn and Warring States periods (722—221 BC). Part of the Qi city wall can still be seen as well as a number of tumuli, thought to be the tombs of notables of the state of Qi. Zibo is today best known for its ceramic and glass production and some specialist groups with a particular interest in either glass or ceramics visit the town for this reason.

The *Glass Factory* produces objects of all sizes from snuff bottles to giant vases and its special characteristic is coloured glass. Most of the vessels are made from layers of different coloured glass, cut through so that red or blue or green silhouettes stand out against a white ground (or vice versa).

The *Ceramics Factory* produces a variety of wares, specialising in dark-ish earthernwares, particularly 'oil spot' glazes. The dark brown or black glaze (whose colour is based on iron oxide) is spotted with tiny, regular silvery spots caused by concentrations of the oxide which appear on the surface during firing.

Satisfactory production of a good base colour and even spotting is extremely difficult and when I last visited the factory in 1983 its administrators were extremely concerned that their only specialist, a very old man, would not last long. He was, apparently, extremely jealous of his secret formula and unwilling to pass on his expertise. They knew that they could make millions if they could increase oil-spot production as it is extremely popular in Japan (Deng Xiaoping had taken a tea-service from Zibo as a gift on an official visit to Japan) and equally attractive to Western visitors.

In the outskirts of Zibo (Zichuan qu) is *Pu Songling's House* (Pu Songling gu ju). Pu Songling (1640–1715) is best known for his collection of short stories, 'Liao zhai zhi yi' (translated long ago by Herbert Giles as 'Strange Stories from a Chinese Studio', 1908, and recently partially translated and introduced by Jonathan Spence in 'The Death of Woman Wang', Penguin, 1979).

Little known in his own time as a writer, Pu Songling passed the *juren* examinations with the highest marks but spent the rest of his life trying to pass the next stage (*xiucai*) without success. He served as secretary to a local magistrate and as secretary to a friend, a retired magistrate, managed the affairs of his family and wrote stories and poems. The 'Liao zhai zhi yi' is a collection of stories and legends, most with some basis in fact though fox fairies mingle with the real-life characters.

Pu Songling's old home is a good example of popular architecture of the Shandong region in the early Qing (though much restored). It is a simple courtyard dwelling of grey brick and tile with courtyard gardens; the furniture is said to be that used by Pu Songling himself. There is an exhibition of translations of his works and manuscript and illustrated woodblock editions as well as many calligraphic inscriptions in his praise by famous people.

24 Qingdao

Qingdao, one of China's major seaports, is on the S side of the Shandong peninsula at the mouth of a natural inlet. Until 1914 it was the 'seat of government of German China'.

Used as a winter anchorage for the Russian fleet in 1895, when the Chinese decided to make it the base for the Beiyang fleet (as Dairen or Port Arthur and Weihaiwei had been lost, the latter to the British). The Germans, however, on the pretext of avenging the murder of two German missionaries in Shandong, took Qingdao on 14 November 1897 and, by a treaty imposed on the Chinese, leased land around the port.

The Germans laid out a new foreign quarter 'under stringent regulations as to sanitation and appearances, with every discouragement to the mere speculator' and the German appearance of the town through its architecture persists to this day. In 1914 the Japanese, anxious to acquire a foothold in China, took advantage of being an ally of the British and demanded that Germany hand over Qingdao. When the demand was ignored, Japan declared war on 23 August 1914 and, with the British, bombarded Qingdao. Despite the German batteries on Mount Bismarck, Qingdao was taken on 7 November and 5000 luckless prisoners taken to Japan.

The 'Japanese Railway Guide' of 1924 naturally devotes much space to 'one of the most fashionable watering-places of the Orient' though it admits that 'being a newly opened district, historic places are scarce, and the parks and other places created by the Germans are still too new to interest visitors' and it recommends trips to the nearby (25km E) Lao shan (mountain), inhabited by Taoist priests and whose springs produce the best-known mineral water in China, Laoshan kuan quan shui; Victoria Bay (the easternmost bathing beach, beyond the piers) and the Governor's Residence on the slopes of Mount Diederich (now Zhongshan gongyuan or Park).

The most interesting part of Qingdao, where the *railway station* (an impressive Teutonic construction celebrating the arrival of the railway from Ji'nan in 1904) and most of the hotels are, is the old **German Concession Area** towards the end of the peninsula. It is an area, like the beaches, simply for wandering in. The Catholic church with its twin spires is to the E of Zhongshan lu, the railway station to the W, and the beach area is lined with fine villas and guesthouses.

The *Museum* (Qingdao shi bowuguan), housed in a welfare institute built in 1931, comprises a collection of Yuan to Qing paintings and an archaeological section which is best known for its large stone Buddha figures produced between 500 and 527. The most impressive weighs 30 tons and is nearly 6m high, accompanied by 3m Bodhisattvas. The heads of the Bodhisattvas were cut off in 1928 by Japanese who moved the sculptures to the railway station for transportation to Japan but the move was foiled and the sculptures restored.

In *Lu Xun Park*, on the tip of the promontory, immediately W of Beach No. 1 (the beaches of Qingdao are numbered 1–6 from W to E) is the *Aquarium* and the 'Museum of Sea Products' (Haichan bowuguan). This was founded in 1932, or at least part of it, set up by the Academia Sinica, was founded in 1932 and amalgamated with the Qingdao Museums

Authority in 1955. The collection is intended both for research and 'to introduce the environment of the oceans, their origins and to popularise the sciences of the sea'.

In the industrial part of the town, E of the main harbour, is the *Qingdao Brewery* which can be visited by arrangement through Luxingshe in the Huiquan Hotel. The brewery was established by the Germans (before the First World War) and hops were planted to supply it. It produces beer known by the old spelling of Qingdao, Tsingtao, which is considered to be the best in China and is now quite widely exported, either in bottles or, more recently, cans. The beer is light and clear though a dark brown stout is also produced (which I have not seen outside the brewery).

25   Yantai

Yantai, known to Westerners of the late 19C and early 20C as *Chefoo*, is a fishing town on the northern tip of the Shandong peninsula.

It was opened to foreign trade in 1858 by the Tientsin treaty though it seemed at the time to be lacking essential amenities as the 'Encyclopaedia Sinica' reports: 'The port lacks a harbour and breakwater but we hope that the want will soon be supplied...It also needs and hopes for railway communication with the interior...'. That last want has been supplied for Yantai is on a railway line from Ji'nan via Weifang, the centre of kite-making with an annual kite-flying festival in March and other handicraft production, notably of yellow striped tiger toys. In the early decades of this century, the chief trade of Yantai was in beancake, vermicelli, groundnuts and silks with 'good business done in pongee, hairnets, lace and fruits' and in the shipment of '100,000 coolies a year to Siberia'. There was also a pioneering winery set up by Singaporean Chinese in 1893.

Apart from the pleasant beaches and harbour, there is also an impressive **Fujian Guild Hall** (Fujian hui guan) in the centre of the town. Started in 1884, it took 22 years to complete. It was financed by Fujianese merchants who used it as a lodging and it was built in the south in the decorative southern style, the pieces being shipped to Yantai for assembly. Its courtyards include a stage (the performance of plays was an important part of trade guild festivals), a main hall, and side wings and the *Yantai Museum* is now housed in it. The timber parts are highly carved and painted.

26   Xi'an

Xi'an (Western Peace) is the modern capital of Shaanxi province and a major industrial centre. It does, however, preserve the Ming city walls in their entirety (they are still being restored) and is one of the most famous tourist centres in China, particularly since the discovery of the spectacular 'buried army' of terracotta warriors.

It served as the capital of China for most of the Han, Sui and Tang dynasties, when it was known as *Chang'an* (Eternal Peace). Particularly during the Han, it was used as a major capital in conjunction with Luoyang (the 'Eastern Capital'), whence the court retreated if Chang'an was menaced by barbarians from the West. Excavations have revealed the huge spread of the Tang city, far beyond the limits of today's Xi'an, and the surrounding countryside is dotted with the tumuli of emperors, empresses and courtiers of the Han and Tang.

Airport: the small airport is not far from the centre of town (though a new airport capable of taking jumbo jets is currently being built in the neighbouring town of Xianyang which will bring ever greater numbers of tourists to Xi'an).

There were at least three flights daily to and from Peking (in late 1987), daily flights from Shanghai, Chengdu, Chongqing, Lanzhou, Guangzhou and Zhengzhou, direct flights from Hong Kong at least once a week as well as less frequent flights to and from Guilin, Hangzhou, Hanzhong, Haerbin, Hefei, Ji'nan, Kunming, Nanjing, Qingdao, Shenyang, Taiyuan, Urumqi, Wuhan, Xiamen, Yan'an, Yinchuan, and Xining and innumerable extra and charter flights, with which the airport and airlines are barely able to cope. I have quite often had to load groups onto more than one flight simply to get them all to Xi'an on the same day—delays are frequent and disastrous owing to the pressure of people.

Rail: the station is in the N of the town, just outside the walls. It is on the main E–W line from Peking or Shanghai to Urumqi and it is possible to get to Xi'an by rail from Nanjing, Qingdao, Zhengzhou, Chongqing, Chengdu, Lanzhou and Taiyuan.

Hotels: hotel building is at last catching up with tourist numbers though many of the new hotels are situated in rather dismal and distant suburbs. The situation has, however improved from the early to mid 1980s when overcrowding meant that groups had to stay in a rather charming (but leaking) hotel in Xianyang.

The best-situated hotels include the *Renmin dasha* (Remin or People's Hotel) on Dongxin jie, just W of the main square. This is a wondrous example of the huge old hotels built sometimes by but invariably for the Russian advisors of the 1950s. Before modernisation, when students were crammed into dormitory rooms for improving summer trips, we used to call it the People's Large Prawn (a daxia, fourth tone, is a prawn, sha, alternative pronunciation xia (fourth tone) means mansion) and it was an unlovely place. It has since been modernised and is well-situated for walks to the city centre. The *Bell Tower Hotel* (Zhonglou fandian), just SW of the Bell Tower, is in the very centre of town and since 1987 has been under Holiday Inn management. There is a smaller, cheaper hotel that is well-situated on Dong da jie, the *Wuyi fandian* (1 May Hotel).

The first 'luxury' foreign-managed (by a Swedish hotel chain) hotel to be opened in Xi'an was the *Golden Flower* on Changle lu which is, unfortunately, a stiff 10-minute walk past a sugarbeet factory and its associated housing blocks from the eastern city wall. It is worth visiting the Golden Flower (if time hangs heavy which is not often in Xi'an where visitors are rushed through and away to allow the next batch in) to see its extraordinary layout. The ground floor is cut in half by a deep channel filled with rushing water. This is quite attractive but it also cuts the dining area in half so that waiters have to walk a long way to the diners. To diminish the communication problem the channel is (or was in late 1987) partially boarded over for breakfast and tables loaded with self-service foods placed over the gully. You do have to be rather careful not to step back from the table and breakfast is a nerveracking affair as incautious guests windmill backwards, arms flailing, over the great divide. At night, a pianist and grand piano are placed over the stream.

Other new hotels such as the *Tangcheng*, the *Xi'an Guesthouse* and the *Tanghua fandian* are all some distance from the city centre.

A development that I have so far only noticed in Xi'an hotels and restaurants serving tourists is the use of self-service catering. A great variety of somewhat indifferent dishes are kept warm on heated tables and visitors can help themselves, ladling their chosen foods into plastic trays. In a country that prides itself on the freshness of its food and that is over-supplied with people to serve it, this seems a great pity and represents one of the threats that tourism brings, reducing Chinese cuisine to a lowest common denominator of what prejudiced packaged travellers will accept, or are thought to be able to accept.

Xi'an's historic importance lies mainly in its use as a capital by the Han and Tang though there were earlier settlements in and near Xi'an. The city's significance in the early part of the 20C derived from its nearness to the Communist Party's 1937–45 headquarters at Yan'an. Travellers such as the American journalist Edgar Snow were smuggled out of Xi'an to Yan'an in the late 1930s and the city is also famous for the Xi'an incident of 1936 when Chiang Kai-shek was captured by his own allies in a vain attempt to make him behave sensibly about the Japanese invasion.

Evidence of early man in the Xi'an area is provided by the discovery in 1963–64 of a skull, jaw and other bones of Lantian man some 38km SE of Xi'an. Lantian man (who was actually almost certainly several Lantian women) exhibited characteristics slightly more 'primitive' than the famous Peking man (or person), such as a thicker skull and smaller cranial capacity, and is thought to lie developmentally somewhere between Pithecanthropus robustus and Pithecanthropus erectus (Peking man is assigned to the latter group). The jawbone of Lantian woman lacked the third molar and this is supposed to be the first known example of agenosis in fossil man though apparently it is not uncommon amongst present-day Asian peoples. Lantian woman appears to have lived about 800,000 BC during a warm interval for the bones were associated with South Chinese Pleistocene faunal species and broadleaf trees. Some stone implements have been found near Lantian but so far there is no definite connection between the human fossil remains and stone implements.

A recent find is that of a considerably later human fossil skull in Dali county, near the Shaanxi-Shanxi border. Dali man is thought to belong to an early subspecies of Homo sapiens of about 300,000 to 200,000 BC.

One of the major sites in the vicinity of Xi'an is the neolithic village of Banpo, discovered in 1953 during excavation for the foundations of a factory. It is known that the fertile valleys of the Wei and Middle Yellow River were the sites of some of the earliest agricultural settlements of the neolithic; Banpo is generally dated to an early stage of the Yangshao (or painted pottery culture) and is thought to have been occupied from c 5000–4000 BC. The village remains are remarkably complete and about 4000 square metres have been roofed over as a site museum.

The Zhou people, who overthrew the Bronze Age Shang dynasty c 1027 BC, had their origins in Western Shaanxi. Two sites near Xi'an have been tentatively identified as capitals—Fengjing (on the W bank of the Feng River) and Haojing on the opposite side. Haojing is supposed to have been the Western Zhou capital from its conquest of the Shang until 771 BC when nomadic tribes forced a move of the capital eastwards to Luoyang. This move from the Xi'an area E to Luoyang was to be repeated in the Han and Tang (when Luoyang was the 'eastern' and secondary capital to Xi'an's 'western' capital). Artefacts unearthed during excavations of the two sites can now be seen in the Xianyang and Shaanxi Provincial Museums.

Similarly, the First Emperor of the Qin, Qin Shi huangdi (Qin was the name of the state in which he rose to power and was used for the dynasty he established after conquering all the other states in 221 BC; huangdi means emperor), established his imperial capital at Xianyang, some 15km NW of Xi'an. As is well known, he was buried in a tumulus in Lintong county, 18km NE of Xi'an, near the many subsidiary pits of his grave which contained, amongst other treasures, the 'Buried Army'.

Remains of the Han dynasty capital of Chang'an (including parts of the city wall) are plentiful and the most spectacular are some of the Han tombs in the surrounding countryside, Mao ling, the tomb of the Wudi (Martial Emperor) of the Han and the tomb of a famous general Huo Qubing. None of the nine Han imperial tombs has yet been excavated.

The Tang capital of Chang'an was, in its time, probably the site of the most advanced culture of the contemporary world, full of traders from all over Central Asia and craftsmen producing wondrous silver and gold vessels for the imperial court, some of whose treasures (gold, silver, jade, silken textiles and ceramics) have been found in hoards buried at the An Lushan rebellion in the mid 8C or in nearby temples that were granted imperial patronage. The Tang tombs of members of the imperial family and their courtiers surround the city with their sculpted 'spirit ways'.

The surviving city walls, bell and drum towers, all date from the Ming when Xi'an was a far smaller centre than it had been in its imperial heyday. Though the first Ming emperor appointed his second son to rule Xi'an, the palace that was built for him no longer survives and there was considerable destruction of the Manchu quarter of the city (a walled section of the NE part of the town) in 1911 when the Qing dynasty was overthrown. In the subsequent Republican era Xi'an was a key communications centre, particularly for those wishing to reach the Communist headquarters at Yan'an.

Xi'an today sprawls out beyond the Ming city walls with cotton mills, electrical-equipment factories, fertiliser factories and many others surrounding the old walled city. It has seen the relocation of various industries from the overcrowded eastern seaboard, with whole factories including workers moved in to promote the development of the relatively backward north-east.

In the early days of visiting the Buried Army (late 1970s), before hotels and restaurants were built in the area to supply the needs of tourists, visitors were often given lunch in a neighbouring sewing-machine factory whose canteen ran a profitable sideline in tourist lunches. The visit was rather uncanny since the factory and its workers had all come from Shanghai (where there were two sewing-machine factories) to Xi'an (where there were none) and in the middle of rough rural Shaanxi, all you could hear was the rather feminine Shanghai dialect. In the last couple of decades, particularly since the discovery of the Buried Army, Xi'an's major industry is that of tourism with ever-expanding numbers of Chinese and foreign visitors being rushed through the major sites.

For most tourists travelling in groups, Xi'an is a 'two-day' stop. One day is spent visiting the Buried Army and Huaqing Hot Springs, usually with a brief stop at the neolithic village of Banpo en route. On the second day, the city walls, the Shaanxi Provincial Museum in the old Confucian temple, the famous mosque and nearby Bell Tower and some rather unlikely 'handicraft factories' are visited. As hotel facilities expand, visitors may be able to stay longer and this is to be recommended for the Han and Tang tombs, in particular, are enormously interesting.

A. The Buried Army, Huaqing Hot Springs, Lintong County Museum, Banpo

With the exception of the Lintong County Museum, this is a standard itinerary of one day, with lunch usually provided, either at the Hot Springs or a nearby hotel or restaurant. Individual travellers can sign up for such a day excursion through CITS.

The **Buried Army** is just under 30km E of Xi'an and forms just a part of the huge grave of the first Qin emperor (reigned 221–209 BC).

Though only 13 when he ascended the throne of the state of Qin in 246, the First Emperor managed to achieve the subjugation of all the other six states in 221 BC, 'as a silkworm devours leaves' as Sima Qian put it, unifying China into one empire for the first time. Naturally a leader capable of such a feat is not generally characterised by historians as a gentle and humane character and Qin Shi huangdi is one of the tyrants of Chinese history, vilified in particular by Confucians throughout the ages for his support of Legalism (a philosophy which assumed that human nature was basically anarchic and evil and required firm government by rule of law rather than the moral precepts and examples of Confucianism).

The First Emperor is most famous for his 'burning of the books' in 213 BC, an event which also included burning (burying alive to be precise) quite a few of their authors. This was an attempt to wipe out all subversive writing and all works inimical to the ruling Legalist philosophy, including poetry and philosophy, historical chronicles and practically everything except manuals on farming and the law. Few works survived.

The Qin empire barely survived the death of its initiator for his equally ruthless advisors eliminated his heir in favour of a more pliable second son but they were finally overthrown in a series of revolts against their tyranny and the Han dynasty replaced the Qin in 206 BC. As part of their attempts to retain power, the First Emperor's ministers are said to have tried to conceal the death of their patron as long as possible, driving his corpse around in an imperial carriage followed by a cart full of rotting fish (to conceal the odour of the decaying corpse). The First Emperor was, however, finally laid to rest in the tumulus he had constructed for himself, beginning in the first year of his reign.

The Buried Army is part of a massive complex of burial pits which surround the **Tumulus** in which the emperor is buried. The tumulus, a grassy mound of considerable size some 1.5km W of the Buried Army, can be climbed by visitors. It has a stepped path constructed to the top, running through stalls where peasants sell anything from appallingly fragile miniature clay warriors to apples and 'ancient coins'. It has not yet been scientifically excavated.

The contents of the mound, or its supposed contents, are well known from the account left by Sima Qian, the Grand Historian, in his 'Shi ji' (Historical Records, 1C BC). He described how 700,000 workmen laboured on the site where a representation of the rivers of China in mercury was made to flow by machinery; the heavens were depicted and the whole was protected by automatic crossbows and arrows designed to fire if the tomb was entered. It is assumed that fantastic gravegoods were also included although it is almost certain that, like almost all others, the tomb was robbed soon after it was closed so precious metals and jewels were probably removed. The description of the contents of the tomb is so extraordinary that some said that Chinese archaeologists were afraid to open it up in case the marvels crumbled before their eyes on exposure to the air. However, a month-long excavation in 1986 revealed extensive damage, probably by Tang and Song robbers, and archaeologists are now concentrating on subsidiary sites in the area.

The **Buried Army**, just further on, is in fact only one of three similar pits, each containing a buried army, and the scale of these subsidiary pits has only served to enhance expectations of the contents of the tomb itself. A huge vault has been built over *Pit No. 1* so that the pit is viewed as it was when finished, with many of the terracotta figures restored and replaced in their original battle formation and the rear section of the pit left as it was when first discovered, with heads of warriors and horses emerging from the yellow earth. Side buildings contain displays of the contents of the three pits and there is an illuminated map of the entire grave area showing the numerous smaller burial pits that have been located. It is known that the First Emperor's paranoia extended beyond the grave. He is said to have ordered that all those who knew of the location and contents of his grave were to follow him into it and a number of pits containing human remains have been uncovered and are presumed to be the tombs of the unfortunate grave-diggers.

Pit No. 1 was discovered in 1974 when local peasants decided to build a well during a drought. They found a vast vault of some 12,000 square metres, about 5m underground, constructed with 11 parallel pits running E to W containing an estimated 8000 terracotta figures. These were drawn up in battle formation with three rows, each of 70 archers as the vanguard, a single column of spearmen facing outwards and a central group of 38 columns of infantry and chariots. The wooden chariots have all but disappeared, except for the terracotta horses which drew them and their metal fittings. The soldiers were provided with real bronze arms: swords, daggers, spears, halberds, axes, crossbows (of wood and of which only the bronze fittings have survived) and arrowheads. Some of the alloys used were quite complex with over ten elements included and the weapons were sharp and untarnished on discovery.

The figures were about 1.8m tall on average and must have been considerably larger than life-size when they were made. The upper part of the body is solid clay, the lower part and legs hollow and, while there is a degree of mass-production about the bodies, the faces in particular were individually modelled, exhibiting a considerable range of facial expressions, hairstyles and head-dresses. It is almost certain that the figures were made in parts—the bodies as one, the legs, hands and head separately—and the different parts were luted together afterwards, enabling variety in the positioning of the hands (which held reins, swords, spears or other weapons in different grasps) and the great variety of facial modelling. All the figures have long hair, dressed in a variety of cloth-wrapped buns on top of the head (the form of masculine hairstyle in China from the Qin until the imposition of the queue by the Manchus in AD 1644). Those on the outside of the formation wear armour, possibly of lacquered leather in small squares whilst those on the inside appear to be unprotected. The figures were all originally painted but few traces of the colours now remain.

The vaults within the pit appear to have been covered with timbers in some form of roof which was burnt in 206 BC when General Xiang Yu (one of the warriors who struggled unsuccessfully for power at the end of the Qin) opened the vault after, it is said, plundering the main mausoleum. The wooden timbers fell in on the contents, preserving them underground for 2000 years.

Pit No. 2, discovered NE of the first pit in 1976, was an L-shaped vault with some 1000 terracotta figures including four chariots, cavalrymen leading horses, foot soldiers and crossbow men. One taller figure (1.95m) is assumed to be a general. *Pit No. 3* lay beside it and contained one chariot with some 70 soldiers.

Some of the figures were removed from the smaller pits for use in the associated museum displays. Though the pits were re-filled, it is now planned to open them to the public in 1989–90, in order to reduce the incredible pressure of visitors to Pit No. 1 where it is true that in high season you have to queue up to see anything at all.

Aside from the major displays relating to the contents of the Buried Army pits (which allow a closer and usually less-crowded view of the figures), there is a small hall to the right of Pit No. 1 where two marvellous *bronze chariots* are displayed. (This hall is likely to be demolished as the other two pits are opened and the chariots displayed elsewhere on the site.)

These two, about half to a quarter life-size, were found near the tumulus, one in remarkably good condition. They have been restored (with colour photographs of the restoration work displayed on the walls of the hall) and are quite extraordinary with all the parts made to move—lattice windows, horse fittings. The four horses that draw each chariot were painted white and have accurately-depicted harness inlaid with gold and silver and decorated with plumes. In one chariot a single figure sits at the front, holding the reins, and behind him is a covered vehicle with a sort of parasol-like roof or awning, little open-work windows that can be opened or closed and a body decorated with swirling cloud-patterns (characteristic of Han lacquer or bronze decoration). The other chariot attendant stands some 91cm high. Both are dressed as 9th grade officials.

An exact replica of one of the chariots was presented to Queen Elizabeth when she visited Xi'an in autumn 1987.

In 1988 the ticketing system at the Buried Army Museum was complex, with separate tickets required for the main hall, museums and chariot hall. For group tourists, this usually means they should try and stick together (which is almost impossible in the overcrowded halls); individuals have to keep buying more tickets.

Outside the enclosure is a vast open market for the peasants of the area have realised the economic potential of tourism. They offer brilliant red embroidered clothes based on traditional children's garments.

The tiger shoes and hats they sell were worn by children as protection against evil spirits; I am not quite so sure about the function of the charming little black pig slippers (perhaps evil spirits were meant to think that the child was a pig and not bother to steal it away). The little parti-coloured padded waistcoats were often decorated (and still are) with the 'five poisonous creatures' (centipede, lizard, scorpion, toad and snake) in the hope that this will prevent them harming the child. Children's pillows of red cotton with two protective tiger-heads at either end were traditionally given when a new baby achieved its first 'hundred days' and stuffed cotton toys were often made in the shape of tigers.

Fengxiang, a town not far from Xi'an, is famous for its painted clay toys, made of soft terracotta with a white slip covered in bright pink and green floral designs. These are often lion-dogs or tigers and usually have a little clay pellet inside to rattle. These traditional toys and garments (the latter all too often now made in giant adult sizes rather than for small children) are characteristic of the area and appropriate purchases but you will have to bargain with the peasant sellers.

The **Huaqing Hot Springs** are c 30km from Xi'an, on the road to the Buried Army. The springs are set beneath the *Li Mountain*, on which there are still Buddhist and Taoist temples of no great significance. Only individual travellers will have time to climb up to them, though the Taoist temples of Laomu (the mother goddess) and Li Er are charming little buildings with the sharply angled roofs characteristic of the area.

The natural springs have attracted Chinese rulers since the Western Zhou when the first palace or villa was built. The First Emperor had a residence here and so did the Wudi emperor of the Han but the major associations of the Huaqing Hot Springs are with the Tang Xuanzong emperor and (rather an incongruous juxtaposition) Chiang Kai-shek.

The first Tang emperor, Taizong (his posthumous name, Taizong, means supreme ancestor), had his palace architect Yan Lide build a palace at the hot springs in 644 and the palace was greatly enlarged by the Xuanzong (Profound Ancestor) emperor (reigned 713–756). He spent the winters here with his fat concubine Yang Guifei whose affections were divided between the emperor and her adopted son, a non-Chinese general called An Lushan who led a nearly disastrous rebellion against the emperor in 755. The adopted son (who was killed by his own son) caused the death of Yang Guifei: popularly held responsible for the uprising, as she and the emperor fled W to Sichuan, the imperial guard insisted that she be killed. This and the emperor's subsequent decline and death form one of the great subjects of Chinese romantic poetry and painting.

The Tang baths at Huaqing are being excavated (and reconstructed) in the 'Tang style' by a team from Nanjing Architectural College (1991).

As you enter the *Huaqing Hot Springs Garden*, straight through the main gates is the major public bath area (to which we will return). To the right is a large hall, one of several rebuilt in 1956 with the original names used in the Tang, the *Hall of 'Flying Clouds'* (Feixia ge). On the far side of the hall is a large pool with a marble boat to the right. Given the opprobrium expressed over the Dowager Empress Cixi's construction of a (rather more vulgar) marble boat at the Summer Palace in Peking, squandering money meant for the Navy in 1888, it is interesting to note that this marble boat was built in 1956. On the far side of the pool is the *Longyin xie* (Pavilion of the Dragon's Song) and behind that, reached by a road that rises slightly up the mountainside, is the *Huaqing Guesthouse*, the most luxurious of the bathing places available.

There are some other sites to see before bathing. Crossing from the Pavilion of the Dragon's Song, along the top of the pool, you reach the major spring area which is now being excavated and 'reconstructed'.

Above the springs is a small, five-bay building, containing the bedroom where Chiang Kai-shek stayed in 1936. Just in front of this, in another building, is a small, elegantly shaped marble bath (in the form of an elongated plum blossom), which, before excavations began, was always said to have been the bath used by the fat concubine Yang Guifei; it must now be described as just another bath. Crossing the *Flying Rainbow Bridge*, you can follow the path up the mountainside to the kiosk marking the spot where Chiang Kai-shek was captured in 1936, according to the popular version, without his false teeth and wearing only a short nightshirt.

One guidebook states that the kiosk was originally erected by the Nationalists to commemorate Chiang's escape and named The Pavilion of National Regeneration; I cannot confirm this though the classical stone pavilion looks more like a pre- than a post-Liberation construction in style.

Chiang had gone to Xi'an to direct an offensive against the Communist forces, despite the threat of a full-scale Japanese invasion which had already led some of his allies to call for negotiations with the Communists to form an anti-Japanese united front. Chiang was chased up the mountain from his bedroom and seized by troops of Zhang Xueliang (the 'Young Marshall'), a warlord allied with the KMT. Zhou Enlai came to Xi'an to mediate, extracting from Chiang the (empty) promise of national unity against Japan. The Young Marshall was in turn taken prisoner by Chiang and held for decades.

The natural springs at Huaqing contain minerals said to be beneficial. The water bubbles up at a comfortable temperature of 43° Celsius. There are various grades of bath: communal and cheap, individual (just below the Tang bath site) and luxurious (with a bedroom and bathroom en suite) in the Huaqing Guesthouse—charges vary accordingly. Towels are provided for the top two grades and the large baths, more like small swimming pools, square and lined with tiles, are very pleasant.

On the mountain behind the springs, the Xixiu Peak, to the W is a restored *beacon tower* said to date from the Western Zhou. It is a tapering square brick tower with a wooden pavilion on top, fired, apparently with wolf dung and the site of a legend similar to the Western one of the 'boy who cried wolf'. The Western Zhou king had a favourite concubine, Bao Si, who never smiled until a court officer suggested the king take her to the beacon tower and summon all his dukes by lighting the fire. They all rushed up when the flames were kindled and Bao Si smiled. However, one year later a real invasion occurred and the beacon fire was kindled but none of the dukes turned up, thinking the king was only trying to amuse Bao Si.

This tower, and the Laomu and Li Er Temples, can be reached by climbing the mountain path that leads W round and behind the springs.

Just up the road (turn right out of the Huaqing Garden) is the **Lintong County Museum**, a small but quite interesting museum. On the way, you pass a small fairground (on your right) and beside it is (1987) a good example of local domestic architecture: a courtyard house with two side wings with single-pitched roofs angled sharply down into the courtyard. The local yellow bricks, black-painted woodwork with a thin red line outlining doors and windows and, above all, the sharp angle of the single-pitched roofs are characteristic of the Xi'an area, a variation on the ubiquitous courtyard house.

The major display in the museum is of the Buddhist relics unearthed in

THE VICINITY OF XI'AN

Buried Army
Lintong
Huaqing Hot Springs
Banpo Museum
Xi'an
Xingjiao temple
Huayan temple
Xiangji temple
Weihe River
Xianyang
Tomb of Huo Qubing
Maoling tomb
Tomb of Yang Guifei
Zhaoling tomb
Tomb of Princess Yongtai
Qinling tomb

the vicinity of the Qinshan Temple on the NE of Li Mountain. In 1985 a group of Buddhist coffins and a reliquary of 741 were found there and are now displayed in the museum. The reliquary is of stone, just over a metre high, in the form of a stupa pagoda, decorated with scenes of Buddhist deities, lotus panels and apsaras with flowing garments in low relief. The reliquary contained two miniature coffins, a silver outer coffin and a gold inner coffin, decorated with gold figures of monks and ropes of baroque pearls and turquoises. The two tiny coffins with their high, boat-like prows are made in the form of the standard wooden coffin still in use.

Other items in the museum include stone pillar bases and carvings from nearby temples and tombs (there is a nice sheep in the courtyard), Tang ceramics and a strange copper ewer decorated with human heads; all locally excavated.

The neolithic village of **Banpo** is on the eastern outskirts of Xi'an. The site was discovered in 1953. Covering some 50,000 square metres, the village site included a dwelling area delineated by a surrounding trench, a ceramic centre and a graveyard (the latter both situated beyond the trench). Forty-five dwellings, six pottery kilns, and 250 graves including 73 ceramic urns containing the remains of small children have been found, together with ceramics, tools, animal bones and the remains of fruit stones, millet and other edibles. Scattered throughout the dwelling area were pocket-shaped pits 1–2m deep, generally called storage pits.

The dwellings of the Banpo people were discovered in more than one stratified layer (it appears from pollen samples that show wild species reappearing after periods of domesticated crop pollens that the settlement was used for several occupations, not occupied continuously) and demonstrate an apparent progression from circular, semi-subterranean to rectangular, ground-level dwellings with a carefully prepared floor surface. Structurally, the houses were similar, with timber columns of varying heights supporting the roof which seems to have been thatched. The small post-holes of short, closely-placed roof supports mark the outer edge of the roof and some of the better-made houses also have larger, central post-holes. The openings to the houses were almost invariably oriented towards the S and inside the entry was a slightly sunken hearth. One much larger floor has been found, in a relatively central position (from a late stage of occupation) and this is usually interpreted as some kind of communal building or meeting place. It appears to have been sacred in some way for the remains of a dog and some ceramics were found beneath the floor.

Fox-tail millet (Setaria indica), cabbage, mustard and hemp (for clothing) were cultivated, pigs and dogs were domesticated and, since the settlement was situated near a river, fish, caught with fine bone hooks, formed part of the diet.

The dead were buried with ceramic bowls and sometimes a few items of adornment, stretched out on their backs and, like their houses, oriented towards the S. Small children, buried in lidded ceramic jars, were interred within the settlement area, otherwise, the cemetery was beyond the ditch, as was the pottery-making area.

The ceramics of Banpo are very fine examples of the Yangshao or 'painted pottery' type. Made by hand from fine red clay, the rims perhaps finished on a turntable of some sort, those that were used in burial were often decorated with black, white and red designs. Ceramics for everyday use—bowls, dishes and fine amphorae with two lug handles—were usually of plain red clay, sometimes decorated with cord, mat or basketwork patterns. The painted pottery shows a clear progression of design from representations of (mainly) fish, human faces and small deer, to an elegant geometric patterning derived from the fish forms.

Chinese archaeologists have argued that Banpo represents a communal society of a primitive sort and ascribe it to a matriarchal state of development. There does not seem to be any material evidence for either communality or matriarchy: the latter theory is derived from Engels' writings on the development of society (and Engels himself was deriving theories from a 19C American anthropologist who drew upon American Indian legends of a matriarchal golden age). The existence of an apparent central building, with its foundation sacrifices, does not necessarily imply communality in terms of shared storage pits though it points to a central belief celebrated communally or a seat of government.

In the two *museum wings* at the front of the Banpo enclosure the daily life of the matriarchy is illustrated in oil paintings, together with illustrations of the development of ceramic designs and the use of fish-hooks, net-weights and spindles.

Of the 50,000 square metres of settlement, some 4000 square metres is now covered over and the outlines of houses, storage pits, part of the surrounding ditch and the occasional ceramic jar burial of a child near a house can all be seen, with diagrams and reconstructions to make the material evidence more comprehensible.

B.   The City of Xi'an

A normal tourist itinerary for a second day in Xi'an takes in the walls, Provincial Museum, mosque and the Bell and Drum Towers, and usually includes some handicraft establishments where items are finished or half-prepared (there seemed to be nowhere to fire the cloisonné, for example) for the benefit of tourists. Depending on where you are staying, the same

Buried Army
Huaqing Hot Springs Golden Flower Hotel

Banpo Museum

East Gate

XI'AN

Big Goose Pagoda

Jiefang lu

Heping lu

Railway station

People's Hotel

Dong dajie

Xixin jie

Provincial Museum
and Forest of Stelae

Small Goose Pagoda

Bell Tower

North Gate

Bei dajie

Nan dajie South Gate

Drum Tower

Mosque

Lianhu lu

Xi dajie

N

West Gate

Tang tombs

sort of itinerary can be organised, to be followed mostly on foot, by individual tourists.

The Shaanxi Provincial Museum is in the S of the city, near the **City Wall** and so provides a suitable opportunity for climbing up onto the wall as well (although the major barbican gates south, east and west are more impressive). The wall dates from the early years of the Ming when the second son of the emperor was appointed to rule the area from his palace in Xi'an. The mass of the the wall consists of rammed yellow earth (loess) on a base of rammed earth, lime and glutinous rice, now mostly faced with grey brick. The east wall is 2590m; the west wall 2631m; the north wall 3244m, and the south wall 3441.6m. It is 12m high and 12–14m wide at the top, 15–18m broad at the base, unadorned on the inside but battlemented on the moat side. There are four corner towers and a tree-lined moat surrounding the whole. There are four major barbicans or double gates in the centre of each side: the eastern *Gate of Extended Joy*, the western *Gate of Settled Peace* (where there is a museum of the city's history, closed late 1988), the southern *Gate of Eternal Tranquillity* and the northern *Gate of Distant Peace*. These are huge barbicans with inner and outer walls and a considerable area within.

Though the wall now looks fine as it and the moat have been cleaned and tidied up and made into a park-like area, only two years ago there was an story in the Chinese press about someone demolishing a part of the wall that irritated him; conservation is not uppermost in the local consciousness.

The **Provincial Museum** consists of two parts. The *Bei lin* or Forest of Stelae, one of the oldest 'museums' in China, is situated in the old Confucian temple, just inside the gate immediately e of the S gate.

Founded in 1090 to protect the Stelae of the 13 Classics which had been carved in stone in 837 during the Tang dynasty, the Forest of Stelae now has six halls in which over 1000 stelae and tomb inscriptions are displayed, covering the period from the Han to the Qing. Some of the stelae, including those of the 13 (Confucian) Classics, are set in the walls of the halls, others (similar to those found in temples, usually standing on the backs of stone tortoises and topped with interknitted dragons) are free-standing, in rows. All have blackened, shiny surfaces where their inscriptions have been rubbed and, if you are lucky, you may see someone taking a rubbing. The stone surface is gently inked with a soft, ink-laden pad, then the fine paper is pasted over the inked stelae and buffed with a pad or a soft brush.

Though the original intention in establishing the museum was to preserve ancient texts (for a text carved in stone is eternal and free from copyists' errors), the Forest of Stelae is today considered as the major museum of Chinese calligraphy for the writing of ancient calligraphers survives only in stone-cut versions. A few of the (mostly later) stelae have line-cut drawings of mountain scenery or the famous monkey figure made out of characters.

One of the stelae of most interest to Westerners (in the past at least) is the 'Nestorian Stele' (Da qin jing jiao liu xing zhong guo bei, or the Jingjiao bei). This is to be found immediately on the left of the entrance in Room 2. It records the arrival of a Nestorian priest in Chang'an and the 781 foundation of a Nestorian chapel. There is a long text on the front of the stele describing the creation and giving an outline of Christian doctrine followed by a shorter inscription in Syriac (estrangelo characters written vertically). The edges of the stone are covered with Syriac names with Chinese equivalents. Though it is now well-known that Nestorianism was known in Chang'an during the Tang, the stelae which was unearthed in 1625, apparently near Zhouzhi outside the western gate of Xi'an, provoked great excitement amongst 17C Jesuit missionaries in China and they used its discovery to prove the early 'conversion to Christianity' of the Chinese during the Rites Controversy.

For Nestorianism see Quanzhou. The church was based on the rather modern-sounding heresy of Nestorius who postulated a dual nature of Christ (human and divine) and refused the title of Holy Mother to the Virgin. Nestorius was condemned at the Council of Ephesus in 431 but his followers survived, especially in eastern Turkey and futher east, converting Khubilai Khan's mother amongst others. I note that the French 'Guide Bleu' states that Nestorianism is today almost 'almost extinct'. As Christian missionaries were all terribly interested in the antiquity of their profession in China (and prepared to overlook the Council of Ephesus' ruling) there are many copies of the Nestorian stele in Europe, brought back by missionaries.

The rest of the museum (a treasury and a chronological arrangement of excavated artefacts) has now been moved to a grand new site (Xiaozhai dong lu, Cuihua lu) considerably S of the city wall, between the two 'Goose' pagodas. The following description of the major contents still stands but their disposition has changed.

The treasury contains the most extraordinary display of bronzes of any Chinese museum. All locally unearthed, it was not simply the quality of the Western Zhou bronzes but the quantity and the way they were arranged. Set out in tiers, matching sets of different implements united by surface decoration, they give a far better idea of the real contents of tombs than the isolated examples seen in other museums. Most bronzes were cast as 'altar sets', groups of utensils for the warming and serving of food to the gods, and this can best be seen in the treasury (unless the arrangement is dramatically altered). Other spectacular pieces in the treasury include silver and gold vessels from Tang hoards buried at the An Lushan uprising, a wonderful little incense-burner with gimbals (to keep the incense upright) in a silver filigree ball, and the agate rhyton with a gold nose, excavated during the Cultural Revolution, that was probably imported from Persia.

The rest of the museum is divided as follows: on the left-hand side of the courtyard the display covers locally excavated items from the Stone Age to the Han, with a vast sculpture gallery at the far end; on the far side of the courtyard the display covers the Tang to the Qing.

In the small drum pavilion before the left-hand gallery is a wonderful, worn horse from northern Shaanxi, AD 424. Inside, the gallery contains the famous bronze ding (tripod) weighing 87.5kg and with two inscriptions, one Shang and one Zhou; the buffalo-shaped zun (wine vessel) from the 9C BC, and the rhinoceros zun (Warring States) which is associated with a number of bronze fittings apparently used architecturally in palaces, perhaps in the legendary Afang Palace built by the First Emperor of the Qin. There is a wonderful bronze horse found near Mao ling (tomb of the Wudi emperor of the Han, 140–81 BC), extraordinary Han lamps, and a representative selection of Han ceramic burial goods with representations of farmyards, pigpens, houses, stoves and other everyday paraphernalia.

To maintain the chronological sequence and retain the striking difference between the ceramic burial goods of the Han, Sui and Tang, cross the courtyard to the N entrance of the opposite gallery. Sui and Tang ceramic tomb models, painted, unpainted, glazed and unglazed (in a far greater variety of treatments than seen in the exhibits in Western museums) are, in subject matter, a long way from their Han predecessors. They depict warriors, guardians, horses and camels laden with goods from the West and, above, all, courtly life—beautiful women, orchestras and dancers. There are copies of some of the murals from the Tang tombs that surround Xi'an—beautiful women in gardens or gentlemen playing polo.

The sculpture gallery is filled with some huge and wonderful pieces, mainly from tombs of the Han–Tang dynasties. There are sinuous, leopard-like bixie from a Western Han tomb; a copy of a horse from the Huo Qubing (Han) tomb, which has some of the most powerful animal statuary anywhere; rhinoceroses and ostriches from Tang tombs (known as exotic gifts from foreign ambassadors to Tang emperors), and four of the six famous high-relief carvings of horses from Zhao ling, the tomb of Li Shimin.

Founder of the Tang dynasty, he loved horses, especially his favourite charger Quanmo, who was one of the six horses portrayed in the stone panels. Unfortunately, two of the panels (including Quanmo) were taken to the University of Philadelphia Museum in 1914 and some of the other panels were broken into four pieces, presumably to facilitate their removal. This (and casts of the two missing panels) can be seen in the museum.

At the angle of the hall (just beside the huge rough rhino) is a charming little stone building, complete in every detail. It is a Sui coffin, made for a small girl, the only daughter of a descendant of the Zhou imperial family who had thrown in his lot with the Sui emperor (unwisely, it turned out, for he was condemned to death by his new master as a result of court intrigue and his wife was poisoned soon after). The child died, just before her parents, in 608, at the age of eight and her coffin, with a rich collection of funerary objects inside (now in Peking), was unearthed in 1957.

The stone coffin is a lovely architectural piece with its curled ridge and details of tiles. There are also a large number of Buddhist stelae, carved with many scenes of deities or events in the life of the Buddha under the elegant, leaf-shaped top.

Just E of the museum, visible from the city wall and standing just S of Shuyuanmen da jie, is a small pagoda, known locally as the *Huata si* (Coloured Pagoda Temple) though its full name was the Baoqing si an d it is said to have been founded in 705. Nothing now remains of the temple except the little pagoda.

The **Bell Tower** in the centre of Xi'an is not far N of the Confucian temple. Either make your way W through the narrow streets to Nan da jie and then turn right (N) until you reach the Bell Tower in the centre of the street, or turn left into Duanlumen jie which runs N–S just outside the Confucian temple, and continue N until you reach Dong dajie where you will see the Bell Tower over to the west.

The Bell Tower originally stood (1384) some two blocks W of its present site. There it was at the centre of the old Tang city but it was moved to its present site in 1582 and restored in 1739. Its bell no longer exists (it used to be rung at dawn). The triple-eaved, two-storey wooden structure (over 27m high) stands on a square brick platform which is 8.5m high.

The *Drum Tower*, pair to the Bell Tower, is just NW of the latter, straddling the second turning on the right (N) along Xi da jie. It stands overlooking the old Moslem quarter of Xi'an with the **Great Mosque** (Qingzhen si) at its centre on Huajue xiang. To reach the mosque follow the paved street, lined with souvenir shops, leading left just beyond the Drum Tower.

The mosque (popularly known as the *Dong da si* or Great Eastern Temple) is one of the most active in metropolitan China for there are said to be some 30,000 practising Moslems in Xi'an. According to a stele, the mosque was founded in 742, during the Tang when Xi'an was full of foreign Moslems. Though most guidebooks now note that the architectural style and present layout is Ming, with restoration work in 1527, 1606 and 1768, the building presents a problem as it has been gradually restored from pillar-bases upwards over the last decade. This restoration was thorough in the extreme, although the new materials were being carved to the earlier forms. Thus the mosque can be said to be Ming in layout and inspiration but every bit of timber is of the late 20C.

The layout is interesting for it is built on an E–W axis, fitting to a mosque, with the great *prayer hall* at the western extremity; it had some particularly fine woodcarving in the coffered ceiling and the front panels of the hall. Walking back from the prayer hall, you will see two stone fountains in the courtyard beneath the terrace on which the prayer hall stands. The courtyard terminates in the *Phoenix Pavilion*. The next courtyard contains the minaret, an octagonal pagoda with a turquoise tiled roof and rooms surrounding the courtyard. These include the imam's living quarters and some exhibits including a Qing illuminated Qu'ran and a Qing Chinese moslem map of the world with the black square of the Kaaba in Mecca at the centre. The entrance to this courtyard is a stelae hall with Ming and Qing stelae in Chinese, Arabic and Persian.

The second courtyard (where visitors enter) contains two free-standing stelae and a stone arch. The stelae are inscribed by two of the most famous calligraphers of China—Mi Fei (or Fu) of the Song, one of the great painting innovators and Dong Qichang of the Ming. The first courtyard contains an elaborate wooden pailou, completely restored during the last decade.

The street that runs under the Drum Tower has some interesting wooden shopfronts with carved fascia (walk N beyond the tower to see these).

A number of temples in the city of Xi'an can be reached on foot, although most are now converted to other uses and may be difficult of access.

The *Chenghuang miao* (Temple of the City God) is just N of Xi da jie (which runs W from the Bell Tower). It is reached by turning N by No. 257 Xi da jie and following the little lane through the Moslem quarter, past a mosque (left). Turn right at the T-junction and right again and the temple gate should be visible on the cobbled lane. The temple was founded in 1433 (it now houses a school and stores) and few of its buildings survive except a main hall built in 1723 with fine bracketing, carved doors and a blue-tiled roof. The two Ming bronze lions (of the Jiaqing period, 1522–67) which used to stand in the temple are now placed outside the main gate of the Provincial Museum.

The *Dongyue miao* (Temple of the Eastern Peak) is just to the NW inside the Eastern Gate, in the grounds of a primary school. It was dedicated to the worship of Tai shan (in Shandong), a major cult in Chinese Taoism, represented by temples in many towns. This one was founded in 1116, restored in the Ming and in 1895. Frescoes still remain on the eastern and western walls of the main hall (an imposing building), depicting female spirits and pavilions in the Yuan and Ming style. There are also stelae recording the restoration of the temple in the Ming and Qing.

The *Guangren si* (Temple of Extensive Humanity), sometimes also called the Lama si or Lama Temple, is in the NW corner of the city wall. Founded in 1705, it is the only example of a Lamaist temple of the Yellow Hat faith in the Xi'an area. In front of the temple is a hexagonal stelae pavilion housing an imperial stele. Inside the temple there are three main halls—the great hall, the sutra hall and the hall where sutras are commented on—and side wings for the kitchen and other offices. The temple is particularly busy every year on the 14th and 15th of the 10th month of the lunar calendar when many Tibetan monks join the crowds that come to celebrate the enlightenment of Tsongkapa, founder of the Yellow Hat sect of Lamaist Buddhism.

Also near the Provincial Museum is the *Wolong si* (Temple of the Recumbent Dragon), reached along a lane between Nos 25 and 27 Baishulin jie. Once one of the richest and best-known temples in Xi'an, founded under the Sui, last restored in 1952, its library of sutras (including a Southern Song example) is now in the Provincial Library. Only part of one hall remains, though it used to contain a stone engraving of Guanyin by Wu Daozi.

The best-known temples in Xi'an are the Little Goose and Big Goose Pagodas and their associated temples. Once well-inside the Tang city walls, they now stand outside the Ming walls, to the S.

The **Big Goose Pagoda** (Dayan ta) and the **Dacien si** (Temple of Great Goodwill) are some 4km S of the city wall.

The pagoda was known as the Jing ta or Sutra Pagoda during the Tang and the source of its (and the Small Goose's) contemporary name is somewhat mysterious. Xuanzang's biography states that as a flock of wild geese flew over a monastery in an Indian kingdom, one bird fell dead to the ground; the monks decided that it was a saint and built a pagoda for its body. If that is the explanation of the name of the (earlier) Great Goose Pagoda, then the Small Goose Pagoda, which resembles it in form but was built later, presumably acquired its name through association.

The Temple of Great Goodwill was built in 647 by a Tang prince (later the Gaozong emperor, reigned 650–684) in honour of his mother. It was originally far bigger than it is now (with 13 courtyards and 300 monks). The temple was destroyed in 907 and the present buildings are Qing (or later; complete resoration from ground level upwards has taken place in recent years). The main hall has a fine series of Qing lohans around the outer walls (which looked rather more dignified in 1976 when their paint was pale and faded).

The pagoda was first built in 652 on the recommendation of Xuan zang, the most prominent monk and translator of the sutras. He had returned to Chang'an and his temple after more than 15 years travelling through the Gobi Desert (via Dunhuang, Gaochang and other ruined cities of the desert) to India and Pakistan where he collected Sanskrit sutras (all this despite an imperial prohibition on foreign travel). On his return he set up a great translation bureau in the temple and recommended the construction of a fireproof store for his precious sutras. A square, five-storey building of rammed earth was constructed but it collapsed and a seven-storey brick structure was built (701–704). A further three storeys were added in 766–779 but they were destroyed. The surviving pagoda was faced with brick in the Ming to strengthen it.

It is square in plan, tapering towards the top with brick eaves marking each storey of the simple but elegant tower. Arched windows in each floor provide a view over the steadily encroaching city (it was set amongst cabbage fields in 1976 when I first saw it). There are important examples of stone carving and calligraphy in the temple: Tang carvings of Buddhist scenes are barely visible on the lintels (that above the W door is clearest, showing the Buddha preaching in a fine open hall); two stone tablets set into the wall on each side of the S door were engraved by a Tang calligrapher, Chu Suiliang. They are of texts by two Tang emperors, Gaozong and Taizong, describing Xuan zang's epic journey to the West (fictionalised in 'Monkey') and his equally epic translation work.

Inside the pagoda is a small exhibition of photographs of Chinese pagodas of all sorts; below, outside and to the left, is a group of stupas housing the remains of the temple's monks (but not Xuan zang whose remains are in the Xingjiao si, outside Xi'an). These are the remains of Qing dynasty monks.

Slightly nearer town is the **Xiaoyan ta** (Small Goose Pagoda) in the **Jianfu si** (Commending Happiness Temple). Previously known as the Xianfu (Presenting Happiness) Temple, this was founded in 684, also by the Gaozong emperor of the Tang. The temple still contains (standing in a courtyard) a large bronze bell cast in 1192, a number of stelae and a small exhibition of Tang Buddhist artefacts, Song and Ming editions of the sutras and a history of the pagoda.

The Small Goose Pagoda was also constructed as a fireproof sutra store in 707. It was built to house the sutras brought back from India by the monk Yi jing who was the first Chinese monk to make the journey by sea, rather than overland across the Gobi (which was the commoner route). Yi jing left for India in 671 and later spent some time on Sumatra before returning in 695 with some 400 sutras. He lived and translated in various monasteries before settling in the Jianfu temple where he died in 713.

The pagoda is built of brick on a square plan and was originally 15 storeys high—earthquake damage has left only 13 storeys and a rather jagged top. It is 45m high, smaller than the nearly 60m of the Big Goose Pagoda and, though similar in plan and construction (with the same simple brick eaves marking the storeys), is more elegantly tapered, in a gentle curve, closer in style to the Tang pagodas in Dali and Kunming than the resolutely angular Big Goose. It has arched doorways on the N and S sides of each storey with fine intaglio carvings of celestials and floral designs over the doorways.

Just S of the Little Goose Pagoda, on Xingshan si jie, in the *Xinfeng Park*, is the *Daxingshan si* (Temple of Great and Flourishing Goodness), founded in the 4C.

During the Sui dynasty a large number of Indian monks came here to teach esotericism and between 716–720 yet more Indian monks came to translate esoteric texts, making the temple one of the three great translation centres of the time. Many Japanese monks also came to the temple to study. The temple was also famous for one monk, Yi xing who made it a centre for the study of astronomy and mathematics (and who calculated the length of the meridian). The temple was destroyed in the late Tang persecution of Buddhism, leaving only some Tang dynasty carved waterspouts and pillar bases; the buildings are all of Ming–Qing date.

Major temples in the vicinity of Xi'an include the Xingjiao si, Xiangji si, Caotang si and Huayan si. The Xingjiao si and Huayan si are both to the S of the city.

The **Xingjiao si** (Temple of Flourishing Teaching) is c 22km SE of Xi'an, beautifully situated on a hillside overlooking the Fan River valley. It was founded in 669 as one of the eight great temples of Fanchuan (the Fan River) in order to provide a home for the ashes of the great travelling and translating monk Xuan zang (602–664). His remains were originally buried at Bailuyuan (The Plain of the White Deer), c 10km SE of Xi'an, where the Ba ling, tomb of Han Wendi (Cultural) emperor and his wife, is also to be found. They were moved to the present site in 669 when the temple was built by the Gaozong emperor.

Three little square stupas contain the remains of Xuan zang (the tallest one) and two of his disciples. The name of the temple was taken from an inscription written on the stupa by the Suzong emperor of the Tang, the two characters for 'flourishing teaching'. *Xuan zang's Stupa* is square in plan and stepped, not unlike the Great Goose Pagoda but with brickwork closely imitating wooden construction. In its present form it is probably 9C. The two smaller three-storey pagodas contain the remains of *Kuiji* (632–82), a translation assistant of Xuan zang's of noble birth (his uncle was a famous general), and (E) the remains of a Korean follower of Xuan zang, *Yuance*. The latter stupa was built later, in 1115. Beside Xuan zang's stupa is a small pavilion with the famous stone carving of Xuan zang bringing back the sutras from India on a sort of backpack frame, carrying a flywhisk and other bits and pieces. The stone carving, which is a charming picture of a loaded traveller, is quite late, probably Qing, although it is remarkably similar to a Tang sketch found at Dunhuang (now in the British Museum).

The stupas were fortunate to survive the constant accidents that destroyed the temple many times over. Apparently first abandoned after the suppression of Buddhism in 839, it was reoccupied and redestroyed many times, and restored in 1922 and 1939. It is now a fairly busy temple with some 30 monks (and some quite interesting sutras in the library). Despite the newness of the buildings, the Great Hall contains a bronze Buddha of the Ming dynasty and, behind, in the Preaching Hall, there is a Ming bronze Amitabha and a Sakyamuni Buddha of 1922.

On the lower floor of the *library* building (the sutras are upstairs) is a fairly modern white jade Buddha, a present from Burma.

The **Huayan si**, another of the eight great temples of Fanchuan, is about 15km outside Xi'an, on the way to the Xingjiao si. It is also very beautifully situated although very little remains of the temple beyond two brick pagodas. It was, however, the birthplace of the popular Huayan sect of Buddhism.

Founded by the monk Du shun (557–640), Huayan followed the Tiantai sect's attempt to classify all the confusingly different sutras by ascribing different doctrines to different periods in the life of the Buddha. Huayan added the (then) new school of Chan (Zen) and also viewed the universe as ordered, the world of principle and phenomena being fused, with everything leading to the centre, the Buddha. The temple was destroyed by an earthquake in the 18C.

The two surviving pagodas include one (E) containing the remains of the Huayan founder. This is a square, seven-storey construction, 13m high, with the characters Yanzhu (Master of Yan) carved on a stone at the top and six characters reading 'the pure, clean and bright precious pagoda' on the third storey. The remains of the fourth patriarch of the Huayan sect are inside the other pagoda which is hexagonal, five-storeyed and 7m high with an inscription reading: 'the miraculous pagoda of the great master of the Tang'. There are brick niches in the lower parts of both pagodas with incised figures and records of late Qing reconstruction. A stele dated 852, recording the life of the first patriarch, has been moved to the Forest of Stelae in Xi'an.

The *Caotang si* (Straw-Hat Temple) is 55km SW of Xi'an, in Hu xian (and c 20km SE of the county town of Hu xian). It is very small and the buildings are comparatively recent, except for the stupa containing the remains of Kumarajiva (384–417).

He was a non-Chinese Buddhist (half-Kuchean, half-Brahmin) who set up a translation bureau of over 1000 monks. His translations are still used today though he himself said that reading a translation was like eating rice that someone else had already chewed. His stupa is small, 2.33m high, with 12 storeys on an octagonal plan and made from 'eight precious jade stones' of different colours, on a Sumeru base and carved with flowers and Buddhas. The stupa is judged to be Tang, on the basis of the figure style and lotus carvings.

In the county town of **Hu xian** an exhibition hall displays paintings by the peasant painters of Hu xian county.

These bright, naive paintings of agricultural scenes with flocks of chickens, rows of pig-stys and trees full of shiny red apples were immensely popular in China in the 1970s, and during the last years of the Cultural Revolution were quite often exhibited abroad. Their popularity at the time was due to the political innocence of the content—themes of bumper harvests and hard work—but the brilliant colours and naive pattern-like effect were also extremely attractive. The painters apparently began painting in 1958, to record the construction of a local reservoir, but their wide reknown came nearly 20 years later (and promoted a general trend towards peasant painting in the late 1970s and early 1980s). Some of the artists (like the apple-grower Wang Jinglong) are now very popular and their works are sold in places like the Alvin Gallery in Hong Kong so the prices are at international heights.

The *Xiangji si* (Temple of Amassed Perfume) is due S of Xi'an, 20km by road, in *Xiangji cun* (Village of Amassed Perfume) which lies near the meeting of two rivers. The temple was originally built by his followers to commemorate Shan dao, the second patriarch of the Pure Land sect, perhaps the most lastingly popular of all Buddhist sects in China. Pure Land preaches salvation through faith rather than esoteric meditation and offers a haven in the Pure Land of Amitabha Buddha for good practitioners. All that remains of the temple today is a Qing dynasty great hall and the 33m Tang brick stupa (imitating timber construction) which is in poor repair. To the E is a far smaller stupa; this is said to contain the remains of Shan dao.

The past glories of the temple were commemorated by the Tang poet Wang Wei who wrote 'Passing the Temple of Amassed Fragrance':

> Hard to find the Temple of Amassed Fragrance, many miles deep in clouds and peaks, ancient trees that no man has touched. Deep in the mountains, the sound of a bell.

Further away is the **Famen si** (Temple of the Gate of the Law) where in 1987 some extraordinary archaeological discoveries were made (which will eventually be exhibited to the public). Over 100km W of Xi'an, the temple itself is 10km N of the country town of *Fufeng xian*. The major feature of the temple is the pagoda which contains a holy relic, one of the fingers of the historic Buddha, placed there by the Huizong emperor of the Tang (reigned 806–21). The existing pagoda is a Ming construction of 1579, an imposing 45m in height, octagonal in plan, with 13 storeys. The pagoda tapers gradually towards the top and the brickwork imitates timber construction.

Recent excavations have revealed a wealth of treasures bestowed on the temple by the Tang imperial house which accorded it considerable patronage (partly because of the finger, it was the most famous temple of the later Tang). Silk garments of all sorts have been found, reliquaries of precious metals and also early tea-drinking implements (spoons, caddies) which are of particular interest because the beginnings of tea-drinking in China were previously only known through literary accounts.

Some of the most splendid sites around Xi'an are the **Imperial Tombs of the Han and Tang**. There was also a considerable chariot burial of the Western Zhou unearthed to the W of the city (complete with horses and full chariots), not far from the tomb of Yang Guifei at Mawei. With the exception of Yang Guifei's tomb, the Tang tombs are grouped c 80–100km NW of Xi'an, in the mountains surrounding the plain, whilst the Han tombs are nearly due W and only 30–40km away.

There are nine Han tombs in the vicinity of Xi'an but none of the imperial tombs has yet been excavated. Two are quite close together: *Mao ling*, the tomb of the Wudi (martial) emperor of the Han (157–87 BC) and the tomb of *Huo Qubing* (140–117 BC), one of Han Wudi's generals. The name of Han Wudi's tomb is composed of a placename, Mao, taken from Maoxiang—the name of the area in which it was situated—and ling, which means tomb. It is a trapezoid mound, 46.5m high, covering 54,054m. The surrounding wall has all but disappeared. The emperor ordered the construction of his tomb as early as the second year of his reign, as was the custom. Literary records describe the contents: the corpse was dressed in a jade suit made of small pieces joined by gold wire (examples of such suits have been excavated: one can be seen in the museum in Nanjing), with a jade cicada in the mouth. Jade boxes were buried with the emperor and many animals were sacrficed to provide food for his spirit. It is also said that his favourite books were buried with him (and many important texts have been uncovered from Han tombs such as that of Mawangdui near Changsha).

Nearby is *Huo Qubing's Tomb* which has a fine series of stone-carved animals that once stood lining the approach to the tomb (they are now under cover) and a museum displaying relics of the Han tombs that have been found in the vicinity. Huo Qubing died young (of disease) but he had already led troops against 'Hun slave-owner intruders' and the emperor ordered that his tomb be constructed 1km away from Mao ling, amidst many other satellite tombs. There is a small brick kiosk on the top of the burial mound but the most remarkable feature was the series of huge stone-carved animals that lay before it. Anticipating the later 'spirit roads' which reached their zenith in the approach to the Ming tombs outside Nanjing and Peking, Huo Qubing's sculptures are not completely in the round as later examples are: the huge horses, tigers, bears and elephants appear to be struggling out of the stone. They are immensely lively, in contrast with the static majesty of later funerary carving, and full of movement: galloping horses, horses trampling 'Huns' and men wrestling with bears. Other items on display include a series of decorated bricks that lined Han tombs, hollow bricks decorated with dragons and tigers, tortoises and snakes (the latter symbols of the North), elegant bronze vessels used for serving wine and food in offerings to the gods, and a range of the rather homely ceramic models found in Han tombs: ducks, sheep, farmyards and houses.

Beyond the Han tombs at *Mawei po* (Mawei Slope) is the tomb of the ill-fated fat concubine Yang Guifei, killed by members of the imperial guard as she and the emperor held the capital during the An Lushan rebellion.

As An Lushan was a general she had adopted and whose career she had fostered, it was ironic that his ambition should cause her death. In the following year the emperor ordered that she should be buried here, under a round mound covering 3000 square metres. The simple stone with the inscription 'Yang Guifei's tomb' has been joined by many others commemorating visits by historical personages, including the 19C opium commissioner Lin Zexu (see Fuzhou). The death of Yang Guifei at Mawei po was one of the great romantic stories of Chinese history, endlessly commemorated by poets and painters.

On the way to the Tang tombs is the **Shanglin Park**. The site of the huge hunting park-cum-garden of the Qin and Han emperors no longer reflects its former glory: it was filled with exotic animals and flora from each province of the empire. All that

remains is a pair of large stone Han figures W of the lake. Said to represent two heavenly lovers, the herd boy and the spinning maid (he a mortal, she a daughter of a
heavenly king, living in the sky on either side of the Milky Way), they look more like
Gog and Magog.

The most impressive group of Tang tombs includes the triple-hilled Qian
ling and the smaller tombs of the Princes Yide and Zhanghuai and
Princess Yongtai. The **Qian ling** is 85km NW of Xi'an and was built for Li
Zhi, the Gaozong (Exalted Ancestor) emperor of the Tang, and his
Empress Wu Zetian.

Though he was the ninth son of the second Tang emperor, he was chosen to succeed
his father in 650 and he died at Luoyang in 683. His wife, Wu Zetian, had been a concubine selected by his father; on the death of the second emperor she became a Buddhist nun and retired to a temple. She was, however, sought out by the Gaozong
emperor in 654 and in 655 he forced his empress Wang to abdicate, though some say
she was murdered by Wu Zetian. Empress Wu's power at court grew and after the
death of the Gaozong emperor, after a few years of controlling a couple of her hap-
less sons as 'emperor', she assumed power in 690. She changed the name of the
dynasty to Zhou and ruled for 21 years with the help of a pair of corrupt courtiers, the
Zhang brothers. She is supposed to have murdered her way to power and, once
enthroned, the killing continued.
    In 701 her granddaughter Princess Yongtai died at the age of 17, officially in child-
birth. Yongtai's half-brother Yide died equally mysteriously (but certainly not in
childbirth) at the same time. It seems probable that Wu Zetian had them put to death
for criticising her favourites. Her second son was ordered (by his mother) to commit
suicide; another was exiled, and one was fortunate enough to succeed his mother
when she was forced into retirement by a palace coup in which the Zhang brothers
were killed. She died in Luoyang in 705, less than a year after the coup.
    She was, in fact, an effective ruler: Korea was successfully conquered during her
reign and the Turkic attacks from the W finally suppressed so that the great prosperity and cultural flowering of the Tang was made possible. Because of her ruthless
elimination of rivals and family members at court, however, she has become one of
the villains of Chinese history, along with the Dowager Empress Cixi of the Qing and
Mao Zedong's wife, all of whom are vilified as negative examples of womanhood.
She was a great Buddhist enthusiast and promoted the growth of temples and monasteries. The Gaozong emperor was buried in the Qian ling in 684 and the tomb
reopened at enormous expense to receive the body of the Empress in 705.

The Qian ling has not been excavated but, externally at least, it is the
grandest of all the Tang tombs. The tomb itself lies in a natural hill which
is approached by a long spirit way (of some 3km) which passes between
two artificial mounds, so that the whole appears to consist of three hills.
The remains of two towers mark the beginning of the spirit way which
passes between the two mounds with tall towers on top. Two obelisks
precede the procession of stone animals beginning with a pair of sturdy
winged horses of great elegance. Then follow a pair of ostrich-like birds
('scarlet birds', symbolic of the South), then five pairs of horses, ten pairs
of large human figures, and then two stelae. That on the left has an
eulogy of the reign of the Gaozong emperor, composed by Wu Zetian and
written by the son who succeeded him but who was deposed by his
mother. That on the right was known as the Stele with No Inscription (it
awaited an eulogy of the empress Wu); it has in fact much later inscriptions of the Song and Jin, the latter written in the language of the Nu zhen
(founders of the Jin), with a Chinese translation.
    Beyond are two towers and large groups of (headless) statues, repre-
senting the foreign envoys and ambassadors who attended the funeral of
the Gaozong emperor. It would be hard to tell that they were foreigners,
were it not for the inscriptions on their backs. Beyond are two colossal
stone lions and the remains of the Hall of Offerings with a stele erected by
the Qianlong emperor. The whole vast enclosure used to be surrounded
by a double wall.

When I first saw the spirit way in 1976 many of the statues had fallen over but they
have now been righted and restored. The sculptures are most impressive, far more
expressive and alive than those of the Ming spirit ways (Nanjing and Peking).

Tomb of the Empress Wu, outside Xi'an

Just beside the winged horses are some of the famous *troglodyte dwellings* of the loess area. You can stand above the courtyard which is cut down into the yellow earth with tunnel-like chambers cut into the earth on three sides, fronted with wooden-framed windows pasted with paper. The wooden frames are painted black with the thin red outline that is so characteristic of domestic architecture of the Xi'an area.

Since 1960 five of the 17 satellite tombs have been excavated, including those of three victims of the Empress Wu: Princess Yongtai, Prince Yide and Prince Zhanghuai. All had been robbed, but only of precious stones and metals, with ceramics and wall-paintings left undisturbed.

Princess Yongtai's Tomb can be entered to provide a view of the underground chambers of Tang tombs. Yongtai was probably murdered by the Empress Wu (or on her orders) in 701 and she was not buried in the Qian ling complex until 706 after her grandmother's death. When the tomb was opened the skeleton of a man was found inside; it is thought to be the body of a Tang tomb-robber, murdered by his accomplices. The tomb is entered down a long sloping corridor with small stepped niches in the walls, filled with rows of pottery tomb figures. It is most interesting to see them arranged in this way (instead of standing as individual works of art in museums). The walls themselves are covered with paintings of women, court attendants and servants (some with the double-bun hairstyle of servants). They carry offerings and candles and flowers.

Their costume, with quite tight bodices to the high-waisted gowns and narrow sleeves and flowing scarves, is characteristic of the early 8C, before the influence of the fat concubine, Yang Guifei. Her bulk altered the idea of female beauty (in the eyes of the emperor at least) and determined new fashions in women's clothing. She introduced the Central Asian style of very loose, baggy, figure-concealing gowns.

Funerary figures of the mid 8C often depict women with very fat faces, vast rolled, turban-like snoods and loose gowns, in contrast with the slim elegance of these early 8C figures.

The dark stone sarcophagus in the tomb chamber (whose ceiling is painted with stars) at the bottom of the long tunnel is carved with figures, birds and flowers.

Prince Yide's Tomb was also constructed in 706, after the death of the Empress, although he died with his sister in 701. It can also be entered and the tunnel, like that of his sister's tomb, is lined with niches and painted with court ladies and eunuchs, palace guards and mounted attendants with a large mural of a procession of guards beneath watch-towers. The ceiling of the tomb chamber is painted with stars.

The *Tomb of Prince Zhanghuai* (second son of the Gaozong emperor, forced to commit suicide by his mother who then buried him with the pomp due to his rank) has a famous wall-painting of polo-playing. In this, as in the other tombs, the original wall-paintings have been removed for safer storage (a closed tomb is one thing, crowds of heavily breathing visitors another) and replaced by extremely exact copies. Two columns and two statues of rams guard the entrance to the tomb, whose ramp is set with niches filled with the *mingqi* (spirit goods), ceramic figures that accompanied the souls of the dead to the other world.

The painting of polo (a game introduced during the Tang from Persia) is immensely vivid. Large, rather stout horses (the cousins of those represented in the ceramic burial figures), their tails tied in neat knots, are depicted at full gallop, ridden by gentlemen wielding sticks that are more like hockey sticks than today's polo mallets. The figures are outlined in black, with colour wash; the painting is sure and swift. On the other wall is a hunting scene with yet another foreign import, falconry. Beyond are a group of officials together with foreign envoys and a palace guard. Two of the animals of the four directions—the green dragon of the E, the white tiger of the W—line the corridor where it joins the tomb chamber and are followed by groups of servants bearing offerings: a cockerel, a pencai (bonsai). Once again the ceiling is decorated with stars.

There is a small *Museum* associated with these satellite tombs displaying Tang funerary ceramics, those of the mid 7C especially, decorated with the three-colour glaze (yellow, green and brown), casually splashed over human figures, horses and vessels.

Zhao ling, the tomb of Taizong, the second emperor of the Tang (reigned 626–649), is to the E of the Qian ling complex. As a group, the Zhao ling and its satellite tombs covers an even greater area than the Qian ling and comprises 177 subsidiary tombs spread across 20,000 hectares. The Zhao ling has not been excavated so the mound may be seen and nearby there is a museum of stelae and excavated ceramics. Taizong was the horse-lover whose tomb contained the beautiful low-relief panels of horses now in the Provincial Museum (and Philadelphia). The stelae are from the surrounding tombs, as are the ceramics. There is a grand series of 163 from a single tomb (that of a high official of Taizong's time), including dancers, officials, entertainers and warriors. There is also a series of copies of wall-paintings from tombs, one of which, unusually, depicts a peasant in a kitchen garden, a more homely picture than most of the more elevated, courtly scenes usually found in Tang tombs.

En route for the Tang or Han tombs, if time allows, the *museum* in the county town of **Xianyang** is filled with mainly Han funerary pieces of considerable interest. The museum is in the old Confucian temple. The greatest collection of funerary ceramics is the army of 2548 pieces from a tomb situated between that of the Gaozu emperor (reigned 206–195 BC) and the Jindi emperor (reigned 157–140). Just like the Qin emperor's buried army, these figures were found in trenches that mimicked the characteristic formation of the Han battlelines. The group also includes entertainers and officials. All the figures are between 48–53cm high (entertainers and officials) and 67–70cm (warriors). There is also a considerable display of jade pieces which were included in large numbers in Han burials because of the strong belief that jade protected the corpse from decay and therefore enhanced the possibilities of longevity of the soul.

27 Yan'an

Rarely visited these days, **Yan'an** in Shaanxi province used to be the major revolutionary tourist centre, closely followed by Shaoshan in Hunan, Mao Zedong's birthplace. Buried deep in the yellow hills, on the bank of the Yan River, Yan'an was the headquarters of the Communist Party during the Anti-Japanese War. Driven out of their previous stronghold in the southern province of Jiangxi, Communist Party members set out on the Long March in 1934, arriving in Yan'an in October 1935, one year later.

Travel: Yan'an is linked to Xi'an by air (two flights a week) and there are also once-weekly flights from Taiyuan and Beijing. These are all in tiny airplanes (the one in which I travelled filled with white clouds at altitude).

It is also possible to take an 8-hour bus ride from the SouthGate in Xi'an, stopping halfway at the *Huang ling*, the 'tomb' of the legendary Yellow Emperor. Traditional founder of the Han race, he is supposed to have ruled from 2698 to 2598 BC and to have invented the wheel, armour, ships and pottery.

Hotel: the Yan'an Hotel was built to cater for the late hordes of revolutionary visitors.

Set in the dry yellow loess hills of N Shaanxi, amongst terraced slopes and troglodyte villages, Yan'an is sparely impressive. As Edgar Snow noted on his arrival in 1937, Yan'an is 'ideally suited for defence. Cradled in a bowl of high, rock-ribbed hills, its stout walls crawl up to the very tops and corner in newly-made fortifications, where machine-guns bristled...' ('Red Star over China', Left Book Club, 1937). The pagoda by the river, the major landmark, has become the symbol of Yan'an which is, itself, a major symbol of the Chinese Communist Party.

It was in Yan'an that Mao Zedong wrote many of his most important speeches, and delivered them from an earthen platform in the Date Garden. It was in Yan'an, during the Anti-Japanese War (1937–45) that the Communist Party began to assume its Chinese (as opposed to Russian) characteristics. As there were no industrialised cities and therefore no proletarians in the vicinity, the Party organised the local peasantry to seize land, collectivise production and, at the same time, assist in guerrilla warfare against the Japanese. Yan'an was visited by a number of distinguished foreign journalists: Agnes Smedley danced with Zhu De (whose biography she later wrote) in the Date Garden and Edgar Snow described life in Yan'an, as well as giving the world the first biographical details of Mao Zedong and other Chinese leaders in 'Red Star Over China'.

Mao's account of his childhood and youth, as told to Snow, revealed his struggles with his autocratic father over his desire for education and his refusal to accept an arranged marriage and the hysterical scenes that ensued with Mao Snr threatening his son with beatings, Mao Jnr standing by the village pond threatening to throw himself in and his mother in tears. His determination to educate himself led him away from home to the Hunan First Normal School (or Teacher Training College) where, once again, his strength of will was revealed in his refusal to co-operate in courses that he thought worthless.

As he told Snow: 'Most of all I hated a compulsory course in still-life drawing. I thought it extremely stupid. I used to think of the simplest subjects possible to draw, finish up quickly and leave the class. I remember once drawing a picture of the "half-sun, half-rock" (a reference to a line in one of Li Bai's poems) which I represented by a straight line with a semicircle over it. Another time during an examination in drawing I contented myself with making an oval. I called it an egg. I...failed.' During this most productive and positive period of his life, when he was writing his most important political essays and planning the way forward for the Chinese Communist Party,

Mao was able to reveal himself to Snow as a humorous and fascinating character.

The Communist Party arrived in Yan'an in force in October 1935, at the end of the Long March (on which 9600km journey some 100,000 had set out but only 8000 made it to Yan'an). There it joined forces with the Shaanxi Soviet. The new arrivals settled in the cave dwellings of the area, Mao Zedong, with his usual impatience, moving house several times during the decade of occupation.

The domestic architecture of Yan'an, characteristic of much of the loess area of Shaanxi and Shanxi, is fascinating and, on that basis alone, Yan'an is worth visiting. In Yan'an the cave houses are usually carved into cliffs, in contrast with the cave houses that can be seen near Xi'an which are dug down from the ground surface. Long caves with rounded roofs were dug into the cliffs in series, each one usually furnished with a kang (brick platform bed) built against the façade with a brick stove beside it. The flue from the stove led under the bed and out through the apron wall of the façade. Above the apron wall, a simple wooden lattice window, covered with white paper, lets light into the cave. The lattice designs are particularly interesting in Yan'an for in many of the caves inhabited by military and political leaders, the five-pointed star of the Red Army uniform has been incorporated.

The **Revolutionary Museum** contains an enormous display of relics of the period: photographs, items of clothing, utensil of all sorts including looms on which the cloth for army uniforms was woven and the white horse that Mao Zedong rode on the Long March (stuffed). The museum is subject to frequent closures and rearrangements.

Similar problems exist in the Revolutionary Museum in Jinggang shan on the Hunan border (the base from which the Long March began). I visited this in 1971, just before the mysterious flight, death and disgrace of Lin Biao. In 1971 Lin Biao's carrying pole was proudly displayed, as evidence of his willingness to do hard work. In 1976, apparently, it had been relabelled as Zhu De's carrying pole and the curator explained, when questioned, that it was indeed Zhu De's carrying pole and always had been but Lin Biao had stolen it. Similar problems dog the Yan'an Museum.

Zao yuan (Date Garden), 10km NW of Yan'an. From 1940 to 1942 and 1944 to 1947, this was the Secretariat of the Central Committee of the Communist Party. Behind the meeting hall and office buildings were the homes of Peng Dehuai (later Minister of Defence, 1954–59, an opponent of the Great Leap Forward which lead to his disgrace and replacement by Lin Biao in 1959) and Liu Shaoqi (Chairman of the People's Republic from 1959 to 1969; the major target of the Cultural Revolution during which he died in prison, refused medical treatment); whilst the great survivors, Mao Zedong, Zhou Enlai and Zhu De (1886–1976, a key military leader) lived on top of the hill.

A Russian doctor lived here, too, and it was here that some of the jollier events of the Yan'an period took place. Agnes Smedley recalled dances held here in the open air, as did members of the ill-fated Dixie Mission of 1944. This was a US Army Observer Group sent to study the military potential of the Communists as part of the Second World War effort to combat Japan. Members of the mission (which was intellectually very high-powered) were impressed with the organisation and spirit they found in Yan'an, in marked contrast to the corruption of Chiang Kai-shek's government, but they later fell foul of Senator Macarthy precisely because they had reported favourably. (The Dixie Mission and, indeed, America's presence in China during the Second World War have been admirably described by Barbara Tuchman in her 'Sand Against the Wind: Stilwell and the American Experience in China 1911–45', London, 1981.)

In 1976 the garden, apart from its flowering trees, also boasted a huge plantation of Indian hemp.

Wangjiaping. NW of Yan'an town is another 'revolutionary site', from 1937 to 1947 headquarters of the Military Commission of the Central Committee of the Communist Party and of the Eighth Route Army. Mao Zedong lived here for a time, as did Peng Dehuai, Zhu De and Ye Jianying (one of the longest-lived Party leaders, his survival through major campaigns suggesting a certain deviousness which was inherited by relatives who achieved high office through nepotism; one nephew was executed for corruption).

Fenghuang shan Revolutionary Site. Inside the North Gate of Yan'an, at the foot of the Fenghuang (Phoenix) Hill, is the first site used by the Party as a headquarters after the Long March in 1837–38. Mao and Zhu De lived here briefly and Mao wrote many of his major political essays here as well as entertaining visitors such as the Canadian doctor who died in the service of the Red Army, Dr Norman Bethune.

The *Yan'an Pagoda*, which stands above the river, existed from the Song dynasty, though the present construction is Ming in date. It is an octagonal brick pagoda, nine storeys and 44m high.

28 Luoyang

Luoyang, in NW Henan, was the capital of nine dynasties from the Eastern Zhou to the Tang, though today's city is industrial and little of its past remains above ground. The nearby site of the Longmen Buddhist cave temples provide the major reason for visiting the city today although during the Cultural Revolution it was famous for its pioneer tractor factory.

Transport: there is no airport, but Luoyang is on the Longhai railway line which runs E to W from Xuzhou in Jiangsu to Lanzhou in Gansu, passing through Zhengzhou and Xian.

Hotels: the main hotel is the Youyi binguan (Friendship Hotel) on Dongfang hong lu in the new, western part of the city. This is one of the hotels built to house Soviet experts who came in the 1950s to help set up the tractor factory, amongst others. It used to offer a Chinese version of Russian cakes, including poppy-seed roll with plum paste instead of poppy seeds. There is another hotel, the Luoyang binguan, in the E of the town, near the old town, but this is not generally open to foreigners. It was a rather charming courtyard construction but somewhat lacking in the amenities (bank, postal counter) usually available, though this may have changed.

Luoyang's ancient glory is disproportionate to its present appearance, especially when viewed from the modern city where the hotel is situated. It was a major capital of the Zhou, made the main capital in 770 BC when a walled city was constructed whose remains have been found in the area now covered by the Wangcheng (Royal City) park. According to legend, Confucius came here to study music and Laozi was in charge of the archives. During the first part of the Han Luoyang was secondary capital (secondary to Chang'an or Xi'an) but it was made the capital of the Eastern Han (AD 25–220). The Han city was to the E of the present city, E of the White Horse Temple. The ramparts can still be seen, running some 4000m N to S and over 2500m W to E, with the Luo river running through the middle of the enclosure. The Han imperial college was to the S of the walls and had over 30,000 students. Here lived Ban Gu, the second great historian of the Han, and Cai Lun, the eunuch who improved the manufacture of paper and reported on his achievements to the emperor in 105. There were two palace complexes within the walls, N and S, linked by a raised and covered avenue with a central path reserved for the emperor. Many of the imperial altars lay outside the city walls.

The same city was occupied by the Wei (220–265) and Jin (265–316). The famous 'Seven sages of the bamboo grove' lived here in the Jin, reclusive scholars who despised politics and devoted themselves to 'pure discussions' (non-political and Taoist in inspiration) when they were not getting drunk, writing poetry or playing music. One was supposed to be permanently accompanied by a servant carrying wine for his master's thirst and a spade to bury him should he suddenly drop dead. Another famous resident was Ma Jun who constructed a 'south-pointing chariot' (a model can be seen in the museum and in the Historical Museum in Peking), which had a wooden figure with a pointing arm which always pointed S, no matter in which direction the chariot was driven, owing to a system of cog-wheels.

The Northern Wei, who had previously established their capital at Datong, in the north, moved their centre of administration to Luoyang (494–534) and, continuing the work they had sponsored at Yungang, began the Buddhist cave-temples at Longmen. Yang Xuanzhi compiled a 'Record of the monasteries of Luoyang' in 547, which is a lengthy description of the city of half-a-million inhabitants during one of its periods of glory. It is an extraordinary text for the grand city, full of monumental buildings was built, rising on ruins, in 493, only to be completely abandoned at three days' notice in 534. The new Wei capital occupied the site of the Han city but the palace was moved to the centre and the rest of the city divided by walls into separate wards, with markets outside the walls (as in the Han). As the Wei were fervent Buddhists, there were 1367 Buddhist temples in the city (for a population of 109,000 families).

When the Wei fell their city was destroyed, and though the Sui emperor chose to site his capital in Luoyang he built it to the W, on a site now comprising the later walled town (which is far smaller). His grand capital, whose walls were some 20km in circumference, covering both banks of the Luo River, was laid out on a checker-board of streets with a main imperial avenue lined with peach and pomegranate trees running N to S. There were over 200,000 families (giving a total population of perhaps one million). Though the first Sui emperor is generally better known for his brutality, he was also said to love literature and music (bringing thousands of musicians to live in Luoyang), to have filled his park outside the town with exotic plants and animals and to have gathered a substantial library of nearly 400,000 volumes. As part of his canal-building projects, the parts of the Grand Canal linking Luoyang with Hangzhou, and Luoyang–Peking were constructed. Grain carried on the canal was stored in surviving granaries.

With the fall of the Sui Luoyang became once more a secondary capital for the Tang; as during the Han, secondary to Chang'an (Xi'an) and, as with the Han, it was mainly in the last years of the Tang that Luoyang became the favoured capital, for it was closer to the major supplies of grain. It was said to be the favoured capital of the Tang Empress Wu who built herself a palace here (outside the old Sui city which continued to serve as the administrative centre) and is supposed to have brought the then-fashionable peonies here. After the Tang, Luoyang was sporadically used as a capital during the Five Dynasties period of disunion but it never regained its former splendour. The current town walls in the E of the city are those of the Song-Qing town, tinier than previous settlements.

Along Yan'an lu, the continuation of Dongfanghong lu (turn left out of the hotel), the **Wangcheng Park** is on the left-hand side of the road. As with all of Luoyang's parks, it is filled with peonies (which flower April–May), but it is also the site of the old Zhou town of *Wangcheng*. In the park two Han tombs and one of the Western Jin are open to the public.

They were moved here to facilitate viewing but their future is uncertain as the site is damp. There are, apparently plans to move them to the Guandi Temple, outside the town and the rumoured 'open-air tomb museum' may well also materialise in the Guandi temple. The tombs were originally excavated elsewhere in the Luoyang area and brought to the park.

The most impressive is the *Western Han Tomb* (206 BC–AD 8). Viewed with the later Eastern Han tomb, it demonstrates the development in the Han from the use of hollow slab bricks, often with impressed and painted designs, towards the use of smaller solid bricks. The central chamber, where the coffin was placed, is constructed from the larger hollow slab bricks and it has a pitched roof supported by columns bearing triangular lintels with painted decorations. The smaller side chambers, originally filled with pottery models and offerings, are constructed from the smaller solid bricks and the roof is vaulted. Later Han tombs are mostly made of the smaller bricks with vaulted roofs. The paintings on the lintels depict an exorcist with a bear's head and his assistants (back wall) and immortals riding on dragons on either side of two doors (central). The second, later tomb (of the Eastern Han, AD 25–220) has sculptured doors and abundant pottery furnishings.

Just E of the park is the **Luoyang Museum** which contains relics excavated in the city and provides a chronological history of the area, beginning with the late neolithic Yangshao and Longshan cultures. Notable are some oracle bones of the Shang and other articles excavated at Erlitou (a major Shang site about 30km E of Luoyang). Erlitou was occupied c 2000–1500 BC, according to radiocarbon dates, and though not definitely identified as a capital, represents a major site. It contained a palace or ceremonial building constructed on a platform c 100m by 100m, jade, bone and pottery artifacts as well as primitive bronzes and workshops in which they were produced. There is some suggestion that this may be a pre-Shang settlement and investigations continue. The Han pottery models of farmhouses, cooking stoves, grain pounders and other scenes from

LUOYANG

White horse temple

Luo He River

to Guanlin and Longmen caves

OLD CITY

Zhou gong temple

Dingding lu

Railway station

Tanggu

Zhongzhou lu

Wanchang Park
and Museum

Shengli lu

Yan an lu

Hotel

N

daily life are very numerous, as well as those representing jugglers, acrobats and musicians. A collection of bronze mirrors with finely decorated backs from the Han anticipates some fine Tang bronze mirrors. The Tang funerary ceramics, like those of the Han, are fine and numerous and the contrasts in colour and technique, but above all, content are interesting. The Han concentrated on scenes from agricultural life whilst the Tang figures are courtly or exotic (camels and foreign attendants from along the Silk Roads). The museum also contains a model of the Sui-dynasty grain silos discovered outside the town, 400 of them built to hold the grain transported via the Grand Canal from Suzhou and other parts of the Yangtse delta to the capital.

Discovered N of the Old Town (where the site can be visited), the silos were underground, some 5–10m deep, the floors hardened by fire, the walls of brick, some recording the number of the pit, its contents and the date of filling, as well as the names of officials in charge. The wide mouths were some 6–18m in circumference. Built during the Sui (605–616), they continued in use throughout the Tang. The whole area was originally walled.

A No. 9 bus will take you from the Youyi binguan to the *Old Town*. This is a pleasant place to wander in and a marked contrast with the brick blocks of workers' apartments that surround the hotel.

In the suburbs of Luoyang, on the Xiangshan (alternatively known as Dongshan), is the *Kanjing si* (Temple for Reading the Sutras), built in the last years of the 7C when the Empress Wu ruled, and it is said that it was built at the order of her consort, Gaozong, whom she dominated. The cave roof is carved with a lotus and with flying apsareses (Buddhist 'angels') of great lightness. Below are 29 lohans, again, carved with considerable skill.

In the same area is the *Tomb of Bai Juyi* (772–846), the great Tang poet. He served as an official in Luoyang until he retired onto the hill and gained the name of the 'scholar who lives on the Fragrant Hill'. There are a grove of cypresses and a stele with the inscription 'Tomb of Master Bai of the Tang'.

The major excursion out of Luoyang is to the Longmen Caves, via the Guanlin.

7km S of Luoyang, on the road to Longmen, are the **Guanlin** (Grove of Guan) and the *Temple of Guandi*, said to be the site of the tomb of Guan Yu, the Shu (Sichuan) general of the Three Kingdoms period (AD 220–280), an historical figure who was popularly canonised as Guan Di, the God of War. The grave mound is surrounded by a cypress grove with a Qing-dynasty stele stating that this is the grave of Guan Yu but as it was erected some 1500 years after the event it cannot be taken as gospel. The temple itself was a Ming construction with a gate, bell and drum towers and main hall. As is often the case in Ming temples, the stone carving (which is original whilst timber work cannot be reliably dated to the period of foundation) of the balustrades is very fine. A wing of the temple houses an exhibition of fine funerary sculpture in stone: the horses and attendants that lined the spirit ways of tombs from the Han to the Qing, sarcophagi and carvings from Longmen. There is also a collection of inscribed stelae.

The **Longmen Grottoes**, with their Buddhist carvings, are amongst the finest in China. Carved into a cliff beside the Yi River (a tributary of the Luo which gives Luoyang its name), the first caves were carved out during the reign of the first Wei emperor to settle in Luoyang in 493 and carving continued to flourish under the Sui and, especially, the Tang. Though two-thirds of the caves are Tang in date, there are a few from the Song and some as late as Ming and Qing. There are, in all, 1352 caves, some 750 smaller niches, comprising 97,306 statues, 3608 inscriptions and 39 pagodas carved into the rock.

LONG MEN CAVES

1. Qian qi si cave
2. Ping yang caves
3. Jing shan si cave
4. Wan fo cave (Ten thousand Buddhas)
5. Lian hua cave (Lotus)
6. Wei zi cave
7. Tang zi cave
8. Ju xian si cave
9. Yao fang cave (Medical prescriptions)
10. Gu yang cave
11. Fire-damaged cave
12. Shi ku si cave
13. Lu dong cave

The most notable carvings are to be found in the following caves, from W to E:

Ludong Cave: carved between 534–550, the cave also includes inscriptions dated to 539, 549, 550 and 572. With a flame ceiling, there are notable low reliefs, of a jataka (life of Sakyamuni) story on one wall and, opposite, a very architectural composition with Buddhas sitting in open halls approached by steps, with detailed roof carvings. The curved figures bearing offerings of long-stemmed flowers are simple but elegant.

Shiku (Stone Room) *Temple Cave:* carved 516–528, with the best adoration scenes remaining in Longmen (after the removal of sections of the Pingyang Cave to the USA in 1935). Processions of figures carved in low relief, Bodhisattvas, elegant court ladies carrying single lotus blossoms with attendants bearing large, long-handled fans and canopy-like parasols, are watched by groups of lohans and Bodhisattvas, their hands clasped together as they stand amongst stylised trees. Small attendants hold up the trailing hems of the loosely-draped, crossover gowns of the nobles who wear high hats and all, lohans and mortals alike, have the elongated earlobes (weighed down by heavy earrings) that are one of the iconographic elements in the Buddha image.

Huoshao (Burnt) *Cave:* built 516–528, its name may come from the flame-decorated ceiling or from the fact of the cave being struck by lightning. The cave contains low-relief carvings of Buddhas in architectural settings, in the Wei style found in the preceding caves and in the Guyang Cave.

Guyang Cave: this has been identified as having been carved out between 488 and 528 and is thus one of the earliest carvings in Longmen. The side walls are covered with carvings: major figures of Maitreya (with crossed legs reaching the ground), sometimes attended by a pair of lithe, snarling lions, and Sakyamuni (legs crossed in the lotus position), in larger niches with silken swags hung above them and smaller figures in niches or small inscriptions between them. Occasionally the niches are topped with an architectural roof rather than the silken swags and lithe apsareses (Buddhist 'angels') fly above them. The major figure at the back of the cave is that of the historic Buddha and the upper parts of the walls are covered with tiny Buddha figures which almost fly up to the ceiling. The figures are characteristic of the Northern Wei, long necked with rather square heads (where they have not been knocked off), scissor-like legs covered with drapery indicated by neat parallel lines, the relative rigidity of the Buddha icons offset by the lithe, sinuous apsareses and lions. Restoration of the head of the major Buddha during the Qing produced a resemblance to the popular conception of the Taoist Laozi so the cave is sometimes known as the Laojun Cave.

Liushi (Six Lions) *Cave:* carved in the Wei (516–528), the cave is noted for its lions, carved in low relief with flat, bushy tails and snarling faces, defenders of the Buddhist law.

Yaofang (Medical Prescription) *Cave*: carved first under the Wei, during the Northern Qi, 120 medical remedies for skin diseases, diabetes, heart disease, madness and other ailments were carved around the entrance to the cave (550–577). The major Buddha figure with two disciples is carved in a fuller, more rounded style than the skinnier Wei figures and is considered to represent the transition from the Wei to the Tang styles. Its stiffness is thought to be due to uncertainty in the transition.

Juxian (Honour to Forebears) *Cave*: carved under the Tang in 675, this is the largest 'cave' carved at Longmen and, as can be gathered from the square holes in the walls into which supporting beams were inserted, was once covered by a large wooden structure. The figures were said to have been paid for by the Tang empress Wu zetian, a great patroness of Buddhism (she is said to have taken an amorous interest in monks), who used 2000 strings of cash from her cosmetics budget. The central Buddha figure is just over 17m high (his ears about 1m long), seated in the lotus position on a lotus throne supported by small figures. The drapery of the robe is schematic but the face is solid and imposing, with sensuous lips in the Indian manner. Immediately to the left and right of the Buddha are smaller figures of the favourite disciples Ananda and Kasyapa (the latter almost completely destroyed), flanked by to Bodhisattvas with elegant headdresses, ropes of pearls and silken cords decorating their more lavish robes and heavy earrings pulling at their lobes. Smaller figures in niches fill the wall. Two of the most impressive figures are the huge guardians to the right of the Buddha figure. One of the four Celestial guardians (Maharaja-devas) stands, hand on hip, one foot crushing a devil-like figure and holding a relic-stupa (or miniature pagoda) in his hand. The sinuousness of the stance and the detail of the carving of his armour is in marked contrast with the stillness of the main icon but is echoed in the protective warrior who stands beside him, again in a naturalistic, challenging pose with his muscular body modelled realistically. These figures represent the best of the Tang carving: lively, naturalistic and extremely decorative (in strong contrast with the static icons of the Wei).

Weizi (Cave of Wei Inscriptions) *dong*: carved 516–528, the cave gains its name from the Wei inscriptions. It is also notable for some very successful (though damaged) Wei carvings where the modelling of drapery is particularly elegant and some of the figures stand in a more natural pose than is commonly found in the Wei. There are also some smaller low-relief depictions of jataka stories.

Lianhua (Lotus flower) *Cave*: carved under the Wei (516–528), the cave's name is derived from the huge, daisy-like lotus flower on the ceiling, the petals flattened to reveal the seed pod in the centre. It is surrounded by flying apsareses and below is a standing Buddha figure, minus head and arms (removed, presumably, for sale to foreign collectors in the 19C and early 20C). The Buddha has a lotus halo and a flame mandorla (the larger 'halo' surrounding the whole body) and there are tiny carvings all over the walls of the cave, which is one of the most impressive for its all-over detail. On the right is an impressive (though headless) figure of the disciple Kasyapa bearing a stave, the drapery of whose robe with its frills and folds is richly detailed (compared with, for example, that of the Buddha's robe). Notice, too, the cap-shaped carving above the entrance with its flame whorls.

Wanshou (Ten-thousand Buddha) *Cave*: completed in 680, under the Tang, this provides a good contrast in styles with the Lianhua (Lotus Flower) Cave, both being richly carved in styles separated by nearly 150 years. The cave's name is derived from the tiny multiple carvings on the side walls. There is also a lotus flower on the ceiling with petals carved more naturalistically than that in the Lotus flower cave. The major figures present the same grouping as in the largest (Juxian) cave: a central Buddha, seated cross-legged on a lotus throne, flanked by two disciples, shaven-headed in monks' robes, and two Bodhisattvas (with tiny attendants between them). Though the figures are Tang, they are not as naturalistic nor as sinuous as those in the major cave but the carving of the lotus throne is particularly fine, with small figures supporting the weight on their shoulders and grimacing with the effort. Underneath the ten-thousand Buddha panels are some elegant musicians, casually seated on cushions with swirling silk behind them, and a dancer with arms raised and waist bent as her silken draperies fly.

Outside the cave is an equally elegant figure of the Bodhisattva Avalokitesvara (Guanyin in Chinese), holding a fly whisk (an essential Buddhist attribute for sweeping flies away to save their lives) and a water bottle which holds the saving 'sweet dew' that Guanyin sprinkles. 85cm high, the figure was carved in 681 by Zhen hui, a monk from Xuzhou. With the head lightly held to one side and the gentle curve to the body, emphasised by the silk drapery and knotted silk girdle threaded with a jade disc, the figure is quintessentially Tang, elegant yet fleshy.

Jingshan si (Veneration of Goodness Temple) *Cave*: carved during the Tang from 650 to 683, this cave has suffered greatly from the depredations of 'head-collectors' but there are two low-relief guardians of the faith, clad in armour and brandishing swords, and a seated figure, smoothed by the elements, that looks rather like a Maitreya Buddha (with feet reaching the ground) but is described as Udayana, King of Kausambi, a contemporary of the historic Buddha, Sakyamuni, who made the first statue of the Buddha.

Nan Pingyang (Southern 'Sun-facing') *Cave*: begun during the Wei, the cave was finished under the Sui (595–616) and the central Buddha figure is, like some others, 'transitional' in style. The drapery of the robe is elegant and realistic and the figure is well fleshed-out, anticipating the Tang style but the head, although with fleshy lips, is rather block-like and elongated in form, reminiscent of the Wei. The ceiling lotus is carved with lotus-shaped petals (unlike the early Wei 'daisy' lotus of the Lotus Flower Cave).

Pingyang zhong (Middle Pingyang or 'Sun-facing') *Cave*: like the Guyang Cave, this was one of the first caves carved at Longmen, c 494–515. An inscription states that the cave took over 20 years to complete and required the labour of over 800,000 workers. It contains 11 large Buddha figures. The figures are set against low-relief carvings of their flaming mandorla haloes and tiny Buddha figures on the walls. The major one is part of a group, again the seated Buddha flanked by small disciples and slightly larger Bodhisattvas and two lions. All the figures are solid with the characteristic thick neck and solid, rather block-like head of the Wei. Details of the clothing, though chunkily carved, are revealing: skirts gathered at the waist and held by a knotted silk tie, overjackets with wide sleeves worn over diaphanous undershirts. Mandorla flames and the flowing robes of apsareses meet in the lotus ceiling.

Pingyang bei (Northern Pingyang) *Cave*: begun under the Wei, the cave was finished during the Tang (627–649) and the figures, roughened by weathering, date from the Tang. There is a Buddha, seated in the lotus position, his feet clearly visible and his upper torso more bare than in many of the other figures so that he looks more like the solitary meditating monk of legend. He is attended by disciples and Bodhisattvas, with guardians at the entrance.

Qianqi si (Qianqi Temple) *Cave*: carved in the Tang, 618–683, as late as 1913 the cave was still protected by a wooden temple (inhabited by monks). The cave contains a seated Buddha figure, the drapery carved in elegant folds, and the attendant Bodhisattva figures are particularly refined and more particularly female than elsewhere (contrary to Indian lore where Bodhisattvas are strictly male).

Nearby is a small four-storey stone *pagoda*, nearly 3m high, built in the early Tang; one of many in the complex.

The **Baima si** (White Horse Temple) is 10km E of Luoyang. Founded in AD 68, the temple is the oldest Buddhist foundation in China.

According to legend, after the Han emperor Mingdi dreamt of a golden figure which was explained to him as being the Buddha, Caiyin and Caijing went off to the west in search of Buddhist sutras and returned to Luoyang on white horses, bringing two Indian monks. A temple was built in the year after their return and it took its name from their horses.

The temple is mainly Ming but has been heavily restored in the 1950s and 1970s.

Before the gate stand two statues of horses, possibly Song in date. Immediately inside the gate, at the eastern and western corners of the surrounding wall are two *tombs*, said to be those of the Indian monks of the Han. On the main axis is the *Hall of Celestial Guardians* where the figure of Weituo (behind, facing the main hall) is said to be Ming. The *Great Hall*, which contains the main Buddha figures, was built in the Ming, apparently using many of the original Han dynasty bricks. The main figure is the historic Buddha, flanked by the Bodhisattvas Manjusri and Samantabhadra. In the hall behind are 18 lohans, said to date from the Yuan dynasty. Steps behind lead up to the *Cool Terrace*, supposedly dating from the Han and built for the two foreign monks to translate the sutras. On the right-hand side of the main axis is the *Hall of the Ancestors* which contains figures of the first six Chan (Zen) masters; the figures are Qing in date. Behind this is the *Meditation Hall*, for the temple, as much as any temple in China can be said to belong to a school of Buddhism, is a Chan (or Zen) temple.

E of the temple is a square brick pagoda built in 1175, 24m high, called the *Qiyun* (Level with the Clouds) *Pagoda*. The spread of dates associated with the temple is considerable; at the height of its power, during the Tang, it had over 1000 monks; these are now reduced to a handful who live at the back of the enclosure and cultivate their own vegetables.

29   Zhengzhou

A. Zhengzhou

Zhengzhou, capital city of Henan province, lies just S of the Yellow River in an area rich in neolithic and bronze age remains. The city was one of the capitals of the Shang dynasty (c 1700–c 1100 BC) and other major Shang city excavations may be visited nearby. Its importance waned after the Shang, not to revive until the early 20C when it regained prosperity after the construction of the Peking–Hankou railway line (1898–1906). Today it is a modern city, a major cotton textile centre, as well as still being a major railway terminus.

Railway: the station is in the SW of the town. As it stands at the nexus of China's railway system, Zhengzhou can be reached from almost all points by train.

Air: there are flights to and from Peking every day except Wednesday, flights every day to Xi'an and less frequent services to Changsha, Guangzhou, Hefei, Ji'nan, Nanjing, Nanyang, Qingdao, Shanghai, Shijiazhuang, Wuhan and Yichang.

Hotels: the major hotel is the Zhengzhou binguan on Jinshui lu, in the NE of the town; it is a large solid building in substantial grounds, originally built for Soviet advisors.

The earliest site yet unearthed in the Zhengzhou area is that of *Dahe cun*, a neolithic village of c 3760–3610 BC whose remains are classified as belonging to the Yangshao or 'painted pottery' culture. The term Yangshao derives from neolithic remains discovered in 1920 in Yangshao village in NW Henan (c 75km W of Luoyang). The Swedish engineer J. Gunnar Andersson was amongst the first to describe the finds in his early classic work on Chinese archaeology, 'Children of the Yellow Earth' (1934). A late neolithic culture characterised by fine red pottery vessels decorated (or 'painted') with designs in black with animal forms gradually developing into geometric derivations, whose remains are widely spread throughout the Yellow River (Huang he) basin, it is still often named the Yangshao Culture, although the original site's stratigraphy is unclear and it may well post-date the neolithic. Perhaps the most famous 'Yangshao' site is that of *Banpo*, on the outskirts of Xi'an, but many later excavations, such as that at Dahe cun, are very rich.

Remains of the painted pottery culture at Dahe cun were overlaid by black pottery kilns of the Longshan culture, a late neolithic culture characterised by burnished black ceramics. The eponymous Longshan site is in Shandong and whilst the red, painted pottery culture tends to be found to the W, with the (generally) later black pottery culture further E, in parts of Henan, such as Dahe cun, the stratigraphic sequence is clear. In 'ideal' sites (which fit a desired pattern of gradual progression), Yangshao is overlaid by Longshan (a culture which includes ceramic forms anticipating bronze shapes and the use of scapulimancy, another bronze age tradition), which is, in turn, overlaid by bronze age remains. If the Zhengzhou area is taken as a whole, this progression can be seen.

Zhengzhou appears to have been the site of one of the Shang (c 16C BC–c 1066 BC) capitals. The Shang kings moved their capital many times before finally settling in Anyang and the Zhengzhou city wall of the Shang (just to the W of Chengdong lu) may well have been Ao, one of the earlier capitals. Though an earlier capital has been unearthed at Erlitou (near Luoyang), that at Zhengzhou represents a considerable expansion, with a city wall of over 7000m, enclosing an area of over 3 square km. Bronze foundries and bone-carving workshops have been found on Huayuan lu, N of the city wall, and pottery kilns to the W, on Minggong lu. Radiocarbon dates suggest that the site was occupied between 2000 and 1500 BC.

The importance of the city at the time may be judged from estimates of the amount of time put into the building of the city wall. It was constructed of 'tamped' earth (or pise), a method still used widely in northern China in domestic architecture where wooden plank frames are set up and earth pounded down inside the frames which are subsequently removed, leaving a hard, firm wall. It was estimated that the wall averaged 10m in height and 20m in width and that if 10,000 workers put in 330 days a year, it would have taken 18 years to build. Though the remains of small, presumably domestic, dwellings have been found outside the wall, those within its perimeter are on the grand scale; thus it is assumed that the wall enclosed the administrative centre as well as aristocratic or palatial dwellings with many ordinary people living outside, near the foundries, potteries and workshops. In the NE section of the city (within the wall) more than 100 human skulls, sawn across the middle, were unearthed and it is suggested that these may have provided the raw material for the bone-carving workshops. A tamped-earth platform, perhaps an altar, was unearthed in the NW corner of the city and many finely carved jade hairpins have been found within the walls (with rare examples unearthed outside, reinforcing the hypothesis that the inner city area was for the rich).

Zhengzhou's importance declined when the capital was moved to nearby Anyang, though the area continued to be occupied. A Han city, enclosing a far smaller area than that of the Shang city, has been unearthed and Han dynasty tombs and an ironworks have been found in Zhengzhou; and a Tang tomb has also been found. Nevertheless, Zhengzhou was outshone, particularly in the Han, Wei, Sui and Tang, by Luoyang, which served as the second capital. In the 17C, Zhengzhou was again walled and the wall, like that of the Han, enclosed an area far smaller than that of the Shang capital.

When the Peking–Hankou railway was built (1898–1906), with later extensions to Guangzhou, as well as the Shanghai–Urumqi line which passes (from W to E) through Zhengzhou, the city became a major terminus. 3000 years after its earlier prominence, it regained a position of importance as a manufacturing centre, particularly of cotton textiles, based on the railway and locally grown raw materials.

Its revolutionary history started early with the famous strike of workers on the Peking–Hankou line which began on 7 February 1923. The railway workers on the line had had 16 local trades unions which they planned to merge but the founding meeting of the 'Unified Syndicate of Railway Workers of the Peking–Hankou Line' was banned by the local warlord, Wu Peifu (1873–1939). His soldiers shot 35 strikers and wounded many more; the strike is now remembered as one of the first struggles of the workers' movement in China. Another recent tragedy in the vicinity occurred when Chiang Kai-shek had the dykes holding back the Yellow River breached in 1938. This was done at Huayankou, 30km N of the city, in order to slow down the advance of Japanese troops. Its major effect was to drown at least 1 million, render 12 million homeless and landless and inundate hundreds of square kilometres.

Railways were of particular importance to the warlords who used them for troop movements: between 200,000 and 300,000 troops were moved annually in the early 1920s on the Peking–Hankou line alone, to the detriment of other traffic. Led by the newly formed Communist Party, the 7 February strike was one of the first events of the 'workers' movement' in China, and railway workers in a modern industry (compared with the more traditional industries such as textiles) were politically further advanced than many others. There are displays of photographs and documents relating to the strike in the city centre's tall monument to the 7 February strike.

Taking Jiefang donglu E from the monument, you will find the **Chenghuang miao** (Temple to the City God) on the N side of the street. This is a Ming foundation, restored in 1502, with side wings added later in the Ming and Qing.

In the past every city had such a temple to the deity alternatively called the god of ramparts and moats, the protector of the city or town. Worship of the Chenghuang is said to date back to the reign of the legendary emperor Yao (2357–2255 BC, according to legend) who instituted a sacrifice in honour of eight spirits, the seventh of which symbolised the city moat and rampart. Later, the deity took the form of a magistrate, a human 'defender of the people'. It was not uncommon for a notable local figure to be deified as the local Chenghuang, and he is usually represented as a magistrate with his official hat, attended by two secretaries, two constables (one with an ox's head, one with a horse's head), two further attendants, one white-faced, one black-faced, and more servants, all of whose duty is to assist him by informing him of what is going on in his area of jurisdiction. Perhaps confounding the Chenghuang's duties as a judge with those of the judges who preside over the Chinese Buddhist hells (where souls are judged), there are often representations of the ten Buddhist hells in City God temples.

The Zhengzhou temple is a complex oriented N–S, comprising a number of buildings including a gateway, main hall and eastern tower, all with glazed tile roofs and striking eaves decorations including dragons, phoenix, lions among lotuses and peonies. The main hall's roof ridge has two animals 'swallowing' its extremities, phoenix and peonies and the hall bears the inscriptions 'eight immortals crossing the sea' and 'Yang Xiang beats the tiger'. A great number of inscribed stone stelae are kept in the temple.

At the far end of the road is the T-junction with Erligang lu where you will find the ruins of the Shang *city wall*, described above. Much of the eastern wall has been unearthed, running parallel to Erligang lu, and the E parts of the northern and southern walls. Turning left into Erligang lu and walking N, you will eventually cross the Jinshui River and then come to the T-junction with Jinshui lu. The hotel is to the right.

The **Henan Provincial Museum** is on Jinshui lu. Turn left out of the hotel; the museum is just beyond the first roundabout, on the right-hand side of the road. As the provincial museum for one of the provinces richest in archaeological sites, the collection is stunning. There are rooms devoted to the neolithic, with many of the finds from Dahe cun, the neolithic village on the outskirts of the city where a number of house-floors were excavated, allowing for reconstruction of neolithic buildings. The collection of bronzes is most notable and the funerary building models of the Han are striking, particularly a huge and unique example which has naked hermaphrodite caryatids instead of columns. Despite the strength of its early collections, there are exhibits from the Tang to Song, including a fine Ming house-model.

Returning to the hotel, on the far side of the roundabout, on the right-hand side of the road is the *Yellow River Exhibition Hall*. Exhibits depict the river itself and its history as well as the engineering efforts devoted to maintaining the dykes and reducing the flow of silt which makes the river particularly difficult to control. So much silt is brought down the river (the yellow earth it carries giving it its name) that in many places the river flows within its dykes up to 10m above the surrounding countryside.

B. Around Zhengzhou

The neolithic village of **Dahe cun**, 12km N of the centre of town, was discovered in 1964. The excavations cover an area of 30 hectares. 28 house-floors unearthed from different periods of habitation reveal varying structural methods. Some are surrounded by a metre-high wall which is unusual in neolithic sites so far discovered. The fine red clay ceramics are decorated, mainly in white or black. Patterns have been identified as representing the sun, moon and stars.

Huayankou: the point where Chiang Kai-shek breached the Yellow River dykes is c 30km N of Zhengzhou.

Dengfeng is either visited from Zhengzhou or from Luoyang. It is 80km SW of Zhengzhou, and c 70km SE of Luoyang. The road from Zhengzhou, however, has extra attractions in the form of Han tombs and a Yuan observatory.

The **Han Tombs** at **Dahu ting** in Mixian, 60km from Zhengzhou, are those of a local official, Zhang Boyan and his wife. *Tomb 1* (that of the official) is made of stone, whilst *Tomb 2* is of brick. Both contain main chambers which contained the tombs, and side chambers for offerings. The tombs are notable for their decoration in carved stone and wall-paintings. In Tomb 1, in particular, they illustrate the preparation of food for the table. Of particular interest to Chinese archaeologists is the apparent depiction of the preparation of bean-curd (doufu or tofu). Literary evidence had suggested that this important protein source had been known from the Han but the evidence was scanty; Henan archaeologists regard the depiction in the late Han tomb at Mixian as confirming the literary account. The left-hand side chamber has depictions of chariots, horses and grain stores, with the official receiving grain, whilst a banquet scene is shown in the right hand chamber. Tomb 2 has a grand banquet scene painted on brick, with entertainers: acrobats, conjurors and fat wrestlers. There are also scenes from Taoist legends.

The **Observatory at Gaocheng zhen**: inside the *Zhougong miao* (Duke of Zhou's Temple), at Gaocheng zhen, near Dengfeng, is a strange brick tower, rather like a pyramid. Built in the Yuan by Gao Shoujing (1231–1314), who was also responsible for the water supply of Peking, it was repaired in 1542, and is China's oldest surviving observatory. The 10m tower is ascended by the two flights of stairs on either side whilst the N side has a runnel down it and a wall at the bottom. These were originally fitted with bronze markers and enabled the calculation of the winter and summer solstices.

Dengfeng lies near the foot of the Song shan (Song Mountain), one of the Five Sacred Mountains (see Tai shan). 2km N of the town is the *Songyang Academy*, one of the four 'great academies'; this one founded in the early Song and housed in a temple founded in 484. It is notable today for its two old pines, survivors of three said to have been seen by the Wudi emperor of the Han in 110 BC when he came to worship at Song shan. He gave them titles as three generals. The second general is 15m high, the first, 6m.

4km E of Dengfeng are two stone *pillars*, all that remains of the Han temple built in 118 at the foot of Song shan. Built of stone in imitation of wooden architecture, they are important architectural relics and also noted for their inscriptions in Han calligraphy (which is comparatively rare).

SONG SHAN itself has a number of temples dotted about its peaks. There are four Buddhist holy mountains but the five antedate them and are associated with the imperial cult and Taoism. Mountains have always had a special place in Chinese belief, their height suggesting proximity to the gods. The five represent the directions with Song shan in the centre. The emperors of the past used to make ceremonial visits to ascend each in turn, both 'beating the bounds' of his territory and sacrificing to the gods. There are many significant temples in the Song shan region and the practice of imperial ascent gave the name to the county town for 'deng' means 'ascend' and 'feng' 'to bestow honours'.

Zhongyue miao (Temple of the Central Peak). At the foot of the famous mountain, ascended by the Han emperor Wudi in 110 and by the Empress Wu (684–704), is a temple, the largest in Henan province, dating to the period of the Qing Qianlong emperor (late 18C) though there were earlier buildings on the site, the first constructed under the Qin (221–207 BC). There are over 30 white pines said to date from the Tang and Song. To the NE of the Chongsheng gate are four 3m-high iron guardian figures cast in 1064, with dates and inscriptions cast on their backs and very fierce faces. They are accurate representations of 11C soldiers and, being cast in iron, link with many other fine iron castings found in northern Henan and southern Shanxi (like the giant Tang Buddha head in Lin Fen). Though iron incense burners and figures are found elsewhere, bronze is more common in other areas. The gate-building with its fantastically decorated roof stands beside a smaller pavilion with temple guardians dating from the Northern Song. On the right in the main courtyard is a stele with carvings of the five peaks. This is in front of the main hall which stands on a high stone platform, with two Ming lions in iron. Inside is a central statue of the god of the mountain.

7km NW of Dengfeng is the 6C **Songyue** (Song Peak) **Pagoda**, a solitary survivor of the numerous religious buildings constructed at Song shan in the Northern Wei, when the area was a particular centre of devotion (perhaps because of its closeness to the capital at Luoyang). It is one of the earliest surviving large brick pagodas in China. It stands amongst the remains of the *Songyue Temple*, also constructed in the Northern Wei (first as an imperial residence, later as a temple). It retained its popularity in the Sui and Tang when the Empress Wu frequently stayed in the temple. The remaining temple structures are Qing in date although there are stone lions and stelae from the Tang. The pagoda is 40m high, hollow and gently curved. It has a substantial base with four arched, lotus-carved openings in the upper part topped by a series of narrower upper storeys separated by layers of corbelled brickwork. There are openings in each of the upper storeys into the rectangular interior whose walls are covered with polychrome Buddha images. Traces of paint indicate that the pagoda was originally whitewashed.

One of the most famous religious establishments in China, which has given its name to a form of the martial arts, the **Shaolin Monastery** is c 15km NW of Dengfeng. It was founded in the Northern Wei, in 495.

The Indian monk, Bodhidharma, founder of the Chan (or Zen) school of Buddhism, is supposed to have come to the Shaolin temple in 527, after seeing the Emperor of the Liang in Nanjing. Disappointed over his failure to persuade the Emperor that all his good works of Buddhist patronage amounted to nothing without an understanding of the nothingness of everything, Bodhidharma crossed the Yellow River on a single reed (thus he is often depicted, with a black curly beard, standing on a slim leaf on the waves) and arrived at the Shaolin Monastery where he sat for nine years facing a wall. Accounts of his subsequent career are equally mystic: dying in the monastery, he was buried there but subsequently returned to India wearing only one sandal (the other remained in his grave). He is seen as the first patriarch of the Chan school which preaches the rejection of doctrine (especially textual study), in favour of meditation alone. The martial art of wrestling (Shaolin fists) practised by the monks, supposedly to help their concentration when meditating, is immensely popular now and many films have been made, both in Hong Kong and China, about the magical powers of the martial monks.

The temple and its subsidiary buildings were destroyed during a persecution of Buddhism (561–77) and restored in 579–80. The foundation flourished during the

Tang, supporting a community of more than 2000 monks. It declined during the late Tang and Five Dynasties. A major renovation took place in 1735 but in 1928 the warlord Shi Yousan set it ablaze and it burned for over 5 weeks. It is still noted for its frescoes: that in the *Thousand-Buddha Hall*, said to be Ming, depicts 500 lohan paying homage to Vairocana (the first of the five celestial Buddhas, the essence of wisdom and absolute purity, whose name means 'shining everywhere'); that in the *White Drapery Hall* shows the rescue of a Tang emperor by 13 martial monks.

W of the monastery is the FOREST OF STUPAS, the monastery's graveyard where over 220 brick stupas (in varying styles, dating from the Tang to the Qing) contain the remains of notable monks. Such large graveyards are rare now, though there is one below the Tanzhe Temple outside Peking. Behind it is the cave in which Bodhidharma was supposed to have sat for nine years and the *Chuzu miao* (Temple of the First Patriarch). In the main hall, constructed in 1125, stone pillars are carved with temple guardians (perhaps an earlier practice, antedating the custom of placing them in a gate-hall), dragons, flying phoenix and other figures. SE of the hall is a pine tree, said to have been planted by the sixth patriarch, Huineng, in the early Tang.

In the *main temple*, stone lions guard the gateway which leads to perhaps the most striking part of the monastery (also impervious to the warlord's fire), the forest of stelae, which includes stones inscribed in 683 and others carved with the calligraphy of the Song artist Mi Fei, the Yuan calligrapher Zhao Mengfu (also noted for his horse paintings) and the Ming calligrapher Dong Qichang. Passing through buildings (which have been in considerable disrepair), the halls at the back of the enclosure, the seven-bay Thousand-Buddha Hall and the White Drapery Hall to its right, contain the well-known frescoes.

The temple is still enormously popular amongst Chinese tourists and the area is now crammed with market stalls, but the cemetery, the forest of stelae with its old trees and the surrounding mountains still retain a certain grandeur.

30 Kaifeng

Kaifeng, E of Zhengzhou, was the capital of China during the Northern Song from 960 to 1127 when the court was forced to flee S in the face of invasion of much of N China. Like Zhengzhou, it has suffered from its proximity to the Yellow River for the dykes were deliberately breached in 1642 though the city was inundated again in 1855 when the river changed course. Thus little remains of its former grandeur. It is also famous for its historic Jewish community which had all but died out by the mid 19C.

Railway: Kaifeng is on the Shanghai–Urumqi line and is most easily reached from Nanjing or Zhengzhou. The station is in the S of the city. There is no *airport* nearer than Zhengzhou.

Hotel: The main hotel, well situated in the centre of the old town, is the Kaifeng Binguan on Ziyou lu, not far from the Xiangguo temple.

Kaifeng's history as a capital begins in the Warring States period (403–221 BC) when it was the capital of the kingdom of Wei. Wei was absorbed by Zhou which, in turn, was absorbed into the Qing empire (221 BC) but one of the major statesmen of Wei was Shang Yang, author of the 'Shang shu' (Book of Lord Shang), one of the major legalist texts. Shang Yang (c 390–338 BC), went to work in Qin (well before it conquered all the other states), where he put his legalist policies into practice, contributing to Qin's success, to the detriment of Wei. Kaifeng became a capital once again in the Five Dynasties period (AD 907–960) but its greatest period of pre-flood glory came when it was the capital of the Song from 960–1127. Little remains of its former glory because of the later floods.

Though Geil in his 'Eighteen Capitals of China' (1911) states categorically, 'Kaifeng is a has-been', the last part of his subsequent description still stands, for

Kaifeng is a pleasant, rather sleepy little place. Geil continues:

> It produces a worse impression than the wretched quarters of Constantino-
> ple. It has no streets, only broad straight stretches which on rainy days are
> seas of mud, on dry days, clouds of dust. 'It has no trade,' said a disap-
> pointed commercial traveller; no manufactures, no imports of any conse-
> quence; a local market-town it may be, but it seems to have the value of a
> big, casual village.

Yet during the Song, the imperial way was 300m wide. On each side there were covered arcades where merchants traded. Barriers, painted black, and a double barrier
painted red, partitioned the route from north to south, leaving a central passage
which was reserved for the emperor and prohibited to people and horses. Traffic was
confined to the arcades, beyond the barriers. Two narrow canals ran alongside the
arcades. They had lotuses planted in them, and were planted with flowering trees:
plum, peach and apricot, so that in spring one got the impression of a brilliantly-
coloured embroidery. (Meng Yuanlao's flowery account of the eastern capital, quoted in Gernet, 'Daily Life in China on the eve of the Mongol invasion'.)

The literary account of Kaifeng's splendour is borne out by a wonderful genre
painting by Zhang Zeduan of the Northern Song, 'Going Up the River at the Qing
Ming Festival', now in the Palace Museum collection in Peking. As it unrolls, Zhang's
scroll takes the viewer up river, through the suburbs where wide barges with
unfurled concertina-like sails and huge steering oars make their slow progress up
river. Kaifeng, with its arched stone bridges and streets lined with tiled-roofed houses (most with a small upper storey), shops open to the street, tea-houses and grand
city gates, is thronged with people, pedlars with their wares slung on shoulder-poles,
donkeys, camel caravans, carts being pushed over the hump-backed bridge, sedan
chairs with ladies peeping from behind patterned curtains, officials on horseback followed by servants on foot, somnolent customers in the tea-houses watching the world
go by. Much of this disappeared when the Jurched (ancestors of the Manchus) over-
ran northern China and captured Kaifeng, taking the emperor and many courtiers
prisoner and driving the remnants of the imperial household S to Hangzhou. The
Jurched established the Jin dynasty, naming Kaifeng 'Nanjing' (Southern Capital), in
deference to their northern roots. The confusing profusion of names continued, for
Kaifeng was known briefly as Beijing (northern capital) under the Ming. The Jurched
were themselves overthrown by the Mongols in 1232, despite their defence of
Kaifeng by grenade (an event of significance in the history of weaponry).

In 1642, when the peasant army led by Li Zicheng threatened Kaifeng, the Yellow
river dykes were breached, according to official sources by the rebel-leader but more
probably by the officials defending Kaifeng, in an attempt to halt his advance. As
with Chiang Kai-shek's action near Zhengzhou (vainly attempting to halt the
Japanese advance), all that happened was that a quarter of a million innocent people
were drowned (and Li Zicheng's uprising ran out of steam as the Manchus swept
down to found the Qing dynasty). This, and the 1855 flood when the Yellow river
changed course of its own volition, having deposited so much silt that its bed was
higher than the dykes, left Kaifeng bereft of many ancient relics.

An aspect of Kaifeng's history that has long fascinated Europeans is its Jewish
community. Jewish relics in China begin with a paper document referring to the sale
of sheep which dates from 718. The document was found near the Buddhist caves at
Dunhuang in 1901 and is now in the British Library. There are records of Jews in
Canton in 877 and later small communities were recorded in Peking, Quanzhou,
Luoyang, Ningbo, Hangzhou, Nanjing and Yangzhou. More is known about the
Kaifeng community than others for several stelae that once stood outside the synagogue there record their history. Though the stelae state that they arrived as early as
the Zhou (c 10C BC), it is now thought that this is a *post-facto* justification, characteristic of the Chinese fascination with ancient history, and that they did not appear until
perhaps the Song. It is thought with that, like the moslem Chinese, their ancestors came to
China from Central Asia and, like the moslem Chinese in China proper (as distinct
from the Uighurs and Kazakhs of Chinese Central Asia), they are physically Han Chinese.

This probable origin is borne out by their division of the Pentateuch into 53 divisions (instead of 54) and their use of 27 letters of the Hebrew alphabet (instead of 22),
characteristics that they share with Persian Jews. The Jesuit missionary Matteo Ricci
(1553–1610) was the first foreigner to note the existence of the Kaifeng Jews and he
sent two Chinese Christian converts to Kaifeng in 1607 where they saw the synagogue and met the Rabbi. Later Jesuit visitors included Jean Domenge (1722) and
Gaulbil (1723). Domenge sketched the synagogue, providing the only illustration of
the whole building that exists. In 1850, the Bishop of Hong Kong, together with missionaries from the London Society for Promoting Christianity among the Jews, visited Kaifeng and obtained a Torah in Chinese (now in the British Library). They found
the community in dire straits (after the great flood following the Yellow river's change

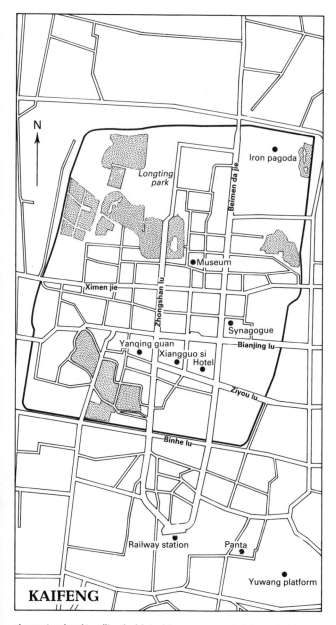

KAIFENG

*Map labels:*

N

Longting park

Iron pagoda

Beimen da jie

●Museum

Ximen jie

Zhongshan lu

● Synagogue

Bianjing lu

Yanqing guan ●
Xiangguo si ● ● Hotel

Ziyou lu

Binhe lu

● Railway station   Panta ●

● Yuwang platform

of course), reduced to selling the fabric of the synagogue as building material.

Bishop White, of the Canadian Church of England, as Bishop of Kaifeng and a considerable sinological scholar, took a great interest in the survivors of the community and wrote about it though his fundamental intention, like that of the London Society, was to teach them 'that Jesus Christ was a Jew, and that he came to save the world' as he stated in 1912. Contemporary attempts were made by the sizable (European and Middle Eastern) Jewish community of Shanghai to help the community through the Society for the Rescue of the Chinese Jews, founded in 1900. In the relaxation that followed the death of Mao articles have begun to appear in Chinese journals which reveal that there are still some 200 Jews in Kaifeng with a smaller community in Yangzhou. Like Chinese Moslems, with whom they have frequently been confused, they do not eat pork but, unlike the Moslems, they trace their descent through the matrilineal line. The site of the synagogue, off Di Jie in the centre of the walled town, is now a hospital garage (though such is the interest of American Jews, in particular, that I would not be surprised if the synagogue were rebuilt, as a tourist attraction) and the three surviving stelae are now in the Kaifeng Museum (see 'Monographs of the Jewish Historical Society of Hong Kong', vol. 2, Hong Kong Jewish Chronicle, 1986).

A.   Within the Walls

Starting from the Kaifeng binguan, turn right into Ziyou lu, past a turning on the right (Madao jie) and you will see the **Xiangguo si temple** (the name, given in the early 8C by a Tang emperor, commemorates one of his pre-imperial titles). One of China's best-known Buddhist temples, it was founded in 555 on the site of the palace of a Wei ruler of the Warring States period. The first temple was destroyed by fire during fighting in the pre-Tang period and was totally destroyed in the 1642 flood. Rebuilt in 1766, the surviving Qing buildings, especially the sutra library (at the far end) and the main hall, are noted for their multiple eaves bracketing and yellow and green tiled roofs.

Entered through a stone pailou gateway, in the *Bell Tower* on your right is a Qing bronze bell 4m high, weighing 10,000kg, which is one of the 'eight sights of Kaifeng'. It is called the Frost Bell of the Xiangguo Temple. In the main hall there is a small exhibition including a fine bronze arhat (Northern Song) and many Ming and Qing porcelains, jades, embroideries (and a parasol formerly belonging to the Dowager Empress Cixi). Behind is the octagonal *pavilion* with uptilted eaves, housing a gilded, four-sided Guanyin of the 1000 arms and 1000 eyes (all-seeing and compassionate). It is said to have been carved from a single piece of gingko wood. Behind that is the two-storey sutra library.

Turn right out of the temple into Ziyou lu and continue until you reach the main N–S road, Zhongshan lu. Cross straight over and continue to the end of the smaller road where it meets Baofukang zhonglu. Diagonally opposite (slightly to the right) is a small road which leads to the **Yanqing guan Taoist Temple** (Temple of Extended Celebration).

Originally founded in the early Yuan, it was given its present name in 1373. All that remains is the *Pavilion of the Jade Emperor*, 13m high. The pavilion survived the flood but its base was covered by nearly 2m of earth, for in 1973 the base was excavated to reveal the bottom of the ironwork windows (which were made in 1549, according to inscriptions). The base is square, the middle and upper parts octagonal, with turquoise tiles above carved bricks imitating wooden construction. The temple was inhabited by a Taoist master, founder of the Quanzhen school which sought to synthesize the theories of 'Laozi', the Confucian classic of filial piety and Buddhist belief.

Return to Zhongshan lu and turn left. At the second crossroads, turn right into Xufu jie, where you will find the *Shanshaangan huiguan* (Fellow Provincials' Association).

Occupied by a school (1983), this was originally a 17C guildhall established by merchants from Shanxi and Shaanxi provinces. These guildhalls, which functioned primarily as hotels for natives of particular provinces, were once scattered throughout China's cities and were useful for travellers of all sorts, if they could prove that they came from the relevant province. Scholars taking official exams in the capital would stay in the appropriate guild hall for very little money.

In the late Guangxu period (1875–1908) this hall was also joined by merchants from Gansu. All the buildings in the enclosure, from the spirit wall at the front, the bell and drum towers, the ornamental arch, to the main halls and side halls, are highly decorated with tiled roofs with elaborate ridge decorations and richly carved wooden panels, all dating from the Qing.

Returning to Zhongshan lu, turn right (N). The second turning on the right, Shuarong jie, brings you to the *Museum* (still under construction in 1985) which promises to display the famous stelae from the synagogue and other items excavated in the area.

Continuing along Shuarong jie, the second crossroads is with the main road Tu Jie; the site of the *synagogue* (in Jiaojing hutong), now a hospital, was formerly reached from Di Jie. Turn right into Di Jie and the next crossroads is with Dongda jie (on the right) and Caizhengting dong jie (on the left). I have not been there but according to the map there is a hospital just off Tu Jie, immediately S of Caizhengting dong jie, which should be possible to find.

Returning to Di Jie, continue S. The third crossroads is where Ziyou lu meets Di Jie. Turn right into Ziyou lu and you will find the Kaifeng Hotel.

Longting (Dragon Pavilion) **Park**. In the NW corner of the walled city is a large park, originally part of the imperial park of the Northern Song. The park was later used under the Ming and the high part on which the Dragon pavilion stands was the only part not to be submerged in the floods of 1642. In 1692 a longevity pavilion was built on top of the prominence and local officials used to come here and offer their respects on the emperors' birthdays. In 1696 it was given the name *Dragon Pavilion*, an inappropriate name for the current building on the site, a Qing dynasty hall with a double-eaved roof, is a majestic structure, closer to a corner tower on a city wall than a pavilion. There are two Song dynasty stone lions in front of the hall and below it, near the entrance to the park, a bronze statue of Sun Yat-sen erected in 1929.

It is said locally (1986) that there are plans to 'rebuild' the old imperial way which ran along today's Zhongshan lu, S from the Dragon Pavilion. I presume that this is part of the tourist thrust which has led to the reconstruction of the Confucian temple area in Nanjing and Liulichang in Peking as 'old-style' quarters.

In the NE corner of the city, the **Iron Pagoda** (Tie ta) stands in the *Iron Pagoda Park*. Kaifeng's major landmark, the pagoda was built in 1049, during the Northern Song, as part of the Youguo (Protect the Country) Temple, which no longer survives. It is said that the pagoda houses relics of the Buddha. It is octagonal, 13 storeys high and almost 55m tall. Its popular name derives from the iron-like colour of the glazed tiles which cover the exterior. Like other early surviving buildings in Kaifeng, its base is buried under a couple of metres of silt deposited during floods. The brick and tile construction imitates timber and the tiles are further decorated with apsareses (Buddhist 'angels'), dragons, qilin (Chinese unicorns), lions and lotuses. It is possible to climb the pagoda. In a small octagonal pavilion just to the S of the pagoda is a Song dynasty bronze Buddha, 5.14m high, weighing 11.7 tons.

B. Outside the Walls

SE of the city, outside the walls is the *Guchui* or *Yu wang Platform*. This elevation is said to have been created by the Great Yu, the legendary tamer of the floods (hence the name Yu wang or King Yu's Platform) and it is also said to have been a place where rulers of the Warring States period came to enjoy music (hence the name Guchui: gu means ancient and chui means to play wind instruments). The park contains buildings housing stelae commemorating the feats of the Great Yu and halls commemorating Tang poets.

Just outside the park, to the W, is a more interesting building, the **Bo ta Pagoda**. It was built in 977 and is the oldest standing building in Kaifeng.

Built of brick, it is hexagonal in plan and now 31.67m high. As it has been deeply buried in silt it must originally have been considerably higher. It was described in the Ming as being nine storeys high but only three remain. Inside are many Buddhist sutras inscribed on stone; outside, the carved brickwork is very fine.

Outside the city, 2km to the NE is the *Iron Rhinoceros*, housed in a *Long miao* (Dragon Temple). It was cast in 1446 to try and ward off floods but it and its temple were submerged in 1642. In 1691 it was dug up and a new temple constructed round it. It is about 2m high with an inscription on its back which reads: '100 smeltings of dark gold, liquidified and transformed into a magical rhino, majestic and brilliant. Set up as a protection against water, stable as Mount Tai, firm as a block of stone...Rain falls and wind blows, men plough and women spin, the four seasons follow each other in order and the 100 spirits do their tasks appropriately.'

It is possible to see the YELLOW RIVER outside the town, to the N, at *Liuyankou Ferry* where there is a tourist lookout point. The river, behind its dykes, flows at a higher level than the flat, flat surrounding countryside and is a rather frightening sight, inexorably bearing the tons of grey-yellow silt which endlessly raise its bed.

31   Anyang

Anyang, a small town on the Zhengzhou–Peking railway, in the N of Henan, was the site of the last Shang capital in the 12–11C BC.

Railway station:to the W of the old walled town.

Hotel: the Anyang binguan is on Jiefang lu, N of the small city wall.

Written records list seven Shang capitals and the ruins at Zhengzhou have been tentatively described as those of the capital of Ao, though this is uncertain and the other earlier capitals, assumed to be in Northern Henan, have yet to be found. The ruins of the capital of Yin, however, are known to lie on the banks of the Huan River, NW of today's Anyang. In the 'Shi ji' (Records of the Grand Historian) by Sima Qian (died c 90 BC) these were described as 'the wastes of Yin' but they were not definitely recognised until the beginning of this century. In 1899 peasants began digging up and selling 'dragon bones', inscribed oracle bones of the late Shang which were ground up and sold as 'dragon bone medicine'. Wan Yirong (1845–1900), an epigrapher and archaeologist, noticed writing on some ground-up bones that he had bought as medicine and investigated their origins. Between 1928 and 1937, many seasons of excavation were undertaken in the area (these have been recorded by one of the leading archaeologists involved; Li Chi, 'Anyang', Seattle, University of Washington Press, 1976. Since 1950 excavations have continued.

The most dramatic finds include palace floors, the remains of large houses, a ceremonial altar and 11 massive royal tombs. In both the major building foundations (perhaps temples) and the royal tombs, human sacrifices have been found. The graves are cross-shaped underground pits (up to 19m by 14m) with ramps leading down to the tomb chamber where human sacrifices, articles of jade, bronze, bone, shell and pottery were laid out around the coffin. It has been estimated that each one might have required 7000 working days to dig out. A recent discovery was that of the tomb of Fuhao, consort of one of the late Shang kings, Wuding. Her tomb was smaller than those of the kings but it is significant for the perfection of its content, including lavishly decorated ritual bronzes with inscriptions and many tiny carved jades. Chariot burials (where chariots complete with horses and grooms) of the Shang have been found in Shandong but not yet in the Anyang area. The buildings, with their carefully prepared floors, seem to have relied greatly on pisé (tamped earth construction), just as at Zhengzhou. As yet, no wall has been found surrounding the Yin ruins; maybe there wasn't one, though the discovery at Zhengzhou and the persistence of walling cities in later dynasties makes this a surprising omission.

The larger houses and palaces were built above ground (smaller houses, assumed to be those of artisans rather than aristocrats were often semi-subterranean, a form that was not uncommon in the late neolithic) with hard floors and stone pillar-bases

ANYANG

(as in later buildings right up to the Qing). Bronze foundry sites, pottery kilns and bone workshops have also been found and under some of the larger floors are complex drainage channels. The Shang capital was burnt by the invading Zhou c 1066 BC, when the last king (whose burial has not been found) was also burnt to death.

The site of **Yin** can be visited by bus (a No. 1 passes the junction of Angang lu and Yinxu lu). Cross the railway line and follow the path which runs beside a bend in the river. Archaeological sites are not wildly exciting to non-archaeologists as they require imagination to recreate from the patches of earth but the walk is pleasant. The building on the site housing a study collection (the majority of the grand finds are to be seen either in the Provincial Museum in Zhengzhou or in the Historical Museum in Peking) is not open to the general public but is often opened to visiting groups.

The old city walls and surrounding moat of the small town still stand and the old town with its narrow streets and walled courtyards lies within. In the NW of the walled town is the *Tianning si ta* (Pagoda of the Heaven's Will Temple). Originally associated with a temple founded in the Sui, its first pagoda, according to literary sources, dated from 952. Popular belief says there was a pagoda in the Sui. The current pagoda is Ming in date. Octagonal in plan, five storeys high and built of brick in imitation of wooden construction with imitation brackets under each of the eaves, the first storey is unusually tall. There are windows for light and ventilation in the upper storeys and the pagoda is decorated in the Ming style with stucco Buddhas, Bodhisattvas and scenes from the life of the Buddha. The pagoda is unusual in that it does not taper towards the top which is adorned with a 10m Tibetan-style stupa. It is possible to climb to the top for a view over the old town.

The *Tomb of Yuan Shikai* is outside the town on the N side of the Huan River.

Yuan Shikai (1859–1916), a general of the late Qing, self-proclaimed emperor (1915), was a native of Xiangcheng in eastern Henan. He led one of the new regional armies founded towards the end of the Qing (which were to become the basis of local warlord power in the early 20C) and first sided with the reformist movement of 1898, only to betray the reformers (and the powerless emperor) to the Dowager Empress, probably because he could see who was strongest. Turning again, he joined the movement for constitutional reform in the last years of the Qing and was declared Premier in 1911. He took over from Sun Yat-sen as President of the Republic of China in April 1911 and was sufficiently confident of his personal power to declare himself Hongxian emperor in 1915, only to die in 1916, when China fell into division as local warlords struggled for power. His tomb is a mixture of the traditional Chinese form and Western influence, not uncharacteristic of the Republican era.

Very recently, the main road leading S out of Anyang has apparently been taken over by the recreational branch of the People's Liberation Army which runs China's first sauna and massage parlour, amongst other attractions.

32   Datong

Datong, the largest town in northern Shanxi, lies on the railway line from Peking to Mongolia and is today best known for its coal mine and China's last steam-engine factory, now going over to the production of diesel engines. Situated between two sections of the Great Wall, Datong was a frontier town for many hundreds of years and as capital of the Northern Wei (386–494) and the Liao (907–1125), two alien dynasties, preserves Buddhist cave temples and two early temple buildings.

Railway: as there is no airport, Datong is usually reached by rail from Peking in c 7–8 hours (it lies on the main Trans-siberian line to Mongolia and the USSR, and the northern line to Urumqi). There is also a line to Taiyuan (7–9 hours). The railway station is in the N of the town. Immediately outside the station there are usually many small stalls and street traders, including fortune tellers and performing monkeys.

Hotel: The Datong binguan is in the S of the town.

Its closeness to Mongolia meant that Datong has long served as a centre of trade with Mongolia. On the edge of the traditional Chinese border (before the full incorporation of Inner Mongolia in 1947), it was frequently overrun by alien groups and was twice made capital, under the Northern Wei and, later, under the Liao.

The Northern Wei, a group of probably Turkic origin, otherwise known as the Tabgatch (sinicised to Tuoba or Toba), established themselves in Datong (then known as Pingcheng) in 368, in a period of Chinese disunion. They later (494) moved their capital S to Luoyang. Fervent Buddhists, the Wei rulers began the great task of carving out cave temples at Yungang, just W of the town. They continued this devotional work after the move to Luoyang by financing the cave temples at Longmen.

Datong's second period of greatness came with the arrival of the Khitan (a Mongol group who had become semi-sedentary) who took advantage of a later period of Chinese disunion to establish the Liao dynasty with its capital in Datong (907–1125). The Liao made constant attempts to overthrow the Northern Song but were themselves swallowed up eventually by the Jin, ancestors of the Manchus. The major monuments remaining from the Liao are the halls, statues and Buddhist library of the Huayan temple. During later periods, when Datong was on the frontiers of Chinese control, it was surrounded by military colonies whose inhabitants, charged not only with the defences of the frontier but also with the maintenance of agricultural supplies on the borders, enjoyed special privileges and status. The town's walls, most of which still stand, were built during the early Ming in 1372. Made of stamped yellow earth (pise), they are some 7.5km in circumference.

A.   Within the Town

It is possible to walk to the temples from the hotel, or get a bus to the major intersection of the town. If you walk, turn right out of the hotel and take the first major turning right. Walk up this road until you come to a

Upper Hua yan temple
Lower Hua yan temple

Nine Dragon screen

●Shan hua temple

Datong Hotel

DATONG

N

major crossroads (about 1km) where on your right you will see a busy market and the huge roofs of the **Huayan Temple** beyond.

During the Liao and Jin this was the most important centre of Huayan (Kegon in Japanese) school of Buddhism, based on the Avatamsakasutra or Garland sutra). Huayan taught the essential sameness of all things, an idea that was close to the Taoist idea of an underlying principle that was to be sought.

The original temple was destroyed by fire in 1122. The layout today, of an upper and lower temple, dates from the Ming and most of the structures are Qing, although the main hall is Jin. The upper temple is unusual in that it faces E instead of S and not for reasons of topography; it is said that the Khitan were sun-worshippers (as well as Buddhists) and this is the reason for the orientation of the building.

The Upper Temple's *Daxiongbao dian* (Mahavira or Powerful Treasure Hall), said to date from 1140 (the only old building left in the ensemble where most are Qing in date), is a rare example of 12C northern building. Set on a high platform (over 4m high), it is a powerful nine-bay hall covering 1560 square metres. The scale of the whole is massive: the walls are well over 1m thick, hinting at freezing winters, and the ridge acroteria (on either end of the ridge) are 4.5m high. The form of the acroteria, a incurved beak (its name in Chinese is owl's beak), is strikingly different from the Ming and Qing acroteria seen on, for example, the roofs of the Forbidden City, where a realistically carved dragon-like head engulfs each end of the roof ridge. The owl's beak form is seen in Tang paintings (and as early as the Northern Wei in reliefs in the Yungang and Longmen caves) and persists in Shanxi (in the Guangsheng temple at Lin fen) into the Yuan and very early Ming. The ridge decoration on the northern end of the roof is an original from the Jin dynasty.

The interior of the hall is similarly massive and constructed on the 'reduced column' principle (with 12 fewer columns than might be expected), allowing for some equally massive Buddha figures. The five Buddhas (of the five directions, including the centre) are Ming, seated on elaborate high thrones, and there are 20 attendants whose figures are elegantly inclined. The three central Buddhas are carved from wood and were made in Peking in 1427, the rest (and the attendants) are of stucco. They are in the Sino-Tibetan style popular in Buddhist images of the 14–15C. The walls are painted with rather gaudy, very late Qing frescoes illustrating scenes from the life of the Buddha. They were painted by a local artist, Dong An, in 1875–1908. When I first visited Datong in 1976, the driver, who had previously taken us to the Yungang caves which are impressively dusty yellow and monochrome, exclaimed with pleasure at the brightness of the wall paintings which are more to the popular taste. The coffered ceiling is decorated with dragons, phoenix, flowers and Sanskrit letters. There is also a 2.5m-high wooden tower in the hall, a model of one of the corner towers of the city wall, made in the Qing by Li Yangui.

The Lower Temple is SE of the Upper Temple; the *library* (Bojiajiao cang dian or Bhagavan Hall), the second hall beyond the entrance, is a survivor from the Liao, built in 1038. It is a five-bay hall, four bays deep, with strong brackets holding up the eaves. It is a rare Liao construction and the architectural style is closer to the solid, simple Tang and Jin style than the more heavily decorated later styles. The interior ceiling is also Liao. On a platform stand 31 Liao stucco figures of great elegance. There are three central Buddhas (past, present and future) and the attendants are in different poses with flowingly modelled garments and inclined bodies.

The walls are lined with wooden bookcases, made to house Buddhist sutras, and constructed like tiny buildings with a wonderful 'suspended palace' at the rear. The architectural detail is minute and accurate and the construction is unique.

Returning to the road and turning right (E), beyond the crossroads, on the right is the Nine-dragon Screen. If you look down to the S at the crossroads, you can see the Drum Tower.

The *Nine-dragon Screen* was built in 1392 and stood, as a spirit wall (keeping out evil spirits) in front of the palace of the Ming founder's 13th son, who was viceroy of Shanxi. The palace was burnt down in the mid 17C, leaving only the ceramic screen. It is 45.5m long, 8m high and just over 2m thick, and covered with glazed tiles in five colours. Just above the base are figures of lions, tigers, elephants, unicorns and other small animals and above these are nine dragons in high relief, rising from waves. The top is modelled on a roof, with tiles and ridge acroteria. Though it stands in roughly its original position, the screen was moved some 10m in 1954. A comparable, though later, screen can be seen in the Forbidden City.

Returning to the crossroads, turn left, towards the Drum Tower and continue until you reach a crossroads with the hotel road, then turn right and you will find first the Friendship Store (on your right), then the hotel.

B.   The Yungang Caves

The **Yungang Caves**, 16km W of Datong, can be reached by taxi or by public bus (the bus station is on the left of the crossroads that lead to the Huayan temples, on the right).

The caves were hollowed out in a S-facing sandstone cliff formed by the Wuzhou River beginning in 453, and probably ending around 525, after the move to Luoyang, though one cave in particular (No. 3) is thought perhaps to be Sui in date. Though some of the caves at Dunhuang are slightly earlier, the Yungang caves are the earliest stone-carved caves in China (those in Dunhuang were decorated with stucco figures and wall paintings). The format came from Indian Buddhism. According to the 'Wei Shu' (History of the Wei), five Indian monks who were also accomplished sculptors arrived in Datong in 455, though the part they played in the carving is not known. There is much Indian influence in the carving, and that itself is heavily influenced by the Graeco-Buddhist style, evidenced in the tridents and acanthus leaves. Other influences came from Iranian and Byzantine sources—lions, weapons, bearded figures—but there is also much that is Chinese in the buildings depicted, the heavily decorated aureoles, and the use of Chinese images—dragons, phoenix, tigers.

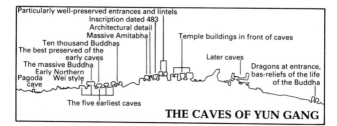

Particularly well-preserved entrances and lintels
Inscription dated 483
Architectural detail
Massive Amitabha
Ten thousand Buddhas
The best preserved of the
early caves
The massive Buddha
Early Northern
Pagoda   Wei style
cave

Temple buildings in front of caves

Later caves

Dragons at entrance,
bas-reliefs of the life
of the Buddha

The five earliest caves

THE CAVES OF YUN GANG

The caves stretch for about a kilometre and are grouped into three main sections: east, central and west. There are four caves in the E section (Nos 1–4), nine in the central section (5–13) and 40 in the west (14–53). Nos 16–20, the 'Five Tan Caves' are the earliest (453–462) and most impressive and were carved under the supervision of a monk called Tan Hao; most of those in the central section were carved between 462 and 495. The majority of the eastern and western caves date from c 495–524; quite a number in the western section were completed after the removal of the Wei capital to Luoyang.

Beginning with the earliest group, *Cave 20* has the largest figure, a seated Buddha with one surviving standing disciple on the right. The front of the cave has collapsed (there are square holes in the back wall indicating that the cave may have had a wooden façade), leaving the huge figure, nearly 14m high, exposed. The mandorla on the wall behind is composed of alternate rows of flames and small figures in low relief, Buddhas and musicians and attendants. The immobility of the figure is characteristic of the early Northern Wei style and the pattern-like effect of the folds, rendered almost like flames across the upper arm, is also characteristic of the early Wei.

The other early caves are all on the same pattern of an enlarged oval niche with a major, central Buddha figure. *Cave 19* is in three parts with a central Buddha over 16m high and two attendant Bodhisattvas with rather Grecian pleats to their robes, particularly that on the left. *Cave 18* is considered to be one of the finest at Yungang; the central Buddha, in the same rigid style, has rows of tiny Bodhisattvas on the folds of his robe and the crowned Bodhisattvas and almost caricatured disciples are extremely lively despite the rigidity of the style. An inscription outside *Cave 17* dates its carving to 480. Apart from the central figure with its standing and sitting attendants, there are bas-relief carvings all over the walls, including Indian apsareses (Buddhist angels) in transparent robes with silken scarves swirling around them. The standing Buddha in *Cave 16* has thick, almost chunkily folded robes and a face which is strongly reminiscent of Northern Wei sculpture at Luoyang, long and block-like, yet the hands are delicately moulded with distinct fingernails.

To take the rest of the caves in numerical order: *Cave 1* is most noted for its bas-reliefs of the life of the Buddha, with funny little Chinese buildings (whose roof acroteria resemble those of the Huayan temples in Datong), and scenes of hunting and horsemanship. In the centre of *Cave 2* is a pagoda-like pillar with interesting architectural detail: the brackets (like Ws) are interspersed with inverted V-shaped props, a form found in buildings from the Tang to the Yuan but which then disappeared. *Cave 3* is the largest of all and was probably once covered with a wooden temple. The figures are fleshier and more plastic than many others and it is thought that they may be as late as the Sui (for in their sensuous fleshiness, they approach the Tang style).

Caves 5, 6 and 7 lie behind the wooden temple and complex of galleries built against the cliff in 1652, and visited by the Kangxi emperor in 1697. He wrote the characters 'the unity of all doctrines' which can be seen at the entrance to Cave 6. The caves behind the wooden temple, protected from the elements, are in very good condition. Inside *Cave 5* is the largest Buddha figure at Yungang, nearly 17m high. It is said to have been carved at the order of the Xiaowen emperor of the Wei (471–500), in honour of his father, and it marks a progression from the stiff early images towards a serene, fleshier form, with more naturalistically modelled garments. The walls are covered with tiny Buddhas in niches and the lively flames of the aureole dart upwards to the ceiling. Serene Boddhisattvas with gently inclined heads stand in attendance.

Cave 6 is equally well-preserved but very different in appearance with its highly carved central tower (a form inherited from Indian cave carvings and ideal for the clockwise perambulating meditation that Buddhists perform), medium-sized Buddha figures in niches and outstanding low-relief depictions of scenes from the life of the Buddha which include Chinese figures (in Chinese dress) riding on Indian elephants. Scenes quite easy to identify are those of the historic Buddha going out on horseback, leaving a minute Chinese building, the hooves of the horse supported by kneeling figures whilst an apsara holds an Indian-style canopy over his head. In a similar scene on the eastern wall, the Buddha (again on horseback) meets an old crippled man with two sticks (in one of the revelations of the existence of human suffering to the previously innocent and over-protected prince). The Buddha's entry into the state of nirvana is also depicted: he lies with his head propped on one arm whilst a female orchestra plays below. In the central column, Buddhas and Bodhisattvas sit in deep niches with architectural roofs, surrounded by flying apsareses with floral garlands and orchestras. This cave, with its incredible variety of lively scenes, is said to have been commissioned by the Xiaowen emperor in honour of his mother (whilst Cave 5 was for his father).

In *Cave 7* the ceiling is particularly fine: a tangle of apsareses surround daisy-like lotus plaques and the female attendants depicted on the rear wall have charming, self-satisfied smiles. The whole reveals a mastery of forms and icons, in marked contrast with the solid rigidity of the early caves.

The entrance to *Cave 8* has extraordinary multi-headed figures: on the left, a five-headed Shiva with six arms clutching a bow and a bird amongst other things, sitting on a huge bird; on the right a three-headed Vishnu holding a bunch of grapes (an Iranian motif) sits on a bull. These figures are regarded as successful fusions of Indian icons with Chinese art forms (the bird, in particular) and the confident carving of these are other figures suggests that sculptors were no longer wrestling with unfamiliar iconography but were enjoying the mastery of their craft.

Caves 9 and 10 are entered through columns and lintels (in the style of the Indian caves) and are noted for the charming orchestra in niches with Chinese-style wooden balustrades in front. In *Cave 10* a particularly fine and elaborate entrance leads to an inner niche; the flat floral scrolls recall Near Eastern metalwork and anticipate Chinese porcelain decoration of later periods.

Cave 11 has an inscription dating its carving to 483 and recording the participation of over 50 donors who dedicated the cave to the Emperor and his family. According to the inscription, they paid for 95 major figures.

The tapering columns at the entrance to *Cave 12* have lush acanthus leaf bases and multiple Buddha figures in tiny niches all over them. The interior of the cave is architecturally divided, providing information on the construction and bracketing of contemporary timber building (none of which survives). Under the beams, above the Buddhas, are complex nets of pearl ropes.

Inside the entrance to *Cave 13* are two wonderful Bodhisattvas, rather flatly carved, the folds of their light silk robes indicated with simple lines.

Yungang Caves near Datong

There is evidence of landscape depiction in the wavelike peaks beside them (which recalls the Tang landscape painting at Dunhuang). A huge figure of Amitabha Buddha has its raised arm supported by a small, four-armed figure standing on the knee of the Buddha. Traces of paint on the walls in this and Caves 9–12 are the remains of paintings paid for by a local landowner during the Qing (as described in a stele erected by his son). Caves 14 and 15 have been rather badly eroded by the wind, owing to the collapse of the fronts.

Cave 21 is considered to be later than many others and may date from the late Northern Wei. It has a central pagoda.

Less attention is generally paid to the remaining caves, many of which are small. *Cave 50*, however, has the most extraordinary ceiling with casually arranged apsareses superimposed on a sketchily coffered ceiling, their trailing silk scarves curling amongst flying elephants and birds. There is another flying elephant on the E wall of *Cave 48*, approaching a reclining figure. This is Maya, mother of Sakyamuni, who dreamt that a white elephant entered her right side and subsequently the Buddha was born painlessly from the same spot.

On the road to the Yungang caves is the Buddhist **Guanyin tang** (Guanyin Hall), c 8km outside Datong, near *Fozi wan*. It was founded in 1038, under the Liao, apparently after the Bodhisattva Guanyin had appeared in the neighbourhood, when devout local people paid for a golden Guanyin figure and four attendant Bodhisattvas with ten guardian figures. It was rebuilt after a fire in 1651. A three-dragon screen of glazed tiles dating from the Ming (and similar to the nine-dragon screen in Datong) stands in front of the temple. The stone figures in the main hall are thought to be the Liao originals; they include Bodhisattvas, celestial guardians and Guanyin figure over 5m high.

In the southern suburbs of Datong is the **Shanhua si** (Temple of Good

Transformations), founded during the Kaiyuan period of the Tang (713–742) but largely destroyed by fire in 1122. Reconstruction took 15 years (1128–43). It was improved during the Ming and given its present name in 1445. Besides its function as a Buddhist temple, it was used by officials to practise and prepare for important ceremonies. The buildings are on the main N–S axis, beginning with the gate which contains the guardian figures. This was originally constructed in 1123-48, in the 'Song style' with 'moon-shaped' (lightly curved) beams. The guardians are Ming stucco figures. Behind is a *Hall of the Three Sages* (San sheng dian), built at the same time as the gateway, but in the Liao-Jin style.

The interior makes use of the 'reduced column' method. The figures, of the Buddha and the Bodhisattvas Manjusri and Samantabhadra, are Jin in origin but repainted and restored in the Qing. A stele records the restoration of the temple in 1176. The main hall, seven bays wide and five bays deep, which contains Liao sculpture (a central Buddha and 29 other figures including a six-armed Guanyin), is said to have been restored in 1123–48. The wall-paintings are Qing but in the 'Yuan style'. One of the side-buildings, to the W, a double-roofed pavilion of apparently two but actually three storeys (this is said to be Tang style), contains an inscription recording its construction in 1154. It is noted that this is only 100 years later than the Yingxian Pagoda (which also has concealed interior storeys; see below).

C.   Around Datong

More than 60km S of Datong is the **Yingxian Pagoda**, the earliest wooden pagoda still standing in China. The trip can be made by public bus or taxi. Built in 1056, on the main axis of the Fogong si (Temple of the Buddha's palace), the pagoda is octagonal in plan and is just over 67m high. Its position on the main axis of the temple is reminiscent of the layout of the Great Goose pagoda temple in Xi'an. The first storey of the pagoda is more substantial than the rest: a mud and earth wall stand back from a columned gallery which is surmounted by a double eaved roof. The upper part of the pagoda is constructed entirely of timber and consists of four galleries with roofs in between.

The actual structure is more complex than it appears as there are four invisible (from the exterior) storeys, making an actual total of nine storeys. The pagoda is topped by an iron spire. 60 different types of bracket have been used in the construction which has been intently studied by the doyen of architectural historians, Chen Mingda, who has linked the construction method to the description of pagoda construction in the 12C architectural manual 'Ying zao fa shi'.

Though there were originally more figures, there remains an 11m-high Liao Buddha inside the pagoda and, in recent repairs, a cache of holy relics was found including manuscript and woodblock-printed Buddhist sutras and coloured Buddhist images printed on silk. Such finds are of particular interest as they are presumably contemporary with the construction (this is reinforced by internal dates), which is early for colour-printing.

A spectacular monastery, c 75km SE of Datong (reached in c 2 hours by either taxi or a CITS tourist bus) is the **Xuankong si** (Temple Suspended in the Void), perched on a cliff in the Heng Mountains. The temple complex was founded in the 6C, during the late Northern Wei, and consists of 40 'rooms', caves in the cliff fronted with timber façades perched perilously on timbers jutting out from the cliff. Over 80 Buddhist figures, in iron, bronze, stucco and stone, are contained in the chambers (not seen by me).

The temple can be visited by CITS tourist excursion (most days) and the *Railway Engine Factory* can also be visited but only by appointment through CITS, whose office is in the Datong Hotel. I believe that the last steam engine was made in 1985 (when I last visited before that they were still being produced) but there may be some still there for enthusiasts.

33 Taiyuan

Taiyuan is the capital of Shanxi province and lies in the Taiyuan basin where some of the world's richest deposits of coal and iron are to be found. It is today a major steel centre, twinned with Newcastle-upon-Tyne, but near the city are some important temples and it is the best starting point for the northern Buddhist mountain, Wutai shan.

Shanxi (West of the Mountains) province, like Shaanxi (capital Xi'an) and Gansu (capital Lanzhou) provinces, is largely covered by a thick deposit of fine wind-laid yellow earth, known as *loess*. The loess deposit, up to 100m thick, creates the characteristic landscape of the area, with rolling yellow hills traversed by deep gullies in which rivers and streams run. These are the characteristic 'vertical' cleavages created by the surface 'cement' which binds the loose grains. In the loess highlands, whole villages are created by tunnelling into the perpendicular loess cliffs, each house tunnel faced with an arched entrance of timber lattice stuck with window paper. Above, in the hillside, are the village fields, sometimes dotted with chimneys 'so that one sees the curious phenomenon of smoke issuing at numerous points in the midst of a field of grain' (George Babcock Cressey, 'China's Geographic Foundations', New York, McGraw Hill, 1934). Loess is very fertile soil but the vertical cleavages make agriculture difficult, except on the highlands which are often difficult of access.

Railway: Taiyuan lies on a main line from Peking and is also linked by rail to Datong, in the N of the province. The station is on Jianshe bei lu, in the E of the town centre.

Airport: 14km S of the town centre; there are daily flights to and from Peking and flights once or twice a week to Xi'an, Guangzhou, Chengdu, Lanzhou and to other centres.

Hotel: The Yingze binguan (perhaps one of the 'two semi-foreign hotels' referred to in the 1924 'Japanese Railway Guide') is on Yingze lu, a 10-minute walk due W from the railway station.

Neolithic remains in the Taiyuan area are mainly of the Yangshao or painted pottery culture, including the late settlement at Dongtaibao zhuang where horse and pig skeletons as well as bone artefacts have been found. When the Zhou dynasty was founded (c 1066 BC) the Fen river valley surrounding today's Taiyuan was made a fiefdom, eventually called Jin, a name that is commemorated in the Jin ci (Jin temple) outside the city, founded in honour of the first Jin ruler. Remains of the city wall of the Jin city built in 497 BC can be seen from the road to the Jin ci.
    Situated in the far north, the Taiyuan area was vulnerable to attack from outsiders: the Huns attacked in 200 BC, and the Tobas (who founded the Wei dynasty with their first capital in Datong, just to the N of Taiyuan) in AD 396. During the Tang dynasty the Taiyuan area was an important part of the frontier defences. In the Five Dynasties period, after the fall of the Tang, the area was repeatedly invaded and the then-major city of Jinyang was completely destroyed in 979 after several attempts to retake it by the founder of the Song dynasty. Not only was the town razed to the ground but the waters of the Fen river and its tributaries were diverted to sweep away the remains. The surviving inhabitants settled in what was to become Taiyuan where the emperor apparently ordered that, instead of the usual regular grid of streets, there should be numerous T-junctions, which look like the character for 'nail' in Chinese, symbolising the 'nailing down' of Jinyang. Several of these junctions can still be seen.
    In the early Ming the founding emperor appointed one of his sons as viceroy to the province, with his headquarters in Taiyuan. This did not prevent the local people (who had suffered under subsequent viceroys) from welcoming the local peasant leader Li Zicheng when he tried to overthrow the Ming in 1644. Members of the Ming royal family were killed (though one escaped and his descendants still live nearby) but when Li Zicheng was defeated the Manchu Qing dynasty captured the city after two assaults. It is said that a local feast day continued to commemorate Li Zicheng until the 20C. Confusingly, the day (18th of the 6th month in the lunar calendar) was called 'Resist Li Zicheng' (apparently to mislead the Qing authorities) but it had become a token of anti-Manchu feeling for all hairdressers, compelled by the Manchus to dress all Chinese men's hair in the pigtail or queue as a sign of submission, took the day off.
    In 1900 Shanxi province, and Taiyuan in particular, became a major centre for anti-missionary activity. The Boxer movement had started in Shandong province and, though originally anti-Manchu, it also focussed its attention on foreigners with isolated missionaries as vulnerable victims. In Taiyuan a mob set fire to the British mission,

killing one woman. The killing led to a massacre when the provincial governor (a Boxer supporter) assembled all the missionaries on the pretext of protecting them and had them publicly killed on 30 June. 44 foreigners, including women and children, were killed together with 17 Chinese converts. This represented the majority of the provincial total of missionary deaths (47 in all in 1901, with another 142 killed elsewhere in China in that year). In a book written by a survivor, 'A Thousand Miles of Miracle in China', by Archibald Glover of the China Inland Mission (London, 1904), the foreigners' import of opium is held almost equally to blame with the anti-foreign Boxer movement, though he also takes an almighty and most unecumenical swipe at the Roman Catholic missionaries in Shanxi province.

Anti-missionary campaigns did not rid the province of foreigners; the railway was half-financed by Russian money and built by French engineers, mines were owned by the British and the post office was partly French-run. The university was largely directed by Timothy Richard, an English Baptist missionary who managed to get some of the Chinese government's reparation for the Boxer damage (the portion of the 'Boxer indemnity' paid by Shanxi province) to found the Shanxi university 'on Western lines' in Taiyuan in 1902.

From 1912 to just before 1949 Taiyuan was the headquarters of one of the most famous of China's 'warlords', Yan Xishan (1883–1960). A loyal supporter of Chiang Kai-shek, when not pursuing military campaigns under the direction of the Generalissimo, he promoted 'the moral and social welfare of his people' and was known by supporters as 'the Model Governor' (for he was Governor of Shanxi province),

Mining, metal-working and coal-mining have a long history in the area, with bronze working dating from the Warring States and the coal mines mentioned in Tang and Song literary accounts. Iron figures have been cast in the area since the Tang and glazed tile works seem to have operated since then if not before, the last two techniques being evident in many temple furnishings and roofing.

The holdings of the **Provincial Museum** are distributed amongst two temples in the city centre, thereby combining architecture and temple visiting with viewing the museum collections.

The nearest part to the hotel is the **Chunyang gong Temple**: turn left out of the hotel along Yingze lu. At Wuyi Square (left) turn left along the side of the square. The Chunyang gong is on the right-hand side of the major turning to the left. Founded during the Ming (in the Wanli reign, 1573–1619), with the three-storey hall added during the Qianlong reign (1736–96), the temple, whose name means Purity of Yang (with yang meaning the masculine, light, positive principle) was a Taoist foundation (as its name of 'gong' rather than the normal Buddhist 'si', suggests).

A member of the Ming ruling family, Zhu Qiugui, wrote a poem, said to be in praise of the beauty of the temple (though the reference to monkeys is obscure):

> The clamour of the world does not reach here,
> Clouds gather within the blue arch,
> White geese gather by the water and green monkeys sleep alone
>   on the sand.
> Old pines block the moonlight,
> Bamboos are blown by the wind and it is said that nothing is worth
>   more than purity and tranquillity.

Within the temple are four courtyards. The major, three-bay hall is the *Lu Hall*, dedicated to Lu Dongbin, an historical figure who has been immortalised (in more ways than one) as one of the eight Taoist immortals.

He is thought to have been born in Yongle county in Shanxi province (not far from Taiyuan), into an official family, and was presented with a magic sword by a fire-dragon when he was 20 years old (still unmarried and on a trip to Lu Shan in Jiangxi province). He spent the rest of his life slaying demons with his magic sword, is worshipped as the God of Inkmakers and usually represented with his sword and a horsetail fly-whisk (also known as a 'cloud-sweeper' and a symbol of the ability to fly through the air and walk on clouds).

Behind the hall are multi-storeyed buildings 'strewn at random, winding and circling in most unusual forms' as the 'Dictionary of Famous Sites' has it; ramshackle and charming country-style temple architecture. The 'Towering Tower' (Weige) of the back courtyard is the tallest building and affords a view of the city. Another building of note in the first courtyard is the octagonal pavilion on a square base. Exhibits scattered in the 'random' buildings include ceramics, bronzes, ivory, bamboo and woodcarving, lacquer, paintings, stone-rubbings, embroidery and enamels, with some marvellous sculpture: stone figures from the Sui and later, bronzes and iron figures, mainly from the Ming.

The other part of the Museum is to be found just beyond the far (eastern) side of Wuyi Square. Cross the square to the far side and take the main road leading E. Just before reaching Jianshe lu (on which the station lies) turn left. The **Confucian Temple** (Wen miao), containing the main part of the Provincial Museum, is on your left. The temple, originally built during the Jin (1115–1234), was expanded in the Ming when it was situated in the W of the town. It was moved to this site in 1881 as the previous location was low-lying and damp.

The main structures from the spirit wall at the southern extremity of the considerable enclosure are: Six-sided Well Pavilion, Lattice Star Gate, Gate of Completeness, Hall of Completeness and the Hall of the Worship of the Sage. The courtyards are broad and filled with trees, and the building style is lively. Exhibits include Shanxi's revolutionary history, Shang bronzes, weaponry, calligraphy attributed to Gu Kaizhi (of the Eastern Jin, 317–420).

Just N of the Museum is the **Chongshan si** (Temple of the Veneration of Goodness), founded under the Tang and previously known as the White Horse Temple, the Zongshan si or Temple of the Emulation of Goodness, gaining its current name in the Ming.

Like the Confucian Temple, this was originally situated outside the old town but when the city moat was enlarged in the mid 14C the temple had to be moved. In 1381 Zhu Gang (third son of the founder of the Ming, Zhu Yuanzhang) enlarged the temple and dedicated it to the memory of his mother. The main hall was nine bays wide and over 30m high. Much of the temple was destroyed by fire in 1864 leaving only the gate, bell tower, side wings and the seven-bay *Dabei dian* (Hall of Great Compassion) with its double-eaved, green and yellow tiled roof, supported by brackets and decorated ceiling inside. Within the hall is a thousand-eyed, thousand-armed Guanyin some 8.5m high, flanked by the other bodhisattvas, Samantabhadra and Manjusri. The figures and the hall itself are all early Ming.

The temple contains an exhibition of Buddhist sutras printed in the Song, Yuan and Ming dynasties, most dated. They include some leaves from a later printing (1108) from the blocks cut in Chengdu for the first printing of the Buddhist canon.

Returning to the square, the hotel is easily regained.

Other sites in the city that can be visited by taxi include the Mosque and the Twin-pagoda Temple.

The *Mosque* is on the E side of Jiefang lu, NW of the hotel. A stele preserved in the mosque states that it was founded in the Zhenyuan reign period of the Tang (785–805) and rebuilt in the Song during the years 1034–38. The surviving buildings include a Ming great hall of timber and brick construction with timber columns sunk in the wall, interior columns decorated with gold and Arab-style decoration. Arabic inscriptions from the Koran are found on the walls. The minaret in the courtyard is Ming with 'flying eaves' and there is a pair of stele pavilions with a 'grass style' inscription by Huang Tingjian and colophons by Zhao Ziang of the Yuan and Fu Qing of the early Qing.

The **Shuang ta** (Twin Pagoda) **Temple** is in the SE suburbs in *Haozhuang* (Hao Village). The pair of *pagodas* which give the temple its popular name (it is actually called the Yongzuo or Eternal Good Fortune Temple) were built in the Wanli period of the Ming (1573–1619) by a monk called Fodeng, who later left for Wutai shan. They are of brick construction, nearly 55m high, with multiple brick eaves with brick brackets underneath and glazed tiles on top. They can be climbed as both have steps inside. The rebel leader Li Zicheng (who succeeded in overthrowing the Ming, only to be overthrown himself by the Qing) wrote a poem in praise of the twin pagodas which includes the line: 'The two pagodas of Haozhuang pierce the sky'.

Beneath the pagodas is the *temple*, with a main hall and two side wings, all made entirely of brick with brick-vaulted ceilings, the bricks used to imitate wooden construction with columns and brackets. The 'beamless brick hall' of Nanjing is the most famous (and southernmost) example of the type; examples such as this and that on Wutai shan are less well-known. Peonies planted in the temple are said to date back to the Ming.

Outside Taiyuan, the major site is that of the *Jin ci* (Jin Temple), 25km SW of the town, but other sites, including the Buddhist cave carvings of *Tianlong shan* (Heavenly Dragon Mountain), 40km SE of the, town are also worth visiting (and are rarely seen). Where the mountains rise from the flat plain, pines and other conifers are thick on the slopes and a number of springs rise in the area. There are eight caves on the eastern peak, 13 on the west, carved at different periods from the Eastern Wei (534–550) to the Tang, with the majority (15) dating from the Tang. The great Buddha of Cave 9 (Tang in date) is now exposed and many of the caves are

Guardian figure at the Jin ci, outside Taiyuan

in rather poor condition, though the traces reveal a high standard of carving. A temple originally stood in front of the caves and the ancient pines were remarked on by a Ming writer.

The **Dafo si** (Great Buddha Temple) is 20km NW of Taiyuan in *Tutang cun* (Earth Hall Village), surrounded by a thicket of fine old pines which provide a major reason for the inhabitants of Taiyuan to visit it. A stele records a local legend that the ground here split during the Han dynasty, revealing a great Buddha figure; a temple was consequently built on the spot. The temple was first constructed in the 6C but the surviving buildings are Ming and Qing, with two stone lions (late 12C or early 13C) the only survivors of earlier works. The storeyed buildings on the E and W sides of the temple are dated to 1541 and they contains groups of clay figures of the Buddha with disciples (the Buddha some 9m high) which also date from the Ming.

The **Jin ci** (Jin Temple) is, today, a large ensemble of buildings from very different dates in a large enclosure crossed by a stream, set against a hill.

The founding date of the temple is uncertain but it is mentioned in a literary account of the Northern Wei (386–534): 'The…temple is surrounded by mountains and rivers. An outdoor pavilion stands by the spring, with its beams reaching out over the water.' The temple, which must therefore have been founded some 1500 years ago, was built to commemorate the founder of the state of Jin, who lived c 1000 BC.

The earliest parts of the temple still standing are found at the back of the temple enclosure, farthest from the entrance. Because of the local topography, the halls, set against the hill, are E-facing (rather than S-facing), and the stream, led through the enclosure, flows in front of them. Inside the gate (the original entrance, the *Jingqing men* or Gate of Pure Landscape, is further to your left), there is a wide open space with an old stage, the *Shuijing tai* (Water Mirror Platform), in the centre, probably dating from the Ming. A stage, for the performance of dramas, often financed by trade guilds, was commonly found in village squares or non-Buddhist temples, and was used particularly by guilds (of carpenters, metal workers, etc) for performances to celebrate their annual festivals. Stages in village squares were also used by itinerant opera troupes.

Behind the stage is a bridge over the stream, the *Huixian qiao* (Bridge of the Gathered Immortals), and behind that is the *Metal Men Platform* (Jinren tai). The iron figures of warriors in armour, slightly larger than life size, were first cast in the Song but, owing to wear and tear, are somewhat composite by now. That in the SW has an inscription on its chest which dates its casting to 1097, that in the NW was cast in the following year though its head was apparently recast in the Ming in 1423. The figure in the SE has an inscription dating its casting to 1089 though its head was remade in 1926, and that in the NE was entirely recast in 1913. According to the gazetteer of Taiyuan ('Tai yuan xian zhi'), the figures were placed here to guard the source of the Jin River.

Behind is the *Xian dian* (Hall of Offerings) where offerings to the Holy Mother were laid out.

The Holy Mother was the mother of Prince Shuyu (the founder of Jin) and her cult gradually eclipsed that of her son. She was believed to be possessed of magic powers, able to bring rain and good fortune and is a good example of the mythicisation of history, not an uncommon feature of Chinese popular religion where historical figures gradually accrued magic powers. The Hall of Offerings was built in 1168, when the cult of the Holy Mother, 'illuminating and helpful', was beginning to overtake that of her son. It was restored in 1594 and 'rebuilt in the original style' in 1955 (though it is not stated which of the two original styles was chosen).

The three-bay hall is two bays deep, its roof ridge decorated with glazed tiles (Shanxi province specialised in fine glazed tiles). The strong, simple brackets supporting the deeply projecting eaves are characteristic of pre-Qing architecture.

Beyond the Hall, in front of the Hall of the Holy Mother (Shengmu dian) is the '*Flying Bridge*' (Fei liang) over one of the three springs in the temple. Though a bridge over the spring was mentioned in Li Daoyuan's 'Shui jing zhu' (Annotations to the Water Classic) of the Northern Wei, the bridge was first built in its cross-shaped form in the Northern Song, when the Hall of the Holy Mother was constructed, and it was restored in 1955. 34 small octagonal pillars with lotus bases stand in the pool as supports for the timber construction of brackets and beams. The crossbeams, known in Chinese as 'fei liang' or 'flying beams' give the bridge its name. Though such cross-shaped 'architectural' bridges were known from literature, this is a rare surviving example.

On the far side of the bridge is the *Hall of the Holy Mother*, one of the earliest timber halls in China. First built in 1023–32 during the Northern Song, it was restored in 1102 and in the Yuan and Ming but restoration in each case did not affect the style or construction of the original. The E-facing hall is seven bays wide, six bays deep with a double-eaved roof with decorative glazed tiles especially on the ridge.

The eight wooden columns at the front of the hall with writhing dragons twisted around them are the earliest surviving examples of a highly decorative form illustrated in the early 12C architectural manual 'Ying zao fa shi' (Building Methods and Styles). In order to increase the internal space, fewer columns are used in the interior of the hall where the roof structure is clearly visible. There are 16 fewer columns than you would expect and the method is called (with little imagination), the 'reduced column style'. Outside, the brackets supporting the eaves (whose projection beyond the columns is considerable) are large and simple, characteristic of earlier timber construction. The eaves are lifted at the extremities, lightening the heavy roof of a most impressive building.

The contents of the building are also extremely important. There is a central image of the 'Holy Mother', surrounded by 42 smaller female figures, most of which are Song in date. The life-size figures are of a clay and straw mixture built up on a wooden frame, with a top layer of finer clay which is brightly painted. Four of the women wear officials' headdresses and costumes, the others, more naturalistically depicted, appear to be attendants. The large pair of temple guardians outside the hall were originally Song in date although that on the right-hand side is a 1950s' replacement.

Other buildings within the enclosure include a *Temple to Taitai*, legendary controller of the Fen river and patron of local agriculture (immediately left of the Hall of the Holy Mother; and the *Mother of Water Tower* (Shuimu lou), a tall structure (a Ming construction of 1545 rebuilt in 1844).

The 'mother of water' legend concerns a young peasant girl whose tyrannical mother-in-law made her spend her whole time fetching water from a distant well. The generous girl nevertheless gave water to an old man who then presented her with a magic horsewhip which she could wave over the water pots and they were magically filled. One day the wicked mother-in-law found the whip and waved it in the house, whereupon water gushed from a pot, threatening a flood. The girl averted disaster by sitting on the water pot. A local saying commemorates the deed: 'The girl of the Liu family sits on the water pot, flourishing a whip she waters the horses'.

In front of the temple is an octagonal pavilion built over the 'Ever Young' (Nanlao) Spring which bubbles with water at 17°C throughout the year. Water from this and the other springs in the Jin ci irrigates the surrounding countryside and helps provide electricity for Taiyuan. In a poem in praise of the Jin Temple, the Tang poet Li Bai wrote the lines: 'Water like green jade flows in the Jin Temple, the waves are like dragons' scales and the banks are green'.

Below the octagonal pavilion, beside the spring, is a small stone boat-shaped pavilion, the *Unmoored Boat* (Buji zhou), near a small stupa-shaped pillar in the water. This is said to mark the grave of Zhang Lang who, according to legend, divided the Jin River.

The river splits near its source and local peasants used to quarrel about sharing the water. In order to solve local disputes, officials put a vat of boiling oil containing ten strings of copper cash near the source of the river and challenged people to remove the money: according to the amount removed, the water would be diverted. Zhang Lang managed to remove seven strings of cash before succumbing to his burns; thereafter seven-tenths of the water has flowed N.

On the N side of the temple complex, just N of the Hall of Offerings, is a *Tang Stele Pavilion* (Tangbei ting), containing a stele dating to 647, inscribed with a text by the second emperor of the Tang dynasty who visited the temple in that year, praising the virtues of the founder of the Jin and asking his protection. The second stele is a copy of the first made in 1773. Further N is a late building (1771), the *Tang Shu yu ci* (Temple to Prince Shu yu) which includes stone-carved inscriptions of poems by Mao Zedong and Zhu De (Commander of the Red Army).

At the back of the enclosure, N of the Hall of the Holy Mother, are several natural caves in the hillside, some decorated with figures of local deities, in one of which lived Fu Shan (1608–84), a calligrapher, painter, poet, philosopher and Ming loyalist, who also wrote a treatise on gynaecology. He became a Taoist when the Ming fell and, despite personal entreaties from the Kangxi emperor, refused to accept official posts and imperial audiences. The cave in which he lived is called *Yun tao* (Staying in the Clouds). There is a small exhibition on the life and work of Fu Shan in a building on the right just inside the entrance (across the stream), in the NE corner of the enclosure.

34   The Wutai Mountain

The **Wutai Mountain**, whose name means 'Five Platforms', rises some 3000m above sea-level roughly between Taiyuan and Datong in Shanxi province, not far from the border with Hebei province. It is the northern Buddhist holy mountain, supposedly once inhabited by the Bodhisattva Manjusri, the god of wisdom. Manjusri is usually represented with a sword (to cleave ignorance) and a flat oblong object, representing a palm-leaf manuscript of the text of the Perfection of Wisdom. He often rides on a lion. Though the centre was huge in the Tang dynasty, at the height of its popularity, today its major temples are concentrated in a depression surrounded by mountains.

Hotels: before 1986 all visitors stayed in one of three hostels; No. 3 (highly recommended) was attached to the Tayuan (Pagoda) Temple in the main village. Visitors were given rooms (with baths and rather leaky central heating in winter) in a series of courtyards, and ate in a communal dining room across a lane. Any other facilities (shops, post office) were available in the village, Tai huai. A new hotel has been built in the Chinese style, S of the village. I haven't stayed in it as it was under construction when I visited Wutai, but it looked quite nice, set amongst fields, and presumably offers the usual facilities.

Transport: it is possible to reach Wutai by public transport, taking a train from Taiyuan or Datong to Xin xian (on the Taiyuan–Datong line) and then a public bus to Tai huai (taking care not to descend at Wutai xian for this is the county town and not the centre of Buddhist temples). If you do this, however, it would be virtually impossible to see the two earliest standing temples in China, which are of great intrinsic beauty, and dramatically sited, as they are isolated and well off the main road. As they are so lovely, it is best to go to Wutai from Taiyuan by car. A taxi can be booked through CITS (in the hotel), for three or four days (c 200 yuan in 1985), the price fixed in advance. Remember that you will have to pay for the driver's accommodation and food, en route and in Wutai, so he counts as an extra person. The trip from Taiyuan, including stops at the Nanchan and Foguang temples, covers some 240km and takes about 8 hours.

The 'platforms' are five peaks, north, south, east, west and central, rising in and around a depression in a now rather bare but imposing mountainous area.

Neolithic implements have been found in the vicinity but its Buddhist history seems to have begun after the Han with the first record of a temple being restored in the area in the Northern Wei (late 5C). By the Northern Qi there were over 200 temples in the mountain area. The Bodhisattva Manjusri was said to have appeared on Wutai,

Landscape with barrel-vaulted mud-brick houses and brick kiln near Wutai shan

hence its consecration, and it became a centre for the study of the Avatamsaka sutra, the principle sutra of the Huayan syncretist school (Kegon in Japanese) which viewed the universe as ordered, the world of principle and phenomena being fused, with everything leading to the centre, the Buddha. The growth of Wutai as a Buddhist centre before and during the Tang period and its subsequent relative retrenchment (as a result of the late Tang persecution of Buddhism) is still evident in the fact that the two earliest surviving buildings, the Nanchan si (782) and Foguang si (857), are today well outside the central circle of peaks where they were once part of a larger centre.

The Japanese monk Ennin made a pilgrimage to China, ancestral home of Japanese Buddhism from 838–847 and left a diary which includes many references to Wutai. He described the five peaks or platforms as looking like 'upturned bowls' and perhaps fancifully described how he was frequently menaced by a lion (associated with the Bodhisattva Manjusri) as he made trips to the peaks. As lions are not native to China, the apparition was viewed as miraculous. He was impressed by the brocade-like covering of alpine flowers on the high peaks which are still to be seen, as well as by the cold of the mountainous area where he claimed there were glaciers (apparently still unmelted since the Ice Age but they have certainly melted since Ennin's visit). Some of the treasured relics he viewed in the temples there included part of the upper skull of a minor Buddha brought from India in the early 7C. Looking like a 'pumice stone', it had 'white hair...about five inches long, apparently grown out since it had been shaved'.

Ennin left very detailed descriptions of relics and icons at Wutai: the portrait of 'Priest Big Shoes' who had been given a pair of miraculous shoes by Manjusri which rather mysteriously enabled him to make 15,000 robes and 75,000 meals for his fellow monks; the revolving sutra library in the Tayuan si (still in existence); the miraculous Manjusri image in the same temple whose lion breathed vapours, emitted light and manifested auspicious signs, all of which were reported to the throne. In the Jinge si (Temple of the Golden Tower) just 8km from Tai Huai, near the Southern Platform, there used to be a relic of a Japanese monk, Reisen, which was of particular interest to Ennin. This was a piece of the skin of his arm, on which Reisen had drawn a picture of the Buddha, in a Buddhist mortification of the flesh that was abhorrent to Confucian or traditionalist Chinese who believed firmly that one did not have the right to destroy or damage one's body and that mutilation would cause problems for the soul after death.

The importance of Wutai in the Tang was evidenced by imperial favour: annually the court sent incense, pearl-covered banners, jade, golden incense-burners, flowered carpets, silk floss, scarves and 450kg (1000lb) of tea, as well as providing annual feasts for thousands of monks.

Despite the late Tang suppression of Buddhism, there was an upsurge of imperial interest in Wutai during the Ming, when some impressive additions were made to many of the temples. By then the mountain had become a special place of pilgrimage for Mongolian Lamaist Buddhists, partly because the mountain is not that far from Mongolia but fundamentally because the Bodhisattva Manjusri had special significance in Lamaism. It became the favoured place for burial amongst Mongolians who could afford to make the pilgrimage bearing the body of a parent. In the summer months of June and July Mongolians and Tibetans still come to Wutai, partly for religious reasons, partly for the animal markets that are held there then, a mixture of trade and faith which was characteristic of medieval religious centres throughout the world but which we in the west have rather lost track of.

On the road to Wutai from Taiyuan, the following temples may be visited: Nanchan si, Yanqing si, Guangji si, Foguang si and Jinge si. If time is short, do not miss the Nanchan si and the Foguang si (you could do the others on the return trip).

The **Nanchan si** (Southern Meditation Temple) is the first temple you reach, before arriving at Wutaixian cheng. It is in *Lijiazhuang*, near Dongzhizhen, in Wutai xian; a turning off the main road to the left. Though there are buildings from various periods in the temple today, the most important is the small main hall, built in 782 and containing a group of figures from the same period. It is thought that it survived the late Tang persecution of Buddhism which involved the dissolution and destruction of many temples because of its isolated position, away from the centre of Wutai. Though much restored, it retains its original proportions and structural features and is the earliest surviving timber-frame building in China. Restoration is evident from comparison with photographs from the early 1950s where the roof is similar but the two façade windows are circular in form; today they are rectangular with a simple lattice of uprights. A lovely little hall of perfect proportions, it is the ideal starting point for anyone interested in Chinese architecture (and I feel that it is always helpful to start with something small; in Suzhou, the gardens make more sense if you start with the tiny Master of Nets Garden).

Standing on a high stone platform, the three-bay hall has an impressive roof with considerable eaves projection supported on simple but massive under-eaves brackets and a ridge decorated with the incurving 'owls' tails' at either end that are characteristic of pre-Ming buildings. An unusual and pleasing feature is the variation in the size of the bays, with the central bay somewhat wider than the two on either side. The variation conveys an impression of grandeur even in a small hall. Bracketing is restricted to simple, inverted W brackets on top of the columns with none of the inter-columnar bracketing that came later. Two elegant bronze urns stand beside the steps, their colour harmonising with the plain dark wood of the façade. The 17 statues inside the hall, set on a platform, comprise a central Buddha on a throne with a mandorla or aureole simply decorated with flowers in relief, and attendants, guardians and Bodhisattvas (including Manjusri on his lion to the Buddha's right), in natural poses, slightly inclined towards the Buddha, forming a composition of great elegance. There is no ceiling inside the hall so the solid timber construction of the roof can be clearly seen.

Beyond the Nanchan si is the *Yanqing si* (Extended Celebration Temple) in *Puwen cun*, whose main hall dates from the Jin (1115–1234). The hall is similar to that of the Nanchan si but the three bays are of even span and intercolumnar brackets are used. The two central columns are topped with horned beasts' heads, an unusual form found also in the Guangji si. In front of the hall is a Northern Song stone sutra pillar (sometimes called a dharani column) dated 1035. Standing on a lotus base, the 7m sutra pillar is a sort of elongated form of the Tang-style stupa or reliquary, with a stupa-shaped top.

The *Guangji si* (Temple of Extensive Succour) is on Xi jie, inside the western city gate of the county town of *Wutai xian*. It was founded in the Yuan, in the Zhizheng reign period (1341–70) but extensively rebuilt during the Qing though the figures inside the hall are thought to be original, and the structure owes more to the Yuan than the Qing, with simple bracketing (columnar and inter-columnar brackets). The columns are all topped with the same horned beast-heads seen in the hall of the Yanqing si, a rather barbaric northern form. There is a fine, if stumpy, sutra pillar just below the hall with Buddhist scriptures carved on the stem, and little figures set under the canopy just below the lotus top.

The **Foguang si** (Temple of Buddha's Glory) is well off the main road to Tai huai, N of the county town of Wutai, in Foguang xin cun, NE of Doucun xiang, set against terraced slopes. It contains a number of early buildings but the Eastern Great Hall dates from 857 and, until the discovery of the small Nanchan si in the early 1950s, was regarded as the earliest surviving timber building in China. It was discovered in 1937 by China's foremost architectural historian, Liang Sicheng (1901–72), a son of the late Qing reformer, Liang Qichao, who found the date of construction recorded in an inscription on an interior beam. The hall is at the back of the temple which, probably because of the mountainous terrain, faces west along a valley.

The temple was founded in 471–499 but largely destroyed in the great Buddhist persecution of 845. The Eastern Great Hall (a comparatively modest building) was built in 857, in a period of relaxation of repression, to replace the grander buildings. Towards the front of the temple, the Manjusri Hall (on the left) is a Jin (1115–1234) construction, whilst the rest of the buildings are Ming or Qing.

You enter the temple through a steeply-stepped, tunnel-like gate which leads to the first courtyard, with tall stone sutra pillars and the *Manjusri Hall* on the left. The hall dates to 1137 and is seven bays wide, still preserving the relatively strong and simple bracketing system. The roof was restored in the Yuan, which accounts for the later style of the ridge acroteria which contrast with the older, incurving owls' tails on the Eastern Hall. The figures within the temple were being entirely remade (by a most effective local craftsman) in 1985.

The *Eastern Hall* stands above the Manjusri Hall and is also a seven-bay, single-storey hall with the most magnificent eaves projection supported on four tiers of cantilevers, clearly seen under the eaves. Though the Nanchan si is perhaps more pleasing and unusual in its general proportions, the structure of the roof and eaves of this hall, with its huge brackets, is incredibly impressive. The roof ridge is finished with a pair of glazed owls' tails and a central pagoda in glazed tile (all of which I suspect are fairly recent but the owls' tails at least are in keeping with the original). In contrast with the chunky structure of the exterior eaves, the interior beams (spanning from front to back) are lightly curved 'moon beams'. Note, too, that the ridge purlin supporting the rafters has no king post (as would be found in Ming and Qing buildings) but is instead supported on a truss in the form of an inverted V. The statues in the hall are also late Tang in date, with the exception of the 500 lohans to left and right which are Ming. There are Tang-dynasty wall paintings of devils and guardians, as well as Song wall paintings (these are mainly in the form of circular cartouches containing Buddhist groups, interspersed with prayers and inscriptions in square cartouches).

Behind the hall, to the right, is the *Zushi* (Founding Teacher's) *Stupa*, a Northern Wei funerary stupa containing the remains of the Meditation master who founded the temple. It is of whitewashed brick, some 8m high, square in base plan and topped with a six-sided pagoda-shaped lotus crown. The interior was hollow, to receive the ashes of the founder. Beside it stands a Tang sutra pillar with a rather bulbous top (a form not uncommon in Japan). Other burial stupas near the temple include some from the Tang and a rather unusual Jin stupa in brick, with a hexagonal base decorated with architectural forms (eaves bracketing) and a complex crown which looks rather like a cabbage stalk with the leaves torn off.

The **Jinge** (Golden Tower) **Temple** is just over the peak that you pass on the road, part of the encircling ring of mountains around Tai huai, and is about 15km S of the village. Founded in 770, the Daizong emperor of the Tang ordered that the roof of the Buddha Hall be covered with gilded bronze tiles, hence the name. Inside the two-storey *Main Hall* (which was being restored in 1985 so it was impossible to see what sort of roof covering it would end up with) is a giant gilded stucco figure of the Bodhisattva Guanyin with 1000 arms, apparently with a bronze figure inside, under the later layers of stucco. Attendants surround the figure. Behind the hall are others, containing up to 1000 figures, with the great hall at the rear containing figures of the past, present and future Buddhas and 18 lohans. Evidence of Tang construction is found in some surviving stone pillar bases, carved with lotus petals, which are originals.

The reconstruction work in 1985 was sensitive, with window lattices being composed of original parts (carved floral motifs) worked in with modern copies.

Within **Tai huai** village it is sometimes difficult to tell where one temple begins and another ends for they virtually run together, and, apart from the main street with its shops, most of the village consists of temple.

The lower part of the village is dominated by the **Tayuan** (Pagoda) **Temple** with its huge, 50m-high whitewashed sarira (reliquary) pagoda in the Tibetan style, which stands between the Great Hall and the Library. Originally part of the Xiantong (Manifest Penetration) Temple, when the sarira pagoda was restored in the Wanli reign period of the Ming (1573–1620), this part of the temple was reconstituted as an independent entity. Approached through a gate with substantial walls pierced with two arched windows and a central arched door (a form often found in the Qing temples at Chengde; very much of the north), the *Daxiong bao dian* Buddha Hall is the main building in the first courtyard, a good, solid five-bay hall of late date, in which services are held quite frequently (often in the late afternoon at 4–5 pm, if getting up before dawn does not appeal). The *pagoda*, behind the hall, is set on a high angular base, its upper part in the characteristic bottle-shape seen in Tibetan Lamaist stupas with a bronze 'umbrella' finial.

The fact that this form is not uncommon in Wutai is probably due to two factors: its importance as a centre for Tibetan and, especially, Mongolian Lamaists for whom this form was important, and also the fact that this smaller centre at Wutai, concentrated around Tai huai, was much patronised, by the imperial house amongst others, in the Ming and Qing when Tibetan styles were popular, almost fashionable, as can be seen in Peking and Chengde. The stupa, constructed of brick and lime and whitewashed, is hung with 252 small bronze wind-bells which tinkle in the breeze.

Behind the stupa is one of the most famous buildings in Wutai, the **Sutra Library**. A two-storey timber-frame building (presumably of Ming foundation but subsequently restored), it was built to house the revolving sutra library case mentioned by Ennin in the 9C. This extraordinary 20-storey wooden structure, hexagonal in plan, narrow at the base and flaring at the top, rises through a hexagonal opening in the coffered ceiling of the library to the upper storey where it is finished with a conical pavilion. It revolves on a wooden lotus base (though being top-heavy owing to its narrow base and wider upper part must have been rather difficult to move when full of books).

There are few volumes now in the pigeon-holes (three to each of the six sides on each storey), as valuable volumes have been moved away for safer storage. There were once Mongolian and Tibetan editions of the 'Tripitaka', as well as Chinese and many smaller editions such as a Ming copy of the 'Avatamsakasutra' written in blood and a Qing scroll of the same sutra written out in the form of a seven-storey pagoda, Ming paintings of Buddhist notables on pipa leaves and a manuscript written in gold by the Qing Kangxi emperor.

Behind the Tayuan Temple is the **Xiantong** (Manifest Penetration) **Temple**, said to be an Eastern Han foundation, dating from 58–75 but, like the

Tayuan or Pagoda Temple, rebuilt in the early years of the Ming. The many halls and wings that survive are mostly of the Ming or Qing and the temple is noted for its bronzes and brick-vaulted halls. Built against a hill, the temple rises ever higher, with a central terrace with two elaborate Ming bronze pagodas on either side. Based on the Tibetan stupa, these have octagonal bases with tapering storeyed tops and are about 8m high. Beautifully cast, covered in images of Buddhas, fat guardian figures holding them up, tiny deities riding on fish or horses amongst waves, pagodas and haloed Bodhisattvas, they are exceptional examples of Ming bronze work. Behind them are a pair of two-storey, three-doored brick-vaulted Ming halls, smaller and more elegant than that at Nanjing or similar constructions in Taiyuan. Another grand example, the *Hall of Immeasurable Splendour*, with seven arched entrances and brick imitations of wooden brackets under the eaves, has fascinating 'bracketed' vaults filled with brightly painted wooden caisson ceilings.

Between the two small brick-vaulted halls is the *Bronze Pavilion*; the best example of this rare form. Cast in the Ming, it is a perfect imitation of timber construction and decoration. The interior is covered with thousands of tiny Buddha figures (and lists of donors) and the structure (apparently timber encased in bronze) of the roof is clear. Outside, the lattice windows and lower panels of the walls, as well as the little balcony surrounding the upper storey, are all cast in perfect imitation of fine timber work. The 'window lattices' include a variety of floral motifs in geometric forms and the panels below depict a wide variety of animals from carp and peacocks to deer in elegant cartouches. The central doors open to reveal the interior.

Some of the treasures of the Wutai temples are exhibited in the Xiantong Temple.

The PUSA DING (Bodhisattva Peak) is behind the Xiantong Temple, up 108 steps which take you to the top of the hill dominating Tai Huai and offering a wonderful view over the temples spread out below.

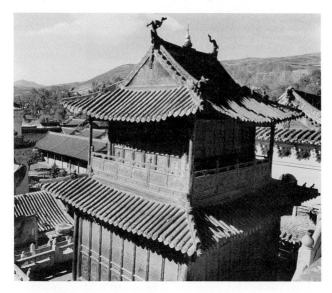

Miniature bronze pavilion, Wutai shan

Founded in the Northern Wei, when Wutai became a great pilgrimage centre for Tibetan and Mongolian Lamaists (especially those of the Yellow Hat sect), from the Yongle reign period of the Ming (1403–25) Lamaist dignitaries used to stay here, as it was said to be where Manjusri stayed on the mountain. The Qing Kangxi and Qianlong emperors also stayed here when they came to pay their respects. Remaining buildings date from the Qing and the stone-carving (of pillar bases and terrace walls) is considered to be of imperial quality. Owing to the number of important visitors, there are many memorial stelae inscribed in Chinese, Manchu, Mongolian and Tibetan.

Down below, to the E of the Tayuan (Pagoda) Temple, is the **Luohou** (Rahu) **Temple**. Rahu is the demon who seizes the sun and moon to cause eclipses and who is reborn as the eldest son of every Buddha. This is described as a 'Lama temple' though there are clear Lamaist elements found throughout Wutai, in the Tibetan-style white stupas and the immensely tall pine trunks with bronze tops set up outside many halls.

Founded in the Tang, it was rebuilt in 1492 and is the temple best preserved in its entirety. On the 14th day of the 6th month of the lunar calendar (thus usually in August though the exact day changes from year to year), on the birthday of Manjusri the monks of the temple perform a devil dance (of the sort also seen in Tibet and Mongolia for the Buddha's birthday and New Year).
Apart from its full range of buildings including meditation hall, hall of guardians and library, the hall at the back of the temple contains the famous circular altar with 18 lohans crossing the sea beneath a great red-petalled lotus flower which contains four Buddha images (Buddhas of the Four Directions) which are revealed when the huge petals (which are moved by means of an underground mechanism) are lowered. This is another temple in which regular services are held.

Behind the Luohou Temple is the **Yuanzhao** (Universally Illuminating) **Temple**, founded in the Ming when an Indian monk came to the area. He died in the meditation position (called 'transformation whilst sitting' in Chinese) and was cremated according to the Buddhist tradition. His ashes were housed in a small white Tibetan-style stupa in the centre of the temple which was built in 1434.

It was in this temple that the founder of the Yellow Hat sect in Tibet, Tsongkhapa, stayed and preached in the early years of the Yongle period (early 15C), bringing the new discipline of Yellow Hat Lamaism to the area. The Yellow Hat sect of Tibetan Buddhism was founded in the early 15C and stressed the need for monastic discipline; its forebears wore red hats. Today's Dalaim Lama is the head of the Yellow Hats whilst the Panchen Lama who lives in Peking with his Tibetan headquarters in Shigatse, is the leader of the older, Red Hats.

The sculptures of the Buddhas, past, present and future, with their attendants in the main hall of the Yuanzhao Temple are considered to be amongst the finest on Wutai. The courtyard in which the white stupa stands (with its holy relic inside) is surrounded by a covered walk and is a favourite place for circumambulation (or walking around sacred buildings or figures), a practice known in Chinese Buddhism but apparently more popular amongst Lamaists; yellow-robed monks can frequently be seen walking clockwise around halls and stupas in the Wutai area.

Behind the Yuanzhao Temple is the *Guangzong Temple*, one of the smallest (one description is 'squashed in') of those in the Tai huai area. Founded in the first years of the 16C, in its centre is the three-bay Bronze-tiled hall (today covered with glazed turquoise tiles said to resemble patinated bronze) with three Buddha figures of wood and 18 iron lohans.

S of the Luohou Temple is the **Wanfo ge** (Ten-thousand Buddha Hall), formerly part of the Tayuan or Pagoda Temple, founded in the Ming and rebuilt under the Qing. The main hall is in the E of the temple, a three-bay, two-storey, triple-eaved timber construction containing a considerable number of Buddhist figures—hence the name. In front of the hall hangs a 3500kg Ming bronze bell. In the SE part of the temple there are two stone Tibetan-style stupas of carved marble, 4m high.

Pailou on Wutai shan

The temple, unusually in this rather strict Lamaist Buddhist stronghold, contains a finely-carved *Dragon-king Hall* (at the back of the enclosure).

The dragon king is not a Buddhist deity; he belongs with Taoism and popular religion as a controller of waters and rain, but it was said that the local dragon king was very fierce and threatened the stability of the temples so a shrine was built to him here. Opposite is a stage for religious dramas, a centre of attraction in the major celebrations of the 6th lunar month.

S of the Wanfo Temple is the **Shuxiang** (Statue of Manjusri) **Temple**, on Yanglin jie. Founded in the Tang, it was restored in the Yuan and subsequently burnt down, to be rebuilt in 1487. It contains a gate-hall, hall of guardians, verandahed courtyards with meditation hall, Manjusri Hall, kitchens and living quarters as well as bell and drum towers. Inside the *Manjusri Hall* is a 9m Ming (1496) figure of Manjusri riding on a lion. Behind are three Buddhas, the Buddha of Medicine (extremely important as a Lamaist icon, frequently seen in Tibet), the historic Buddha, Sakyamuni, and Amitabha Buddha, who presides over the Western Paradise, with 500 lohans on either side.

Outer temples that are best visited by car (the driver can have a day off when you walk around Tai huai) include the Longquan, Zhenhai, Nanshan, Puhua and Bishan Temples and the Guanyin Cave.

The **Bishan** (Azure Mountain) **Temple** is just 2km N of Tai huai on the slopes of the northern platform, set in a forested area well supplied with water. It is thought to have been founded in the Northern Wei when the famous teacher Fa cong preached there. It was rebuilt in the Chenghua reign period of the Ming (1465–87) and restored in the Qing. On the central axis of the large temple are the Hall of Guardians, bell and drum towers, Thunder Sound Hall, Hall of the Ordination Altar and side wings, with a 'hanging flower gate' marking the back part of the main axis where the library is situated. Most of the buildings in the front part are single storeyed whilst those behind are multi-storeyed and multi-eaved. All the sculptures are Qing, including a 1.5m white jade Buddha presented by Burmese Buddhists set in front of the Historic Buddha figure in the Vairocana hall. Out in the wooden surroundings are a number of white stupas containing the ashes of notable monks.

On the far side of the river that runs just E of Tai huai is the **Nanshan** (Southern Mountain) **Temple** which is made up of three temples: *Youguo* (Protect the Nation) *Temple, Jile* (Extreme Joy) *Temple* and *Shande* (Goodness and Virtue) *Temple* which were joined together early this century. The complex was founded in 1296, rebuilt in 1541 and restored in the Qing. Built against the mountain, the temple is reached, like the Pusa ding, by 108 steps; the significance of 108 being that it is the number of beads on the Buddhist rosary (also the 108 passions or delusions, the 108 karmic bonds and the 108 tolls of temple bells at dawn and dusk) so that the rosary can be said *en route*. A fine brick spirit wall marks the entrance to the temple which is full of further steps and decoratively carved stone railings and there is much decorative cut-brick work and stone-carving depicting spirits, scenes from drama and history as well as Buddhist scenes. In the *Main Hall* the 18 lohan figures which date from the Ming are thought to be the best lohans on Wutai. Each very different, with separate attributes, they are not as caricatured as many of the Qing assemblages (which enjoy greater popularity) but, set under their carved wooden canopy, retain a certain dignity. Behind them are wall paintings of scenes from the life of the Buddha, who is depicted as a Chinese gentleman; these also date from the Ming.

Beyond is the *Guanyin Cave* where a six-armed Guanyin figure of no great note is set in a cave behind a main hall which is reached up a stepped path.

The *Puhua* (Universal Transformation) *Temple* is of uncertain founding date; it was rebuilt during the Ming. It lies beyond the Nanshan temple and Guanyin cave. Many of the halls and canopies over the figures are decorated with elaborate carvings, brightly painted and there is a lot of decorative cut-brick work.

The **Zhenhai** (Calm Sea) **Temple** is 5km S of Tai huai, beautifully set beside a spring (called the spring from the bottom of the sea), surrounded by pines and poplars. The temple as it stands today was founded in 1711. It has a fine stupa in the centre, built in 1786 and carved with scenes from the Buddha's life, above which are four Buddhas. Around the courtyard are covered walks with paintings of Bodhisattvas. The temple, which is still very active (though the monks, many of whom are from Mongolia, were very elderly in 1985), was the home of a famous 'living Buddha' of the Qing and is an important pilgrimage site for Mongolian and Tibetan Buddhists.

The **Longquan** (Dragon Spring) **Temple**, SW of Tai huai, is an extraordinary mixture of styles. It was founded in the Song, rebuilt in the Ming and most notably in the late Qing and early Republican period. Reached by the inevitable 108 steps, the first edifice is a stone pailou (arch) dating from the early Republican period, lavishly carved, partly in imitation of timber construction but covered with dragons and foliage. The temple buildings appear greatly restrained beside the stone carving, not only on the pailou but also on the two carved stone stupas, especially the Puji (Universal Succour) Pagoda, with fat, smiling Maitreya (Future) Buddhas on four sides, beneath an elaborate mock-timber pagoda top, above a series of fat, supporting guardian figures, the whole set behind an elaborately carved railing. In the W of the temple is a 10m three-storey, hexagonal pagoda said to contain the relics of a Song notable.

In the outer temples, but also from a lot of the temples in Tai huai which is small and quiet, many birds can be seen. The most numerous in early winter are red-legged choughs who tumble above. They have a nerve-wracking habit of 'free-falling', apparently hurtling to a certain death before they flap upwards at the last moment.

35   The Yongle gong

The **Yongle gong** (Palace of Eternal Joy) is a major Taoist temple near Rui cheng in the SW corner of Shanxi province. It lies in an area that is rich in well-preserved architectural remains which can be reached from the town of **Lin Fen**, on the railway line S of Taiyuan.

Lin Fen is a small, rather bleak town, interesting in that, despite its bleak northernness, it was chosen as an area for resettlement of a large number of Indonesian Chinese who fled Indonesia during anti-Chinese riots there in 1960 (when Zhou Enlai sent boats to rescue them) and again when Sukarno took over in 1965 and there was considerable persecution of Overseas Chinese.

Its major monument is a *pagoda* built in 1715, originally part of the Dayun si (Great Cloud Monastery), founded in the Tang. The pagoda (built to replace one which was destroyed by an earthquake in 1695) has a square base and six square storeys above, topped with an octagonal storey and decorated with poorly preserved glazed tiles (characteristic of Shanxi buildings) made by craftsmen in Yangcheng xian, depicting Buddhist figures. It was built over a magnificent iron Buddha head which fills the base. The head, which has a large hole in the back, was cast in parts, in sand (which ran out of the hole) and is very thick at the base. It is 5m high and very imposing, sitting on its chin in the pagoda. The *Drum Tower*, said to be the largest of its kind in China (at 43.5m high) and to be over 1000 years old, was opened to visitors in November 1987.

In Yuncheng xian, about 100km S of Lin Fen, is **Jiezhou** which has a fine Qing **Temple** dedicated to Guan di (Guandi miao), the god of war. The temple was founded in 589, rebuilt in 1017; destroyed by an earthquake in 1555 and rebuilt, only to be destroyed by fire in 1702. Over the subsequent ten years it was rebuilt, apparently with faithful attention to its previous form.

Though there are many temples and shrines to the god of war throughout China, this one is the most important (apart from being a very fine piece of Qing building) because Jiezhou was the birthplace of Guan Yu who was deified by the Wanli emperor of the Ming (after many previous posthumous honours). He was a great hero of the Three Kingdoms period (220–280), a follower of Liu Bei who became first emperor of the Minor Han or Shu dynasty (221–263) and one of the great folk-heroes of China, celebrated in the 'Romance of the Three Kingdoms' ('San guo zhi', which reached its final form as a novel by Luo Guanzhong in the 14C). Plays celebrating the life and legendary accomplishments of Guan yu (or Guan di) were performed inside the fist main gate at festivals.

The temple, which is built to the same plan as most temples in China, has a main axis with subsidiary buildings to E and W. It is most noted for its fine glazed tile work (all locally produced and characteristic of southern Shanxi) seen on the roofs, on the dragon screen (at the front of the temple) and on the wooden pailou. The stone carving is also very fine: the carved pillar bases are very good examples of Qing stone carving which is not to be dismissed lightly as 'late'; and the stone-carved pailou is extremely interesting.

Some 25km N of Lin Fen is *Hongdong*. 17km NE of the town is the **Guangsheng si** (Temple of Widespread Victory). This has a famous glazed-tile *pagoda* (with a very strange staircase inside) and some extremely early buildings as well as an unusual wall painting depicting a temple play. The temple is divided into three parts: upper, lower and the Yongshen miao (which contains the wall painting). The temple was founded in AD 147 and rebuilt in 769. In 1303 it was destroyed by a major earthquake and rebuilt soon after; sections that date to that last rebuilding—in the last years of the Yuan or the first years of the Ming—are quite rare early survivals. The upper temple has three main halls and the spectacular *Feihong ta* (Soaring Rainbow Pagoda).

The halls, built soon after the 1303 earthquake, preserve the Yuan style of building, solid and massive, closer to the earlier Tang examples (on Wutai shan) than the more decorative and lighter examples of Ming and Qing building (the Forbidden City, for example). There are fewer brackets under the eaves, those that there are usually sit on top of the columns (rather than forming in effect a decorative frieze as in the Forbidden City); the ridge acroteria consist of simple inturned 'owls' tails' rather than the highly elaborate later versions. The halls and their sculptures are all fine surviving examples of early building: the figures of Amitabha and his attendants in the Front Hall being Yuan whilst this and the other halls and sculptures are early Ming.

One of the early printed versions of the Buddhist Tripitaka, or canon, was still in this part of the temple in 1942 and narrowly escaped being taken to Japan; soldiers of the Chinese 8th Route Army rescued the volumes from the occupying Japanese. Most of the canon is now in the National Library in Peking (4330 scrolls were sent by the 8th Route Army and further finds brought the total to 4541) with 152 scrolls in the Shanxi Provincial Museum.

This edition of the Tripitaka was published during the Jin dynasty (1115–1234) and published in nearby Jiezhou. It is known as the Zhaocheng Tripitaka. The woodblocks for printing it were cut between 1148 and 1173. This length of time is not surprising when you consider that the full set consisted of about 7000 printed scrolls (each of which would have been printed from a considerable number of blocks), printed on mulberry paper and mounted on red rods. A set was stored in the temple and re-discovered in 1934. The scrolls have handsome frontispieces and the printing is unusual for it relied for finance upon donations from local Buddhists (printing the entire Buddhist canon of well over 1000 titles was usually dependent upon imperial finance as it was so expensive; this happened with the first printing—in Sichuan, 972–983—and most subsequent reprintings). In the early Yuan the blocks were removed to Peking for storage where they were used as a model for the Yuan dynasty edition of the Tripitaka.

The *pagoda* is on the central axis of the temple (a feature common to early Chinese temple layouts; it may be compared with the two Goose Pagodas and their associated temples in Xi'an). Thirteen storeys high, octagonal in plan and covered with lively glazed-tile decorations, the pagoda was built in 1527 and the verandah on the ground level was added in 1622. It is 47.3m high, built of 'green brick' with tiled eaves (imitating timber-bracketed construction) at each storey and decorative tilework depicting Buddhist figures, plants and animals in between. The finial is very fine, with a central stupa-shaped 'diamond finial' and four tiny pagodas surrounding it so that it forms a five-stupa group which is said to have Lamaist connections.

The interior is hollow and has the most extraordinary steps which can be climbed with great difficulty. Leaving aside the height of the steps, the fact that the opening gets narrower and narrower as you ascend, and the total lack of illumination, the steps mount in a gradual zig-zag with a yawning gap in between so that you have to keep climbing over a black hole below you. I climbed some of the way up behind a wonderful but stout expert in architectural history from Taiyuan who was too tubby to get terribly far up (she said that in her youth she had managed it) and in descending in total darkness tended to land heavily on the fingers of those behind her. The glazed tilework, which is in very fine condition, is a local speciality.

The *lower temple* is built on a single axis; the rear hall (built in 1309) is particularly fine, as are the three Buddhas and Manjusri and Samantabhadra figures in the upper part. The Yuan dynasty wall paintings in the temple were removed in 1928 and are now in the Nelson Atkins Museum in Kansas City.

Beside the lower temple is the *Shuishen miao* (Temple of the Water God), said to be the site of worship of the god of the Huo spring. In the Hall there are wall paintings, the most famous of which depicts Yuan dynasty drama (on the eastern part of the S wall). The painting was made in 1324 and depicts a troupe in performance, showing the scenery, orchestra, props and actors on a brick-paved stage (of the sort that might be found in temples). The 11 actors are shown in the ritualised roles of sheng (older male), dan (female), jing (painted face) and mo (young male) with the appropriate make-up, embroidered costumes and beards. The musical instruments include bamboo flute, drum and clapper for keeping time. It is an extremely rare illustration from the golden age of the Chinese drama.

In the town of Hongdong there is a *Ming prison* (the earliest to survive in China) with high surrounding walls and two gates with cave-type cells inside. There is a tiger-headed stele in the back courtyard with a list of the criminals held.

Some 240km S of Lin Fen in the SW tip of Shanxi province is *Ruicheng*; 3km N of Ruicheng is the present site of the **Yongle gong** (Palace of Eternal Joy), one of the major centres of northern Taoism.

Its name sounds appropriate but it derives from the fact that the temple (or palace) was originally located in Yongle village. First built as a memorial temple, later a monastery, the temple commemorated one of the Eight Taoist Immortals, Lu Dongbin, who was a native of the village. Lu Dongbin (born 755) came from a family of officials. He is a fine example of the historicisation of myth and/or the mythicisation of history. As E.T. Chalmers Werner has it, Lu 'was 5 feet 2 inches in height and at 20 he was still unmarried' but he met a dragon on Lu shan who gave him a magic sword with which he could hide himself and also fly. He met a general in Chang'an who had discovered the secret of immortality (which all Taoists sought) and had successfully survived from the Zhou until the Tang, a period of some 2000 years. He passed the secret on to Lu Dongbin who was then subjected to ten temptations but survived to do good deeds through magic for the next 400 years. This is but one version of the many legends about him and the temple which was built on the site of his house (according to a stele of 1262 in the Yongle gong) and called the Temple of Mr Lu.

The temple today is most famous for its wall paintings and for the fact that in 1959–60 it was transported with the help of Eastern European experts from its original site in Yongle on the banks of the Yellow River to just N of Ruicheng when the Sanmen gorge dam of the Yellow River was built and Yongle submerged. The buildings were moved stone by stone (with each brick and roof-tile numbered for reinstatement) and the frescoes were cut up into blocks and remounted. An exhibition at the rear of the temple describes the work.

The layout of the temple is interesting for it reflects a peculiarity of the period in which it was originally constructed (1232–1358). The main buildings are aligned on a single N–S axis, standing high off the ground on a series of terraces linked by walkways. The Chinese would describe the layout of the buildings linked by raised walkways as resembling the character 'gong' (work) which consists of two horizontal strokes joined by one vertical stroke; this form of layout has also been found in excavations of Yuan dynasty domestic architecture. It can also be seen in palace architecture of the Ming and Qing (in the Forbidden City).

The first building on the central axis is the *Wuji men* (Gate of the Unfathomable) with wall paintings of door gods and celestial generals and armies (characteristically protective in this first building in the temple). Behind is the *Sanqing dian* (Hall of the Three Pure Ones) with its huge murals of the three pure ones or major Taoist deities surrounded by all the other Taoist deities—the complete pantheon. In this representation of the entire pantheon and the paintings of door gods in the gatehouse the Taoists are borrowing from the Buddhist tradition. The figures are immensely tall and portrayed in rows four deep, with strong outlining and rich colours of bronze, red, brown, pink, light blues and greens. In the third building, the *Chunyang dian* (Hall of Essential Yang—as in yin-yang—one of Lu Dongbin's Taoist names), 52 extraordinary episodes from his long life are depicted in misty, mountainous landscape settings which serve to frame and separate the episodes (like the frames in a comic strip). Behind is the *Zhongyang dian* (Hall of Zhongyang), dedicated to Wang Zhongyang, c 1120–1170, founder of a Taoist sect called the Teaching of True Integrity (Quanzhen jiao) which was particularly strong during the Yuan.

The life of Wang and his seven disciples is depicted in the frescoes of the hall which are not considered to be quite up to the standard of those in the Chunyang dian. All the frescoes were painted between 1325 and 1368 with the Zhongyang dian frescoes finished last, in 1368.

36   The Silk Road

The **Silk Road** or **Roads** is the name given to tourist itineraries that take you out into Gansu and Xinjiang provinces, to many of the oasis towns that stand on what was the ancient silk route, a trading route across the Gobi Desert to Central Asia and thence to the Western world. Though the route is named after its most famous commodity, the Silk Road, and indeed the whole of Central Asia, have been vital meeting points of west and east, a place of changing governments and peoples (particularly in the first millennium AD when kingdoms rose in importance in different parts of the area, only to be supplanted by the rise of another group), and, despite the physical barriers, a corridor, not only for trade but also for the movement of ideas. Religions such as Nestorian Christianity, Manichaeism and, above all, Buddhism and Islam travelled across the deserts permanently to influence the Far East and far western China respectively.

The Chinese silk which gave the trade route its name was carried by camel trains across the deserts and transported to ancient Rome, though not by Chinese merchants for the loads changed hands in the Pamirs and Persian traders took the cargo onward. Just as porcelain was to puzzle the world less than a thousand years later, silk was a fabulous mystery in the western world where people struggled to reproduce the raw material. The Chinese have been traditionally supposed to have guarded the secret of the manufacture of silk and, later, porcelain; folklore relates how a Chinese princess, sent to be married to the King of Khotan in the 5C and forewarned that there was no silk in Khotan, smuggled silk-moth eggs in her piled-up hair and established the silk industry on the far side of the Gobi. The story continues with the smuggling of eggs to Constantinople in 552 by two Persian monks who travelled to China as Christian missionaries. Whether or not this is true, these luxury products were concealed from most travellers for they were made in the hinterland, far from visitors' eyes and above all far from the west.

Fantastically light and delicate (sometimes considered a bit too light and flimsy for decency; the Roman emperor Tiberius banned men from wearing silk in AD 14), silk was a mystery to its enthusiastic wearers. Pliny described how silk grew, as 'wool' in the 'forests' and Virgil described the harvest, 'the Chinese comb off leaves their delicate down'; not much wider of the mark than a 16C English entrepreneur and would-be silk producer who started a moth farm (but was cultivating the wrong moth).

The Silk Road started from the Han and Tang capital of Xi'an (known as Chang'an in those times) and led almost due W to Lanzhou and Dunhuang where it divided just beyond Dunhuang at Yumen guan or the 'Jade Gate'. A northern loop took in the fertile oasis towns of Turfan and Hami; the central (most direct) route passed through Loulan and on through Kucha and Aksu to Kashgar, whilst a southern route, following the southern rather than the northern edge of the Taklamakan Desert (or Tarim Basin), passed through Miran, Niya, Khotan and Yarkand before reaching Kashgar. From Kashgar, too (though here we are outside Chinese territory) there were northern and southern routes, through Samarkand and Bokhara or, alternatively, through Balkh.

For many centuries much of the Silk Road was also a pilgrimage route to India, home of the Buddhist faith. Monks would turn southwards from Yarkand, down through Leh and Srinagar into India in search of sacred texts and images which they carried back to China. Their route, like that of the merchant caravan trains, skirted the edge of the Taklamakan for it was an 'abomination of desolation', believed to be full of demons who led men and animals astray, quite apart from the wind-blown and shifting sands which made it almost impossible to find the way through. The routes were also bounded by high, freezing mountain ranges, the Pamirs to the W, the Tian shan or Heavenly Mountains to the N, and the Kunlun range to the S of the Taklamakan.

The trade route was first opened up during the reign of the Han emperor Wudi (the 'Martial Emperor'). He sent Zhang Qian, an official at his court, on an expedition in 138 BC to seek an alliance with the peoples of Yuezhi (sometimes identified as Indo-scythians, they later migrated to NW India and founded the Kushan kingdom) against the Xiongnu of the steppe who presented a real threat to the westwards expansion of the Han empire.

The Xiongnu are often tentatively identified as Huns; their language was part of the Turkish group. It took Zhang Qian 13 years (which included being taken prisoner twice by the Xiongnu) to get back to the Chinese capital with a wealth of information about the kingdoms of Central Asia. One of his greatest finds were the 'heavenly' horses of Ferghana (just N of Kashgar), larger, faster and stronger than the small native horses the Chinese knew (Prjevalsky's horse, now only to be seen in zoos, I believe), ideal for pursuing Huns. The Han emperor expended many men on expeditions along the Silk Road to acquire these large beasts.

Han Wudi reinforced Chinese control over the Silk Road by extending the Great Wall westward and establishing a series of beacons and garrisons out into the Gobi (where the beacon towers made of tamped earth can still be seen outside Dunhuang) protecting, as far as was possible, the chain of oasis towns where travellers could rest and change their animals before continuing westwards. Chinese control over the area continued during the Tang dynasty when China was at its most cosmopolitan, open to the luxuries of the West (grapes, silver vessels, glass, ivory, coral and amber, saffron, fragrant timbers, parrots, peacocks, leopards and carpets) and relatively liberal about Western ideas which came with them (like the Buddhist, Manichean and Nestorian faiths all of which were celebrated in Xi'an and other parts of China, the latter on a small scale). Large numbers of non-Chinese traders and craftsmen came to live in Xi'an and many influential citizens had non-Chinese blood, like the General An Lushan and, perhaps, the poet Li Bai who was born in what was, until a few months ago, Soviet Central Asia.

The end of the Silk Road as a major route of transportation came gradually over the centuries and the decline of the Tang (which collapsed in 907) which meant the end of cosmopolitan openness in China for succeeding dynasties were inward-looking and generally suspicious of the outside world and most of its goods) was only one factor. The desert moved inexorably and now and then would claim an oasis like the settlement at Niya which was explored (I hesitate to say excavated) by Sir Marc Aurel Stein in 1901, revealing numbers of wooden tablets with clay seals inscribed in Prakrit in Kharoshthi script and some fine pieces of carved wooden furniture now in the British Museum. Niya had been suddenly abandoned in the 3C AD when the water supply failed. Another factor in the decline of free travel along the Silk Road was the rise of Islam which gradually spread to influence the entire Taklamakan area. In the 9C, too, marauding Tibetans threatened the small pockets of Chinese settlers and it is believed to be in response to this last threat that the library of the great cave-temple complex at Dunhuang was walled up for safety, remaining sealed for some 900 years.

The Silk Road area today remains largely Islamic in faith, inhabited by some of China's 'national minorities', mainly the Uighurs and Kazakhs. The importance of the Uighurs, in particular, to the Chinese of the metropolitan area, has been crucial at many times. Inhabiting border areas, they have held the key to national defence but have frequently been somewhat unamenable to control from distant Peking. The Song and Ming dynasties were too preoccupied with threats from the north and northeast to try and regain control of the Gobi region but the Qing emperors devoted much of their time, money and military resources to the area. Threatened by the Russian empire which was interested in territorial expansion, by Uighur uprisings and by the Mongols who were eager to win control of Tibet (with which area their shared

Lamaist Buddhist faith made a strong link), the Qing were hard pressed to control the area and by the end of the 19C had almost lost it.

The Kangxi emperor was keen to take Mongolia into the Chinese empire, a task in which he was helped by dissention between the Eastern and Western Mongols in particular. When, in 1688, an Eleuth or Western Mongol leader sought to conquer the Eastern Mongols in Outer Mongolia, the latter appealed to the Qing court for assistance, which was readily granted. By 1696 the Qing army, personally led by the Kangxi emperor, had beaten the Eleuths and incorporated Outer Mongolia into the empire. The struggle was not over for it was only in 1720 that the Chinese succeeded in eliminating and replacing Eleuth influence in Tibet. The Kangxi emperor's grandson, the Qianlong emperor, had to have a second war against the Eleuths in 1755–57, his success resulting in the extension of Qing control into NW Xinjiang. In 1758, the area controlled reached the Pamirs, as it had done nearly 2000 years previously, after the conquest of the Uighurs of Eastern Turkestan.

Later, in 1862, came one of many uprisings against the Qing, that of the moslems of Gansu and northern Shaanxi, followed by that of Kashgaria and Dzungaria (areas to the S and N of the Tian shan) under Yakub Beg, who also moved N towards Urumqi (where his progress was blocked by invading Russians). His rebellion and conquests were only really ended by his death in 1877 and were complicated by the fact that the Russians and the British both supported him against the Qing (Xinjiang being an area involved in 'the Great Game' where both hoped to set up puppet, buffer states against the other). The Chinese managed to take Xinjiang again in 1878 but as central power declined, so did control over the border regions of Xinjiang (and Tibet).

In the early years of the 20C, and for several decades after that, though most of Xinjiang was nominally under Chinese rule, as contemporary travellers', spies' and archaeologists' accounts relate, there were many other contenders for power as Peter Hopkirk describes in the prologue to his 'Setting the East Ablaze: Lenin's dream of an empire in Asia' (Oxford University Press, 1986). He starts with Lenin and his ambitions for British India (reached across the Taklamakan Desert) but notes that:

> …three other would-be Genghis Khans were to arise in Central Asia, the battlefield of the new Great Game. The most notorious by far was a psychopathic White Russian general named Ungern-Sternberg, 'the Mad Baron', whose dreadful atrocities are still remembered with a shudder in Mongolia.

The next to try his luck was Enver Pasha, Turkey's flamboyant but defeated wartime leader, then in exile in Central Asia…The last of these dreamers was a young but charismatic warlord called Ma Chung-yin, sometimes known as 'Big Horse'. A Chinese Moslem visionary barely out of his teens, he was to leave a trail of blood across the Gobi desert before fleeing west along the Silk Road in a stolen lorry, pursued by Soviet bombers.

Whilst all this was going on, a minor archaeological 'great game' was being played out in the same area, graphically described by Peter Hopkirk in his first book on the area, 'Foreign Devils on the Silk Road: the search for lost cities and treasures of Chinese Central Asia' (John Murray, London, 1980). In the 'Great Manuscript Race', as he describes it, the Swede Hedin, Sir Marc Aurel Stein, a Hungarian working for the British Government, the Japanese Baron Otani, Paul Pelliot of the Ecole Francaise d'Extreme-Orient, Von le Coq of the Indian section of the Ethnological Museum in Berlin and (later) Langdon Warner seeking exhibits for the Fogg Museum at Harvard, raced across the desert in search of manuscripts and other buried treasure.

At the same time, two lady missionaries, Mildred Cable and Francesca French, were plodding steadily across the desert, distributing Bibles and taking notes on the warlord General Ma amongst others for their book, 'The Gobi Desert' (Hodder and Stoughton, London, 1942) and Peter Fleming and Ella Maillart, a British journalist and a Swiss ski champion were compelled (for reasons of convenience) to travel across the Gobi together, a trip recorded separately in 'News from Tartary' by Fleming (London 1936) and 'Forbidden Journey' by Maillart (London 1937), the title of the latter hinting at one of the fundamental difficulties they encountered.

Even in recent years, the Chinese have found Xinjiang difficult to control. Most of the nationality peoples have cousins across the border which, even if the Russians and Chinese officially close it, does not preclude contact. In the late 1950s, when conditions in China became too hard, some thousands of Kazakhs simply crossed into the Soviet Union, and the problems of racial and religious tension never entirely disappear. Though the Chinese have populated the area, both by means of great state farms (there is a huge sugar-beet state farm and factory out beyond Urumqi, peopled and worked entirely by Shanghainese) and individual settlement (like a Sichuanese taxi-driver in Turfan who had lived there since the 1950s but still did not know enough Uighur to make a satisfactory purchase in a local store), the Uighurs are still numerically superior though administratively and politically inferior.

Tension occasionally reaches boiling point and incidents involving the military are not unknown. In the years of greater relaxation since the Cultural Revolution the Uighurs are now abandoning the romanised alphabet the Chinese helpfully insisted upon during the 1960s and 1970s, in favour of a return to the old Arabic script which is familiar to the old and to the post-Cultural Revolution young but something of a problem for those educated in the period 1966–76. The Islamic faith is still extremely strong (perhaps partly as a rallying point against the Chinese, as Lamaist Buddhism serves in Tibet) and the Chinese authorities are torn between a desire to control it and the knowledge that they are powerless to do so if they wish to avoid more confrontation in the border areas. They are quite reasonably worried by the rise in Islamic fundamentalism in Iran and Afghanistan, which in Central Asian terms are not far away.

Tourist itineraries in the Silk Road area are now expanding. Some ten years ago they usually took in Lanzhou, Dunhuang, Turfan and Urumqi, all on the northern silk route. Some now continue as far as Kashgar, often taking in part of the southern silk route via Hetian (Khotan). Backpackers and some tourist groups now continue from Kashgar over the Pamirs into Pakistan (by bus), and recent tour-group innovations have included crossing by rail from the Soviet Union in the far NW.

There is a new railway line from Turfan to Korla which may well be extended as far as Kashgar but most travel beyond Urumqi is still by bus. Tourist buses are reasonably comfortable, public buses are extremely uncomfortable (unpadded and overcrowded seats) and distances are enormous so travellers should be prepared for discomfort and very long hours spent bouncing over rough roads, with stops in somewhat primitive oasis hotels.

A. Lanzhou

Lanzhou, capital city of Gansu province, lies on the upper reaches of the Yellow River (Huang he). Now a major transport and industrial centre, Lanzhou was once a stopping place on the old Silk Road, near the end of the Great Wall proper (whose major westernmost fort is that at Jiayuguan, some 450km NW of Lanzhou).

Railway: Lanzhou is on the Xi'an–Urumqi line and it is not uncommon for tour groups travelling out on the Silk Road to stop in Lanzhou.

Airport: the airport is c 72km outside town (the trip can take up to 90 minutes by car or bus). There are daily flights to Peking, Xi'an and Jiayuguan, fairly frequent departures for Dunhuang, Guangzhou and Shanghai, and departures twice or three times a week to Chengdu, Guilin, Taiyuan, Urumqi and Xining.

Hotels: one of the solid old hotels, the Lanzhou fandian, is on Tianshui lu in the centre of town. Just up the road is the new Jincheng Hotel; right out in the W of town is another big, old Russian-style hotel, the Youyi binguan (Friendship Hotel) on Xinji lu.

The discovery of oil in the desert has brought petrochemical industries to Lanzhou which is now a major industrial centre with two pleasant parks set on hillsides and the Yellow River flowing between. It also has a very good Provincial Museum. A possible day excursion from Lanzhou is to the Buddhist Caves at Binglingsi.

In the S of the city, on the far side of the railway line, is **Wuquan shan** (Five Springs Mountain), some of whose springs descend the mountain in waterfalls. The steep slopes with rocks and buildings are quite impressive, containing all the required elements of a Chinese garden (water, rocks, pavilions, plants) but in an unusually dramatic setting.

The mountain, with its abundant water supply, is said to have been where the Han dynasty general Huo Qubing (whose tomb can be visited at Xi'an) encamped with his cavalry in 120 BC on his way out to the west.

The major buildings on the mountain include the **Chongqing si** (Temple of Lofty Celebrations), founded in 1372, while the *Qianfo ge* (Tower of the Thousand Buddhas), *Mani si* (Mani Temple), *Dizang si* (Ksitigarbha Temple) and the *Sanjiao dong* (Cave of the Three Teachings) are all later, and much restored after 1868.

In the Chongqing si is preserved an iron bell, cast in 1202. It is 3m high, with a diameter of 2m and weighs nearly 10,000 jin (a jin is half a kilogram) with a longish inscription cast on it, beginning: 'When the immortals hear it they rejoice, when ghosts hear it, they cease their wickedness. It strikes at the gates of hell and saves from a myriad sufferings…'

Five Springs Mountain was opened in 1955. It is one of the most interesting modern parks in China because of the rather imaginative use of concrete in both traditional and modernistic garden forms. Decorative gates, a major design feature of traditional gardens, are made in brick and concrete, some pure moon gates, others more fanciful: quatrefoil (or plum blossom) moon gates, moon gates with concrete lotuses set in a vase neck above the circular opening (so that the whole looks like a vase with two ring handles on the neck, filled with lotus flowers), a strange opening in a wall framed with entwined blossoming cherry trees in concrete, and so on.

On the N bank of the Yellow River, opposite the *Iron Bridge*, is the Baita shan (White Pagoda Mountain). The bridge (Tie qiao) which leads to it is said to be situated at the oldest bridging point on the Yellow River for it was first built during the Ming in 1368–98.

At a crucial point on the Silk Route, the Yellow River had to be crossed. According to the 'Lan zhou fu zhi' (Gazetteer of Lanzhou) of the late 19C, in the past this was done from the late Ming by making a floating bridge of 24 boats chained together across the river, a method which was set up every spring and abandoned every winter. In winter, when the ice was thick enough the 'ice bridge' method was used (people simply crossed the frozen river), and it was the latter method that the Han armies had used to get across to the Gobi Desert and Central Asia. In 1907 the floating bridge was replaced by a proper iron bridge with concrete supports (based on 'foreign construction methods') which lasted for 30 years. The bridge was restored and improved in 1954.

The **White Pagoda Mountain** takes its name from the *White Pagoda* (of the Lamaist stupa type) on top of the mountain. This was constructed (as part of a Buddhist temple) during the Yuan, restored between 1450 and 1456 and again in 1980. It is some 17m high and stands amongst many other temple halls built against the mountain on terraces. The whole area is now a park.

The **Gansu Provincial Museum** (Gansu sheng bowuguan) is in the W of the town on Xixin xi lu, opposite the Youyi fandian (Friendship Hotel). Its major collections include a tremendous display of the Yangshao or red pottery of the late neolithic of which many sites have been excavated in Gansu.

One of the pioneers of neolithic archaeology in China was a Swedish engineer called J.G. Andersson, a mining consultant employed by the Chinese government in the early years of the Republic who also discovered painted pottery in Henan province. In 1923–24 he found a cemetery area in the Banshan Hills in eastern Gansu where the dead were buried with great red pottery urns decorated mainly in black, with some white, in swirling bands of geometric patterns along the broadest part of the body up to the neck. He later excavated similar vessels in the vicinity of Lanzhou.

The Gansu painted pottery culture is thought to date from c 3000–1850 BC, and is later than the metropolitan painted pottery culture (which begins c 5000 BC) and is presumed to have been brought from eastern China by settlers. The museum contains the finest group of these late neolithic pots in China. There is also a major display of Silk Road artefacts including the wood slips used for documentation and records by the soldiers of the Han garrisons and beacons along the Silk Road.

Tombs in Gansu of different periods have yielded various interesting

LANZHOU

finds: Western Zhou bronze harness pieces and fine Han bronzes. There is a 'cortège' of 14 chariots, 17 horses and 45 attendants from the Eastern Han (AD 25–220) tomb of a General Zhang in Wuwei which was also the site of the Eastern Han tomb which contained the famous 'flying horse' of Gansu, a small bronze horse at full gallop, one hoof delicately mounted on a swallow's back.

The piece was exhibited in the great travelling exhibition of Chinese archaeology which was seen in London, Paris and New York in the early 1970s (London in 1973; see William Watson, 'The Genius of China', London, Times Newspapers, 1973). It is interesting to note that the title chosen (in London) caused absolute fury at the time in China because 'genius' was considered to be a class-ridden concept in the Cultural Revolution period when egalitarianism ruled.

The 'flying horse' is one of the many major archaeological discoveries whose actual whereabouts is the subject of much discussion: like the Mawangdui banner of Changsha, the original may be in the museum vaults or perhaps in Peking—the exhibit is almost certainly an exact replica.

Slightly later tombs in the Jiayuguan area (c 220–316) were lined with fine painted bricks with scenes from daily life including much butchery of oxen and pigs, chicken plucking, as well as agricultural scenes. One of the similar tombs discovered near Jiuquan (not far from Jiayuguan) has been reassembled in the museum's garden.

A rather long day's excursion from Lanzhou is to the Buddhist caves at **Binglingsi** c 100km from the city. The journey includes some 2 hours by bus and nearly 2 hours by boat. If you go with a tourist group, whether a foreign one, or a tour group arranged from Lanzhou by the China Travel Service, you will almost certainly stop at the **Liujiaxia Dam** en route where (as long as the water level allows, and this is most certain in autumn), you embark in a boat for the caves.

The **Liujia Gorge Dam** is one of five planned with the help of Soviet advisors in the mid 1950s. It is one of the biggest hydroelectric power stations in China and was completed in 1974. It has five turbo-generators, the first of which began operation in 1969, the last in 1974 and the generating equipment (as may be gathered from the operating dates) is not Russian but Chinese. The barrage itself (147m high, 840m long) was finished much earlier, within the period of Sino-Soviet co-operation which ended in 1960. The output is now 5.7 billion kilowatt hours, more than the entire national electrical output before 1949 and power is transmitted to Lanzhou and Tianshui, to Xi'ning (capital of Qinghai province upstream) and to the Wei River area in neighbouring Shaanxi province.

A major problem in the construction of all the Soviet dams on the Yellow River is silting, the yellow earth (loess) it carries giving it its name (and the subsequent flooding its other name, 'China's Sorrow'). The river brings more silt with it than any other in the world (its silt concentration being, for example, 34 times higher than that of the Nile) and this problem has dogged the dam builders anxious both to exploit and control its flow. The nearby Sanmenxia Dam's reservoir was almost completely clogged by the time the barrage was finished and the dam had to be rebuilt.

The **Bingling si** (Temple of the Bright Spirit) **Caves** spread along 2km of the stone cliff on the N bank of the Yellow River, some 50km W of the dam and accessible only by water. There are 34 caves and 149 niches containing (for those numerically inclined) 679 stone-carved Buddha figures, 82 of clay and 900 square metres of wall painting. The largest Buddha figure is 27m high and there are also four clay pagodas and one in stone.

The earliest caves were carved in the Northern Wei (368–534) and work continued through to the Ming and Qing, with the greatest period of activity being the Tang dynasty and the Tang cave carving, probably of Cave 169, being recorded in the 'Notes to the Water Classic' ('Shui jing zhu'), where the cave's dimensions tally with those described. The style of carving resembles that of contemporary carvings at Yungang and Longmen.

Much of the wall painting dates from the Northern Song and Ming and it is most impressive in Caves 3 (where the figures are Tang in date), 4, 10 and Cave 11 where a landscape with palm trees is depicted, 70, 82 (Song paintings) and 114 (immediately to the left of the largest Buddha figure) where the somewhat crude paintings date from the Tang. The largest Buddha is a Maitreya figure rather similar to that at Leshan in Sichuan and probably Tang in date. Maitreya, The Buddha of the Future, is usually depicted, as here, seated with feet on the ground.

B. Jiayuguan

Jiayuguan, the site of the fort that marks the western extremity of the Great Wall proper, is c 600km NW of Lanzhou, at the far end of the Gansu corridor (the province of Gansu is squashed between mountains which force it into a narrow pass). It is on the main railway line from Xi'an through Lanzhou westwards to Urumqi.

The fort was constructed in 1372 under the Ming, from tamped earth. Whether seen simply from the train across the flat desert or close to, it is a spectacular construction, the same colour as the surrounding land but with long lines of battlements from which elegant, tiled roofed and red-pillared gate towers rise. The circumference of the fortress' walls is 733m, enclosing 33,500 square metres; the walls are some 10m high. The fort has been substantially reconstructed (1988) with the gate towers being substantially renewed: they are very much in the same style as the surviving gates in Peking like the Desheng Gate, Qian men and the Drum Tower.

20km NW of Jiayuguan are the stone-carvings of **Hei shan** (Black Mountain). Over about 1km, figures have been carved into the side of the mountain, about 3m above ground level. The figures are depicted dancing, riding horses (and shooting with bows and arrows), hunting and at military drill. There are no scenes of agriculture and on the basis of this, the stress on hunting (and the absence of knives and spears in the hunting and military scenes), these are thought to be carvings of some of the local nomadic peoples, perhaps the Qiang, a minority group of herdsmen found in the NW; first mentioned in oracle bone inscriptions, they flourished in Gansu, Qinghai and Sichuan from the Han to the Song after which they seem to have disappeared through intermarriage with Chinese. They were charitably known by the Chinese as one of the 'Five Barbarians' and may have been connected with the (later) Tanguts. Other possible groups are the Xiongnu (Huns) or the Dayuezhi, another minority group that flourished in the Han period around the Dunhuang area. Whoever painted them, the rock paintings must presumably date from about the Han period or between the Han and Tang.

The painted bricks (of which there are many examples in the Lanzhou Museum) that lined local tombs of the Western Jin (AD 265–316) were mainly unearthed c 20km NE of Jiayuguan town. In 1972 a group of eight tombs was excavated, six of which had wall paintings of agricultural, herding, hunting, building, cooking, banqueting and musical scenes. One feature is the depiction of mulberry trees and sericulture which proves that mulberries and silk production had moved 'west of the river' (ie beyond the Yellow River into the far west) by this period. There are also depictions of ploughs with two yoked oxen. Tomb 1 was that of a local notable of the Yin family which, according to the 'Jin shu' (History of the Jin) was famous in the west.

C. Maiji shan

Maiji shan (Corn Rick Mountain) is the site of a major Buddhist cave carving group in Tianshui xian, c 30km SE of *Tianshui*, a town on the major Xi'an–Urumqi railway c 300km SE of Lanzhou.

The caves are best reached by bus from Tianshui and individual travellers are warned that here (as in Dunhuang), it is best to join a group with an official guide (which is quite possible to do at the caves themselves). Otherwise the caves which have locked doors will not be opened for you.

The mountain is an amazing tump, reminiscent of a haystack, hence its name. Of all the Buddhist sites and holy mountains in China it most resembles Sumeru, the mythical mountain of the Buddhists which rises from the seven seas as a single peak.

The earliest inscription on Maiji shan is dated AD 502 but, according to literary records, the first caves were carved out during the Later Qin (384–417) a short-lived dynasty, one of the 'Sixteen Kingdoms' (304–439), founded in the NW by the Qiang minority. Carving of caves and images continued during the Wei, when some of the balustrades were repaired, and the Northern Zhou (557–581), when the local military commander Li Chongxin had seven caves carved out in memory of his father. A contemporary poet described the mountain where: 'The walls are covered with inscriptions from holy texts, multiple images of Buddha fill the niches...'. The caves were carved some 30–80m above the foot of the mountain and reached by series of wooden steps and ladders. The cliff face was split in two (E and W) by an earthquake in 734.

There are now 54 surviving caves on the E cliff, 140 on the W, dating from the Northern Wei (386–584) to the Qing dynasty; over 7000 Buddha figures either in clay or stone and 1300 square metres of wall painting. Surprisingly, there was little activity during the Tang, though the poet Du Fu passed by in 759 and wrote a poem on mountain temples: 'High narrow paths, Musk deer sleeping amongst bamboo and cockatoos amongst golden peaches...Cells ranged across the hanging cliffs, Tiered chambers to the very peak...'.

The largest figure is a 16m-high Amitabha Buddha which now stands exposed to the air in the middle of the series of galleries which hang high up on the side of the mountain. It stands in a major triad with Avalokitesvara (Guanyin) on the right and Mahasthamapraptna on the left.

The **Western Cliff Caves** have apparently been left untouched since the Tang and Song and date mainly from the Northern Wei–Northern Zhou (4–6C AD). When the famous painter Zhang Daqian visited Maiji shan in 1943 he could only see the eastern caves because he would have had to pay for the construction of ladders and galleries to reach the western caves. In Cave 100 the direct influence of the Hellenistic West is apparent in the features, shoulders and general bearing of the Northern Wei figures; much of the early Buddhist iconography in China is Hellenistic, influenced by Gandharan sculptures by way of Central Asia. The light treatment of drapery and slender bodies of the figures are Chinese rather than Hellenistic features.

Cave 133 is recognised as Maiji shan's finest, containing sculptures and 18 engraved stones, the latter in a hard stone which must have been brought to the mountain from elsewhere. The stone engravings date from the Western Wei and Northern Zhou. One is particularly graceful, a depiction of a Buddha flanked by two others with hands raised and sleeves and garments falling in elegant folds. In the centre of the cave are two standing Buddha figures of the Tang dynasty. Cave 121 has two clay Buddhas apparently Western Wei (534–550) in date and Cave 165 is a Song work (960–1279) with very realistically depicted figures.

The **Eastern side** of the mountain has always been easier of access and the caves are in poorer condition, with more restoration. Cave 4 has apparently escaped restoration, though it is so tiny that the fine wall paintings are difficult to see properly. They are probably late Tang or early Song in date with some fine Bodhisattvas and pavilions against an ornamental ground. Cave 7, known as Niu er tang (Calf Cave or Cave of the Son of the Cow), contains a well-observed statue of a calf.

Notable caves include 13 with the colossi, probably dating from the Sui and repaired in the Ming, surrounded by a great number of square holes in the cliff face for galleries and protective buildings which have since disappeared. Cave 4 has a magnificent Song guardian figure to the W; Cave 72a has wall paintings from the 5C and Cave 93 has a mysterious grouping of the Historic Buddha with Maitreya (with pendant legs), mysterious since they are never normally associated. It may be that the sculptor has exercised license in borrowing the common Wei grouping of

Sakyamuni with Prabhutaratna and is characteristic of the rather free treatment of iconography often found in China.

Cave 102 has a very fine Wei seated Buddha with the characteristic Wei long head, small features and beautifully draped gown. In the open niche of *Cave 169* there is a very pretty Sui Maitreya and there are elegant figures of very young worshippers on the left and right walls of *Cave 123* (6C). In *Cave 127* the halo of the seated Buddha is most unusual—a lotus halo with floral scrolling (reminiscent of Tang silver decoration) is surrounded by a halo of elegant little apsaras (Buddhist angels). *Cave 133* is full of stelae; no-one knows quite why they have been gathered into the one cave but it is a fine collection of 6C carvings. The Bodhisattvas outside *Cave 191* are remarkably elegant (and of uncertain date).

Though there are fewer of them, and they are less well-preserved and less well-known, the *cave paintings* at Maiji shan have been compared usefully with those at Dunhuang, which is generally held to be a more important site. By contrast, the clay carvings are generally far more lively than those at Dunhuang. Maiji shan is set in some delightful scenery and with its rickety ladders and balconies has a dramatic charm of its own.

D. Dunhuang

Dunhuang, a small oasis town in Gansu, is the most important site on the Silk Road itinerary. Its name, 'Blazing beacon', is old, dating back to the Han dynasty when it was sited at the virtual end of the line of communication beacons and fortifications of the Great Wall that stretched W from the last major fort on the Wall (at Jiayuguan, near Lanzhou).

Dunhuang's importance lies in the cave-temple complex outside the town which contains the greatest grouping of early Chinese Buddhist painting to survive. Once the last stop in China for the great pilgrim monks of the Tang on their way to India in search of sutras and sculptures, the cave-temple, carved into a cliff with a small stream running in front of it, served as a lodging for them but was also a major Buddhist centre and a storehouse of local documents and papers.

Hotels: pretty much a one-street town (though in the 1930s it boasted the sobriquet of 'little Peking' and was one of the most lively and sprightly towns on the trade route), there are two hotels opposite each other at the eastern end of the main street. The older one, the small Dunhuang Binguan, is in a pleasant garden; opposite is a taller, newer tourist hotel.

Transport: Dunhuang is about 2 hours by tourist bus (over 3 hours in a public bus) from the nearest station, *Liuyuan* on the Lanzhou–Urumqi line.

Air: there are now flights in planes called Y97, to Jiayuguan and Lanzhou on Mondays, Tuesdays, Thursdays, Saturdays and Sundays and to Urumqi on Tuesdays and Saturdays.

Bus: the tougher individual traveller may well use buses in the Gobi: 12 hours to Golmud (in Qinghai) or 9 hours to Jiayuguan.

Equipment: everywhere in China a torch is a very useful thing but it is *essential* when visiting caves filled with paintings (and not otherwise illuminated).

Dunhuang was made a prefecture in 117 BC under Han Wudi and was then on the very edge of 'China' or the territory roughly controlled by China. Some of the beacons made of tamped yellow earth can be seen on the road between Dunhuang and the railway station at Liuyuan: these were part of the Han extension of the Great Wall (whose westernmost fort is at Jiayuguan), used for signalling between garrisons.

Buddhism entered China sometime around the beginning of the Christian era, making its way along the Silk Route which passed through the Dunhuang oasis. In AD 366 the first caves were carved by Buddhist monks in a long cliff some 25km outside the oasis town. The caves are known to the Chinese as Mogao ku (the Mogao Caves, Mogao being an old name for the administrative district during the Tang) or Qianfo dong, Thousand Buddha Caves. The conglomerate cliff into which the caves were cut was an oasis in itself for the River Da (fed from glaciers in the distant mountains) runs along in front of the cliff, enabling a sizable community of monks and pilgrims to live in the caves.

As the caves were carved out, between 366 and the last years of the 10C, they were filled with wall paintings and stucco figures, all of which were extremely well-preserved, partly because they were left virtually forgotten and undisturbed for nearly 1000 years, and partly because of the dry climate of the desert. The painters who worked in the caves ranged from well-known figures who travelled out to the oasis to local jobbing-painters. Their rates of pay and supply of materials have been described in some of the manuscripts found in the caves: famous painters were often paid 'by the painting' whilst others were on day (or weekly or monthly) rates and some of the more expensive pigments used were measured out carefully and their distribution recorded.

'Mass-production' techniques were used, especially in some of the 'Thousand-Buddha' friezes. Figures were drawn on paper and the outlines pricked out. The paper pounces were then placed on the wall and red chalk blown or rubbed through the holes to produce a dotted outline which could be reproduced ad infinitum; one of these pattern pounces survives in the British Museum's Stein Collection. A later step was the production of small stamps (presumably of clay, perhaps metal) of Buddhha figures which could similarly be repeated endlessly. This repetition of figures probably had quite a lot to do with the beginnings of printing and most of the earliest surviving Chinese examples of printing come from Dunhuang.

Despite its distance from metropolitan China, it is clear that famous painters were happy to come and work in the caves during their period of pre-eminence in the Tang. For much of the 1000 years after the fall of the Tang, however, Dunhuang was known by the name of Sha zhou, 'Sand City', a more appropriate description of the oasis that had slipped from prominence into desert oblivion. As manuscripts discovered in the caves testify, Dunhuang was an extremely important centre, from the 4C to the 10C; although distant , it was by no means cut off from metropolitan China for the monks had a ready supply of good paper (still probably quite rare and expensive in the 4th and 5Cs) made in central China on which devoutly to copy sutras. Fragments of calendars printed in the capital Chang'an and in Sichuan have also been found in the library.

Dunhuang's importance as a Buddhist centre survived the 8C Tang persecution of Buddhism, perhaps because of its distance from Chang'an, but it did not survive for long. As the Tang declined, it was isolated and threatened by invading Tibetans, by the spread of Islam in Chinese Central Asia and by the Tanguts or Xi Xia, a people of the Tibetan-language group (who used a form of script based on Chinese characters) who founded the Xi Xia kingdom in NW China (Gansu province and neighbouring areas), 1038–1368. It was probably in response to the last threat that, before they themselves dispersed, the remaining monks at the Dunhuang cave temples closed up one cave which they had filled with documents from the temples which were not to be rediscovered until the last years of the 19C. The documents, virtually all written on paper, consist mainly of Buddhist sutras, copied out as an act of devotion by monks, include a dated sutra copied on paper in AD 406 (this some 800 years before paper was widely known in Europe). The last date on a document is 1004.

Though the Buddhist sutras often provide dates and form the majority of the manuscripts from Dunhuang, there are also a very large number of secular documents including census returns, tax documents, bills of sale (including some relating to slaves). These may have been placed in the temple for safe-keeping, rather as one might deposit important papers in a bank today. Though the majority are manuscripts on paper, the cave library has also thrown up the world's earliest printed 'book', a paper scroll some 8m long, printed with the text of the Diamond Sutra and with a colophon giving a date of AD 868. Slightly earlier examples of printing have survived in Japan (and possibly Korea) but they are simple, stamped incantations: the Diamond Sutra from Dunhuang is a long, complete text, with beautifully carved characters and a complex frontispiece.

The technique used was woodblock printing, with one block for the frontispiece and all the other sheets of paper printed from blocks carved with text. A scribe first wrote out the text on thin paper which was laid face down on a block of (probably) pearwood and the text cut out. Produced some 500 years before the first printing in Europe, the Diamond Sutra is clearly not the first printed book made in China for the elegance of the frontispiece and calligraphy demonstrates that it must have been the product of a long period of development; it is a lucky survivor of the dry, dark walled-up cave. The Diamond Sutra was purchased by Sir Marc Aurel Stein and is now in the British Library in London.

The contents of the cave library are now scattered about the world, the majority of the manuscripts being in the British Library, the Pelliot Collection in the Bibliothèque Nationale in Paris, the Academy of Sciences in St Petersburg, and in Peking, with some ex-Otani examples now in Scandinavia. Stein was the first Westerner to reach the caves, in 1907, followed by Pelliot and Otani. Stein found that the caves were being 'looked after' by a self-appointed curator, a Taoist priest called Wang Yuanlu, who had discovered the hidden library and who spent his time collecting money to restore the caves' sculptures. After much bargaining Stein persuaded the priest to let him buy silken painted banners (now in the British Museum, London) and manuscripts with money that Wang was to use for his restoration work. Stein was in a hurry and, knowing no Chinese, though he had a Chinese helper with him, bought in bulk. The collection he brought back to England, consisting of some 7000 virtually complete scrolls and a similar number of fragments, consisted mainly of copies of major sutras, of little interest in terms of content (though the paper, ink and calligraphy, especially of the dated items, has been invaluable in establishing a chronology) but his bulk buy happened to include the Diamond Sutra, other printed items including very rare calendars (some of which were privately printed in the early 10C, in defiance of a law prohibiting the private publication of calendars and almanacs) and a number of secular texts which are still providing scholars with research material. Paul Pelliot, a sinologist, made a more careful selection so that the Paris collection is full of precious items.

Because of these Western intrusions there are no documents to be seen at Dunhuang (though some copies are displayed in the local museum), but the caves still contain a wealth of statuary and painting, mainly from the Wei to the end of the Tang (with some later over-painting and additions by such as Wang Yuanlu). The paintings are on the walls and ceilings of caves carved out of the conglomerate cliff. The surfaces were plastered with mud, then successive layers of plaster, dung and animal hair or straw. The surface was then smoothed and dressed with white kaolin (china clay) to provide a smooth surface for painting. Pigments were mixed with water and painted onto the dry plaster surface; the major pigment colours were malachite green, azurite blue, orpiment yellow, iron oxide or earth red, cinnabar vermillion, red ochre, kaolin white, white lead, lampblack (using soot from oil lamps), and powdered and leaf gold and silver. These same pigments were used to paint the statues in the caves. Chemical changes have occurred, especially in the earlier caves of the Wei and Sui periods: pink flesh tones have oxidised to dark grey and brown, and the dark, Rouault-like outlines to some of the figures were originally pale, perhaps invisible. The figures in the caves were made in different ways: smaller, free-standing figures were probably made on a wooden frame, wrapped in straw and plastered, whilst the figures on the walls and pillars were roughly rock-cut and then plastered.

The caves were excavated from AD 366 by monks who carved themselves plain caves to live in at the northern (right-hand) end of the cliff. Most of them are square and some of the earlier caves have a square stone pillar left in the centre which is carved with figures and provides (as do central sculptures) a focus for perambulating, clockwise meditation. They either have a door to the outside or a passage leading to an antechapel leading to the cliff face. The whole of the interior, every bit of wall and ceiling, was painted with icons, scenes from the life of the Buddha, paradise paintings and donor portraits in a palette dominated by green, blue, black and white with some reds (though more reds appear on silken banners), almost blinding to the viewer. There are various forms to the ceilings of the cave, some are 'tent-shaped' (in an inverted V), though most have lantern-shaped or coffered, with a series of smaller squares, one on top of the other, each set at an angle to the last.

The cliff face was limited in size; by the end of the Tang there was no space left to carve new caves so 'later' caves are reworkings of earlier ones, raising a dating problem that is eternal to China: a cave may be described as 'Wei' but have a large number of much later figures in it and it is difficult to know how far the earlier date remains valid. Of the surviving caves, 23 are described as Wei (Northern Wei 386–534, Western Wei 535–557), 95 as Sui (581–618), 213 as Tang (618–907), 33 from the Five Dynasties (907–960), 98 as Song (960–1279), three are Tangut or Xi Xia, nine date from the Yuan.

Access to the upper caves may have been easier in the past for wind and sand erosion have affected much of the façade but wooden ladders and balconies must have existed from very early on. These have now been largely replaced by pebbledash and concrete (safer) though there is still a nine-storey wooden pagoda-like building rising in the centre of the cliff in front of Cave 96 which houses a 33m high Buddha.

Though there are hundreds of caves, only some 40 are generally open to the public (at present). Those in the centre of the cliff are amongst the earliest, and those to each end are roughly the latest. Scholars and specialists may be able to see others through contacts with the Bureau of Cultural Relics or the local Research Centre; any group of people hoping to see specific caves other than those listed should apply well in advance through their host organisation, with a greater chance of success of this is also a relevant specialist organisation. Closure of the caves is done to preserve them. They are also closed for lunch and quite early in the afternoon (hours being c 8.30–11.30 and 2–4). Many groups return to Dunhuang for lunch but it is possible to eat just outside the cave complex entrance.

Caves known to have been open in 1987–88 are listed below in rough chronological order from the Northern Wei to the Xi Xia or Tangut period of 1036–1227.

Chinese art historians divide the Tang period caves into the following divisions: *Early Tang 618–712; High Tang 712–781; Middle Tang 781–848; Late Tang 848–907.*

Northern Wei

Cave 246. This cave is Northern Wei in form only; the wall paintings and figures are of the Xi Xia or Tangut period (early 11C). The cave is square with the central pillar and has an inverted V ceiling with lotus flowers.

Cave 257. Another Northern Wei cave with pillar (with a Buddha in the niche with a very elaborately painted halo), this is famous for the unrestored wall-paintings depicting the jataka story ('birth story'—stories about the previous life of the historical Buddha) of the Deer King.

The nine-coloured deer king rescued a man (shown wearing an Indian dhoti) from drowning in a river but made the man promise to tell no-one. The Queen of Benares wanted the skin of a nine-coloured deer; the man told the King of Benares where to find the deer but it was alerted to the danger by a swallow and explained the treachery to the King of Benares. The deer king (representing Buddha) stands quite unafraid. The man who betrayed him falls ill and is depicted covered in spots before he dies. The story, which is depicted at the back of the cave on the W wall, rather confusingly starts at both ends as it were and finishes in the middle, its episodes divided by saw-toothed mountains (one of the earliest landscape depictions surviving in China). An interesting feature is the deep red used as a background colour which apparently occurs in the jataka text for the treacherous man explains that the deer is to be found 'within yonder clump of flowering sal and mango, where the ground is as red as cochineal' and apparently the earth around Benares is a deep red colour. The artist was presumably working with the text in mind.

Other wall paintings include Northern Wei Buddhist angels (apsareses), vigorous, blackened figures with looped drapery and haloes, flying amongst bands of flame. There is also a fine depiction of a garden and garden buildings (used by architectural historians). Figures sit on cross-legged stools in an open-fronted hall in a walled garden filled with clumps of flowers. Beside the hall is a four-storey tower of a slightly impossible type; the artist has not quite mastered the intricacies of structure though the style is credible. Each storey has a roof (like that of the pavilion) with curled acroteria at the end of the ridge, between which the next storey rises, though the combination of ridge acroteria and upper storey is unlikely. In other construction details the tower is exactly like the ceramic burial models of towers found widely during the Han and suggests the continuity of the form, as well as putting it in a context.

Amongst the sculpture, a meditating Bodhisattva with one leg crossed over the other and one hand held pensively to the chin shows strong Indian influence in the bodily form and especially the face. The narrow, almost hooked nose and chiselled, curved lips are in the Indian tradition (more characteristic Northern Wei figures have slightly block-shaped heads, high, thin arched eyebrows and rather tiny smiling lips and eyes).

Cave 259. A Buddha figure in this cave is very characteristic of the Wei. Seated with three folds of its lower garment concealing the lower part of the body, the figure is slightly stiff and upright with a block-shaped head, the curving linear eyebrows and small, slightly self-satisfied features. One of the earliest caves, this does show strong Indian influence in the form of the niches with their elegant, wide and lightly pointed arches and Buddhas with very Indian features.

The major figures are a pair (reminiscent of the common pairing of small Northern Wei Buddhist bronzes), the historic Buddha and Prabhubaratna (the 'ancient' Buddha, who had been in nirvana for long but who reappeared to hear the historic Buddha, Sakyamuni, preach the Lotus sutra. His presence revealed that nirvana did not mean annihilation and also affirmed that the Lotus doctrine was the Buddha-gospel). The cave's ceiling resembles a tiled ceiling with beams.

Western Wei (535–556)

Cave 249. The major Buddha figure of Maitreya (the Buddha of the future) shown, as almost always, sitting with both feet firmly on the ground, has been altered, the head and hands replaced during the late Qing, but the paintings are original. The ceiling with its square painted coffer ceiling has fine pictures including a four-armed, four-eyed figure supporting the sun and moon; he stands with his feet in a river from which a red deer drinks. On the N ceiling face is a hunting scene which includes a beautifully drawn outline (unfinished) of a wild ox and a leaping wild cat amongst the saw-toothed mountains, trees and clouds.

This landscape style with the real (ox, hunting scene, trees and mountains) mixed with the heavenly (dragons, flying angels, human-headed birds) is reminiscent of Han painting and decoration in content and, to some extent, in style. Han incense burners in the form of mountains have the same grouping of animals and mountains and clouds and the swirling linear style is like that found on lacquer wares. On the E wall are musicians and a tumbler.

Northern Zhou (557–581)

Cave 428. The cave is of the central pillar type with an inverted V-shaped roof. The niches around the pillar have the same wide, lightly-pointed arches as in Cave 259. Under the figures in the niches (repaired in the late Qing) runs a row of donor figures, men and women in elegant stances, the women in long dark outer robes with paler underdresses, the men in knee-length gowns.

Paying for holy paintings was a devout act, which would help the donor to pass quickly through courts of judgement into Amitabha's paradise and small figures of the donors were frequently included in wall paintings and silken banners from Dunhuang. The largest group of donors (4200) are found in this cave, a crowded group to be seen under a triple-row version of the Mahasattva jataka (a story from the former life of the historic Buddha) at the northern end of the eastern wall.

This is a fascinating painting, with its fan-shaped trees and frequent depiction of open-fronted halls with roof-ridges terminating in curled owls'-tail acroteria (which are of great interest to architectural historians since no actual timber buildings survive from the period). The scenes are broken up by saw-toothed mountains and the open-fronted halls and there are small cartouches for entitling the scenes so that the whole is a sort of cartoon-strip version of the tale in which three brothers go hunting. Before they leave they do some target practice (top row). When hunting, they find a starving tigress and her cubs and one brother stays and lies down in front of the tiger so that she may eat him and feed her cubs. She doesn't so he climbs a cliff and drops dead in front of her to save her the effort. When his brothers return, they build a stupa for him to commemorate his unselfishness (bottom right) and he is later reborn as the Buddha (bottom left).

Notice the lotus ceiling, whose design is also strongly reminiscent of floor tiles.

Sui Dynasty (581–618)

Cave 244. This includes some later painting—Five Dynasties painting on the W wall and some Xi Xia overpainting of the Five Dynasties paintings in the passage and on the W wall—otherwise the Buddha figures (past on the S wall, historic on the W wall and future (Maitreya) on the N wall), bodhisattvas and flying angels are of the Sui.

Cave 410. The niche with five figures is original; behind is a tunnel-like passage.

Cave 420. A Sui cave, this has one of the most original compositions amongst the ceilings at Dunhuang, a huge grouping of buildings. Encircled by zigzag walls which are topped with rooflike tiling, a variety of halls are depicted—simple open halls with gable half-hip roofs or double-roofed halls. There are taller, pagoda structures and rather fine gates with double roofs. Bracketing is indicated by a a zigzag line under the eaves and the whole busy temple complex (perhaps based on a major centre like Wutai shan which is and was filled with temples) is a fascinating survival from a period from which no timber building still stands. The sculptures are also rather fine, with a rather Indian cast to the features, especially of the attendant Bodhisattvas, but a greater confidence in modelling which anticipates the plastic freedom of the Tang.

Cave 427. This has a Song antechamber with two guardian figures repainted in the Qing. Song-dynasty donors paid for the roofbeams of the antechamber which bear dates. The inner cave is Sui with the same grouping of Buddhas as in Cave 410 though the garments of the Bodhisattvas and attendant figures show strong Persian influence in their decoration. It is said that gold leaf on the ceiling was stolen by Russian soldiers in 1920.

Early Tang (618–712)

Cave 202. The sculptures are of the Qing period, the wall paintings original. On the E wall is the Buddha teaching, on the N wall Buddhas of the ten directions, and on the S wall is Maitreya and a very agricultural painting of a paradise of plenty (with two harvests from one sowing). Heavenly kings guard the four corners and the farmers' clothes have been hung in the trees whilst they work.

Cave 209. Here again the figures were replaced or restored in the Qing and only the paintings are original. The coffered ceiling is decorated with grapes and pomegranates, the former, in particular, often found on Tang silverware and ceramic decoration. The cave contains some of the best Tang landscapes. Some of the distant mountains are reminiscent of the patterned saw-toothed Wei mountains in form but they rise from clouds, are mountain-coloured and generally more in a landscape tradition. Foreground mountains are outlined by different sorts of trees treated in a variety of ways, with little curlicued clouds floating above. A group of women with piled-up hair listen to a preaching Buddha.

Cave 323. This contains paintings that are very highly regarded and considered to be by the hand of a great master. The landscapes include a scene of a boat containing Buddhist figures being rowed through a landscape of small mountain peaks. It may represent the arrival in

Guangzhou of a famous sandalwood statue sent to an emperor of the Liang dynasty by an Indian king in the 6C. The mountains are not inappropriate to the Guangzhou area. The detail of the painting is charming: a man carrying a lotus rides on an ox with a small boy mounted behind him and tiny attendant figures are amongst those shown welcoming the arrival of the boat.

Cave 329. This has a painting of Amitabha Buddha and the western paradise over which he presides on the W wall; paradise scenes such as this were immensely popular in Dunhuang and a large number have been found painted on silken banners (of which there are many examples in the British Museum).

Though the landscape scenes found at Dunhuang have excited more interest (for their social and architectural content and their links with the enormously important tradition of landscape painting on silk and paper), the paradise paintings are complex and beautiful. Amitabha's western paradise was not the only one depicted, though it is probably the most popular, but other Buddhas presided over other paradises which were also painted. Amitabha's paradise usually has a lotus pond in the foreground, with ducks and small babies sitting on lotus leaves; beside the Buddha is a crowd of saints and Bodhisattvas; above are landscape scenes with temples amongst clouds.

Cave 332. The most dramatic painting in this cave is the cavalry charge on the S wall.

Cave 387. A niche-type cave (with the major figures grouped in a niche, rather than around a central pillar as in the earlier caves), the central figures are probably Qing.

High Tang (705–781)

Cave 96. This cave, with its giant 33m Buddha, lies behind the nine-storey pagoda-like structure which rises the full height of the cliff.

Climbing to the top of the cliff, above the pagoda, onto the sands above, is highly recommended. It allows a view over the valley with the poplars and the river close against the cliff, the wide expanse in front dotted with the small stupa-graves of monks, and dark mountains in the distance. The rolling sand dunes behind contrast with the stark mountains in front; thus the Gobi, not one desert but many with extraordinarily varied topography and geology.

The giant Buddha is Maitreya, the Buddha of the future, seated with his feet on the ground; the figure has a rock core (and the tunnel behind is hollowed out of the rock), covered with clay. Though originally Tang, the figure was much restored under the Republic and the left hand was last restored in 1987.

Cave 130. This contains the second-largest Buddha at Dunhuang, 26m high, which can be seen at three viewing levels. The head is 7m high with 2m ears. The elegant left hand over the left knee is the original Tang hand; the right hand is a Song replacement. Behind the Buddha are an elegant ceiling and halo, painted in black, red and green in brocade patterns. 15m-high Bodhisattvas stand beside the Buddha and there are beautifully painted Bodhisattvas in the passageway.

Cave 148. The cave was carved in AD 775 and contains a 17m 'sleeping Buddha' (the Buddha on his deathbed about to enter Nirvana) whose robes were overpainted in the Qing. Lines of disciples stand behind the figure and on the E wall is a painting of Amitabha and the western paradise. The date of the cave is recorded on a stele in the antechamber in which stand large guardian figures. Paintings echo the sculpture with five scenes showing Sakyamuni entering Nirvana.

Cave 172. The cave is dated AD 781 and the paintings are of the Tang, though the figures are Qing in date. On the N and S walls are Amitabha and the western paradise, including some startling architectural detail in the upper register, an open-fronted hall with incredibly complex and deeply projecting bracketing (similar to that on the 9C Foguang si on Wutai shan and presumably not uncommon on contemporary buildings). There is also the most marvellous canopy over the head of the Buddha.

Details in the painting include a tiny landscape of Queen Vaidehi sitting on a mat beside a fast-flowing stream. She sits with a silver censer in her hand, meditating on the rising sun (which has been, like her face, blackened by chemical action). Queen Vaidehi was imprisoned by her son but sustained by Amitabha Buddha who appeared to her in prison and recommended 16 subjects for meditation. The way she sits on the mat is interesting, not only because mats are still used for meditation, especially in Japan, but the painting antedates the common use of chairs in China (chairman, as in Chairman Mao, translates as 'chief mat' in Chinese). The leafless trees on the riverbank, with hints of blossom in the distance and the cold blue of the rippling water, all convey the chill of an early spring dawn. The 1000-armed Guanyin figure in the antechamber is of Xi xia (11C) date.

Cave 320. The Tang figures in the cave were originally covered in gold and one (Ananda) is missing, taken by Langdon Warner in 1924, together with 12 paintings from the walls and now in the Fogg Museum. The Amitabha's paradise painting has children emerging from lotus leaves in the pool beneath the pantheon. There are, as always, intriguing vignettes beside the more systematised central depiction. Here one is of monks meditating before the setting sun. They sit on mats, some in front of small pools lined with bright tiles of blue, green, red and brown, some under pine trees or bushes, against a rocky cliff with the red setting sun slowly sinking behind distant blue mountains.

Cave 328. The cave was also visited by Langdon Warner and one figure is missing: the statues are Tang, the wall and ceiling paintings are Song.

Middle Tang (781–848)

Cave 321. The paintings are Tang in date, the statues are Qing and, in the passageway, Song paintings cover the Tang originals. A heavenly palace depicted in one painting is a broad expanse, in effect on three axes, with gardens on either side and several courtyards within a walled enclosure. Octagonal garden pavilions stand amid flowering trees and the bracketing of the open-fronted halls is very impressive.

Cave 237. Again, Qing statues (Sakyamuni accompanied by Samantabhadra on his white elephant and Manjusri on his lion) accompany Tang paintings of the western Paradise (S wall), the Buddha with orchestra and dancers (N wall) and the Buddha teaching (E wall). In the centre of the painted coffered ceiling is a triangle enclosing three rabbits. Some of the painting, the quick, fluent outlining of feet and the silken folds of garments, is very attractive in its liveliness, with portraits of Buddhist notables set in frames of brightly coloured lozenges.

Cave 365. The cave has a barrel-shaped roof and a row of seven Buddhas along the W wall. Of the 1000 Buddhas on the walls, many have had their faces scraped off by Moslem iconoclasts objecting, according to Koranic prohibitions, to the depiction of human form (prohibited because no-one could equal the work of god).

There was relatively little destruction at Dunhuang, especially when compared to the fate of some of the caves nearer to Uighur (rather than mainly Chinese) settlements like Bezeklik, but the occasional Moslem and then a group of White Russians (interned in Dunhuang after escaping from China from Russia in 1922) ruined some of the paintings. It was the Russian desecration that persuaded Langdon Warner that he was quite justified in removing figures and paintings from Dunhuang although the desecration is hardly as widespread as he suggests (and removal, in consequence, hardly as easily justified).

Late Tang (848–906)

Caves 16 and 17. *Cave 16* is a large cave with a sizable platform on which stand nine Qing figures. One of the most interesting features is that the floor of patterned tiles still survives (a rare example of a flooring seen in the frontispiece to the printed Diamond Sutra of AD 868). The long entrance passage to Cave 16 is painted with Song Bodhisattvas and the tiny *Cave 17* is off the passageway. It was in Cave 17 that Wang Yuanlu discovered the hidden library of the temple, whose contents have now been scattered over the world.

The cave has an interesting assemblage of wall paintings of trees covered with creepers from whose branches a satchel and water-bottle have been suspended and by which an attendant, holding a crook, waits patiently. An attractive sculpture of the monk Hong Bian seated in the meditation position, his limbs invisible, wrapped in the patchwork robe of a monk, is inside the small cave. Today's monks' robes are made of several squares of cloth joined together (imitating the patchwork of poverty); in Dunhuang, in both drawings and sculpture like this one, the patchwork is suggested by a black criss-cross line so that Hong Bian rather looks as if he has been trussed up. The sculpture is an impressive combination of icon (upright, with slightly Indian or classically Buddhist features) and portrait (lines at the corners of the eyes, the angle of the neck).

Five Dynasties (907–960)

Cave 16. On a platform in the cave there was once a huge figure of the Bodhisattva Manjusri seated upon his lion but all that remains is the tail of the lion at the back of the platform. Behind the platform, the entire W wall is covered by a painted map of Wutai shan in Shanxi province, the Buddhist holy mountain sacred to the worship of Manjusri.

It is possible that the painting was based on a sort of pictorial pilgrim's map (of the kind still sold) for a monk from Dunhuang is known to have made the pilgrimage to Wutai shan at about the time the painting was made. The cave was built and decorated (according to the inscription) by the third daughter of the King of Xinjiang and there is a fine series of donor paintings by the E wall, a whole family richly dressed. In the Wutai painting the temples and the surrounding mountains are laid out and labelled and dark-plumed birds fly over the mountains (just as red-legged choughs do today).

Cave 98 contains some of the best 10C painting at Dunhuang, including very varied forms: a fine, rather formal, portrait series of the King of Khotan and his family with the king wearing a very complicated hat with the imperial rows of beads hanging down on either side; a lively hunting scene amongst mountains, and a richly painted, jewel-like assemblage of all-girl orchestra and dancer.

Cave 146. The statues are Qing in date. The ceiling is covered with most of the paintings including a fine central design and some lively but slightly crude guardian figures in the four corners and the 1000 Buddhas on the walls with large donor paintings (the donors do appear to get proportionally bigger as time passes in Dunhuang).

Cave 385. A niche-type cave, this has some beautiful Bodhisattvas in it.

Northern Song (960–1127)

Cave 55. The statues and paintings are all original. The major figures are of the past, present and future Buddhas with the statue of a king on the S side; there are four guardians in the corners. There is a dragon in the centre of the coffered ceiling.

The paintings, particularly the screen-like series on the lower surface of the walls, are interesting as they are close in style (but slightly superior in technique) to a small illustrated booklet of part of the Lotus sutra now in the British Library (originally from Cave 17). The scenes include one which is usually interpreted as Prince Siddharta (the Buddha) riding out on a white horse, leaving the haven of his father's palace for the first time (this preceding his first view of the old, poor, sick and dying citizens of his father's kingdom, a sight which was to shock him profoundly). The horses with their neatly tied tails are well painted, as is the solid fortress with its imposing entrance gate. Other parts of the painting include agricultural scenes of ploughing and animal husbandry and of a boat with a beehive-shaped canopy being beset by crocodiles and demons as those on board call upon the Bodhisattva Guanyin for protection (as instructed in the Lotus sutra).

Cave 152. The long passageway into the cave has Song floor tiles still in place and Song paintings on the ceiling although the wall paintings are later (Xi Xia).

Cave 256. The cave's ceiling paintings have fallen down so that the chisel marks of the monks who hollowed out the cave can now be seen; the statues are Qing. Paintings include donors who are non-Chinese minority peoples on the E walls and some highly decorative Bodhisattvas under jewelled and silken canopies.

The Bodhisattvas are interesting for they are moustached: Bodhisattvas in Indian Buddhism are invariably masculine but in China, Guanyin (Avalokitesvara), in particular, assumed a somewhat ambivalent but increasingly female form as he was associated with the 'female' qualities of mercy, provision of children for the childless and the rescue of those in distress. Some of the earlier Indian-influenced figures are also slightly female in form but here (as in some of the silken banners from Dunhuang in the British Museum), although the jewelled robes could be somewhat female, the thin, curly moustache is unambiguous.

Cave 454 has served as a sort of 'Lady Chapel' for women came in to pray to the Qing Guanyin figure, apparently perambulating around the figures in one direction if a boy was required, the other for a girl (a highly unlikely thing to wish for in traditional China). The floor tiles and four heavenly kings in the corners are original, as are the Song paintings on the walls, some of which have been blackened by fires lit by the White Russian soldiers so abhorred by Langdon Warner. There is a particularly fine procession of minority leaders in striped under-robes and gowns richly patterned with flowers.

Though the figures (including Guanyin) are Qing in date, they are said to have been made before Wang Yuanlu arrived; perhaps this was the only cave that was still in use by those wishing to pray to Guanyin for the boy-girl perambulation sounds characteristic of late traditional popular religion.

Xi Xia (1036–1227)

Caves 354 and 367. Later caves apparently show a greater Tantric influence, not surprising given the Tibetan influence over the area. Mandalas (mystic meditational diagrams) have been found amongst the paper documents in the caves, probably dating from the 10C and it is said that some of the Yuan caves such as No. 465 include tantric paintings of sexual union, a form of enlightenment.

The above (with the exception of No. 465) are caves that are or have been generally open to the public, under supervision. Virtually every cave has something to offer and once the eye is in, it is not too difficult to distinguish roughly between the narrow iconic figures of the Northern Wei with their wedge-shaped heads, the increasing confidence of the Sui figures and the supreme confidence of the Tang; to enjoy the glimpses of the landscape revealed in paintings and appreciate the genre figures.

Other caves that might be requested could include (Early Tang) Cave 431 which includes a scene of some finely drawn horses, some with long natural tails, others with their tails tied up decoratively, and a small groom or ma fu (the 'mafoo' of expatriates and expatriate novels set in the 1920s and '30s) resting with his head on his knees. High Tang caves include 23 and 148 with genre scenes of ploughing in the rain and a flock of oxen, simply, almost crudely drawn; Cave 45 with its illustrations of Chapter 25 of the Lotus Sutra (describing how those in various sorts of distress should call upon the Bodhisattva Guanyin for salvation. A marvellous boat with striped sails is beset by demons and some travellers meet with thieves in a landscape, all very beautifully drawn. *Cave 217* has some marvellous Bodhisattvas in outline (unfinished) and drawings and paintings signed by various artists. *Cave 39*, as well as many others, has some wonderfully confident apsaras in swirls of cloud and trailing silks, the 'flying angels' sometimes used as a sort of logo for Dunhuang.

Mid Tang caves include a herd of softly painted oxen in *Cave 238*; Late Tang caves of interest include *156* with a huge cavalry force drawn up with banners and armour, and *Cave 85* where a series of scenes from the life of the Buddha (in a Chinese setting) includes genre scenes of a butcher at work and a couple playing the qin under a tree.

Outside the caves, far across the river are scattered stupas, burial places for the ashes of some of the monks who lived at Dunhuang. Near the road back to the oasis is the *Stupa of Wang Yuanlu*, a rather tall and ornate structure with a long inscription.

Behind the cliff face and caves are extensive sand dunes and in the dunes some 7km S of Dunhuang town is the *Crescent Lake*, a small, new-moon-shaped pool fed by a spring and which used to have temples and rest-houses for pilgrims on its S side (of which some ruined walls remain). Now there is a gate with camels and drivers ready to take tourists around the dune to the lake. You can climb to the top of the dunes (on the previously inhabited side of the lake, I believe) and slide down on your bottom in an attempt to make the sands 'sing' or roar like thunder (I have never succeeded). Trees growing beside the lake include tamarisk and saksaul (*Anabasis ammondendron*); coots swim and dive on it, and the intrepid missionaries Cable and French reported in the 1940s that they found the sweet-scented sand jujube (*Eloeagnus latifolia*), a silver-leafed plant with small fragrant flowers growing by the lake in early summer.

In the town of **Dunhuang**, on the S side of the main road by the traffic roundabout, there is a small *museum*, run by the *Dunhuang Research Institute* (founded in 1943; the main building is on the road to the caves). It includes a display of facsimiles of manuscripts found in the caves (including a brightly coloured version of the famous Star Map of the early 10C now in the British Library) and interesting items excavated in and around Dunhuang like reed torches for the beacons and some of the bamboo slips on which records were kept during the Han dynasty.

E. Turfan

Turfan or **Turpan** (a Uighur word for 'lowland'), an oasis town on the northern silk route between Hami and Korla, lies in the Turfan depression which reaches 154m below sea level at its lowest point at Lake Aydingkol. Unlike Dunhuang which is in appearance and population a 'Chinese' oasis, Turfan is very much Uighur and Islamic today. It is, however, surrounded by ruins of previous oasis cities which, though Uighur rather than Chinese, date from before the Islamic influence on the area and include many Buddhist sites.

N are the 'Flaming Mountains' and the water which flows from the melting snows there is supplied to Turfan by man-made underground channels or 'karez' which prevent the water from evaporating in the summer desert heat before it reaches the town. The karez system (there are said to be 1600km of underground channels in Turfan county) is thought to have been introduced from Persia some 2000 years ago. The gradient down from the mountains enables the water to flow naturally throughout the system. Every so often there is a well cut from the surface down into the karez to allow ventilation and access in order to keep the channels

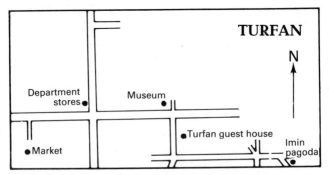

clear. The water is used to irrigate grapevines, a feature of the oasis.

Railway: the nearest station is Daheyuan on the Lanzhou–Urumqi line, 32km N of the town.

Buses: tourist groups are often brought by bus from Urumqi or Dunhuang; long-distance public buses ply the same routes.

Hotels: the Turfan Binguan is a very pleasant old hotel, once a caravanserai with vine trellises in the garden; it is a short walk (or donkey ride) from the Museum and the market. Some distance N is the Er Binguan (No. 2 Guesthouse), a modern tourist hotel.

Turfan itself is a pleasant, small market town with no enormous history of its own (though the Imin Mosque dates back to 1777) but it is close to the ancient capital of the Uighurs and some early cave-temples.

The Uighurs, still numerically dominant in the area, are descended from nomadic Turkic tribes from the Lake Baikal/Lake Balkash area who grouped themselves together as a political unit in the 7C AD, after defeating the Xiongnu. They speak a Turkic language, much of which is intelligible to speakers of modern Turkish: many words being identical. Between the 9C and 12C the Uighurs settled and began to farm, establishing themselves from 840–1209 in the area with their capital at what is now called Gaochang (c 45km SE of Turfan, near the village of Karakhoja) but which was known in Turkish as Kocho (Chotscho to German archaeologists like Von Le Coq who excavated in the area in the 1920s), also as Idikut Shahri.

The Uighurs were converted to Islam from the 9C as the faith was carried into Central Asia, just as Buddhism in Chinese territories was anyway beginning to lose its sway in the face of imperial prohibitions and persecution. Islam has had its effect on the Uighur way of life: the women wear chiffon headscarves and trousers under dresses (which are sometimes made of ikat-weave silk with its different-coloured stripes fading into each other) and men wear small squared skull-caps of black cotton with white embroidery in the sort of curled leaf-shape found on paisley shawls.

The town today is very different in appearance from Dunhuang and other 'Chinese' oases. The streets are lined with poplars and the distinctive mud-brick houses of the Uighurs. These are square, often with dark, cool semi-subterranean rooms and a yard in which there is usually a high round bread oven built of clay, the yard covered with timbers over which vines are grown to provide both grapes and shade from the sun. The windows of the houses are very small and some use is made of open-work brick windows for ventilation. Cable and French describe how the inhabitants of Turfan in the 1930s slept on high beds because of the 'large and virulent scorpions which creep under sleeping mats, drop onto the unconscious sleeper from the beams or hide themselves in his shoes. One jumping spider with long legs and a hairy body as large as a pigeon's egg leaps on its prey and makes crunching noises with its jaws…Turfan cockroaches are over 2 inches in length with long feelers and red eyes which make them a repulsive sight…'.

Many of the houses have open-brick towers attached, for drying grapes. The gateways to the mosques are brightly painted with little minarets and some of the modern municipal buildings have very distinctive façades of an architectural type I can only describe as Communist Central Asian. The market stalls show the difference of culture: they are piled high with dried raisins and sultanas; food-stalls sell large flat loaves of unleavened bread, mutton kebabs, mutton pasties and pilau made from rice, mutton, carrots and sultanas. Mildred Cable and Francesca French described the dried-fruit market in Turfan as:

> ...one of the most varied and certainly the cheapest in the world. The vendor sits amid piles of sultanas of varying quality—the dark, the pale, the golden and the jade-green...dried black plums and apricots...there are also piles of sweet apricot kernels...so sweet as to be almost indistinguishable from the almond; it is used in making an emulsion which is served as a drink at feasts...there are also dried peaches, nectarines and mulberries, piles of shelled walnuts and dried jujube fruit.... Sellers of cotton goods are numerous...some of this material is very cleverly dyed, for the women know how to knot little bunches in the length of stuff before it goes to the dyer, so that when it comes back they open it out and find a pattern of flowers or butterflies scattered at regular intervals over the material.... The silk merchants exhibit skeins of floss silk dyed in every colour and Turfan silk is highly prized by the women of Turkestan for embroidering caps. Each city has its own characteristic skull-cap, and men from any locality can be recognised by their head-dress. For example, the Aqsu men wear a handsome cap of black velvet heavily embroidered with gold and silver thread, the Hami and Turfan men wear variegated silk embroideries, but the pattern and design is different in each....

They also mention carpet weaving, the leather merchant and the leather boots he sells, melon sellers (from Hami), herbalists and the food-sellers with their kebabs and pilau.

Outside the town, on the road out to Gaochang, you pass the *cemetery* with its distinctive graves, the finer ones like small domed houses in whitewashed brick.

Sites to visit in Turfan itself include the market, the Museum, grape farms and the karez system and the Imin (or Emin) Minaret.

The Museum is easily reached from the old guesthouse on foot, as is the market. Turn right out of the guesthouse and walk up the road to the first main crossroads where the **Museum** is diagonally opposite (on the NW corner), approached through a poplar-filled garden. It contains exhibits excavated from some of the Tang tombs in the desert (Astana) which include some fine examples of Tang silks and a single (apparently fossilised) stuffed dumpling or jiaozi. This is insufficiently publicised for it should put paid to the argument about whether Marco Polo found spaghetti and ravioli (or jiaozi) in China or introduced them from Italy. This dumpling antedates Marco Polo whether or not he went to China. There are also exhibits from the old Uighur capital at Gaochang, including documents relating to land tenure in the early 7C.

Turn right out of the Museum, go straight over the next major intersection (on whose corners are the main department store and a *Minorities Store* where you may find some of the traditional items like leather boots, skull-caps and ikat cloth) and take the next turning on the left for the centre of the *market* (described above). It is open every day but, as elsewhere in Xinjiang, Sunday is the busiest day.

The **Imin Minaret** is also walkable (about half an hour) from the old guesthouse (or you could travel on one of the tiny donkey carts controlled by small boys who hang around outside the guesthouse if the weather is terribly hot). Turn left out of the guesthouse, turn left again at the first crossroads and the road takes you to the fine brick minaret.

The minaret is the most striking building of the now disused mosque. It was built in 1778 by the then local ruler, as a Chinese work on architectural history has it, 'Prince Sulaiman of Turfan', in honour of his father Prince Emin, a Hajji. Most European

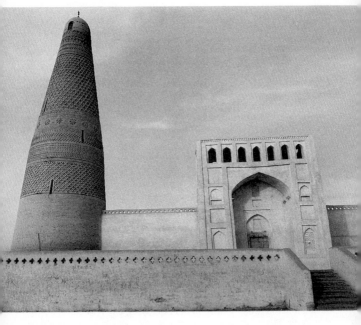

Turfan: the Imin Mosque

guidebooks call it the Imin Minaret; the name of the man to whom it was dedicated is rendered in Chinese as 'Emin' and the local name for the minaret is Sugong ta (Prince Su's pagoda).

The minaret is constructed entirely of brick, in the style of the pre-Safavid architecture of Iran, and is a lovely example of decorated brickwork. 44m or 36m high, depending on whether you follow the 'Zhongguo mingsheng cidian' or Qinghua University's 'Historic Chinese Architecture' (1985). The minaret is broad at the base and tapers markedly. Broad bands of bricks set in different patterns, of the sort that Robert Byron described as 'tweed' or zig-zags, here herringbone, lozenges, crosses and daisies, give a wonderful texture to the warm yellow bricks.

Grape farms and the karez can be visited by arrangement with China Travel Service (office in the old guesthouse).

Trips outside Turfan can be made to Jiaohe (the ruins of Yarkhoto), c 9.5km W, and to the cave temples of Bezeklik (48km NE), the cemetery at Astana (40km SE) and the ruins of Gaochang (c 45km SE, just beyond Astana). These huge ruined settlements are difficult for the layman to understand (or reconstruct) except in scale: their size and number, however, convey something of the importance of the Silk Road and the oases of Central Asia in earlier times.

Jiaohe (Meeting of Rivers), the Chinese name for *Yarkhoto* (which in Turkish means the same thing), is thought to have been a Han foundation as a Chinese garrison town, taken over in the 6C by the Uighurs. The ruins of Jiaohe are clearer and slightly easier to comprehend than those at Gaochang which was the more important town. Jiaohe was a rectangular, unwalled settlement about 1000m N–S, 300m E–W, with a strongly marked central avenue running from N to S. Different quarters have been distinguished within the town on the basis of excavated artefacts and architectural remains: the NW corner was mainly filled with Buddhist temples with Buddhist figures, stupas and pagodas, whilst the NE corner was filled with courtyard dwellings. The grander architectural remains with multi-courtyard buildings of the SE corner suggest that this was the governmental centre of the town. There was also a grand Buddhist temple at the northern end of the central avenue, built, like everything else, in brick with Tang-period tile ends decorated with lotuses.

Much pottery was found in Jiaohe, mainly unglazed with stamped and impressed decoration or crude, red-bodied glazed wares. A Tang dynasty copy of the Lotus Sutra copied in 722 was unearthed here in 1901. The settlement was abandoned in the Yuan period, for reasons which are not yet clear: some suggest that Moslem fanatics destroyed it for its Buddhist remains, others assume that the water supply failed.

Some 48km NE of Turfan are the *Cave Temples* of **Bezeklik** where 57 caves were carved on a river terrace high above the Sengim River in a striking setting, approached across the desert and up a barren gorge. The monastery existed from the 6C to the early 14C, abandoned (as were so many of the settlements in the area) at the beginning of the Yuan period. In Eastern Turkish, Bezeklik means 'place of paintings and ornaments'.

The caves, which were originally protected by wooden constructions in front, were badly damaged by centuries of use as shelters by goatherds (who blackened many of the walls with their fires) and there are few wall-paintings remaining for many were removed by a series of German archaeological expeditions (1902–03, 1904–05, 1905–07, 1913–14) led by Albert Grunwedel (1856–1935) and Albert von le Coq (1860–1930) whose finds were brought back to the Museum fur Indische Kunst, Staatliche Museen Preussischer Kulturbesitz, Berlin.

It is ironic that Grunwedel's intention, to save the wall paintings from the Moslem population of local villages which had 'got into the habit of breaking off pieces thereof to fertilise their fields', was thwarted by Allied bombers whose raids on Berlin between November 1943 and January 1945 destroyed 28 of the largest wall paintings, almost all from Bezeklik, and damaged many others brought back from Central Asia on the four expeditions. The remains are on display in Berlin, many in pocket-handkerchief-sized fragments.

In contrast with the Chinese style of the Dunhuang cave paintings, those at Bezeklik show distinct Western influences mixed with Chinese and are often described as being in an Indo-Iranian style, still apparent in the faces and figures of *Caves 37* (which includes pictures of Mongolians and an Indo-Iranian Bodhisattva) and *39* where many local rulers are depicted making offerings. The mixed influences are also apparent in the inscriptions which are frequently bilingual in Chinese and Uighur (written in the Central Asian Brahmi script).

Gaochang and the cemetery of Astana are some 45km and 40km SE of Turfan respectively. Like Jiaohe, **Gaochang** was founded by the Han Chinese in the 1C BC as a garrison town and as a base for grain production to supply the frontier troops.

By the 4C AD, during the Eastern Jin, it had become the capital of the 'Western Territories' and the centre of Gaochang prefecture. As the Chinese lost control of the western territories, it became the capital of various local kingdoms until 640 when the Chinese regained control of the area and reinstated Gaochang as capital of the western territories. The great pilgrim Xuan zang came through Gaochang in 630 on his way to India in search of Buddhist sutras and the local king, having heard him preach, wanted to keep this savant permanently in Gaochang. After Xuan zang resorted to a hunger strike he was allowed to go with a promise to return (which he did not but since it was 16 years before he returned on the southern silk route, Gaochang was by then in Chinese hands again). In this second period of Chinese rule, Gaochang was a true local economic, religious and cultural centre, with a population of 37,000. The German archaeologist Von le Coq found substantial Manichean and Nestorian remains, as well as Buddhist relics.

The Nestorian remains (chiefly wall paintings) found in a three-room temple northeast of the city walls, excited the eurocentric archaeologists of 100 years ago for the 'Nestorian heresy' was part of the history of Christianity (based on the views of Nestorius, patriarch of Constantinople who was deposed by the Council of Ephesus on 431, the ideas were transmitted to Persia by 485 and thence to Central Asia and China). Sacred writings of the Manicheans, thought to have been lost in the savage persecutions of the religion in the Middle East and the Balkans, were found in some numbers (though Von le Coq was appalled to hear that five years before the first expedition, a local peasant had thrown five cart-loads of writings in 'small characters' into the river as he was 'fearful of the sinister nature of the writings'. Nevertheless, the expedition recovered texts in 24 scripts in 17 different languages, including Manichean texts.

From 840 to 1209, Gaochang became the Uighur capital and it was eventually abandoned or destroyed in the 14C, at the beginning of the Ming. At its height, it was a roughly rectangular double-walled city covering 2 million square metres, the outer wall being some 5km in circumference.

The remains are less clearly defined than those at Jiaohe. In the SW area just outside the wall, a *Buddhist Temple*'s remains were quite well-preserved (and have been reconstructed recently). The temple covered c 10,000 square metres, with a gate, courtyard, hall and pagoda. Inside the town walls the only clear surving remains are those of a high platform and wall, built of sun-baked bricks and pise (and where Xuan zang is said to have preached in public).

Astana (which means 'Capital City' in Kazakh) is the site of a major *graveyard* whose contents can be dated on the basis of inscriptions and artefacts to between 272 and 778. Family graves in the cemetery were divided by stones and mostly consisted of earthen chambers surmounted by earth mounds.

The graveyard, as the 'Zhongguo mingsheng cidian' states, was visited in the late 19C and early 20C by predatory archaeologists from Russia, England, Japan and Germany and 'elsewhere'. Official Chinese excavations began only in 1959, revealing well-preserved bodies (preserved by the dryness of the atmosphere) wrapped in silks and provided with grave goods (many of which can be seen in the Provincial Museum in Urumqi, some in the Turfan Museum) of wood and pottery, documents and coins and paintings. The documents which relate to all aspects of life: military, political and private, have been extensively studied and published in China. Three of the caves can be visited, two containing Tang paintings and one two effectively mummified bodies (with, when I last saw them, the extra protection of mothballs stuffed into various orifices).

As Cable and French reported, destruction of the remains was considerable in the 1930s when the area was simply known to cart-drivers and camel caravanners as 'er pu', second stage, in their assessment of mileage. Local farmers used the earth to fertilise fields and ploughed within the city walls, their irrigation channels causing further havoc, though their ploughshares constantly turned up little treasures, 'we came away with a seal, an old metal horse, a fragment of an Uighur manuscript, and other small relics. Many beads are collected by children as they play among the ruins, and any old pots which are unearthed are taken into immediate use by the women, to save the expense of buying others.'

Other sites in the Turfan area listed in the 'Zhongguo mingsheng cidian' are: the *Shengjinkou Buddhist Caves* (Shengjinkou qian fo dong), 40km NE of Turfan, a collection of 10 caves dating from the 7C to the 14C which sound similar to those at Bezeklik in style, with wall paintings which include Chinese and Uighur inscriptions; the *Yaerhu qian fo dong* (Thousand-Buddha Caves of Yaerhu), c 10km NW of Turfan, said to date from the Tang and Song periods. There are seven caves, six of which are said to be 'mausoleum caves or relic caves', the seventh a monk's cave. There are wall paintings to be seen and an inscription in Turkish in Cave 5 on the W wall.

F. Urumqi

Urumqi is the capital of Xinjiang province and the Uighur Autonomous Region. It is situated on the northern part of the old Silk Route at the N end of a corridor between the E and W Tianshan mountains which separate the Dzungarian basin (N) from the Tarim basin (S). Just E of Urumqi is one of the highest peaks in the Tianshan range, the 5000m Bogdo Ola.

The major site in the city is the Provincial Museum; outside, tourists are often taken to the Heaven Lake and the Kazakh settlements there. Carpet-weaving factories are also often on tourist itineraries.

Railway: the station is in the W of the town; the line is on the end of a spur off the main line across the Gobi. Long-distance travel to Peking (3 days) or Xi'an (2 days) gives an impressive view of the ever-changing Gobi and then the loess areas nearer Xi'an.

Air: the airport is 15km outside Urumqi. There are twice-daily flights to Peking and less frequent departures to Chengdu, Guangzhou, Lanzhou, Shanghai and Tianjin (metropolitan or relatively metropolitan centres) and fairly frequent flights to closer locations including Altay, Dunhuang, Jiayuguan, Fuyun, Hetian, Karamay, Kashgar (Kashi), Korla, Kuqa and Qiemo. There are also international departures to Istanbul and Bahrain.

Hotels: the Youyi binguan is a long way S of the town, the Kunlun Hotel on Fanxiulu, somewhat closer in (but still not close enough to walk to the centre). The Huaqiao binguan is on Xinhua nanlu and is the most central.

Urumqi (whose name is said to mean 'beautiful pastures' in Mongolian) is not a city with a very long history of significance. During the Tang dynasty, it was merely an en-route stop to the administrative centre of the region at Jimusaer (to the NE of Urumqi). In 1760 the Qianlong emperor defeated the Mongols and regained Chinese sovereignty over the NW and gave Xinjiang ('New dominions') its name. In 1884 Urumqi became the capital of this new province. Moslem rebellions against Chinese rule were common and in 1911, after the overthrow of the Qing dynasty, Xinjiang was ruled by a series of warlords.

From 1911 to 1928, 'Marshall' Yang Zhengxin controlled the area despite border problems with the Soviet Union (during which he allowed a large number of White Russians to settle in Urumqi). His ferocity made him unpopular and his habit of inviting his enemies to banquets and beheading them caught up with him when he was shot at a banquet in 1928. His successor did not last long for his policy of giving land that belonged to local Moslems to Chinese settlers led to a revolt in 1931. This was led by the young Moslem Ma Chongying who managed to take much of Xinjiang. In 1934, he and his 'Tungan' troops (see below) were beaten back from Urumqi for a third time, by Soviet Russian troops summoned by the desperate Governor of Xinjiang, Sheng Shicai. Mysteriously, ironically perhaps, Ma Chongying took refuge in the Soviet Union where he eventually disappeared, presumed to have been killed on Stalin's orders.

The influence of the Soviet Union in Urumqi had grown considerably since the opening of a consulate there (together with others in Kashgar and other parts of Xinjiang) in 1922. Though Sheng Shicai, the provincial Governor was to turn his allegiance to the KMT government in Nanking in the 1940s, the distance and isolation of Urumqi from metropolitan China meant that allegiance with and assistance from the neighbouring Soviet Union was much easier to obtain. The varied foreign residents of the town in the 1930s were divided between the walled Chinese town and separate Russian and Uighur or Moslem quarters and the most often-cited description of the town by Mildred Cable and Francesca French was unpromising: 'The town has no beauty, no style, no dignity and no architectural interest. The climate is violent, exaggerated and at no season pleasant…'.

Architecturally, Urumqi remains somewhat unprepossessing and its situation (in a rare part of the Gobi that looks like a large slag-heap) similar. What charm it has derives from an attractive population of cheerful Uighurs and their bustling street markets. The residents are divided between Chinese (50 per cent) and 50 per cent minority peoples of which the Uighurs are the most numerous but which also includes Hui, Kazakh, Tatar, Uzbek, Khalka, Mongolian, Tahur, Tajik, Manchu and Sibo (descendants of Manchu soldiers) and Russians.

The Hui, formerly often referred to as Tungans, are Chinese-speaking Moslems of mixed racial origin who live mainly from sheep-farming in Gansu, Ningxia and Qinghai provinces (though there are quite a number in China proper, especially the NW provinces). The name 'Hui', which is applied to all Chinese Moslems, means 'to return' and one explanation of the term is that when these Moslem Chinese first appeared in China proper they were unwanted and so promised to return from whence they came. Uighurs, Kazakhs, Uzbeks and Tatars all speak Turkic languages and are found on both sides of the Sino-Soviet border.

Manchus and Sibo both originated in the NE whilst Mongols and Tahurs originate in Mongolia. The Khalka (or Kalmuck or Torgot) are a Mongolian tribe who left Mongolia in the early 17C to settle on the Volga in Russia. In 1770, however, because they wished to practise their Buddhist religion in freedom, they made a mass exodus back to the newly reclaimed northwest territories of China where they were welcomed by the Qianlong emperor and settled W of Urumqi at Karashahr and in Mongolia.

Distances in Urumqi (particularly from most hotels into town) are considerable and most visits for individuals will be best made by taxi rather than on foot.

The *Xinjiang Provincial Museum* (Xinjiang sheng bowuguan) is on Xibei lu, not very far from the Kunlun Hotel. It consists of two parts, one displaying archaeological and historical relics unearthed in the province, notably in the Turfan region (including some of the sand-preserved bodies from the Astana graveyard and the charming little multi-coloured clay grave figurines). There are also numerous examples of silk textiles (from the old Silk Route) including Tang silk paintings from Turfan. The other section of the museum is devoted to the local minorities and includes a Kazakh yurt of felt, Mongolian riding boots and decorated saddles, heavy silver jewellery and the bizarre hats of the Daur made from animal heads.

The finest example of Qing architecture surviving in Urumqi is the **Shaanxi da si da dian** (the Great Hall of the Great Temple of Shaanxi province) on Yonghezheng xiang. Its main hall is constructed in two parts, the front a simple pitched roof structure; behind a pavilion-style building with a complex roof.

In the S of the city, in *Yanerwo gongyuan* (Yanerwo Park), is the *Martyrs' Memorial Hall*. It stands behind the tomb of the local Communist martyrs who included Mao Zemin, younger brother of Mao Zedong, executed in 1942 by Sheng Shicai, the Provincial Governor who had then just allied himself with the KMT government in Nanjing for he claimed he had just uncovered a plot by his erstwhile ally Stalin to take over Xinjiang. In front of the tomb is a stele inscribed in Chinese, Uighur, Mongolian and Kazakh.

In *Hongshan gongyuan* (Hongshan Park) in the centre of the city, just N of the roundabout at the northern end of Xinhua bei lu, a place where the Qing army's horse troops were stationed, there was once a large temple to the Jade emperor. It was burnt down in 1929–30 and now only a small nine-storey brick pagoda, the *Zhenlong ta* (Pagoda of the Tranquil Dragon), remains. It is said to have been built in a place where dragons endlessly appeared and needed calming. Its date is uncertain but it can be no earlier than the Qing and it is a 'fengshui'-type pagoda, one not associated with a Buddhist temple but built on a hill to improve the local fengshui. It is solid and has shallow eaves marking each storey.

Outside the park, just to the W of the entrance is the main department store in Urumqi (Hongshan department store) with a major market area in front of it. If you walk S down Xinhua bei lu, the fifth major turning on the left is a road with another major bazaar on it.

I do not know the address but the Provincial Song and Dance Troupe (Xinjiang sheng wudao tuan) is said to be situated in the building that was the old Russian consulate in Urumqi.

A frequent excursion from Urumqi is to **Tian chi** (Heaven Lake), some 112km across the desert to the E of the city. Situated at 1800m up in the Tianshan (Heavenly Mountains), the 3.2km-long lake lies in scenery reminiscent of the Swiss Alps with steep green pastures, conifer forests and snowy mountain peaks above, and would be a marvellous place for walks if time permitted.

Individual travellers can reach Tian chi by public bus (tickets available from a small booth on the N side of Renmin gongyuan or People's Park which is diagonally opposite Hongshan Park: buses leave from the same spot) and stay overnight in the guesthouse there. Nearby are Kazakh yurt settlements, now set up for tourist visits.

G. Hetian

On the southern Silk Road, S of the *Taklamakan Desert*, is **Hetian** (the modern Chinese name) or *Khotan*. S are the foothills of the Kunlun Mountains where two rivers rise to flow past Hetian to join the Tarim River. They are the Black Jade River (Karakash) to the W and the White Jade River (Yurungtash) to the E and they bring boulders of jade down from the mountains.

Khotan was the source of Chinese jade (nephrite), probably since neolithic times. Nephrite is only one of a group of hardstones that the Chinese carved and polished. The group includes chalcedony, saussurite, soapstone, serpentine, bowenite, jadeite and others and is collectively known as yu (usually translated as jade), with only nephrite singled out as zhen yu ('true jade'). The recovery of jade boulders from the rivers and their subsequent trade was noted by Zhang Qian on his mission of exploration for the Han emperor in 125 BC and Chinese tradition had it that jade was best found by women who had an affinity for the stone. Technological works such as the 'Tian gong kai wu' (Creations of Nature and man, by Song Yingxing, late 16C) contain illustrations of ladies diving for jade in the rivers of Khotan although the material was being more systematically mined in the Kunlun mountains by that time.

Khotan was the capital of the kingdom of Yutian and traditionally maintained trading links with China, at times, especially during the Han and Tang dynasties, being incorporated into the Chinese empire. Like many of the other oasis kingdoms of the western Gobi, it was a Buddhist centre, following the Hinayana tradition rather than the later Mahayana which was followed in China. The pilgrim monk Xuan zang visited Khotan in about 645 on his way back to China from India and noted the jades of light and dark colours in the market and also the fine silks that were locally produced (according to tradition, only since AD 440 when a Chinese princess arrived with silk-moth eggs smuggled in her hair). These were, and still are, woven into the distinctive ikat weave with wave-like stripes produced by tie-dying the warp threads so that the pattern is in the warp. Xuan zang was greeted by the king of Khotan and escorted in a procession with musicians, flowers and incense to a nearby monastery where he stayed for several months. Marco Polo also claimed to have passed through Khotan and, with his usual unerring ability to miss the point, failed to note either jade or silk.

It was from Khotan that the first rumours of buried cities and lost civilisations reached Western archaeologists and explorers in the late 19C, again as a result of preliminary moves in the 'Great Game'. The British in India were keen to map and survey the Taklamakan and the eastern fringes of the Pamirs. In the 1860s the head of the Survey of India had the idea of sending Indians out secretly to survey the area, posing as simple travellers through Yarkand to Ladakh. The first Indian surveyor died before he reached home but his notes were retrieved by an English surveyor, William Johnson, who was, to his surprise, invited to visit Khotan by the Khan who had heard of his surveying trips and who, apparently, wished to try and hold him hostage to force the British to arm Khotan against the Russians. Whilst in Khotan, Johnson heard of the sale of excavated tea-bricks dug up from the desert and managed to acquire one. Frugal local people, whose supply of tea from China had dried up, were using the old bricks of pressed tea dust that they found in ruins in the desert (just as in Gaochang where excavated pots were used in local households to save the expense of buying new ones). Johnson was followed by Sir Douglas Forsyth in 1870. He went to Yarkand (between Khotan and Kashgar) to try and forge an anti-Russian alliance with a local ruler Yakub Beg who had seized much of Chinese Turkestan. Forsyth (whose missions to Yakub Beg met with mixed success) later read a paper to the Royal Geographic Society in London 'On the buried cities in the shifting sands of the great desert of the Gobi' which, with its mention of Bactrian gold coins and Buddha figures, started the great archaeological race which first centred on Khotan.

A sidelight on the effect of the sudden arrival of numerous competing archaeologists in a small oasis town on the fringes of the Taklamakan is the story of Islam Akhun and the lost languages of Central Asia. Birch-bark manuscripts that had filtered back to Calcutta from Kucha in the 1890s were deciphered by Dr Augustus Rudolph Hoernle. He was so excited by their antiquity that he had all sorts of people looking out for manuscripts, including the British Consul at Kashgar, George Macartney, who purchased a number from Islam Akhun in Khotan. These caused Hoernle considerable headaches as he attempted to decipher the 'lost languages' until Sir Marc Aurel Stein managed to catch Islam Akhun in 1901 and proved what had begun to be suspected, that he had been making his own 'ancient' manuscripts (many of which are still in the British Library in London).

Sites in the vicinity of Khotan include *Yotkan* (Yuetegan), c 10km W of the town. The remains, which include potsherds, are said to be those of an important town of Khotan, occupied from the 3–8C AD. It has not yet been systematically excavated.

The remains of an ancient city, variously known as *Malikewate* or *Shensibier* to the Chinese, lie c 25km S of Hetian and include architectural remains such as pillar bases, platforms and a Han dynasty pottery kiln (excavated in 1978). Parts of the site have been tentatively identified as a royal residence.—10km S are the remains of a stone *stupa*, some 60m in circumference and only 6m high (now), associated with small pottery fragments including Buddha heads.

Further away is the site of **Niya**, excavated by Stein in 1901 and 1906. The site is considerable, some 10km N–S and 2km E–W.

The houses there were large, made mainly of wood and plaster. A number of beams carved in the Gandharan style were found by Stein, together with bits of furniture, also of carved wood (and examples can be seen in the British Museum). The most significant finds were of wooden tablets inscribed in Prakrit with much Sanskrit mixed in, in the Kharosthi script. Both script and language are thought to have originated in the extreme NW of the Punjab. These gave some credence to the local belief that the area was colonised by Indians from Taxila in the 1st and 2C AD. Chinese wooden documents dated to AD 269 confirm that the area was under Chinese control in the late 3C. The site of Niya was apparently abandoned in the late 3C, perhaps because the Chinese withdrew, perhaps because of a shortage of water.

H. Kuqa

Kuqa (known to early Western travellers as *Kucha* and to Chinese today as *Ku che*) is the second largest town in southern Xinjiang, second only to Aqsu, and is a major oasis on a tributary of the Tarim River. It may be reached by bus from Urumqi or Turfan, or by rail from Turfan, on the northern Silk Route. Arriving by bus involves an overnight stop in Korla or Bugur.

Korla is 480km W of Urumqi and Turfan, just beyond the site of *Karashahr* (modern *Yan chi*), one of the Han garrison towns later visited by Xuan zang on his way to India in 630.

After being robbed by bandits, Xuan Zang was happy to reach the peaceful haven of Karashahr where the 'air is soft and agreeable' and the soil suitable for 'red millet, winter wheat, scented dates, grapes, pears and plums'. Karashahr was excavated by the German archaeologists Von le Coq and Grunwedel, who brought back a number of ceramic Buddha figures with very round faces and unmodelled backs (for they were made to fit into niches), and by Sir Marc Aurel Stein.

W of Korla is *Bugur*, an oasis town believed by Stein to be the site of ancient Luntai, seat of the Chinese Protector General of the Tarim Basin in the Han dynasty, but he could find no trace of it.—W of Bugur many of the old Han watchtowers or beacon towers that were built along the northern Silk Route can still be seen, their tamped-earth (pisé) construction resistant in the dry atmosphere and only weathered by wind. Around such watchtowers, which were garrisoned during the Han, Stein found masses of the bamboo and woodslips which served as the writing material for army documents and letters and which have provided a surprisingly vivid picture of the life of the army garrisons.

Written up by Michael Loewe in his 'Records of Han Administration' (Cambridge University Press, 1967), and listed by the French scholar Henri Chavannes, 'Les documents chinois decouverts par Aurel Stein dans les sables du Turkestan oriental' (Oxford, Clarendon Press, 1913) and 'Les documents de la troisième expedition de Sir Aurel Stein en Asie centrale' (London, British Museum, 1953) (catalogues of the woodslips in the British Library's collection), they are mostly dull accounts of military life (c 100 BC–AD 100) spent counting and tidying the piles of brushwood for the beacons or rounding up the local civilians or stray dogs, but there are also some stray poems, letters, calendars and doodles that enliven the picture.

Kuqa, once the capital of the independent kingdom of Qiuci that flourished until the mid 7C when its ruler accepted Chinese rule, was a town with many contacts with India and the West. It also had a long history of communication and co-operation with China from the Han when a Chinese garrison was stationed in the town to help protect the trade route and when a Prince of Qiuci had married into the Han imperial family (in 69 BC). After 658 it became one of the four garrisons of the Chinese western territories. It had long been a centre of Buddhism and was the birthplace of one of the greatest translators of Sanskrit Buddhist works into Chinese, Kumarajiva (344–c 431). Son of a Princess of Kuqa and a Brahmin father, Kumarajiva eventually settled in China as a Buddhist monk and headed a translation bureau of some 1000 monks. He was admired for the faithfulness of his translations which were yet extremely elegant in style. Despite his industry he was said to have believed that no translation could capture the flavour of the original Sanskrit and that reading translations was like eating rice that someone else had already chewed.

Xuan zang passed through after visiting Karashahr and noted that the air here, too, was 'soft'. He found the population clothed in ornamental silks and the children with their heads flattened 'by the pressure of a wooden board'. The inhabitants of Kuqa were then Hinayana Buddhists (of a tradition perhaps closer to the original canon, offering salvation only to an elevated few, less philosophically developed than the later Mahayana which also offered the possibility of salvation to all), whilst Xuan Zang followed the Mahayana tradition and refused to eat the meat offered him, also (according to his version) thoroughly defeating the King of Kuqa in a theological debate. Evidence of the Buddhist faith in Kuqa and its neighbourhood has been found in the nearby caves, most notably at Kizil.

Kizil was excavated by Von le Coq and the French sinologist Pelliot and, apart from wall paintings, it also yielded manuscripts on palm leaves, birch-bark, paper and wood, including the earliest Sanskrit manuscript and many items written in Kuchean (or Tocharian), an entirely independent branch of the Indo-European family, lost for 1000 years until these mansucripts were found and deciphered by Sylvain Levi in Paris at the turn of the century.

The caves at **Kizil** are a 1½-hour drive from Kuqa and are situated in cliffs on the banks of the Muzart River. They date from 500–700 and are strongly in the Indo-Iranian style with no trace of Chinese influence (non-existent in the region during almost all the time the cave paintings were being made). The Indian element of the style is found in the basic iconography and depiction of the Buddha and subjects from the Buddhist canon. The Iranian element is identified in decorative details, either as borders or on dress and furniture depicted in the murals. Scrolls and friezes of circular medallions with elegant stylised birds, ribbons and flower-strewn grounds are derived from similar patterns on Sassanian silks and metalwork and painting.

The caves are now numbered but were originally named by Grunwedel and Von le Coq after the subject matter of the wall paintings: Cave of the Musicians, Stairs Cave, Prayerwheel Cave, Foot-washing Cave and so on. Earthquake damage to the caves has been frequent but the worst problem for the visitor is that the best frescoes (or the wartime survivors thereof) are all in Berlin. Those interested are referred either to the Museum fur Indische Kunst in Dahlem or to the catalogue of a travelling exhibition, 'Along the Ancient Silk Routes: Central Asian Art from the West Berlin State Museums' (New York, Metropolitan Museum of Art, 1982).

There are 236 caves at Kizil of which only 74 still have reasonably well-preserved wall paintings. Chinese art historians, stressing the non-religious side of the paintings (in an atheist state) single out the musicians in Cave 38 and the scenes of ploughing and pottery-making in Cave 175.

Other cave sites that may open to visitors in the vicinity are the *Kahar* and *Kizdora Caves* which are contemporary with those at Kizil; the *Kumtura Caves* (Kumutula qian fo dong) c 30km SW of Kuqa which include some later, 8C caves, showing a marked Chinese influence in contrast with the earlier Indo-Iranian style, and the *Subashefo si* (Buddhist Monastery), 4–9C.

I. Kashgar

Kashgar (*Kashi* in modern standard Chinese), in the far W of Xinjiang province, is situated at an altitude of some 1200m above sea level, in the foothills of the ring of mountains that surround the Taklamakan Desert, with the Tian shan (Heavenly Mountains) to the NE and the Pamirs to the SW. It was the point at which the southern and northern silk routes joined, and the 'gateway to the west' for the mountain passes through the Pamirs and Karakorum mountains, leading to Pakistan, Afghanistan, India and Russia, lie just S of Kashgar. Though remote, Kashgar's strategic position has given it importance throughout history and it remains a major transport centre especially since the construction during the Cultural Revolution of the Karakorum highway linking China and Pakistan.

Airport: there are daily flights to and from Urumqi.

Bus travel: individual travellers will probably arrive by bus; the long-distance bus station is in the SE of town, near the W side of the East Lake. Buses take 3 days to Tur-

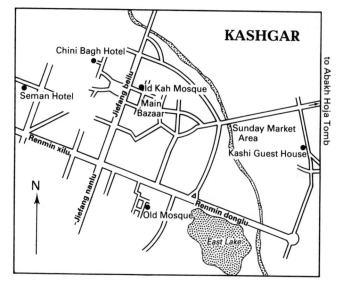

KASHGAR

Chini Bagh Hotel

Seman Hotel

Id Kah Mosque

Main Bazaar

Jiefang beilu

Renmin xilu

Jiefang nanlu

N

Old Mosque

Renmin donglu

East Lake

Sunday Market Area

Kashi Guest House

to Abakh Hoja Tomb

fan, about a day to Aksu and about 3 days to Rawalpindi.

Hotels: the best hotel in Kashgar is the Kashi binguan, well outside the centre of town, E of the Sunday market area on the E side of the Kashgar Darya River. The Seman Hotel is in the old Russian Consulate (see below) on the opposite side of town. The Chini Bagh Hotel (in the old British Consulate) is now a somewhat run-down hostel used by long-distance lorry-drivers from Pakistan. It is just NW of the Id Kah Mosque.

In AD 78 the Chinese set up a garrison in Kashgar to guard the western frontier but the area was over-run by the Western Turks until the Chinese once more assumed control in the early Tang dynasty, though this sovereignty was soon challenged by the rise of Islam. In 747 a Chinese army was sent out across the Hindu Kush to repel the Arab threat. The army was eventually defeated in 751 at the Battle of Talas River (NE of Tashkent) and Central Asia was gradually opened to Islam. The Battle of Talas River is also supposed to have marked the beginning of paper-making in the West, with the capture of Chinese paper-makers by the Turkic-Tibetan forces. These paper-makers were supposed to have been moved to Samarkand to start a paper industry there (though paper fragments dated back to some 900 years earlier have been found at sites along the Silk Road so the spread of material and technique was probably more gradual).

Kashgar had become a Moslem centre by the 10C and did not come under Chinese control again until the 18C. In the interim it may have been visited by Marco Polo whose book contains a description of the vineyards, cotton, hemp and flax fields and 'close-fisted' inhabitants, as well as the importance of the place as the 'starting point from which many merchants set out to market their wares all over the world'.

Chinese control from the 18C was constantly threatened, by the local Moslem inhabitants and by outside powers. In 1865 Yakub Beg (c 1820–77), a Moslem apparently from Soviet Central Asia, proclaimed himself Khan of East Turkestan and by 1873 was 'master of the entire Tarim region', attracting 'the attention of Delhi, London, St. Petersburg and Constantinople', with both Russia and Britain signing treaties of friendship with him. Yakub Beg apparently committed suicide in 1877 when Turfan fell to the Chinese but outside interest in the area continued for this was the beginning of the Great Game: the Russians occupied Western Turkestan in 1860 and were viewed as a threat to British India, hence the interest of Delhi and London. Kashgar was a major centre of information-gathering: in 1882 the Russians opened a Consulate in Kashgar (their consulate now occupied by the Seman Hotel), ostensibly to control trade, and in 1890 the British opened a 'listening post' which was elevated to Consular level in 1909 and which controlled Indian (British) representatives in every oasis of the Silk Road.

The extraordinary comings and goings on both sides of the Pamirs have been described by Peter Hopkirk in 'Setting the East Ablaze: Lenin's Dream of an Empire in Asia', Oxford University Press (paperback edition), 1986, in which he relies in part on many of the memoirs of British Consuls in Kashgar. Lady Macartney, wife of the first British Consul in Kashgar (Sir George Macartney who was there from 1909–18) has left a charming account of the early days in her 'An English Lady in Chinese Turkestan', 1931 (reprinted by Oxford University Press, Hong Kong, 1984). She describes the Consulate, Chini Bagh (the name means Chinese garden) which had originally been a flat-roofed courtyard house when her husband and Colonel Younghusband (of the Indian Army and the Lhasa expedition of 1904) first arrived in 1890 but which had been rebuilt (1913) as an 'imposing European house'.

Some idea of intra-consular relations may be gathered from the problem of glazing the windows, for glass was almost unknown in Kashgar but the Russian Consul, Monsieur Petrovsky 'had, as a great mark of friendship, lent my husband a large pane of glass in a frame for one window, but unfortunately before long they had a quarrel, and the precious piece of glass had to be returned.' The garden at Chini Bagh was famous for its fruit trees grown from cuttings from England, and the family house (with a pet gander who lived in the drawing room) was a haven for travellers like Peter Fleming and Ella Maillart who arrived in summer 1935 to enjoy baths after 5½ months crossing the deserts.

Peter Fleming's chapter on Kashgar in 'News From Tartary' (1936) is even entitled 'Kashgar-les-Bains'. He describes Chini Bagh as 'a pleasant house with a lovely garden, standing on a little bluff outside the city' and Kashgar itself as 'very prone to spy-fever' though he went swimming in the pool at the Russian Consulate and played 'tennis with the Russians'. For his travelling companion, Ella Maillart, Chini Bagh was also a source of sybaritic memories: 'Hot water in the bath up to one's neck', 'the gleam of crystal and silver and flowers on the mahogany table … the luxurious sense of black coffee … morning slices of bread drowned under butter and honey'—as well as playing football with the Hunza guards of the British Consulate ('Forbidden Journey', London, Heinemann, 1937). As frequently occurs in their books (they were unwilling travelling companions for both would have preferred to explore the Gobi alone but the complications and dangers were too great), whilst Peter Fleming mentions playing tennis with the Russians, Ella Maillart states that neither she nor Fleming could actually play tennis (hence her indulgence in football). Since 1949, when the Chinese reassumed full control, Kashgar has been altered somewhat, Chinese settlers bringing a statue of Chairman Mao (on Renmin lu, just E of the junction with Jiefang lu), wide streets and department stores, though the town remains essentially as Turkish as it always was. Uighurs are in a majority although the population also includes Kirghiz, Uzbeks and Tajiks.

The markets are some of the best ways of seeing the Uighur way of life. As in all the oasis towns of Xinjiang, the major market is on Sunday and is held on open ground just E of the river in the E of the town. Camels, horses, donkeys, melons, grapes, hats, goats, articles of furniture and knives are amongst the items on sale. At other times, the main bazaar area is just to the E of Jiefang bei lu (the main north–south street), due E of the Id Kah Mosque. Boots, hats of all kinds, saddles and fast food of all muttony sorts can be found there.

The **Id kah Mosque** (*Aiti ka qingzhen si* in Chinese) in Id kah Square (Aiti ka gongchang) is the largest mosque in Xinjiang. It is said to have been founded in 1738 and repaired and altered through the succeeding century, achieving its present form in 1838. Two minarets over 10m high stand beside the imposing main gate built in yellow brick with brilliant white tiling patterns. Inside the gate is an octagonal gate pavilion and there is a pool in the courtyard. The main hall is 160m by 16m and there is room for some 6000–7000 worshippers. 140 carved green pillars support the white roof of the hall.

In the S of the town is the *old mosque*, reached by a lane which leads S off Renmin lu, almost opposite (slightly to the E) of the Mao statue. The old mosque, about which there is little concrete information, is a mud-brick construction with traces of coloured tilework remaining. On the outskirts of the town are the Abakh Hoja Tomb, the San xian Buddhist caves and the ruins of Aisikeshaer.

The **Abakh Hoja Tomb**, Aba hejia mazha (mu) in Chinese, is in the suburbs of the town, to the E. Said to have been constructed in the 17C, it is surrounded by plane trees and covered with green glazed tiles. The tombs, which have been damaged, contain the remains of Abakh Hoja and five generations of his family, 72 people in all. The tomb was renovated and enlarged in 1807 but was apparently vandalised during the period before Liberation when the gold leaf on the ceiling was removed, as was a board personally inscribed by the Qianlong emperor.

Abakh Hoja was a man of great saintliness and reknown but the tomb is also said to contain the body of the probably legendary 'fragrant concubine', said by some to have been the daughter of Abakh Hoja. The story was that a Moslem princess was captured in the mid 18C and taken to Peking as an imperial concubine where she was known as 'fragrant' because she naturally emanated perfume. She pined for the desert and refused to let the emperor near her; despite this he (Qianlong) was supposed to have built her Turkish baths and a tower in the imperial gardens in Peking for her to look towards her homeland. In the end, the emperor's mother, who feared that the concubine would kill her son, is supposed to have forced her to commit suicide by 'self-strangulation'. Two oil portraits by Castiglione of a woman in armour (in the Palace Museum collection) are supposed to be of the 'fragrant concubine' of whom Hummel's 'Dictionary of the Eminent Chinese of the Qing Perod' says '... while there is little doubt that such a person actually lived, many of the stories about her are probably legendary.'

The *San xian dong* (Buddhist Caves of the 'Three Immortals') are c 10km N of Kashgar. Their origin is somewhat doubtful; non-one knows when they were carved and restoration during the Qing period appears to have effaced virtually all that remained of the frescoes and figures. Seventy tiny Buddha figures remain in one cave with traces of a lotus ceiling.

The remains of the ancient town of *Aisikeshaer* in the SE suburbs of Kashgar are thought to be those of the Chinese Tang dynasty settlement. Little work has been done on the site where some coins have been found. Legend has it that when the Arabs came, bringing Islam with them, the ruler of this place resisted them; on his defeat the town was destroyed.

There is apparently the *tomb* of a noted Uighur poet inside Kashgar's No. 12 Primary School. Information (gathered from Chinese sources) is not terribly illuminating. His name, in Chinese, was Yusipu Hasi Hajimazha. He was a scholar, poet and writer whose most famous work was an epic poem called (in Chinese) 'Fule zhi hui' which means something like wisdom through joy. He was apparently first buried elsewhere but river damage to his tomb caused ti to be moved to its present site.

37 Chengdu

Chengdu, capital of Sichuan province, is a city which manages to preserve some of its traditional flavour despite very recent improvements (the old Ming viceroy's palace was only knocked down to make way for the major department store during the Cultural Revolution, 1966–76). The history of the city dates back to the Spring and Autumn period (220–475 BC), though its greatest glory came when it was capital of the state of Shu during the Three Kingdoms (AD 221–263). From the Han, it was known for its production of silk brocade (its major river is still known as the Jin jiang or Brocade River), lacquer and salt.

Sichuan province in SW China has the highest population of any province, over 100 million, and, though one of the largest provinces, contains much mountainous, sparsely populated terrain. In the eastern part of the province is the Sichuan Basin (at about 1000m) of which the most fertile and highly populated part is the Chengdu Plain, irrigated by the Min River which has been artificially controlled since the 3C BC to improve the agricultural water supply. Sichuan is ringed by mountains, with the Yangtse passing through the narrow gorges to the E and the western part of the province (amalgamated into the present province in 1955) rising sharply to meet the Himalayan massif.

Sichuan province

Historically, because of its mountainous isolation, Sichuan has been a
semi-independent province at many periods of Chinese history. It was
first incorporated into the empire in the 4C BC; before that, its connections with the separate cultural area of Yunnan and the fringes of southeast Asia appear to have been stronger. A report in the summer of 1987
described the discovery of an extraordinary hoard of about 1000 bronze
figures, some nearly 3m high and weighing about 300kg, with strange,
barbaric, mask-like faces. Found at Sanxingdui, N of Chengdu, these
early figures, quite distinct from contemporary bronzes of metropolitan
China, emphasise the difference of Sichuan at the time, as well as its
advanced technology.

In the period after the Han, the state of Shu in Sichuan produced semi-
legendary heroes like Zhuge Liang, Liu Bei and Wang Jian, whose historical exploits have been embroidered into myth. The independence and
initiative of the Sichuanese has persisted to the present day. Deng Xiaoping is a native of the province and most of those associated with Deng
and the post-Mao economic reforms are from Sichuan (to the point that
after the 'Gang of Four', there was talk of the 'Sichuan Gang').

The Sichuan basin is very beautiful in an intensely cultivated way—
hillsides carved and sculpted with terraced fields, softened by feathery
giant bamboo, much silvery water, citrus groves and a remarkable natural flora which, together with that of neighbouring Yunnan, attracted the
19th and early 20C plant-hunters from the west. Apart from the primulas,
buddleias, rhododendrons and azaleas of the Himalayan slopes, the
province is also the home of the Giant panda, now protected in a few
reserves, most notably Wolong in western Sichuan (which can be visited),
and its faster-moving relative the Lesser, or Red, panda. As well as the
panda reserve at Wolong, which is not far from Chengdu, a newly opened
area in Sichuan, close to the border with Gansu province, is Jiuzhaigou,
some 200km NW of Chengdu. There, the main attraction is dramatic
scenery, including waterfalls, the Pearl Rapids, lakes and the slopes of
Mount Zanglong.

The weather varies according to area and altitude: the basin has mild
winters and hot summers with most of the plentiful rain falling in July and
August. The sky is frequently, almost permanently, overcast and it is said
locally that the dogs bark when the sun comes out (as it is such an unusu-

al event). The damp and warm conditions are ideal for agriculture with all-year cultivation of a variety of vegetables and fruit as well as two grain crops, but it can be a bit uncomfortable for the visitor who is recommended to bring (or acquire) a light mackintosh, waterproof footwear and fast film.

Food: for those who like spiced food, Sichuan cuisine is the best in China. It is usually described as 'hot', meaning peppery, but this is not entirely accurate. There is much use of chilli, though it is rarely as palate-burning as in some Indian dishes, but the great local spice is Sichuan pepper which imparts a lemony pepper flavour. Hotels tend to underplay flavouring for foreign visitors and the food may be blandly acceptable but unexciting. When I was in Chengdu with three friends (forming a 'cultural delegation'), our most important morning task was to order three good local dishes rather than the usual hotel fare provided for lunch and supper. Hui guo rou, a stewed pork dish with pepper, coriander and lemon balm, Ma po doufu, chilli-hot, spiced beancurd, dumplings or Dandan mian (noodles in spicy soup) with a plate of fresh green vegetables was a favourite menu.

Air: Chengdu's airport is 18km from the centre of town (to the SW) and there are daily flights from Peking, Lhasa, Chongqing, Shanghai, Kunming, Guangzhou and Xi'an and slightly less frequent arrivals and departures from Changsha, Guilin, Guiyang, Hefei, Lanzhou, Nanjing, Shenyang, Taiyuan, Urumqi, Wuhan and Xichang.

Rail: The railway station in the N of the city connects with Kunming, Chongqing and Guiyang (also Xi'an and Lanzhou). From Peking it takes about 4 days to reach Xian.

Hotels: The main hotel in Chengdu is the Jinjiang Hotel, 180 Renmin lu, beside the river. It has been refurbished with overseas help (American Standard bath fittings) and, though large, is no longer invariably used for tour groups. It is well situated, with the old quarters of town reached in a short walk up Renmin lu (turn left out of the hotel and take sidestreets on either side of Renmin lu). Another hotel, originally for Chinese only but now used for tour groups, is the Chengdu, way out in the E of the city, a tower block in a grey residential area of concrete blocks.

The city of Chengdu was first walled in 311 BC and was made the state capital of Shu some 500 years later. In the 1920s its heart was the square walled and moated enclosure of the old palace. Hemmed in by two rivers, the Nanhe and the Fuhe, a street map still shows how the irregular rectangle of the outer city was contained by the two with the small rectangle of the palace quarter (correctly oriented N–S) in the centre.
    There are varying accounts of Chengdu in the 1920s and 1930s. The 1924 'Japanese Railway Guide' states: 'The only buildings of any consequence in the old palace quarter are the bazaar and the examination hall…to the west…is a separate quarter, surrounded by walls, which is occupied by Manchu bannermen and their families. The busiest quarter is inside the East Gate where a street, 50ft wide, is lined with rows of silk shops, whose signboards with their gilt inscriptions will at once attract the eyes of a stranger.' In the 1933 'Handbook for China' by Carl Crow the 14.5km outer city wall is described and the broad streets, well-paved and well-produced are also remarked upon whilst the palace quarters in the centre are described as being occupied by a teacher training college.
    The city has long been an important trade centre. During the late Tang and Song it was a major printing centre, with the entire Buddhist canon printed from 130,000 woodblocks in Chengdu between 971 and 983 and, in an amalgamation of the business and printing enterprises, printed paper money first appeared in Chengdu in the early 11C.

Apart from wandering in the narrow streets, lined with wooden-fronted shops on either side of Renmin lu (near the huge statue of Mao, if it still stands in front of the vast and rather thinly filled main department store), distances between cultural sites in Chengdu are considerable so they are best visited in groups by taxi or bus.

South of the centre.
The **Sichuan Provincial Museum** is on Renmin nan lu, S of the Jinjiang Hotel.

It contains a rich collection of artefacts unearthed in Sichuan, and is very strong in graphic arts of the Han dynasty. There are a number of pottery models of houses, models of entertainers of all sorts and an array of the local incised ceramic bricks used to line Han tombs (including copies of some in the Chongqing Museum) depicting buildings, chariots, archery and hunting, salt-mining and banquet scenes. There is a fine bronze 'money tree' (another example is in the Nanjing Museum), with coins amongst the branches, a concept which has given rise to a popular opera about a celestial maidservant whose passion for the good things in life (on earth) was so troublesome she had to be recalled to heaven. Many of the Han tomb figures (in greyish clay) are larger than the green-glazed figures from metropolitan China; characteristic of Sichuan are large females with flowers in their hair and rather daft smiles. The museum also holds some fine Eastern Han Buddhist reliefs and a large Ming funerary cortege in clay. Later exhibits of articles unearthed in Sichuan from the Ming and Qing reveal the widespread use of porcelain from Jingdezhen in Jiangxi; there is also a Qing brocade loom of great complexity.

In the SW of the city is the **Wuhou ci** (Temple of the Military Marquis), founded in the early 5C in honour of Zhuge Liang.

Zhuge Liang (181–234) was a military genius, native of Shandong, who assisted Liu Bei (161–223) who proclaimed himself emperor of Shu (based in Chengdu) when the Han fell in AD 220. Zhuge Liang is a good example of a man becoming a myth; a wealth of folklore has grown up around him and he is credited with the invention of various odd military machines as well as military strategies. One story tells of how he promised to acquire 100,000 arrows in four days for a battle against Cao Cao (155–220), founder of the State of Wei, arch-eneny of the State of Shu and therefore of Zhuge Liang and Liu Bei. For three days Zhuge Liang did nothing, on the fourth he filled ships with bales of straw and sent them out towards Cao Cao's fleet in the foggy night. Safely concealed below deck, soldiers made a great noise and Cao Cao's fleet let loose with their arrows. The ships returned home, the straw bales filled with reusable arrows, 'borrowed' from Cao Cao, against whom they were to be turned.

The temple was originally linked with one commemorating Liu Bei which stood beside it. Both were destroyed by fire and the existing complex was substantially rebuilt in 1672. The Tang poet Du Fu described the temple in the Tang: 'Where is the temple of the famous minister to be found? In a pine forest outside Brocade City (Chengdu). Spring grass covers the steps and birds sing in the trees. He answered the third call to affairs of state and gave his all to two generations. Before he could achieve conquest, he died and since then, heroes have wet their sleeves with tears'.

The temple is still quite green and full of trees. It has red surrounding walls topped with green tiles. It encloses a hall dedicated to Liu Bei with some famous pieces of congratulatory calligraphy, statues of Liu Bei and (E and W) red-faced Guan Yu (the god of war, one of those who helped Liu Bei to establish Shu, subsequently elevated to the status of god of war and justice), Zhang Fei, another noted general, and others.

Galleries contain brightly-painted stucco figures of military heroes of the Three Kingdoms period. In the *Zhuge Liang Hall* (inside the second gate, beyond a courtyard filled with stone stelae) there is a gilded figure of Zhuge Liang with, to one side, an inscription of Zhuge Liang's memorial on setting out on a campaign in calligraphy by Yue Fei (the famous Song general whose own temple is in Hangzhou) and, on the other, a carving recording a meeting with Liu Bei in his retreat. In front of the figure (encased in glass) are three bronze drums, in a form that recalls the bronze-casting of Yunnan, said to have been cast during Zhuge Liang's lifetime.

On either side of the Zhuge Liang Hall are smaller halls containing statues of the red-faced Guan Yu (the god of war, one of those who helped Liu Bei to establish Shu, subsequently elevated to the status of god of war and justice), and Zhang Fei, another noted general. In covered galleries there are statues of noted officials and military figures, each with a small stone stele recording his life and deeds.

To the W of the enclosure is a walled area enclosing the high, grassy mound said to be *Liu Bei's Tomb* (which has yet to be excavated).

Just N of the Wuhou ci, in the western suburbs, just to the W of Xi cheng bian jie, is the **Qingyang gong** (Green Sheep Hall) in a park of the same name. Founded in the Tang, the surviving buildings of this Taoist temple date from the Qing. In the main hall (*Sanqing dian* or Hall of the Three Pure Ones—the Jade Emperor, ruler of heaven, the 'mystic jewel', a god who lives beyond the North Pole, and Lao zi) are gilded figures of the trinity as well as other gods. In front of the altar table are two bronze sheep. The one-horned sheep has an inscription dating it to 1723 and stating that it was brought from the capital to Chengdu to add to the relics of Lao zi. It is said to incorporate the attributes of all the 12 animals of the Chinese zodiac—rat ears, ox nose, tiger claws, rabbit back, dragon horn, snake tail, horse lips, sheep whiskers, monkey neck, chicken eyes, dog belly and pig buttocks. The two-horned sheep was cast in 1829.

A flower festival is held in the park every year in the 2nd month of the lunar calendar (late February–March).

Further W of the Green Sheep Hall, outside the main ring road, is the **Du Fu cao tang** (Thatched Cottage of Du Fu), a bamboo-filled park built on the supposed site of a small rustic retreat inhabited by the poet Du Fu (712–770) in the mid 8C after the rebellion of An Lushan (756) had disrupted life in the capital.

Many of Du Fu's poems refer to the 'Brocade City' of Chengdu and the 'Brocade River' beside which he lived, as well as to the local heroes Liu Bei and Zhuge Liang and their associates. His stay outside Chengdu seems to have been a peaceful respite in a life of considerable difficulty. Du Fu constantly failed the civil service exams, partly because of general corruption and his own lack of patronage, partly because his extraordinary literary skills may have seemed threatening to the examiners. His personal difficulties were compounded by the disaster of the An Lushan rebellion (756) which laid waste to the capital. Du Fu's family frequently faced starvation (one of his children effectively starved to death) and this, combined with his great sensitivity to the suffering of others (and a keen sense of social injustice) has made him a favoured poet of contemporary China where correct social content is an important aspect of literary evaluation.

The tranquil poems written in his 'thatched cottage' refer to natural images far from the war-torn capital, willows carpeting the path with white fluff (a common sight in spring when the seeds with their fluffy coating are released in white clouds), pheasants among the thick bamboo stems, ducklings sleeping pressed against their mothers on the riverbank, peach and plum petals falling on dark pools and swallows nest-building and midge-hunting over the water.

Du Fu's poems have been widely translated but the best versions are to be found in Arthur Cooper's 'Li Po and Tu Fu', Harmondsworth, Penguin Books, 1986 (1973) and David Hawkes' 'Little Primer of Tu Fu', Oxford University Press, 1967.

Whatever it was that Du Fu actually lived in, on the banks of the 'Washing Flowers Stream', the site was venerated and replicas of various sorts of thatched cottages have been built on the site site since the early 11C. Today there is a sizable park with various buildings apart from the thatched garden-house. There are exhibition halls with displays relating to Du Fu's life, paintings illustrating scenes from the poems and examples of the multiple editions of his works, including translations. The park itself is well-planted with huge bamboos in thick groves and trees including peach and cedar, and small garden-areas with flowering plants, pen cai (bonsai) and pen jing (pot 'scenes' with rocks, water and flowers).

Outside the gate, there is a Gaudi-like four-character inscription, 'Thatched cottage of Du Fu', made from bits of broken decorated porcelain.

Just NE of the Thatched Cottage is **Wang Jian mu** (Wang Jian's Tomb), inside the ringroad at Santong qiao. Excavated in 1942, the tomb contained the remains of Wang Jian (847–918), ruler of the semi-independent kingdom of the Former Shu during the Tang dynasty. The earth mound is 15m high and more than 80m in diameter. A brick-vaulted construction with three chambers, there are fragmentary wall paintings in the first chamber, a stone-carved portrait of Wang Jian in the back hall and and a great stone-carved platform (on which the coffin rested) in the middle chamber.

Artefacts in the tomb included a jade belt and silver and iron items, including an iron cow. Many of these are displayed in two exhibition halls in front of the tomb. The carved figures around the stone platform are the most interesting items. Warriors hold up the platform, their faces distorted by the effort (like some of the figures at Dazu, they are depicted from the waist up), and a female orchestra is also depicted. The small figures, in varying life-like postures with elegant, wind-tossed robes, play drums, cymbals, various sorts of wind-instruments and the pipa (lute), accompanying elegant dancing figures (on the front of the platform). The small group illustrates the lively style of Suchuan sculpture in the late Tang and Song (as seen also at Dazu).

In the E of the city, on Dongfeng lu (not far from the Chengdu fandian) is the **Daci si** (Temple of Great Benevolence). This now houses the City Museum in late Qing buildings which are all that remain of a Tang temple once famous for its wall paintings. These were praised by Su Shi and Li Zhicun who said 'The best (and most numerous) Tang wall paintings in the world are in Chengdu and those in the Daci Temple are the most numerous'.

SE of the Daci si is the large compound of **Sichuan University** (once the missionary West China Union University) and the Wang jiang lou (River-viewing Pavilion). The university houses one of the most remarkable small *museums* in China, strongest in archaeology and local crafts but also very interesting for its cheerful display. This may be visited by appointment (through China Travel Service, or if they are spectacularly unhelpful, just try and see it by turning up). The museum's history goes back to missionary days when the finds of archaeological expeditions were collected and the anthropology department also sent out expeditions to collect artefacts.

There is a lively display of folk crafts, costumes and handicrafts of all sorts and, remarkably (for the art of display is still in its infancy in China), imaginative presentation of the collections. Sculptures have been placed in 'niches' as if in a cave-temple, peasant lan bu (blue and white indigo-dyed cotton with wax resist patterns) has been used as a background to the anthropological displays. There is a shadow-puppet theatre which is still used (or was a few years ago as the museum's director, archaeologist and ex-science-fiction writer Tong Enzheng, was recording puppet play scenarios with the help of a very old local puppetteer).

The **River-viewing Pavilion** is on the banks of the Brocade River in the SE corner of the university campus. The building that stands today is a late Qing pagoda-like tower with sharply up-turned eaves, 30m high, square at the base, octagonal in plan on the two upper storeys.

It is associated with one of the few famous women poets of China, Xue Tao (died c 834). A native of Chang'an (present-day Xi'an), she came to Chengdu with her family and, after her father's death, lived in poverty. She is said to have written her poems on red-dyed paper and a well in the park is traditionally supposed to have been where she washed her poem-paper after dyeing it.

North of the centre.
In the N of the city are the Wenshu yuan (Manjusri Temple), the Tomb of Meng Zhixiang and the Zoo.

The **Wenshu yuan** (or *Manjusri Temple*) is just E of Renmin bei lu, on Wenshu yuan jie. It is a thriving religious centre: the path leading to the temple is lined with stalls selling a mixture of religious necessities (firecrackers for scaring evil spirits), candles and incense, holy pictures and rosaries, mixed in with spiced noodles and cotton knickers. This sort of approach to a temple by means of a street of stalls is reminiscent of the surroundings of cathedrals and shrines in medieval Europe.

The temple is the headquarters of the Sichuan (and Chengdu) Buddhist Association and bursts with old ladies lighting incense sticks in bronze burners. The temple dates back to the Nan chao (Southern Kingdoms Period, 420–589) but was destroyed in military action during the Ming. It was rebuilt in 1691 and renamed Manjusri Temple. It encloses five linked halls and contains over 100 bronze Buddha figures of different sizes, many cast by famous craftsmen of the Qing. In the *Hall of the Law* (towards the rear) are 10 iron figures of the Song period. The stone used for pillar bases and platforms is local.

The **Chengdu Zoo** is in the N of the city and is naturally best-known for a large number of pandas, both giant and lesser. The giant pandas, at feeding time, do seem to be less lethargic and bored in their home province than elsewhere. When they hear the keeper coming, they occasionaly push, shove and fight, growling and honking in a very un-panda-like way. There are fairly frequent births so quite a number of young pandas can often be seen. Beside the giant panda enclosure is that of the Lesser red pandas who are always lively and jolly.

7km N of the city at *Moban shan*, is the *Tomb of Meng Zhixiang* (893–934), excavated in 1971, which yielded a similar array of artefacts as that of Wang Jian (jade belts and tablets and decorative items), but it is otherwise noted for the wall-paintings of figures and carvings of dragons.

Outside Chengdu are two major sites, the Baoguang si (Divine Light Monastery) to the NW in Xindu xian county town, and the Dujiangyan Irrigation Scheme and Qingcheng Mountain in Guan xian to the W.

Guan xian is c 60km from Chengdu, reached by a road of considerable interest which runs through green paddy fields, past half-timbered farmhouses hidden in damp, dark groves of bamboos towering over the thatched roofs. Some of the villages on the road are very picturesque, the main street lined with wooden-fronted shops, open to the street to display their brightly-coloured wares.

Hardware stores sell choppers, wooden buckets, birdcages, basketwork fishtraps, baskets and scoops; teahouses (very popular in Sichuan), with their low bamboo chairs spilling out onto the roadside, are full of tradesmen, their loads piled outside, and street-traders include butchers and toffee toy-makers with special tables. Small children pay a few cents to spin a pointer on a board surrounded by paintings of animals and then the toffee is dribbled onto a marble slab in the form of a dragon, goldfish or monkey, according to the animal that the pointer indicated. Traffic on the road includes huge pigs, immobilised by being tied with a plank along the spine, being taken to market on the back of a bicycle.

In 1986 the road was apparently being widened (like almost every road in Sichuan, from the point of view of traffic control, not a moment too soon) as the volume of trucks, cars, slow-moving hay-carts, pig-laden bicycles and handcarts had reached saturation point. However, the road may now include detours round the villages, which would be a pity. In the county town of Guan xian, a road to the left leads to **Qingcheng shan** (Green City Mountain), one of the lesser Taoist mountains; climbable in a day. During the Han the 'Heavenly master' Zhang Daoling ascended the mountain and built a thatched hut for himself and since then the mountain has been a Taoist centre. You can see old Taoists, dressed in short black robes, their legs bound in cloth leggings, their hair in a small bun (in the Ming man's hairstyle which antedates the Qing imposition of the queue or 'pigtail') in the Guan xian market or on the mountain.

The highest temple is the *Shangqing gong* (Hall of Supreme Purity) at 1600m above sea-level. Though most of the temples are Tang (or earlier) foundations, the damp, dank atmosphere is not conducive to timber preservation and those now standing are mostly late Qing (or later). The mountain contrasts with Buddhist holy mountains in its stress on nature and natural appearance. The small thatched shelters at resting points on the steps are unpainted, built of timber and thatch, blending with the trees that tower over them. In some, twisted, curling branches have been attached just under the eaves, in imitation of the complex brackets found on grander buildings.

As one of the Taoists greatest tenets was reverence for nature and a refusal to inter-fere with natural processes, the mountain, with its rustic shelters almost indistin-guishable from their surroundings, is a fine illustration (and remarkable in contrast with Emei where the Buddhist temple buildings stand out from their setting).

About half-way up the mountain is the *Tianshi dong* (Cave of the Heavenly Master), headquarters of the Taoist Association, the site where Zhang Daoling used to deliver his sermons. There is a stone-carved por-trait of the master on the rock and statues of three emperors of the Tang dynasty in the main hall (which is late Qing in date). The buildings, rick-ety wooden halls perched on the rocks, with windows framing misty views and verandah seats, have a dark charm. There is a huge gingko, said to have been planted by Zhang Daoling in the Han dynasty (described in a local guidebook as 'doddering, whirling and imposing'), a palm that is said to date from the Tang, nine Song dynasty pines and a 'fairy pine' of the Ming. Small stone carvings on the balustrades depict small boys in unusual postures.

Outside the gate of the Shangqing gong (near the summit) are two gingkos, believed to be several hundred years old and on either side of the hall are two springwater wells, one square, one round, known as the 'Mandarin Duck Wells' (meaning that they are a male and female pair).

The **Dujiangyan Irrigation Scheme** on the outskirts of Guan xian is one of China's earliest irrigation schemes, begun in about 250 BC when the local prefect Li Bing and his son diverted the waters of the Min River to irrigate the plain.

Guan xian stands at the point where the Chengdu plain meets the mountains of W Sichuan, and the Min River reaches the plain. The river was divided into two chan-nels (the 'inner' and 'outer' river) by means of a 'fishmouth' dyke, constructed of stones held in bamboo nets, with a further movable dyke to divert the water in case of flood (and to prevent excessive silting). The 'outer' river is the natural course of the Min. The scheme brought water to some 1300 square km (an area expanded to 5300 square km after 1949 with the aid of some slightly more modern methods).

The scheme is best viewed from the **Fulong** (Subdued Dragon) **Temple**,

The Two Kings temple, Guan xian

first built in the Song, to commemorate Li Bing and his son, on a promontory where the river divides. Approached through a park, the Qing-dynasty temple buildings, dark-roofed with up-turned eaves, now contain relics relating to Li Bing and his son. The highest part, overlooking the division of the river waters, is the *Guanlan ting* (Looking Out Over the Waves Pavilion). In the main hall is a large (nearly 3m, weighing 4.5 tons) stone statue of Li Bing carved in AD 168. This was excavated from the river in 1974 and is thought to have been cast into the river in a superstitious gesture (to ensure the maintenance of successful irrigation).

As the 'Mingsheng cidian' records, the posterior hall contains an electric, movable model of the dam for the edification of visitors; these days there is also a video.

Some distance from the Fulong Temple, on the E bank of the Min River, above the division, is the **Erwang miao** (Two Kings Temple), dedicated to Li Bing and his son. This is usually approached from above, from the road leading up through the mountains from Guan xian. Seen from above, the Two Kings Temple is wonderfully sited: grey-tiled roofs with extravagantly upturned eaves and tiled decoration sit amongst a sea of green trees on the high bank above the racing river and the chain-bridge below.

The temple was founded in the Nanchao period (420–589), though the surviving buildings are Qing. As you descend the steep steps to the temple, notice the roofs with their tiled figures: elephants, cats, dragons, horses and phoenix. Inside the temple halls are modern stucco figures of the two kings as healthy heroes (despite or because of the filmstar looks of the younger Li in particular, old ladies still burn incense in the temple). There are many stone-carved inscriptions in the temple including Li Bing's famous dictum 'Dig canals deep, make embankments low' (which was later half-hijacked by Mao Zedong in regard to planting rice). Though lavish in its roof decoration, as you reach the lower parts of the temple, the use of whitewash and dark wood in the 'half-timbered' Sichuan style is restrained and attractive. Note, as you descend, a sort of cage with sculpture in it, including some fine iron pieces.

Below the temple is the *Anlan* (Pacifying the Waves) *Bridge*. This is an iron chain version of a common form of low-slung (originally on bamboo ropes) bridge common in the SW of China.

The first bridge was built here before the Song but it was destroyed by fire in the Ming and rebuilt in the Qing. A local story says that a local tutor's wife proposed the rebuilding of the bridge and gave some money but, because of the corruption of the local officials (who took the money), nothing happened. The tutor exposed the corruption and was killed for his pains so local people, enraged by this, helped his wife to continue with the bridge-building.

You can cross the 500m bridge though a major tourist pastime seems to be to jump up and down on it which makes it feel very unlike a 'wave-pacifying' bridge.

The **Divine Light Monastery** is c 19km NW of Chengdu, in a small market town.

It is said to have been founded in the Eastern Han. In 881, when the Yellow Turbans uprising laid waste to the Tang capital, the emperor fled to Sichuan (as his ancestor had done during the An Lushan rebellion over 100 years earlier) and stayed in this temple. At his orders the temple was restored and renamed the Divine Light Temple. It flourished during the Ming and the Qing (with a major restoration in 1670).

Today it comprises a (leaning) pagoda, five halls and 16 courtyards (and a figure of over 400 stone columns involved in the buildings is given). The *pagoda* appears to be Tang in date (whilst the rest of the temple is Qing), with close-packed eaves in 13 storeys above a square base. The slightly upturned eaves are probably a later addition (Tang pagodas of this type do not tend to have upturned eaves). An early feature of the pagoda is its position in the heart of the temple (common in Tang layouts). It has a pronounced lean.

In the large and flourishing temple, the most popular attractions are trying to hit the centre of the spirit wall (outside the main gate) with your eyes shut (for luck) and a gaudy collection of 500 lohans (of the Qing period). If you notice people wandering past the lohans and laughing uproariously, it is probably because they have been practising another local custom which is to set off past the lohans, counting the years of their age. The lohan they reach at the appropriate moment is a form of fortune-telling. As they all have 3m eyebrows or other grotesque attributes, this gives rise to hilarity.

In the small courtyards at the back of the temple where tea is offered, there are some charming 'sunken' gardens. The buildings are raised above the open courtyards (because of the heavy rainfall in Sichuan) and these lowered stone courts are filled with marvellous pot-plants. There are also some interesting and rather baffling old photographs of famous monks of the temple who were known for their meditational acrobatics (balancing on one finger on a tiny teacup, levitation, etc).

A town rarely visited, some 200km SE of Chengdu (or 200km W of Chongqing) is **Zigong**, famous since the Han for its salt production. The rock salt is found in wells, deep beneath the earth, drawn up by water-buffaloes. There is a *Museum of Salt Production* set up at Deng Xiaoping's suggestion in 1959, housed in the lavish *Xiqin Guild*. This was the salt-producers' guildhall, sometimes known as the 'Shaanxi Temple' built in 1736 for the salt-merchants who came to trade in Zigong. Built in the traditional courtyard style, the guildhall is particularly extravagant in construction, from the incredibly complex gate through to the rear. It was said of it: 'Every five paces a tower, every 10 paces a pavilion, with covered walks all round, eaves projecting like teeth and brackets and corners', suggesting palatial construction. The columns, whether of wood or stone, are mostly carved and there is hardly a surface left uncarved or unembellished. It is one of the most extraordinary buildings in China and a fine example of merchant ostentation.

38 Dazu

The small town of **Dazu** is just N of the Chengdu–Chongqing railway line, roughly equidistant between the two. Set in beautiful, lush countryside, it is famous for its stone carvings which date from the last years of the Tang to the Qing, with the majority carved during the southern Song. The carvings are largely Buddhist in theme but combine elements of Confucianism and Taoism (as well as being fairly eclectic within the Buddhist tradition).

Road: Dazu is 160km NW of Chongqing and the easiest way to get to Dazu is by car or bus from Chongqing (a journey of c 5 hours through green hilly country, carved out with paddy-fields. There is a regular bus service from Chongqing's northwest bus station (on the far side of the Jialing River bridge), with buses usually leaving just after 7 am.

Rail: the nearest station to Dazu is Youtingpu (5 hours from Chongqing, 7 hours from Chengdu). From Youtingpu, public buses take c 1 hour to get to Dazu.

Hotel: there is one small guesthouse in Dazu, with some 40 rooms; not a luxury hotel but quite comfortable (though some complain of damp beds, a perennial problem in Sichuan, best remedied by a hot water bottle).

The **stone carvings** of Dazu represent the last great group of stone carvings in China but, compared with Yungang and Luoyang, they also represent a strong local tradition, with no imperial connections. Sculpture in Sichuan is everywhere remarkably plastic and lively, nowhere more so than in Dazu, where strict iconography is subservient to movement and story-telling. There are two major groups of sculpture around Dazu, the Bei shan (North Hill) and Baoding shan (Precious Summit), with other smaller groups scattered in the hills.

The sculptures were begun in 892, just before an independent kingdom was set up in Sichuan (Earlier Shu, 907–971), presaging the general breakup at the end of the Tang. The North Hill group was started in 892 by Wei Junjing, the local Commander-in-Chief and Governor of Changzhou (representative of the imperial Tang government in the area). He presided over the early Buddhist carvings which were continued through the collection of donations by local gentry, Buddhist monks and nuns over the succeeding 250 years, resulting in some 10,000 carved figures.

The Baoding group centred on a monastery 15km NE of the town. A local monk, Zhao Zhifeng, who returned to Dazu after years of study of Tantric Buddhism, worked for 70 years (1179–1249) to collect money to finance the carving of a similar number of figures. He became known as the 'Sixth Patriarch of Tantric Buddhism'. Another name for Tantric Buddhism is Esoteric Buddhism; it relied on incantations and meditational techniques (including meditation on mandalas or diagrams of the disposition of deities) to achieve union with the Buddha. This is another method of 'simplifying' or shortening the process of enlightenment, an important aspect of Buddhism in China with its frequent anti-monastic movements.

North Hill is just 2km N of Dazu, with 290 caves carved into a 500m cliff. The first figure (*Cave 2*) is a statue of the founder, Wei Junjing, with an inscription dated to 895 recording the making of the sculptures as well as a contemporary peasant uprising. The earliest caves (of the Wei Junjing period) are *Cave 3* (containing a Vajra Bodhisattva), *5* (a Vaisravana-devaraja), *9* (Thousand-armed Guanyin) and *10* (Historic Buddha), and the solid, smooth-faced figures are more simply disposed than some of the later figures. In *Cave 245* there is a sort of mandala or meditational diagram in low relief, based on the Pure Land sutra (which relates to the Pure Land or paradise of Amitabha).

In an assemblage of over 650 figures, there are three levels: at the top, in a mixture of palace buildings and ribbon clouds is the Western Paradise or 'World of Extreme Joy', the Chinese Buddhists' heaven; in the centre are the three deities of the Western Paradise, with Amitabha Buddha in the centre, Guanyin on the left and Mahasthamaprapta on the right (the last is a Bodhisattva who represents the Buddha-wisdom of Amitabha and this grouping is characteristic of all representations of the Western

Paradise); at the bottom is a section of the sutra where rulers request the Buddha's help, a request which resulted in an apparition of the paradise, also the 16 paths to be cultivated. As with almost all the sculpture at Dazu, this is elegantly designed and positioned, framed by a stepped series of square-framed Buddha images, the architectonic base adds strength and grandeur to the more fluid crowd and cloud-filled upper section where straight lines give way to swirls and circles.

In *Cave 273* is a rather stubby Thousand-armed Guanyin with almost caricatured attendants; *Cave 101* has a fine example of Song calligraphy by Cai jing; and *Cave 279* has another beautifully designed, asymmetrical niche with the Buddha of Medicine, Bhaisajyaguru as its centre. To the left a pagoda, to the right, shelf-like niches of Bodhisattvas with (headless) attendants, above a row of Buddhas sitting on lotuses, below, the 12 protectors of Bhaisajyaguru above a row of naturalistic lotus buds and leaves. The somewhat stolid carving of the main figures and the Viennese whorl clouds below the protectors do not detract from the balanced design of the whole.

The different representations of the Bodhisattva Guanyin in *Caves 125* and *113* (sometimes said to be the work of one sculptor) reveal a more confident phase; here the figures themselves are elegantly designed (rather than being like some of the others mentioned, stumpy icons in elegant frames). In *Cave 125* the Guanyin with a rosary is an elegant woman with swirling sleeves and scarves standing on a lotus against a plain oval halo. In *Cave 113* the Bodhisattva is depicted in the pose called 'royal ease', one knee drawn up, the other dangling carelessly, ribbon-drapery flowing around the casually disposed limbs, pearls and silks decorating the impressive headdress and loose robes.

The largest cave on the North Hill is *Cave 136*, carved between 1142 and 1146. In the centre is an octagonal 'Cart of Mental Divinity' resting on a huge dragon. There is a Buddha figure and several representations of Guanyin: seated in the lotus position with meticulously carved draped robes, four arms, two in a mudra, two holding up discs representing the sun and moon, beside, a standing Guanyin, casually holding a rosary, with an extraordinary crown with two crossed ribbons floating ceilingwards; another standing figure with flame-halo, holding a sprig of willow and the bottle of sweet dew which is one of Guanyin's more common attributes. Another seated Guanyin in the cave, with crisp robes and a beautifully detailed headdress, holds up a jade seal, a standing Guanyin, with a veil partially covering the headdress, holds a strange, ethereal version of a ruyi 'sceptre': a ball from which a ribbon swirls up and over the deity's shoulder. A very female-looking Bodhisattva Samantabhadra with a flaring headdress, sitting on an elephant whose trunk is missing, is matched by Manjusri, in a petalled headdress, sitting on a lotus throne on a lion's back.

In *Cave 130*, a slender, rather threatening figure brandishing swords and spears in her eight arms, is the 'bright-eyed daughter', or Prabhacaksadevi, a former incarnation of Ksitigarbha, the Bodhisattva who presides over the underworld. She is surrounded by monster-headed protectors. In the *Thousand-Buddha Cave* (155) where the walls are lined with tiny Buddha figures, there is a four-armed Buddha figure on the back of a giant peacock, a representation of the 'peacock king', a former incarnation of Sakyamuni who, as a peacock, sucked water with healing power from a rock. Like the 'Cart of Mental Divinity', this central figure provides a focus for perambulating meditation.

The rather squat figure of Ksitigarbha (dressed as a lama) seated on a square plinth in *Cave 177* was carved by the same man who made the Peacock King, You Yuanjun, not perhaps the most skilled of the Dazu sculptors. The grotesque attendants to Ksitigarbha in Cave 177 are more skilfully carved, dismally representing the terrors of judgement, and the figures on the walls in lama robes, looking varyingly serene and disturbed, are metamorphoses of Kistigarbha. In *Cave 180* there are 13 representations of Guanyin, elongated and serene, with filigree head-dress-es, very characteristic of Song art at its most elegant.

The *Many-Treasure Pagoda* (Duobao ta), 1148–54, an octagonal, multi-eaved pagoda 31m high, stands over the cliff, above some large Buddha figures carved against the rock.

The **Baoding** carvings, (15km NE of Dazu), reached by a road that runs up through neat terraced slopes towards misty mountains, are more exposed, carved in a a horseshoe-shaped gully. Above the gully are some temple buildings, totally rebuilt in the 1980s, and steps leading down to the sculptures below. These were almost all carved between 1179 and 1249. At the bottom of the steps, turn right (towards the huge 'sleeping' Buddha, No. 11). On your right are 'a fierce tiger coming down the moun-tain' (*1*) and a series of guardians (*2*) and in *Niche 3*, a great 'wheel of the law'.

In the centre is the monk Zhao Zhifeng who founded the site, above him a pavilion representing the Western Paradise. The two outer rings contain the animals of the cycles of re-births and the deeds that lead either to paradise or hell or re-birth as a lower animal. The wheel is gripped in the teeth of a monster and supported below by more human attendants; ribbons of Buddha figures emanate from the centre.

A little further along are three large (7m) figures, flanked by pagodas and with 1000 small Buddha images carved into the rock behind (*Niche 5*). These are the Three Saints of Huayan or Avatamsaka Buddhism (which viewed the universe as ordered, classifiable, with everything leading to the centre, the Buddha): Vairocana Buddha in the centre, flanked by Manjusri and Samantabhadra, all bearing pagodas (Vairocana Buddha's has disappeared). Further on, *Cave 8*, which is fronted by a timber façade set further into the cliff than most of the Baoding sculptures, contains China's largest 1000-armed Guanyin figure. The central figure is about 3m high but the assemblage of 1007 hands, each with an eye in the palm (the Bodhisattva is 'all-seeing' as well as 'all-succouring'), covers 88 square metres. The popularity of Guanyin as a saviour is evident from the number of scarves and offerings draped over the hands.

The 'Reclining Buddha', actually entering nirvana, filling the E cliff and measuring 31m from head to knees, forms a backdrop for an extraor-dinary sculptural ensemble. The Buddha who, instead of dying, is enter-ing a state of non-being (nirvana, which should not be confused with heaven), is surrounded by smaller figures that emerge, waist-high, from the rock. They include Bodhisattvas bearing the symbols of their attributes; at the central altar, topped with more Bodhisattvas, three officials in official hats, preside over the offerings. The grouping of these figures, some with their backs firmly turned, others facing this way and that, is remarkably naturalistic.

At the far end of the nirvana scene, *Niche 12* contains a fountain drip-ping from the mouth of one of nine dragons into a pool below where the baby Buddha is being bathed. In *Niche 13* there is another peacock king cave, with inscriptions from the Mayurasanasutra. *Niche 14*, where Vairocana Buddha is depicted preaching, is the centre of Tantric or eso-teric worship in Dazu. Disciples are depicted listening to the Buddha and the elegance of the carving is considerable.

Niche 15, which depicts parental care and the consequent debt owed by all to their parents, is an interesting mixture of the Confucian stress on filial piety (which is a fundamental tenet of Chinese society) and its takeover by Chinese Buddhism. Non-canonical Buddhist texts presented virtually the same contents as the Confucian texts on filial piety. In Dazu, the representation of childbirth, suckling and childcare, is in the form of a three-dimensional comic-strip, with text included. From the top are scenes of praying for a son, pregnancy, childbirth (the mother, standing, is about to give birth, the kneeling midwife rolls up her sleeves), suckling, washing babyclothes, lying with the child, the concern of the father about to depart on a journey, arranging a marriage for a child and killing a pig to celebrate, and 100-year-old parents still worrying about their 80-year-old offspring.

In *Niche 16* are the deities of wind (holding an inflated bladder), rain (riding on a dragon, for dragons are associated with water, both in rivers and clouds), lightning (holding two mirrors) and thunder (a pig-headed figure banging a drum).

Niche 17 returns to the theme of filial piety, essentially Confucian, here showing how Sakyamuni, the historic Buddha, repaid the kindness of his parents, a distinctly Chinese embroidery on the few facts. Beside a large figure of the Buddha, the stories are told, as in Niche 15, in a three-dimensional comic-strip, with blocks of text (from the apocryphal sutra on Mahopaya Buddha requiting the kindness of his parents) set between the scenes.

The Buddha offers his own flesh to nourish his parents (a story that is duplicated in the Confucian Twenty-four Examples of Filial Piety when, during a famine, a daughter-in-law thoughtfully cuts off her finger to feed her elderly parents-in-law); the Buddha's parents bend over a skeleton, that of their child devoured by a tiger, but the infant miraculously reappears; below, brahmins accuse the Buddha of being unfilial; to the right of the major statue, Sakyamuni helps to carry his father's coffin and, further on, when a doctor prescribes a human eye as the only remedy for his father's blindness, the Buddha offers his own.

In *Niche 18* the Western Paradise theme is illustrated, with the presiding Buddha and attendant Bodhisattvas apparently looking down over the scene, with tiny pavilions representing heaven between them. Below, meritorious believers who will enter heaven stand before the judges who preside over heaven and hell, and small boys, emerging from lotuses (symbols of purity) tumble over the balustrade. By contrast with the relative calm of Niche 18, *Niche 21* has a three-tier representation of judgement resulting in relegation to hell. Above is the Bodhisattva Ksitigarbha who sits in judgement over the souls of the dead; in the centre are the judges and below are the tortures of hell. As in other sections at Dazu, isolated figures set between the major scenes tell stories by themselves: the scenes of husbands and wives, brothers and sisters unable to recognise each other (because they are drunk) foretell inevitable consignment to hell; even the charming 'hen-wife', a gently-smiling woman tending her chickens, is doomed (presumably because the chickens are to be killed and eaten).

Crossing by the bridge, or returning to the bottom of the steps, a number of late Taoist images (*Niches 24, 25*) from the late Ming and Qing can be seen and a lion guards the entrance to *Cave 29*, the *Cave of Perfect Enlightenment*, deeply carved into the rock and filled with a pantheon of the three Buddhas (past, present and future) with attendant Bodhisattvas. Typically, there is a sculpted kneeling figure, with his back to the visitor, recalling the interesting placing of the attendant figures to the reclining Buddha and illustrating the difference of Dazu where straightforward icons are rare. Finally, beside the steps in *Niche 30*, cowherds are shown tending their oxen, taking them out to pasture (where the cowherd can rest or play the flute).

The Buddhist significance of cowherding relates to the 'taming' of one's nature. There is a charming Chinese Buddhist work with illustrations that depict the ox turning from black, through half-black, half-white, to white as the cowherd manages to tame it. At first it must be led by means of the ring through its nose; when it knows what it is meant to do, the cowherd need no longer lead it it, it follows him docilely; thus should Buddhists tame their passions.

39 Emei shan

Emei shan (Lofty Eyebrow Mountain), 3099m above sea-level, is the western Buddhist holy mountain, the abode of Samantabhadra, the Bodhisattva of pervading goodness, patron of followers of the Lotus sutra, who is usually depicted on a white elephant. The mountain, rising on the SW of the Sichuan basin, is thickly wooded almost all the way to the Thousand-Buddha and Golden Summit and frequently covered with cloud, often in several levels. It is said locally to be 'Beautiful, like moth's eyebrows, long and fine', perhaps because the soft outline of the summit can occasionally be seen above the thick cloud. It is c 50km from the foot to the summit; a Ming poet said, 'Emei is lofty, piercing heaven; a hundred miles of mist, built in the void where birds whirl and turn, lotuses open amongst the strange peaks'. The earliest temples were built here during the Eastern Han (AD 25–220) though those that stand today have all been very recently restored.

Railway: the Emei station on the Chengdu–Kunming line is some distance (c 4km) from Emei town, and the mountain itself is 7km SW of Emei town.

Hotel: there are frequent local buses from the station to the Baoguo (Protect the Nation) Temple which is close to the major hotel, the *Hongzhushan Hotel*. This is a collection of buildings in the thick woods of the foot of the mountain, due S of the Baoguo si. The Dining Hall (whose existence precludes the need to bring cooking stove, pots, pans, charcoal, chickens, vegetables and sugar as suggested in the 1924 'Japanese Railway Guide') and the Post Office (open rather unreliably and unhelpfully) are in separate buildings in the complex. Owing to the weather in Sichuan and the over-shadowing trees, beds tend to be damp and Building No. 2 was famous for its rats (in 1983, perhaps a cat has been acquired since). There is not much you can do about the rats except avoid keeping food in your room and try wearing earplugs. Laundry is not worth attempting unless the weather is good; as clothes are left to dry naturally, they never do.

Climbing the mountain.

Emei is the most arduous of the Buddhist mountains (those with heart conditions should remember that it is over 3000m high and consult a doctor; it might be wiser to stay lower down), though it only takes a couple of days to either ascend or descend and there are now minibuses which run from the Baoguo Temple to the *Jieyin dian* (Welcoming Hall), at 2540m, near the summit. In bad weather, or for those not accustomed to climbing slippery steps, one day could be spent taking the bus to the Jieyin dian (individual travellers may find that the fare involves considerable bargaining) and walking to the summit from there, returning to take the bus back to the Baoguo Temple.

On the second day take the bus to the *Wannian* (Ten-thousand Years) *Temple*, about half-way up the mountain, and either explore at this level (and bus back) or descend to the Baoguo Temple on foot. The third day can be spent in the temples on the foot of the mountain. Obviously the plan can be reversed (though waiting for clear weather for the peak is not a very profitable planning method as it so rarely comes). Better climbers may prefer to take a bus to the Jieyin dian and then walk the whole way down the mountain, staying overnight in a temple.

Those wishing to see the famous monkeys in their natural surroundings should descend via the *Xianfeng* (Fairy Peak) *Temple* and remember not to tease the monkeys which are said to have rushed the odd visitor off a cliff before now.

Because of rain and cloud, the mountain is very damp: a light waterproof cape with a hood is useful and a stick is helpful on the slippery stepped paths (these can usually be bought from persistent salespersons dotted about the mountain). If you are to stay overnight in temples, you may have to hire extra bedding or a thick padded coat as it is very cold and damp at high altitudes.

There are porters on the higher slopes of the mountain, above the Jieyin Hall. They carry everything up the mountain: all the equipment for the cable-car which was being built near the Jieyin Hall (1983) was carried by teams of porters. Though very small (as are most people in Sichuan), they are used to their job. They have a wooden contraption on their backs with a sort of shelf, and carry T-shaped sticks. When resting, they place the stick under the load, to take the weight. They are quite keen to carry visitors, for about 10 yuan, though they very much object to being photographed doing so. In 1983 a cable-car was being built, with one station near the Jieyin Hall and vast pieces of machinery carried by porters. This should relieve the problems of those who find the muddy, leaf-covered steps difficult.

From the Jieyin Hall, follow the stepped path to the *Golden Summit* (3077m). The climb is steep, with occasional flat parts for relief, the steps rising through thick forests of conifer and rhododendron, mist and cloud. When you emerge from the forest, the summit lies along a steep cliff. Some stay overnight at the summit to see the dawn, others wait for the 'Buddha light' (3–4 pm, October–November, weather permitting, which it rarely does) when rainbows appear above the cloud below the cliff and, if the sun is in the right place, giant shadows may be cast on the cloud. Railings were set on the cliff as early as the Song dynasty, for ecstatic believers cast themselves into the cloud at the sight of the miraculous light.

The temple has been completely rebuilt (1983).

The original temple at the Golden Summit was constructed in the Eastern Han and was the most important of the 100 or so that flourished from the 6C on the mountain. Apparently the summit was often struck by thunderstorms and buildings were frequently destroyed by lightning. There was a temple, much decorated in gold (popularly known as the Golden Temple) housing a bronze Buddha and a Ming bronze stelae (of the Chenghua reign period, 1465–87), recording one reconstruction in the calligraphic style of Wang Xizhi. The stelae was said (in 1981) to be housed in the Woyun (Sleeping Clouds) Hermitage (with the corrugated iron roof just below the site of the Golden Temple), but it may reappear in the Golden Temple when rebuilding is completed.

For those making the full descent, retrace your steps to the Jieyin Hall and continue down the stepped path until you reach the *Xixiang chi* (Elephant Bathing Pool), at 2100m above sea level, said to be where the Bodhisattva Samantabhadra's elephant bathed. Beside the pool is a small *hermitage*, founded in the Ming, enlarged in the Qing (1699). In the hall are figures of Guanyin, Ksitigarbha and Mahasthama. The rare sight of the 'nightmoon in the elephant's pool', as the Tang poet Li Bai put it, is one of the famous views of Emei. It is round about the Elephant Bathing Pool that you may first see the troupes of 'wild' monkeys that live on the mountain (and off tourists), begging for food. They can be very persistent and quite dangerous if teased.

The next major building below the Elephant Bathing Pool, at 1752m, is the *Xianfeng* (Fairy Peak) *Temple*, built by a Ming dynasty monk in 1612. The original buildings were said to have been constructed with lead planks and iron tiles. On the hillsides nearby grow Dove trees (*Davidia involucrata*) and more monkeys.

Descending from 1120m, the *Hongchun* (Tall Tree of Heaven) *Temple* was also founded by a Ming monk (a Chan or Zen follower) but rebuilt in 1790 by another Chan monk. The temple takes its name from the Trees of Heaven in front of it. Inside the hall is a late Qing 'thousand-Buddha lotus lamp' carved with seven dragons and 100 Buddha figures.

At 710m is the *Qingyin* (Clear Sound) *Pavilion*, about 15km from the foot of the mountain (those descending from the summit may wish to stay overnight here, or in the Hongchun Temple). The White Dragon and Black Dragon Streams meet just below the pavilion, where a large black shiny rock projects; this is known as the *Oxheart Rock*, from its shape. Nearby is the *Flying Rainbow Bridge* spanning the two streams. The local gazetteer describes the scene: 'Clear sounds are heard near the lofty pavilion, as if Buddhist spirits were playing musical instruments; incline your ear near the double bridge where the water strikes the ox's heart.'

Those who have made the descent from the summit may then climb up to the **Wannian** (Ten-thousand-year) **Temple** at 1020m, slightly to the W of the Qingyin Pavilion. (Those who returned to the foot of the mountain should take a bus up to near the Wannian Temple which is not quite half-way up the mountain.) This is the major surviving temple on the mountain. In 1983 many subsidiary buildings were being reconstructed (when I first visited the mountain in 1981 there was virtually nothing except the square brick building enclosing the Bodhisattva riding on his elephant).

The temple was founded during the Jin (3–4C AD) and greatly expanded in the Wanli reign period of the Ming (1573–1620) when there were seven great halls. With the exception of the brick building (also Ming in date), these were destroyed by fire in 1946.

The brick building, with a beamless vaulted ceiling, is 16m high and each side is 15.7m long. Inside is a Northern Song figure (cast in 980) of the presiding Bodhisattva on his white six-tusked elephant. Cast from bronze, the whole is 7.3m high and weighs over 60 tons. As the figure has been plastered with stucco and painted, no traces of the casting technology are visible; it must have been a complex task. Around the central figure there are 24 niches on the lower part of the walls, containing small iron Buddha figures; above are six rows of niches containing 307 small bronze Buddha figures.

In pools on the mountain nearby and in front of the hall lives another animal speciality of the mountain, the 'lute frog' whose croaking on summer nights is said to sound like lute music.

Just below the Wannian Temple is the *Cave* (or Temple) *of the White Dragon*, Bai long dong. This is locally said to be the place where the legend of the White Snake took place (though the story is also associated with Hangzhou's Leifeng Pagoda).

A white snake which had turned itself into a beautiful girl married a young man. He was eventually persuaded by a Buddhist monk that she was fundamentally evil and she was incarcerated alive, either here or in the Leifeng Pagoda. Around the temple building are many huge old nanmu cedars, said to have been planted by a Ming monk. He planted them whilst reciting the Lotus sutra, planting a tree for every character he uttered. Though he is said to have planted 69,777 trees, only a few stand today.

Following the path downwards, you reach the Qingyin Pavilion (see above). From there, head S along the ridge towards the *Chunyang* (Pure Brightness) *Hall* (920m), first built in 1585, restored in 1633. This was originally a Taoist temple, transformed into a Buddhist temple in the early Qing. In front of the hall is a stone, said to be the place where Samatabhadra rested when he arrived on the mountain.

Either retrace your steps to the bus near the Wannian Temple or continue down the mountain past the *Leiyin* (Thunder-sound) *Temple*, founded in the Ming. In the Qing it was known as the 'casting off' hermitage for it was said that pilgrims to the mountain cast off the dust of the world here.

Below is the *Fuhu* (Crouching Tiger) *Temple* (which can also be visited, by those based at the foot of the mountain, by climbing up from the hotel). It was founded in the Tang and gained its name either from the hills behind looking like a crouching tiger or because the monks here in the Song suffered from the depredations of tigers and prayed in the temple for protection. The temple was rebuilt in 1651. Surrounded by nanmu cedars, the temple was described by the Qianlong emperor as 'the garden far from impurity'; the inscription can still be seen.

The lowest temple on the mountain is the **Baoguo** (Protect the Nation) **Temple**, just N of the hotel. Founded in the Ming, it was restored in the Qing and the inscription over the gate (with the three characters of the name of the temple) is in The Qianlong emperor's handwriting. The main halls rise, one above the other, and comprise a *Maitreya Hall, Main Hall, Seven-Buddha Hall* and *Sutra Library*. The greatest treasure of the temple is a Ming ceramic Buddha dated 1415, 2.4m high, and the *Huayan* (Garland) *Pagoda*, a 7m, 14-storey dark bronze pagoda, also dating from the Ming. This has the complete text of the Garland Sutra (Avatamsaka-sutra) cast on it, as well as 4700 tiny Buddhas.

In the side wing before the main hall there is an exhibition of the stuffed animal life of Emei—including bearded frogs, lesser pandas and small deer—its geology and history.

40 Leshan

Leshan, 167km S of Chengdu, is famous for its giant Buddha, carved out of a cliff in the Tang dynasty.

Railway: Leshan is some distance from the railway; the most convenient station is Emei, near Emei shan (Mount Emei), where buses run to Leshan (about 90 minutes).

Hotel: the Jiahou Hotel may be singled out as one of the rare hotels in China that is wonderfully situated. It stands high above the confluence of two rivers, the Dadu and the Qingyi, offering a fine view of river life and, in the misty distance, the giant Buddha. A new block has been constructed, behind the old one, and it is worth trying to get a room with a view (some in the old hotel have balconies overlooking the river).

Three rivers converge at Leshan, the Dadu, Qingyi and Min, and the Buddha sits against a cliff on the bank of the Min. Though the town has grown, sprawling down hills away from the rivers, the Jiayou Hotel is in the old town which is pleasant to wander in with its open-fronted timber-frame shops and restaurants.

The giant **Buddha**, carved between 713 and 803, the largest of its kind in China, is 71m high. The head alone is 14.7m high and 10m broad with 7m-long ears (all Buddha figures have long ears, the lobes dragged down by earrings). It is said to have been built with funds raised by a monk who gouged out one of his own eyes to impress potential donors. One of his motives was to subdue the river floods—hence the position of the figure, dominating the rivers.

According to Chinese sources, it is the largest stone-carved Buddha in the world and a local saying states: 'the mountain is a Buddha, the Buddha is a mountain'. Impressive rather than beautiful, it is a figure of the Buddha of the Future, Maitreya, sitting as if on a chair, with hands on knees. A local guide says that it 'is deeply impressive not only because of its perfect proportion, but also the advanced scientific principles it embodies. For example, it has a complete hidden drainage system…to prevent its surface from weathering'.

To the right of the Buddha a narrow series of steps with nine turnings has been cut into the rock to enable visitors to descend to the feet and the riverside (100 people are supposed to be able to sit on one foot). As the steps are very narrow and have to accommodate those ascending and those descending, it is something of a struggle but the feet are worth it.

Above the Buddha are temple buildings and the *Lingbao* (Spirit Treasure) *Pagoda*, first built in the Song and restored in the Ming and Qing. It is built on a square base, with 13 close-eaved storeys built in brick.

If you walk past the Buddha along the river (away from the town), you will see in the distance a low-slung suspension bridge and you will pass a number of tombs built in natural caves along the cliff. Low down, near the river, is one dating from AD 159 with a roughly-carved Buddha figure in the lintel. This is a very early example of a Buddha figure, dating from the first years of the introduction of Buddhism to China.

LESHAN

Han tombs

Wu long temple

Giant Buddha

Dadu river

Min river

Dongda jie

Yutang jie

Shaan xi jie

Ziyun jie

Jiahou Hotel

N

Further along is the **Wulong** (Black Dragon) **Temple**, founded in the Tang, with a *Guardian King Hall, Maitreya Hall, Tathagata Hall* and *Mahavira Hall*, all of the Ming and Qing. The last houses 3m figures of Sakyamuni, Manjusri and Samantabhadra carved from camphor wood. In the temple is the 'Er ya' platform, supposed to be the place where the text of the 'Er ya'—a 3C BC 'dictionary' of glosses on early texts, the forerunner of the tradition of dictionary-making and literary exegesis—was first expounded. The original text by Guo Sheren was lost but much survived in Guo Pu's work of some 500 years later.

Another Guo, whose family home is c 35km E in Shawan, is Guo Moruo. The house is a fine example of local domestic architecture. Three courtyards and a garden formed the home of one of the most extraordinary figures of 20C China. Guo Moruo (1892–1978) studied medicine in Japan but never practised. He became a prominent member of the political and literary establishment from his discovery of Marxism in the 1920s. He was also a major historian, literary critic, scholar of early texts, translator and poet and playwright. His political position meant that his literary talents have not really been critically assessed but his tendency to flaunt his wide reading, dotting his works with foreign names and terms (which had to be written sideways to fit in with Chinese typography) has provided amusement for students of Chinese; an unforgettable line: 'Wo tebie xihuan Spinosa, yinwei wo ai tade pantheism' (I especially like Spinosa because I love his pantheism).

Those who have reached Leshan from Chengdu by coach or car may stop at the **San Su ci** (Memorial Temple to the Three Sus), pretty well half-way between the two. Set in a huge park which is itself of passing interest as it contains in one section some concrete walls, quite effectively modelled on the pierced walls of Suzhou gardens (here openings filled with bamboo to enhance the view beyond are all in concrete, rather than tile), an interesting development. The park and halls commemorate three generations of poets.

The most famous poet in the Su family was Su Shi or Su Dongbo (Su Tung-po; 1037–1101), whose family lived in this part of Sichuan. His father and younger brother were also well-known poets. Su Shi passed the civil service exams in 1057 but his career as a bureaucrat was blighted by his opposition to the reigning reformer, Wang Anshi. He was endlessly exiled, as far away as Hainan Island on one occasion. Also a noted painter of bamboo (the all-round cultivated scholar of the Chinese ideal), he is said to have been able to turn the lyric form to an incredible variety of themes.

41 Chongqing

Chongqing, wartime capital of Nationalist China, is dramatically situated at the meeting place of the Yangtse and the Jialing Rivers in Sichuan province. The city, Sichuan's largest, is situated on the SE edge of the Red Basin of Sichuan which is surrounded by high mountains. The rivers that meet at Chongqing are fed by the snows of the Qinghai plateau and swell dramatically in the spring, rushing through deep gorges that cut the city into three.

Until the bridges were built after liberation, the separate parts of the city were accessible only by ferry. Ferries can still be seen, viewed best from the Chaotianmen Point where, when the river is high and fast, they are pulled at top speed downstream before struggling back against the flood to reach the jetties. Mainly used as a starting point for a boat trip through the Yangtse Gorges, Chongqing has a good museum, some picturesque stepped streets lined with rickety, dark-tiled houses on stilts, and sinister wartime relics.

Airport: there are daily flights (except Saturdays) from Chengdu and Guangzhou, Peking and Xi'an (not Tuesdays) and less regular flights from Kunming, Shanghai, Changsha, Guiyang and Wuhan. The airport is 25km W of the city and as Chongqing is famous for its damp and fogs (it is known in Chinese as 'foggy Chongqing' though Sir Archibald Clark Kerr, British Ambassador during the war, described the climate with some enthusiasm as being like that of Scotland), flights are frequently delayed.

Railway: the station is in the SW of the town, near the N bank of the Yangtse, and connects Chongqing with Chengdu (an overnight trip), also Guiyang and Wuhan.

Boats for the Yangtse Gorges (and beyond—Wuhan and Shanghai) leave from Chaotianmen Point. The booking office is just nearby, at the end of Shaanxi lu.

Hotels: the major hotel is the Holiday Inn but the Renmin Dalitang, set back from Renmin lu in the W of the town, is unmissable for its Temple of Heaven design.

The old part of town is situated on a spur of land or 'high rocky bluff' above the fast-running rivers below, giving it another of its epithets, 'mountain city'. It was a centre of trade, standing at the head of the Yangtse Gorges through which the Yangtse flows down to the ports of Wuhan and Shanghai and much of Sichuan's trade with the rest of China passed through the town (for the Red Basin is surrounded by mountains which made overland trade difficult). Its present name (Repeated Celebrations, which derives from the Song emperor's subjugation of the area, an event quickly followed by his ascent to the throne) dates from the Song dynasty and it was declared a 'city' as late as 1927.

It had attracted the interest of Western entrepreneurs anxious to reach the markets of the hinterland of Sichuan, somewhat earlier, and Archibald Little's steamer 'Leechuan' was the first to make the up-river trip to Chungking (as the city's name used to be romanised) in the low-water season of 1898. This was after the town had been opened to foreign trade by an Additional Article of 1890 to the Chefoo Agreement of 1876. The Chefoo Agreement followed the murder of the British Consul, Augustus Raymond Margary (1846–75) in Yunnan where he had gone to meet Colonel Browne's mission from Burma. The intention of the agreement (on the British side) was to open trade routes between Yunnan (and eventually Sichuan, too) and British-ruled India.

The difficulties of Yangtse navigation were (and still are) complicated by the annual rise of the river—between 21m and 33m—the height and volume of water being most marked in late summer and early autumn after summer rains and melting snow.

After the opening of the city and the start of regular steamer trade the foreign population grew rapidly, with some 180 residents in 1920 (British, American, French and Japanese, all with their own consulates) and all the major firms: Butterfield & Swire, Jardine & Matheson, Asiatic Petroleum, the British-American Tobacco Company, Standard Oil and the India and Eastern French Trading Company, dealing in yellow silk, goatskin, hides, bristles, musk, rhubarb, insect wax and wool (from Tibet).

Chongqing's greatest period of population expansion came in October 1938 when Chiang Kai-shek's Nationalist government moved from Nanjing which was captured by the Japanese on 13 December 1938. Over 2000km inland, protected by the gorges and mountain ranges, Chongqing quickly filled as government officials and refugees of all sorts flooded in to the walled city. The population spilled out to fill the other small walled city on the N bank of the Jialing River, described in 1920 as 'occupying a space less than 1 mile square...built on solid rock with no possible chance for drainage, and consequently reeks with odours even more pronounced than in most Chinese cities'.

With grander houses perched on top of the city (when the American General Stilwell arrived in 1942 to try and clarify his position in relation to Chiang Kai-shek and the command of the Chinese armies in Burma, he had to climb 365 stone steps up to his Western-style house near the Chaotianmen promontory), poorer houses were clustered on stilts along the stepped lanes. Transport within the city was mainly by sedan-chair for the lanes were impassable to motor vehicles—even today, Chongqing is virtually empty of bicycles because of the steep inclines.

During the brief and rather unsuccessful 'united front' (of Nationalists and Communists against the Japanese invaders) in 1937–41, the overcrowded city was home to leaders of both parties and, as a consequence, simply bursting with secret agents and spies. Soaring inflation and corruption meant that coolies carried $50 notes, according to General Stilwell, and it was generally agreed by foreign correspondents that government salaries were so low (and infrequently paid) that there were no fat Chinese under the rank of Minister of Finance. The miseries of overcrowding were complicated by Japanese bombing raids which devastated the unprotected city whenever the fogs lifted. Bomb-shelters were carved out of the rocks wherever possible but the flimsy wooden houses of the city were flattened in their thousands.

It was described in the 1890s (by 'The Times' correspondent, Morrison) as a city full of temples and pagodas and spacious public buildings whose grandeur was said to be due to opium revenues: these have all disappeared, together with the city walls. The city today has been much rebuilt, in concrete, and only sections, which escaped the Japanese, still reveal what it was like in the 1930s.

To see the town at its most dramatic, at the point where the two rivers meet, go to the **Chaotianmen Point**, at the easternmost end of the city. This can be reached by taxi or by a No. 12 bus (from outside the hotel) which takes you to the junction of Minzu lu and Xinhua lu. From the terminus, walk towards the point (NE along Xinhua lu. From the point, where once you could see the gunboats of foreign nations at anchor ready to protect trade and the interests of foreign nationals, as well as more junks than anywhere else on the upper Yangtse, you can watch the cable-car crossing the Jialing River (to the left) as well as the many ferries struggling against the currents.

Returning to the bus terminus area, just off Minzu lu on the S side, opposite where the road is joined by Cangbai lu, is the **Luohan Temple**, virtually the only surviving temple in Chongqing. Founded in the Song, it was heavily restored in 1752, only to be burnt down during the Japanese bombing raids and restored in 1945. In front of the gate is a stele dated 1623, bearing, rather mysteriously, the inscription 'Ancient traces of the West Lake'. Inside, on either side are Buddhist carvings in the rock, of Buddhas and lohans, rather weather-worn. The 500 stucco lohans that once stood in the main hall and gave the temple its name have been destroyed.

Pipa Park and the Museum.

S of the hotel is the *Loquat Park* (Pipa shan gongyuan), named after the loquat trees that grow there. Before 1949 it was the site of the private residence of a family named Wang and was therefore called the Wang Garden.

Take Zaozi gangya S of the hotel until you reach the junction with Zhongshan er lu; turn right for the entrance to the park which stands (as you will already be aware) at Chongqing's highest point, offering a view of the city, fog permitting. The tea-houses of the park are popular with the elderly.

The **City Museum** is on the S side of the park and contains most notably one of the best collections of carved tomb-bricks (from the Han dynasty), a small but rare ethnographical exhibit including puppets and woodblock prints, and paintings mainly by the local painter Zhang Daqian, born in 1898 (who spent his later life in Brazil and Taiwan). When they are not travelling the world, some of Sichuan's dinosaur remains, including the skeleton of the world's largest beast, Mamenchisaurus, are displayed here, too. The Han tomb-bricks are displayed with photographs of *que* pillars (also of the Han), which have been quite widely found in Sichuan.

Erected in front of major buildings, these usually have timber architectural details reproduced in brick or stone. The tomb-bricks, made of incised and stamped earthenware, were used to line the interior of local tombs and bear a variety of designs, many of which illustrate daily life under the Han—chariots and horses, courtyard houses, acrobats and tumblers performing at banquets, and hunting scenes, fulfilling the same function as wall paintings in Egyptian tombs. These bricks were peculiar to Han tombs in Sichuan.

A number of sites in Chongqing recall the days of the anti-Japanese war and the 'united front', mostly those sanctified by the presence of well-known Communists. The best known is **Hongyan cun** (Red Crag Village), near the S bank of the Jialing River, just NW of the hotel. Directly behind the hotel, a small turning to the left off Renmin lu takes you to the forbidding brick-red building, No. 50 Zengjiayan, just off Zhongshan si lu.

In 1938 the Eighth Route Army (part of what was to become the People's Liberation Army) set up its southern headquarters in Chongqing, together with the office of the 'Xinhua Ribao' (New China Daily News, forerunner of the People's Daily). Zhou Enlai was in charge of this southern headquarters, assisted by such notables as Dong Biwu, Deng Yingchao (Zhou Enlai's wife) and Ye Jianying. Their first office was destroyed by Japanese bombs so this three-storey building was built by officers of the

southern headquarters themselves. Together with the nearby Gui yuan (on Zhongshan si lu), and the New China Daily Office at 208 Minsheng lu, the whole grouping is known as 'Red Crag Village'. The new headquarters building backs onto the river and to the left, the KMT established their police headquarters (non-secret variety) whilst the headquarters of Dai Li, head of the secret police, were moved to the right.

Dai Li—described by Barbara Tuchman as 'China's combination of Himmler and J. Edgar Hoover' and his 'organisation' by General Stilwell as a 'Gestapo'—can hardly have been a reassuring neighbour. Not a very confidence-inspiring landlord, either: it was he who supplied General Stilwell with lodgings on Chaotianmen Point, a building which was presumably bugged by whatever means, electronic or human, he had at his disposal, As well as being surrounded by buildings full of police and spies, it appears that every street-hawker and tea-stall proprietor in the road outside was suspect. The red building, with its wooden walls and verandahs, seems curiously flimsy and unsafe, even today, and it is easy to imagine the enemy outside.

Mao Zedong stayed here when he arrived in August 1945, to negotiate with Chiang Kai-shek, after the Japanese had been defeated. The Chongqing negotiations, a vain attempt to stave off the inevitable civil war, involved substantial concessions from the Communists (withdrawal from their southern 'liberated' zones and a huge reduction of their armed forces) in return for greater democracy in the Nationalist government, did not long survive. In 1947, under threat, the Communists left the Red Crag Village for Yan'an.

Returning to Zhongshan si lu, turn right along it until you reach the *Gui yuan* (Cassia Garden) on your right, just before the roundabout. The small two-storey Western-style house was the home of Zhang Zhizhong (1890–1969), who had served as director of the Huangpu (Whampoa) Military Academy in Guangzhou and was an important Nationalist general.

He was a KMT delegate at the Chongqing negotiations and later led the KMT delegation which made peace with the Communists in 1949 (in Chiang Kai-shek's absence). After 1949 he remained in China, serving as a Deputy Chairman of the National People's Congress and on defence committees. He let Mao Zedong use the house during the negotiations, moving, with his family, to another residence. On 10 October 1945, the Chongqing negotiations were concluded in the house and the next day, Zhou Enlai wrote a poem for Zhang Zhizhong: 'We are hoping for brightness, ten thousand miles ahead; the new China will belong to our young people'.

From the roundabout, the turning on the right leads to one of the two bridges of Chongqing, the *Jialing Bridge*, high above the river, constructed in 1963–66. The road opposite, Renmin lu, leads back to the hotel.

Outside Chongqing.

Sites to be seen outside Chongqing include two hot springs and the US-KMT joint prison site at *Gele shan*. The latter is in the NW suburbs and consists of an exhibition hall displaying photographs and manacles. The prison, established by the KMT in 1943, was where a number of Communists and KMT opponents were killed, particularly on the eve of the liberation of the city on 27 November 1949, when over 300 inmates were killed.

The northern hot springs are in **Beipei**, a suburb in the NW of the city, an area of pretty mountain and river scenery including a *temple* with a main Buddha hall built in 1432. Spring-water baths may be taken, where the water arrives naturally warmed to 32–37°C.

The southern hot springs are some 20km from the city on the S bank of the Yangtse, again set in a pretty, cliffside garden.

42 The Yangtse River

The upper reaches of the **Yangtse River** have been navigated for thousands of years despite difficulties. Rising on the high Qinghai plateau, on the border with Tibet, the river flows fast down through Sichuan province, swelled in the late summer by melting snow from the highlands and the summer rains. Near the border of Sichuan and Hubei provinces, the Yangtse flows through a series of narrow gorges where the river level falls 150m. Now valued for their attraction to tourists, until 1898, the gorges were navigable only by small boats.

Determined to gain better access to the riches of Sichuan province (silks, goatskins, hides, bristle, minerals, timber) and those of Tibet, distributed via Sichuan (musk, rhubarb, medicines and wool), Archibald Little (1838–1908) first got a steamer up the Yangtse through the gorges to Chongqing. Downstream navigation involved riding the treacherous rapids which were particularly dangerous since there were numerous obstacles, hidden at high water, but it was upstream navigation that was hardest and slowest. It was particularly difficult during the high-water season as the water flow was so rapid. Boats had to be dragged by trackers, usually teams of 80 to 100 men hauling on a 400m-long rope of twisted bamboo. In the gorges they frequently used narrow trackers' paths cut into the rock many metres above the water level which made their task all the more difficult and dangerous. These paths can still sometimes be seen although the generally higher level of the water has covered many parts. In the late 19C these were described thus:

> Narrow, steep flights of steps are in many places cut into the rock to facilitate tracking, as well as rock paths a foot or so wide, some only fifteen or twenty feet above the river, others at a giddy height on which the trackers looked no bigger than flies…On all of these, and indeed for much of the upward journey, the life of the tracker is in continual peril from losing his foothold owing to the slipperiness of the rock after rain, and from being dragged over and drowned by the backward tendencies of a heavy junk tugging at the end of 1200 feet of a heavy bamboo hawser as thick as an arm…

Travellers described how the trackers, the rope on their calloused shoulder, were bent double with effort, their fingers touching the ground. Apparently even Archibald Little's steamer required trackers to guide it through the gorges. His boat was only 16.5m long and he travelled at low water when many dangerous rocks were at least visible.

In her book, 'The Yangtse Valley and Beyond' (1899), Isabella Bird describes the organisation of the tracking team, their work directed by a rapid beating of gongs and drums on board ship when they were required to pull hard, their pace slowed by a slower drumbeat. There was also a flag-signalling system operated from boat to shore with the trackers' foreman communicating the message to his men. The need for these subtleties of direction was due to the complex water-flow through rapids with whirlpools and eddies that threatened to take a boat off-course. The many semi-submerged rocks in the rapids added to the dangers; some of these can still be seen at low water though, since the construction of the Gezhou Dam just above Ichang (1970–81), the water above Ichang is never as low as it was in Mrs Bird's day.

A British naval commander who served on the Upper Yangtse in 1926–28 and 1932–34 wrote a book called 'Excelsior: being an inadequate description of the Upper Yangtse compiled by "Charon"' (Shanghai, 1934), describing the late summer high water:

> Vast volumes of water come pouring down from Tibet in the form of 'freshets' raising the level of the river by leaps and bounds. In their struggle to fight their way through the 'bottleneck' formed by the Gorges in the last hundred miles above Yichang, they turn these hitherto peaceful reaches into boiling, seething infernos of tumbling, tossing water, whirlpools, eddies, backwaters and sudden vertical 'boils'.

Mrs Bird watched a junk falling foul of such conditions:

> A great cargo junk was being hauled up with two hawsers, over 200 trackers, and the usual enormous din, the beating of drums and gongs, the clashing of cymbals, and the incessant letting off of crackers to intimidate the spirit of the rapid, when both ropes snapped, the trackers fell on their faces, and four hours' labour was lost for in a flash the junk was at the foot

of the rapid, and the last sight I had of her was far below twirling round in a whirlpool with a red lifeboat in attendance…

(Apparently one junk in ten was stranded and one in 20 lost annually.) Mrs Bird noted that all this 'climbing over the huge angular boulders of the river banks, sliding on their backs down spurs of smooth rock, climbing cliff walls on each other's shoulders, or holding on with fingers and toes, sometimes on hands and knees, sometimes on shelving precipices where only their grass sandals save them from slipping into the foaming race below…on a narrow track cut into the rock…on which narrow and broken ledge a man unencumbered and with a strong head would need to do his best to keep his feet…' was accomplished on a diet mainly of rice.

Travellers today generally embark at Chongqing and, after 2½ days, disembark at Wuhan. Though it is possible to continue to Shanghai or Nanjing, beyond Yichang the river is flat and immensely broad and not terribly exciting. It is also possible to see the gorges by going upriver from Wuhan to Chongqing (which is cheaper) but it takes 4½ days against the current.

Boats: there are six luxury-class liners which accommodate foreigners only in 1st-class (single) cabins. More commonly used are the boats of the Dongfang hong (East is Red) line which offer 2nd, 3rd, 4th and 5th-class accommodation. 2nd class means a neat two-berth cabin with its own washbasin (hot and cold water), desk and chair. 2nd-class passengers may use the lounge at the front of the boat (where they sometimes fight in an ugly manner for the best photographic vantage points). 3rd-class passengers are accommodated in rooms with ten berths (two-tiered bunks); 4th class is similarly arranged with space for 12 or more, and 5th class is a vast area of three-tiered bunks. There is a dining room, available to all, at the back of the upper deck (at the opposite end to the lounge).

Departure from **Chongqing** is in itself impressive: the confluence of the two rivers (Yangtse and Jialing) adds to the volume of water swirling eastwards; the many ferries swing out in wide circles as they cross from bank to bank and the city stands high above. As you leave the city, most of the boats that you pass are either steamers, loaded with passenger, or small sailing vessels on short-haul, often loaded with rock, presumably for building.

If possible, it is interesting to get onto the deck at the prow (on the boats I have travelled on, this was officially reserved for the crew but our crews did not seem to mind). From there you can look back, up to where the captain or pilot directs the course and communicates with other vessels. Though the river level is higher than it was, his activities still indicate the dangers that lurk. He is constantly scanning the river and the course may appear peculiar for he has to navigate past many hidden shoals and rocks which may not be visible at high water.

The towns and villages that you pass also indicate the perils of river life. They are perched high, 'scattered on carefully terraced heights' reached by steep flights of hundreds of slippery steps for the river may rise as much as 40m in the summer.

The first major sight on the river, c 280km from Chongqing, is *Shibao zhai* (Stone Treasure Storehouse), a 30m-high rock which is said to look like a stone seal (inscribed stone, rather than animal).

This the first of thousands of stones said to look like other things that you encounter on the Yangtse; these, combined with folk legends attached to peaks and caves, can seriously interrupt study of the scenery. The narrative is, however, the way the Chinese see the gorges and hence the way the scenery is presented or explained.

A temple was built at the top of the Stone Treasure Storehouse during the Qianlong emperor's reign (1736–96) and the pagoda-like structure of 11 storeys concealing a spiral staircase leading to the temple was built during the reign of Jiaqing (1797–1821). This tapering multi-eaved structure with its up-turned eaves and porthole windows is most impressive.

50km beyond is **Wan xian**, where most boats moor for the night. If the current is particularly strong, this is an impressive moment. Often, the anchor has to be laid near the far bank, and the anchor chain fed through the boat to enable it to resist the pull of the water and moor in Wan xian (rather than miles downstream). Wan xian, a county seat, is perched high above the river, reached by a broad sweep of steep stone steps, beneath which a multitude of boats are moored. Passengers can usually disembark and fight their way up to the town whose streets are lined with stalls selling lidded baskets (a Sichuan speciality: most have black and red patterns) which you can fill with other local products, tangerines and pomeloes. Sometimes, groups of tourists are taken to factories where silk is spun and woven.

Historically, Wan xian was known as 'the gateway to east Sichuan'. Situated between the two river ports of Chongqing (in Sichuan) and Yichang in Hubei where the river broadens for easier navigation, it was an important centre of riverine commerce, and still is. It became a foreign treaty port in 1902 for that reason. Mrs Bird was impressed by it: 'Graceful pagodas and three-storeyed pavilions guard the approaches. The Feng Shui of Wan xian is considered perfect. Rich temples on heights above the river... retain their hold on the people. The wealth of vegetation is wonderful...'.

For Charon, the stalls in the markets were of interest: 'All sorts of quaint objects of local manufacture can be bought.... Such weird items as flea-traps for carrying in the sleeves of gowns (these one must buy in the spring), prayer mats (a joy to upper deck sleepers), cow-horn opium boxes, bamboo baskets...'. He noted that: 'The foreign community, except for missionary bodies, is practically non-existent. A Danish chemical expert and his wife live at the Standard Oil installation...In years gone by there was quite a large community, mostly engaged in the "Wood-oil" trade".' He does not

mention the 'Wan-hsien incident' when two British gunboats opened fire on the city
in 1926 because the local warlord had taken to seizing foreign ships to load his own
goods. This led to a lengthy boycott of British goods and a refusal to load or unload
British ships.

The next day is that on which the boat passes through the famous gorges.
I have to admit to a slight disappointment, due to the relative height of the
river since the construction of the dam downstream but on one trip, when
the weather was particularly cloudy, the steep cliffs of the gorges were
impressively cloaked in mist and looked very much like a Chinese painting.

After passing the town of *Fengjie* (119km downstream from Wan xian),
the first gorge appears. This is **Qutang Gorge**, known to earlier Western
travellers as 'Windbox Gorge'. 'Charon' waxes lyrical: 'Try and picture a
mountain 3000 feet high split down the centre by a titanic axe…'. The
gorge is 8km long and is entered through the *Chijia* (Red Shoulder)
Mountain to the N and the *Baiyan* (White Salt) *Mountain* to the S.

At low water it is sometimes possible to see great 2m-high iron pillars in the water on
either side, formerly used to attach chains which traversed the river. During the
Tang, these were defensive barriers but by the Qing they were used to stop vessels
in order to collect taxes, most notably the 'likin', an inland tax on the transport of
goods, supposedly fixed (in the mid 19C) at one-tenth of one percent their value but
often as much as 20 percent in certain areas.

On the side of the White Salt Mountain, a zig-zag series of square holes
cut into the cliff is known as *Meng Jiang's Ladder.*

A Song dynasty general, Yang Jiye, was said to have been buried high up on the cliff,
far from his home. One of his comrades, Meng Jiang, decided to collect Yang's bones
and take them home for reburial in his native place. He was hewing steps out of the
cliff when a monk discovered him and began to crow like a cockerel at dawn. Fear-
ing discovery by daylight, Meng Jiang gave up but he later discovered the monk's
ploy and hanged him from a rock further up the cliff, known as the Monk Hanging By
His Feet (and it is said to look like a monk hanging by his feet).
     Meng Jiang's stairway is probably the remains of a form of access to a city of the
6C AD, the remains of whose walls have been found on top of the White Salt Mountain. Right at the top of the cliff, above the suspended monk rock, is a cave, *Kuangjia*
(Armour) *Cave,* so-called because a Tang dynasty woman general was supposed to
have used it as an armory. 30 years ago archaeologists discovered three wooden
coffins in the cave (their siting and dating to c 1000 BC similar to the boat burials high
up in the Wuyi mountains in Fujian province).

For those who are good at the Chinese game of seeing things in rocks,
there is a 20m stalactite visible on the White Salt Mountain called the
Drinking Phoenix because it is said to resemble a phoenix drinking from
a spring. Nearby, the *Fengbi tang* (Chalk Wall Hall) is easier to spot with
inscriptions carved on the rock face (previously smoothed and enhanced
as a writing surface by the application of chalk or whitewash) by Song
dynasty calligraphers.

Opposite, on Red Shoulder Mountain, is the *Fengxiang* (Windbox or
Bellows) *Gorge,* named after some more square indentations on the rock,
supposed to have been used as a bellows by Lu Ban, the magical carpen-
ter and great inventor (and patron saint of all woodworkers and masons).
These were recently (1971) discovered to contain more of the wooden
coffins like those found opposite. High up along the N face of the cliff of
the gorge is the old towpath. On both sides of the gorge there are deep
holes (visible only at low water) used when boatmen used to pole or punt
their boats up the river.

Just beyond the Armour Cave, on the S side, a huge stone on top of a black rock is
known as the 'Rhinoceros Looking at the Moon' because that is what it is supposed to
look like.

The end of the first gorge is marked by the appearance of the town of
Daixi on the S bank. Two dark peaks can be seen on the S bank of the

river; they are said to be the remains of two dragons that used to block the river.

They had been playfully whipping up tornadoes and hurricanes and wreaking destruction when Yao Ji, youngest daughter of Xi wang mu (Queen Mother of the West) caused a thunderbolt to stop them in their tracks. As they were then blocking the river, the Great Yu, legendary founder of the Xia dynasty (21C–16C BC), 'tamer of the floods', came rushing to unblock the waters. A muddle ensued since the goddess and the flood-tamer moved the dragon-rocks the wrong way at first, thus the two peaks are known as *Cuokai* (Wrongly Opened) *Gorge*.

Some 20km downstream, the town of **Wushan** is on the N bank; behind lie mountains where there are many Tong trees from whose fruit is derived the wood-oil mentioned in connection with foreign trade at Wan xian. Tong oil has been widely used in China for treating timber (caulking boats, bringing out the grain in fine hardwood furniture) and it was traditionally incorporated in the mixture of pig blood, clay and straw that was painted onto wooden columns in palaces and temples to protect the timber from the elements. Some stop here for an excursion up the Da ning River to see the three 'mini gorges'.

Not far beyond Wushan is the second gorge, **Wu xia** (Wu Gorge). This is 44km long and lined with 12 peaks, six on either side of the river. Here, 'Charon' felt 'the littleness of Man and the wonder of Nature. One felt as if one had been caught "blowing a bine" in Westminster Abbey'. Just at the beginning of the gorge on the S side is a small valley called the *Valley of the Golden Helmet and Shining Armour*, apparently named because the walls of the valley are lined with a grey folded limestone formation which looks like ancient armour. The rounded mountain top is coloured yellow-brown by iron in the local water and is thus said to resemble a golden helmet above the armour. On the N bank of the gorge are: *Goddess Peak, Dragon Peak, Holy Spring Peak, Facing the Clouds Peak, Pine Ridge Peak* and *Gathered Immortals Peak*. On the S side are: *Gathered Cranes Peak, Cloudy Screen Peak* and *Flying Phoenix Peak* with *Pure Altar Peak, Rising Cloud Peak* and *Soaring Peak* behind.

The requisite accompanying legend states (in one version authorised by the Yangtse Branch of the China International Travel Service) that the Goddess Peak represents Yao Ji, youngest daughter of the Queen Mother of the West (who made the mistake over the 'Wrongly Opened Gorge'). Bored with life in heaven, she secretly descended to earth with her 11 sisters. At Wushan she met Yu the Great, tamer of the floods, who was fighting 12 dragons who had caused a flood. The 12 maidens killed the 12 dragons and then helped Yu to organise China's waterways. They failed to remove all the obstacles to river transport in the Wu Gorge and so stayed there (as the 12 peaks) to assist sailors 'and to help the peasants bring in bumper harvests'.

Two lines in Mao Zedong's poem 'Swimming' refer to Yao Ji: 'The mountain goddess, if she is still there, Will be startled to find her world so changed'.

The Gathered Immortals Peak appears almost in the middle of the river at one bend. On its side is a pale rock, the *Kong Ming Rock*, with an inscription which reads: 'The Wuxia gorge has peaks rising higher and higher'.

The inscription is supposed to have been written by Kong Ming who was better known as Zhuge Liang, Prime Minister of the State of Shu during the Three Kingdoms (220–280; see Chengdu). Further inscriptions recorded Zhuge Liang's masterly handling of the alliance between the states of Shu and Wu against Wei. It is said that during a later battle between Shu and Wu (Zhuge Liang's alliance proving shortlived), the Wu general was in hot pursuit of the army of Shu when he passed the rock. Moved by the inscription and its exhortation to unity, he abandoned the chase. It is thought that all the inscriptions are Ming or later in date.

5km further along the S bank is the small town of **Beishi** where as the poet-historian-epigrapher-playwright-politician (and native of Sichuan; see Leshan) Guo Moruo (1872–1978) said, 'When the bow of my boat enters Hubei province, the stern is still in Sichuan'.

A few km beyond, on the N bank, is the *Iron Coffin Peak*, said to be shaped like a man kneeling by a coffin, a symbol of filial piety. The gods were so moved by the son's devotion to his mother that he was turned to stone.

Some 45km beyond, on the N bank is the town of **Zigui**, famous as the home town of Qu Yuan (c 3C BC), the loyal but falsely betrayed minister of the state of Chu.

He had always advocated resistance to the advance of the state of Qin but his advice was unheeded and he was banished. His despair at his treatment, and at the seizure of Chu by Qin in 278 BC, was such that he drowned himself. It is said that the local people venerated him so much, they did not want fishes to eat his body (but wanted to preserve it whole for burial) so they threw food into the river to feed the fish and this is the origin of the lotus-wrapped sticky-rice bundles that people eat on the 5th day of the 5th month of the lunar calendar. The festival is known as the Dragon Boat Festival when gloriously decorated boats with dragon prows are raced (apparently to commemorate the search for Qu Yuan's body, by boat).

Just beyond Zigui, on the N side of the river (where the next gorge begins) is a small stream, the *Fragrant Stream*.

Though many will be weary of the interminable folk-tales associated with every pebble (and the attributes of form mysteriously assigned to every boulder), they may not be surprised to know that a romantic tale is associated with the Fragrant Stream. It flows by the birthplace of Wang Zhaojun, one of the concubines of the Yuandi emperor of the Han dynasty (reigned 48–32 BC). It is said that once the concubine washed her face in the stream and dropped a pearl from her head-dress; ever since the water has been fragrant.

Every year, small fish appear in the stream at peach-blossom time and they are called Peach-blossom Fish. They recall the time that Wang Zhaojun was sent off to the north to marry a barbarian chieftain. She sailed down the stream singing so plaintively that even the peach trees were moved to shed their blossom. The petals dropped into the water and turned into little fish which swam alongside Wang Zhaojun's boat.

Immediately beyond is the last of the three gorges, **Xiling Gorge**, 75km long and full of folklore…It comprises four smaller gorges: the Gorge of the Sword and the Book on the Art of War; the Gorge of the Ox's Liver and Horse's Lung; the Kongling Gorge and the Gorge of Shadowplay.

The *Sword and the Book on the Art of War Gorge* is said to be the place that Zhuge Liang stored grain for his troops in a cave, where he also placed his book on military strategy for safe-keeping. There is a small cave on the N bank, near a stratified layer of rock, that is supposed to look like a stack of paper; beside it is a narrow rock 'resembling a sword thrust into the river'. An alternative story is that the book and the sword belonged to Zhang Liang, a follower of Liu Bang (founder and first emperor of the Han dynasty), whose book and sword were stored here after his death. Between this and the next gorge is the *Blue* (or *New*) *Shoal*, formed by the collapse of a cliff.

Invisible at high water, the rocks, despite dredging and clearing, are still something of a hazard at low water. In the past, ship's passengers would disembark here and walk, such was the danger and it was after numerous accidents at this spot in particular that the red lifeboats (described by Mrs Bird) were established here in 1854 by public subscription amongst local merchants who were losing cargoes.

The *Ox's Liver and Horse's Blood Gorge* is named after stones that look like ox liver (N bank) with a lung-shaped rock above. According to the official guide, imperialist warships invaded the gorge in 1900 and destroyed half the Horse's Lung Gorge with their bombardment.

Beyond is the *Kongling Gorge* and the *Kongling Shoal*, with a hidden rock, 220m long, which divides the bed into two channels. There are other boulders of danger here such as the 'big pearl' and its three smaller pearls, a hazard which is clearly illustrated in the woodblock pilot's guides published in Chinese ('Charon' describes the boulders as being the target of blasting in 1933 by the Chinese Maritime Customs).

The small *Yellow Ox Gorge* (named after a low rock on the S shore said to look like a person leading an ox) leads to the *Huangling Temple*, dating from the Ming, though originally supposed to have been a Spring and Autumn period (770–476 BC) foundation dedicated to the Great Yu and his yellow ox which cut channels for water with its horns.

The *Shadowplay* or *Bright Moon Gorge* follows: its double name refers to the way the rocks shine in the moonlight and also to the appearance of four rocks on the right which, viewed preferably from Yichang (ie from downstream), against the setting sun, look like the silhouettes of the four major characters in the Ming novel 'Journey to the West' by Wu Cheng'en (c 1500–80; translated by Arthur Waley as 'Monkey'). The monkey king stands at the front as a lookout; behind is the pig, leading a horse. The monk-pilgrim Xuan zang sits straight whilst his assistant Sha carries the Buddhist sutras on a shoulder-pole.

Beyond is another small gorge, the *Yellow Cat Gorge*, named after a yellow rock that looks like a cat.

Then the river widens and the next event is the lock on the *Gezhou Dam*. 70m high, with three shiplocks, the dam cuts the Yangtse in two, which is good for electricity but not for ecology and some rare species such as the freshwater dolphin are in even greater danger since its construction. It was built in two parts, the first (1970–81) was the major construction across the river, the second, completed in 1986, is said to provide an annual production of 14 billion kilowatt hours. It was a fascinating sight to watch, particularly at night when the site was illuminated by pink and pale blue acetylene flares. The dam's locks are also impressively high and all ships must pass through them before reaching Yichang.

Yichang was an important entrepôt on the Yangtse and was therefore made a Treaty Port by the Cheefoo Convention of 1876.

The Cheefoo (proper name Yantai) Agreement or Convention followed the murder of Margary in Yunnan in 1875 when he was attempting to meet Captain Browne's mission from Burma. Wuhu, Yichang and Wenzhou (on the coast) were opened to foreign trade. In 1917 Yichang was described as having a population of 40,000 with 187 foreigners supervising the transit of beans, grain, sesame seed, vegetable tallow and wood (or Tong) oil. It was also noted that in 1910 work had begun on a railway between Yichang and Wan xian which, as it does not exist, must have been abandoned.

The riverfront still has a number of European buildings and three more can be seen in the grounds of the Taohualing Hotel. Otherwise, the city is a neatly laid-out modern one with quite pleasant blocks of flats lining straight streets, most recent development being due to the construction of the dam and its hydroelectric power station.

43 Wuhan

Wuhan, capital of Hubei province, is a modern city, with a major iron and steel industry. The city is made up of three older cities lying on two sides of the Yangtse where the Han River joins it. Wuchang lies on the south bank of the Yangtse, whilst Hanyang and the later settlement of Hankou (a treaty port) are on the other side of the river, divided by the Han. Wuhan is a mainly modern city with much rather fine treaty-port architecture and a famous university; it is a centre of communication but it also has a very important collection of recently unearthed bronzes in the Provincial Museum.

Hubei province is a Qing creation, established in the early 18C when the previous province of Huguang was divided. It was the site of one of the most distinctive of the Warring States (403–221 BC), the kingdom of Chu whose wood carvings (composite animal forms with deer antlers and long tongues) and bronzes covered in lost-wax tangles, more like worms than dragons, can be seen in the Provincial Museum. When central control disintegrated at the end of the Han, another independent kingdom, Wu, was established in the area and the province saw some of the epic battles described in the 'San guo yan yi' ('Romance of the Three Kingdoms').

Industrial development of the Wuhan complex began in the late 19C and Wuhan is noted by historians of the Communist movement for its proletarian uprisings.

The province, named 'North of the [Dongting] Lake', has a population of 49,310,000.

Airport: 19km from Wuhan city centre. The central position of Wuhan is evident from the number of flights from Peking, Changsha, Chengdu, Chongqing, Fuzhou, Guangzhou, Guilin, Hangzhou, Hefei, Nanchang, Nanjing, Shanghai, Shashi, Shenyang, Xi'an, Yichang and Zhengzhou.

Railway: there are two stations, one in Wuchang (for Guilin, Guangzhou, Chongqing, Xi'an and Zhenjiang), one in Hankou for Anyang, Peking, etc, though the situation is not as clear-cut as it sounds as many trains cross from one station to the other on the Yangtse Bridge.

Boat: many passengers on Yangtse Gorges steamers disembark or embark at Wuhan. It is possible to reach other destinations on the Yangtse by boat and some places, such as Nanjing and Shanghai, are more easily accessible by water than by rail since the train goes N to Zhengzhou before heading E. The jetty and ticket office are on the waterfront in Hankou.

Hotels: the nicest hotels are old foundations in Hankou: the Shengli, 11 Siwei lu, built in the German concession in the 1930s and near the waterfront; the Xuangong Hotel (45 Jianghan lu) in the old British Concession which dates from the 1930s and is in the centre of the commercial district, and the Jianghan (245 Shengli lu) (old French concession) near Hankou railway station.

Wuhan's legendary history begins with the Great Yu, tamer of the floods, who is supposed to have done some work in the Hanyang area, vulnerable to floods. There was a Shang-dynasty settlement to the NE of Wuhan, Panlong cheng, excavated in 1950–60 and 1974, where a palace and a city, surrounded by a wall and moat, were uncovered. A middle-Shang site, it also comprises tombs (including one with human sacrifices) and evidence of local bronze production. The latter finds are of interest since Panlong cheng was some distance from the metropolitan Shang centre; other non-metrolitan Shang finds often include bronzes thought to have been imported but here they were locally produced.

Settlement continued in the area and Wuchang was briefly used as a capital by the state of Wu during the Three Kingdoms (222–280) before power was transferred to Nanjing in 229. It later served as a provincial capital under the Yuan and Ming (although the provincial boundaries were different from those of today: in the Yuan the area was larger, incorporating Hubei, Hunan, Guangdong and Guangxi; in the Ming, only Hubei and Hunan were included). As late as 1924, as the 'Japanese Railway Guide' demonstrates, both Wuchang and Hanyang were surrounded by walls (Wuchang's being far more extensive than those of the smaller settlement at Hanyang.

The town of Hanyang on the other side of the river was founded under the Sui (581–618) and saw great expansion in the 19C when the Hanyang arsenal was founded and Zhang Zhidong promoted the development of the iron and steel works, cotton mills, silk factories and tanneries amongst other industrial enterprises. Zhang Zhidong (1837–1909), an official and reformer, was appointed governor general of Hubei and Hunan (still administratively regarded as one in the Qing), with his headquarters in Wuchang, in 1889, after his energetic promotion of the construction of the Peking–Hankou railway line (completed in 1906). Hummel's 'Eminent Chinese of the Ch'ing Period' (US Government Printing Office, 1943–44) notes that many of his projects in Hanyang were 'riddled with graft and conducted at a loss, but it is largely to his great initiative that the Wu-Han cities owe their subsequent position as the "Chicago" of China.'

The third of the three cities, Hankou, developed as a treaty port with the British arriving in 1861, the French, Russians and Japanese in 1896. With river transport plus the railway from 1906, Hankou 'boomed' as a trading town with sesame and goat-skins from Hunan, beans, silk, cotton, hides and gypsum from the Hubei plains, and nutgalls, varnish, wood-oil and vegetable tallow from the western mountain regions (according to the 'Encyclopaedia Sinica', 1917). Its factories, second in importance to those of Shanghai, processed some of these raw materials and the 'Chicago' reputation was based on the arsenal, the mint (in Wuchang), the Hanyang iron and steel works, the railway and electric light works, etc.

Wuhan's revolutionary history is perhaps due in part to the arrival of the railway for railway workers were amongst the earliest of China's small number of proletarians to become politicised. The 1911 revolution which overthrew the Qing started in Wuhan, gathering strength as it spread to other cities until it succeeded. Much of Hankou was destroyed in the weeks of fighting between revolutionaries and imperial troops, but it was rebuilt under the Republic. From 1926–27 Wuhan was the headquarters of part of the the KMT, the faction which opposed Chiang Kai-shek. Wang Jingwei (who later associated himself with the Japanese and finally set up a puppet government in Najing in 1940) was one of the leaders of the 'left KMT' which maintained an alliance with the Communist Party after April 1927 and claimed to adhere more closely to Sun Yatsen's principles than his successor, Chiang Kai-shek. Sun's widow, Song Qingling, was associated with the Wuhan Left KMT government, as were Russian advisors such as Mikhail Borodin (described rather threateningly by a recent American biographer as 'Stalin's man in China'). The Wuhan government's alliance with the Communist Party did not survive for long; in July 1927 Wang Jingwei turned on his former allies just as Chiang Kai-shek had done, killing some 100,000 communist supporters in Wuhan and the surrounding countryside. Song Qingling just managed to escape with her life.

In 1957, the bridge across the Yangtse was built, effectively joining the two halves of China (north and south) in the centre and improving rail links dramatically.

The major sites in Hanyang are Gui shan (see below), N of the old (originally walled) city and just S of the Hanyang iron and steel works and the old arsenal (to the left of the iron and steel works), and the **Guiyuan si** (Temple of the Return to the Fundamental Principle) at the western end of Cuihui jie in the W of Hanyang. The temple was founded in the first reign of the Qing (1644–62) by a monk, Bai guang, on the site of a Ming garden. Owing to 'economic and military vicissitudes' (Zhongguo mingsheng cidian), the present buildings date from the late Qing (1864, 1895) and the Republican period. Though it is a Buddhist temple, it has preserved something of the garden layout but its 500 luohan figures are the most famous part of the temple, sculpted in 1822–31. It contains a few earlier relics such as a Northern Wei Buddha (4–5C) with strong Indian influence in the attitude of the figure and the delineation of its robes. Some Ming bronzes are also on display and there is a group of 17C stucco figures on wooden frames.

Gui shan, Turtle Mountain, where Yu tamed the local floods, was named after a magic turtle which emerged to help the deity by imposing its body between the waters of the Han and the settlement at Hanyang. It was covered with pavilions and temples which had virtually all disappeared by 1949. Reconstructions include the *Guqin tai* (Guqin Terrace) at the western end of the mountain, near *Yue hu* (Moon Lake) where the most famous musician of antiquity, the legendary Bo Ya, used to play his zither-like instrument. When his favourite listener, Zhong Ziqi, died Bo Ya broke his guqin and never played again. The terrace was said to have existed during the Northern Song and to have been restored in the Qing and again after 1949.

On the E end of the mountain is the *Yugong ji* (Breakwater Built by Yu) and a couple of tombs survive on the mountain; that of *Lu Su* (172–217), was once at the southern foot of the mountain and moved higher up the southern slope in 1955 in the course of water works. Lu Su was a general of the state of Wu (of which Wuchang was briefly the capital) during the Three Kingdoms period. The tomb of *He Jingyu* (1895–1928), one of the earliest women leaders of the Communist movement, killed when Wang Jingwei turned on the Wuhan Communists, is at the western end of the mountain.

There used to be a *Qingchuan lou* (Pavilion of the Clear Sky and the River) on Gui shan, a pair to the tower on She shan (Serpent Mountain) in Wuchang on the opposite side of the Yangtse. Built by Fan Zizhen, a prefect of Hanyang during the Ming, the two towers were named after references in a Tang poem by Cui Hao (early 8C), 'Climbing the yellow crane tower', '... the clear sky and the river are eternal, and the trees of Hanyang...' (the poem is said to have left Li Bai, one of the greatest of Tang poets, silent in admiration). The tower was repaired many times during the Qing, and the last repair was made by Zhang Zidong who wrote a pair of couplets to commemorate the act but it did not survive the fighting during the 1911 revolution. There are plans to rebuild it (this may already have happened).

Over the river, in the old Wuchang, the She shan (Snake Mountain), Hong shan (Vast Mountain), and the Dong hu (East Lake) area which

Museum

Dong hu

Zhongshan lu

Luoyu lu

WUHAN

includes the Provincial Museum, are all quite close together. If you are pressed for time make straight for the museum which is quite small (but closes at lunchtime when some rather nice mice emerge in the quiet rooms).

She shan (Snake Mountain) is on the riverbank, once used as a stronghold by local rulers like Huang Wu of Wu who built a castle on it in AD 223. It was, however, much praised for its beauty by innumerable poets: 'In winter, blossom dances over the stones, thick forests and a line of tall pavilions', 'Thick with peach blossoms, soft clouds floating, when the leaves are red, a green pavilion towers over them'. The *Huang he lou* (Yellow Crane Pavilion) is said to have been first built in the 3C AD, but much restored in the Qing, most recently after a fire in 1884. Images of earlier towers have survived in Song and Yuan paintings, and in Qing silks and late Qing photographs.

The name (commemorated in the Tang poem) is supposed to have derived from a stopover made on the mountain by a Taoist Wang Zian who was riding on a yellow crane. Another version of the name is that a family called Xin used to sell wine here; a Taoist priest often came to drink it and they didn't like to ask him for money. The Taoist used a piece of orange peel to draw a picture on the wall of a yellow crane with the inscription: 'The guest comes to drink wine and make obeisance; the yellow crane comes down to dance' and the Xin family grew rich. The Tang poem by Cui Hao, also supposed to have been the derivation of the name, describes how 'in ancient times, a man flew in on a yellow crane to the place that was bare of buildings apart from the Yellow Crane Pavilion; the yellow crane flew off, never to return, white clouds float for ever and ever. The clear sky and the river are eternal, and the trees of Hanyang…' The pavilion was also central to a poem by Cui Hao bidding farewell to his friend, another poet, Meng Haoran: 'You leave me in the west at the Yellow Crane Pavilion, amongst the cloudy flowers of April you sail to Yangzhou; the single sail, a distant form, disappears in the blue of the horizon and I can see nothing but the Great River as it flows towards the sky.'

The last pavilion was burnt down in 1884, though its foundations remain and a new one is being built.

On the W end of Snake Mountain is the *Shengxiang bao ta*, a 'bottle'-shaped or Lamaist-stupa-style pagoda, moved to this site in 1957 because of work on the bridge over the Yangtse. Built in 1343, restored in 1394, the pagoda is over 9m high and rather wonderfully carved.

There is also a tomb on the southern slopes, that of *Chen Youjing* (1320–63) who had declared an independent kingdom in the area in the confusion of the late Mongol period, only to be conquered (and killed) by Zhu Yuanzhang, future founder of the Ming dynasty. Showing a magnanimity that was apparent in his early years and lacking in his later life when paranoia appears to have set in, Zhu Yuanzhang himself wrote the four characters for the tomb stele: 'Man builds but Heaven determines'. The stele actually in front of the tomb reads 'Tomb of the King of Han, Chen Youjing'.

Also on Snake Hill is the late Qing *Baobing tang* (Hall to Cherish the Ice), built in 1907, restored in 1953, apparently first erected in memory of Zhang Zhidong.

Near the foot of the mountain or hill, on Minzhu lu, at the northern corner of Yuema chang Square, is the red-brick building, the *Hong lou* (Red Building), with a statue of Sun Yatsen outside it. This was the headquarters of the 1911 uprising and now contains an exhibition relating to it. The square was originally used by the Qing troops to exercise their horses, hence the name which means drilling-horses square. On the banks of the river not far from the square is a tall square tower, the 'Nine Women's Grave' (Jiu nu dun) which commemorates nine women who participated in the Boxer uprising.

Beyond Snake Hill, before you reach Dong hu (East Lake) and the university and museum area, there is *Hong shan* (Vast Hill) with the *Lingji* (Universal Spirit) *Pagoda* behind the *Baotong zhan si* (Temple of Precious Communication). The temple, whose surviving buildings date from 1865 and 1879 (though it was founded under the Southern Song), is built against the mountain; the pagoda, first built in 1307, was rebuilt in 1865. It is an octagonal, seven-storey pagoda, 43m high. The exterior is brick, being modelled on timber construction.

Another, smaller, pagoda can be found on the SW slopes (it was moved in 1963 from the eastern slope of the hill). This is the *Xingfu si Pagoda* (Pagoda of the Temple of Flourishing Good Fortune). It is just over 11m high and was built in 1270, again in brick imitating timber construction, with lively carving around the mock doors.

Also in Wuchang, in Huang xiang, is the site of the *Central Peasant Movement Insti-tute* (Zhongyang nongmin yundong jiangxi suo), founded in January 1927 and housed in what had formerly been part of a school founded by Zhang Zhidong, later the Hubei Province No. 1 Commercial School. Over 800 students came here in the brief period that it was open (by the end of the year Wang Jingwei had turned on the Communists who were running the Institute) and Mao Zedong taught here. There is now an exhibit relating to the Insitute and its teachers and pupils.

The most important site in Wuchang is the **Provincial Museum**, on the shore of Dong hu (East Lake) in a pleasantly wooded area which also con-tains the university (part of which is apparently modelled on the Temple of Heaven) and many of Wuhan's institutes of higher education. The museum is almost entirely devoted to the display of articles discovered in a local tomb unearthed at Sui xian which contained lacquer vessels and a complete set of musical instruments of the day, and a quite extraordinary collection of bronzes. The tomb was that of a Prince Yi of the state of Zeng who was buried in 433 BC. Pride of the collection is the set of 64 graded bronze bells, displayed on a three-tiered rack supported by six bronze figures carrying swords. The decoration on the rack, more startlingly obvious on the complex ritual vessels also found in the tomb, is of extraor-dinarily intricate lost-wax spaghetti. Even the dragons that crawl over the spaghetti-covered vessels have interlaced bodies and curling limbs. The bells were struck from outside (they don't have internal clappers) and there is also a set of 16 musical stones which were similarly hung on a frame and struck to sound.

Other buildings around the lake include the *Xingling ge*, a hall built to commemorate Qu Yuan, the great poet of the 3C BC, author of the Li sao and the Songs of the South (Chu ci) who drowned himself in despair when his warnings to his ruler were disre-garded and in whose honour the dragon boat festival was created.

Hankou, the old treaty-port section of Wuhan, was bounded on the N by the railway line. Between the railway and the river it was divided between the British whose concession lay between Jianghan da dao and the railway station, the French concession which was separated from the British by a couple of Russian streets, the Germans whose concession began at roughly Sanyang da dao and ran for some six streets NE, and the Japanese whose concession lay beyond that of the Germans.

Along the waterfront (from just N of the Han river, heading down river) were the Customs House, Butterfield and Swire, Nippon Yusen Kaisha, Yokohama Specie Bank, Hongkong and Shanghai Bank, British Consulate, Nishin Kisen Kwaisha, Litvinoff and Co., (of the Shun-fung brick tea manufactory), the Russian Consulate, the American Consulate, Terminus Hotel, German Consulate, Melcher's Wharf, Arn-hold Karberg and Co., wharf, Swedish Consulate, British-American Tobacco Com-pany, Italian Consulate, Mitsubishi Co., the Japanese Consulate and the Hsieh-chang match factory.

In the 1924 'Japanese Railway Guide' the visitor to Hankou is recommended to visit various 'manufactories—Brick-tea factory, Match factory, Albumen factory (Societé Anonyme Belge pour l'Industrie des Oeufs)' on the first day, the Hankow Iron and Steel Works, Hanyang Government Arsenal and Powder Factory on the sec-ond day and rounding off the third with the Cotton Spinning and Weaving Factories and a hemp factory.

In the old days, visitors to Wuhan found themselves disembarking 'at the hulk' and could always find rickshaws though they had to telegraph ahead for motor vehicles in order to visit the tree-lined Bund with its 'handsome modern buildings, automobile boulevards and beautiful residences policed by turbaned Sikhs'. The beautiful resi-dences were provided with a 'thorough system of sewerage' though Hankou was not considered a 'healthy place to live in' in 1924.

In Hankou, on Poyang jie is the site of the 'Eight-seven' meeting (Ba qi huiyi hui zhi) of 7 August 1927, at which Mao Zedong and others includ-ing Qu Qiubai and Li Weihan argued that 'political power grew out of the barrel of a gun' and that the Communist Party should arm itself. The meeting, however, 'succumbed to the right-opportunist line of Chen Duxiu' and continued to support Stalin's line of unity with the KMT against the northern warlords (a mistaken choice as the KMT turned on its Communist allies and killed them).

Also in Hankou on Changchun jie is the site of the Eighth Route Army headquarters in 1937 (before the army moved to Nanjing) where Zhou Enlai, amongst others, worked briefly.

44 Lu shan

Lu shan is c 30km from Jiujiang, a sizable town on the south bank of the Yangtse River (see below). Lu shan is a mountain without particular religious associations; it has always been appreciated simply for its beauty: its sheer cliffs and twisted pines, its mists and peaks.

It was a favourite, perhaps the favourite, hill resort for the foreign community in China at the turn of the century (opened as a resort in 1895) and later, and the town of Guling is almost entirely composed of foreign architecture: villas, guesthouses and sanatoria. Chiang Kai-shek also had a villa on Lu shan and a training centre for KMT officials but its fame in recent years is due to the Lu shan plenums of 1959 and 1970; two extremely bitter conferences of the Central Committee of the Communist Party which were held in these charming surroundings. At the first, in 1959, Defence Minister Peng Dehuai (1898– 1974) strongly criticised the Great Leap Forward of 1958.

The Great Leap had been an attempt rapidly to increase production, notably of coal and steel. Production quotas were raised everywhere and 'backyard furnaces' (inefficient and dangerous) sprang up throughout the country. In agriculture the same increase in production was required, at the same time as the implementation of the commune policy, increasing the size of the agricultural production units. It is now recognised that the policy was not successful, partly because it was implemented in far too much of a hurry, partly because figures were falsified (giving rise to ridiculous expectations) by local officials trying to curry favour with the centre. Peng Dehuai's criticism was prescient (the ensuing years of natural disasters compounded the problems already existing in the new communes) but, at the time, it led to his dismissal and disgrace. He has only been rehabilitated since the death of Mao in 1976.

Similarly, the second plenum of 1970 developed into a bitter, and eventually fatal, struggle, in this case between Mao and Lin Biao (also Minister of Defence at the time). This split is less clear, even today, though it was ostensibly over the vacant post of State Chairman, which Lin coveted. Chen Boda (1904–), Mao's secretary and speech-writer, strongly associated with Cultural Revolution policies, was the sacrificial victim of the second plenum but in the following year, Lin Biao, apparently having plotted to kill Mao, died in a plane shot down over Mongolia (assumed to be heading for sanctuary in the USSR).

There are famous photographs of Mao at Lu shan, relaxing in a wicker chair on a grassy peak. They were taken by his wife Jiang Qing, who amused herself with photography on the mountain, dropping glycerine dewdrops on roses for greater effect.

The bus to Lu shan from Jiujiang takes about 2 hours and stops at **Guling**.

In the past, missionaries and their families, coming up for the cool mountain air, would be carried up on sedan chairs, with all their luggage. In 1917 there were 320 houses and a foreign population of 1731.

The streets of Guling are interesting for the foreign resort architecture and occasional transformations (church into cinema). The *Lu shan Museum*, next to the theatre where the plenums were held, is housed in Chiang Kai-shek's library and some of the villas inhabited by celebrities are now open to the public.

There are major 'scenic spots' on the mountain—the *Dragon-Head Peak*, the *Floral Path* (wild azalea and peach blossom in April and May), the *Fairy Cave*, the *Three Waterfalls* and the *Five Immortals Peak*, near the Rujin Lake, or the *Three Ancient Trees*, *Black* and *Yellow Dragon Pools* near the Lulin Lake—but as these are almost invariably dramatically overcrowded, wandering on smaller paths is recommended. As there are few temples and religious sites remaining after the devastation by the Taiping rebels, the scenery can be enjoyed in tranquillity.

One temple at the foot of the mountain is of note, the **Donglin si** (Temple of the Eastern Grove).

It was the home of the founder of the Pure Land sect, Hui Yuan, built for him as a school in 381. Pure Land Buddhism, with its stress on the possibility of salvation in the 'pure land' of Amitabha Buddha, was to have a profound effect on popular Buddhism in China for it offered a view of a 'life' or state after death for the faithful. Such was the popularity of Hui Yuan and the Pure Land that many visitors came from China and abroad and during the Tang there were 'halls, courtyards and pagodas numbering over 310'. The monk Jian Zhen passed by on his way to Japan from Yangzhou and took two monks with him, taking the Pure Land to Japan where Hui Yuan is also revered as the founder of the sect.

In front of the temple is the *Tiger Pool* where Hui Yuan would bid farewell to guests. He practised his devotions nearby when, it is said, he had no shadow, 'it did not cleave to his body'.

Here he discussed Buddhist doctrine with such as the poet Tao Yuanming. Hui Yuan was supposed never actually to cross the bridge over the pool. Once, when seeing Tao Yuanming and the Buddhist Lu Xiujing off, he inadvertently crossed the bridge, at which point the tiger spirit in the water began howling ceaselessly and the three men laughed, giving rise to the saying: 'three (men) laughing on the tiger pool'.
The temple buildings were frequently destroyed, most recently by the Taipings, so they are all now late Qing in date. The site was visited by a great number of famous people including Li Bai, Lu You and Bai Juyi (Tang poets), Wang Yangming, the Ming Buddhist and others, their visits commemorated by stelae.

Jiujiang, starting point for a visit to Lu shan, was opened to foreign trade in 1861, when the previously flourishing town had, like so many others in the area, been devastated by the Taiping uprising, much of the land within its walls reduced to weed-covered rubble. It became a major centre for the foreign tea-trade, with Russian factories producing tea bricks for the home market (powdered tea compressed into solid bricks) before 1917. Tea still produced on the slopes of Lu shan and other hills is known as Yunwu ('Misty Clouds'), and is a green tea. Known to Westerners as Kiukiang, Jiujiang (which in Chinese means Nine Rivers) was the major port for shipment of the porcelain of Jingde zhen. Jiujiang's previous prominence as a Buddhist centre is marked by the *Ningren Temple* (founded in 502–49) but the surviving buildings are all post-Taiping (ie late 19C).

45   Jiuhua shan

The southernmost of the four Buddhist holy mountains, **Jiuhua shan** (Nine Glories or Nine Flower Mountain) is over 100km SW of Wuhu on the Yangtse River, upstream from Nanjing.

Dedicated to the Bodhisattva Ksitigarbha who rules over the underworld and delivers souls from hell, the mountain has long been the prime place of pilgrimage for the recently bereaved who came (and still come) to pay for a series of masses to be held for the soul of the departed. At the eastern end of a ridge of mountains with the more picturesque (and therefore more popular) Huang shan (Yellow Mountain) to the E, Jiuhua shan is, nevertheless, quite pretty and, at 1342m above sea-level, is easily climbed in a day.

Access: Jiuhua shan is easily reached from Nanjing, either by rail and bus or by boat and bus. The former method is quicker but less picturesque. A branch line runs from Nanjing Station to Tongling (on the Yangtse), 12 stops in all and the slow-moving train stops at all of them. There is only one class (hard seats, very crowded) and the journey takes 5–6 hours. From Tongling, a bus (hard seats, very crowded) takes several hours to reach Jiuhua shan.

A pleasant way to reach the mountain is to take a small boat upriver on the Yangtse from Nanjing to Wuhu. The river port of Nanjing is in the NW of the town, at the river end of Zhongshan bei lu, within sight of the extraordinary *Yangtse River Bridge*, its piers topped with red concrete revolutionary 'flames'. The bridge was built between 1960 and 1968, begun with Russian assistance and blueprints, both of which were almost immediately withdrawn with the Sino-Soviet split of August 1960. It is a matter of national pride that the inexperienced Chinese managed to finish the bridge themselves and decorate it with revolutionary flames and streetlamps in the form of magnolia buds.

The boat from Nanjing to Wuhu takes the greater part of a day; such small boats stop at all the river ports (in this case only Ma'an shan and Wuhu), loading and unloading passengers and cargo. The boat I travelled on, the 'Red Flag No. 7', was British-built (pre-1949) with much decorative marquetry in the saloon (reserved for cabin-class passengers) where a cocktail shaker in the form of a penguin and glasses with elaborately folded napkins in the shape of birds and flowers stood in a glass-fronted cabinet. The small, two-berth cabins with fitted sink and tiny cupboard and well-polished elderly fittings made it the sort of boat that Evelyn Waugh's Gilbert Pinfold might have had his ordeal on.

On arrival at **Wuhu** (literally 'weed-filled lake'), make for the hotel which is on the left-hand side of the main street. Before settling in, buy tickets for the bus to Jiuhua shan for the following day in the bus station as the bus departs early and fills up quickly.

If stuck in Wuhu, there are a number of sites to visit and some quaint thatched cottages to be found even along the main streets, with round thatched roofs and thick mud walls pierced with tiny windows, rather like the toadstool houses of pixies in children's books. Wuhu is also the home of a particular form of Chinese handicraft, the 'iron picture' where thin strips of iron are twisted to make silhouettes, mainly of landscape scenes.

The **Guangji si** (Temple of Universal Rescue) is on the SW slopes of Zhe shan (Red Mountain) and, as a traditional stopping place for pilgrims on their way to Jiuhua shan, is sometimes known as 'Little Jiuhua'. Built against the mountain, with anterior halls 10m above those in front, the temple was founded in 894–97, destroyed by fire in the Xianfeng reign period (1850–61), presumably by the Taiping rebels, and rebuilt in the Guangxu era (1875–1908).

The *Zhe Pagoda* behind is one of the 'Eight Sights of Wuhu' (I have been unable to find a list of the other seven). There are a number of 'mountains' in the town: **Zhe shan**, 86m high, of reddish earth, where a pavilion built in 1522–66 stands on top, affording a view of the town and the river and **Shen shan** (Spirit Mountain), where, according to the local gazetteer, swords were forged by Gan Jiang the magical sword-maker of Chu (one of the Warring States, 8–4C BC).

On Shen shan are the *Tomb of Gan Jiang*, the *Sword-honing Stone* and the *Forging Pool*, as well as the remains of a Luohan *Temple*. In the centre of the town is the *Jinghu* or Mirror Lake whose clear waters bear little relation to the weed-filled lake from which the town takes its name.

The bus journey from Wuhu to **Jiuhua shan** takes almost a whole day in a crammed, hard-seat bus which stops for lunch at a roadside café where, at risk of seeming fussy, it might be wise to use your own bowl and chopsticks. Although the food will be freshly cooked and therefore bacteria-free, washing-up facilities are primitive.

As the bus approaches the mountain from the plains you can see the start of the stepped pilgrim path which leads from the *Yitian men* (First Heavenly Gate) past the *Ganlu si* (Sweet Dew Temple, named for the ambrosial nectar of immortality dispensed by the gods) and the *Ertian men* (Second Heavenly Gate). The Ganlu si, founded in 1667 in an area where 'sweet dew' was said to drip from the bamboos and pines, was rebuilt in the Tongzhi reign of the Qing (1862–75) after destruction by the Taiping rebels. The golden-tiled buildings are constructed high against the mountain slopes.

The bus stops below the *Huacheng Temple*, beside which there is a new guesthouse. Ideally, walk on and around a bend to a long white-washed building, the *Zhantanlin si* (Temple of the Sandalwood Grove) and try to get a bed there.

Behind the main temple hall are other halls, above which, reached by steep, ladder-like steps (which are agonising to ascend after a day on the stepped mountain path) are dormitory rooms for pilgrims, simply furnished with mosquito-netted beds and basins. Cold water may be drawn from the well, hot water is available in vacuum flasks and vegetarian meals are served communally for pilgrims, visitors and monks in the main courtyard.

The mountain area, which covers some 100 square km, was originally known as the *Jiuzi shan* (Nine Mountains) after the nine peaks behind the village. These are also sometimes known as the 'brush-rest' peaks as they resemble the zigzag of brush-rests used by calligraphers and painters. A rather banal explanation for the Nine-mountain name is given in the local gazetteer (compiled in the Tang dynasty): 'These mountains are strange and beautiful, with peaks reaching the clouds, rising and falling. There are nine in number therefore they are called the Nine Mountains.

However, the great poet Li Bai visited the area in the Tianbao reign period of the Tang and he regarded the nine peaks as resembling lotus flowers, describing them in a poem: 'Once, I stood by the nine rivers and gazed at the nine splendid peaks in the distance; nine lotus flowers rising from the blue waters of the Milky Way...' and henceforth they were known as the Nine Splendid Peaks (Jiuhua shan). Famous visitors after Li Bai include the Tang poet Du Mu, Su Dongpo, the Song poet, and Wang Anshi, the great tax reformer of the Song, the philosopher Wang Yangming and the painter and art theorist Dong Qichang of the Ming. Poems that they wrote to commemorate their visits tended to follow the lotus flower image of Li Bai.

It is said that in the 3–5C AD there were Taoist and Buddhist temples on the mountain. In the 5C a Buddhist monk called Huai Du (a name which means 'embrace the crossing of the ocean') came to live on the mountain in a thatched hut where he read the sutras. In 643 a member of the royal family of Korea, Jin Qiaojue, crossed the sea (an event prophesied in the religious name of the earlier monk) and came to Jiuhua shan. For 75 years he led a life of asceticism and mortification of the flesh, dying whilst meditating at the age of 99. His body was miraculously preserved and closely resembled the icons of the Bodhisattva Ksitigarbha, to the point that he was acknowledged as a reincarnation. Thus Jiuhua shan is the only one of the Buddhist holy mountains (Putuo, Emei and Wutai are the others) which has an historical figure as its incarnation; on the other mountains, visions of the presiding deity sufficed to sanctify the area.

Imperial favours to the mountain were evident in the gold seals and calligraphic inscriptions of the Tang, Song, Yuan, Ming and Qing emperors once preserved on the mountain. The Ming Wanli emperor visited the mountain in 1586 and 1599; the last emperor of the Ming wrote the inscription 'the incarnate Bodhisattva' for the Bai sui gong (Hundred-year Hall); the Qing Kangxi emperor visited in 1705 and later sent a carved inscription in his own hand, 'the magical scenery of Jiuhua', for the Huacheng Temple, which temple was also graced with calligraphy by the Qianlong emperor after his 1766 visit. Owing to lavish gifts (including two of over 40,000 taels of silver from the Kangxi emperor), the monastic population of monks and nuns grew to more than 5000 in over 300 temples during the Qing.

Very little survives of its former grandeur for the area was devastated by the Taiping uprising (which centred on Nanjing) in 1850–64 and all existing temples have been rebuilt since. Rebuilding probably started quite early for a Buddhist Association was set up on the mountain in 1914, to organise work on the mountain, set up educational institutes and organise lectures and visits by famous monks from within China and abroad (a level of organisation not seen on other holy mountains at the time). For those interested in Republican-period ceramics, a number of unusual blue and white porcelain incense burners with Republican inscriptions can be found in temples and halls.

The religious life of the mountain is still intense, more than at any of the other Buddhist holy mountains. A substantial number of monks are congregated in the major temples, and the tiny halls dotting the mountain itself and the village are all inhabited by elderly monks and nuns who provide locally grown tea for visitors (and should be rewarded with a small donation). Services are held most evenings in the main hall of the Zhantanlin Temple and the Huacheng Temple.

In general, the bereaved pay for two ceremonies, held on consecutive evenings. The first, longer, ceremony fundamentally takes the soul of the departed through the ten Buddhist hells. The abbot of the temple, wearing the red crown-like hat of Ksitgarbha, takes the soul through the ten hells, interceding on its behalf. The abbot scatters grains of rice and flicks water (sweet dew), expressing the benevolence of the Bodhisattva, and the assembled monks mumble their way through prayers for some hours. The members of the family of the dead person stand at the threshold of the hall, kneeling and kowtowing as instructed by a monk. The second ceremony on the second evening is much shorter and is intended to welcome the soul into the western paradise of Amitabha Buddha. Having passed through the ordeals of the hells (each intended for specific crimes such as meat-eating or unfiliality), the soul is given a cheerful send-off as those present join in a conga-like file weaving through the temple hall, chanting 'O-mi-tuo-fo' (Amitabha Buddha). In the ceremonies that I watched, the widow in question, who had travelled nearly 2000km in the company of a young monk from Guangdong province, was solemn and serious on the first evening, cheerful on the second and positively radiant at breakfast next morning, having ensured her husband a safe trip to paradise.

Such ceremonies are not connected with burial or cremation but, according to the Buddhist belief that the soul is present on earth for 49 days after death, should be carried out within the 49 days after a death. Grander ceremonies can be held, it very much depending on the means of the bereaved family. It is clear that holding such ceremonies on the mountain where the Bodhisattva who presides over the underworld was incarnated is seen to provide a particularly powerful guarantee of salvation.

The major temples in the village below the mountain are the Huacheng si (Illusion City Temple, a reference to a state of temporary or incomplete nirvana referred to in the Lotus Sutra) and the Roushen si (Temple of the Physical Body).

The **Huacheng Temple**, just N of the Zhantanlin Temple, is built against the mountain and comprises four courtyards, rising with the terrain.

One of the most impressive of all the temples on the mountains, it is said that it was built in 757 as a residence for the Korean prince. In 781 it began to be used for funeral rituals and was therefore given the name 'Illusion City' by the emperor. It was visited by the Ming emperors Xuande and Wanli and both Kangxi and Qianlong of the Qing, most of whom left gold-carved inscriptions in commemoration.

Many times destroyed by fire, only the *Sutra Tower* (or Library) is considered to be of early 15C date. The temple is famous for its great bell; that too is a recent replica, made in the last years of the 19C to replace an earlier one. The names of the dead are often written on paper and placed under the bell which is rung during religious ceremonies.

The **Roushen Temple**, also known as the *Roushen bao dian* (Precious Hall of the Physical Body), stands on the far side of the village, reached by a steep flight of 81 steps. The temple hall contains a 17m-high wooden *pagoda* (reconstructed in 1862–78 after the Taiping rebellion) with eight niches on each storey holding tiny golden Ksitigarbha figures. On either side of the pagoda are figures of the ten kings of hell (each presiding over one hell). Behind the hall is a semicircular stone platform with a great iron incense burner.

Climbing the mountain.

The first temple at the base of the eastern ridge, is the **Qiyuan si** (Temple of the Garden of Veneration), E of the Huacheng si. Founded in the Ming (1522–66) but rebuilt several times since, it is the biggest of Jiuhua's temples. It has a tall main hall, covered with yellow tiles, the roof combining upturned eaves and stepped gables. In common with much of the local architecture, the edges of the stepped tops of the gable end walls are painted in white and decorated with cartouches enclosing landscape and other scenes in black on white. Figures in the main hall include the trinity of Amitabha, Avalokitesvara and Mahasthamaprapta, who receive souls into the western paradise.

Above, on the ridge, is the **Baisui gong** or Hundred-Year Hall, a deceptively small building which, because of the topography, comprises five-storeyed towers and numerous 'heaven-well' courtyards and, according to one source, can hold 5000 people. In front of the whitewashed hall is an inscribed stele recording the arrival here (from Wutai shan in the north), during the Wanli reign of the Ming (1573–1620), of a monk called Hai Yu (Sea Jade). When he died, at the age of 100, his body was found to remain in a state of perfect preservation and his remains can still be seen. A small, seated figure (the size of a small monkey and much lacquered) is the precious 'Hundred-year' relic which gives the hall its name. There are also three 'blood sutras' preserved in the hall (sutras written in human blood by Buddhist devotees).

In 1983 the middle-aged Shanghainese monk who looked after the hall described to a small group (including two disapproving members of the People's Liberation Army) how, on hearing of the Cultural Revolution on their transistor radios, the monks buried the precious relics and retired to the top of the mountain, expecting the arrival of Red Guards. They never came and 10 years later the monks descended, disinterred their relics and recommenced their religious life. A brief guide to Jiuhua shan published in 1980 states that there was some destruction during the Cultural Revolution and Colin Thubron, who visited the mountain and described his visit in 'Beyond the Wall', also heard long stories of Red Guard atrocities, so the Shanghainese monk's earlier version may not be accurate. The number of Republican-period relics suggests that Cultural Revolution destruction was considerably less thorough than that of the Taipings, a hundred years earlier.

At the southern end of the ridge on which the Baisui gong stands is a tiny *Bell Tower*. In 1983 this was inhabited by an elderly monk who came down to the Zhantanlin Temple early in the morning carrying a Buddhist pilgrim staff (with a leaf-shaped bronze head with a couple of loose, clinking bronze rings) and basket for his provisions. He sat in the tiny tower surrounded by his meagre possessions (a stove, condiments, wellington boots, warm padded winter coat and alarm clock), holding a string that he pulled (to activate the wooden clapper of the huge bell) when the mood took him, sending a sonorous boom out across the valley below.

Descending the ridge's eastern slope, the 'brush-rest' mountains and the peak usually climbed, the **Tiantai** (Heavenly Platform) **Peak**, are ahead. The path leads beside, and occasionally through, small temples and tiny halls, inhabited by little old ladies or gentlemen, who sleep beside the images they care for, burn incense and provide tea (often with sugar added as you near the top, for extra energy).

The climb is not too strenuous, though the steps are uncomfortable, narrow for large western feet; the scenery provides views of twisted pines and handsome rocks, with dog roses scenting the air in spring.

46 Hefei

Hefei, capital city of the province of Anhui, which straddles the Yangtse, is in the northern part of the province and has few partisans (except those who live there). If you pass through it does have a fine museum (the *Anhui Provincial Museum*) with one of the rare Han dynasty jade body-suits (another is to be found in the Nanjing Museum).

Anhui province is crossed by both the Huai and Yangtse Rivers and has a population of some 51,560,000. It is a fairly recent creation (1662), made by the Qing who subdivided the Jiangnan ('South of the Yangtse') region. Though a relatively fertile area, with irrigation making rice-cultivation possible in what was previously a wheat area, and famous during the Ming for its rich salt merchants whose elegant houses can still be seen in

She xian, it is currently regarded as a backward area, the 'Appalachians' of China, with all that that implies.

Currently known for its production of domestic servants for Peking, where recent economic and political changes have made it possible for the urban rich to employ domestics, it was previously known for the Red Turban uprising (1344) lead by a charismatic bandit who claimed to be the Buddha of the Future, Maitreya, and as the birthplace of the first Ming emperor, Zhu Yuanzhang (1328–98), an equally charismatic character who rose through the White Lotus rebel band to overthrow the Mongol Yuan dynasty. It was originally his intention to establish the capital of China in his birthplace in Anhui (Fengyang) but some years into construction he was persuaded that Nanjing was a more logical choice.

Hefei is a possible starting point for long car journeys to the two major sites in northern Anhui, the Tomb of Li Bai, China's foremost poet, near Ma'an shan on the S bank of the Yangtse, and the first of the Ming imperial capitals near Fengyang, c 100km NE of Hefei.

The **Tomb of Li Bai** (also accessible by car from Ma'an shan or Wuhu on the Yangtse though both of these are, as yet, less well-organised for tourists and car-hire may be problematic), is c 7km from Ma'an shan, near *Caishiji* (Coloured Stone Boulder), the place where the poet is said to have drowned whilst drunkenly trying to catch the moon reflected in the river below.

Li Bai (701–762), together with his near-contemporary Du Fu (see Chengdu, Sichuan) is perhaps China's major poet. He was born in distant Central Asia, in Sujab, near Lake Balkash, but when he was 5 his family moved to Sichuan province. Despite his origin, he came to be viewed as the master of the brief lyric, his most famous example being that in which he invites the moon and his own shadow to drink with him. He was a famous drunk, unlike the sober and socially-concerned Du Fu, and has therefore sometimes been regarded with less favour during more puritannical episodes in China's recent past. It is said that when he fell into the river, all that fishermen could retrieve were his gown and cap which were buried at Caishi village and later reinterred in the present tomb.

Though there have been memorial halls on the site since the early 9C, the present buildings date from the reign of the Guangzu emperor of the Qing (1875–1908), reflecting a last major destruction during the Taiping uprising. The base of his tomb is of azurite, topped by the grassy mound and the inscription on the stele (which would normally just record the name of the deceased) reads 'Robes and cap of the great Tang poet Li Bai'.

More impressive are the sculptures from the imperial **Mausoleum of Zhong du** (Middle Capital), virtually all that remains of the first great capital built at the order of the first ruler of the Ming in 1369–75. These are to be found near Fengyang in northern Anhui and can be reached from Hefei or perhaps from Fengbu which is on the railway line N of Hefei and consequently closer though transport, other than public buses, will be harder to find.

All that remains of the vast construction of Zhongdu—the palace and city walls built for the first emperor—are some foundation floors, bases of walls, stone balustrades and remnants of stone carvings, NW of Fengyang. Construction had begun here at imperial order because this was the home base of the emperor who came from a poor local family; he was later convinced that Nanjing was a more appropriate seat for the imperial capital (though the Ming finally shifted its capital yet again to Peking in the early 15C).

The spirit way, marking the approach to the tomb of his parents, which was intended originally to serve as an imperial mausoleum for the entire dynasty, is 5km SW.

It is said that when Zhu Yuanzhang's parents died in poverty, they were buried here on a small plot provided by a kind neighbour. When their son eventually became emperor he was loth to move the bodies for fear of disturbing their spirits so he began the construction of the imperial mausoleum around his parents' grave. The vast enclosure was attacked and virtually destroyed at the fall of the Ming; all that survives is the avenue of stone animals and figures, more numerous than in any other surviving spirit way in China and rare examples of the period (1369–80).

47 Huang shan

Huang shan (Yellow Mountain), in Anhui province, is famous for its spectacular scenery and is therefore spectacularly crowded. It is part of the range which includes the southern Buddhist mountain Jiuhua shan (see above) which is infinitely more peaceful though its peaks and pines are less spectacular.

Huang shan may be reached by bus from Nanjing, Hangzhou (c 9 hours) or Wuhu (c 5 hours) or Tunxi on the railway line from Nanjing (90 minutes).

Hotels: there is a CITS hotel at the foot of the mountain and the Beihai Guesthouse (full to bursting in the season from May to late October) at the summit.

Huang shan is considered to be the most beautiful mountain in China, ascended by emperors in sedan chairs, by poets and by Chinese travellers. Li Bai wrote: 'Huang shan is 9666 metres high, with 32 lotus peaks. Rock pillars press against red cliffs, luxuriant golden lilies; Ancients ascending the matchless peak looked down on the sky and the pines'. The height of Huang shan was somewhat exaggerated, the highest peak being less than 1900m, but Li Bai used poetic licence (and actually said it was 4000 ren; a ren being an ancient measure equivalent to 7 or 8 chi, a chi being about a third of a metre).

Paths of steep stone steps up the mountain are easily followed: it is recommended that you take the eastern path upwards and the steeper western path down. There is a cable car. Near the top of the eastern path is a view of the 'brush-rest peaks', a number of pointed peaks rising from the mist. Just off the western path, about half-way down, near the *Yuping lou* (Jade Peak Tower) is the *Huang ke song* (Welcoming Pine) which is reproduced on hundreds of thousands of paintings in restaurants and hotels, to 'welcome guests'.

74km S of Huang shan is **She xian** where the best-preserved group of *Ming dynasty houses*, once the home of the 'Huizhou' salt merchants, can be seen. Massive, whitewashed, closed to the exterior, they have richly carved interior timbers and internal courtyards of the closed 'heaven-well' type characteristic of the warm south. The narrow opening in the roof (the heaven well) allows some ventilation whilst preventing the sunshine from heating the cool, dark interior. The whitewashed exterior walls, with their elegant stepped gable-end walls, are decorated with grey 'cut-brick' work, like that of Suzhou (also to be seen, though in less lavish forms, in Peking).

48 Nanchang

Nanchang, capital city of Jiangxi province, is a city that has existed (under different names) since the Han. In the last years of the 16C the pioneering Jesuit missionary Matteo Ricci (1553–1610) came to stay in the flourishing city full of merchants and alchemists. For Chinese Communists the city is famous for the Nanchang Uprising of 1 August 1927 (a date which has provided Army Day, 1 August). In that difficult year when the Nationalists, under their new leader Chiang Kai-shek, turned bloodily on their former allies, the Communists, Zhou Enlai, Zhu De, He Long, Liu Bocheng and others led a peasant army to seize the city. The seizure was part of a protest against Chiang's attack on the Shanghai Communists in April. The city was held for three days before the Nationalist army retook it and what was to become the Red Army fled to the provincial borders and the mountains of Jinggang shan. The formation of the Red Army was one result of the abortive uprising; another was the beginning of Mao Zedong's firm conviction that the Soviet line (armed insurrections, work in cities) was wrong for China.

Railway: the station is in the E of the city. Nanchang is on a branch line (to Jiujiang), off the Shanghai–Yunnan/Guangzhou line but a number of Shanghai–Guangzhou express trains make the detour to Nanchang.

Air: there are daily flights to Ganzhou, Fuzhou, Guangzhou and Wuhan; flights to Shanghai every day except Thursday, four a week to Peking, and three to Hefei, Xiamen and Jingdezhen.

Hotel: the major hotel for foreigners is the Jiangxi binguan on the corner of Bayi da dao (the main N–S thoroughfare) and Changzheng lu. (In 1985 service was strikingly awful; I trust things have improved.)

There are a surprising number of things to see in Nanchang, a city whose centre has been extensively modernised. Most people simply pass through on the way to Jingdezhen or Jiujiang, in which case, the major things to see are the Provincial Museum and Ba da shan ren (or Zhu Da)'s Residence and, for those interested in revolutionary history and revolutionary interior design, the Revolutionary Memorial Hall.

The two museums are easily reached on foot from the hotel. The **Provincial Museum** (Jiangxi sheng bowuguan) is on the S of Bayi gongchang (1 August Square): turn left down Bayi da dao, past Renmin gongchang (People's Square). In the middle of 1 August Square is a tower commemorating the uprising. The museum contains funerary remains of local cultures during the Spring and Autumn Period, a considerable display of

Jingdezhen ceramics from the 4C to the end of the Qing and a good collection of Ming funerary wares: jade belts, filigree jewellery and funerary figures from the tomb of the 16th (or 17th; there is some confusion) son of the Ming founder and his son, enfeoffed in Nanchang.

The *Revolutionary Museum* (Nanchang bayi qiyi jinianguan) is on Zhongshan lu (which runs along the E side of 1 August Square). Turn right out of the museum and left at the far side of the square, continue up Zhongshan lu. The five-storey grey building used to be a hotel (with 96 rooms). It was used as a headquarters by the leaders of the uprising who held meetings in the main hall. In 1957 it was made into a memorial museum; the museum's name inscribed in the calligraphy of another major military figure, Chen Yi, and the displays consisting of old furniture in recreations of rooms used by notables (Zhou Enlai, Liu Bocheng) and as dressing stations, and photographs.

To return to the hotel, turn right out of the museum up Zhongshan lu. The next major crossroads is with Changzheng lu; turn left, cross Bayi da dao to the hotel.

The **Qingyun pu** (Blue Cloud Text), is a country retreat where the wandering painter Zhu Da or Ba da shan ren (the 'Man of Eight Great Mountains'; 1626–1705), one of the most innovative of Chinese painters, lived for a while. Near *Dingshan qiao* in the southern suburbs, about 10km from the city centre, it can be reached by suburban bus from Bayi da dao or by taxi.

Set beside a pool, the Qingyun pu was first built as a country retreat- cum-Taoist retreat by the Taoist adept Xu Sun (also known as Xu Zhenchun and the 'True Prince of Miracles') in 321. It was then known (perhaps because of the pool) as the 'True Mirror of Brilliance' and later named the 'View of Heavenly Peace'. After Zhu Da had stayed here it was renamed Qingyun pu or Garden of Blue Clouds and, for some reason, in the Kangxi era the last character 'pu' (meaning garden) was changed to 'pu' (meaning text).

Zhu Da was a ninth-generation descendant of a member of the Ming royal house (surnamed Zhu). At the fall of the Ming he went into hiding, partly for fear of persecution by the Qing, partly because he was reclusive. He lived in various (mainly Buddhist) monasteries and stayed here in the Taoist retreat from 1661 to 1687 with disciples including Qiu Yue (whose studio name was 'The Wisdom of the Stone Ox').

Zhu Da's paintings (of which there is a fine collection in the Shanghai Museum), here only displayed in reproduction, are strikingly modern. Painted in the Chan (or Zen) style, with a few, immensely strong strokes, they frequently depict, in a Chinese minimalist way, fish beneath rocks, birds on rocks, or just rocks. Like their creator, the birds, in particular, often look wild and hunted, on the brink of a nervous breakdown. Zhu Da's influence on 20C Chinese painters such as Pan Tianshou has been enormous for he anticipated 20C Western modernism.

The complex retains its part-religious, part-secular feeling: the rooms used by Zhu Da have been preserved whilst reproductions of his works and those of his followers have been added to the display; there are also figures of popular deities including the Jade Emperor, Xu Sun and the God of War, with Ming bronze altar pieces (vases, incense burners and bell) and in the 'heaven well' courtyard at the rear is a cassia tree and four other trees said to have been planted in the Tang dynasty. There are a number of tombs in the vicinity.

If time allows, the **Bayi Park** contains much water, and relics both ancient and modern. It was the site of the provincial examination halls and also encloses a small square garden known as *Old Man Su's Vegetable Plot* (for it was originally cultivated by Su Yunliu of the Song dynasty.

Zhou Enlai and Zhu De's Residence during the 1927 uprising was close by at 2 Huayuan jiao and opposite the North Gate (29 Huanhu lu) is the **Youmin** (Assist the People) **Temple**, founded in 502–519. One of the most famous temples in the province, it has a sizable bronze Buddha in the rear hall, a bronze bell of the Wanli period of the Ming and, most notably, a bronze bell cast in 967 at the order of a general of the Southern Tang.

Other temples include the *Daan* (Great Peace) *Temple* (just inside the Desheng Gate in Yuzhang hou jie), built on the site of the headquarters of a local general in 398 and possessing an iron incense burner said to have been cast during the Three dynasties (220–280); and the *Wanshou* (10,000-year) *Temple* in Cuihua jie with its iron pillar, said to have been cast by the Taoist Xu Sun (of the Qingyun pu). Another revolutionary site is the former *Residence of Ye Ting*, another of the famous generals of the 1927 uprising, in the No. 2 Middle School beside the Huazhou dong hu.

Almost nothing now remains of the old *Headquarters of Zhu Quan* (the 16th or 17th son of the founder of the Ming dynasty, enfeoffed here) except carved stones on Xinghuo lu but there is still a fine *Drum Tower* on the W bank of the East Lake (S of the Guangji Bridge) and the fine *Shengjin* (Gold Restraining) *Pagoda*, near Zhishi jie, first built in the 10C but entirely rebuilt in 1708–88. Part of the temple which lies beneath it, this particular pagoda has also an association with geomancy; the belief that disasters could be averted by the construction of a pagoda for it was constructed (after collapse) because of a series of disastrous fires in the locality. A golden tripod vessel was placed at the top of the pagoda to try to avoid more fires. The pagoda is 59m high, octagonal and seven-storeyed, of brick construction imitating timber, with upturned eaves on each storey.

49 Jingdezhen

Jingdezhen in Jiangxi province has long been the ceramic centre of China. There have been ceramic kilns in operation here since before the Tang, though it was with the development of porcelain, manufactured from locally produced clays (based on feldspathic rocks), that the town came to occupy its dominant position from the Five Dynasties (907–979). It is still one of the major porcelain centres of China.

Railway: Jingdezhen is on a branch line from Guixi (in Jiangxi) to Tongling in Anhui, best joined from Shanghai or Nanchang at Guixi. The station is in the E of the town.

Air: there are flights of 50 minutes on Mondays, Wednesdays and Fridays to the very small airport from Nanchang. The aircraft used (in 1985) were tiny, twin-winged propellor planes with room for about six passengers (tightly squeezed), straight out of 'They Flew By Night'. The pilot stood up at the front in a leather flying cap and the plane was steered by wires through the cabin. We flew very low over the Poyang Lake and landed in Jingdezhen, scattering chickens. I'd recommend this method of travel as it was very exciting although I understand that flights are often cancelled if there is any cloud at all. According to the CAAC timetable, the plane used (1987) is a Yun 5.

Road: Jingdezhen is about 300km from Nanchang; it is possible to make the journey by taxi quite comfortably.

Hotel: the Jingdezhen binguan is in the N of the town, beyond a small lake, in forested hills, an easy walk from the town centre.

Textual evidence suggests that there were kilns operating in Jingdezhen during the Eastern Han. During the 4C the local court at Nanjing ordered various pottery items for use in palace building, a practice which continued under the Sui. The kiln sites that survive in and around Jingdezhen mostly contain shards from the Five Dynasties onwards. The Five Dynasties shards are mostly of white-bodied wares with the characteristic glassy Qingbai glaze, transparent with a blue colour where it collects thickly. Those of the Yuan dynasty and the Ming are predominantly underglaze blue for which Jingdezhen is renowned and it was blue and white from the many kilns here which made its way by river to the coast and was eventually exported to SE Asia, Japan and, increasingly, to Europe, from the 17C.

One of the most famous accounts of Jingdezhen and its porcelain manufacture was that of the Jesuit Père D'Entrecolles in 1712 (published among the 'Lettres edifiantes et curieuses de Chine par des missionaires jesuites 1712–1776', Garnier-Flammarion, 1979). His description of the town, a veritable inferno at times when all the kilns were firing, is still applicable as the methods are still very much labour intensive and unmechanised. 'Jingdezhen stands on the banks of a beautiful river (the Nan jiang)…and contains a prodigious multitude of workers; it is said that there are more than a million souls and they eat daily more than 10,000 catties of rice and more than 1000 pigs…There are now over 3000 kilns and it is not surprising that fires are frequent; for this reason there are several temples to the god of fire.' He mentions the number of ships on the river, tied up three-deep at the quays and 'the whirlwinds of smoke and flame that rise from different parts, illustrating the size and spread of the town; at dusk these create the impression of a large town fully ablaze or a huge furnace with many vents. Surprisingly, this populous place is not walled and is the province of a single mandarin…but policing is admirable.'

D'Entrecolles continues with a description of the raw materials of porcelain which has confused experts for centuries since: he distinguishes between two forms of local clay, suggesting that they are chemically distinct (kaolin and petuntse), though it is now thought they are different forms of the same material. 'The clay is first refined and broken up and then formed; larger pieces being made in one or more parts and then luted together.' He stresses the number of hands through which each piece passes, which is most remarkable when the pieces are painted (before glazing). 'One simply traces the lines at the rim; another outlines flowers which are painted in by a third. This one does mountains and water, that birds and other animals.' He mentions the variety of colours, though at the time 'In Europe, we only see blue on a white ground, though I believe our merchants have brought other sorts. Some have mirrored grounds, some are red all over…and there are porcelains where the painted scenes are a mixture of all possible colours, enlivened by gilding.' He describes a particularly successful type of vessel: 'I saw a cat, painted quite naturally. A tiny lamp was placed inside it, the light shining out of the eyes and I was assured that it frightens rats at night. A couple of such pieces, small nightlights in the form of a crouching cat decorated in blue and white, were found in the recent wreck of an East Indiaman, the 'Geldermaasen', whose contents were sold in Amsterdam in 1985 (one is now in the British Museum).

From the Song onwards, the court took a great interest in the production of Jingdezhen. The town takes its name from a reign period of the Song, Jingde (1004–07), when pieces destined for the court were marked 'made in the Jingde reign period'. Imperial kilns were established at the beginning of the Ming and continued through the Qing, with occasional special orders as when the Kangxi emperor ordered paintings by Jiao Bingzhen to be copied onto porcelain and Yongzhen and Qianlong later took especial interest in the production of fine tiny pieces of overglaze enamelled wares called Guyue xuan (Pavilion of the Ancient Moon), production which came to an end with the death in 1753 of Tang Yin, the last of the great superintendents of the imperial kilns.

In the past (as today), high-class or imperial production went side by side with the production of lesser pieces in smaller, private kilns. The kilns in the south of China, including Jingdezhen, were 'dragon kilns', multi-chambered constructions, usually built up hills and fired with wood. Around the hotel, you can see great stacks of timber for the kilns and it is still fascinating to watch a wood-firing. The kiln supervisor keeps his eyes fixed on a vent, in which two balls of clay (between golf-ball and tennis-ball in size) are placed, and with minimal hand gestures controls a team of young men stripped to the waist in the heat who toss logs into the kiln. Elsewhere in the factory, workers still paint by hand and pass pots from one to the next, though the cheaper wares are often stencil-decorated.

A visit to Jingdezhen is best organised through the China Travel Service or, for those professionally interested, ceramic connections. It is possible to visit the Taoci guan (Ceramic Exhibition Hall) without an introduction but factories and old kiln-sites are out of bounds. A factory visit is extremely interesting as are the great mounds of thousand-year-old mistakes (waste sites associated with ancient kilns).

The **Taoci guan** is on Lianshe bei lu (pass the two lakes in front of the hotel and turn right). It includes a small historical exhibition of production at Jingdezhen, as well as a display of currently produced ceramics, many of which are based firmly on past production.

If you turn left out of the hotel and take the curving Fengjing lu (which leads to Zhonghua bei lu, one of the town's pleasant main streets), you pass small factories and can often find white porcelain golf-ball-like testers in the gutters. When you reach Zhushan dong lu, turn left and you will reach the centre of the town. Alternatively, turn right and you will reach the river which, if not quite as busy as in the days of Père D'Entrecolles, still bustles.

Surrounding the town (and inaccessibly underneath it) are many kiln sites. These consist of huge hills, now apparently natural, rounded in contour, but actually artificial, made from hundreds of thousands of kiln wasters (broken or faulty pots), thrown out from the kilns. If you get permission to visit them, by all means pick up pieces to look at them, but try and replace them where you find them (and resist the temptation to take them home) for you are standing on an archaeological site.

Ancient kiln sites to be seen out of town include the *Baihu wan* (White Tiger Bend) remains, 9km E of Jingdezhen, off the Jingwu road. This includes remains from the Five Dynasties, Northern and Southern Song. Further out is the *Liujia wan* (Willow Family Bend) kiln site, 22km from Jingdezhen, 10m high, covering over 10,000 square metres. Finds here are mostly middle to late Northern Song qingbai or yingqing white wares with incised decoration under the blue-tinged glassy glaze. Nearby is the Nanshijie site.

Just over 7km E of the town, on a hill behind the Huangnitou primary school, is a site covering 5000 square metres. To the W are Five Dynasties shards (grey-bodied, white-glazed and white-bodied, white-glazed wares) and to the E, yingqing of the Northern Song. The *Hutian* kiln site, E of Jingdezhen in Hutian village, covers the broadest time span, from Five Dynasties to the mid-Ming.

One of the most fascinating places in Jingdezhen is the **Ceramic Research Institute** which has been sited in one of several rare surviving Ming houses in Jingdezhen. Entered from the side, past a whitewashed, grey-tiled stepped gable (characteristic of southern building), the tall hall with its small, almost enclosed courtyard (the small opening in the roof is called a 'heaven well'), in dark, carved wood with elegantly curved beams, reveals the wealth of local merchants in the Ming. Exhibits in the hall (which may not be open to the public without introduction) include reconstructed vessels from some of the imperial kilns now buried under modern housing estates and photographs of the excavations.

50 Changsha

Changsha, capital of Hunan province, is a city of enormous historical and archaeological significance but little of its past remains to be seen outside the Provincial Museum.

Hunan province, 'South of the [Dongting] Lake', is one of China's major tea-producing areas. Created at the same time as Hubei, in the early 18C, by the division of Huguang, its history is similar for the Chu kingdon of the Warring States period (403–221 BC) also occupied present-day Hunan and had its capital at Changsha. Long regarded as a border region (the Chu did not, apparently, speak Chinese), Hunan was, nevertheless, linked to the north through the network of canals and rivers that allowed rice to be transported north.

The revolutionary history of Hunan is important. Mao Zedong was born in *Shaoshan,* just over 100km SW of Changsha. Shaoshan is a small village which, at the height of the personality cult during the 1960s, apparently saw some 8000 pilgrims a day. Now relatively deserted, the village—with its ancestral hall, and the pond where Mao threatened suicide when faced with an arranged marriage—has considerable charm and is worth a visit for anyone with time on their hands in Changsha. The natal house is a substantial yellow brick farmhouse beyond a lotus pool, entered through a room where the family altar stands with ancestral tablets. In the kitchen, an image of the stove god stands above the stove and the rooms arranged around the interior courtyard include Mao's bedroom, those of this parents and younger brother, and the stables.

Airport: S of the city. There are daily flights from Peking and Guangzhou, with less frequent departures to and from Chengdu, Wuhan, Shenyang, Xi'an and Zhengzhou, and extremely sparse (once or twice a week) departures for Nanjing, Shanghai, Shijiazhuang and Yichang.

Railways: the station is in the E of the city. Changsha is something of a major intersection with lines to Shanghai and Beijing and S to Guangzhou as well as W to Yunnan, Guizhou and Sichuan.

Hotel: the Xiang Jiang on Zhongshan lu in the centre of the city is open to foreigners.

During the Eastern Zhou (771–256 BC) the state of Chu, on the Yangtse, with Changsha (then known at Qingyang) at its centre, was one of the strongest of the Warring States, and one of the major texts of the period, the 'Zhan guo ce' (Intrigues of the Warring States, a 'work of fiction in a magnificent prose style'), is greatly taken up with the battles for supremacy between Qin (the eventual victor) and Chu. As well as battling against its neighbours, taking over the southern state of Yue in the 4C BC, the State of Chu developed a system of administration by which ministers' offices were regularly changed to prevent the growth of corruption, hereditary offices were decreased and officials were fairly strictly controlled.

The separateness of Chu is evident in its artefacts: the bronzes of Chu, in the 'Huai' style, were decorated with knobbly, high-relief coiled dragons; the use of lacquered wood in sculpture (including funerary sculpture) was distinctive, and a rare literary survival, the 'Chu ci' (Songs of Chu), which describes the beliefs and feelings of the Chu people who lived (at the time) on the frontiers of China and who were regarded as hardly Chinese by the northerners. Shamanistic beliefs and descriptions of the haunted horrors of the underworld (echoed in somewhat mysterious paintings and jade monsters) are described.

Even after its subjugation to the Qin and the establishment of the first empire, Chu, with its capital at Changsha, remained to some extent detached from the centre, a principality under the Han and part of the southern border regions that to those from the north and centre of China were foetid realms of exile. Until 187 BC, when a series of rebellions compelled the emperor to revise policy, Chu was ruled by nobles who were not members of the imperial clan—one of the famous Mawangdui tombs is that of a Marquis and his wife who were not related to the imperial Li family. The town's population more than quadrupled between AD 2 and 140 (years of census) because of a population influx from the troubled north; the population was over a million at the second census. A second Chu state was declared from 906–923 before the empire was reunited and Changsha grew steadily throughout the succeeding centuries.

Its second period of glory (in retrospect) was when Mao Zedong studied at the Teacher Training College here between 1912 and 1918, a period of great importance to him as he developed his interest in social matters. The first meeting of the provincial Communist Party Committee was held in Changsha in 1921. After considerable destruction during the Sino-Japanese war Changsha was rebuilt after Liberation and is today a modern city with few traces of its past visible outside the museum which is full of evidence of fascinating excavations relating in particular to the state of Chu and the city during the Han period.

The city lies mainly on the E bank of the Xiang River with a narrow island (*Juzi zhoutou* or Orange Island) in the centre. On the W bank of the river is *Hunan University*, built on part of Yuelu Mountain which is a favourite 'scenic spot'. The mountain, which is only 297m high, was nevertheless considered as one of the 72 peaks of the old southern state of Yue and described as such in the 'Account of Southern Yue' in the Nan bei chao period (420–581).

The area has a history: the university includes the site of the Yuelu Academy of the 10C, one of the four major scholastic establishments of the Song. Major figures including the philosopher Zhu Xi (1130–1200) taught here. Zhu Xi was a statesman and historian whose commentaries on the classics became the set texts for the imperial examinations for the succeeding centuries; he is very much associated with the revival of interest in Confucianism (Neo-Confucianism) of the Song period which was later to become something of a philosophical and educational straitjacket. In 1903 the academy was transformed into a teacher training college and in 1918, the Hunan Provincial Technical College also moved to the site so that in 1925 these diverse academies were joined to form the Hunan Provincial University.

The earliest surviving buildings on the site date from the Qing, though there is a stele left of the academy carved in 730 with a description of the Lushan temple written by the famous calligrapher Li Yong. The stele was later further embellished by other calligraphers including Mi Fei of the Song in 1080.

Just behind the University is the two-storey *Aiwan ting* (Love of the Evening Pavilion) with its exaggeratedly upswept eaves. It is also known as the Red Leaf Pavilion and the Love of Maples Pavilion, the latter name taken not only from the trees that surround it but also from a line in a poem by the Tang poet Du Fu: 'In the evening I stop and sit in the grove of the love of maples; the frost reddens the leaves and in the second month they flower'. The name of the pavilion was written out by Mao Zedong after restoration in 1952 and on the columns are couplets reflecting its importance in poetry written by students of the nearby academies in the late Qing period. They read: 'Staying at night in the red house on the side of the mountain, surrounded by 500 newly planted peach trees. The clouds wreathing the peaks are deep and the greenery drips and I bring two tame cranes in a basket'.

On the summit of the mountain, N of the University, is the *Yunlu gong* (Misty Hill Hall), now just a pavilion built in 1863 to replace an 18C original which was destroyed during the Taiping rebellion in 1852. Below, half-way up the mountain is the *Lushan si* or temple, over whose gate are the words: 'First famous in the Han and Wei, the first in Hunan'. It was indeed the first Buddhist temple in Changsha, founded in 268. The main hall was destroyed in 1944 and only the gate and library now remain.

There are two graves on the mountain, those of *Huang Xing* (1874–1916), a leader of the 1911 revolution, and *Cai E* (1882–1916), a military leader who led an unsuccessful rising in Hankou in 1900. Huang Xing's grave is just above the road, a three-stepped structure (wide, stepped graves are characteristic of the south) and Cai E's, also stepped, is above the White Crane Spring on the mountain.

Three sites in the S of the city may be visited together, either by taxi or on foot. These are the Tianxin Park, the Hunan No. 1 Teacher Training College and the *Headquarters of the local communist party* (Zhonggong xiangqu weiyuanhui jiuzhi, also known as Clearwater Pool or Qing shui tang) which is virtually opposite the hotel (just to the E), at No. 22 Qingshui tang. This was where the first meeting of the Provincial Party Committee, with Mao as Party Secretary, was held in July 1921 and where Mao and his first wife Yang Kaihui (executed by the KMT in 1930: she was the daughter of one of Mao's former teachers in Changsha; they married in 1920 and had three sons) lived from 1921 to 1923. The room in which they lived has been reconstructed and forms part of the exhibition on Mao's life and achievements.

Heading W along Zhongshan lu, turn left (S) down Jiangxiang lu and after a major crossroads (with Wuyi lu) you will find a park on your right, the *Tianxin gongyuan* (Park of the Heart of Heaven). This used to mark the SE angle of the city wall, just inside which were the Tianxin ge (Pavilion of the Heart of Heaven) and the Wenchang ge (Pavilion of the Flourishing of Literature). During the Taiping uprising the park was occupied by a local Taiping leader, the Western Heavenly King, who executed a large number of Qing imperial troops here. In 1930, when the Red Army attacked Changsha, Peng Dehuai held a meeting here.

The *Hunan No. 1 Teacher Training College* (or Normal School) is on Shuyuan lu: leaving the park, turn right along Chengnan lu (marking the southern line of the old city wall) and take the second major turning on the left, Shuyuan lu. The old college is not far down the road on your right. Mao studied here from 1913 (when he was 19 years old) to 1918, impressing his student colleagues and teachers (including his future father-in-law) by his activity, organising student societies, a night-school and becoming 'Student of the Year' in 1917 despite his varied application. It was here that he failed his art exam (by drawing a circle and calling it 'an egg'), and he also consistently got practically no marks for maths and none at all for English which he must have seen as being as useless as art to a man who wanted to change society.

You could return to the hotel by retracing your steps to Chengnan lu and turning left. The road (which changes its name to Yanjiang da dao) runs along the riverside. The first major turning on the right after Wuyi lu (which crosses the bridge over to Orange Island) is Zhongshan lu. Turn right into it to find the hotel.

Not far NW of the hotel is the **Kaifu si** (Opening to Luck Temple) on Xiangchun jie. Leaving the hotel, turn right into Zhongshan lu, cross Jianxiang lu and take the next major turning on the right, Dazhai lu. The second major turning on the left is Xiangchun jie which runs W–E from the river. Founded in the Five Kingdoms period (907–960) by Ma Yin, then king of Chu, the temple was added to by his son and extensively rebuilt in succeeding dynasties, the main hall most recently rebuilt in 1923. Its great stone pailou with highly decorated roof tiles stands in front of a temple whose roofs are decorated in the lavish southern style.

The greatest glories of today's Changsha are to be found in the **Provincial Museum** which is just N of the hotel, in the NW corner of the *Martyrs' Park* (Hunan lieshi gongyuan). It can be reached by taking the first street heading N towards Jingdu lu (which runs along the southern edge of the park).

The museum contains an important collection of red-painted neolithic pottery and bronzes from the Shang and Zhou, as well as a chronological display of artefacts from the Han to the Qing unearthed in Hunan. The major display is that referring to the three tombs at Mawangdui in the E suburbs of the town (where Tomb 3 can still be seen).

Tomb 1, excavated in 1973, is that of a woman, the wife of the Marquis of Dai; Tombs 2 and 3, discovered in the following year, contain the bodies of her husband and son. The Marquis of Dai, Li Cang, was appointed prime minister to the King of Changsha in 193 BC and died in 186 BC. The third tomb, containing the body of a younger son of the Marquis, is dated by an inscription to 168 BC. Tomb 1 was constructed later than the other two, slightly damaging them during construction. Li Cang appears to have been the last prime minister appointed by the King of Changsha; his successor was appointed by the central Han government.

All the tombs were vertical shafts cut into the ground and surmounted by a cone-shaped mound. This southern form contrasts with the hollow brick chambers of the north, the brick chamber serving as a sort of outer coffin. The Mawangdui tombs contained a 'nest' of four inner coffins within a wooden outer coffin. The outer coffin was surrounded by a layer of charcoal and a layer of white clay which preserved the contents admirably. The inner coffins were: a black-painted coffin containing a black-lacquered coffin, painted with mythological animals and figures, containing a red-lacquered coffin decorated with auspicious emblems which in turn contained the inner coffin housing the dead body.

The bodies were dressed in up to 20 thin silk garments. The body of the woman in Tomb No. 1 was remarkably well-preserved, her flesh still reasonably elastic to the touch (as can be seen in a rather gruesome film of the excavation and subsequent autopsy). She appears to have died from some sort of seizure shortly after eating melon (pips and all) and had TB, a slipped disc, intestinal worms, marked arthritis and arteriosclerosis though she was only about 50.

The coffins, some of which are on display, are beautifully painted with swirling clouds in which tiny animals sit on the black-lacquered versions, the whole outlined with almost art-nouveau interlocked cloud swirls, whilst on the end of the red-lacquered coffin a pair of prancing deer, heraldic in appearance, are surrounded by swirling cloud scrolls and bordered by a geometric interlocking pattern with fleur-de-lys. The same sort of swirling linear designs are seen on the huge quantity of grave goods, some life-size and everyday like the double-lugged lacquer cups and bowls, compartmented toilet boxes and combs and food containers, the others miniaturised and symbolic like the small painted wooden statuettes of servants.

The dual nature of the funerary furnishings have been interpreted as intended to serve the two souls that the Han believed in, the *hun* and the *po* (there were thought to be three hun and seven po). On death, the hun soul leaves the body and makes its way to heaven and the place of the spirits whilst the po souls stay around in the tomb (hence the food and drink provided) before descending to the Yellow Springs in the centre of the earth. It was (and still is) considered important to keep the po souls happy and well fed lest they leave the tomb early and come to create havoc for the deceased's descendants. Foods provided in the 48 bamboo food baskets and 51 ceramic food containers in Tomb 1 alone included wheat, barley, rice, soya, kidney beans, lotus roots, melon, chives, lentils, ginger, pears, plums, peaches, oranges, persimmons, water-chestnuts, beef, mutton, pork, dog, chicken, pheasant, duck, quail, sparrow, bream, perch, carp, salt, sugar, honey, vinegar, cinnamon, alcohols and fruit juices. Many of the foods provided were salted, smoked or pickled in vinegar.

There were musical instruments in the tombs and fabrics of silk, notably a fine gauze, figured and embroidered silks and a variety of colours used in dying and painting the fabrics. Designs on the textiles echo those on the lacquered and painted coffins and lacquered utensils.

For the Chinese, some of the most important finds in the tombs were those of books and documents. These included a text of the 'Zhan guo ce' (Intrigues of the Warring States), the 'Yi jing' (Book of Changes), the Taoist classic 'Dao de jing' (with its sections reversed to read De dao jing), and texts on punishments, astronomy, meteorology, divination, horse physiognomy, maps of the Changsha area and an exercise chart. The last is very charming, showing various figures bending and stretching and touching their toes. The texts appeared either on narrow wooden strips or painted on silk (in the case of the illustrated works such as maps and charts).

Apart from the still-fascinating bodies in the tombs, one of the most significant pieces to emerge was the T-shaped silk banner from Tomb 1 which serves as a graphic illustration of Han beliefs about the world.

At the base is the subterranean world, the realm of water and darkness represented by two fish. From there two dragons ascend, their bodies interlocked in a jade *bi* disc (the disc, with a hole in the centre, is decorated with characteristic raised circles and has a silken thread knotted through it). Below the *bi* disc hangs another decorative jade (the *heng*, an inverted V form, part of a characteristic series of jade pieces that were threaded with silken cords and hung from the belt in the Han), and below that a picture of the sorts of food vessels containing offerings that were left in the tomb. The dragons were believed to assist the *hun* soul on its journey to heaven so it must be assumed to be rising with them from the depths. Above the *bi* is a platform with figures, that of a woman assumed to be the Marquess of Dai in whose tomb the hanging was found. An owl flies above, supporting a canopy upon which two birds stand. These have been interpreted as phoenixes, birds of good omen who escort the hun soul to the heavens (just as the nice spotted leopards beneath the figures are thought to be protective of the soul on its journey upward).

Above the canopy is an opening into the heavens presided over by two gentlemen (seen by some as representatives of the celestial king, come to greet the hun soul). Beside them are two more protecting leopards and above them hangs a bronze bell. At the top left is the moon with the toad and the hare who live there and, to the right, the red disc of the sun and the black crow, symbolic of the sun. At the top, in the centre, is a female figure enlaced in a snake which, mermaid-like grows from her own body. She is thought to be Nu gua, ancestress of mankind, here representing the celestial gods, ready to welcome the soul to this upper realm.

This physical depiction of the realms of the spiritual world (otherwise known only from literary accounts which are necessarily less graphic and difficult to interpret) is one of the great treasures from Mawangdui and you can amuse yourself not only in trying to penetrate the Han mind but also in trying to decide whether that which is displayed in Changsha's museum is the banner, or has Peking won and the example in the Historical Museum there is in fact the real thing? Or is the real thing locked away for preservation in rather better storage conditions?

51   Fuzhou

Fuzhou is the capital of Fujian province.

Fujian province (Fukien in the old Postal Service romanisation, Fu-chien in Wade-Giles) is on China's SE coast, the southern part of the province facing the island of Taiwan. It is a very beautiful province, in general, fitting the Chinese term for landscape which is *shan shui*, meaning 'mountains and water'. They say that there are more mountains and water in Fujian than almost anywhere else, therefore more 'landscape'.

The province has a semi-tropical or tropical climate with winter average temperatures (in Fuzhou) of nearly 11°C and July averages of nearly 29°C. The mountainous areas inland are rather cooler and there is a considerable rainfall (1500mm to 2000mm a year) with typhoons on the coast in the summer months. The mountains have made communications difficult inland though two railways lines connecting Fuzhou and Xiamen with the interior were built in 1955. Much transport goes by road or by sea along the coast for Fujian has a long maritime tradition.

Before the Tang, Fujian lay outside the Chinese empire, part of the kingdom of Min-yue, and, despite loose integration under the Jin (AD 265–420), it was not really settled by the Chinese until the Tang dynasty. From the early days, the province's prosperity grew on the basis of maritime trade.

Local products, fine teas from the N of the province and cane sugar from the S, were exported to N China and as early as the 1C AD, ships came from SE Asia seeking Chinese produce. The protected harbours of Fuzhou, Quanzhou and Xiamen (essentially protected against typhoons by being situated up-river from the sea or sheltered by off-shore islands) were major trading centres with Japan, SE Asia and beyond, shipping Fujian lead and tin, ceramics from neighbouring Jiangxi, silks from Zhejiang, Fujian lacquer (highly polished lacquer vessels made on a hemp base formed over a wooden mould), cotton and tea, and returning with luxury goods: ivory, amber, spices and rare timbers. In the 13C Quanzhou was known as 'Zaytun', the name eventually applied to satin which was shipped to Manila and thence (in the 16C) to Mexico. Fuzhou in the 13C presented the scene of 'large numbers of ships, loaded with goods' mentioned in Marco Polo's dubious 'Description of the World'. The famous eunuch Zheng He, who led the grand series of maritime expeditions in the early Ming (1405–33), set off from Zhejiang but stopped in Fuzhou to replenish provisions and recruit sailors.

The ports of Xiamen (Amoy) and Fuzhou were opened to foreign trade and residence by the Treaty of Nanjing after the Opium War of 1842, and, because of the favourable trading conditions and pleasant climate (except for the hot, humid summers), were favourite places of residence for traders and missionaries. The name for tea, one of the early trade items, derives from the pronunciation of the character in the Xiamen or Amoy dialect: 'te'. In modern standard Chinese it is pronounced cha. In the middle of the 19C, each vessel to leave for North America carried an average of 1000 tons of tea, though as late as 1910 the trans-shipment of opium through Xiamen was still a major aspect of trade. The writer who noted the movement of opium in 1910 was the Reverend Philip Wilson Pitcher ('In and Around Amoy, Shanghai and Foochow', 1910, 1912) who also noted that 'the great export from this port is labour. Many thousands go abroad every year to Singapore, Java, Borneo and Manila.'

One of the distinguishing attributes of Fujian is its enormous contribution to the Chinese diaspora; Overseas Chinese communities in Singapore, Malaysia and Manila in particular, virtually all originate in Fujian (including the ancestors of Cory Aquino). They are linked by language, the communities overseas still speaking the distinctive local dialects, a link emphasised by Reverend Pitcher's praise for the English Presbyterian missionary Carstairs Douglas' 'inestimable Dictionary of the Vernacular or Spoken Language of Amoy—the joy and delight of every one living in this region, across the Channel [i.e. on Taiwan], or in the Straits Settlements, fortunate enough to possess a copy'. Some 45 per cent of the Chinese on Taiwan are said to have originated in the town of Quanzhou. Probably the oldest Overseas Chinese settlement was in the Philippines in the 16C when successful Chinese traders (from Fujian), made their money in silver which originated in the New World mines of the Spanish conquistadores. Silver from the Philippines was remitted to China in considerable quantities where it was used as currency in the Ming.

The impact of the Overseas Chinese on Fujian is considerable. Money is remitted to relatives and, since the relaxation following the death of Mao (1976), Overseas Chinese have been returning for visits in greater numbers than ever. Many Buddhist temples in Fujian have been rebuilt with money from Overseas Chinese and their incredibly lavish decoration (together with a considerable structural use of concrete) sets them apart from the more sober buildings of the North. In late 1987 the first Taiwanese visitors since 1949 were finally permitted (by the Taiwanese authorities who had held out against it) to return, through the Chinese Red Cross. People had been returning during the 1950s, particularly following anti-Chinese government regulations and bloody riots in places such as Indonesia. Many were settled in 'Overseas Chinese farms' in Fujian though some younger people have now left the farms and found employment elsewhere in China.

One of the earliest Overseas Chinese to pour money back into his home town was Chen Jiageng (whose name in Amoy dialect is rendered Tan Kah-kee, which underlines the extremely different pronunciation of this dialect), 1874–1961. From the Xiamen area, he spent much of his life in Singapore where he made his money in rubber. Between 1913 and 1920 he established primary and middle schools, a teacher-training college, business, agricultural, marine-engineering and fisheries colleges in Jimei, on the outskirts of Xiamen. The architecture of Jimei, a startling combination of western and Chinese in the early 20C style, survives, as do the institutions he founded. He died in Beijing, having returned to China where he held many important posts, including membership of the Committee for Overseas Chinese Affairs.

The proximity of Taiwan has meant that for many decades Fujian has been a military centre. It was only opened to foreign tourism in 1979 and tourists are still very restricted there. The coast is generally open, the interior mostly closed, for military reasons. It seems likely, as tourism con-

tinues to develop, that many significant sites currently in military zones may yet be opened. In late 1987, the word seemed to be that 'in a couple of years' various sites that were still closed would finally be opened. Tourist maps are somewhat misleading as they indicate sites (such as a cave in which Zhu Xi may have taught, in Xiamen) which lie smack in the middle of barracks and are therefore inaccessible. The major list of sites of cultural interest, 'Zhong guo ming sheng ci dian' (Dictionary of Famous Sites), produced by the Bureau of Cultural Relics which supervises their preservation, also lists a number of protected sites (such as the tombs of Lin Zexu and Yan Fu outside Fuzhou) which are still out of bounds to foreigners. I will list them, with a caution, in the hope that they will eventually be accessible. The military presence in Fujian is not obvious but it is obtrusive when you search for out-of-the-way tombs, and taxi-drivers, who seem to have been instructed not to tell the simple truth, appear both cretinous and obstructive at times.

Fuzhou lies on the Min River, some 40km from the coast. The wide river, protected from coastal typhoons, has provided a safe anchorage for over 1000 years and Fuzhou has long been a major port. It was given its name during the Tang dynasty (in 725) when the state of Min came under central Chinese control and Minzhou (Min City) became Fuzhou (Happy City). The 'fu' comes from the Fu mountains to the northwest. The city is beautifully situated, the river Min passing through dark mountains, the plain lush and green with subtropical foliage including banyans (Fuzhou is sometimes called Banyan City). As provincial capital, it houses Fujian University and industries including chemicals, machine-building, paper-making, timber and foodstuffs (including jasmine and other teas) with handicrafts (lacquer, wood, stone, notably a local stone related to pyrophyllite, and ivory carving).

Airport: S of the city, 30–40 minutes by bus from the hotel area (at the northern end of Wusi lu). There are daily CAAC flights to Beijing, Nanchang and Wuhan, flights to Shanghai every day except Wednesday and Guangzhou every day except Saturday; twice weekly flights to Hefei, Hangzhou and Nanjing and an increasing number of charter flights from Hong Kong and local flights on local airlines (Xiamen International Airlines which also run the Hong Kong charters).

Railway: the station is in the N of the city, only about 10 minutes by bus from the major hotel area. The line to Fuzhou, one of only two in Fujian, breaks off from major E–W and N–S lines at Yingtan in Jiangxi province. Within Fujian, the line branches again at Waiyang, splitting into a Xiamen and Fuzhou branch. It is therefore possible to reach the interior of China from Fuzhou or Xiamen by rail but travel within Fujian by rail is impractical for Fuzhou–Xiamen by road is some 250km but it is almost twice as far by rail.

Buses: the most comfortable buses can be booked and boarded from major hotels and these represent the best way for individuals to travel down the Fujian coast. It takes just over 2 hours to get to Quanzhou and about 7 hours to get to Xiamen.

Boats: Shanghai and Xiamen can be reached (rather slowly) by boat: the passenger terminals are near the Jiefang bridge.

Hotels: The Overseas Chinese Hotel, the Foreign Trade Hotel and others are near the N end of the 'middle section' of Wuyi lu. This is a convenient area to stay in. The Xi hu (West Lake) Hotel is near the lake, convenient for that and the provincial museum but is otherwise a bit far from the town centre.

As Fuzhou lay outside China proper before the Tang, little is known about it. When the Min kingdom was absorbed the safe, inland port of Fuzhou on the Min River quickly became prosperous. It was described in Marco Polo's late 13C 'Description of the World'. Polo says that the city is full of idolators, ready to rise against the Mongol rulers, and they therefore garrisoned a large number of imperial troops there (just as large numbers are still stationed in Fujian owing to the proximity of Taiwan). 'Through the midst of the city flows a great river…It is crossed by a very fine bridge resting on huge pontoons', this last, an accurate description of the city divided by the Min, with a small island in the centre, dividing the bridge in two. Polo also mentioned the quantities of sugar cane, still to be seen in the area, and the trade of the city in pearls and precious stones by 'merchants who traffic in the Indies'. A long passage with no apparent basis in fact describes the lions said to infest the neighbourhood which were lured into pits by means of howling white dogs.

As one of China's major ports, used for provisioning by the great eunuch admiral Zheng He in the 15C, Fuzhou was also attractive to Western traders and was one of the first ports opened to foreign trade and residence by the earliest of the 'unequal treaties' signed in Nanjing in 1842. The new foreign residents settled on the south bank of the Min, building their fine houses and offices on the sloping land facing the old, walled Chinese city on the north bank. By the time they arrived, the river was crossed by a stone bridge (now called Jiefang or Liberation Bridge), in two parts, built originally in 1297.

The Ming city walls have disappeared (they were still present, with their six gates, two sluice gates and frequent gun-towers, in 1924) though their position can be traced along Huancheng lu (W), Wushan lu and Gutian lu (S), Dongshui lu and the Puan River (E), cutting across to Hualin lu (N) with the West Lake lying just outside the ramparts. The city has filled out: in the mid 19C there were many open spaces, those within the E wall the result of devastating fires, to the SW, the Wushan area (currently the seat of local government), a parkland full of temples '…houses cease to appear and the domain of temples begins. The silence deepens.' Elsewhere, the common noise and bustle of a Chinese city was apparent to an American missionary in the 1850s: '…blacksmith shops, brasier shops and a variety of other noisy trades each congregated in its own locality…the dwellings have one room open to the street and two or three back of it…with dirt floors and pigs and chickens common tenants with the inhabitants. Handicrafts of various descriptions are prosecuted by the inmates.'

Xi hu. It is possible to walk to the lake from the hotel area, cutting through to Guping lu, turning N to the next major crossroads and turning W into Hubin lu where the entrance to the park is on the N side of the road. Cross the lake by the bridge and cross the central island. On the far side of the lake is the **Fujian Provincial Museum**, divided into two parts, one of revolutionary, one of pre-revolutionary history.

In the pre-revolutionary, archaeological exhibition, one of the most striking exhibits is that of the boat coffin from Wuyi shan excavated (if removing a wooden coffin from a cave high up on a cliff can be called excavation) in 1978. The full-size covered boat, with raised prow and stern, was made from nanmu cedar and the Carbon-14 date ascribes it to 3445 years ago. Iron tools and implements including cog-wheels and crossbow fittings were found in a Western Han city in Fujian and there is a large collection of locally produced green wares of the Tang, including some small tiger-headed, almost gargoyle-like pots, described as having 'hygienic function'. They are not dissimilar to (though much smaller than) the flattish, wide-spouted ceramic chamberpots still sold today.

Another good collection is that from the Five Dynasties when the kingdom of Min controlled the area. A stone- and brick-lined tomb of the period produced a sizable collection of ceramic figures, some half life-size, others smaller, grouped in a central case. There is an interesting group of Song bronzes and some charming iron cattle and pig sculptures as well as many funerary jars with tall, elaborately decorated covers. These were used for secondary burials when the bones were dug up some two years after burial, cleaned and broken to fit into the jars which were then placed in final resting places. There are a number of stone-carved Nestorian crosses from Quanzhou (described in more detail under Quanzhou). A variety of locally produced Song ceramics show the well-known Fujian black wares (known in Japanese as *temmoku*) with hare's-fur iron patterning in the glaze. Many kilns, such as that as Dakou, produced both black and white wares. Evidence of Song overseas trade is clear in the boat excavations (mainly from around Quanzhou). There are good Yuan celadons and blue-and-white export wares from the Anxi and Dehua kilns (the latter most famous for its white Buddhist figurines and altar pieces from the Ming).

There is an interesting collection of metal filigree wares from the tomb of Zhang Hai, a contemporary of Qi Jiguang (1528–88), a major military strategist of the Ming who was for many years responsible for local coastal defences.

Fujian's revolutionary history was one of struggle, with a failure of the Chinese Soviet government to carry through an alliance with a KMT rebellion against Chiang Kai shek (over his failure to resist Japan), led by the commander of the KMT's 19th Route Army, Cai Tingkai. The rebellion was suppressed brutally by Chiang Kai shek in 1933. The exhibition of revolutionary relics in the museum has a certain charm for it comprises all sorts of objects used by famous Communists when passing through the area, and other items produced by local guerrillas for their own use. There are Qing dynasty handcuffs and false-bottomed buckets used for carrying messages past enemies; Qu Qiubai's binoculars (Qu Qiubai, 1899–1935, served briefly as CCP general secretary from 1927–28 and was a prominent writer and translator associated with the League of Left-Wing Writers, translating Gorky and Tolstoy as well as Marxist works until his execution by the KMT when he was already half dead of TB), and He Shuheng and Mao Zedong's hurricane lamps. Articles used and produced by guerrilla groups in Fujian (which was close to the Jiangxi Soviet) include conch shells (used as bugles), printing plates and locally made banknotes with Marx and Lenin on them, straw and bamboo sandals and cloth bags for carrying grain rations. The most charming item of all (in the first row of cases on the right, 1987), next to a group of crankshafts, is a small bamboo cup with a handle, carved with a simple figure of a horse, used by guerrillas in northern Fujian.

The LAKE itself is artificial, dug in 282 to collect water from the nearby hills to irrigate local fields. From the period of the State of Min (in the Five Dynasties) it has been a local park, embellished by buildings. By the early 19C the lake was in a poor state when one of the best-known Qing officials, Lin Zexu, returned to Fuzhou to observe the Confucian ritual of mourning for his father.

Lin (1785–1850) was born just outside Fuzhou and was best-known for his moral stand against the opium trade for which he was made Imperial Commissioner with plenipotentiary power to investigate the opium question at Canton (1839–40). Despite his failure to withstand the massed might of the West placed behind the opium traders, he remains an heroic figure of Chinese history for his principled letter to Queen Victoria requesting the end of the opium trade, and for his destruction of the over 20,000 chests of opium confiscated at Canton, which sparked off the first Opium War. On his filial return to Fuzhou in 1827 (when he was Financial Commissioner in Nanjing), Lin noted the disrepair of the lake and local officials, prompted by his observations, spent a year clearing and restoring it. One of the first buildings to be restored was the old memorial hall to Li Gang of the Tang, behind the Lotus Pavilion, where there were two cassia trees; after his death the Gui zhai (Cassia Study) was constructed there in his memory. In 1929 it was designated the *Lin Zexu Memorial Hall*, but it gradually crumbled and was rebuilt in 1985 to commemorate the 200th anniversary of his birth. It is a pretty site with open courts, moon gates and cool dark halls in the southern style.

Leaving the West Lake, take the road straight ahead (leading S), Tonghu lu; turn left into the first main road, Guxi lu. Continue E, crossing five small crossroads until you come to a big main road (with bus routes) which at this crossroads is called Guping lu to the N and Bayiqi bei lu to the S. Cross straight over and take the third turning on your left to find the **Kaiyuan Temple** (Kaiyuan si). Straight ahead of you is a primary school (Kaizhi xuexiao): turn right past it, following the narrow lane (when you pass by some sort of noisy metalworking factory) and, as the road turns again, the Kaiyuan Temple is ahead of you. This consists of two main halls, the second way above the first.

It is said to be a Liang (early 6C) foundation and according to the old monk who lives there, the major Buddha figure is Tang dynasty in date and made of iron, weighing about 40 tons. Over 5m high, seated on a lotus throne, the figure was thought to have been one of the late Tang bronze Buddhas cast on the order of the King of Min but when the temple was restored in the early Qing (1659) it was discovered that the figure was made of iron and a small silver pagoda was found under the Buddha with an inscription dating to 1083, in the Northern Song. It is now gilded. On the platform in front of the hall behind are two wonderful Song stone troughs with lotuses growing in them (Buddhist emblems of purity).

Retrace your steps to the main road, turn left and then, when you reach the main road at the end, turn right. Very soon on your left you will see a narrow lane leading into a free *market*, overhung with trees and filled with stalls selling vegetables and fruit. Not far along the market street (Qingcheng si lu), there is a highly decorated *temple* frontage on the left.

Still under restoration in late 1987, the temple, with its elaborately carved façade and roofline, was dedicated to the ruler of the Min state (862–925). At the end of the Tang an independent kingdom of Min was proclaimed in Fujian and the ruler is said to have promoted culture and the economy with success so that he was called the 'King who Developed Min' (Kaimin wang). The temple is built on the site of his palace which in 946 was turned into a commemorative hall. From the Song to the Qing it was here that the local officials came at the Spring Festival to ceremonially initiate the spring ploughing by making little mud figures of the 'spring oxen' which pull the ploughs. In the temple there is a great stele almost 5m high, carved in 906 and describing the achievements of the King of Min and his family and the successes of the early years of his reign in the economy, culture, military affairs and foreign trade.

If you walk right through the market to the E end (where a notice describes it as the 'Fuzhou Cultural Market' although it consists entirely of edibles), you are on Wuyi lu. Turn left and you will soon see the Overseas Chinese Hotel on your left and the Foreign Trade Hotel further up on your right.

It is also possible to walk from the hotel area to the White Pagoda on Yu shan, the Black Pagoda, the mosque and Li Zexu's Memorial Hall.

To reach the White Pagoda, turn left out of the hotel and head S down Wuyi lu. Cross straight over the major crossroads (with Dong da jie) and continue, passing a small, tree-draped stream (visible on the right-hand (W) side of the road). Soon after this, there is a shop on the same side of the road, selling seals, brushes and white plaster busts of Marcus Aurelius and others. Next to the shop a lane leads to steps winding up and over YU SHAN (Yu Mountain), a rocky, tree-covered eminence. As you climb the steps you pass the abandoned Wangtian Temple and reach the summit of the hill where the White Pagoda is visible ahead, like a lighthouse.

The W side of the mountain boasts over 100 stone-carved inscriptions dating from the Song to the present day and several temples.

It has traditionally been the favourite place for local inhabitants to climb during the mid-autumn festival (which falls on the 15th of the 8th lunar month, usually some time in late September). Described in the 1920s, the festival involves admiring the full moon and 'it is believed that if a mountain is not ascended, evil spirits will visit the home and consequently the whole family packs off to the nearest mountain, making the event a sort of picnic.'

As you descend from the summit, on your right, a solid red wall with steps beside it leads up to the site of the *Dashi Hall* (or Guanyin Hall) and the *Huguo Temple*, built side by side up the slope. The Huguo Temple was closed (late 1987) but formerly housed an exhibition on relations between Fuzhou and Japan. The Dashi Hall was a Song foundation, rebuilt in 1713 as the Ten-thousand-year Pavilion where all the officials in the city (the 'hundred officials') prayed for good fortune. In 1737 it was renamed the Dashi Hall (Hall of Great Men). During the 1911 uprising which established the Republic, the Dashi Hall was the headquarters of the uprising. On 9 November 1911 a beacon was fired here by the revolutionary forces to launch the attack on government forces and captives were executed near a well W of the hall. Today the building houses the *city museum* of Fuzhou, with a special exhibition in the left wing of a Southern Song tomb excavated in 1986 in the suburbs of Fuzhou at Chayuan shan.

The tomb, underground and lined with stone slabs, contained the bodies of a man and a woman, both of which can be seen in formaldehyde baths in the exhibition. The grave goods included a number of miniature silver foliate dishes and bowls, like a doll's tea set, silver chopsticks and serving tongs, legal documents and a quantity of well-preserved silk garments which are of considerable interest since they demonstrate clearly the distinction between clothing of the Song and later dynasties.

The bodies were wrapped in silken shrouds which were neatly knotted around them, and silk shoes and purses were found on them. There are silk wrap-around 'apron' skirts, one with 'Fortuny' pleats, cross-over under and outer jackets, some with bands of embroidery at the edges or edged with darker silk. Robes have a distinct waist, where the panelled skirt is joined to the cross-over top and either wide, square sleeves or bulging, gourd-shaped sleeves. Both corpses had good sets of teeth with the front teeth filed down which is assumed in the commentary to have been a contemporary burial practice.

In the main hall is an exhibit of articles excavated in the Fuzhou area, from the neolithic to the Qing. This mainly consists of ceramics, from Sui and Tang Yue wares (greenish southern stonewares), Southern Song and Yuan Yue and brown wares and many examples of the white porcelain of Dehua (some 70km NW of Quanzhou) from the Ming. There is a particularly interesting floor tile of the Five Dynasties with quite high relief decoration strikingly similar to the frontispiece of the 868 (printed edition) Diamond Sutra (British Library) and presumably representative of contemporary temple and palace floors (impossible to dust and not very hard-wearing). The Qing items are a rather motley gathering of ceramics with a fine wooden document box and there is a guqin (zither-like instrument) with instruction manuals donated by a local inhabitant. On the far right is a display of ceramics unearthed on the sea-bed at the mouth of the Min River, downstream from Fuzhou, an example of the sea-trade with SE Asia, Japan and Korea by which China shipped silks and ceramics to these eager markets.

Behind the main halls, up the hill, is a courtyard with a central pool surrounding a mock mountain sprouting a creeper-draped tree. Behind is an almost smooth *stele* of 1779 with a nearly invisible depiction of a rather masculine Bodhisattva Guanyin. The stele apparently describes the story of Guanyin 'turning from a man into a woman'.

Scripturally inaccurate (for in Indian Buddhism it was naturally assumed that all Bodhisattvas and any figures of importance were masculine), this change is typical of Chinese Buddhism which in its popular aspects paid little attention to doctrinal niceties. In early Buddhist iconography, the Bodhisattvas were depicted according to Indian concepts of beauty as sinuous, fleshy, soft figures and this, combined with the 'female' attributes of Guanyin as the succourer, bringer of children, the deity of mercy, caused the gradual but incomplete change of sex in Chinese Buddhism. That it was not a complete change is evident in the natural (unbound) form of the bare feet that are often evident, particularly in the Ming and Qing blanc de Chine porcelain figures from Dehua.

Descending the W side of the hill to the base of the pagoda, you pass a small stone Tang pagoda. On the E side of this is the *Qi Gong Memorial Hall*, dedicated to Qi Jiguang (1528–87), a major military strategist of the Ming.

A native of Penglai (Shandong), Qi led an army in support of the Fujian garrison when menaced by the Japanese in 1562 and inflicted three major defeats. When he was about to return to Zhejiang a banquet was held in his honour on the Pingyuan platform on Yu shan where a hall in his honour was later built. The present structure dates from 1918, built beside five green pines, with the Pingyuan platform in front of it. Beside the hall is a rockery with a great stone inscribed with two characters which mean 'Drunken stone', supposedly where Qi slept when drunk after the banquet.

Below is the *Pagoda*. Its proper name is *Dingguang* (Certain Brightness) but for obvious reasons it is popularly known as the White Pagoda. The present structure is a seven-storey brick octagon, 41m high, with a wooden internal structure. It was first constructed in 904 and owed its name to a brilliant pearl concealed in the foundations.

The pagoda was originally built the other way round, with a brick core and wooden exterior, but it was destroyed by lightning in 1534 and reconstructed with a brick exterior in 1548. The temple building below was constructed in 905 but the present structures, used as a children's library and meeting rooms, are Qing. They have characteristically decorated columns of local stone, carved with high-relief dragons curling some two-thirds of the way up. The facility with which the local stone can be carved into such high-relief designs adds to the generally highly decorated appearance of much architecture of Fujian.

Leaving Yu shan by the exit on Gutian lu, turn right and take the first major turning on the right, Bayiqi bei lu (for those who recognise Chinese numerals, Eight One Seven Road North, which I think refers to the Nanchang uprising of 1 August 1927. This, though not successful, marked the beginning of the Communist Party's independent leadership of the revolutionary war and is usually referred to as the First of the Eighth without the seven). Cross the road. Not far up on the W side is a narrow lane with a wirework archway over it. Take this lane and soon, on your right, you will see a turning, again with the entrance marked by a green concrete deer and crane archway, with the 'Black' Pagoda visible beyond. This smaller stone pagoda, with fine carvings of protective guardians on the lower register, was built in 799 and was originally part of a temple which has since disappeared.

The **Mosque** is a little further N up Bayiqi bei lu, reached by a lane near No. 247, on the W side of the road.

A stele records its foundation as being in 628 although the area was subsequently occupied by the palace of the King of Min in the Five Dynasties and in 936 the buildings were apparently taken over by Buddhists and called the Ten-Thousand-Year Temple. It reverted to Islam in the mid 13C. It was commonly known as the 'Weekly Worship' Temple, a name often given to Islamic temples because of the weekly service on Fridays. Chinese religions did not have a weekly service, or a special day: services, whether Buddhist or Taoist, were held daily and people attended when they could; temples also set great store by special festivals. The buildings were destroyed by fire in 1541 and subsequently rebuilt.

The main hall was large and square and built in the Chinese style (as opposed to the Islamic style of the old Quanzhou mosque). It had a five-ridged roof and was five bays deep and five bays wide in the characteristic Chinese mosque style. Unlike Chinese temple buildings, whose 'great hall' was usually built on a larger scale than the others, with a higher roof, taller columns and wider bays, the main hall in mosques built in the Chinese architectural style (with the exception of the Xi'an mosque) is often low-roofed but deep and wide. However, this main hall was rebuilt in 1955 and transformed in shape. Steles include an imperial edict of Yongle (early 16C) and one recording the rebuilding in the mid 16C.

Continue N a little way up the main road and take the first main turning on the left, Jibi lu, which runs beside a small stream. At the other end of Jibi lu is Xiamen lu; turn left into it. Not far down on the W side of the road is the *Lin Zexu Memorial Hall*. Said to be built on the site of Lin's house, the recently rebuilt, traditional-style complex in a series of courtyards surrounded by white-walled and dark-wood halls is now a sort of domestic museum to the 'upright official' of the Qing.

Lin Zexu (1785–1850) served as secretary to the governor of Fujian after passing his zhuren exams in 1810. In 1811 he passed the higher examinations in the capital and was selected as a member of the Hanlin Academy. In 1819 he was chief examiner for Yunnan province, later serving as a local official in Zhejiang, Jiangsu and Shanxi and as financial commissioner in Nanjing, Hubei and Henan. In 1832 he became Governor of Jiangsu, later Governor-general of Hunan and Hubei. In 1838 he reported to the throne on the measures he was taking to eradicate the opium habit by confiscating smokers' equipment, providing prescriptions for cures and requiring them to be followed within a time limit, and by drastically punishing smugglers and dealers. Such was his success in Hunan and Hubei that in 1838 he was appointed Imperial Commissioner to try and stamp out the problem at its root, with the European importers of (illegal) opium in Canton.

Though its import was officially prohibited, with the ending of the East India Company's trade monopoly in 1834 the trade had grown to vast proportions and made enormous profits both for the foreign importers and Chinese dealers, none of whom was prepared for the drastic action undertaken by Lin Zexu. He deprived the Hong merchants (those licensed to trade with foreigners) of their buttons of rank, ordered all Chinese servants and traders out of the 'factories' (or foreign warehouses and residences) in Canton and demanded the surrender of all opium. The British Superintendent of Trade, Captain Elliot, refused to sign a paper promising non-importation of opium in future although nearly 2.5 million catties were handed over and destroyed. The Opium War of 1840 grew out of this and further complicating events.

In July a Chinese was killed in a brawl involving British and American sailors in Kowloon. Captain Elliot refused Lin's demand to hand the culprit over to the Chinese for punishment. Unable to determine a single offender, Elliott held a trial of those most likely to be involved and sentenced them to imprisonment in England. Lin then expelled the British from Macau (whence they went to Hong Kong which was no great hardship) though he compounded this by refusing to allow the British to buy food in Kowloon. Skirmishes were followed by an imperial edict prohibiting all trade with Britain on 13 December 1839.

When the Opium War broke out Lin Zexu was dismissed from office and eventually banished to Chinese Turkestan where he distinguished himself (as he had done previously in his official career) particularly by opening the area to agriculture. Recalled to Peking in 1845, he served with particular success in Yunnan where he managed to lessen considerably the tension between local resident Chinese and Moslems. Though he had been appointed Imperial Commissioner to suppress the

Taiping rebels in 1850, he died before he could take up the task.

The epitome of the 'upright' official, one of Lin's most interesting contributions is his letter to Queen Victoria of August 1839 (apparently never received, certainly never acknowledged), a letter couched in the standard language of the Chinese official edict:

> We find that your country is 20,000 miles from China. Yet there are barbarian ships that strive to come here for trade for the purpose of making a great profit. The wealth of China is used to profit the barbarians...By what right do they in return use a poisonous drug to injure the Chinese people?...Let us ask where is your conscience? I have heard that the smoking of opium is very strictly forbidden by your country; that is because the harm that is caused by opium is clearly understood. Since it is not permitted to do harm to your own country, then even less should you let it be passed on to the harm of other countries—how much less to China! Of all that China exports to foreign countries there is not a single thing which is not beneficial to people: they are of benefit when eaten, or of benefit when used, or of benefit when they are resold: all are beneficial...Take tea and rhubarb for instance: foreign countries cannot get along for a single day without them...Suppose there were people from another country who carried opium for sale to England and seduced your people into buying and smoking it; certainly your honourable ruler would deeply hate it and be bitterly aroused...

Lin also raised the vexed question of legal process in his letter:

> Suppose a man of another country comes to England to trade, he still has to obey the English laws; how much more should he obey in China the laws of the Celestial dynasty? Now we have set up regulations governing the Chinese people. He who sells opium shall receive the death penalty and he who smokes it also the death penalty. Now consider this: if the barbarians do not bring opium then how can the Chinese people resell it, and how can they smoke it? The fact is that the wicked barbarians beguile the Chinese people into a death trap. How then can we grant life only to those barbarians? He who takes the life of even one person still has to atone for it with his own life; yet is the harm done by opium limited to the taking of one life only? Therefore in the new regulations, in regard to those barbarians who bring opium to China, the penalty is fixed at decapitation or strangulation. This is what is called getting rid of a harmful thing on behalf of mankind...

(Based on Fairbank and Teng, 'China's Response to the West.')

Lin Xexu's lack of success is not reflected in the heroic paintings in the Lin Zexu Hall which also displays photographs relating to other famous sons of Fuzhou (such as a photograph of Yan Fu's tomb). Inside the gate a small series of Qing funerary statues of animals (tiger, horse, sheep) and military and civil officials in the local green stone line the path. These are not from Lin's grand tomb.

To return to the hotel area, retrace your steps up Xiamen lu until you reach Jibi lu (running alongside the stream). This can be followed, across Bayiqi bei lu as far as Wuyi lu where the hotels are to the N (turn left across the bridge). The narrow street is lined with houses on the right and on the left, the stream is overhung with trees growing out of cracks in the stone-lined banks with wooden houses perched above.

A pleasant area to wander in is the river bank, across the stone bridge with its central island to the old 'FOREIGN CONCESSION' AREA on the S bank.

One of the most distinguished inhabitants was the poet and writer Paul Claudel, who served as French vice-consul (1896–1904, and subsequently in Tianjin, 1906–07). He noted that, as the area allocated for foreign residence had previously been used for tombs, it was very difficult to keep servants, since they feared the ghosts. Though better known for his imaginative writing, Claudel wrote consular papers with such diverse titles as 'The olive oil business at Fuzhou' (1986) and 'The packaging of biscuits for export' (1901), and became involved with an unsuccessful French entrepreneur, Monsieur Vetch, with whose wife Claudel fell in love.

Claudel supported Vetch in ventures such as the supply of Fuzhou coolies to Madagascar and Réunion (most of them died). In 1905 Claudel broke off relations with Madame Vetch (who was to serve as the model for Ysé in 'Partage de Midi'), reassumed relations with God, and married before taking up his post in Tianjin.

The Foreign Concession Area can be reached by public transport from the hotel area: take a No. 2 bus S down Wuyi lu to its terminal and then continue walking S until you reach the river. The bridge will be to your right. It is divided by a small island, *Zhong zhou*. On the S bank were the major foreign banks, businesses, consulates and residences. If you turn left along Guanjing lu, the Hong Kong and Shanghai Bank was near the corner with Liuyi nan lu.

Continuing up Liuyi nan lu, take the fourth on the right which wiggles until it joins Gongyuan lu where, turning left and continuing S a little way, you will find the *Sports Ground*, built on the old racecourse of the foreigners. Retracing your steps back down Gongyuan lu towards the river, you will pass the old *Trinity College* on your right and on the slopes on your left, above the park, were the Foochow Club, the British and American Consulates with the Japanese and French Consulates higher up the hill behind. The majority of the domestic buildings reflect the colonial style (out of renaissance Italy by way of Portuguese Macau): solid, square, verandahed houses with windows on all four sides so that cooling breezes can be created during the worst of the summer heat when missionaries slept on Chinese mats rather than hot stuffed mattresses and 'the lives of hundreds of natives are sacrificed daily through the ravages of bubonic plague and cholera'.

To return to the hotel area, either take a No. 2 from the same terminus or any of the small 'free enterprise' buses that are going to the railway station (huochezhan), for they also travel right up Wuyi lu.

The **Hualin Temple Hall and the Xichan Temple**.
The *Hualin Temple Hall* is inconveniently situated just inside the Provincial Government compound on Hualin Road, at the NE corner of the Xihu Park.

Founded as a Buddhist temple in 964, the description in the 'Zhong guo ming sheng ci dian', compiled in 1981, states that the great hall, the only surviving building of the temple, preserved the architectural style of the Tang and Song and that it was three bays wide, four bays deep, with brackets and beams in a very early style. In late 1987 it was being rebuilt from the foundations upwards and, unlike some of the restoration work on, for example, Wutai shan or in the mosque at Xi'an, there did not appear to be a single old timber incorporated; this was rebuilding rather than restoration. In Fuzhou and Quanzhou rebuilding seems more common than restoration, which is to be regretted. The hall was officially inaccessible in late 1987 (and the gate to the Provincial Government compound is guarded by soldiers) but rebuilding presumably implies an eventual opening of the 'new' hall on an old site.

The **Xichan** (Western 'Zen') **Temple** is best reached by taxi, although it is on a No. 14 bus route. The intrepid could take a No. 2 S to its terminus near the Min River and, from the same terminus, take a No. 14 to the western suburbs, getting off at the eighth stop. Just S of Fujian University campus, in a district called Yi shan (Yi Mountain), the Xichan Temple is unfortunately also suffering from an excess of complete rebuilding and is now mainly interesting as an example of contemporary architectural taste and the effect of funds supplied by devout Overseas Chinese on ancient buildings.

The temple site was first (in the early 6C) that of a palace of a local ruler, but later abandoned. In 867 Buddhists settled on the site in a settlement first called 'Pure Meditation', later 'Extended Longevity'. In 933 the temple was renamed Changqing (Lengthy Celebration) which remains its official name though it is popularly known as Xichan Temple. It covers a considerable area (100 Chinese mou or over 260 hectares) and comprised over 40 buildings. There is a grove of over 100 old lychee trees beside the temple and the monks are said to hold 'lychee meetings' annually when poems are recited and paintings painted—'Eating Yi mountain lychees' means participating in a cultural event.

The recent history of the temple has been one of close connections with Overseas Chinese. Most of the buildings surviving in 1981 were of the Guangxu period of the Qing (1875–1908) when a monk named Wei miao (Subtle Wonder) went abroad to collect money from Overseas Chinese originally from Fuzhou to pay for restoration. Though it is unlikely that any monks have been abroad in the last five years with begging bowls, the temple had been almost entirely rebuilt by 1987, presumably with much Overseas Chinese help, so that virtually nothing remains even of the late Qing construction.

Gu shan (Drum Mountain), about 9km E of the city centre, on the N bank of the Min, rises nearly 1000m above sea level and is perhaps the most famous site in the Fuzhou area. The mountain is covered with stone-carved inscriptions from various periods. The Buddhist inscriptions are most numerous to the E of the **Yongquan** (Gushing Spring) **Temple** in the Lingquan (Spirit Spring) Cave.

The temple is one of the most famous in Fujian, partly because of its site, half-way up the pine-covered mountain. Founded in 908, the buildings have been constantly repaired, restored and rebuilt, and there is a distressing amount of painted concrete on the mountain. The temple was favoured in the past with imperial patronage and there is a fine collection of early Qing sutras presented by the Kangxi and Qianlong emperors. In front of the first major hall (of three), the *Hall of the Heavenly Kings*, is a pair of Northern Song ceramic pagodas (dated by inscription to 1082) of nine storeys, almost 7m high, with ceramic bells dangling from the eaves and 1078 Buddha figures decorating each. They were apparently made and fired in separate storeys and finally joined together. They originally stood in the Longrui temple in Fuzhou itself and were moved here in 1972.

2500 stone steps above the temple (just over 1km) is the summit of the 'drum-shaped' mountain, a recommended point for viewing the sunrise.

Two tombs outside the city, but still (late 1987) in forbidden military zones, may well be opened to visitors within the next couple of years and, judging by photographs, they are well worth visiting.

Compared with the simple earth mounds of the N, southern tombs are lavish. Built against hillsides, they are often called 'horseshoe-shaped' tombs as the central chamber is surrounded on either side by walls which curve around, but do not completely enclose a flat area in front of the tomb itself.

The *Tomb of Lin Zexu*, the Opium Commissioner, is stepped on four levels (still in the horseshoe) and has a pair of lions before the tomb. It was originally built by Lin for his father and has six chambers (which contain the remains of Lin Zexu and his wife, and his brother and his wife as well as his parents). The tomb is in the northern suburbs of Fuzhou on the slopes of *Jinshi* (Golden Monkey) *Mountain*, opposite Wufeng (Five Phoenix) Mountain near *Maan cun* (Horsewhip Village).

The *Tomb of Yan Fu* (1853–1921) is in the suburbs of Fuzhou at *Yangqi cun*. Yan Fu was born in Houguan, now part of Fuzhou city, and studied at the Fuzhou Shipbuilding School which, together with the Fuzhou Arsenal, was one of the first 'modern' (Western-style) institutions set up in the wake of the Taiping uprising and the Opium War to try to bring China's defences up-to-date.

The Fuzhou arsenal was founded by Monsieur Giquel in 1866, three years after the first modern arsenal was established in Nanjing by Sir Halliday Macartney who was serving under Li Hongzhang against the Taiping rebels and was 'painfully making better shells, powder and guns than the Chinese could produce alone'. In pursuit of modern technology, Yan Fu was sent to England to study (1877–79), first in Portsmouth, subsequently at the Greenwich Naval Academy where, though his class performance was good, he was far more interested in the theoretical basis of Western wealth and power and the British political and legal systems. He used to discuss these late into the night with China's first ambassador to the UK, Guo Songtao, who informed Peking that Yan Fu was better qualified than himself for his job; a message regarded as absurd by his superiors. Yan Fu returned to China to run the Tianjin Marine Academy and from 1911 until 1916 he was head of Peking University.

He is, however, best known for his translations from the English of John Stuart

Mill, Adam Smith's 'The Wealth of Nations', T.H. Huxley's 'Evolution and Ethics', Darwin's 'The Origin of the Species', and Herbert Spencer's 'The Study of Sociology'. He had his own tomb built in 1910, from stone with a stone-carved inscription: 'This is the longevity domain of Mr Yan Jidao of Houguan of the Qing period'.

52   The Wuyi Mountain Natural Reserve

The **Wuyi Mountain Natural Reserve**, covering some 60 square km, is inland to the north of Fujian, near the border with Jiangxi province. There is an airport at *Chishi* with flights from Xiamen and Fuzhou. Chishi is less than 10km S of *Chongan*, the nearest town of any size. Wuyi may also be reached from the Jiangxi side of the border where the nearest railway station is at Shangrao, some 60km to the N. It is just over 50km NNW of Shaowu on the railway line to Fuzhou (and buses run from Shaowu).

Communications and accommodation are likely to be improved within the next few years as Wuyi is now being developed as a major tourist centre.

The major aspects of the local scenery are described as the *Three Times Three Crooked Stream* (Jiuqu xi or Nine-bend Mountain Stream) and the *Six Times Six Surrounding Mountain Peaks* (or the Thirty-six Peaks). The scenery is spectacular, and best viewed first from a bamboo raft (down-river from Xingcun or up-river from Wuyigong). Peak-like mountains rise individually from the riverside, some draped with spectacular waterfalls, peaks and slopes softened by bamboo clumps.

Many of the peaks can be climbed, notably the **Dawang feng** (Great King Peak) at the mouth of the stream, of which it is said: 'If you haven't climbed the Great King Peak, you have not undertaken a trip to the Wuyi Mountains', and from where you can see virtually the whole area. Another is the **Tianyou feng** (Travelling in the Heavens Peak), near the fifth bend in the river, praised by the great Chinese tourist and geographer of the Ming (1586–1641) as 'the first peak in the area, affording a view of the glories of the nine bends in the river'. 840 stone steps from the bottom, you reach the the *Tianyou guan*, a two-storeyed building with upturned eaves, surrounded by 'Red bean trees' (? Ormosia). Higher up, on the top of the peak are smaller buildings including a small temple.

Though it tends to dry up in winter, the *Shuilian* (Water Curtain) *Waterfall* in the NE is the most dramatic in the area, falling in a sheet down a cliff and viewed from a small teahouse set against the rock behind the water curtain. The whole area is covered in the low, rounded bushes of tea plantations and Wuyi tea (a 'black tea', one of the Wulong or Oolong types) is well-known.

A locally produced (and locally translated) description says it has 'a strong taste which is famous worldwide. Since Song dynasty it has been appreciated by culturists. In Yuan dynasty, Wuyi tea was used to entertain the emperor. Wuyi tea is a general term for Wulong tea from Chongan county. The tea leaves turned golden with red edges. After drinking Wulong tea people feel moist in throat and sweet between teeth. It will help people's moral, digestion and avoid sickness of heat and intoxication.'

Your morals improved by tea, turn next across the nearby bridge to the *Eagle Beak Rock*, named for the shape of the summit.

One of the most interesting features of the area is the presence of 'boat-shaped coffins' pushed into depressions in the cliffs high above the river. Remains can be seen best above the fourth bend but they have been found all along the river.

The wooden coffins, nearly 5m long, carved out of a solid log of nanmu cedar (perhaps imported from Yunnan province), with a wooden cover, are placed some 50m above the ground in the cliffs. They contain individual burials, the bodies wrapped in cloth made from hemp, silk and cotton, similar to those of the Warring States period found in river cliffs in north-central Sichuan province. There is an excavated example of a Wuyi boat burial in the Provincial Museum in Fuzhou.

These burials appear to antedate those of Sichuan although there is some controversy over the date. Carbon-14 dating suggests that they may be over 3000 years old although comparison with the later bronze age examples from Sichuan and the possibility that iron tools were used in their construction has led some to suggest they may be slightly later. Owing to their odd position, local people have, in the past, called them 'hanging' or 'suspended' coffins and 'immortal coffins'. How the coffins were raised into their cliff homes remains somewhat mysterious. The great Song dynasty philosopher Zhu Xi thought that the area might have been flooded at the time and the coffins simply rowed into place but archaeologists discount this early hypothesis. The local annals record grave robbers of 500 years ago lowering themselves by winches from the top of the cliffs to get at the coffins. Remains of planking along the sides of the cliffs suggest that there were wooden walkways built along the sides of the cliffs in the past which may have been used to move the coffins.

53   Fuzhou to Quanzhou

The road from Fuzhou to Quanzhou offers two very different types of scenery with very differing domestic architecture. Near Fuzhou the countryside is lush and green, dark mountains tower in the background and water is plentiful. The houses have highly elaborate gable end walls and highly decorated roof ridges. The gable end walls are stepped and curved at once and are vaguely reminiscent of (though unconnected with) tent profiles. Nearer Quanzhou the mountains recede but the earth itself is rocky and far less verdant. Rock seems close to the surface, with little topsoil, and houses and even fences are built of stone slabs. The scarcity of topsoil in the Quanzhou area helps to explain the incredible migration from the area. It seems apparent, even to the naked eye, that the land can only support a limited population which may have driven surplus people to seek their fortunes overseas.

A roadside custom described by a friend is that of hanging dead cats on fences. We have not been able to decide whether this is to encourage mice or to discourage cats.

Quanzhou was the foremost port in China during the Song and Yuan. With its cosmopolitan population, at the time it was almost a later equivalent of the Tang capital Chang'an. It has perhaps the most interesting mosque in China and relics of Nestorian Christianity as well as China's only museum dedicated to the overseas trade that made Quanzhou so important. Today the city, with perhaps a quarter of a million inhabitants, is hardly any bigger than it was in the Qing.

Hotel: the Overseas Chinese Hotel on Baiyuan lu is apparently the only one open to foreigners. It has a huge, multi-storeyed wing (cheaper rooms) and a new lower luxury wing. Though the rooms in the luxury wing are comfortable, service and food in the restaurant are not to be recommended; the restaurants on the top floor of the taller block are preferable.

Transport: it is only possible to get to Quanzhou by road. The long-distance bus station is at the southern end of Hongwu xiang. Soft-seater buses from Fuzhou drop passengers at the E end of Jiuyi lu. Walk W along Jiuyi lu for 10 minutes until you come to a small park on your left and then turn left into Baiyuan lu where you will see the towering hotel. There is a *tourist office* on the ground floor of the taller block and buses booked there (for Xiamen, Shantou or Fuzhou) leave from the hotel forecourt.

Within the town itself, taxis refuse to take tourists to many destinations as the streets are mainly stone-paved lanes, too narrow for cars. If possible, hire a bicycle from the lobby of the taller block of the Overseas Chinese Hotel (and be prepared to spend time in a bicycle-repair shop: the nearest is on Houcheng gujie xiang (turn

to Lingshan

N

Zhongshan beilu

Hong clan hall

Museum of Overseas
Communication History

Kaiyuan temple●   ●
                Xi jie   Dong jie
            Shi Lang's house●
          ●Chentian temple

Xinhua lu

Nanjun xiang

Jiuyi lu
              ● ●Tong fo Hall
Overseas Chinese hotel ●
                Baiyuan lu
        Tu men jie   ●Mosque

Zhongshan nanlu

Dongda lu

          ●Tianfei gong

Jin River

QUANZHOU

right out of the hotel and first right), and there is another just beyond the mosque.

Known as a settlement of some size since the Tang, it was in the Song and Yuan and
early Ming that Quanzhou was at its peak. Like Fuzhou, the port is situated some way
from the coast, up the Jin River which afforded protection from the coastal typhoons.
Quanzhou was known to Arab geographers as Zayton (or Zaiton) from which our
word 'satin' derives. The origin of Zayton is somewhat mysterious: some suggest it
may derive from the citong tree (a prickly tree that grows in the area) or from Ruitong,
an early name for Quanzhou. The account in Marco Polo's 'Description of the World'
gives an idea of its contemporary importance:

> ...the splendid city of Zaiton, at which is the port for all the ships that arrive
> from India laden with costly wares and precious stones of great price and
> big pearls of fine quality. It is also a port for all the merchants of...all the
> surrounding territory, so that the total amount of traffic in gems and other
> merchandise entering and leaving this port is a marvel to behold...And I
> assure you that for one spice ship that goes to Alexandria or elsewhere to
> pick up pepper for export to Christendom, Zaiton is visited by a hundred.
> For you must know that it is one of the two ports in the world with the
> biggest flow of merchandise.

Trade brought foreign residents in the Song and Yuan whose origins are still evident in the large number of Moslem gravestones in Arabic script and the Nestorian Christian crosses carved in stone to be found in the Museum.

Quanzhou remained an important port in the early Ming when its contacts with the Philippines were important though ports further up the coast were used for Zheng He's voyages of exploration. It was threatened in the mid 15C by Japanese pirates who made sea travel dangerous and even occupied Quanzhou as a base for attacks on local shipping.

Quanzhou is still a town of narrow winding streets, paved with the stone that is everywhere (and fences of stone are to be found in the town as well as outside).

Opposite the hotel in the small park is a single hall of the *Tong fo si* (Bronze Buddha Temple); despite its small size, quite an active shrine about which no details appear to be available.

Turning right out of the hotel and taking the second turning on the left (Tumen jie), you can reach the mosque in a few moments (on your left). Called the **Qingzheng** (Pure Truth, another name often given to Islam in China) **Temple**, according to an Arabic inscription in the mosque it was built in 1009 and restored in 1309. According to a Chinese stele it was further repaired or restored in 1350 and 1609. The surviving buildings include the great gate which is strongly reminiscent of Islamic architecture with a pointed arch and scooped-out vaulting. In its solid stone construction and vaulting as well as the form of the entrance, it owes nothing to Chinese architecture. In this it is quite unique, for other mosques in metropolitan China are fundamentally Chinese buildings (with pagoda-shaped minarets) adapted for the purpose. Particularly in Fujian where architecture is highly decorated, the mosque is extremely restful in its restrained elegance.

For the moment, the rest is roofless, a wooden roof presumably having disappeared. Inside there is a small museum display explaining Quanzhou's importance as a centre of foreign trade and the non-Chinese writers who mention it, including an Iranian, Khajha Rashid E-din (1247–1317), a Syrian, Abul Fedha (1273–1331) and the Moroccan traveller Ibn Battuta (1304–97).

During the Song and Yuan there were apparently tens of thousands of foreigners, the majority of whom were Moslems. An honorary title was bestowed on a Moslem merchant who brought vast quantities of frankincense to Quanzhou and another was made Superintendent of Customs; they helped to finance the building of the city wall during the Southern Song. The name of the major (Chinese) Moslem clan in the city was Ding and a notable, Ding Gongchen of the Qing, is mentioned as having written a book, 'Gunnery Through Diagrams'. All the medieval settlers took sinicised surnames: Pu, Ge, Shang, Mi, Zhang, Guo, Yang, Huang, Lin and Li. There were ten communal burial grounds N of the city which contain the remains of thousands of Moslems who died here, the earliest dated tombstone being of someone called Hussain who died in 1171.

There is a famous 'holy tomb' (not yet open to non-believers) said to be that of two sages who visited China in the Tang (618–626), a site of pilgrimage (visited by Zheng He, who erected a stele there in 1417). All these tombs are situated on *Lingshan*, a hill to the E of the town which is probably open to *bona fide* Moslems and may well eventually be opened to all foreign tourists.

Walking back from the mosque, continue past the hotel road going W until you reach the main N–S artery of Quanzhou, Zhongshan lu. Turn right up Zhongshan lu with its arcaded shops, for some 5–10 minutes until you come to the major crossroads with Xi lu and Dong lu. Turn left into Xi lu and soon you will see the tree-filled enclosure of the major temple in Quanzhou, the **Kaiyuan Temple**.

It is said that this was a mulberry grove during the early Tang. When white lotuses miraculously appeared on the mulberry trees (since the lotus grows in beauty out of mud it represents purity in the midst of the mire, to which we should all aspire) the landlord gave the land for a temple which was first called the White Lotus Temple. In 738, during the Kaiyuan reign period, it was renamed. It covers an area of 50 mou.

The *Great Hall* is in the Ming style with a double-eaved roof. Standing 20m high, it is nine bays wide and six bays deep. The central columns are of stone carved in high relief with dragons. The floor is covered in red terracotta tiles. The interior beams are carved with birds. There is a five Buddha group with 18 lohans behind assembled around a Guanyin figure. At the back of the main hall, two columns in the local green stone are carved with acrobats, multi-armed wrestlers, elephants and phoenixes. Topiary is found on either side of the main hall; a hedge pierced with 'windows' like a decorative garden wall and two lions behind. To the W of the Great Hall is a mulberry, said to be the Tang tree that sprouted lotuses. Behind the Great Hall is a second, the *Sweet Dew Vinaya Hall*, originally a Song construction (1018) but much restored since. Set amongst huge poinsettia trees, this has a complex ceiling with a square topping the rectangle and a figure of the Bodhisattva Ksitigarbha (who presides over the world of death) sitting high on a throne. The third hall behind is clearly inhabited by monks and nuns (judging by the washing).

To right and left of the main axis with its huge, wide halls, stand two *pagodas*, 200m apart. That on the E side was built in wood in 865 and then rebuilt in brick in the Southern Song (1225–28) and finally rebuilt in stone as an octagonal, five-storeyed structure imitating wooden construction between 1238 and 1250. It is just over 48m high. Near the base scenes from the life of the historic Buddha are carved. The western pagoda was also first built in wood in 916 and rebuilt in stone between 1228 and 1237. It is 44m high and very similar to the eastern pagoda. Both are considered to be monuments of considerable national importance owing to the skill of the carving and construction.

Also within the temple enclosure, on the E side, are two museum halls. The main one, a new building, houses the *Museum of Overseas Trade*, built round the preserved hull of a Song boat.

During the Song ships left Quanzhou, exporting all the way to the Gulf, along the coast of Africa, to India, SE Asia, Korea and Japan. They carried porcelain, silks, lacquerware, medicines, handicrafts, cloth, wine, silver, gold and iron ore, and imported spices and medicinal herbs, semi-precious stones like amethysts, rhinoceros horn, ivory, glass and precious woods and dyestuffs. Pagodas were used, not as lighthouses but as coastal and up-river landmarks (as can also be seen near Fuzhou). The Song ship was discovered during dredging in 1973. It is 24m long by 9m wide and was originally higher though some parts have been destroyed, probably by shipworm. It dates from about 1274; the hull planking is of cedar and is constructed in a mixture of carvel and clinker with separate bulkheads (an early Chinese safety invention). It had sails of woven bamboo and hempen cords. Near Fuzhou in 1982 a similar boat was found with a sail of woven bamboo. There are various shipboard items displayed, a squashed straw hat, bucket and game of Chinese chess. Illustrations from the Song painting 'Qing ming shan he tu' (Going Upriver on the Eve of the Qingming Festival) by Zhang Zeduan (fl. late 11C–early 12C) depicting river boats at Kaifeng are used to reconstruct the ship. Unfortunately for ceramic historians who have been most interested in the dating of Chinese ceramics from underwater excavations (and in the spread of Chinese export wares), this particular ship was on its way home, carrying tortoise-shell, frankincense, mercury, rare woods and various desiccated herbs, many of which are displayed.

The other part of the museum is to be rehoused (closed to the public 1987, said to reopen in two years) and contains stone carvings which illustrate the cosmopolitanism, particularly of religious belief in the area during the Song. There are a number of Moslem inscriptions including many of the tombstones mentioned in the mosque, all inscribed in arabic script. There are also stone carvings related to Manichean beliefs and Nestorian Christianity. A Manichean temple has been found not far from Quanzhou, a rare survival of the 'religion of light' close to Persian Zoroastrianism and there are a number of Nestorian crosses.

The Nestorian schism is named after Nestorius (died c 451), a Syrian ecclesiastic born in Antioch who was Patriarch of Constantinople (428–431) until he clashed with Cyril, Patriarch of Alexandria. Cyril got the Roman Pope to condemn Nestorius (in his absence) at the Council of Ephesus in 431, and he was subsequently exiled by Emperor Theodosius II. He represented the Antiochene school of historical exegesis (of which the best exponent was said to be Theodore of Mopsuestia, 350–428) which opposed the allegorical and speculative school of Alexandria. Nestorius denied the validity of the title 'Bearer of God' to the Virgin Mary and also held that Jesus possessed a genuine human nature, connected with his equally genuine divine nature by means of free human will. Cyril denied this, saying that it made Jesus into two people. The rather modern-sounding heresy survived in Syria, Persia and China until the Mongol period and the Nestorian crosses with funny little angels are evidence of its survival in Quanzhou.

There are also 14C Franciscan fragments (it is said that there were three Franciscan bishops in Quanzhou following the embassy of John of Montecorvino who died in Peking in 1328). Whilst the new museum is under construction, some fragments are visible to the E side of the main halls (1987).

An excursion to the river past the Tianfei gong and Li He's house.

Turn right out of the hotel and right into the first turning (Houcheng gu jie). Walk W until you reach the main road, Zhongshan lu. Turn left into it and continue S (about 10 minutes) until you come to a wide stretch where Zhongshan lu virtually ends. Turn left into Tudi lu and almost immediately on your left you will find the *Tian fei gong* (Palace of the Heavenly Concubine) built in memory of a filial daughter of the Lin family in 1196, a girl who had become a sort of 'sea spirit' and saviour of sailors. It has the same green stone carved pillars as other Quanzhou temples.

It was said that this was a 'gathering place of boats' (for it is close to the shore) and the temple was restored in 1415 at the express wish of the sea-going eunuch admiral, Zheng He. During the Ming, whenever ships left for the Ryukyu islands or more distant parts, the sailors would all come here first to offer sacrifices for a safe journey. It is now a wireless factory and institute and not open to visitors.

Turning back to the end of Zhongshan lu, immediately opposite it, leading S, is a small road (Street of 10,000 Longevities, Wanshou lu). At No. 159 is the '*House*' of Li He (1527–1602), a philosopher of the late Ming, one of the leaders of the 'feudal enlightenment'. The house is now said to be late Qing in style but Li He lived on the same spot as a child and youth.

If you continue down Wanshou lu as it curves round to the W (notice on the curve, a small Buddhist altar on your right), turn left and then first right (into Zhushu gang), you will eventually reach the river (and note that the last building on the right before the quayside road is a combination temple hall and old persons' club with tea, chess, music and occasional story-tellers). The quayside is no longer the bustling place it must have been some 600 years ago but boats are loaded with gravel and other heavy cargoes for shipment.

The **Chengtian Temple** is NE of the hotel: turn left and walk up Baiyuan lu to the intersection with Dingxi lu (left) and Jiuyi lu (right). Continue N up Nanjun lu (the continuation of Baiyuan lu) and the entrance to the temple (not very obvious while it is under reconstruction) is not far up on your right.

The site was originally a garden belonging to a local official in the Wudai period. Between 957 and 958 a temple was constructed there and named the Nan chan (Southern Meditation) temple though the name was changed to Cheng tian (Carrying Heaven). The large complex (not much smaller than the Kaiyuan Temple enclosure) was frequently restored and rebuilt through the centuries. The most important stone carvings, including the stone-carved 'ten scenes', have been moved to the stone-carving museum housed in the Kaiyuan Temple.

In 1938 the Central Fujian Red Army stayed in the temple enclosure for 'training and consolidation' preparatory to moving N to participate in the Anti-Japanese War. The army was surrounded by KMT troops and five Red Army soldiers were killed in the 'Quanzhou incident'.

As with so many other temples in Fujian, the Chengtian Temple was being rebuilt from the ground up in 1987, including completely new stone foundations (the implication of these is that the temple buildings will not even be the same size as their ancestors for if the same pillar bases are not used proportions are liable to change). The fine trees of the enclosure are being carefully preserved, however, and much of the extremely heavy sawing and timber work was being carried out by slim girls from Huian, less than 25km NE of Quanzhou.

In Huian a slender waist is considered very beautiful and it is emphasised by local costume. Women wear short, bright-blue tops whose hems dip in the centre and rise at the sides. Their wide black trousers are cut tight at the hips and bound tightly with brightly coloured braid and silver belts. As the girls work their slim waists are clearly visible. They also wear light, flowery headscarves tied over a frame which holds them out from the head, and with red braided and embroidered decorations.

From the Chengtian Temple, turn back to Nanjun lu and head back towards the hotel. Take the first turning on the left (Guitan xiang) and then the second on the left, Dongbian xiang. Not far along on your right, you will see a large gateway which is the entrance to the local *Agricultural College*. Inside, not really officially open, is the *Residence of Shi Lang* (1621–96), a general who supported the Qing.

He led attacks on the Ming loyalists on Taiwan in 1683, apparently also to establish a Qing military presence on the island to fend off the Westerners who were beginning to threaten invasion. His house, across the top of the playing field and obvious as an old building amongst the new dormitory blocks, is a charming example of Fujian domestic architecture: built with much of the local red brick streaked with black creating a sort of herringbone effect, and characteristically upswept eaves-lines, and consisting of buildings grouped around a low stone courtyard.

As in the major temples (like the Kaiyuan Temple), the floor of the splendid, open-fronted main hall which stands above the others is of red terracotta tiles though these, according to the current inhabitant, were deliberately smashed by Red Guards during the Cultural Revolution. Picking around outside Shi Lang's house were splendid white chickens with thickly feathered legs and bright blue skin around the eyes, apparently an expensive type of chicken favoured (in the past) by emperors.

There are a number of other sites around Quanzhou which are preserved but not really open to the public although from the outside, at least, they give a good impression of the fine domestic architecture of the town in the past. One is the *Ancestral Temple and Home of the Hong Clan*, like Shi Lang's house, a low red and black striped brick building with elaborately curved and decorated roofs, enclosing a large courtyard. This is not far from Shi Lang's Residence. Turning left into Dongbian xiang, take the first left (Feng chi) which leads to the main road on the E of the town, Dong da lu. Turn left into Dong da lu and cross over the road. Not far N of the junction with Feng chi is a narrow lane on your right where you will find the Hong clan hall on your right (with a block of flats on your left).

A slightly longer trip, N up Zhongshan bei lu which runs through the centre of the town, will take you (c 45 minutes on foot) to *Qingyuan shan*, a hill which overlooks the town and where the only surviving relic of a Taoist temple built here in the Song is a giant statue of the bearded sage Lao zi, one of the founders of Taoism. 7m broad at the base, it is just over 5m tall and was carved from a single rock. It is a rare example of Song stone carving in Fujian.

54   Xiamen

Xiamen, known in the 19C West as *Amoy*, is an island off the Fujian coast which, in 1956, was linked to the mainland by a road and rail causeway 5km long. The town dates from the Ming dynasty and has been of significance in coastal trade (whether piratical, imperialist or local) ever since. Opened to foreign trade by the Treaty of Nanking in 1842, it had a substantial foreign population until the Japanese invasion, mostly concentrated on the small island of Gulangyu.

Railway: the station is in the E of the town; Xiamen is the terminus of the short Longyan–Xiamen line which joins the line to Fuzhou well inland.

Airport: also to the E, the airport is about 30 minutes by taxi from the city centre. There are flights to and from Beijing, Guangzhou, Guilin, Hangzhou, Nanchang, Nanjing, Shanghai and Xi'an (although only those to Beijing, Guangzhou and Shanghai are daily, the rest once or twice a week). There are weekly CAAC flights to and from Manila and daily scheduled flights from Hong Kong.

Boats: there are twice-weekly boats to Shanghai and to Hong Kong, as well as shorter trips to nearby Shantou (whence you can get an overnight boat to Guangzhou).

Buses: there are minibuses and air-conditioned buses to and from Quanzhou and 20-hour buses to Guangzhou (enquire at the hotel desk).

Hotels: the Xiamen binguan is at 16 Huyuan lu, near the Botanic gardens, E of the town, is pleasant and quiet. The cheaper Huaqiao Dasha (Overseas Chinese Hotel) is in the centre of town, just E of the junction of Zhongshan lu and Siming lu. There is also a rambling and sleepy guesthouse with billiard tables and 1920s' dark wood panelling on the W side of Gulangyu Island (25 Huangyan lu, tel. 22052). That is perhaps the most atmospheric but it is hopelessly inconvenient if you have much luggage as it is only accessible by ferry and then by foot (and it is on the far side of the island from the ferry pier). The best hotel to stay in is the Lujiang binguan, on the quay opposite the ferry pier (at the far W end of Zhongshan lu). The noise and bustle of the quay is silenced at night, the hotel is comfortable (medium price-range) and immensely popular with locals, especially louche taxi-drivers, their pockets bulging with money.

The city was founded during the Ming at the end of the 14C, and at the end of the Ming it was a stronghold of Zheng Chenggong (1624–62) who is often referred to as Koxinga. This is a Dutch version of Guo xing ye (Lord of the Imperial Surname), a title granted to Zheng by one of the surviving members of the Ming royal family which he supported loyally after the Manchu invasion of 1644 which proclaimed the Qing dynasty. Zheng and his family were fierce supporters of the Ming, and he led an attack (which failed) on Nanjing in 1659, retreating in 1661 to the island of Taiwan which is off the coast near Xiamen. There he finally forced the Dutch (who had settled on Taiwan in 1624) to withdraw to Batavia. The Qing government, in an effort to cut him off, ordered all the coastal inhabitants of Fujian and much of Guangdong province to withdraw at least 16km inland, but they only managed to gain control of Taiwan after Zheng committed suicide in 1662.

Xiamen's troubles were not simply due to the Ming loyalist for in the middle of the 16C the area was occupied by Japanese pirates who ravaged the eastern seas as far as the Philippines and Borneo. When western traders arrived after 1842, they settled in the main on the tiny island of Gulangyu, a few minutes by boat from Xiamen proper. Gulangyu became the 'international concession' though there was also a British concession in the town of Xiamen, just N of the Lujiang Hotel, along the quayside where the Customs Building and several major banks were situated. During the Taiping rebellion (1850–64) Xiamen was occupied by the rebels in 1853 and held for a year, despite attacks by government troops and a naval battle offshore. In 1864, nearly 10 years after they had been driven out, the Taipings reappeared and were soon joined by the American General Burgevine who had previously commanded the joint foreign-imperial 'Ever-victorious army', subsequently led by General Gordon. Burgevine apparently wished to go over to the rebels and made his way to Xiamen, then to Taiwan, then back to the mainland. At some point on his way N he appears to have been betrayed by his black servant and subsequently drowned.

As in so many other cities in Fujian, a vast number of people left to work in plantations in SE Asia or tin-mines or on the American railways, and Xiamen, in particular, has been a favourite place to return to and is full of rather grand mansions built by Overseas Chinese for their retirement. The most notable local is Tan Kah-kee (1874–1961; Chen Jiageng in putonghua; the Amoy dialect version of his name revealing how wildly different Amoy dialect is from the Northern standard), whose home town of Jimei, some 10km E of Xiamen, near the new causeway, is full of grand buildings in a mixture of Western and Chinese architectural styles built to house the educational institutes that he endowed.

In recent years the industrial area to the E of Xiamen has been declared a 'special economic zone', open to foreign investment to attract more patriotic Overseas Chinese funds and the grand exhibition halls and tall office buildings can be seen on the way to the airport.

With their usual care for health, the foreign inhabitants of **Gulangyu** (Drum Wave Island), installed sewerage works and, as a Japanese guide of the 1920s noted, 'The authorities carefully inspect all foodstuffs for sale, including milk. In the native town, however, conditions are very differ-ent—dirty water lies about, and rubbish, piled up in the streets, gives out most offensive odours; cholera and plague often break out.' The island officially became an international concession in 1903 and 'buildings in foreign style, consulates of various nations, schools, churches, a hotel, hospitals and residences are situated amid luxuriant groves and strangely-shaped rocks'.

Reached by a ferry (which takes about 10 minutes and runs from 5 am to midnight, for which a single fare is paid for a two-way journey), the island is entirely traffic-free and also bicycle-free so it is extremely pleas-ant to wander in. The residences are large and spacious for in 1912 there were only 250 foreign residents. The major business houses and banks were located on the Amoy side of the island and, running S from the ferry jetty, were the British Consulate, German Consulate, King George Hotel and the Amoy Telephone Company.

Follow Zhangzhou lu to the S along the waterfront. The road then turns N and eventually arrives at the *Sports Ground*. Immediately behind the Sports Ground, on Huangyan lu, is the *Gulangyu Hotel*, and if you con-tinue on Huangyan lu past the hotel you reach the 1962 building (clearly architecturally inspired by some of the grander surrounding mansions) which houses the *Zheng Chenggong Memorial Museum*. The museum offers a marvellous view of surrounding houses, many of which closely resemble those found in Macau (where they are described as typical old Portuguese houses)—square, brick buildings with verandahs all round and large rooms with windows on either side, presumably to allow a through draught in the hot, humid summers. That immediately below the museum closely resembles the Amoy Club which was situated nearby.

Zheng Chenggong was born of a Chinese father and a Japanese mother in Japan. At the age of seven he returned to China with his parents. He early gained favour with the last of the Mings and, though his father openly accepted the new Qing regime, he initiated a long campaign along the Fujian coast from his base on Gulangyu. He was said to have had a fleet of 8000 war junks, 240,000 fighting men, 8000 Ironsides and 'with all the pirates that infested the coast of Southern China under his command he claimed to have a combined force of 800,000 men.' His personal bodyguards were selected by a test of strength: any who could lift a stone lion weighing 270kg (600lb) were selected for his 'Tiger Guards'. Another name for them was the 'Ironsides' and they wore iron masks and protective iron aprons, and carried red and green striped bows and arrows, and long-handled swords for killing horses.

In 1661 he drove the Dutch from Taiwan and from this new base attempted to induce the Spanish in Manila to accept his suzerainty. He had endless trouble with his family: his father went over to the Qing early on but was subject to endless pres-sure to bring his son to his senses (and was eventually executed by the Qing); in 1650, he killed his cousin and took over his troops and in 1651 he killed his uncle whom he had left in charge of Xiamen but who had been overcome by the Qing troops. His death in 1662 on Taiwan was believed to be suicide when enraged by a series of set-backs: the execution of his father and brothers in 1661 by the Qing court, the failure of his mission to Manila and a massacre of the Chinese there, and the refusal of his own generals to execute his son 'who had illegally consorted with a nurse'.

The memorial museum contains paintings and impressions of scenes from his life and a number of gunpowder bottles and double-dragon can-non weighing over 82kg as well as items depicting the ancient history of Taiwan.

Behind the garden and the museum is the main *bathing beach*, a clean, sandy shore with a view of further off-shore islands, most obviously Jin-men (Quemoy) which is still occupied by Nationalist forces. The more expensive ferry to Gulangyu (which costs 1 yuan instead of a few cents) first takes visitors on a circuit of Gulangyu and provides binoculars for hire (as well as cups of coffee) so that the Nationalist-occupied islands (between Gulangyu and Taiwan) can be observed at leisure. Around the corner from the beach, near the southern tip of the island are a small pen-cai (bonsai) garden and a small enclosure with a pool and a few pavilions, the *Shuzhuang Garden* built by a rich merchant from Taiwan, Lin Erjia, in 1913. He had fled Taiwan when it was occupied by the Japanese (1895).

Walk N from the museum along Yongchun lu, take the second on the left and just beside the next crossroads at 71 Anhai lu is the *Sanyi Protestant Church*, a large, plain hall, probably that of the London Missionary Society (said to seat 1000 in 1912 although the current guide suggested several hundreds). This was built in 1904 to replace several smaller chapels on the mainland.

If you continue on down Anhai lu (towards the Xiamen side of the island), turn right into Gushan lu and then take the first turning on the left from where you can see the *Xiamen Museum* (in the Bagua lou) on top of a hill, a substantial domed building near the site of the old Anglo-Chinese college which was a square, arcaded building. The museum, said to be a general historical museum serving the area, has been closed for renovation.

Turn back into the centre of the town (take Guxin lu and its continuation, Longtou lu) and, as in all other parts of Gulangyu, there are fine residences amongst the banyans, poinsettia, bougainvillea and bauhinia. Fine stucco doorways have blank ovals where enamelled coats of arms have been removed. *27 Guxin lu* has a gate with Corinthian columns which are echoed in the massive two-storey porch but modernism is more evident at 18 Guxin lu where the gateway, built in 1935, recalls militaristic modernism in contemporary Germany. *Nos 261* and 227 Longtou lu provide the same contrasts between old-style curlicues and eagle-topped modernism whilst *151 Longtou lu* is in the Chinese baroque style with lions, grapes, swathes and swags in stucco and curly balconies. Faded lettering announces the Hok Heng Hoat Chinese and Foreign restaurant, tea and bathrooms (and it is still a restaurant).

Following Longtou lu round, near the junction with Huangyan lu is the *Roman Catholic Church*, said to be about 100 years old and built in the charming, whitewashed wedding-cake style often found in Chinese churches.

The roads on Gulangyu wind impossibly so that it is difficult to follow street names and house numbers but the traffic-free whole (with a single, immobilised pre-war American car—a Plymouth—found round one corner) is a delightful place to simply wander in and the fresh prawns and other seafood served in tiny roadside cafés are also highly recommended.

Returning to Xiamen, in the E of the city, at the top of Huyuan lu, visible from the Xiamen binguan, is a very fine **Botanic Garden** which also contains (just on the far side of the lake) the site where Zheng Chenggong killed his cousin. A huge grey stone (apparently pocked with machine-gun bullets) marks the spot. The garden is rich in southern Chinese and SE Asian plants and trees with a number of the eucalypt variants (all natives of Australasia) that are planted quite widely in Fujian, including ghostly white-barked examples planted in a slightly sinister clump and others with bark like elephant skin. There is a huge bamboo plantation (with over 100 varieties), a grove of palms (*Arenga pinata*) at the head of the lake, and plenty of Bauhinia (native to China) with its sweet-scented flowers and half-split leaves), *Delonix* (native to SE Asia but seen widely in Fujian), *Malvaviscus pendulifloris*, *Ficus microcarpa* with its thread-like roots trailing from branches (also seen in the Hong Kong Botanic Gardens) and *Thunbergias*. Just inside the gate, on the right, is a grassy slope with small trees set in paved plots, including a small cassia and a *Cinnanmomum gladuliferum* (a native of Yunnan) planted by Deng Xiaoping in 1982. In late winter paper narcissus bulbs are on sale at the gate, very popular native bulbs which are grown in beautiful bowls filled with colourful pebbles and water, to flower and scent rooms in winter.

Within easy reach of the Botanic Garden and the Xiamen binguan is the

Wuli cannon
Lujiang lu
Xiahe lu
Datong
Lujiang Ho
Zhongshal
Sanming lu
Bishan lu
Neicuao lu
Fuzhou lu
Longtou lu
Lujiao lu
Zhonghua lu
Gusheng lu ·Koxinga Museum●
Gulangyu Hotel●
Zhangzhou lu
Tianwei lu
Gulangyu Island
South China Sea
XIAMEN

White Tiger Cave, said to have been a place where Zhu Xi (1130–1200), a native of Fujian, expounded on the Confucian classics.

Zhu Xi was the foremost exponent of Neo-Confucianism, a Song re-examination and re-interpretation of the Confucian Classics, a sort of revival of State orthodoxy through Confucianism. His commentaries became the standard for exams until this century.

The White Tiger Cave was called a 'university' but it is now unfortunately in the middle of a military camp and is thus described unseen. To reach it, take the road opposite the entrance to the Xiamen Binguan, Bai lu lu, and follow it upwards until you reach a gateway with army buildings beyond (identifiable from the khaki washing on the balconies). Ahead, there is a basketball pitch, occasionally used for high-speed, baked earth croquet by old ladies. Beyond, in the wooded hill, is the White Tiger Cave.

It is easy to retrace your steps, or return to the Botanic Garden.—In the latter case, instead of taking the right fork where Bai lu lu turns towards the main road, take the left fork (Huyuan lu) which leads to the entrance to the Botanic Garden. Immediately beside the entrance to the Botanic Garden (N) is the tall column of the memorial to the revolutionary martyrs, on a stepped approach.

The Overseas Chinese Museum, Nan putuo Temple and Xiamen University are easily reached by bus from the city centre.

From the Ferry Pier, take a No. 2 bus (the Ferry is the terminus) and get off at the fourth stop, the *Huaqiao* or *Overseas Chinese Museum* (closed Mondays). Built with Overseas Chinese money, it contains three floors of exhibits: the first (or ground floor) exhibit is devoted to the history of the Overseas Chinese, with many reproductions of newspaper photographs and artists' impressions; the second (Western first) floor has the most extraordinary collection of (mostly late) Chinese bronzes and a less extraordinary collection of ceramics; the third floor has an exhibition of paintings.

The exhibit on the Overseas Chinese runs through the early Chinese settlements in Japanese cities (for trade) and the trade routes to Europe and SE Asia and beyond. Oil paintings depict coolie labourers on ships; opium dens and slave-drivers beating slaves with whips on plantations. Perhaps owing to the concentration on the Overseas Chinese in SE Asia, less attention is paid to the coolies sent to Europe to work behind the lines in the First World War, many of whose graves can still be seen in War Cemeteries in Northern France. There are sections depicting with illustrations the transmission of Chinese words into Indonesian and other SE Asian languages, and items used by the Overseas Chinese: puppets, shadow puppets, straw shoes, pewter tea-cups and other handicrafts. Famous Overseas Chinese including the first Chinese astronaut are illustrated from newspaper articles and there is a bust of Mr Tan Kah-kee, benefactor of Xiamen University and Jimei township.

The bronzes are the most interesting group on the next floor, though some of the altar groups in ceramic are also unusual in a museum. The bronzes are interesting in that they must have come from private collections (presumably of Overseas Chinese) and they cover an unusually broad time-span, from the Shang, over 3000 years ago, to the Republican period (1911). It is the latter period that is of especial interest as it is relatively unknown in the West—the substantial deer settling itself (Song) and the vast Song vessels, the enormous (1m) Ming vessels covered with rings, the inlaid and gilt Republican bronzes, all these are rare in the West and little-studied as yet.

Take the No. 2 (or a No. 1) bus, in the same direction (S, away from the city centre) for one stop and you reach the **Nanputuo Temple**. Set against a mountain, the surroundings are pretty. To the eastern side of the temple there are rocks carved with calligraphic inscriptions (the largest reading 'yuan tong' or perfect communication), concrete lions and the tombs of two eminent monks, both erected in 1982, in the characteristic stupa style, that on the left containing the remains of a late Qing monk from Anhui and that on the right the remains of a monk from the Ming dynasty.

The temple itself, as with virtually all in Fujian, has been extensively rebuilt: two highly decorated bell towers stand in the first courtyard and in front of the Three-Buddha Hall is an iron incense burner dated 1982, made in the Suzhou Min feng iron works and donated by pious Buddhists whose names are cast on the vessel. Inside the hall, which is filled with sculpture including 18 rather horrible lohans, there are many items of dark wood furniture and an important-looking grandfather clock. There is a small octagonal hall with a thousand-armed Guanyin.

Behind are buildings including a two-storey, triple-roofed Fa dian (Hall of the Law) which was under restoration in late 1987.

The bus station is to the E of the temple and just beyond is the entrance to *Xiamen University* (founded by Tan Kah-kee over 70 years ago). Turning right inside the entrance, heading towards the sea, there is a small exhibition commemorating the short stay of Lu Xun (1881–1936) the most prominent writer of the early 20C. He taught in the university from 1926–27, before going on to Zhongshan University in Guangzhou.

Set up in the building he lived in at the time, the first two rooms contain material including photographs relating to Lu Xun's life, among them pictures of him and colleagues from the University relaxing in the hills behind the Nanputuo temple. The third room is arranged ostensibly as it was when he lived and taught in the University. This contains a mosquito-netted bed, tables, chairs and desk with an Yixing (dark red terracotta ware) teapot and four cups, and a number of cases and wicker baskets. There are also some faded cloth banners carried at his funeral.

On the shore road, near the SE corner of the University, is the *Huli Cannon*, set there in 1891. Of German manufacture, nearly 14m long and weighing nearly 49,000kg, it is set up in a favourite spot for hiring binoculars to peer at the off-shore islands.

To return to the centre of town, take a No. 1 or 2 bus from the bus station at the gate. Where the road passes over a railway line there is an interesting old *hall* just where the road crosses a railway line (beside a bus stop). Now a shoe factory, it retains remnants of finely carved timbers and swooping roof.

55 Guilin

Guilin or **Cassia Forest**, in Guangxi province, is surrounded by the best-known scenery in China, the narrow mountains that rise, one by one, from the flat banks of the *Li jiang (Li River)*. The scenery remains magnificent and the trip along the Li jiang to Yangshuo does offer the most wonderful peaceful views of the river—'a belt of fine green silk'—and the mountains—'like kingfisher jade hairpins', as the poet and essayist Han Yu (768–824) described them—but it is generally agreed that Guilin has been pretty well ruined by tourism. Hordes of hawkers and touts surround visitors, and 'planes and buses are overloaded so that frequent delays ensue; prepared for the worst, it is possible that the scenery can still be enjoyed.

Airport: the airport is 14km S of the city of Guilin. There are 50 flights a week from Guangzhou alone and daily flights from Peking, Chengdu, Shanghai and Chengdu, with less frequent flights from Chongqing, Guiyang, Hangzhou, Kunming, Lanzhou, Nanjing, Nanning, Xiamen and Xi'an, not to mention the innumerable flights from Hong Kong. These may give you some idea of the volume of tourist trade.

Railway: the station is in the N of the city. Guilin is on the line that runs from SE China (Shanghai, Hangzhou) to the SW (Nanning, Kunming).

Boat: it is possible to take a boat from Guangzhou to Wuzhou, then a bus to Yangshuo which is just S of Guilin on the Li River. From Yangshuo (which individual travellers recommend as less rapacious and overrun than Guilin), you could take the Li jiang boat trip to Guilin (or a bus, c 1½ hours).

Hotels: the Sheraton and Guishan hotels are well-situated and offer good service; others of note include the Rongchang Hotel (near Seven Star Hill/Qixing shan) as well as several cheaper hotels on Zhongshan lu in the centre of town (Bangui fandian, Yinshan fandian, Nanxi fandian and Guilin Hotel).

Guilin (this name dates back only to the Ming for before that it was called Shian and then Guizhou), was established as a commandery under the first emperor of the Qin when he made his southern expedition to Guangzhou in 214 BC. At the same time the Lingqu canal was begun, linking the river networks of the Pearl and the Yangtse and Guilin's importance as a regional trading centre grew. From the Ming until 1914 it was the capital of Guangxi province (in 1914 Nanning replaced it). In the early Ming it was made the capital of a principality ruled by Zhu Shouqian, a nephew of the founding emperor of the Ming, who established himself there in 1369, building a residence which he had walled in 1393.

The walled enclosure was converted into the provincial examination hall during the Qing and now encloses the provincial teacher training college. At the end of the Ming, Zhu Youlang, who had been holding Guangzhou against the Qing, was forced to leave Guangzhou and he set up his capital in Guilin in 1647–60, before the Qing troops drove him onwards to Yunnan.

During the Sino-Japanese war the population of Guilin was enormously increased by refugees from the N (who also moved to Kunming in large numbers where one of

GUILIN

the major university centres was temporarily established) and the city was bombarded by the Japanese; this destruction is part of the reason for the enormous amount of
new building since 1949.

Guilin's famous scenery, the 'best under heaven', was well-known from the Tang
as Han Yu's poem illustrates. The peaks are part of the karst topography of much of
Guangxi (and the Stone Forest in neighbouring Yunnan), limestone formations of
peaks and pot-holes, underground waterways and caverns filled with stalactites and
stalagmites. The formation dates from about 200 million years BC when the land
began to push up from under the sea that had previously covered it and the gradual
erosion of the limestone began, leaving the needle-like points of harder rock sticking
up out of the plain. Numbers of painters and poets came to the city and some of them
have left inscriptions carved onto the rock-faces of the famous mountains; the long-
held Chinese view that nature is greatly improved if you carve an inscription on it is
evident in the more than the 'more than 2000 stone-carved inscriptions' mentioned in
the 'Zhongguo mingsheng cidian'.

The highlight of a stay in Guilin is a trip on the Li River. The trip takes
about 6 hours to cover the 85km stretch between Guilin and Yangshuo.
Some 60 boats depart at about 8 am from the boat dock on Binjiang lu,
just S of *Jiefang qiao* (Liberation Bridge). Most tourist groups then return
by bus and, to avoid overcrowding, some are first taken to Yangshuo and
make the trip upriver instead. The scenery along the river is at its most

spectacular with the breadloaf peaks rising from the flat green paddy-fields: fishermen, some with cormorants, fishing from flat boats of bamboo stems lashed together, water buffaloes and workers in the paddy fields are amongst the other rural sights.

In and near Guilin are many groups of mountains that can be visited. In the centre of the town is the *Duxiu feng* (Peak of Solitary Splendour, also known as the Pillar under the Southern Sky). The Duxiu feng is just E of the northern part of Zhongshan lu, inside the old Ming palace. It was described by the poet Yan Yanzhi of the Song dynasty of the Nan bei chao (420–479) as 'unrivalled in its solitary beauty; towering, it floats in the middle of the town'. It can be climbed (306 steps) and it has many cliffs and caves, bridges, small pavilions and stone inscriptions, including that written by Huang Guocai of the Qing—'a pillar of the southern sky'—and Zheng Shuji of the Tang's 'record of the reopening of the stone chamber of solitary splendour'.

The *Ming Palace* (Wang cheng or 'King's Palace') is in the very centre of town, with Zhongshan lu running along its W side. It was constructed on the site of a Song temple, the Tieniu si or Temple of the Iron Cow. Nothing now remains of the buildings constructed by the 'King' of Guilin, nephew of the first Ming emperor in 1369, but one of the gates and some of the floors of the halls.

Just NE of the palace is *Fubo shan* (Sleeping Wave Hill), beside the river with a small garden planted with bamboos, palms and flowers on its S side. The Song dynasty pavilions built on its S side were burnt down and all constructions are now post-1949. On the eastern side, at the base, is the famous **Huanzhu dong** (Cave of the Returned Pearl) which can be entered by boat from the Li River. It has a 3m stalactite inside, said to resemble something hacked away by a sword (the Han-dynasty general Fu Bo is supposed to have sharpened his on it), also described as 'hanging in the void, looking like a floating pillar'. The cave is supposed to have been the home of a dragon which, like those in paintings and on ceramics, used to play with a pearl. The pearl was once stolen by a fisherman but he returned it almost at once.

On the *Thousand-Buddha Cliff* nearby are more than 200 Buddha figures carved in the Tang (in 853). Inside the cave are some of the best of the numerous stone carvings in Guilin, the earliest dating from 863 with colophons by local officials; they include a self-portrait by the famous Song painter Mi Fei.

Further N, at 98 Zhongshan lu is the reconstructed *Headquarters of the Eighth Route Army* (part of the Red Army which was commanded by Zhu De and Peng Dehuai). The brick and timber, two-storey building was destroyed in 1944 and has been reconstructed as a museum. It served as the office in Guilin from 1938 and was three times visited by Zhou Enlai before operations were moved back to Yan'an in 1941. It is worth visiting for its urban architecture (despite being a reconstruction).

Just N is **Diecai shan** (Pleated-silk Mountain) which has numerous small peaks. All the present pavilions and walkways are post-1949 constructions, replacing earlier ones, and the cassia planting is also post-1949 though the old path up the peak (on the S) still remains. The *Feng dong* (Wind Cave) is open at both ends and cool and breezy throughout the year. The view from the top, celebrated since the Five Dynasties (10C AD) when the King of Chu built a pavilion, is spectacular, 'the place where mountains and water meet'.

There are many stone carvings on the mountain, of which the most notable are the Record of the Pleated-Silk Mountain and Record of the Four-View Mountain by Yuan Hui of the Tang, the poems 'Visiting the Pleated-Silk Mountain' by Zhu Xiyan of the Song, 'Pleated-Silk Mountain' by Liu Tai of the Ming, 'Enjoying the Wind Cave' and 'Climbing Up to Watch the Magical Birds Amongst the Gathered Peaks by the Light of the Bright Moon' by Yuan Mei of the Qing (a well-known exquisite, poet, essayist and gourmet whose life has been written up in English by Arthur Waley). There are also stone-carved pictures such as Li Bingshou's orchids and bamboo and Tang and Song Buddhist figures carved into cliffs.

Just NE of the Pleated-Silk Mountain, by the river, is the *Mulong dong ta* (Pagoda of the Wooden Dragon Cave), a tripartite pagoda (with separate base, body and top) made of stone. The base (a 'sumeru base') is carved with lotuses and supports a rounded, bottle-shaped body with Buddha figures in niches to E and W, Bodhisattvas N and S, and the top of the pagoda has a 'gourd-shaped' finial. It is said to be Tang in date and the date of 1885 carved on the S side relates to waterworks on the river, rather than to the pagoda.

Almost due W of the pagoda, on Zhongshan bei lu, is *Baoji shan* (Precious-Pile Mountain); it is said that during the Northern Song the city wall stretched between this and the Pleated-Silk Mountain. S of the mountain is the *Kongming tai* (Platform of Emptiness and Brightness) and on the N side of the mountain, behind the *Tiefo si* (Temple of the Iron Buddha) is the *Huajing dong* (Cave of the Beautiful View) which leads, twisting and turning, through to the platform on the other side. Stone carvings include some by Li Shizhong, Lu Yuanzhong and Zhang Ziming of the Song. In 1979 two fossilised human teeth, together with stone tools and animal fossils, were found in the mountain.

Further N, on the banks of the Li, just past a small island, is *Yu shan* (Yu Mountain, also known as Shun shan), on the E side of Beiji lu. This is a 'solitary' mountain and the Tang and Song buildings on it were destroyed by Japanese bombardment.

According to legend, the good emperor Shun, chosen by Yao as his successor in the 2nd millennium BC, canonised as one of the 24 examples of filial piety, possessor of double pupils in both eyes, often visited this mountain on his travels in the south and because he was of the Yu clan (his full name being Yu Shun), the mountain was named after him and a temple was constructed here in his honour.

There is a stele—'Shun miao bei' or 'Stele of Shun's Temple'—the three simple characters apparently the joint work of three notables of the Tang dynasty: Han Yunliu selected the characters, Han Xiushi wrote them and Li Yangbing wrote the seal.

On the W is the *Shaoyin dong* (Cave of the Beautiful Sound), so-called because the wind in the trees and the noise of the nearby water is supposed to sound like a performance of music for the Emperor Shun. Inside the cave are the three characters Shaoyin dong written by a Song calligrapher, the Record of the Shaoyin Cave by Zhang Shi, and orchid and bamboo paintings by Li Bingshou (other examples can be seen on the Pleated-Silk Mountain).

In the S of the town are the small lakes (*Rong hu* or Banyan Lake and *Shan hu* or Fir Lake) which Zhongshan lu crosses on the Green Belt Bridge; surrounded by bamboos, willows, kumquat and peach trees, once part of the city moat, they are now part of a small park.

Further S is a bridge which crosses the Taohua jiang (Peach River) which comes in from the W to join the Li in the S of the town; just SW of that is the **Sheli ta** (Relic Pagoda). The 'relic' was a stone box, encased in the brick pagoda which is part of the **Wanshou si** (Ten-thousand-year Temple), the earliest Buddhist foundation in Guilin though the present temple buildings are Ming, Qing and 'later'.

The temple existed in the Sui when it was called the 'Greening Temple' (Luhua si); its subsequent names were Flourishing Goodness, Longevity and Eternal Longevity. The present name dates from the Ming. The pagoda was first built in the Tang, when it was said to be a seven-storey brick construction. This gradually decayed and was rebuilt in its present form in 1385. It is a lamaist stupa (bottle-shaped) pagoda set on a high square base or platform. The base has four doors and over the main entrance are the four characters 'she li bao ta' (precious relic pagoda). Above, the base of the pagoda itself is octagonal with Buddha figures in the eight openings, and the top part of pagoda is in the characteristic bottle-shaped form.

On the E side of the road, right against the Li River (where the Taohua joins it) is another single mountain peak, the **Xiangbi shan** (Elephant's Trunk Mountain), said to look like an elephant bending to drink the river water through its trunk. The peak can be climbed by a path which starts on the W side and leads up to the flat summit. There is a Ming pagoda on the N side, the *Puxian ta* (the Samantabhadra Pagoda; I don't know if the name is coincidental or whether it refers to the fact that the Bodhisattva Samantabhadra is usually depicted on the back of a white elephant) which is said to look like a precious flask from a distance. The *Moon and Water Cave*, at the base of the mountain on the riverside, can be entered by (small) boat.

The Song poet Jibei chushi is supposed to have written his 'In Praise of Moonlit Nights' about the cave and mountain: 'The bright moon is far below the water's surface; the bright moon floats on the water's surface. The water flows where the moon cannot go; when the moon goes, the water cannot flow.'

The cave is full of stone-carved inscriptions including the 'Added preface to the poem on the pavilion facing the sun' by the Song poet Zhang Xiaoxiang, Fan Chengda's 'On the inscriptions in moon and water cave' and the Tang poet Lu You's 'Poetic notes'.

Much further S, best reached by bicycle or taxi, is the **Nanxi shan**. Nanxi shan can be reached by continuing S along Zhongshan nan lu until you reach the bridge over the Nan xi (Southern Stream), another tributary of the Li River; on your left, on the S bank of the Nan xi, is the Nanxi peak. This is actually a double-peaked mountain, whose stone is a greyish colour said to shine after rain. The caves on the mountain are considered to have particularly fine baroque stalactites and stalagmites and the multiple caves have almost 200 stone-carved inscriptions in their praise.

Out to the W of the town are the Hudi shan (Reed Flute Mountain), Xi shan (West Mountain) and Yin shan. The last two are not far apart, reached by following Lujun lu W from the centre of town. Just after crossing the railway, **Yin shan** can be seen on your right. Once entirely surrounded by water (now by fields), this mountain (whose name is the yin of yin and yang, meaning dark, shady, the female principle) is particularly famous for its many caves and grottoes, many water-filled, but it also includes a stone-carved drawing of the Bodhisattva Guanyin by the famous Tang painter Wu Daozi and, most notably, carvings of the 16 worthies originally made by a monk of the Five Dynasties (10C), Shi Xiu, recut during the Qianlong period by Li Yimin. Shi Xiu was noted for his Buddhist figure depiction and the carving, in the Huagai an (Parasol Hut), is very highly prized.

Beyond, further W, is **Xi shan** (Western Hills), a collection of peaks where a number of temples were built during the Tang and Song—they have since disappeared. The hills, however, are scattered with niches containing Buddhist figures, over 200 in all, most dating from the Tang. In their lightness and vivacity they are considered by some to be amongst the best Tang carvings in China and are of some importance in the study of Buddhist iconography in south China (for most of the major sites are northern). They range in height from 2m to 20cm.

Following the road round (it turns N just beyond the Xi shan), you come to a bridge on your left (W) which crosses the Taohua River. Turn left (W) here and the road takes you to *Hudi yan* (Reed Flute Cliff) on *Guangming shan* (Brightness Hill). The cliff takes its name from the reeds growing nearby which are used in the making of musical instruments. The vast cave in the cliff can be visited on a guided tour which takes you past peculiar limestone formations, all with names. The lighting in the cave has been described in the 'Rough Guide to China' as making it look 'like Indiana Jones' Temple of Doom'.

Concentrated in the E of Guilin, across the Li River are a number of mountain peaks in a large park, perhaps the best site to visit if your walking time is limited. Take Jiefang dong lu heading E across the Li River. The first, modern bridge is Jiefang qiao but the second, roofed bridge (which crosses the Xiao dong jiang (Little Eastern River) is the *Hua qiao* or Flowery Bridge, first built in the Song dynasty. It was washed away by floods during the Mongol Yuan dynasty and a wooden bridge built on the site in 1456. In 1540 a stone bridge with four arches replaced the wooden one and the bridge was extended (with seven extra arches). It is now 125.2m long and 7.2m broad. The extra seven 'dry' arches are useful at times of flood when they help to disperse water that might otherwise affect the main structure.

Immediately ahead is the great **Putuo shan** (named like the Buddhist holy mountain off the coast S of Shanghai for the abode of the Bodhisattva Guanyin), part of the **Qixing Park** (Seven-Star Park) where the rocks are said to be laid out in the form of the seven-star or Great Bear constellation. This also has a cave on its W slope called the *Yuan feng dong* (First Windy Cave), open at both ends, described in a poem by the Ming poet Yu Anqi: 'The deep cave is truly dark and shady, Cool winds blow unceasingly. Water falls endlessly on the stone and in the hot months, breath turns to snow.' In 1974 a pavilion was built beside the cave to house the three characters in calligraphy by Yan Zhenqing of the Tang, which read 'Xiao yao lou' (Carefree Tower), the 'Account of the tower south of the river' by Li Yanbi of the Song and the 'Account of the repair of the stele' by Bao Gu of the Ming, amongst others.

The inscription on the cliff—'Bixu yan'—(Cliff of the Azure Void) was written by a Ming Taoist Pan Changjing (Cliff of the Azure Void was the old name for the Seven-Star Cliff). The Putuo 'stone forest' of strangely-shaped rocks lies below where a Tang building was supposed to have stood, named 'View of the Celebration of the Forest' (Qinglin guan), which three characters are supposed to have been written in the hand of the founding emperor of the Tang, Li Shimin.

The *Seven-Star Cliff* is to the left of the Putuo Hill and contains caves of some size, the largest being 43m wide and 27m high. This large cave used to contain an underground river and is full of strange rock formations including the elephant with the rolled trunk, the lion playing with a ball, the gate of heaven and the magpie bridge (a reference to a famous folk story about lovers' separation, the herd boy and the spinning girl. Fated to be separated on earth, they flew to heaven where they became the stars Altair and Vega, separated by the Milky Way except for one day a year when a flock of magpies formed a bridge across the Milky Way). The cave has been a tourist site since the Sui dynasty and the earliest stone-carved inscription in it dates from 590.

S of Putuo shan in the park is the *Luotuo shan* (Camel Mountain), so-called because it is said to resemble a crouching camel. It is also said to resemble an ancient wine pot and is sometimes called 'pot mountain' (Hu shan), and the two characters for pot mountain are carved on its S side.

Close to the Xiao dong jiang (Small Eastern River), S of Putuo shan is the *Yueya shan* (Crescent Moon Hill), made up of the three remaining peaks of the seven-star constellation. Seen from the Hua qiao (Flowery Bridge), a cliff on the mountain is said to resemble a crescent moon. The *Longyin dong* (Dragon Darkness Cave) is near the foot of the Crescent Moon Hill, opening onto the river. The roof of the cavern is said to look as if the imprint of a dragon's body has been left after it flew away and an inscription reads: 'It broke down the wall and flew off'. Fang Yanru of the Song said 'There are living dragon scales in the rock and its eyes suddenly open', and Zhou Jinlong of the Ming described it as 'Having flown off many thousands of years ago, the dragon's scales remain to this day'. There are stone-carved inscriptions from the Tang and Song.

56 Kunming

Kunming, the capital city of Yunnan province, is situated in the centre of the eastern Yunnan plateau on a large plain. South of the city is the largest lake in the province, *Lake Dian* (Dian chi in Chinese; Dian is an alternative name for Yunnan province).

Yunnan province is situated on the southwestern tableland, a spur of the Tibetan plateau. Much of the province is high, with an average altitude of 1800m above sea level. The plateau is divided by deep river valleys and high mountains, all of which make large-scale agriculture and communications difficult. Owing to its height, the temperature of what would otherwise be a semi-tropical region is tempered. Even in winter frosts are rarely heavy; Kunming is known as the Spring City for the temperature remains pleasant virtually throughout the year.

The area is rich in minerals, tin and copper in particular: during the Qing (1644–1911) much of China's copper cash was made from Yunnanese ore although the difficulties of transport meant that a considerable proportion was exported through Burma, rather than directly overland to the capital in Peking. Much of the province is too mountainous to allow cultivation. Such soil as there is is a rich red laterite and major crops include rice (only one harvest per year), wheat, oil seeds of various sorts and tobacco, tea, hemp, a variety of vegetables throughout the year and fruits including peaches, pears, apricots, persimmons, oranges, lemons, walnuts and chestnuts. Recent agricultural innovations are leading to over-cultivation and soil erosion is likely to become a serious problem as peasants are currently growing crops on plots that stretch down the hillsides rather than the erosion-preventing (but labour-intensive and time-consuming) terraces built along the contours of the slopes.

The name of the province means 'South of the Clouds', referring to the mist and cloud which constantly covers the neighbouring province of Sichuan, to the N. Though now part of China proper, Yunnan was only brought into the Chinese empire during the Mongol Yuan dynasty (1279–1368). Before that it had been ruled by independent kings. One of the most interesting kingdoms in Yunnan was that of Dian. The Dian ruled during the 2C and 1C BC and in 109 BC the Dian ruler submitted to Han Chinese suzerainty, the gesture made concrete in a fine golden seal which used to be on display in the Yunnan Provincial Museum in Kunming. Dian tombs excavated S of Kunming in the late 1950s have revealed a complex bronze-working culture whose artefacts are quite different from those of contemporary China. Most impressive are the bronze drums which stand 55cm or 85cm high and have scenes of daily life, animal herding, battle and human sacrifice on their tops. The fine horned cattle represented are unlike any cattle found in China today and it may well be that the cultural contacts of the Dian were stronger with other SE Asian peoples than with the Chinese. Despite the treaty of sovereignty, Chinese control of Yunnan remained tenuous for the next 1000 years.

During the Tang dynasty (618–907) a new kingdom rose to power in Yunnan. This was the Nan chao kingdom with its centre in the town of Dali, some 200km W of the present provincial capital, Kunming. The Nan chao rulers are thought to have been Thai though they followed the Chinese pattern of government. The Nan chao kingdom successfully defeated a Chinese army near Dali in 751, one of the first presages of the mid-Tang collapse.

It was not until the Mongols invaded China to establish the Yuan dynasty (1279–1368) that the Nan chao were subjugated (in 1253) and Yunnan finally brought under Chinese control. During the Ming dynasty (1368–1644) the Chinese began seriously to colonise the province by voluntary and forced settlement. Many of the Han Chinese living in Yunnan today can trace their origins back to the Ming when their families arrived from other provinces in China proper. In the final defeat of the Ming ruling house by the invading Manchus, who took the dynastic name Qing (meaning 'bright' or 'pure'), one of the last of the Ming princes fled to Yunnan, pursued by a Chinese general, Wu Sangui, who had him strangled in 1662. Though most histories record the strangling as having taken place on the Burmese border, a stele erected in the first year of the Republic (1912) records his death within the city of Kunming.

During the Qing (1644–1911), revolts against the ruling house persisted, the most long-lived and disastrous being the Moslem uprising of 1857–72, connected with the Taiping uprising. The uprising decimated the considerable Moslem population of the province and some of the surviving Yunnanese Moslems still remember it with bitterness. The self-proclaimed Sultan of Yunnan, Tu Wenxiu, who had led the uprising, is said to have offered his sultanate to Queen Victoria when he despaired of maintaining resistance to Peking, but the offer was, apparently, declined. The uprising was only quelled when the Imperial house persuaded the French in neighbouring Indochina to send an expeditionary force.

Because of their colonial interest in the area, the French were the first to bring a railway to Yunnan, breaking its physical isolation. A narrow-gauge railway was constructed in 1904–10, running between Kunming and Haiphong, via Hanoi. The route is still in use and the trains can be seen from the road from Kunming to the Stone Forest. Travellers by rail from Peking to Hanoi have to change at Kunming because of the different gauge. During the Cultural Revolution Red Guards made specific attacks on some of the surviving Moslem communities.

One of the most striking aspects of Yunnan is its population. Half of the 50-odd minority races of China live in this province, making a third of the total population (the remaining two-thirds are Han Chinese). The minorities include Tibetans and Miao who cross the inter-provincial borders and the national border, as do the Yi who also live in Sichuan. The Yi are the majority 'minority', followed by the Tai, the Bai and the Na Xi in the region of Dali, and the Li Su, Wa and Jing po in the Burmese frontier area. In the past these separate cultural and racial groups survived because of the relative isolation of Yunnan and even within the province the difficulty of transport made contact rare. Today, official Chinese policy is to promote the cultural and linguistic heritage of the different groups. Many are exempt from the strict population control methods to which the Chinese are subject, because their numbers are low. Those that have a script have books translated and published in that script at the Yunnan Provincial Publishing House. Tourism has had its effect in promoting the interests of minority groups, who are encouraged to perform traditional dances for visitors and sell their handicrafts to them.

Visitors to Yunnan in the late 19C were drawn by the incredible variety of plant life. Some 80 per cent of European and North American garden flowers were originally native to China, and Yunnan and the highlands of neighbouring Sichuan were perhaps the most fertile provinces for plant-hunters. One of the most beautiful of Yunnan's native plants is the Camellia and *Camellia japonica* was one of the first Chinese plants to be introduced into Europe by the East India Company in the 17C. In Chinese the camellia is called cha hua or 'tea flower' and though Linnaeus originally separated camellia and tea (he named the tea plant *Thea sinensis*) it has now been renamed *Camellia sinensis*. Another major species from Yunnan and Sichuan is the rhododendron; more than half of the nearly 400 species of rhododendron originate there and plant-hunting in China was once described as a 'hectic hunt for rhododendrons'. Chinese rhododendrons are all of the azalea group and, as with tea and camellia, the Chinese simply have one name for both rhododendron and azalea. Despite the difficulties of transportation (azaleas couldn't stand sea-water and perished en voyage until John Dampier Parks suggested transporting them under glass bell-jars) and the dangers of the frontiers (Soulie, who introduced *Rhododendron souliei, Primula souliei* and *Buddleia variabilis*, was murdered by Tibetan monks in 1905, as was Dubernard [*Primula dubernardiana*] though Forrest, who introduced 22 rhododendrons and nine primulas, managed to escape), *Rosa banksiae* and others, *Lilium regale, henryi* and *sargentiae*, viburnum, mallow, hibiscus and hollyhock all made their way from Yunnan and Sichuan to the gardens of the world.

By the 1C BC Kunming had become the centre of the Dian kingdom and in 109 BC the Dian rulers acknowledged Chinese suzerainty. At the end of the 8C, however, the Nan chao kingdom, based at Dali, took control of Kunming and made it the secondary capital, later the main capital when a palace was constructed there in 871. When the Mongols took power in Yunnan, deposing the Nan chao rulers, Kunming became the provincial capital in 1288 and has remained the principal city of the province. With the construction of the French railway linking Kunming and Haiphong in Vietnam, and the Burma Road during the Second World War, Kunming developed as a supply centre, a role which continued during the Vietnam War when railway links were maintained, despite the growing border conflict between China and Vietnam.

In the past gold and silver were mined around the lake and today there is a major smelting industry and ironworks, as well as textile, electrical, chemical and food-processing industries.

Airport: Kunming airport is to the E of the town; a bus ride to the centre takes approximately 10 minutes. Internal flights, including flights direct to Hong Kong, can be booked at the CAAC booking office which is on Dongfeng donglu, immediately beside the Kunming Hotel (and this is where the airport bus drops passengers).

Railway: the station is to the S of the city, at the S end of Beijing lu.

One of the most beautiful railway trips in China is that between Chengdu (Sichuan) and Kunming. The line was built during the Cultural Revolution (1966–76), following first the Dadu and then the Anding River valleys through the Xueshan (or Snow Mountain) range. The line traverses the home of the Lolo national minority, once fierce warriors jealous of territory who terrified missionaries and other would-be travellers. The Lolo have their own script which can be seen used in conjection with Chinese for station names and they are a handsome people with high-bridged noses, large silver and coral earrings and dark fringed capes. The only problem with the scenic beauty of the line is that, owing to the terrain, it is 50 per cent tunnel. If you take the early morning departure from Chengdu (c 9 am), by about 1 pm the train has reached the Lolo area which is not only distinctive for the people and script at the stations but also for the way they cut their rice straw higher and nearer the ear than the Chinese and then stack it in long narrow piles raised above the ground, in contrast with the circular Chinese haystack which is usually built around a wooden pole.

Hotels: most tourist groups now use the Golden Drangon Hotel; the two other main hotels are the Kunming Hotel in the town centre on Dongfeng dong lu and the Cuihu Guesthouse on Cuihu nan lu in the NW. Both provide cheap, dormitory accommodation and 'middle'-level accommodation. There is little to choose between the two: the Kunming Hotel is central, near shops, government buildings, etc; the Cuihu is opposite a pleasant park with a lake (cui means green, hu means lake), near the Yuantong Temple and behind it is an interesting group of narrow lanes lined with small shops.

Buses: the long-distance bus station for buses to Dali is in the W of the city at the terminus of the Nos 1, 2 and 5 bus routes.

Food: rice is the Yunnanese staple and perhaps the most sought-after local product for visiting Chinese is Yunnan ham, which is rather like prosciutto. Cheese made from buffalo milk (rather rubbery, resembling something between gouda and mozarella) is eaten as a side-dish, often with hot pepper sauce. The use of cheese is unusual for most Chinese abhor it and it is generally associated only with Mongolians and Tibetans. Its occurrence in Yunnan may owe something to the Tibetan inhabitants of NW Yunnan.

The two most famous dishes from Yunnan are stewed chicken, which is boiled with medicinal roots in a special ceramic pot and produces wonderfully soft meat and delicately flavoured soup, and 'crossing the bridge noodles', a southern version of the Mongolian hot-pot, where side-dishes of vegetables, meat and noodles are provided to be cooked in the boiling pot of chicken stock set in the centre of the table. The dish is said to date from antiquity when a young scholar retired to an island to concentrate on his studies, hoping to pass the civil service examinations. His young wife felt that he should be nourished during his ordeal but found that food cooled when she took it across the bridge to him. Finally she discovered that a good chicken stock kept warm enough and she would take it, together with raw noodles and other delicacies, across the bridge.

The present name of Kunming (Generations of Brilliance) is only one of many that were used in the past. The earliest town on the site was founded by the Dian in the 1C BC and called Yizhou jun. Remains of the Dian civilisation have been unearthed in the hills around Lake Dian (on Mt Shizhai and Mt Lijia) and the best of these are on display in the Yunnan Provincial Museum in Kunming. The Dian established a slave-owning society based on agriculture and produced marvellous bronzes by the lost-wax method which, in the earliest phase (4C BC) sets them apart from bronzes of China proper. The latter were mainly cast in ceramic moulds although lost-wax was beginning to gain favour. The forms of the Dian bronzes, great drums and drum-shaped cowrie containers with fine, thin walls and three-dimensional scenes of hunts, warfare and human sacrifice or groups of long-horned cattle (a type no longer seen in the area) are also very different from those of contemporary China. There is virtually no physical evidence in Kunming of the Nan chao rulers who established their second capital there in 809, although it is possible that the two pagodas of the East and West Temples were Nan chao foundations for they are very similar in form to the largest of the three pagodas at Dali.

After the Mongols seized Kunming (and made it the headquarters of the Zhongqing district) a description remains in Marco Polo's 'Travels' which mentions the sizable Moslem population, the cultivation and consumption of rice and, surprisingly, the persistence of the cowrie shell as an object of value.

In 1382 the Ming armies conquered Kunming and, as in so many other towns, built an enclosing wall and gave the town the name of Yunnan fu (a name still current in the 1920s as can be seen from Gabrielle Vassall's 'In and Around Yunnan fou', Heinemann, 1922). When the Qing dynasty of Manchu origin invaded China, Yunnan fu was one of the last towns to submit, retaining allegiance to the Ming until almost 40 years after the Qing established themselves at Peking. Nothing now remains of the walls that surrounded the city as late as 1922 although many of the small narrow streets in the N and W (behind the Cuihu Guesthouse) convey something of what the city must have been in the Ming and Qing.

There was considerable damage during the long Moslem revolt (1857–72) which had begun with disputes in the silver mines and was continued by arms supplies from Burma until the French helped to put it down bloodily. Quite a few buildings in the centre and near the Cuihu and Dian Lakes show influence of the French colonial style with mansard roofs and green or grey tiling for the French, established in the late 19C in neighbouring Indochina, had a strong presence in Kunming before the Second World War.

During the Anti-Japanese War (1937–45) Kunming was one of the major places of exile, most notably for the two major universities of Peking, Peking University and Qinghua University, which, together with Nankai University from Tianjin, established a campus in 1938 in Kunming called the Southwest Associated University (the campus they occupied is now that of Kunming Teachers College on Huancheng bei lu—literally the North Circular Road). Students had to move from a temporary refuge in Changsha (Hunan province), the men on foot, the women by rail first to Haiphong and then back into Kunming. The male students, accompanied by, amongst other distinguished academics, the poet Wen Yiduo, covered some 1900km (1200 miles) in 68 days, a sort of mini Long March. Though most of the teachers from Peking came to Kunming, Wen Yiduo is remembered for his increasing participation in the Democratic League (which advocated civil liberties, avoidance of civil war, nationalisation of the Chinese armed forces and convocation of an elected national congress) which led to his assassination in 1946 by agents of Chiang Kai-shek's Guomindang. Wen was killed immediately after a memorial meeting commemorating the assassination of one of his closest friends in the Democratic League. His writings and activities reflected the increasing politicisation of intellectuals appalled at the state of the Guomindang army, with soldiers starving to death before their eyes, as well as Guomindang attacks on patriotic students.

Kunming was affected not only by the arrival of thousands of refugees fleeing the

KUNMING

Yuantong temple

Yuantong jie

Cuihu Park

Cuihu Guest House
Stele
Government buildings

Double pagodas

Huashan nanlu

Wucheng lu

Confucian temple

Minsheng jie

Changchun lu

Weiyuan jie

Bird market

Qingyun jie

Nantaiqiao

Kunming Department Store

Kunming Hotel

Dongfeng donglu

Yunnan Provincial Museum

Jinbi   lu

Tuodong lu

N

West temple pagoda

East temple pagoda

to Railway station

Japanese, but also by the American presence. In order to supply the Anti-Japanese War, Stilwell, in charge of the China-Burma-India theatre, oversaw the building of the Burma Road, from Yunnan across the border. When the Japanese closed the road Kunming's airport became a major factor in the replacement flights across 'the Hump'.

Kunming today is marked by the traditional city, French influence and post-'49 civic architecture. The city centre, with its open parade ground surrounded by government buildings, is not very different from any other modern Chinese city centre; only the back streets and the mixed population with the colourful clothes of the national minorities single it out.

From the Kunming Hotel to the Pagodas of the East and West Temples.
The trip can be made by taxi. Taxis are to be found at every major hotel (hence the starting point) but many taxi-drivers are not very familiar with cultural sites. If in doubt get an English-speaking receptionist to confer with the driver. Maps, which whether in Chinese or English show the points of interest (including the two pagodas), can be used easily.

Turn right out of the hotel along Dongfeng dong lu. The first major crossroads is Beijing lu. Carry on across on Dongfeng dong lu. At the crossroads with Huguo lu the People's Bank of China is on the right and later, as you approach the large roundabout where Zhengyi lu crosses Dongfeng lu (dong lu means east road, xi lu means west; Zhengyi lu is considered to be the central N–S axis so here Dongfeng lu changes from dong lu to xi lu), the Nationalities Trade Store and then the Yunnan

Antique Store are on the left near the roundabout. At the roundabout turn left (S) down Zhengyi lu until it reaches Jinbi lu. Turn left along Jinbi lu until you reach the second major right turn, Shulin jie. Past Houxin jie, on the left, the pagoda will soon be visible near No. 64 Shulin jie.

The *East Temple* no longer stands; all that remains is the *Pagoda*. This, like many other late Tang pagodas, has a square base, the top is stepped, rising to a slightly rounded top, like a head of lilac. According to the 'Zhongguo mingsheng cidian' (Dictionary of Famous Sites in China), the pagoda originally stood in the Changle temple (Temple of Constant Joy), which was also known as the Eastern Temple. It was thought to have been built during the Nan chao period and is thus related to the Dali pagodas and dates from the 8C. It was badly damaged by an earthquake in 1833 and rebuilt (preserving the 8C form) in 1882. No reference books refer to the four extraordinary bronze birds which are placed on the top. They look rather like turkeys and resemble bird forms on Ming ceramics and fabrics. It is possible that they are original, though they may have been added later.

To reach the West Temple Pagoda, the twin of the East Temple example, you can either retrace your steps up Shulin jie and take the first major turning on the left (before Houxin jie) which will lead you across Sima Xiang to Dongsi jie, or go S down Shulin jie to the next major turning on the right which will also take you to Dongsi jie. The pagoda should be visible. The *West Temple Pagoda* is now, unfortunately, within an army barracks. The sentries will not allow photographs and are unsympathetic to lovers of architecture. There is quite a good view from a lane further up the street (to the N). The West Temple, which no longer stands, was originally called the Huiguang Temple (Temple of Brilliant Wisdom) and was built between 824 and 859. There is no record of its having suffered earthquake damage like the Eastern Pagoda but it probably did. Almost identical in form to the Eastern Temple Pagoda, this is 36m high and has Buddhist texts in Chinese and Sanskrit carved on the bricks. It has the same four bronze birds and finial as the Eastern Temple Pagoda.

Local people say that the Eastern Temple is intimately connected with the fate of the inhabitants of Kunming and that they protected it during the Cultural Revolution from Red Guards who wished to destroy it. They believe that Kunming itself would be destroyed by an earthquake if anyone toppled the East Temple Pagoda.

To return to the Kunming Hotel go N up Dongsi jie until you reach the junction with Jinbi lu. Turn right into Jinbi lu until you reach Zhengyi lu on the left. Go left into Zhengyi lu as far as the roundabout (with the Kunming Department Store on the N side), turn right into Dongfeng dong lu and carry on until you reach the hotel on the left-hand side of the road.

From the Cuihu Guesthouse to the Confucian Temple, Ming Emperor's Stele and the Yuantong Temple.
It is simplest to leave the guesthouse by the back entrance which leads to Huashan xi lu. If this is not possible, turn right out of the guesthouse and take the first right off Cuihu nan lu and the first right again which is Huashan xi lu. Not far to the right of the back entrance of the guesthouse, near No. 156 Huashan xi lu, is an undecorated concrete *stele* erected in memory of the last prince of the Ming dynasty who was strangled near the spot at the order of Wu Sangui (1612–78), a general who, after a complicated series of shifts in loyalty, backed the Manchu invaders who set up the Qing dynasty (1644).

Invested with the title 'the Generalissimo who pacifies the West', Wu was given civil and military control of Yunnan in 1657. Zhu Yulang (1623–62), grandson of the Ming Wanli Emperor, led the remnants of the Ming forces to Yunnan where they were defeated by Wu Sangui at Dali in 1669 and Zhu Yulang fled to Burma. Pursued by Wu Sangui, he and his young son (born 1648) were taken back to Yunnan fu (Kunming) and put to death by strangulation with a bowstring on 2 March 1662. The stele commemorating this simply gives Zhu's name and titles and the date of erection, 1912. This is interesting in itself for during the Qing it would have been virtually treasonable to mention the deposed Ming dynasty, but once the Qing had been overthrown the Ming became respectable again.

Continue down Huashan xi lu (the road changes its name at the point where Huashan nan lu leads off to the left and becomes Minquan jie). At the bottom of the hill, where Minsheng jie crosses the road, there is the old *Confucian Temple* set back from the road on the left. Little remains of the temple buildings but there is a garden in the enclosure with a small pool.

There is little information on the original buildings but Gabrielle Vassall's account of her visit (published in 1922) provides a picture of what was already a temple in decay. In the past, every town and city had its temple to Confucius, the presiding spirit behind the imperial ideal, but the Republic, founded in 1911, discarded the Confucian ideology:

> …we made our way to the central building. It was dark and cool inside but we were disappointed to find it nearly empty. There was one single Buddha behind a piece of wire netting in a corner, but the whole place had evidently been neglected for a long time. Our Chinese guide…informed us that during the Revolution in 1911 the temple had been pillaged and all the Buddhas beheaded. The ancient cult was apparently unpractised and all that remained of former glories were one or two bronze incense burners which had evidently resisted destruction and been too heavy to carry away. The carved columns and the ceiling with its highly coloured and ornamented beams were all that had been left intact…In the middle of the garden was a small pond with a round Chinese bridge stretching across it.

The garden, with a small garden pavilion, remains but the enclosure is now the *Masses' Arts Centre* and exhibitions are sometimes held there. Mrs Vassall mentions in her account of trying to find the Confucian Temple how the cats belonging to shopkeepers along Huashan xi lu wore 'collars and were chained up like dogs'; they can still be seen, crouched on stools in the sun but firmly attached. She received the explanation that cats were valued for they brought good luck to merchants. This may still be the case but there is an added incentive to keeping a cat in Kunming today; apparently after the destruction of dogs and cats before and during the Cultural Revolution the rat problem became uncontrollable and now people are paid a small subsidy for keeping a cat.

Retrace your steps up Minquan jie and turn right at the first major turning (Huashan nan lu). To the N (on your left) are myriad charming little lanes with courtyard houses, potted plants, caged birds and other domestic scenes. They are all cut off to the N by a group of government buildings and anyway bear no names in romanisation but they are interesting to wander in before you return to Huashan nan lu.

At the end of Huashan nanlu turn left into Huashan dong lu which climbs a steep hill. About half-way up, on the right (opposite No. 40 Huashan dong lu) there is a painting of a pair of *pagodas*, the twin pagodas of the *Da de Temple* (Temple of Great Virtue). Miniature versions of the East and West Temple pagodas, presumably originally of Tang date because of their form, they have been rather brutally restored in concrete and are hidden within the housing estate associated with a pharmaceutical enterprise. You can, however, get in to see them.

Continuing up Huashan dong lu, which at the next crossroads changes its name to Pingzheng jie, you eventually reach Yuantong jie. Turn left into it at the T-junction and soon, on your right, you will see the entrance to the **Yuantong Temple** (Temple of Universal Penetration; my translation based on the Buddhist significance of the characters; on the tourist map of Kunming it is called the Full and Smooth Temple), headquarters of the provincial Buddhist Association. Founded in the Tang, restored during the Yuan, Ming and Qing, apart from its impressive gateway, the most charming part of this temple is the back courtyard with an octagonal pavilion set in a pool with four bridges, the whole surrounded by cool walkways with whitewashed walls cut by fancifully-shaped openings with bamboos planted behind. It is one of the finest temple gardens in China. In the first hall behind the entrance gateway is a white jade Buddha which was presented in 1985 by Thai Buddhists, emphasising both the outside support that Chinese Buddhists receive from Buddhist countries and Yunnan's special SE Asian connections.

When you leave the temple turn right and Yuantong lu will bring you down to the Cui hu lake. Turn left at the lake to return to the hotel.

The Provincial Museum is easily reached from the Cuihu Guesthouse. Turn left out of the guesthouse and follow Cuihu nan lu until you reach the T-junction with Dongfeng xi lu; turn left into Dongfeng xi lu until you reach a major junction with Wuyi lu (on your left). To the right, set back from the road at the junction is the **Yunnan Provincial Museum**. It was built in 1951 and the two major exhibits are the excavated finds of the Dian kingdom (excavated between 1956 and 1960 S of the city) and an exhibition of the national minorities of the province. The *Dian Exhibit* contains bronze drums and cowrie containers (cowries had value as currency as late as the Qing dynasty) with scenes representing warfare, agriculture and sacrifice on their tops.

The famous gold seal of 109 BC which cemented the suzerainty of the Han Chinese over the Dian is no longer on display—or at least the original is no longer there. It is rumoured that a theft took place in the museum sometime in the late 1970s and the gold objects of the Dian culture were stolen. In the *National Minorities Exhibit*, clothing, photographs and cultural artefacts depict the life of the minorities.

Some of Kunming's most famous sites lie outside the town. These are best visited by taxi and may be grouped as follows: to the W, Daguan Park, Xi shan (Western Hills) and the Qiongzhu (Bamboo) Temple; to the N, best visited separately, is the Jin dian or Golden Temple.

Daguan Park (which can also be reached by public bus; it is at the end of the No. 4 route) lies beside the huge Lake Dian, 2km W of the city. There has been a park here since the Ming dynasty. After the construction of a Guanyin temple on the site (1682) it became an increasingly popular beauty spot and in 1690 the park was enlarged by the construction of the *Daguan lou* (Tower of the Magnificent View) and many other small pavilions. In 1828 a third storey was added to the tower. It was burnt down in the Moslem uprising (1857) and the existing structure was built in 1869. It became a public park in 1913. The tower with its whitewashed walls and curving eaves is best known in China for the pair of carved inscriptions on its main pillars.

All gardens and places of interest in China have been decorated for centuries with carved inscriptions extolling their significance but this pair of couplets is known as the 'finest long pair of inscriptions in China'. The couplets were originally carved in 'grass' or running hand but these were destroyed with the original tower and those you can see now were inscribed in regular hand by Zhao Fan at the order of the provincial governor in 1888 and carved in gold on blue. Roughly translated, they read:

> The 500 li Lake Dian stretches before my eyes, spread out like a garment, The banks its headdess, a vast expanse. To the east gallops a spirit horse, magic birds fly west, a snake-like wriggle to the north and gossamer hovers in the south. Who could prevent us approaching the crab peninsula and snail island, wind in the hair, spray on the temples; reeds cover the ground, spotted wings amongst red sunset clouds. I am not alone surrounded by green rice fields, a vast expanse of clean sand, nine summers of lotuses and three springs of willow.

> (No. 2) Several thousand years of history in my heart, wine cools in the pot. Heaving sighs for absent heroes, I think: the Han built tall ships, the Tang set up iron pillars, the Song wielded jade axes, the Yuan rode with leather saddle-bags. The exploits of their heroes were glorious, inspired by the

spirit to move mountains, they respected the pearl curtains and painted
ridgepole [the emperor and the state], through endless evening rains and
morning clouds. But the stelae recording their exploits are cracked and
broken, gone to ashes, scattered; all they achieved, a double line of autumn
geese, a frosted pillow.

Sun Ran, the late 17C–early 18C poet who wrote these lines, was a reclusive scholar
from Kunming who often met with other poets at the Daguan lou. Though some 26 of
his poems are included in a Qing collection of Kunming poetry, he lived in great
poverty, surviving by casting Yijing predictions in the Yuan tong temple. He is said
to have been a Ming loyalist who refused to seek office under the invading Manchu
Qing dynasty.

The couplets are by no means untypical of one strand in Chinese poetry whereby
the poet points to the glories of the past to highlight present decay. The Tang poet Bai
Juyi (Po Chu-i) wrote many poems in this vein; in one he complains that the present
emperor is not up to the last one and this is evident because the elephants in the
imperial zoo are dying, something which never happened under the previous glorious administration. Sun Ran uses the locality—the lake—to set the mood of nostalgia
for past glories.

The Western Hills, Longmen (Dragon Gate). The Western Hills overlooking the lake are 15km SW of the city. The best view of the huge lake
is obtained from the Dragon Gate near the top of the hill. The lake itself
is the sixth largest in China and an impressive sight for it covers some
297sq km. Though there is anxiety about recent pollution, it still looks
clear and blue and is crossed by a variety of small boats and junks. The
Dragon Gate is approached up stone steps starting from the *San qing ge*
(Pavilion of Three Purities), first built as a summer resort for the King of
Liang in the Yuan dynasty and then converted into a Taoist temple in the
Ming. The present buildings are an amalgam of Yuan, Ming and Qing.
Beyond, the path leads up through caves and steps carved out of the rock,
the walls of the caves also carved, often with Buddhist figures. The carv-
ings were made between 1751 and 1853. At the top, beyond the Dragon
Gate is a tiny moon-viewing platform with stone railings looking out over
the lake.

Below the Sanqing ge is the *Taihua Temple* (named after the Tai hua
Hill, one of the Western Hills, on which it stands). Originally a Yuan foundation, it was rebuilt in the Qing (1688) and much restored after 1949. It
is most notable for the carved Dali marble balustrades and for the trees
and plants in its courtyards, particularly an ancient magnolia; the camellias are also fine.

The **Bamboo Temple**, c 10km NW of the city, which also has some
magnificent trees in its courtyards, has an inscription in the main hall
dated 1316, written in both Chinese characters and Mongolian, asking
that officials, soldiers and the local population protect the temple and the
copy of the Tripitaka it houses. The temple was believed to be the first
place where Chan (Zen) Buddhism was brought to Yunnan from central
China.

According to a legend, during the Northern Song period (960–1126) two of the
princes of the kingdom of Dali were hunting and they followed a horned bull as far as
the Yu'an hill (on which the Bamboo Temple stands), where it disappeared. Through
the cloud they saw a monk. Soon afterwards the staff of bamboo the monk has been
holding grew into a clump of bamboo which gave the temple its name; the only concrete evidence for the date of construction remains, however, the inscription.

The temple is now best known for the painted clay figures of the 500
lohans and guardian kings. These were made between 1883 and 1890 by
Li Guangxiu and his five assistants. Li was from Sichuan, a Buddhist lay
brother. The figures, about 1m tall, are almost caricatured in their (greatly admired) variety, as is common in these multi-lohan assemblages.

The **Jin dian** or Golden Temple is 7km NE of Kunming, also in wooded
hills. Its most distinctive feature is a small bronze hall which stands at the

back of the main temple enclosure (there is an exhibit featuring the bronze temple bell, cast in 1423 in a hall to the left before you reach the bronze hall). The bronze hall stands in a courtyard that is surrounded by a crenellated wall of grey bricks, like a toy fort protecting the bronze pavilion within.

Bronze pavilions are not uncommon in China; the original one in this temple was said to have been based on one in Wudang shan in Hubei, a slightly smaller example than this, built in 1416. Another can be seen on Wutai shan (Shanxi), also of Ming date, inscribed inside with long lists of donors' names arranged by province, and in the Summer Palace, Peking. There used to be a Qing example at Chengde (Hebei) but that was apparently melted down by the Japanese in the 1930s.

The Jin dian bronze hall is like others in that it faithfully reproduces timber architecture in cast bronze. A small square pavilion, 6m wide, 6.7m high, it has a double roof, lightly curved eaves, standard timber-style construction with columns (these consist of bronze wrapped around real timbers, presumably to support the weight of the roof; elsewhere, little timber appears to be used) and the walls consist of panels, carved below and with open-work lattice windows above. It is a perfect miniature of a highly carved timber construction. The original bronze temple here was made in 1602 but was apparently moved to Bingquan (c 200km NW of Kunming) in 1637. The present bronze hall was donated by Wu Sangui, who had driven the last of the Ming from the province, in 1671. The other surviving bronze halls are not surrounded by castle walls, but they seem appropriate here in view of the military donor. As in many other Kunming temples, the trees are important. They include two camellias said to date from the Ming.

THE STONE FOREST. A limestone karst formation of extraordinarily tightly packed pillars of grey stone weathered into fantastic shapes, this lies 126km SE of Kunming and can be reached by bus or taxi in about 3 hours although the narrow road through the hills is, like so many in China, inadequate for the variety and quantity of traffic now found so the journey may be longer. There is a new hazard—an immensely successful duck restaurant about two-thirds of the way along the road. Long-distance lorry drivers have been known to leave their enormous vehicles in the middle of the road and stop for lunch with the result that anyone else on the road has to stop too.

Along the road, the distinctive local houses are made with timber frames, often with a narrow, open upper storey for storing hay. Their brick walls are of sun-baked red clay and enclose a small courtyard in front of the house. Near a large lake, about 1 hour out of Kunming, the narrow-gauge railway track to Vietnam can be seen and slightly further along the road a new form of local transport, horse buses, appear. These are open or canopied carts where some ten passengers sit facing each other and they are drawn by minute horses or donkeys. As you approach the Stone Forest you can see the beginnings of pointed limestone rocks protruding from the soil on either side of the road. The sharp karst peaks were apparently formed under the sea some 270 million years ago. The softer earth between the peaks has been gradually eroded since the sea retreated, leaving the limestone.

To visit the Stone Forest from the guesthouse: turn left out of the guesthouse and along the road until you pass a small pool on the left (*Lion Pond*). Turn left after the pond, up to the *Lion Pavilion* from which the forest can be seen.

For the Chinese much of the interest of the Stone Forest lies in finding pictures or similarities in the rock formations: submerged rocks that look like baby water buffalo, strangely placed stones atop columns that look either like two birds feeding each other or two birds kissing (depending upon the prurience of your guide), a stone that looks like a profile of Napoleon and so on. Thus maps and points of identity rest upon these anthropomorphic interpretations.

From the Lion Pavilion, follow the path until you reach the stone screen. This serves as the main 'gate' into the Stone Forest and the name of the site has been carved upon it. This is another aspect of the Chinese attitude to nature; as in gardens where poetic names for pavilions and calligraphic inscriptions are seen as integral to the garden, in places such as the Stone Forest the carving of inscriptions on the rock enhances the beauty and significance of the area. Take the right-hand path towards *Sword Peak Pond* where the rocks have begun to close in and tower over you, occasionally with a jagged boulder apparently poised on the edges of two knives above your head. The pond, like others, deep between grey walls, is supposed to have been formed by the sweep of a giant sword. From this point you can take which path you like, the shorter cut leading directly to the pavilion 'commanding a view of the whole' then back towards the Lion pond, or further round on the southern route.

The *Minor Stone Forest*, immediately E of the guesthouse, is often quieter than the main one and has some very fine giant bamboos.

The local people are called Sani or Hani and are a branch of the main Yi minority. The women wear colourful dresses over trousers, with aprons, all embroidered and sewn with ribbon. They also wear flat headbands or scarves.

The advent of tourism has transformed the local economy; you are likely to be followed round the forest by a horde of very high-pressure salesmen masquerading as women and children. If you want to buy things, like embroidered aprons or the typical canvas cross-stitched bags appliqued with bright cotton, a certain amount of bargaining is possible, particularly if you buy several items, but prices seem to have been mutually agreed and are fairly immovable. The guesthouse has been expanded recently to accommodate the numbers of tourists (this is a very popular place with the Japanese and for weekenders from Hong Kong). In the evening a Sani entertainment is offered with local people singing and dancing. This is surprisingly good fun as it remains spontaneous and reasonably authentic and the Sani, apart from blowing on leaves to produce a comb-and-paper effect, have a remarkable, if high-pitched, way of singing.

57 Yunnan to Dali

Dali, once the capital of the Nan chao rulers of Yunnan (c 740–1253), is a pretty little town set beside another of Yunnan's large lakes, the Er hai (Ear-shaped Sea), and beneath a long high mountain, Cang shan (the Green Mountain), which has snow on its peaks as late as June for they are as high as 4000m above sea-level. The lake itself and the town of Dali are at almost 2000m above sea-level. Quiet, pretty, offering marvellous walks from the picturesque town through rice-fields to the incredibly blue lake, Dali is well worth visiting, though rather exhausting of access.

Dali is on the BURMA ROAD, built as a vital supply route for the India-Burma-China theatre in the Second World War. The road departs from Yunnan and Dali lies c 250km (as the crow flies) W of Kunming. As it passes over many hills and down into valleys, the road is full of hairpin bends, not wide enough for the current volume of traffic, and the journey, with a break for lunch, takes about 11 hours. For almost all of its length the road is lined with eucalyptus trees, presumably imported during the period of French influence (for they are common in Sichuan province, too, but are not native to China). Tall and ragged, frequently suffering from stripping of the lower branches, they give a rather French air to parts of the road. The area between Kunming and Dali is clearly one of substantial tobacco production for tall ragged tobacco plants can be seen in the fields and almost every house has a high, windowless tower which looks almost military but is used for drying and curing the tobacco leaves.

The first part of the road (c 100km) follows the route of the Kunming–Chengdu railway which was built in the late 1960s and early 1970s (dates of their construction can be seen on the tunnels). The road then descends towards **Chu xiong** where most buses (tourist or public) stop for lunch. For tourist buses, there is a good meal arranged in the Chu xiong hotel. Once a walled, town, Chu xiong is now resolutely modern, the administrative capital of an autonomous county (autonomous regions are national minority areas, Chu xiong county is an Yi county). Notices, shop and hotel names are often written in a combination of Yi and Chinese. Though the town centre is quite new and furnished with a fine white concrete municipal statue of an Yi maiden in the middle of the main roundabout, the street markets (down both the first and second turnings on the left out of the hotel) are pleasant to walk in.

A visitor in the 1930s gives a very different account of the arriving in the town:

> It is a walled town. The gates are so narrow that the car could barely squeeze through...It is quite likely that a private car had never been seen before in the shopping street of Chu-Hsiung. Several hundred gaping people began to pack themselves into a tube behind and in front of us. A single policeman tried to control their helpless movements. Our ephebe lost his head and ran backwards into a wall. Subsequent manoeuvres showed that he had not yet learnt how to reverse the car. Local feeling began to surge against him as a possible child murderer...

(Gerald Reitlinger, 'South of the Clouds', Faber, 1939).

Beyond Chu xiong the road follows the bed of the Longquan jiang (Dragon Spring River) before crossing a broad plain, a high pass and descending towards Xia guan.

Xia guan is c 10km S of Dali, at the southern tip of the lake. The town (with the standard tourist hotel which visitors to Dali stay in, rather to their annoyance because of the distance) is more of an administrative and commercial centre than Dali and not terribly prepossessing (even in the 1930s, Reitlinger described it as 'a long gloomy street like a Welsh mining village') though it does have a good market beside the river, and over the bridge on the slope of a hill a narrow street lined with traditional shops leads up to an imposing bell tower.

The relationship between Xia guan and Dali seems to have been problematic in the early part of the century, 'When the Government carried the new road through to Tali, the inhabitants of Hsia Kuan, a mushroom town with no history, feared that Tali, the old western capital, would recover the trade monopoly which had once been wrested from it. So they claimed that the stone bridge in the middle of the town, crossing the torrential Hsia Kuan river, was unfit for heavy traffic...the lorries therefore stop short of the bridge.' The same resentment felt by Reitlinger, who had to break his journey to Dali at Xia guan, is felt by many of today's visitors, anxious to stroll to the lake from the attractive town of Dali, not to be marooned in Xia guan.

It is, however, worth walking from the hotel (which backs onto the river) into the centre of the town to inspect the offending bridge and markets alongside it and walk up to the bell tower on the other side of the bridge. (Start by turning right out of the hotel; turn left off this street down to the river and follow it upstream until you reach the bridge.) If you are with a tour group your bus will take you to Dali; if not, there are very frequent buses between the two towns.

Dali is approached from Xia guan by a road which arrives at the *South Gate*, one of two gates (the North Gate is at the end of the main street, Fuxing lu). These are the major remnants of the old city wall. The buildings as they stand are in the Qing style, brightly painted towers surmounting a battlemented gateway (like miniature versions of the surviving gates, the Desheng Gate for example, that can still be seen in Peking), but they have been heavily restored in the last decade. Further along the main street lies the central bell tower, the *Tower of the Five Glories* (Wuhua lou), once, apparently the S gate of the town before its

to 3 pagodas

DALI

North gate

Fuxing lu

Yu'er lu

Huguo lu

Renmin lu

Bo'ai lu

to Lake

N

South gate

to Xiaguan

enlargement some time in the past. The main street has small shops open to it, many selling bits of Dali marble which is quarried in the hills to the NW of the town (scars of quarries can be seen high up on the slopes).

The marble has long been popular in China; during the Qing, in particular, the 'land-scape' effect of the dark corrugated veins against the white was used to create land-scape pictures, slabs of marble mounted in mahogany frames, resembling a painted landscape of mountain peaks rising above mist. Slabs of landscape marble were also set into darkwood furniture, chairbacks and tabletops and tablescreens; examples can be seen in the mosque at Xi'an, many of the Suzhou garden buildings and the Summer Palace. Local stone is also used to make distinctive gravestones, visible in undertakers' shops, often adorned with a photograph of the deceased (possibly through French influence).

Local traders also sell embroidered clothes and bags made by the Bai people who live in an around Dali. The Bai, a branch of the Yi, have a distinctive language whose affinities are still problematic; one of the major authorities on the Bai, Fitzgerald, writing in 1941, saw it as quite unique, unrelated to any of the neighbouring languages or dialects, although apparently Japanese anthropologists now claim that it and the Bai culture have distinct similarities to Japanese. The Bai culture is in some ways very different from that of the Chinese, perhaps most notably in that they stress affinity on the basis of friendship, rather than kinship (which was and still is the most important affinity for the Chinese). Many Bai women, in bright tunics, head-dresses with embroidered ribbons and black cloth shoes with red trimmings, often carrying a baby strapped to their backs, can be found in the street markets and at tourist sites, selling vegetables, garlic and spices, embroidered bags, marble pestles and mortars and household goods like little earthenware stoves.

A turning off Fuxing lu, to the right, Yuer lu (just past the Bank of China, also on the right), leads down to the lake, as do all the right turns. This one goes past a marble-cutting factory (right) where thin slabs of marble are sliced and polished in the open yard. Two of Dali's best restaurants, the Happy and the Garden, are further down the road on the right.

Dali is a charming place to wander in, down any of the small narrow streets towards the lake and back up to the North Gate.

The major sites lie just out of town. The most famous, the **Three Pagodas**, are N of Dali. They once stood inside a temple which was destroyed under the Qing. The tallest is the earliest, built under the Nan chao (824–839); it stands over 69m tall, with 16 storeys, each embellished with small Buddha figures of Dali marble and openings on each side. In form it resembles the East and West Temple Pagodas of Kunming. The smaller pair are probably slightly later, though still of the Nan chao; they are more than 42m tall, ten-storeyed and more elegantly proportioned than the bulbous earlier form, closer to the classic pagoda with its evenly tapered line. They are beautifully carved with Buddhas, lotuses and cloud scrolls. Unlike the larger pagoda which is hollow, they are solid. On top they have bronze finials which were added in the Five Dynasties period (907–979).

The **Butterfly Spring** (Hu die quan), 20km N of Dali, has been mentioned in Chinese guidebooks as early as the Ming; it is a pool enclosed by a railing of Dali marble, overhung by a large old tree which is said to flower in the fourth month of the lunar calendar and its flowers look like butterflies. To make up for the absence of butterflies or butterfly flowers at other times of the year, a small museum displaying moths and butterflies as well as handicrafts (paintings, etc.) made from butterfly wings, has been built beside the spring.

One is also told that this is a favourite meeting place of the Bai youth and that young women come here to choose their mates. Bai women are supposed to take the lead in choosing a marriage partner although Fitzgerald's account of marriage practices in the 1930s sounds exactly like those of the Chinese, with parents and go-betweens deciding everything and women, in particular, lacking any rights. Women certainly still do much of the heavy work, carrying huge loads strapped to their backs, the weight supported on the forehead by a woven band which passes over the forehead and around the load on the back.

Though the Butterfly Spring has very fine trees and, once you have escaped the ladies selling embroidered bags at the gate, is quite peaceful, its main attraction is that reaching it involves getting out into the countryside (which you can also achieve by walking from the centre of Dali down to the lake).

Going back towards Dali, the first small village you pass after the Butterfly Spring is **Zhou cheng**, with a few shops on the main road, and a fine market square just off the main road. Turn up the road (away from the lake, towards the mountains) at the N end of the village and you will reach the square, shaded by a huge old tree under which the market traders sit with meat, spices, garlic and fruit spread out before them. At the E end of the square is a fine old stage (probably Qing in date) on which travelling operatic troupes would perform and where performances would have been held at special festivals.

Fitzgerald describes one Bai festival usually held in late May or early June, roughly between the wheat harvest and rice planting, when young men from Bai villages travelled about performing special dances in series of villages, ending up at the lake shore with a special dance in honour of the local village god. Such performances must have taken place on the stage and open-air stages in village squares used to be a major feature of village life in China but are now very difficult to find.

In autumn it is interesting to note the way the Bai thresh their rice in the fields. Apparently a new type of rice, called 'dropping rice' was introduced, perhaps in the early 1930s, and this had to be threshed in the fields when cut because the grain falls very readily when ripe. Thus Fitzgerald described it in 1941 and the same type of rice must still be used for in the fields you can see huge baskets with everted rims like vast inverted sun-hats, into which the Bai thresh the rice by hand, as they harvest it.

Villages by the lake live by both agriculture and fishing. Fishing with tame cormorants is still practised, although much fishing is now done with nets and some villages have invested in processing plants where fish can be canned for export. Where cormorants are used, they have rings around their necks to prevent them actually swallowing fish; they get their food from their master. Fish caught this way are necessarily smaller than those caught in nets and may be damaged, thereby lowering their market price.

II HONG KONG AND MACAU

Hong Kong Island in the foreground, and the Kowloon Peninsula in the background

58 Hong Kong

HONG KONG, until 1997 still a British colony and one of the great maritime entrepôts of the Far East, lies at the mouth of the Pearl River delta, just N of the Portuguese colony of Macau. It consists of Hong Kong Island, an archipelago of some 230 smaller islands, most uninhabited, and a stretch of the Chinese mainland called Kowloon (on the shore) and the 'New Territories'. The island was ceded to Britain in 1842 under the Treaty of Nanking; the stretch of the Kowloon shoreline was ceded in 1860 as part of the Treaty of Peking and the New Territories were leased to Britain (until 1997) under the second Treaty of Peking in 1898. Before the arrival of the British, Hong Kong and the New Territories area came under the jurisdiction of the Chinese Governor of Guangdong province.

The total land area is some 1064 square km with a population of 5.5 million living in extremely cramped conditions (possibly the densest urban concentration in the world) for much of the land is very hilly and both uninhabitable and unfarmable. Its free-port status means that Hong Kong for the tourist is usually a shopping stop but in recent years a greater interest in culture and local history has led to the opening of a number of museums (though the interest has, alas, come too late to save many buildings).

Visas: visa requirements vary. UK citizens with valid passports are usually issued with a visa on arrival permitting a stay of 6 months (which is easily extended); US citizens can stay for a month without a visa and Commonwealth citizens up to 3 months. Most Western Europeans are automatically granted 1–3-month visas.

Airport: Kai Tak Airport is in Kowloon, on the mainland. Surrounded by crowded public housing bristling with washing, the runway was built out into the bay by French engineers in 1959 so that the descent, at first apparently into the sea then with the aeroplane wings practically brushing the washing, is spectacular (and though apparently difficult, only two planes have half-toppled into the sea so far). The view before you reach the airport of the hundreds of tiny islands dotting the sea like green mushrooms is lovely. There is an airport tax of HK$150 payable on departure.

There are buses from the airport into the Central District of Hong Kong Island (through the Cross Harbour Tunnel) and to Tsim Sha Tsui, the waterfront area of Kowloon where there are many tourist hotels. Most major hotels have buses from the airport. If you take a taxi, bear in mind that the tunnel is a toll tunnel (HK$20; the toll fee and return fare will be charged to you.

Though the airport is not far from Hong Kong Island, taking about half an hour by car if traffic allows, the traffic is often very bad, especially in heavy rain or at race time so check with your hotel before deciding when to leave for the airport.

Railway: the railway station for China (and the New Territories) is also in Kowloon, not far from the airport, so the same traffic considerations apply.

The New Territories were inhabited by various groups mainly of rice-farmers or fishermen, Cantonese, Holkos, the Hakka ('Guest People' who seem to have originated in Sichuan and migrated to Guangdong and Fujian), whose women still wear flat straw hats with curtains of black cotton, and the Tankas or 'egg people'. The last are sometimes supposed to have been so-called because the awnings of the boats on which they live are supposed to be egg-shaped. Couling, in his 'Encyclopaedia Sinica' (1917) says this view is mistaken though he offers no other explanation save to say that these are the traditional 'boat people' of Canton, forbidden to marry Chinese or to take the civil service exams, allowed since 1730 to live in seashore villages though many still prefer to live on their boats. Apart from the Tankas, the inhabitants of the New Territories lived mainly in fortified 'walled towns' (some of which can still be visited: Shan La Wai near Shatin, the Luk Keng-Fanling area, Kat Hing Wai, Wing Lung Wai and Shui Tau Tsuen in Kam Tin) because of the pirate raids which devastated the area: it was not for nothing that the Portuguese called the islands of the area (including pre-British Hong Kong) the Ladrones (meaning pirates).

In 1277, the last 'emperor' of the Song dynasty, a small boy of nine, spent a year in the area, driven S with the remnants of an army and court by the Mongols. His death (as the Mongols approached, his Chief Minister is said to have taken the child in his arms and jumped into the sea with him) is commemorated by a rock inscribed 'Song huang tai' (Song Emperor's Terrace) in a garden beside Kai Tak Airport. Government impinged in the area hundreds of years later when, at the beginning of the Qing dynasty, the Manchus ordered a scorched-earth evacuation of the entire area (moving some 16,000 people) to prevent any foothold being gained by the anti-Manchu loyalists on Taiwan. There were defences built, mostly against pirates, but in general the clans in their walled villages were left largely alone to farm and fish by the provincial government as long as taxes were collected regularly.

Whilst Hong Kong was a relative backwater, the great port of Guangzhou, up the Pearl River, was besieged by foreign traders from the late 17C. Forced by Chinese government regulations to move backwards and forwards between Portuguese Macau and Canton, the British were looking for a territorial base. Before any treaty had been drawn up following the first Opium War of 1840, a British naval party landed and raised the Union Jack on Hong Kong island on 26 January 1841. Charles Elliot, the Chief Superintendent of Trade, was impressed by the deep-water harbour in the Kowloon Strait but Lord Palmerston in London felt that Elliot could have done better and sent him off to Texas to be the British chargé d'affaires.

In the Treaty of Nanking Palmerston's grander designs (of access to Chinese ports) were recognised but Hong Kong—'deep water and a free port for ever'—was also ceded 'in perpetuity'. It was to become, as its first Governor, Sir Henry Pottinger (1789–1856), proclaimed, '...a vast emporium of commerce and wealth'. The territory was expanded to take in the *de facto* cricket ground on the tip of the Kowloon peninsula (1860) and the 'New Territories'(1898), securing the harbour's sea approaches.

The treaty that gave Hong Kong to the British also served to diminish its importance for some 100 years for as Shanghai developed, Hong Kong remained in its shadow. As Jan Morris has pointed out in 'Hong Kong' (1988), it was the Chinese revolution of 1949 and the effective closure of China (including Shanghai) that promoted the incredible growth to prosperity of Hong Kong.

There was one anomaly in the treaties: the 'Walled City of Kowloon' just N of Kai Tak Airport, bounded by Tung Tau Tsuen Road. Built in 1847 as a defence against the British on Hong Kong island, the Chinese officials who lived there, protected by 5m-thick walls and a garrison of 500 soldiers, were ejected by the British after the acquisition of the New Territories, but they never actually managed to control the area within the walls. It became a no-go area with its very narrow lanes, tightly-packed buildings and reputation as a Triad stronghold. Its walls disappeared during the Second World War when the Japanese occupation force used the stones to extend Kai Tak's runway and now the whole area is gradually being razed to the ground, its population rehoused and the site destined to become a public park. There is therefore no need to reiterate the warning given to tourists to stay away.

The Japanese invaded Hong Kong in the Second World War and the tiny garrison of British, Indian and Canadian troops and local volunteers surrendered on Christmas Day 1941, not before losing some 2000 men (and 4000 civilians). Civilians were imprisoned in an internment camp at Stanley (on Hong Kong Island), soldiers in prisoner-of-war camps in Kowloon whilst the Japanese administration set up office in the Hong Kong and Shanghai Bank building. They rebuilt the Governor's residence to the designs of a 26-year-old engineer, they set up torture cages on the balconies of the Supreme Court building on Statue Square and the barber of the Hong Kong Hotel turned out to have been a Japanese Naval Commander under cover. Hong Kong was liberated in August 1945.

1949 and the preceding years of civil war brought a huge influx of refugees into Hong Kong, their numbers swelled by Shanghainese factory-owners and entrepreneurs, some of whom brought their entire factories with them. By 1956 (when there was a further wave of immigration from China) the population was 2.5 million, by 1988 it was 5.5 million. The latter figure comprises 98 per cent Chinese, of whom the vast majority are refugees themselves or the children of refugees. Crises of fire and flood in squatter camps, like that on Christmas Day 1953 which left 53,000 homeless, promoted the government's housing programme, first of crowded blocks of flats in Kowloon, more recently seen in the construction of elegant clusters of tower-blocks (which are still crammed with tiny flats) in the new towns of the New Territories built in the late 1970s and 1980s. By the end of the 1980s, it is estimated, half the population will be accommodated in public housing.

A further major wave of refugees arrived in 1962 as a result of the famines in China that followed the 'Great Leap Forward' of 1958 and a series of natural disasters. This group was virtually encouraged to leave by the Chinese authorities (for they left fewer mouths to feed) but the Hong Kong border patrols tried to send them back. Later the police began to operate a 'touch base' policy, allowing refugees who managed to reach the urban areas and find relatives there to remain: this policy was discontinued in 1980 not long after the beginning of the last major wave of refugees, the second group of 'boat people', ethnic Chinese fleeing Vietnam.

During the Vietnam War Hong Kong became a major holiday place for GIs on leave (some 3000 a month) but the relative peace of the rest of the colony was interrupted by the Cultural Revolution in China. Riots broke out in Hong Kong in 1967 in support of the sacking and burning of the British Embassy in Peking and the arrests of Hong Kong rioters led to the imprisonment of Reuters' correspondent in Peking, Antony Grey. In the previous year Hong Kong had been shocked by the disappearance of the Chief Superintendant of the Police Force Special Branch, John Tsang, who had been one of the highest ranking Chinese policemen in Hong Kong at the same time as being a spy. He remerged as Chief of Security for Guangdong Province, just across the border from his old beat.

The 1970s saw the opening of the Cross Harbour Tunnel (1972), and the beginnings of the famous ICAC (Independent Commission Against Corruption) which sought to root out corruption, particularly in the police force. At its lower levels this was said to be infiltrated by Triads and to those at higher levels it offered handsome opportunities (one policeman granted immunity after testifying against his superior boasted of having made US$1 million during his short career as a not-very-well-paid officer in the Hong Kong Police).

Confidence in the future of Hong Kong fluctuated throughout the 1970s and early 1980s with uncertainty over the appropriate length of property leases and the amount of time required to repay an investment. These uncertainties have to some extent been settled (or one might say brought to a head) by the negotiations over the Draft Agreement on the future of Hong Kong. The Draft was signed on 26 September 1984 after two years of preliminary negotiation which included considerable opposition by the British Prime Minister Margaret Thatcher to the cession of Hong Kong island, which according to the Treaty of Nanking was British 'in perpetuity'. The Chinese government refused to recognise this and other 'unequal treaties' (forced upon China) but it took the Prime Minister a while to see that Hong Kong on its own (with a very limited water supply and no agriculture) was hardly a viable colony. Detailed negotiations on the details of the future administration of Hong Kong and the New Territories continue.

Expressions of confidence in the future are seen in the new buildings (the Hong Kong and Shanghai Bank's new headquarters by Norman Foster was completed in 1986; I.M. Pei, whose father was the bank's first manager in the 1930s, has built the new Bank of China) and the changing pattern of investment with China taking a small interest in Cathay Pacific Airlines, in garages, in shoring up rocky banks and sharing with the Hong Kong-based China Light and Power Company in the joint Daya Bay nuclear project which will supply electrcity to both Hong Kong and Guangdong province. Expressions of doubt can be seen in the removal of the headquarters of Jardine Matheson (the oldest European trading company) to Bermuda and the enormous number of people applying to leave for Canada, the USA and Australia (or anywhere that will take them). As negotiations continue, rival interest groups contend: there are those who believe that nothing should rock the boat, there are those, led by the lawyer Martin Lee, who believe that it is essential to establish some constitutional rights before the Chinese take over in 1997 as there is far less likelihood of achieving them thereafter.

Hong Kong Island presents a very different appearance from the barren rock that was first taken by the British in 1841. Victoria Peak, the top of the island, has been covered with trees, including some dozens of varieties of Australian eucalyptus. The Peak remains less thickly inhabited than the lower levels, partly because of its topography but also because it is frequently veiled in cloud in the rainy season of the summer when everything smells of mildew. Below the Peak on the N side of the island are the 'Mid-levels' where tall blocks of grand flats house the expatriate workers in considerable luxury (with a tiny hut for the maid on the balcony). Below the Mid-levels is the Central District where most of the major institutional buildings are to be found.

Walking is not very easy in Hong Kong, except in the small streets above Queens Road Central; even there you are endangered by fast-moving buses and vans. On more major streets, particularly those which lead to the few monuments of interest, there appear to be virtually no concessions made to pedestrians, except in the downtown shopping area where you can cross from one vast business/shopping centre to another. Shoppers must be protected.

A. Flagstaff House, Government House, Botanic Gardens, Peak Tram, Hollywood Road and Man Mo Temple, Queens Road Central, Anglican Cathedral

Flagstaff House (open daily 10 am–5 pm; closed on Wednesdays) is on the E side of Cotton Tree Drive, just beside the Hilton Hotel. Cotton Tree Drive is, unfortunately, a major motorway with, at this point, very little in the way of pedestrian facilities. Flagstaff House contains a Museum of Tea Drinking. One of the finest surviving colonial buildings in Hong Kong, with a colonnade, cool verandah and shuttered windows, it was built in 1845 as the residence of the General in charge of the Hong Kong garrison. Nearby, where the huge new Bank of China building rises on the far side of the road (I.M. Pei's new bank is 70 storeys high, higher than anything else in Hong Kong as yet) there was once an associated group of colonial buildings, Murray Barracks. It was demolished to make way for the bank and earlier plans to reconstruct it somewhere appear to have been abandoned.

The displays in the Flagstaff House Museum change from time to time but are usually associated with tea and its accoutrements. There is a very fine collection of the (usually) brick-red Yixing ware, favoured by connoisseurs of tea. Yixing teapots are small and often quite amusing, produced in a variety of forms—cloth-wrapped bundles, peaches complete with stone, lotus buds, and sometimes speckled with gold dust, rimmed with metal or polished. According to the portrayal of gangsters in Chinese films, tea was drunk (by gangsters) straight from the spout, with no time for cups. There is a pictorial display on the history of tea and the tea trade.

Head up Cotton Tree Drive towards the Peak (away from the Harbour). On your right is the *Peak Tram Terminus*. Cross the road with care. Before taking the tram to the Peak, you could look at the *Botanical and Zoological Gardens* which lie ahead of you on Garden Road, a dark green haven between the motorways. (*St. Joseph's Church* (RC), built for the English-speaking Catholic community in 1876 (replacing a building that had been destroyed in the typhoon of 1874) is on your left, on Garden Road.)

Botanical specimens in the gardens include those native to Hong Kong and China, as well as many tropical varieties that have been established for over 100 years. The gardens have a considerable history, featuring in the 1893 'Hong Kong Guide' (when they were merely botanical, not yet zoological) where it was recommended that 'many a spare hour may be profitably spent'—they remain a quiet retreat on the noisy, overcrowded island.

Returning to the Peak Tram Terminus beside the US Consulate, you can take the tram (actually a funicular railway) up to the Peak (9-minute journey) at any time between 7 am and midnight for a few dollars. The funicular was built in 1888 by a Scottish railway engineer and its green cars with mahogany-slatted seats have been climbing the 45° incline ever since without a single accident. There are five intermediate stations, all pleasant little Victorian halts, before you reach the Upper Peak Terminus.

There, cloud permitting, various walks are possible. The normal 3.2km 'circuit' is Lugard Road–Harlech Road past the spacious mansions that still exist, for the Peak was the 'hill station' of this Victorian colony.

In 1847 the Colonial Surgeon recommended residence on the Peak for reasons of health. At that time, before the funicular, everything had to be carried up to the fine residences on the backs of coolies, some of whom were mere children, hauling loads of coal up the incline for some ten hours a day, seven days a week. The inhabitants themselves had to be carried up in palanquins but now the early trams are often filled with uniformed schoolchildren and dark-suited businessmen.

If it isn't too hot and the hill isn't too much, Mount Austin Road (which also starts from the Upper Peak Terminus) leads up to the **Peak** itself (554m above sea level) through the gardens of what was once the Governor's Summer Residence, *Mountain Lodge* (destroyed by the Japanese during their occupation). The view of the island below with its crammed skyscrapers and yellow beaches, the shipping out on the blue, island-dotted sea, is spectacular. At quiet times, there is still some remaining wildlife on the Peak. I'm not sure I believe that there are still barking deer lurking amongst the rhododendrons, tallow trees and jasmine, but kites and blue magpies abound.

Returning by tram to the Lower Terminus, walk up to Upper Albert Road for a peer through the gates of **Government House**, the residence of the Governor of Hong Kong.

It used to stand in splendid isolation on the hillside beside the Botanic Gardens, a white neo-classical building, colonnaded and surrounded by a sloping garden and five tennis courts. It was extended by the Japanese during the Occupation when the tower was added. Its view of Central District is gradually being eroded as buildings rise around it.

If you walk back round the grounds, with the US Consulate on your right, the road twists round until it joins Wyndham Street. At the bottom of Wyndham Street turn left into Hollywood Road which takes you through some of the older residential and commercial areas of Hong Kong, above Queens Road Central. This sort of mix of buildings antedates the post-Second World War International style of high-rise buildings in reinforced concrete that has come to dominate the Central area (partly because of the lack of space for building). The verandahs, balconies and shuttered windows of the older mixed areas reflect considerable Portuguese influence (from Macau) but the interiors are usually Chinese. Some of the more interesting older buildings lie beyond the end of Hollywood Road and the Man Mo Temple; you may care to leave these for another outing.

The **Man Mo Temple** at the W end of Hollywood Road is a Taoist temple, built in two sections with a 'smoke hole' for incense in between. A bell in the temple records a date of 1847 which is generally assumed to be the year of its foundation. The buildings were enlarged in 1850.

The temple is dedicated to the twin deities of Literature and Martial Matters. The God of War is the deified general of the Three Kingdoms, Guan yu, whilst the God of Literature (or Civil Matters) was supposed to have lived in the 3C AD and to have had jurisdiction over the lives of government officials. It was not uncommon to find shrines to these two on either side of a temple dedicated to Confucius (a feature of most Chinese towns) and this temple is in effect the 'city temple' of Hong Kong.

There is lavish use of Shekwan (or Suiwan) ceramic tiles on the roof and stucco relief work, and the gables are arched in the curved 'cat's back' shape characteristic of the decorated roofs of the south. The two stone lions in the forecourt were presented to the temple by the Pork Butchers'

Guild in 1851. In the first hall there are some gilded, highly carved sedan chairs, dating from 1885 and 1862, used to carry the deities in religious processions. On the right are the bell and drum used in temple cere-monies and in the centre is the open 'smoke hole' courtyard with large censers for incense. Beyond is the main hall. The major figures of the Gods of War and Literature are straight ahead; to the right is the shrine of the Earth God (the locality deity).

Not far away is the *Lo Pan Temple* on Ching Liu Terrace, dedicated to the God of Carpenters (Lu Ban in putonghua). It has fine stepped gables and black and white painting around the eaves in an architectural style found in south central China.

Just S of Hollywood Road, centred on Tai ping shan Street (one down), the whole TAI PING SHAN AREA was demolished and replanned after the plague of 1894 (which killed 2500, including the Governor's wife, though most victims were the tenement-dwelling Chinese). Despite this, the incessant rebuilding that goes on everywhere else in Hong Kong means that the area still includes some of the earliest surviving tenement buildings in Hong Kong. *103–107 Hollywood Road*, for exam-ple, is a narrow, balconied tenement with a rare Chinese tiled roof; and just round the corner (to the left) from the Man Mo Temple is Ladder Street where *No. 2–6* has shuttered, full-length windows.

The area below Hollywood Road is worth exploring for the occasional older building and Chinese shops: the roads down to Queens Road Cen-tral are often stepped 'ladder streets' lined with small stalls.

The extreme western end of the built-up area, KENNEDY TOWN, is the area in which the first British landfall was made, where the old waterfall that ships used for fresh water and which figures so prominently in early photographs and engravings of the island, reached the sea. The street names, including Possession Street, record the early landing, as does Belcher Street, named for the Captain of HMS 'Sulphur', whose crew was the first to step ashore.

Some quite interesting older buildings are to be found on Caine Road, which turns into Bonham Road (at its western extremity) and Robinson Road, above it. They are best reached from Aberdeen Street which runs upwards from Hollywood Road. On Caine Road, the *Cathedral of the Immaculate Conception* is No. 16 (built during the 1880s and described in 1893 as a 'handsome modern cruciform construction in the gothic style'); *Nos 66–69* have enclosed verandahs above shops; *No. 99*, with its cupo-las and plaster ornamentation, cast-iron panel balustrades and grand 'Chinese' windows, was Buxey Lodge, built in the 1870s for the promi-nent Parsee merchant Hormusjee Mody (of Mody Road). *No. 115* Caine Road has a rusticated ground floor with an arched door and keystones above the windows (repeated on the third floor) and Doric columns, but the Police Quarters at 150–156 Caine Road, built in the 1920s, have already gone.

On Bonham Road, *No. 44–46* was the mansion 'Euston' with a grand iron gateway, built in 1931; *No. 63*, with its 1930s' curved frontage, was built in the garden of Ball's Court which was the residence of Judge Ball in the 1860s; it was once used as a home for St. Stephen's Boys School. *No. 90* once belonged to the Church Mission Society but was integrated into the University of Hong Kong in 1918. It boasts classical features, assembled in a non-classical fashion with fluted Corinthian columns.

Back-tracking to Caine Road, at the junction with Peel Street, you can climb upwards towards Robinson Road, passing the Old Mosque on the way. The *Ohel Leah Synagogue* (1901) on Robinson Road is a late foun-dation despite the early arrival of prominent Jewish citizens such as the Sassoon family in 1857. They later founded the synagogue, Jacob Elias Sassoon paying for the construction, his brothers for the land. The archi-tects were Leigh and Orange (the firm which established itself in Hong

Kong in 1874 and also built the Mandarin Hotel in 1963) who chose an hispanic style with red-brick and whitewashed walls. The synagogue was dedicated to Leah Gubbay Sassoon, mother of the brothers who provided the funds. Also on Robinson Road, *No. 62* is an eclectic building with baroque, classical and renaissance motifs and an interior court; *No. 68* is a grand residence with ceramic bamboo decoration and baroque iron grill balconies. There is a Chinese gateway to No. 88B.

The **University of Hong Kong**, founded in 1911 but incorporating a number of older buildings such as 90 Bonham Road, stands above the Western District. The *Vice-Chancellor's Residence* at 8 University Path was built of brick and stone in 1911.

There is an art gallery in the University which may be visited by the public: the *Fung Ping Shan Museum*, 94 Bonham Street (10 am–6 pm daily except Thursdays, Sundays 2–6 pm). This is the oldest museum in Hong Kong, founded in 1953. It contains a good chronological display of Chinese art including archaic bronzes, ceramics of all periods and some Ming and Qing paintings. It is a fine collection, established to assist in the teaching of Chinese art to the students and its most unusual feature is the largest collection of Chinese Nestorian Christian crosses in the world (966 of them, dating from the Yuan dynasty).

Returning to the eastern part of Central District, **St. John's Cathedral** stands below Government House, on the W side of Garden Road. It was built in the Gothic style between 1847 and 1849, replacing a temporary mat-shed church.

It has seen many services, including some strange ones like that of the thanksgiving after the bread-poisoning incident of 1857. The major supplier of bread to the British, Cheong Ah Lum, decided to free Hong Kong of the colonial yoke by poisoning all his customers with arsenic in the bread. He put in far too much so that they vomited before ingesting a lethal dose. Acquitted for lack of evidence, Cheong Ah Lum was deported to China and the Governor of Hong Kong, Sir John Bowring, himself composed a hymn of thanksgiving for the cathedral service.

B.   Hong Kong and Shanghai Bank, Statue Square, Star Ferry, Kowloon

The unmissable grey building at No. 1 Queens Road Central is the new headquarters of the **Hong Kong and Shanghai Bank**, completed in 1986 to designs by the British architect Sir Norman Foster. Hung between a criss-cross exterior scaffolding of dull grey steel girders, it contrasts with the other glassy skyscrapers and towers over the old Bank of China, a '30s building next door. The ground floor is open to the street, with crossing escalators taking clients up to the airy halls above. In front stand the two old bronze lions named Stephen and Stitt after two bank officials of the 1930s (when the previous building was erected).

The first bank building was designed in 1886 by the local architects Palmer and Turner, who built the next in 1935, a skyscraper (the tallest building between Cairo and San Francisco) equipped with squash courts and helipads and with a fine mosaic ceiling by a Russian artist from Shanghai. This was taken down to make way for Foster's new building.

Not to be outdone, the **Bank of China** has moved to new headquarters just diagonally across the road (beside the Hilton), designed by I.M. Pei.

In front of the two banks is STATUE SQUARE, now rather devoid of statues as the massed royal group with Queen Victoria and her family was taken down by the Japanese during the Occupation. The cenotaph, erected after the First World War, still stands but the only remaining statue, in bronze, is that of Thomas Jackson, manager of the Hong Kong and Shanghai Bank at the end of the 19C.

The gothic *Hong Kong Club* which used to stand on the eastern side of the square was demolished in 1981 and replaced with a small white skyscraper (of which the Club occupies four floors) which stands next to the *Legco Building*. This, with its dome and Ionic columns, was designed for the Supreme Court in 1900 by Sir Aston Webb, the architect of the Victoria and Albert Museum. It was previously separated from the Club by a cricket pitch.

The Supreme Court now meets elsewhere and the building is occupied by Legco, the Legislative Council, which since 1985 has been composed of 24 members elected by functional constituencies (or interest bodies). Above Legco is the Governor's Executive Council, composed of civil servants, the Commander of the British Forces and ten 'unofficial' Governor's appointees mostly selected from the business community. Below Legco is the directly-elected Urban Council, 'the politically toothless' equivalent of a municipal authority in the West. The lack of direct elections to the Legislative Council is one of the problems raised by those worried by the future of democracy after 1997.

Immediately S of Statue Square, on the waterfront, is the *Star Ferry Terminus* for Kowloon. To the E, set back from Queen's Pier, is **City Hall** where there is a small *Museum of Art* in the high block (open daily 10 am–6 pm, except Thursdays, Sundays and Public Holidays, 1–6 pm). It has a considerable permanent collection covering Chinese art from the earliest times but exhibitions vary so check newspaper listings.

The *Star Ferry* is the best way to reach **Kowloon** from Central District (4.30 am–11.30 pm) in a few minutes, with a fine view of the harbour. The old open green and white double-ended diesel ferries, all with stars in their names, have been in operation since 1868. Founded by an Indian, the ferry company belonged to the shipping magnate from Ningbo, Sir Y.K. Pao (died 1991; he also owned Lane Crawford's department store).

Walk along Salisbury Road (along the waterfront in Kowloon), past the old YMCA and the Peninsula Hotel to Nathan Road which runs inland along the far side of the Peninsula. The *Peninsula Hotel*, built in the early years of the 20C, remains perhaps the grandest hotel in Hong Kong with its fleet of eight green Rolls Royces and its famous tea-lounge and restaurants; it is certainly the oldest hotel building since the lamented demolition of the Repulse Bay Hotel in the early 1980s.

NATHAN ROAD is the major shopping street of Kowloon and stretches for miles past Boundary Road (which marks the boundary between Kowloon and the New Territories). Some three blocks up, on the far side of Haiphong Road on the left-hand side of the street, is *Kowloon Park* with the **Hong Kong Museum of History** (closed Fridays, open daily 10 am–6 pm, Sundays and Public Holidays 1–6 pm). Housed in 'pre-war' buildings, the museum has a fairly permanent exhibition on Hong Kong before 1841 with fine models of sea-going junks and good use of photographs and other illustrative material. Its other exhibitions change from time to time but are usually concerned with aspects of the traditional culture of southern China: weddings, puppet theatres, etc. They are well-researched and beautifully presented. There are occasional visiting exhibitions (check newspaper listings).

There is now a *Museum of Space* in the domed planetarium (which blocks the harbour view from the Peninsula) on Salisbury Road. Its exhibitions change fairly regularly so check newspaper listings.

C.   The New Territories

You can take the new *Mass Transit Railway* (opened in 1979 but still expanding), either from Hong Kong island or from Tsin Sha Tsui on the tip of Kowloon to Sham Shui Po. The underground railway is easy to use from the point of view of maps and directions, but the tickets are a bit confusing. The ticket machines take the exact money only but there are

machines to enable you to change notes. Ticket machines issue magnetic
plastic cards which you are instructed to look after carefully, not bending
or 'flicking' them or they won't let you through the automatic barriers.
One small drawback to the trains is the long, polished seats which are
extremely slippery: as the train starts up passengers tend to slide together.

The **Lei Cheung Uk Museum** in Sham Shui Po (closed Thursdays, open
daily 10 am–1 pm, 2–6 pm, Sundays and Public Holidays 1–6 pm) is based
around a Han dynasty tomb which was discovered when the vast area of
squatter housing was cleared following a devastating fire in 1954. It is in
the middle of the oldest group of public housing blocks in Hong Kong,
Shek Kip Mei, at 41 Tonkin Street.

The Han tomb is dated to AD 100–200 and comprises three chambers with shards; a
separate exhibition hall has drawings and contemporary rubbings illustrating life in
the Han, rubbings from the carved bricks of the tomb, and bronze and ceramic artefacts unearthed in it. It is interesting for it illustrates Chinese control of the area as
early as the Han, contrary to the assertion of early British settlers: 'the Colony has
grown to its present position and importance within the last half century, as a result
of the necessities of English trade with China' (1893).

Staying on the MTR, changing at Prince Edward Station, you could travel
on to *Wong Tai Sin* where there is a very new (1973) 'multi-faith' temple
just beside the station, with shrines to the Buddha, and a central hall
devoted to the Taoist Deity Wong Tai Sin who heals the sick. The tap
water in the temple is believed to be efficacious. You could then take the
MTR to Yaumatei to see the *Yaumatei Typhoon Shelter* where many
Hoklo and Tanka boat people live. The shelter is three blocks E of the
Portland Street exit from Yaumatei Station.

It was built in 1915 after a terrible typhoon and is now virtually self-sufficient, with
shop sampans, medical and educational facilities. Some of the larger junks are lovely
but all serve as home for the Tanka (who wear flat-brimmed straw hats) and Hoklo
(possibly from Fujian province) who have hats that look like huge solar topees with
angled brims. There is often a tiny shrine to Tin Hau, Empress of Heaven, roughly the
same deity as A-Ma of Macau. Though some guidebooks describe Tin Hau as a
Taoist deity, I think it likely that she is a version of the Buddhist Avalokitesvara or
Guanyin, thoroughly female (unlike the Buddhist original) and specifically associated
in this area with protection of boats and sailors at sea as one aspect of her compassion. There are, of course, Taoist aspects to the deity and her worship; just one being
her sex.

If time allows, more far-flung trips into the New Territories are interesting. They are easily made by tourist bus (arranged through the hotel or
any travel agent) although tourist buses necessarily mean tourist stops,
such as the amazingly kitsch *Sung Dynasty Village*—certainly an experience. Some of the walled villages (see above) are also fascinating,
although they are full of old ladies demanding money for photographs.
For those interested in botany, the *Kadoorie Experimental and Extension
Farm*, in Lam Tsuen Valley, has fine botanical gardens attached; a group
of columns on a hill are all that remain of the fine central *Post Office* that
used to stand on Statue Square (see above).

Another enterprise of the Kadoorie family is the *Taipo Carpet Factory*, in **Taipo**,
which can be visited by arrangement. There you can see mechanised weaving of carpets whose designs are based on traditional Chinese carpets: the weavers use what
look like power drills and the designs are finally cut and carved (with electric clippers
rather than scissors) in the traditional manner.

A trip that can be made by public transport is to the Museum of the Chinese University, and the Temple of Man Fat in Shatin. Take a train to
Shatin from the Kowloon Station.
    The *Temple of Ten Thousand Buddhas* and the *Man Fat Temple* are
reached by climbing 431 steps up from the railway station, and a further
69 for the Man Fat Temple. The former temple was founded in 1950 and

boasts a pink pagoda, 12,800 Buddha figures and a small fairground for children. The Man Fat Temple above contains the preserved body of the Reverend Yuet Kai who was buried in a sitting position (Buddhist adepts attempt to emulate the sages who died sitting in the meditation position) at the age of 87 in 1965. Eight months after his death his body was discovered to be still in perfect condition and covered in gold leaf, leaving his hair and beard still visible. The body, and its treatment, is reminiscent of that on Jiu hua shan in Anhui.

On the next hill, Tao Fong Shan, is the *Lutheran Chinese Mission to Buddhists*, founded by Karl Reichelt, a Scandinavian missionary who arrived in the area in 1929 after teaching Christianity to Buddhists in China (and becoming an expert on the religion, writing a number of useful books about it). He employed a Chinese Buddhist architect to design the mission whose foundations were laid in 1931. It now has a guesthouse and a pottery in which converted Buddhist monks do overglaze enamel painting on porcelain.

The **Chinese University** is a bus or taxi ride from Shatin Station, magnificently sited on hills above the sea. It was founded in the 1960s with Chinese as its main (though not entirely exclusive) teaching language and the campus incorporates some earlier colleges. Its *museum* was founded to assist in the teaching of Chinese art history but its collections are sometimes displayed and it often houses loan exhibitions of interest (especially since its relations with the art historians and museums of China are very good). The museum is open 10 am–4.30 pm on weekdays and you can find listings of its exhibitions in newspapers.

You can catch buses back to the railway station or to Kowloon from just outside the university gates (be careful that the bus does go to Tsimshatsui) or you may find a passing taxi if you are lucky.

D.   Hong Kong Island

Apart from extended walks in the old Chinese areas of Western and Kennedy Town, there are some places of interest to the east of Central (although this eastern district is in general newer than Western and Kennedy Town; much use has been made of reclaimed land to build apartment blocks on the extended waterfront in Causeway Bay and North Point).

Wanchai, famous as the red-light district in the 1950s and through the Vietnam War period, is not quite the single-minded bar district of fiction ('The World of Suzie Wong') and its *Post Office* has just been singled out for preservation.

Take the Mass Transit Railway to Wanchai and go up O'Brien Road, across Johnston Road and straight ahead for Queens Road East. Before land reclamation, this was the harbour front.

I haven't seen it; according to reports it is a white, Dutch-influenced building and its gables, shuttered windows and brick-arched doorway are perfect examples of turn-of-the-century architecture in Hong Kong. It was built between 1912 and 1913 and became a post office in 1915. It may be used by the Hong Kong Philatelic Society in the future and it stands next door to the *Wu Chung Building* (Hopewell Holdings).

Next to the Hopewell Centre (64 storeys high) is a temple, variously known as the *Hung Shing Temple* or the *Pak Tai Temple*, a single-storeyed temple to the god of seafarers with a fine line of Shekwan ceramics along the roof (added at the turn of the century). The temple was built in 1860 although the shrine inside is dated 1847–48 and the copper image is said to date to 1604.

On the other side of the Hopewell Centre is the narrow Tik Loong Lane which leads up steps to a row of 19C houses and the *Sui Pak* or *Chai Kung Woot Fat* (Living Buddha) *Temple* (c 1870) whose deities have proved efficacious in the control of disease as the many inscribed mirrors (presented by those whose prayers were answered) testify.

The side streets off Queens Road East contain many shops selling traditional goods: paper offerings, birds and birdcages and crickets. *Wanchai Market* (which runs from Queens Road East to Wanchai Road) is quite interesting.

Walk E along Queens Road East. Just beyond the point where Stubbs Road (named after the Governor from 1919 to 1925, Sir Reginald Stubbs, who attended Council meetings on Thursday mornings and afternoons and said he might as well have tripe for lunch on Thursdays, too) leads upwards towards the Peak, are the European cemeteries. On the corner is the *New China News Agency Building*, until the signing of the Joint Declaration and open discussion on Hong Kong directly with Peking, viewed as a sort of unofficial Chinese embassy in Hong Kong. It is interestingly situated for its proximity to the cemeteries would make it a rather unattractive piece of real estate to any but the atheist Communists. There is also a Sikh temple near the corner.

The cemeteries include a *Moslem Cemetery* with a mosque, then the *Catholic Cemetery* (1847) and beyond that the *Colonial Cemetery* (1845). Beyond that is the *Parsee Cemetery* (1852). On Shan Kwong Road is the *Jewish Cemetery*, consecrated in 1855; its earliest headstone is dated 1859.

The Colonial Cemetery is not as fascinating as the Protestant Cemetery in Macau, nor is it as old, but it contains the remains of all sorts of people from Lord Napier (who died in Macau in 1834 after presiding over the opening of trade that followed the ending of the East India Company's monopoly in the same year that he died of fever) to Karl Friedrich August Gutzlaff (died 1851), a Pomeranian missionary who travelled the China coast by junk, writing religious tracts in Chinese and deploring the idolatry of Putuo shan and other Buddhist centres. He worked as an interpreter during the negotiation of the Treaty of Nanking and became Chinese Secretary to the Hong Kong Government from 1834 to 1851. He was apparently 'very greatly deceived by his native helpers but his zeal never failed'.

The cemetery, which covers a large sloping area, is also very peaceful and full of well-tended plants and birds. It can be entered from Queens Road East or you could climb up Stubbs Road and descend through the quiet cemetery.

On the far side of the island, reached by bus or taxi from Central, are Stanley, Repulse Bay and Aberdeen.

Stanley beach and village lie on the SE tip of the island, near Stanley Prison (all named after Lord Stanley, Secretary of State for the Colonies at the time of Hong Kong's annexation). This was also the area in which military prisoners were cruelly interned by the Japanese during their occupation, the death rate commemorated in Stanley Military Cemetery nearby. Stanley is most famous for its *street market* which, though open every day, is most crowded on Sundays. The street is lined with shops and stalls selling rattan, porcelain and, above all, cheap casual clothing, much of it 'designer label'.

There is a **Temple** dedicated to Tin Hau, the Heavenly Empress, sometimes identified as a Taoist deity but who appears also be one of the incarnations of Avalokitesvara, the Bodhisattva of Mercy in (his) sinified (and feminised) incarnation of Guan Yin. Tin Hau is the same as A-Ma of Macau and the Tian hou of the temple in Tianjin (a young female deity, protector of seafarers). The temple lies at the end of Stanley Main Street (turn right at the bottom of the market and continue along a narrow lane at the end of the main street).

The temple is thought to have been founded by the pirate Chang Po Chai some 200 years ago, making it the oldest temple on the island. Chang Po Chai captured the island of Hong Kong in 1770 and set up his headquarters in Stanley, when he wasn't forced to retreat to a cave on Cheung Chau (see below). A drum and bell that he is supposed to have used to signal to his ships are now in the temple; the bell with an inscription dating it to 1767, the drum with a maker's inscription from Guangzhou. An interesting collection of little wooden, gilded deities is ranged on a ledge that runs round the inner wall of the temple. The deities include the City God, the God of War, the barefoot Emperor of the North, the Dragon Mother (who hatched a dragon from an egg) and Guan yin. The front doors of the temple are painted with door gods (whose paper images are pasted on household doors throughout China at the lunar New Year) and a tiger skin said to have been shot very close to the temple by the Japanese during the Second World War.

The next bay is REPULSE BAY, named after HMS 'Repulse' which attempted to keep pirates down in the 19C. Its most famous landmark, the Repulse Bay Hotel, with a long verandah and glass fan-shaped porch, was built in 1918 and demolished some 10 years ago (just before the bottom dropped out of land prices so it was really a mistake to demolish it anyway). Apparently a Repulse Bay Restaurant has been built there now in an attempt to recreate the gracious dining room on the verandah.

DEEP-WATER BAY, filled with mansions and a golf course, lies next to **Aberdeen** (named after Lord Aberdeen, Foreign Secretary in the mid 19C at the time of Hong Kong's annexation) which, unlike the constructed Yaumatei Typhoon Shelter, has been a natural typhoon shelter and home to some 20,000 of Hong Kong's original boat people (as opposed to the more recent sea-going arrivals from Vietnam). Life on board the boats that cram the harbour is the main attraction for visitors.

You can also go (by ferry or by road) to the nearby island of *Apleichau*, the main boat-building centre of the island where junks are made beside luxury cruisers.

There is a *Tin Hau Temple* in Aberdeen (naturally, for the goddess protects fishermen), built in 1851 and one of the most crowded during the Tin Hau festival in April.

The other islands of the archipelago can be visited by ferry (from the Outlying Districts Ferry Pier on Connaught Road, Central, just along from the Star Ferry Pier). The three major islands are Lamma, Lantau and Cheung Chau—others can be explored at will.

Lamma is sparsely inhabited and lovely to walk in—it only takes a couple of hours to get from one end to the other, though it is the third largest of the islands. Depending on where you land, visit the *Tin Hau Temple* in *Sok Kwu Wan*.

Lantau is the largest of the outlying islands—about twice as big as Hong Kong. It is still fairly rural and unspoilt, in contrast to its smaller neighbour. The imminent construction of a proposed new airport on the island will change this. Most ferries land at *Silvermine Bay*, where buses take tourists to the *Po Lin Monastery*, a rather theatrically bright red and gold building (1970) on a hillside N of the reservoir.

The temple was founded in 1927. The images in the main hall are of Sakyamuni, the Buddha of Medicine (left) and Amitabha (right). In the hall above are figures of Guan yin, Bodhisattva of Mercy, Manjusri on his lion, symbol of wisdom, and Samantabhadra on a white elephant, the patron siant of Mount Emei in Sichuan. On a hilltop near the monastery is the only *cremation-tower* in Hong Kong where the bodies of Buddhists, monks, nuns and lay-believers are cremated in the open air.

You could walk on W to the *Yin Hing Monastery*, closer to the sea, or visit the *Lantau Tea Gardens* (opened in 1959 to recultivate disused tea terraces) just by the Po Lin Monastery.

On the N side of the island is the *Tung Chang Fort*, built in 1817 against pirates; with solid ramparts and six cannon.

On the E side of the island is the Trappist *Monastery of Our Lady of Joy* where the monks, who have taken a vow of silence, serve simple meals and run a guesthouse as well as caring for a fine herd of dairy cattle which supply milk to the top hotels in Hong Kong. You can reach the monastery on foot from Silvermine Bay (heading NE around the bay); alternatively, some of the ferries stop at *Peng Chau Island* just opposite whence a sampan will take you across the narrow stretch of water between Lantau and Peng Chau.

Cheung Chau is an island with far more houses on it; more town than boat, the main urban area concentrated on a narrow strip linking two rounded and wooded hills. There is, however, no traffic so that wandering in the narrow streets of the little town is still restful. The oldest temple on Cheung Chau, the *Pak Tai Temple*, is on the waterfront, just left of the ferry pier. It was founded in 1783 and contains a Song sword found in the sea nearby.

Pak Tai is the local God of the Sea, also known as the Emperor of the North. He is supposed to have been a scholar, immortalised for his courage and brilliance. Appointed to stop a demon king from threatening the earth, he defeated the demon and the tortoise and snake (symbols of the north) summoned by the demon, hence his title of Emperor of the North. He is depicted in the temple in his usual form, barefooted and with flowing black hair. Before his altar are two figures of assistant generals, Thousand-li Eye and Favourable-wind Ear.

The temple is the centre of the famous Cheung Chau Bun Festival (held annually between the last 10 days of the 3rd lunar month and the first 10 days of the 4th, usually in late April or early May). The festival originated after the discovery of skeletons, probably pirates' victims, which precipitated a series of natural disasters on the island. A Taoist priest recommended that the hungry spirits of the dead be placated by offerings of food. During the festival, huge bamboo towers, 20m high, are completely covered with about 5000 buns which are eventually donated to the thousands of visitors (after the spirits have partaken of their essence during the days of the festival) to bring them good luck. They are said to cure disease so that bits of dried bun are used throughout the year, boiled with water and drunk in search of a cure for headaches, backaches and other ailments. There used to be rather dangerous fights amongst the young men who clambered up the towers to reach the top buns (the luckiest) and one tower collapsed so that now the buns are more sedately distributed by Taoist priests.

Cantonese operas are performed in the streets on temporary stages and a strange procession includes tiny children dressed up in all sorts of things from mermaid costumes to dinner jackets and bow ties. They are tied into metal frames so that they appear to float on air, unsupported, as they are carried through the streets atop wooden poles.

On the SW tip of the island is the *Cheung Po Tsai Cave*, supposedly the hideout of the most famous local pirate of the 18C (who is also supposed to have founded the Tin Hau Temple at Stanley). He is said to have had an English mistress with whom he hid in the cave.

The *Tin Hau Temple* on **Tap Mun** is perhaps the most important of all as it is the last temple before junks reach the open sea with all its dangers. The 100-year-old temple is thus visited by fishermen to pray for a safe return and successful voyage before they leave the archipelago.

59 Macau

The Portuguese colony of **Macau**, on a peninsula linked by a narrow isthmus to Guangdong province on the Chinese mainland, lies just S of Hong Kong Island, an hour away by hydrofoil. Filled with Hong Kong visitors who come to gamble in the casinos (forbidden in Hong Kong) at holidays and weekends, it is on weekdays a comparatively quiet place filled with pretty colonial buildings in flower-filled gardens and baroque churches.

Access: *Jetfoils* (55 minutes) and *Hydrofoils* (75 minutes) depart at half-hourly intervals (c 7 am–6 pm daily) from the modern *Macau Ferry Pier* on Connaught Road (beyond all the other ferry jetties for the outlying islands).

There is an official *Tourist Information Office* between the pier and the seashore where you can buy maps and a variety of fascinating publications about Macau's history (almost all of them by the indefatigable Father Teixeira). It is quite possible to see most of Macau in reasonable comfort in a day. You can buy quite useful 1:6000 maps of Macau with street names in Chinese and 'English'; these are to be recommended if you speak neither Cantonese nor Portuguese as communication, especially with taxi-drivers, can be a bit difficult.

Visas: for a three-day stay visas are no longer required for nationals of the USA, Philippines, Japan, Australia, Canada, New Zealand, Malaysia, Thailand, Brazil, Austria, Belgium, France, Denmark, Spain, Greece, Italy, Norway, the Netherlands, Sweden, UK, Germany, and Hong Kong.

Currency: the Macau *pataca* is worth about the same as the Hong Kong dollar. It is not necessary to change money before a trip as Hong Kong notes and coins are accepted in Macau (though pataca are only accepted in banks or moneychangers' establishments in Hong Kong).

Hotels: there are a number of luxury hotels in Macau, most clustered near the Hong Kong Ferry Pier because of their casino facilities. One of the most charming (of the luxury class) is the *Pousado de Sãotiago* in what was once the 17C Barra Fort, Fortaleza da Barra, Avenida Republica. It stands high on the shore, overlooking the sea, and has been tastefully converted (it also has a fine restaurant serving Macanese food). The most famous of Macau's hotels is the *Bela Vista* (see below), 8 Rua Comendador Kuo Ho Neng, perched high above the sea, a lovely, if slightly crumbling, example of Portuguese colonial architecture with verandahs overlooking the sea. This is being converted to a super-luxury hotel by the Mandarin Group.

The name of Macau (first mentioned in 1555) is derived from Ma-kan-ngao (or Ma-ngao), meaning port or bay of Ma in Fujian dialect. The local waters were said to be sacred to Ma (known to the Cantonese as Tin-hua), merciful goddess of the sea, and since the peninsula was frequently used by fishermen from Fujian province, further up the Chinese coast, the use of Fujian dialect is not surprising. Macau in fact consists of the peninsula and Taipa and Coloane islands (linked by bridges), though the major historical sites are on the peninsula.

Before the arrival of the Portuguese, there was a small village on the peninsula and the temple dedicated to A-Ma, Goddess of the Sea, was founded during the reign of the Ming Wanli emperor (1573–1621). The first Portuguese to approach Macau were traders based in Malacca in the early 15C. Their numbers grew when in 1542 they discovered Japan where, owing to Japanese pirate activities, the Chinese emperor had forbidden direct trade between China and Japan and the Portuguese were able to act as middlemen. Owing to the distance and the dangers of the seas during the typhoon season, the Portuguese were anxious to establish a secure foothold in China. They set up a number of somewhat insecure trading posts in the coastal provinces of Guangdong, Zhejiang and Fujian. Relations with Chinese officials remained extremely difficult until in 1556 a Portuguese fleet under Leonel de Souza forced an agreement out of the Admiral of Guangzhou giving the Portuguese the right to trade at various places in the vicinity of Guangzhou. The Portuguese settlement in Macau is generally thought to have begun in 1557, against payment of a lease.

By the end of the 16C there were 900 Portuguese based in Macau, with their retinues of servants and Bantu slaves (who were to play a considerable part in the repulsion of a Dutch attack in 1622), and the small number of Chinese inhabitants was swelled by the arrival of pedlars, traders, shopkeepers and craftsmen, despite an imperial prohibition on their residence in Macau. In 1573 the Chinese built the first wall across the isthmus. Attacks by the Dutch led to the appointment of a Captain-General or Governor in 1623 (previously, Macau's administration had been entrusted to an annually-appointed Captain-Major, in fact the commander of the Japan trading fleet), although his existence did not end the attacks which continued throughout the 17C.

Macau's importance declined with the decline of the Portuguese empire, complicated by local problems like the loss of Malacca to the Dutch and the rebellions in Timor which put an end to the lucrative sandalwood trade in which Macau had participated, though there were moments of glory, as in the 1760s during the early European passion for tea. The Kangxi emperor, perturbed by the demands of foreign traders and missionaries, reversed previous prohibitions and ordered that henceforth the Chinese should trade only with the Japanese. This had the effect of re-routing Dutch tea through Macau, to its profit. By the beginning of the 19C, however, the bulk of foreign trade was conducted through Guangzhou (Canton). As the Chinese refused the traders permission to reside there permanently (and embargoed all family members), Macau eventually became the residence of the families of the Canton traders and, for the same reason, missionaries and their families. This was only after Portuguese restrictions on the residence of foreigners had been relaxed in 1757.

After the Opium Wars and the forced opening of the Chinese hinterland to trade and religion, and the rise of Hong Kong, Macau's importance declined once again to the point that it was described in 1917 as 'a quiet retreat and a sanatorium'. It had, however, seen a small revolution in the early 19C, reflecting events in Portugal itself. Conflicts between the Portuguese-appointed Governor and the locally elected Senate led to the formation of a Liberal Party in Macau which drafted a petition to the Portuguese King in 1822 (even though the King had seen his absolute power curtailed), demanding the restitution of the Senate's privileges, the reservation of senior posts for Macanese and a suspension of subsidies to other distant colonies. The Governor, Jose Ozorio de Cabral, refused any compromise and was asked to resign when the Liberals won the elections. He refused and was deposed but he led several attempts to regain power.

The Liberals were eventually deposed by the arrival of a gunboat sent from Goa in 1823, driving the editor of the *Abelha da China* ('China Bee', the first printed newspaper in the Far East and a mouthpiece of the Liberals) into exile and unfortunately re-establishing the rather sinister Judge Miguel de Arriaga. Arriaga only survived a year after his reinstatement, leaving a huge pile of debts and willing his opium connections to his son-in-law. Arriaga had been in illegal partnership with Thomas Beale, for many years Macau's foremost opium trader (though his dealings in the illicit drug were concealed behind his 'general agency'). Beale was one of the notables of early 19C Macau, living in a fine old Portuguese house with a marvellous garden and an aviary of rare birds, collected for him by his agents throughout East Asia. When the Governor of Guangdong imprisoned Chinese opium dealers and searched ships, Beale was caught with several hundred chests of unsaleable opium (for which he owed the British East India Company thousands of pounds). His partner, Arriaga (who as a judge was not supposed to trade at all), offered Beale little assistance and, after many years in hiding, Beale committed suicide on Cacilhas Bay in 1841, 17 years after the hypocritical Arriaga had died in his bed.

Despite the machinations of politics and opium dealers and the expulsion of the religious orders in 1834 following the 'revolution', Macau has a long religious history and some of its greatest monuments are associated with religion. It began with St. Francis Xavier's dream of the conversion of China. Francis Xavier (1506–52) had been a founding member of the Jesuit order. Sent to Goa, he made thousands of converts before travelling to Japan in 1549. His main ambition was to enter China and in 1552 he travelled to Sheungchuen Island (just SW of Macau) where he died as he prepared for the great trip. His body was later transferred to a temporary resting place in the nave of the (now-ruined) church of São Paulo before being sent to its final grave in Goa. His proximity to Macau at the time of his death lent credence to the view that the eventual Portuguese occupation of Macau was a miracle, willed by the saint.

The 'rites controversy' that divided the Catholic Church in the late 17C also divided Macau. A sort of religious power struggle, it centred on the appropriate approach to traditional Chinese practices of ancestor worship and the state cult of Confucius. The Jesuits held that these were not idolatrous but the Franciscans and Dominicans (partly out of jealousy over the Jesuits' success in penetrating the Chinese court) disagreed and 'reported' the Jesuits to the Pope. The dispute began in the mid 17C and was revived under Pope Clement XI in the early 18C when he sent an envoy to the Chinese court to investigate the problem. Tournon, in his turn, gained temporary favour with the Kangxi emperor but was eventually ordered out of the country (he had already instructed missionaries to reject the Chinese rites). When he arrived in Macau, Tournon was imprisoned in the Santo Agostinho monastery for the Bishop of Macau disagreed with his view, moreover, Portugal was concerned that the Pope was ignoring the padroado (Portuguese prerogative regarding the China missions). Tournon died in Macau in 1710 (but not before the Pope had made him a cardinal).

The churches of Macau were immensely impressive as mid 17C chroniclers record: Father Alexander of Rhodes felt that São Paolo was equal to all the best churches in Italy, with the sole exception of St. Peter's, and the surviving examples, including the facade of São Paolo and the Church of São Jose, illustrate the Macanese taste for the baroque and rococo. The survival of 17C churches and a number of 18th and 19C villas and gardens is in marked contrast to the fate of Hong Kong's older buildings which have almost all vanished. There, even skyscrapers are razed to build bigger and higher and little attention is paid to conservation whilst the 'quiet retreat' of Macau still preserves much of its 18th and 19C charm (despite an ever-increasing traffic problem).

During the Cultural Revolution, following the liberation of Portugal from Salazar, the new government of Portugal offered to return Macau to Chinese rule. The offer was not accepted but now, after the negotiations over Hong Kong, it has been decided that Macau will also revert to Chinese rule at the end of the 20C. It will be interesting to see what happens to the casinos, her major source of income.

Macau: the A-Ma Temple

Unless you are a racing-car enthusiast, a time to avoid Macau, if possible, is the second or third weekend in November when the *Macau Grand Prix*, which races through the streets, cuts the peninsula in half, making transport difficult. Part of the circuit runs behind the Lisboa Hotel, between the centre and the ferry piers, completely cutting road access from the piers to the centre. Taxis can only take you as far as the Lisboa Hotel, when you have to get out and walk on flimsy bamboo walkways, over the roads. As half the taxis are marooned on one side of the island, they become extremely scarce on the other side.

Though the peninsula only covers 520 hectares, the monuments are rather scattered and are perhaps best visited by a combination of taxi and walks. Use a taxi to take you to the outer monuments: the A-Ma Temple on the southernmost point, the Porta do Cerco and Lin-Fong Temple at the northernmost point, near the isthmus and the Chinese border, Sun Yat-sen's House and the Kun-Yam Temple NE of the centre of the peninsula. If the taxi then drops you at the Camões Museum in the centre, you can walk to most of the other central monuments.

The **A-ma Temple** (Ma-kok-miu), is just beyond the Barra Fort (now the *Posada de São Tiago Hotel*), on the western side of the southern tip of the peninsula, at the entrance to the inner harbour.

A-Ma, who has given her name to the peninsula of Macau, appears to be one of the manifestations of the Bodhisattva of Mercy, Guanyin (Avalokitesvara in Sanskrit, Kun Yam in Cantonese). The temple devoted to her is said to date from the Ming and the present buildings are of Wanli (1573–1621) foundation, with major restorations (commemorated in an inscription over the gateway to the first pavilion) in the Daoguang period (1824–56). This last major restoration was funded by merchants from Fujian province and Macau and an 'Association of Piety and Benevolence', apparently founded during the Ming to upkeep the temple and support one priest to conduct services, maintain a school for the poor (which still exists), all within the context of the desire to 'worship the Buddha, spread good doctrine, practise charity and keep a school for the poor' as set out in the aims of the Association.

The feast-day of A-Ma is the 23rd day of the third lunar month (effectively late April–early May) and celebrations in the A-Ma Temple are followed by a noisy celebration the next day with firecrackers set off on junks moored outside the A-Ma Temple on the Macanese island of Coloane.

The major legend relating to the foundation of the temple recounts how a young woman begged a lift on a fleet of junks about to set off from Fujian province for Macau. The richer junks were all fully laden but the captain of the poorest junk allowed her on board. In a terrible storm, all but the poorest junk were sunk and the young woman steered the latter safely to port, whereupon she climbed up a hill and disappeared. When the junk passengers searched for her, all they found was the image of a goddess. A temple was built on the site and a junk carved in the rockface (which can still be seen).

The temple is built against a rocky slope with steps carved out of the rock leading from one hall to the next. Topography dictates this piled and stepped plan, different from the usual layout of local temples, but the halls themselves have the typpical exaggerated southern upturn to the eaves. The lower three are dedicated to Tian hou (Tin hau in Cantonese; the Heavenly Empress), the highest to Guanyin (Kun Yam or Avalokitesvara), thus effectively separating deities who are effectively fused in the folk-stories, but such is the complexity of popular religion. The *gate* is guarded by two stone lions whose teeth are in very poor condition, apparently because they used to escape at night and eat the tender rice sprouts in the paddy-fields of Lapa Island until the peasants broke their teeth.

Inside the gate on the right is a *courtyard* between the two lower temples; the courtyard is surrounded by a wall with stone carvings. It contains banyan trees (a major feature of temples of the far south of China), two small 'ovens' (one of brick, one of iron) for burning paper offerings, and painted carvings of junks on two large rocks. The small flag on the stern of the junk reads 'Crossed the great river in safety', for these are pictures of the junk rescued by A-Ma. Beside the steps (to the left of the junk-carved rocks) is a niche dedicated to the earth spirit (Tu di) who guards the place. Two stone archways are carved with inscriptions reading: first arch, top: Temple of the Heavenly Goddess; right side: Virtue changes the whole universe; left: Benevolence nourishes the living; behind: Her mercy is as boundless as Heaven; second arch: Calm sea of the south; behind: Pavilion for contemplating sadness and Swallows and herons offer congratulations.

Behind is the first hall, called *Tian hou miao* (Temple of the Heavenly Empress), with inscriptions on the lintel recording the foundation and repairs to the temple. On the altar, the figure of the goddess is dressed as a bride in red, her attendants carved on the walls. Apart from the usual altar table with incense burners and candle-sticks, there is a smaller table with cylindrical bamboo tubes which are filled with bamboo sticks by which fortunes can be told.

Worshippers light three incense sticks, ke tou three times (kneel with head on the ground) and then shake the bamboo tube until a stick falls out. This is exchanged for a slip of yellow paper inscribed with characters revealing the fate which will be interpreted by the temple attendant. Another form of fortune-telling which, interestingly, is a major feature of temples in Fujian (whose connection with Macau through sea-junk trade is clear), is the pan (pooi in Cantonese), pairs of small pieces of wood or bamboo. These are thrown to the ground in pairs (the musical clatter can constantly be heard in Fujian temples) and the temple assistants interpret the future from the way they have fallen.

The second **Temple**, devoted to the same goddess, has been painted by many foreign artists, including Chinnery (see below), John Webber (Captain Cook's draughtsman) and Auguste Borget (1808–77). Higher, with a fine view of the sea and the hills of Lappa, it also has an image of the Goddess as a Chinese bride and is covered with inscriptions relating to her mastery of the sea: 'Can use her intelligence to control the rough sea with her bare hands', 'Under her protection when I go sailing in springtime, the sun rises and sets appropriately and the sea is calm', 'Under her protection my ship can sail safely on the enormous sea', etc. A side altar on the right is dedicated to Dizang wang (Ksitigarbha, ruler of the underworld) and on the left, Weituo, the ubiquitous guardian of the Buddhist law and Buddhist temples (usually found in Chinese temples facing towards the main hall).

Weituo is a somewhat mysterious Chinese invention, although the characters in his name are also used for Vitasoka or Vigatasoka, younger brother of King Asoka, who did so much to promote Buddhism in the 2C BC.

In the left corner of the circular window, near a dried swordfish, is a junk model, claimed to be 400 years old and to replicate that which brought the goddess from Fujian. On the left wall of the hall is a drum, on the right a drum and bell with the inscription 'favourable wind and seasonable rain', referring to agriculture. It is at this level that the entrance to the Buddhist Association's school for children is to be found, as well as a winding stepped path, 'the path of enlightenment', through a moon gate (inscribed 'touching the clouds') which leads to a tiny chapel called the *Hall for Increasing Virtue*, dedicated to the same goddess. Above, up a path is the fourth hall, the *Guanyin ge* (Tower of Guanyin), with a major image, crowned with pearls, flowers and a veil, seated on a throne behind two smaller images that are used in processions. A small altar on the left is dedicated to Wei tuo, protector of the faith; on the left wall is a painting of Guan gong (or Guan Yu), the God of War, dated to 1887.

Guan Yu is part of Chinese popular religion and his presence is another example of the eclecticism of Chinese popular religion which here has elevated a manifestation of Guanyin, at the same time as celebrating Guanyin unmanifested.

At the northern extremity of the peninsula is the **Porta do Cerco**, the bat-tlemented border gate, built in 1870 (on the site of previous barriers, the first of which was put up by the Chinese in 1573 to control the flow of goods into Macau—it was at first opened only twice a month—and to remind the settlers of the temporary and uncertain nature of their sojourn).

It was the scene in 1849 of the murder of the Governor, Joao Ferreira do Amaral. His instructions from Lisbon were to make Macau a free port and consolidate Portuguese control of the island. This he did by expelling the Chinese customs officials (the 'Hoppo') and destroying their residences and offices on the Rua de Nossa Senhora do Amparo. His schemes upset more than the Chinese authorities for he cleared graveyards near the Porta (to build a road), upsetting local inhabitants, and he managed to upset the distant Lord Palmerston by imprisoning James Summers, an English chaplain who had come for the Macau regatta but refused to remove his hat during a Corpus Christi procession. A British mission was sent to rescue Summers and one man was killed before Foreign Secretary Palmerston intervened. It was the Guangdong authorities who were most upset and posters were stuck up in Guangzhou offering a price for Amaral's head. Seven assassins disguised as beggars attacked him near the Porta and took his head and left hand across the border for their reward. It seems that he had already lost his right hand.

Not far S of the Porta do Cerca, at the junction of the Avenida do Almirante Lacerda and the Estrada do Arco, is the Buddhist **Lin Fong** (Lotus) **Temple**, founded in 1592, which used to serve as a guesthouse for officials travelling between Macau and Guangzhou.

It is a typical Guangdong temple (similar to the Chen family temple in Guangzhou, for example), quite different from the northern temples with their long, deep N–S axis. These southern temples have broad E–W buildings, arranged in rows so that there are, in fact, three parallel N–S axes (much shorter than those of the north) but the effect is of three long, broad E–W buildings with open courtyard-gardens between. The same variation is also seen in Guangdong housing where houses are ranged in terraces with a communal courtyard in a long strip running between the terraces.

The façade of the Lin Fong Temple is grand and lavishly decorated with glazed tiles. There are many halls in the three E–W rows, with A-Ma (known in Hong Kong as Tin-hau) presiding over the main hall.

At the back, on the right-hand side is a *temple garden* with some squiggly bonsai, and near the vegetarian temple kitchen is an altar for family use. These altars, decorated with paper flowers and photographs of the recently deceased, are set up for 40 days after death (regardless of date of burial) for the spirit of the dead needs feeding and placating in that period according to the popular version of Buddhism.

The temple's collection of bronze bells includes examples dating back to the early years of the 17C; they were donated by grateful inhabitants of the Pearl River delta to the boat-builders of Macau.

The **Kum Iam** (Guan yin) **Temple** is on the Avenida do Coronel Mesquita, SE of the Lin Fong Temple. It is a smaller, plainer temple built to the same E–W plan as the Lin Fong Temple but its façade is decorated with more sober (but rather fine) grey cut-brick work, rather than lavish glazed tile decoration.

The temple was the scene of the signing of the first treaty between America and China on 3 July 1844. The signing took place at a stone table in the Kum Iam temple. Caleb Cushing, the American Minister to China, was sent to try and negotiate the same terms ('extra-territorial rights' and the right to trade and send missionaries) for America as Great Britain had recently obtained through the Opium War.

Cushing was prevented from travelling to Peking but placated somewhat by the news that Qi Ying (sometimes romanised as Kiying), the Manchu official who had ratified the British Treaty of Nanking, had been appointed Governor of Guangdong and would come to negotiate a treaty with him in the south. Qi Ying (died 1858) was an imperial clansman, probably descended from the Qing founder Nurhaci, and whilst in Macau he stayed in the Kum Iam Temple. On a circular stone table in the forecourt of the temple, the Treaty of Wanghia (Wangxia in pinyin, Mong Ha in Cantonese pronunciation) was signed. The treaty was named after the district of Macau in which the temple stands. Its name, Wangxia, means 'looking towards Xiamen', reflecting the Fujianese origins of many Macanese.

Extra-territoriality arose from the incompatibility of laws and the question of whether a traveller 'carried his own law with him', a problem that dates back to Roman times and the extension of Roman dominions. The first Europeans to arrive in the Far East were subject to *lex loci* or local laws but conflict soon arose over the executions of Europeans and Americans for causing the death of Chinese in the foreign settlements. The principle, that the law of the defendant's nationality should apply in trial and administration of justice, had been accepted in the earliest treaties made by the Russians with the Chinese (Nerchinsk, 1689, and Kiakhta, 1727) but was not extended to other powers until one by one they forced it upon the Chinese during the mid 19C.

In the *main hall* of the temple are fine figures and banners used in A-Ma processions in front of the carved and gilded altar to A-Ma (or Tian hou or Tin-hao). The temple is two 'terraces' deep with a lotus pool at the back.

At the back, left-hand side, is the *Hall of the 'Golden Flower Mother'* who appears to give protection from smallpox and other diseases. There are some strange figures in the temple including an official with two pairs of eyes, as well as some fine stone carving.

S of the Kum Iam Temple, on the corner of the Estrada Adolfo Loureiro (an engineer who first drew up the plans for the Inner Harbour in 1884) and the Avenida do Conselheiro Ferreira de Almeida is the **Lou Lim Ieoc Garden**. Described as the 'grandest example' of the late neo-classical phase in Macau, it is a Chinese garden with a pavilion supported on Corinthian columns and it belonged to a family of officials from Guangzhou, the Lous. Dating back to the 19C, it takes its name from Lou Lim-Yeoc (or Ieoc), a merchant and diplomat of Macau who was awarded the Order of Christ by the Portuguese Government in 1925. The garden was restored and made public after his death.

Just a few hundred metres E of the garden is the *house* in which Sun Yat-sen lived whilst working at the Kiang Vu Hospital on the Estrado do Repouso during one of his many periods of exile from China before 1911. There is a small exhibition devoted to his life in the house which is an imposing yellow Victorian villa. There is some doubt as to whether this is the actual house or a more recent construction.

The **Camões Grotto and Gardens** with the adjoining Protestant Cemetery are on the W side of the peninsula, off the Rua Palmeira, high above the harbour.

Luiz Vaz de Camões (1524–78), one of Portugal's great poets, was supposed to have spent some time in Macau in the year of its foundation (1557) when he wrote his most famous work, the epic poem 'Os Lusiades' on Vasco da Gama's voyage, a poem that is seen as a commemoration of the golden age of discovery. The tradition that he visited Macau, and even held an official post as Trustee for the Dead and Absent, is an old one, dating back to the early 17C, and is a little difficult but not impossible to square with what is known of his extraordinary life.

Exiled from Lisbon for his political lampoons, he lost an eye in the Portuguese campaigns in North Africa and, on his return to Lisbon, was banished to Goa for duelling over a lady. His political views got him exiled (with the suggestion that he had better go as far away as possible, perhaps to Japan or China) from Goa. He travelled widely, gaining inspiration for his exotic poem, but died in great poverty in Lisbon some six years after its publication.

The Camões Grotto (where he is supposed to have taken the evening air after a hard day acting for the dead and absent) now stands in the **Camões Garden**, formerly known as the Casa Garden, which houses the **Casa Villa**, a fine colonial house (now containing the Museum) which used to belong to the British East India Company and where Lord Macartney stayed in 1794 on his return from Peking.

The house has seen many changes since the middle of the 18C when it was first built as a country villa by the Jesuits, just N of the 'Christian city's' walls. The first Portuguese settlers lived at the foot of São Paolo do Monte, with the Monte Fort (built by Jesuit priests) high above them to defend them from land or sea attacks with its cannon. The Chinese city, Mong Ha (Looking towards Xiamen), lay to the N, and the Casa Villa was off to the W. In the 1780s it was rented by an East India Company supercargo called William Fitzhugh and later by another British East India Company merchant, James Drummond. It was during his tenancy that Macartney came and his botanist James Stromach examined the plants in the garden.

In 1796 it became the property of the Leal Senado (the 'Loyal Senate', Macau's governing body) and in 1815 Senator Manuel Pereira bought it. He rented it for some time to the Dents, owners of a major opium firm, before giving it to his daughter as part of her wedding present. Pereira's daughter married Lourenco Marques who installed the classical canopy over the rocks of Camões and had a bust of the poet (a much-prettied portrait of the one-eyed satirist) installed in the 'grotto'.

The Casa Villa has been altered considerably through out its history though its basic plan remains the same, like that of other mansions in Macau, 'large, roomy, two-storeyed structures composed of piano nobile and basement'. A classical balustrade with urns was added in the early 20C but has almost disappeared. The neo-classical interior hints at what the building might have been like in the 18C and the cool, breezy interior is typical.

The *Luis de Camões Museum* inside contains some especially interesting Ming bronzes and a collection of Chinese furniture (ornate beds, tallboys and chests) which is not very often seen outside the Victoria and Albert Museum in London.

Opening off the front garden to the Casa Villa is the old **Protestant Cemetery**, on two terraces below the villa, a calm and pleasant garden area with some very interesting gravestones.

There is a new Protestant cemetery, on the Rampa dos Cavaleiros, just off the Avenida do Coronel Mesquita to the E of the Kun Ian Temple (it is called the *Bela Vista Cemetery* because it is S of the Estrada de Bela Vista, but is not to be confused with the Bela Vista Hotel which is near the southern tip of the Peninsula).

The earliest graves in the cemetery date to the 1770s but the cemetery was not formally opened until some time later. Some of the earliest stones in this cemetery were in fact moved here from Meesenberg Hill (named after William Meesenburg of the Dutch East India Company, first to be buried there) under the supervision of Sir Lindsay Ride (1898–1977), Professor of Physiology and Vice-Chancellor of the University of Hong Kong, who was passionately interested in the Protestant Mission to the Far East and also in the history of Macau (his ashes are now in the cemetery).

The formal opening date of the Protestant Cemetery remains a mystery which is not helped by the inscription above the gate which reads 'Protestant Church and Old Cemetery (East India Company 1814)', the date most likely referring to the year of the new charter of operation of the EIC. The most probable date is 1821, the year in which the wife of Robert Morrison died.

From the beginning, none but Catholics were permitted by the ecclesiastical authorities to be buried in Macau, for it was Catholic soil; non-Catholics had to be buried in the area between the walls of the 'Christian city' and the Porta do Cerco. A complication to non-Catholic funerals was the resistance of the Chinese to foreign burials, which sometimes required armed guards for burials of foreigners amongst Chinese graves (and from the fate of Amaral it is known that there were Chinese burial grounds in the area).

Robert Morrison (1782–1834), first Protestant missionary in China and translator of the Bible into Chinese, was appalled at the prospect of a hasty burial of his wife and her unborn child ('Mary died! and our little baby alas found a grave in her mother's womb') in front of hostile crowds, and pushed the Committee of the English Factory into buying a piece of land 'to lay the remains of my beloved wife in a place appropriated to the sepulture of Protestant Christians, denied a place of interment by the Romanists'. He had already tried to reach the grave of his firstborn son on a nearby hilltop, so that he could bury his wife with him, but had been driven away by Chinese squatters there. He was eventually able to move the remains of 'James Morrison Born and Died March 5th 1811' to a place beside his mother in the cemetery.

Beside the cemetery entrance is a small *chapel* (often closed; I've never seen inside), built by the British East India Company in 1831 and reconstructed and reconsecrated in 1921. There is a memorial to Endicott, a missionary buried at Happy Valley in Hong Kong, two of whose children are 'sleeping here' (Fidelia and Rosalie in graves Nos 33 and 34). The graves on the upper terrace include that of George Chinnery, the painter who was born in 1774 at Gough Square in London (where Dr Johnson lived) and who died in Macau in 1852, after working there for 27 years.

Chinnery was a competent jobbing painter who had worked for 23 years in India before arriving in Macau in 1825 (owing £40,000 in Calcutta), declaring that he had come to escape from his wife, 'the ugliest woman I ever saw'. At one point a rumour arose that Mrs Chinnery was on her way to Macau from Calcutta and Chinnery decamped to the safety of Canton where one of the Chinese government's regulations vis à vis foreign residents ran 'Neither women, guns, spears nor arms of any kind can be brought in to the factories'. Chinnery made his living by painting the notables of the area (including Morrison) in great numbers, travelling to other parts of the Far East to paint, but he also left a number of lively sketches of Macau, showing the city and its people as they were in the early 19C. Though Macau's fortunes were beginning to wane as Hong Kong developed in the early 19C, Chinnery never moved from peaceful Macau, only ever visiting Hong Kong once.

Also on the upper terrace is the tomb of Lieutenant Joseph H. Adams of the US Navy (died 1853), a grandson of President John Adams and nephew of President John Quincy Adams and that of the American who 'assisted in setting up the first magnetic telegraph in Japan in 1854'.

Most of the memorials on the upper terrace are simple headstones commemorating American, French, German and Danish missionaries and seamen who died in the area. George Henry Brady, a seaman of New York, was 'murdered on board by pirates' in 1974; in the era of sail, several seamen died from falls from the rigging, like John P. Griffin, 'seaman born in New York and died on board the US ship 'Plymouth', Macao Roads, by a fall from aloft, June 10, 1849' and the unfortunate apprentice boy Thos. Pennington, 'Through the effects of a fall into the hold', and the US frigate 'Brandywine' lost its musician in October 1844. No. 60 is the grave of Anders Ljungstedt, Knight of Wasa, Scholar and Philanthropist, his tomb erected by 'A Mournful Friend'.

Ljungstedt wrote the first history of Macau, published in 1834 on the basis of a series of articles he had written in the 'Canton Miscellany' magazine, though Father Manuel Teixeira SJ, who is the oldest Portuguese in Macau (having arrived in 1924) and its most prolific historian, does not appear to approve Ljungstedt's early effort.

On the *lower terrace* are the three monuments to infant Colledges, the increasing despair of their parents evident in the increasingly grim epitaphs chosen for the babies' graves, and the memorial to Edmund Roberts who died in Macau in 1836 on his way to Japan where he was to sign a treaty for the US Government. The stone records how 'He devised and executed to their end under instructions from his government treaties of amity and commerce between the United States and the courts of Muscat and of Siam'. Winston Churchill's great-great-uncle Henry Spencer Churchill, 4th son of the 5th Duke of Marlborough, was 'Captain of Her Britannic Majesty's ship 'Druid' and senior officer in the China Seas' when he died off Macau in 1840 and his successor Sir Humphrey Le Fleming Senhouse died on board HMS 'Blenheim' (curiously named after the seat of the Dukes of Marlborough) 'at Hong Kong on the 13th June 1841 aged 60 years from the effects of fever contracted during the zealous performance of his arduous duties at the capture of the heights of Canton in May 1841'.

Thus naval involvement in the first Opium War is commemorated in the graveyard, as are the vexations of free trade in the drug which seems to have dogged the career of James Innes (1787–1841)—'Haud procul ab esto, mari terraque, litibus multo vexatus' (...Vexed by much discord by land and by sea...)—who had declared himself an independent trader (in opium) in defiance of the East India Company's monopoly. Morrison's grave, together with those of his wife and sons, dominate the lower terrace but there are numerous other graves of interest.

The *Church of São Antonio* lies just below the Camões Gardens and if you walk round the church on the Largo da Companhia, you will soon find on your right the *Calcada de São Paolo* which leads to the symbol of Macau, the wonderful baroque façade of the **São Paolo Church**, all that survives of the old Jesuit college and Church of Madre de Deus, standing above a flight of 70 steps.

Peter Mundy, who visited Macau in 1637, saw São Paolo just two years after the carved stone façade had been put up with the help of Japanese Jesuit converts. He remarked particularly on the rest of the church (burned to the ground in 1835) '...of excellentt worckemanshippe, Carbed in wood, curiously guilt and painted with exquisite collours', and for Mundy's contemporary Father Alexandre de Rhodes, it was more beautiful than any Italian Church except St Peters. It is believed that the architect of this (the second Jesuit Church to be built in Macau) was an Italian Jesuit, Carlos Spinola and that the work took place between 1602 and 1638.

The façade of local granite is European in design, its inspiration taken either from late 16C churches in Genoa and Milan or from Spanish retable-façades according to your source, but it incorporates Chinese decoration amongst the European Christian imagery. The design is separated into three major horizontal planes, the major figure of the Virgin in a niche in the centre, surrounded by angels. Binoculars are required to make out the lines of Chinese characters running beside the columns: other details include a figure of the Virgin stamping on a chimera, a Portuguese carrack (very similar to the carved Chinese junk in the A-Ma Temple which makes one wonder if the latter were not a Portuguese carving, or directly inspired by Portuguese boat carvings?), a ladder, crown of thorns and a supine skeleton, a memento mori beside the fat scaly chimera and a line of Chinese characters.

The wooden part of the building suffered a series of fires, but the last, in 1835, left only the façade standing. It occurred the year after the dissolution of the religious orders in Macau when the buildings were used as a barracks by Portuguese soldiers and is said to have started in their kitchen.

Overlooking the façade of São Paolo, to the E, is the old **Monte Fortress and Observatory**. Bronze cannon, some dating back to the early 17C when Manuel Bocarro's foundry supplied the best weapons in Asia, still stand in position.

Monte Fort was half built when the Dutch launched a major attack in 1622 with three warships in the front line (and a following fleet of 13 with over 1000 men). They would have had two more boats and an ally had the British not pulled out of the engagement through a disagreement about the proposed invasion and looting of Macau. Jesuits manned the Monte Fort and one of their cannon shots blew up a barrel of the Dutch gunpowder, forcing a retreat during which the fleeing Dutch were attacked by the African slaves of the Portuguese (which assistance led to their freedom from slavery).

In the following year Francisco Mascarenhas was appointed Captain-Major (effectively military governor) of Macau and his first task was to complete the construction of Monte Fort and other defences. One of his successors, Governor Diego de Pinho Teixiera, had a major disagreement with the Leal Senado in 1710 and turned the cannon of Monte Fort on his opponents who had decamped to the College of São Paolo below but the Bishop's intervention prevented major bloodshed. The same thing happened during the revolution of 1822 when the guns (used by the Liberals) failed to prevent the arrival of a fleet come to overthrow them.

Returning to the façade of São Paolo, take the Rua São Paolo (which leads down, due S from the church) until it joins the Rua Palha. Continue S and a narrow street with a market on the left leads to **São Domingos Church and Monastery** (founded in 1588) with a fine yellow and white baroque façade (but which is often shut). Its silver and mother-of pearl tabernacle with Solomonic columns, made in 1683, is one of the finest surviving examples of the rich church furnishings of the 17C when Portuguese colonies and overseas trade flourished.

Returning to the Rua Palha, take the second turning on the left beyond the church and you are in the Largo do Senado with the building of the Leal Senado in front of you. The LARGO DO SENADO, broad with central gardens, is lined with arcaded commercial buildings, mostly dating from the 19C and early 20C. Despite their recent construction, the style is characteristic of the colonised cities throughout southern China where buildings with cool verandahs are built out over the streets so that their upper storeys, supported on columns, shade the street and the shops below, and the whole, from a distance, is elegantly arcaded. The design harks back to Italian city planning of the Renaissance.

The **Leal Senado** itself is part of the design of the triangular 'square' of the Largo do Senado which was originally laid out in the 1580s. The building as it stands today was dedicated in 1784 though the façade was not completed until 1876 (and much restoration was undertaken in 1939). Today the building has been half converted to house art exhibitions.

Behind the elegant classical façade is a charming garden with blue and white tile plaques set into the walls. There is some fine carved woodwork in the library and council chamber and the before the entrance is a stone tablet inscribed 'City of the name of God, there is none more loyal', dating from 1654, placed there by the Governor, Joao de Souza Periera, at the order of the King of Spain to commemorate Macau's loyalty to Portugal during the Spanish Hapsburg rule of the home country. The title of 'Leal' (Loyal) was also granted in recognition of the same fealty, much later, in 1809.

The new *Cathedral* is just NE of the Senate, reached by taking the turning on the E of the square (on the right if the Senate is behind you). This leads round to the Largo da Se and the Cathedral which no longer bears any resemblance to the 17C Santa Casa da Misericordia. If you return to the Largo do Senado, on the right is a highly decorated building with an internal courtyard, the Chinese 'Holy House of Mercy', a privately endowed clinic and pharmacy with much green-painted wrought-iron.

From the Largo do Senado, turn E along the major road that runs in front of the Senate (Avenida Almeida Ribeiro) and take the first major turning on the left, Rua Central. This takes you along past the bottom of a raised square in which the pretty *Dom Pedro V Theatre* stands. Built in 1858, during the reign of King Pedro V of Portugal, the designer was the Macanes e Pedro Marques. The present façade was built some 20 years later and the tiny theatre is now restored to its former elegance (after being occupied until 1985 by the 'Crazy Paris' strip show which is now in the Hotel Lisboa).

Behind the theatre is the *Sir Robert Ho-tung Cultural Centre*, once the summer residence of the Hong Kong philanthropist after whom it is named since he donated it to the Portuguese government. With its light, airy rooms and pleasant garden, it is a fine example of late 19th–early 20C regional domestic architecture. The arcaded lower floor is open so that you can see through to the green of the garden behind.

To the right behind the theatre is the church of **Santo Agostinho**, founded in 1586, another yellow and white baroque façade whose interior with rosettes on the blue wooden ceiling and suffering Christ is faintly reminiscent of Mexico.

The monks of Santo Agostinho were partisans of the Papal envoy Tournon in the first decade of the 18C (when he ignored the advice of the Jesuits and instructed missionaries to reject the Chinese rites under pain of excommunication) and Tournon was held under 'church arrest' in the church at the order of the Viceroy of Goa after his expulsion from China. The same viceroy ordered that the monks of Santo Agostinho be deported to Goa for a decade for he believed that the Pope was flouting the agreement that the Portuguese and not the Vatican were responsible for the China mission.

To the left, on the slope of the hill is **São Jose Church and Seminary**, founded by the Jesuits in the early 17C.

Built on land donated by the Senate to the Jesuits, its foundations were laid in 1730 and the church was finished in 1758; its domes are unique in Macau. It now looks rather modern and concretey with a Chinese tile roof. The seminary was built expressly to train missionaries for China so its classrooms are rather empty now (though it is the home of Father Manuel Teixeira, the great historian of Macau). The church is only used once a year, on New Year's Eve.

It used to house St. Francis Xavier's humerus (now in the Chapel of St. Francis on Coloane Island), together with relics of the 'Japanese martyrs', killed in the anti-Christian persecution of the shogun Hideyoshi in the last years of the 16C (instigated mainly because Hideyoshi feared that religious faith might be put to political use). It still, however, houses many of the fine polychrome wooden figures, probably locally made in the 17C, that were rescued from the destructive fire of São Paolo.

Beyond the theatre, where the Rua Central changes its name to the Rua de S. Lourenco and past the *Imprenca Nacional* or Government Printing Press on the corner of the Rua Prata and Rua de S. Lourenco, is the church of **São Lourenco** (St Lawrence) whose construction, funded by the Jesuits, began between 1550 and 1570. The painter, Chinnery, lived behind São Lourenco, on the Rua of the same name, for most of his stay in Macau. São Lourenco's last major reconstruction was in 1897–98, to designs by the architect Augusto Cesar d'Abreu Nunes in the late neo-classical Macanese style (though the pair of towers to the E and the single nave were earlier features that can be distinguished in some Chinnery drawings).

I have not seen the interior except through the doorway, which offered a view of grand Corinthian columns and chandeliers in contrast with the Doric exterior.

If time allows, you could continue W towards the *Penha Church* and *Bishop's Residence* (not open to the public) on the Colina da Penha ahead of you, and the Bela Vista Hotel, otherwise you could turn down towards the bay along the Travessa Padre Narciso (left, just behind the church) and then back eastwards along the Praia Grande towards the Lisboa Hotel and the Macau–Taipa Bridge.

For the Hotel Bela Vista, continue W along the Rua São Lourenco which changes its name to the Rua Padre Antonio. The second major turning on the left is the Rua Penha, which then joins the Rua Boa Vista. As the Rua Boa Vista approaches the bay, the **Hotel Bela Vista** is on your left.

It was founded in the late 19C by an English couple, a sea-captain William Edward Clarke and his wife, who named it the Boa Vista (good view). When Clarke wished to sell it in the early years of the 20C, interest was expressed in making it a sanatorium and hospital for French soldiers (mostly recuperating victims of marsh fever caught in the French Indo-Chinese colonies). This plan was vetoed by the British, who were extremely concerned about the growth of French influence in the Far East and the threat this posed to British interests and they managed to persuade the Portuguese administration to expropriate the whole area, including the hotel. The matter had, apparently, reached the British Houses of Parliament where, according to Fr Teixeira's entertaining history of the Bela Vista, the matter served to 'substantiate the fear that it was part of a deep-laid plot of the French to exchange Macao for some part of the Congo.'

The history of the hotel in the subsequent decades was complex, though it remained a hotel until 1917 when it became a secondary school, the Liceu Central. In 1923 the Government took it over, only to sell it to a Chinese lady in 1932 but her debts to the Caixa Economica Postal de Macau were such that it became the property of the Caixa. It was rented as a language school for the study of Cantonese by recruits to the Hong Kong Civil Service and after the Japanese invasion of China it was filled with refugees from north China and Shanghai. When the Japanese occupied Hong Kong Portuguese residents forced to flee the British colony occupied it. From 1946 to 1950 it was rented to the Hong Kong government as a NAAFI for British servicemen stationed in Hong Kong.

In 1948 the Caixa had sold the hotel to three ladies, 'Mesdames Kwok Chi Chan, Chan Sok Fong (represented by Ho Yin) and Ng Tong Ying (now the widow of Chong Chi Kong)', as Fr Teixeira puts it. Under their ownership, the Bela Vista (which acquired its new name of Bela or Beautiful Vista round about the same time) has once again opened as a hotel. It is a fine colonial building with the characteristic arcaded verandahs offering breezy and shaded views over the Baia da Praia Grande (or 'a surprising look over the harbour' as the historian has it).

Traffic on the PRAIA GRANDE, the 'Bund' of Macau, is unfortunately rather noisy but at siesta time it is a pleasant, tree-shaded street which leads back towards the Lisboa Hotel, the Macau–Taipa Bridge and, beyond, the hydrofoil piers for the return trip to Hong Kong. The Praia Grande is lined with grand villas on its western end, including the pink *Gover-*

nor's Residence, marked by the Portuguese flag flying over it and a tennis court in front. Nearer the point where it leaves the bay and runs into th e town, the buildings are similarly grand, tall arcaded structures with classical columns and urns decorating the façades, but these apparently conceal a Chinese heart behind the classical Western exterior. Hidden, inner courtyards are surrounded by symmetrical dwellings arranged according to traditional principles.

At the angle of the Praia Grande and the Avenida Amizade (which leads to the Lisboa Hotel and Taipa Bridge) is the stone *Jorge Alvares Monument*, commemorating the first European to reach China in 1513 (the place he landed is usually supposed to be Tuen Mun in Hong Kong). Just in front of the Taipa Bridge is the *Ferreira do Amaral Monument*, an equestrian statue in bronze in which the one-handed Governor appears to be flogging his horse without mercy. This is the Amaral who was murdered at the Porta do Cerco in 1849; the statue was erected in 1940.

The other islands, Taipa and Coloane, can now be reached by taxi or bus.

Taipa is linked to the peninsula by the impressive arching bridge. It boasts a very popular restaurant which serves Macanese food (wonderful salt cod or bacalhau and spiced African chicken) in an open courtyard roofed by trees (*Pinocchio*, 4 Rua do Sol, Taipa). There is apparently a museum on Taipa's own Praia, in one of the fine 19C houses, filled with furniture and fittings of the period (*Casa Museu*).

Coloane is accessible by ferry or the Taipa–Coloane causeway. It has fine beaches and many pine plantations which scent the island.

On *Kao Ho Beach* is the *Chapel of St. Francis Xavier* where the precious relic of the saint (his humerus) and those of the Japanese martyrs once housed in the São Jose Seminary are now preserved.

INDEX

Personal names are printed in *italic* type; ancient sites and monuments are in SMALL CAPITALS; places of minor importance and subjects are in Roman type; **bold** and **BOLD CAPITALS** are used for places of successively greater importance.

PHYSICAL MAP OF CHINA

☐	−200m
▒	200–1000
▓	1000–2000
■	2000–

PAKISTAN

N

NEPAL

BHUTAN

INDIA

BANGLADESH

0   km   500

BURMA

LAOS

Bay of Bengal

THAILAND

U.S.S.R.

U.S.S.R.

MONGOLIA

NORTH KOREA

SOUTH
KOREA

YELLOW SEA

JAPAN

EAST CHINA SEA

HONG KONG
MACAO

VIETNAM

PACIFIC OCEAN

SOUTH CHINA SEA

PHILIPPINES

THE PROVINCES OF CHINA

0   km   500

Lake Balkhash

U.S.S.R.

MON

● Ürümqi

XINJIANG UIGHUR AUTONOMOUS REGION

GANSU

PAKISTAN

Xining

QINGHAI

TIBET AUTONOMOUS REGION

● Lhasa

SIC

NEPAL

BHUTAN

N

INDIA

BANGLADESH

Kunming

YUNNAI

BURMA

Bay of Bengal

THAILAND